Business Organizations
Law in Focus

Focus Casebook Series

Business Organizations Law in Focus

Deborah Bouchoux

Georgetown University

Christine Sgarlata Chung

Associate Professor, Albany Law School
Director, Institute for Financial Market Regulation

 Wolters Kluwer

1 2 3 4 5 6 7 8 9 0
ISBN 978-1-4548-6807-1

Library of Congress Cataloging-in-Publication Data

Names: Bouchoux, Deborah E., 1950- author. | Chung, Christine Sgarlata, author.

Title: Business organizations law in focus / Deborah Bouchoux, Christine Sgarlata Chung.

Description: New York : Wolters Kluwer, [2016] | Series: Focus casebook series

Identifiers: LCCN 2016025072 | ISBN 9781454868071

Subjects: LCSH: Business enterprises — Law and legislation — United States--Cases. | LCGFT: Casebooks.

Classification: LCC KF1355 .B685 2016 | DDC 346.73/065 — dc23

LC record available at https://lccn.loc.gov/2016025072

About Wolters Kluwer Legal & Regulatory US

Wolters Kluwer Legal & Regulatory US delivers expert content and solutions in the areas of law, corporate compliance, health compliance, reimbursement, and legal education. Its practical solutions help customers successfully navigate the demands of a changing environment to drive their daily activities, enhance decision quality and inspire confident outcomes.

Serving customers worldwide, its legal and regulatory portfolio includes products under the Aspen Publishers, CCH Incorporated, Kluwer Law International, ftwilliam.com and MediRegs names. They are regarded as exceptional and trusted resources for general legal and practice-specific knowledge, compliance and risk management, dynamic workflow solutions, and expert commentary.

This book is dedicated to the memory of Philip John Sgarlata

The first member of his family to go to college
The first member of his family to get a law degree
The winner of the Albany Law School Prize for Highest Standing in
Corporation Law
An expert on health law
And, the best father in the world

and

to Donald Robert Bouchoux

The most wonderful husband to me and most loving father to his children and
grandfather to his grandchildren

Summary of Contents

Table of Contents

The Focus Casebook Series

Help students reach their full potential with the fresh approach of the **Focus Casebook Series**. Instead of using the "hide the ball" approach, selected cases illustrate key developments in the law and show how courts develop and apply doctrine. The approachable manner of this series provides a comfortable experiential environment that is instrumental to student success.

Students perform best when applying concepts to real-world scenarios. With assessment features, such as Real Life Applications and Applying the Concepts, the **Focus Casebook Series** offers many opportunities for students to apply their knowledge.

Focus Casebook Features Include:

Case Previews and Post-Case Follow-Ups — To succeed, law students must know how to deconstruct and analyze cases. Case Previews highlight the legal concepts in a case before the student reads it. Post-Case Follow-Ups summarize the important points.

Case Preview

In re Hlavin

As the hypothetical of Mary Jones and her loaves of bread illustrates, the number of potential disputes about the kinds of debt that are or are not to be considered consumer debts is simply limitless. The lawyer has to recognize when the issue matters and can be contested. As you read In re Hlavin, a case involving the 11 U.S.C §707(b) dismissal for abuse provision, consider the following questions:

1. Why is it the debtors and not the bankruptcy trustee who are arguing that their home mortgage is not a consumer debt?
2. What does this court s[...]
   gage is or isn't a consu[...]

Post-Case Follow-Up

Is this opinion making a distinction between the repossessor himself disturbing the peace and his committing an act that motivates another to disturb the peace once the repossessor is gone? Would the result in this case have been different if the activities of the repossessors had awakened the debtor or the neighbor and the one awakened had shouted at them out of a window something like, "Stop, thief! I've called the police"? See Robinson v. Citicorp National Services, Inc., 921 S.W.2d 52 (Mo. Ct. App. 1996), and Chrysler Credit Corp. v. Koontz, 661 N.E.2d 1171 (1996). If the debtor's husband had raced outside with a firearm while the repossessors were pulling away from the property? If he or the neighbor had fired a firearm at the fleeing repossessors? If a sleeping child had been in the car unseen by the repossessor when the car was driven off? See Chapa v. Traciers & Associates, 267 S.W.3d 386 (Tex. App. 2008)? If the repossessor had violated a driving ordinance in the course of repos-

The Focus Casebook Series

Real Life Applications — Every case in a chapter is followed by Real Life Applications, which present a series of questions based on a scenario similar to the facts in the case. Real Life Applications challenge students to apply what they have learned in order to prepare them for real-world practice. Use Real Life Applications to spark class discussions or provide them as individual short-answer assignments.

In re Hlavin: Real Life Applications

1. Would the result in *Hlavin* have been different if the loans secured by their home had originally been taken out to fund a failed business venture? What if they had been taken out for home improvement or a vacation but then actually used to fund a business venture? Would it matter if they told the bank the money was being borrowed for home improvement or vacation but intended it to be used to fund a business venture? What if the home loans had been taken out for mixed personal/business reasons?

2. If the debtors in *Hlavin* had 30 different consumer debts totaling $75,000 and only one business debt totaling $76,000, would that court find that they had "primarily consumer debts" under §707(b)(1)? What would be the result if a court utilized one of the alternative approaches to this question mentioned in *Hlavin*?

Applying the Concepts — These end-of-chapter exercises encourage students to synthesize the chapter material and apply relevant legal doctrine and code to real-world scenarios. Students can use these exercises for self-assessment or the professor can use them to promote class interaction.

Applying the Concepts

1. Assume you are consulted by the following potential bankruptcy clients. Which of these appear at first blush to be candidates for a consumer bankruptcy filing as opposed to a non-consumer or business filing?

   a. The individual owners of an unincorporated video rental store whose business has plummeted due to the popularity of Internet movie-streaming services.

   b. A married couple both employed but who have abused their credit card spending and now owe more than they make together in a year.

   c. A recently divorced woman with two children whose ex-husband is unemployed and not contributing child support and who is having trouble paying her monthly living expenses.

   d. A married couple, one of whom has suffered major health problems resulting in medical expenses in excess of what they can expect to earn in ten years.

Preface

Ensure student success with the Focus Casebook Series.

THE FOCUS APPROACH

In a law office, when a new associate attorney is being asked to assist a supervising attorney with a legal matter in which the associate has no prior experience, it is common for the supervising attorney to provide the associate with a recently closed case file involving the same legal issues so that the associate can see and learn from the closed file to assist more effectively with the new matter. This experiential approach is at the heart of the *Focus Casebook Series*.

Additional hands-on features, such as Real Life Applications, Application Exercises, and Applying the Concepts provide more opportunities for critical analysis and application of concepts covered in the chapters. Professors can assign problem-solving questions as well as exercises on drafting documents and preparing appropriate filings.

CONTENT SNAPSHOT

This text is intended to provide readers with a thorough understanding of the forms of organization that business people use when establishing and operating for-profit businesses in the United States. Chapter 1 sets the stage for our study by providing an overview of each of the various forms of organization, focusing on key attributes, advantages, and disadvantages of each form. Chapter 1 also discusses considerations that drive choice of form decision making, including management and governance structures, liability risks and rules, tax considerations, and funding and financing needs. Chapter 2 focuses on agency law issues. Chapters 3 to 5 focus on general partnerships and partnership variants. Chapters 6 to 11 focus on corporations, including formation basics (Chapter 6), corporate finance basics (Chapter 7), corporate governance (Chapters 8 and 9), shareholder rights and closely held corporations (Chapter 10), and changes in corporate structure and corporate combinations (Chapter 11). Chapter 12 covers the limited liability company form. Chapter 13 addresses issues arising under the federal securities laws, including issues associated with the Sarbanes-Oxley Act of 2002 and the Dodd-Frank Wall Street Reform and Consumer Protection Act. In several chapters, we address "hot topics" arising under business organizations and the federal securities laws. We have also included "spotlight" sections addressing corporate inversions, so-called "unicorns" (i.e., a start-up business, usually in the technology space, with a valuation of at least $1 billion), and insider trading. The text also includes charts and diagrams demonstrating key principles of business organizations, sample forms that illustrate the topics discussed, and excerpts of documents from well-known companies such as General Electric Company and Microsoft Corporation to highlight critical business concepts.

RESOURCES

Casebook: The casebook is structured around text, cases, and application exercises. Highlighted cases are introduced with a *Case Preview,* which sets up the issue and identifies key questions. *Post-Case Follow-Ups* expand on the holding in the case. *Real Life Applications* present opportunities to challenge students to apply concepts covered in the case to realistic hypothetical cases. *Application Exercises* offer a mix of problem solving and research activities to determine the law of the state where the student plans to practice. State law application exercises better prepare the student to actually handle cases. The *Applying the Concepts* feature demands critical analysis and integration of concepts covered in the chapter.

Other resources to enrich your class include: Practice Skills Exercises, or supplementary material such as Business Organizations by J. Mark Ramseyer. Ask your Wolters Kluwer sales representative or visit the Wolters Kluwer site at *wklegaledu.com* to learn more about building the product package that's right for you.

Acknowledgments

As an initial matter, I want to thank my family — James, Connor, and Caitlin. You make everything possible, and I am grateful for your love and support.

I also want to thank my dear colleagues at Albany Law School, especially Dean Alicia Ouellette, Dean Connie Mayer, and Professors Mary Lynch, James Redwood, Nancy Maurer, Melissa Breger, Danshera Cords, and David Pratt. You are all brilliant, of course. But, equally as important, you were kind, supportive, and patient with me throughout this project. I am lucky to count you as colleagues, mentors, and friends.

Many thanks to all of my students at Albany Law School over the past nine years, as well. Your hard work and dedication has taught me so much, and I owe a debt of gratitude to all of you — especially my research assistants and teaching assistants. I know the materials on *Caremark*, in particular, will bring back memories of our time together in business organizations!

A special word of thanks to Deborah Bouchoux, my co-author, Jane Hosie-Bounar, our editor, and Richard Mixter from Wolters Kluwer. Deborah was a joy to work with, and her drafting skills and seemingly limitless patience with me made this book so much better. Jane likewise was a joy to work with — and endlessly patient. And, I am grateful to Rick and Wolters Kluwer for getting me involved in this project. Thank you also to The Froebe Group and Andrew Blevins for their enormous help in editing and producing this text.

Thank you also to the reviewers of early drafts of these chapters for their invaluable comments, suggestions, and candid critiques.

And finally, a note of appreciation to Corbis Images for the photograph of Ferdinand Pecora in Chapter 13; NYSE Regulation for allowing us to include excerpts from the New York Stock Exchange Listed Company Manual; the National Venture Capital Association for allowing us to include references to and excerpts from sample documents; the states (including Delaware, California, Arizona, the Commonwealth of Virginia) for the use of relevant business organizations forms; the Uniform Law Commission for the Uniform Acts cited in this text; and the American Bar Association for the Model Business Corporation Act provisions cited herein, as well.

Business Organizations Law in Focus

Introduction to Business Organizations

Welcome to the study of business organizations! During this course, we will study forms of organization that business people use when establishing and operating for-profit businesses in the United States. We will focus on several forms of organization common in the for-profit world: (i) sole proprietorships; (ii) partnerships (and partnership variants); (iii) corporations; and (iv) limited liability companies. We will also discuss specialized forms of organization often available only to professions such as law and accounting. In this first chapter, we provide an overview of each of these forms of organization, focusing on key attributes, advantages, and disadvantages of establishing and operating a business in each form. We also discuss considerations that drive choice of form decision making, focusing on management and governance structure, liability risks and rules, tax considerations, and funding and financing needs.

A. HOW IS BUSINESS CONDUCTED IN THE UNITED STATES?

Many people imagine that business in the United States is conducted mostly by and between large corporations. This may be because large, well-known corporations sell products and services that people use every day—for example, kitchen appliances, home mortgages, cars and trucks, cell phones, social media platforms, etc. It also may be because millions of

Key Concepts

- Overview of forms of organization common in the for-profit world, including a discussion of key characteristics of each form, and key advantages and disadvantages of establishing and operating a business in each form
- Factors that influence choice of form, including management and governance structure, liability risk and rules, tax treatment, and funding and financing plans

Americans work for or have ownership stakes in large corporations, giving many an incentive to keep track of these businesses. Corporations may also draw our attention because they are a regular feature of popular media and popular culture commentary. During the recent financial crisis, for example, national newspapers, magazines, online sites, academic journals, social movements, and even Hollywood movie makers examined complex financial instruments developed and marketed by large, well-known financial institutions organized as corporations.

The focus on corporations speaks to their power and influence in economic, political, and social life in the United States. In addition to employing millions of Americans, corporations account for a disproportionately large share of reported business revenues in the United States, far outstripping revenues reported by sole proprietorships, partnerships, and other unincorporated forms of organization. See Exhibit 1.1. Corporations also engage with political and social issues, in part because they enjoy rights to engage in electioneering communications. *See Citizens United v. Federal Election Comm'n*, 558 U.S. 310 (2010) (holding law that prohibited corporations from spending general treasury funds on certain electioneering communications violated corporation's First Amendment rights). Some corporations even appear to enjoy rights and protections derived from their owners' religious beliefs. *See Burwell v. Hobby Lobby Stores, Inc.*, 134 S. Ct. 2751 (2014) (holding corporations are "person[s]" for purposes of the Religious Freedom Restoration Act of 1993's (RFRA) protection of a person's religious exercise rights, and further holding that United States Department of Health and Human Services regulations that required corporations to provide health insurance coverage for certain methods of contraception violated RFRA, where the contraceptive methods at issue violated the sincerely held religious beliefs of the corporations' owners).

And yet, though undeniably important, large, well-known corporations do not tell the "whole story" of business in the United States. First, not all businesses are organized as corporations. In 2012, for example, there were approximately 23 million sole proprietorships, 3.3 million partnerships (including general partnerships, limited partnerships, and limited liability companies), and only 5.8 million business corporations in existence, according to Internal Revenue Service (IRS) data.[1] Second, not all businesses organized as corporations are the large, powerful behemoths that we read about in the news. Instead, as Exhibit 1.2 reflects, nearly 90 percent of all U.S. corporations employ fewer than 20 employees. See Exhibit 1.2. Third, small businesses (defined to include businesses with fewer than 500 employees, and including both incorporated and unincorporated entities) play an important role in the domestic economy, despite their comparatively low profile, accounting for (i) 99.7 percent of U.S. employer firms; (ii) 63 percent of net new private sector jobs; (iii) 48.5 percent of private sector employment; (iv) 42 percent of private sector payroll; (v) 46 percent of private sector output; (vi) 37 percent of high-tech employment; (vii) 98 percent of firms exporting goods; and (viii) 33 percent of exporting value, according to the Small Business Administration.[2]

---

[1] *See* SOI Tax States, Integrated Business Data, Table 1, available at https://www.irs.gov/uac/SOI-Tax-Stats-Integrated-Business-Data.
[2] *See* Small Business GDP: Update 2002-2010, www.sba.gov/advocacy/7540/42371.

As these facts and figures suggest, business in the United States occurs by and between incorporated and unincorporated entities, both large and small. Consequently, as lawyers and lawyers-in-training, we must examine all of the different forms of organization common in the for-profit world to understand how to form and operate businesses in the United States in compliance with the governing law. The goal of understanding how for-profit businesses are organized and how they operate from a legal perspective thus animates our study of business entity forms in this book.

EXHIBIT 1.1 **Business Receipts (2012) by Entity Type (in Billions of U.S. Dollars)**

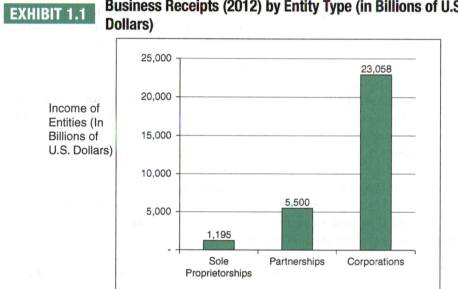

Source: SOI Tax States, Integrated Business Data, Table 1, available at https://www.irs.gov/uac/SOI-Tax-Stats-Integrated-Business-Data.

EXHIBIT 1.2 **Corporations Indexed by Numbers of Employees (2012) (in Thousands)**

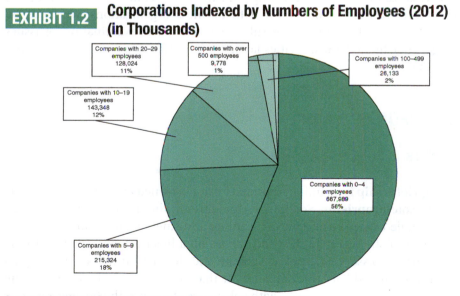

Source: United States Census Bureau, https://www.census.gov/econ/susb.

B. INTRODUCTORY PRINCIPLES

As we begin our study of business organizations, we offer a few "rules of the (legal) road" that you may want to keep in mind as you work through the remaining chapters of this book:

- The study of business organizations involves a healthy dose of statute-based learning. In fact, compared to many of your first year courses, you will be spending a great deal more time in this course delving into codes — for example, your state's general partnership act, limited partnership act, limited liability company act, and corporations code. Business entity statutes contain important and oftentimes quite specific rules. You must know and comply with these rules when representing clients, so be sure to engage with both statutory and common law rules when working through the course material.
- We will study model and uniform acts in this course, and (in some cases) particularly prominent state statutory and common law rules and principles. Our purpose in using model and uniform acts is to introduce you to rules and concepts. Remember, however, that states are not bound by uniform laws or model acts, and state legislatures may accept, reject, or accept but modify uniform or model act language when drafting and enacting state law. Consequently, you should make it your practice to check statutory and common law rules in your home jurisdiction, and any other jurisdictions identified by your professor, as you work through the course materials.
- Be aware that the study of business organizations involves both state and federal law. As a general rule, state statutory and common rules speak to the formation and governance structures of business entities, as well as to relations among stakeholders. The federal securities laws contain rules governing the offer, purchase, and sale of corporate securities (e.g., the stock of publicly traded corporations), the mechanics of shareholder voting, and the like. While this book discusses federal securities law issues relevant to business organizations, we focus on state statutory and common law rules. For a detailed examination of issues arising under the federal securities laws, consider taking a course in securities regulation.

C. SOLE PROPRIETORSHIPS

1. What Is a Sole Proprietorship?

A **sole proprietorship** is an unincorporated business owned and conducted by one person, the **sole proprietor**. Sole proprietorships are the default form of organization for single-owner businesses — meaning, a business owner will form a sole proprietorship if she (i) establishes and carries on a business; and (ii) fails to file the paperwork necessary to create a separate and distinct business entity (e.g., a corporation or limited liability company) for that business with the relevant state **secretary of state**. As this suggests, with sole proprietorships, the business is not a separate legal entity, and there is no legal distinction between the business and its individual owner.

Almost any kind of business can be conducted as a sole proprietorship: a restaurant, an auto repair service, a web design business, etc. From 2008 to 2012, the number of sole proprietorships grew from approximately 22.6 million to approximately 23.5 million.[3] Because of the liability risks associated with sole proprietorships (discussed in subsection 5 below), however, lawyers rarely recommend that a business be operated as a sole proprietorship. Consequently, we discuss sole proprietorships in this chapter only.

2. Governing Law

Because a sole proprietorship is not a separate legal entity, there is no body of sole proprietorship law setting forth the rights and obligations of the owners of sole proprietorships. This also means that there is no separate body of law governing the formation, organization, operation, or dissolution of sole proprietorships.

3. Management

Sole proprietorships are characterized by a single owner with ultimate decision-making authority over business operations. In many instances, it is easy to determine when a business is operating as a sole proprietorship. For example, assume Sandy Smith owns a barbershop. Further assume that Sandy has not filed any formation paperwork with the secretary of state. As long as Sandy is the sole owner and ultimate decision maker with respect to the business, Sandy is a sole proprietor, even if Sandy employs other barbers or allows other barbers to "rent" chairs as independent contractors. As a sole proprietor, Sandy would own the assets of the business (e.g., shaving equipment, supplies) in the same way that Sandy owns non-business property (e.g., Sandy's furniture at home), and Sandy would have authority to decide how to operate the business.

In some situations, however, it may be difficult to determine whether a business is operating as a sole proprietorship or as a partnership (the default form of organization for multi-owner businesses). Determining whether a business is operating as a sole proprietorship or partnership can be particularly tricky with family businesses. Often with family businesses, one spouse may work in the shop while the other spouse does the accounting and bill paying. Children or other relatives

> ### What Is a Secretary of State?
>
> A secretary or department of state office is the arm of state government charged with (among other things) processing, filing, and maintaining documents relating to businesses formed or operating in the state. Many states have a specific division or office charged with overseeing business entity formation and operation: New York has the "Division of Corporations, State Records and UCC," Delaware has the "Corporations Division," California has a "Business Entities Section," and so forth. For ease of reference, we will use the term "secretary of state" to refer to these offices.

---

[3] *See* http://www.irs.gov/uac/Tax-Stats-2.

may work in the business or fill in as employees during summer vacations. In such circumstances, it may be difficult to determine whether one person is "in charge." To determine the nature of such an enterprise, examine how decisions are made. If one person makes key business decisions, such as whom to hire and fire, what products and services to offer, and whether additional shops will be opened, it is likely a sole proprietorship. If more than one person makes key decisions, or has authority to enter into key contracts, then the business is likely a partnership (discussed in Section D below and in Chapter 3).

4. Taxation

Because there is no legal distinction between sole proprietors and their businesses, sole proprietorships are not recognized as separate tax-paying entities under the Internal Revenue Code. Sole proprietorships thus do not pay any federal income tax at an entity level (because there is no entity as a legal matter), nor are they required to file a federal income tax return. Instead, income earned from the business is reported on a separate form called Schedule C (see Exhibit 1.3), which is attached to the sole proprietor's individual income tax return, and the sole proprietor (not the business) pays tax on business income as an individual, based on individual tax circumstances. Subject to governing tax rules, the sole proprietor may declare and deduct various business expenses such as advertising, rent, business insurance, and interest paid, and use these to offset income. Taking such deductions may be especially helpful in the first few years of the business when losses may be expected as the business is developing.

5. Characteristics: Advantages and Disadvantages

Ease of Formation and Power of Control

Sole proprietorships offer two potential advantages. First, because there are no statutory formalities associated with forming a sole proprietorship, sole proprietorships are easy to form and generally inexpensive (focusing on administrative expenses) to operate. Second, sole proprietorships offer the owner the power of ultimate control over business activities.

Unlimited Personal Liability

The principle disadvantage of the sole proprietorship form is that the owner of a sole proprietorship has no **liability shield** — meaning, the owner may be held personally liable for business debts. Because sole proprietors shoulder the burden of unlimited personal liability for business debts, most lawyers and business people engaged in entity selection and business planning do not consider the sole proprietorship a truly viable option for most clients.

Assume, for example, that a sole proprietor operates a restaurant. If the sole proprietor purchases wine or food for the restaurant, but the restaurant is unable to pay debts owed to these vendors, the restaurant's creditors are not limited to the restaurant's business accounts for debt repayment. Instead, creditors may look

EXHIBIT 1.3 **IRS Schedule C**

SCHEDULE C (Form 1040)	**Profit or Loss From Business** (Sole Proprietorship)	OMB No. 1545-0074
Department of the Treasury Internal Revenue Service (99)	▶ Information about Schedule C and its separate instructions is at *www.irs.gov/schedulec*. ▶ Attach to Form 1040, 1040NR, or 1041; partnerships generally must file Form 1065.	20**14** Attachment Sequence No. **09**

Name of proprietor	Social security number (SSN)

A	Principal business or profession, including product or service (see instructions)		B Enter code from instructions ▶
C	Business name. If no separate business name, leave blank.		D Employer ID number (EIN), (see instr.)

E Business address (including suite or room no.) ▶ _____
City, town or post office, state, and ZIP code

F Accounting method: (1) ☐ Cash (2) ☐ Accrual (3) ☐ Other (specify) ▶ _____

G Did you "materially participate" in the operation of this business during 2014? If "No," see instructions for limit on losses . ☐ Yes ☐ No

H If you started or acquired this business during 2014, check here . . . . ▶ ☐

I Did you make any payments in 2014 that would require you to file Form(s) 1099? (see instructions) . . . . ☐ Yes ☐ No

J If "Yes," did you or will you file required Forms 1099? . . . . ☐ Yes ☐ No

Part I **Income**

1	Gross receipts or sales. See instructions for line 1 and check the box if this income was reported to you on Form W-2 and the "Statutory employee" box on that form was checked . . . . ▶ ☐	1	
2	Returns and allowances	2	
3	Subtract line 2 from line 1	3	
4	Cost of goods sold (from line 42)	4	
5	**Gross profit.** Subtract line 4 from line 3	5	
6	Other income, including federal and state gasoline or fuel tax credit or refund (see instructions)	6	
7	**Gross income.** Add lines 5 and 6 . . . . ▶	7	

Part II **Expenses.** Enter expenses for business use of your home **only** on line 30.

8	Advertising	8		18	Office expense (see instructions)	18	
9	Car and truck expenses (see instructions)	9		19	Pension and profit-sharing plans .	19	
				20	Rent or lease (see instructions):		
10	Commissions and fees .	10		a	Vehicles, machinery, and equipment	20a	
11	Contract labor (see instructions)	11		b	Other business property . . .	20b	
12	Depletion	12		21	Repairs and maintenance . . .	21	
13	Depreciation and section 179 expense deduction (not included in Part III) (see instructions).	13		22	Supplies (not included in Part III) .	22	
				23	Taxes and licenses	23	
				24	Travel, meals, and entertainment:		
14	Employee benefit programs (other than on line 19) . .	14		a	Travel	24a	
15	Insurance (other than health)	15		b	Deductible meals and entertainment (see instructions) .	24b	
16	Interest:			25	Utilities	25	
a	Mortgage (paid to banks, etc.)	16a		26	Wages (less employment credits) .	26	
b	Other	16b		27a	Other expenses (from line 48) . .	27a	
17	Legal and professional services	17		b	Reserved for future use . . .	27b	

28	**Total expenses** before expenses for business use of home. Add lines 8 through 27a . . . . . . ▶	28	
29	Tentative profit or (loss). Subtract line 28 from line 7	29	
30	Expenses for business use of your home. Do not report these expenses elsewhere. Attach Form 8829 unless using the simplified method (see instructions). **Simplified method filers only:** enter the total square footage of: (a) your home: _____ and (b) the part of your home used for business: _____ . Use the Simplified Method Worksheet in the instructions to figure the amount to enter on line 30	30	
31	**Net profit or (loss).** Subtract line 30 from line 29. • If a profit, enter on both **Form 1040, line 12** (or **Form 1040NR, line 13**) and on **Schedule SE, line 2.** (If you checked the box on line 1, see instructions). Estates and trusts, enter on **Form 1041, line 3.** • If a loss, you **must** go to line 32.	31	
32	If you have a loss, check the box that describes your investment in this activity (see instructions). • If you checked 32a, enter the loss on both **Form 1040, line 12,** (or **Form 1040NR, line 13**) and on **Schedule SE, line 2.** (If you checked the box on line 1, see the line 31 instructions). Estates and trusts, enter on **Form 1041, line 3.** • If you checked 32b, you **must** attach **Form 6198.** Your loss may be limited.	32a ☐ All investment is at risk. 32b ☐ Some investment is not at risk.	

For Paperwork Reduction Act Notice, see the separate instructions. Cat. No. 11334P Schedule C (Form 1040) 2014

EXHIBIT 1.3   **IRS Schedule C (continued)**

Schedule C (Form 1040) 2014   Page **2**

| **Part III** | **Cost of Goods Sold** (see instructions) |

33 Method(s) used to
value closing inventory: **a** ☐ Cost **b** ☐ Lower of cost or market **c** ☐ Other (attach explanation)

34 Was there any change in determining quantities, costs, or valuations between opening and closing inventory?
If "Yes," attach explanation . . . . ☐ Yes ☐ No

35 Inventory at beginning of year. If different from last year's closing inventory, attach explanation . . .	**35**	
36 Purchases less cost of items withdrawn for personal use	**36**	
37 Cost of labor. Do not include any amounts paid to yourself	**37**	
38 Materials and supplies	**38**	
39 Other costs	**39**	
40 Add lines 35 through 39	**40**	
41 Inventory at end of year	**41**	
42 **Cost of goods sold.** Subtract line 41 from line 40. Enter the result here and on line 4	**42**	

| **Part IV** | **Information on Your Vehicle.** Complete this part **only** if you are claiming car or truck expenses on line 9 and are not required to file Form 4562 for this business. See the instructions for line 13 to find out if you must file Form 4562. |

43 When did you place your vehicle in service for business purposes? (month, day, year) ▶ _____/_____/_____

44 Of the total number of miles you drove your vehicle during 2014, enter the number of miles you used your vehicle for:

a Business _____ **b** Commuting (see instructions) _____ **c** Other _____

45 Was your vehicle available for personal use during off-duty hours? . . . . ☐ Yes ☐ No

46 Do you (or your spouse) have another vehicle available for personal use? . . . . ☐ Yes ☐ No

47a Do you have evidence to support your deduction? . . . . ☐ Yes ☐ No

b If "Yes," is the evidence written? . . . . ☐ Yes ☐ No

| **Part V** | **Other Expenses.** List below business expenses not included on lines 8–26 or line 30. |

--		
--		
--		
--		
--		
--		
--		
--		
48 **Total other expenses.** Enter here and on line 27a	**48**	

Schedule C (Form 1040) 2014

to the sole proprietor's personal assets to satisfy the business's debts. Likewise, if one of the restaurant's employees commits a tort or civil wrong while acting in the course of his employment, the tort victim may look to the sole proprietor's personal assets to satisfy a judgment.

Sole proprietors are not altogether without recourse. In some states, there are statutes that protect certain property from attachment by creditors. For example, household furnishings, appliances, and other personal effects may be exempt if they are personally used by the sole proprietor and are reasonably necessary. Similarly, certain heirlooms, jewelry, artworks, and other items of personal property may be exempt to the extent they do not exceed some stated statutory value, often $3,000. In addition, many states have homestead exemptions to protect one's residence from creditors' claims, and exemptions for certain retirement benefits may exist, although the nature and extent of these exemptions can vary from state to state. Sole proprietors also may seek out insurance to protect against the disadvantage of unlimited personal liability or may seek to enter into contractual arrangements with creditors whereby, in return for obtaining the proprietor's business, the creditors agree not to look to the sole proprietor's personal assets to satisfy debts.

While potentially available, however, there are limits to statutory and negotiated protections. For example, depending on the business, general liability insurance may be prohibitively expensive, or not available to cover all types of risk. In addition, counterparties may not be willing to enter into contractual arrangements designed to insulate sole proprietors from personal liability, or they may seek to exact additional money or other onerous terms in exchange for agreeing to limit a sole proprietor's personal liability via contract. Rather than go through machinations to obtain protections that may turn out to be uncertain, expensive, or unavailable, business owners are well advised to consider forms of organization (e.g., a limited liability company or corporation) that offer a liability shield. While these forms of organization may be marginally more expensive to form and operate in the first instance, the benefits of liability protection typically outweigh the additional expense.

Lack of Continuity

Lack of continuity is another disadvantage of the sole proprietorship form. Because the sole proprietorship is merely an extension of the sole proprietor, with no separate and independent legal existence, the sole proprietorship generally terminates with the death of the sole proprietor. While a sole proprietor may sell her business to a new owner, a change in ownership may affect the operation of the business or its value as an ongoing concern. This is because the value of a sole proprietorship often is tied to the identity, skill, and reputation of the individual owner, and if the individual owner is no longer involved, the business may be less attractive to potential customers or worth less to a potential buyer.

Difficulties in Raising Capital

The sole proprietorship form also can make it difficult to raise **capital** — that is, money or other assets raised to fund operations, meet unforeseen needs, or grow the business. Because sole proprietorships have only one owner, a sole proprietor can look only to his own funds for additional equity investment. A sole proprietor may seek a loan from a bank or other lender, of course, but potential creditors may be reluctant to lend to a sole proprietorship if they do not believe the business has a proven track record or if they are concerned that the business is too dependent on the identity, skill, and continued involvement of the sole proprietor.

Dependence on Owner and Difficulties Attracting Talent

Relatedly, although the sole proprietorship form gives owners the benefit of control over business affairs, a single-owner structure can be a disadvantage, especially if the business needs special assistance or expertise as it grows. Partnerships and multi-member limited liability companies can leverage the skills, knowledge, and resources of multiple owners to respond to business challenges. A corporation can call upon the skills and knowledge of its board of directors and executive team and the resources of its shareholders. If a sole proprietor lacks skills or resources needed to respond to a changing economy, a changing market, or a growing business, she may need to hire employees in exchange for compensation or call upon advisors who, by definition, do not have an ownership interest in or managerial authority over the business. A sole proprietorship may find it difficult to attract skilled, high-level employees because outsiders cannot become owners of a business operating as a sole proprietorship, nor can they exercise ultimate authority over business affairs. Advisors likewise may be unwilling to help out without the possibility of an ownership stake or formal governance or managerial role.

6. Rules and Requirements Relating to Formation

Fictitious Name Statements

Although sole proprietors do not need to create or file any particular documents to form their business as a matter of business organizations law, there are certain administrative requirements associated with doing business in any form, including a sole proprietorship. For example, many sole proprietors choose to operate their businesses under a name other than their own. This is often referred to as an *assumed name, trade name,* or a **fictitious name**. For example, assume Susan Sullivan intends to operate a web design business. She prefers to call the business SS Web Design rather than Susan Sullivan's Web Design. Because SS Web Design is a fictitious name, Susan must generally file a document with her local or state authority informing the public that she intends to "do business as" or "trade as" SS Web Design. Sometimes this document is referred to as the **DBA** statement (for "doing business as"). An example of a **fictitious business name statement** is shown in Exhibit 1.4. This document protects consumers by allowing them to identify the

EXHIBIT 1.4   **Example of a DBA Statement (TEXAS)**

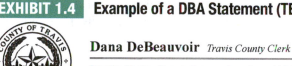

Dana DeBeauvoir *Travis County Clerk*

Mailing Address: P.O. Box 149325, Austin, Texas 78714-9325
Phone: (512) 854-9188
www.traviscountyclerk.org

Recording, Elections, Computer Resources, Accounting, and Administration Divisions   5501 Airport Boulevard, Austin, Texas 78751
Misdemeanor Records, Civil/Probate/Commissioners Court Minutes, and Records Management Divisions   1000 Guadalupe, Austin, Texas 78701

ASSUMED NAME CERTIFICATE FOR CERTAIN UNINCORPORATED PERSONS

ASSUMED NAME under which the business or professional service is or is to be conducted (print clearly):

PHYSICAL ADDRESS OF BUSINESS (print clearly):

Address _____

City _____   State _____   Zip Code _____

I hereby state that this registrant is:

☐ **AN INDIVIDUAL.** Below is my full name and residence address.

☐ **A PARTNERSHIP.** Below is the name and office address of the venture or partnership; the full name of each joint venture or general partner; and each joint venturer's or general partner's office address, if the venture or partner is not an individual.

☐ **AN ESTATE.** Below is the name and address (if any) of the estate; the full name of each representative of the estate; and each representative's residence address if the representative is an individual, or the representative's office address, if the representative is not an individual.

☐ **A REAL ESTATE INVESTMENT TRUST.** Below is the name and address of the trust; the full name of each trustee manager; and each trustee manager's residence address, if the trustee manager is an individual, or the trustee manager's office address, if the trustee manager is not an individual.

☐ **COMPANY OTHER THAN A REAL ESTATE INVESTMENT TRUST.** Below is the name and office address of the company. The state, country, or other jurisdiction under the laws of which this company was organized is _____

And further state that this registrant is **not** a limited partnership, limited liability company, limited liability partnership, or foreign filing entity.

Information required as listed above (print clearly):

Name _____   *Signature* _____

Address _____

Name _____   *Signature* _____

Address _____

Name _____   *Signature* _____

Address _____

FOR USE BY NOTARY AND CLERK OF THE COURT, DEPUTY. The State of Texas and County of Travis:

Before me, the undersigned authority, on this day personally appeared: _____
known to me to be the person(s) whose name(s) is/are subscribed to the foregoing instrument and acknowledged to me that he/she/they signed the same purpose and consideration therein expressed. Given under my hand and seal of office, on _____

_____
Signature of Notary Public in and for the State of Texas or Clerk of the Court, Deputy

Seal of the Notary Public or Clerk of the Court, Deputy

INFORMATION WHERE DOCUMENT SHOULD BE RETURNED
(to be completed by applicant):
In the spaces below, clearly print the name, address, city, state, and zip code where this document should be returned

_____
_____
_____

Form of identification presented: _____

actual owner of a given business, if a lawsuit must be filed against the sole proprietor. Most jurisdictions provide a standard form, which is generally quite simple to complete, and filing fees are minimal.

Tax-Related Obligations

If the sole proprietorship will be making sales, arrangements must be made to pay sales tax to the appropriate authority. The business should contact the relevant state's taxing agency to obtain a sales tax permit. A sole proprietor who hires employees also must apply for an employer identification number to make arrangements to withhold federal income tax. Application for the number is made by obtaining Form SS-4 with the IRS. There often are similar requirements associated with state tax obligations.

Licensing Obligations

In addition to tax-related requirements, many businesses also have licensing requirements under state consumer protection statutes and public health and safety laws. For example, individuals who wish to provide real estate brokerage services, insurance agent services, barber or cosmetology services, etc., may need to comply with licensing requirements applicable to those professions as a matter of state law. To determine whether a business is one that requires a license, you should review your state's business entity, consumer protection, and public health and safety statutes and your state's administrative code (which generally will include all information relating to any testing for the license or other prerequisites that must be met). For example, the New York Department of State Division of Licensing Services website provides licensing requirements for 32 different occupations and businesses. California likewise provides its professional licensing requirements on the California Department of Business Oversight website.

In addition to profession-based licensing requirements, some jurisdictions also require businesses to obtain a basic license simply to do business. For example, New York City requires most businesses to file an application to conduct business within the city, whether the business operates as a sole proprietorship, a partnership, a corporation, etc.

D. GENERAL PARTNERSHIPS

1. What Is a General Partnership?

A **general partnership** is an association of two or more persons to carry as co-owners a business for profit. (This somewhat awkward phrasing is taken from uniform partnership statutes.) General partnerships are the default form of organization for multi-owner businesses — meaning, a partnership will be formed whenever two or more persons (i) associate together to carry on their business as co-owners; and

(ii) do not file the paperwork necessary to create a corporation, limited liability company, or other business entity with the secretary of state. As discussed in detail in Chapter 3, business associates may form a partnership via an express oral or written partnership agreement or they may form a partnership through the act of associating as co-owners of a for-profit business. Partnerships formed through conduct (rather than an express oral or written agreement to form a partnership) are known as **inadvertent partnerships**, and business associates may form an inadvertent partnership even if they do not appreciate or intend the legal consequences of their actions under partnership law.

As discussed below, because general partnerships do not offer a liability shield, this form of organization tends not to be attractive to lawyers and business people engaged in entity selection and business planning. Even so, partnership law remains important because there continue to be many inadvertent partnerships, and because newer forms of organization (e.g., the limited liability company) draw upon partnership law principles while also providing a liability shield. Consequently, we introduce general partnerships here, and study this form of organization in detail in Chapter 3.

2. Governing Law

Under default rules, general partnerships are usually governed by the partnership law of the state in which the partnership was formed or the state in which the partnership has its principal office. As discussed in Chapter 3, with the exception of Louisiana, state partnership law is based on one of two versions of the Uniform Partnership Act adopted by the Uniform Law Commission (ULC). The ULC is a non-partisan body of lawyers that researches, drafts, and promotes the enactment of uniform state laws.

Under state partnership statutes, the partnership agreement plays a key role in partnership governance. This is because state partnership statutes contain default rules that function as a safety net, applying when (i) the partnership agreement is silent; (ii) the partners fail to agree on a modification of default rules; or (iii) the matter at issue involves a limited list of non-waivable or non-modifiable statutory rules. Apart from these limited circumstances, partners have considerable freedom to tailor default rules to meet business needs, and as between the partnership agreement and statutory default rules, the partnership agreement generally governs.

3. Management

A key feature of general partnerships is that each partner has an equal right to participate in management under default rules. Partners participate in management by voting, and under default rules, partners generally vote on a **per capita** basis (meaning one partner, one vote). In most states, when partners disagree as to ordinary course matters, majority rule usually governs. Non-ordinary course matters generally require unanimous consent. That said, partnership statutes tend to allow partners to customize many voting and governance rules to meet business needs. As discussed in Chapter

3, common approaches to customization include (i) using pro rata rather than per capita voting so that voting power is tied to ownership interest; and (ii) appointing a managing partner or management committee to make certain decisions.

4. Taxation

As a default matter, partnerships are taxed under Subchapter K of the Internal Revenue Code (IRC). Under Subchapter K, the partnership itself is not a separate tax-paying entity for purposes of federal income tax liability, thus the partnership is not required to pay federal income tax at the entity level. Instead, the partnership allocates any profits or losses to individual partners according to the terms of the partnership agreement (or, according to default statutory rules if the partnership agreement is silent). Each partner reports his share of profits or losses on his individual tax return — usually by attaching Schedule E (Form 1040) to his federal income tax return. This sort of taxation is referred to as **pass-through taxation**, because the partnership's profits or losses are allocated, and passed through, to individual partners and recorded on the partners' individual tax returns. To facilitate partners' tax filings, the partnership should prepare an informational return (Schedule K-1 Form 1065) that specifies the partnership's income, deductions, and each partner's allocation of profits or losses. While partnerships may opt out of Subchapter K taxation and elect to be taxed as a corporation (discussed below), this is not typical.

> **Pass-Through Taxation**
>
> Pass-through taxation refers to the tax treatment in which profits and losses of the business are allocated, and "passed through" to the owners of the business. Profits and losses are reflected on the owners' returns, and the owner (not the business) pays federal income tax according to the owner's applicable rate or "bracket."

5. Characteristics: Advantages and Disadvantages

Ease of Formation and Power of Control

Like sole proprietorships, general partnerships have the advantage of being easy and generally inexpensive (focusing on administrative expenses) to form and operate. Also, like sole proprietorships, general partnerships offer partners the power of ultimate control over partnership business and partnership affairs.

Unlimited Personal Liability

As with sole proprietorships, however, partners in a general partnership suffer the disadvantage of unlimited personal liability for partnership debts, making the general partnership form less attractive than newer forms of organization (e.g., limited liability companies) which offer many of the legal attributes of partnerships but also a liability shield. The lack of a liability shield means, for example, that if a partnership fails to pay a vendor invoice, the vendor may be able to sue any or all of the partners to collect on its debt. Likewise, if one partner or a partnership employee commits a tort, the tort victim may be able to sue and recover from any or all of the partners until the debt is satisfied. While creditors generally must exhaust partnership resources first, before seeking redress from individual partners, this so-called **exhaustion doctrine** offers little protection to individual partners when a partnership fails, leaving behind unpaid debts and insufficient tangible assets. While the same property protection statutes, insurance opportunities, and negotiated protections available to sole proprietors also may be available to partners in a general partnership, the same risks, limitations, and expenses associated with these tools are present, too. For all of these reasons, lawyers and business people engaged in business planning and entity selection tend not to choose the general partnership form when advising clients.

Lack of Continuity

As with sole proprietorships, lack of continuity is another disadvantage of the general partnership form. A partnership is a voluntary association, and partners can elect to leave a partnership at any time for any reason. Depending on state law, a partner's departure can cause the partnership to dissolve as a legal matter, and the remaining partners may be required to wind up and shut down the business. Even if the partnership is able to continue as a legal matter, the departure of one or more partners may have an impact on the partnership's reputation, operations, or business prospects, making it difficult for the partnership to thrive going forward, or reducing the value of the partnership's business as a going concern.

Potential Difficulties in Raising Capital

Like sole proprietorships, the general partnership form also may make it difficult to raise capital. Although partnerships may have the legal and contractual right to call upon the partners to contribute additional capital, partners may — or may not — have additional resources to contribute to the business when needed. Moreover, depending on relations between partners, the partnership agreement, and the state of the partnership's business, a partnership may find it difficult to attract and admit new partners as a means of raising additional capital. As with sole proprietorships, some lenders may be unwilling to lend to partnerships due to concerns about the legal or economic fragility of partnerships, dependence on individual partners, and the like. Note, however, that some lenders may prefer lending to a partnership because of partners' unlimited personal liability for partnership debts. *See, e.g., Cheesecake Factory, Inc. v. Baines*, 964 P.2d 183 (N.M. Ct. App. 1998) (holding individual liable as partner by estoppel based on evidence that (i) individual consented to another's representation that he was partner; and (ii) seller reasonably relied on representation in extending credit).

Dependence on Owners

Like sole proprietorships, partnerships are uniquely dependent upon the skills and talents of individual partners. If a key partner dies or elects to leave the business, the partnership may find it difficult to hold onto customers, employees, etc. (This can happen even if partners are able to continue the partnership business as a legal matter and do not have to wind up and terminate the partnership's business and affairs.) In addition, rules relating to the admission of new partners and restrictions on the transfer of partnership status and partnership governance rights may make it difficult or even impossible to bring new partners into an existing business or to sell the business of a partnership as a going concern.

Management Difficulties

While partners enjoy the right of ultimate control over partnership affairs, governance rules can be a challenge if partners disagree. Both majority and unanimous voting requirements can lead to disagreements and even deadlock among partners, especially when partners have not customized default voting rules to mitigate such risks.

E. LIMITED LIABILITY PARTNERSHIPS

1. What Is a Limited Liability Partnership?

A **limited liability partnership** (LLP) is a for-profit business with two or more owners that has filed a "statement of qualification" with the relevant state's secretary of state office. States created the LLP form by adding LLP provisions to state general partnership statutes. This means that LLPs are general partnerships (for purposes of management, taxation, etc.) that have elected LLP status under state law. As discussed below, the key difference between general partnerships and limited liability partnerships relates to liability: Unlike partners in a general partnership, partners in an LLP do not suffer the disadvantage of unlimited personal liability for all partnership debts. We discuss LLPs in detail in Chapter 4.

2. Governing Law

LLPs generally are governed by law of the state in which the LLP organized — that is, the state in which the LLP files its statement of qualification. As with general partnerships, state partnership statutes contain default rules that apply to LLPs when (i) the partnership agreement is silent; (ii) the partners fail to agree on a modification to a default rule; or (iii) the issue involves a limited list of non-waivable, non-modifiable rules. Apart from these circumstances, as between the partnership agreement and the default rules, the partnership agreement governs.

3. Management

Because LLPs are a type of general partnership, the management rules applicable to general partnerships apply with equal force to LLPs. This means that LLPs are governed by default management rules set forth in the relevant state's partnership statute, unless the partners customize these rules in their partnership agreement.

4. Taxation

Limited liability partnerships are taxed in the same manner as general partnerships.

5. Characteristics: Advantages and Disadvantages

Liability Shield

As noted above, LLPs are distinguished from general partnerships by the liability shield available to owners. Many states originally provided only a limited liability shield to partners in a limited liability partnership. Under limited shields, LLP partners were not liable for partnership debts arising from the negligence or misconduct of a fellow partner (i.e., debts associated with tort liability arising from the acts of co-partners) but remained liable for other partnership obligations, including contractual obligations.

Over time, the rules have changed. Today, all but two states (Louisiana and South Carolina) have amended the LLP language in their state partnership statutes to provide LLP partners with a full liability shield. Partners in LLP full shield states are not liable for partnership debts, whether arising in tort or contract, based solely on partner status. Partners do, however, remain liable for their own negligence, wrongful acts, and misconduct. The LLP liability shield makes the LLP form well suited to legal, medical, and accounting practices in many jurisdictions. This is because partners in one office of an LLP will not be held liable for acts of other partners or other offices, simply because of the co-partner relationship.

Note that there are potential nuances to the LLP form and the LLP liability shield in both full shield and partial shield states. For example, three states — California, New York, and Oregon — limit the LLP form to certain professional practices, such as law and medicine. Although a non-professional practice operating in one of these states may choose to organize as an LLP in another state that does not have a professional practice restriction, the state with the restriction may treat the LLP as a general partnership for liability purposes, meaning the partners may not enjoy the protection of a liability shield. In addition, it is unclear whether an LLP that operates in a partial shield state but forms in a full shield state will get the benefit of the full shield, and thus protection against personal liability for both contract and tort debts. More generally, because states may have forms of organization available only to professional practice businesses, be sure to check relevant state codes before recommending a form of organization to professional services clients.

F. LIMITED PARTNERSHIPS

1. What Is a Limited Partnership?

A **limited partnership (LP)** is a partnership with one or more general partners, and one or more limited partners, that has filed a certificate of limited partnership with the relevant secretary of state office. In a limited partnership, the **general partner** has the same rights and obligations as a partner in a general partnership, meaning the general partner has the right to manage and control partnership affairs but suffers the disadvantage of unlimited personal liability for partnership debts. **Limited partners**, on the other hand, have no management rights but have the benefit of a liability shield, meaning that limited partners may not be held liable for the debts of the partnership based solely on their limited partner status. In effect, the LP form allows limited partners (typically, individuals with money, but not time, expertise, or an interest in managing day-to-day partnership affairs) to act as passive investors in a business without putting personal assets at risk, while entrusting management to a skilled general partner. We discuss LPs in detail in Chapter 5.

2. Governing Law

Limited partnerships generally are governed by the limited partnership statute of the state in which the partnership is organized. Each state (with the exception of Louisiana) has its own limited partnership statute based on some version of the Uniform Limited Partnership Act (ULPA). As with general partnership statutes, limited partner statutes are composed largely of default rules, giving partners flexibility to customize their relationship via a partnership agreement to meet business needs.

3. Management

The key distinguishing feature of the limited partnership form is the distinction between the general and limited partners. As noted, the general partner in a limited partnership has the right to exercise control over partnership affairs. Limited partners typically are passive investors with no right to control partnership business.

4. Taxation

The Internal Revenue Code treats limited partnerships and general partnerships in the same fashion — meaning that Subchapter K, with its pass-through taxation rules, is the default tax treatment.

5. Characteristics: Advantages and Disadvantages

Cost

As there are more statutory requirements associated with limited partnerships compared to general partnerships, LPs tend to be more expensive to form and operate (focusing on administrative expenses) compared to their general partnership "cousins." LP partnership agreements and LP taxation also tend to be more complex, and thus more expensive, compared to those for general partnerships.

Limited Liability for Limited Partners, Unlimited Liability for General Partners

As discussed above and in Chapter 5, general partners face unlimited personal liability for partnership debts, while limited partners enjoy a liability shield. Limited partners are, however, responsible for their own negligence or intentional torts, and they can lose their liability shield in some (but not all) jurisdictions if they participate in the control of the limited partnership or become too involved in day-to-day decision making. To address the general partners' risk of unlimited personal liability, lawyers have long recommended forming an entity to serve as general partner — say, a limited liability company or corporation — so that the individual decision makers behind the general partner can enjoy the benefit of a liability shield.

Dependence on General Partner

Although the general partner's power of control eliminates many intra-partner disputes, dependence on the general partner is a potential issue for limited partnerships. Lenders may be unwilling to lend due to concerns about dependence on the general partner. In addition, if the general partner becomes unwilling or unable to serve, limited partners may seek to withdraw funds, and the business may have difficulty retaining capital or attracting new capital.

G. CORPORATIONS

1. What Is a Corporation?

A corporation is a business that has filed **articles of incorporation** (also known as a **certification of incorporation** or **corporate charter**) with a state's secretary of state office. Compared to partnerships and limited liability companies, corporations are characterized by a higher number of mandatory statutory rules. Corporations also are characterized by their **centralized management structure**. Centralized management means that the authority to manage a corporation is vested in its **board of directors**. The directors, in turn, are charged with acting in the best interest of the corporation and its shareholders when carrying out board duties. Indeed, board members owe the corporation and its shareholders **fiduciary duties of care and loyalty**. (We introduce fiduciary duty concepts in Chapter 2 and discuss fiduciary concepts at length throughout this book.) The corporation's owners, called **shareholders** or **stockholders**, do not (in their role as shareholders) have managerial authority over corporate affairs, nor are they authorized (as shareholders) to act on behalf of the corporation or to participate in day-to-day decision making. We discuss corporations in detail in Chapters 6-11 and 13.

2. Governing Law

The formation and internal affairs of a corporation are governed principally by the law of the state in which it is **incorporated** — that is, the state in which the corporation files its charter. Each state has its own corporations code. As discussed in Chapter 6, thirty-two states model their corporate statutes on some form of the Model Business Corporations Act (MBCA): Alabama, Alaska, Arizona, Arkansas, Connecticut, Florida, Georgia, Hawaii, Idaho, Indiana, Iowa, Kentucky, Maine, Massachusetts, Mississippi, Montana, Nebraska, New Hampshire, New Mexico, North Carolina, Oregon, Rhode Island, South Carolina, South Dakota, Tennessee, Utah, Vermont, Virginia, Washington, West Virginia, Wisconsin, and Wyoming. The remaining 17 states (including California, Delaware, Texas, and New York) have developed their own statutes, with many including some (but not all) aspects of the MBCA.

What Is the MBCA?

The MBCA was released in 1950 by what is now the Business Law Section of the American Bar Association. The Business Law Section puts out new versions of the MBCA from time to time and promulgated an extensive revision in 1984. The latest major edition (incorporating prior amendments) dates to 2007.

3. Management

Under state corporation statutes, the **board of directors** has ultimate authority over the business affairs of the corporation. The corporation's owners — that is, its stockholders or shareholders — "weigh in" on corporate affairs by electing directors, and by voting on a limited number of "big ticket" items such as certain amendments to the company's articles of incorporation or bylaws (key governance documents), certain important transactions (e.g., most mergers, sales of substantially all assets), and the like. Shareholders do not have statutory authority to manage the affairs of the corporation. As noted, this separation of ownership and control, together with the allocation of managerial power to the board, is referred to as centralized management because authority is concentrated, or centralized, in the hands of the board rather than decentralized among the owners of the business.

In large corporations, the board of directors typically does not "get into the weeds" on day-to-day decision making. Instead, the board appoints officers to run the business day to day, subject to board oversight. In corporations with relatively few shareholders (so-called close or closely held corporations), a single individual may wear multiple "hats"—serving as director, officer, and shareholder at the same time. Recognizing that the centralized management approach of corporate law may not apply in exactly the same fashion to both large, publicly held corporations and smaller, closely held corporations, some state corporations statutes include management rules and related provisions that apply only to closely held corporations. For example, a number of states allow corporations with fewer than a specified number of shareholders to be managed by their owners rather than under the direction of a board of directors. We discuss closely held corporations in more detail in Chapter 10.

4. Taxation

Under the Internal Revenue Code, corporations are taxed according to **Subchapter C** under default rules, unless the corporation is eligible for and elects to be taxed under Subchapter S. A corporation that is taxed under Subchapter C is commonly referred to as a C-Corporation (or C-Corp) for taxation purposes, whereas a corporation that elects **Subchapter S** taxation is commonly referred to as an S-Corporation (or S-Corp). Note that the C and S designations have to do with tax law and regulations. These designations generally are not significant as a matter of state corporations law.

How does C-Corp taxation work? In contrast to the pass-through regimes that we have studied thus far, C-Corporations are treated as separate tax-paying entities under the IRC. This means that C-Corporations must file a federal income tax return (usually on Form 1120) reporting income, deductions, and credits for the relevant year, and they must pay any taxes due on income at corporate income tax rates. If a C-Corporation distributes money or property to its shareholders (e.g., pays **dividends**, or makes a distribution of earnings to shareholders), shareholders must include the distribution in their income and must pay tax on any such distribution. As this suggests, a C-Corporation's profits thus are taxed twice—once at the level of the corporation, when earned, and again at the shareholder level, when distributed. This taxation structure is commonly referred to as **double taxation**.

Subchapter S taxation is different. As with a partnership taxed under Subchapter K, an S-Corporation is not required to pay income taxes at the entity level under applicable federal tax law. Instead, S-Corporations pass profits and losses through to shareholders based on their ownership interests: Shareholders report these profits and losses on their individual returns and pay any resulting tax liability according to their individual tax situations. The IRS does require S-Corps to file informational returns (Form 1120S) reflecting the corporation's income and deductions and each shareholder's allocation of profits or losses.

It is important to understand that an entity that wishes to elect Sub-S tax treatment may do so only if it meets the following requirements:

- It is a domestic entity, meaning that it is organized or incorporated in one of the 50 states or the District of Columbia;
- It has fewer than 100 owners;

■ All of its owners are individuals, estates, certain types of trusts, or tax-exempt organizations;

■ None of its owners is a non-resident alien;

■ It has only one class of ownership interests outstanding; and

■ The entity is not publicly traded.

See IRC § 1361.

Under pertinent Treasury Regulations, an entity is considered to have only one class of stock if "all outstanding shares of stock of the corporation confer identical rights to distribution or liquidation proceeds." *See* Treas. Reg. § 1.361-1(l)(1). An entity must satisfy these requirements at all times to retain S-Corp taxation eligibility. This makes Sub-S taxation fragile, because Sub-S status may inadvertently be lost if the business becomes ineligible under even one of the criteria listed above. For example, if a corporation acquires even one non-resident alien owner, it is no longer eligible for Sub-S tax treatment, and its tax classification will revert to the relevant default treatment — here, Subchapter-C .

5. Characteristics: Advantages and Disadvantages

Liability

Unlike sole proprietorships and general partnerships, corporations offer business owners the benefit of a liability shield, meaning that shareholders are not personally liable for the debts or obligations of the corporation by virtue of their status as shareholders. Thus, even if a corporation's business fails and it becomes unable to pay its debts, and the shareholder's ownership interest (**stock or shares**) become worthless, creditors still may not reach shareholders' personal assets to satisfy corporate debts under default liability rules. Directors and officers are not liable for corporate debts based solely on director or officer status, either. As discussed in Chapter 9, directors and officers may, however, be held individually liable if they breach fiduciary duties of care or loyalty or violate other substantive laws.

Continuity of Existence

For the most part, corporations have a perpetual life, which means that once a corporation is properly formed, and assuming all required fees or taxes are paid, a corporation will continue in existence unless and until dissolved in compliance with the relevant state's corporations code. Corporations thus tend to be more legally "durable" than sole proprietorships and general partnerships.

Transferability

In addition to their perpetual life, rules regarding the transfer of ownership interests make the corporate form more durable and flexible compared to sole proprietorships and partnerships. Unlike partners, corporate stockholders generally can transfer their ownership stake (and shareholder status and governance rights) to third parties, subject to restraints on alienation arising under the federal securities laws or shareholder agreements. Shares of large, economically healthy, publicly traded companies tend to be both liquid and easily transferrable, allowing public company stockholders to sell their shares without undue delay or expense. The market for shares in smaller, closely held companies tends to be less liquid, due to transfer restrictions, questions about valuation, and the corresponding lack of a robust market with ready buyers. Even so, the transferability of corporate stock (and all of the rights associated with stock ownership) contrasts sharply with the restrictions on the transferability of the bundle of rights composing a partnership interest.

Raising Capital

The corporate form is well suited to raising capital. Corporations that wish to raise funds may have several options, including issuing additional debt or equity securities, or both, to existing or new bondholders or shareholders, respectively. While there are rules relating to securities offerings under state and federal securities laws, and potentially restraints on alienation set forth in shareholder agreements and other documents, the management structure, continuity of life, comparatively easier ownership transfer rules, and liability shield available through the corporate form make corporations an attractive form or organization from a capital-raising perspective.

Management

Unlike sole proprietorships and partnerships, corporations are not dependent — at least as a structural matter — on the expertise and efforts of a single owner or owners or a single manager. Instead, the corporate form provides that the affairs of the corporation will be managed by the board of directors, which in turn may delegate responsibility for day-to-day decision making to a skilled executive and management team. Of course, the separation between ownership and control is more pronounced in large corporations compared to smaller, closely held corporations. Even so, the corporate form tends to be less dependent upon the skills, talents, and efforts of a single person or small group, as both a legal and practical matter, compared to unincorporated entities.

Complexity and Cost

Most of the disadvantages of the corporate form have to do with complexity, and its close relation, cost. Because of the separation of ownership and control in corporate governance, shareholders incur costs associated with monitoring and overseeing the corporation's officers and directors. In addition, publicly held corporations are subject to a robust (and potentially very expensive) registration and reporting regime under the federal securities laws. More generally, accounting, legal, and tax issues may be more complex, and thus more expensive, for corporations compared to unincorporated entities. Finally, the double taxation rule applicable to C-Corps may be more expensive for certain businesses and shareholders, compared to the pass-through regime available to partnerships and limited liability companies.

H. LIMITED LIABILITY COMPANIES

1. What Is a Limited Liability Company?

A **limited liability company** is a business that has filed "**articles of organization**" (or a similarly named document) with the secretary of state office. The owners of an LLC typically are called "members" under state law. The LLC is a relatively new form of organization that combines attractive features of a partnership (e.g., opportunities to customize default management rules) with those of a corporation (e.g., limited liability for owners, perpetual existence). Currently, most new businesses in the United States that choose to operate via a legal entity (and not as a sole proprietorship or general partnership) choose the LLC form. LLCs are discussed in detail in Chapter 12.

2. Governing Law

A limited liability company typically is governed by the law of the state in which the LLC is formed. As discussed in Chapter 12, although the Uniform Law Commission released a Uniform Liability Company Act (ULLCA) in 1995 and a revised version in 2006, neither version has been widely adopted — at least as a verbatim matter. Consequently, you should be sure to investigate the LLC statute in jurisdictions in which you practice to confirm governing rules. As with partnership statutes, LLC statutes consist of default management rules, many of which can be customized to meet business needs via a carefully drafted **operating agreement** (also known as a **limited liability company agreement**).

3. Management

As with partnerships, LLC management is governed in the first instance by the LLC operating agreement, with state LLC statutes providing default rules to fill in gaps in the operating agreement in much the same way that partnership statutes fill in gaps in partnership agreements. With respect to default rules, most state LLC statutes provide that an LLC will be member-managed (meaning managed by the members of the LLC) unless its articles of organization provide that the LLC will be manager-managed. Member management is similar to partner management in a general partnership in that members in a member-managed LLC generally have equal rights to participate in the management of partnership affairs. As with partners in a partnership, members in an LLC participate in management by voting. Voting in LLCs may be either pro rata or per capita as a default matter, as state laws vary.

4. Taxation

The Internal Revenue Service treats LLCs with more than one member as general partnerships for federal tax purposes under default rules, unless the LLC affirmatively elects (by filing a specific tax form) to be taxed as a corporation. This means that pass-through taxation is the default tax treatment for multi-member LLCs. Single-member LLCs are treated as **disregarded entities** for federal tax purposes unless the LLC affirmatively elects to be treated as a corporation for tax purposes. This means that under default rules, a single-member LLC will be disregarded as an entity separate from its owner for federal income tax purposes. As with sole proprietorships, the tax consequences of a single-member LLC thus should be reflected on the sole member/owner's tax filings under default rules.

5. Characteristics: Advantages and Disadvantages

As a hybrid form of organization, LLCs combine aspects of both the partnership and corporate forms. For example, as with partnerships, LLC statutes give member/owners freedom to customize many default rules to meet business needs. At the same time, drawing upon corporate law, the LLC form provides a liability shield for owners. Opportunities for customization mean that LLC costs may vary widely, depending on the degree of complexity of the parties' operating agreement. The more complex and customized the agreement, the more expensive the LLC will be to form and potentially to operate.

I. OTHER FORMS OF ORGANIZATION

In addition to the forms of organization discussed above, you should be aware that there are other business structures that may be available to your clients.

1. Statutory Close Corporation

A **statutory close corporation** is a corporation that has elected to be governed by the state's close corporation statute. Typically, statutes permit eligible corporations to elect statutory close corporation status by including language in the charter to that effect — for example, language stating "this corporation is a statutory close corporation." Statutory close corporations statutes vary widely from state to state. Eligibility typically is tied to having no more than a specified number of shareholders. Close corporation statutes are more flexible than regular corporate statutes with respect to governance in that they generally permit stakeholders to adjust certain governance rules to address the needs of corporations with a small number of shareholders. Not all states have statutory close corporation statutes, and few eligible corporations historically have elected this status. We discuss statutory close corporations (and non-statutory close corporations) in more detail in Chapter 10.

2. Professional Corporations

A professional corporation, or PC, is a business incorporated under a state professional corporation statute. States enacted PC statutes to address the liability concerns of the owners of professional firms (e.g., medicine, law, accounting), as governing rules historically prohibited these types of businesses from incorporating under regular corporations law statutes. Typically, professional corporations must be organized to provide the professional services at issue, and all owners/ shareholders must be licensed to provide those services. Professional corporations have become less popular in recent years with the rise of LLPs and PLLCs (professional services limited liability companies).

3. Professional Limited Liability Company

A professional services limited liability company, or PLLC, is a business organized under a state PLLC statute. As with a PC, a PLLC can be organized only for the purpose of providing eligible professional services, and all member/owners must be licensed to provide that service.

4. Benefit Corporations

Benefit corporations are corporations incorporated in a state with a benefit corporation statute. Corporations that wish to elect benefit corporation status must do so in conformity with their state's benefit corporation statute. The idea behind benefit corporations is that they have as their purpose the creation of a "public benefit." According to model benefit corporation legislation, a general public benefit is a "material positive impact on society and the environment, taken as whole, assessed against a third-party standard, for the business and operations of a benefit corporation." Benefit corporation statutes generally require directors to consider not only the best interests of shareholders in making decisions, but also those of employees, customers, community and society, and the local and global environment. By way of example, outdoor gear and apparel manufacturer and retailer Patagonia Corp. was one of the first corporations to elect benefit corporation status. As of March 2015, 26 states and the District of Columbia have adopted benefit corporation statutes: Arizona, Arkansas, California, Colorado, Connecticut, Delaware, District of Columbia, Florida, Hawaii, Illinois, Louisiana, Maryland, Massachusetts, Minnesota, Nebraska, Nevada, New Hampshire, New Jersey, New York, Oregon, Pennsylvania, Rhode Island, South Carolina, Utah, Vermont, Virginia, and West Virginia. In 2012, Washington state created Social Purpose Corporations. An additional ten states have introduced legislation to adopt a benefit corporation statute: Alaska, Idaho, Indiana, Iowa, Kentucky, Montana, New Mexico, North Dakota, Oklahoma, and Tennessee.

5. Low-Profit Limited Liability Company

A low-profit limited liability company (or L3C for short) is an LLC whose primary purpose is to pursue a socially beneficial objective, not to earn a profit. In effect, L3Cs are the LLC analog to the benefit corporation discussed above. As of this writing, eight states have L3C statutes: Illinois, Louisiana, Maine, Michigan, Rhode Island, Utah, Vermont, and Wyoming.

6. Nonprofit Corporation

Nonprofits are corporations formed under state nonprofit corporation statutes. Nonprofits generally must be organized for public benefit, religious purposes, or the mutual benefit of relevant stakeholders. Nonprofits typically do not issue stock and are exempt from federal taxation. We list nonprofit corporations last in this section merely to reflect the fact that this text focuses on business organizations in the for-profit context. Rules governing the creation, operation, and taxation of nonprofits are worthy of their own course.

J. CONSIDERATIONS FOR ENTITY SELECTION

Determining which form of business enterprise is the most advantageous for a client involves careful consideration of a number of factors, including tax treatment and tax planning objectives, risks and liability exposure, and funding and financing plans. We discuss each of these factors in the following subsections.

1. Tax Treatment

For many businesses, federal tax treatment is one of the most important considerations influencing entity selection. Here, we focus on two tax issues with implications for entity selection — i.e., minimizing federal income tax liability and allocating profits and losses. Please be aware that there are other tax-related considerations that may be important to your clients, as well — for example, minimizing federal employment tax liability. Students who wish to practice business law are well advised to take upper-level business entity taxation classes, including corporate and partnership tax. Our coverage here is intentionally at a basic level.

Federal Income Tax Liability

The federal income tax liability of a business depends largely on how the business is classified for tax purposes. Tax classification, in turn, depends on (among other factors) the form in which the business is operated. As you know from our earlier discussion, possible classifications relevant here include (i) disregarded entity; (ii) partnership (Subchapter K); and (iii) association taxable as a corporation under either Subchapter C (Sub-C) or Subchapter S (Sub-S). While a business may be able to elect from among certain of these classifications, each form or organization has a default tax treatment, and certain tax classifications (e.g., Sub-S) have eligibility rules and requirements. The chart in Exhibit 1.5 summarizes federal income tax classification and possible tax classifications options for the forms of organization that we are studying here. The default option for each form of organization is the choice in bolded text. As noted previously, if an entity does not wish to use the default classification it must file a form with the Internal Revenue Service electing the desired tax classification.

EXHIBIT 1.5   **Business Entity and Tax Treatment**

Business Entity	Tax Classification
Single-member LLC	**Disregarded entity** Association taxable as a corporation
Multi-owner unincorporated entity	**Partnership (Sub-K)** Association taxable as a corporation
Corporation	**Association Taxable as a Corporation (Sub-C)** Sub-S (if eligible)

Allocating Profits and Losses

As noted earlier, both Sub-S and Sub-K taxation provide for pass-through taxation, meaning that the business calculates its profits and losses for the relevant tax year and then allocates those profits and losses to the owners of the business for reporting on the owners' federal tax returns. For a Sub-S entity, allocations are based on percentage ownership: meaning, if you own 20 percent of the entity, you will be allocated 20 percent of the profits (or losses, as applicable) each year. For Sub-K tax treatment entities, allocation can be based on something other than ownership stake. Allocations made on a basis other than ownership interest (or default rules) are commonly referred to as **special allocations**, and businesses that want to make special allocations must (i) be formed as an unincorporated entity; and (ii) stick with Sub-K taxation. This is because corporations are taxed under either the Sub-C or Sub-S regime, and neither the Sub-C nor the Sub-S regime permits special allocations.

In response to concerns about potentially abusive tax shelters and other tax-related concerns, the IRS has implemented rules targeting special allocations. (These rules are enormously complicated and beyond the scope of our study here. This is yet another reason why you should take corporate and partnership tax classes.) For purposes of this class, you should understand the following *grossly simplified* points: (i) a special allocation is valid for tax purposes only if it has "substantial economic effect" (*see* IRC § 704(b)); and (ii) an allocation has substantial economic effect if it creates an economic consequence to the owners (usually judged at liquidation), and not solely a tax consequence.

Even if special allocations have substantial economic effect, however, an individual may not be able to deduct losses allocated to her due to the **basis**,

at-risk, or **passive loss limitation**. The **basis limitation** limits the deduction a partner can take for partnership losses allocated to her in any particular year to the partner's adjusted basis in her partnership interest, before taking into account a partner's share of the loss. In general, a partner's initial basis equals the amount of money and the value of any property contributed to the partnership. A partner's basis will increase if, among other things, the partner makes additional capital contributions or if the partnership allocates income to the partner. A partner's basis will be reduced if, among other things, the partnership distributes money or property to the partner, or it will be reduced by any losses allocated to the partner. Adjusted basis refers to initial basis, plus any increases, minus any decreases.

For example, assume that you contributed $10,000 in initial capital to a partnership. During the first year, the business does not earn a profit, and thus makes no distributions, so there are no increases to capital. The partnership does, however, allocate $2,000 in losses to you. Your adjusted basis would be $8,000 ($10,000 – $2,000). In year two, the partnership again does not earn money, and an additional $6,000 in losses is allocated to you. You would be able to deduct the entire $6,000 (subject to the at-risk and passive loss limitations), resulting in an adjusted basis of $2,000. If, however, you are allocated $3,000 in losses in year three, you would only be able to deduct $2,000 (subject to any other applicable limitations), and your adjusted basis would drop to zero. IRS rules provide that your adjusted basis can never be less than zero, but further state that you may be able to carry forward your losses and deduct them in a future year in which your adjusted basis is greater than zero.

The **at-risk limitation** limits the deduction that a partner can take for losses allocated to her to the amount the partner has "at-risk." While the concept behind the basis and at-risk limitations is similar, the amount at risk can differ from the adjusted basis due to loan guarantees, nonrecourse loans, and other similar arrangements. As with the basis limitation, a partner can carry forward losses that are disallowed under the at-risk rules to future years when the partner has additional amounts at-risk.

The **passive activity loss limitation** allows taxpayers to deduct losses from "passive" activities only to the extent of the taxpayer's income from other passive activities for the year. Passive activities include (i) ownership of a business in which the taxpayer does not materially participate during the year; and (ii) rental activities, even if the taxpayer materially participates, unless the taxpayer is a real estate professional. Treasury regulations identify a number of different tests for what constitutes material participation. *See* Treas. Reg. § 1.469-5T9. As with the other deduction limitations that we have studied, a taxpayer may carry forward unused passive losses to deduct against future passive income.

It is important to understand that this is an area where you should consult with a tax expert! This material is complicated and ever-changing, and our very brief, simplified summary is intended only to alert you to the danger of proceeding without expert advice.

2. Risk and Liability Exposure

Liability Shields: Comparing Entities

Risk and liability exposure also should influence choice of entity. As discussed above, two forms — sole proprietorships and general partnerships — do not offer any liability shield for owners. For many lawyers and business people, the lack of a liability shield is a non-starter, especially since there are forms of organizations (e.g., LLPs, corporations, and LLCs) that offer many of the advantages of the sole proprietor and partnership forms, but also offer the protection of a liability shield.

Veil Piercing

Even when a form or organization has a liability shield for owners, there are exceptions and nuances that you should consider when advising clients as to both formation and operational issues. **Veil piercing** is one such exception. Veil piercing is an equitable, judicially created exception to limited liability under which a claimant asks the court to treat an entity and its owner(s) as one for purposes of liability. In **traditional veil piercing**, a tort or contract creditor of a business entity seeks to collect from the entity's owner(s) (in addition to collecting from the entity itself). *See, e.g., Sea-Land Servs., Inc. v. Pepper Source*, 993 F.2d 1309 (7th Cir. 1993) (holding contract creditor could pierce corporate veil to hold sole shareholder personally liable for unpaid bills where shareholder treated corporation and related entities as "playthings" and corporation's assets were not sufficient to satisfy the debt). Another traditional veil piercing fact pattern involves parent/subsidiary matters. *See, e.g., Fletcher v. Atex, Inc.*, 68 F.3d 1451 (2d Cir. 1995) (declining to hold a parent corporation liable for injuries allegedly caused by computer keyboards manufactured by a wholly owned subsidiary under veil piercing theory where plaintiffs could not establish that the parent dominated and controlled subsidiary to extent that it would be unjust and unfair to uphold separate corporate existence). In **reverse veil piercing cases**, a claimant owed a debt by an individual (typically, a controlling corporate shareholder) seeks to hold the corporation liable for the individual's debt. The related doctrine of **enterprise liability** speaks to situations where a creditor-plaintiff asks the court to disregard the separate legal existence of multiple corporations under common ownership to satisfy a liability owed by one entity. (For example, in the *Sea-Land Services* case referenced above, the creditor-plaintiff sought to reach the assets of sister corporations owned by the defendant shareholder in addition to the defendant shareholder's personal assets.)

There is no single test for veil piercing (or reverse veil piercing, for that matter) used across or even within jurisdictions. Instead, jurisdictions use different language and different names for veil piercing tests — for example, the **alter ego** test, the **instrumentality** test, and the **identity** test. Despite differences in nomenclature and phraseology, however, veil piercing tests tend to speak to two core issues: namely, (i) did the owners of the business dominate and control the business to a degree that the business no longer functioned as a legal entity separate and apart from its owners; and (ii) did the owners use their domination and control of the entity to commit a fraud or a wrong resulting in injury to the plaintiff such that it would be unjust or unfair to allow the defendant to hide behind the entity's liability shield.

While there is no single, definitive list of veil piercing factors, courts frequently consider the following when deciding whether to pierce the veil of limited liability:

- inadequate capitalization;
- failure to adhere to formalities or to recognize and maintain the separate legal status of the entity or entities whose liability shields are at risk;
- commingling of personal and business assets;
- use of entity funds for personal matters;
- nonobservance of corporate formalities;
- absence of business records;
- nonfunctioning of managers, officers, or directors;
- use of the business for transactions of the dominant owners; and
- use of the business to promote fraud or perpetuate a wrong.

Drilling down on capitalization, there is no single "magic" amount of capital that will justify—or prevent—veil piercing. Instead, courts consider the type of business at issue and risks associated with that type of business to determine whether the business was adequately capitalized upon formation. If owners make a good faith attempt to provide sufficient initial capital, mindful of business needs and liability risk, they may be able to overcome veil piercing arguments even if the business later falls upon hard times. Insurance may be helpful in this regard. If, however, the amount of initial capital appears "trifling compared to the business to be done and the risks of loss . . . ," *see Automotriz del Golfo de California S.A. de C.V. v. Resnick*, 306 P.2d 1, 4 (Cal. 1957) (internal citation omitted), a court may be more willing to disregard separate legal entity status and pierce the veil. As the reference to "initial" capital suggests, capitalization levels generally are judged as of formation: Owners are not required to contribute additional capital to an entity that has fallen on hard times merely to avoid veil piercing. *See Truckweld Equip. Co., Inc. v. Olson*, 618 P.2d 1017 (Wash. Ct. App.) (1980).

Drilling down on the question of formalities, while more may be required of larger, more sophisticated entities, even smaller businesses should be sure to keep accurate and complete records relating to the finances and operations of the business to avoid becoming vulnerable to veil piercing arguments.

Finally, as to the requirement that the defendant misuse the corporate form to commit a fraud or wrong, be aware that there is a strong equitable component to veil piercing. Courts generally will permit veil piercing only when it appears that it would be unjust or unfair to the plaintiff to do otherwise.

Case Preview

Midland Interiors, Inc. v. Burleigh

In the following case, a trade creditor (Midland Interiors, Inc., a carpet installer) sought to recover from the sole owner and stockholder of Window Treatment & Carpet, Inc. (a corporation formed to sell and install carpets and window treatments). Window Treatment had hired Midland to install carpet on a number of jobs but then failed to pay for the work. After Window Treatment collapsed, leaving unpaid debts, Midland asked the court to pierce the corporate veil and hold Window Treatment's sole stockholder-employee individually liable for Window Treatment's debt. When reading the case, consider the following questions:

1. What test does the court use in deciding whether to pierce the corporate veil?
2. What factors does the court consider in deciding whether veil piercing is warranted?
3. Do you think it is easy for plaintiffs to obtain veil piercing?

Midland Interiors, Inc. v. Burleigh
CIV.A. 18544, 2006 WL 3783476 (Del. Ch. Dec. 19, 2006)

PARSONS, Vice Chancellor.*

At issue in this case is whether a judgment creditor can "pierce the corporate veil" of the judgment debtor corporation to reach the assets of the sole stockholder-employee of the debtor. Plaintiff, Midland Interiors, Inc. ("Midland"), contracted with Defendant Window Treatment & Carpet, Inc. ("Window Treatment") to install carpet for Window Treatment's clients. Window Treatment failed to pay Midland for many of the carpet installations. On December 9, 1997, Midland obtained a stipulated judgment against Window Treatment in the amount of $7,180.37 (the "December 9 Judgment"). Midland has not collected on this judgment, in part because Window Treatment has no assets. Therefore, Midland seeks equitable relief in the form of piercing the corporate veil of Window Treatment so as to enforce the December 9 Judgment against its owner and sole stockholder, David Burleigh, personally. For the reasons set forth below, the Court will disregard the corporate status of Window Treatment and enter judgment against Burleigh and in favor of Midland.

I. FACTS AND PROCEDURAL HISTORY

A. The "Corporate Form" and History of Window Treatment

On February 25, 1994, Burleigh formed Window Treatment as a corporation under Delaware law to engage in the sale and installation of carpet and window treatments. To assist him in incorporating the company, Burleigh hired McBride, Shopa & Company ("Shopa"), an accounting firm.* Throughout Window Treatment's existence, Burleigh was the sole stockholder, director, president and employee. Burleigh never held any corporate meetings of Window Treatment or kept corporate minutes.

Financially, Window Treatment never owned any assets, although it did maintain a corporate checking account. Burleigh wrote all checks drawn on Window Treatment's account. Window Treatment did not carry workers' compensation for its subcontractors or maintain a general liability insurance policy. It never paid Burleigh a salary, in part because the company was losing money and unable to generate new

---

*For purposes of brevity, the footnotes have been omitted from this case.

business. In 1996, Window Treatment remained undercapitalized and its expenses exceeded its revenue to the point that it ceased to be a viable business.

On March 1, 1996, the Secretary of State proclaimed Window Treatment inoperative and void effective May 30, 1996 for failure to pay its annual franchise taxes. When Burleigh received actual or constructive notice of this voidance constituted the primary factual dispute at trial. In an August 2001 interrogatory response, prepared with assistance from his attorney, Burleigh answered that Window Treatment ceased doing business in or around June 1996. At trial, however, Burleigh testified that he continued to operate Window Treatment until he closed the corporate bank account in September 1996, and he could not remember why he would have told his attorney June. Burleigh therefore disavowed his interrogatory response as mistaken. He also testified that the Shopa firm would have processed any notices sent to the corporation.

Notwithstanding the failure of Window Treatment to generate any net income, Burleigh started a new company, Window Treatments Unlimited, Inc. ("Window Unlimited") in March 1997. Window Unlimited purportedly engaged in the same general business as Window Treatment, except that it also tinted windows. Burleigh served as its sole stockholder, director, president and employee. Like Window Treatment, Window Unlimited did not maintain an insurance policy or have any assets other than a corporate bank account. Ultimately, Window Unlimited proved no more successful than Window Treatment, and it, too, went out of business.

B. The Midland Contracts

During its existence, Window Treatment used subcontractors to fulfill its carpet installation orders. One of these subcontractors was Midland. Upon receiving a carpet order, Burleigh would contact Vito Delloso, Midland's president. Midland would then order the carpeting and perform the installation. After completing the work, Midland would bill Window Treatment, and Window Treatment would pay Midland with a company check. Window Treatment initially paid Midland without incident for the jobs Midland performed.

Shortly after the relationship began, however, Window Treatment became delinquent in its payments to Midland. In total, Midland presented uncontested evidence that Midland performed nine contracts in 1996 for which Window Treatment either did not pay or only partially paid (collectively, the "1996 Contracts"). Six of the nine contracts began on or after June 1, 1996, and the final contract between the two companies began on August 12, 1996. As of December 4, 1996, Midland calculated that Window Treatment owed $9,680.37 on the 1996 Contracts.

C. Midland Sues in Justice of the Peace Court

In May 1997, Midland filed suit against Window Treatment in Justice of the Peace Court 12 to recover the $9,680.37 Window Treatment owed on the 1996 Contracts. On June 9, 1997, Burleigh handwrote a letter to the court asking for a bill of particulars because he disputed the total amount of the debt. He signed this letter "Window Treatment & Carpet Inc."

On December 9, 1997, Burleigh appeared in court for a hearing on Midland's claim. Before the hearing began, Burleigh asked Delloso and his attorney to speak with him. Delloso recounted this conversation as follows:

> Mr. Burleigh approached Mr. Freibott and I and asked us to please step outside, he wanted to talk to us, and I had no problem with that. When we stepped outside, Mr. Burleigh said, "Listen, this is going to be very short because I'm going to tell the judge that *the company owes the money and we fully intend to pay for it,* and when we go in, I'm going to tell the judge that." I said, "I have no problem with that." We said okay. We went back inside, the judge came out, and . . . he called the hearing to order, and Mr. Burleigh stood up, and he said, "Your Honor, I'd like to make a comment," and he said, "Go right ahead," and he stated the same thing that he told Mr. Freibott and I outside. At that point, I'm not sure how the terminology was, but the judge had said, "Okay, fine, if you understand what you're saying and you want to say this, then I'll enter judgment for Midland Interiors," as I understood it, and that was the gist of the conversation.

Although Burleigh did not recall the specifics of this discussion during his trial testimony, he did state that he questioned the amount claimed and whether Delloso was mistaken in his figures. Before returning to the courtroom, the parties negotiated the amount Window Treatment owed to $7,180.37, which Delloso felt would satisfy the 1996 Contracts in full. During the hearing, Burleigh stated that he represented the corporation and recognized that the judgment was going to be entered against Window Treatment, but he did not advise the court or Midland that Window Treatment was void and no longer in operation or that it had no assets or income from which to pay the judgment. As a result of the proceeding, Midland obtained a stipulated judgment against Window Treatment for $7,180.37.

D. Midland Files This Action in the Court of Chancery

Midland transferred the December 9 Judgment to the Superior Court on October 26, 1999. On July 17, 2000, Midland deposed Burleigh to determine what assets, if any, were available to satisfy the judgment. Finding Window Treatment to be insolvent, Midland sued Window Treatment and Burleigh in this Court on December 12, 2000, seeking to pierce the corporate veil. Midland seeks to hold Burleigh personally liable for the December 9 Judgment and also requests a determination as to whether a fraudulent conveyance occurred when Burleigh formed Window Unlimited.

This Court held a trial on the merits of those claims on May 10, 2006. This is the Court's post-trial opinion.

II. ANALYSIS

Having considered the parties' positions, the Court is satisfied that Midland has established, both factually and legally, adequate grounds to disregard Window Treatment's separate corporate existence and hold Burleigh personally liable on the December 9 Judgment.

A. Legal Standard

At the outset, this Court realizes that persuading a Delaware court to pierce the corporate veil is a difficult task. Absent compelling cause, a court will not disregard the corporate form or otherwise disturb the legal attributes, such as limited liability, of a corporation. Although the legal test for doing so "cannot be reduced to a single formula that is neither over nor under-inclusive," our courts have only been persuaded to "pierce the corporate veil" after substantial consideration of the shareholder-owner's disregard of the separate corporate fiction and the degree of injustice impressed on the litigants by recognition of the corporate entity.

"Beyond according respect for the formalities some weight, however, the cases inevitably tend to evaluate the specific facts with a standard of 'fraud' or 'misuse' or some other general term of reproach in mind." As the Supreme Court stated in *Pauley Petroleum Inc. v. Continental Oil Co.*, "[Disregarding the corporate entity] may be done only in the interest of justice, when such matters as fraud, contravention of law or contract, [or] public wrong . . . are involved." Thus, the evaluation of corporate formalities must be performed in conjunction with consideration of any fraudulent action committed under the guise of the corporate form.

Implicitly, the legal status of the corporation also factors into the analysis. "[A] Delaware corporation is not dead for all purposes following forfeiture of its charter." Further, 8 Del. C. § 278 continues the existence of a voided corporation for three years for purposes of lawsuits. These provisions operate to provide a corporate creditor a remedy against the corporation and to protect individual corporate officers against personal liability if they contract on behalf of a voided corporation. Because Burleigh never reinstated Window Treatment's corporate status, these provisions have limited relevance to this case.

B. Factors Relevant to Whether Burleigh Used the Corporate Status of Window Treatment to Perpetrate a Fraud

The issue here is whether Burleigh's negotiation of the 1996 Contracts and his subsequent representations to Delloso and the Justice of the Peace Court amount to a fraud, contravention of contract, or public wrong sufficient to justify this Court setting aside the protections of incorporation and holding Burleigh personally liable. This Court concludes that the question must be answered in the affirmative due to the frauds committed by Burleigh in the name of the defunct Window Treatment.

1. Lack of Corporate Formalities

Corporations such as Window Treatment, like any other business incorporated in this State, are required to conform to the requirements of the law in order to invoke fully its protections. Although the failure to observe corporate formalities does not, by itself, warrant piercing the corporate veil, this Court notes Window Treatment's disregard of those formalities. On one hand, Burleigh maintained a separate corporate bank account and hired an accountant to assist him with the incorporation. On the other, Burleigh failed to adhere to other formalities traditionally associated with the corporate fiction, such as holding corporate meetings and keeping minutes of them. Further, Burleigh's operation of Window Treatment ensured that it never had any economic worth, insurance policy, or assets that could be attached by a judgment creditor.

Insolvency is another factor that may be relevant in veil piercing cases. In *Mason v. Network of Wilmington, Inc.*, this Court determined that insolvency, like respect for corporate formalities, is just part of the entire determination:

> Clearly, mere insolvency is not enough to allow piercing of the corporate veil. If creditors could enter judgments against shareholders every time that a corporation becomes unable to pay its debts as they become due, the limited liability characteristic of the corporate form would be meaningless. . . . [I]nsolvency is one factor to be considered in assessing whether the corporation engaged in conduct that unjustly shields its assets from its creditors. If so, and especially if particular shareholders benefited from and controlled that conduct, then justice would require the piercing of the corporate veil in order to hold the benefiting shareholders responsible.

While Window Treatment's disregard of many of the corporate formalities and its insolvency support Midland's position, Burleigh should not be deprived of the protections of incorporation merely by a balancing of what he did right and what he did wrong in these respects. Instead, the Court must consider Burleigh's substantial lack of adherence to corporate attributes in conjunction with the actions he took under the guise of his corporation in connection with the 1996 Contracts and the proceeding before the Justice of the Peace in December 1997.

2. Business Practices After Window Treatment Became Legally Void

On March 1, 1996, Window Treatment was proclaimed inoperative and void effective May 30, 1996, pursuant to 8 Del. C. § 510, for failing to pay its annual taxes as a Delaware corporation. Window Treatment, through Burleigh, however, continued to order carpet from Midland after this date. Specifically, from June 1, 1996 until August 12, 1996, Burleigh, on behalf of Window Treatment, negotiated six of the nine contracts comprising the 1996 Contracts. Midland argues that it entered into these contracts because Burleigh gave Midland the false and mistaken impression that Window Treatment could fulfill its end of the contracts without incident.

Having considered Burleigh's explanation of the circumstances regarding the 1996 Contracts, I find that Burleigh knew Window Treatment had become inoperable for failing to pay its taxes by the end of June 1996. In reaching this conclusion, I credit Burleigh's August 2001 interrogatory response on this very issue, which was prepared with help from his attorney five years after the fact. I do not believe his contrary trial testimony in 2006 that he was mistaken in 2001 and give that testimony no weight, particularly considering that he gave it ten years after the formation of the 1996 Contracts and presented no evidence that he ever previously controverted or corrected his earlier interrogatory response as mistaken. Because I find that Burleigh knew about the voided status of Window Treatment when he secured the last of the 1996 Contracts, I conclude that at least some of those contracts were fraudulently negotiated.

Burleigh's actions in the year immediately following the March 1996 declaration that Window Treatment would become void effective May 30, 1996 further corroborates the conclusion that it is more likely than not that Burleigh knew the corporation was void by the end of June 1996. For example, the closing of Window Treatment's bank account in September 1996 evidenced Burleigh's intent to accept the voiding of the company without trying to cure its tax delinquencies. Similarly, his formation of a new and different corporation in March 1997 to carry on essentially the same business as the voided corporation reflects little or no concern for his previous suppliers or the obligations he undertook to them in his capacity as the sole person behind Window Treatment.

3. The Misrepresentations Made in the Justice of the Peace Court

Burleigh's conduct in connection with the December 1997 hearing in the Justice of the Peace Court also favors piercing the corporate veil. Burleigh admitted having a conversation with Midland's president, Delloso, before the hearing. Burleigh testified that he did not recall the details of that conversation, but he did remember negotiating a reduction of the amount Midland claimed. Delloso had a more detailed recollection of the conversation, and I accept his description of what transpired. In particular, I find that Burleigh said to Delloso and his attorney, "I'm going to tell the judge that the company owes the money and we fully intend to pay for it."

Burleigh's statement cannot be reconciled with the fact that he knew the company had ceased to exist in June 1996, more than a year earlier, and that it had no assets. In making such a statement in the course of discussions with Midland, Burleigh intentionally misled Midland into believing Window Treatment would be able to satisfy the stipulated December 9 Judgment. There is no dispute that Window Treatment was legally void when Burleigh acquiesced to the entry of judgment against it, and Burleigh understood as much. Burleigh also failed to present any evidence to suggest that he had any reason to believe in December 1997 that Window Treatment could pay the judgment. Under these circumstances, permitting Burleigh to invoke the corporate form of Window Treatment to avoid any personal liability would compound the fraud.

4. The Degree of Injustice to Midland If the Corporate Status Is Upheld

The facts that Window Treatment ceased to be legally operative on May 30, 1996, that Burleigh knew this fact in June 1996, that he closed the corporate bank account in September 1996, and that Burleigh failed to disclose these facts in 1997 when he stipulated to the December 9 Judgment show that Burleigh intended to use Window Treatment's flawed corporate form to shield himself from personal liability to Midland in 1997 and, by inference, during the negotiation and performance of the 1996 Contracts as well. To uphold Burleigh's attempt to hide behind Window Treatment's corporate status in the face of his false representation to a judge and Midland in 1997 that Window Treatment fully intended to pay the amount due would encourage similar fraudulent behavior. The interests of justice, together with Burleigh's failure to adhere substantially to the corporate formalities, mandate piercing Window Treatment's corporate veil and imposing the December 9 Judgment against Burleigh personally.

III. CONCLUSION

For the foregoing reasons, the Court grants Midland's claim to pierce the corporate veil of Window Treatment. Judgment shall be entered for Midland and against defendant Burleigh, individually, in the amount of $7,180.37.

. . .

Post-Case Follow-Up

As *Midland Interiors* recognizes, veil piercing requires a fact-intensive analysis and the balancing of competing concerns. On one hand, the doctrine of veil piercing recognizes that business people form limited liability entities (as opposed to sole proprietorships and general partnerships) specifically to avoid personal liability for entity debts. The idea is that limited liability encourages business people to engage in productive risk taking — for example, starting new businesses — without having to fear that their personal assets are at risk at every turn. On the other hand, veil piercing doctrine recognizes that we do not want business owners to abuse the privilege of limited liability. That is why courts typically allow veil piercing only when the defendant misuses a business's separate legal entity status to commit a fraud or wrong, and only when it would be unjust or unfair to allow the defendant to hide behind that entity's liability shield.

Midland Interiors, Inc. v. Burleigh: Real Life Applications

Ollie Owner is the founder and sole owner of Sportswatch, Inc., an early-stage company that hopes to develop and sell multi-sport watches to triathletes, marathoners, and other endurance athletes. Initially, there was a great deal of enthusiasm for Sportwatch's product — an early version of the watch sold out quickly, and Ollie paid himself a handsome salary from the sale proceeds. Over time, however, users began to notice issues with the watch's performance. The watch's touchscreens began to fail, and users reported errors and inaccuracies with the watch's GPS mapping software. While Sportswatch tried to send replacement units, and continued working on its GPS software, it was unable to address the problems before running out of money. The company ceased operations last week, leaving many customers with unfulfilled orders or malfunctioning watches. The company's lawyers have discovered that as problems mounted, the company's record keeping fell by the wayside, leaving salaries unpaid, bills overdue, and litigation deadlines long past. The lawyers also discovered that Ollie was transferring assets between several different companies (including Sportswatch), all of which are subsidiaries of Ollie's holding company, Ollie's Endurance Sports, Inc.

a. A group of disgruntled customers who ordered watches but who did not receive them seeks to hold Ollie personally liable for Sportswatch's debts. Will the customers prevail? Why or why not? What additional facts (if any) would you want to know to assess the likelihood that a court would pierce the veil and hold Ollie personally liable for Sportwatch's debts?

b. Barry Biker claims that he was injured when the watch's touchscreen shattered and cut his arm. Can Barry hold Ollie personally liable for his injuries? Why or why not?

c. Are the assets of Ollie's parent company available to cover Sportwatch's debts? Why or why not? What about the assets of the other subsidiaries of Ollie's Endurance Sports, Inc.?

Veil Piercing and LLCs

Veil piercing initially appeared in the context of corporations. When LLC statutes first began to appear, many experts questioned whether legislatures and courts would permit veil piercing (or reverse veil piercing) in the LLC context, as well. States have taken a variety of approaches to this issue. Some states provide for veil piercing in their LLC statutes, often referencing the common law concerning veil piercing in the corporations context. *See, e.g.,* Colo. Rev. Stat. Ann. § 7-80-107(1) (West 2015); Minn. Stat. Ann. § 322B.303(2) (West 2015); Wis. Stat. Ann. § 183.0304 (2) (West 2015).

Other states permit veil piercing in the LLC context as a matter of common law. For example, in *Colonial Surety Co. v. Lakeview Advisors, LLC*, 941 N.Y.S.2d 371 (App. Div. 2012), the court allowed veil piercing where O'Brien (the manager and sole principal of the LLC) admitted that he dominated the LLC at issue. In addition, the evidence in the record demonstrated that O'Brien established the LLC after the judgment at issue was entered against him in order to shield his assets from petitioner, and after he fraudulently attempted to have the debt discharged in bankruptcy. The evidence also established that O'Brien used LLC funds to pay personal expenses, make payments to his wife in lieu of his salary, and contribute to his personal IRA account. O'Brien also used LLC checks to pay his personal bills. Based on these facts, the court concluded that inequitable consequences would result if O'Brien were permitted him to shield his assets from petitioner, his judgment creditor, by misusing the LLC in this manner. *Id.* at 374.

In jurisdictions where the legislature or courts have permitted veil piercing in the LLC context, courts tend to consider the same (or similar) factors (referenced above) in both corporation and LLC veil piercing cases. That said, the Uniform LLC Act, some courts, and some legislatures have suggested that the veil piercing analysis should be customized for LLCs, which often have fewer owners and a less formal governance structure compared to their corporate counterparts. *See, e.g., D.R. Horton Inc.-New Jersey v. Dynastar Dev., L.L.C.*, No. MER-L-1808-00, 2005 WL 1939778, at *30-36 (N.J. Super. Ct. Law Div. Aug. 10, 2005) (holding veil piercing factors from cases involving corporations should not be mechanically applied in cases involving LLCs). For example, the ULLCA and some state statutes affirmatively state that failure to comply with formalities is not, by itself, grounds for veil piercing in the LLC context. *See, e.g.,* ULLCA § 304(b) ("The failure of a limited liability company to observe any particular formalities relating to the exercise of its powers or management of its activities is not a ground for imposing liability on the members or managers for the debts, obligations, or other liabilities of the company."); Wyo. Stat. Ann. § 17-29-304(b) ("The failure of a limited liability company to observe any particular formalities relating to the exercise of its powers or management of its activities is not a ground for imposing liability on the members or managers for the debts, obligations or other liabilities of the company."). As statutes and case law vary from jurisdiction to jurisdiction, you should be sure to investigate applicable governing rules when advising clients.

Single-Member LLCs: Veil Piercing and Charging Orders

Although case law is sparse, be aware that single-member LLCs may present particular risks and concerns with respect to veil piercing. As a practical matter, owners of single-member LLCs may not observe the same degree of formality in the operation of their business compared to entities with more than one owner. (Think of it this way: Is the sole owner of an LLC likely to engage in the same degree of formality with respect to calling a meeting of owners compared to an LLC or corporation with many owners?) In a limited number of decisions, courts have allowed veil piercing with single-member LLCs on arguably thin facts, without much attention to the differences between single-owner and multi-owner LLCs. *See, e.g., Kosanovich v. 80 Worcester St. Assocs., LLC*, No. 201201 CV 001748, 2014 WL 2565959 (Mass. App. Div. May 28, 2014) (piercing veil based primarily upon LLC's failure properly to maintain business records); *Martin v. Freeman*, 272 P.3d 1182 (Colo. App. 2012) (allowing veil piercing without the sort of proof of fraudulent or wrongful conduct typically seen in veil piercing cases). Given the potentially greater risk of veil piercing with single-member LLCs, you should remind your single-member LLC clients to identify and comply with formalities relating financial records (e.g., separate bank accounts, financial books and records, etc.) and governance rules.

There also may be caveats to **charging order** protections for single-owner LLCs. A charging order is a court order directing an LLC to redirect distributions intended for a debtor-member to a creditor to satisfy a debt of the debtor-member, if and when the LLC makes a distribution. If the LLC does not make a distribution, the creditor gets nothing. In *In re Albright*, 291 B.R. 538 (Bankr. D. Colo. 2003), Ashley Albright, the sole member of Western Blue Sky, LLC, filed for Chapter 7 bankruptcy protection. The LLC owned real property in Colorado, and it was not a debtor in the bankruptcy proceeding. Albright's interest in the LLC was transferred to the Chapter 7 trustee as part of the bankruptcy proceeding, and as substituted member, the Trustee made arrangements to sell the property. Albright argued that the Trustee was entitled to a charging order against distributions only, and that the Trustee therefore should not have been permitted to act as substituted member in arranging for the liquidation of the property. The court rejected Albright's arguments, holding that charging order protection exists to protect non-debtor LLC members from having to share governance responsibilities with someone whom they did not choose, or from having to accept a debtor-member's creditor stepping in as member/manager. The court held that since Albright was the sole member of the LLC at issue, these considerations did not apply. *Id.* at 541.

3. Funding and Financing Plans

In addition to tax and liability concerns, funding and financing plans also impact choice of entity. Businesses need money to survive and grow. Sometimes, this money comes from the business's own coffers — for example, profits from operations. Sometimes, a business may obtain a loan from a bank or other lender. Businesses also may raise money by selling debt (e.g., bonds) or equity securities (e.g., corporate stock). We provide an introduction to corporate finance topics in Chapter 7. For present purposes, we want briefly to mention how funding and financing plans can influence choice of business form.

Spotlight: Start-Up Businesses

The term **start-up** is commonly used in the business world to refer to a new business venture. Start-up businesses — especially those that seek to develop and commercialize a new technology — may require thousands or even millions of dollars of **seed money** for research and development simply to get their product to market. For these companies, the needs and desires of potential investors will have a significant impact on choice of entity.

After exhausting "friends and family" funders, start-up businesses often seek funding from two main types of investors — **angel investors** and **venture capitalists**. Angel investors tend to be wealthy individuals who invest personal funds in early-stage start-ups. Angel investors often are serial entrepreneurs who enjoy providing seed capital and advice to the next generation of founders. Venture capital firms also provide funding to emerging growth companies, but VC firms tend to invest at a later stage in the lifecycle of a business compared to angel investors. Venture capital firms typically raise funds from institutional investors such as pension funds, insurance companies, endowments, etc., and deploy those funds by investing in a portfolio of emerging companies.

As a general rule, venture capitalists prefer to invest in C-Corps. There are several reasons for this. First, Sub-C classification allows the corporation to issue different classes of stock — and venture capitalists generally will insist upon preferred stock. Second, venture capitalists generally want to avoid potential complications associated with pass-through taxation, and may also wish to take advantage of favorable tax rules applicable to gains on the sale of C-Corp stock. Finally, the S-Corp tax treatment may be unavailable, anyway, because S-Corps cannot have certain entities as owners, and VC funds generally are organized as LLCs or LPs.

4. Spotlight: Ethics Issues

One final, important "spotlight" note about legal ethics. Helping clients form a new business is incredibly rewarding work! You have the opportunity to help your clients take an idea from their garage, dorm room, or basement and make it into a real business, generating wealth and creating jobs for founders and other members of your community. As lawyers, however, you must remain mindful of ethical rules when helping your clients achieve their business goals. For example, recognizing that founders may have different concerns, especially when it comes to issues like taxes, you should be on the lookout for potential conflicts of interest between founders or business owners at the formation and entity selection stage. Family businesses may present particular planning challenges, as relatives across generations may be involved in the formation and operation of the business. Remember that you should make sure to address issues relating to potential conflicts of interest (including those associated with joint representation, if applicable) in your engagement letter and in careful conversations with your clients. You should also be on the lookout for situations in which it is best for founders or business associates to consult with personal counsel. Be sure to consult your state's ethics rules to ensure compliance.

Chapter Summary

- There are several forms of organization commonly used for for-profit businesses, including (i) sole proprietorships; (ii) partnerships (and partnership variants); (iii) corporations; and (iv) limited liability companies.
- In deciding what form of organization to use, lawyers and business people typically consider (among other factors) management and control structures and rules, risks and liability rules, tax treatment, and funding and financing objectives.
- Generally speaking, business owners are well advised to use a form of organization that provides a liability shield — that is, a "shield" that protects owners from personal liability for the debts of the enterprise.
- Veil piercing is an equitable, judicially created exception to limited liability under which a claimant asks the court to treat an entity and its owner(s) as one for purposes of liability.

Applying the Concepts

1. Smith, a famous scientist and inventor, has obtained a patent for a new kind of electric battery for cars. Smith decides that he would like to manufacture and sell his batteries to car manufacturers. To get the business off the ground, Smith orders component parts from Supplier, Inc. via a written contract signed by "Smith on behalf of Smith Industries." Smith has not filed any paperwork with

the secretary of state respecting Smith Industries, though he did open a bank account to use for Smith Industries business. After the parts are delivered, but before they are paid for, Smith has a change of heart and decides that he no longer wants to launch the business. Is Smith personally liable to Supplier for the cost of the parts?

2. A corporation serves as the landlord for an apartment building in northern New York State. The corporation provides the usual landlord services: repairs, maintenance, collecting all rents due, etc. Although the corporation started out flush with funds, it has fallen on hard times because of the recent recession and the failure by some tenants to pay their rent when due.

   Martha is a model tenant who has always paid her rent on time. As a result of heavy snowfall this past winter, the ceiling of Martha's apartment, which is on the top floor of the building, has buckled. She has asked the corporate landlord several times to repair the roof, but because of the corporation's shaky financial situation and delays in the negotiations between the landlord and its insurance carrier for funds to pay contractors, the landlord has not yet completed the necessary repairs. Assume that the corporate landlord is obligated to repair Martha's apartment. Martha does some research and learns that the landlord's president, Dana, owns all of the landlord's stock. Martha wishes to sue Dana to force Dana to pay for repairs to her ceiling. Is Martha likely to prevail?

3. Ollie Owner owns and operates Paris Bistro, a small but beloved restaurant that operates as a general partnership. (Owner's mother, who is not actively involved in the business, is the only other partner.) Due to a combination of luck and good management, Paris Bistro has never been sued. Owner is aware, however, that other restaurants have paid substantial judgments to patrons who choked on chicken bones, had allergic reactions to undisclosed nuts in desserts, and the like. Owner knows that a lawsuit of this magnitude would be devastating for Paris Bistro, since the liability easily could exceed the value of Paris Bistro's limited assets.

   Although Owner has always maintained liability insurance to protect against these sorts of risks, the insurance has become very expensive. Last week, after hearing about limited liability companies from a friend in the restaurant business, Owner tells Lawyer that he would like to (i) convert his business into a single-member LCC (his mother wants to retire and no longer wishes to be involved); (ii) serve as the managing member of the LLC; and (iii) drop the liability insurance. What advice should Lawyer give?

Business Organizations in Practice

1. Four clients — college roommates — have asked you to help them form a business entity for the purpose of developing and selling their new smartphone app. One of the roommates is personally wealthy, having inherited millions from his

parents. This roommate wants to invest but does not anticipate being involved in day-to-day management. This roommate would prefer a form of organization that will minimize his tax liability during the research and development phase. The second roommate invented the technology at issue. This roommate wants to contribute technology to the venture, and to serve as the business's chief technology officer. The third roommate has excellent management skills, but no money. The clients want the third roommate to run the business side of things, while roommate two works on the technology. The fourth roommate has deep connections to the likely purchasers of this product, but no money or technological expertise.

   a. Make a list of questions to ask the clients to determine which form of organization is best suited to their needs and goals. Apart from choice of entity–related questions, what other questions might you ask?
   b. Are there any ethical issues associated with representing all four clients at the entity formation stage? Can you represent both the founders and the to-be-formed business?
   c. What form of organization would you recommend? Why?
   d. What tax treatment would you recommend? Why?

2. Your client — a brilliant physician, teacher, and inventor — comes to your office and tells you that she has invented a new drug to treat diabetes. She has developed a plan to get through the new drug approval process at the Food and Drug Administration, and she estimates that it will take $30 million over the next several years to complete testing, obtain FDA approval, and begin manufacturing and marketing the drug. She explains that her mentor, a wealthy and successful biotechnology entrepreneur, has already agreed to invest $10 million in start-up capital through the mentor's venture capital business, Nia Ventures, L.P. Your client also explains that she wants to contribute the intellectual property behind the drug (including certain patents) to the business that she would like you to form. Your client recognizes that it will take an enormous amount of money and work to get the product to market, and she is not yet sure whether she wants to license the technology to a third-party manufacturer (and collect royalty fees) or whether she wants to rent or build a manufacturing facility to make the product.

   a. What questions would you ask to determine which form of organization to recommend to your client? Apart from choice of entity–related questions, what other questions might you ask?
   b. What form of organization would you recommend? Why?
   c. What tax treatment would you recommend? Why?

3. Abel and Cain, two siblings, hire you to form a business organization for their new business — a sports bar. Abel made a killing in the stock market a few years ago, allowing him to invest in a number of different ventures over the past couple years. Abel presently earns a substantial amount of passive income from his investments that he would like to reduce or eliminate with losses associated with

the sports bar start-up. Abel will not be involved in the day-to-day operations of the bar, but is willing to invest 100 percent of the start-up capital needed to get the business off the ground. Cain is a former minor league baseball pitcher whose career was cut short after he sustained an elbow injury. Cain does not have much money, but he will run the bar day to day.

a. What form of organization would you recommend? Why?
b. What tax treatment would you recommend? Why?

Agency Law and Agency Relationships in Business Organizations

As legal and economic entities, businesses rely upon people to get work done. They need people to enter into and perform contracts. They need people to make decisions about business strategies and goals. And, they need people (e.g., lawyers and accountants) to take care of legal issues, financial reporting, and other technical requirements. This is where agency law comes into play. When a person agrees to work on behalf of a business, subject to the business's control, that person becomes an **agent** of the business. When a business authorizes a person to work on its behalf, subject to its control, the business acts as a **principal**. Under agency law principles, an agent who acts with **authority** has the power to bind the principal to contracts. Agents also may subject their principals to liability for certain torts. To explore these rules, and how agency law works in the context of business organizations, we will study the following issues in this chapter: (i) how agency relationships are formed; (ii) when an agent has authority, and thus the power to bind a principal to a contract; (iii) when a principal will be liable for an agent's torts; and (iv) other rights and obligations associated with the principal-agent relationship.

Key Concepts

- The definition and meaning of the term "principal"
- The definition and meaning of the term "agent"
- When a principal is liable on a contract that an agent entered into on the principal's behalf
- When a principal is liable for an agent's torts
- When an agent is liable on a contract that the agent entered into on the principal's behalf

A. WHAT IS AN AGENCY RELATIONSHIP?

According to the Restatement (Third) of Agency, agency is a "**fiduciary relationship** that arises when one person (a '**principal**') manifests assent to another person (an '**agent**') that the agent shall act on the principal's behalf and subject to the principal's control, and the agent manifests assent or otherwise consents so to act." Restatement (Third) of Agency § 1.01. Agency relationships exist across different types of business relationships, and across different types of business entities. So, for example, when a client asks a law firm organized as a professional services corporation to prepare a will, the law firm is the agent and the client is the principal. Likewise, when an employee of a retail business organized as a limited liability company sells goods to customers, the employee is the agent and the business is the principal. When a partner in a general partnership signs a contract, the partner acts as an agent of the partnership, and the partnership is the principal.

B. HOW ARE AGENCY RELATIONSHIPS FORMED?

According to the Restatement (Third) of Agency, an agency relationship is formed when one person (the principal) "manifests assent" to another person (the agent) that "the agent shall act on the principal's behalf and subject to the principal's control" and "the agent manifests assent or otherwise consents so to act." Restatement (Third) of Agency § 1.01. As this definition suggests, agency relationships are both consensual and contractual in nature. Consequently, as is true of contract formation generally, a principal and agent may "manifest[]" their asset to, and thus create, an agency relationship, through "written or spoken words or other conduct." *Id.* § 1.03. For example, if a homeowner decides to sell her house and lists it with a real estate agency, the homeowner is the principal and the broker is the agent. If, as is likely, the parties enter into a written agreement setting forth the parties' respective rights and obligations relating to the sale of the house, they have entered into an **express agency relationship**, as memorialized by an **express agency agreement**. Certain agency relationships must be memorialized in a writing as a matter of state law.

In contrast to express agency agreements, **implied agency agreements** arise when one party (the agent) demonstrates through conduct that he has agreed to act on the principal's behalf, subject to the principal's control, and the other party (the principal) demonstrates through conduct that she has agreed that the agent may so act. For example, individuals employed by small retail stores or restaurants may not have formal employment agreements, and thus may not be in an express agency relationship with their employers. The employees have (at least) an implied agency relationship with their employers, however, as established through the employers' act of hiring the workers and directing their conduct, and the employees' act of working for their employers, subject to the employers' direction and control.

In addition to express and implied agency relationships, obligations associated with agency relationships also may arise under **estoppel** principles. Suppose that

Jean, an interior decorator, visits the home of a customer. Sam, a new employee who is just learning the business, accompanies Jean to the customer meeting. At the customer's house, Jean repeatedly tells the customer, "We can supply all your needs," and "We are the best decorators in the county." If the customer calls an order in to Sam, Jean will be estopped from denying that Sam is her agent. This is because Jean created the reasonable impression that Sam was her agent when she repeatedly used the term "we" when dealing with customers and engaged in conduct that led customers reasonably to believe that Sam had authority to act for Jean and the business. Having created this impression through her words and conduct, Jean will be estopped from denying the existence of agency relationship.

Case Preview

Shiplet v. Copeland

In the following case, plaintiff Billy Shiplet (a car buyer) sought to hold Larry and Judith Copeland (d/b/a C & C Car Sales) and Bob Lees (d/b/a Auto Body Plus) jointly and severally liable for damages allegedly incurred in connection with Shiplet's purchase of two cars from Bob Lees's son. Shiplet's theory was that C & C and Auto Body were in an agency relationship, because the two businesses shared an address and cooperated in certain business matters. In reading the case, think about the following questions:

1. Why does Shiplet want to establish an agency relationship?
2. What legal rules does the court apply to determine whether the Copelands and Bob Lees were in an agency relationship?
3. What facts does the court point to in deciding whether an agency relationship exists under the rules that you identified in response to Question 2?
4. The court mentions actual and apparent authority. What do these terms mean? What is the legal significance of actual or apparent authority under agency law?
5. What legal standards and facts does the court consider in deciding whether actual or apparent authority was present in this case?

Shiplet v. Copeland
450 S.W.3d 433 (Mo. Ct. App. 2014)

CYNTHIA L. MARTIN, Judge.*

Billy Shiplet ("Billy") sued Larry Copeland ("Larry") and Judith Copeland ("Judith")[1] (collectively the "Copelands"), d/b/a C & C Car Sales, and Bob Lees ("Lees"), d/b/a Auto Body Plus, alleging violations of the Missouri Merchandising

---

*Most footnotes have been omitted for purpose of brevity.
[1]Because Billy Shiplet and Julie Shiplet share the same surname, we refer to each by their first name for purposes of clarity. The same is true for Larry Copeland and Judith Copeland. No familiarity or disrespect is intended with respect to any of the parties.

Practices Act ("MMPA") in connection with the sale of two vehicles. After suit was filed, Billy died, and his personal representative, Julie Shiplet ("Julie"), was substituted as plaintiff. Following a bench trial, the trial court entered judgment in favor of Julie and against the Copelands and Lees, jointly and severally, in the amount of $9,000 in connection with the sale of one of the vehicles. The trial court entered judgment in favor of Julie and against Lees in the amount of $5,705.73 in connection with the sale of the second vehicle. The trial court did not award Julie attorney's fees. Julie appeals, alleging error in the failure to award attorney's fees and in the calculation of the $9,000 damage award. The Copelands cross-appeal, alleging they were not legally liable for Lees's sale of a vehicle to Billy. We affirm.

FACTUAL AND PROCEDURAL BACKGROUND

The Copelands are the owners of C & C Car Sales, a used car dealership licensed in the state of Missouri. C & C Car Sales originally operated from a location located at 100 South Madison in Raymore, but on the 2001 motor vehicle dealer license application, the Copelands indicated that the physical location of C & C Car Sales had moved to 202 Evans in Raymore. That address is also home to Lees's automobile body repair business, Auto Body Plus.

Before completing the 2001 license application for a motor vehicle dealer, Larry approached Lees with a business proposition regarding the physical location of C & C Car Sales. Larry and Lees never reduced their agreement to writing, but the testimony at trial established that the two men struck a deal in which C & C Car Sales would be physically located at Auto Body Plus for the purpose of motor vehicle dealer licensing, and in exchange, Larry would allow Lees to use dealer tags allotted to C & C Car Sales. Larry and Lees took several actions that demonstrated their agreement, including (1) installing a "C & C Car Sales" sign in front of the Auto Body Plus building; (2) printing business cards that listed Lees as an owner of C & C Car Sales; (3) using sales made by Lees to meet the requirements of C & C Car Sales for motor vehicle dealer licensing; (4) authorizing Lees to act as a representative of C & C Car Sales for the purpose of inspections by the Department of Revenue or law enforcement; and (5) naming Lees as an owner of C & C Car Sales on the applications for a motor vehicle dealer license.

In 2008, while Larry and Lees's business arrangement regarding C & C Car Sales remained in place, Billy attempted to purchase two vehicles located at 202 Evans in Raymore. The first vehicle Billy purchased was a 1993 Pontiac owned by Lees's son. The Pontiac was in a wrecked condition and required automobile body repair. Billy gave Lees's son cash and personal property valued at $5,705.73 in exchange for the Pontiac. Testimony at trial was conflicting as to whether the purchase price included the parts and labor required for the Pontiac's repair. Nonetheless, Lees never completed the repairs on the Pontiac, and Billy never took possession of the Pontiac.

The second vehicle Billy purchased was a 2002 Volkswagen also owned by Lees's son. Billy agreed to purchase the Volkswagen for $12,000. Billy gave Lees a cashier's check in the amount of $10,500 made payable to C & C Car Sales and promised to pay the remaining $1,500 at a later unspecified date. Billy took possession of the Volkswagen, and Lees provided Billy with a temporary permit to use until he could license the vehicle. Billy did not, however, receive the title to the Volkswagen at the time of purchase. When Billy attempted to license the Volkswagen, the Department of Revenue rejected his application because he did not have the title. Billy talked to Lees about receiving the title to the Volkswagen. Lees did not deliver the title, but offered Billy a C & C Car Sales's dealer tag to use on the Volkswagen. Billy accepted the dealer tag and continued driving the Volkswagen.

The Volkswagen started having mechanical issues following Billy's purchase of it. Lees repaired the Volkswagen once. Approximately four months after Billy's purchase, the Volkswagen again had mechanical problems. Billy returned the Volkswagen to Lees. Billy demanded return of the $10,500 he paid for the vehicle, as he had never paid the $1,500 balance of the purchase price. While the vehicle was in Billy's possession, it was driven approximately 3,500 to 4,000 miles.

Billy filed suit alleging, *inter alia*, that the Copelands d/b/a C & C Car Sales and Lees d/b/a Auto Body Plus violated the MMPA in connection with the sale of the Pontiac and the sale of the Volkswagen. The petition asserted that, with respect to the sale of each vehicle, the "Defendants made certain false or misleading representations and led [Billy] to believe certain falsehoods about the vehicle, specifically [that the] Defendants would pass clear title to [Billy] [and] [t]he condition of the vehicle." The petition also asserted two counts alleging negligence per se and two counts alleging common law fraud. . . .

On April 24, 2013, the trial court noted its decision by docket entry. With respect to the sale of the Pontiac, the docket sheet notation reflects the entry of judgment in favor of Julie and against Lees in the amount of $5,705.73 on one of Julie's MMPA claims. With respect to the sale of the Volkswagen, the docket sheet notation reflects the entry of judgment in favor of Julie and against the Copelands and Lees, jointly and severally, in the amount of $9,000 on the second MMPA claim. The remaining counts of the petition were shown as dismissed. . . .

. . .

THE COPELANDS' CLAIM ON APPEAL

The Copelands' single point on appeal argues that the trial court erred in concluding that the Copelands and Lees were jointly and severally liable with respect to the sale of the Volkswagen. The Copelands contend that there was insufficient evidence to establish that Lees was an agent of the Copelands so that they could be found vicariously liable for Lees's actions. The Copelands assert that the evidence presented at trial did not support a finding of agency because there was no evidence that Lees had either actual authority or apparent authority to act on the Copelands' behalf. Without the agency relationship, the Copelands argue, they cannot be found liable for the MMPA violation in connection with the sale of the Volkswagen so that the entry of judgment finding the Defendants jointly and severally liable constituted error.

"Whether an agency relationship exists is generally a factual question. . . ." *West v. Sharp Bonding Agency, Inc.*, 327 S.W.3d 7, 11 (Mo. App. W.D. 2010). Because this appeal arises from a bench trial, we will review the trial court's finding of an agency relationship between the Copelands and Lees and will affirm that finding unless it is not supported by the evidence, is against the weight of the evidence, or is based on an erroneous application of the law. *Williams*, 99 S.W.3d at 557.

"Agency is the fiduciary relationship resulting from the manifestation of consent by an agent to a principal that the agent will act on the principal's behalf and subject to his control." *Bach v. Winfield-Foley Fire Prot. Dist.*, 257 S.W.3d 605, 608 (Mo. banc 2008). An agency relationship requires the existence of three elements: (1) an agent must have the authority "to alter legal relations between the principal and a third party"; (2) the agent must be "a fiduciary with respect to matters within the scope of the agency"; and (3) the principal must have "the right to control the conduct of the agent with respect to matters entrusted to the agent." *State ex rel. Ford Motor Co. v. Bacon*, 63 S.W.3d 641, 642 (Mo. banc 2002). The absence of any of the three elements defeats the purported agency relationship. Id. The Copelands argue that the first element is absent in that Lees had no authority from the Copelands to act on their behalf.

There are two types of authority sufficient to create an agency relationship: actual and apparent. Lynch v. Helm Plumbing & Elec. Contractors, Inc., 108 S.W.3d 657, 660 (Mo. App. W.D. 2002). Actual authority relates to the *agent's* understanding of the principal's intent to give power to the agent to act on the principal's behalf. See id. Actual authority can be either express or implied. Id. Actual express authority occurs when the principal expressly indicates that the agent has power to act on behalf of the principal. Id. Actual implied authority exists when a reasonable person would interpret the principal's conduct as desiring the agent to act on the principal's behalf. Id. Apparent authority, on the other hand, relates to *third persons'* understanding of the principal's intent to give power to the agent to act on the principal's behalf. " 'Apparent authority is authority which a principal, by its acts or representations, has led third persons to believe has been conferred upon an agent.' " *Id.* (quoting *Stitt v. Raytown Sports Ass'n, Inc.*, 961 S.W.2d 927, 932 (Mo. App. W.D. 1998)). "Generally, any conduct by the principal which, if reasonably interpreted, would cause a third person to believe that the principal consents to the acts of the agent is sufficient to create apparent authority." Id. The Copelands argue that the evidence presented at trial does not support either a finding of actual authority or apparent authority. We disagree.

The evidence presented at trial concerned the business arrangement that Larry and Lees had with one another regarding the physical location of C & C Car Sales. In exchange for allowing the Copelands to designate the address of Auto Body Plus as the physical location for C & C Car Sales for the purpose of motor vehicle dealer licensing, Larry would allow Lees to use dealer tags allotted to C & C Car Sales. In furtherance of this business arrangement, Larry authorized Lees to act as a representative of C & C Car Sales for the purpose of inspections by the Department of Revenue, and Larry issued business cards to Lees that listed Lees as an owner of C & C Car Sales to give to the inspectors. Larry listed Lees as an owner on C & C Car Sales' yearly applications for a motor vehicle dealer license. Further, Larry and Lees installed a C & C Car Sales sign in front of the Auto Body Plus building and posted C & C Car Sales' motor vehicle dealer license and business license in the Auto Body

Plus building. Some of Lees's car sales were attributed to C & C Car Sales for purposes of reporting to the Department of Revenue. In connection with the sale of the Volkswagen, paperwork identified the seller as C & C Car Sales, and Billy made his initial payment with a cashier's check made payable to C & C Car Sales. When an issue arose about title to the Volkswagen, Lees offered Billy, and Billy accepted, a C & C Car Sales dealer tag for use on the vehicle.

This evidence could be reasonably interpreted to support either a finding of actual authority or apparent authority. Lees plainly had the authority to hold himself out as C & C Car Sales with Larry's consent, and to use C & C Car Sales dealer tags. Moreover, the circumstances surrounding the sale of the Volkswagen would reasonably lead a third party to believe that Lees was acting on behalf of C & C Car Sales.

The Copelands argue that even if evidence supports a finding of actual or apparent authority between Lees and C & C Car Sales, no evidence established an agency relationship between Lees and the Copelands. This argument conveniently ignores that as a sole proprietorship, C & C Car Sales was indistinguishable from the Copelands. Though Billy never met or communicated with the Copelands, Billy plainly could have believed that he was dealing with C & C Car Sales. The Copelands cite no authority for the proposition that a third party must interact with the sole proprietors/owners of an unincorporated business to establish apparent authority of another to act for the business. "The failure to cite relevant authority supporting a point or to explain the failure to do so preserves nothing for review." *Jay Wolfe Used Cars of Blue Springs, LLC v. Jackson*, 428 S.W.3d 683, 689 (Mo. App. W.D. 2014) (internal quotation marks omitted).

The trial court did not err in assigning joint and several liability to the Copelands and Lees for the MMPA violation concerning the sale of the Volkswagen.

The Copelands' point on appeal is denied. . . .

Post-Case Follow-Up

To avoid legal consequences associated with agency relationships, parties may seek to disclaim the existence of an agency relationship through contractual provisions like the following:

No Agency, Partnership, or Joint Venture. The parties understand and agree that neither party is an agent, employee, or servant of the other for any purpose. Each party agrees to conduct its business in its own name, with each party solely responsible for (i) its own acts, omissions, and expenses of any kind; and (ii) the acts, omissions, and expenses of any kind associated with its own employees, independent contractors, or other agents. Nothing in this agreement shall create an agency relationship, partnership, or joint venture between the parties.

Although a provision like this is relevant to determining whether an agency relationship exists, such a provision is neither controlling nor dispositive. Instead, the question under agency law is whether the parties' relationship (as reflected in words and conduct) meets the legal definition of agency. If it does, the parties will be subject to agency law rules, whether or not they used particular words (like agent or principal) in forming their relationship or sought to disclaim an agency relationship through a contractual provision like the one set forth above. As the Restatement (Third) explains, "[t]he parties' agreement may negatively character-ize the relationship as not one of agency, or not one intended by the parties to create a relationship of agency or other employment. Although such statements are rele-vant to determining whether the parties consent to a relationship of agency, their presence in an agreement is not determinative and does not preclude the relevance of other indicia of consent." Restatement (Third) of Agency § 1.02 cmt. b. *See also Morris Oil Co. v. Rainbow Oilfield Trucking, Inc.*, 741 P.2d 840, 843 (N.M. Ct. App. 1980) (finding agency relationship despite contractual provision that stated that party was "not appointed and shall not become" an agent). *See also* Restatement (Third) of Agency § 1.02 ("An agency relationship arises only when the elements stated in § 1.01 are present. Whether relationship is characterized as agency in an agreement between the parties or in the context of industry or popular usage is not controlling.").

Shiplet v. Copeland: Real Life Applications

Jay is a pizza delivery person for Pizza Pie, LLC ("Pizza Pie"). Last year, while Jay was driving a car delivering a pizza to a Pizza Pie customer, Jay struck and injured Sandy Jones, a pedestrian. Jay and Pizza Pie have acknowledged that Jay was neg-ligent and that both Jay and Pizza Pie are liable for Sandy's injuries. (Jay is directly liable for his own negligence. Pizza Pie is vicariously liable under the doctrine of respondeat superior, which is discussed below.) Anxious to ensure that she is able to cover her medical bills, Sandy has decided to sue Pizza Pie Franchising, LLC ("Franchising"), as well. Franchising and Pizza Pie are in a franchisor/franchisee relationship. Sandy claims that the language of the franchising agreement, together with the parties' conduct, make Pizza Pie an agent of Franchising. If true, this would make Franchising vicariously liable for Sandy's injuries. Following discovery, the following facts are both undisputed and supported by competent evidence:

a. The franchise agreement contains a "no agency" clause, which states that Pizza Pie and Franchising are not in an agency or independent contractor relationship.

b. Pizza Pie (not Franchising) controlled the day-to-day activities of Pizza Pie's pizza delivery workers.

c. The franchise agreement requires Pizza Pie to name Franchising as an additional insured on all general liability and non-owned auto insurance policies, including the policies at issue in this case. Pizza Pie did so, and Franchising was listed as an additional insured during all periods relevant to this action.

d. The franchise agreement requires Pizza Pie to adhere to Franchising's listed operational guidelines when hiring, supervising, and terminating pizza delivery drivers.

e.   Franchise reserved the right to terminate the franchise if Pizza Pie did not comply with listed operational rules, including rules relating to wait staff and pizza delivery drivers.

f.   Franchising audited and supervised Pizza Pie to ensure compliance with operational rules, including rules relating to the hiring, training, and supervision of delivery staff.

g.   Franchising regularly provided technical expertise and in-store assistance to Pizza Pie to ensure compliance with operational rules.

Are Pizza Pie and Franchising in an agency relationship, such that Franchising may be held vicariously liable for Sandy's injuries? Why or why not?

C. AGENTS, AUTHORITY, AND CONTRACT LIABILITY

Under agency law rules, a principal will be bound to a contract made by the agent on the principal's behalf if (i) the agent acted with **actual, apparent,** or **inherent** authority; (ii) the principal is **estopped** from denying the existence of an agency relationship; or (iii) the principal **ratifies** a contract entered into by a purported agent (even if the agent initially lacked authority).

1. Actual Authority

According to the Restatement (Third) of Agency, an "agent acts with actual authority when, at the time of taking action that has a legal consequence for the principal, the agent reasonably believes, in accordance with the principal's manifestations to the agent, that the principal wishes the agent so to act." Restatement (Third) of Agency § 2.01. To see how this rule might play out in practice, assume that Ellis is the sole owner and managing member of Green Lawns, LLC, a landscaping business. Last month, Ellis hired Terry as a crew chief, and told Terry that (i) he should stop by Hank's gas station each morning to fill gas cans for the crew to use when fueling up and operating landscaping equipment at job sites; and (ii) he should charge the gas to Green Lawns's account at Hank's. In so doing, Ellis manifested to Terry that he had authority to charge gas. As Ellis is the sole owner and manager of Green Lawns, Terry's belief that Ellis gave him permission to charge gas (and that Ellis has the power to do so) appears reasonable. Terry has actual authority under these facts, and Green Lawns will be obligated to pay for gas that Terry charges on Green Lawns's behalf.

Actual authority can be **express** or **implied.** Terry has **express actual authority** in our example because Ellis specifically told Terry that he was authorized to charge the gas. **Implied actual authority** arises when an agent reasonably believes that he has authority to perform acts that, while not explicitly discussed, are necessary to achieve the principal's goals. *See* Restatement (Third) of Agency § 2.01 cmt. b; § 2.02. For example, assume Ellis tells Terry that part of his job as crew chief is to make sure that the truck that Terry and the crew drive to job sites is gassed up and ready to go each morning. Also, assume that Ellis waves good-bye to Terry as

Terry walks out of the office holding keys to the truck every morning. Terry has implied actual authority to drive the truck to the gas station on these facts and likely has implied actual authority to purchase windshield wiper fluid and other sundries necessary to keep the truck on the road, along with gas. As Terry has implied authority under these facts, Green Lawns will be obligated to pay for Terry's reasonable charges at Hank's.

2. Apparent Authority

Apparent authority is a different animal. According to the Restatement (Third) of Agency, "[a]pparent authority is the power held by an agent or other actor to affect a principal's legal relations with third parties when a third party reasonably believes the actor has authority to act on behalf of the principal and that belief is traceable to the principal's manifestations." Restatement (Third) of Agency § 2.03. As this definition suggests, unlike actual authority (which depends on the principal's manifestations to the agent), apparent authority depends on (i) the principal's manifestations to third parties; and (ii) the reasonableness of a third party's belief that the agent is authorized to act on behalf of the principal.

For example, continuing with our fact pattern from the prior section, assume that Ellis calls Hank's and tells the manager that Terry is authorized to charge gas for Green Lawns's landscaping equipment and trucks to Green Lawns's account. Green Lawns will be obligated to pay for Terry's gas charges on these facts because Ellis had apparent authority: Ellis told Hank's that Terry was authorized to charge gas, and Hank's reasonably believed that Ellis had the power to authorize Terry's charges. Likewise, Green Lawns will be bound due to apparent authority if Ellis tells Hank's that crew chiefs are authorized to charge gas, and Terry drives up in his crew chief uniform, fills gas cans, and loads the cans onto a Green Lawns truck. In both cases, Green Lawns's obligation to pay derives from (i) Ellis's representations to Hank's respecting Terry's (or a crew chief's) authority; and (ii) Hank's reasonable belief, given Ellis's representations, that Terry had authority to charge gas to Green Lawns's account.

Case Preview	***Themis Capital, LLC v. Democratic Republic of Congo***

In the next case, Plaintiffs (successors in interest to certain debt-related agreements) sued the Democratic Republic of the Congo (DRC) and the Central Bank of the Democratic Republic of the Congo for failure to repay debts, which had been in default for approximately two decades. Don't be put off by the unusual defendants in this case. We have included the case because, at its heart, it involves a contract dispute between a debtor and creditor where the debtor's liability turns on agency law issues — namely, (i) whether the people who signed the relevant agreements were agents of the debtor; and (ii) whether the signers had (or lacked) authority to bind the debtor. This case thus speaks to the risks of both empowering — and relying upon — agents.

Here is a nutshell version of the facts to get started. Back in 1980, officials of the Republic of Zaire (now known as the DRC) entered into agreements with creditors whereby the creditors agreed to restructure and refinance certain of Zaire's debts in exchange for Zaire's promise to make payments according to a repayment schedule ("the 1980 Agreement"). Then-President Mobutu Sese Seko signed an ordinance directing government and bank officials to sign the agreements.

Zaire initially made payments according to the schedule set forth in the 1980 Agreement. Beginning in the mid-1980s, however, Zaire began missing payments. Then, in 1990, Zaire stopped making payments altogether. In response to the default, certain creditors negotiated agreements with the DRC and its Central Bank whereby government and bank personnel purported to acknowledge the debts in a manner designed to avoid any risk that the six-year prescription period established by New York statute of limitations law would bar the creditors from moving against the DRC and its Central Bank to recover payments then in default. Government and bank officials signed a series of debt acknowledgment letters memorializing the parties' agreement in 1991, 1997, and 2003.

In 2009, plaintiffs Themis and Des Moines (assignees of debts consolidated under the 1980 Agreement) filed suit against the DRC and its Central Bank alleging that defendants had breached the 1980 Agreement by failing to pay the principal and interest owed and acknowledged in the debt acknowledgment letters. Ordinarily, the plaintiffs' lawsuit would have been time-barred under New York's six-year statute of limitations governing breach of contract claims. Citing the debt acknowledgment letters, however, the plaintiffs argued that their suit was timely. In response, the defendants argued that the officials who had signed the letters had acted without authority. The portion of the opinion that we have excerpted focuses on apparent authority. When reading this section, consider the following questions:

1. What is the test for apparent authority?
2. What facts does the court consider in deciding whether the officials had apparent authority to bind their country?
3. What do you make of the court's discussion of whether or not Citibank had a duty to inquire respecting the officials' authority to enter into the tolling agreements at issue?

Themis Capital, LLC v. Democratic Republic of Congo
35 F. Supp. 3d 457 (S.D.N.Y. 2013)

PAUL A. ENGELMAYER, District Judge.*

Plaintiffs Themis Capital, LLC ("Themis") and Des Moines Investments, Ltd. ("Des Moines") (collectively, "plaintiffs" or "Themis") bring this claim for breach of

---

*Footnotes omitted for purposes of brevity.

contract against the Democratic Republic of the Congo (the "DRC") and the Central Bank of the Democratic Republic of the Congo ("Central Bank of the DRC") (collectively, "defendants"). Themis and Des Moines are successors-in-interest to portions of debt that the DRC restructured in 1980, which have been in default since 1990. Plaintiffs' lawsuit seeks to recover on this debt.

Plaintiffs' lawsuit would ordinarily be time-barred under New York's six-year statute of limitations governing breach-of-contract claims. To sustain this claim, plaintiffs rely on a series of debt acknowledgment letters that purport to have been signed by officials of the DRC and Central Bank in 1991, 1997, and again in 2003. These letters, by their terms, tolled the statute of limitations, and, if effective, would make this lawsuit, brought in 2009, timely.

Defendants, however, assert that the signatories to these letters lacked actual or apparent authority to bind the DRC and the Central Bank. Thus, they argue, the statute of limitations expired long ago. Whether defendants are liable to pay the debts at issue here therefore turns on whether the debt acknowledgment letters are legally binding.

. . .

A. LIABILITY

1. Actual Authority

If the signatories had actual authority to sign the 2003 Acknowledgment Letter, then Themis's lawsuit is timely, and the DRC is liable for breach of contract.

"Under New York law, an agent has actual authority if the principal has granted the agent the power to enter into contracts on the principal's behalf, subject to whatever limitations the principal places on this power, either explicitly or implicitly." *Highland Capital Mgmt. v. Schneider*, 607 F.3d 322, 327 (2d Cir. 2010) (citing *Ford v. Unity Hosp.*, 32 N.Y.2d 464, 346 N.Y.S.2d 238, 299 N.E.2d 659 (1973)). Actual authority "may be express or implied," and in either case "exists only where the agent may reasonably infer from the words or conduct of the principal that the principal has consented to the agent's performance of a particular act." *Minskoff v. Am. Express Travel Related Servs.*, 98 F.3d 703, 708 (2d Cir. 1996). Regardless, "[t]he existence of actual authority depends upon the actual interaction between the putative principal and agent, not on any perception a third party may have of the relationship." *Merrill Lynch Capital Servs. v. UISA Fin.*, No. 09 Civ. 2324(RJS), 2012 WL 1202034, at *6 (S.D.N.Y. Apr. 10, 2012). "[T]he extent of the agent's actual authority is interpreted in the light of all circumstances attending those manifestations, including the customs of business, the subject matter, any formal agreement between the parties, and the facts of which both parties are aware." *Peltz v. SHB Commodities, Inc.*, 115 F.3d 1082, 1088 (2d Cir. 1997) (citation omitted).

In its previous opinion, the Court held that DRC law governs whether Luongwe and Masangu had actual authority to bind the DRC and the Central Bank to a commercial contract, *see Themis I*, 881 F. Supp. 2d at 521—here, an agreement to toll the running of the statute of limitations for an action to collect upon an unpaid debt. . . .

1. *Apparent Authority*

In the alternative, Themis argues that the signatories to the 2003 Acknowledgment Letter had the apparent authority to bind the DRC and the Central Bank.

Even where an agent lacks actual authority, it is well settled under New York law that an agent may "bind his principal to a contract if the principal has created the appearance of authority, leading the other contracting party to reasonably believe that actual authority exists." *Highland Capital*, 607 F.3d at 328; *see also Goldston v. Bandwidth Tech. Corp.*, 52 A.D.3d 360, 859 N.Y.S.2d 651, 655 (1st Dep't 2008) ("[A]n agreement entered into within the exercise of a corporate officer's apparent authority is binding on the corporation without regard to the officer's lack of actual authority."). This Court has previously held, in this case, that "apparent authority can bind foreign governments whose acts are private," including entering into "commercial transactions on apparent behalf of a sovereign state." *See Themis I*, 881 F. Supp. 2d at 526. Here, the governmental acts in question—restructuring debts owed to creditors and entering into tolling agreements regarding the dates on which collection actions may be brought—are quintessentially private. Accordingly, if the Court finds that the signatories—Luongwe and Masangu—had apparent authority to sign the 2003 Acknowledgment Letter, then the DRC and Central Bank are bound to honor that acknowledgment.

Apparent authority authorizes an agent to bind its principal when the "principal, either intentionally or by lack of ordinary care, induces a [third party] to believe that an individual has been authorized to act on its behalf." *Merrill Lynch*, 2012 WL 1202034, at *6 (citing *Highland Capital*, 607 F.3d at 328); *see also Reiss v. Societe Centrale du Groupe des Assurances Nationales*, 235 F.3d 738, 748 (2d Cir. 2000) ("[A]pparent authority depends on some conduct by the principal, communicated to a third party, which reasonably gives the appearance that the agent has authority to conduct a particular transaction."). In this case, there are thus two requirements to finding apparent authority: First, Citibank must have reasonably believed, based on the DRC's conduct, that the Finance Minister and Central Bank Governor had authority to sign the 2003 Acknowledgment Letter; Second, Citibank must have, considering the relevant circumstances, fulfilled its duty of inquiry. *See First Fidelity Bank, N.A. v. Government of Antigua & Barbuda—Permanent Mission*, 877 F.2d 189, 193-94 (2d Cir. 1989).

The Court evaluates each requirement in turn.

a. The DRC's Conduct

To find apparent authority, the DRC and the DRC's Central Bank (the principals) must have made a representation—upon which a third party (Citibank) could reasonably have relied—that certain agents (the Finance Minister and Central Bank Governor) were acting on the principals' behalf. Whether a party reasonably relied on a representation by the principal turns heavily on the circumstances surrounding both the representation and the reliance, and "requires a factual inquiry into the principal's manifestations to third persons." *Id.* at 193 (citing *General Overseas Films, Ltd. v. Robin Int'l, Inc.*, 542 F. Supp. 684, 689 (S.D.N.Y. 1982), *aff'd*, 718 F.2d 1085 (2d

Cir. 1983)). This maxim applies equally to representations made by foreign states. *See id.* ("[A]n ambassador's actions under color of authority do not, as a matter of law, automatically bind the state that he represents."). Accordingly, in assessing whether a government official's act binds a sovereign on the basis of apparent authority, courts must consider "whether the affected parties reasonably considered the action to be official." *Id.* (quoting Restatement (Third) of Foreign Relations §712(2) cmt. h).

Here, the document at issue—the 2003 Acknowledgment Letter—was signed by the DRC's Vice Minister of Finance and Governor of the Central Bank. The Court has already held, *supra* Part II.A.1, that these two officials had actual authority to sign the letter. But even if they lacked actual authority, it was eminently reasonable for Citibank to *believe*, based on the powers vested in these officials and on the conduct of the principals, that the signatories possessed such authority. That is so for two independent and mutually reinforcing reasons.

First, the Finance Minister and Central Bank Governor are national-level officials charged with safeguarding the DRC's monetary and fiscal health. These two officials had been vested with the authority to execute the Credit Agreement, *see* Ordinance No. 80-073, and to prevent that agreement from becoming unenforceable, *see* Credit Agreement §8.01(b). Particularly in light of that authority, it would not have been unreasonable at all for Citibank to conclude that these same two officials had also been given the authority to enter into a tolling agreement that deferred the deadline for filing breach-of-contract lawsuits to collect debts owed under the Credit Agreement, and that served to deter creditors from filing such lawsuits. Indeed, given the role these two officials played in the national government, Citibank was completely reasonable in concluding that these two officials could act on behalf of the DRC and Central Bank in signing the 2003 Acknowledgment Letter.

Second, the Finance Minister and Governor had signed, without incident or objection, debt acknowledgment letters in 1991 and 1997. This would have also led a reasonable party to believe that these same two officials had the authority to sign a substantively identical letter in 2003. As noted, there is no evidence that anyone from DRC or the Central Bank had ever claimed, before this case was filed in 2009, that these officials lacked the authority to sign either the 1991 or 1997 letter. And there is no evidence that anyone from the DRC had ever disclaimed the authority of these officials to sign an identical letter in 2003. *See Parlato v. Equitable Life Assur. Soc. of U.S.*, 299 A.D.2d 108, 749 N.Y.S.2d 216, 222-23 (2002) ("[A] third party who . . . previously dealt with the principal through the principal's authorized agent, is entitled to assume that the agent's authority continues until the third party receives notice that the principal has revoked the agent's authority.") (citing *McNeilly v. Cont'l Life Ins. Co.*, 66 N.Y. 23, 28 (1876)); *Seetransport Wiking Trader Schiffarhtsgesellschaft MBH & Co. Kommanditgesellschaft v. Republic of Romania*, 123 F. Supp. 2d 174, 190 (S.D.N.Y. 2000) (in concluding that sovereign officials possessed apparent authority, stating that "defendant's failure to make any representation during the entire course of negotiations that would at all suggest that the Finance Minister did not have such authority, made it entirely reasonable for plaintiff to have relied upon such representations").

Based on the previous course of dealing, the signing in 2003 of a debt acknowledgment letter that served to further toll the expiration of the statute of limitations would have seemed, from Citibank's perspective, entirely routine and uncontroversial.

It was thus reasonable for Citibank to believe that the Finance Minister and Governor maintained the authority, in 2003, to bind the DRC and the Central Bank to an acknowledgment of their debt under the Credit Agreement.

b. Duty to Inquire

Defendants argue, however, that even if it was reasonable for Citibank to assume that the two officials who signed debt acknowledgment letters in 1991 and 1997 were also authorized to sign the same letter in 2003, Citibank failed to satisfy its duty to inquire. *See* Def. Br. at 41-49. Under the apparent authority doctrine, this duty is triggered when " '(1) the facts and circumstances are such as to put the third party on inquiry, (2) the transaction is extraordinary, or (3) the novelty of the transaction alerts the third party to a danger of fraud.' " *Republic of Benin v. Mezei*, No. 06 Civ. 870(JGK), 2010 WL 3564270, at *7 (S.D.N.Y. Sept. 9, 2010) (quoting *FDIC v. Providence Coll.*, 115 F.3d 136, 141 (2d Cir. 1997)). "[T]he duty of inquiry amounts to an alternative way of asking whether the third party reasonably relied on the representations of the agent that he possessed authority to bind the principal." *C.E. Towers Co. v. Trinidad and Tobago (BWIA Int'l) Airways Corp.*, 903 F. Supp. 515, 525 (S.D.N.Y. 1995) (quoting *Herbert Constr. Co. v. Cont'l Ins. Co.*, 931 F.2d 989, 995-96 (2d Cir. 1991)).

Here, it was unnecessary for Citibank to inquire into whether the Finance Minister and/or Central Bank Governor had the authority to sign the 2003 Acknowledgment Letter. As the Court has noted, the transaction was not extraordinary—it involved the execution of a tolling agreement, substantively identical to those signed in 1991 and 1997. And there were no facts or circumstances known to Citibank that put it "on inquiry" or alerted it to the danger of fraud. To the contrary—all of the circumstances surrounding the 2003 Acknowledgment Letter made the signing of that letter seem utterly routine, and the DRC's claim to lack authority was made only years later, after plaintiffs filed this lawsuit. Citibank, in fact, sent a draft of the 2003 letter to both the Vice Minister of Finance and the Central Bank Governor, explaining that the draft was similar to the one that had been signed in 1997. Both officials, in short order, returned the letters signed. *See Herbert Construction Co. v. Continental Ins. Co.*, 931 F.2d 989, 995 (2d Cir. 1991) ("a recovery based on the doctrine of apparent authority does not require that the third party have inquired into the scope of the agent's authority"; only in cases where seemingly actual authority is placed in doubt by a transaction that is "extraordinary" or patently fraudulent does a duty to inquire into the state of that authority arise); *see also Am. Nat. Fire Ins. Co. v. Kenealy*, 72 F.3d 264, 269 (2d Cir. 1995) (same). Although defendants assert that the duty of inquiry was triggered by the political turmoil present in the DRC in 2003, the same, if not more serious, turmoil beset Zaire in March 1997. And there was no question in 2003 that the 1997 Acknowledgment Letter had been validly signed and executed.

Based on these circumstances, Citibank did not have a duty to inquire into the Finance Minister and Central Bank Governor's authority to sign the 2003 Acknowledgment Letter. Because these officials had the apparent authority to bind the DRC and the Central Bank to that letter, this lawsuit, filed in 2009, is timely. . . .

Post-Case Follow-Up

As *Themis Capital* suggests, to determine whether a purported agent has authority to bind a purported principal to a contract, you should consider both actual and apparent authority (along with, potentially, the estoppel and ratification doctrines discussed below). Sometimes, an agent has *both* actual and apparent authority. For example, going back to the example of Terry, Ellis, and Green Lawns from earlier in the chapter, Terry would have both actual and apparent authority if (i) Ellis told Terry that he had authority to charge gas to Green Lawns's account; and (ii) Ellis also told Hank's that Terry was authorized to charge gas to Green Lawns's account. Other times, an agent may lack actual authority, but may still have apparent authority, and thus the power to bind the principal to a contract. For example, assume that Ellis told Terry that he did not have authority to charge gas, despite being a crew chief, because he was a new hire and was subject to a three-month probationary period. Further assume that Ellis told Hank's that crew chiefs have permission to charge gas, but failed to tell Hank's about Terry's probation. If Terry arrives at Hank's in his crew chief uniform and charges gas, Green Lawns will be obligated to pay under the doctrine of apparent authority, because Ellis told Hank's that crew chiefs were authorized to charge gas — even though Ellis specifically told Terry that he did not have authority to charge gas to Green Lawns's account.

Themis Capital v. The Democratic Republic of Congo: Real Life Applications

Periodic Table, Inc. is a manufacturer of industrial chemicals. On January 2, Ted Dolby contracted with Periodic Table to act as the exclusive sales agent in California for Periodic Table's products. The contract stated that Dolby was authorized to make sales of chemicals in Periodic Table's name, in accordance with current price lists, and also provided that Dolby would be paid a commission of 20 percent on all sales.

Tube, Inc. is a manufacturer of industrial tubing with a plant located outside Los Angeles, California. On January 15, the manager of Tube's plant visited Periodic Table's website to obtain information about purchasing Periodic Table's products. On the website, Dolby was identified as the exclusive sales agent for Periodic Table in California. The website listed Dolby's name and contact information and directed potential customers to contact Dolby with any purchasing inquires. Tube's plant manager contacted Dolby, who thereafter visited Tube's plant and quoted prices on several chemicals for Tube.

On January 30, in a contract signed by the Tube plant manager and "Periodic Table, by Ted Dolby," Tube agreed to purchase 25,000 gallons of one of Periodic Table's products at a price of $10 per gallon for delivery on April 1. At the time the contract was signed, the price list Periodic Table provided to Dolby listed the price for that product as $13 per gallon. Although Dolby was aware that the contract with

Tube provided for a lower price than was indicated on Periodic Table's price list, he hoped to persuade Periodic Table to honor the lower price in order to make the sale to Tube, a new customer.

Upon receiving Tube's order form and a copy of the contract, Periodic Table refused to deliver the chemicals to Tube for $10 per gallon. (Periodic Table told Tube that Dolby was not authorized to enter into a contract at that price on Periodic Table's behalf.) Tube thereafter contracted with another supplier to purchase the product for $12 per gallon.

(a) Tube claims that Periodic Table and Dolby are jointly and severally liable for the difference between the contract price ($10) and the price it paid to obtain the chemical from an alternative supplier ($12). If Tube sues Periodic Table, who will prevail? Why?

(b) Assume that Tube and Periodic Table are able to work out an agreement on pricing, and further assume that Dolby is charged with bringing the first shipment of chemicals to Tube as a gesture of good faith. Unfortunately, while making the delivery, Dolby negligently spills some of the chemical, injuring a Tube worker. If the worker sues Periodic Table, along with Dolby, will the worker prevail? Why or why not? (Hint: Read Section E below.)

3. Estoppel

As set forth in the Restatement (Third) of Agency, a principal also may be liable under an **estoppel** theory if the principal intentionally or carelessly allows a third party to believe that the principal has appointed an agent to act on the principal's behalf:

> A person who has not made a manifestation that an actor has authority as an agent and who is not otherwise liable as a party to a transaction purportedly done by the actor on that person's account is subject to liability to a third party who justifiably is induced to make a detrimental change in position because the transaction is believed to be on the person's account, if:
>
> (1) the person intentionally or carelessly caused such belief, or
> (2) having notice of such belief and that it might induce others to change their positions, the person did not take reasonable steps to notify them of the facts.

Restatement (Third) of Agency § 2.05.

For example, assume that Ollie (the owner of a used car dealership) has an on-site manager-agent — Bobby — who runs the business day to day. Further assume that Bobby's significant other Terry often stops by the dealership to help out Bobby. Terry is not an employee. Six weeks ago, Ollie learned that Terry has been at the dealership regularly over the past few months, often meeting with customers and negotiating deals. Ollie also learned that Bobby, acting without actual or apparent authority, falsely represented to a customer that Terry had authority to sell cars at 20 percent off list price. If a customer agrees to purchases a car from Terry at a 20 percent discount after Bobby became aware of Terry's actions, and the customer makes a down payment and presses Ollie to honor the deal, Ollie may be obligated under estoppel principles. Ollie's problem is that (i) he was aware of Bobby's and Terry's conduct; (ii) the customer justifiably and detrimentally relied upon Terry's purported authority in agreeing to purchase a car and making a down payment; and (iii) Ollie did not take steps to notify customers of the true facts. Note that the customer would not be able to rely upon the doctrine of actual authority to hold Ollie responsible because Ollie did not tell Bobby or Terry that Terry was authorized to act for the dealership. Apparent authority might not work for the customer, either, because Ollie did not represent to the customer that Terry was an employee, nor did Ollie suggest to the customer that Terry was authorized to offer a 20 percent discount. Estoppel is the customer's best argument, given Ollie's knowledge of Terry's conduct, his failure to put a stop to it, and the customer's detrimental reliance.

4. Inherent Authority and Inherent Agency Power

A business also may be bound on a contract under the doctrine of **inherent agency power**. Inherent agency power is discussed in the Restatement (Second) of Agency, which describes the doctrine as follows:

> Inherent agency power is a term used in the restatement of this subject to indicate the power of an agent which is derived not from authority, apparent authority or estoppel, but solely from the agency relation and exists for the protection of persons harmed by or dealing with a servant or other agent.

Restatement (Second) Agency § 8A. *See also* Restatement (Second) Agency §§ 161, 194, 195. The Restatement (Third) of Agency does not use the term "inherent agency powers" but the concept may be embedded (*see, e.g.*, Restatement (Third) of Agency §§ 2.01, 2.02(1) and (2)). Inherent agency power functions as something of a stop-gap, arising in situations where fairness requires holding the principal liable on the contract, even though the agent lacked authority as to the specific matter at issue.

For example, assume that a landlord has a policy that rent must be delivered by mail to the landlord by the first of every month. One tenant who does not get paid until the last day of each month begins personally delivering the monthly rent check to the on-site manager. The manager accepts the checks and delivers them to the landlord. This continues for several months. Although the landlord never gave the manager or the tenant permission to handle rent in this fashion, the landlord did gave the on-site manager broad authority to interact with tenants on range of issues relating to the apartment — including issues relating to rent.

One month, the on-site manager allows the check to fall into the hands of another before turning it over to the landlord. The landlord insists that the tenant repay the rent, on the theory that the manager was never authorized to receive rent checks. The tenant will not be able to avoid payment using the doctrine of actual authority, because the landlord did not give the manager permission to receive checks. The tenant will not be able to rely upon apparent authority either, because the landlord never represented to the tenant that the manager was authorized to accept rent checks. Estoppel may be problematic for the tenant as well, since the existence of an agency relationship is not in dispute. Inherent agency power may be available, however, if the tenant can establish that the manager appeared to have authority to accept rent checks by virtue of the manager's title, role, and prior conduct.

5. Ratification

Finally, even if an agent is not authorized to perform an act under actual, apparent, or inherent authority theories, or as a result of estoppel, the principal may nevertheless be liable if the principal **ratifies** the agent's act. *See* Restatement (Third) of Agency § 4.01 (defining ratification as the "affirmance of a prior act done by another, whereby the act is given effect as if done by an agent acting with actual authority"). The Restatement states that a person ratifies an act by (a) manifesting assent to be bound by the act, or (b) through conduct that justifies a reasonable assumption that the person so consents. *See id.* For example, if a homeowner instructs her real estate agent not to present any offers with a proposed purchase price of less than $300,000, but the agent nevertheless presents an offer for $290,000, which the homeowner accepts, the homeowner will be deemed to have ratified her agent's act. Ratification occurs whenever a principal accepts an agent's act — even if the agent had no authority to do the act in the first place or the act exceeded the scope of the agent's authority. Ratification may be express or implied.

D. CONFIRMING AGENT AUTHORITY IN BUSINESS DEALINGS

To avoid confusion over the existence and scope of a purported agent's authority, businesses and their customers and vendors may choose to use verification systems. In our earlier example involving Ellis, Terry, and Green Lawns, for example, Hank's might call or e-mail Ellis to confirm Terry's authority to charge gas to Green Lawns's account. Similarly, Ellis could call or e-mail Hank's with a list of people authorized to charge gas, or give only those authorized to charge access to a Green Lawns credit card. Of course, verification systems are not perfect: Ellis might be unavailable when Hank's calls or e-mails; Ellis might forget to update his list of authorized agents after Terry quits or is fired; or Hank's could forget to check Ellis's list of authorized chargers before allowing someone wearing a crew chief uniform to charge gas to Green Lawns's account. Even under the best of circumstances, mistakes can happen and principals can become bound.

For these reasons, when dealing with significant transactions (e.g., the purchase or sale of a business, significant contracts, etc.), lawyers and their clients are well advised to confirm the authority of purported agents. In the context of corporations, for example, parties to a significant transaction may require a **secretary's certificate** stating that the officers who sign transaction documents on behalf of the corporation are in fact authorized to do so. Such certificates typically (i) confirm that the corporation has resolved to enter into the transaction at issue; (ii) confirm that the corporation has authorized the named officers to execute and deliver the necessary transaction documents; and (iii) confirm that the officers directed to execute and deliver the necessary documents were duly elected, are qualified, and hold the titles stated in the transaction documents. Most corporations provide for the office of the secretary in their bylaws. In addition, parties also may require an **opinion letter** stating that the execution and delivery of the required documents and the performance of all obligations connected to the transaction have been duly authorized by the corporation. Certain corporate codes also contain statutory provisions relating to the authority of officers. *See* Cal. Corp. Code § 313. In the partnership context, the Revised Uniform Partnership Act (discussed in Chapter 3) permits a partnership to file an optional statement of partnership authority with the secretary of state setting forth the actual authority of partners. A counterparty may require a partnership to file a statement of authority with respect to a transaction or other material agreement. The Uniform Limited Liability Company Act (discussed in Chapter 12) takes a similar approach.

E. AGENTS, PRINCIPALS, AND TORT LIABILITY

When you took Torts during your first year of law school, you may have studied the doctrine of **respondeat superior** — Latin for "let the master answer." Under this doctrine, employers are **vicariously liable** for torts committed by their employees if the employee committed the tort while acting within the scope of her employment. *See, e.g.*, Restatement (Third) of Agency § 2.04 ("An employer is subject to liability for torts committed by employees while acting within the scope of their employment.") The Restatement (Third) of Agency defines an **employee** as "an agent whose principal controls or has the right to control the manner and means of the agent's performance of work." Restatement (Third) of Agency § 7.07(3)(a). An employee acts within the scope of employment for agency law purposes "when performing work assigned by the employer or engaging in a course of conduct subject to the employer's control." *Id.* at § 7.07(2). So, under the respondeat superior rule, if an employee of a restaurant accidentally spills scalding coffee on a patron, the restaurant may be vicariously liable for the customer's injuries because this act was performed in the routine course of duties by the employee-agent for her employer-principal. On the other hand, if the employee *throws* scalding coffee on a patron, the employer-principal is not as likely to be held vicariously liable to the person harmed. Note that the agent remains responsible for her own torts, whether or not the principal is liable under respondeat superior, so our coffee-challenged employee is not "off the hook" merely because her employer is (or is not) vicariously liable for the customer's injuries. *See* Restatement (Third) of Agency § 7.01.

In addition to being vicariously liable, a principal also may be held directly liable for an agent's torts if the principal was negligent in selecting or supervising the agent, as may be the case when an employer hires an obviously unqualified person for a position or hires a person with a known history of criminal activity. Assume, for example, that Terry (our Green Lawns crew chief from earlier in the chapter) broke into the home of one of Green Lawns's customers last week while the crew was performing landscaping work and stole property and money. Further assume that Green Lawns did not perform a background check before hiring Terry, and that if it had, it would have discovered that Terry has been arrested and convicted of breaking and entering and theft on several occasions over the past few years. Green Lawns may face direct liability for the homeowner's losses under a negligent hiring or negligent supervision theory on these facts. Similarly, an employer may be liable for wrongful retention of an employee if the employer allows an employee to remain employed after the employee threatens others or commits violent acts at the workplace.

Finally, note that while a principal is liable for the torts of his agent committed in the course and scope of the agency, a principal is usually not held liable for torts committed by **independent contractors**, unless the principal directed or authorized the wrongful act. Independent contractors are individuals performing services for another who are not employees, and who exercise independent discretion and control over their own activities. Be aware that this is an area of some complexity. There are several different bodies of law (e.g., tax, labor, and employment) and different legal tests that speak to whether a worker is an independent contractor or an employee. For our purposes, understand that employers cannot avoid liability for contracts, torts, or other legal obligations associated with, or resulting from, a worker who qualifies as an employee under applicable law simply by calling the worker an independent contractor.

F. FIDUCIARY DUTIES OF AGENTS

Agency relationships are fundamentally fiduciary in nature. As fiduciaries, agents are required to act with due care and also must "act loyally for the principal's benefit in all matters connected with the agency relationship." Restatement (Third) of Agency § 8.01; *see also* § 8.08. Among other obligations, agents owe their principals the specific duties outlined in the following subsections.

1. Performance

An agent must perform work or duties required by the principal. These duties may be set forth in the agency agreement (whether written or oral) or may be implied from the nature of the agency relationship. The duty of performance is sometimes called the duty of obedience, because the agent has a duty to obey the principal's directions. Agents must perform required duties with the care, competence, and diligence normally exercised by agents in similar circumstances. *See* Restatement (Third) of Agency § 8.08. For example, attorney-agents will be held to standards of care and loyalty set forth in professional responsibility rules.

2. Notification and Disclosure

An agent must disclose all information relating to the agency to his principal. For example, assume a real estate agent has been hired by a family to sell their home. The agent has a duty to notify the sellers, the principals, of all offers on the house. The agent cannot decide for himself, "This offer is so low I won't bother telling the family about it." In agency law, it is presumed the principal knows all that the agent knows, and the agent has an affirmative obligation to share information with his principal.

3. Loyalty

An agent also must act solely for the benefit of the principal. This means, for example, that an agent cannot use her position to make a secret profit for her own benefit. *See* Restatement (Third) of Agency § 8.02. Agents also cannot disclose the principal's confidential information to third parties or use the principal's information or resources for any purpose except for those related to the principal's business. *See* Restatement (Third) of Agency §§ 8.03, 8.04, 8.05. Agents also cannot deal with their principals as adversaries, compete with their principals, or represent anyone whose interests conflict with those of the principal, unless the principal agrees. *See* Restatement (Third) of Agency §§ 8.03, 8.04.

4. Accounting

An agent must account to the principal for all money or property paid out or received on the principal's behalf. Under this rule, for example, an attorney cannot settle a case and keep an extra $10,000 for herself by telling the principal that the settlement was $10,000 less than it actually was. Agents also must keep records and maintain separate accounts for the principal's funds and cannot commingle funds.

5. Agent's Liability for Breach of Fiduciary Duty

If an agent breaches his fiduciary duty, the principal may have several potential remedies. In appropriate circumstances, a principal may be entitled to an injunction or other similar equitable remedy. *See* Restatement (Third) of Agency § 8.01 cmt. d. The principal also may have a basis for voiding or rescinding a contract with a third party. *Id.* A breach also may subject the agent to liability for actual losses caused to the principal, and, potentially, punitive damages as well. *Id.* Finally, a principal may seek disgorgement in cases involving breaches of fiduciary duty, even if the principal cannot establish that the agent's breach damaged the principal. *Id.* *See also Sokoloff v. Harriman Estates Dev. Corp.*, 754 N.E.2d 184, 189 (N.Y. 2001) (holding "[if] an agent receives anything as a result of his violation of a duty of loyalty to the principal, he is subject to a liability to deliver it, its value, or its proceeds, to the principal") (internal quotations and citations omitted).

G. THE PRINCIPAL'S DUTIES

Principals typically owe three duties to their agents, in addition to those arising under express and implied terms of the agency contract between the principal and the agent.

1. Compensation

Principals must pay agents for their services. Sometimes, the compensation is fixed in a written agreement. An example is the standard real estate listing agreement that obligates sellers of a dwelling to pay a 6 percent commission based on the purchase price of the property. If no sum certain is stated, the agent is entitled to compensation in a reasonable and customary amount, unless the agent has agreed to act without pay.

2. Reimbursement and Indemnification

The principal must reimburse the agent for costs and expenses reasonably incurred in the course of performance by the agent. Oftentimes, parties address reimbursement in their agency agreement: For example, an employer may require an employee to obtain advance approval before incurring expenses above a certain dollar amount. The principal also generally must indemnify the agent if the agent makes a payment that is within the scope of the agent's actual authority, or is beneficial to the principal, or if the agent suffers a loss that fairly should be borne by the principal. *See* Restatement (Third) of Agency §§ 8.14, 8.15. For example, assume a real estate agent provides an offer to homeowners for their house. The homeowners accept the offer and agree to vacate the house by the first of the next month. If the homeowners fail to vacate on time, the buyers may be required to incur costs for staying in hotels and eating in restaurants. The homeowners, as principals, are required to indemnify the real estate agent for this liability if the buyers attempt to hold the agent responsible.

3. Cooperation

The principal must not hinder the agent in the performance of his duties and must deal with the agent fairly and in good faith. Building upon our real estate example above, assume the homeowners have a change of heart and decide not to sell their house. Because they have listed the house with an agent, they are required to cooperate with the agent so the agent can perform his duty to sell the house. If the homeowners refuse to show the house, purposefully ruin the appearance of the house, or destroy appliances so that the house will not be attractive to buyers, the agent may sue for breach of contract. Similarly, the homeowners generally cannot list the house with two agents. Finally, the duty to cooperate encompasses a duty to provide the agent with what he will need to perform duties. This could include a credit card, an office, or equipment. (See Exhibit 2.1 for chart of duties owed in agency relationships.)

EXHIBIT 2.1   Duties Owed in Agency Relationships

Duties Owed by Agent
Performance (using due care and diligence)
Notification (duty to inform principal)
Loyalty
Accounting of profits

Duties Owed by Principal
Compensation
Reimbursement and indemnification
Cooperation

H. CONTRACTUAL LIABILITY OF AGENTS

When an agent enters into a contract with a third person on behalf of a principal, the agent's liability depends in first instance on whether the principal is bound. If the agent has actual, apparent, or (traditionally) inherent authority to enter into the contract, so that the principal is bound, the agent's liability will turn on whether the principal is disclosed, undisclosed, or partially disclosed or unidentified.

A **disclosed principal** is a principal whose existence and identity are known to the third party. Thus, a truck driver who introduces himself by saying, "I'm Sam, the driver for Ace Movers," has disclosed both the principal's existence and identity. Generally, agents are not personally liable to third parties if disclosed principals do not perform their contractual duties. *See* Restatement (Third) of Agency § 6.01.

A **partially disclosed** or **unidentified principal** is a principal whose existence is known to the third party, but whose specific identity is not known. For example, the owner of a house might tell her real estate agent not to disclose her identity to potential buyers to protect her anonymity. The potential buyers of the house would know that a seller-principal exists, but would not know her specific identity. Because the third parties do not have an opportunity to conduct any investigation of the unidentified principal, and cannot judge her trustworthiness, an agent is usually liable for contracts made on behalf of such a partially disclosed principal, even though the principal is bound as well. *See* Restatement (Third) of Agency § 6.02.

An **undisclosed principal** is a principal whose existence and identity are unknown to third parties. For example, a real estate agent might not disclose that he represents a buyer and might appear to be negotiating for the purchase of a home on his own behalf. Because the third party, the seller of the home, has no way of assessing the unknown principal's credibility and indeed believes the agent is acting on his own behalf, the agent will retain liability for contracts made for such undisclosed principals. The principal may also retain liability because the contract was made for her benefit. *See* Restatement (Third) of Agency § 6.03.

I. DEFINING AND LIMTING AUTHORITY AND POWER

Parties to an agency agreement may attempt to limit their potential liability for unauthorized acts, fiduciary breaches, etc., by using exculpatory language in their contract. For example, the contract might state that the agent is not authorized to make certain statements or representations on behalf of the principal and that the agent will be liable if any such representations are made to the third party. Contracts also may contain a so-called **merger** or **integration clause**, which provides that the signed writing constitutes the full and final statement of the agreement between the parties and that any prior or contemporaneous statements made by an agent/employee are not part of the deal unless contained in the written agreement. Although merger clauses come in many forms, they often look something like this:

> This Agreement represents the Parties' entire understanding regarding the subject matter expressed herein. None of the terms of this Agreement can be waived or modified, except by an express written agreement signed by an authorized representative of the Parties. There are no promises, representations, covenants, warranties, or undertakings between the Parties other than those expressly set forth in this Agreement.

The purpose of both authority and merger clauses is to reduce the likelihood that the principal will be bound by a statement made by an agent during the sales process that is not part of the final, approved deal. Finally, the agent and principal also may reduce uncertainty by agreeing in writing as to which party will be liable for certain acts or obligations.

J. TERMINATION OF AGENCY RELATIONSHIP

Upon termination of the agency relationship, an agent no longer has the authority to bind the principal. Agency relationships may be terminated when the stated time period expires if the agreement provides a period of duration (such as a six-month listing period for a real estate agent), when the purpose of the agency has been fulfilled, by mutual agreement, by death or bankruptcy of either party, or by either party upon reasonable notice to the other. If the parties have agreed that the agency will exist for some specified time period, a termination by one party prior to this period may constitute a breach of contract and subject the breaching party to damages proximately caused by early termination. If the parties have no agreement specifying a termination date for the agency, it is usually held that the agency relationship will expire after a reasonable time. Agency relationships also terminate if an event occurs that makes it impossible for the agent to perform, such as destruction of property that is the subject of the agency.

Chapter Summary

- An agent is a person who acts on behalf of a principal and is subject to the principal's control.
- A principal is a person who agrees that another person may act on his behalf, subject to the principal's control.
- An agent acting with actual, apparent, or (traditionally) inherent authority has the power to bind a principal to a contract.
- A principal also may be bound to a contract under the doctrines of estoppel or ratification.
- A principal may be held vicariously or directly liable for an agent's torts under doctrines such as respondeat superior. Under this doctrine, an employer is liable for the torts of its employees, provided the employee was acting within the scope of her employment.
- A principal may be held directly liable for an agent's tort if the principal was negligent in appointing or retaining the agent.
- Agents owe fiduciary duties of care and loyalty to principals.
- An agent's liability on a contract entered into on a principal's behalf depends on whether the principal is disclosed, partially disclosed, or undisclosed.

Applying the Concepts

1. A successful business, Acme Diversified, was established by its founder many years ago. The founder spoiled his only child, who grew up to live an undisciplined and dissolute life. Nevertheless, the child inherited Acme upon the founder's death and became its president. The child was in fact a poor manager and was widely regarded as such. An experienced and competent officer of Acme devised a new business strategy and loyally presented it to the president. The president, aware of his own deficiencies, adopted the strategy and publicly presented it as his own, claiming credit for his business acumen and giving the experienced officer no recognition or reward. The officer felt mistreated and, as the president imperfectly understood and executed the new strategy, the experienced officer was able, on his own time, to found another business, which used the new strategy very effectively to compete with Acme. The officer remained employed by Acme at all times, operating the new business on his own time and through agents of his own. Acme seeks an order directing that the new business's profit be turned over to Acme, while the new business seeks to resist such an order. Will Acme prevail? Why or why not?

2. Abel, Betty, and Connor are each owners of English Gardens, LLP, a landscape architecture and design business organized as a limited liability partnership. Betty owns 80 percent of the partnership; Abel and Connor each own 10

percent. The partnership agreement contains a provision that states that "[n]o partner shall engage in any of the following acts or transactions without the prior written consent of the other two partners: (i) make or incur any expenditure on behalf of the partnership in excess of $10,000; (ii) lease, purchase, rent, sell, mortgage, or otherwise create a lien upon any partnership real estate or any interest therein, or enter into any contract for such purpose; and (iii) borrow money on behalf of the partnership, except in the ordinary course of partnership business."

Last week, Betty purchased a new, high-end truck in the name of the partnership for $50,000. Betty dealt with the dealership by herself, taking a loan out in the name of the partnership to finance the purchase. She did not seek permission for the transaction from Abel or Connor, nor has she disclosed the purchase to them. Although Betty initially intended to use the truck for partnership business, since taking possession of the truck she has kept it in her driveway and used it exclusively for personal matters.

a. Is English Gardens obligated to repay the loan?
b. Would the result be different under § 301(1) of the Uniform Limited Liability Company Act?

3. You represent Bank Corp., a commercial lender. Two years ago, Bank loaned money to Road Racer, Inc., a company that designs and builds custom road racing bicycles. Although Road Racer's business historically has been strong, several years of mismanagement and economic stress have taken their toll. Concerned about protecting Bank's interests in Road Racer as a lender, an employee of Bank has been stopping by the bike factory every day for the past several months to check on the status of orders, etc. Recently, Bank's employee also has begun to interact directly with customers while on site at the factory — for example, taking orders and receiving payments. Bank's employee is convinced that unless she helps out, Road Racer's business will fold.

Last week, Peter Plaintiff, a customer, placed an order for a custom bike. Bank's employee took the order from the customer. Unfortunately, however, Road Racer never finished the order — Road Racer's CEO and master builder fled the jurisdiction under a cloud of suspicion arising from financial improprieties related to Road Racer's vendor relationships.

Customer has sued Road Racer and Bank for breach of contract. Is Bank liable for customer's losses?

4. Hereford College would like to acquire additional land near its current campus to build a new science lab. The land currently is owned by residents of the town that surrounds Hereford. For a number of reasons, "town-gown" relations between Hereford and the surrounding community are tense. First, while the town depends on Hereford economically, it spends a significant amount every year on public safety issues (e.g., parties with underage drinking, fire alarms) associated with Hereford's student population. Every year, the college and town officials engage in difficult discussions regarding payments that Hereford makes

to the town for these public services. Second, some residents of the town believe that the college's land purchases have driven up real estate prices throughout the town, "pricing out" long-time residents. Third, the college believes that whenever it seeks to purchase land openly, sellers jack up the price, believing (correctly) that the college has deep pockets.

For all of these reasons, the college decided to hire Sam Smith to act as Hereford's agent in the purchase of property for the science center. Sam's contract states that Sam cannot tell anyone that Hereford is the real purchaser.

Sally Seller owns a piece of prime real estate near the Hereford campus. Last week, Sally negotiated a deal with Smith whereby Sally agreed to sell, and Smith agreed to purchase, an undeveloped parcel of land for $15 million. Sally and Smith signed the land sale agreement. Hereford was not mentioned.

Last night, Smith told Hereford about the deal. Hereford's president yelled at Sam, telling him the price was too high. The president also made it clear that he would not honor the $15 million price term. Sally, who now knows about Hereford's involvement, has sued Hereford and Smith for breach of contract. Is Hereford liable? What about Smith? Why or why not as to both questions? (For purposes of this question, ignore issues relating to the availability of specific performance.)

5. Terry is a crew chief for Green Lawns, LLC, a landscaping architecture and design firm. Terry's job include managing work crews, making sure equipment is gassed up and in good working order, driving crews to job sites, and the like. Terry has no responsibility for purchasing plants or other landscaping material.

Last night, on the way back from a job, Terry noticed a "pop-up" stand where a local farmer was selling apple seedlings. Based on his work over the years, Terry believes the seedlings are of high quality and that they are being offered at a good price. He decides to purchase some and bring them back to Ellis, the owner of the business, having assured the farmer that Ellis would pay for the trees. Is Ellis bound by Terry's purchase? Why or why not? What if Ellis takes a look at the trees and says, "Thanks for picking them up, we can use them on the Sawyer job next week"?

Business Organizations in Practice

1. You represent Acme Auto Repair. Acme's CEO tell you that her long-time friend Uma (who owns Uma's used cars) would like to rent space at Acme for her used car dealership. Acme would like to help out Uma, and also would like Uma to send customers needing car repairs to Acme. Write a memo advising Acme's CEO as to potential risks and benefits associated with allowing Uma to set up a used car dealership at Acme's location. What (if anything) can Acme do to mitigate any of the risks that you identify?

2. You represent a business that is purchasing a factory from a partnership. Your client has asked for a statement of authority to ensure that Paula Partner (the partner who will sign the relevant transaction documents) has authority to do so. Draft a statement of authority for your client's review.

3. You represent minor children who were sexually abused by a religious figure. In addition to suing the religious figure, you seek to hold the national organization directly and vicariously liable for damages resulting from the abuse. What will you need to prove as a matter of agency law to hold the national organization directly liable for the offender's conduct? Vicariously liable? What evidence will you seek in discovery to support your claims?

3

General Partnerships

A general partnership is an association of two or more persons to carry on as the co-owners of a for-profit business. Partnerships are the default form of organization for multi-owner businesses — meaning, partnerships are formed whenever (i) two or more persons associate and carry on as the co-owners of a for-profit business; and (ii) the founders do not file the paperwork necessary to form or operate their business using some other business entity form. Business associates may form partnerships through an express oral or written agreement partnership agreement or through the act of associating with one another as partners (i.e., as the co-owners of a for-profit business). Partnerships formed through conduct rather than through an express oral or written agreement are known as inadvertent partnerships, and business associates can form an inadvertent partnership even if they do not intend to enter into a legal partnership or do not appreciate the legal consequences of their action under partnership law. As we discussed in Chapter 1, the general partnership form is not as popular as it once was, largely because partners in a general partnership suffer the disadvantage of unlimited personal liability for partnership debts. Nevertheless, partnership law remains important because business associates still regularly form inadvertent partnerships, and because newer forms of organization (e.g., the limited liability company) draw upon partnership law principles.

A. WHAT IS A GENERAL PARTNERSHIP?

A **general partnership** is an association of two or more persons to carry on as co-owners a business for profit. Uniform Partnership Act (UPA) § 6 and Revised

Key Concepts

- Formation and characteristics of general partnerships
- Partners' rights and obligations with respect to partnership, each other, and third parties
- Advantages and disadvantages of the partnership form
- Partner exit and partnership dissolution

Uniform Partnership Act (RUPA) §§ 102(11) and 202(a). (The uniform acts are discussed in Section B.)

- The element of **association** means that the partners have agreed (orally, in writing, or through their conduct) to associate with one another as the co-owners of a for-profit business. As noted, partnerships formed through conduct (i.e., through the act of associating to carry on as co-owners) rather than through an express oral or written partnership agreement are known as **inadvertent partnerships**. As noted, business associates can form an inadvertent partnership even if they did not intend to form a partnership or were unaware of the legal consequences of their actions under partnership law. *See* RUPA § 202(a).

- The **two or more persons** requirement excludes sole proprietorships from the definition of a general partnership. The **"persons"** in the partnership may be individuals, or they may be other business enterprises, such as a partnership (either general or limited) or a corporation.

- **Co-ownership** means that the partners have equal rights to participate in the management and conduct of partnership business.

- The word **business** refers to every trade, occupation, or profession. As Exhibit 3.1 reflects, there are far more partnerships devoted to finance, insurance, and real estate than any other businesses.

- The **for-profit** requirement excludes charitable, civic, fraternal, or other not-for-profit organizations from using the partnership form. With respect to profit, so long as there is the expectation of earning a profit, an enterprise may use the partnership form. A business does not actually have to make money to qualify for partnership status.

EXHIBIT 3.1   Partnerships by Type of Business (2012-2013)

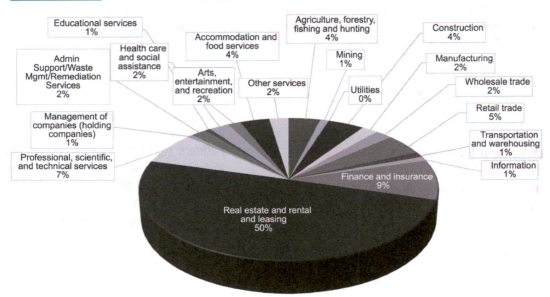

B. WHAT LAW GOVERNS A GENERAL PARTNERSHIP?

1. Choice of Law

As a general rule, the internal affairs of a partnership and the liability of a partner as a partner for a debt, obligation, or other liability of the partnership are governed by: (1) the law of the state of formation in the case of a limited liability partnership (discussed in Chapter 4); and (2) the law of the jurisdiction in which the partnership has its principal office in the case of a non-limited liability partnership. *See, e.g.,* RUPA § 104. The reference to internal affairs in § 104 is thought to include interpretation and enforcement of the partnership agreement, relations among the partners as partners, and relations between the partnership and a partner as a partner. The reference to the law of the state in which the partnership has its principal office is a default rule, and the partnership may change this rule via the partnership agreement. *See* RUPA § 104 cmt. Note, however, that other bodies of law may limit a partnership's choice of law options. *See* Restatement (Second) of Conflict of Laws §§ 294 (1971) (Relationship of Partners Inter Se), 187(2) (stating the limited bases for disregarding a contractual choice of law).

2. The UPA and RUPA

With the exception of Louisiana, state partnership statutes are based on either the Uniform Partnership Act (UPA) or the Revised Uniform Partnership Act (RUPA). The UPA dates to 1914, when members of the Uniform Law Commission (ULC) (also known as the National Conference of Commissioners on Uniform State Laws, or NCCUSL) proposed the UPA as a means of encouraging uniformity among the states in their treatment of partnerships. All of the states except for Louisiana adopted a UPA-style statute into law following the ULC's proposal of the 1914 Uniform Act, and UPA-style statutes dominated the landscape for many years.

In 1992, however, the ULC adopted and proposed a revised Uniform Partnership Act (RUPA) to address certain issues associated with the UPA regime. Additional changes were incorporated in 1994, 1996, 1997, and, most recently, in 2011 and 2013. The ULC refers to the revised act as the "Uniform Partnership Act (1997) (Last Amended 2013)," but for ease of reference, this text refers to the 1914 act as the UPA and the revised 1997 (with amendments) act as the RUPA.

Although the RUPA retains many features of the UPA, there are a number of important distinctions between the two regimes. For example, under the RUPA, a general partnership is a distinct entity that operates independently of its partners. RUPA § 201(a)

RUPA and the Harmonization of Business Entity Acts

The RUPA was amended in 2011 and 2013 as part of the **Harmonization of Business Entity Acts** project. The Harmonization of Business Entity Acts (HBEA), also referred to as the "hub," harmonizes the language of all of the uniform unincorporated entity acts and permits their integration into a single code of entity laws. The HBEA is Article 1 of the Uniform Business Organization Code (UBOC) proposed by the Uniform Law Commission. The UBOC includes the HBEA, along with the seven harmonized unincorporated entity acts (including the RUPA), and revises the language of each of the harmonized acts in a manner that permits their integration into a single code of entity laws. The latest amendments to the RUPA were intended to expand the comprehensiveness of the act, incorporate statutory and case law developments since its initial promulgation, and harmonize the language in the provisions that are similar to the other uniform and model unincorporated entity acts, according to the Uniform Law Commission's website. The UBOC has only been adopted in a couple of jurisdictions as of the date of this writing. The Uniform Law Commission website contains information respecting states' adoption of both the RUPA (stand-alone) and the HBEA and UBOC. In this text, we cite to the most recent version of the RUPA as published on the ULC website, which is currently located at www.uniformlaws.org.

("A partnership is an entity distinct from its partners."). As a consequence, in RUPA regimes, partnerships can own property, sue or be sued, and enter into contracts or other obligations in the name of the partnership. This differs from the UPA approach, which treats a partnership as an aggregate collection of its partners and not as a separate legal entity with the capacity to own property, to sue or be sued, or to incur contract or other obligations in the name of the partnership. Some UPA jurisdictions have enacted "common name" statutes to address complications associated with the UPA's aggregate (not entity) approach. *See, e.g.,* N.Y. C.P.L.R. § 1025 (stating two or more persons conducting business as a partnership may sue or be sued in the partnership name). Other significant differences between the UPA and RUPA are discussed in Section M and Exhibit 3.9 below.

At the time of this writing, 38 states and the District of Columbia have enacted RUPA-style regimes. The remainder of the states (except for Louisiana) continue to follow UPA-style regimes. See Exhibit 3.2 for a list of which states follow each act. Because U.S. jurisdictions are divided as to which act they follow, lawyers should have a thorough understanding of both the UPA and RUPA regimes. Moreover, because states are free to make changes to the uniform acts when enacting state law, and may choose to adopt (or not adopt) amendments proposed by the ULC, you should always consult applicable state partnership law statutes and associated case law before advising clients as to their rights and obligations.

3. The Partnership Agreement

The **partnership agreement** plays a key role in partnership governance. *See* RUPA § 105 (reflecting in text and comments primacy of partnership agreement in establishing *inter se* relations among the partners and partnership). This is because under both the UPA and RUPA, state partnership statutes contain default rules that function as a safety net, applying when (i) the partnership agreement is silent; (ii) the partners fail to agree on departures from default rules; or (iii) the matter at issue involves a limited list of non-waivable or non-modifiable rules. *See id.* Apart from the limited list of non-waivable or non-modifiable rules, both the UPA and the RUPA afford partners considerable freedom to tailor governance rules to meet business needs, and as between the partnership agreement and statutory default rules, the partnership agreement generally governs. This relationship between the partnership agreement and default rules is spelled out in RUPA §§ 105(a) and (b):

EXHIBIT 3.2   **Table of Jurisdictions Following UPA and RUPA**

UPA (1914 Act)	RUPA (1997 Act)
Georgia	Alabama
Indiana	Alaska
Massachusetts	Arizona
Michigan	Arkansas
Missouri	California
New Hampshire	Colorado
New York	Connecticut
North Carolina	Delaware
Pennsylvania	District of Columbia
Rhode Island	Florida
South Carolina	Hawaii
	Idaho
	Illinois
	Iowa
	Kansas
	Kentucky
	Maine
	Maryland
	Minnesota
	Mississippi
	Montana
	Nebraska
	Nevada
	New Jersey
	New Mexico
	North Dakota
	Ohio
	Oklahoma
	Oregon
	South Dakota
	Tennessee
	Texas
	Utah
	Vermont
	Virginia
	Washington
	West Virginia
	Wisconsin
	Wyoming

(a) Except as otherwise provided in subsections (c) and (d), the partnership agreement governs:

(1) relations among the partners as partners and between the partners and the partnership;

(2) the business of the partnership and the conduct of that business; and

(3) the means and conditions for amending the partnership agreement.

(b) To the extent the partnership agreement does not provide for a matter described in subsection (a), this [act] governs the matter.

See also UPA § 18.

To see how this system of default rules and private ordering works in practice, consider how profits are allocated as between partners. Both the UPA and the RUPA provide that partners in a general partnership are entitled to share equally in partnership profits (and are chargeable with an equal share of partnership losses) even if the partners make unequal contributions to capital or spend unequal amounts of time working on partnership business. *See* UPA § 18(a); RUPA § 401(a) (referencing partnership distributions rather than profits). If the partners agree to adjust that allocation of profits, they may do so as a matter of partnership law, keeping in mind the allocation of profits and losses also is subject to constraints and requirements arising under tax law. If the partnership agreement is silent as to the allocation of profits or losses, however, the default rules will apply, and both profits and losses will be allocated equally despite differences in partners' investment of capital or time spent working on partnership business.

C. TAXATION OF PARTNERSHIPS

Although a partnership is an entity and can sue and be sued in its own name under the RUPA, a general partnership is not a separate tax-paying entity under the federal tax code. Instead, under default rules, partnership income and losses are **passed through** to the partners, with each partner's respective share of partnership income or losses reported on a separate form called Schedule K-1 (see Exhibit 3.3). In this way, the taxation of partners is much like the taxation of sole proprietors: The partners simply include their share of any partnership income or losses on their individual tax returns and pay tax based on their individual tax circumstances and according to the personal income tax rates or "brackets" established by the Internal Revenue Service.

Note that partners must declare and pay taxes on any income allocated to them, whether or not that income is actually distributed. For example, assume that a two-person partnership had profits of $20,000 for 2015. Further assume that the partners decided to reserve an emergency account of $10,000 for anticipated repairs to partnership property. Each partner must declare and pay tax on his respective share of the allocated profits (50 percent, or $10,000 each under default rules), even if the partnership elects not to distribute 100 percent of allocated profits to each partner. This rule is discussed below in Section J.2. Similarly, losses experienced by the partnership should be declared on each partner's individual tax return, potentially offsetting other income and lowering tax liability. Although the partnership does not pay federal income tax, it does file an information return, Form 1065 (see Exhibit 3.4).

EXHIBIT 3.3   IRS Schedule K-1

651113

☐ Final K-1 ☐ Amended K-1	OMB No. 1545-0123

**Schedule K-1
(Form 1065)**

Department of the Treasury
Internal Revenue Service

2015

For calendar year 2015, or tax
year beginning _____ , 2015
ending _____ , 20 ____

**Partner's Share of Income, Deductions,
Credits, etc.**   ▶ See back of form and separate instructions.

Part I   Information About the Partnership
A   Partnership's employer identification number
B   Partnership's name, address, city, state, and ZIP code
C   IRS Center where partnership filed return
D   ☐ Check if this is a publicly traded partnership (PTP)

Part II   Information About the Partner
E   Partner's identifying number
F   Partner's name, address, city, state, and ZIP code

G ☐ General partner or LLC member-manager   ☐ Limited partner or other LLC member

H ☐ Domestic partner   ☐ Foreign partner

I1 What type of entity is this partner? _____

I2 If this partner is a retirement plan (IRA/SEP/Keogh/etc.), check here . . . . ☐

J Partner's share of profit, loss, and capital (see instructions):

	Beginning	Ending
Profit	%	%
Loss	%	%
Capital	%	%

K Partner's share of liabilities at year end:

Nonrecourse	. . . . . .	$ _____
Qualified nonrecourse financing	.	$ _____
Recourse	. . . .	$ _____

L Partner's capital account analysis:

Beginning capital account . . .	$ _____
Capital contributed during the year	$ _____
Current year increase (decrease) .	$ _____
Withdrawals & distributions . .	$ (_____)
Ending capital account	$ _____

☐ Tax basis   ☐ GAAP   ☐ Section 704(b) book
☐ Other (explain)

M Did the partner contribute property with a built-in gain or loss?
☐ Yes   ☐ No
If "Yes," attach statement (see instructions)

Part III Partner's Share of Current Year Income, Deductions, Credits, and Other Items		
1 Ordinary business income (loss)	15	Credits
2 Net rental real estate income (loss)		
3 Other net rental income (loss)	16	Foreign transactions
4 Guaranteed payments		
5 Interest income		
6a Ordinary dividends		
6b Qualified dividends		
7 Royalties		
8 Net short-term capital gain (loss)		
9a Net long-term capital gain (loss)	17	Alternative minimum tax (AMT) items
9b Collectibles (28%) gain (loss)		
9c Unrecaptured section 1250 gain		
10 Net section 1231 gain (loss)	18	Tax-exempt income and nondeductible expenses
11 Other income (loss)		
	19	Distributions
12 Section 179 deduction		
13 Other deductions	20	Other information
14 Self-employment earnings (loss)		

*See attached statement for additional information.

For IRS Use Only

For Paperwork Reduction Act Notice, see Instructions for Form 1065.   IRS.gov/form1065   Cat. No. 11394R   **Schedule K-1 (Form 1065) 2015**

EXHIBIT 3.4   **IRS Form 1065**

Form **1065**		**U.S. Return of Partnership Income**		OMB No. 1545-0123

Department of the Treasury
Internal Revenue Service

For calendar year 2015, or tax year beginning _____ , 2015, ending _____ , 20 ____

▶ Information about Form 1065 and its separate instructions is at *www.irs.gov/form1065.*

2015

A Principal business activity		Name of partnership	D Employer identification number
B Principal product or service	Type or Print	Number, street, and room or suite no. If a P.O. box, see the instructions.	E Date business started
C Business code number		City or town, state or province, country, and ZIP or foreign postal code	F Total assets (see the instructions) $

G   Check applicable boxes: **(1)** ☐ Initial return **(2)** ☐ Final return **(3)** ☐ Name change **(4)** ☐ Address change **(5)** ☐ Amended return
   (6) ☐ Technical termination - also check (1) or (2)

H   Check accounting method: **(1)** ☐ Cash   **(2)** ☐ Accrual   **(3)** ☐ Other (specify) ▶ _____

I   Number of Schedules K-1. Attach one for each person who was a partner at any time during the tax year ▶ _____

J   Check if Schedules C and M-3 are attached . . . . ☐

Caution. *Include **only** trade or business income and expenses on lines 1a through 22 below. See the instructions for more information.*

Income	1a	Gross receipts or sales	1a	
	b	Returns and allowances	1b	
	c	Balance. Subtract line 1b from line 1a	1c	
	2	Cost of goods sold (attach Form 1125-A)	2	
	3	Gross profit. Subtract line 2 from line 1c	3	
	4	Ordinary income (loss) from other partnerships, estates, and trusts (attach statement) . .	4	
	5	Net farm profit (loss) (attach Schedule F (Form 1040))	5	
	6	Net gain (loss) from Form 4797, Part II, line 17 (attach Form 4797)	6	
	7	Other income (loss) (attach statement)	7	
	8	**Total income (loss).** Combine lines 3 through 7	8	
Deductions (see the instructions for limitations)	9	Salaries and wages (other than to partners) (less employment credits)	9	
	10	Guaranteed payments to partners	10	
	11	Repairs and maintenance	11	
	12	Bad debts	12	
	13	Rent	13	
	14	Taxes and licenses	14	
	15	Interest	15	
	16a	Depreciation (if required, attach Form 4562)	16a	
	b	Less depreciation reported on Form 1125-A and elsewhere on return	16b	16c
	17	Depletion **(Do not deduct oil and gas depletion.)**	17	
	18	Retirement plans, etc.	18	
	19	Employee benefit programs	19	
	20	Other deductions (attach statement)	20	
	21	**Total deductions.** Add the amounts shown in the far right column for lines 9 through 20 .	21	
	22	**Ordinary business income (loss).** Subtract line 21 from line 8	22	

Sign Here

Under penalties of perjury, I declare that I have examined this return, including accompanying schedules and statements, and to the best of my knowledge and belief, it is true, correct, and complete. Declaration of preparer (other than general partner or limited liability company member manager) is based on all information of which preparer has any knowledge.

May the IRS discuss this return with the preparer shown below (see instructions)? ☐ **Yes** ☐ **No**

▶ _____
Signature of general partner or limited liability company member manager

▶ _____
Date

Paid Preparer Use Only	Print/Type preparer's name	Preparer's signature	Date	Check ☐ if self-employed	PTIN
	Firm's name ▶			Firm's EIN ▶	
	Firm's address ▶			Phone no.	

For Paperwork Reduction Act Notice, see separate instructions.   Cat. No. 11390Z   Form **1065** (2015)

This form is used to report the income, deductions, gains, and losses from the operation of the partnership and each partner's distributive share of taxable income.

A 1996 change to the tax code (*see* 26 C.F.R. §§ 301.7701-1 et seq.) allows partnerships to "check the box," or elect how the business wishes to be classified for federal income tax purposes (i.e., as a partnership or as an association taxable as a corporation) on a designated IRS form (Form 8832). See Exhibit 3.5. According to tax regulations, if the partners do not make an affirmative election as to tax treatment, the default tax treatment for partnerships — i.e., pass through taxation — will apply. Any partnership desiring to be classified as an association taxable as a corporation must file the election. See Exhibit 3.5. The election is made by attaching IRS Form 8832 to the partnership's informational return or to a corporate tax return. Generally, once the election is made, it cannot be changed for five years. Because taxation is a complex issue, and the election to be taxed as either a partnership or a corporation might not be equally beneficial to all partners, lawyers should be sure to consult with clients, and also with taxation experts, before making an election.

D. HOW ARE GENERAL PARTNERSHIPS FORMED?

As with sole proprietorships, there are few legal formalities involved in creating a general partnership. This is because the essence of a general partnership is the partners' voluntary association as co-owners.

1. Partnership Formation and Inadvertent Partnerships

When business associates enter into an express partnership agreement (especially a written partnership agreement), partnership formation generally is not in question. But when business associates do not expressly agree (either orally or in writing) to form a partnership, formation is a more complicated question. In a nutshell, when there is no express oral or written partnership agreement, we examine the parties' objectively manifested intentions, as reflected in their words, conduct, and in the nature and context of their business relationship, to determine whether the parties' association meets the definition of a legal partnership. *See* UPA §§ 7, 18(e); RUPA § 202.

The presence — or absence — of equal rights to manage and control partnership affairs is a key factor in partnership formation cases. As the Official Comments to RUPA § 202 suggest, the power of ultimate control is a key concept in partnership formation because control rights serve to distinguish the partnership relationship from other relationships involving ownership, but not control – e.g., passive co-ownership of property, as distinguished from using the property to carry on a business, without the right to control its use or disposition.

Profit sharing is another key issue in partnership formation cases. At common law, "profit sharing was the most important factor in shedding light on the intention to establish a partnership." *See, e.g., Ingram v. Deere*, 288 S.W.3d 886, 893-94 (Tex. 2009) (citations omitted). Under both the UPA and the RUPA, profit sharing remains an important factor: It is prima facie evidence that a partnership has been formed

EXHIBIT 3.5	Excerpt, IRS Form 8832

Form **8832**
(Rev. December 2013)

Entity Classification Election

OMB No. 1545-1516

Department of the Treasury
Internal Revenue Service

▶ Information about Form 8832 and its instructions is at *www.irs.gov/form8832*.

	Name of eligible entity making election	Employer identification number
Type or Print	Number, street, and room or suite no. If a P.O. box, see instructions.	
	City or town, state, and ZIP code. If a foreign address, enter city, province or state, postal code and country. Follow the country's practice for entering the postal code.	

▶ Check if: ☐ Address change   ☐ Late classification relief sought under Revenue Procedure 2009-41
☐ Relief for a late change of entity classification election sought under Revenue Procedure 2010-32

Part I	Election Information

1   **Type of election** (see instructions):

a ☐ Initial classification by a newly-formed entity. Skip lines 2a and 2b and go to line 3.
b ☐ Change in current classification. Go to line 2a.

2a Has the eligible entity previously filed an entity election that had an effective date within the last 60 months?

☐ **Yes.** Go to line 2b.
☐ **No.** Skip line 2b and go to line 3.

2b Was the eligible entity's prior election an initial classification election by a newly formed entity that was effective on the date of formation?

☐ **Yes.** Go to line 3.
☐ **No.** Stop here. You generally are not currently eligible to make the election (see instructions).

3   Does the eligible entity have more than one owner?

☐ **Yes.** You can elect to be classified as a partnership or an association taxable as a corporation. Skip line 4 and go to line 5.
☐ **No.** You can elect to be classified as an association taxable as a corporation or to be disregarded as a separate entity. Go to line 4.

4   If the eligible entity has only one owner, provide the following information:

a Name of owner ▶ ....
b Identifying number of owner ▶ ....

5   If the eligible entity is owned by one or more affiliated corporations that file a consolidated return, provide the name and employer identification number of the parent corporation:

a Name of parent corporation ▶ ....
b Employer identification number ▶ ....

For Paperwork Reduction Act Notice, see instructions.   Cat. No. 22598R   Form **8832** (Rev. 12-2013)

EXHIBIT 3.5   (continued)

Form 8832 (Rev. 12-2013)   Page **2**

| **Part I** | **Election Information** (Continued) |

6   Type of entity (see instructions):

a ☐ A domestic eligible entity electing to be classified as an association taxable as a corporation.
b ☐ A domestic eligible entity electing to be classified as a partnership.
c ☐ A domestic eligible entity with a single owner electing to be disregarded as a separate entity.
d ☐ A foreign eligible entity electing to be classified as an association taxable as a corporation.
e ☐ A foreign eligible entity electing to be classified as a partnership.
f ☐ A foreign eligible entity with a single owner electing to be disregarded as a separate entity.

7   If the eligible entity is created or organized in a foreign jurisdiction, provide the foreign country of organization ▶ --

8   Election is to be effective beginning (month, day, year) (see instructions) . . . . ▶ _____

9   Name and title of contact person whom the IRS may call for more information | **10** Contact person's telephone number

Consent Statement and Signature(s) (see instructions)

Under penalties of perjury, I (we) declare that I (we) consent to the election of the above-named entity to be classified as indicated above, and that I (we) have examined this election and consent statement, and to the best of my (our) knowledge and belief, this election and consent statement are true, correct, and complete. If I am an officer, manager, or member signing for the entity, I further declare under penalties of perjury that I am authorized to make the election on its behalf.

Signature(s)	Date	Title

Form **8832** (Rev. 12-2013)

under UPA, and it creates a rebuttable presumption of partnership formation under RUPA. There are nuances to this rule, however, as reflected in RUPA § 202(c):

> (c) In determining whether a partnership is formed, the following rules apply:
>
> (1) Joint tenancy, tenancy in common, tenancy by the entireties, joint property, common property, or part ownership does not by itself establish a partnership, even if the co-owners share profits made by the use of the property.
>
> (2) The sharing of gross returns does not by itself establish a partnership, even if the persons sharing them have a joint or common right or interest in property from which the returns are derived.
>
> (3) A person who receives a share of the profits of a business is presumed to be a partner in the business, unless the profits were received in payment:
>
> (A) of a debt by installments or otherwise;
>
> (B) for services as an independent contractor or of wages or other compensation to an employee;
>
> (C) of rent;
>
> (D) of an annuity or other retirement or health benefit to a beneficiary, representative, or designee of a deceased or retired partner;
>
> (E) of interest or other charge on a loan, even if the amount of payment varies with the profits of the business, including a direct or indirect present or future ownership of the collateral, or rights to income, proceeds, or increase in value derived from the collateral; or
>
> (F) for the sale of the goodwill of a business or other property by installments or otherwise.

RUPA § 202(c). *See also* UPA § 7.

Other factors relevant to formation include the presence (or absence) of (i) an agreement to share losses; (ii) joint liability to creditors; (iii) contributions of capital to the enterprise; and (iv) the extension of loans to the enterprise. *See, e.g., Brodsky v. Stadlen*, 526 N.Y.S.2d 478 (App. Div. 1988).

Case Preview

Fredianelli v. Jenkins

In *Fredianelli v. Jenkins*, a member of the band Third Eye Blind (Fredianelli, a guitar player and song writer) alleged that he and Stephan Jenkins (the lead singer) and other band members had created and entered into a legal partnership through their conduct, which included writing songs together, performing, and touring. As you read *Fredianelli*, consider the following questions:

1. Why does Fredianelli want to establish that a partnership existed? What rights would Fredianelli have as a partner? What duties would Jenkins owe?
2. What legal standards does the court apply in deciding whether a partnership existed?

3. What evidence does Fredianelli offer to support his claim that a partnership existed? How does this evidence match up (or not) with the definition of a legal partnership?
4. Does it matter that the parties allegedly referred to Fredianelli as a "member" and "officer" of the band?
5. There appears to have been a fair amount of "paperwork" in this case — documents relating to corporations, song-writing credit, etc. How does the absence of a formal, written partnership agreement play into this case, if at all?

Fredianelli v. Jenkins
931 F. Supp. 2d 1001 (N.D. Cal. 2013)

EDWARD M. CHEN, District Judge.*

I. INTRODUCTION

Defendants Stephan Jenkins; Bradley Hargreaves; Third Eye Blind, Inc.; 3EB Touring, Inc.; and Stephan Jenkins Productions, Inc. bring the current motion for summary judgment or, alternatively, partial summary judgment of Plaintiff Anthony Fredianelli's First Amended Complaint ("FAC"). Plaintiff's complaint includes six causes of action stemming from his participation as lead guitarist for the rock group Third Eye Blind ("the Band") from 1993 to 1994 and from 2000 to 2009, and his alleged co-ownership of the Band and related entities. Jenkins is the founder, singer, and leader of the Band, and Hargreaves its drummer. The six causes of action in the FAC are for (1) breach of contract; (2) reasonable value of services performed (Plaintiff's "quantum meruit" claim); (3) constructive trust; (4) accounting; (5) declaratory relief regarding ownership of copyrights; and (6) declaratory relief regarding ownership of trademarks. Defendants now move for summary judgment on each cause of action.

For the reasons stated herein, the Court GRANTS Defendants' motion for summary judgment in its entirety except to the extent Plaintiff's claims for breach of contract and an accounting are based on his not receiving his full share of net touring revenues, irrespective of his status as a co-owner of the Band, as discussed further below . . .

. . .

IV. FACTUAL AND PROCEDURAL BACKGROUND

The following facts are viewed in Fredianelli's favor. Nearly all are based on Fredianelli's declaration except where it is barred by Defendants' evidentiary objections. Where the declaration is silent as to an issue and does not rebut Defendants' proffered evidence, such facts are considered undisputed.

---

* Most footnotes and record cites have been omitted for purposes of brevity.

A. *Fredianelli's Beginnings with Third Eye Blind*

Plaintiff Anthony Fredianelli met Eric Godtland and Defendant Stephan Jenkins in early 1993, helping Jenkins form the band Third Eye Blind ("the Band"). Godtland served as the Band's manager and funded the Band's startup costs. *Id.* From 1993 to 1994, Fredianelli traveled back and forth from Nevada, where he lived, to San Francisco, California, where the Band was based, to rehearse, record, write songs, and play gigs. *Id.* However, Jenkins eventually told Fredianelli that the Band was going to go forward with Kevin Cadogan as its guitar player. *Id.*

It is undisputed that, in or about 1996 to 1997, after Fredianelli was no longer in the Band, Jenkins formed three corporate entities: Third Eye Blind, Inc., which was to handle various financial aspects of the band including receipt of music royalties; Stephan Jenkins Productions, Inc., which was to handle the various expenses associated with recording and producing the recording of songs; and 3EB Touring, Inc., which was to handle the financial aspects of the Band's touring and merchandise activities. It is undisputed that Jenkins was the sole shareholder of these corporations, as well as the president and chairman of their boards.

In late 1999, Jenkins asked Fredianelli if he would consider touring with the Band as a utility musician. Fredianelli became a "hired musician" of the Band in approximately January 2000, and considered himself an employee. Once Fredianelli began rehearsing with the Band, the Band voted to fire Cadogan. Brad Hargreaves, drummer for the Band, recounted to the rest of the Band, including Fredianelli, how he let Cadogan know that he was being fired, citing the "3eb band agreement." Fredianelli was immediately promoted to lead guitarist of the band. *Id.* Cadogan subsequently sued the Band. As lead guitarist, Plaintiff earned $1750 per week with a $1000 weekly retainer for weeks when there was no work.

At the time Fredianelli was hired by the Band, Arion Salazar, the Band's bass player, Jenkins, and Godtland told him that he would have to "pay [his] dues" during a two-year "probationary period," after which he would officially be a Band member like they were and participate as a full fledged member and co-owner of the Band. Salazar explained that "the band made big decisions together, like firing Kevin Cadogan for example, and that each member had an equal vote."

B. *The Agreement*

In or around late 2002 or early 2003, Salazar told Fredianelli that "the band[']s agreement ['the Agreement'] was affirmed through the closing of the Cadogan litigation." Godtland confirmed this fact. *Id.* Salazar told Fredianelli that "he had a lawyer who was working out 'vesting the shares' of 3eb to the shareholders, i.e. the band members." *Id.* Godtland told Fredianelli that the rest of the band agreed that Fredianelli "could begin being se[n]t all corporate and shareholder documentation from David Rawson, [the Band's accountant,] which began, and [Fredianelli] was told by Eric Godtland was information no different from Stephan Jenkins (sic)."

Subsequently, Godtland set up a meeting with Plaintiff "in or around early March of 2003, where he walked [Plaintiff] through his management agreement, and the interim agreement, going over his management agreement line by line, but also going over general dynamics of the band[']s two pass through corporations, that all members, including Stephan Jenkins, were employees of the corporations as well as owners and that [Plaintiff] in essence was agreeing to sharing the expenses of funding the business, which would include making records, to which [Plaintiff] would receive an equal share of proceeds." "Eric Go[d]tland, 3eb's manager and representative to the outside world, told [Plaintiff] he had consulted with the band by conference call and that the points of [Godtland and Plaintiff's] conversation were approved by the band." Regarding the Band's agreement, Godtland testified in the *Godtland* case that

> [a]t each stage of band members, they agreed that they would take the shareholder agreements, sign them and distribute the shares. That happened while Cadogan was in the band, that happened again when Cadogan was out of the band with Arion, and that happened again when Tony joined.
>
> What the band members said to each other with me there was that they were going to distribute these shares and they were going to sign off on these documents, and Stephan would distribute the shares to each of them.

Although Plaintiff alleges in his complaint that "[d]uring the Meeting, Plaintiff accepted the Band's offer to become a full partner according to the terms of the Agreement, as that offer was conveyed to him by the Band's manager and agent, Eric Godtland," he did not testify to such in his declaration. Fredianelli submitted no admissible evidence that he accepted the Band's offer.

Defendants have submitted a document produced by Plaintiff in this matter titled "Third Eye Blind Inter Party Agreements" (the "Agreement"), which is presumably the "interim agreement" referenced by Plaintiff. The Agreement consists of two separate sections, titled "Business Structure (entities)" and "Employment Agreements." The Business Structure section provides that the Band members "shall be the sole owners in equal economic shares of any and all issued and outstanding shares of any corporation(s) or other business entities conducting business for or on behalf of the Group . . . including but not limited to Third Eye Blind, Inc. and Third Eye Blind Touring, Inc." It then states that each member "shall have voting interests equal to their economic interests in the Corporation(s)" and requires majority approval "with respect to business and creative decisions of the Corporation(s) or the Group," such as "approval of recording budgets." Towards the end of the Business Structure section, it states in handwriting that touring revenue will be split evenly, such that 25% goes to each of Salazar, Hargreaves, Fredianelli, and Jenkins. It also provides that merchandise royalties would be divided such that 28% would go to Salazar, 19% to Hargreaves, 10% to Fredianelli, and 43% to Jenkins.

The Employment Agreements section of the Agreement provides that each Band member is entitled to an "[a]mount equal to their respective Economic Interest in the net profits of the Corporation(s)," among other forms of compensation. The Agreement contains different provisions for compensation following terminations based on whether the termination was "for cause" or without cause.

C. Operation of Band Following Plaintiff Becoming a Member

In line with the Agreement, upon his becoming a full-fledged member of the Band, Plaintiff ceased receiving the weekly retainer he had received since joining the Band in 2000 and began to receive 25% of touring revenue. However, contrary to the Agreement and as admitted at his deposition in the *Godtland* case, Plaintiff did not begin to have a role in the decision-making process of the Band and did not have a say in business decisions, where to tour, legal matters, creative decisions, or what expenses to incur. Rather, Jenkins "would make those decisions because he was the leader." In characterizing the decision-making structure of the Band, Plaintiff testified that it was not a "democracy." Rather, Jenkins told Plaintiff that Plaintiff "would have no role in the final decisions, in the decision making of the band." "[Jenkins] made an analogy as if he would be the United States and [the rest of the Band] would be smaller countries and he would — if he wanted to ask for advice, he would ask." "At the end of the day, he would reserve the right to make the decision and that that would not change." Plaintiff conceded that, although "[f]iring someone in a band is a big decision," Jenkins had the authority to fire him. Moreover, Plaintiff does not dispute that shares in the corporations conducting business for the Band were never distributed to Plaintiff or any member of the Band other than Jenkins.

A February 23, 2008 email from Plaintiff to the Band's business manager corroborates his testimony about the Band's decision-making structure. In the email, Plaintiff indicates that Jenkins, not the collective Band, was negotiating each Band member's share of the touring income, writing that "SJ and I sat down and had a talk" regarding a new agreement as to touring income, that "Stephan [Jenkins] has this same plan in mind for Brad [Hargreaves] — but as of right now they don't have an agreement," that Plaintiff was "going to be asking Eric [Godtland] — for a little bit of breathing room in regards to [Plaintiff's] management commission," and that he did not "know what Stephan [Jenkins] has in mind for [Godtland] in general."

Furthermore, it is undisputed that contrary to the Agreement, Fredianelli did not initially share in the merchandising royalties. Rather, Jenkins took the net proceeds from merchandise sales, and only came to share such revenue four years later, in 2007, at which point Jenkins received 50% of net merchandise proceeds, Hargreaves received 35%, and Plaintiff received 15%, terms which were not consistent with the Agreement.

D. Changes Following Plaintiff Becoming a Band Member

Shortly after Plaintiff's March 2003 meeting with Godtland, Godtland arranged a band meeting in Miami where he explained to each Band member that, since the Band no longer had a record company, all expenses would be paid from the Band's touring revenue, including non-touring expenses such as the Band's recording expenses. The Band agreed to the decision to pay non-touring expenses out of the net touring revenue.

From 2004 to 2007, Jenkins all but abandoned the Band. Plaintiff stepped into the void and took over the leadership role for the Band, engaging in a variety of marketing activities on behalf of the Band, such as building the Band's first Myspace and Facebook pages as well as reaching out to the Band's fanbase through the "Village Churchyard" website.

In 2005, Jenkins changed Salazar's share of the net touring revenue to less than 25%, with the remaining funds shared equally by Plaintiff, Jenkins, and Hargreaves.

It is undisputed that, in June 2006, Salazar left the Band, and the remaining three musicians continued to share the net touring revenue equally, such that each member took home one-third of the net touring revenue.

In or around early 2008, Jenkins replaced Godtland as manager for the Band. In his first act as manager, Jenkins approached Fredianelli in January 2008 about reducing his share of the touring revenue back to 25%. Fredianelli told Jenkins that he "would tentatively agree to making this one change to the deal [they] had in place, but told him strictly that it would be the only point [Fredianelli] would be willing to negotiate upon." Plaintiff told Jenkins he would make that one concession "contingent on [his] income not going down" from the $292,000 he earned touring in 2007.

E. Godtland Litigation and Plaintiff's Termination from the Band

Following Godtland's ouster as manager for the Band, Jenkins wished to sue him. Jenkins threatened that if Plaintiff and Hargreaves "did not agree to sue Godtland, Jenkins would pursue other projects, leaving the band without a lead singer and mak[ing] it impossible for 3eb to deliver the new album Jenkins had been promising [Plaintiff], Hargreaves and Third Eye Blind fans for years." *Id.* Jenkins indicated on several occasions "that he already was rich and did not need Third Eye Blind anymore, but that [Plaintiff] and Brad Hargreaves did, so [Plaintiff] had better go along, as he had convinced Brad [Hargreaves] to do, or [Plaintiff and Hargreaves] would lose everything." *Id.* Ultimately, the Band decided to proceed with the litigation against Godtland. In his deposition, Plaintiff testified he had no say in legal decisions of the band.

During the course of the *Godtland* litigation, Plaintiff gave a deposition in March 2009, in which he testified that he had never seen a management contract with Godtland and that he had effectively no control over the Band. Approximately nine months later, in December 2009, he contacted Godtland to apologize about his testimony and expressed a desire to make changes to his deposition. About a week after Plaintiff's conversation with Godtland, Plaintiff perceived that Jenkins was angry with him for the recantation of his deposition testimony. Plaintiff played his last show with the Band on December 31, 2009, after which he was effectively frozen out of the Band. *Id.* He was never formally terminated for cause or any other reason.

. . .

V. DISCUSSION

A. Breach of Contract (First Cause of Action)

This cause of action involves two separate legal theories: (1) that there existed an express contract between the parties conferring on Plaintiff co-ownership of the Band; and (2) that the parties' course of conduct evidenced an intent for Plaintiff to be a partner even absent an express partnership agreement. In addition, Plaintiff argued, but did not plead in his complaint, that Defendants breached a profit-sharing agreement with him, regardless of his status as a co-owner of the Band.

1. Express Contract

First, Defendants dispute Plaintiff's allegation that he entered an express contract, the Agreement, to become a co-owner of the Band. While both parties use the term "partner" and "partnership" throughout their briefs, this terminology appears to be inapposite with respect to the Agreement; the Agreement, as produced by Defendants, contemplates that Plaintiff will be a *shareholder* in "any corporation(s) or other business entities conducting business for or on behalf of the Group. . . ."

. . .

In sum, there is no evidence the written Agreement was consented to by all parties. Nor was it executed in a manner suggesting its existence as a binding contract. Plaintiff has not met his burden of producing evidence from which a reasonable jury could conclude that the Band consented to be bound by the terms of the Agreement.

c. Agency Authority

If Plaintiff's reliance on Godtland's representations regarding the Agreement were sufficient to create a contract, such reliance is problematic for another reason: Godtland did not have the authority to bind the Band to the Agreement's terms. An agent may bind a principal to a contract if he has either actual or ostensible authority to do so, or, if the agent is unauthorized to do so, the principal ratifies the agent's unauthorized action. *See* Cal. Civ. Code §§ 2307, 2330.

i. Actual Authority

Actual authority "is such as a principal intentionally confers upon the agent, or intentionally, or by want of ordinary care, allows the agent to believe himself to possess." Cal. Civ. Code § 2316. In other words, actual authority may be either express, whereby a principal gives it to an agent orally or by writing, or implied, whereby the conduct of the principal indicates an intent to confer actual authority or causes the agent to believe he possesses such authority. *See* 3 Witkin, Summary of Cal. Law (10th) Agency § 134. "[A] general manager ... may not, in the absence of express authority, contract to distribute to employees a portion of the profits of a business. . . ." *Howard v. Winton Co.,* 199 Cal. 374, 379, 249 P. 511 (1926). Similarly, a general manager does not have implied authority to sell the business. *See London v. Zachary,* 92 Cal. App. 2d 654, 657, 207 P.2d 1067 (1949).

Here, Plaintiff has submitted no admissible evidence showing that Godtland had express authority to bind Jenkins or the Band to the Agreement with Plaintiff. While Plaintiff testifies in his declaration that Godtland told him "he had consulted with the band by conference call and that the points of [their] conversation were approved by the band," this statement is inadmissible hearsay evidence for the point that the Band did in fact approve of Godtland entering the agreement on its behalf. Significantly, Plaintiff did not submit direct non-hearsay evidence from Godtland that he had actual authority. Moreover, Godtland could not have had implied authority to either enter into a profit-sharing agreement with Fredianelli or grant him an ownership stake in the Band, as general managers may not contract to distribute the profits of a business or sell a business absent express authority. *See Howard,* 199 Cal. at 379,

249 P. 511; *London,* 92 Cal. App. 2d at 657, 207 P.2d 1067. Thus, Fredianelli has not set forth a claim based on Godtland's actual authority to make him a co-owner of the Band.

ii. *Ostensible Authority*

Ostensible authority "is such as a principal, intentionally or by want of ordinary care, causes or allows a third person to believe the agent to possess." Cal. Civ. Code § 2317. In order for an agent to bind a principal to a contract based on the agent's ostensible authority, (1) "[t]he person dealing with the agent must do so with belief in the agent's authority and this belief must be a reasonable one"; (2) "such belief must be generated by some act or neglect of the principal sought to be charged"; and (3) "the third person in relying on the agent's apparent authority must not be guilty of negligence." *Ass'd Creditors' Agency v. Davis,* 13 Cal. 3d 374, 399, 118 Cal. Rptr. 772, 530 P.2d 1084 (1975).

As to the first factor, Plaintiff testifies in his declaration that Godtland told him "he had consulted with the band by conference call and that the points of [their] conversation were approved by the band." Although this point of Fredianelli's declaration is inadmissible to prove that the Band actually did approve of Godtland entering into the Agreement with Fredianelli on behalf of Jenkins or the Band, it is admissible for the limited purpose of establishing Plaintiff's belief that Godtland had that authority and suggests that Plaintiff's belief may have been reasonable.

On the other hand, Plaintiff has not submitted any admissible evidence that conduct of the principals—*i.e.,* Jenkins or the Band—would lead him to believe that Godtland had the authority to bind them to the Agreement. In fact, he testifies to the opposite, that Hargreaves told him that "Godtland . . . did not have the authority to act unilaterally specifically when it came to changing any member[']s financial position in the band." Although Salazar, Jenkins, and Godtland did tell Plaintiff that he would eventually become a full-fledged member and co-owner of the Band around the time that he began playing with them in 2000, they never indicated that Godtland would be the one to make that arrangement. In fact, Salazar said that "the band made big decisions together, like firing Kevin Cadogan for example. . . ." Absent admissible evidence showing that other members of the Band led Plaintiff to believe that Godtland would have the authority to enter into the Agreement on their behalf, Plaintiff cannot demonstrate that Godtland had ostensible authority to do so.

iii. *Ratification*

Even if Godtland's offering Plaintiff to enter the Agreement was unauthorized, Defendants may still be bound to it if they ratified the Agreement. "A ratification can be made . . . where an oral authorization would suffice[ ] by accepting or retaining the benefit of the act, *with notice thereof.*" Cal. Civ. Code § 2310 (emphasis added). "[R]atification may be proved by circumstantial as well as direct evidence," and "[a]nything which convincingly shows the intention of the principal to adopt or approve the act in question is sufficient." *StreetScenes v. ITC Entertainment Group, Inc.,* 103 Cal. App. 4th 233, 242, 126 Cal. Rptr. 2d 754 (2002) (quotation marks and citations omitted). On the other hand, ratification "may also be shown by implication," meaning that, "where an agent is authorized to do an act, and he transcends his authority, it is the duty of the principal to repudiate the act as soon as he is fully informed of what has been thus done in his name, else he will be bound by the act as having ratified it by implication." *Id.* (alterations, quotation marks, and citations omitted).

Here, Plaintiff does not submit any admissible evidence that the Band knew Godtland had presented Plaintiff with the Agreement. Moreover, circumstantial evidence suggests they did not have notice of Plaintiff being offered with and accepting the Agreement, as he was never treated in accordance with the Agreement, aside from his taking a twenty-five percent share of the net touring revenues. As admitted by Plaintiff in his deposition, once he became a member, he did *not* gain a role in the decision-making process of the Band, did not have a say in the Band's business decisions, and did not have a say in the Band's creative decisions, despite the Agreement's explicit provision that "[m]ajority approval of the voting interests of the Corporation(s) will be required with respect to business and creative decisions of the Corporation(s) or the Group. . . ." *See* Fredianelli Dep. 78:2-80:15; Greenberg Decl. Ex. B at 2. In addition, he did not take a share of the band's merchandise proceeds until 2007, despite the Agreement's statement that he would immediately take a ten percent share of such revenue. Such treatment is inconsistent with any ratification theory and thus this argument in favor of contract formation fails, too.

Thus, no contract may be found based on Godtland's putative role as agent.

2. Partnership

The parties devote the lion's share of their briefing on Plaintiff's first cause of action to the question of whether or not Defendants created a partnership with Plaintiff by way of their conduct.[4] Under California law, "the association of two or more persons to carry on as coowners a business for profit forms a partnership, whether or not the persons intend to form a partnership." Cal. Corp. Code § 16202(a). Whether a partnership exists depends primarily on the intention of the parties, determined from the terms of the parties' agreement or from the surrounding circumstances. *Greene v. Brooks*, 235 Cal. App. 2d 161, 165-66, 45 Cal. Rptr. 99 (1965). "It is immaterial if the parties do not designate their relationship as a partnership or if they do not know that they are partners, for intent may be implied from their acts." *In re Lona*, 393 B.R. 1, 14 (Bankr. N.D. Cal. 2008). "Ordinarily, the existence of an actual partnership is evidenced by the right of the respective parties to participate in the profits and losses of the business, the contribution by the partners of either money, property or services and some degree of participation by the partners in the management and control of the business." *Id.*

---

[4]The legal entities that appear to comprise the Band — 3EB Touring, Inc., Stephan Jenkins Productions, Inc., and Third Eye Blind, Inc. — are all corporations. Thus, it is not clear how a partnership theory fits into this scheme, *i.e.* whether Plaintiff is a partner with the other members of the Band in the operation of the Band as some separate entity from these corporations, whether Plaintiff is a partner with these corporations in the operation of the Band, whether Plaintiff is a partner with Jenkins in the operation of some aspects of the Band, and so forth. In any event, as discussed herein, Plaintiff has not produced sufficient evidence from which a reasonable jury could conclude he was a partner in the Band or any of its related enterprises.

"To participate to some extent in the management of a business is a primary element in partnership organization, and it is virtually essential to a determination that such a relationship existed." *Dickenson v. Samples,* 104 Cal. App. 2d 311, 315, 231 P.2d 530 (1951). However, where partners have designated a particular partner to manage the partnership, "the making of the agreement to relinquish control is itself an exercise of the requisite *right to control.*" *Dills v. Delira Corp.,* 145 Cal. App. 2d 124, 132, 302 P.2d 397 (1956) (emphasis in original).

Here, while some of the hallmarks of a partnership were present (*e.g.,* sharing of profits), Plaintiff was effectively shut out of the Band's decision-making process. Rather, Jenkins had the final say as to all creative and business decisions of the Band. There is no evidence that Plaintiff relinquished any control he had in the Band or that Plaintiff ever took part in a decision that Jenkins did not favor.

Aside from aspects of his own declaration and alleged deposition corrections prohibited by the sham affidavit rule,[6] Plaintiff puts forth two admissible pieces of evidence supporting his claim he had some control over the Band: (1) Jenkins's deposition admission that he was not the only person to make the decision to hire Mandlebaum as an attorney; and (2) Jenkins's deposition admission that he made the decision to change the touring revenue split with Hargreaves "in consultation with" Plaintiff. However, neither of these facts suggests that Plaintiff had any say in the final decision, nor has Plaintiff offered evidence suggesting that he did. Jenkins's admission that he was not the only person to make the decision to hire Mandlebaum as an attorney does not, on its own, suggest that Plaintiff was involved in the decision to hire Mandlebaum, especially in light of Plaintiff's deposition testimony that he had no say in the Band's legal matters. That the decision to change the touring revenue split was made "in consultation with" Plaintiff does not imply that Plaintiff had the power to change the outcome. In fact, such a characterization comports with Plaintiff's deposition testimony that he "renegotiated" his touring split with Jenkins and that Jenkins had previously told Fredianelli "if he wanted to ask for advice, he would ask," but "[a]t the end of the day, he would reserve the right to make the decision. . . ." Obviously, a reduction of an employee's compensation would involve some degree of consultation with the employee, even if just presented as a "take it or leave it" offer. However, just because an employee has the power to accept reduced compensation, negotiate for a different compensation, or leave his job, does not mean that the employee has power over the employer's ultimate decision of what compensation to offer. Thus, there is no record evidence before the Court that Fredianelli ever had any control in a decision by the Band.

Several other facts cited by Plaintiff to support the existence of a partnership, such as sharing of net touring revenues, Plaintiff's participation as a party in the *Godtland* case, and Plaintiff's being referenced as a "member" and "officer" of the Band, are insufficient to give rise to a genuine issue of fact as to which Plaintiff was a partner.

---

[6]For example, Plaintiff's declaration and deposition contain statements suggesting that he did take part in the decision-making structure of the Band and was told by Jenkins that he could have voted to terminate Jenkins as the Band's manager, which are directly contradicted by statements in his deposition that he effectively had no control over the Band and was told by Jenkins that he would have no role in the decision-making of the Band.

First, as discussed above, it is undisputed that Plaintiff took between a quarter and a third of the Band's net touring revenue from the time he was made a member in 2003 to the time he was ousted in 2009. Sharing of net touring revenues with Plaintiff is not inconsistent with Defendants' assertion that Plaintiff's share of net touring revenues constituted wages for his employment with the Band, especially where Defendants support the contention by introducing testimony that the Band's accountant made wage payments to Plaintiff, issued W-2 and 1099 tax forms for such payments, and never filed partnership tax returns or made partner draw payments. [S]ee also Cal. Corp. Code § 16202(c)(3)(B) (profit-sharing as form of wages does not create presumption of partnership). Moreover, Plaintiff did not share in the net merchandise proceeds until 2007, demonstrating that Plaintiff did not even participate in a full profit-sharing agreement, as would be expected of a co-owner of a business.

Second, the complaint in the *Godtland* case alleges that Plaintiff was a party to a contract with Godtland by which Godtland took a commission based, in part, on "the band members' songwriting income" for, among other tasks, "us[ing] [his] best efforts to promote the band's *careers* and *efforts* in the entertainment industry." While Plaintiff did take part as a party to the *Godtland* case, his participation was premised, at least in part, not on his being a partner in the ownership of the band, but on his allegedly being an individual party to a management contract with Godtland. Plaintiff's individual participation in such a contract comported with its covering "the band members' songwriting income," which would naturally vary for each member of the Band based on their individual contribution to the Band's songwriting, as well as with Plaintiff's representation in an email that Godtland and Plaintiff had an individual agreement regarding Godtland's management commission for Plaintiff. *cf. Love v. The Mail on Sunday,* 489 F. Supp. 2d 1100, 1106-07 (C.D. Cal. 2007) (recognizing that songwriting collaboration does not in and of itself create partnership and that each collaborator is individually entitled to royalties). Plaintiff's individual participation in the *Godtland* case also comports with the allegation therein that part of Godtland's role as manager was to promote Plaintiff's career and efforts in the entertainment industry, giving rise to individual rights against Godtland.

Lastly, Plaintiff was at various times referred to as a "member" and "officer" of the Band. However, such designation does not necessarily make him a legal partner in the Band's operation, especially in light of the evidence showing that Plaintiff had no effective control over the Band. Being a band "member" does not necessarily denote ownership. *Cf. Bartels v. Birmingham,* 332 U.S. 126, 127-28, 67 S. Ct. 1547, 91 L. Ed. 1947 (1947) (members of "name bands" are employees and leader is employer); *Far Out Productions, Inc. v. Oskar,* 247 F.3d 986, 998 (9th Cir. 2001) (recognizing band members being hired as employees). Regarding Plaintiff being labeled an "officer" of the Band, there is only one document referring to him as such, a one page balance sheet under the header of 3EB Touring, Inc. This one document does not establish a genuine dispute as to whether Fredianelli was, in fact, an officer of the Band. However, even construing the evidence in the light most favorable to Plaintiff, his being an "officer" would not make him a "partner" in the Band in light of his undisputed lack of control over management of the band. *Cf. GAB Bus. Servs., Inc. v. Lindsey & Newsom Claim Services, Inc.,* 83 Cal. App. 4th 409, 420-21, 99 Cal. Rptr. 2d 665 (2000) *overturned on other grounds by Reeves v. Hanlon,* 33 Cal. 4th 1140, 1153-54,

17 Cal. Rptr. 3d 289, 95 P.3d 513 (2004) (recognizing that corporations may have nominal officers without control over business). Plaintiff has not offered evidence from which the Court may reasonably infer a partnership existed between him and the Band members.

Thus, the Court GRANTS Defendants' motion for summary judgment as to Plaintiff's first cause of action except to the extent it is based on his not receiving his full share of net touring revenues irrespective of ownership, as discussed below.

. . .

VI. CONCLUSION

In sum, the Court GRANTS Defendants' motion for summary judgment as to all of Plaintiff's causes of action permits except to the extent his causes of action for breach of contract and accounting are based on his not receiving his agreed-to share of net touring revenues.

This order disposes of Docket No. 171.

IT IS SO ORDERED.

Post-Case Follow-Up

In *Fredianelli*, the court acknowledged that Fredianelli was at various times referred to as a "member" and "officer" of the band, but held that these designations did not necessarily make him a legal partner in the band's operation, especially in light of the evidence showing that he had no effective control over the band. *Fredianelli*, 931 F. Supp. 2d at 1022. This discussion speaks to issues that may arise when business people use terms with legal meanings — for example, member, partner, partnership, etc. — in non-legal ways. For example, business people may use the terms "partner" or "partnership" to denote a close, cooperative relationship between commercial counterparties without intending to refer to a legal partnership. Business people also may decline to use the word partnership while associating in ways that meet the legal definition of a partnership.

To avoid confusion and misunderstandings, lawyers are well advised to speak with clients about when and how partnerships — particularly inadvertent partnerships — are formed. Clients who do not wish to enter into partnerships should take a number of steps to avoid forming an inadvertent partnership, including the following: (i) taking care not to use words like "partner" or "partnership" if they do not intend to form a legal partnership; (ii) ensuring role clarity — and preventing role "creep" — through careful conversations, early and often, about the nature and status of associates' business relationships; and (iii) entering into formal, written agreements that clearly state rights and obligations.

Fredianelli v. Jenkins: Real Life Applications

1. Sandy James invested $50,000 to purchase plastic injection molding manufacturing equipment used to produce small fishing boats for James Marine, a family business. James Marine has never drafted or filed formation paperwork with the secretary of state. Sandy receives 25 percent of the profits every year and does most of the day-to-day work. Sandy's three siblings share the remaining profits of the business and weigh in on business matters once in a while, as they choose. Are the James siblings partners, and is James Marine a partnership?

2. James Marine owes Molding Tech $20,000 for raw materials used to manufacture its fishing boats. Sandy and Molding Tech have had a mutually beneficial commercial relationship for the past 20 years, and both entities regularly refer to each other in promotional materials as business partners and members of the angler community. Sandy James directs James Marine to pay Molding Tech $25,000 from James's profits each quarter to pay for raw materials. Are James Marine and Molding Tech partners?

3. Fran Johnson works in James's manufacturing facility. As a long-time employee, Fran serves as a production manager, and has considerable flexibility with regard to staffing the production line and supervising manufacturing operations. Fran receives an hourly wage plus a bonus of 1.5 percent of James's profits for her annual compensation. Is Fran a partner in James Marine?

4. Don and Sue retired from James Marine last year after many years of service. James Marine pays Don and Sue $1,500 each per year from its annual profits as retirement benefits. Are Don and Sue partners in James Marine?

As both *Fredianelli* and RUPA § 202 suggest, the parties' characterization of their relationship as a partnership — or not a partnership — is relevant to questions of partnership formation, but it is not dispositive. If parties associate as co-owners, they will form a legal partnership, whether or not they use certain words or titles. If they do not associate in this fashion, they will not form a legal partnership, even if they call themselves partners, or act as non-legal "partners" in some contexts. *See, e.g., Love v. The Mail on Sunday*, 489 F. Supp. 2d 1100, 1106-07 (C.D. Cal. 2007) (holding that alleged song-writing partnership between members of the Beach Boys did not give rise to legal partnership); *Holmes v. Lerner*, 88 Cal. Rptr. 2d 130, 142 (Ct. App. 1999) (finding agreement to associate as co-owners, and thus partnership, based on statements including the following: "[I]t's going to be our baby, and we're going to work on it together." . . . "We will hire people to work for us." . . . "We will do . . . everything we can to get the company going, and then we'll be creative, and other people will do the work, so we'll have time to continue riding the horses.").

Fredianelli thus demonstrates that parties seeking to prove the existence of a legal partnership cannot simply allege in conclusory language that a partnership was formed; rather, they must allege specific facts demonstrating association as co-owners. *See, e.g., Peed v. Peed*, 325 S.E.2d 275, 279 (N.C. Ct. App. 1985) ("We stress that the determination of whether a partnership exists, and whether the parties are co-owners, involves examining all the circumstances. . . . Partnership is a legal concept but the determination of the existence or not . . . involves inferences drawn from an analysis of all the circumstances attendant on its creation and operation.") (citations and internal quotations omitted). Conclusory allegations of ownership, control, profit sharing, etc., are not enough. *See Love*, 489 F. Supp. 2d at 1106-07 (holding that conclusory allegations of partnership status did not establish that a legal partnership existed).

Relatedly, *Fredianelli* shows that while proof of profit sharing is relevant to partnership formation, it is not always dispositive. *See Fredianelli*, 931 F. Supp. 2d at 1020 (finding that while some of the hallmarks of a partnership were present, such as sharing of profits, a partnership was not formed because plaintiff was shut out of the band's decision-making process). For similar reasons, the absence of an express profit-sharing agreement is not fatal to a partnership claim. *See Holmes v. Lerner*, 88 Cal. Rptr. 2d at 132 ("[A]n express agreement to divide profits is not a prerequisite to prove the existence of a partnership.").

Finally, be aware that litigants do not need to prove that every statutory factor set forth in the RUPA or the UPA respecting partnership formation is present to establish that a partnership exists. *See, e.g., Ingram v. Deere*, 288 S.W.3d at 896 (holding that "[t]he TRPA factors seem to serve as a proxy for the common law requirement of intent to form a partnership by identifying conduct that logically suggests a collaboration of a business's purpose and resources to make a profit as partners. After examining the statutory language and considering that TRPA abrogated the common law's requirement of proof of all five factors, we determine that the issue of whether a partnership exists should be decided considering all of the evidence bearing on the TRPA partnership factors.").

2.   Administrative Formation-Stage Requirements

A final few points are worth keeping in mind at the partnership formation stage. While partners do not have to file formation documents with state or local officials to create a partnership as a matter of partnership law, they may have to comply with other administrative rules lawfully to operate their business. For example, similar to a sole proprietorship, a partnership may choose to operate under a fictitious name. The general rule is that if all of the partners' surnames are included in the business name, then it is not fictitious. For example, suppose a partnership of Dave Adams, Susan Baker, Alan Carr, and Geri Dolan is formed. If the partnership operates as Adams, Baker, Carr & Dolan, no fictitious business name filing need be made. If, however, the business operates as Adams & Baker or Adams & Associates, then a fictitious business name statement must be filed. The use of signals such as "and Associates" makes the name fictitious in many states, because the signal implies the existence of other partners. In jurisdictions that permit the use of certain types of fictitious names, the partnership **fictitious business name statement** is highly similar to, or in some instances, identical to, that required of a sole proprietor. The goal of fictitious name statements is to protect consumers, so they know who is responsible for operating the business and who can be sued for a debt or other obligation. Failure to file the appropriate fictitious business name statement, when required, will result in the same penalties being imposed on a general partnership as are imposed on a sole proprietorship — generally, fines or inability to maintain an action in that jurisdiction until the defect is cured.

In addition, just as with sole proprietorships, if the business is one that is subject to licensing requirements, the partnership must comply with these requirements. Thus, a real estate sales agency, a liquor store, or a general construction business may all have to comply with various statutes relating to the licensing of these businesses. Similarly, if the business will sell goods, it must obtain a sales tax license; and if it will hire employees, it must obtain an employer identification number and make arrangements to comply with laws relating to Social Security, withholding taxes, and workers' compensation.

Finally, in many instances, a partnership may be able do business in a state other than the one in which it was formed without filing any documents or notices. Thus, a partnership operating in Maryland may be able to expand and offer its services in Virginia and Delaware without any formal requirements (although it must comply with each state's licensing and name requirements). You should check the rules in jurisdictions in which a partnership plans to operate, however, to be sure that an out-of-state partnership does not need to qualify to do business within the borders of states in which the partnership offers services. In this regard, note that other forms of organization (including limited partnerships, limited liability companies, and corporations) generally must qualify to do business in states other than the one in which the enterprise at issue was formed.

E. VOTING AND GOVERNANCE RULES

1. Equal Rights to Participate in Management, Per Capita Voting

Under both the UPA and the RUPA, each partner is a co-owner with the right to participate equally in the management of partnership affairs and the conduct of partnership business. UPA § 18(e); RUPA § 401(h). Partners exercise their right to participate in management by voting. Unless the partners agree otherwise, voting typically is on a per capita basis — meaning, each partner gets one vote, even if partners have made unequal contributions to capital or spent more (or less) time compared to co-partners working on partnership business. For example, assume that Ellen and James are partners. Ellen contributed $60,000 to the partnership and works full time on partnership business, whereas James contributed $40,000 and spends less time on a day-to-day basis working on the partnership's behalf. Ellen may think because she has contributed more than James to the partnership, her voting and management rights should be greater. This is not the case under default rules. Unless Ellen and James agree otherwise, the UPA and the RUPA both provide that Ellen and James have equal voting rights notwithstanding disparities in their capital or other contributions to the business.

2. Ordinary Course versus Non-Ordinary Course Activities

Under both the UPA and the RUPA, ordinary course and non-ordinary course activities are treated differently when it comes to partner voting. Differences concerning matters within the ordinary course of partnership business generally may be decided by a majority. UPA § 9; RUPA § 401(k). For matters outside the ordinary course of partnership business, the approval of all partners typically is required. *See* UPA § 9; RUPA § 401(k). Amending the partnership agreement requires the unanimous consent of the partners. *See* RUPA § 401(k); UPA § 9. UPA § 9 states that the following extraordinary matters also require the unanimous consent of all partners:

- assigning the partnership property in trust for creditors;
- disposing of the goodwill of the business;
- performing any act that would make it impossible to carry on the ordinary business of the partnership;
- confessing a judgment (permitting a judgment to be entered against one without the necessity for instituting legal proceedings); and
- submitting a partnership claim or liability to arbitration.

Although the RUPA does not contain a corresponding list (and instead references only acts outside the ordinary course of a partnership and the amendment of the partnership agreement as requiring unanimity), the acts set forth in UPA § 9 arguably are not in the ordinary course of partnership business, suggesting that unanimous approval for such acts would be required under a RUPA regime, as well. *See* RUPA §§ 301(2) (stating an act of a partner which is not apparently for carrying on in the ordinary course the partnership's business or business of the kind carried on by the partnership binds the partnership only if the act was actually authorized by all other partners).

3. Customizing Voting Rules

As noted above, both the UPA and the RUPA permit partners to customize statutory default voting rules to meet business needs. For example, in a partnership with a large number of partners, it may be impractical for all partners to participate equally in managing the business. To address this issue, some partnerships appoint a managing partner or a committee of partners to address particular issues — for example, a compensation committee, a hiring committee, and a marketing committee. These committees may study various proposals and make reports to the full partnership, which will then vote on these matters. Alternatively, the committees may have some limited authority to act on their own. For example, the hiring committee may be able to hire anyone whose salary will be less than $40,000, while individuals who will be hired at salaries in excess of $40,000 may need to be approved by a majority vote of all partners. Keep in mind that the partners' decision to appoint a managing partner or management committee, or otherwise to empower certain partners to make certain decisions, does not mean that non-managing partners forfeit their right to participate in management. In one representative New York case, for example, the court recognized that each partner has the right to participate in management, even if the partnership designates a partner as managing partner. *See Krulwich v. Poster*, 738 N.Y.S.2d 315, 317 (App. Div. 2002). The court reasoned that if the parties had wanted to relieve a particular party of management authority, "they had merely to organize as a limited partnership, designating only Robert [the managing partner] as general partner." *Id.*

In addition to appointing a managing partner or committee, other common variations in default voting rules include the following:

■ Requiring super-majority votes for certain decisions or categories of decisions. For example, a partnership agreement could require that expenditures or borrowing over a certain amount require a super-majority vote.

■ Allocating voting power based on contributions to capital (and thus ownership stake) versus the default per capita rule. Under this rule, for example, a partner who contributes 51 percent of the partnership's capital would enjoy 51 percent of the voting power.

■ Changing the approval requirement for decisions (all decisions, certain categories of decisions, etc.) outside the ordinary course to something less than unanimous approval.

Note that any tweaks to default governance and voting rules ought to be spelled out in a written partnership agreement.

Case Preview

Summers v. Dooley

In *Summers v. Dooley*, Summers (one partner in a two-person partnership) hired a worker over the objections of Dooley, his co-partner. Summers paid the worker out of his own pocket and then filed suit against Dooley, seeking reimbursement. When you read *Summers v. Dooley*, consider the following questions:

1. What does *Summers* tell us about the risks of a two-person partnership under default management and voting rules?
2. How might Summers and Dooley have customized default voting rules to avoid a stalemate over the hiring of a worker and the associated expenses?
3. What are your options if you disagree with your co-partners as to how best to manage partnership affairs?

Summers v. Dooley
481 P.2d 318 (Idaho 1971)

DONALDSON, J.*

This lawsuit, tried in the district court, involves a claim by one partner against the other for $6,000. The complaining partner asserts that he has been required to

---

*Most footnotes have been omitted for purposes of brevity.

pay out more than $11,000 in expenses without any reimbursement from either the partnership funds or his partner. The expenditure in question was incurred by the complaining partner (John Summers, plaintiff-appellant) for the purpose of hiring an additional employee. The trial court denied him any relief except for ordering that he be entitled to one half $966.72 which it found to be a legitimate partnership expense.

The pertinent facts leading to this lawsuit are as follows. Summers entered a partnership agreement with Dooley (defendant-respondent) in 1958 for the purpose of operating a trash collection business. The business was operated by the two men and when either was unable to work, the non-working partner provided a replacement at his own expense. In 1962, Dooley became unable to work and, at his own expense, hired an employee to take his place. In July, 1966, Summers approached his partner Dooley regarding the hiring of an additional employee but Dooley refused. Nevertheless, on his own initiative, Summers hired the man and paid him out of his own pocket. Dooley, upon discovering that Summers had hired an additional man, objected, stating that he did not feel additional labor was necessary and refused to pay for the new employee out of the partnership funds. Summers continued to operate the business using the third man and in October of 1967 instituted suit in the district court for $6,000 against his partner, the gravamen of the complaint being that Summers has been required to pay out more than $11,000 in expenses, incurred in the hiring of the additional man, without any reimbursement from either the partnership funds or his partner. After trial before the court, sitting without a jury, Summers was granted only partial relief[1] and he has appealed. He urges in essence that the trial court erred by failing to conclude that he should be reimbursed for expenses and costs connected in the employment of extra help in the partnership business.

The principal thrust of appellant's contention is that in spite of the fact that one of the two partners refused to consent to the hiring of additional help, nonetheless, the non-consenting partner retained profits earned by the labors of the third man and therefore the non-consenting partner should be stopped from denying the need and value of the employee, and has by his behavior ratified the act of the other partner who hired the additional man.

The issue presented for decision by this appeal is whether an equal partner in a two man partnership has the authority to hire a new employee in disregard of the objection of the other partner and then attempt to charge the dissenting partner with the costs incurred as a result of his unilateral decision.

The State of Idaho has enacted specific statutes with respect to the legal concept known as "partnership." Therefore any solution of partnership problems should logically begin with an application of the relevant code provision.

In the instant case the record indicates that although Summers requested his partner Dooley to agree to the hiring of a third man, such requests were not honored. In fact Dooley made it clear that he was "voting no" with regard to the hiring of an additional employee.

---

[1]The trial court did award Summers one half of $966.72 which it found to be a legitimate partnership expense.

An application of the relevant statutory provisions and pertinent case law to the factual situation presented by the instant case indicates that the trial court was correct in its disposal of the issue since a majority of the partners did not consent to the hiring of the third man. I.C. § 53-318(8) provides:

> "Any difference arising as to ordinary matters connected with the partnership business may be decided by a *majority of the partners* * * *." (emphasis supplied)

It is the opinion of the Court that the preceding statute is of a mandatory rather than permissive nature. This conclusion is based upon the following reasoning. Whether a statute is mandatory or directory does not depend upon its form, but upon the intention of the legislature, to be ascertained from a consideration of the entire act, its nature, its object, and the consequences that would result from construing it one way or the other. *In re McQuistons Adoption*, 238 Pa. 304, 86 A. 205 (1913).

The intent of the legislature may be implied from the language used, or inferred on grounds of policy or reasonableness. . . . A careful reading of the statutory provision indicates that subsection 5 bestows equal rights in the management and conduct of the partnership business upon all of the partners.[4] The concept of equality between partners with respect to management of business affairs is a central theme and recurs throughout the Uniform Partnership law, I.C. § 53-301 et seq., which has been enacted in this jurisdiction. Thus the only reasonable interpretation of I.C. § 53-318(8) is that business differences must be decided by a majority of the partners provided no other agreement between the partners speaks to the issues.

A noted scholar has dealt precisely with the issue to be decided.

> "* * * if the partners are equally divided, those who forbid a change must have their way." Walter B. Lindley, A Treatise on the Law of Partnership, Ch. II, § III, 24-8, p. 403 (1924). See also, W. Shumaker, A Treatise on the Law of Partnership, § 97, p. 266.

. . .

In the case at bar one of the partners continually voiced objection to the hiring of the third man. He did not sit idly by and acquiesce in the actions of his partner. Under these circumstances it is manifestly unjust to permit recovery of an expense which was incurred individually and not for the benefit of the partnership but rather for the benefit of one partner.

Judgment affirmed. Costs to respondent.

McQuade, C.J., and McFadden, Shepard and Spear, JJ., concur.

---

[4] In the absence of an agreement to the contrary. . . . In the case at bar, there is no such agreement and thus I.C. § 53-318(5) and each of the other subsections are applicable.

Post-Case Follow-Up

Summers speaks to the difficulties that can arise when voting rights are allocated equally in a two-person partnership. Under applicable default rules, neither partner may be able to act without the consent of the other on matters as to which they disagree. In the event of a stalemate, each partner may have to choose between walking away from the partnership (and being subject to the partnership "breakup" rules discussed in Sections M and N below) or simply going along with the other partner. The possibility of a stalemate, and the costs associated with unplanned partnership "divorces," speak to the importance of making sure the partners address voting rules, partnership departures, and partnership "divorce" in a written partnership agreement.

Summers v. Dooley: Real Life Applications

1. Summers has decided to form a new partnership with Jones. Summers has retained you as counsel, and he wants to know what he might do differently this time around to avoid disputes over hiring workers. Draft provisions for the Summers/Jones partnership agreement that might reduce the risk of stalemate.

2. Summers asks you why Dooley had the right to object to his decision to hire a worker in the first place. Write a letter to Dooley explaining whether and why Dooley had the right to object to Summers's hiring decisions.

F. PARTNER AS AGENT

1. Partners Owe Duties of Care and Loyalty

At both common law and under the UPA and the RUPA, partners are agents of the partnership for purposes of partnership business. *See* UPA § 9; RUPA § 301. As agents, partners owe duties of care and loyalty to the partnership and co-partners. *See* RUPA § 409; UPA §21. This means, for example, that partners may not engage in activities that are detrimental to or competitive with the partnership (unless they disclose this conflict and receive consent from the other partners) or otherwise act disloyally toward the partnership. *See, e.g.,* RUPA § 409(b). Similarly, partners must act with due care when carrying out partnership business and must deal with each other and the partnership consistent with a contractual obligation of good faith and fair dealing. *See* RUPA §§ 105(c)(6), 409(a) and (d).

Case Preview

Meinhard v. Salmon

Meinhard v. Salmon contains one of the most famous articulations in all of business associations law of the fiduciary duty of loyalty. When reading *Meinhard*, consider the following questions:

1. Why is *Meinhard* cited as an example of fiduciary duties in the partnership context, when Salmon and Meinhard are described as co-adventurers (joint venturers)?
2. How does Judge Cardozo describe the duty of loyalty?
3. Did Salmon violate an express provision of his agreement with Meinhard?
4. Would the result have been different had Salmon waited until after his business relationship with Meinhard had ended?
5. What if Salmon had disclosed the new opportunity to Meinhard prior to proceeding with the opportunity at issue?
6. Do you think Meinhard should have taken steps to protect himself? If so, what steps?
7. Would the result have been different had this case been decided under a RUPA regime? Why or why not?

Meinhard v. Salmon
164 N.E. 545 (N.Y. 1928)

CARDOZO, C.J.*

On April 10, 1902, Louisa M. Gerry leased to the defendant Walter J. Salmon the premises known as the Hotel Bristol at the northwest corner of Forty-Second street and Fifth avenue in the city of New York. The lease was for a term of 20 years, commencing May 1, 1902, and ending April 30, 1922. The lessee undertook to change the hotel building for use as shops and offices at a cost of $200,000. Alterations and additions were to be accretions to the land.

Salmon, while in course of treaty with the lessor as to the execution of the lease, was in course of treaty with Meinhard, the plaintiff, for the necessary funds. The result was a joint venture with terms embodied in a writing. Meinhard was to pay to Salmon half of the moneys requisite to reconstruct, alter, manage, and operate the property. Salmon was to pay to Meinhard 40 per cent of the net profits for the first five years of the lease and 50 per cent for the years thereafter. If there were losses, each party was to bear them equally. Salmon, however, was to have sole power to "manage, lease, underlet and operate" the building. There were to be certain pre-emptive rights for each in the contingency of death.

---

*Most internal citations have been omitted for purposes of brevity.

The two were coadventures, subject to fiduciary duties akin to those of partners. As to this we are all agreed. The heavier weight of duty rested, however, upon Salmon. He was a coadventurer with Meinhard, but he was manager as well. During the early years of the enterprise, the building, reconstructed, was operated at a loss. If the relation had then ended, Meinhard as well as Salmon would have carried a heavy burden. Later the profits became large with the result that for each of the investors there came a rich return. For each the venture had its phases of fair weather and of foul. The two were in it jointly, for better or for worse.

When the lease was near its end, Elbridge T. Gerry had become the owner of the reversion. He owned much other property in the neighborhood, one lot adjoining the Bristol building on Fifth Avenue and four lots on Forty-Second street. He had a plan to lease the entire tract for a long term to someone who would destroy the buildings then existing and put up another in their place. In the latter part of 1921, he submitted such a project to several capitalists and dealers. He was unable to carry it through with any of them. Then, in January, 1922, with less than four months of the lease to run, he approached the defendant Salmon. The result was a new lease to the Midpoint Realty Company, which is owned and controlled by Salmon, a lease covering the whole tract, and involving a huge outlay. The term is to be 20 years, but successive covenants for renewal will extend it to a maximum of 80 years at the will of either party. The existing buildings may remain unchanged for seven years. They are then to be torn down, and a new building to cost $3,000,000 is to be placed upon the site. The rental, which under the Bristol lease was only $55,000, is to be from $350,000 to $475,000 for the properties so combined. Salmon personally guaranteed the performance by the lessee of the covenants of the new lease until such time as the new building had been completed and fully paid for.

The lease between Gerry and the Midpoint Realty Company was signed and delivered on January 25, 1922. Salmon had not told Meinhard anything about it. Whatever his motive may have been, he had kept the negotiations to himself. Meinhard was not informed even of the bare existence of a project. The first that he knew of it was in February, when the lease was an accomplished fact. He then made demand on the defendants that the lease be held in trust as an asset of the venture, making offer upon the trial to share the personal obligations incidental to the guaranty. The demand was followed by refusal, and later by this suit. A referee gave judgment for the plaintiff, limiting the plaintiff's interest in the lease, however, to 25 per cent. The limitation was on the theory that the plaintiff's equity was to be restricted to one-half of so much of the value of the lease as was contributed or represented by the occupation of the Bristol site. Upon cross-appeals to the Appellate Division, the judgment was modified so as to enlarge the equitable interest to one-half of the whole lease. With this enlargement of plaintiff's interest, there went, of course, a corresponding enlargement of his attendant obligations. The case is now here on an appeal by the defendants.

Joint adventurers, like copartners, owe to one another, while the enterprise continues, the duty of the finest loyalty. Many forms of conduct permissible in a workaday world for those acting at arm's length, are forbidden to those bound by fiduciary ties. A trustee is held to something stricter than the morals of the market place. Not honesty alone, but the punctilio of an honor the most sensitive, is then the standard of behavior. As to this there has developed a tradition that is unbending and inveterate. Uncompromising rigidity has been the attitude of courts of equity when petitioned to undermine the rule of undivided loyalty by the "disintegrating erosion" of particular exceptions. *Wendt v. Fischer*, 243 N.Y. 439, 444, 154 N.E. 303. Only thus has the level of conduct for fiduciaries been kept at a level higher than that trodden by the crowd. It will not consciously be lowered by any judgment of this court.

The owner of the reversion, Mr. Gerry, had vainly striven to find a tenant who would favor his ambitious scheme of demolition and construction. Baffled in the search, he turned to the defendant Salmon in possession of the Bristol, the keystone of the project. He figured to himself beyond a doubt that the man in possession would prove a likely customer. To the eye of an observer, Salmon held the lease as owner in his own right, for himself and no one else. In fact he held it as a fiduciary, for himself and another, sharers in a common venture. If this fact had been proclaimed, if the lease by its terms had run in favor of a partnership, Mr. Gerry, we may fairly assume, would have laid before the partners, and not merely before one of them, his plan of reconstruction. The pre-emptive privilege, or, better, the pre-emptive opportunity, that was thus an incident of the enterprise, Salmon appropriate to himself in secrecy and silence. He might have warned Meinhard that the plan had been submitted, and that either would be free to compete for the award. If he had done this, we do not need to say whether he would have been under a duty, if successful in the competition, to hold the lease so acquired for the benefit of a venture then about to end, and thus prolong by indirection its responsibilities and duties. The trouble about his conduct is that he excluded his coadventurer from any chance to compete, from any chance to enjoy the opportunity for benefit that had come to him alone by virtue of his agency. This chance, if nothing more, he was under a duty to concede. The price of its denial is an extension of the trust at the option and for the benefit of the one whom he excluded.

No answer is it to say that the chance would have been of little value even if seasonably offered. Such a calculus of probabilities is beyond the science of the chancery. Salmon, the real estate operator, might have been preferred to Meinhard, the woolen merchant. On the other hand, Meinhard might have offered better terms, or reinforced his offer by alliance with the wealth of others. Perhaps he might even have persuaded the lessor to renew the Bristol lease alone, postponing for a time, in return for higher rentals, the improvement of adjoining lots. We know that even under the lease as made the time for the enlargement of the building was delayed for seven years. All these opportunities were cut away from him through another's intervention. He knew that Salmon was the manager. As the time drew near for the expiration of the lease, he would naturally assume from silence, if from nothing else, that the lessor was willing to extend it for a term of years, or at least to let it stand as a lease from year to year. Not impossibly the lessor would have done so, whatever his protestations of unwillingness, if Salmon had not given assent to a project more attractive. At all events, notice of termination, even if not necessary, might seem, not unreasonably, to be something to be looked for, if the business was over the another tenant was to enter. In the absence of such notice, the matter of an extension was one that would naturally be attended to by the manager of the enterprise, and not neglected altogether. At least, there was nothing in the situation to give warning to any one that while the lease was still in being, there had come to the manager an offer of extension which he had locked within his breast to be utilized by himself alone. The very fact that Salmon was in control with exclusive powers of direction charged him the more obviously with the duty of disclosure, since only through disclosure could opportunity be equalized. If he might cut off renewal by a purchase for his own benefit when four months were to pass before the lease would have an end, he might do so with equal right while there remained as many years. He might steal a march on his comrade under cover of the darkness, and then hold the captured ground. Loyalty and comradeship are not so easily abjured.

Little profit will come from a dissection of the precedents. None precisely similar is cited in the briefs of counsel. What is similar in many, or so it seems to us, is the animating principle. Authority is, of course, abundant that one partner may not appropriate to his own use a renewal of a lease, though its term is to begin at the expiration of the partnership. The lease at hand with its many changes is not strictly a renewal. Even so, the standard of loyalty for those in trust relations is without the fixed divisions of a graduated scale. There is indeed a dictum in one of our decisions that a partner, though he may not renew a lease, may purchase the reversion if he acts openly and fairly. . . . It is a dictum, and no more, for on the ground that he had acted slyly he was charged as a trustee. The holding is thus in favor of the conclusion that a purchase as well as a lease will succumb to the infection of secrecy and silence. Against the dictum in that case, moreover, may be set the opinion of Dwight, C., in *Mitchell v. Read*, where there is a dictum to the contrary. 61 N.Y. 123, at page 143, 19 Am. Rep. 252. To say that a partner is free without restriction to buy in the reversion of the property where the business is conducted is to say in effect that he may strip the good will of its chief element of value, since good will is largely dependent upon continuity of possession. Equity refuses to confine within the bounds of classified transactions its precept of a loyalty that is undivided and unselfish. Certain at least it is that a "man obtaining his locus standi, and his opportunity for making such arrangements, by the position he occupies as a partner, is bound by his obligation to his copartners in such dealings not to separate his interest from theirs, but, if he acquires any benefit, to communicate it to them." Certain it is also that there may be no abuse of special opportunities growing out of a special trust as manager or agent. If conflicting inferences are possible as to abuse or opportunity, the trier of the facts must make the choice between them. There can be no revision in this court unless the choice is clearly wrong. It is no answer for the fiduciary to say "that he was not bound to risk his money as he did, or to go into the enterprise at all." "He might have kept out of it altogether, but if he went in, he could not withhold from his employer the benefit of the bargain." A constructive trust is, then, the remedial device through which preference of self is made subordinate to loyalty to others. Many and varied are its phases and occasions.

We have no thought to hold that Salmon was guilty of a conscious purpose to defraud. Very likely he assumed in all good faith that with the approaching end of the venture he might ignore his coadventurer and take the extension for himself. He had given to the enterprise time and labor as well as money. He had made it a success. Meinhard, who had given money, but neither time nor labor, had already been richly paid. There might seem to be something grasping in his insistence upon more. Such recriminations are not unusual when coadventurers fall out. They are not without their force if conduct is to be judged by the common standards of competitors. That is not to say that they have pertinency here. Salmon had put himself in a position in which thought of self was to be renounced, however hard the abnegation. He was much more than a coadventurer. He was a managing coadventurer. For him and for those like him the rule of undivided loyalty is relentless and supreme. A different question would be here if there were lacking any nexus of relation between the business conducted by the manager and the opportunity brought to him as an incident of management. For this problem, as for most, there are distinctions of degree. If Salmon had received from Gerry a proposition to lease a building at a location far removed, he might have held for himself the privilege thus acquired, or so we shall assume. Here the subject-matter of the new lease was an extension and enlargement of the subject-matter of the old one. A managing coadventurer appropriating the benefit of such a lease without warning to his partner might fairly expect to be reproached with conduct that was underhand, or lacking, to say the least, in reasonable candor, if the partner were to surprise him in the act of signing the new instrument. Conduct subject to that reproach does not receive from equity a healing benediction.

A question remains as to the form and extent of the equitable interest to be allotted to the plaintiff. The trust as declared has been held to attach to the lease which was in the name of the defendant corporation. We think it ought to attach at the option of the defendant Salmon to the shares of stock which were owned by him or were under his control. The difference may be important if the lessee shall wish to execute an assignment of the lease, as it ought to be free to do with the consent of the lessor. On the other hand, an equal division of the shares might lead to other hardships. It might take away from Salmon the power of control and management which under the plan of the joint venture he was to have from first to last. The number of shares to be allotted to the plaintiff should, therefore, be reduced to such an extent as may be necessary to preserve to the defendant Salmon the expected measure of dominion. To that end an extra share should be added to his half.

Subject to this adjustment, we agree with the Appellate Division that the plaintiff's equitable interest is to be measured by the value of half of the entire lease, and not merely by half of some undivided part. A single building covers the whole area. Physical division is impracticable along the lines of the Bristol site, the keystone of the whole. Division of interests and burdens is equally impracticable. Salmon, as tenant under the new lease, or as guarantor of the performance of the tenant's obligations, might well protest if Meinhard, claiming an equitable interest, had offered to assume a liability not equal to Salmon's, but only half as great. He might justly insist that the lease must be accepted by his coadventurer in such form as it had been given, and not constructively divided into imaginary fragments. What must be yielded to the one may be demanded by the other. The lease as it has been executed is single and entire. If confusion has resulted from the union of adjoining parcels, the trustee who consented to the union must bear the inconvenience.

Thus far, the case has been considered on the assumption that the interest in the joint venture acquired by the plaintiff in 1902 has been continuously his. The fact is, however, that in 1917 he assigned to his wife all his "right, title and interest in and to" the agreement with his coadventurer. The coadventurer did not object, but thereafter made his payments directly to the wife. There was a reassignment by the wife before this action was begun.

We do not need to determine what the effect of the assignment would have been in 1917 if either coadventurer had the chosen to treat the venture as dissolved. We do not even need to determine what the effect would have been if the enterprise had been a partnership in the strict sense with active duties of agency laid on each of the two adventurers. The form of the enterprise made Salmon the sole manager. The only active duty laid upon the other was one wholly ministerial, the duty of contributing his share of the expense. This he could still do with equal readiness, and still was bound to do, after the assignment to his wife. Neither by word nor by act did either partner manifest a choice to view the enterprise as ended. There is no inflexible rule in such conditions that dissolution shall ensue against the concurring wish of all that the venture shall continue. The effect of the assignment is then a question of intention.

Partnership Law (Cons. Laws, c. 39), § 53, subd. 1, is to the effect that "a conveyance by a partner of his interest in the partnership does not of itself dissolve the partnership, nor, as against the other partners in the absence of agreement, entitle the assignee, during the continuance of the partnership, to interfere in the management or administration of the partnership business or affairs, or to require any information or account of partnership transactions, or to inspect the partnership books; but it merely entitles the assignee to receive in accordance with his contract the profits to which the assigning partner would otherwise be entitled." This statute, which took effect October 1, 1919, did not indeed revive the enterprise if automatically on the execution of the assignment a dissolution had resulted in 1917. It sums up with precision, however, the effect of the assignment as the parties meant to shape it. We are to interpret their relation in the revealing light of conduct. The rule of the statute, even if it has modified the rule as to partnerships in general . . . is an accurate statement of the rule at common law when applied to these adventurers. The purpose of the assignment, understood by everyone concerned, was to lower the plaintiff's tax by taking income out of his return and adding it to the return to be made by his wife. She was the appointee of the profits, to whom checks were to be remitted. Beyond that, the relation was to be the same as it had been. No one dreamed for a moment that the enterprise was to be wound up, or that Meinhard was relieved of his continuing obligation to contribute to its expenses if contribution became needful. Coadventurers and assignee, and most of all the defendant Salmon, as appears by his own letters, went forward on that basis. For more than five years Salmon dealt with Meinhard on the assumption that the enterprise was a subsisting one with mutual rights and duties, or so at least the triers of the facts, weighing the circumstantial evidence, might not unreasonably infer. By tacit, if not express approval, he continued and preserved it. We think it is too late now, when charged as a trustee, to come forward with the claim that it had been disrupted and dissolved.

The judgment should be modified by providing that at the option of the defendant Salmon there may be substituted for a trust attaching to the lease a trust attaching to the shares of stock, with the result that one-half of such shares together with one additional share will in that event be allotted to the defendant Salmon and the other shares to the plaintiff, and as so modified the judgment should be affirmed with costs.

Post-Case Follow-Up

Although the *Meinhard* case involves co-adventurers — or parties to a joint venture, to use more modern terminology — the case is widely cited as an example of partnership fiduciary duties. Why is this? A joint venture exists when two or more persons (individuals or businesses) combine resources to pursue a particular business opportunity or venture. In *Meinhard*, that opportunity was to reconstruct, operate, and manage the Bristol Hotel for 20 years. Under partnership law, relations that are called 'joint ventures' are partnerships if they otherwise fit the definition of a partnership. *See* RUPA § 202, cmt. 2. Arguably, the Meinhard/Salmon relationship fits both the UPA and RUPA definitions of partnership cited at the beginning of this chapter. (Specifically, the relationship likely constitutes a partnership for a definite term of 20 years.) *See* RUPA § 102(13), which provides that there are three types of partnerships: (i) partnerships for a definite term; (ii) partnership for a particular undertaking (partnership agreement states that partnership will end upon completion of specified task); and (iii) partnership at will (in which partners form a partnership, but do not agree that the partnership will terminate upon expiration of term or completion of task). (A form of joint venture agreement is provided in Appendix A.)

Meinhard v. Salmon: Real Life Applications

1. You represent Salmon. Assume that Salmon comes to you before entering into an agreement with Meinhard respecting the Bristol Hotel. Further assume that the RUPA applies. Review RUPA §§ 105 and 409. Can you draft a provision for the Meinhard/Salmon agreement that might allow Salmon more easily to pursue opportunities like the one involved in the case? Do you think such a provision would be a defense to a breach of fiduciary duty claim?

2. You represent Salmon. Assume that Salmon comes to you with news of the Midpoint Realty opportunity at issue in the *Meinhard* case. Salmon explains that he does not want to speak with Meinhard about the opportunity because he is concerned that Meinhard will get in the way of the deal. He also says that he has been doing all of the work respecting the Bristol Hotel project and that Meinhard has been largely absent. What advice, if any, might you give Salmon respecting any obligation to disclose the Midpoint deal to Meinhard?

As you probably gathered from Question 1 immediately above, RUPA speaks to partners' duties of care and loyalty in two related sections of the act — § 409 and § 105. Section 409 states that partners owe duties of care and loyalty to the partnership and their co-partners, and further states that partners must discharge duties owed to the partnership and their co-partners in a manner consistent with the contractual obligation of good faith and fair dealing:

§409. Standards of Conduct for Partners

(a) A partner owes to the partnership and the other partners the duties of loyalty and care stated in subsections (b) and (c).

(b) The fiduciary duty of loyalty of a partner includes the duties:

(1) to account to the partnership and hold as trustee for it any property, profit, or benefit derived by the partner:

(A) in the conduct or winding up of the partnership's business;

(B) from a use by the partner of the partnership's property; or

(C) from the appropriation of a partnership opportunity;

(2) to refrain from dealing with the partnership in the conduct or winding up of the partnership business as or on behalf of a person having an interest adverse to the partnership; and

(3) to refrain from competing with the partnership in the conduct of the partnership's business before the dissolution of the partnership.

(c) The duty of care of a partner in the conduct or winding up of the partnership business is to refrain from engaging in grossly negligent or reckless conduct, willful or intentional misconduct, or a knowing violation of law.

(d) A partner shall discharge the duties and obligations under this [act] or under the partnership agreement and exercise any rights consistently with the contractual obligation of good faith and fair dealing.

(e) A partner does not violate a duty or obligation under this [act] or under the partnership agreement solely because the partner's conduct furthers the partner's own interest.

(f) All the partners may authorize or ratify, after full disclosure of all material facts, a specific act or transaction by a partner that otherwise would violate the duty of loyalty.

(g) It is a defense to a claim under subsection (b)(2) and any comparable claim in equity or at common law that the transaction was fair to the partnership.

(h) If, as permitted by subsection (f) or the partnership agreement, a partner enters into a transaction with the partnership which otherwise would be prohibited by subsection (b)(2), the partner's rights and obligations arising from the transaction are the same as those of a person that is not a partner.

Relatedly, RUPA § 105 speaks to partners' ability to clarify the scope and reach of partners' duties of care and loyalty and partners' obligation to discharge partnership duties and responsibilities in a manner consistent with the contractual obligation of good faith and fair dealing through contract. In this regard, § 105 provides that partners may not (i) alter or eliminate the duty of loyalty or the duty of care, except as otherwise provided in subsection (d); or (ii) eliminate the contractual obligation of good faith and fair dealing under § 409(d), but the partnership agreement may prescribe the standards, if not manifestly unreasonable, by which the performance of the obligation is to be measured. *See* §§ 105(c)(5) and (6).

RUPA § 105(d) provides that a partnership agreement may specify the method by which a specific act or transaction that would otherwise violate the duty of loyalty may be authorized or ratified by one or more disinterested and independent persons after full disclosure of all material facts. Subsection (d) further provides that, if not manifestly unreasonable, a partnership agreement may (i) alter or eliminate the aspects of the duty of loyalty stated in § 409(b); (ii) identify specific types or categories of activities that do not violate the duty of loyalty; (iii) alter the duty of care, but may not authorize conduct involving bad faith, willful or intentional misconduct, or knowing violation of law; and (iv) alter or eliminate any other fiduciary duty. *See id.* Section 105(e) provides that the court shall decide as a matter of law whether a term of a partnership agreement is manifestly unreasonable under subsection (c)(6) or (d)(3). Subsection (e) further provides that the court shall make its determination as of the time the challenged term became part of the partnership agreement and by considering only circumstances existing at that time; and may invalidate the term only if, in light of the purposes and business of the partnership, it is readily apparent that the objective of the term is unreasonable or the term is an unreasonable means to achieve the term's objective. RUPA § 105(e).

While the UPA does not contain a list of non-waivable rules and permissions, courts have restrained general partners from eliminating the fiduciary character of the general partner/partnership relationship via contract. *Cf. Labovitz v. Dolan,* 545 N.E.2d 304, 310-12 (Ill. 1989) (holding general partner in limited partnership "still owed his limited partners a fiduciary duty, which necessarily encompasses the duty of exercising good faith, honesty, and fairness in his dealings with them and the funds of the partnership. . . . Indeed, at least one of the authorities relied upon by defendants is clear that although "partners are free to vary many aspects of their relationship *inter se,* . . . they are not free to destroy its fiduciary character.") (internal citations omitted). (Note that although *Labovitz* involved a limited partnership, the case is instructive here because a general partner's obligations to a limited partnership and its limited partners are identical to those owed by a general partner in a general partnership.)

2. Partners' Authority to Bind the Partnership

Because partners are agents of the partnership, the act of any partner in carrying out the usual business of the partnership will bind the partnership, unless the partner had no authority to so act, and the person with whom the partner was dealing knew or received notice that the partner lacked authority. *See* UPA § 9(1); RUPA § 301(1). Note that there are fine differences between the UPA and RUPA formulations of this rule, so you should be sure to consult the applicable law in your jurisdiction.

The partner/partnership agency relationship is a **general agency**, which means that each partner has the authority to take action on the partnership's behalf—for example, sign contracts, execute documents, and make purchases—that will bind the partnership. And, as you know from our discussion of agency law in Chapter 2, a partner may have either actual or apparent authority to bind his principal. So long as a partner has authority, the partnership will be bound.

For example, assume Patricia, Allen, and Doug are partners in Autoparts, a general partnership engaged in selling auto supplies and performing automotive services. Patricia routinely buys supplies for Autoparts at Cars R Us using an Autoparts credit card, with the approval of her co-partners. Patricia's co-partners even caused the partnership to give Autoparts a form identifying Patricia as an authorized purchasing agent. One day, however, using her Autoparts credit card, Patricia buys a CD player, car phone, and spoiler for her own use. Patricia's co-partners did not authorize these purchases. As we discussed in Chapter 2, Autoparts is likely to be liable to Cars R Us for Patricia's purchases on these facts under the doctrine of apparent authority, even though Patricia did not have permission (actual authority) to purchase items for personal use. Because Patricia exceeded her actual authority, and potentially violated her fiduciary duties to the partnership, however, her co-partners partners may be able to sue her for this breach and recover the money the partnership had to pay on her account.

If a partnership is aware that one of its partners is acting without authority — for example, by purchasing unneeded items for the partnership, or purchasing items for personal use — the partnership should (in addition to considering whether and how to remove the partner from the partnership) send written notices to as many of its suppliers and creditors as possible, stating that the partner no longer has the authority to bind the partnership. Those creditors who sell items or provide credit to the partnership after receiving such a notice likely do so at their own risk, and they will have to look solely to that partner, rather than the partnership or other partners, for payment.

To avoid "rogue partner" issues, third parties (e.g., banks) may not be willing to enter into a commercial deal with a partnership without first (i) reviewing the partnership agreement to ensure that such an act is authorized by the agreement; (ii) examining any filings relating to partner authority; and (iii) requiring the partnership to execute a document confirming the authority of any signatories. RUPA § 303 allows partnerships to file an optional **Statement of Authority** with state officials to provide public notice of the specific partners who are authorized to execute instruments transferring real estate. For a statement to be effective for real estate transfers, a certified copy of the statement issued must be recorded in the office for recording transfers of real property. The statement may also grant or limit partners' authority to enter into other transactions (see an example in Exhibit 3.6). Filing the statement thus provides a partnership an opportunity to limit liability that might arise from certain unauthorized acts of its partners. The statement also assures third parties who deal with partners that those partners have authority to act.

Another new document, allowed by RUPA § 304, is the **Statement of Denial**, typically filed by a partner to deny information given in the Statement of Authority, often filed by a withdrawing partner to provide notice that the partner denies his status as a partner or filed to deny another partner's authority (see Exhibit 3.7).

Information in the Statement of Authority and Statement of Denial is imputed or charged to members of the public because it is a public record available to all.

EXHIBIT 3.6   **California Statement of Partnership Authority**

	GP-1	File # _____

State of California
Secretary of State

Statement of Partnership Authority

Document # _____

A $70.00 filing fee must accompany this form.

IMPORTANT – Read instructions before completing this form.

This Space For Filing Use Only

Partnership Name

1. Name of Partnership

Office Addresses   (Do not abbreviate the city. Items 2 and 3 cannot be P.O. Boxes.)

	City	State	Zip Code
2. Street Address of Chief Executive Office	City	State	Zip Code
3. Street Address of California Office, if any	City	State **CA**	Zip Code
4. Mailing Address of Chief Executive Office, if different from Items 2 or 3	City	State	Zip Code

Names & Addresses of Partners   (Complete Item 5 with the names and mailing addresses of all the partners (attach additional pages if nee OR leave Item 5 blank and proceed to Item 6. Any attachments to this document are incorporated herein by this reference.)

5. Name	Address	City	State	Zip Code
Name	Address	City	State	Zip Code
Name	Address	City	State	Zip Code

Appointed Agent   (If Item 5 was not completed, complete Item 6 with the name and mailing address of an agent appointed and maintained partnership who will maintain a list of the names and mailing addresses of all the partners. If Item 5 was completed, leave Item 6 blank and proceed to

6. Name	Address	City	State	Zip Code

Authorized Partners   (Enter the name(s) of all the partners authorized to execute instruments transferring real property held in the name partnership. Attach additional pages if necessary. Any attachments to this document are incorporated herein by this reference.)

7. Partner Name:	Partner Name:
Partner Name:	Partner Name
Partner Name:	Partner Name

Additional Information

8. Additional information set forth on the attached pages, if any, is incorporated herein by this reference and made part of this docume

Execution   (This form must be signed by at least two partners. If additional signature space is necessary, the dated signature(s) with verification(s) made on an attachment to this document. Any attachments to this document are incorporated herein by this reference.)

9. I certify under penalty of perjury that the contents of this document are true.

Signature of partner	Type or Print Name of partner
Signature of partner	Type or Print Name of partner

GP-1 (REV 01/2013)	APPROVED BY SECRETARY C

EXHIBIT 3.7 **California Statement of Denial**

State of California
Secretary of State

Form GP-2

STATEMENT OF DENIAL

A $30.00 filing fee must accompany this form.
IMPORTANT – Read instructions before completing this form.

1. NAME OF PARTNERSHIP	2. SECRETARY OF STATE FILE NUMBER

3. FACT DENIED, WHICH MAY INCLUDE DENIAL OF AUTHORITY OR STATUS AS A PARTNER:

4. NUMBER OF PAGES ATTACHED, IF ANY:

5. I DECLARE UNDER PENALTY OF PERJURY UNDER THE LAWS OF THE STATE OF CALIFORNIA THAT
THE FOREGOING IS TRUE AND CORRECT.

THIS SPACE FOR FILING USE ONLY

DOCUMENT # _____

_____
SIGNATURE OF PARTNER

_____
DATE EXECUTED

_____
TYPE OR PRINT NAME OF PARTNER

_____
COUNTY AND STATE EXECUTED

6. **RETURN TO:**

NAME:

ADDRESS:

CITY: STATE: ZIP CODE:

G. PARTNER LIABILITY RULES

Unlimited Personal Liability

A notable disadvantage of doing business as a general partnership is that each partner shoulders unlimited personal liability for debts and obligations of the partnership. Because partners are agents of the partnership, and thus have the authority to act for and bind the partnership, one partner may find herself facing personal liability for an obligation that she did not know was incurred by another partner. Under the RUPA, partner liability is joint and several. RUPA § 306(a). Under the UPA, partner liability is joint and several as to everything chargeable to the partnership due to wrongful acts (*see* UPA § 13) and breaches of trust (*see* UPA § 14), and joint for all other debts and obligations of the partnership (*see* UPA § 15).

As you know from Torts, joint and several liability means that a creditor can sue all partners for the wrongful act, can sue the partnership itself for the wrongful act, or may pick and choose among the partners as to which ones may be sued. Thus, a wealthy partner may find he is the sole target in a lawsuit arising because of other partners' misconduct. The theory used by courts to justify this potentially harsh rule is that outside third parties injured by a partner's misconduct or breach of trust should be protected. If the wealthy partner is "targeted," and he must pay the entire damages sum, he may later seek indemnification from his co-partners. RUPA § 401(c); UPA § 18(b). If the partnership is not able to cover the reimbursement obligation (which is likely, if a creditor sought recovery from an individual partner), then the other partners will be obligated to cover the reimbursement obligation in accordance with loss-sharing rules. The applicable loss-sharing rule would depend upon the partnership agreement, or, if the agreement is silent, the default statutory rule. *See* RUPA § 401(a); UPA § 18(a). In essence, the message is that the innocent third party will be protected first, and it is up to partners to sort out the true allocation of responsibility and damages among themselves later on, according to their partnership agreement, or, if the partnership agreement is silent, according to the default rules of the relevant partnership statute.

A judgment obtained by a creditor against a partnership is not by itself a judgment against any individual partner. Thus, to maximize the avenues of ultimate collection on a judgment, creditors likely will name both the partnership and all of its partners as defendants in any lawsuit. In general, the judgment must be satisfied from partnership assets first and thereafter from individual partners' assets on the basis of joint and several liability. (Note that under RUPA § 504, a creditor may obtain a **charging order** from the court that directs the partnership to pay to the creditor any distributions that would ordinarily have been paid to the partner until the judgment is fully satisfied. *See also* RUPA § 504; UPA § 28. Charging orders make the most sense where a judgment creditor of a partner seeks to collect from the partner, and not based on a claim against the partnership.)

As with sole proprietorships, partners can attempt to protect themselves against this unlimited personal liability by obtaining insurance or by attempting to secure agreements from third parties so they will not look to a partner's personal assets to satisfy partnership obligations. Using a corporation as a general partner will also minimize the risk of personal liability for the owners of the corporate partner, because corporate shareholders generally enjoy a liability shield as to corporate obligations. Additional protection is derived from the **marshaling of assets doctrine** (also called the **exhaustion rule**), requiring partnership creditors to first exhaust all partnership assets before they can attack the personal assets of any partner. *See* RUPA § 307(d). That said, as set forth in § 307(d) (reproduced in pertinent part below), personal assets remain vulnerable to seizure by partnership creditors in situations where the partnership's assets are insufficient to satisfy a debt and where no statutory exemptions exist to protect individual assets:

> A judgment creditor of a partner may not levy execution against the assets of the partner to satisfy a judgment based on a claim against the partnership unless the partner is personally liable for the claim under Section 306 and:
>   (1) a judgment based on the same claim has been obtained against the partnership and a writ of execution on the judgment has been returned unsatisfied in whole or in part;
>   (2) the partnership is a debtor in bankruptcy;
>   (3) the partner has agreed that the creditor need not exhaust partnership assets;
>   (4) a court grants permission to the judgment creditor to levy execution against the assets of a partner based on a finding that partnership assets subject to execution are clearly insufficient to satisfy the judgment, that exhaustion of partnership assets is excessively burdensome, or that the grant of permission is an appropriate exercise of the court's equitable powers; or
>   (5) liability is imposed on the partner by law or contract independent of the existence of the partnership.

H. THE PARTNER'S INTEREST IN THE PARTNERSHIP

1. Distribution Rights Transferable, Governance Rights Not Transferable

A partner's interest in a partnership is composed of a bundle of rights, including (i) the right to receive distributions; and (ii) partnership status and management and governance–related rights. *See* RUPA §§ 502-503; UPA §§ 24-27. Under default rules, partners *may* transfer financial distribution rights associated with their partnership interest. *See* RUPA § 503(b). Transfer entitles the transferee to receive whatever distributions the partner is entitled to under the partnership agreement or, where applicable, default rules. *See id.* (providing that transferee of a partnership interest has the right to "receive, in accordance with

Limited Liability Partnerships

To address liability concerns, general partnerships may choose to operate as a limited liability partnership (LLP) in jurisdictions which recognize this form of organization by filing a notice of election in the office of the secretary of state or the equivalent state filing office. The effect of such a filing is to eliminate partners' personal liability for any partnership obligation incurred while the partnership was an LLP. *See* RUPA § 306. In an LLP, the partners generally are not vicariously liable for the obligations of the partnership. *Id.* Partners in an LLP are, however, liable for their own malfeasance. Limited liability partnerships are discussed in detail in Chapter 4.

the transfer, distributions to which the transferor would otherwise be entitled"). *See also* UPA § 27 (1) (providing conveyance of partnership interest merely entitles assignee to receive in accordance with his contract the profits to which the assigning partner would otherwise be entitled.) The transferor retains the status of partner and the rights and duties of a partner, however, such as the right to participate in management and personal liability for partnership obligations. *See* RUPA §§ 503(a)(3); 503(f), UPA § 27. As discussed in Sections M and N below, the transfer of distribution rights does not **dissolve** the partnership (i.e., cause it to cease to exist as a legal matter) under a UPA-style regime (*see* UPA § 27), nor does it cause the **dissociation** of the partner (i.e., the departure of the partner from the partnership) or the dissolution of the partnership or winding up of the partnership business under the RUPA. *See* RUPA § 503(a)(2).

In contrast to distribution rights, partners *may not* assign or transfer partnership status, partnership governance rights, or partner informational rights without the consent of all other partners. RUPA § 503 makes this clear by providing that the transfer of a partner's transferable interest in a partnership does not entitle the transferee to participate in the management or conduct of the partnership's business, nor does it entitle the transferee to have access to records or other information concerning the partnership's business except in connection with matters relating to the dissolution and winding up the partnership. *See also* UPA § 27(1) (providing that conveyance by a partner of his interest in the partnership does not entitle the assignee to interfere in the management or administration of the partnership business or affairs, or to require any information or account of partnership transactions, or to inspect the partnership books).

The following example shows how these principles might play out in practice. Assume Terry (a partner in a partnership) owes support payments to his ex-spouse and decides to assign the right to receive distributions from the partnership to the ex-spouse to satisfy the debt. Terry can have the partnership write a check to his ex-spouse each month for his share of the partnership profits rather than writing a check directly to the ex-spouse. Similarly, Terry's share of earned profits can be reached by his individual creditors (such as a landlord or utility company) and will descend to his heirs upon his death. But, while the ex-spouse may have a contractual claim to Terry's distributions, receipt of distributions does not make the ex-spouse a partner, nor does it give the ex-spouse informational rights or rights respecting the management of partnership business.

The non-transferability of governance rights, together with the default rule that the admission of new partners requires unanimous consent of all the partners (*see* RUPA § 402(b)(3); UPA § 18(g)), speaks to the **"pick your partner" principle**, which is a core concept of partnership law. While partners may, if they wish, modify or waive their right to approve the admission of any new partners, or change other governance rules, the default rule is that no one may become a partner in an existing partnership, or exercise informational or governance rights, without the consent of all other partners. In our example, Terry's partners "picked" Terry as their co-partner. They cannot be forced to go into business with Terry's ex-spouse merely because Terry elected to assign away his distribution rights.

2. Allocations, Distributions, and Compensation Are Not the Same

Note that while partners are entitled to an allocation of profits per the partnership agreement (or default rules), the allocation of profit and the distribution of any profits to partners is not the same thing as paying a salary or other compensation to a partner for work performed on behalf of the partnership. As co-owners, partners are not entitled to compensation for work performed on behalf of the partnership under default rules, except for work associated with winding up the partnership. *See* UPA § 18(f); RUPA § 401(j). This is because partners are supposed to devote their undivided loyalty to the partnership business and to work in good faith to advance the partnership's interest. A partner having special responsibilities, such as a managing partner, may negotiate to be paid a stated salary as a partnership expense. Partners who wish to receive a salary should take care to spell out any agreements regarding compensation in the partnership agreement and in a separate employment agreement. Partners should not engage in "self-help" (here, unilaterally deciding to pay oneself a salary) without obtaining the consent of all partners.

To manage cash flow and meet obligations that may arise over the course of a year, some partnership agreements provide that partners will receive a monthly **draw** against the anticipated profits of the partnership. At the end of the year, the draw is deducted from that partner's percentage of profits. A monthly draw is a payment in anticipation of profits, not a salary. Draws are not mandatory, and some partnerships adhere strictly to the rule that partners are paid only from profits via an end-of-year reckoning.

I. PARTNERSHIP PROPERTY

1. Partnership Capital and Partnership Property

Generally speaking, there are two categories of partnership property: (i) **partnership capital**, or property or money contributed by each of the partners for the purpose of establishing and carrying on the business of the partnership; and (ii) property owned by the partnership, consisting of both capital contributed and property subsequently acquired. Partnership property should be distinguished from each partner's separately owned property — meaning, property each partner owns separate and apart from the partnership.

As to partnership capital, partners may contribute almost anything — for example, cash, real estate, office furniture, a car, a trademark, and services such as legal, accounting, or decorating services — to the partnership. Any such **capital contribution** should be documented during the partnership formation process through a schedule to the partnership agreement and (particularly with intellectual property) a separate contribution agreement whereby the owner of the property contributes that property to the partnership. Once contributed, and unless a partner specifies otherwise, the property then becomes the property of the partnership itself. The partner who contributed it cannot change her mind and tell the remaining partners, "Remember that car I provided as my $15,000 contribution? Well, I want it back." The car is no longer owned by that partner; it has become the property of the partnership. If something other than cash is contributed, the value of this contribution should be determined. If the partners cannot agree among themselves as to the value of a contribution, they should retain an expert to value the contribution.

When it is not clear whether property belongs to the partnership or to some individual partner, a court will look to the parties' intentions. This is another example of why a written partnership agreement clearly setting forth the rights and duties of all partners is important. If a partner intends to retain some right to property contributed, his rights should be clearly set forth in the agreement. The money or value of any property contributed by a partner forms the partner's **capital account**. A partner's capital account is increased if a partner makes additional contributions and decreased as distributions are made to the partners.

2. Rights in Partnership Property

Under the UPA, each partner has an equal right with co-partners to possess partnership property for partnership purposes, but partners have no right to possess partnership property for any other purpose without the consent of co-partners. Thus, a car purchased for a UPA-style partnership is co-owned by the partners under a theory entitled **tenancy in partnership**. *See* UPA § 25(1) and (2). Ownership rights to specific partnership property (cars, inventory, accounts receivable, promissory notes) under the tenancy in partnership theory are very limited. A partner cannot use the specific property for her own benefit without the consent of the other partners; the property cannot be seized by a creditor of a partner; a partner cannot transfer or assign the specific property to another; and upon the death of a partner, the partner's heirs have no rights to such property. *See id.*

Section 203 of the RUPA eliminates the theory of tenancy in partnership and provides that property acquired by the partnership is owned by the partnership itself, rather than by the individual partners who therefore cannot assign or transfer that property. RUPA § 203. This determination avoids the conflict inherent in the UPA, which provides in § 24 that a partner has "rights in specific partnership property" and then in § 25 essentially cancels almost all of the rights one expects to flow from "ownership" (e.g., the right to use or transfer property and the right to leave it to one's heirs). In fact, RUPA § 501 expressly states that an individual partner is not a co-owner of partnership property and thus has no interest in partnership property that can be transferred, either voluntarily or involuntarily. RUPA § 501.

Property acquired in the name of an individual partner, without an indication of partnership capacity and without use of partnership funds, is presumed to be owned by the individual partner, even if the property is used by the partnership. RUPA § 204(d).

J. ALLOCATION OF PROFITS AND LOSSES

1. Distributions and Losses Shared Equally Under Default Rules

According to UPA § 18(a) and RUPA § 401(a), unless the partners agree otherwise, each partner is entitled to an equal share of the partnership profits (and is chargeable with a share of losses in the same proportion as profits). *See* UPA § 18(a); RUPA § 401(a). Note that whereas the UPA references partners' right to share equally in profits and surplus, the RUPA references partners' entitlement to an equal share of partnership distributions. *See* UPA § 18(a); RUPA § 401(a). In practical terms, this means that absent an agreement to the contrary, each partner shares equally in profits and surplus remaining after all liabilities, including those owed to partners, are satisfied. Losses likewise are shared equally under default rules. If the parties vary the allocation of profits in their partnership agreement, but the agreement is silent as to losses, the default rule is that the allocation of losses will follow the allocation of profits.

The per capita allocation of profits and losses under default rules may make sense if each partner makes substantially similar contributions to the partnership's capital. Because this is not always the case, partnership agreements often modify these default rules. Typical provisions include:

- an agreement to allocate profits and losses on a pro rata basis;
- provisions specifying that losses caused by reckless conduct or fraud be borne solely by the partner committing such acts; and
- subject to limitations arising under tax law, special allocations of profits and certain losses.

Once again, all such modifications to default rules should be spelled out in a written partnership agreement.

2. Allocations versus Distributions

As referenced earlier, it is important to remember that there is a difference between allocating profits to an individual partner and actually distributing profits to that partner. An allocation of profits relates to the amount of partnership profits that a partner has to include on her individual income tax return. A partnership distributes profits when it actually pays out profits to a partner. For example, assume that Terry and Fran are partners in a two-person partnership that uses the default rule respecting the allocation of profits and losses — that is, a 50/50 split. Further assume that the partnership generates $100,000 in profits over the course of a year. Fran and Terry decide to distribute $60,000 ($30,000 to each partner, based on the default 50/50 rule), and further agree that they will use the remaining $40,000 in profits to purchase equipment for the partnership business. Under default rules, Fran and Terry each will have to include $50,000 on their individual tax returns (representing 50 percent of the partnership's total profits allocated to each partner), even though Terry and Fran each received distributions of only $30,000 in cash.

3. Tax Burden Distributions

In many cases, profit distributions will be sufficient to satisfy individual partner's tax liability. In some cases, however, distributions may fall short — for example, when a partnership earns profits (and thus allocates profits to each partner), but does not distribute any profits to partners. In this scenario, partners may owe taxes due to the allocation of profits, but may not have cash on hand to satisfy tax obligations. To avoid this problem, partnership agreements frequently include a provision requiring the partnership to distribute to each partner funds sufficient to satisfy partners' tax liabilities resulting from the allocation of profits. The following is sample language relating to tax burden distributions:

> As soon as practicable following the end of each calendar year, the Partnership shall distribute to each Partner an amount sufficient for the partner to pay taxes owed by the Partner from income of the Partnership allocated to the Partner for that year.

The purpose of these provisions is to assist partners in paying taxes associated with the allocation of partnership's earnings to the partners. In the absence of such a provision, the partnership agreement's management rules (or default rules where the partnership agreement is silent) govern the decision whether to distribute profits to partners.

K. PARTNERS' INFORMATIONAL RIGHTS, RIGHT TO AN ACCOUNTING

All partners have the right to inspect and copy the partnership's books of account, which should be kept at the principal place of business of the partnership. *See* RUPA §§ 408(a) and (b). Partners also have a duty to supply information on matters affecting the partnership to their co-partners. *See* UPA §§ 19, 20; RUPA § 408(d). Finally, under UPA § 22, a partner can demand a formal accounting if he is wrongfully excluded from the partnership affairs or whenever circumstances render such an accounting reasonable and just. The RUPA also provides for the remedy of an accounting, though the UPA and RUPA formulations are slightly different. *Compare* UPA § 22 and RUPA § 410.

L. ENTERING AND WITHDRAWING FROM THE PARTNERSHIP

Under default rules, no one can be admitted to a partnership without the unanimous consent of partners. UPA § 18(g); RUPA § 402(b)(3). As noted above, this rule expresses the pick your partner principle, or the idea that partners have the right to decide with whom they wish to associate. Rules regarding admission to the partnership are customizable, though, so if partners wish to allow the admission of new partners upon less than unanimous consent, they may do so via the partnership agreement. In any event, newly admitted partners should sign the existing partnership agreement, thereby acknowledging their agreement to be bound by its terms. An incoming partner will not be held personally liable for debts or obligations arising before his admission to the partnership; this liability can be satisfied only out of partnership property. *See* UPA § 17; RUPA § 306(b). The new partner will have personal liability only for debts or obligations incurred after admission. RUPA § 306(b).

M. DISSOLUTION, DISSOCIATION, AND WINDING UP

The nature of partnerships can create confusion and complexity when a partner leaves the enterprise. In part, this is because the success of a partnership often depends on personal relationships, with the result that partnerships can be thrown into turmoil following the death, bankruptcy, or withdrawal of a partner from the enterprise. There are legal complexities to partner exit, as well. Under the UPA, a partnership **dissolves** as a legal matter whenever a partner departs the partnership. *See* UPA § 31(b) ("Dissolution is caused . . . [b]y the express will of any partner when no definite term of particular undertaking is specified"). Unless the partners (i) negotiated a **continuation agreement** at the time of formation (i.e., an agreement among partners providing that non-dissolving partners may continue the partnership business post-dissolution); or (ii) agree post-dissolution that the remaining partners may carry on the business, the non-dissolving partners may be forced to **wind up** the partnership's business and **terminate** the partnership following the departure of a partner. *See* UPA §§ 33-42.

The RUPA attempts to provide more stability and continuity to partnerships by providing that most partner departures (called "**dissociations**" under the RUPA) result in a buyout of the withdrawing partner's interest. *See* RUPA § 701. Only certain partner departures trigger a winding up and termination of partnership business under the RUPA. *See* RUPA § 801. We review both the UPA and RUPA regimes below.

1. Dissolution, Winding Up, and Termination Under the UPA

Dissolution Under the UPA

Under the UPA, **dissolution** is the change in the relation of the partners caused by any partner's ceasing to be associated in the carrying on of the business. UPA § 29. Dissolution thus designates the point in time when the partners cease to carry on the business together. Termination is the point in time when all the partnership affairs are wound up. "Winding up" is the process of terminating all partnership business, satisfying all obligations, selling assets, collecting debts, and distributing any remaining assets to the business owners.

The UPA dissolution regime is set forth in §§ 31 and 32. UPA § 31 provides that dissolution will occur in the following circumstances:

(1) Without violation of the agreement between the partners,
    (a) By the termination of the definite term or particular undertaking specified in the agreement,
    (b) By the express will of any partner when no definite term or particular undertaking is specified,
    (c) By the express will of all the partners who have not assigned their interests or suffered them to be charged for their separate debts, either before or after the termination of any specified term or particular undertaking,
    (d) By the expulsion of any partner from the business bona fide in accordance with such a power conferred by the agreement between the partners;
(2) In contravention of the agreement between the partners, where the circumstances do not permit a dissolution under any other provision of this section, by the express will of any partner at any time;
(3) By any event which makes it unlawful for the business of the partnership to be carried on or for the members to carry it on in partnership;
(4) By the death of any partner;
(5) By the bankruptcy of any partner or the partnership;
(6) By decree of court under section 32[.]

Under UPA § 32, dissolution also can occur via a court decree:

(1) On application by or for a partner the court shall decree a dissolution whenever:
    (a) A partner has been declared a lunatic in any judicial proceeding or is shown to be of unsound mind,
    (b) A partner becomes in any other way incapable of performing his part of the partnership contract,
    (c) A partner has been guilty of such conduct as tends to affect prejudicially the carrying on of the business,
    (d) A partner wilfully [sic] or persistently commits a breach of the partnership agreement, or otherwise so conducts himself in matters relating to the partnership business that it is not reasonably practicable to carry on the business in partnership with him,
    (e) The business of the partnership can only be carried on at a loss,
    (f) Other circumstances render a dissolution equitable.
(2) On the application of the purchaser of a partner's interest under sections 28 or 29:
    (a) After the termination of the specified term or particular undertaking,
    (b) At any time if the partnership was a partnership at will when the interest was assigned or when the charging order was issued.

As § 31 of the UPA reflects, a partner may exit a partnership, and thereby dissolve the partnership, in a manner and under circumstances that are consistent with the partnership agreement, or in a manner and under circumstances that violate the partnership agreement. Because partnerships are a type of voluntary association, partners cannot force a fellow partner to remain associated against her will, nor can they prevent a partner from exiting, even if the exit violates the partnership agreement. Exit in violation of the partnership agreement can, however, subject the departing partner to liability and other sanctions, as described in the wrongful dissolution section below.

However caused, dissolution has consequences as between and among partners, and as between partners as a group and third parties. These consequences are set forth in the following UPA sections:

- § 33 (General Effect of Dissolution on Authority of Partner);
- § 34 (Right of Partner to Contribution from Co-Partners After Dissolution);
- § 35 (Power of Partner to Bind Partnership to Third Persons After Dissolution);
- § 36 (Effect of Dissolution on Partner's Existing Liability);
- § 37 (Right to Wind Up);
- § 38 (Rights of Partners to Application of Partnership Property);
- § 39 (Rights Where Partnership Is Dissolved for Fraud or Misrepresentation); and
- § 40 (Rules for Distribution).

These provisions are detail-filled and technical, but they are well worth a careful read if you are operating in a UPA jurisdiction. We discuss some of the consequences of wrongful dissolution below.

Spotlight: Winding Up and Termination Under the UPA

One of the most important issues associated with dissolution under a UPA regime relates to the ability of surviving partners to continue the partnership business. Following dissolution, the default path under the UPA provides for the winding up and termination of the partnership and the partnership's business. As noted above, this means that unless the partners negotiated a continuation agreement at the time of formation, or agree post-dissolution to allow the remaining partners to continue the partnership business, default rules may require that the remaining partners wind up the partnership and terminate the partnership's business despite a desire to continue the business. This can result in a poorly timed closure of the business and a "fire sale" of partnership assets, netting far less for the partners than if they had continued with the business or arranged for winding up and termination in a more orderly fashion.

If a partnership is required to be wound up and its business terminated, the UPA provides for a distribution of partnership assets. Section 40 provides that once partnership assets are marshalled, third-party creditors are to be repaid first, partners are then reimbursed for loans or advances to the partnership, partners are returned their capital, and only then do partners receive profits. The distribution of profits after winding up is generally in accord with the percentage of capital contribution. If the partnership is unable to satisfy its third-party creditors, the partners must make the appropriate personal contributions to pay these debts.

Case Preview

Creel v. Lilly

Creel v. Lilly explores tensions that may arise when dissolution occurs under a UPA-style regime. When reading *Creel*, consider the following questions:

1. How could the partners in *Creel* have avoided or reduced the risk of litigation?
2. Having failed to negotiate a continuation agreement, what steps did the surviving partners take in *Creel* to improve their chances of being able to buy out the surviving spouse and continue the partnership's business?
3. Would *Creel* come out the same way under a RUPA regime (discussed below)?

Creel v. Lilly
729 A.2d 386 (Md. 1999)

CHASANOW, J.*

The primary issue presented in this appeal is whether Maryland's Uniform Partnership Act (UPA), Maryland Code (1975, 1993 Repl. Vol., 1998 Supp.), Corporations and Associations Article, § 9-101 *et seq.*, permits the estate of a deceased partner to demand liquidation of partnership assets in order to arrive at the true value of the business. Specifically, Petitioner (Anne Creel) maintains that the surviving partners have a duty to liquidate all partnership assets because (1) there is no provision in the partnership agreement providing for the continuation of the partnership upon a partner's death and (2) the estate has not consented to the continuation of the business. Respondents (Arnold Lilly and Roy Altizer) contend that because the surviving partners wound up the partnership in good faith, in that they conducted a full inventory, provided an accurate accounting to the estate for the value of the business as of the date of dissolution, and paid the estate its proportionate share of the surplus proceeds, they are under no duty to liquidate the partnership's assets upon demand of the deceased partner's estate.

As discussed in more detail in Part II.A., *infra*, UPA, which has governed partnerships in this State for the past 80 years, has been repealed since this litigation commenced. The Act that now governs Maryland partnerships is the Revised Uniform Partnership Act (RUPA), Maryland Code (1975, 1993 Repl. Vol., 1998 Supp.), Corporations and Associations Art., §9A-101 *et seq.*, which was adopted in July 1998 with a phase-in period. Therefore, until December 31, 2002, both UPA and RUPA will coexist, with § 9A-1204 determining which Act applies to a particular partnership's formation, termination, and any other conflict that may arise.

---

*Most footnotes have been omitted for purposes of brevity.

At the outset we note there is a partnership agreement in the instant case that, while somewhat unclear, seems to provide for an alternative method of winding up the partnership rather than a liquidation of all assets. The circuit court and intermediate appellate court both found the agreement unclear as to dissolution and winding up of the business upon the death of a partner and correctly turned to UPA as an interpretative aid. In looking specifically at the trial court's order, the trial judge referred to the partnership agreement and UPA but was not explicit as to which one he primarily relied on in holding that a forced sale of all assets was not required in this case. Regardless, the trial judge's interpretation of the partnership agreement and holding are in conformity with UPA.

Due to our uncertainty as to whether the trial court's holding was based primarily on the partnership agreement or UPA, and also because clarification of the liquidation issue implicates other aspects of partnership law, we will examine not only the partnership agreement itself, but also Maryland's UPA and applicable case law, the cases in other jurisdictions that have interpreted the liquidation issue under UPA, and the newly adopted RUPA. For the reasons stated in this opinion, we concur in the finding of the courts below that Respondents are under no duty to "liquidate on demand" by Petitioner, as UPA does not mandate a forced sale of all partnership assets in order to ascertain the true value of the business. Winding up is not always synonymous with liquidation, which can be a harsh, drastic, and often unnecessary course of action. A preferred method in a good faith winding up, which was utilized in this case, is to pay the deceased partner's estate its proportionate share of the value of the partnership, derived from an accurate accounting, without having to resort to a full liquidation of the business. To hold otherwise vests excessive power and control in the deceased partner's estate, to the extreme disadvantage of the surviving partners. Thus, on this issue, we affirm the judgment of the Court of Special Appeals.

In this appeal, Petitioner also asks us to award the estate its share of the partnership profits generated by the Respondents' alleged continued use of the partnership assets for the period of time during which Petitioner claims the Respondents neither liquidated the business nor agreed to pay the estate its proper percentage share of the partnership. . . . We reject Petitioner's request and agree with the courts below that there is no basis for damages because Good Ole Boys Racing (Good Ole Boys) is a successor partnership and not a continuation of Joe's Racing, which was properly wound up and terminated before the new partnership began operations.

I. BACKGROUND

On approximately June 1, 1993, Joseph Creel began a retail business selling NASCAR racing memorabilia. His business was originally located in a section of his wife Anne's florist shop, but after about a year and a half he decided to raise capital from partners so that he could expand and move into his own space. On September 20, 1994, Mr. Creel entered into a partnership agreement — apparently prepared without the assistance of counsel — with Arnold Lilly and Roy Altizer to form a general partnership called "Joe's Racing." The partnership agreement covered such matters as the partnership's purpose, location, and operations, and stated the following regarding termination of the business:

"7. TERMINATION

(a) That, at the termination of this partnership a full and accurate inventory shall be prepared, and the assets, liabilities, and income, both in gross and net, shall be ascertained: the remaining debts or profits will be distributed according to the percentages shown above in the 6(e).

* * *

(d) Upon the death or illness of a partner, his share will go to his estate. If his estate wishes to sell his interest, they must offer it to the remaining partners first."

The three-man partnership operated a retail store in the St. Charles Towne Center Mall in Waldorf, Maryland. For their initial investment in Joe's Racing, Mr. Lilly and Mr. Altizer each paid $6,666 in capital contributions, with Mr. Creel contributing his inventory and supplies valued at $15,000. Pursuant to the partnership agreement, Mr. Lilly and Mr. Altizer also paid $6,666 to Mr. Creel ($3,333 each) "for the use and rights to the business known as Joe's Racing Collectables." The funds were placed in a partnership bank account with First Virginia Bank-Maryland. All three partners were signatories to this account, but on May 19, 1995, unknown to Mr. Lilly and Mr. Altizer, Mr. Creel altered the account so that only he had the authority to sign checks. It was only after Mr. Creel's death that Mr. Lilly and Mr. Altizer realized they could not access the account funds, which were frozen by the bank upon Mr. Creel's passing. Moreover, on approximately February 20, 1995, Mr. Creel paid a $5,000 retainer to an attorney without his partners' knowledge. He wanted the attorney to prepare documents for the marketing of franchises for retail stores dealing in racing memorabilia.

Joe's Racing had been in existence for almost nine months when Mr. Creel died on June 14, 1995. Mrs. Creel was appointed personal representative of his estate. In this capacity, and acting without the knowledge of the surviving partners, Mrs. Creel and the store's landlord agreed to shorten the lease by one month so that it expired on August 31, 1995. June, July, and August's rent was paid by Mr. Lilly and Mr. Altizer.

In accordance with § 9-602(4),[3] Joe's Racing was automatically dissolved upon Mr. Creel's death and because the partnership agreement did not expressly provide for continuation of the partnership nor did his estate consent to its continuation, the surviving partners were required under UPA to wind up the business. *See* § 9-601 and § 9-609(a). In order to pay debts and efficiently wind up the partnership affairs, Mr. Lilly and Mr. Altizer requested that Mrs. Creel and the bank release the funds in the partnership account ($18,115.93 as of July 13, 1995). Their request was refused and it was at this point that litigation commenced. We adopt the following procedural history of this case, as detailed in the unreported opinion of the Court of Special Appeals:

"Not receiving a favorable response, the surviving partners, on behalf of Joe's Racing, brought an action in the District Court against Mrs. Creel, individually and as

---

[3]Section 9-602 states in pertinent part:

"Dissolution is caused:
* * *
(4) By the death of any partner[.]"

personal representative of her late husband's estate, and First Virginia Bank-Maryland. Mrs. Creel filed a demand for a jury trial, which brought the case to the circuit court. By way of a counterclaim, the bank filed a complaint for interpleader. The court authorized the bank to deposit with the court the money in the partnership account, dismissed the bank from the suit, and ordered that the conflicting claims of the parties be transferred to the funds on deposit, with the case to proceed as one between the Joe's Racing partnership and Ann [sic] Creel, individually and as Personal Representative of the Estate of Joseph Creel.

In the meantime, [Mrs. Creel] had filed in the circuit court a complaint seeking an accounting and a declaratory judgment against Messrs. Lilly and Altizer, individually and doing business under the name 'Good Ole Boys Racing.' She asserted that, instead of winding up the affairs of Joe's Racing in accordance with her demand, Lilly and Altizer continued the partnership business under a new name, using the assets of the partnership. Lilly and Altizer, as general partners of Joe's Racing, and Joe's Racing had also filed in the circuit court a complaint against Mrs. Creel, the Estate of Joseph Creel, and the bank, seeking to recover the $18,115.93 that was in the partnership's checking account. [Mr. Lilly and Mr. Altizer] later filed an

Amended Complaint/Counter Complaint for Declaratory Relief, naming Mrs. Creel, as Personal Representative, as the sole defendant, seeking, *inter alia,* a declaration as to the amounts the Estate of Joseph Creel was entitled to by way of return of capital contributions and as Joseph Creel's share of the net value of the partnership as of the time of dissolution.

Rejecting [Mrs. Creel's] request to refer the matter to an auditor for an accounting as (a) untimely (and therefore likely to delay final resolution of the case) and (b) unnecessary, the court[, after a four-day trial,] determined that Joseph Creel had a 52% interest in the partnership instead of a 36% interest as claimed by [Mr. Lilly and Mr. Altizer]; that Joseph Creel's expenditure of $5,000 of partnership funds for legal assistance was an expense chargeable to the partnership and did not justify reduction of his capital contribution by [$]5,000 as contended by [Mr. Lilly and Mr. Altizer]; and that effecting a change in the partnership bank account so that only he could sign checks was not a breach of fiduciary duty by Mr. Creel.

The court also found that the surviving partners sought to wind up and close out the partnership and took all reasonable steps to do so, and that there was no breach by them of any fiduciary duty to the Estate. The lease on the store premises occupied by the partnership expired on 31 August 1995, and on that date Mr. Lilly conducted an inventory of all merchandise in the store. Based on that inventory, an accountant computed the value of the partnership business; Mrs. Creel was invited to review the books and records and retain her own accountant or appraiser if she questioned [Mr. Lilly or Mr. Altizer's] figures. *She declined to do so. After 31 August 1995, Messrs. Lilly and Altizer ceased doing business as Joe's Racing and began doing business together under the name 'Good Ole Boys Racing.'*

The court accepted the valuation prepared by [Mr. Lilly and Mr. Altizer's] accountant as the correct value of the partnership assets as of 31 August 1995, and found that the surviving partners fully disclosed and delivered to the Estate all records of the financial affairs of the Joe's Racing partnership up to 31 August 1995, which the court took to be the end of the winding up period. Rejecting [Mrs. Creel's] assertions (1) that [Mr. Lilly and Mr. Altizer] were obligated to liquidate the partnership assets in order to *wind up the partnership; (2) that [Mr. Lilly and Mr. Altizer], instead of winding up the partnership by liquidating its assets, misappropriated partnership assets, i.e., inventory to make a profit, for which they were obligated to account; and (3) that the Estate was entitled to 52% of such profits, the court declared that the Estate was entitled to a total of $21,631....*

* * *

On the basis of those findings, the court ordered that [Mrs. Creel] could withdraw the funds deposited in court by the bank and that [Mr. Lilly and Mr. Altizer] should pay [Mrs. Creel] the difference between the amount of those funds and $21,631.00." (Emphasis added).

The Court of Special Appeals affirmed the judgment of the Circuit Court for Charles County, finding that under UPA "winding up" does not always mean "liquidate"; therefore, Joe's Racing had no duty to sell off all of its assets in a liquidation sale. The court also held that Good Ole Boys was not a continuation of Joe's Racing, and as such the Creel estate was not entitled to damages equal to a share of the profits allegedly made by the successor partnership. Mrs. Creel filed a petition for certiorari in May 1998, which we granted.

II. DISCUSSION AND ANALYSIS

A.

We begin our analysis by reviewing the law of partnership as it pertains to the issues in this case. Maryland enacted UPA in 1916. *Shafer Bros. v. Kite,* 43 Md. App. 601, 607, 406 A.2d 673, 677 (1979). Section 9-101(g) defines a partnership as "an association of two or more persons to carry on as co-owners [of] a business for profit." There is no requirement that the partnership be formally established with a writing; so long as this definition is met, a partnership exists whether the parties intend it to or not. However, the "general rule is that the partnership agreement governs the relations among the partners and between the partners and the partnership. The provisions of [UPA] govern to the extent the partnership agreement does not provide otherwise." John W. Larson et al., *Revised Uniform Partnership Act Reflects a Number of Significant Changes,* 10 J. Partnership Tax'n 232, 233 (1993) (footnote omitted).

A partnership is either (1) for a definite term or a particular undertaking or (2) at will, which means the business has no definite term or particular undertaking. 59A Am. Jur. 2d *Partnership* §§ 89 & 90 (1987). *See also* § 9A-101(k). An at-will partnership continues indefinitely and can be dissolved by the express will of any partner or automatically by the happening of a specific event as mandated by UPA, such as the death of a partner. 59A Am. Jur. 2d *Partnership* § 89 (1987). *See also* § 9-602(4). Under UPA, partners may avoid the automatic dissolution of the business upon the death of a partner by providing for its continuation in their partnership agreement. *See Gerding v. Baier,* 143 Md. 520, 524, 122 A. 675, 677 (1923). Sophisticated partnerships virtually always use carefully drafted partnership agreements to protect the various partners' interests by providing for the continuation of the business, the distribution of partnership assets, etc., in the face of various contingencies such as death. *See* Judson A. Crane & Alan R. Bromberg, Law of Partnership § 73, at 417-19 (1968). Less sophisticated partnerships, however, are often operating under oral terms or a "homemade" agreement that does not contain protections for the partners or the business.

While the death of a partner automatically dissolves the partnership unless there is an agreement stating otherwise, the partnership is not terminated until the winding-up process is complete. *Miller v. Salabes,* 225 Md. 53, 59, 169 A.2d 671, 672 (1961). *See also* § 9-601 ("On dissolution, the partnership is not terminated, but continues until the winding up of partnership affairs is completed.") Winding up is generally defined as "getting in the assets, settling with [the] debtors and creditors, and appropriating the amount of profit or loss [to the partners]." *Comp. of Treas. v. Thompson Tr. Corp.,* 209 Md. 490, 501-02, 121 A.2d 850, 856 (1956) (quoting *Lafayette Trust Co. v. Beggs,* 213 N.Y. 280, 107 N.E. 644, 645 (1915)). The surviving partners have the right to wind up the partnership or the deceased partner's representative may obtain a winding up through the courts. *See* § 9-608. Section 9-609 details the winding-up procedures and whether Subsection (a) or (b) applies depends on whether dissolution was caused in contravention of the partnership agreement or not, wrongfully, etc. The winding-up procedure that applies in this case is found in § 9-609(a), which states in pertinent part: "When dissolution is caused in any way . . . each partner . . . unless otherwise agreed, may have the partnership property applied to discharge its liabilities, and the surplus applied to pay in cash the net amount owing to the respective partners."

Historically, under many courts and commentators' interpretation of UPA, when a partner died and the partnership automatically dissolved because there was no consent by the estate to continue the business nor was there a written agreement allowing for continuation, the estate had the right to compel liquidation of the partnership assets. *See Gianakos Ex'r v. Magiros,* 238 Md. 178, 183, 208 A.2d 718, 721 (1965) (noting surviving partners' right to continue the business "if he has the consent of the representative of the deceased partner and there is no agreement to the contrary"). Reducing all of the partnership assets to cash through a liquidation was seen as the only way to obtain the true value of the business. *Dreifuerst v. Dreifuerst,* 90 Wis. 2d 566, 280 N.W.2d 335, 338 (Ct. App. 1979). However, while winding up has often traditionally been regarded as synonymous with liquidation, this "fire sale" of assets has been viewed by many courts and commentators as a harsh and destructive measure. Consequently, to avoid the drastic result of a forced liquidation, many courts have adopted judicial alternatives to this potentially harmful measure. *See Fortugno v. Hudson Manure Company,* 51 N.J. Super. 482, 144 A.2d 207, 219 (App. Div. 1958) (court approved an alternative proposal to the complete liquidation of the partnership, stating that it "recogniz[ed] that a forced sale of the partnership will destroy a great part of the value of the business. . . ."). *See also* full discussion on judicial alternatives to liquidation in Part II.B., *infra.*

Over time, the UPA rule requiring automatic dissolution of the partnership upon the death of a partner, in the absence of consent by the estate to continue the business or an agreement providing for continuation, with the possible result of a forced sale of all partnership assets was viewed as outmoded by many jurisdictions including Maryland. The development and adoption of RUPA by the National Conference of

Commissioners on Uniform State Laws (NCCUSL) mitigated this harsh UPA provision of automatic dissolution and compelled liquidation.

RUPA's underlying philosophy differs radically from UPA's, thus laying the foundation for many of its innovative measures. RUPA adopts the "entity" theory of partnership as opposed to the "aggregate" theory that the UPA espouses. Thomas R. Hurst, *Will the Revised Uniform Partnership Act (1994) Ever Be Uniformly Adopted?*, 48 Fla. L. Rev. 575, 579 (1996). Under the aggregate theory, a partnership is characterized by the collection of its individual members, with the result being that if one of the partners dies or withdraws, the partnership ceases to exist. *See* Joan E. Branch, Note, *The Revised Uniform Partnership Act Breakup Provisions: Should They Be Adopted?*, 25 Creighton L. Rev. 701, 701 (1992). On the other hand, RUPA's entity theory allows for the partnership to continue even with the departure of a member because it views the partnership as "an entity distinct from its partners." Section 9A-201.

This adoption of the entity theory, which permits continuity of the partnership upon changes in partner identity, allows for several significant changes in RUPA. Of particular importance to the instant case is that under RUPA "a partnership no longer automatically dissolves due to a change in its membership, but rather *the existing partnership may be continued if the remaining partners elect to buy out the dissociating partner.*"[4] *Will the Revised Uniform Partnership Act (1994) Ever Be Uniformly Adopted?*, 48 Fla. L. Rev. at 579 (emphasis added) (footnote omitted). In contrast to UPA, RUPA's "buy-out" option does not have to be expressly included in a written partnership agreement in order for it to be exercised; however, the surviving partners must still actively choose to exercise the option, as "continuation is not automatic as with a corporation." *Will the Revised Uniform Partnership Act (1994) Ever Be Uniformly Adopted?*, 48 Fla. L. Rev. at 579-80 (footnote omitted). This major RUPA innovation therefore delineates two possible paths for a partnership to follow when a partner dies or withdraws: "[o]ne leads to the winding up and termination of the partnership and the other to continuation of the partnership and purchase of the departing partner's share." *Will the Revised Uniform Partnership Act (1994) Ever Be Uniformly Adopted?*, 48 Fla. L. Rev. at 583 (footnote omitted). Critically, under RUPA the estate of the deceased partner no longer has to consent in order for the business to be continued nor does the estate have the right to compel liquidation.

Like UPA, RUPA is a "gap filler" in that it only governs partnership affairs to the extent not otherwise agreed to by the partners in the partnership agreement. *See* [§ 9]A-103(a), which states: "[R]elations among the partners and between the partners and the partnership are governed by the partnership agreement. To the extent the partnership agreement does not otherwise provide, this title governs relations

---

[4]RUPA uses the term "dissociation" rather than dissolution. "Dissociation" is viewed as having a less significant impact on the partnership than dissolution, which is in line with RUPA's entity theory of partnership of continuing the business whenever possible. John W. Larson et al., *Revised Uniform Partnership Act Reflects a Number of Significant Changes*, 10 J. Partnership Tax'n 232, 236 (1993). *See also* § 9A-601, which describes the events causing a partner's dissociation, including death. Under RUPA, a dissociation may result in dissolution and a winding up of partnership business. *See* §§ 9A-801 through 9A-807, which provide for the winding up of partnership business. Even after a dissociation leads to a dissolution, RUPA offers a final opportunity for the partners to continue the partnership if they so choose. *See* § 9A-802(b).

among the partners and between the partners and the partnership." There are certain RUPA provisions, however, that partners cannot waive, such as unreasonably restricting the right of access to partnership books and records, eliminating the duty of loyalty, unreasonably reducing the duty of care, and eliminating the obligation of good faith and fair dealing. *See* § 9A-103(b).

Along with 18 other states, Maryland has adopted RUPA, effective July 1, 1998, with a phase-in period during which the two Acts will coexist. As of January 1, 2003, RUPA will govern all Maryland partnerships. *See* § 9A-1204. In adopting RUPA, the Maryland legislature was clearly seeking to eliminate some of UPA's harsh provisions, such as the automatic dissolution of a viable partnership upon the death of a partner and the subsequent right of the estate of the deceased partner to compel liquidation. In essence, the NCCUSL drafted RUPA to reflect the emerging trends in partnership law. RUPA is intended as a flexible, modern alternative to the more rigid UPA and its provisions are consistent with the reasonable expectations of commercial parties in today's business world.

B.

As discussed earlier, the traditional manner in which UPA allows for the continuation of the partnership upon the death of a partner is to either obtain the consent of the deceased partner's estate or include a continuation clause in the partnership agreement. *Gianakos,* 238 Md. at 183, 208 A.2d at 721. There have been several cases in other jurisdictions, however, where neither of these conditions was met and the court elected another option under UPA instead of a "fire sale" of all the partnership assets to ensure that the deceased partner's estate received its fair share of the partnership. *See Cutler v. Cutler,* 165 B.R. 275, 278 (Bankr. D. Ariz. 1994) ("The winding up process does not necessarily mean that the assets of the partnership must be liquidated, although that is one option."). These jurisdictions have recognized the unfairness and harshness of a compelled liquidation and found other judicially acceptable means of winding up a partnership under UPA, such as ordering an in-kind distribution of the assets or allowing the remaining partners to buy out the withdrawing partner's share of the partnership.

While the following cases have not involved the specific situation that we are faced with here — dissolution upon the death of a partner — the options the various courts have adopted to avoid a compelled liquidation of all partnership assets are equally applicable to the instant case. A dissolution is a dissolution and a winding-up process is a winding-up process, no matter what the underlying reason is for its occurrence. The reason for the dissolution is relevant when liabilities are being apportioned among partners, such as in a wrongful dissolution, but such is not the concern in the instant case. Many of these cases also involve a continued partnership, as opposed to a successor partnership like Good Ole Boys, but again the various courts' reasons for not compelling a sale of all assets in order to arrive at the true value of the business are equally applicable to the instant case.

We look to the case law of other jurisdictions because this is a case of first impression in Maryland. The Maryland cases cited by Petitioner and Respondent in their briefs and during arguments are inapposite and offer little assistance in the task before us. We now turn to a discussion of out-of-state cases that have confronted the issue of whether, under UPA, a compelled liquidation in a dissolution situation is always mandated or whether there are other judicially acceptable alternatives.

1. In-Kind Distribution

We first examine the cases where the court elected to order an in-kind distribution rather than a compelled liquidation in order to ascertain the true value of the partnership. An in-kind distribution is the actual division and distribution of the physical assets themselves. *See* Black's Law Dictionary 475 (6th ed. 1990) (defining "[d]istribution in kind" as "[a] transfer of property 'as is' ").

. . .

2. Buy-Out Option

We turn to the line of cases where the court allowed the remaining partners to buy out the withdrawing partner's interest in the partnership, rather than mandate a forced sale of assets to derive the true value of the business.

In *Gregg v. Bernards,* 250 Or. 458, 443 P.2d 166 (1968), Gregg appealed from a decree that dissolved the partnership and vested in Bernards the title to a race horse, the main partnership asset, upon payment by Bernards to Gregg the value of his partnership interest and also his share of the profit. The Supreme Court of Oregon affirmed the trial court's alternative resolution — a buy-out option — to a forced sale of the race horse. *Gregg,* 443 P.2d at 167.

Goergen v. Nebrich also involved a court refusing to order a public sale of the partnership assets in a dissolution situation and instead mandating a buy-out option. 12 Misc. 2d 1011, 174 N.Y.S.2d 366 (N.Y. Sup. Ct. 1958). Dissolution of the two-person partnership was sought on the basis of one partner's incompetency due to illness. After the decree was entered, the incompetent partner died and his estate wanted a public sale of all partnership assets. The New York court held that the partnership assets must be properly appraised to ascertain the true value of the business, but stated that "this does not mean that there must be a ... sale of the partnership assets." *Goergen,* 174 N.Y.S.2d at 369. The court held that because the surviving partner wanted to continue the business, "it would be inequitable and unfair to the surviving partner to have a public sale." *Goergen,* 174 N.Y.S.2d at 369. The court then went on to outline its alternative proposal to a sale of the assets:

> "The legal representative of the deceased partner will be fully protected by a disinterested appraisal of the assets of the former partnership and by receiving decedent's share on the purchase of the deceased partner's assets by the surviving partner at the appraisal price. For this purpose, the Court will appoint two qualified, disinterested appraisers to make an appraisal of the firm's assets and upon the filing with the Court of such appraisals and the final accounting ... *the Court will approve the sale of the deceased partner's interest to the surviving partner* providing that cash is paid for said interest. If the surviving partner is unable to do this, then it will be necessary, in the interest of justice to order a public sale." (Emphasis added).

Goergen, 174 N.Y.S.2d at 369-70.

Similarly, in *Fortugno* the court adopted what it called a "novel" alternative to a forced sale of the partnership assets. 144 A.2d at 219. As in *Goergen,* the New Jersey court was willing to adopt the alternative proposal, but if it was not executed properly by the partners, then a liquidation sale would be ordered. The court held:

> "[R]ecognizing that a forced sale of the partnership will destroy a great part of the value of the business[,] we approve the alternative proposal. . . . If the opposing partners will agree to the entry of an order for the appraisal of the partnership under the direction of the court and directing them to pay [the withdrawing partner] one-eighth of the valuation determined upon, such an order will be entered. Otherwise, there will be a liquidation by sale of all the partnership assets. . . ." (Emphasis added).

Fortugno, 144 A.2d at 219.

Another case in which the court ordered a buy-out option rather than a forced sale of assets is *Wanderski v. Nowakowski,* 331 Mich. 202, 49 N.W.2d 139 (1951). Nowakowski was not required to liquidate the partnership's assets, pay off creditors, and then settle accounts between himself and the withdrawing partner, Wanderski. Instead, he was entitled to continue operations, provided that he paid Wanderski the fair value of his interest in the partnership as of the date of dissolution. The Supreme Court of Michigan allowed Nowakowski this alternative to a forced sale, even though their partnership agreement did not contain any provision regarding the continuation of the business after dissolution. *Wanderski,* 49 N.W.2d at 142-44. *See also Dow v. Beals,* 149 Misc. 631, 268 N.Y.S. 425, 427 (N.Y. Sup. Ct. 1933) (refusing to order liquidation sale of partnership assets and instead mandating that Dow pay to his former partners their proportionate shares of the business).

C.

In applying the law discussed in Part II.A. and B. to the facts of this case, we want to clarify that while UPA is the governing act, our holding is also consistent with RUPA and its underlying policies. The legislature's recent adoption of RUPA indicates that it views with disfavor the compelled liquidation of businesses and that it has elected to follow the trend in partnership law to allow the continuation of business without disruption, in either the original or successor form, if the surviving partners choose to do so through buying out the deceased partner's share.

In this appeal, however, we would arrive at the same holding regardless of whether UPA or RUPA governs. Although our holding departs from the general UPA rule that the representative of the deceased partner's estate has a right to demand liquidation of the partnership, as we discuss in this subsection, *infra,* our position of "no forced sale" hardly represents a radical departure from traditional partnership law. The cases discussed in Part II.B., *supra,* many of which arose early in UPA's existence, illustrate the lengths other courts have gone to in order to avoid a compelled liquidation and adopt an alternative method for ascertaining the true value of a partnership. With that background, we turn to a discussion of the two issues Mrs. Creel raises in this appeal.

1. Compelled Liquidation Issue

The first issue is whether the Creel estate has the right to demand liquidation of Joe's Racing where its partnership agreement does not expressly provide for continuation of the partnership and where the estate does not consent to continuation. Before we move on to our analysis of the compelled liquidation issue, we point out that our finding that Good Ole Boys is a successor partnership, rather than a continuation of Joe's Racing, does not negate the need for a complete discussion of this issue. Unless there is consent to continue the business or an agreement providing for continuation, upon the death of a partner the accurate value of the partnership must be ascertained as of the date of dissolution and the proportionate share paid to the deceased partner's estate, no matter if we are dealing with a subsequent new partnership or a continuation of the original business. If a compelled liquidation of all partnership assets is seen as the only way to arrive at its true value, then property from the original partnership will have to be sold whether the present business is a continuation or a successor business; regardless, the potential harm of such a "fire sale" affects both equally. *See* Part II.C.2., for a full discussion of our characterization of Good Ole Boys.

a.

Because a partnership is governed by any agreement between or among the partners, we must begin our analysis of the compelled liquidation issue by examining the Joe's Racing partnership agreement. We reiterate that both UPA and RUPA only apply when there is either no partnership agreement governing the partnership's affairs, the agreement is silent on a particular point, or the agreement contains provisions contrary to law. *See* §§ 9-401, 9-608, 9-609, 9-611, 9-613, and 9-614, which contain phrases such as "subject to any agreement between [the partners]," "unless otherwise agreed," "subject to any agreement to the contrary," and "in the absence of any agreement to the contrary." *See also* § 9A-103(a). Thus, when conflicts between partners arise, courts must first look to the partnership agreement to resolve the issue:

> "The agreement, whatever its form, is the heart of the partnership. One of the salient characteristics of partnership law is the extent to which partners may write their own ticket. Relations among them are governed by common law and statute, but almost invariably can be overridden by the parties themselves. As one court has long put it, *the agreement is the law of the partnership.*" (Emphasis added) (footnote omitted).

Seattle-First Nat. Bank v. Marshall, 31 Wash. App. 339, 641 P.2d 1194, 1199 (1982) (quoting Judson A. Crane & Alan R. Bromberg, Law of Partnership § 5, at 43 (1968)).

The pertinent paragraph and subsections of the Joe's Racing partnership agreement are as follows:

"7. TERMINATION

(a) That, at the termination of this partnership a full and accurate inventory shall be prepared, and the assets, liabilities, and income, both in gross and net, shall be ascertained: the remaining debts or profits will be distributed according to the percentages shown above in the 6(e).

* * *

(d) Upon the death or illness of a partner, his share will go to his estate. If his estate wishes to sell his interest, they must offer it to the remaining partners first."

Even though the partnership agreement uses the word "termination," paragraph 7(a) is really discussing the dissolution of the partnership and the attendant winding-up process that ultimately led to termination. Paragraph 7(a) requires that the assets, liabilities, and income be "ascertained," but it in no way mandates that this must be accomplished by a forced sale of the partnership assets. Indeed, a liquidation or sale of assets is not mentioned anywhere in 7(a).

In this case, the winding-up method outlined in 7(a) was followed exactly by the surviving partners: a full and accurate inventory was prepared on August 31, 1995; this information was given to an accountant, who ascertained the assets, liabilities, and income of the partnership; and finally, the remaining debt or profit was distributed according to the percentages listed in 6(e).[6]

Mrs. Creel argues that the partnership agreement does not address the winding-up process and that we should look to UPA's default rules to fill in this gap. Her contention is incorrect. We only turn to UPA and its liquidation rule if there is no other option, and such is clearly not the case here. While this partnership agreement was drafted without the assistance of counsel and is not a sophisticated document that provides for every contingency, if it states the intention of the parties it is controlling. As we stated in *Klein v. Weiss*:

> "A partnership is, of course, a contractual relation to which the principles of contract law are fully applicable. . . . One of the essential elements for formation of a contract is a manifestation of agreement or mutual assent by the parties to the terms thereof; in other words, to establish a contract the minds of the parties must be in agreement as to its terms." (Citations omitted).

284 Md. 36, 63, 395 A.2d 126, 141 (1978).

Thus, when we look to the intention of the parties as reflected in 7(a) of the partnership agreement, the trial judge could conclude that the partners did not anticipate that a "fire sale" of the partnership assets would be necessary to ascertain the true value of Joe's Racing. Paragraph 7(a) details the preferred winding-up procedure to be followed, to include an inventory, valuation, and distribution of debt or profit to the partners.

---

[6]Paragraph 6(e) of the partnership agreement states "[t]hat the net profits or net losses be divided as follows:

Joseph Creel	28%
Arnold Lilly	24%
Joseph Cudmore	24%
Roy Altizer	24%"

As determined by the trial court, the interest of Joseph Cudmore, who never signed the partnership agreement, reverted to Joseph Creel, who was entitled to a 52 percent share.

Moreover, paragraph 7(d), which discusses what happens to a partner's share of the business upon his death, also makes no mention of a sale or liquidation as being essential in order to determine the deceased partner's proportionate interest of the partnership. On the contrary, 7(d) appears to be a crude attempt to draft a "continuation clause" in the form of a buy-out option by providing that the deceased partner's share of the partnership goes to his estate, and if the estate wishes to sell this interest it must first be offered to the remaining partners. *See* § 9A-701, which details the purchase of the dissociated partner's interest. In contrast to consenting to the continuation of the business, Mrs. Creel made it plain that she wanted the business "dissolved and the affairs of the company wound up"; however, this does not mean a liquidation was required. Particularly in light of Maryland's recent adoption of RUPA, paragraph 7(d) of the partnership agreement can be interpreted to mean that because Mrs. Creel did not wish to remain in business with Lilly and Altizer, they had the option to buy out her deceased husband's interest.

In short, when subsections (a) and (d) of paragraph 7 are read in conjunction, it is apparent that the partners did not intend for there to be a liquidation of all partnership assets upon the death of a partner. Paragraph 7(a) delineates the winding-up procedure, which was methodically followed by Lilly and Altizer. Paragraph 7(d) dictates what happens to the partnership in the event of a partner's death, and it can be interpreted as allowing a buy-out option if the deceased partner's estate no longer wishes to remain in business with the surviving partners, as was clearly the case here. Therefore, the trial judge could have concluded that Lilly and Altizer exercised this 7(d) buy-out option, and subsequently began a new partnership, when they followed the winding-up procedure dictated by 7(a) and presented the Creel estate with its share of Joe's Racing.[7]

Assuming *arguendo* that the Joe's Racing partnership agreement cannot be interpreted as outlining an alternative to liquidation in winding up the partnership in the event of a dissolution caused by a partner's death, we still find that a sale of all partnership assets is not required under either UPA or RUPA in order to ascertain the true value of the business. Support for this is found in Maryland's recent adoption of RUPA, which encourages businesses to continue in either their original or successor form, and also the holdings of out-of-state cases where other options besides a "fire sale" have been chosen when a partnership is dissolved under UPA. *See* full discussions in Part II.A. and B., *supra*.

We agree with the trial court and the intermediate appellate court that there is nothing in Maryland's UPA, in particular §§ 9-608 and 9-609, or any of our case law that supports an unequivocal requirement of a forced sale in a situation akin to the instant case. The one case Mrs. Creel relies on, *Comp. of Treas., supra*, is inapposite for the following reasons, as succinctly stated by the Court of Special Appeals:

"Finally, appellant relies on a sentence in [*Comp. of Treas.*]: 'A liquidation is generally defined as the winding up of a business or enterprise.' Such reliance is a classic example of the fallacy of assuming that a word, phrase, clause, or sentence used in one

[7]Lilly and Altizer originally offered Mrs. Creel a share based on a 36 percent interest of the partnership; however, this percentage was later adjusted to 52 percent by the trial court and applied retroactively to the August 31, 1995, wind up and termination date of Joe's Racing. Neither Lilly nor Altizer dispute this percentage in this appeal.

context will have the same meaning in a totally different context. The issue in [*Comp. of Treas.*] was whether a certain transaction was subject to the Maryland retail sales tax or exempt as a casual and isolated sale 'by a vender who is not regularly engaged in the business of selling tangible personal property.' The sale in question was one of equipment formerly used by the vendor who was liquidating all of his business assets with the intention of retiring. The comptroller pointed out that the liquidation of assets process was drawn out, but the court held that the sale was 'in conjunction with a complete liquidation of a person's business' and was therefore not taxable. *To rely on a statement that a liquidation is generally defined as a winding up of a business or enterprise, in the context of determining whether a sale of a business['s] assets is a taxable transaction as equivalent to a holding that winding up the affairs of a dissolved partnership means liquidation is patently ludicrous.*" (quoting *Comp. of Treas.*, 209 Md. at 501, 121 A.2d at 856) (Emphasis added).

b.

We find it is sound public policy to permit a partnership to continue either under the same name or as a successor partnership without all of the assets being liquidated. Liquidation can be a harmful and destructive measure, especially to a small business like Joe's Racing, and is often unnecessary to determining the true value of the partnership. *See Arnold v. Burgess,* 113 Idaho 786, 747 P.2d 1315, 1322 (Ct. App. 1987) ("A forced sale of partnership assets will often destroy a great part of the value of the business and may prevent the continuation of a valuable source of livelihood for former partners."). We now explore the "true value of the partnership" issue and whether liquidation is the only way to obtain it.

In the instant case, per paragraph 7(a) of the partnership agreement and § 9-614 of UPA,[8] the Creel estate had the right to ask the surviving partners for an accounting of Mr. Creel's interest in Joe's Racing as of the date of dissolution. We agree with the Court of Special Appeals when it stated, however, that "*[t]he right to an accounting is not a right to force the winding up partners to liquidate the assets.* The personal representative of a deceased partner is entitled to receive, on behalf of the estate, as an ordinary creditor, the value of the decedent's partnership interest as of the date of dissolution, *i.e.*, the date of the decedent's death." (Emphasis added).

In accordance with both the partnership agreement and UPA, Lilly and Altizer provided Mrs. Creel with an accounting, which was based on the valuation performed by the accountant they hired. Mrs. Creel contends that this accounting did not reflect the true value of Joe's Racing, and as a result the estate did not receive its proportionate share of the partnership.

First, we note that Mrs. Creel did not contest the figures that the surviving partner's accountant derived until approximately a year and a half after her husband's death and one month before trial. At this late date, Mrs. Creel made a request for a court-appointed auditor per Maryland Rule 2-543(b) but the trial court correctly

---

[8]Section 9-614, "Accrual of right to account," provides:

> "The right to an account of his interest shall accrue to any partner, or his legal representative, as against the winding up partners or the surviving partners or the person or partnership continuing the business, at the date of dissolution, in the absence of any agreement to the contrary."

found that "where a request for an auditor is made one month before trial in an action pending in excess of one year, such a referral would cause unnecessary delay in the resolution of this case. Furthermore, the Court ... finds that the interests of the parties can be properly determined by the Court." Moreover, if Mrs. Creel was so concerned that the accounting rendered by Lilly and Altizer's accountant was incorrect, then she should have immediately hired her own appraiser to review the accountant's work and/or make an independent valuation of Joe's Racing. As the *Rinke* court so aptly stated:

> "[W]e think the failure on the part of cross-plaintiffs to offer evidence as to the value of the assets used by plaintiffs, or either of them, precludes them from now contending that the decree from which they have appealed should be set aside on this ground. *The trial court determined the issues before him on the basis of the proofs of the parties. This court is necessarily governed by the record before us.*" (Emphasis added).

48 N.W.2d at 207.

Second, we disagree as to Mrs. Creel's argument that the accountant's valuation was in error and that the trial court subsequently arrived at an incorrect distribution of Mr. Creel's interest in the partnership. Mrs. Creel maintains that the only way to ascertain the true value of her deceased husband's interest in Joe's Racing is to liquidate all of its assets but we agree with the trial court, which held: "The surviving parties under the Code and existing case law had to account for the inventory and pay to the Estate its appropriate share, *but not sell off the assets in a liquidation sale.*" (Emphasis added). In making his findings, the trial judge looked to paragraph 7(a) of the partnership agreement and also § 9-611 of UPA, which outlines the rules of distribution in settling accounts between partners after dissolution. The court held:

> "The Court finds that directions of Section 9-611 are similar to clause 7 (termination) of the Partnership Agreement and the Court will now apply that analysis. The partnership assets are $44,589.44. The Court accepts the valuation prepared by Mr. Johnson [the accountant] as the correct statement of value. The Court determines the debts to creditors to be the accounting fees due Mr. Johnson in the amount of $875.00. The debts owed to partners are: (1) $495.00 to Mrs. Creel; (2) $2,187.00 to Mr. Lilly[;] and (3) $900.00 to Mr. Altizer. The capital contributions are determined to be $15,000.00 to Mr. Creel and $6,666 each to Mr. Altizer and Mr. Lilly. The Estate is also due 52% of the balance of the $11,800.00 or $6,136.00. *The total due to the Estate, therefore, is declared to be $21,631.00 ($15,000.00 + $495.00 + $6,136.00).*"

Finally, Mrs. Creel contends that the accountant's valuation improperly considered only the book value of the business and not its market value. "Book value" refers to the assets of the business, less its liabilities plus partner contributions or "equity." "Market value" includes the value of such intangibles as goodwill, the value of the business as an ongoing concern, and established vendor and supplier lines, among other factors. Again, we concur with the trial court's findings as to the valuation of Joe's Racing.

In making no finding of goodwill value, for example, the trial court likely considered the fact that Joe's Racing had only been operating a little over a year before the partnership was formed, and after Lilly and Altizer became partners with Mr. Creel the business was only in existence for nine months before Mr. Creel died. On these facts, it is reasonable for the trial court to conclude — without any evidence presented to the contrary — that a small business selling NASCAR memorabilia, which had been operating for barely two years, did not possess any goodwill value.

c.

Our goal in this case, and in cases of a similar nature, is to prevent the disruption and loss that are attendant on a forced sale, while at the same time preserving the right of the deceased partner's estate to be paid his or her fair share of the partnership. With our holding, we believe this delicate balance has been achieved. For the reasons stated, we hold that paragraph 7, subsections (a) and (d), of the partnership agreement should be interpreted as outlining an alternative method of winding-up Joe's Racing and arriving at its true value other than a "fire sale" of all its assets. Even if there were no partnership agreement governing this case, however, we hold that Maryland's UPA — particularly in light of the legislature's recent adoption of RUPA — does not grant the estate of a deceased partner the right to demand liquidation of a partnership where the partnership agreement does not expressly provide for continuation of the partnership and where the estate does not consent to continuation. To hold otherwise vests excessive power and control in the estate of the deceased partner, to the extreme disadvantage of the surviving partners. We further hold that where the surviving partners have in good faith wound up the business and the deceased partner's estate is provided with an accurate accounting allowing for payment of a proportionate share of the business, then a forced sale of all partnership assets is unwarranted.

. . .

III. CONCLUSION

We hold that Maryland's UPA does not grant the estate of a deceased partner the right to demand liquidation of a partnership where the partnership agreement does not expressly provide for continuation of the partnership and where the estate does not consent to continuation. Winding up is not always synonymous with liquidation, which can be a harsh and unnecessary measure towards arriving at the true value of the business. A preferred method in a good faith winding up is the one used in this case — the payment to the deceased partner's estate of its proportionate share of the partnership. Thus, we further hold that where the surviving partners have in good faith wound up the business and the deceased partner's estate is provided with an accurate accounting allowing for payment of a proportionate share of the business, then a forced sale of all partnership assets is generally unwarranted. Finally, we hold that because Good Ole Boys is a successor partnership and not a continuation of Joe's Racing, the Creel estate is not entitled to a share of any profits generated by the surviving partners' alleged continued use of the partnership assets.

Judgment of the Court of Special Appeals affirmed. Costs in this Court and the Court of Special Appeals to be paid by Petitioner.

Post-Case Follow-Up

Creel highlights the importance of planning for the withdrawal of a partner — particularly in a UPA-style regime. First, partnership agreements should contain rules and procedures respecting the withdrawal of partners and the admission of new partners. Second, partnership agreements should include a continuation agreement so that non-dissolving partners can continue the partnership business post-dissolution. Third, partners should consider including a **buy-sell agreement** in their partnership agreement as well, or an agreement providing that upon the withdrawal or death of a partner (or other agreed-upon trigger), that partner's interest in the partnership must be offered and sold to the partnership. Buy-sell agreements typically identify events that will trigger the obligation to transfer the partnership interest, outline the plan for buying out the departing partner's interest, set the cost or valuation method for the buyout, and identify any other procedural or substantive requirements for the buyout. To fund such a provision, the partnership may purchase life insurance policies, sometimes called **key person policies**, for each partner, naming the partnership as beneficiary. Then upon the death of a partner, the partnership will have sufficient funds to pay to the deceased partner's estate to buy out the decedent's interest in the partnership. The buy-sell agreement also should include a method of payment (e.g., installment payments) if there is not enough cash to pay off the withdrawing partner.

Creel v. Lilly: Real Life Applications

1. Terry, Fran, and Sandy retain you to draft a partnership agreement. All three partners agree that they want to be able to continue the business should one partner die, withdraw, be expelled, or seek bankruptcy protection. Assume that a UPA-style regime applies. Write a letter to Terry, Fran, and Sandy explaining the purpose of a continuation agreement, and draft key terms of that agreement.

2. Terry, Fran, and Sandy ask you what will happen to their interests in the partnership should any one of them choose to withdraw. Draft a letter explaining what is likely to happen assuming a UPA-style regime applies. Draft another letter assuming a RUPA-style regime applies. Include a section in your letter discussing the possibility of a buy-sell agreement and its key terms, tailoring your discussion to the UPA and RUPA regimes, as appropriate.

3. Two years into the partnership, Terry withdraws. One week later, an employee of the partnership hits a pedestrian in a crosswalk while making a delivery of partnership goods. Is Terry personally liable for damages associated with the accident?

Spotlight: Wrongful Dissolution

Although partners can withdraw from a partnership at will under the UPA, triggering dissolution, there are consequences for wrongfully withdrawing partners. *See* UPA § 38. Whereas the departure of a partner that is not wrongful typically triggers winding up and termination under a UPA-style regime (at least in cases where there is no continuation agreement), the remaining partners may be able to continue the partnership business when a partner wrongfully dissolves a UPA-style partnership, and thus may avoid having to wind up partnership affairs, even if they failed to negotiate a continuation agreement. *See* UPA § 38(2). In addition, although a wrongfully departing partner will not forfeit his economic interest in the partnership entirely, he will be subject to a claim for damages, and may see the value of his interest in the partnership calculated without considering the goodwill of the business under the default rules. *See, e.g.,* UPA § 38(2)(b)(II); *Drashner v. Sorenson*, 63 N.W.2d 255 (S.D. 1954).

Application Exercise 1

Acme is a general partnership formed in a jurisdiction with a partnership statute that tracks the UPA. Acme has three partners. Abe and Benjie are hardworking, and have spent the past ten years building up the partnership's business. Formerly a hard worker, Carl (the third partner) has become increasingly unreliable over the past year. Bartenders around town have called Abe and Benjie expressing concern over Carl's behavior — Carl stays out late every night drinking to excess. Customers have reported that Carl has left long and nonsensical voicemails during his late night drinking binges. Carl rarely reports to work anymore, and when he does, he appears hungover and disheveled.

Two days ago, Carl walked into Acme's offices and demanded his share of the partnership, declaring that he was sick and tired of being nagged by Benjie and Abe to clean up his act. Carl said (correctly) that Acme's partnership agreement does not contain a continuation agreement, and he made it clear that he would not agree to a continuation of the partnership's business in his absence. Horrified, Benjie and Able call you for advice, asking the following questions. Prepare to discuss these questions at a meeting with Benjie and Abe:

1. For purposes of this question only, assume that you have represented Acme in the past in business matters. Are there any ethical issues associated with fielding questions from Abe and Benjie respecting Carl's behavior and the legal status of the partnership?
2. Can Carl simply walk away from the partnership without consequence?
3. What is the legal status of Acme today, given Carl's decision to walk away?
4. If Acme is dissolved as a legal matter, can Carl block Benjie and Abe from continuing the partnership's business?
5. If Benjie and Abe are able to continue the business, are they required to buy Carl out? What will (and will not) be considered in calculating the value of Carl's share, if buyout is in fact an option?

2. Dissociation, Dissolution, Winding Up, and Termination Under the RUPA

Dissociation

RUPA was intended to change the law governing partnership breakups and dissolution. Specifically, the RUPA seeks to avoid the harsh UPA approach that any withdrawal from a partnership for any reason triggers a dissolution, and likely winding up and termination, by creating a new concept of **dissociation** and by making it clear that not every dissociation causes dissolution of the partnership, or necessitates winding up and termination of the partnership and its business.

Under the RUPA, a dissociation is a withdrawal of a partner from a partnership. *See* RUPA § 601. According to RUPA § 601, a dissociation occurs whenever a partnership receives notice of a partner's express will to leave the partnership, when a partnership agreement provides for events that cause dissociation, upon a partner's expulsion, upon court decree (usually initiated by the partnership because a partner's misconduct threatens the partnership business), or upon a partner's death or bankruptcy. Upon a partner's dissociation, the partner's right to participate in the management of the business terminates, as does the duty of loyalty (unless the partner is participating in winding up the partnership's business). *See* RUPA § 603(b).

Effect of Partner Dissociation Under the RUPA

The key difference between the UPA and the RUPA is that under the RUPA, not every partner dissociation causes a dissolution of the partnership, or requires the winding up and termination of the partnership, under default rules. Instead, a partnership will be dissolved, and its business must be wound up, only upon the occurrence of one of the events listed in § 801. If § 801 is not triggered, dissolution does not occur; rather, the dissociating partner's interest will be bought out according to statutory rules, and the partnership and its business may continue. *See* RUPA § 701 (providing that "[i]f a person is dissociated as a partner without the dissociation resulting in a dissolution and winding up of the partnership business under Section 801, the partnership shall cause the person's interest in the partnership to be purchased for a buyout price determined pursuant to subsection (b)"). RUPA thus ameliorates the harsh effects of the UPA by allowing partnerships and partnership businesses to survive the dissociation of their members in many instances.

Application Exercise 2

1. Return to the example of the Acme general partnership with Abe, Benjie, and the rogue partner Carl. Now, assume that the events described above took place in a jurisdiction with a partnership statute that follows the RUPA model. Would the answers to the questions posed by Benjie and Abe change under a RUPA-style approach?

2. Assume for purposes of this question only that Carl has been a model partner for the past ten years, but has expressed a desire to withdraw from the partnership so that he can spend more time addressing health concerns.
   a. Under the RUPA, what is the legal term for Carl's exit from the partnership?
   b. Will Carl's departure dissolve the partnership?
   c. Will Acme be forced to wind up and terminate the partnership following Carl's withdrawal?
   d. What will happen to Carl's financial interest in the partnership following his departure?

In the case of a dissociation that does not cause a dissolution and winding up, and in order to protect innocent third parties, a continuing partnership remains bound for two years for the dissociating partner's acts before dissociation if the other party did not have notice of the partner's dissociation or reasonably believed the dissociated partner was still a partner. *See, e.g.,* RUPA §§ 702, 703. The dissociating partner has the same liability. The partnership or the dissociating partner may, however, file a voluntary **Statement of Dissociation** with its state agency, identifying the partner who dissociated. Under RUPA § 103, third parties will be deemed to have notice of the dissociation 90 days after the statement becomes effective, thereby reducing the two-year period of potential liability for the dissociating partner's acts to 90 days (see Exhibit 3.8).

If the partnership does dissolve and its business must be wound up, creditors must be paid prior to partners. Although the UPA requires third-party creditors' claims to be paid in full prior to claims of partners and requires partners to be repaid their contributions before they receive profits, the RUPA draws no such distinctions and merely requires creditors' claims (including those of partners) to be paid in full before partners receive any assets. *See* RUPA § 806(a). A **Statement of Dissolution** may be filed to cancel an earlier filed Statement of Authority and to provide notice to the public that the partnership has dissolved and is winding up its business. RUPA § 303(h).

3. Opportunities for Private Ordering

Because both the UPA and the RUPA contain mostly default rules, nearly all procedures relating to dissociation and dissolution can be varied or limited by the terms of the partners' agreement.

N. DISSOLUTION, WINDING UP, TERMINATION, AND SERVICE PARTNERS

Under UPA §§ 18(a), 40(b), and 40(d), so-called service partners (partners who contribute services to the partnership, but not capital) arguably are not entitled to

EXHIBIT 3.8 **Florida Statement of Dissociation**

STATEMENT OF DISSOCIATION FOR PARTNERSHIP

Pursuant to section 620.8704, Florida Statutes, I hereby submit the following statement of dissociatic

FIRST: The name of the partnership is:_____

_____

SECOND: (CHECK ONE)

☐ The partnership was registered with the Florida Department of State on _____

 and assigned registration number GP_____ .

☐ The partnership has not registered with the Florida Department of State.

THIRD: The purpose of this document is to state that

_____ has dissociated as a partner
(Partner's Name)

_____ .
(Partnership Name)

FOURTH: Effective date, if other than the date of filing: _____.
(Effective date cannot be prior to the date of filing nor more than 90 days after the date of filing.)

The execution of this statement in compliance with s. 620.8105(6) constitutes an affirmation und
penalties of perjury that the facts stated herein are true.

I am aware that any false information submitted in a document to the Department of State const
a third degree felony as provided for in s. 817.155, F.S

Signed this _____ day of _____, _____.

_____
(Signature)

_____
(Typed or printed name of person signing above)

Filing Fee:	$25.00
Certified copy:	$52.50 (optional)
Certificate of Status:	$ 8.75 (optional)

Make checks payable to Florida Department of State and mail to:
Division of Corporations P.O. Box 6327 Tallahassee, FL 32314

EXHIBIT 3.9   **Comparison of UPA and RUPA Provisions**

	UPA	RUPA
Nature of partnership	Partnership is an aggregation of individuals.	Partnership is an entity for nearly all purposes.
Acts requiring unanimity	Lists certain acts requiring unanimous consent	No list of acts requiring unanimous consent
Public filing of Statements of Authority, Denial, Dissociation, Dissolution, Merger, and Conversion	Not provided for	Statements may be filed with state officials.
Fiduciary duties	Generally provides only that partners are accountable as fiduciaries	Provides that partners are subject to the duties of loyalty and due care, which cannot be waived or eliminated; partners must exercise their duties consistent with good faith and fair dealing
Right to accounting	Partners have a right to formal account of partnership affairs.	Partner may bring an action for an accounting.
Property rights	Partner is a co-owner with his partners of specific partnership property (the theory of tenancy in partnership).	Abolishes concept of tenancy in partnership and provides that partnership property is owned by the entity and not by individual partners
Withdrawal by partner	Withdrawal of a partner for any reason causes a dissolution of the partnership.	Provides for dissociation of partner, which causes a dissolution and winding up only in certain situations; otherwise, partnership buys out dissociating partner's interest and continues unaffected by dissociation
Settlement of accounts upon dissolution	Outside third-party creditors are paid first, followed by partners' claims, followed by return of partners' capital, and then distribution of profits.	Creditors' claims are paid first (including claims by partners who separately hold the status of creditor) and then surplus is paid to partners.
Limited liability partnerships	Not provided for	Provided for under RUPA
Conversion and mergers of partnerships	Not provided for	RUPA allows the merger of two or more partnerships and the conversions of general partnerships to limited partnerships (and the reverse).

a share of partnership capital in the event of dissolution, unless the partners have agreed otherwise, and they may even be required to contribute to losses. The RUPA takes a similar position. *See* RUPA § 401(b). Although some courts have gone to great lengths to mitigate the potential harshness of this rule, the RUPA Official Comments note that partners contributing services ought to take advantage of their power to vary by agreement the allocation of capital losses. *See* RUPA § 401(a) cmt. As this suggests, to avoid problems, partners should work out in advance whether services will "count" as a contribution to capital, and if so, how those services will be valued. If services are to be considered a contribution to capital, the value assigned to those services ought to be recorded on the balance sheet as an intangible asset offset by an increase in the service-contributing partner's capital account.

Chapter Summary

- A general partnership arises when two or more persons associate to carry on a for-profit business as co-owners.
- Partnership agreements can be oral, written, or implied through conduct; written agreements are recommended to minimize confusion over relationships and governance.
- With a limited number of exceptions, partnership statutes contain default rules, or gap fillers, that partners may modify to meet business needs. As between the partnership statute and the partnership agreement, the partnership agreement generally governs.
- In deciding whether business associates have formed a partnership inadvertently (i.e., through the act of associating as co-owners, rather than through an express oral or written partnership agreement), courts consider the parties' intentions as expressed through their words, conduct, and actions, and the circumstances surrounding their business relationship, to decide whether a partnership was formed. Among other factors, courts examine whether the parties (i) carried on as co-owners, with equal rights to control the business; (ii) shared profits; (iii) shared losses; and (iv) contributed capital (cash or other property) to the business.
- All partners have equal rights to manage and control partnership affairs.
- Partners exercise their right to participate in management by voting: Disputes regarding ordinary course matters typically are decided by a majority of partners; disputes regarding non-ordinary course matters typically require unanimous approval.
- Partners are agents of the partnership and owe duties of care and loyalty. Partners also must discharge partnership duties in a manner that is consistent with the contractual duty of good faith and fair dealing.
- As agents, partners can bind the partnership and subject the partnership and co-partners to liability, according to agency law rules.
- Partners in a general partnership suffer the disadvantage of unlimited personal liability for partnership debts.

- If a partner withdraws from a UPA-style partnership, the partnership is dissolved as a legal matter, and unless the partners have negotiated (or agree to) a continuation agreement, the partnership may have to be wound up and terminated.
- By contrast, under a RUPA-style regime, only certain partner departures result in winding up and termination of the partnership. More often, the remaining partners are able to buy out the departing partner's interest in the partnership and continue with partnership business.

Applying the Concepts

1. Jack Ellis and Laura Bond are business associates and former romantic partners. When Jack and Laura first met three years ago, Jack was operating a personal endurance sports training business under the name Triathlon Training ("Training"). Jack had just purchased a building that he intended to transform into an exercise studio and apartment for his business, and he was busy obtaining a mortgage and financing for this project when he and Laura began dating.

   Within six months of beginning their relationship, Laura began to help Jack with Training. Laura established credit accounts in her name to help fund construction, and Laura's parents loaned the couple money for the project. Laura also began working in the business. At Jack's direction, Laura accompanied Jack to fitness-related expos, helped him promote his personal training services to potential clients, assisted with various office tasks, installed a new computer system, and paid various expenses to support the business. Laura received compensation for this work in the form of wages, and she followed Jack's instructions on all matters relating to the business. Jack and Laura operated in this fashion for two years, as the construction project dragged on.

   During the third year of their relationship, Laura became concerned about her rights and obligations respecting Training. Laura drafted, and the parties both signed, a one-page document that was intended to establish and clarify the parties' "financial and personal relationship." The stated purpose of the agreement was to reduce Laura's "personal financial liability for debts incurred in the course of the construction of the studio." The agreement identified three revolving credit accounts that had been established in Laura's name, which were exclusively used for expenses relating to the construction of the studio and for operating expenses incurred by Training. The agreement provided that in the event of Jack's death or disability, the assets of Training would be used to repay (i) debts associated with the revolving credit accounts; and (ii) any outstanding balance owed on any loans extended by Laura or her parents.

   Two weeks ago, Jack and Laura had a personal and professional falling out. Laura has filed a lawsuit seeking (i) a declaration that the parties were legal partners; (ii) damages for breach of the partnership agreement; (iii) an accounting of the profits, losses, and assets of Training for the past three years; and (iv) a constructive trust upon the assets of Training and its real property. Will Laura prevail on any or all of these claims? Why or why not?

2. Tess, Fran, and Taylor have formed a general partnership to provide interior design and decorating services. Although they have a written partnership agreement, the agreement does not discuss division of profits or losses, nor does it discuss how the partnership will be managed. It does provide that the partnership will last for five years. Tess contributed $30,000 to the partnership, Fran contributed $45,000 to the partnership, and Taylor contributed $25,000 to the partnership. Answer the following questions applying both UPA and RUPA rules.

   a. Last year the partnership made profits of $200,000, but decided to retain $50,000 for future expansion. How will the remaining $150,000 be divided among the partners? What share will each partner declare on his or her tax return?

   b. Without the knowledge or consent of the other partners, Tess has engaged the services of a marketing company to promote the partnership's business. Who is liable to pay for these services? What remedies, if any, do Fran and Taylor have if they object to the expenditure?

   c. Without the knowledge or authority of the other partners, Tess signs a contract on behalf of the partnership to provide landscaping design services to a longstanding client. Is the partnership obligated to honor the contract?

   d. Tess believes that it is important for the partnership to diversify its business. Tess approaches Fran and Taylor with the idea of providing landscape design services in addition to decorating services. Fran agrees with Tess. Taylor believes that they should stick with decorating services. Whose preferences will prevail?

   e. Assume for purposes of this question only that Tess owns 75 percent of the partnership, and that Fran and Taylor own 12.5 percent each. Further assume for purposes of this question that the partners have agreed to allocate voting power based on their ownership interest (pro rata) rather than a per capita basis.

      (i) Tess approaches Fran and Taylor and proposes that the partnership take on a decorating job for a new clothing store. The job is similar to work that the partnership has taken on in the past. Nevertheless, Fran and Taylor are reluctant to take on the work. Can Tess commit the partnership over the objections of co-partners?

      (ii) Tess approaches Fran and Taylor and proposes that the partnership take on a landscaping design job for a longstanding client of the firm. Fran and Taylor are reluctant to take on the work. Can Tess commit the partnership over the objections of her fellow partners?

   f. The partnership owes $40,000 to one of its furniture suppliers. The supplier has sued the partnership and all of the partners. The partnership has $30,000 in its accounts. Who is liable for payment of the money owed to the supplier?

   g. Tess would like to transfer her interest in the partnership to her sibling, Morgan. If Tess transfers her interest, does the partnership dissolve under a UPA regime? What about under the RUPA? What rights will Morgan have, if any, respecting the partnership following transfer?

h. Assume that the partnership has decided to convert to a limited liability partnership. Is this permitted under the statute in effect in your home state? If so, are there any conditions, limitations, or requirements of note? Assuming the partnership is able to convert to a limited liability partnership, what effect would this have on an existing lawsuit pending against the general partnership?

Business Organizations in Practice

1. You are an associate at a law firm. Anna, Ben, and Carly retain you to draft a written partnership agreement for their web design and database development business. Anna plans to contribute $30,000 to the partnership, Ben plans to contribute $100,000 to the partnership, and Carly plans to contribute $20,000 to the partnership. Carly also plans to contribute several servers (a type of computer that the business will use to store and manage data and provide web services) to the venture. Ben, Carly, and Anna tell you to allocate voting power based on their initial contributions to the business. Draft provisions for the partnership agreement that will accomplish this goal.

2. After you finish meeting with Anna, Ben, and Carly, Anna pulls you aside to explain that she wants voting control because she thinks that Ben and Carly are wonderful designers, but terrible business people. She is worried that Ben and Carly will spend partnership profits unwisely and demand excessive distributions, so she asks you to make sure that she has voting control over all matters, whether ordinary course or not.

   a. What ethical issues, if any, does this conversation raise under your state's ethical rules?

   b. If you allocate voting according to ownership interest, and say nothing about ordinary course versus non-ordinary course activities, will Anna have voting control over all matters?

   c. Assume for purposes of this question that Ben and Carly agree with Anna's assessment of their business skills, and further agree (upon advice of personal counsel) that Anna should have voting control over all matters, whether ordinary course or not. Draft provision(s) for the partnership agreement that will accomplish this goal.

3. During your private meeting with Anna, Anna explains that she has developed a new computer-aided design (CAD) software program that will allow web and database design customers to explore possible architecture and design ideas "virtually" through software, before committing to a development plan. Anna would like to contribute the software to the partnership. After performing legal research, draft a letter to Anna discussing ownership and/or valuation issues that may arise when a partner contributes intellectual property to a partnership.

4. Anna, Ben, and Carly call you up two weeks after the initial meeting to explain that they want to bring Isaac into the partnership. Isaac is a brilliant designer, and is beloved by clients, but has no capital to contribute to the partnership. The

parties all anticipate that Isaac will work at the partnership's offices and at client work sites every day. Anna, Ben, and Carly ask whether Isaac can receive a salary for his work. They also ask whether Isaac's work on behalf of the partnership could "count" as his contribution to capital. After performing legal research, provide advice to the parties respecting whether and under what circumstances Isaac's labor could "count" as his capital contribution. Suggest language for the partnership agreement that would accomplish this goal.

5. What happens if Anna decides unilaterally to pay Isaac a salary?

Registered Limited Liability Partnerships

4

A registered limited liability partnership is a relatively new form of business organization. Recognized in all states and the District of Columbia, the LLP modifies a fundamental principle of general partnership law relating to liability. You will recall that under general partnership law (both the UPA and RUPA regimes), a partner in a general partnership has unlimited personal liability for the debts or obligations of the partnership. In a limited liability partnership, partners are not subject to unlimited personal liability for tort-based claims (e.g., the negligence or incompetence of fellow partners). In nearly all states, partners in an LLP are insulated from personal liability for the contractual obligations of the partnership as well. The registered limited liability partnership thus continues a trend in modern business law of creating new forms of organization that offer partnership-style flexibility in governance rules and pass-through taxation and limited liability. In this chapter, we focus on formation of LLPs and differences between LLPs and general partnerships.

A. WHAT IS A REGISTERED LIMITED LIABILITY PARTNERSHIP?

The LLP form originated in Texas in 1991 as a response to lawsuits against lawyers and accountants arising out of the collapse of the real estate and energy markets in the late 1980s. *See* Conrad S. Ciccotello & C. Terry Grant, *Professions as Commercial Institutions: An Analysis of Evolving Professional Forms*, 7 J. Legal Stud. Bus. 1, 16 (2000). In the late 1980s, a number of savings and loan institutions failed. Injured investors could not bring effective causes

Key Concepts

- Definition and characteristics of limited liability partnerships
- Differences between limited liability partnerships and general partnerships

Growth in LLPs

LLPs have seen enormous growth since Texas first recognized this form of organization in 1991. For example, the growth in LLP registrations from 1994-1996 was almost fivefold and far exceeded that for corporations and limited partnerships. *See* Conrad S. Ciccotello & C. Terry Grant, *Professions as Commercial Institutions: An Analysis of Evolving Professional Forms*, 7 J. Legal Stud. Bus. 1, 19 (2000). Because lawsuits are significant threats for many professionals, the LLP form has been of particular interest to professional partnerships. In fact, professional service firms dominate the types of businesses that register as LLPs, with law firms making up the largest single category of businesses formed as LLPs, followed by medical firms and then accounting firms. *Id.* at 23-24. In states that limit LLPs solely to the practice of professions such as these, other types of businesses must operate in some other form (often as a limited liability company). Be sure to check the law in your home jurisdiction.

of action against the institutions because those institutions were insolvent. Seeking some recovery, investors began to bring malpractice actions against the law firms that had provided legal advice and against the accounting firms that had provided accounting services to the institutions. Many of those firms were general partnerships. Because partners in a general partnership have unlimited personal liability for the debts and obligations of the partnership, partners in one office found themselves subject to unlimited personal liability for advice given by partners in another office, perhaps thousands of miles away. In many cases, the savings and loan institutions had been represented by only a few attorneys or accountants in a firm, and only those individuals had provided any professional services to the failed institutions; yet hundreds of other partners across the country and around the world found themselves facing unlimited personal joint and several liability for advice they had not given to clients of whom they had never heard.

The **registered limited liability partnership** (RLLP), often called a **limited liability partnership**, was created in response to this situation. In brief, an LLP is a general partnership that files a statement electing LLP status with the secretary of state. *See* RUPA § 901.[1] Filing this statement changes one critical feature of general partnership law—instead of unlimited personal liability for partnership debts, partners enjoy the protections of a liability shield. American jurisdictions take two different approaches to the LLP liability shield:

■ *Partial shield states.* In two states (Louisiana and South Carolina), a partner in an LLP generally will not have personal liability for the wrongful acts or omissions of her partners. Partners in partial shield states retain personal liability for other partnership obligations, however, such as those arising from contract. *See* La. Rev. Stat. Ann. § 9:3431(A) and (D); S.C. Code Ann. § 33-41-370(B), (C), and (D).
■ *Full shield states.* In the remaining 49 jurisdictions, a partner in a limited liability partnership is not personally liable for either the wrongful acts or omissions of her partners or for commercial, contractual, or other obligations of the partnership. Whether partnership obligations arise in contract or tort, they remain solely the obligations of the partnership in full shield regimes.

Although the LLP was created with professional businesses in mind (e.g., law and accounting firms), many states allow other types of business partnerships to

---

[1]As in Chapter 3, we cite to the most version of the Uniform Partnership Act (1997) (last Amended 2013) (RUPA) currently available on the ULC website. This version includes revisions associated with the Harmonization of Business Entity Acts.

use the LLP form. A few jurisdictions, however, including California, New York, and Oregon, limit LLPs solely to the practice of specified professions.

B. GOVERNING LAW

In 1996, the RUPA (discussed in Chapter 3) was amended to add provisions relating to limited liability partnerships. By 2001, all 51 U.S. jurisdictions recognized the LLP form via state statute. Although many states and the District of Columbia have adopted the RUPA, many have modified its provisions as they relate to LLPs. In addition, a number of state statutes relating to LLPs preceded the adoption of LLP provisions in the RUPA. Consequently, because LLP statutes vary from jurisdiction to jurisdiction, and may depart from the uniform act, it is essential that you research relevant state law to determine requirements associated with forming and operating using the LLP form.

As is true of general partnerships, state LLP statutes (many of which are based on the RUPA) serve as default rules, applying only when (i) the partnership agreement is silent; (ii) the partners fail to agree to a modification of a default rule; or (iii) the matter involves a limited list of non-waivable or non-modifiable terms identified under state law. Otherwise, as between the state statute and the partnership agreement, the partnership agreement governs.

As a general rule, the law of the state where the LLP files its statement of qualification governs the internal affairs of the partnership (e.g., relations between and among partners). Depending on state law, the law of the state of formation may govern the liability of the partners for debts and obligations of the partnership as well. In this regard, § 1001 of RUPA provides, in pertinent part, as follows respecting choice of law and foreign limited liability partnerships:

> (a) The law of the jurisdiction of formation of a foreign limited liability partnership governs:
> (1) the internal affairs of the partnership; and
> (2) the liability of a partner as partner for a debt, obligation, or other liability of the foreign partnership.
> (b) A foreign limited liability partnership is not precluded from registering to do business in this state because of any difference between the law of its jurisdiction of formation and the law of this state.

RUPA § 1001. As always, you should check your home state's law, and think carefully about choice of law when drafting an LLP agreement, as discussed below.

C. TAXATION OF LLPS

LLPs are treated as general partnerships for purposes of taxation. The tax forms used by general partnerships and general partners (shown in Chapter 3) are also used for LLPs and their partners. Thus, under default rules, the income earned (whether distributed or not) is passed through (i.e., allocated) to the individual partners, who pay taxes at whatever rate is appropriate to them. The LLP itself does not pay federal income tax at the entity level, but it must file the informational tax form required of all partnerships. In addition, as discussed in Chapter 3, partners must attach Form K-1 to individual returns. While pass-through taxation is the default rule, an LLP may elect to be treated as an association taxable as a corporation by "checking the box" on the appropriate tax form.

D. HOW ARE LLPS FORMED?

Because LLPs are creatures of state statute, they cannot be created by a simple oral or written agreement, or through conduct, as can a general partnership. Instead, an LLP can only be created by complying with registration requirements found in applicable state statutes. Those requirements generally include filing a statement of qualification with the secretary of state. *See* RUPA § 901. States have statement of qualification or application forms of varying length. In Delaware, for example, the statement of qualification need contain only the following six elements:

- Name of the limited liability partnership, which must include a designation of its LLP status, such as "L.L.P.";
- The address of its registered office in the state and the name and address of the agent for service of process;
- The number of partners the LLP will have;
- The effective date of formation;
- An actual application statement reading as follows: "The partnership elects to be a limited liability partnership"; and
- The signature of an authorized partner.

See Exhibit 4.1 for the application form required in Texas. Most states require amendment of the application to reflect any later changes in the LLP.

E. OTHER REQUIREMENTS

1. Insurance, Financial, and Other Reporting Requirements

In addition to registration requirements, some states also impose insurance or financial requirements upon LLPs. (In some jurisdictions, only LLPs doing business in certain professions, such as law, medicine, or accounting, must meet insurance requirements.) These requirements are designed to protect injured parties who previously would have been able to sue or recover from all partners. (As discussed below, because only malfeasing partners generally have unlimited personal liability for their wrongful acts, a tort claimant may be limited to the limited liability partnership's assets, which may be depleted by distributions to partners and thus unavailable to claimants, and to the assets of the individual partner or partners who performed the wrongful act.) If an LLP does not carry and maintain the requisite insurance, it will not be recognized as an LLP in those states that condition the existence and maintenance of an LLP upon insurance. Instead, it will be viewed as a general partnership, in which case all partners will have unlimited personal liability

| EXHIBIT 4.1 | **Texas Application for Registration of Limited Liability Partnership** |

| **Form 701**
(Revised 12/15)
Submit in duplicate to:
Secretary of State
P.O. Box 13697
Austin, TX 78711-3697
512 463-5555
FAX: 512 463-5709
Filing Fee: See instructions | **Registration of a
Limited Liability Partnership** | This space reserved for office use |

Entity Information

1. The name of the partnership is:

_____

Name must contain the phrase "limited liability partnership" or an abbreviation of that phrase. If the partnership is a limited partnership, the entity name may include the phrase "limited liability limited partnership" or an abbreviation of that phrase.

2. The federal employer identification number of the partnership is: _____

☐ The partnership has not obtained a federal employer identification number at this time.

Number of Partners

3. The number of general partners at the date of registration is: _____

The number of general partners in a general partnership must be at least two.

Principal Office

4. The address of the partnership's principal office in Texas or outside of Texas, as applicable, is:

_____

Street Address   *City*   *State*   *Country*   *Zip Code*

Statement of Partnership's Business

5. The partnership's business is:

```



```

Effectiveness of Filing (Select either A or B)

A. ☐ This document becomes effective when the document is filed by the secretary of state.

B. ☐ This document becomes effective at a later date, which is not more than ninety (90) days from the date of signing. The delayed effective date is: _____

Execution

The undersigned signs this document subject to the penalties imposed by law for the submission of a materially false or fraudulent instrument and certifies under penalty of perjury that the undersigned is authorized under the provisions of law governing the entity to execute the filing instrument.

Date: _____

_____

_____

For a general partnership, signature of a majority-in-interest of the partners or signature of one or more of the partners authorized by a majority-in-interest. For a limited partnership, signature of one general partner.

for the obligations of the partnership, including those arising from the conduct of their fellow partners.

State law also may require an LLP to file an annual or biennial report with the secretary of state. *See* RUPA § 913. Under the RUPA, this report must contain (1) the name of the partnership or registered foreign partnership; (2) the name and street and mailing addresses of its registered agent in the state; (3) the street and mailing addresses of its principal office; (4) the name of at least one partner; and (5) in the case of a foreign partnership, its jurisdiction of formation and any alternate name adopted under § 1006. *See id.*

2. Licensing Requirements and Fees

LLPs also may be subject to local licensing laws, fees, and tax-related obligations. For example, in California, an LLP that provides professional legal services is not entitled to limitation of liability for legal malpractice unless it maintains a certificate of registration issued by the State Bar. See Exhibit 4.2 for the California State Bar application form. State statutes generally impose filing fees as well.

3. Naming Requirements

LLPs also must conform to naming rules. The name of the LLP generally must contain the words "Registered Limited Liability Partnership," "Limited Liability Partnership," or the abbreviation "L.L.P.," "R.L.L.P.," LLP, or RLLP. *See* RUPA § 902. The purpose of this requirement is to afford notice to those dealing with the entity that, at a minimum, the partners are shielded from personal liability for tort obligations of the partnership. All letterhead, envelopes, business cards, websites, signs, directory listings, brochures, and advertisements should also carry this designation to afford such notice to third parties.

4. Foreign LLP Registration

An LLP formed in one state can operate as an LLP in another. For example, a law firm registered as a California LLP can operate as an LLP in Dover, Delaware; Dallas, Texas; and Washington, D.C., provided the firm complies with rules relating to foreign LLP registration, and (of course) relevant rules of professional responsibility. The procedure for operating in another state is much the same as that for a general or limited partnership: The partnership must complete and file an application with the new state asking it to recognize the partnership as a foreign limited liability partnership. *See* RUPA §§ 1002, 1003. A certificate of good standing from the jurisdiction in which the LLP was originally formed will also generally be required so that the new state has some assurance that the organization is law-abiding. Filing fees will be required. (See Exhibit 4.3 for the form used in Arizona to register as a foreign limited liability partnership.)

| **EXHIBIT 4.2** | **California State Bar Limited Liability Partnership Application** |

THE STATE BAR OF CALIFORNIA
LIMITED LIABILITY PARTNERSHIPS
180 Howard Street · San Francisco, CA 94105-1617
(888) 800-3400 · llp@calbar.ca.gov

Application for Issuance of a Certificate of Registration as a Limited Liability Partnership (LLP)

FOR OFFICIAL STATE BAR USE ONLY   # _____

Amt Rcvd $ _____ Chk #_____

___ No Check

Initials: _____

- - - - - - - - - - - - - - - - - - -

Application #: _____

1) LLP INFORMATION

Name of Limited Liability Partnership (LLP): _____
(The LLP name must comply with Rule 1-400 of the California Rules of Professional Conduct)

Address 1: _____

Address 2: _____

City: _____ State: _____ Zip: _____ + _____

Contact Name: _____

E-mail: _____ Phone: _____

The following partners are authorized to act on behalf of the LLP:

Partner Name: _____ Attorney License or Member #: _____

Partner Name: _____ Attorney License or Member #: _____

Partner Name: _____ Attorney License or Member #: _____

2) ATTACHMENTS

Complete and Attach the following:

☐ **Attachment 1**: LLP List of Partners.

☐ **Attachment 2**: LLP List of Non-Partners.

☐ **Attachment 3**: Declaration of Compliance with Rule 1-400, Rule of Professional Conduct of the State Bar of California.

☐ **Attachment 4**: Declaration of Compliance with California Corporations Code Section 16956 (a)(2).

☐ **Secretary of State Certification**: Attach an **original** certified copy of the Secretary of State's Registered Limited Liability Partnership Registration (LLP-1) including Secretary of State date-stamp. The form is available from the Office of the Secretary of State.

☐ **Payment**: A $50 per partner (minimum of $100 up to a maximum of $2500) non-refundable fee must accompany this Application. Make checks payable to: The State Bar of California.

3) DECLARATION

I am _____ and I am authorized to act on behalf
(Name of partner authorized to act on behalf of the LLP)

of _____ and as such make this declaration
(Full Name of Limited Liability Partnership)

for and on behalf of said partnership. I have read the foregoing and all attachments thereto and know the contents thereof and the same are true of my own knowledge. I declare under penalty of perjury under the laws of the State of California that the foregoing application and all attachments are true and correct and that the applicant is an existing Limited Liability Partnership and that its affairs will be conducted in compliance with the State Bar Act, and the applicable provisions of the Corporations Code, The Rules of Professional Conduct of the State Bar, the Limited Liability Partnership Rules of the State Bar and such other laws, rules and regulations as may be applicable.

Executed On: _____

Signature:

Print Name: _____

4) SUBMISSION INFORMATION

Submit completed application with all attachments and payment to:

**The State Bar of California
Limited Liability Partnerships
Department #05017
PO Box 39000
San Francisco, CA 94139-5017**

LLPApp-0211

| EXHIBIT 4.3 | **Statement of Foreign Qualification of Foreign Limited Liability Partnership** |

State of Arizona – Office of the Secretary of State
Statement of Foreign Qualification of a Foreign Limited Liability Partnership *A.R.S. § 29-1106*
SEND BY MAIL TO:
Secretary of State Michele Reagan, Atten: Limited Partnerships
1700 W. Washington Street, FL. 7, Phoenix, AZ 85007-2808
OR return this application in person:
PHOENIX - State Capitol Executive Tower,   **TUCSON -** Arizona State Complex,
1700 W. Washington Street, 1st Fl., Room 103   400 W. Congress, 1st Fl., Suite 141
Office Hours: Monday through Friday, 8 a.m. to 5 p.m., except state holidays.
IN-PERSON ONLY - We accept major credit
cards and bank debit cards.

PLEASE NOTE: All correspondence regarding this filing will be sent to the principal office identified on this statement. This application must be submitted with a self-addressed, stamped envelope with applicable filing fees.

DO NOT WRITE IN THIS SPACE

FOR OFFICE USE ONLY
SOSBS ARS291106 REV. 3/12/2015

INSTRUCTIONS

Before transacting business in this state, a foreign limited liability partnership must file a statement of foreign qualification. A.R.S. § 29-1106

Be Accurate: Complete all applicable fields on this form. Write legibly; or fill out this application online at www.azsos.gov and print it.

Submission: Submit this certificate in duplicate (one original, one copy) with a self-addressed, stamped envelope with payment. Any other matters, please attach additional sheets with filing.

Filing Fee and Payment: $3.00 Filing Fee; Plus $10.00 Authority to Transact Business; Plus $3.00 per page. If filing by mail, make checks or money orders payable to the: Secretary of State.
Processing: 2-3 weeks; expedited service, fee $25 (24-48 hours).
Website: All forms are available on the Secretary of State's website, www.azsos.gov.
Questions? Call (602) 542-6187; in-state/toll-free (800) 458-5842.

1. Partnership information

Name of the Foreign Limited Liability Partnership *End the name with the words "Limited Liability Partnership" or "L.L.P."*

The state or country under whose laws the FLLP was formed or created	**Date of formation**	Month	Day	Year

The authorizing agency (optional)	Registration number (optional)

The address of the office maintained in the state of organization:

Address	City	State	Zip

The Arizona street address of the office used by the Foreign Limited Liability Partnership in this state:

Arizona address of chief executive office (P.O. Box or C/O are unacceptable)	City	State AZ	Zip Code

2. Agent for service of process information

Agent for service of process	Phone number (include area code) ( )

Arizona address of agent (P.O. Box or C/O are unacceptable)	City	State AZ	Zip Code

3. Delayed Effective Date, If Any

Month	Day	Year

4. Signatures of general partners:

Name of General Partner

Signature	Month	Day	Year

Name of General Partner

Signature	Month	Day	Year

Name of General Partner

Signature	Month	Day	Year

Before filing the application in the foreign jurisdiction, carefully review that state's statutes to ensure the LLP is in fact required to qualify to do business in the foreign state. Many states and the RUPA (*see* RUPA § 1005) have statutes providing guidance as to what activities constitute "doing business," such as to require businesses formed in other states to qualify to do business therein. For example, merely holding meetings, maintaining a bank account, or engaging in an isolated transaction in a state may not be considered "doing business" under applicable state law.

One question that has arisen is whether the limitations imposed on liability in one jurisdiction will be followed by another jurisdiction in which the LLP does business. For example, if an LLP is formed in a full shield state and begins doing business in a partial shield state in which there is a breach of contract, are all partners jointly and severally liable for breach of the contract as they would be in the partial shield state, or is there no liability imposed on the partners for the breach of contract, as would be the case in the home state that is a full shield state? This is another area where it is important for you to research state law. For example, California Corporations Code § 16958 provides that the laws of the jurisdiction under which a foreign limited liability partnership is organized shall govern its organization and internal affairs *and* the liability and authority of its partners. In jurisdictions where the law of the state where the LLP is formed governs the liability of partners for partnership obligations, selecting a full shield state for formation is critical because it may protect all partners from liability for any contractual obligations. At a minimum, LLPs should be scrupulous in inserting "choice of law" provisions in their contracts, providing that the law of a certain jurisdiction (namely, a full shield jurisdiction in which the LLP is organized or doing business) applies in any action relating to the contract, thus affording a credible argument that the full shield law governs so as to bar joint and several personal liability for contractual obligations, no matter where the breach of contract occurred or the parties reside. As more and more states adopt full shield status, this issue is becoming less important as to liability. Still, you should be sure to check the partnership statutes and case law in relevant jurisdictions when forming LLPs, drafting LLP agreements, and drafting contracts between LLPs and third parties.

F. VOTING AND GOVERNANCE RULES

Because limited liability partnerships function as general partnerships with respect to voting and governance, we will not review all of the rules associated with these topics here, as they are covered in Chapter 3. As a quick review, note that (i) LLP agreements may be oral or in writing (written agreements are strongly preferred, and the statement of qualification must be in writing and filed with the secretary of state); (ii) LLP partners owe fiduciary duties to each other and the partnership; (iii) each partner in an LLP is an agent of the partnership in the same way that partners in a general partnership are agents of a partnership; (iv) in the absence of agreement to the contrary, profits will be shared equally (with losses treated the same as profits); and (v) each partner has an equal right to participate in the management of partnership affairs and the conduct of partnership business. Finally, as contemplated by the RUPA, in many states, statements of authority and statements of denial (discussed in Chapter 3) may be filed to provide public notice regarding an LLP partner's authority to act or limitations on that authority.

G. LIABILITY RULES

The following principles apply to LLPs with respect to liability:

1. Partners in LLPs always retain personal liability for their own negligence, incompetence, omissions, misconduct, or wrongful acts.
2. LLP partners retain personal liability when they have agreed to do so via contract, for example, if a partner agrees via contract to personally guarantee repayment of a loan made to the LLP itself.
3. The LLP itself is liable for both tort claims (e.g., acts of malpractice) and contractual obligations of the partnership.
4. LLP partners are protected against personal liability for the debts and obligations of the partnership as set forth in the liability shield language (partial or full) of the relevant state's LLP law.

1. Partial Shield States

As noted previously, in the two partial shield states (Louisiana and South Carolina), partners in a LLP generally are not personally liable for debts or obligations arising from the wrongful acts and omissions of a fellow partner, but they remain liable for other debts and obligations incurred by a partner or the partnership, such as money borrowed, contractual commitments, rent, insurance, etc. For example, assume a law firm is organized as a partnership in South Carolina, and has offices in Cleveland, Chicago, and Charleston, South Carolina. The partnership is composed of 100 attorneys employed throughout these offices. Two partners in the Charleston office begin working on a case. As a result of legal malpractice, they miss a statute of limitations deadline, and their client therefore cannot bring an action. No one else in the Charleston office is aware of the case, and the partners in the other cities have never worked on the case, seen any files relating to this matter, or even heard of the client. If the law firm is a general partnership, the partnership itself and all 100 partners in all the offices would have unlimited personal and joint and several liability for this claim of malpractice. If the partnership filed the paperwork (and met all other requirements) necessary to become a South Carolina LLP, however, only the partnership itself and the two attorneys who actually committed the act of malpractice would face liability on those claims. The individual assets of the other partners in Charleston, Cleveland, and Chicago could not be reached to satisfy the claim of malpractice. The other partners would, however, remain liable on contract-related obligations associated with the law firm's business, such as rent, according to partnership law principles.

Note that it is important to check state law respecting the nature and scope of partnership liability. For example, in South Carolina, a partner may be held liable for the wrongful acts or omissions of a fellow partner if the partner directly supervised or controlled the wrongdoer or if the partner was at fault in appointing, supervising, or cooperating with the wrongdoers. South Carolina's limited liability partnership law provides as follows, in pertinent part:

> (A) Except as provided by subsection (B), all partners are liable jointly and severally for everything chargeable to the partnership.
>
> (B) Subject to subsections (C) and (D), a partner in a registered limited liability partnership is not liable directly or indirectly, including by way of indemnification, contribution, or otherwise, for debts, obligations, and liabilities chargeable to the partnership arising from negligence, wrongful acts, or misconduct committed while the partnership is a registered limited liability partnership and in the course of the partnership business by another partner or an employee, agent, or representative of the partnership.
>
> (C) Subsection (B) shall not affect the liability of a partner in a registered limited liability partnership for his own negligence, wrongful acts, or misconduct, or that of a person under his direct supervision and control.
>
> (D) Each individual who renders professional services on behalf of a registered limited liability partnership is liable for a negligent or wrongful act or omission in which he personally participates to the same extent as if he rendered the services as a sole practitioner. A partner of a registered limited liability partnership which renders professional services, as defined in Section 33-19-103(7), is not liable for the negligence, wrongful acts, misconduct, or omissions of other partners, agents, or employees of the registered limited liability partnership unless he is at fault in appointing, supervising, or cooperating with them.

S.C. Code Ann. § 33-41-370(D).

2. Full Shield States

In the 49 American jurisdictions that follow the full shield approach, a partner in an LLP is not, solely by reason of being a partner, personally liable for any obligation of the LLP, whether arising in tort, contract, or otherwise. *See* RUPA § 306(c), (d), and (e). Partners remain liable for their own misconduct, of course. In addition, in some states, partners may be held liable if they know of a tortious act by another and fail to stop it or prevent the act or if they directly controlled or supervised the tortious act at issue. Recognizing that supervisory duties may lead to liability, some LLPs provide additional compensation to supervisors or agree to indemnify them if they are found liable for a subordinate's negligence. This may be particularly important if a limited liability partnership has operations in a partial shield state.

For example, assume that an accounting firm is organized in and operates as an LLP in New York (a full shield state). Dana, an accountant in the firm, will not be personally liable for acts of malpractice committed by her partners. She also will not be personally liable for the partnership's obligation to pay its rent, its bank loan, or its car leases. If, however, Leigh, another accountant, is employed by an LLP's South Carolina office (South Carolina being a partial shield state), Leigh would not be personally liable for acts of malpractice committed by her partners (unless she engaged in conduct giving rise to liability under the South Carolina statute cited above). Leigh might, however, be held personally liable (jointly and severally) for the partnership's South Carolina rent, bank loan, car lease, and other contractual obligations, if a South Carolina court refuses to recognize the full shield available under New York law. Dana and Leigh also would be personally liable for their own acts of malpractice, negligence, and misconduct.

Full shield statutes have steadily gained in popularity over the years, due to concerns that the entire justification for LLP statutes could be eviscerated simply by styling pleadings as breach of contract claims, rather than claims sounding in tort, in partial shield jurisdictions. Full shield statutes avoid such circumvention. Thus, § 306(c) of the RUPA flatly states "A debt, obligation, or other liability of a partnership incurred while the partnership is a limited liability partnership is solely the debt, obligation, or other liability of the limited liability partnership." This language provides a true corporate-styled liability shield, protecting partners from vicarious personal liability for any obligations incurred by the LLP, corresponding with the approach taken by most states. Some states have language that tracks the previous version of the RUPA and provide that an obligation of a partnership incurred while the partnership is a limited liability partnership, *whether arising in contract, tort, or otherwise*, is solely the obligation of the partnership. Such language also makes it clear that partners in an LLP have no personal liability for acts of the partnership or their co-partners, whether those acts arise in tort or contract. Some states have statutory provisions that may be less clear. For example, West Virginia's statute provides that a partner in an LLP is not liable for "debts, obligations and liabilities of or chargeable to the partnership, whether in tort, contract or otherwise, *arising from omissions, negligence, wrongful acts, misconduct or malpractice* committed while the partnership is a registered limited liability partnership. . . ." W. Va. Code § 47B-3-6(c) (emphasis added). (Language in other states, such as Michigan, New Hampshire, and Pennsylvania, is similar.) Reviewing applicable statutory language and case law is essential to understanding the statutory provisions in these (and indeed all) jurisdictions.

Case Preview

In re Promedicus Health Group, LLP

In the following case, a New York court considered the nature and extent of the liability shield available to LLP partners. In reading this case, consider the following questions:

1. What is the New York rule concerning liability of partners in a limited liability partnership for wrongful acts committed by those under the "direct supervision and control" of a partner?
2. How does this rule play out in bankruptcy?

In re Promedicus Health Group, LLP
416 B.R. 380 (Bankr. W.D.N.Y. 2009)

MICHAEL J. KAPLAN, Bankruptcy Judge.

The question before the Court is that of what definition of "insolvent" applies to a debtor that is a New York registered limited liability partnership. The defendants argue that it is 11 U.S.C. § 101(32)(B) that applies, and more particularly subparagraph (ii) thereof, which requires that "the sum of the excess of the value of each general partner's non-partnership property" is to be added to the asset side.

The Plaintiff argues that it is 11 U.S.C. § 101(9)(A)(ii) that applies, which declares that the term "corporation" includes a "partnership association organized under a law that makes only the capital subscribed responsible for the debts of such association," and consequently § 101(32)(B)(ii) is of no moment here.

At the core of this disagreement is the fact that the protection from personal liability afforded to the members of a registered limited liability partnership ("RLLP") in the State of New York does not extend to "any negligent or wrongful act or misconduct committed by [any partner, employee or agent of the RLLP] or by any person under his or her direct supervision and control while rendering professional services on behalf of such registered limited liability partnership." New York Partnership Law § 26(c). Thus the Defendants argue that New York Law does not make "only the capital subscribed responsible for the debts of such association." Instead, they argue, New York Partnership Law § 2 states that a " 'registered limited liability partnership' means a partnership without limited partners operating under an agreement governed by the laws of this state, registered under § 121-1500 of this Chapter and complying with § 121-1501 of this Chapter." And in their brief, Defendants argue that "contrary to the wishful thinking of the Plaintiff, a 'partnership without limited partners' can only consist of general partners, clearly putting [the debtor]" within the purview of § 101(32)(B)(ii). Defendants' Sur-reply Memorandum of Law page 5.

For his part, the Trustee argues as follows: "Defendant seizes upon the fact the partners of a limited liability partnership are members of a 'general partnership' under New York Partnership Law, but labeling such partners as 'general partners' does not further the analysis." Citing other relevant State Law, the Trustee argues "the liability of the partners of a registered limited liability partnership is, as the name would imply, limited. It would be irrational to contend that a limited liability partnership is solvent, even though the net assets which make it so are beyond the reach of creditors." Plaintiff's Reply Memorandum pages 14, 15.

Addressing limited liability partnerships, Collier states "these entities are partnerships with at least some degree of limited liability protection, such as protection against claims of professional negligence against other partners. The protection varies depending upon State Law, which in some jurisdictions gives protection to partners similar to that of corporate shareholders. The degree of protection from liability will determine whether the entity is a corporation under the definition in § 101. If the protection is more like that given to corporate shareholders, the entity is more likely to be found to meet the Code's definition of 'corporation.' If the protection is more limited, the entity is likely to be found to be a partnership under § 101." 2 Collier on Bankruptcy 5th Ed. ¶101.09.

However difficult the question may be in a different state, it is not difficult at all under the New York Statutes.

It is simply incorrect to think of the "universe" of partnerships in the State of New York as consisting only of general partnerships and limited partnerships. Consequently, it is incorrect to think of the universe of *partners* as being only general partners and limited partners. Rather, it has been stated that "effective October 1, 1994, Article 8-B [§§ 121-1500 to 121-1503] was added to the Partnership Law to permit a general partnership engaged in professional service activities in New York *to become a Registered Limited Liability Partnership.*" Rich, Bruce A., Practice Commentary to Article 8-B, 38 McKinney's Consolidated Laws of New York Annotated, introduction to § 121-1500. [Emphasis added.]

This Court emphasizes the words "to become." Indeed, examining § 121-1500, the operative language is found to be this: "a partnership without limited partners each of whose partners is a professional authorized by law to render a professional service within this state and who is or has been engaged in the practice of such profession in such partnership or a predecessor entity, or will engage in the practice of such profession in the registered limited liability partnership within thirty days of the date of the effectiveness of the registration provided for in this subdivision ... *may register as a registered limited liability partnership* by filing with the Department of State a registration which shall" provide specific required information. After that language, Article 8-B uniformly refers to such a registered entity as a "registered limited liability partnership," not as a "general partnership," or even as a "partnership that has no limited partners." Therefore, the universe of types of partner in New York, consists of general partners, limited partners, and partners in a registered limited liability partnership.

The Defendants here being of the last type, § 101(32)(B)(ii) cannot avail them, because that calls only for the addition of the personal assets of each "general partner."

Furthermore, even if the statutory language were not so clear, this Court would reach the same conclusion were it to examine only the test offered by the above-cited language from Collier on Bankruptcy. Turning again to the practice commentary by Bruce Rich, we find the following: "LLP Statutes in other states vary from the New York Statute [as] to limitations on liabilities of partners for contractual and tort obligations of their partners and to mandated insurance and financial requirements on the RLLP. A multi-state professional partnership should consider which of the states in which it has offices has the most favorable LLP provisions as well as the most favorable general partnership law provisions when selecting or changing its state of formation. . . . The amended New York law differs from the provisions in most other jurisdictions which since 1991 enacted legislation authorizing limited liability partnerships, in that under New York Law (1) only a professional service general partnership may elect such status and (2) the 'liability shield' of a partner protects him not only for negligence, wrongful acts or misconduct of another partner and employees or agents of the partnership, but also for all other debts and liabilities of the partnership."

Hence, the Court concludes that under the language of the pertinent New York statute, the partnership definition of insolvency does apply, but that there are no "general partners" in a registered LLP. And alternatively, examining the substance of the protection that New York has given to partners in an RLLP, leads the Court to conclude that the corporate definition would apply, to identical effect.

The Court will address other aspects of the Trustee's Rule 56 Motion in a separate decision, filed herewith.

SO ORDERED.

Post-Case Follow-Up

As *Promedicus* suggests, state law matters. To avoid surprises, be sure to research the law in your home jurisdiction, and educate your clients respecting rights and obligations associated with the LLP liability shield.

In re Promedicus Health Group, LLP: Real Life Applications

1. Susan and Fran, the owners of a website design and hosting business, have just retained you to help them with business planning. Susan and Fran live in Albany, New York. They have been operating the business for six months, and they have not filed any registration or other formation materials with state officials. They have asked you to form a limited liability partnership for their business. May Susan and Fran use the LLP form? What if they lived and worked in California? Washington State?

2. Rob and Dot live in Louisiana and operate a sport-fishing business in Louisiana and Mississippi. To date, they have not filed any registration or other formation documents with state officials. During your initial meeting, Rob and Dot ask you to form a limited liability partnership for the business.
   a. Where would you recommend forming the LLP? Why?
   b. Do you recommend including a choice of law provision in contracts between the business and its customers? If so, draft such a provision.
   c. Is there any risk that Rob and Dot could face personal liability for debts or obligations of the LLP?

H. DISSOLUTION AND LIQUIDATION OF LLPS

Dissolution of LLPs is similar to that of general partnerships. LLPs, however, must generally renew their applications or certificates filed with the state on an annual basis. Failure to renew the application or certificate will result in the would-be LLP being viewed as a general partnership. Many states and RUPA § 904 allow reinstatement of LLPs that have been revoked for failure to file annual reports once the defect is cured.

The partnership agreement likely will provide the events that will cause a dissolution of the LLP. If terms are not provided, state partnership law provides the terms and conditions for dissociation (where applicable) or dissolution. Recall from

Chapter 3 that under the RUPA, not every dissociation of a partner triggers a dissolution, winding up, and termination. If dissolution, winding up, and termination are not required, the LLP generally will be able to buy out the dissociating partner's interest. When an LLP dissolves, and is wound up in preparation for termination, it must collect any debts due it, satisfy all obligations, liquidate assets, and distribute the proceeds to third-party creditors and then to the partners. A certificate of withdrawal or cancellation should be filed with the state of formation and in any state in which the LLP is operating.

Chapter Summary

- In the jurisdictions that follow the full shield model, LLP partners generally have no personal liability for either the wrongful acts of their co-partners or for contractual obligations of their co-partners or the partnership.
- In jurisdictions that follow a partial shield model, LLP partners generally do not have personal liability for wrongful acts or torts of their co-partners but generally do have personal liability for contractual obligations.
- Partners in LLPs retain personal liability for their own wrongful acts, and (depending on state law) may be held personally liable for the wrongful acts of those they direct or supervise, as well. The LLP itself is also liable for such acts.
- LLPs may be formed only by complying with state statutes that require the filing of an application with the appropriate state agency.
- Some states require the LLP to carry insurance or meet financial responsibility standards.
- LLPs are taxed as partnerships under default rules, meaning pass-through taxation.
- LLPs continue the modern trend of business structures that allow their members flexibility and freedom of contract with respect to management and governance rules but also provide a liability shield.

Applying the Concepts

1. Robertson & Walker, a law firm of 20 attorneys located in Charleston, South Carolina, is considering changing from a general partnership to a limited liability partnership. Using the RUPA, draft a memo to the managing partner answering the following questions:

   a. What are the primary advantages and disadvantages of such a change?
   b. What vote is required?
   c. What must the partnership do to effect the change from general partnership to LLP?

2. Assume that the partnership has become an LLP. After this change, Anthony, one of the LLP partner-attorneys in the litigation group, commits an act of

malpractice. Draft a memo to the managing partner answering the following questions:

a. Who has liability for this act?
b. Would your answer be different if the partnership had remained a general partnership?
c. Assume that Anthony was being supervised by Olivia, the head of the litigation group. Does Olivia have exposure?

3. After the change of the partnership to LLP status, and without partnership authority, Anthony arranged for the partnership to lease ten cars for a period of three years.

a. Discuss the liability of all partners and the partnership for this act.
b. Would your answer be different if this LLP had been formed in California?

4. The LLP would like to open a bank account in Georgia and would like to purchase property in Florida. Identify any formalities the LLP would need to undertake to engage in such acts.

Business Organizations in Practice

You represent Susan Stein, a business person who wishes to form a limited liability partnership with Stan and Beverly. Once formed, the partnership will operate a white water rafting business in Oregon, California, and New York. Susan is an expert guide but does not have cash or other assets to contribute to the business. Stan and Beverly have money to put into the business but are new to whitewater rafting. The parties anticipate that Susan will teach Stan and Beverly the business, and supervise their activities, for several years.

a. Where do you recommend that the parties form their entity? Where should the business maintain its principal office?
b. Draft a memo to Susan, Stan, and Beverly respecting what it means to "do business" in a foreign jurisdictions. In your memo, identify all requirements associated with registering to do business in any foreign jurisdiction(s) you believe to be relevant here.
c. Are there any issues associated with forming an LLP for this business, given the parties' intention to operate in New York?
d. What, if anything, can Susan do to mitigate risks associated with supervising Stan and Beverly?

5

Limited Partnerships and Limited Liability Limited Partnerships

Limited partnerships are a unique kind of partnership. As you will recall from Chapter 3, in a general partnership, all partners stand on equal footing; they all have equal rights in the management and conduct of partnership business, and they all suffer the disadvantage of unlimited personal liability for partnership obligations and debts. In a limited partnership, there are two types of partners — general partners and limited partners. Like their general partnership counterparts, general partners in a limited partnership have equal rights in the management and conduct of partnership business and suffer the disadvantage of unlimited personal liability for partnership obligations and debts. Limited partners are different. They are passive investors and do not have statutory management or control rights. They also do not suffer the disadvantage of unlimited personal liability for partnership obligations and debts. In this chapter, we discuss the limited partnership form, along with several limited partnership variants, focusing on when this form of organization is used, formation requirements, and the rights and obligations associated with the general partner and limited partner roles.

Key Concepts

- Definition and key characteristics of limited partnerships
- Formation requirements for limited partnerships
- General partners' rights and obligations with respect to the partnership, other partners, and third parties
- Limited partners' rights and obligations with respect to the partnership, other partners, and third parties
- Definition and key characteristics of limited liability limited partnerships
- Family limited partnerships

A. WHAT IS A LIMITED PARTNERSHIP?

A **limited partnership** is a partnership formed by two or more persons pursuant to a limited partnership statute, having as its members one or more **general partners** and one or more **limited partners**. *See* RULPA § 101(7); ULPA-2001 § 102(12). (We identify and discuss these uniform acts in Section B.)

■ **"Persons"** in this context includes natural persons, and general partnerships, limited partnerships, trusts, estates, associations, corporations, and limited liability companies, among other entities. RULPA § 101(11); ULPA-2001 § 101(15).

■ The **general partner** in a limited partnership functions identically to and has the same rights, obligations, and risks as a general partner in a general partnership. This means that the general partner has the right to manage and control the limited partnership, has the power to bind the limited partnership according to agency law principles, owes duties of care and loyalty to the partnership and the other partners, and also faces the risk of unlimited personal liability for limited partnership debts and obligations. *See* RULPA § 403 (addressing powers and liabilities of general partner) and ULPA-2001 § 402 (addressing agent status of general partner); § 403 (limited partnership liable for general partner's actionable conduct); § 404 (general partner's liability); and § 406 (management rights of general partner). As discussed below, for liability reasons, partners often choose to appoint an entity with limited liability for its stakeholders (e.g., a corporation or LLC) as general partner. Every limited partnership must have at least one general partner.

■ The **limited partner** in a limited partnership differs from a general partner in the same entity in three critical respects. First, limited partners are not agents of the partnership, and they do not have statutory authority to manage partnership business or exercise control over partnership affairs. *See* RULPA §§ 303(a) and 303(b); ULPA-2001 § 302 (stating limited partner not agent of the limited partnership solely by virtue of being limited partner). Second, limited partners do not suffer the risk of unlimited personal liability for the debts or obligations of the limited partnership solely by virtue of their status as limited partners. *See* RULPA § 303(a); ULPA-2001 § 303. Instead, a limited partner's risk of loss usually is limited to the amount of his investment in the limited partnership. Third, while limited partners must discharge any duties owed and exercise rights available under the limited partnership statute or the limited partnership agreement in a manner consistent with the contractual duty of good faith and fair dealing, limited partners do not owe duties of care or loyalty to the limited partnership or the other partners under default rules. *See* ULPA-2001 § 305.

■ The phrase referring to the formation of the entity **under the laws of [a state]** confirms that the creation of a limited partnership is governed by state limited partnership statutes. Unlike general partnerships, which can be formed through conduct (and even in the absence of an express oral or written partnership agreement, as you know from Chapter 3), compliance with statutory formation requirements set forth in the relevant state's limited partnership statute is required to form a limited partnership. When presented with a multi-owner entity not in compliance with limited partnership statutory formation requirements, a court may determine that the entity is not a limited partnership, and that it instead must be treated as a general partnership (in which case, all partners have unlimited personal liability for obligations of the partnership).

B. WHAT LAW GOVERNS LIMITED PARTNERSHIPS?

1. Uniform Limited Partnership Acts

Each state except Louisiana has adopted a limited partnership statute based on some version of the Uniform Limited Partnership Act proposed by the Uniform Law Commission (ULC). The earliest version of the **Uniform Limited Partnership Act** (**ULPA**) was approved in 1916. The ULC revised the 1916 Act extensively in 1976 and approved additional revisions in 1985. As of this writing, a majority of states (31) have enacted a limited partnership statute that is based on ULPA-1976, with many (but not all) of these states adopting some or all of the 1985 amendments. We refer to the 1976 version of the Uniform Act (with the 1985 amendments) in this text as the **RULPA**. The remaining 19 states (Alabama, Arkansas, California, Florida, Hawaii, Idaho, Illinois, Iowa, Kentucky, Maine, Minnesota, Mississippi, Montana, Nevada, New Mexico, North Dakota, Oklahoma, Utah, and Washington) plus the District of Columbia follow the **ULPA-2001**, a newer version of the uniform partnership act, which was drafted by the ULC "for a world in which limited liability partnerships . . . and limited liability companies . . . can meet many of the needs formerly met by limited partnerships." Uniform Law Commission, The Uniform Limited Partnership Act (2001) (Last Amended 2013), A Summary. The 2001 Act is significantly more complex and substantially longer than its predecessor (the RULPA), and it targets two types of enterprises that seem largely beyond the scope of LLPs and LLCs, according to the ULC: (i) sophisticated, manager-entrenched commercial deals whose participants commit for the long term, and (ii) estate planning arrangements (family limited partnerships). *Id.* Because both the RULPA and ULPA-2001 serve as models for existing limited partnership statutes, we discuss both in this chapter. In addition, for reference, we have included a chart summarizing important differences between the RULPA and ULPA-2001 Act in Exhibit 5.7.

> **Limited Partnerships versus LLCs and LLPs**
>
> Limited partnerships have fallen out of favor in some circles in recent years due to the rise of limited liability partnerships and limited liability companies — two newer forms of organization that offer limited liability, management rights for owners, and partnership-style pass-through taxation without the risk of exposure to entity obligations that can occur in certain jurisdictions under the so-called control rule, which is discussed in Section F below. Current data confirm the waning popularity of limited partnerships. In 2014, for example, only 615 limited partnerships were formed in the State of Georgia. By contrast, nearly 73,000 limited liability companies were formed during the same time period. That having been said, there are two contexts in which the limited partnership form remains an entity of choice. First, private investment funds (e.g., venture capital funds, hedge funds, private equity funds) still tend to use this form of organization. Second, attorneys may recommend so-called family limited partnerships for tax and estate planning purposes in certain circumstances.

Status of the Uniform Act

In 2011 and 2013, amendments to ULPA-2001 were enacted as part of the Harmonization of Business Entity Acts (HBEA) project. Those amendments harmonize the language in ULPA-2001 with similar provisions in the other uniform unincorporated entity acts. When citing to ULPA-2001, we use the latest version of the Uniform Limited Partnership Act (post-HBEA amendments) and comments currently available at the ULC's website, www.uniformslaws.org. As always, because limited partnership statutes vary from jurisdiction to jurisdiction, a thorough review of state-specific statutes is necessary.

2. Governing Law

The law of the state where the limited partnership is formed typically governs the internal affairs of the limited partnership and the liability of a partner as partner for debts, obligations, or other liabilities of the limited partnership. *See* ULPA-2001 §§ 104, 1001 (governing law for foreign limited partnerships); RULPA § 901 (governing law for foreign limited partnership).

3. The Limited Partnership Agreement

Like general partnership statutes, limited partnership statutes consist largely of default rules, most of which can be customized to meet business needs. RULPA uses a provision-by-provision approach, whereby particular provisions specify whether they can be modified via the partnership agreement. *See, e.g.*, RULPA § 301(b) (stating that a person who acquires a limited partnership interest from an existing limited partner may be admitted as an additional limited partner upon compliance with the partnership agreement, or if the agreement is silent, with the unanimous written consent of all partners). The ULPA-2001 permits customization as a general rule, but also contains a limited list of non-waivable or non-modifiable provisions. *See* ULPA-2001 § 105. Under both regimes, the state limited partnership statute provides default rules, applying only when (i) the limited partnership agreement is silent; (ii) the partners fail to agree on a modification to a default rule; or (iii) the matter involves a limited list of non-waivable or non-modifiable terms identified under state law. As between the state statute and the partnership agreement, the limited partnership agreement generally governs. *See* ULPA-2001 § 105(a) and (b).

Although both the RULPA and ULPA-2001 recognize that limited partnership agreements may be written or oral, *see* RULPA § 101(9); ULPA-2001 § 102(14), you should always prepare a written limited partnership agreement setting forth partners' rights and responsibilities to reduce the risk of uncertainty, discord, and litigation.

C. TAXATION OF LIMITED PARTNERSHIPS

Like general partnerships, limited partnerships are not separate tax-paying entities for purposes of federal income tax law; thus, they do not pay federal income tax at the entity level under default rules. Instead, profits and losses are passed through to the general and limited partners, who then pay taxes according to their appropriate tax brackets and individual tax circumstances. Although losses of the limited partnership generally can be used to offset other income at the partner level, specific loss-limitation rules come into play. As with general partnerships, limited partnerships complete an informational return. Both general and limited partnerships use IRS Form 1065 for this purpose. See Exhibit 3.4. Individual partners in a limited partnership attach Schedule K-1 forms to their individual tax returns. *See* Schedule K-1, shown in Exhibit 3.3.

Note that while limited partnerships do not pay federal income taxes under default rules, they may be subject to taxation on income under state law. In addition, while pass-through taxation is the default tax treatment for limited partnerships, a limited partnership can elect to be classified as an association taxable as a corporation for federal income tax purposes by "checking the box" on the appropriate tax form. (See Chapter 3 and Exhibit 3.5.)

D. HOW ARE LIMITED PARTNERSHIPS FORMED?

1. The Limited Partnership Certificate

To form a limited partnership, a **limited partnership certificate** must be prepared, signed, and filed with the secretary of state (or an equivalent official) of the state in which the partnership seeks to organize. RULPA § 201; ULPA-2001 § 201. Some states may also require that the certificate be filed in the county in which the limited partnership will principally conduct its business.

The applicable state's limited partnership act lists information that must be included in the limited partnership certificate. RULPA § 201(a); ULPA-2001 § 201(b). Under § 2 of the original 1916 ULPA, the certificate needed to provide 14 items, including the nature of the business, an identification of each limited partner's contribution, how additional contributions were to be made, and each limited partner's share of the profits. RULPA § 201 streamlined the contents of the certificate, recognizing that the limited partnership agreement, not the certificate of limited partnership, is the authoritative governance document for a limited partnership. Thus, only the following must be included in the certificate governed by a RULPA-style statute:

- The name of the limited partnership;
- The address of the office and the name and address of the agent for service of process (namely, litigation summonses and complaints);
- The name and business address of each general partner;
- The latest date on which the limited partnership is to dissolve; and
- Any other matters the general partners determine to include.

RULPA § 201(a). We review each of these required elements below. The ULPA-2001 takes a similar approach, but also requires the certificate to indicate whether the partners have elected to form a limited liability limited partnership (a limited partnership variant available under the ULPA-2001 Act). *See* ULPA-2001 § 201(b).

Name

The rule that sole proprietorships and general partnerships may not select names that are indistinguishable from or deceptively similar to that of another business also applies to limited partnerships. *See* RULPA § 102(3) (deceptively similar standard); ULPA-2001 § 114(d)-(i) (distinguishable standard). In addition, according to RULPA § 102(1), the name of a limited partnership must include without abbreviation the words "limited partnership," although most states allow abbreviations such as "L.P." *See also* ULPA-2001 § 114. The purpose of these requirements is to afford the public notice that the partnership is not a general partnership and that the personal assets of certain partners (the limited partners) generally will not be available to satisfy the claims of creditors of the business. Finally, in RULPA regimes, the name of the limited partnership may not include the name of a limited partner unless a general partner shares that name or unless the limited partnership operated under that name prior to the admission of the limited partner. *See* RULPA § 102(2). Barring that narrow exception, a limited partner who knowingly permits her name to be used in the name of the limited partnership is liable to those who extend credit to the limited partnership without actual knowledge that the limited partner is not a general partner. *See* RULPA § 303(d).

Registered Office and Agent

The limited partnership must designate an office in the state to which documents and notices can be sent. This need not be the limited partnership's principal place of business; however, an address must be provided so that notices and documents can be sent to the limited partnership. RULPA § 105 provides that certain records must be kept at the office, including alphabetical lists of all partners, copies of tax records and financial statements for the three most recent years, copies of any partnership agreements, and information relating to the contributions made by each partner and their right to receive distributions. Equally important, an **agent for service of process** must be identified so those who sue the entity will know who will accept the summons and complaint. RULPA § 201(a)(2); ULPA-2001 § 201(b)(3).

Names and Addresses of General Partners

The name and business address of each general partner must be identified. RULPA § 201(a)(3); ULPA-2001 § 201(b)(4). Because the limited partners generally do not participate in the control of the business, they should be able to conduct due diligence to investigate the background of the general partner(s). The identification of the general partner(s) not only provides an official address for correspondence with the limited partnership, but also provides sufficient information that the limited partners, if they desire, can conduct some investigation into the general partner(s) to determine whether the general partner has been involved in previous lawsuits, has filed a petition for bankruptcy, or has engaged in other conduct that would influence the decision of a limited partner to invest money in this enterprise.

Dissolution Date

The latest date for dissolution of the limited partnership is given to provide notice to limited partners so they know when final distributions may be made and when their involvement with the limited partnership ends.

Other Matters

The general partner may include other items in the limited partnership certificate, including events triggering dissolution, names and addresses of limited partners, information regarding additional contributions that may need to be made by limited partners, and specifics regarding the return of contributions. Because the certificate of limited partnership is a public document, however, most general partners comply narrowly with the requirements of their state statute to avoid making unnecessary disclosures about partnership matters. Certificates tend to be "bare bones" for the additional reason that changes may trigger onerous or undesirable certificate amendment rules. For both of these reasons, partners tend to address issues of governance, partnership finances, etc., in the partnership agreement rather than in the certificate. As always, because states may modify default rules, you should check the limited partnerships statute in your home jurisdiction when completing and filing a limited partnership certificate. Exhibit 5.1 shows the form required by the State of Delaware, which requires even fewer than the four items required by the RULPA.

2. Errors or Deficiencies in the Certificate of Limited Partnership

If there is an error or deficiency in the certificate of limited partnership, and a litigant challenges the limited partnership's legal status based on the error, the court will examine whether the partners substantially complied with the pertinent state statutes when they attempted to form the limited partnership. If the partners were in substantial compliance with the state statute, the court may decide to treat the entity as a limited partnership despite the error, and thus may allow the limited partners to enjoy the protection of the limited partnership liability shield despite imperfect compliance with formation rules. If the substantial compliance standard is not met, however, the court may treat all of the owners of the enterprise as if they were partners in a general partnership, with the resulting risk of unlimited personal liability for partnership obligations.

Sometimes, individuals invest in a business enterprise believing they are limited partners, but the general partner, through mistake, inadvertence, or willfulness, fails to file the limited partnership certificate or mistakenly identifies a limited partner as a general partner. Individuals who erroneously believe they are limited partners are not subject to liability as general partners to creditors of the business if, upon discovering the mistake, they cause the appropriate certificate to be filed or if they renounce their future profit in the enterprise. *See* RULPA § 304(a); ULPA-2001

EXHIBIT 5.1   **Delaware Certificate of Limited Partnership**

STATE OF DELAWARE
CERTIFICATE OF LIMITED PARTNERSHIP

- **The Undersigned,** desiring to form a limited partnership pursuant to the Delaware Revised Uniform Limited Partnership Act, 6 Delaware Code, Chapter 17, do hereby certify as follows:

- **First:** The name of the limited partnership is _____

    _____ .

- **Second:** The address of its registered office in the State of Delaware is _____

    _____ in the city of _____ .

    Zip code _____ . The name of the Registered Agent at such address is

    _____ .

- **Third:** The name and mailing address of each general partner is as follows:

    _____
    | |
    | |
    | |
    | |
    |_____|

- **In Witness Whereof,** the undersigned has executed this Certificate of Limited Partnership as of _____ day of _____ , A.D. _____ .

                          By: _____
                                  General Partner

                          Name: _____
                                      (type or print name)

§ 306. If the certificate contains a false statement, one who suffers loss by reliance on the statement may be able to recover damages from anyone who signed the certificate and knew the statement was false or from any general partner who knew or should have known the statement was false. *See* RULPA § 207; ULPA-2001 § 205.

3. Amending the Limited Partnership Certificate

In the event of certain changes in the limited partnership, a certificate of amendment must be prepared and filed with the secretary of state. *See* RULPA § 202; ULPA-2001 § 202. RULPA § 202(b) provides that an amendment to the certificate of limited partnership must be filed within 30 days after any of the following events:

- admission of a new general partner;
- withdrawal of a general partner; or
- the continuation of the business after the withdrawal of a general partner.

Under ULPA-2001 § 202, a certificate of limited partnership may be amended or restated at any time and must be amended upon the occurrence of listed events. *See also* RULPA § 202(a) (discussing amendment rules and logistics under the RULPA). In the event that a general partner becomes aware that the certificate of limited partnership contains a false statement, or that any other facts set forth in the original certificate of limited partnership have changed, the general partner must promptly amend the certificate. *See* RULPA § 202(c); ULPA-2001 § 202(e). Amending the original certificate generally requires preparation of the appropriate form designated for use in that state, signature by a general partner and any new general partner, and payment of a filing fee. See Exhibit 5.2 for a sample certificate of amendment.

E. VOTING AND GOVERNANCE RULES

1. General Partners: Agents and Fiduciaries

Under default rules, general partners have equal rights in the management and conduct of partnership business. In this regard, ULPA-2001 provides, in pertinent part, as follows:

> Each general partner has equal rights in the management and conduct of the limited partnership's activities and affairs. Except as otherwise provided in this [act], any matter relating to the activities and affairs of the partnership is decided exclusively by the general partner or, if there is more than one general partner, by a majority of the general partners.

ULPA-2001 § 406(a). *See also* RULPA § 403. If there is more than one general partner, each general partner's specific duties and responsibilities should be set forth in the limited partnership agreement. If the agreement fails to provide specific duties

EXHIBIT 5.2 **Certificate of Amendment**

State of Arizona – Office of the Secretary of State
All Limited Partnerships *A.R.S. §§ 29-309 & 29-1103(H)*
Amendment to Certificate; Restatement
SEND BY MAIL TO:

Secretary of State Michele Reagan, Atten: Limited Partnerships
1700 W. Washington Street, FL. 7, Phoenix, AZ 85007-2808
OR return this application in person:

PHOENIX - State Capitol Executive Tower, **TUCSON -** Arizona State Complex,
1700 W. Washington Street, 1st Fl., Room 103   400 W. Congress, 1st Fl., Suite 141
Office Hours: Monday through Friday, 8 a.m. to 5 p.m., except state holidays.
Questions? Call (602) 542-6187; in-state/toll-free (800) 458-5842.
IN-PERSON ONLY - We accept major credit
cards and bank debit cards.

MICHELE
REAGAN
Secretary of State

PLEASE NOTE: All correspondence regarding this filing will be sent to the principal office identified on this certificate. This application must be submitted with a self-addressed, stamped envelope with applicable filing fees.

DO NOT WRITE IN THIS SPACE

FOR OFFICE USE ONLY
SOSBSPARTNERSHIPAMEND REV. 3/12/2015

INSTRUCTIONS

When to use this form: Partnerships already registered with the office shall use this form to AMEND a certificate.

Be Accurate: Complete all applicable fields on this form. Write legibly; or fill out this application online at www.azsos.gov and print it.

Submission: Submit this amendment to certificate in duplicate (one original, one copy) with a self-addressed, stamped envelope with payment. Any other amendments not listed, please attach additional sheets with filing.

Filing Fee and Payment: $10, plus $3 per page; If filing by mail, make checks or money orders payable to the: Secretary of State.

Processing: 2-3 weeks; expedited service (24-48 hours) available for an additional $25.

Website: All forms are available online at www.azsos.gov.

1. PARTNERSHIP INFORMATION *(As on your current certificate on file with the Secretary of State)*

A. Name of Partnership ON FILE

Where applicable end with "Limited Partnership" or "LP" | "Limited Liability Partnership" or "LLP" | "Limited Liability Limited Partnership" or "LLLP"

B. Secretary of State File Number	C. Date Certificate was Filed		
Registration Number:	Month	Day	Year

2. AMENDMENT INFORMATION -- *Check and fill in all that apply. The amendment to the certificate of the LP/LLP/LLLP is as follows:*

☐ **A. Name Change:** End with "Limited Partnership" or "LP"; "Limited Liability Partnership" or "LLP"; "Limited Liability Limited Partnership" or "LLLP"

☐ **B. Office Address Change:**

Former Mailing Address (P.O. Box or C/O are unacceptable)	City	State	Zip Code
New Mailing Address (P.O. Box or C/O are unacceptable)	City	State	Zip Code

☐ **C. Other**

D. General Partner(s) Amendments

☐ **Admission:** Name of NEW General Partner	Signature of General Partner	Date admitted as General Partner / /
Mailing Address	City	State	Zip Code
☐ **Admission:** Name of NEW General Partner	Signature of General Partner	Date admitted as General Partner / /
Mailing Address	City	State	Zip Code
☐ **Withdrawal:** Name(s) of FORMER General Partner(s)		Date ended as General Partner(s) / /

E. ☐ **Agent for Service of Process Change** ☐ **Agent for Service of Process Address Change** ☐ **Agent for Service of Process Phone Change**

Agent for service of process	Phone number (include area code) *optional* ( )		
Address of agent (P.O. Box or C/O are unacceptable)	City	State	Zip Code

3. GENERAL PARTNER(S) - Signature(s)

Current General Partner (Printed)	Current General Partner (Printed)	
1st Signer's Signature	Date	2nd Signer's Signature	Date

Arizona Department of State   Office of the Secretary of State   Michele Reagan, Secretary of State and responsibilities, management and control will be shared equally between general partners, just as in a general partnership, under default rules.

As RULPA § 403 and ULPA-2001 § 406(a) suggest, a general partner's management rights and obligations are the same as those of general partners in a general partnership. This means, for example, that a general partner of a limited partnership is an agent of the partnership and thus has broad authority to bind the partnership with respect to contract matters according to agency law principles. Section 402 of ULPA-2001 provides, in pertinent part, as follows:

> (a) Each general partner is an agent of the limited partnership for the purposes of its activities and affairs. An act of a general partner, including the signing of a record in the partnership's name, for apparently carrying on in the ordinary course the partnership's activities and affairs or activities and affairs of the kind carried on by the partnership binds the partnership, unless the general partner did not have authority to act for the partnership in the particular matter and the person with which the general partner was dealing knew or had notice that the general partner lacked authority.
>
> (b) An act of a general partner which is not apparently for carrying on in the ordinary course the limited partnership's activities and affairs or activities and affairs of the kind carried on by the partnership binds the partnership only if the act was actually authorized by all the other partners.

As agents, in addition to having authority to bind the partnership according to agency law rules, general partners also owe duties of loyalty and due care to the other partners and to the limited partnership. *See* RULPA § 403 (stating that a general partner of a limited partnership has the same rights and powers and is subject to the same restrictions of a partner in a partnership without limited partners); ULPA-2001 § 409 (stating general partner owes to limited partnership duties of care and loyalty as referenced in §§ 409(b) and 409(c).) Although limited partnership law allows partners some freedom to customize governance obligations, ULPA-2001 § 105(c)(6) provides that a limited partnership agreement cannot eliminate the duty of loyalty or the duty of care except as provided for in § 105(d). Section 105(d) provides, in pertinent part, that subject to § 105(c)(8) (discussed below), a partnership agreement may (i) specify the method by which acts or transactions that would otherwise violate the duty of loyalty may be authorized or ratified by one or more disinterested and independent persons after disclosure of material facts; and (ii) if not manifestly unreasonable, alter or eliminate aspects of the duty of loyalty, identify certain types or categories of activities that do not violate the duty of loyalty, and alter the duty of care within statutory limits. Section 105(c)(8) provides, in pertinent part, that a partnership agreement cannot relieve or exonerate a person for liability for conduct involving bad faith, willful or intentional misconduct, or knowing violations of law. ULPA-2001 § 105(c)(8).

Apart from their duties of care and loyalty, general partners in a limited partnership also must discharge duties and obligations owed under the state's limited partnership law or the limited partnership agreement and must exercise any rights available under the law or the limited partnership agreement in a manner that is consistent with the contractual obligation of good faith and fair dealing. ULPA-2001 § 409(d). As with the duty of loyalty, a limited partnership agreement may prescribe the standards by which the performance of the obligation is to be measured, if the standards are not manifestly unreasonable, but may not eliminate this obligation, according to ULPA-2001 § 105(c)(7).

Two states — Delaware and Alabama — permit partners in a limited partnership to expand, restrict, or even eliminate fiduciary duties owed by the general partner via contract. The Delaware Limited Partnership Act § 17-1101(d) states as follows:

> To the extent that, at law or in equity, a partner or other person has duties (including fiduciary duties) to a limited partnership or to another partner or to another person that is a party to or is otherwise bound by a partnership agreement, the partner's or other person's duties may be expanded or restricted or eliminated by provisions of the partnership agreement; provided that the partnership agreement may not eliminate the implied contractual covenant of good faith and fair dealing.

See also Alabama Business and Non-profit Entities Code § 10A-9-1.10(2). While other states permit private ordering respecting rights and obligations of general partners, most state statutes do not provide for the outright elimination of fiduciary duties via contract at this time. *See, e.g.,* N.J. Stat. Ann. § 42:1A-24.

Case Preview

Norton v. K-Sea Transportation Partners L.P.

In Delaware, the ability to modify duties via contract reflects a deeply rooted commitment to freedom of contract as an organizing principle for unincorporated business entities. In the following case, the Delaware Supreme Court considered the interplay between statutory default rules and provisions in a limited partnership agreement that purported to specify, via contract, certain rights and obligations. In reading the case, consider the following questions:

1. Did the general partner owe statutory fiduciary duties of loyalty and care to the partnership and the other partners in this case? Why or why not?
2. What role, if any, did the parties' contract, as expressed in the limited partnership agreement, play in determining the nature and scope of the general partner's obligations?
3. What is the implied covenant of good faith and fair dealing? When and how do concepts of good faith and fair dealing apply (if at all) to limited partnerships formed under the Delaware Limited Partnership statute?
4. Did the conflict of interest provisions in the limited partnership agreement at issue affect the outcome of this case? How and why?
5. Why did the general partner obtain a fairness opinion? What impact, if any, did the fairness opinion have on the outcome of this case?

Norton v. K-Sea Transportation Partners L.P.
67 A.3d 354 (Del. 2013)

STEELE, Chief Justice:*

In this appeal, we consider a general partner's obligations under a limited partnership agreement. The plaintiffs allege that the general partner obtained excessive consideration for its incentive distribution rights when an unaffiliated third party purchased the partnership. Importantly, the plaintiffs do not allege that the general partner breached the implied covenant of good faith and fair dealing. We conclude that the limited partnership agreement's conflict of interest provision created a contractual safe harbor, not an affirmative obligation. Therefore, the general partner needed only to exercise its discretion in good faith, as the parties intended that term to be construed, to satisfy its duties under the agreement. The general partner obtained an appropriate fairness opinion, which, under the agreement, created a conclusive presumption that the general partner made its decision in good faith. Therefore we AFFIRM the Court of Chancery's dismissal of the complaint.

I. FACTUAL AND PROCEDURAL BACKGROUND

A. *The Parties*

This case arises out of the Merger of K-Sea Transportation Partners L.P. (K-Sea or the Partnership) and Kirby Corporation. K-Sea operates a barge and tugboat fleet that transports refined petroleum products between American ports. Before the Merger, K-Sea was a publicly traded Delaware limited partnership. The Fourth Amended and Restated Agreement of Limited Partnership (the LPA) created K-Sea's governance structure. Plaintiffs Edward F. Norton III and Ken Poesl (Norton) represent a class consisting of K-Sea's unaffiliated former common unitholders.

K-Sea's general partner is K-Sea General Partner L.P. (K-Sea GP), which is also a Delaware limited partnership. K-Sea GP's general partner is K-Sea General Partner GP LLC (KSGP), a Delaware limited liability company that ultimately controls K-Sea. Anthony S. Abbate, Barry J. Alperin, James C. Baker, Timothy J. Casey, James J. Dowling, Brian P. Friedman, Kevin S. McCarthy, Gary D. Reaves II, and Frank Salerno served on KSGP's board of directors (the K-Sea Board) during the Merger negotiations. Directors Abbate, Alperin, and Salerno comprised the K-Sea Board's Conflicts Committee. K-Sea, K-Sea GP, KSGP, and the K-Sea Board members are the Defendants in this action.

B. *K-Sea's Capital Structure and Ownership*

At the time of the Merger, K-Sea's equity was divided among K-Sea GP, the common unitholders, and a class of preferred units held by KA First Reserve, LLC (KAFR). The common unitholders held 49.8% of the total equity, KAFR held 49.9%, and K-Sea GP's general partner interest comprised the remaining 0.3%.

---

* For purposes of brevity, footnotes (the bulk of which are case cites) have been omitted.

In addition to its general partner interest, K-Sea GP held incentive distribution rights (IDRs) through a wholly owned affiliate. These IDRs entitled K-Sea GP to increasing percentages of K-Sea's distributions once payments to the limited partners exceeded certain levels. K-Sea GP would not receive payments on the IDRs until *quarterly* distributions reached $0.55 per unit. K-Sea's conservative estimates indicated that *annual* distributions would not reach $0.55 per unit until 2015. Norton extrapolates these projections to show that K-Sea would not reach the $0.55-per-unit quarterly threshold until the mid-2030s. Based on these projections, the IDRs were worth as little as $100,000.

C. The K-Sea Board Issues Phantom Units to the Conflicts Committee Members

In December 2010, the K-Sea Board approved incentive compensation for the Conflicts Committee members, each of whom received 15,000 phantom K-Sea common units. These phantom units vested over five years, but became immediately payable if a change of control occurred. These phantom units represented a significant component of Abbate's, Alperin's, and Salerno's equity interests in K-Sea. The LPA, however, prohibited Conflicts Committee members from holding any ownership interest in K-Sea other than common units.

D. Kirby Approaches K-Sea and Negotiates the Merger

Shortly after the phantom unit grant, Kirby's CEO communicated with McCarthy, who also served as a director designee of KAFR, to discuss a strategic transaction between Kirby and K-Sea. On February 2, 2011, McCarthy informed Dowling, the K-Sea Board's Chairman, of those discussions. K-Sea and Kirby then extended a confidentiality agreement they had previously signed, and K-Sea provided Kirby with due diligence.

On February 9, 2011, Kirby offered to pay $306 million for K-Sea's common and preferred units. After discussing the offer with the K-Sea Board, McCarthy rejected it and informed Kirby that future offers should include consideration for K-Sea GP's general partner interest and its IDRs. Kirby responded the next day with a $316 million offer for all of K-Sea's equity interests, but McCarthy again rejected the offer as inadequate. On February 15, 2011, Kirby offered $329 million for K-Sea, which included an $18 million payment for the IDRs (the IDR Payment).

E. K-Sea Activates Its Conflicts Committee to Consider the Merger

When the K-Sea Board met to consider Kirby's new offer, it acknowledged that the IDR Payment created a "possible conflict of interest" and referred the proposed Merger to the Conflicts Committee for a recommendation. Under the LPA, the Conflict Committee's approval of a transaction would constitute "Special Approval," which purportedly would limit the unitholders' ability to challenge the transaction.

The Conflicts Committee hired Stifel, Nicolaus & Co. (Stifel) and DLA Piper LLP as its independent financial and legal advisors, respectively. Stifel valued K-Sea's common units using a distribution discount model based on K-Sea's internal projections. After valuing the common units, Stifel opined that the consideration K-Sea's unaffiliated common unitholders received was fair from a financial viewpoint. The fairness opinion expressly did not consider "the fairness of the amount or nature of any compensation to any of the officers, directors or employees of K-Sea or its affiliates . . . relative to the compensation of the public holders of K-Sea's equity securities."

F. The K-Sea Board Approves the Merger and the Transaction Closes

After reviewing Stifel's fairness opinion, the Conflicts Committee unanimously recommended the Merger to the K-Sea Board, which also approved it. Like Stifel's fairness opinion, the Conflicts Committee's recommendation did not refer to the IDR Payment. K-Sea and Kirby then entered into a definitive merger agreement and disseminated a Form S-4 recommending that the common unitholders vote in favor of the Merger. A majority of K-Sea's unitholders voted in favor of the transaction, and the Merger closed on July 1, 2011. As finally negotiated, K-Sea's common unitholders received $8.15 per unit and K-Sea GP received $18 million for the IDRs. The consideration represented a 26% premium over K-Sea's March 11, 2011 closing price.

G. Procedural History

Shortly after K-Sea announced the Merger, Norton filed a class action complaint in the Court of Chancery. As amended, the Complaint contained four counts. Count I alleged that the Conflicts Committee members breached their fiduciary duties by recommending the Merger without evaluating the IDR Payment's fairness. In Count II, Norton contended that K-Sea GP, KSGP, and the K-Sea Board members breached the LPA by proposing, approving, and participating in an unfair transaction based on an inadequate review process. In Count III, Norton accused K-Sea GP, KSGP and the K-Sea Board of breaching the LPA by approving the Merger in reliance on the improperly constituted Conflicts Committee's Special Approval. Count IV alleged that K-Sea GP, KSGP, and the K-Sea Board breached their duty of disclosure by authorizing the dissemination of a materially misleading Form S-4. The Vice Chancellor denied Norton's motion for expedited discovery.

After the parties submitted initial briefing on Defendants' motion to dismiss, the Vice Chancellor contacted the parties and advised them that he had reached a preliminary decision to grant the Defendants' motion. His rationale relied upon an interpretation of the LPA that neither party had argued nor briefed, and so he invited supplemental briefing. After reviewing the parties' submissions, the Vice Chancellor dismissed Norton's Complaint. Norton appeals from the Vice Chancellor's dismissal of Counts I, II, and III of that Complaint.

. . .

III. ANALYSIS

A. What Contractual Standards Apply to the Merger?

Limited partnership agreements are a type of contract. We, therefore, construe them in accordance with their terms to give effect to the parties' intent. We give words their plain meaning unless it appears that the parties intended a special meaning. When interpreting contracts, we construe them as a whole and give effect to every provision if it is reasonably possible. A meaning inferred from a particular provision cannot control the agreement if that inference conflicts with the agreement's overall scheme. We consider extrinsic evidence only if the contract is ambiguous. A contract is not ambiguous "simply because the parties do not agree upon its proper construction," but only if it is susceptible to two or more reasonable interpretations. If the contractual language at issue is ambiguous and if the limited partners did not negotiate for the agreement's terms, we apply the *contra proferentem* principle and construe the ambiguous terms against the drafter.

The Delaware Revised Uniform Limited Partnership Act (DRULPA) gives "maximum effect to the principle of freedom of contract and to the enforceability of partnership agreements." Parties may expand, restrict, or eliminate any fiduciary duties that a partner or other person might otherwise owe, but they "may not eliminate the implied contractual covenant of good faith and fair dealing."

B. The LPA's Provisions Governing Mergers and Creating Contractual Fiduciary Duties

Unfortunately, limited partnership agreements that attempt to modify, rather than eliminate, fiduciary duties often create a Gordian knot of interrelated standards in different sections of the agreement. This LPA requires us to parse several provisions to determine which standards apply to the Merger. The LPA creates procedures for mergers in Article XIV. Section 14.2 of Article XIV establishes that K-Sea GP must approve any proposed merger. K-Sea GP may consent to a merger "in the exercise of its discretion." Section 7.9(b), which attempts to clarify the nebulous "discretion" standard, provides:

> Whenever this Agreement . . . provides that [K-Sea GP] . . . is permitted or required to make a decision (i) in its "sole discretion" or "discretion," . . . except as otherwise provided herein, [K-Sea GP] . . . shall be entitled to consider only such interests and factors as it desires and shall have no duty or obligation to give any consideration to any interest of, or factors affecting, the Partnership . . . [or] any Limited Partner . . . [and] (ii) it may make such decision in its sole discretion (regardless of whether there is a reference to "sole discretion" or "discretion") unless another express standard is provided for. . . .

Therefore, when K-Sea GP decides whether to consent to a merger, it may "consider only such interests and factors as it desires and shall have no duty or obligation to give any consideration to any interest of, or factors affecting" K-Sea or its limited partners. The limited partners' ultimate right to reject a merger under Section 14.3 practically limits that discretion however.

The LPA limits Section 14.2's broad grant of discretion in Section 7.10(d), which provides:

> Any standard of care and duty imposed by [the LPA] or [DRULPA] . . . shall be modified, waived or limited, to the extent permitted by law, as required to permit [K-Sea GP] to act under [the LPA] . . . and to make any decision pursuant to the authority

prescribed in [the LPA], *so long as such action is reasonably believed by [K-Sea GP] to be in, or not inconsistent with, the best interests of the Partnership.*

If K-Sea GP were subject to common law fiduciary duties, it could not consent to a merger in its sole discretion. Therefore, Section 7.10(d) eliminates any duties that otherwise exist and replaces them with a contractual fiduciary duty—namely, that K-Sea GP must reasonably believe that its action is in the best interest of, or not inconsistent with, the best interests of the Partnership.

Finally, the LPA broadly exculpates all Indemnitees (which no party disputes includes all the Defendants) so long as the Indemnitee acted in "good faith." Although the LPA regrettably does not define "good faith" in this context, we cannot discern a rational distinction between the parties' adoption of this "good faith" standard and Section 7.10(d)'s contractual fiduciary duty, *i.e.,* an Indemnitee acts in good faith if the Indemnitee reasonably believes that its action is in the best interest of, or at least, not inconsistent with, the best interests of K-Sea. If we take seriously our obligation to construe the agreement's "overall scheme," we must conclude that the parties' insertion of a free-standing, enigmatic standard of "good faith" is consistent with Section 7.10(d)'s conceptualization of a reasonable belief that the action taken is in, or not inconsistent with, the best interests of the Partnership. In this LPA's overall scheme, "good faith" cannot be construed otherwise.

Thus, while the LPA does not require K-Sea GP to consider any particular interest or factor affecting the Partnership when exercising its discretion, K-Sea GP still must reasonably believe that its ultimate course of action is not inconsistent with K-Sea's best interests. Therefore, unless another provision supplants this standard, in order to state a claim that withstands Rule 12(b)(6), Norton must allege facts supporting an inference that K-Sea GP had reason to believe that it acted inconsistently with the Partnership's best interests when approving the Merger.

C. Does Section 7.9(a) Impose Additional Obligations that Supplant Section 14.2's Discretion Standard?

Norton contends that the LPA's generally applicable discretion standard for mergers must yield to Section 7.9(a), the provision governing conflicts of interest, which he argues requires K-Sea GP to establish that the Merger was fair and reasonable. The LPA contemplates that conflicts of interest may arise, and Section 7.9(a) establishes procedures for curing these conflicts. Section 7.9(a) provides:

> Unless otherwise expressly provided in [the LPA], . . . whenever a potential conflict of interest exists or arises between [K-Sea GP], on the one hand, and the Partnership . . . on the other, any resolution or course of action by [K-Sea GP] in respect of such conflict of interest shall be permitted and deemed approved by all Partners, and shall not constitute a breach of [the LPA] . . . or of any duty stated or implied by law or equity, if the resolution or course of action is, or . . . is deemed to be, fair and reasonable to the Partnership. [K-Sea GP] shall be authorized but not required . . . to seek Special Approval of such resolution. Any . . . resolution of such conflict of interest shall be conclusively deemed fair and reasonable to the Partnership if such conflict of interest or resolution is (i) *approved by Special Approval* . . . , (ii) on terms no less favorable to the Partnership than those generally being provided to

or available from unrelated third parties or (iii) fair to the Partnership. . . . [K-Sea GP] shall be authorized . . . to consider (A) the relative interests of any party to such conflict, agreement, transaction or situation and the benefits and burdens relating to such interest . . . and (D) such additional factors as [K-Sea GP] . . . determines in its sole discretion to be relevant, reasonable or appropriate under the circumstances. Nothing contained in [the LPA], however, is intended to nor shall it be construed to require [K-Sea GP] (including the Conflicts Committee) to consider the interests of any Person other than the Partnership. . . .

If Section 7.9(a) requires K-Sea GP to establish that the Merger was fair and reasonable to K-Sea, we must consider whether the grant of phantom units to the Conflicts Committee tainted the Special Approval process. If, however, Section 7.9(a) does not impose that affirmative obligation on K-Sea GP, we do not need to reach the issue unless Norton has pleaded a violation of the LPA's more lenient discretion standard.

Section 7.9(a) applies "whenever a potential conflict of interest exists or arises." Norton alleges that the IDR Payment created a conflict of interest because K-Sea GP did not share the IDR Payment with any other unitholder. The IDR Payment motivated K-Sea GP to increase the amount of consideration K-Sea GP received at the expense of the consideration paid to the other unitholders. Accepting these well-pleaded allegations as true, the IDR Payment created a conflict of interest and Section 7.9(a) applies by its terms. Section 7.9(a)'s applicability does not necessarily mean that it displaces Section 14.2's discretion standard, however. If Section 7.9(a) is only a safe harbor, the phrase "whenever a potential conflict of interest exists or arises" merely means that the safe harbor is available whenever there is a potential conflict of interest.

The provision's plain language indicates that if K-Sea GP's resolution of a conflict of interest is fair and reasonable or is deemed to be fair and reasonable, that resolution is not a breach of the LPA. This statement's contrapositive is that if K-Sea GP's resolution of a conflict of interest is a breach of the LPA, then it is not fair and reasonable. Norton arrives at his construction by inverting Section 7.9(a), *i.e.,* he argues that a resolution of a conflict of interest that is not fair and reasonable *is* a breach of the LPA. Unlike the contrapositive, Section 7.9(a)'s inverse does not necessarily follow.

Recognizing that Section 7.9(a)'s text does not mandate his construction, Norton argues that other portions of the section and the LPA weigh in its favor. Section 7.9(a) states that "[K-Sea GP] shall be authorized but not required . . . to seek Special Approval." Norton contends that, because under the LPA Special Approval is optional, that implies that Section 7.9(a) as a whole is mandatory. We disagree. Read in context, this language means that K-Sea GP is not required to obtain Special Approval in every case where a conflict of interest arises. For example, K-Sea GP may determine that the transaction is "on terms no less favorable to the Partnership than those . . . available from unrelated third parties" or "fair to the Partnership" to resolve the conflict. That example underscores that K-Sea GP does not need to resolve a conflict of interest through the Conflicts Committee. The language does not make the entire Section mandatory by implication.

Other LPA provisions support the Vice Chancellor's construction of Section 7.9(a). Section 7.6(d) governs transactions between K-Sea GP and the Partnership, which necessarily involve a conflict of interest. That Section begins by stating that "[n]either [K-Sea GP] nor any of its Affiliates shall sell . . . any property to, or purchase any property from, the Partnership . . . except pursuant to transactions that are fair and reasonable to the Partnership." This language creates an affirmative obligation — K-Sea GP may not engage in a transaction with the Partnership unless the transaction is "fair and reasonable." Section 7.6(d) indicates that the LPA's drafters knew how to impose an affirmative obligation when they so intended, and that Section 7.9(a)'s language does not result from sloppy drafting.

Section 7.9(c) also weighs against Norton's interpretation. That Section provides that "[w]henever a particular . . . resolution of a conflict of interest is required . . . to be 'fair and reasonable' . . . the fair and reasonable nature of such . . . resolution shall be considered in the context of all similar or related transactions." This language indicates that not all resolutions of conflicts of interest are required to meet a "fair and reasonable" standard.

. . .

Therefore, the Vice Chancellor correctly held that Section 7.9(a) is "a permissive safe harbor." Our construction of the LPA indicates that Section 14.2's "discretion" standard applies to mergers generally, and that K-Sea GP may (if it so chooses) take advantage of Section 7.9(a)'s safe harbor provisions to resolve any conflict of interest relating to a merger. A resolution of a conflict of interest that is actually, or is deemed to be, fair and reasonable is deemed approved and is not a breach of the LPA. If K-Sea GP does not meet that standard, however, that does not automatically put K-Sea GP in breach of the LPA.

. . .

Because Section 7.9(a) does not impose any additional affirmative duties on K-Sea GP, our analysis focuses on the otherwise controlling standard — whether K-Sea GP exercised its discretion to approve the Merger in good faith, (*i.e.*, with a reasonable belief that its actions were in, or not inconsistent with, the best interests of K-Sea).

. . .

Here, Norton has alleged that the IDR Payment created a conflict of interest between K-Sea GP and the Partnership because K-Sea GP obtained consideration that did not flow to the common unitholders. At the motion to dismiss stage we must draw all inferences in Norton's favor. We therefore could conclude that K-Sea GP used its position to extract an excessive amount of consideration for its IDRs at the expense of the limited partners. That permits us to infer that K-Sea GP may not have acted in good faith when it approved the Merger and submitted it to the unitholders for approval. That raises the next issue, which is whether Norton has pled a cognizable claim that K-Sea GP did not act in good faith.

D. Did the Investment Banker's Fairness Opinion Create a Conclusive Presumption of Good Faith?

In addressing that issue, we must consider yet another LPA provision addressing K-Sea GP's obligation to act in "good faith." That provision creates a conclusive presumption that K-Sea GP has acted in good faith if K-Sea GP relies on a competent expert's opinion. Section 7.10(b) provides that

[K-Sea GP] may consult with . . . investment bankers . . . and any act taken or omitted to be taken in reliance upon the opinion . . . of such Persons as to matters that [K-Sea GP] reasonably believes to be within such Person's professional or expert competence *shall be conclusively presumed to have been done or omitted in good faith* and in accordance with such opinion.

The Conflicts Committee obtained Stifel's opinion that the consideration that Kirby paid to K-Sea's unaffiliated common unitholders was financially fair. No party alleges that Stifel lacked the requisite expertise to render that opinion. Norton nowhere claims that the opinion did not state that the Merger was fair, nor does he allege that the analyses underlying the fairness opinion were flawed. Rather, he alleges that K-Sea extracted a larger portion of the consideration than the IDRs' value justified. We note also that Norton does not claim on appeal that Defendants' actions breached the implied covenant of good faith and fair dealing.

Norton argues that K-Sea GP is not entitled to a conclusive presumption of good faith because Stifel did not specifically address the IDR Payment's fairness — the reason why K-Sea GP activated the Conflicts Committee. He concedes that the unaffiliated unitholders received a fair price, and he correctly notes that a limited partnership's value is not a single number, but a range of fair values. While we understand Norton's frustration, the LPA's provisions control.

The LPA does not require K-Sea GP to evaluate the IDR Payment's reasonableness separately from the remaining consideration. Section 7.9(a) explicitly states that nothing in the LPA shall be construed to require K-Sea GP to consider the interests of any person other than the Partnership. That Section authorizes (but does not require) K-Sea GP to consider the "relative interests of any party to such conflict." These provisions indicate that K-Sea GP was not required to consider whether the IDR Payment was fair, but only whether the Merger as a whole was in the best interests of the Partnership (which included the general partner and the limited partners). Because of those clear provisions, Norton had no reasonable contractual expectation that K-Sea GP or the Conflict Committee's retained investment banker would specifically consider the IDR Payment's fairness.

Because Stifel's opinion satisfied the LPA's requirements, we next address whether that opinion entitles *K-Sea GP* to a conclusive presumption of good faith. Although the Conflicts Committee of the K-Sea Board actually obtained the fairness opinion, it is unreasonable to infer that the entire K-Sea Board did not rely on the opinion that a K-Sea Board subcommittee obtained. Similarly, because K-Sea GP is a "pass-through" entity controlled by KSGP, the only reasonable inference is that K-Sea GP relied on the fairness opinion. K-Sea GP is therefore conclusively presumed to have acted in good faith when it approved the Merger and submitted it to the unitholders for a vote. That process satisfied K-Sea GP's contractual duty to exercise its discretion in "good faith" (as this LPA defines the term).

Norton willingly invested in a limited partnership that provided fewer protections to limited partners than those provided under corporate fiduciary duty principles. He is bound by his investment decision. Here, the LPA did not require K-Sea GP to consider separately the IDR Payment's fairness, but granted K-Sea GP broad discretion to approve a merger, so long as it exercised that discretion in "good faith." Reliance on Stifel's opinion satisfied this standard. By opining that the consideration

Kirby paid to the unaffiliated unitholders was fair, Stifel's opinion addressed the IDR Payment's fairness, albeit indirectly. Kirby presumably was willing to pay a fixed amount for the entire Partnership. If K-Sea GP diverted too much value to itself, at some point the consideration paid to the unaffiliated unitholders would no longer be "fair."

Furthermore, the LPA does not leave K-Sea's unitholders unprotected. K-Sea GP's approval merely triggered submission of the Merger to the unitholders for a majority vote. If the unitholders were dissatisfied with the Merger's terms, "their remedy [was] the ballot box, not the courthouse." Here K-Sea GP is conclusively presumed to have approved the Merger in good faith, and a majority of the unitholders voted to consummate it. The LPA required nothing more.

. . .

IV. CONCLUSION

For these reasons, Norton has not stated a claim for relief that survives Defendants' Rule 12(b)(6) motion. Accordingly, the Court of Chancery's judgment is AFFIRMED.

Post-Case Follow-Up

As *Norton* suggests, lawyers must take care when drafting partnership agreements. Although Delaware is particularly committed to principles of freedom of contract in the context of unincorporated business entities, all jurisdictions afford partners significant freedom to customize partnership agreements to meet business needs, and courts tend to enforce these agreements when there are disputes. As the *Norton* court observed, without careful drafting, efforts to contract around default rules can become a trap for the unwary.

Norton v. K-Sea Transportation Partners L.P.: Real Life Applications

1. You represent Nanotech Investment Research and Management, LLC (NIRM), a venture capital firm formed in Delaware. Over the next few years, NIRM intends to form a series of investment funds, organized as Delaware limited partnerships, to invest in nanotech-related businesses. For each of these funds, NIRM will serve as the general partner, while individual and institutional investors will serve as limited partners and passive investors.

NIRM's representative explains that NIRM is concerned that some limited partners might raise issues respecting the nature and extent of NIRM's duties of care and loyalty to each of the funds and its investors. For example, NIRM wants to be sure that each of its funds has the freedom to invest in start-up business of their choosing, even if those businesses compete with one another, potentially causing some businesses (and the funds that invest in those businesses) to out-perform other NIRM-supported businesses and funds. What language might you include in the partnership agreement to avoid or mitigate the risk of claims alleging breaches of the duty of loyalty arising from NIRM's investment activity? To what extent can NIRM modify any statutory duties of loyalty owed to each of the funds?

2. NIRM's representative also explains to you that NIRM intends to invest in start-up businesses, which often involve a high degree of risk. While some of NIRM's investments might earn millions for NIRM and its investors, others may fail, leaving behind unpaid debts. Draft risk disclosures and a limitation of liability provision for the limited partnership agreement.

3. The Garcia family asks you to form a family limited partnership (discussed below) for estate and tax planning purposes. The family explains that Marisol, a family member with an MBA degree and experience in investing and financial planning, will make investment decisions for the family limited partnership. Marisol is in charge of several investment partnerships apart from her family-related work, and she would like to be sure that she can continue working with these other partnerships even after the Garcia Family Limited Partnership is formed.
   a. What ethical issues, if any, are presented by this engagement?
   b. Assume that all of the Garcias are on board with having Marisol manage the Garcia Family Limited Partnership, along with the other investment funds mentioned above. What provisions might the Garcias want to include in the family limited partnership agreement respecting Marisol's rights and obligations?
   c. Should Marisol serve as the general partner in her individual capacity? Why or why not?

2. Limited Partners

In contrast to general partners, limited partners generally do not manage or control the limited partnership business, nor do they owe duties of care and loyalty to the limited partnership or any other partner (limited or general) under default rules. ULPA-2001 305(b) and (c); *see* RULPA §§ 303(a) and (b). (In this regard, John McMullen, who sold his interest in the New York Yankees to buy the Houston Astros in 1979, reportedly said that there was nothing more limited than being a limited partner of George Steinbrenner in the New York Yankees!) Note that under ULPA-2001 § 305(a), limited partners do owe an obligation of good faith and fair dealing when discharging duties to the partnership and the other partners under the partnership agreement and when exercising any rights arising under the limited partnership act or the partnership agreement. *Id.* The 2001 Act further provides that this obligation cannot be waived or eliminated by contract. *See* ULPA-2001 § 105(c)(7).

F. LIABILITY RULES

1. Unlimited Personal Liability for General Partners

As noted above, a general partner in a limited partnership suffers the disadvantage of unlimited personal liability for the debts and obligations of the business. If there is more than one general partner, liability will be joint and several. To address the general partner's risk of unlimited personal liability for entity debts, limited partnerships may choose to appoint an entity as general partner — say, a corporation or limited liability company. Corporations and limited liability companies provide owners with a liability shield, meaning that the only funds and assets available to creditors are those owned by the corporation or LLC itself. The owners of the corporation or LLC serving as a general partner generally have no personal liability for the debts and obligations of the entity, because the corporation and LLC forms provide owners with a liability shield. Thus, if a corporation or limited liability company is the general partner of a limited partnership, neither the limited partners of the partnership nor those holding an equity interest in the partnership's general partner have personal liability for the limited partnership's debts and obligations. Assuming there has been no fraud or other inequitable conduct giving rise to a claim for breach of fiduciary duty or veil piercing at the general partner level, the only assets available to satisfy creditors would be those of the limited partnership itself and those owned by the corporate or LLC general partner. The personal assets of the owners of the corporation or LLC general partner would not be at risk. *See In re USACafes, L.P. Litig.*, 600 A.2d 43 (Del. Ch. 1991) (denying motion to dismiss limited partners' complaint for breach of fiduciary duty against individual owners of all of the stock of corporate general partner where individual owners allegedly used control over partnership property to advantage general partner — and its director/owners — at the expense of the partnership, and thus personally participated in the general partner's alleged fiduciary breach).

2. Limited Liability for Limited Partners

RULPA's Control Rule

As discussed above, in contrast to general partners, limited partners are not liable for the debts and obligations of the limited partnership based solely upon their status as limited partners. ULPA-2001 § 303(a); RULPA § 303. There are, however, two potential wrinkles to the limited partner liability shield. The first applies in RULPA regimes. Under RULPA's so-called **control rule**, a limited partner may lose her limited liability status if she acts like a general partner — that is, participates in the control of partnership business. *See* RULPA § 303. (In particular, RULPA provides that a limited partner who participates in the control of the business may become personally liable to those who transact business with the limited partnership while reasonably believing, based on the limited partner's conduct, that the limited partner was a general partner. RULPA § 303(a).) The general prohibition against a limited partner claiming the benefit of the limited partnership liability shield while still "controlling" the business or having her name in the business name seems to be based on what third parties and creditors are likely to perceive. If a third party sees an individual engaged in the management and control of a business or notes that person's name in the partnership name, the third party is likely to believe that person is a general partner whose personal assets are available to satisfy obligations of the limited partnership. (Note: As discussed below, the ULPA-2001 Act drops the control rule.)

While RULPA does not specifically define what constitutes "participating in the control of the business," RULPA § 303(b) provides that a limited partner may engage in the following "safe harbor" activities without subjecting himself to personal liability:

1. being a contractor for or an agent or employee of the limited partnership or an officer, director, or shareholder of a general partner that is a corporation;
2. consulting with and advising a general partner with respect to the limited partnership business;
3. acting as a guarantor of partnership obligations;
4. bringing a derivative action in the name of the limited partnership;
5. requesting or attending a meeting of partners;
6. proposing, approving, or disapproving one or more of the following matters:
   - the dissolution and winding up of the limited partnership;
   - the sale, transfer, lease, or mortgage of all or substantially all of the assets of the limited partnership;
   - the incurrence of indebtedness by the limited partnership other than in the ordinary course of its business;
   - a change in the nature of the business;
   - the admission or removal of a general or limited partner;
   - a transaction involving an actual or potential conflict of interest between a general partner and the limited partnership or limited partners;
   - an amendment to the partnership agreement or certificate of limited partnership; or
   - matters related to the business of the limited partnership not otherwise enumerated that the partnership agreement states may be subject to the approval or disapproval of limited partners;
7. winding up the limited partnership; or
8. exercising any right or power permitted to limited partners under the RULPA and not specifically enumerated in RULPA § 303(b).

RULPA § 303(b). The RULPA also specifies that conduct or activities undertaken by limited partners that are not specifically enumerated in the preceding list, often referred to as the **safe harbor** list, do not necessarily constitute an act of control by a limited partner that would render him subject to personal liability. RULPA § 303(c). Thus, a limited partner may perform some act not on this list, and it will not necessarily be viewed as an act of control that would subject him to personal liability. That having been said, limited partners subject to control rule regimes should proceed with caution when performing non–safe harbor acts to reduce the risk of being held personally liable for entity debts.

Case Preview

Shimko v. Guenther

In *Shimko v. Guenther*, a lawyer (Shimko) and his firm sought to recover legal fees for services allegedly provided to two limited partnerships. The organic documents of both limited partnerships listed Guenther as a limited partner, not a general partner. Citing the control rule set forth in the relevant state statute, Shimko argued that Guenther should be held personally liable for the legal fees (despite his limited partner status) because Shimko reasonably believed Guenther to be a general, rather than a limited, partner. As you read *Shimko v. Guenther*, consider the following questions:

1. What does the Arizona statute at issue say respecting the potential liability of limited partners for obligations of a limited partnership?
2. Under what circumstances will a limited partner be deemed to have participated in the control of limited partnership business, according to the statute and the opinion?
3. Under what circumstances will a third party be found to have "reasonably" believed that a limited partner was a general partner?
4. What lessons might you take from this case respecting Shimko's knowledge of Guenther's limited partner status?

Shimko v. Guenther
505 F.3d 987 (9th Cir. 2007)

MILAN D. SMITH, JR., Circuit Judge:*

Appellants Milton and Kathi Guenther (collectively, "the Guenthers"), appeal a judgment awarding $359,668.00 in attorneys' fees to Appellees Timothy Shimko, and his law firm, Shimko & Piscitelli (the law firm and its partners collectively, "Shimko") in payment for certain legal services allegedly provided to Arizona limited partnerships, Comprehensive Outpatient Rehabilitation Facility ("CORF") Licensing Services, L.P., and CORF Management Services, L.P. (collectively, "CORF entities"), and their limited partners. The organic documents of both the CORF entities list Milton Guenther (individually, "Guenther") as a limited partner, not as a general partner.

On appeal, Shimko argues that it reasonably believed Guenther to be a general, rather than a limited partner, and that, as a result, the Guenthers are liable for the legal fees of the CORF entities under Arizona Revised Statutes ("A.R.S.") § 29-319. We disagree. Shimko is not an ordinary creditor.

Shimko is a law firm hired to defend the CORF entities and its limited partners against a significant number of multimillion dollar claims filed across the country,

---

* Most footnotes have been omitted for purposes of brevity.

primarily alleging fraud. We hold that because Shimko owed a fiduciary duty of care to its clients, it is chargeable under the facts of this case with knowledge of the contents of the CORF entities' organic documents, whether or not it actually examined them, and, consequently, that it was not reasonable for Shimko to believe that Guenther was a general partner of either of the CORF entities. Accordingly, Shimko may not recover from the Guenthers the legal fees owed by the CORF entities to Shimko.

We reverse in part, affirm in part, and remand for further proceedings on the Guenthers' liability for legal fees incurred as a result of Shimko's representation of the Guenthers personally.

I. BACKGROUND AND PRIOR PROCEEDINGS

Richard Ross, David Goldfarb, Paul Woodcock, and Guenther (collectively, "Defendants") were limited partners of the CORF entities. The CORF entities offered clients consulting and management services to help them establish and operate Medicare-compliant outpatient treatment facilities. Upon commencement of the CORF entities' operations, Guenther was in charge of field operations, actively lectured at CORF marketing seminars, and helped find locations and medical directors for CORF clients.

During the period from late 2001 to 2003, a number of the CORF entities' clients located in various parts of the country threatened to file or did file complaints against the CORF entities, as well as against the Defendants in their individual capacities, alleging fraud and other causes of action.

According to Shimko's Response Brief filed in this case, "Shimko was asked to advise Dr. Guenther and the other owners on the extent of their individual and personal exposure, if any, beyond the protection offered to them by the limited partnership structure under which they owned and operated [the CORF entities]." Although the district found otherwise, Shimko claims it did not represent the CORF entities and billed them only because it was requested to do so by the Defendants. Neither the CORF entities nor the Defendants paid Shimko for its services during the period from October 2002 to April 2003. In April 2003, Shimko stopped representing the CORF entities and the Defendants, and shortly thereafter, it filed suit in district court, alleging "action on an account, breach of contract, passing bad checks, and quantum meruit and fraud" and seeking payment of legal fees in the sum of $359,668.00. . . .

Shimko's remaining claims against the Guenthers for breach of contract, action on account, and quantum meruit then proceeded to trial. Following a one day bench trial, the district court held that Guenther, as a limited partner in control, and his spouse, were liable for the entirety of Shimko's unpaid attorneys' fees.

In its Findings and Conclusions, the district court found that Shimko was retained to represent the CORF entities as well as its individual principals. It found that the Guenthers were personally represented by Shimko, that they personally agreed to this representation, and that they were liable for legal services performed for them personally. The district court also found that Guenther participated in the control of the CORF entities as a general partner, along with his colleagues, and that due to his substantial involvement in the operations of the CORF entities, "it was reasonable for Shimko to believe that he was dealing with a general partner." The court then found in favor of Shimko on the action on account and contract causes of action and found the Guenthers liable for all unpaid legal fees charged to the CORF entities, mooting the claim for unjust enrichment. . . .

The Guenthers filed a motion for reconsideration and/or a new trial, which the district court denied. The Guenthers now appeal both the judgment and the denial of their post-trial motion.

. . .

III. DISCUSSION

A. *Arizona Revised Statutes § 29-319*

A.R.S. § 29-319(A) states, in pertinent part:

> [A] limited partner is not liable for the obligations of a limited partnership unless he is also a general partner or, in addition to the exercise of his rights and powers as a limited partner, he participates in the control of the business. However, if the limited partner participates in the control of the business, he is liable only to persons who transact business with the limited partnership reasonably believing, based on the limited partner's conduct, that the limited partner is a general partner.

Thus, a limited partner may be held liable to a third party for the debts of the partnership if the limited partner is either a general partner or a participant in the control of the business and the third party reasonably believes that the limited partner is a general partner. A.R.S. § 29-301(5) defines a general partner as "a person who has been admitted to a limited partnership as a general partner in accordance with the partnership agreement and named in the certificate of limited partnership as a general partner." Guenther was not a general partner, as defined by A.R.S. § 29-301(5), of either CORF entity. The district court found, however, that Guenther participated in the control of the business. We review this factual finding for clear error, and we find none.

This determination, however, does not complete our inquiry. Guenther can only be held liable as a general partner to persons who "transact business with the limited partnership reasonably believing, based on the limited partner's conduct, that the limited partner *is* a general partner." A.R.S. § 29-319(A) (emphasis added). This statute, derived from § 303 of the Revised Uniform Limited Partnership Act ("RULPA"), is related to the same legal principle as the agency concept of apparent authority. *See, e.g.,* Restatement (Third) of Agency §§ 2.03, 3.03. Someone who actually knows (or should know, by virtue of the nature of his relationship with the person) that a person is not a general partner cannot transmute that person into a general partner of the limited partnership based upon that person's conduct. Both the evolution of A.R.S. § 29-319 and § 303 of the RULPA (amended 1985) on which it is based support this reading of the statute. The original version of A.R.S. § 29-319 was almost identical to the 1976 version of RULPA § 303(a). *Gateway Potato Sales v. G.B. Inv. Co.,* 170 Ariz. 137, 822 P.2d 490, 496 (Ariz. App. 1991). In 1982, the second sentence of A.R.S. § 29-319(a) provided:

> However, if the limited partner's participation in the control of the business is not substantially the same as the exercise of the powers of a general partner, he is liable only to persons who transact business with the limited partnership with actual knowledge of his participation in control.

Thus, under the 1982 statute, if a limited partner exercised substantially the same powers as a general partner, he could be liable as a general partner. *See Gateway Potato Sales,* 822 P.2d at 497.

Following *Gateway Potato Sales,* however, the Arizona legislature amended A.R.S. § 29-319(A) to conform with the 1985 version of § 303(a) of RULPA. The current version substantially changed the second sentence of the former statute. The drafters of RULPA explained:

> [The 1985 version of § 303] was adopted partly because of the difficulty of determining when the "control" line has been overstepped, but also (and more importantly) because of the determination that it is not sound public policy to hold a limited partner who is not also a general partner liable for the obligations of the partnership except to persons who have done business with the limited partnership reasonably believing, based on the limited partner's conduct, that he is a general partner.

RULPA § 303 cmt. By adopting the language "reasonably believing . . . that the limited partner is a general partner," the drafters restricted the liability of limited partners to third party creditors to situations where the third party was misled about the limited partner's actual status and potential liability.

Were a different creditor involved, Guenther's conduct may have been enough to support the conclusion that a third party reasonably believed that he was a general partner of the CORF entities. Here, however, such a holding would be perverse because Shimko acted as legal counsel to both the CORF entities and the Guenthers, and owed a fiduciary duty of care to each.

Timothy Shimko and other members of his law firm are members of the Ohio State Bar Association, but the record shows that at least Timothy Shimko was also admitted *pro hac vice* in Arizona to defend the CORF entities and the Defendants. According to A.R.S. Rules of the Supreme Court of Arizona, Rule 46(b), by being admitted *pro hac vice,* Timothy Shimko and Shimko agreed to abide by the rules applicable to members of the State Bar of Arizona.

It is well-settled under the rules of both the Arizona and Ohio bars that a lawyer owes his or her client a fiduciary duty. *See, e.g., In re Piatt,* 191 Ariz. 24, 951 P.2d 889, 891 (1997) ("A lawyer is a fiduciary with a duty of loyalty, care, and obedience to the client."); *Adams v. Fleck,* 154 N.E.2d 794, 799-800 (Ohio Prob. 1958) ("The very existence of the relationship of attorney and client raises a presumption that relations of trust and confidence exist between the parties, and a presumption of invalidity arises where an undue advantage is obtained by an attorney over his client."). The contours of this duty are laid out in the ethical rules governing the State Bar of Arizona and the Ohio State Bar Association, and, particularly relevant here, address competent representation, diligence, and necessary disclosures when conflicts of interest arise. *See, e.g.,* Arizona ER 1.1, 1.3, 1.7; A.R.S. Sup. Ct. R. 46(b); Ohio Rules Prof'l Conduct 1.1, 1.3, 1.7.[4]

---

[4]We note, without deciding, that the relevant state bar rules of ethics may preclude recovery where an attorney fails to adequately disclose a conflict of interest among clients. The record in this case is not clear whether Shimko obtained written waivers of conflict from the Guenthers, the CORF entities and the other Defendants in this case. The district court may wish to take these ethical rules into consideration when determining the recovery to which Shimko is entitled, if any.

In this case, Appellees' Response Brief states: "Shimko was asked to advise Dr. Guenther and the other owners on the extent of their individual and personal exposure, if any, beyond the protection offered to them by the limited partnership structure under which they owned and operated [the CORF entities]." One of the first acts of any competent lawyer or law firm hired under those circumstances should have been to review the organic documents of the potentially liable limited partnerships to determine whether all legal formalities had been followed and whether any limited partner, by his previous or current actions, might have exposed himself to liability under A.R.S. § 29-319. Had Shimko examined the CORF entities' organic documents, it would have observed that Guenther was listed as a limited partner, not as a general partner. Although Timothy Shimko claimed at trial that he never examined those documents, Shimko is chargeable with the knowledge of their contents. An attorney or law firm may not breach their fiduciary duty of care to their client and then hide behind their failure to fulfill that duty in order to qualify for a monetary recovery against their former client. Shimko knew (or by discharging the duty of care it owed to Guenther, would have known) that Guenther did not meet the definition of general partner as set forth in A.R.S. § 29-301(5).

Because Shimko knew, or should have learned by the discharge of his duty of care to his client, Guenther's actual status as a limited partner, we hold that Shimko could not have reasonably believed that Guenther was a general partner, whatever role Guenther played in the control of the business. We reverse the district court's finding that Guenther is liable as a general partner of either of the CORF entities. Accordingly, Guenther and his spouse are not personally liable for those attorneys' fees properly chargeable to the CORF entities.

. . .

IV. CONCLUSION

We reverse the district court's holding that the Guenthers are liable for legal fees owed by the CORF entities. We remand to the district court for further proceedings consistent with this opinion regarding Shimko's claims against the Guenthers for unjust enrichment and quantum meruit. We affirm the district court's denial of the Guenthers' motion for a new trial.

The parties shall each bear their own costs on appeal.

REVERSED in part, REMANDED in part, and AFFIRMED in part.

Post-Case Follow-Up

The control rule is a feature of RULPA-style regimes. Section 303 of the ULPA-2001 Act drops the control rule, stating in pertinent part as follows:

A limited partner is not personally liable, directly or indirectly, by way of contribution or otherwise, for a debt, obligation, or other liability of the limited partnership solely by reason of being a limited partner, even if the limited partner participates in the management and control of the limited partnership.

The Official Comments to this section explain this change, in part, by noting that, "in a world with LLPs, LLCs and, most importantly, LLLPs," the control rule has become an "anachronism." RUPA § 303 cmt. These Official Comments further note that the Act takes the next logical step in the evolution of the limited partner's liability by eliminating the control rule and providing a full shield against limited partner liability for obligations of the entity, whether or not the limited partnership is an LLLP or a 'standard' limited partnership formed under the 2001 Act.

Shimko v. Guenther: Real Life Applications

You represent Tom, a limited partner in Ace Auto, L.P., a limited partnership that operates a car repair shop. Fran is the general partner and is in charge of day-to-day operations. For most of the partnership's existence, Fran has been an exemplary general partner, spending long hours at the garage dealing with customers and repairing cars. Six months ago, however, Fran's work began to suffer due to personal problems. In response, Tom began spending long hours at the garage, looking over the business's books and records, and assuring customers that Ace would complete work on their cars. Two months ago, after Tom confonted Fran, Fran stopped working on cars and stormed out of the garage. Fran has not been seen since. Since that time, Tom has been working at the garage every day to try to keep the business afloat.

Carrie dropped her car off at Ace three months ago. (She owns a vintage car that Fran promised to restore.) For the first month, Carrie dealt with Fran, and was satisfied with Fran's progress. After Fran stormed off, however, Carrie became concerned. When she called for information, she spoke with Tom, who assured her that Ace would complete the job on time. For the past two months Tom has worked on Carrie's car (along with other Ace employees). During this time, Tom repeatedly assured Carrie that Ace would complete the job.

Unfortunately, it now appears that Ace will be unable to complete work on Carrie's car.

a. What risks, if any, did Tom take with his work at the garage and his dealings with Carrie?
b. Is there anything that Tom could have done to mitigate any risks?
c. Does Carrie's understanding of Tom's role at Ace matter? Why or why not?
d. Does it matter whether the relevant state's limited partnership statute follows RULPA or ULPA-2001? Why or why not?

Potential for Contractual Liability

A second wrinkle in limited partners' limited liability exists under both RULPA and ULPA-2001 style regimes, and it arises from the contractual nature of limited partnerships. A limited partner may incur personal liability as a result of contractually assumed obligations, despite the presence of a statutory liability shield. *See, e.g., In re LJM2 Co-Investment, L.P.*, 866 A.2d 762 (Del. Ch. 2004) (citing Delaware limited partnership act's policy of freedom of contract and maximum flexibility to deny motion to dismiss action against limited partners to recover monies owed on unsatisfied capital calls where general partner made capital calls pursuant to contractual provisions in partnership agreement).

G. PARTNERS' INTEREST IN THE LIMITED PARTNERSHIP

Distribution Rights Transferable, Status, Governance and Informational Rights Not Transferable

Under default rules, a partner's interest in a limited partnership is personal property. *See* RULPA §§ 701, 702 (discussing assignment of partnership interest); ULPA-2001 §§ 701, 702 (discussing transfer of transferable interest). That having been said, as is true of general partnerships, the assignment of an interest in a limited partnership does not entitle the assignee to become or to exercise any rights of a partner. *See* RULPA § 702; ULPA-2001 §§ 702(a)(3)(A) and (B). Instead, the assignee merely becomes entitled to receive any financial distributions that the original limited partner is (or becomes) entitled to receive. *See* ULPA-2001 § 702; RULPA § 702. The assignee may become a new limited partner if all other partners agree, if admission as a limited partner is allowed by limited partnership agreement, or as otherwise provided in the limited partnership statute. RULPA § 301; ULPA-2001 § 301. Just as with general partnerships, a judgment creditor of either a general or limited partner may obtain a charging order from a court so that any partner's distributions will be paid to the creditor until the judgment is satisfied. *See* RULPA § 703; ULPA-2001 § 703.

H. ALLOCATION OF PROFITS, LOSSES, AND DISTRIBUTIONS

Section 503 of the RULPA provides that the profits and losses shall be allocated among the partners in the manner provided in writing in the partnership agreement, and if the partnership agreement does not so provide in writing, profits and losses shall be allocated on the basis of value, as stated in partnership records, of the contributions made by each partner. RULPA § 503. While the ULPA-2001 does not contain a default rule referencing the allocations of profits and losses, it does contain a default rule regarding financial distributions. This rule provides that "[a]ny distribution by a limited partnership before its dissolution and winding up must be shared among the partners on the basis of the value, as stated in the required information when the limited partnership decides to make the distribution, of the contributions the limited partnership has received from each partner, except as necessary to comply with a transfer effective under Subsection 702 or charter order in effect under Subsection 703." ULPA-2001 § 503. As the allocation of profits and losses or distribution implicates tax, accounting, and other regulatory requirements, lawyers should be sure to consult rules from these substantive areas before making allocation decisions.

Limited Partnerships and Tax Shelters

To ensure that limited partnerships are not used solely (and, potentially, improperly) as tax shelters (vehicles which create losses for tax purposes, or that focus on tax savings rather than on profit making), provisions of the Tax Reform Act of 1986 limited the ability of limited partners to take advantage of losses sustained by the limited partnership. Losses of the partnership that are allocated to general partners may be used to offset income from any other source, whereas losses allocated to limited partners can now be used to offset only income received from other similar passive investments and only to the extent that limited partners are at risk, meaning to the extent of their contributions to the limited partnership entity. These rules are complicated, so be sure to obtain advice from an expert in partnership taxation before drafting limited partnership agreements or advising clients with respect to distributions.

I. ACTIONS BY LIMITED PARTNERS

If a limited partner has been directly injured by the limited partnership—for example, she is refused her statutorily granted right to inspect the books—the limited partner may institute an action to seek redress for the injury to her. This type of action is called a **direct action** because the limited partner has been directly injured. In some instances, however, the limited partnership itself is injured, but it refuses to enforce its own cause of action. For example, assume that a limited partnership loans $50,000 to one of the friends of a general partner. If the loan is not paid, the general partner may be reluctant to enforce a claim against his friend. The failure to enforce a claim, however, deprives the limited partnership of capital. In such a case, a limited partner may institute a **derivative suit** to enforce the obligation due to the limited partnership. The action is referred to as derivative because the limited partner is not suing for herself, but rather to enforce rights held by the partnership.

There are several requirements associated with derivative actions. For example, to ensure that individuals do not join partnerships solely to litigate actions, both the RULPA and the ULPA-2001 provide that the plaintiff partner must have been a partner at the time of the transaction at issue and must also be a partner at the time the action is commenced. *See* RULPA § 1002; ULPA-2001 § 903. In addition, a limited partner may institute a derivative action only if (i) the limited partner plaintiff first makes a demand on the general partners requesting that they cause the partnership to bring an action to enforce the right at issue, and the general partners wrongfully refuse to bring the action, or (ii) if the limited partner is able to demonstrate that efforts to cause the general partner(s) to bring the action are likely to be futile. *See* RULPA §§ 1001, 1003; ULPA-2001 § 902. (We discuss requirements associated with derivative actions in more detail in our chapter on corporations and shareholder actions (Chapter 9). If the derivative action is successful, the recovery will belong to the limited partnership, although the limited partner who brought the action may be reimbursed for expenses and attorneys' fees. RULPA § 1004.

J. PARTNER WITHDRAWAL AND DISSOLUTION AND WINDING UP OF LIMITED PARTNERSHIPS

1. Partner Withdrawal

Withdrawal of Limited Partners

According to RULPA § 603, a limited partner may withdraw from a limited partnership in accordance with the provisions of the limited partnership agreement. If the agreement does not specify such events, a limited partner may withdraw from the partnership upon giving six months' written notice to each general partner. *Id.* At the time of withdrawal, the withdrawing partner is entitled to receive any distribution to which she may be entitled under the terms of the agreement, and, if not otherwise provided, may receive the fair value of her interest in the limited partnership within a reasonable time after withdrawal, so long as partnership assets exceed liabilities (to ensure creditors are fully paid before distributions are paid to a limited partner). RULPA § 604. Because six months is a fairly lengthy notice period, the agreement may provide for a shorter period. The agreement may provide that a limited partner who wishes to sell her interest must first offer it to other existing partners. The limited partnership does not dissolve upon the death or withdrawal of a limited partner. Because limited partners are merely passive investors, their membership in the limited partnership is not critical to the operation of the partnership business, and thus they generally may withdraw from a limited partnership without causing a dissolution.

Under ULPA-2001, a limited partner does not have an automatic right to dissociate as a limited partner before the completion of the winding up of the limited partnership. *See* ULPA-2001 § 601. Instead, limited partner dissociation is addressed in ULPA-2001 § 601, which provides that dissociation occurs in the following circumstances:

(b) A person is dissociated as a limited partner when:

    (1) the limited partnership knows or has notice of the person's express will to withdraw as a limited partner, but, if the person has specified a withdrawal date later than the date the partnership knew or had notice, on that later date;

    (2) an event stated in the partnership agreement as causing the person's dissociation as a limited partner occurs;

    (3) the person is expelled as a limited partner pursuant to the partnership agreement;

    (4) the person is expelled as a limited partner by the affirmative vote or consent of all the other partners if:

        (A) it is unlawful to carry on the limited partnership's activities and affairs with the person as a limited partner;

        (B) there has been a transfer of all the person's transferable interest in the partnership, other than:

            (i) a transfer for security purposes; or

            (ii) a charging order in effect under Section 703 which has not been foreclosed;

        (C) the person is an entity and:

            (i) the partnership notifies the person that it will be expelled as a limited partner because the person has filed a statement of dissolution or the equivalent, the person has been administratively dissolved, the person's charter or the equivalent has been revoked, or the person's right to conduct business has been suspended by the person's jurisdiction of formation; and

            (ii) not later than 90 days after the notification, the statement of dissolution or the equivalent has not been withdrawn, rescinded, or revoked, the person has not been reinstated, or the person's charter or the equivalent or right to conduct business has not been reinstated; or

(D) the person is an unincorporated entity that has been dissolved and whose activities and affairs are being would up;

(5) on application by the limited partnership or a partner in a direct action under Section 901, the person is expelled as a limited partner by judicial order because the person:

(A) has engaged or is engaging in wrongful conduct that has affected adversely and materially, or will affect adversely and materially, the partnership's activities and affairs;

(B) has committed willfully or persistently, or is committing willfully and persistently, a material breach of the partnership agreement or the contractual obligation of good faith and fair dealing under Section 305(a); or

(C) has engaged or is engaging in conduct relating to the partnership's activities and affairs which makes it not reasonably practicable to carry on the activities and affairs with the person as a limited partner;

(6) in the case of an individual, the individual dies;

(7) in the case of a person that is a testamentary or inter vivos trust or is acting as a limited partner by virtue of being a trustee of such a trust, the trust's entire transferable interest in the limited partnership is distributed;

(8) in the case of a person that is an estate or is acting as a limited partner by virtue of being a personal representative of an estate, the estate's entire transferable interest in the limited partnership is distributed;

(9) in the case of a person that is not an individual, the existence of the person terminates;

(10) the limited partnership participates in a merger under [Article] 11 and:

(A) the partnership is not the surviving entity; or

(B) otherwise as a result of the merger, the person ceases to be a limited partner;

(11) the limited partnership participates in an interest exchange under [Article] 11 and, as a result of the interest exchange, the person ceases to be a limited partner;

(12) the limited partnership participates in a conversion under [Article] 11;

(13) the limited partnership participates in a domestication under [Article] 11 and, as a result of the domestication, the person ceases to be a limited partner; or

(14) the limited partnership dissolves and completes winding up.

ULPA-2001 § 601. If a limited partner dissociates (or is dissociated), the limited partner generally will not have further rights as a limited partner (though a deceased partner's representative may exercise certain rights). *See* ULPA-2001 §§ 602, 704. In addition, the limited partner's contractual obligation of good faith and fair dealing ends with regard to matters arising and events occurring after dissociation. ULPA-2001 § 602. Dissociation does not, however, discharge the former limited partner from any debt, obligation, or other liability to the limited partnership or the other partners that the dissociating limited partner incurred while still a limited partner. *Id.*

Withdrawal of General Partners

According to RULPA § 402, unless agreed otherwise by all partners in writing, the following are **events of withdrawal** of a general partner that will cause a dissolution of the partnership and its affairs to be wound up (as discussed below):

1. The general partner withdraws by giving written notice to the other partners; however, if this withdrawal violates the terms of the partnership agreement, which might specify a definite date of duration, the limited partnership can recover any damages from the general partner caused by this breach of agreement;

2. The general partner assigns all of her interest to an assignee;

3. The general partner is removed from the partnership in accordance with the terms of the partnership agreement (such as removal by a certain percentage of the limited partnership interests);

4. Unless allowed in writing in the partnership agreement, the general partner
    a. makes an assignment for the benefit of creditors;
    b. is adjudicated bankrupt; or
    c. files a petition under the Bankruptcy Act or consents to the appointment of a receiver for her property; or

5. The general partner dies (if she is a natural person) or is terminated or dissolved (if it is an entity).

See RULPA § 402.

An event of withdrawal of a general partner will not cause a dissolution if there is at least one other general partner and the written partnership agreement permits the business to be conducted by the remaining general partner or, if within 90 days after the withdrawal, *all* partners agree in writing to continue the partnership business and a new general partner is appointed, if needed. RULPA § 801. (Otherwise, the withdrawal of the general partner will cause a dissolution of the limited partnership and its affairs to be wound up, unless the partnership agreement provides otherwise. *Id.*) If the general partner withdraws in violation of the terms of the limited partnership agreement, she may be held liable for damages caused by this breach of agreement. *See* RULPA § 602.

Dissociation of general partners is discussed in §§ 603 and 604 of the ULPA-2001. Section 603 provides that a person is dissociated as a general partner in the following circumstances:

(1) the limited partnership knows or has notice of the person's express will to withdraw as a general partner, but, if the person has specified a withdrawal date later than the date the partnership knew or had notice, on that later date;

(2) an event stated in the partnership agreement as causing the person's dissociation as a general partner occurs;

(3) the person is expelled as a general partner pursuant to the partnership agreement;

(4) the person is expelled as a general partner by the affirmative vote or consent of all the other partners if:

(A) it is unlawful to carry on the limited partnership's activities and affairs with the person as a general partner;

(B) there has been a transfer of all the person's transferable interest in the partnership, other than:

(i) a transfer for security purposes; or

(ii) a charging order in effect under Section 703 which has not been foreclosed;

(C) the person is an entity and:

(i) the partnership notifies the person that it will be expelled as a general partner because the person has filed a statement of dissolution or the equivalent, the person has been administratively dissolved, the person's charter or the equivalent has been revoked, or the person's right to conduct business has been suspended by the person's jurisdiction of formation; and

(ii) not later than 90 days after the notification, the statement of dissolution or the equivalent has not been withdrawn, rescinded, or revoked, the person has not been reinstated, or the person's charter or the equivalent or right to conduct business has not been reinstated; or

(D) the person is an unincorporated entity that has been dissolved and whose activities and affairs are being wound up[4];

(5) on application by the limited partnership or a partner in a direct action under Section 901, the person is expelled as a general partner by judicial order because the person:

(A) has engaged or is engaging in wrongful conduct that has affected adversely and materially, or will affect adversely and materially, the partnership's activities and affairs;

(B) has committed willfully or persistently, or is committing willfully or persistently, a material breach of the partnership agreement or a duty or obligation under Section 409; or

(C) has engaged or is engaging in conduct relating to the partnership's activities and affairs which makes it not reasonably practicable to carry on the activities and affairs of the limited partnership with the person as a general partner;

(6) in the case of an individual:

(A) the individual dies;

(B) a guardian or general conservator for the individual is appointed; or

(C) a court orders that the individual has otherwise become incapable of performing the individual's duties as a general partner under this [act] or the partnership agreement;

(7) the person:

(A) becomes a debtor in bankruptcy;

(B) executes an assignment for the benefit of creditors; or

(C) seeks, consents to, or acquiesces in the appointment of a trustee, receiver, or liquidator of the person or of all or substantially all the person's property;

(8) in the case of a person that is a testamentary or inter vivos trust or is acting as a general partner by virtue of being a trustee of such a trust, the trust's entire transferable interest in the limited partnership is distributed;

(9) in the case of a person that is an estate or is acting as a general partner by virtue of being a personal representative of an estate, the estate's entire transferable interest in the limited partnership is distributed;

(10) in the case of a person that is not an individual, the existence of the person terminates;

(11) the limited partnership participates in a merger under [Article] 11 and:

(A) the partnership is not the surviving entity; or

(B) otherwise as a result of the merger, the person ceases to be a general partner;

---

[4]The version of the Uniform Limited Partnership Act posted to the ULC as of the date of this writing contains the word "would" instead of "wound." The authors have confirmed with ULC staff that this provision should contain the word "wound."

(12) the limited partnership participates in an interest exchange under [Article] 11 and, as a result of the interest exchange, the person ceases to be a general partner;

(13) the limited partnership participates in a conversion under [Article] 11;

(14) the limited partnership participates in a domestication under [Article] 11 and, as a result of the domestication, the person ceases to be a general partner; or

(15) the limited partnership dissolves and completes winding up.

As set forth in ULPA-2001 § 605, if a person is dissociated as a general partner, that person's right to act as general partner is terminated:

(a) If a person is dissociated as a general partner:

(1) the person's right to participate as a general partner in the management and conduct of the limited partnership's activities and affairs terminates;

(2) the person's duties and obligations as a general partner under Section 409 end with regard to matters arising and events occurring after the person's dissociation;

(3) the person may sign and deliver to the [secretary of state] for filing a statement of dissociation pertaining to the person and, at the request of the limited partnership, shall sign an amendment to the certificate of limited partnership which states that the person has dissociated as a general partner; and

(4) subject to Section 704 and [Article] 11, any transferable interest owned by the person in the person's capacity as a general partner immediately before dissociation is owned by the person solely as a transferee.

(b) A person's dissociation as a general partner does not of itself discharge the person from any debt, obligation, or other liability to the limited partnership or the other partners which the person incurred while a general partner.

The liability of a dissociating general partner is discussed in ULPA-2001 § 606 (power to bind and liability of person dissociated as general partner) and ULPA-2001 § 607 (liability of persons dissociated as general partner to other persons).

2. Dissolution

There are two types of dissolution of a limited partnership — nonjudicial and judicial. As the names indicate, nonjudicial dissolution occurs without the involvement of a court, and judicial dissolution involves court action. As noted above, limited partnerships do not automatically dissolve upon the withdrawal of a limited or even a general partner. *See* RULPA § 801. Instead, a limited partnership is dissolved, and its business affairs must be wound up under RULPA, only when one of the following events occurs:

1. at the time specified in the certificate of limited partnership;
2. upon the happening of events specified in writing in the partnership agreement;
3. written consent of all partners;
4. an event of withdrawal of the general partner unless there is at least one general partner to conduct the business and the written provisions of the partnership agreement permit the business of the limited partnerhsip to be carried on by the

remaining general partner and that partner does so, but the limited partnership is not dissolved and is not required to be wound up by reason of any event of withdrawl, if, within 90 days after withdrawal, all partners agree in writing to continue the business of the limited partnership and to the appointment of one or more additional general partners if necessary or desired; or

5. entry of a decree of judicial dissolution under § 802.

RULPA § 801.

Unless a general partner has wrongfully caused a dissolution (e.g., by withdrawing before the term set in the agreement), the general partner may wind up or liquidate the limited partnership by collecting its assets and completing its obligations. *See* RULPA §§ 803, 804. Otherwise, a court may oversee the winding up upon the application of any partner. *Id.* After creditors are paid (including partners' claims for reimbursement for expenses incurred or loans made on behalf of the partnership), partners and former partners will then receive any outstanding distributions. *See* RULPA § 804. Then partners will receive a return of their contributions and, finally, their profits. *Id.*

ULPA-2001 § 801(a) provides that a limited partnership is dissolved, and its activities and affairs must be wound up, upon the occurrence of any of the following events:

(1) an event or circumstance that the partnership agreement states causes dissolution;

(2) the affirmative vote or consent of all general partners and of limited partners owning a majority of the rights to receive distributions as limited partners at the time the vote or consent is to be effective;

(3) after the dissociation of a person as a general partner:

(A) if the partnership has at least one remaining general partner, the affirmative vote or consent to dissolve the partnership not later than 90 days after the dissociation by partners owning a majority of the rights to receive distributions as partners at the time the vote or consent is to be effective; or

(B) if the partnership does not have a remaining general partner, the passage of 90 days after the dissociation, unless before the end of the period:

(i) consent to continue the activities and affairs of the partnership and admit at least one general partner is given by limited partners owning a majority of the rights to receive distributions as limited partners at the time the consent is to be effective; and

(ii) at least one person is admitted as a general partner in accordance with the consent;

(4) the passage of 90 consecutive days after the dissociation of the partnership's last limited partner, unless before the end of the period the partnership admits at least one limited partner;

(5) the passage of 90 consecutive days during which the partnership has only one partner, unless before the end of the period:

(A) the partnership admits at least one person as a partner;

(B) if the previously sole remaining partner is only a general partner, the partnership admits the person as a limited partner; and

(C) if the previously sole remaining partner is only a limited partner, the partnership admits a person as a general partner;

(6) on application by a partner, the entry by [the appropriate court] of an order dissolving the partnership on the grounds that:

(A) the conduct of all or substantially all the partnership's activities and affairs is unlawful; or

(B) it is not reasonably practicable to carry on the partnership's activities and affairs in conformity with the certificate of limited partnership and partnership agreement; or

(7) the signing and filing of a statement of administrative dissolution by the [secretary of state] under Section 811.

ULPA-2001 § 801(a). The ULPA-2001 winding up regime is set forth in § 802 of the 2001 Act. It provides as follows, in pertinent part:

(b) In winding up its activities and affairs, the limited partnership:

(1) shall discharge the partnership's debts, obligations, and other liabilities, settle and close the partnership's activities and affairs, and marshal and distribute the assets of the partnership; and

(2) may

(A) amend its certificate of limited partnership to state that the partnership is dissolved;

(B) preserve the partnership activities, affairs, and property as a going concern for a reasonable time;

(C) prosecute and defend actions and proceedings, whether civil, criminal, or administrative;

(D) transfer the partnership's property;

(E) settle disputes by mediation or arbitration;

(F) deliver to the [Secretary of State] for filing a statement of termination stating the name of the partnership and that the partnership is terminated; and

(G) perform other acts necessary or appropriate to the winding up.

ULPA-2001 § 802(b).

When a limited partnership is dissolved and wound up, a certificate of cancellation must be filed with the secretary of state. It will contain basic information about the limited partnership, including the reason for discontinuance of the business. The certificate must be filed and signed by all general partners and must usually be accompanied by a filing fee. (Exhibit 5.3 provides a certificate of cancellation of limited partnership.) If the partnership is doing business in any other states, it should cancel or withdraw any applications in those foreign states.

EXHIBIT 5.3 Certificate of Cancellation of Limited Partnership

COMMONWEALTH OF VIRGINIA
STATE CORPORATION COMMISSION

LPA-73.52:4   **CERTIFICATE OF CANCELLATION**
(07/10)   **OF A VIRGINIA LIMITED PARTNERSHIP**

The undersigned, on behalf of the limited partnership set forth below, pursuant to Title 50, Chapter 2.1 of the Code of Virginia, state(s) as follows:

1. The name of the limited partnership is

    _____.

2. The effective date of the filing of the limited partnership's certificate of limited partnership with the State Corporation Commission was _____.

3. The certificate of cancellation is submitted for filing for the following reason(s):

    _____

4. The limited partnership has completed the winding up of its affairs.

5. Other information that the partners have determined to include herein, if any:

    _____

Signature(s) of **ALL** general partners:

_____	_____
(signature)	(date)
_____	_____
(printed name and title)	(telephone number (optional))
_____	_____
(signature)	(date)
_____	_____
(printed name and title)	(telephone number (optional))
_____	_____
(signature)	(date)
_____	_____
(printed name and title)	(telephone number (optional))

_____
(limited partnership's SCC ID No.)

PRIVACY ADVISORY: Information such as social security number, date of birth, maiden name, or financial institution account numbers is NOT required to be included in business entity documents filed with the Office of the Clerk of the Commission. Any information provided on these documents is subject to public viewing.

SEE INSTRUCTIONS ON THE REVERSE

Provide a name and mailing address for sending correspondence regarding the filing of this document. (If left blank, correspondence will be sent to the registered agent at the registered office.)

_____
(name)

_____
(mailing address)

K. FAMILY LIMITED PARTNERSHIPS

During the 1990s, following an IRS Revenue Ruling relating to valuation discounts (*see* IRS Rev. Rul. 93-12), so-called **family limited partnerships** gained attention as an estate planning tool. Family limited partnerships (sometimes called "FLiPs") and **family limited liability companies** are like any other partnership or LLC as a legal matter. The reference to "family" simply reflects the fact that partners/members are family members (or spouses of family members). In most cases, parents act as general partners, and children and other family members are limited partners. With FLiPs and family LLCs, partners/members place property (e.g., a family farm, rental property, or securities) in the partnership or LLC, then claim a **minority discount** for the gifts of limited partner interests to children. *See* Ray D. Madoff, Cornelia R. Tenney & Martin A. Hall, *Practical Guide to Estate Planning* § 807[b] (Aspen Publishers 2001). From a tax and estate planning perspective, FLiPs and family limited liability companies are attractive because they have the potential to reduce the transfer tax burden of passing property to children. *See, e.g., Estate of Jones v. Comm'r*, 116 T.C. 121 (2001). Lawyers recommending these structures should proceed with care, however, and should be well versed in topics such as partnership and gift taxation, due to the potential for complexity and IRS scrutiny. (For example, while transferring minority interests in a family limited partnership can be an effective way to reduce the gift tax value of transferred property, the IRS may challenge taxpayers' valuation of the property if the transfer lacks economic substance and occurs solely for tax planning purposes. *See* Madoff, Tenney & Hall, *supra*.) So, once again, we urge you to take advanced business entity tax classes before working with FLiPs or family LLCs.

L. MASTER LIMITED PARTNERSHIPS

Another relatively new variation of limited partnership is the master limited partnership (MLP), which

FLiPs versus Family LLCs

To avoid the risk of unlimited personal liability, parents serving as general partners are well advised to consider using an entity general partner. The family LLC form arguably is simpler in this regard, in that parent-members enjoy the protections of the LLC liability shield even if they manage the affairs of the family LLC. Lawyers and clients choosing between the limited partnership and LLC forms should consider tax, estate planning, and any other relevant goals.

What is a Minority Discount?

For present purposes, the term minority discount refers to a discount applied when valuing a minority or non-controlling interest in a closely held enterprise. When valuing an interest in a partnership, LLC, closely held corporation or other similar business entity, the first step typically is to calculate the fair market value of the underlying assets held by the entity. For highly marketable securities (e.g., the stock of a publicly held company), the analysis is fairly straightforward — i.e., examine the price at which the security trades on the day or during the period called for by an appropriate valuation methodology. For a closely held business, however, it can be more difficult to determine fair market value. This is because interests in closely held enterprises generally are not highly marketable due to statutory and negotiated restrictions on transfer. Once the fair market value of the underlying assets has been determined, a discount analysis is performed to arrive at the fair market value of the interests being gifted, typically the limited partnership interests. The two discounts applied most often in the family limited partnership context are (i) minority interest (also called the non-controlling interest), and (ii) lack of marketability. The minority interest discount reflects the degree of control or influence inherent in the transferred interest. Put simply, a minority or non-controlling interest in a closely held enterprise tends to be worth less than a controlling interest in the enterprise. The lack of marketability discount corresponds to the transferred interest's degree of liquidity. A minority or non-controlling interest in a closely held enterprise tends to be harder to sell, and thus less marketable, than a controlling interest.

is a limited partnership (or, less commonly, a limited liability company) formed under state law that is publicly traded and listed on a national securities exchange. MLPs were first recognized in 1981. In 1987, Congress passed legislation restricting MLPs, the effect of which was to limit MLPs to certain types of industries (primarily those in the energy and natural resources fields). The general partner manages the entity and typically owns a 2 percent interest in the entity with a right to receive additional distributions if the entity performs well. The limited partners, who are often called "unitholders," provide capital and receive quarterly distributions. The MLP has the pass-through taxation of a partnership and is a popular vehicle because of its ability to raise capital from a broad range of investors who then receive regular cash distributions. Because the entities are publicly traded, they must comply with securities laws. (See Chapter 13.) As of 2013, there were about 130 publicly traded MLPs with a total market capitalization of $445 billion. Nearly 90 percent of the MLPs are in the energy and natural resources industries.

M. LIMITED LIABILITY LIMITED PARTNERSHIPS

Under new statutory provisions in the ULPA-2001 Act, several states allow a limited partnership to file a registration statement with the secretary of state to elect to be classified as a **limited liability limited partnership** (LLLP). The usual procedure is that the certificate of limited partnership requires the filer to state whether the entity is being organized as a "standard" limited partnership or as a limited liability limited partnership. See Exhibit 5.4 for a sample filing. This requirement is intended to force the organizers to affirmatively decide whether the entity is to be a conventional limited partnership or an LLLP, the effect of which is that the general partners then have limited liability for partnership debts and obligations, making their liability equivalent to that of limited partners. Alternatively, a limited partnership may convert or change its status to an LLLP.

If such an election is made, the general partners are relieved of any personal liability for the limited partnership's debts or obligations, which then must be satisfied solely from the assets of the limited partnership itself. These changes are significant and substantive and are designed to ameliorate the effects of current

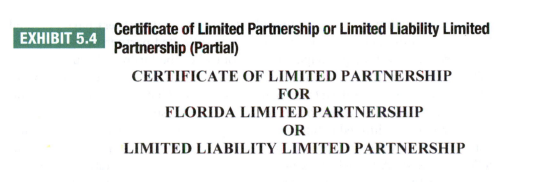

EXHIBIT 5.4 **Certificate of Limited Partnership or Limited Liability Limited Partnership (Partial)**

CERTIFICATE OF LIMITED PARTNERSHIP
FOR
FLORIDA LIMITED PARTNERSHIP
OR
LIMITED LIABILITY LIMITED PARTNERSHIP

1._____.

(Name of Limited Partnership or Limited Liability Limited Partnership, *which must include suffix*)
Acceptable Limited Partnership suffixes: Limited Partnership, Limited, L.P., LP, or Ltd.
Acceptable Limited Liability Limited Partnership suffixes: Limited Liability Limited Partnership, L.L.L.P.
or LLLP.

2._____

(Street address of initial designated office)

_____

3._____

(Name of Registered Agent for Service of Process)

4._____

(Florida street address for Registered Agent)

_____

5. *I hereby accept the appointment as registered agent and agree to act in this capacity. I further agree to comply with the provisions of all statutes relative to the proper and complete performance of my duties, and I am familiar with and accept the obligations of my position as registered agent.*

_____

Signature of Registered Agent

6._____

(Mailing address of initial designated office)

_____

7. If limited partnership elects to be a limited liability limited partnership, check box ☐

Page 1 of 2

limited partnership laws, which provide that (i) general partners have personal liability for entity debts and obligations; and (ii) limited partners may lose their protected status if they participate in the control of the business in jurisdictions following the control rule discussion in Section F.2 above. The election to be an LLLP recognizes the modern trend of limiting personal liability and places general partners and limited partners on an equal footing with shareholders in a corporation, partners in a limited liability partnership, and members of a limited liability company, all of whom are protected from personal liability. In jurisdictions that follow the RULPA (which does not contain specific statutory authorization for LLLPs), partners may choose to register their limited partnership as a limited liability partnership (LLP) to ensure that all partners will enjoy the protection of a liability shield.

N. FOREIGN LIMITED PARTNERSHIPS

A limited partnership formed under the laws of one state may decide to expand its operations and conduct business in another state. A limited partnership formed in one state and doing business in another is referred to as a **foreign limited partnership** by the second state, inasmuch as it was not originally created in the second state. In its original state of formation, it is referred to as a **domestic limited partnership**.

To protect its citizens, a state can require that a foreign limited partnership apply to do business within its borders. *See* RUPA § 902; ULPA-2001 § 1002 (requirement of registration), § 1003 (foreign registration statement). Many activities, such as bringing or defending a lawsuit, holding meetings, or engaging in an isolated transaction may not be considered "**doing business**" such that an application must be filed in the other state. ULPA-2001 § 1005. As always, check state statutes to determine which activities require the foreign limited partnership to apply to do business.

In the application, the foreign limited partnership generally must appoint an agent for service of process so that any citizens injured by acts of the limited partnership in that state will be able to bring claims against the limited partnership. RULPA § 902 sets forth the elements to be included in an application. *See also* ULPA-2001 § 1003. In many respects, the application mimics the requirements of a certificate of limited partnership. Further, a limited partnership conducting business in another state generally will be required to comply with all of that state's laws, for example, any laws relating to the requirement of the words "limited partnership" or the abbreviation "L.P." in the business name. Exhibit 5.5 provides a sample application for registration of a foreign limited partnership. Amendment of the

EXHIBIT 5.5 **Foreign Limited Partnership Application**

060203

BARBARA K. CEGAVSKE
Secretary of State
202 North Carson Street
Carson City, Nevada 89701-4201
(775) 684-5708
Website: www.nvsos.gov

Application for Registration of Foreign Limited Partnership
(PURSUANT TO NRS CHAPTER 87A)

USE BLACK INK ONLY - DO NOT HIGHLIGHT   ABOVE SPACE IS FOR OFFICE USE ONLY

1. Name of Foreign Limited Partnership:	
2. Name Being Registered with Nevada: (see instructions)	
3. Date and State or Country of Formation:	Date Formed State or Country where Authorized ☐ This entity is in good standing in the jurisdiction of its incorporation/creation.
4. Registered Agent for Service of Process: (check only one box)	☐ Commercial Registered Agent: Name ☐ Noncommercial Registered Agent (name and address below) **OR** ☐ Office or Position with Entity (name and address below) Name of Noncommercial Registered Agent **OR** Name of Title of Office or Other Position with Entity Street Address City Nevada Zip Code Mailing Address (if different from street address) City Nevada Zip Code This Foreign Limited Partnership hereby undertakes to keep a list of the names and addresses of the limited partners and their capital contributions at this office until its registration in Nevada is canceled or withdrawn. In the event the above-designated Agent for Service of Process resigns and is not replaced or the agent's authority has been revoked or the agent cannot be found or served with exercise of reasonable diligence, then the Secretary of State is hereby appointed as the Agent for Service of Process.
5. Street Address of Principal Office: (see instructions)	Street Address City State Zip Code
6. Name and Business Address of each General Partner: (attach additional page if more than 2)	1) Name Business Address City State Zip Code 2) Name Business Address City State Zip Code
7. Name and Signature of General Partner Making Statement:	I hereby declare and affirm under the penalties of perjury that I am a General Partner in the above-named Foreign Limited Partnership and that the execution of this application for registration is my act and deed and that the facts stated herein are true. I also declare, to the best of my knowledge under penalty of perjury, that the information contained herein is correct and acknowledge that pursuant to NRS 239.330, it is a category C felony to knowingly offer any false or forged instrument for filing in the Office of the Secretary of State. **X** Name Authorized Signature
8. Certificate of Acceptance of Appointment of Registered Agent:	*I hereby accept appointment as Registered Agent for the above named Entity.* **X** Authorized Signature of Registered Agent or On Behalf of Registered Agent Entity Date

This form must be accompanied by appropriate fees.

Reset

Nevada Secretary of State NRS 87A FLP Registration
Revised: 1-5-15

application will be required in the event of changes in the foreign limited partnership that make the application inaccurate, and the application should be canceled or withdrawn when the foreign limited partnership ceases to do business in the foreign state.

O. UNIFORM LIMITED PARTNERSHIP ACT OF 2001

As discussed above, the ULC substantially revised the limited partnership model act in 2001, when it adopted the ULPA-2001 Act. For reference, we have summarized certain provisions of the 2001 Act below:

- *Full liability shield for general partners with LLLP election.* As discussed above, one of the disadvantages for a general partner in a limited partnership under the RULPA is the unlimited personal liability for debts and obligations of the limited partnership. The 2001 Act provides for the possibility of a liability shield for general partners through the election of the limited liability limited partnership (LLLP) form. *See* ULPA-2001 § 201(b)(5). If such an election is made, the general partners will be shielded from any personal liability, and any debts or obligations of the limited partnership, whether arising in tort or in contract, must be satisfied solely by the limited partnership itself. ULPA 2001 § 404(c).
- *Full liability shield for limited partners; control rule dropped.* Whereas the RULPA position is that a limited partner is shielded from personal liability only if he does not participate in the control of the limited partnership, the 2001 Act provides that a limited partner is not personally liable for any obligation of the limited partnership even if the limited partner participates in the management and control of the business. *See* ULPA-2001 § 303(a). This full shield for limited partners applies whether or not the limited partnership has elected to be a limited liability limited partnership.
- *Perpetual duration.* Under the RULPA, the latest date for dissolution of the limited partnership is required to be set forth in the certificate of limited partnership. *See* RULPA § 201(a)(4). Under the 2001 Act, a limited partnership has perpetual duration (although the partnership agreement can vary this by providing for an express term or by specifying events that would cause dissolution).
- *Use of limited partner's name.* The RULPA prohibits the use of a limited partner's name in the business name except in certain narrow circumstances. The 2001 Act, however, allows the use of any partner's name in the limited partnership's name. *See* ULPA-2001 § 114(a).
- *Annual report.* The 2001 Act requires the limited partnership to file an annual report with the secretary of state providing basic information about the limited partnership. *See* ULPA-2001 §§ 212, 811, and 1010. No such annual report is required under the RULPA.

■ *Dissolution by consent.* The RULPA allows a limited partnership to dissolve and wind up at any time upon the written consent of all partners. The 2001 Act provides that the limited partnership may be dissolved and wound up upon consent of all general partners and of limited partners owning a majority of the rights to receive distributions as a limited partner at the time the vote or consent is to be effective. *See* ULPA-2001 § 801(a)(2).

■ *Transfers of interests.* The provisions of the RULPA relating to transfers of partnership interests are substantially the same in the 2001 Act; thus, a partner's rights to financial distributions are fully transferable, although the transferee does not become a partner with rights to manage or control merely by virtue of the transfer. *See* ULPA-2001 § 702.

We also have included a chart highlighting some of the distinctions between RULPA and ULPA-2001 in the quick reference section below.

P. QUICK REVIEW: SUMMARY CHARTS

EXHIBIT 5.6   **Quick Guide to Partnership Forms**

General Partnerships	Limited Partnerships	Limited Liability Limited Partnerships
Most states follow 1997 Revised Uniform Partnership Act (RUPA in this text); a minority follow 1914 Act (UPA in this text).	Most states follow Revised Uniform Limited Partnership Act of 1976 (with 1985 Amendments) (RULPA in this text).	Twenty jurisdictions follow ULPA-2001. Some other states recognize the LLLP form without adopting the 2001 Act.
Formed by agreement (written or oral)	Formed by filing certificate of LP	Formed by filing certificate of LP
All partners are general partners.	Has general and limited partners	Has general and limited partners
All partners may control.	Only general partners may control.	All partners may control.
All partners have unlimited joint and several personal liability.	Only general partners have personal liability.	No partners have personal liability.
NOTE: Partners in limited liability partnerships enjoy a liability shield as discussed in Chapter 4.		

EXHIBIT 5.7	Quick Guide to Differences Between Limited Partnership Uniform Acts

	RULPA	2001 Act
Relationship to general partnership act	Linked, RUPA §§ 1105, 403; UPA § 6(2)	De-linked, though many RULPA provisions are incorporated
Status of entity	Entity must be a limited partnership with full liability for general partners.	Entity may elect to be a limited liability limited partnership and thereby eliminate personal liability of general partners and provide full liability shield to both general and limited partners.
Duration	Certificate of limited partnership must provide latest date for dissolution.	A limited partnership has perpetual duration.
Limited partner's name	Limited partner's name cannot be used in name of entity except in limited circumstances.	Any partner's name may be used in entity's name.
Annual report	There is no requirement of filing an annual report.	An annual report must be filed with secretary of state.
Profits and losses/ distributions	Unless agreed in writing otherwise, profits and losses will be divided according to contributions of partners made and not returned.	Unless agreed in writing otherwise, distributions will be divided according to contributions of partners.
Liability of general partners	General partners have full, inescapable personal liability for obligations of the limited partnership.	If the entity elects to be a limited liability limited partnership, the general partner will not be personally liable for obligations of the limited partnership.
Liability of limited partners	Limited partners are protected from personal liability for entity debts unless they "participate in the control of the business" and a person "transacts business with the limited partnership reasonably believing . . . that the limited partner is a general partner. . . ."	Limited partners are protected from personal liability even if they participate in management and control of the business.

EXHIBIT 5.7 (continued)

	RULPA	2001 Act
Limited partner duties	None specified	No fiduciary duties "solely by reason of being a limited partner," but each limited partner is obligated to "discharge duties . . . and exercise rights consistently with the obligation of good faith and fair dealing."
Transfer of interests	Rights to distributions are fully transferable although transferee does not become a partner by virtue of the transfer.	Rights to distributions are fully transferable although transferee does not become a partner by virtue of the transfer.
Dissociation of limited partner	Limited partner may withdraw upon six months' notice unless partnership agreement provides a term or provides otherwise.	Limited partner does not have absolute right to dissociate before termination of the limited partnership. Limited partner may give notice of will to withdraw, but such withdrawal is wrongful.
Dissolution	Withdrawal of limited partner does not automatically cause dissolution and winding up. Withdrawal of a general partner does not cause dissolution if agreement allows continuation or if all partners agree in writing to continue.	Dissociation of limited partner does not automatically cause dissolution and winding up. Dissociation of a general partner does not cause a dissolution if, generally within 90 days, majority agree to continuation of business.
Partner access to information; required records information	All partners have right of access, with no requirement of good cause. Act does not state whether partnership agreement may limit access.	The list of required information is slightly expanded compared to RULPA. Act states that partners do not need to show good cause for inspection; however, the partnership agreement may set reasonable restrictions on access to and use of required information.

EXHIBIT 5.8	Comparison of General and Limited Partnerships	
	General Partnerships Under RUPA	**Limited Partnerships Under RULPA**
Formation	Informal formation, no formal state filings required; agreement may be oral or written.	Must file certificate of limited partnership with secretary of state. Agreement may be oral or written, although it is usually written.
Ownership	Unlimited number of general partners permissible	Must have at least one general partner and one limited partner
Management	Unless otherwise agreed, all partners share equal rights to management.	Only general partners manage the business. Limited partners may not manage or control the business or they risk loss of limited liability status.
Profits and losses	Unless otherwise agreed, profits and losses are divided equally among all partners.	Unless otherwise agreed in writing, profits and losses are divided according to contributions to limited partnership.
Liability	All general partners have unlimited, joint and several personal liability.	Only general partners have personal liability. Limited partners are liable only to the extent of their contributions to the entity.
Dissolution	Many events of dissociation merely trigger a buyout of the dissociating partner's interest and partnership continues.	Death or assignment of limited partner does not dissolve entity. Entity can survive withdrawal or death of general partner if agreement provides or if all partners agree in writing to continue the entity.
Taxation	Pass-through tax status afforded to all partners.	Pass-through tax status afforded to all partners.

Chapter Summary

■ Limited partnerships are partnerships with two different types of partners — general partners and limited partners.
■ General partners in a limited partnership are like general partners in a general partnership — they have equal rights in the conduct of partnership affairs, and they suffer the disadvantage of unlimited personal liability for partnership obligations and debts.

- Limited partners are passive investors: They do not have the right to manage partnership affairs, and they do not have personal liability for the limited partnership's obligations (so long as they do not participate in the control of the business under RULPA-style regimes). RULPA-2001 drops the control rule.
- Formation of limited partnerships requires filing a certificate of limited partnership with the appropriate state agency.
- Limited partnerships must have at least one general partner and one limited partner.
- Limited partnership statutes give partners flexibility to customize most rules to meet business needs, and as between the limited partnership statute and the partnership agreement, the partnership agreement generally governs.
- Limited partnerships are eligible for pass-through taxation under default rules.

Applying the Concepts

Mia, Amanda, Alex, and Daniel have formed a limited partnership in compliance with the relevant state's LP act. Mia is the general partner, and Amanda, Alex, and Daniel are the limited partners. Mia contributed $40,000 to the limited partnership, and each of the limited partners contributed $20,000. Although the partners have a limited partnership agreement, it is silent on several issues. Use the RULPA and the ULPA-2001 Act to answer the following questions.

a. The agreement does not discuss the admission of new partners. If the limited partnership would like to admit a new general partner, how would this be accomplished?

b. Alex has begun dropping by the partnership office and has engaged in the following acts: informing Mia that the partnership should hire additional employees; contacting the partnership's customers to inquire whether they need additional services; and proposing that the limited partnership certificate be amended. Discuss whether these activities are permissible, and whether Alex could incur liability for any of these acts.

c. Daniel would like to transfer or assign his partnership interest to his sister, Emily. The partnership agreement is silent on the issue of assignments. May Daniel assign his interest? If so, what rights will Emily have?

d. The partnership agreement is silent on the issue of division of profits and losses. The partnership made $200,000 in profits this year. How will those profits be allocated? Is the partnership required to distribute profits to the partners? Who has the right to decide whether distributions will be made?

e. Assume that the partnership owes a creditor $500,000. The partnership has $60,000 in its bank accounts. From which sources may the creditor recover the debt?

f. Are your answers to Questions b and e different depending on whether you use the RULPA on the ULPA-2001? Why or why not? Discuss.

Business Organizations in Practice

1. You are an associate at a law firm. You represent Bill, a wealthy and successful business person who is considering investing in Ventures, L.P., a new investment fund being established by Ventures, LLC, a venture capital firm. Although Bill is fabulously wealthy, he is new to venture capital investing and to the limited partnership form. Bill wants to invest capital in Ventures, L.P., but does not anticipate serving as the General Partner. (Ventures, LLC will serve in this role.) Draft a memo to Bill explaining the governance and liability rules of limited partnerships in your home jurisdiction, addressing at least the following questions: (i) will Bill have the right to weigh in on partnership business; (ii) how will profits and losses be allocated to Bill and the other limited partners; (iii) what happens if Bill wishes to withdraw from the partnership; (iv) can Bill invest in other venture capital funds, even if those funds end up competing with Venture, L.P.?

   For extra credit, research the governance and liability rules in California, Connecticut, New York, Texas, Washington (State), and North Carolina, as these are jurisdictions where the venture capital and private equity industries are particularly robust.

2. After you and Bill meet to discuss your memo, Bill asks you what due diligence, if any, he should do before committing his capital to Ventures, L.P. What do you suggest?

3. After performing due diligence, you discover that Ventures, L.P. intends to invest heavily in the biotechnology sphere, with a particular focus on gene and stem cell therapies. Bill is excited about this type of business because he has worked in biotechnology for more than 20 years, but he is mindful of the fact that investing in new and unproven medical technologies can be risky for investors. Bill also is aware of potential risks to patients who participate in medical trials. Bill explains that he is concerned that he will become a target for tort claims, given his wealth, should he invest in Ventures, L.P. Is Bill right to be concerned? Are there circumstances under which Bill could become personally liable for entity debts or obligations? What advice, if any, would you give Bill to mitigate his risks? Does it matter whether Ventures, L.P. is a RULPA-style limited partnership? A ULPA-2001-style partnership? A limited liability limited partnership?

4. For purposes of this question, you represent Ventures, LLC. Ventures wishes to preserve its ability to form future venture capital funds to invest in the biotechnology sphere. These future funds could compete with Ventures, L.P. for investment opportunities. Recommend a state of formation for Ventures, L.P. in your role as Ventures, LLC's counsel. Draft proposed language for the limited partnership agreement concerning Ventures, LLC's fiduciary obligations, if any, to Ventures, L.P.

5. After Bill invests in Ventures, L.P. (which was formed as a Delaware limited partnership), he learns that Ventures, LLC intends to form several additional venture funds, all of which are likely to invest in early-stage biotechnology companies. Bill is concerned that Ventures, LLC might prefer its newer funds. Does Ventures, LLC owe fiduciary duties of loyalty or care to Ventures, L.P.?

Introduction to Business Corporations

As you will recall from Chapter 1, a business corporation is a for-profit enterprise that has filed articles of incorporation with a state secretary of state office. In this first chapter on corporations, we focus on key characteristics of the corporate form and formation mechanics — for example, selecting a jurisdiction for incorporation, choosing a name, preparing and filing articles of incorporation, holding the first organizational meeting, and so forth. We discuss corporate finance basics, corporate governance, closely held corporations, minority shareholder protections, and public company regulation in subsequent chapters.

A. WHAT IS A CORPORATION?

A **corporation** is a business enterprise that has filed a **certificate of incorporation** (also known as **articles of incorporation** or **corporate charter**) with the appropriate state office — typically, the state secretary of state. Although there are many different types of corporations — for example, not-for-profit corporations and professional corporations — we will focus on business corporations in this chapter. To provide some

Key Concepts

- Definition and attributes of business corporations
- Taxation of business corporations
- Law governing the formation and internal affairs of business corporations
- Mechanics of forming a business corporation

context for our discussion, we begin with a brief description of key attributes of business corporations:

- Corporations have a legal status, or **legal personality**, that is separate from the legal identity and personality of the corporation's owners, who are known as **shareholders** or **stockholders**. (In fact, the root word for *incorporate* is *corpus*, Latin for *body*.) Indeed, even a corporation with a single shareholder exists as a "legal person" separate and apart from its shareholder/owner. The attribute of legal personality means that corporations enjoy (i) continuity of existence, or the ability to remain in existence even if owners die, sell their shares, file for bankruptcy protection, etc.; and (ii) legal capacity, including the right to hold assets in the name of the corporation, to enter into contracts, to sue or be sued, etc.

- Corporations have a **centralized management structure** whereby the business and affairs of the corporation are managed by a **board of directors**. The corporation's **shareholders** have the power to elect directors, but they do not (in their role as shareholders) have the right to control the business or affairs of the corporation or participate in day-to-day management of the enterprise.

- Directors and officers owe **fiduciary duties of loyalty and care** to the corporation and its shareholders.

- Shareholders enjoy **limited liability**. Absent fraud or other wrongful conduct justifying piercing the corporate veil (as discussed in Chapter 1), a corporation's shareholders are not personally liable for the debts or obligations of the enterprise.

- Corporations are **creatures of statute**. They must be formed (and dissolved) in accordance with statutory requirements, and they are subject to a range of statutory rules having to do with management and governance, many of which are mandatory.

Along with these attributes, here are a few other terms and definitions to get started:

- A corporation is a **domestic corporation** in the state in which it is incorporated. For example, See's Candy Shops, Inc. was incorporated in California. In California, See's is a domestic corporation.

- A corporation formed in one state and doing business in a state other than or in addition to its state of incorporation is a **foreign corporation** in the second state. Thus, See's Candy Shop, Inc. is a domestic corporation in California, where it was formed (and also transacts business), but a foreign corporation in Nevada, where it transacts business.

- A corporation that wishes to transact business in states other than its state of incorporation does not have an automatic right to operate in those other states. Instead, the corporation must **qualify to transact business** in those states. This generally involves filing paperwork with the secretary of state in the other states, paying filing and other fees, appointing an agent for service of process within the foreign jurisdiction, and the like.

- **Public corporations** (also known as **publicly held** or **publicly traded** corporations) are corporations that have offered their securities for sale to the public in accordance with the federal securities laws, and whose securities trade on the open market. For example, in May 2012, Facebook, Inc. conducted an initial public offering (IPO) of its shares—a process colloquially referred to as "going public." Shares of Facebook now trade on the open market, making Facebook a publicly traded corporation.

■ A **privately held** corporation is a corporation that has not offered its stock for sale to the public at large, and whose shares do not trade on the open market. It is usually the case that privately held corporations have fewer shareholders compared to publicly held corporations.

Corporations and the U.S. Economy

Corporations are enormously important to the U.S. economy. In 2011, for example, corporations reported approximately $28.3 trillion in business receipts, compared to $6 trillion for partnerships and $1.3 trillion for sole proprietorships. See Exhibit 6.1 for a chart showing corporate profits in the United States.

■ While not statutorily defined, the term **closely held corporation** (or **close corporation**) is used to refer to a corporation (i) with relatively few shareholders; (ii) whose shares are not freely traded; and (iii) whose shareholder/owners also control the business and affairs of the enterprise. *See, e.g., Donahue v. Rodd Electrotype Co.*, 328 N.E. 505, 511 (Mass. 1975). A **statutory close corporation** is an entity with a small number of shareholders (typically 50, or even fewer) formed pursuant to a state close corporation statute. *See, e.g.,* Del. Code Ann. tit. 8, §§ 341, 342. In general, statutory provisions and common law rules applicable to closely held corporations and statutory close corporations give these enterprises comparatively greater flexibility with regard to formalities and governance compared to non-closely held corporations—for example, by providing that the business and affairs of the corporation may be managed by its shareholders rather than a board of directors. *See, e.g., id.* § 351.

■ A corporation that creates another corporation—often to operate a particular business—is called a **parent corporation**. Typically, the parent will own all or the vast majority of the stock of the **subsidiary** (the corporation that it formed). The expression **wholly owned subsidiary** refers to a subsidiary corporation whose stock is owned entirely by its parent.

EXHIBIT 6.1   **Corporations: Profits (Before Tax in $ Billions)**

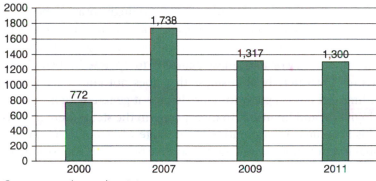

Corporations: Profits (Before Tax in $ Billions)

Source: www.irs.gov/taxstats.

B. GOVERNING LAW

1. The State of Incorporation

The formation and internal affairs (discussed below) of a corporation are governed by the laws of the state of incorporation. Each of the 50 states and the District of Columbia has its own statutes governing corporations formed in or doing business in that jurisdiction. Many of these state statutes are based on the 1950 Model Business Corporation Act, drafted by the Business Law section of the American Bar Association and completely revised in 1984. This text refers to the 1984 **Model Business Corporation Act** (with its later amendments) as the **MBCA**. The following 32 states have corporate law statutes based on some form of the MBCA: Alabama, Alaska, Arizona, Arkansas, Connecticut, Florida, Georgia, Hawaii, Idaho, Indiana, Iowa, Kentucky, Maine, Massachusetts, Mississippi, Montana, Nebraska, New Hampshire, New Mexico, North Carolina, Oregon, Rhode Island, South Carolina, South Dakota, Tennessee, Utah, Vermont, Virginia, Washington, West Virginia, Wisconsin, and Wyoming.

Other states — including the important corporations law jurisdictions of Delaware, New York, and California — have developed their own corporations law statutes, in some cases incorporating select MBCA provisions. In addition, a few jurisdictions have proposed or adopted unified business entity legislation that brings disparate state business entity statutes into one "hub and spoke" system. For example, in 2012 the District of Columbia combined all of its business statutes into one title. The "hub" or basic provisions apply to all entities. The "spokes" are separate chapters within the title that apply only to specific entities. To illustrate, Chapter 1 (the "hub") relates to names of entities and registered agents and includes more than 50 definitions that apply to each business entity, whereas Chapter 3 (a "spoke") covers Business Corporations (and is based on the MBCA), Chapter 6 (a "spoke") covers General Partnerships, and Chapter 8 (a "spoke") covers LLCs. Along with Washington, D.C., Washington state also has taken this approach.

2. Choosing a State of Incorporation

As a general rule, businesses are free to choose any U.S. state, or even a non-U.S. jurisdiction, for incorporation. Deciding where to incorporate depends on a number of factors, including the nature, scope, and location of business operations; the capital needs, funding, and financing plans of the business; and plans (if any) for growth and expansion. For a business planning to operate in a single state — particularly a small, privately held business that does not anticipate seeking venture capital funding and has no plans to "go public" — it generally makes sense (for reasons both logistical and financial) to incorporate in the state where the business will operate. This is because incorporating in one state while operating in another adds an additional layer of expense and administrative burden. Businesses generally have

---

[1] At the time of this writing, the American Bar Association Corporate Law Committee has proposed a revision of the MBCA. This text reflects the current edition of the MBCA in effect at the time of this writing.

to maintain an office and appoint a registered agent in the state of incorporation. If a corporation transacts business in a state other than the state of incorporation, it will have to maintain the required presence in the state of incorporation *and* also qualify to do business in the foreign jurisdiction. This typically involves paying filing and other fees to the foreign jurisdiction, establishing an office in the foreign jurisdiction, and appointing an agent in the foreign jurisdiction. For example, in California, all corporations pay a minimum annual tax rate of the greater of 8.84 percent of their net income or $800 just for the privilege of being incorporated or qualified to do business in California, whether or not they are active or operate at a loss. For a small, non-public business with operations in a single state, the costs and burdens associated with these sorts of obligations may outweigh the benefits associated with incorporating in a state other than the state in which the business operates.

If a business plans to operate in multiple states, seek venture capital funding, or sell shares to the public, however, it may make sense to incorporate in the state where it maintains its headquarters, or in Delaware. The state in which the business maintains its headquarters may be a good choice for incorporation, as the business will already have an office and agents in the jurisdiction. As for Delaware, it has long been the leading non-home jurisdiction in which to incorporate a business. Delaware takes great pride in referring to itself as being the "Incorporating Capital of the World." More than one million businesses and 70 percent of the Fortune 500 companies are incorporated in Delaware, including more than half of the corporations whose stock is publicly traded. For example, McDonald's Corporation, Alphabet Inc. (the company formed upon the reorganization of Google Inc.), and Facebook, Inc. are all Delaware corporations.

Why Delaware? Lewis S. Black, Jr., an expert on Delaware corporate law, offers the following explanation for Delaware's preeminence in a pamphlet available on the Delaware Secretary of State's website:

> So what is the source of Delaware's prestige — even cachet? Why do corporations choose Delaware? I think the answer is not one thing but a number of things. It includes the Delaware General Corporation Law which is one of the most advanced and flexible corporation statutes in the nation. It includes the Delaware courts and, in particular, Delaware's highly respected corporations court, the Court of Chancery. It includes the state legislature which takes seriously its role in keeping the corporation statute and other business laws current. It includes the Secretary of State's Office which thinks and acts more like one of the corporations it administers than a government bureaucracy.
>
> There are other, less tangible, factors that go into the mix that make Delaware appealing to corporations and other business forms. There is the fact that Delaware is a small state whose populace is generally probusiness. The people of Delaware are aware that the income received from corporation franchise taxes is an important part of the state budget and that Delaware law firms that specialize in business law matters employ significant numbers of people. As a result, the Delaware citizenry supports the legislature in keeping Delaware's business laws state-of-the-art. There is the fact that lawyers all over the country feel comfortable with Delaware corporation law. Many lawyers have learned Delaware corporation law in law school. Delaware cases are studied in almost every corporations course; hence, American lawyers generally are knowledgeable about Delaware business law. It provides a *lingua franca* for lawyers and an instant credibility that facilitates business transactions. Perhaps the most important element

is also the most difficult to articulate. It is the history and tradition that surrounds the Delaware corporation law and, in particular, the Court of Chancery, that invests the law with a predictability and respect that cannot be matched. A law school professor friend of mine was once asked about the merits of creating a national corporation law. He replied: "We already have a national corporation law. It's called the Delaware corporation law." He meant, of course, not just the statute but the case by case development of a common law of corporations that is widely accepted as American corporation law.

Lewis S. Black, Jr., Why Choose Delaware (2007).[2]

As Black's comments suggest, Delaware is a popular choice for incorporation because it is thought to have a state-of-the-art, business-friendly corporations code and a robust body of common law relating to business entities. In addition, jurisdiction over questions arising under Delaware's corporation laws is vested in the Delaware Court of Chancery, which has more than 220 years of legal precedent in business entity law. These features of the Delaware system are thought to lend a degree of certainty — or, at least, predictability — to business and legal planning and the resolution of disputes involving corporations. Certainty and predictability are attractive to businesses seeking to identify and plan for legal and business risks, costs, and opportunities. Delaware also has no sales tax and does not impose state income tax on corporations that do not conduct business in Delaware. For these and related reasons, many venture capitalists, investment bankers, and other sophisticated market participants prefer Delaware as the state of incorporation, and businesses that intend to seek venture capital funding, or sell shares to the public, may have to incorporate in Delaware or re-incorporate in Delaware (if the business was initially organized elsewhere), as a condition of receiving funding from these sources.

In an effort to emulate Delaware and thereby attract incorporation business, other jurisdictions have amended their corporations statutes and made other changes to legal, taxation, or regulatory regimes. For example, Nevada has amended its corporations code to align it with the Delaware corporations code in certain instances, and it also eliminated state income tax. In the last few years, incorporations in Nevada are reported to have increased 25 to 30 percent. Because California is thought to be a comparatively costly state in which to incorporate, attorneys in California have been the target of an advertising campaign to encourage them to incorporate their clients in Nevada. Some experts have questioned whether the competition among states to attract corporations is in the best interest of shareholders or is a "race to the bottom." Also, some have questioned whether there is, in fact, an empirically supported, economic basis for Delaware's appeal in the market for company incorporations. Robert Anderson IV & Jeffrey Manns, *The Delaware Delusion*, 93 N.C. L. Rev. 1049, 1067-87 (2015).

Despite these developments and critiques, however, Delaware continues to have a dominant share of the market for incorporation business. A 2012 study released by the United States Chamber of Commerce Institute for Legal Reform ranked Delaware (for the eleventh year in a row) as having the most favorable legal system and litigation environment, meaning one that is favorable to business. For

---

[2] https://corp.delaware.gov/pdfs/whycorporations_english.pdf.

these and related reasons, Delaware corporate law continues to cast a long shadow over corporations codes nationwide.

3. Spotlight: Corporate Inversions

A previous trend among some American corporations was to reincorporate in Bermuda (or certain other jurisdictions thought to be tax havens), primarily to avoid taxation in the United States. Congress and public opinion were so strongly against such reincorporations that at least one company abandoned its reincorporation plans after activists protested the plan. Congress closed this tax loophole in 2004. In a more recent trend, called inversions, American corporations have been acquiring or merging with foreign corporations, with the resulting entity selecting the foreign corporation's jurisdiction (which has a lower tax rate) as its official tax residence, even while leaving its executive team in America.

In September 2014, the U.S. Treasury issued rules to make inversions more difficult. Under the 2014 reforms, an inverted company was subject to potential adverse tax consequences if, after the transaction (i) less than 25 percent of the new multinational entity's business activity is in the home country of the new foreign parent; and (ii) the shareholders of the former U.S. parent end up owning at least 60 percent of the shares of the new foreign parent. If these criteria were met, the tax consequences depended on the size of the continuing ownership stake of the shareholders of the former U.S. parent. If the continuing ownership stake was 80 percent or more, the new foreign parent would be treated as a U.S. corporation (despite the new corporate address), thereby nullifying the corporate inversion for tax purposes. If the continuing ownership stake was at least 60 but less than 80 percent, U.S. tax law would respect the foreign status of the new foreign parent, but other potentially adverse tax consequences could follow. Although some pending inversion deals reportedly were canceled, many experts believed that either legislation or tax reform was needed to prevent inversions.

On November 19, 2015, the Treasury Department issued a notice modifying this regime for transactions in the continuing ownership range of 60 to 80 percent. The November 19, 2015 notice included a number of reforms intended to make it more difficult for U.S. companies to effect an inversion:

■ *Strengthened the requirement that the former owners of a U.S. company own less than 80 percent of the new combined entity.* In certain cases where the foreign parent is a tax resident of a third country, the new rules provided that stock of the foreign parent issued to the shareholders of the existing foreign corporation is disregarded for purposes of the ownership requirement, thereby raising the ownership attributable to the shareholders of the U.S. entity, possibly above the 80 percent threshold. The intent of this provision was to prevent U.S. firms from "cherry picking" a tax-friendly country in which to locate their tax residence.

■ *Limited the ability of U.S. companies to inflate the new foreign parent corporation's size as a means of avoiding the 80 percent threshold.* Existing rules had permitted a company to invert when the U.S. entity has a value of up to 79 percent, and the foreign "acquirer" has a value of 21 percent of the combined group. In some inversions, however, the foreign acquirer's size may be inflated by "stuffing" assets into the foreign acquirer. The 2015 notice clarified that "anti-stuffing" rules apply to any assets acquired with a principal purpose of avoiding the 80 percent rule.

- *Strengthened the substantial business activities exception.* Under then-existing law, a U.S. company could invert if, after the transaction, at least 25 percent of the combined group's business activity was in the foreign country in which the new foreign parent is created or organized. This was the rule regardless of whether the new foreign parent was a tax resident of that foreign country. The standard for determining the tax residence of a corporation for U.S. income tax purposes is where the entity is created or organized. This standard may not align with standards of foreign countries that, for example, consider the location in which the entity is managed or controlled when determining tax residence. The 2015 notice stated that the combined group cannot satisfy the 25 percent business activities exception unless the new foreign parent is a tax resident in the foreign country in which it is created or organized. In so stating, the new rules limited the ability of a U.S. multinational corporation to replace its U.S. tax residence with a tax residence in another country in which it does not have substantial business activities.

- *Expanded the scope of inversion gain for which current U.S. tax must be paid.* Under current law, U.S. multinationals owe U.S. tax on the profits of their controlled foreign corporations (CFC), although they typically do not have to pay tax until those profits are paid to the U.S. parent as a dividend. Profits that have not yet been repatriated are known as deferred earnings. However, to the extent a CFC has passive income, the U.S. parent is treated as if it received a taxable deemed dividend from the CFC. Under current law, an inverted company must pay current U.S. tax on inversion gain (i.e., gain recognized when the inverted company transfers stock in its CFC or other property to the new foreign parent) without the benefit of otherwise applicable tax attributes (e.g., net operating loss carryovers) to offset the gain. The new rules imposed penalties on post-inversion transactions that are designed to remove income from foreign operations from the U.S. taxing jurisdiction. The November 2015 notice expanded the scope of inversion gain to include certain taxable deemed dividends recognized by an inverted company.

- *Required that all built-in gain in CFC stock be recognized, without regard to the amount of deferred earnings, upon a restructuring of a CFC.* After an inversion, the new foreign parent may acquire CFC stock held by the former U.S.-parented group, with the result that the CFC is no longer under the U.S. tax net. Under then-current law, the former U.S. parent recognized built-in gain in the CFC stock as a result of the transfer, but not in excess of the deferred earnings of the CFC. The November 2015 notice provides that all built-in gain must be recognized as a result of the post-inversion transfer, regardless of the amount of the CFC's deferred earnings.

On April 4, 2016, Treasury Department and the Internal Revenue Service (IRS) issued additional temporary and proposed regulations relating to inversions. These latest reforms include several provisions designed to further reduce the benefits of, and limit the number of, corporate tax inversions:

- *Disregarding foreign parent stock attributable to recent inversions or acquisitions of U.S. companies.* This reform is intended to prevent a foreign company (including a recent inverter) that acquires multiple American companies in stock-based transactions from using the resulting increase in size to avoid the current inversion thresholds for a subsequent U.S. acquisition.

- *Addressing earnings stripping.* The reforms target transactions that generate large interest deductions by simply increasing related-party debt without financing new investment in the United States.

- *Allowing division of instruments into debt and equity.* The new regulations allow the IRS on audit to divide debt instruments into part debt and part equity, rather than the current system that generally treats them as wholly one or the other.

- *Facilitating improved due diligence and compliance.* The regulations are designed to improve due diligence and compliance by requiring certain large corporations to do up-front due diligence and documentation with respect to the characterization of related-party financial instruments as debt. If these requirements are not met, instruments will be treated as equity for tax purposes.

- *Formalizing Treasury's two previous actions.* The new regulations formalize actions associated with the September 2014 and November 2015 reforms.

4. The Internal Affairs Doctrine

Under the **internal affairs doctrine**, the law of the jurisdiction of incorporation governs a corporation's internal affairs. The internal affairs doctrine is a conflict of law doctrine, with a constitutional dimension, which is based on the idea that "only one State should have the authority to regulate a corporation's internal affairs — matters peculiar to the relationships among or between the corporation and its current officers, directors, and shareholders — because otherwise a corporation could be faced with conflicting demands." *Edgar v. MITE Corp.*, 457 U.S. 624, 645 (1982) (citing Restatement (Second) of Conflict of Laws § 302 cmt. b at 307-08 (Am. Law Inst. 1971)). The doctrine seeks to avoid the uncertainty and costs that could arise if a business entity operating in multiple states were subject to different, and potentially conflicting, rules. It also reflects a presumption that those who choose to form their entity in a particular state desire to have their legal relations governed by the laws of that state.

In practical terms, the internal affairs doctrine means that disputes involving the relationship between and among corporate stakeholders — officers, directors, and shareholders — tend to be governed by the law of the state of incorporation. For example, if a shareholder brings a lawsuit relating to a Delaware corporation's bylaw provisions concerning shareholder meetings, Delaware law likely will govern resolution of the dispute, even if the plaintiff files suit in a different jurisdiction. Similarly, if a shareholder alleges that a director of a Delaware corporation breached his fiduciary duty to the corporation — for example, by acting disloyally or by failing to exercise due care in carrying out directorial responsibilities — Delaware law will apply, even if the corporation has little or no contact with Delaware beyond minimum organizing activity.

Case Preview

VantagePoint Venture Partners 1996 v. Examen, Inc.

In the following case, litigants clashed over whether voting rights ought to be determined according to California or Delaware law. VantagePoint Venture Partners, Inc. was an Examen, Inc. Series A preferred stockholder. After Examen entered into a merger agreement with a Delaware subsidiary of the company Reed Elsevier, Inc., VantagePoint argued that the Series A preferred stockholders should have class voting rights (i.e., the right to vote as a class separate and apart from other classes of stockholders) with respect to the proposed merger, citing § 2115 of the California Corporations Code. Examen, on the other hand, took the position that Delaware law controlled voting rights under the internal affairs doctrine. Delaware provided for voting by all shareholders together (not class voting), whereas California § 2115 provided for class voting rights. In reading the case, consider the following questions:

1. What does § 2115 say respecting the right of shareholders to vote separately, by class?
2. What does Delaware law say respecting the right of shareholders to vote separately, by class?
3. As a practical matter, why does VantagePoint want class voting?
4. As a practical matter, why does Examen want all shareholders to vote together, as one class?

VantagePoint Venture Partners 1996 v. Examen, Inc.
871 A.2d 1108 (Del. 2005)

HOLLAND, Justice:*

This is an expedited appeal from the Court of Chancery following the entry of a final judgment on the pleadings. We have concluded that the judgment must be affirmed.

DELAWARE ACTION

On March 3, 2005, the plaintiff-appellee, Examen, Inc. ("Examen"), filed a Complaint in the Court of Chancery against VantagePoint Venture Partners, Inc. ("VantagePoint"), a Delaware Limited Partnership and an Examen Series A Preferred shareholder, seeking a judicial declaration that pursuant to the controlling Delaware law and under the Company's Certificate of Designations of Series A Preferred Stock ("Certificate of Designations"), VantagePoint was not entitled to a class vote of the

---

*Most footnotes have been omitted for purposes of brevity.

Series A Preferred Stock on the proposed merger between Examen and a Delaware subsidiary of Reed Elsevier Inc.

CALIFORNIA ACTION

On March 8, 2005, VantagePoint filed an action in the California Superior Court seeking: (1) a declaration that Examen was required to identify whether it was a "quasi-California corporation" under section 2115 of the California Corporations Code[1]; (2) a declaration that Examen was a quasi-California corporation pursuant to California Corporations Code section 2115 and therefore subject to California Corporations Code section 1201(a), and that, as a Series A Preferred shareholder, VantagePoint was entitled to vote its shares as a separate class in connection with the proposed merger; (3) injunctive relief; and (4) damages incurred as the result of alleged violations of California Corporations Code sections 2111(F) and 1201.

DELAWARE ACTION DECIDED

On March 10, 2005, the Court of Chancery granted Examen's request for an expedited hearing on its motion for judgment on the pleadings. On March 21, 2005, the California Superior Court stayed its action pending the ruling of the Court of Chancery. On March 29, 2005, the Court of Chancery ruled that the case was governed by the internal affairs doctrine as explicated by this Court in *McDermott v. Lewis*. In applying that doctrine, the Court of Chancery held that Delaware law governed the vote that was required to approve a merger between two Delaware corporate entities.

On April 1, 2005, VantagePoint filed a notice of appeal with this Court. On April 4, 2005, VantagePoint sought to enjoin the merger from closing pending its appeal. On April 5, 2005, this Court denied VantagePoint's request to enjoin the merger from closing, but granted its request for an expedited appeal.

MERGER WITHOUT MOOTNESS

. . .

We have concluded that this appeal is not moot.

FACTS

Examen was a Delaware corporation engaged in the business of providing web-based legal expense management solutions to a growing list of Fortune 1000

---

[1]Section 2115 of the California Corporations Code purportedly applies to corporations that have contacts with the State of California, but are incorporated in other states. *See* Cal. Corp. Code §§ 171 (defining "foreign corporation"); and Cal. Corp. Code §§ 2115(a), (b). Section 2115 of the California Corporations Code provides that, irrespective of the state of incorporation, **foreign corporations' articles of incorporation are deemed amended to comply with California law and are subject to the laws of California if certain criteria are met.** *See* Cal. Corp. Code § 2115 (emphasis added). To qualify under the statute: (1) the average of the property factor, the payroll factor and the sales factor as defined in the California Revenue and Taxation Code must be more than 50 percent during its last full income year; and (2) more than one-half of its outstanding voting securities must be held by persons having addresses in California. *Id.* If a corporation qualifies under this provision, California corporate laws apply "to the exclusion of the law of the jurisdiction where [the company] is incorporated." *Id.* Included among the California corporate law provisions that would govern is California Corporations Code section 1201, which states that the principal terms of a reorganization shall be approved by the outstanding shares of each class of each corporation the approval of whose board is required. *See* Cal. Corp. Code §§ 2115, 1201.

customers throughout the United States. Following consummation of the merger on April 5, 2005, LexisNexis Examen, also a Delaware corporation, became the surviving entity. VantagePoint is a Delaware Limited Partnership organized and existing under the laws of Delaware. VantagePoint, a major venture capital firm that purchased Examen Series A Preferred Stock in a negotiated transaction, owned eighty-three percent of Examen's outstanding Series A Preferred Stock (909,091 shares) and no shares of Common Stock.

On February 17, 2005, Examen and Reed Elsevier executed the Merger Agreement, which was set to expire on April 15, 2005, if the merger had not closed by that date. Under the Delaware General Corporation Law and Examen's Certificate of Incorporation, including the Certificate of Designations for the Series A Preferred Stock, adoption of the Merger Agreement required the affirmative vote of the holders of a majority of the issued and outstanding shares of the Common Stock and Series A Preferred Stock, *voting together as a single class*. Holders of Series A Preferred Stock had the number of votes equal to the number of shares of Common Stock they would have held if their Preferred Stock was converted. Thus, VantagePoint, which owned 909,091 shares of Series A Preferred Stock and no shares of Common Stock, was entitled to vote based on a converted number of 1,392,727 shares of stock.

There were 9,717,415 total outstanding shares of the Company's capital stock (8,626,826 shares of Common Stock and 1,090,589 shares of Series A Preferred Stock), representing 10,297,608 votes on an as-converted basis. An affirmative vote of at least 5,148,805 shares, constituting a majority of the outstanding voting power on an as-converted basis, was required to approve the merger. If the stockholders were to vote by class, VantagePoint would have controlled 83.4 percent of the Series A Preferred Stock, which would have permitted VantagePoint to block the merger. VantagePoint acknowledges that, if Delaware law applied, it would not have a class vote.

CHANCERY COURT DECISION

The Court of Chancery determined that the question of whether VantagePoint, as a holder of Examen's Series A Preferred Stock, was entitled to a separate class vote on the merger with a Delaware subsidiary of Reed Elsevier, was governed by the internal affairs doctrine because the issue implicated "the relationship between a corporation and its stockholders." The Court of Chancery rejected VantagePoint's argument that section 2115 of the California Corporation Code did not conflict with Delaware law and operated only in addition to rights granted under Delaware corporate law. In doing so, the Court of Chancery noted that section 2115 "expressly states that it operates 'to the exclusion of the law of the jurisdiction in which [the company] is incorporated.' "

Specifically, the Court of Chancery determined that section 2115's requirement that stockholders vote as a separate class conflicts with Delaware law, which, together with Examen's Certificate of Incorporation, mandates that the merger be authorized by a majority of all Examen stockholders voting together as a single class. The Court of Chancery concluded that it could not enforce both Delaware and California law. Consequently, the Court of Chancery decided that the issue presented was solely one of choice-of-law, and that it need not determine the constitutionality of section 2115.

VANTAGEPOINT'S ARGUMENT

According to VantagePoint, "the issue presented by this case is not a choice of law question, but rather the constitutional issue of whether California may promulgate a narrowly-tailored exception to the internal affairs doctrine that is designed to protect important state interests." VantagePoint submits that "Section 2115 was designed to provide an additional layer of investor protection by mandating that California's heightened voting requirements apply to those few foreign corporations that have chosen to conduct a majority of their business in California and meet the other factual prerequisite of Section 2115." Therefore, VantagePoint argues that "Delaware either must apply the statute if California can validly enact it, or hold the statute unconstitutional if California cannot." We note, however, that when an issue or claim is properly before a tribunal, "the court is not limited to the particular legal theories advanced by the parties, but rather retains the independent power to identify and apply the proper construction of governing law."

. . .

INTERNAL AFFAIRS DOCTRINE

In *CTS Corp. v. Dynamics Corp. of Am.*, the United States Supreme Court stated that it is "an accepted part of the business landscape in this country for States to create corporations, to prescribe their powers, and to define the rights that are acquired by purchasing their shares." In *CTS*, it was also recognized that "[a] State has an interest in promoting stable relationships among parties involved in the corporations it charters, as well as in ensuring that investors in such corporations have an effective voice in corporate affairs." The internal affairs doctrine is a long-standing choice of law principle which recognizes that only one state should have the authority to regulate a corporation's internal affairs-the state of incorporation.

The internal affairs doctrine developed on the premise that, in order to prevent corporations from being subjected to inconsistent legal standards, the authority to regulate a corporation's internal affairs should not rest with multiple jurisdictions. It is now well established that only the law of the state of incorporation governs and determines issues relating to a corporation's internal affairs. By providing certainty and predictability, the internal affairs doctrine protects the justified expectations of the parties with interests in the corporation.

The internal affairs doctrine applies to those matters that pertain to the relationships among or between the corporation and its officers, directors, and shareholders. The Restatement (Second) of Conflict of Laws § 301 provides: "application of the local law of the state of incorporation will usually be supported by those choice-of-law factors favoring the need of the interstate and international systems, certainty, predictability and uniformity of result, protection of the justified expectations of the parties and ease in the application of the law to be applied." Accordingly, the conflicts practice of both state and federal courts has consistently been to apply the law of the state of incorporation to "the entire gamut of internal corporate affairs."

The internal affairs doctrine is not, however, only a conflicts of law principle. Pursuant to the Fourteenth Amendment Due Process Clause, directors and officers of corporations "have a significant right ... to know what law will be applied to their actions" and "[s]tockholders ... have a right to know by what standards of accountability they may hold those managing the corporation's business and affairs." Under the Commerce Clause, a state "has no interest in regulating the internal affairs of foreign corporations." Therefore, this Court has held that an "application of the internal affairs doctrine is mandated by constitutional principles, except in the 'rarest situations,'" *e.g.,* when "the law of the state of incorporation is inconsistent with a national policy on foreign or interstate commerce."

CALIFORNIA SECTION 2115

VantagePoint contends that section 2115 of the California Corporations Code is a limited exception to the internal affairs doctrine. Section 2115 is characterized as an outreach statute because it requires certain foreign corporations to conform to a broad range of internal affairs provisions. Section 2115 defines the foreign corporations for which the California statute has an outreach effect as those foreign corporations, half of whose voting securities are held of record by persons with California addresses, that also conduct half of their business in California as measured by a formula weighing assets, sales and payroll factors.

VantagePoint argues that section 2115 "mandates application of certain enumerated provisions of California's corporation law to the internal affairs of 'foreign' corporations if certain narrow factual prerequisites [set forth in section 2115] are met." Under the California statute, if more than one half of a foreign corporation's outstanding voting securities are held of record by persons having addresses in California (as disclosed on the books of the corporation) on the record date, *and* the property, payroll and sales factor tests are satisfied, then on the first day of the income year, one hundred and thirty five days after the above tests are satisfied, *the foreign corporation's articles of incorporation are deemed amended to the exclusion of the law of the state of incorporation.* If the factual conditions precedent for triggering section 2115 are established, many aspects of a corporation's internal affairs are purportedly governed by California corporate law to the exclusion of the law of the state of incorporation.[22]

In her comprehensive analysis of the internal affairs doctrine, Professor Deborah A. DeMott examined section 2115. As she astutely points out:

> In contrast to the certainty with which the state of incorporation may be determined, the criteria upon which the applicability of section 2115 hinges are not constants.

---

[22]If Section 2115 applies, California law is deemed to control the following: the annual election of directors; removal of directors without cause; removal of directors by court proceedings; the filing of director vacancies where less than a majority in office are elected by shareholders; the director's standard of care; the liability of directors for unlawful distributions; indemnification of directors, officers, and others; limitations on corporate distributions in cash or property; the liability of shareholders who receive unlawful distributions; the requirement for annual shareholders' meetings and remedies for the same if not timely held; shareholder's entitlement to cumulative voting; the conditions when a supermajority vote is required; limitations on the sale of assets; limitations on mergers; limitations on conversions; requirements on conversions; the limitations and conditions for reorganization (including the requirement for class voting); dissenter's rights; records and reports; actions by the Attorney General and inspection rights. *See* Cal. Corp. Code § 2115(b) (1977 & Supp. 1984).

For example, whether half of a corporation's business is derived from California and whether half of its voting securities have record holders with California addresses may well vary from year to year (and indeed throughout any given year). Thus, a corporation might be subject to section 2115 one year but not the next, depending on its situation at the time of filing the annual statement required by section 2108.

INTERNAL AFFAIRS REQUIRE UNIFORMITY

In *McDermott,* this Court noted that application of local internal affairs law (here California's section 2115) to a foreign corporation (here Delaware) is "apt to produce inequalities, intolerable confusion, and uncertainty, and intrude into the domain of other states that have a superior claim to regulate the same subject matter. . . ." Professor DeMott's review of the differences and conflicts between the Delaware and California corporate statutes with regard to internal affairs, illustrates why it is imperative that only the law of the state of incorporation regulate the relationships among a corporation and its officers, directors, and shareholders. To require a factual determination to decide which of two conflicting state laws governs the internal affairs of a corporation at any point in time, completely contravenes the importance of stability within inter-corporate relationships that the United States Supreme Court recognized in *CTS.*

In *Kamen v. Kemper Fin. Serv.,* the United States Supreme Court reaffirmed its commitment to the need for stability that is afforded by the internal affairs doctrine. . . . In *Kamen v. Kemper,* the Restatement (Second) of Conflict of Laws was cited for the proposition that "[u]niform treatment of directors, officers and shareholders is an important objective which can only be attained by having the rights and liabilities of those persons with respect to the corporation governed by a single law." . . .

STATE LAW OF INCORPORATION GOVERNS INTERNAL AFFAIRS

In *McDermott,* this Court held that the "internal affairs doctrine is a major tenet of Delaware corporation law having important federal constitutional underpinnings." Applying Delaware's well-established choice-of-law rule — the internal affairs doctrine — the Court of Chancery recognized that Delaware courts must apply the law of the state of incorporation to issues involving corporate internal affairs, and that disputes concerning a shareholder's right to vote fall squarely within the purview of the internal affairs doctrine.

Examen is a Delaware corporation. The legal issue in this case — whether a preferred shareholder of a Delaware corporation had the right, under the corporation's Certificate of Designations, to a Series A Preferred Stock class vote on a merger — clearly involves the relationship among a corporation and its shareholders. As the United States Supreme Court held in *CTS,* "[n]o principle of corporation law and practice is more firmly established than a *State's authority* to regulate domestic corporations, including the authority to *define the voting rights of shareholders.*"

In *CTS,* the Supreme Court held that the Commerce Clause "prohibits States from regulating subjects that 'are in their nature national, or admit only of one uniform system, or plan of regulation,'" and acknowledged that the internal affairs of a corporation are subjects that require one uniform system of regulation. In *CTS*, the Supreme Court concluded that "[s]o long as each State regulates voting rights *only in the corporations it has created,* each corporation will be subject to the law of only one State." Accordingly, we hold Delaware's well-established choice of law rules and the federal constitution mandated that Examen's internal affairs, and in particular, VantagePoint's voting rights, be adjudicated exclusively in accordance with the law of its state of incorporation, in this case, the law of Delaware.

. . .

CONCLUSION

The judgment of the Court of Chancery is affirmed. The Clerk of this Court is directed to issue the mandate immediately.

Post-Case Follow-Up

Companies incorporated outside of California but with significant California contacts (so-called quasi-California corporations) have long struggled with § 2115 of the California Corporations Code. Although some questioned the validity of § 2115 in the face of conflicting state of incorporation rules — particularly in the wake of the *VantagePoint* decision in Delaware — California courts were not quick to conclude that § 2115 reached too far. Things changed a bit in May 2012, when a California appeals court signaled that it might be unwilling to enforce § 2115. In *Lidow v. Superior Court*, 141 Cal. Rptr. 3d 729 (Ct. App. 2012), the Second Appellate District of the California Court of Appeal, in the published portion of an opinion, stated in dicta that matters of internal corporate governance (such as the voting rights of shareholders) fall within a corporation's internal affairs, and that the law of the state of incorporation should govern such matters. *Lidow* involved the purported wrongful termination of the chief executive officer of International Rectifier Corporation. In moving for summary judgment, International Rectifier cited the internal affairs doctrine, and argued that because it was a Delaware corporation, Delaware law should govern the wrongful termination claim. Lidow, the former chief executive officer, opposed the motion, arguing that the circumstances underlying his claim did not implicate the internal affairs doctrine, and thus that California law (and not Delaware law) ought to govern. The court sided with Lidow, and in so doing, agreed with key portions the Delaware Supreme Court's analysis in *VantagePoint*. Citing the internal affairs doctrine, the court stated that the voting rights of shareholders, the payment of dividends to shareholders, and the procedural requirements for shareholder derivative suits all involved matters of internal corporate governance and thus the corporation's internal affairs. Because the court ultimately determined that the issue in dispute did not involve "corporate internal affairs," the court held the internal affairs doctrine did not dictate the choice of law applicable to Lidow's claim. In so holding, the *Lidow* court did not expressly reject § 2115. Nevertheless, *Lidow*'s favorable treatment of *VantagePoint* left open the possibility that California courts could be disinclined to enforce the long-arm statute in future litigation involving a corporation's internal affairs. That having been said, although the California Assembly passed legislation in 2012 to repeal § 2115, the Senate Judiciary Committee rejected the legislation. Thus, § 2115 remains on the books as of this writing.

VantagePoint Venture Partners 1996 v. Examen, Inc.: Real Life Applications

The continued existence of § 2115 and the internal affairs doctrine means that there are (or can be) situations involving potential conflicts between the requirements of California and Delaware law. For the following questions, identify the applicable rules under both California and Delaware law:

a. Election of directors: Is cumulative voting the default rule? Is cumulative voting permitted, if the charter provides for it?
b. Director removal without cause: Under what circumstances, if any, may directors be removed without cause? May directors be removed without cause if the board is staggered?

The internal affairs doctrine does not mean that every lawsuit involving a corporation is governed by the law of the state of incorporation. For example, if a California-based employee of a Delaware corporation headquartered in California negligently hits a pedestrian in California while driving to a business meeting, the plaintiff's personal injury claim likely will be governed by California law under traditional choice of law principles. This is because if the corporation's internal affairs are not at issue, traditional choice of law rules dictate which jurisdiction's law should apply. *Compare VantagePoint*, 871 A.2d at 1109 (holding voting rights of stockholders in California-based, Delaware corporation should be adjudicated according to Delaware law (which did not call for vote), despite existence of California statute (which called for vote)), *with Bell Helicopter Textron, Inc. v. Arteaga*, 113 A.3d 1045 (Del. 2015) (holding law of Mexico, not Texas or Delaware, applied to products liability action against Texas-based, Delaware corporation, which was a manufacturer of component parts for helicopters, where Mexican citizens were killed in a helicopter crash in Mexico).

Case Preview

American International Group, Inc. v. Greenberg

As you will recall from your Civil Procedure classes, forum non conveniens refers to the court's discretionary power to dismiss a case where another forum is better suited to hear the dispute. In the following case, the founders of American International Group, Inc. (AIG) — the insurance company/financial institution that attracted attention in 2008 in the wake of the financial crisis — sought to stay or dismiss an action in New York state court pending resolution of proceedings in a different jurisdiction involving many of the same players. Citing the internal affairs doctrine, the defendants argued that Delaware law ought to apply to the claims at issue and that Delaware therefore was the most appropriate forum for the case. While this case does not have the most detailed examination of the internal affairs doctrine — check out the *VantagePoint* case excerpted and cited above for such a review — we have included it because it speaks to the interplay between the internal affairs doctrine, traditional choice of law rules, and doctrines that speak to forum and venue. When reading the case, consider the following questions:

1. What factors do New York courts consider when deciding whether to dismiss an action under the doctrine of forum non conveniens?
2. What doctrines determine which state's law will apply to this action?
3. What doctrines determine whether New York is an appropriate forum for this case?
4. How does a foreign state of incorporation play into choice of law under the internal affairs doctrine and dismissal (or not) under the doctrine of forum non conveniens?

American International Group, Inc. v. Greenberg
877 N.Y.S.2d 614 (Sup. Ct. 2008)

CHARLES E. RAMOS, J.*

In motion sequence 001, defendant Ernest E. Stempel moves to stay this action pending the resolution of an action in the Southern District of New York, captioned *Starr International Company, Inc. v. American International Group, Inc.* (Federal Court Action), and alternatively to dismiss the complaint.

. . .

BACKGROUND

In this action for damages, plaintiff American International Group, Inc. (AIG) seeks to remedy alleged breaches of fiduciary duty by certain of AIG's founders, and former officers and directors, for their alleged misappropriation of a special block of AIG shares, worth approximately $20 billion in 2005.

The seven individual defendants are Greenberg, Smith, Matthews, Stempel, Murphy, Roberts and Freeman (collectively, Defendants). In addition to serving as AIG's founders, directors and officers, Defendants were all voting shareholders of AIG affiliate and non-party Starr International Company, Inc. (SICO).

The genesis of the alleged fiduciary relationship between AIG and Defendants is AIG's formation in 1967 by C.V. Starr, as a wholly owned subsidiary of American

---

*Footnotes have been omitted for purpose of brevity.

International Reinsurance Co. (AIRCO). Starr hand-picked nine men, that included defendants Greenberg, Stempel, Roberts and Freeman (Control Defendants), to be his successors and to direct and control the four principal companies that comprised Starr's global network of insurance operations, including AIG, SICO, and non-party C.V. Starr & Co.

AIG alleges that Starr's vision for his insurance organization was that a unique entrepreneurial culture be perpetuated, that included a compensation philosophy that management should have an ownership stake in the business and share in the profits.

In 1970, shortly after Starr's death, the four main entities of Starr's network, including AIG and SICO, were reorganized under the direction of Greenberg. As part of the reorganization, most of the insurance operations were transferred to AIG, indirectly through AIRCO, in exchange for AIRCO stock, that was exchanged for AIG common stock when AIRCO merged into AIG. Approximately $130 million worth of AIG stock was transferred to SICO (the Shares).

As part of the reorganization, SICO allegedly agreed to continue funding a profit participation and deferred compensation plan to its employees, who became AIG employees in the 1970 reorganization. At this time, the Control Defendants, as Starr's hand-picked successors, agreed that the value of the Shares would be preserved solely for the benefit of current and future AIG employees and used to fund the incentive compensation plan maintained by SICO, in addition to protecting AIG from a hostile takeover attempt.

As part of this alleged agreement, the Control Defendants expressly agreed to serve as the fiduciaries of the Shares, that represented the wealth created by past generations. As part of this pledge, they allegedly promised that the value of the Shares would never be used for the personal enrichment of SICO, and the individual SICO voting stockholders, including the Control Defendants.

Moreover, in order to fulfill the purposes of the alleged trust and to ensure that Defendants' fiduciary duties to AIG to safeguard the Shares were not violated, it was agreed by AIG directors also serving as SICO voting shareholders, that AIG management would always control SICO. Consistently, from October 1970 to March of 2005, AIG officers and directors always comprised the voting shareholders and directors of SICO. Defendants were all officers and directors of AIG and voting shareholders and directors of SICO.

In addition to the Control Defendants, remaining defendants Smith, Matthews, Murphy, and Freeman, who each became either an AIG officer or director or SICO voting shareholder at a subsequent point in time, each adopted and reaffirmed the pledge to serve as fiduciaries of the value and use of the Shares for the benefit of AIG and for future generations of AIG employees.

The Shares were placed in a segregated account with restricted access at Chase Manhattan Bank in New York for over thirty-five years. The Shares were withdrawn only to fund AIG's deferred compensation plan, until March of 2005, when AIG, Greenberg and Smith were under investigation by state and federal officials for accounting fraud.

At that time, Greenberg resigned as AIG's Chief Executive Officer (CEO), and Smith was terminated as AIG's Chief Financial Officer (CFO). Greenberg and Smith remained directors of AIG until June of 2005.

On March 28, 2005, AIG alleges that Defendants, at Greenberg's request, seized control of SICO by causing nine of the AIG executives, then serving as SICO directors, to be removed from the SICO board. The following month, Greenberg informed AIG, through Matthews, that SICO was reneging on the 2005/2006 compensation plan, and that there would be no more compensation plans in the future. All of the Defendants allegedly participated in this decision.

The Defendants then caused SICO to formally cancel the compensation plan, and announced their intention of selling the Shares. Since that time, Defendants allegedly caused SICO to sell portions of the Shares, the proceeds of which have allegedly been used to invest in a venture capital and private equity firm. AIG commenced this action in March 2008, asserting three causes of action for breach of fiduciary duty against Greenberg and Smith in their capacity as AIG directors, breach of fiduciary duties against all Defendants, and aiding and abetting breach of fiduciary duty against Defendants.

DISCUSSION

I. Forum Non Conveniens

Defendants move to dismiss this action on the ground of forum non conveniens. They contend that the internal affairs doctrine, AIG's improper claim splitting, in addition to other relevant factors, render Delaware the most appropriate forum for this action.

AIG asserts that Defendants have not met their heavy burden of demonstrating that New York is an inappropriate forum.

Defendants' motion to dismiss under the doctrine of forum non conveniens fails for two primary reasons. Defendants offer no persuasive reason why New York is an inconvenient forum for an action involving former directors of a corporation headquartered in New York, several of which are already defending against a pending action here. Additionally, New York is already the forum for another pending, related action. Further, Defendants fail to persuade that Delaware, AIG's state of incorporation, is more convenient than New York, thereby warranting dismissal of the present action in its favor.

The common law doctrine of forum non conveniens, codified in CPLR 327, permits a court to dismiss an action if it would more properly be heard in another forum. Whether to dismiss in favor of another forum is left to the sound discretion of the court (*Shin-Etsu Chemical Co., Ltd. v. 3033 ICICI Bank*, 9 A.D.3d 171, 175-176, 777 N.Y.S.2d 69 [1st Dept. 2004]).

Although no one factor is controlling, courts should balance factors including the factual nexus between New York and the action, the burden on New York courts, the potential hardship to the defendant of litigating here, the availability of an alternative forum in which the plaintiff may bring suit, and the residency of the parties (*Kinder Morgan Energy Partners, L.P. v. Ace American*, 55 A.D.3d 482, 482, 866 N.Y.S.2d 191 [1st Dept. 2008]; *Kuwaiti Eng'g Group v. Consortium of Intl. Consultants, LLC*, 50 A.D.3d 599, 600, 856 N.Y.S.2d 101 [1st Dept. 2008]). Ultimately, the plaintiff's choice of forum should not be disturbed unless the balance strongly favors the jurisdiction in which the defendant seeks to litigate the claims (*Anagnostou v. Stifel,* 204 A.D.2d 61, 611 N.Y.S.2d 525 [1st Dept. 1994]).

The complaint alleges facts sufficient to establish a factual nexus between New York and the underlying dispute. Defendants' allegedly reaffirmed their fiduciary duties to preserve the value of the Shares in New York on numerous occasions. The decision to allegedly repudiate these duties and cancel the compensation plans occurred at a meeting attended by Defendants in New York. Further, Defendants allegedly directed an agent to enter this state to remove the Shares from where they have been held for thirty-five years. Greenberg and Smith allegedly decided to step down as AIG executives as the result of events that occurred in New York, including investigations by the New York Attorney General and the Securities and Exchange Commission into several transactions entered into during their tenure.

Notably, Defendants do not contend that litigating this action here would cause hardship to them. AIG is headquartered in New York, and consequently, key documents and witnesses are located within the state (*Georgia-Pacific Corp. v. Multimark's Intern. Ltd.,* 265 A.D.2d 109, 112, 706 N.Y.S.2d 82 [1st Dept. 2000]).

Further, three of the defendants, Greenberg, Smith and Matthews, reside or are employed here. The remaining four defendants, Stempel, Murphy, Roberts and Freeman, do not reside in Delaware but in Bermuda, Hawaii and Maryland, respectively.

Moreover, Defendants have not established that litigating this action here would burden New York courts. The Commercial Division of this State frequently resolves disputes of this nature, and this court is fully capable and frequently called upon to apply Delaware law.

Defendants rely heavily on the fact that AIG is incorporated in Delaware, and the so-called internal affairs doctrine as the primary factor that renders Delaware the most suitable forum for this action.

Generally, issues concerning the internal affairs of a corporation and the conduct of its directors are governed by the laws of the state of incorporation (*Hart v. Gen. Motors Corp.,* 129 A.D.2d 179, 182, 517 N.Y.S.2d 490 [1st Dept.], *app. denied* 70 N.Y.2d 608, 521 N.Y.S.2d 225, 515 N.E.2d 910 [1987]). Although the state of incorporation undoubtedly has an interest in the outcome of such actions, incorporation in a foreign state, does not, by itself, necessitate dismissal in favor of another forum (*see Broida v. Bancroft,* 103 A.D.2d 88, 90-91, 478 N.Y.S.2d 333 [2d Dept. 1984]; *In re Topps Co., Inc. Shareholder Litig.,* 19 Misc. 3d 1103(A), 2007 WL 5018882, *4-5 [Sup. Ct., N.Y. County 2007]; *Berger v. Scharf,* 11 Misc. 3d 1072(A), 2006 WL 825171, *2 [Sup. Ct., N.Y. County 2006]; Restatement [Second] of Conflict of Laws § 84, comment d).

Rather, a New York court may properly retain jurisdiction over an action involving the internal affairs of a foreign corporation if a majority of other factors indicate that New York is an appropriate forum (*accord Broida,* 103 A.D.2d at 90-91, 478 N.Y.S.2d 333; Restatement [Second] of Conflict of Laws § 313, comment c).

A foreign state of incorporation generally weighs heavier in favor of dismissal on the ground of forum non conveniens where related actions are already being litigated in that state (*see e.g. Carroll v. Weill,* 2 A.D.3d 152, 152, 767 N.Y.S.2d 627 [1st Dept. 2003], *lv. denied* 2 N.Y.3d 704, 780 N.Y.S.2d 310, 812 N.E.2d 1260 [2004]; *Sturman v. Singer,* 213 A.D.2d 324, 325, 623 N.Y.S.2d 883 [1st Dept. 1995]; *see also Hart,* 129

A.D.2d 179, 517 N.Y.S.2d 490 [dismissal in favor of Delaware, the state of incorporation, was proper where multiple and virtually identical actions were already pending there]).

The court already determined that a number of relevant factors indicate that New York is an appropriate forum. Further, there is no related action pending in Delaware.[6] As indicated above, there is an action pending in the Southern District of New York against SICO, the Federal Court Action, that involves similar factual issues present here, making it likely that discovery exchanged in that action is located in New York and will be relevant to this action (*Rostuca Holdings, Ltd. v. Polo,* 246 A.D.2d 475, 475, 667 N.Y.S.2d 250 [1st Dept. 1998]).

Defendants additionally argue that AIG has engaged in improper claim splitting that weighs in favor of forum non conveniens dismissal, because it should have brought the causes of action asserted here in the Delaware Derivative Action.

However, the doctrine against claim splitting does not apply, because the causes of action in the Delaware Derivative Action do not arise out of the same transaction or series of transactions at issue in this action (*Barrett v. Delma Properties, Inc.,* 35 A.D.3d 279, 279, 825 N.Y.S.2d 911 [1st Dept. 2006]; *Brown v. Lockwood,* 76 A.D.2d 721, 739-40, 432 N.Y.S.2d 186 [2d Dept. 1980]).

In the Delaware Derivative Action, AIG is challenging Greenberg and Smith's alleged involvement in accounting improprieties that ultimately led do their departure from AIG. The conduct at issue here is the Defendants' alleged failure to safeguard the Shares, and improper cancellation of AIG's compensation plans, that occurred subsequent to Greenberg and Smith's resignation as AIG executives.

Therefore, because Defendants failed to demonstrate private and public interest factors that militate against retaining New York as the forum to litigate this action, the motions to dismiss on the ground of forum non conveniens are denied.

. . .

Post-Case Follow-Up

As the *AIG* case suggests, litigation involving business entities (and individuals who own or lead those organizations) can touch many different jurisdictions — the jurisdiction where the entity was formed, jurisdictions where the business has substantial operations, and (in some cases) jurisdictions where plaintiffs reside. For this reason, lawyers representing business organizations may be called upon to examine forum selection bylaws, the internal affairs doctrine, and civil procedure doctrines relating to forum and venue when helping clients plan for, and navigate through, disputes.

---

[6]There is a shareholder derivative action (Delaware Derivative Action) pending against Greenberg and Smith in the Delaware Chancery Court, that arises out of unrelated transactions that are not at issue in this action, namely, their alleged involvement in accounting improprieties in several large reinsurance transactions. These transactions are also the subject of an action brought by the Attorney General of the State of New York, that is currently pending before this Court. The Delaware Derivative Action is currently stayed.

American International Group, Inc. v. Greenberg: Real Life Applications

1. Zed, Inc. is a Delaware corporation. You represent Sandra, a shareholder of Zed. Sandra lives in New York, where Zed maintains its corporate headquarters. Zed recently restated its results of operations for 2014 after discovering that the company's former (and recently fired) chief financial officer engaged in financial reporting irregularities. (A restatement is a revision and republication of previously reported results.) Sandra has asked you to prepare a complaint alleging breach of fiduciary duty against the chief financial officer and other officers and directors and to file the complaint in a court in New York State.

   a. What law is likely to govern this case?

   b. Will the choice of a New York forum dictate the choice of law?

   c. If the court concludes that Delaware law applies, does that mandate dismissal of any claims filed in New York?

2. You represent Zed, Inc., a Delaware corporation. After examining the *Boilermakers Local 154 Retirement Fund* case and subsequent Delaware legislative developments referenced in the "Internal Affairs and Forum Selection Bylaws" sidebar immediately below these questions, draft a forum selection bylaw for Zed.

5. Corporations Codes and Mandatory versus Default Rules

One final point on the law that governs corporations: As you will recall from Chapters 3, 4, and 5 (dealing with various types of partnerships), state partnership statutes consist largely of default rules. Compared to partnerships (and limited liability companies, as you will learn in Chapter 12), corporations are subject to many more mandatory rules than default rules. A mandatory rule is one that is not subject to private ordering—meaning it cannot be modified by agreement between the parties, and indeed will apply even if the parties seek to contract around it. For example, state corporations codes contain rules respecting directors' fiduciary duties of care and loyalty owed to the corporation and its shareholders. Directors' fiduciary obligations are not subject to private ordering, meaning (for example) that a director cannot "opt out" of owing fiduciary duties via contract. Even when corporations codes allow for private ordering, there often are substantive or procedural requirements or limits on the

Internal Affairs and Forum Selection Bylaws

In *Boilermakers Local 154 Retirement Fund v. Chevron Corp.*, 73 A.3d 934 (Del. Ch. 2013), shareholders of two Delaware corporations challenged the validity of forum selection bylaws (we discuss bylaws below) that stated that litigation relating to the corporation's internal affairs should be brought in Delaware courts. The plaintiffs alleged that the forum selection bylaws were beyond the board's statutory authority and contractually invalid due to the manner of adoption. The Chancery Court rejected these challenges, holding that the bylaws were valid as a matter of both Delaware corporate law and contract law. Following this decision, the Delaware State Legislature approved amendments to the Delaware General Corporation Law that (i) authorize forum selection clauses in the charters or bylaws of Delaware corporations specifying

Delaware as an exclusive forum for litigating internal corporate claims; and (ii) prohibit clauses designating only courts outside of Delaware as the exclusive forum for internal corporate claims. The Delaware governor signed these amendments into law on June 24, 2015, and the amendments became effective on August 15, 2015. Forum selection bylaws and related issues are discussed in more detail in Chapter 8.

power to customize the rule. For example, some corporate law rules can be modified only by a provision in the corporation's charter (articles of incorporation), others can be amended via the charter or the corporation's bylaws, while still others can be amended via the corporation's bylaws or a resolution of the board of directors. (We define and discuss corporate charters, bylaws, and board resolutions below.) As we work through our materials on corporation, keep an eye out for mandatory versus default rules, and be sure that you keep track of how to modify those few corporate law rules that allow for at least some private ordering.

C. TAXATION OF CORPORATIONS

1. Subchapter C

As discussed in Chapter 1, corporations are taxed under Subchapter C of the Internal Revenue Code unless they elect (and are eligible to elect) to be taxed as a small business corporation under IRC Subchapter S. Subchapter C tax classification carries with it the burden of **double taxation**. As you will recall, double taxation means that corporate profits are taxed twice — once at the entity level and once at the shareholder level. How does this work in practice? After paying taxes on its income according to rates applicable to corporations, a corporation may distribute these earnings/profits (or some portion thereof) to the shareholders. Money received by shareholders, even $1, must be declared as income by the shareholder, and thus is subject to taxation at the shareholder level, as well. Thus, under Subchapter C taxation, the same money is taxed once when the corporation receives it, and then again when it is distributed to the shareholders.

The imposition of tax at both the corporate level and the individual shareholder level under Subchapter C taxation contrasts sharply with the default taxation regime applicable to sole proprietorships, general and limited partnerships, registered limited liability partnerships, and limited liability companies, all of which "pass through" all the income earned by the business to the owners, who then pay tax at whatever rate is applicable to them. Note, however, that if an entity that would otherwise enjoy pass-through tax treatment elects to be taxed as a corporation under the IRS "check the box" provisions, then the double taxation regime will apply.

2. Avoiding or Minimizing the Effects of Double Taxation

Various measures can be taken to avoid or minimize the effects of double taxation, including the techniques discussed here. As with any matter involving federal and state taxation, one should review applicable rules carefully and consult with an expert before deploying any strategy intended to manage or reduce tax-related obligations.

S-Corporations

As noted above, some corporations avoid the burden of double taxation by electing to be S corporations, as Subchapter S provides for pass-through taxation. As you will recall from our earlier discussion, a corporation that wishes to elect Subchapter S treatment may do so only if it meets the following requirements: (i) it is a domestic entity, meaning that it is organized in one of the 50 states or the District of Columbia; (ii) it has fewer than 100 owners; (iii) all of the owners are individuals, estates, certain types of trusts, or tax-exempt organizations; (iv) none of its owners is a non-resident alien; (v) it has only one class of ownership interests outstanding; and (vi) its stock is not publicly traded.

Small Corporations Whose Shareholders Are Employees

Small corporations whose stock is held by a few family members or friends, all actively employed by the corporation, may seek to reduce the burden of double taxation by choosing not to distribute dividends to the shareholders. Instead, if all of the shareholders are employed in the business, each might receive a merit bonus or holiday bonus or salary increase rather than a "dividend" as a way of sharing in the corporation's profits. The recipient of the bonus or salary must still pay tax on that money received, but the payment of salaries or bonuses is a deduction for a corporation that can be used to offset income and reduce tax liability. (Note, however, that the IRS may challenge such transactions as being constructive distributions, and thereby deprive the corporation of a deduction, in certain circumstances.) This technique is not available to larger or publicly traded corporations whose stock is owned by nonemployees.

Section 1244 Stock

Section 1244 of the Internal Revenue Code was enacted to allow shareholders of small domestic business corporations to deduct as ordinary losses (as opposed to capital losses) losses sustained on the sale or other taxable disposition of stock. To receive this favorable tax treatment, the Internal Revenue Code contains specific requirements for (i) the corporation issuing the stock; (ii) the stock itself; and (iii) the shareholders of the corporation. As these requirements are quite technical, what follows is a greatly simplified summary.

The corporation issuing the stock must qualify as a domestic small business corporation. For § 1244 purposes, to qualify as a "small business," the corporation's aggregate capital must not exceed $1 million at the time the § 1244 stock is issued to shareholders. The corporation also must derive more than 50 percent of its receipts from sources other than passive investment income (e.g., collecting rent on an investment property is an example of a passive investment activity). This requirement ensures § 1244 tax relief is available only to a small business actively engaged in a trade or business. With respect to the stock itself, IRC rules provide that both common stock and preferred stock may qualify for § 1244 treatment. In order to qualify for § 1244 stock treatment, however, the stock must be issued and the consideration paid must consist of money or other property, but not services. Stock and other securities do not qualify as "other property" for this purpose. Finally, with respect to the shareholders, § 1244 is available only for shareholders who are individuals. Losses on shares held by a corporation, for example, are not eligible.

If the requirements of § 1244 of the Internal Revenue Code are met, losses on the sale or other taxable disposition of § 1244 stock will be treated as ordinary loss (and not as capital loss), subject to an annual limitation and certain other requirements. The current limitation is $50,000 per year for individuals and $100,000 in the case of spouses filing joint returns. Such losses can then be used to offset ordinary income (such as salaries), up to allowable limits. Confirmation of the desire to access the tax relief available under § 1244 can be accomplished at a meeting of the corporation's directors. In many cases, confirmation takes place at the corporation's first organizational meeting.

Qualified Small Business Stock

Another way corporations can avoid or minimize the effect of double taxation is through the provisions of § 1202 of the Internal Revenue Code (26 U.S.C. § 1202), enacted to allow individuals who hold qualified small business stock (QSBS) for more than five years to exclude all of the gain they realize on the sale of such stock. (By way of history, in tax years 2011 through 2013, all of the gain could be excluded from one's taxes. Then, for a period of time, only one half of any gain was excludable; the remaining one half of the gain was taxed as a capital gain. In December 2015, the Protecting Americans from Tax Hikes Act of 2015 ("PATH Act") was passed by Congress and signed into law. The PATH Act made several tax breaks permanent, including § 1202. The PATH Act thus made permanent the exclusion of 100 percent of the gain on the sale or exchange of qualified small business stock acquired after September 27, 2010, and held for more than five years.) A qualified small business must have total gross assets of less than $50 million at the time the stock is issued, and at least 80 percent of its assets must be used in certain trades and businesses (and generally *not* in businesses involving the performance of services, such as law or medicine).

Limited Liability Companies

Choosing to form as a limited liability company, discussed in Chapter 12, rather than a corporation, also avoids double taxation while providing limited liability to the members, as LLCs are eligible for pass-through tax treatment under default rules.

Limited Liability Partnerships

Like limited liability companies, limited liability partnerships (discussed in Chapter 4) also are eligible for pass-through tax treatment. Recall, however, that personal liability in a limited liability partnership is somewhat unresolved (with 49 jurisdictions providing full shield protection from liability and two providing only partial shield protection from negligence and misconduct). For this and other reasons, the limited liability partnership form might not be suitable for a large business intending to operate on a nationwide basis.

3. Other Taxes

In addition to income tax, corporations may also be subject to various state fees and taxes, including real estate and **franchise taxes**, which are taxes imposed by states on businesses for the privilege of being able to conduct business in the state.

D. FORMATION: PRE-INCORPORATION ACTIVITIES BY PROMOTERS

1. Duties of Promoters to One Another

Oftentimes, when founders approach a lawyer for help forming a corporation or other business entity, they have already taken preliminary steps to establish their business. For example, the founders may have entered into a lease for office space, purchased equipment on credit, etc. A person who engages in this type of pre-incorporation activity is referred to as a **promoter**. Although that term may have a slightly unsavory connotation in other contexts, in the context of pre-incorporation activities, it refers solely to the persons who plan and organize the corporation.

During the process of planning and forming the corporation, promoters are usually viewed as joint venturers/partners who have undertaken one particular activity, that of forming a corporation. The promoters may have a written agreement defining their rights and responsibilities, but because a joint venture can be created without a written agreement, one is not required. That said, reducing the parties' agreement to writing is generally a good idea. Especially if the parties contemplate making substantial contributions to the corporation or will be engaging in extensive activities on behalf of the proposed corporation, the promoters should have a formal written agreement defining their rights and obligations to each other and to the proposed corporation.

As joint venturers/partners, promoters owe obligations of good faith and fiduciary duties of care and loyalty to each other and to the proposed corporation. This means that promoters must deal with each other and with the proposed corporation in good faith, loyally, and with due care. Under these standards, a promoter may be liable for failing to disclose pertinent information, for example, or for secret profits obtained. To see how this might play out in practice, assume one promoter is charged with the responsibility of finding a lot on which to build the corporate offices. If the promoter owns real estate and wishes to sell it to the proposed corporation, he must disclose all material information about the property. Failure to disclose known defects about the lot, such as drainage or access problems, would be a violation of the fiduciary duties owed by the promoter. Disclosure should be made to the other promoters and to any prospective shareholders or others who may be interested in the corporation. Similarly, full disclosure must be made if a promoter might stand to gain by a transaction (such as owning the lot next to the one he proposes the corporation buy and build on when construction would enhance the value of his lot).

2. Pre-Incorporation Contracts by Promoters

In addition to obligations owed to one another and to the proposed corporation, promoters may incur obligations to third parties through **pre-incorporation contracts**. For example, assume Carlos, Ellen, and Amanda are the promoters for a proposed corporation (Basketia) that will engage in making and selling gift baskets. Carlos may be assigned the task of finding office space for the corporation, Ellen may be in charge of hiring a receptionist and a secretary, and Amanda may be responsible for ordering stationery and advertising and promotional brochures and contracting for development of a website for the new business. In carrying out these tasks, Carlos might approach a landlord and seek to lease space. Based upon Carlos's representations, the landlord might enter into a lease agreement with Carlos, take the property off the market, and prepare to remodel the space pursuant to Carlos's instructions. Ellen might advertise for employees and hire two individuals who leave their present jobs in reliance on getting jobs at the new business. Amanda might order the stationery and brochures printed by a local company at great expense and engage a website developer to build a site for Basketia.

If everything goes as planned, Basketia will honor these pre-incorporation contracts once the corporation is formed. What happens, though, if there is a falling out among Basketia's promoters, causing them to abandon the enterprise or to refuse to honor pre-incorporation contracts? The landlord could be left with a remodeled space that has not been on the market for several weeks; the would-be employees might have quit their former jobs; the printer could have prepared materials never to be used by anyone; and the website developer may have created design templates and content for a site that will never be launched. All of these third parties will want compensation for their services and losses. The possibility of debts and obligations to third parties thus raises two important legal questions: (i) are Carlos, Ellen, and Amanda personally liable on pre-incorporation contracts? and (ii) is Basketia, if formed, liable on pre-incorporation contracts?

Promoter Liability

As a general rule, promoters are personally liable on pre-incorporation contracts, and remain liable on those contracts, even after the corporation is formed. Courts have used a variety of theories to hold promoters liable for their pre-incorporation agreements. If a promoter signs a written agreement in his individual capacity, the promoter is personally bound under contract law principles. So, in our example, if Carlos signed the lease in his own name, he would be bound under traditional contract law principles. If a promoter signs a contract in the name of the proposed corporation, but the third party is not aware that the corporation does not yet exist, the promoter will be personally liable under the agency law principle that an agent who acts on behalf of a non-existent principal is personally liable. So, if Carlos signed the lease in the name of the corporation yet to be formed, but the landlord was not aware that the corporation did not yet exist, Carlos would be personally liable on the lease. Section 2.04 of the MBCA is consistent with these rules:

> All persons purporting to act on behalf of a corporation, knowing there was no incorporation under this Act, are jointly and severally liable for all liabilities created while so acting.

Things become more complicated if Carlos signs the lease as a promoter on behalf of "Basketia, a corporation to be formed." This is because courts have held that a promoter will not be held personally liable on a pre-incorporation contract if the promoter can establish that the other party (here, the landlord) was aware that the promoter was signing on behalf of an entity to be formed, and agreed to look solely to the corporation on the contract. Thus, while § 2.04 of the MBCA refers only to promoter liability, the Official Comments to this section recognize that § 2.04 does not foreclose the possibility that persons who urge promoters to execute contracts in the name of the corporation knowing that no steps to incorporate have been taken may be estopped to impose personal liability on the promoter. If there is any ambiguity respecting the third party's knowledge or intentions, the trend is to hold promoters personally and jointly and severally liable on contracts entered into before the corporation is formed.

Corporation Liability on Pre-Incorporation Promoter Contracts

In contrast to promoters, corporations generally are not liable on pre-incorporation contracts, unless (i) the corporation adopts the contract; or (ii) the contract is assigned to the corporation, and the corporation is substituted in as the responsible party, a process also known as a **novation**. We discuss these doctrines in turn.

A corporation may adopt a pre-incorporation contract by manifesting an assent to be bound. A corporation may adopt a contract expressly (e.g., by a vote of board of directors), or it may be deemed to have impliedly adopted the contract (e.g., by accepting goods or services under the contract, and thereby manifesting assent to being bound). Continuing with our earlier example, Basketia could adopt the pre-incorporation contracts discussed above through a board vote (once the company is formed), or by moving into the leased spaces, accepting the employees' work, and using the stationery, brochures, and website. As a general rule, a corporation becomes bound on a pre-incorporation contract via adoption as of the date of the adoption.

In addition to adoption, a pre-incorporation contract also may be assigned from the promoter to the corporation. The assignment can be made effective as of the date the contract was entered into so that it is as if the corporation was always a party to the contract. Such an assignment may be called a nunc pro tunc (literally "now for then") assignment in certain jurisdictions, meaning that although the assignment document is executed on one date, it is effective as of a prior date.

Some jurisdictions use the concept of **novation**, a term meaning substitution, to describe the process of assignment and substitution of parties. In novation, the promoter is released and the corporation is substituted in place of the promoter as a party to the contract in all respects. Be aware that unless the promoter is released from contractual obligations via a novation, she will remain personally liable on pre-incorporation contracts — even if the corporation also becomes liable as a result of assignment. A well-advised promoter thus will include novation language in pre-incorporation contracts, if possible, to avoid remaining personally liable on pre-incorporation contracts after the corporation is formed.

In addition to assignment and novation, some courts have held that a corporation may be bound on a pre-incorporation contract if the corporation **ratifies** the contract. As with adoption, ratification can be express (e.g., through a board vote to ratify) or implied (e.g., by accepting benefits under the contract). Ratification is thought to "relate back" to the date the contract was entered into, so a corporation will be bound to a ratified contract as of the original date of execution. The problem with the doctrine of ratification is that under agency law principles, ratification can only occur if the principal existed at the time the contract was made. *See* Restatement (Second) of Agency §§ 84(1), 86(1); Restatement (Third) of Agency § 4.04. Since that is not the case when dealing with pre-incorporation contracts, it may be that a later-formed corporation lacks the legal power to ratify a pre-incorporation contract. The availability (or not) of the doctrine of ratification has legal significance, because ratification would retroactively validate a contract from the time the contract was made (the "relates back" doctrine cited above), whereas adoption makes a corporation a party to the contract only from the moment of adoption. Given the potential for confusion respecting these doctrines, lawyers should consider advising clients to manifest their intentions respecting pre-incorporation contract clearly, in written agreements and through board votes, using the doctrines of adoption, assignment, substitution, and novation.

Case Preview

Ratner v. Central National Bank of Miami

In the next case, the court considered whether a self-identified promoter ought to be held personally liable for unauthorized, forged sales drafts that a bank provisionally credited to the account of a later-formed corporation. The question on appeal was who should bear the loss for the forged drafts — the bank, the corporation, or the promoter? When reading the case, consider the following questions:

1. Promoters are individually liable for pre-incorporation contracts under default rules. Under what circumstances will promoters be relieved of personal liability?
2. Assume a corporation adopts a pre-incorporation contract. Is the promoter automatically off the hook?
3. Why did the court grant summary judgment in favor of the bank and find Ratner (the promoter) personally liable for the forged drafts?
4. What are the de facto corporation and de jure corporation doctrines? (Hint: Take a look at Section I.)

Ratner v. Central National Bank of Miami
414 So. 2d 210 (Fla. Dist. Ct. App. 1982)

Ferguson, Judge.*

Joel S. Ratner appeals from a summary judgment entered in favor of appellee, Central National Bank of Miami, plaintiffs below. Ratner contends that the trial court erred in granting summary judgment and finding Ratner personally liable for $32,756.56 in unauthorized sales drafts which Central National Bank had provisionally credited to the account of The Stereo Corner, Inc., pursuant to a merchant's Mastercharge agreement. The question on appeal is who should bear the loss for forged sales drafts — the bank, the corporation, or the promoter.

The facts are briefly these. On November 3, 1978, Central National Bank of Miami entered into a merchant's Mastercharge agreement with The Stereo Corner, Inc. The agreement was signed, The Stereo Corner, Inc., by Joel S. Ratner. Under the terms of the agreement the merchant warranted each sales draft and agreed to be liable for certain improper sales drafts including those executed or accepted fraudulently. The Stereo Corner, Inc. was not incorporated until July 10, 1979, eight months after the contract was signed. From April 21, 1979 to October 1, 1979, there was a series of deposits in Stereo Corner's account with Central National Bank and a corresponding series of charge-backs against the account by the bank pursuant to Section 674.212, Florida Statutes (1979). Central exercised its right of charge-back when it was unable to collect from the Mastercharge Center of Southeast First National Bank on the sales drafts forged by Stereo Corner's employee. When Central was unable to recoup its losses by charge-back to Stereo Corner's account, Stereo Corner having become insolvent, Central sued Ratner claiming Ratner was individually liable on the contract.

On appeal Ratner contends that questions of fact and law remain as to the following issues precluding entry of summary judgment: (a) whether Central intended to contract with the corporate entity and not hold Ratner individually liable, (b) whether Central Bank breached its statutory duty of ordinary care and is thereby estopped to assert its claim, and (c) whether Central satisfied the conditions of Section 674.212, Florida Statutes (1979), entitling it to a right of charge-back against Stereo Corner's account. We have determined the other issues raised by Ratner to be without merit.

We find no merit in Ratner's contention that there are material questions of fact and law as to whether he can be held personally liable for the corporate debt pursuant to Section 607.397,[1] Florida Statutes (1979). In an affidavit in opposition to the motion for summary judgment, Ratner states that he acted as a promoter for The Stereo Corner, Inc. Ratner contends, however, that he is not liable because his acts

---

*Most footnotes have been omitted for purposes of brevity.
[1]Section 607.397 provides:

> All persons who assume to act as a corporation without authority to do so shall be jointly and severely liable for all debts and liabilities incurred or arising as a result thereof.

as promoter were subsequently ratified by Stereo Corner on July 25, 1979 and, in addition, that The Stereo Corner was a de facto corporation.

We do not determine whether the Corporation Act of 1975, Chapter 607, Florida Statutes (1975), abrogated the doctrine of de facto corporation because there can be no de facto corporation where the filing of papers was not even attempted until eight months after the entity held itself out to be a corporation. . . .

The Florida law and general rule is that the promoter of a corporation is liable on his contract although the contract was made on behalf of the corporation to be formed, unless the other party agrees to look to another fund for payment. . . . The later formation of the corporation and subsequent adoption or ratification of the contract by the corporation does not necessarily release a promoter from liability, but may result in joint liability of the promoter and corporation, absent a novation or express release by the other party to the contract. *Vodopich v. Collier County Developers, Inc., supra. See also* Fletcher 1 Cyclopedia Corporations § 190 (perm. ed.) (1981 cum. supp.). Moreover, where the promoter does not make it clear that he is acting as a promoter and misrepresents — even if unintentionally — that the corporation is already in existence, thereby causing the other party to enter the contract without knowledge that the entity had not yet been incorporated, the later formation of the corporation and subsequent ratification of the contract, will not by itself, relieve the promoter of liability. . . .

In this case, Ratner stated in an affidavit that he was acting as promoter. There is no evidence that Central agreed to look solely to the corporation, and there is no evidence of novation or release of Ratner after the alleged ratification.

We also find no merit to Ratner's second issue on appeal. In his answer below, Ratner pled as an affirmative defense that Central Bank had by its actions either waived its rights or was estopped to assert its claims. We find no legal basis for Ratner's assertion on appeal that breach by Central of its statutory duty of ordinary care pursuant to Section 674.202, Florida Statutes (1979), estops Central from asserting its claim against Ratner. Nor is Section 674.202, *supra*, a defense to the bank's right to charge-back. It is, instead, the basis for affirmative relief by complaint or counterclaim. *See* Section 674.212(4)(b), Florida Statutes (1979), providing that a bank's right to charge-back is not affected by failure of bank to exercise ordinary care with respect to any item but any bank so failing remains liable. *See, e.g., Wells Fargo Bank v. Hartford National Bank and Trust Co.*, 484 F. Supp. 817, 822-23 (D. Conn. 1980).

. . .

Affirmed.

Post-Case Follow-Up

In addition to speaking to the liability of promoters (and corporations) on pre-incorporation contracts, the *Ratner* case also demonstrates why it is important to investigate the legal entity status of counterparties, and why it is important to be very clear about the liability of promoters and later-formed corporations. If you represent the founder of a business, it is best to create the legal entity through which the founder will do business (e.g., a corporation, limited liability company, etc.) before entering into any contracts. Otherwise, the founder (as promoter) is liable (and will remain liable absent a novation) on pre-incorporation contracts. As this suggests, to the extent that there are any pre-incorporation contracts in existence, it is important that you discuss with your client whether the corporation intends to adopt the contracts post-formation. If the corporation will adopt the contract, it is important to attend to the corporate formalities necessary to accomplish adoption (e.g., a board vote adopting the contract) to avoid confusion. It also is important to examine what agreements, if any, exist with counterparties respecting the liability of the founder/promoter and the liability of the corporation post-formation. Particularly if a business is new, counterparties may not be willing to consent to a novation, or otherwise release the promoter from personal liability. This is another reason why it is best to delay contracting until after formation.

Ratner v. Central National Bank of Miami: Real Life Applications

1. Sam is a recently retired police officer who is in the process of forming his own security services business. Sam intends to perform background checks on potential employees prior to extending an offer of employment but has not yet filed articles of incorporation with the secretary of state. Yesterday, Sam negotiated an agreement with Background Checkers, Inc., a company that provides finger printing and background check services. Sam signed the agreement as follows: "Sam, on behalf of Sam's Security Services, Inc." Sam explained that he was in the process of finalizing the paperwork for the business.

   For the next two weeks, potential employees reported to Background Checkers for finger printing and background checks. Background Checkers issued a bill to Sam, care of Sam's Security Services.

   One month after signing the agreement, Sam submitted formation papers to the secretary of state. The secretary of state accepted the papers and issued all necessary approvals relating to the formation of the company.
   a. Is Sam personally responsible for the bill submitted by Background Checkers? What about bills submitted by Background Checkers for expenses incurred after Sam's Security Services, Inc. was formed?
   b. Is Sam's Security Services, Inc. automatically responsible for the Background Checkers bill?

2. At the first regularly scheduled board meeting, Sam and the other directors review and approve the reports prepared by Background Checkers. The directors direct the company bookkeeper to prepare and mail a check to Background Checkers paying the bill in full.
   a. Is Sam excused from having to pay the Background Checkers bill?
   b. Is Sam excused from having to pay future bills from Background Checkers?
   c. Is Sam's Security Services responsible for paying future Background Checkers bills?

E. FORMATION: INCORPORATION MECHANICS

Choosing a Corporate Name

Selection

Selecting a name is one of the first tasks that a business should tackle when forming a corporation. Most state statutes require that the name of the corporation include some signal to the public that the business is a corporation and therefore the personal assets of shareholders may not be available to creditors. Generally, states require that the name include the word "corporation," "company," "incorporated," or "limited," or an abbreviation of one of these words. This is also the position taken by MBCA § 4.01. A few states prohibit the use of "limited" in a corporate name on the basis that it signals a limited partnership or a limited liability company. Delaware allows a wide variety of signals, including "association," "club," or "society."

Other guidelines might be set forth in state statutes. For example, most states prohibit the corporation from selecting a name implying the corporation is organized for a purpose other than that stated in its articles of incorporation. Similarly, most states prohibit the corporation from using certain words in the corporate name that would imply some association with a state or federal agency. Thus, a private corporation could not use the name "Federal Mortgage Lending, Inc.," as it implies some affiliation with the U.S. government. Similarly, many corporations codes prohibit certain selected words such as "bank," "trust," "bond," or "insurance," without prior approval from the state commissioners of banking or insurance. Finally, various federal statutes prohibit the use of certain words such as "Olympic," or "Red Cross," as they suggest an affiliation with the well-known organizations using those names.

A corporation also may not select a name that is the same as or confusingly similar to that used either by another domestic corporation or that used by a foreign corporation qualified to do business in that state. If a name is identical or confusingly similar to another (either a domestic corporation or a foreign corporation qualified to do business in the state), the secretary of state will refuse to allow incorporation of the corporation under that name. In nearly 40 states, if the secretary of state rejects the name as being too similar to that of another, it is possible to obtain the name if the other party consents in writing and the consent is delivered to the secretary of state (and, in many states, the other party agrees to change its name).

Finally, it is essential to examine whether the proposed name risks infringing upon the name or trademark of another. A **trademark** is a word, phrase, symbol, or design (or combination thereof) that identifies and distinguishes the source of the goods or services offered under the mark. Registering a trademark with the U.S. Patent and Trademark Office provides the trademark owner with the nationwide exclusive right to use the mark on or in connection with the goods or services listed in the registration materials. Approval of a corporate name by a secretary of state is no defense to a claim of trademark infringement. While preliminary trademark searching can be done through the website of the U.S. Patent and Trademark Office at www.uspto.gov, it is important to obtain advice from intellectual property counsel to confirm name availability.

A corporation — especially one that intends to offer its goods or services nationwide at some point — should give careful and deliberate thought to the corporate name early on in the formation process, to avoid devoting resources to a name that ultimately turns out to be unavailable or subject to challenge. Highly descriptive names such as "Medical Supplies, Inc." are so common that they are likely to be "taken" in at least some jurisdictions, thus precluding a potential corporation from doing business under the name in all jurisdictions. They also are likely to be given a very narrow scope of protection by courts, potentially hindering the corporation in its attempts to stop infringers from using the same or a highly similar name. Highly original names are much more likely to be available, and they are both less likely to infringe upon the intellectual property rights of another and more likely to receive protection in the courts. Such names may not be intuitive for consumers of the corporation's goods or services, however, and thus may require greater investment of time and money to build name recognition. These considerations point to the need to consult with both the corporation and intellectual property counsel early in the naming process, particularly if the proposed corporation intends to have a national footprint.

Reservation

If the name is available, it should be reserved for the prospective corporation during the period of time the articles of incorporation are being prepared. Some states allow the proposed corporation to reserve the name by phone call or online and will charge a modest fee to a credit card. Other states require that the **name reservation** be made in writing and accompanied by a fee. The fee will vary from state to state, with Arizona charging $10 to reserve a name to an average of approximately $25. Many states offer online name reservation. See Exhibit 6.2 for a sample name reservation form.

The reservation will be limited in its duration. MBCA § 4.02 allows for a nonrenewable 120-day period. Some states, such as Georgia, afford only a 30-day reservation period. Other states, such as Michigan and Washington, allow reservations for six months. During the period the reservation is in existence, the name may not be used or taken by any other corporation seeking to incorporate in that state or to qualify to do business in that state. In some states, the reservation might be renewable. Other jurisdictions have a nonrenewable reservation period, aiming to spur businesses to incorporate promptly and to clear the state's corporate rolls of unused names so they can be made available for use by others. You must be sure to docket the date the reservation expires to ensure timely filing of the incorporation papers during the period of the reservation (or to renew the reservation, if possible).

Registration

A procedure somewhat similar to reservation of a name is **registration** of a name. Registration is used by foreign corporations to preserve the corporate name in a state in which the corporation plans to do business. For example, assume a corporation is formed in New Jersey to operate a restaurant. After a period of time, the

EXHIBIT 6.2 **New York Application for Reservation of Name**

Application for Reservation of Name
Under §303 of the Business Corporation Law

NYS Department of State
Division of Corporations, State Records and Uniform Commercial Code
One Commerce Plaza, 99 Washington Avenue Albany, NY 12231-0001
www.dos.ny.gov

PLEASE TYPE OR PRINT

APPLICANT'S NAME AND ADDRESS

NAME TO BE RESERVED

RESERVATION IS INTENDED FOR (CHECK ONE)

☐ New domestic corporation (The name must contain "Incorporated" or "Inc." or one of the other words or abbreviations in §301 of the Business Corporation Law.)

☐ New domestic professional service corporation (The name must end with "Professional Corporation" or "P.C.")

☐ Foreign corporation intending to apply for authority to do business in New York State*

☐ Proposed foreign corporation, not yet incorporated, intending to apply for authority to conduct business in New York State

☐ Change of name of an existing domestic or an authorized foreign corporation*

☐ Foreign corporation intending to apply for authority to do business in New York State whose corporate name is not available for use in New York State*

☐ Authorized foreign corporation intending to change its fictitious name under which it does business in this state*

☐ Authorized foreign corporation which has changed its corporate name in its jurisdiction, such new corporate name not being available for use in New York State*

X_____   _____
Signature of applicant, applicant's attorney or agent   *Typed/printed name of signer*
(If attorney or agent, so specify)

INSTRUCTIONS:

1. Upon filing this application, the name will be reserved for 60 days and a certificate of reservation will be issued.

2. The certificate of reservation must be returned with and attached to the certificate of incorporation or application for authority, amendment or with a cancellation of the reservation.

3. The name used must be the same as appears in the reservation.

4. A $20 fee payable to the Department of State must accompany this application.

5. Only names for business, transportation, cooperative and railroad corporations may be reserved under §303 of the Business Corporation Law.

*If the reservation is for an existing corporation, domestic or foreign, the corporation must be the applicant.

restaurant might become well known and the corporation might consider opening branches in the neighboring states of Pennsylvania and New York. During the period in which the corporation is planning its expansion, conducting market surveys, and so forth, it should register its name in Pennsylvania and New York. A name registration keeps a corporate name available for a substantial length of time, often one year. During this period, no other corporation can be formed in or qualify to do business in those states using an identical or deceptively similar name.

Name registrations are thus used by corporations considering expansion into other jurisdictions and serve to save the name during the process of planning and development. Otherwise, the corporation might establish its reputation under one name, and then be "beat out" in another state by another company operating under that name and thus be unable to capitalize on consumer recognition of the original name. Most states provide specified forms for name registration and impose filing fees therefor. See Exhibit 6.3 for a sample registration of corporate name form. The name registration is generally effective for 12 months or until the end of the calendar year in which the application for registration is filed and is often renewable.

Not all states permit name registration. In those states that do not, in order to preserve a name for future use, a corporation might have to incorporate another corporation (a subsidiary corporation) solely for the purpose of holding the corporate name. Name reservation is not effective for this purpose because reservations are often for such short periods of time (30-120 days). The subsidiary will have few assets and will conduct no business. Nevertheless, it will be subject to regulation and taxation in the state of formation. Thus, this is a far more expensive and cumbersome route than name registration. It might be necessary, however, if the corporation plans to expand into other jurisdictions. Subsidiaries formed for these purposes are sometimes called **name-savers** or **nameholders**. Because corporations exist perpetually, there is no need to renew any forms when a name-saver is formed (although annual reports are required in all jurisdictions, and annual taxes and fees may be imposed on the name-saver corporation). When the parent is ready to conduct business in the state, the subsidiary can be merged into the parent.

Assumed Names

Just as sole proprietors and general partnerships often operate under an **assumed name** (or *fictitious name*), corporations can also be formed under one name and then elect to operate under another. A corporation might wish each of its separate divisions to operate under its own name. Alternatively, there could be certain marketing and consumer-related issues that necessitate operation under an assumed name. Most states provide forms for corporations to adopt an assumed name and will charge a filing fee therefor. In some states, the form used by sole proprietors and partnerships for fictitious names can also be used by corporations.

EXHIBIT 6.3 Illinois Application for Registration of Foreign Corporate Name

FORM **BCA 4.25** (rev. Aug. 2014)
**APPLICATION FOR REGISTRATION,
RENEWAL OR CANCELLATION OF
FOREIGN CORPORATION NAME**
Business Corporation Act

Secretary of State
Department of Business Services
501 S. Second St., Rm. 350
Springfield, IL 62756
217-782-9520
217-782-6961
www.cyberdriveillinois.com

Payment must be made by check or money
order payable to Secretary of State.

Filing fee $ _____ File # _____ Approved: _____

– – – – **Submit in duplicate** – – – – **Type or Print clearly in black ink** – – – – **Do not write above this line** – – – –

1. Corporation Name: _____

2. State or Country of Incorporation: _____

3. Date of Incorporation: _____

4. Business in which Corporation is engaged: _____
   _____

5. Post Office Address of Corporation to which the Secretary of State may mail notices:
   _____
   _____

6. The corporation desires to register its corporate name pursuant to Section 4.25, and it is not transacting business in the State of Illinois at this time.

7. Attached to this application is a certificate setting forth that the corporation is in good standing under the laws of the state or country wherein it is organized, executed by the proper officer of the state or country wherein it is organized, and which certificate shall not be more than 90 days old.

8. Check appropriate box:
   ☐ $50 registration fee
   ☐ $50 renewal fee
   ☐ $25 cancellation fee

9. Such registration or renewal of registration is effective from the date of filing by the Secretary of State until the first day of the 12th month following such date.

10. Cancellation is effective upon filing with the Secretary of State.

11. The undersigned corporation has caused this statement to be signed by a duly authorized officer who affirms, under penalties of perjury, that the facts stated herein are true and correct.

Dated _____ , _____   _____
            Month & Day   Year   Exact Name of Corporation

by   _____
            Any Authorized Officer's Signature

       _____
            Name and Title (type or print)

Printed by authority of the State of Illinois. January 2015 — 1 — C 197.11

F. FORMATION: THE ARTICLES OF INCORPORATION

Having selected a name, the next step is to prepare and file **articles of incorporation** with the secretary of state or similar agency. Some states, including Delaware, use the term **certificate of incorporation**, and others use the term **charter**, but most states and the MBCA use articles of incorporation. We will use these terms interchangeably to help you get familiar with all three of them. The state's corporations code will specify what must be included in the articles of incorporation. States generally provide forms for articles of incorporation, although use of the forms is not, of course, mandatory. By way of example, see Exhibit 6.4, which contains Delaware's certificate of incorporation form.

1. Elements of Articles of Incorporation

As a general rule, a business should include in the charter only (i) required provisions; and (ii) any desired optional provisions that the statute requires to be set forth in the articles, if they are to be adopted and implemented by the corporation. Articles of incorporation tend to be "bare bones" because corporate charters are public documents, and businesses often do not want to spell out every non-essential detail in a public document. In addition, because it may be difficult or costly to amend the charter, due to approval requirements, committing the corporation to non-essential rules, provisions, etc., in the charter may be unadvisable for governance and business reasons, as well.

Although there is some variation from state to state, the provisions described below generally must be included in articles of incorporation.

Name and Address

The corporation's name must be set forth in the articles. If it has been reserved, the articles of incorporation should be filed during the reservation period so that the name is "locked up" for the corporation. As noted above, review your state statute to ensure the corporate name complies with any requirements that the name include a designation of corporate status such as "Company," "Inc.," or "Corp."

The corporation also must set forth an address (usually called the **registered office** or **registered address**) in the state of incorporation so there will be a public record showing how and where the corporation can be reached. Nearly all states require a street address rather than a mere post office box. If the corporation does not intend to do business in that state and has incorporated there only for the purpose of incorporating under a permissive and flexible corporations code, it can make arrangements with various corporate service companies to maintain a registered office in the state. (For example, CT Corporation and Corporation Service Company will, for a fee, agree to serve as the registered office or address in the state of incorporation.) State secretary of state websites often list corporate service

State of Delaware Certification of Incorporation

STATE *of* DELAWARE
CERTIFICATE *of* INCORPORATION
A STOCK CORPORATION

- **First:** The name of this Corporation is _____
  _____.

- **Second:** Its registered office in the State of Delaware is to be located at _____
  _____ Street, in the City of _____
  County of _____ Zip Code _____. The registered agent in
  charge thereof is _____
  _____.

  Third: The purpose of the corporation is to engage in any lawful act or activity for
  which corporations may be organized under the General Corporation Law of
  Delaware.

- **Fourth:** The amount of the total stock of this corporation is authorized to issue is
  _____shares (number of authorized shares) with a par value of
  _____ per share.

- **Fifth:** The name and mailing address of the incorporator are as follows:
  Name _____
  Mailing Address_____
  _____Zip Code_____

- **I, The Undersigned,** for the purpose of forming a corporation under the laws of the
  State of Delaware, do make, file and record this Certificate, and do certify that the
  facts herein stated are true, and I have accordingly hereunto set my hand this
  _____day of _____, A.D. 20 _____.

BY:_____
(Incorporator)

NAME:[_____]
(type or print)

companies, as well. For example, the California and Delaware secretary of state websites contain lists of private service companies.

Agent for Service of Process

In nearly all states, the corporation must designate an individual residing in the state of incorporation or a domestic corporation or qualified foreign corporation that will receive service of legal process (the summons and complaint that initiate legal action). Once again, if the corporation is not actually doing business in the state of incorporation, and no individual residing in the state will agree to accept service of process, the corporation may enter into an agreement with one of the corporation service companies. For an annual fee, they will agree to accept service of process and immediately notify the corporation thereof so it can respond to the complaint and ensure that a default judgment is not entered against the corporation. In most states, the secretary of state is also authorized to accept service of process on behalf of the corporation. In New York, the articles must designate the secretary of state as the agent and need not appoint any other. Generally, changing the registered office or agent for service of process is fairly easy and does not require the complex process required for amending the articles. See Exhibit 6.5 for a sample form for changing the registered agent or registered office address. Many states require that the agent for service of process be located at the registered office.

Under MBCA § 14.20, failure to have a registered agent or registered office for 60 days is grounds for administrative dissolution of a corporation. The websites of most of the secretaries of state provide identification of agents for service of process for corporations incorporated in or doing business in the state. Enter a company's name in the search box and you will be informed of its date of incorporation, status (active, suspended, or dissolved), and the identity of its agent who will accept service of process.

Corporate Purposes

Many states require the corporation to set forth its purposes in the articles. A **corporation purpose clause** is a statement that describes the business the corporation is to conduct. Most states allow the corporation to use a **broad purpose clause** rather than setting forth in detail its actual purpose(s). A broad purpose clause typically provides that "the purpose of the corporation is to engage in any lawful act or activity for which a corporation may be organized under the laws of this state." The advantage of using such a clause is that it does not limit the corporation to any specific activity, and the corporation thus has room to grow and develop into other endeavors in the years ahead without requiring an amendment of its articles. Moreover, because the articles are open to public inspection, the corporation might not wish to set forth a detailed description of its business purposes.

If a state does require that the purposes be specifically set forth, the drafter of the articles should allow room for expansion by setting forth the specific purposes, and then adding a clause such as "and may transact any business or perform any act reasonably necessary to accomplish such purposes." As noted, modern corporations

EXHIBIT 6.5 **Florida Statement of Change of Registered Office or Registered Agent**

STATEMENT OF CHANGE OF REGISTERED OFFICE OR REGISTERED AGENT OR
BOTH FOR CORPORATIONS

*Pursuant to the provisions of sections 607.0502, 617.0502, 607.1508, or 617.1508, Florida Statutes, this
statement of change is submitted for a corporation organized under the laws of the State of _____
_____ in order to change its registered office or registered agent, or both, in the State of Florida.*

1. The name of the corporation:_____

2. The principal office address:_____

_____

3. The mailing address (if different):_____

_____

4. Date of incorporation/qualification: _____ Document number: _____

5. The name and street address of the current registered agent and registered office on file with the
   Florida Department of State: (If resigned, enter resigned)

   _____

   _____

   _____

6. The name and street address of the new registered agent (if changed) and /or registered office
   (if changed):

   _____

   _____
   P.O. Box NOT acceptable

   _____

The street address of its registered office and the street address of the business office of its registered agent,
as changed will be identical.

Such change was authorized by resolution duly adopted by its board of directors or by an officer so
authorized by the board, or the corporation has been notified in writing of the change.

_____   _____
Signature of an officer or director   Printed or typed name and title

*I hereby accept the appointment as registered agent and agree to act in this capacity.
I further agree to comply with the provisions of all statutes relative to the proper and complete
performance of my duties, and I am familiar with and accept the obligation of my position as registered
agent. Or, if this document is being filed merely to reflect a change in the registered office address, I
hereby confirm that the corporation has been notified in writing of this change.*

_____   _____
Signature of Registered Agent   Date

If signing on behalf of an entity:

_____
Typed or Printed Name

* * * **FILING FEE: $35.00** * * *

MAKE CHECKS PAYABLE TO FLORIDA DEPARTMENT OF STATE
MAIL TO: DIVISION OF CORPORATIONS, P.O. BOX 6327, TALLAHASSEE, FL 32314

CR2E045 (03/12)

statutes also permit the articles to authorize the corporation to engage in "any lawful purpose," and modern purpose clauses often include catch-all language to this effect, as well. The MBCA and many states do not require a purpose clause.

Description of Stock

A corporate charter must describe the corporation's shares. For example, the charter must state the number of **authorized shares,** or the number of shares that the corporation has the authority to issue. This number forms an upper limit on the number of shares the corporation can issue. If the corporation wishes to issue stock in an amount greater than this number, the articles will need to be amended. To eliminate this potential difficulty, the articles should provide for a large enough number to accommodate any anticipated growth. Be aware, however, that in some states, filing fees are based on the number of shares the corporation will issue. For example, in Delaware, a filing fee tax is based on the number of shares the corporation will issue. For stock with no par value (discussed below), the filing fee tax is one cent per share on the first 20,000 shares of stock issued ($200), and a half-cent for the next 1,980,000 shares to be issued ($9,900). For this reason, while it is important to "leave room" for growth, smaller corporations should remain mindful of fees associated with issuing a large number of shares.

In addition to stating the number of authorized shares, this section of the articles must also describe any privileges, preferences, or restrictions imposed on any class of stock. If there is only one class of stock, that stock is usually called the **common stock** of the corporation. Common and preferred stock will be fully discussed in Chapter 7, but at this point it is sufficient to know that **common stock** is stock of a corporation having no special features or privileges, whereas **preferred stock** generally has some privilege(s) (typically, a liquidation preference or dividend preference, or both, as discussed in Chapter 7). If the corporation will issue more than one class of stock, the charter must state the number of authorized shares in each class and the rights and preferences of each class.

In some states, this section also must state the par value of the stock, if any, or include a statement that the stock has no par value. **Par value** is the nominal or face value of each share of stock, which is generally quite low. Par value is the minimum amount for which a share of stock may be issued. Stock that has no par value may be issued for any amount per share that the directors of the corporation deem appropriate. When required, the statement in the articles describing the stock of the corporation can be quite simple: "The corporation has the authority to issue 20,000 shares of common stock with a par value of $1 per share." By way of example, see the articles of incorporation of Microsoft Corporation, which state as follows:

Article IV — Capital Shares
3.1 **Authorized Shares**

The total number of shares of stock that the Corporation shall have authority to issue is 24,100,000,000 shares, which shall consist of 24,000,000,000 shares of common stock, $0.00000625 par value per share ("Common Shares") and 100,000,000 shares of preferred stock, $.01 par value per share ("Preferred Shares"). Except as otherwise provided in accordance with these Articles of Incorporation, the Common Shares shall have unlimited voting rights, with each share being entitled to one vote, and the rights to receive the net assets of the Corporation upon dissolution, with each share participating on a pro rata basis.

The MBCA approach and that of most states is to eliminate any requirement of referring to par value in the articles. We discuss par value in more detail in Chapter 7.

Incorporators

The name (and usually the address) of each **incorporator** (those preparing the articles) must be provided. The incorporators must also sign the articles of incorporation. In many instances, the attorney or paralegal preparing the articles will sign as the incorporator. Some states require the incorporator to formally acknowledge the truth of the contents of the articles.

Other Elements as Required by State Law

There may be other elements required for the articles of incorporation in certain states. For example, in New Jersey, the certificate of incorporation must set forth the names and addresses of the initial directors of the corporation. N.J. Rev. Stat. § 14A:2-7(1)(h). By way of comparison, MBCA § 2.02 requires only the following elements to be included in the articles of incorporation: the corporate name; the number of authorized shares; the street address of the corporation's registered office and the name of its registered agent at that office; and the name and address of each incorporator.

2. Optional Provisions in Articles of Incorporation

There are two kinds of optional provisions that may be included in a corporate charter. First, certain provisions must be included in the articles of incorporation if the corporation desires to adopt or invoke the rule at issue. For example, under MBCA § 7.25, *unless the articles of incorporation provide otherwise*, a majority of votes constitute a quorum. *See* MBCA § 7.25 (emphasis added). Similarly, MBCA § 8.08 provides that shareholders may remove directors with or without cause, *unless the articles provide that directors may be removed only for cause* (meaning for a reason, such as fraud or dishonesty). *See* MBCA § 8.08 (emphasis added). In the absence of provisions in the articles of incorporation modifying the statutory default rules referenced in these sections, the default statutory provisions will apply, so if a corporation wishes to depart from the default, it must do so via a charter provision.

Second, most states and the MBCA allow the inclusion of purely optional provisions in the articles of incorporation. The following items are among the more common optional provisions found in articles of incorporation:

- number, names, and addresses of the initial board of directors and a statement as to how directors are to be elected or appointed;
- the period of duration of the corporation (the articles often provide that the corporation is to exist perpetually, although there is no reason a specific date of termination cannot be set);
- provisions requiring greater than majority vote for certain corporate action, such as requiring two-thirds approval by shareholders for a merger;
- provisions regarding managing the business of the corporation;
- provisions imposing personal liability on shareholders (under specified conditions), if desired;
- provisions eliminating or restricting the personal liability of directors for money damages in the event of a breach of duty by the directors (other than disloyal acts, including intentional misconduct, willfully reckless, or criminal acts);
- provisions permitting the corporation to indemnify directors or officers if they incur liability (such provisions usually require that these corporate managers have acted in good faith); or
- any provisions that may be set forth in the corporation's bylaws.

3. Preemptive Rights

The articles of incorporation may include a provision allowing preemptive rights for the shareholders. A **preemptive right** is the right of a shareholder, when new shares are being issued, to purchase as much of the newly issued stock as is needed to maintain her then-current ownership interest in the corporation. In essence, a preemptive right is a kind of right of first refusal. Before the corporation can sell stock to any outsiders, the current shareholders must be given the opportunity to purchase stock in an amount equal to their present percentage of ownership in the corporation.

Assume that when a corporation is formed, Chris, Sean, and Kevin purchase 37 percent, 42 percent, and 21 percent, respectively, of the stock of the corporation. The corporation has the authority to issue additional shares and wishes to do so to raise capital. If the shareholders have preemptive rights, Chris would have the opportunity to purchase 37 percent of any later stock to be issued, Sean would have the opportunity to purchase 42 percent of any later stock to be issued, and Kevin would have the right to purchase 21 percent of any newly issued stock. Only when the shareholders elect not to exercise their rights to make such purchases can the corporation offer the stock to third parties. Thus, preemptive rights allow shareholders to maintain their proportionate interest and control in a corporation. When preemptive rights exist, the corporation cannot flood the market with shares and thereby unilaterally reduce existing shareholders' power and control.

In most states, if preemptive rights are to be given, they must be included in the articles of incorporation. A common preemptive provision is as follows: "Shareholders shall have the right to purchase their pro rata interest in shares of any new stock that may be issued by the corporation." Failure to specify that preemptive rights exist typically means that they do not exist. This is the approach in Delaware and of the MBCA. Other states have contrary statutory provisions. Statutes that provide that preemptive rights exist unless denied in the articles are often referred to as **opt out provisions**; whereas statutes that provide that preemptive rights exist only if the corporation elects them in its articles are called **opt in provisions**. Shareholders who have preemptive rights must be given notice and an opportunity to purchase newly issued stock. This notice and waiting period may delay the corporation in raising money. Preemptive rights generally exist for shareholders only when new stock is issued for cash and not when stock is issued under employee stock option plans or other similar plans.

The general trend is that preemptive rights are disfavored because they tend to restrict the flexibility of a corporation that might need to issue stock to raise capital. Furthermore, preemptive rights are generally seen only in smaller corporations in which maintaining ownership and control is important to a small group of shareholders. For an example of a charter provision expressly stating that preemptive rights do not exist, see the following excerpt from General Electric Company's charter:

1. Preemptive Rights

No present or future holder of any shares of the corporation of any class or series, whether heretofore or hereafter issued, shall have any preemptive rights with respect to (1) any shares of the corporation of any class or series, or (2) any other security of the corporation (including bonds and debentures) convertible into or carrying rights or options to purchase such shares.

4. Filing of Articles of Incorporation

Once drafted, the articles of incorporation must be filed with the appropriate state agency, usually the secretary of state, in the state of incorporation. Each state's filing requirements vary slightly, and failure to comply with the state's requirements will likely result in refusal of the articles of incorporation. In some instances, the incorporator simply mails the articles of incorporation to the office of the secretary of state with an appropriate cover letter and the required filing fee. Some states, such as Florida, provide a sample cover letter. Most states now permit online filing of the articles of incorporation with payment of fees by credit card. The secretary of state will then review the articles to ensure they comply with the state's requirements. The secretary of state might then return a copy of the articles to the incorporator stamped "Approved" or "Filed" along with a date, might issue a formal certificate of incorporation confirming the date of incorporation, or might send an electronic notice verifying incorporation. Some states require that additional copies of the articles be provided; one copy is retained for the state's files and another is file-stamped and returned to the incorporators to verify incorporation.

Some states require that other formalities be observed. For example, Florida requires that the registered agent sign the articles, accepting the appointment as registered agent for the corporation and confirming that the agent understands her duties in connection with acting as the corporation's agent (see Exhibit 6.6). Pennsylvania requires that the incorporators advertise their intention to file the

EXHIBIT 6.6   **Florida Articles of Incorporation and Registered Agent Acceptance Statement**

ARTICLES OF INCORPORATION
In compliance with Chapter 607 and/or Chapter 621, F.S. (Profit)

ARTICLE I   NAME
The name of the corporation shall be:_____

ARTICLE II   PRINCIPAL OFFICE

Principal **street** address   Mailing address, if different is:

_____   _____

_____   _____

_____   _____

ARTICLE III   PURPOSE
The purpose for which the corporation is organized is: _____

_____

_____

_____

_____

_____

_____

_____

ARTICLE IV   SHARES
The number of shares of stock is:_____

ARTICLE V   INITIAL OFFICERS AND/OR DIRECTORS

Name and Title:_____   Name and Title:_____

Address   _____   Address: _____

               _____   _____

               _____   _____

Name and Title:_____   Name and Title:_____

Address   _____   Address: _____

               _____   _____

               _____   _____

Name and Title:_____   Name and Title:_____

Address   _____   Address: _____

               _____   _____

               _____   _____

EXHIBIT 6.6 **(continued)**

Name and Title:_____   Name and Title:_____

Address   _____   Address: _____

_____   _____

_____   _____

ARTICLE VI   REGISTERED AGENT
The **name and Florida street address** (P.O. Box **NOT** acceptable) of the registered agent is:

Name: _____

Address: _____

_____

ARTICLE VII   INCORPORATOR

The **name and address** of the Incorporator is:

Name: _____

Address: _____

_____

ARTICLE VIII   EFFECTIVE DATE:
Effective date, if other than the date of filing: _____. (OPTIONAL)
(If an effective date is listed, the date must be specific and cannot be more than five business days prior or 90 business days after the filing.)

Note: If the date inserted in this block does not meet the applicable statutory filing requirements, this date will not be listed as the document's effective date on the Department of State's records.

Having been named as registered agent to accept service of process for the above stated corporation at the place designated in this certificate, I am familiar with and accept the appointment as registered agent and agree to act in this capacity

_____   _____
Required Signature/Registered Agent   Date

I submit this document and affirm that the facts stated herein are true. I am aware that the false information submitted in a document to the Department of State constitutes a third degree felony as provided for in s.817.155, F.S.

_____   _____
Required Signature/Incorporator   Date

articles or advertise the actual filing of the articles. Proofs of publication of such advertising must be kept with the minutes of the corporation. A careful reading of the pertinent state statutes is required to ensure that any other miscellaneous formalities are completed.

In most states, and according to the MBCA, corporate existence begins upon filing of the articles of incorporation. Some states, however, provide that corporate existence begins upon issuance of a certificate of incorporation by the secretary of state. Many states and the MBCA permit the articles to provide that they will not become effective until some date after the filing date. It might be necessary to determine the date the corporation comes into existence for tax reasons or for determining when promoters' obligations for pre-incorporation obligations end and corporate responsibility begins.

G. CORPORATE PURPOSE VERSUS CORPORATE POWERS

1. Corporate Purpose

Although not a formation issue, we want to clarify the difference between corporate purpose and corporate powers at this point to avoid confusion. Whereas corporate purpose refers to the business the corporation intends to conduct, **corporate powers** refer to the methods the corporation may use to achieve its purpose. For example, if a corporation's purpose is to buy and sell real estate, it needs the power to enter into contracts for the purchase and sale of real estate to achieve its business goals and objectives. Each state's corporation statute grants certain **powers** to the corporation to enable it to conduct business. MBCA § 3.02 provides a list of corporate powers. Among the powers typically granted to a corporation by state law are the following:

- to sue and be sued and to defend in the corporation's own name (rather than in the names of the officers, directors, or shareholders);
- to make and amend bylaws for regulating the business of the corporation;
- to purchase, acquire, own, hold, improve, sell, lease, or mortgage real or personal property;
- to enter into contracts, incur liabilities, borrow money, issue bonds, and lend money;
- to elect directors and appoint officers, employees, and agents;
- to establish pension and other benefit plans for its directors, officers, agents, and employees;
- to make donations for the public welfare;
- to make payments or donations that further the business of the corporation (such as those for political purposes);
- to purchase and hold shares or other interests in other entities;
- to be a member or manager of a partnership or other entity;
- to have and use a corporate seal;
- to transact any lawful business; and
- to exist perpetually.

2. The Ultra Vires Doctrine

Years ago, when corporations were required to state their specific purposes, and when corporate powers were to be exercised in service of a specifically identified corporate purpose, corporations would occasionally exceed or act beyond their purposes or powers as stated in their articles or under state law. Such acts were said to be ***ultra vires***, literally acts "beyond the powers" of a corporation. The early view was that corporations had no capacity to act beyond their powers; that any act that exceeded the corporation's powers was null and void; and that either party to a contract that exceeded a corporation's powers could disaffirm the contract, even if the other party had already performed its duties under the contract. Apart from disputes over contracts, unhappy shareholders would cite the *ultra vires* doctrine when challenging corporate acts such as charitable contributions and the creation of employee education, training, or benefits programs. *See, e.g., Dodge v. Ford Motor Co.*, 170 N.W. 668 (Mich. 1919); *A.P. Smith Mfg. Co. v. Barlow*, 98 A.2d 581 (N.J.), *appeal dismissed*, 346 U.S. 861 (1953).

Over the past one hundred years, courts have chipped away at the *ultra vires* doctrine. For example, starting in approximately 1900, courts began recognizing the unfairness of the application of the *ultra vires* doctrine and began to refuse to apply it in situations where one of the parties had substantially performed its duties under a contract. In addition, as state statutes and cases began broadening corporate powers, the *ultra vires* doctrine was further eroded as a meaningful constraint on corporate activity. The theory is that if a corporation has the power to perform any lawful act, then few acts can be challenged on the basis that they are *ultra vires*, or beyond the power of the corporation.

The MBCA reflects the modern approach to the *ultra vires* doctrine: Neither the corporation nor any third party doing business with the corporation can escape its respective duties on the theory that the corporation lacked authority to enter into the contract or power to act as necessary to perform contractual duties. The MBCA also lists as default corporate powers specific acts previously subject to challenge, including charitable contributions and employee assistance programs. MBCA §§ 3.02(12), 3.02(13). (Such expenditures should, however, be connected to the corporation's current or prospective welfare. Approval by directors or shareholders, where appropriate, is advisable.)

That said, there are still three actions that can be taken with regard to a transaction that allegedly exceeds the corporation's powers: A shareholder can sue to enjoin the transaction, the corporation can sue the directors and officers for taking the unauthorized action, and the attorney general can seek dissolution of the corporation. MBCA § 3.04. And, it may be that there are categories of acts that are *ultra vires* even today, such as illegal conduct. *See* Kent Greenfield, *Ultra Vires Lives! A Stakeholder Analysis of Corporate Illegality (With Notes on How Corporate Law Could Reinforce International Law Norms)*, 87 Va. L. Rev. 1279, 1281-82 (2001) ("Because unlawful acts are ultra vires — 'beyond the power' of the corporation — such activities become subject to the enforcement powers of corporate law, in addition to the enforcement powers of whatever governmental or private entity is charged with enforcing the underlying, substantive legal requirement.").

H. POST-INCORPORATION ORGANIZATIONAL ACTIVITIES

Once the corporation has been formed by the filing or the acceptance of the articles of incorporation, a few basic activities must be undertaken to organize the corporation. Bylaws must be drafted, supplies must be ordered, and an initial organizational meeting must be held.

1. Bylaws

Drafting **bylaws** is an important step in getting a newly formed corporation off the ground. Corporate bylaws contain rules governing the operation and management of a corporation. They should be presented and adopted at the first organizational meeting of the corporation. According to MBCA § 2.06(b), the bylaws of a corporation may contain any provision for managing the business and regulating the affairs of the corporation that is not inconsistent with law or the articles of incorporation. Bylaws are adopted by either the incorporators or the initial board of directors. We will discuss the substance of certain bylaw provisions in our chapter on corporate governance. For now, we will note typical items commonly provided for in corporate bylaws.

Introductory Information

The first few sections of the bylaws will set forth the name of the corporation and the address of its principal office and any other office locations. The bylaws may designate one office as the address to which notices and communications must be provided.

Information About Directors

The bylaws should contain various provisions relating to the board of directors, including the following:

- *Requirements for position.* Any specific requirements that must be met by directors (such as being residents of the state of incorporation or being shareholders in the corporation) should be set forth.

■ *Number, tenure, and compensation.* The bylaws should provide how many directors the corporation will have and when and how they will be elected, replaced, or removed from office. Compensation of directors and reimbursement of their expenses should be addressed.

■ *Authority to manage.* The bylaws should provide the directors with the authority to manage the corporation. If any limitations are desired (e.g., limitations on any one director's ability to incur indebtedness), they should be specified. Authority to declare and pay distributions to shareholders should be granted to the directors. If the board will have any committees, such as compensation committees, executive committees, or audit committees, their membership and duties should be described in full.

■ *Meetings.* The bylaws should provide when regular meetings of the directors will be held (weekly, monthly, quarterly, and so forth), where those meetings will be held, and any minimum advance notice required to be given to the directors. Provisions should be made for calling **special meetings** of the directors (any meeting between regularly scheduled meetings) and the appropriate notice therefor. The bylaws should establish how many directors constitute a **quorum** (the minimum number of directors who must be present to transact business), how meetings will be conducted and adjourned, and whether directors may take action without a formal meeting (i.e., by unanimous written consent or by conference call).

■ *Liability.* Because few individuals would agree to serve as directors if they believed they could be held liable for any mere error in business judgment, bylaws may (if permitted by state law) contain provisions exculpating directors from liability for money damages for certain types of fiduciary breaches, and provisions indemnifying the directors for any costs or expenses incurred in defending any lawsuit arising out of their ordinary business activities. Directors are not usually indemnified against criminal acts or intentional acts of recklessness. (Director exculpation and indemnification are discussed in more detail in Chapter 9.)

Information About Officers

The bylaws should identify the corporate officers. The most typical offices are president, vice president, secretary, and treasurer. A corporation may opt to have additional officers and can create additional titles and positions. The bylaws should confirm that the officers are to be appointed by the directors to carry out whatever management functions are delegated to them by the directors, and, similarly, that the directors may remove officers. The manner of filling officers' vacancies should be discussed. Specific duties for each officer can be set forth, as should information pertaining to their salaries and reimbursement of expenses incurred by them on behalf of the corporation.

Information About Shareholders

Just as the bylaws should contain all information pertaining to directors and officers of the corporation, so should they also include information relating to the owners of the corporation, the shareholders. Provisions regarding the holding and location of regular annual meetings as well as the manner for calling special meetings should be set forth. The method of voting and the authority of shareholders to vote in person or by proxy should also be detailed. The manner in which notice of meetings is to be provided should be specified, as well as information as to how many shareholders constitute a quorum to conduct business (typically, a quorum is a majority of shares outstanding), how elections of directors will be held, any particular provisions regarding voting, and any items that will require a **super-majority** (typically a two-thirds vote) rather than a simple majority. Any restrictions or limitations on voting rights of any classes of stock should be set forth. If the shareholders have the authority to act outside of a meeting, for example, by written consent, this should be indicated. Shareholders should be given the authority to inspect the shareholders' list and other corporate records.

Miscellaneous Information

The bylaws should also approve a form of stock certificate (typically attached to the bylaws) as well as the form for the corporate seal (often impressed upon the bylaws). Provisions relating to inspection of corporate records, how amendment of the bylaws will be effected, and the **tax year** of the corporation, which may be the **calendar year** (January 1 through December 31) or a **fiscal year** (a 12-consecutive-month period), should be set forth. A tax year is an annual accounting period for keeping records and reporting income and expenses. A tax year is adopted when the corporation files its first income tax return and generally requires IRS permission to change. (A form of bylaws for a non-public corporation is provided in Appendix B.)

Application Exercise 2

You have been asked to prepare and draft bylaws for Sheila and Sandy's crepe and sorbet business. Prepare an agenda for a meeting with Sheila and Sandy to discuss matters that you believe should be addressed in the bylaws. What questions should you highlight in your conversations with Sheila and Sandy? Assume that you have already prepared and filed articles of incorporation for the business.

---

2. Corporate Supplies

As soon as the corporation is formed, the necessary supplies for the corporation should be ordered. These supplies should be ordered only after formation of the corporation has been assured, because the seal (and often the stock certificates) might display the date of incorporation.

The **seal** is a device used to impress the corporation's name on certain documents. Just as kings of England used a specific seal to attest to the validity of documents, corporations are often required to impress their seal upon certain documents to verify their authenticity. Use of a seal is uncommon now, although it might be required on bids for government contract work, requests to open bank accounts, and various other official documents.

The **minute book** is usually a three-ring binder divided or tabbed into different sections. In one section, the corporation may place its articles and in another its bylaws. The minute book is best known for containing the minutes of meetings of directors and shareholders.

The **stock certificate book** resembles a large checkbook. Rather than checks, however, it contains certificates that are completed and provided to purchasers of the corporation's stock. Each certificate is required to include certain information (the name of the corporation, the type of stock being issued, the number of shares being issued, restrictions on transfer of the shares, if any) and must be signed by the corporate officers, typically, the president and secretary of the corporation. A rosette, or place for impressing the corporate seal, is usually found on the certificate. When the appropriate consideration for the stock has been received, the corporation will issue the certificate to the owner of the shares. A tear-off slip attached to the certificate will be completed and maintained by the corporation to provide a ledger or accounting of those to whom stock has been issued, the date of issuance, and the number of shares issued. The reverse side of the certificate typically includes endorsement information so that an owner of the stock can transfer it to another person by merely endorsing the certificate over to the new owner. These days, large corporations seldom use paper stock certificates. See Exhibit 6.7 for a sample stock certificate.

EXHIBIT 6.7   **Sample Stock Certificate**

3. Organizational Meeting

Although a corporation is legally formed upon the filing or acceptance of its articles of incorporation, some basic organizational activities must be undertaken to complete the process and start the corporation on its way. Accomplishing these goals occurs at the corporation's first meeting, usually referred to as the **organizational meeting**. Most states require that a corporation hold an organizational meeting. MBCA § 2.05(a)(1) provides that if initial directors are named in the articles of incorporation they shall call and hold an organizational meeting to complete the organization of the corporation by appointing officers, adopting bylaws, and carrying on any other business. If initial directors are not named in the articles of incorporation, the MBCA requires that the incorporators hold the organizational meeting to elect directors and complete the organization of the corporation.

Carefully review the statutes in the state of incorporation to determine if there are any requirements for the organizational meeting. For example, must the organizational meeting be held in the state of incorporation or can it be held elsewhere? Must written notice of the organizational meeting be given? Oftentimes, attorneys will hold the organizational meeting at their offices to ensure the corporation, its directors, officers, and shareholders are aware of various requirements imposed on them by the state and to emphasize the need to act in compliance with all statutory requirements relating to corporations in that state. The organizational meeting is usually attended by the incorporators, the initial board of directors, the initial officers, and (potentially) any anticipated shareholders. For small corporations, the meeting may therefore be attended by a mere handful of people. The items typically acted on at the organizational meeting are discussed below.

Election of Directors

If directors have not already been named in the articles of incorporation, they will be elected by the incorporators. If a "dummy" board was identified in the articles (such as the attorney, paralegal, and legal secretary), these "**dummy directors**" will resign one at a time and be replaced with the actual initial directors. The directors will "take over" and run the meeting. The role of the incorporator is now complete. The initial board of directors will serve until the first meeting of shareholders, at which time their successors will be elected.

Appointment of Officers

The directors of the corporation will appoint the officers of the corporation. The most typical offices of smaller corporations are those of president, vice president, secretary, and treasurer. Large corporations will have numerous other officers, such as a chief financial officer and chief operating officer.

Adoption of Bylaws

The bylaws drafted by the attorney will be presented and adopted.

Acceptance of Pre-Incorporation Stock Subscriptions

If parties have made offers to purchase stock upon the formation of the corporation, these offers or pre-incorporation share subscriptions should be accepted. The officers will be directed to issue stock certificates upon receipt of the amount offered in the subscription.

Acceptance of Pre-Incorporation Contracts

The directors should formally consider and ratify or adopt action taken by the promoters or contracts, if any, entered into by the promoters prior to incorporation. The promoters should be expressly relieved of their liability under those contracts. The corporation will then be a party to the various contracts with the right to enforce the terms and conditions of those contracts. For example, ratification or adoption of a lease for corporate offices entered into by a promoter will allow the corporation to demand that the premises be repaired or maintained. Ratification will also allow for reimbursement of the costs, including legal fees, incurred by the incorporators in preparing and filing the articles of incorporation and drafting the bylaws.

Approval of Corporate Seal and Form of Stock Certificate

The directors should approve the seal and the form of stock certificate obtained from the corporation's supplier. A sample or specimen of the stock certificate is often attached to the minutes of the meeting. Similarly, the seal is often impressed upon the minutes of the organizational meeting to demonstrate its form.

Banking and Accounting Information

The directors should discuss where the corporation's accounts will be held and the types of accounts to be opened, as well as any restrictions on banking. For example, the directors can require that for any expenditure in excess of $10,000, two officers must approve the transaction or must sign the check rather than merely one. The accountants to be used by the corporation may be designated. The directors can establish a fiscal year for the corporation (assuming it is not set forth in the bylaws). The most common fiscal year is the calendar year (January 1 through December 31), but other possibilities may be desired for particular businesses. For example, a corporation operating a resort with its peak season in the summer may elect a fiscal year of September 1 through August 31.

S Election

The directors should discuss whether it is desirable, if feasible, for the corporation to elect to become an S-Corporation. Because all shareholders must agree to the election, the directors' recommendation on this issue should be discussed with the shareholders if they are all present at the meeting or should be voted on at the first meeting of shareholders (sometimes held immediately following the organizational meeting). To obtain S status for a corporation, the filing must generally be made with the Internal Revenue Service within certain time limits to be effective for that tax year. Thus, election of S status is commonly discussed at the organizational meeting held shortly after incorporation.

Confirmation of § 1244 Stock

A "small business corporation" is automatically eligible for the benefits of § 1244 of the Internal Revenue Code. Although qualified corporations are not statutorily required to take affirmative action to achieve the tax benefits of § 1244, directors or incorporators often specifically confirm at organizational meetings that it is the corporation's intent that its stock qualify under § 1244 for the favorable tax treatment provided by that provision.

Issuance of Stock

The directors should authorize the officers to begin issuing stock and should fix the consideration to be paid per share.

Other Actions Taken at Organizational Meetings

Other actions taken at organizational meetings include the following:

- presenting the filed articles of incorporation to the attendees and placing the articles in the corporation's minute book;
- adopting employee benefit plans, including health and insurance plans, retirement plans, or other similar benefits;
- discussing whether the corporation will commence doing business in other states and, if so, making plans to qualify as a foreign corporation in those other states; and
- instructing the officers to apply for an Employee Identification Number (required for all corporations), if not already obtained.

If the shareholders are present at the organizational meeting, they will likely vote on only two issues: the election of directors and approval of the S-Corporation election. If the shareholders' initial meeting immediately follows, the shareholders will likely approve the election of the directors by the incorporators and will also vote on S-Corporation election.

After the organizational meeting, the corporate secretary will prepare minutes of the meeting reflecting the various actions taken at the meeting. These are signed by the secretary of the corporation and placed in the minute book. (In some cases, the attorney who handled the formation will prepare the initial set of minutes, which should be reviewed and signed by the corporate secretary and then filed in the minute book.)

Some states do not require that an actual formal organizational meeting be held. In those states, all of the activities that would be undertaken at an actual meeting can be done by unanimous written agreement. MBCA § 2.05(b) allows for action by unanimous written consent of the incorporators in place of an organizational meeting. The incorporators waive their right to notice and attendance at a formal meeting and unanimously agree in writing to all of the matters that would ordinarily be discussed at the organizational meeting. The **written consent** sets forth the names of the directors to be elected, the appointment of certain individuals as officers, approval of the pre-incorporation share subscriptions, and the like. Each director or incorporator will sign his name and date the document. The consent is placed in the minute book. (A form of written consent in lieu of organizational meeting is provided in Appendix C.)

Although acting by written consent may be easier than getting all of the principals of the corporation together for a meeting, it precludes the attorney from giving advice to the principals regarding their duties and obligations to the corporation and responding to questions regarding notice of meetings, preparing minutes of meetings, and the like. Thus, even though a state statute might allow for action to be taken by unanimous written consent rather than by a formal in-person organizational meeting, many attorneys prefer that the organizational meeting be held "in person" as an opportunity to emphasize corporate responsibilities and to respond to questions. Also, it is important to ensure compliance with formalities associated with written consents—for example, confirming that *unanimous* written agreement is required, ensuring that all of the covered stakeholders return signed, dated written consents to the company, etc.

Application Exercise 3

Create an agenda for the organizational meeting of Sheila and Sandy's corporation.

4. Annual Report

Although it is not due immediately after incorporation, most state statutes and MBCA § 16.21 require a corporation (both domestic and foreign corporations authorized to do business in the state) to submit an **annual report** providing basic information about the corporation. The MBCA requires the following information:

- name of the corporation and state of incorporation;
- address of the corporation's registered office and name of the registered agent at that office in the state;
- address of the corporation's principal office;
- names and business addresses of the corporation's directors and principal officers;
- brief description of the nature of the business;
- total number of authorized shares; and
- total number of issued and outstanding shares.

Although the secretary of state will usually automatically mail the report form (or a reminder that it is due) to the corporation to be completed, it is a good idea to docket the due dates for annual reports for any law firm corporate clients. For a large corporation that does business in numerous jurisdictions, calendaring, completing, and filing the annual reports is often nearly a full-time job. The annual report is usually accompanied by a filing fee and various state tax payments. Nearly all states now allow (and many require) electronic filing of annual reports.

I. DEFECTS IN INCORPORATION PROCESS

On occasion, there are defects in the incorporation process. For example, assume that a creditor is owed $50,000 by a corporation having three individuals as the directors, officers, and shareholders. If the corporation has only $30,000, the creditor might suffer a loss of $20,000 because the corporation protects the shareholders from personal liability for corporate debts and obligations. In such a case, the creditor might begin investigating various corporate documents in an effort to defeat the shareholders' limited liability and hold them personally liable for the remaining $20,000 owed to the creditor.

Assume that the creditor obtains a copy of the articles of incorporation from the secretary of state and notices that, due to an error, the address given for the corporation's registered office in the state is incorrect. The creditor might attempt to argue that because the state statutes relating to incorporation were not complied with, the corporation has been defectively formed and the shareholders are not entitled to protection from corporate debts. Other "defects" can include failure to have the requisite number of directors, failure to publish articles in newspapers or record them after filing (if required), failure to adopt bylaws, or failure to hold an organizational meeting. In such cases, courts typically examine the nature of the defect and then classify the corporation as de jure or de facto.

A **de jure corporation** (literally, one "of right") is a corporation that has substantially or strictly complied with the appropriate state statutes. For example, a mere typographical error in an address in the articles would likely be viewed as so minor that substantial compliance with the statutes is acknowledged. The corporation would be classified as de jure. The significance of achieving de jure status is that the corporation's existence and validity cannot be attacked or challenged by any party, including the state in which it was incorporated.

A corporation that fails to achieve de jure status can be classified as a **de facto corporation** (literally, one "in fact"), if the de facto corporation doctrine is recognized under state law. The significance of being classified as a de facto corporation is that the corporation cannot be attacked by any third party, such as a creditor. It can, however, be challenged by its creator, the state, which may bring an action to declare the corporation invalid. To achieve de facto status, there must be some good faith attempt by the corporation to comply with the laws of the state of incorporation and some good faith conduct of business as if a corporation existed. Some courts have held that failure to file the articles in the county in which the corporation does business (although they have been filed with the secretary of state) results in a de facto corporation.

If a corporation is neither de jure nor de facto, or if the jurisdiction does not recognize the de facto corporation doctrine, the business entity can be attacked by a third party who may then recover from individual would-be shareholders. Having failed to form a corporation, the would-be shareholders will, in effect, be deemed sole proprietors (if one shareholder) or partners (if two or more shareholders), and thus subject to unlimited personal liability for the business's debts and obligations. There are situations in which courts hold that the attacking party or creditor is **estopped** (or precluded) from challenging the validity of the corporation. In such cases, the corporation is said to be a **corporation by estoppel**. If creditors have dealt with the entity believing it was a corporation, they will generally be estopped from later claiming that it is not a valid corporation. Similarly, if an entity has held itself out as being a corporation, *it* will later be estopped from claiming that it is not liable for debts and obligations because it is not a validly formed entity.

Modern statutes and the MBCA have eliminated or lessened the use of the de jure and de facto doctrines. For example, MBCA § 2.03(b) provides that the secretary of state's filing of the articles of incorporation is "conclusive proof" that the incorporators satisfied all conditions required for incorporation (except that the state can challenge the validity of the corporation). Many states have similar statutes. These statutes preclude a third party from attacking the corporation based on defects in the formation process. Under these statutes, even if the articles included an error, once the articles are filed, a valid corporation exists, and it cannot be attacked by anyone but the state of incorporation. The secretary of state's filing of the articles is the demarcation point under this approach: Before this, the promoters have personal liability; after this, the corporation is viewed as validly formed (and can be attacked only by the state).

J. QUALIFYING TO DO BUSINESS IN OTHER STATES

As noted above, most states require foreign corporations (corporations formed outside the state) that transact business within the state to obtain a certificate of authority from the secretary of state qualifying the corporation to do business in the state. To obtain a certificate, the corporation must fill out a form and pay a fee. Typically, these forms require the corporation to specify a registered officer and designate a registered agent. Qualifying to do business in the state has consequences for the corporation. The corporation will have to pay the annual franchise tax charged by the state, it will be subject to service of process in the state, and it will have to file an annual report with the state.

To avoid these costs and burdens, a corporation may wish to argue that it is not conducting business in the state and thus need not register. The problem with this approach is that if the corporation fails to qualify, but is later deemed to be conducting business, it (and in some instances the individual who directed or engaged in the activities at issue) may become subject to penalties, its contracts with in-state parties may be voided, and it may forfeit the right to maintain an action in the foreign state's court system. State corporations statutes generally provide that a foreign corporation will not be considered to be transacting business based on isolated acts within the jurisdiction. Some statutes provide a list of activities that will not result in the business having to qualify in that jurisdiction. For example, MBCA § 15.01 provides that the following activities, among others, do not constitute transacting business for purposes of determining whether the business needs to obtain a certificate of authority to do business in a state other than the one in which it was formed:

> (b) The following activities, among others, do not constitute transacting business within the meaning of subsection (a):
> (1) maintaining, defending, or settling any proceeding;
> (2) holding meetings of the board of directors or shareholders or carrying on other activities concerning internal corporate affairs;
> (3) maintaining bank accounts;
> (4) maintaining offices or agencies for the transfer, exchange, and registration of the corporation's own securities or maintaining trustees or depositaries with respect to those securities;
> (5) selling through independent contractors;
> (6) soliciting or obtaining orders, whether by mail or through employees or agents or otherwise, if the orders require acceptance outside this state before they become contracts;
> (7) creating or acquiring indebtedness, mortgages, and security interests in real or personal property;
> (8) securing or collecting debts or enforcing mortgages and security interests in property securing the debts;
> (9) owning, without more, real or personal property;
> (10) conducting an isolated transaction that is completed within 30 days and that is not one in the course of repeated transactions of a like nature;
> (11) transacting business in interstate commerce.
> (c) The list of activities in subsection (b) is not exhaustive.

But, while courts generally look to whether the activities by the business are permanent, continuous, and regular in the foreign jurisdiction, there is no universally accepted definition of "doing business," and cases that exist tend to be highly fact-dependent. *See, e.g.,* New York Bus. Corp. Law § 1301(b) (containing non-exclusive list of what does not constitute doing business but failing to define standard for doing business). Thus, when advising clients whose business crosses state lines, be sure to research the law of doing business and qualifying as a foreign corporation in all potentially relevant states.

Chapter Summary

- A business corporation is an enterprise that has filed a certificate of incorporation (also known as articles of incorporation or corporate charter) with the appropriate state office.
- Corporations must be formed in compliance with statutory formalities.
- Corporations are characterized by centralized management whereby the business and affairs of the corporation are managed by a board of directors.
- Corporate shareholders enjoy limited liability.
- The incorporation process and the internal affairs of a corporation are governed by the state of incorporation.
- Corporations seeking to do business outside their jurisdiction of incorporation generally must qualify to do business in the foreign jurisdictions.

Applying the Concepts

1. Nicki and Doug are in the process of forming a corporation. They engage the services of a law firm on July 1 to prepare various documents, including bylaws for the proposed corporation. The corporation is never formed. Discuss whether the law firm may recover payment for its services.

2. Assume that the corporation discussed in Question 1 is formed on September 1.

   a. What actions may be taken to ensure that Nicki and Doug are relieved of liability for the law firm's services?
   b. If you were the law firm, would you consent to a novation? Why or why not?
   c. What is (or should be) the effective date of the contract between the law firm and the corporation? Why?

3. Indicate whether the following names would likely be valid corporate names:

   a. Home Lending, Inc.
   b. Federal Home Lending, Inc.
   c. Home Lending, Inc. dba Budget Home Loans

4. Discuss whether the following items are better placed in a corporation's articles of incorporations or in its bylaws:

   a. A provision setting par value for the company's stock at $1.00 per share
   b. The names and addresses of all directors and officers
   c. Duties of the corporate secretary
   d. A provision allowing preemptive rights

5. What is the fee in Minnesota to reserve a corporate name?

6. Is the corporate name "Bennett Furniture, Inc." available in Illinois?

7. Review the form for filing articles of incorporation in Pennsylvania. What information is called for in § 4 of the form?

8. Access the website for the Delaware Division of Corporations.

   a. Who is the agent for service of process for Facebook, Inc.?
   b. Use the New Company Filing Fee Calculator. What is the filing fee for a company that will issue 90,000 shares of stock with a par value of $1.00 per share?

9. Access the website for Alphabet Inc. Select the "Investors" tab. Review the company's certificate of incorporation. Answer the following questions and indicate which provisions of the certificate of incorporation govern your answer.

   a. What is Alphabet's state of incorporation?
   b. Compare Alphabet's charter to the Delaware form certificate of incorporation. Are they the same? Different?
   c. How many classes of shares has Alphabet authorized?
   d. What are the differences between the various classes of authorized shares? In answering this question, please focus on voting and governance rights.
   e. What is the minimum number of directors the company may have?
   f. May directors act by written consent?

10. Access the Governance Section of the Investor Relations Section of the General Electric Company website. Review the company's certificate of incorporation. Answer the following questions and indicate which provisions of the certificate of the incorporation govern your answer.

    a. What is GE's state of incorporation?
    b. How does GE's charter compare to the list of required items set forth the New York Business Corporations law?
    c. How many classes of shares has GE authorized?
    d. What are the differences between the various classes of authorized shares?
    e. Do shareholders have preemptive rights?
    f. What is the minimum number of directors the company may have?
    g. May directors act by written consent?

11. Locate and review the bylaws for Alphabet Inc., available on the company's website. Answer the following questions, citing applicable bylaws provision(s) and any relevant provision(s) of the Delaware General Corporation Law:

    a. Do Alphabet's bylaws permit stockholder action by written consent?
    b. Do Alphabet's bylaws permit director action by written consent?
    c. Do Alphabet's bylaws require advance notice of stockholder business at stockholder meetings? What rules, if any, govern the conduct of stockholder business?

    d. What rules, if any, govern the nomination of candidates for election as a director?

    e. Do the bylaws call upon Alphabet's board to establish any board committees?

    f. Do the bylaws call for the appointment of any specific officers of the company?

    g. Do the bylaws address whether and under what circumstances Alphabet will indemnify any of its directors or officers?

12. Locate and review the bylaws for General Electric Company. Answer the following questions, citing applicable bylaws provision(s) and any relevant provisions of the New York Business Corporation Law:

    a. Do GE's bylaws permit stockholder action by written consent?

    b. Do GE's bylaws permit director action by written consent?

    c. Do GE's bylaws require advance notice of stockholder business at stockholder meetings? What rules, if any, govern the conduct of stockholder business?

    d. What rules, if any, govern the nomination of candidates for election as a director?

    e. Do the bylaws call upon GE's board to establish any board committees?

    f. Do the bylaws call for the appointment of any specific officers of the company?

    g. Do the bylaws address whether and under what circumstances GE will indemnify any of its directors or officers?

13. Paula, one of the promoters of Lion Inc., sent to New York's Department of State complete incorporation documents on January 31. Due to a major storm, the documents do not reach the Department of State's corporations office until February 5. On January 17, Paula entered into a lease contract with Zara for office space for Lion Inc. Paula signed the lease agreement on behalf of Lion, Inc. Zara had no knowledge that Lion Inc. had not yet been incorporated at the time of signing.

    At the first board meeting of Lion Inc. on February 21, the board discussed the lease contract and authorized the first payment. A few months later Lion Inc. defaulted on the lease. Who is liable for the lease obligation? Why?

14. You represent Deborah, a technical genius who has invented a groundbreaking technology relating to the wireless transfer of energy from power sources to devices requiring power. Deborah would like to form a corporation to commercialize her technology. Venture capitalists are clamoring to invest in the business. Deborah is interested in electing Subchapter S tax treatment for her venture. If Deborah agrees to allow Sergei, a well-known venture capitalist from Moscow, to invest in her business, may she elect Subchapter S tax treatment?

Business Organizations in Practice

1. You have assisted your client in forming a corporation under Texas law. The company's headquarters and principal operations are in Texas today. The company has plans to expand into New Mexico, Arizona, and California within two years. What actions should the corporation take to ensure that expansion proceeds smoothly, from a legal perspective?

2. You have been retained to form Golazo Sports Bar, a proposed corporation that will operate sports bars in New York, New York and Los Angeles, California. The founders, former professional soccer players from the United States and Europe, hope to expand to other U.S. cities and, ideally, overseas as well, if they can raise sufficient capital. The founders anticipate that they will be the public face of Golazo, but will hire professional managers to run the business. You are meeting with the founders next week to discuss the formation process. Prepare an agenda and draft questions to ask your clients so that you can address the following issues:

   a. What steps, if any, should you take to determine whether Golazo is a good choice for the name of the business?
   b. Where should the business incorporate?
   c. Should the corporation consider authorizing both preferred and common stock? (Or, alternatively, should it authorize only common stock?)

3. In January, Adam entered into a contract with Bill, a local craftsman, for the purchase of hand-made, stained-glass windows for his home. The windows were to be made with a special lining to prevent leakage. The contract included an express warranty against leakage for three years.

   Before executing the contract, Bill told Adam that he was in the process of incorporating his window business, which he intended to name Windows of Wonder, Inc. Bill signed the contract as follows:

   "Bill, for Windows of Wonder, Inc."

   Bill completed the delivery and installation of Adam's windows on June 15, at which time, at Bill's request, Adam issued his check for the full amount due payable to Windows of Wonder, Inc. On July 1, as soon as the incorporation process for Windows of Wonder was finalized, Bill opened a bank account in the name of the corporation, and deposited Adam's check in the corporate account.

   Adam first noticed problems with water leakage around the windows in August. Upon inspection, Adam determined that the windows had been improperly manufactured and installed. Adam immediately complained to Bill, who refused to repair or replace the windows.

   Last week, Adam sued Bill and Windows of Wonder for breach of the warranty. Windows of Wonder has moved for summary judgment dismissing the action against it on the grounds that the contract was between Adam and Bill.

Bill simultaneously moved for summary judgment on the grounds that he was merely acting as an agent for Windows of Wonder.

a. How should the court rule on Bill's motion?

b. How should the court rule on Windows of Wonder's motion?

c. What, if anything, could Adam have done to increase his chances of being able to recover against both Bill and Windows of Wonder?

d. What, if anything, could Bill have done to reduce his risk of being held personally liable for losses caused by the leaky windows?

e. What, if anything, could Windows of Wonder have done to reduce the risk of being held responsible for Adam's losses?

4. You are a lawyer licensed in New York, with an office in New York, New York. Last week, you were retained by Acme, a California corporation based in Cupertino, California to handle a contract dispute between Acme and Beta Corp., which is organized in California and based in Cupertino. For a two-month period, you travel back and forth between New York and California on several occasions to handle settlement negotiations. You also perform work on the case while in New York.

Although the matter ultimately settled on terms that you believed to be favorable to Acme, Acme has refused to pay your bill, arguing that you practiced law in California without a license when negotiating the settlement agreement. You would like to sue to recover your fee.

Research California Business and Professions Code § 6125. What does it mean to practice law in California, for purposes of § 6125? Is a California court likely to require Acme to pay 100 percent of your bill under this section? Compare § 6125 to Model Rules of Professional Conduct 5.5.

5. You represent Seattle Software, Inc., a New York corporation. Bill Bridges is the founder, director, and largest individual stockholder of the company. At a regularly scheduled board meeting in September, the board unanimously approved a motion proposed by Bridges to give a corporate donation amounting to US $50 million toward efforts to combat the spread of HIV/AIDS in Africa. The company's certificate of incorporation is silent on whether gifts to charity could be made.

In the discussion leading up to the vote on the motion, Bridges told the board of directors that it was a shame that thousands of the most productive members of West African society were dying and little was being done about it, yet there were drugs available for HIV/AIDS patients that enabled those infected to live longer lives in dignity. He proposed that of the $50 million, $25 million be devoted to buying drugs and facilitating educational programs to prevent the further spread of the scourge. He also proposed that the other $25 million be devoted to research on finding a malaria vaccine in light of the fact that there was little spending on this curable disease that kills at least one child every 30 seconds in Africa. The well-designed plan was to be exclusively located in Mozambique initially, as a pilot program, to ensure that it was as effective as possible. In the financial year prior to the $50 million donation,

Seattle Software had made after tax profits in excess of $50 billion. However only 0.0005 percent of its profits came from business in Mozambique and less than 4 percent of its profits were made in sub-Saharan Africa.

Andrew Richards is a Seattle Software stockholder. He has just read the story of the $50 million gift to Mozambique and he is enraged. He files an *ultra vires* suit challenging the gift. Write a memo to the board discussing the likely outcome of Richards's lawsuit.

Introduction to Corporate Finance

When a corporation is first formed, it needs capital (i.e., money and property) to get the business off the ground. Corporations obtain initial capital from investors who commit funds or property in exchange for equity (i.e., an ownership stake) in the business. Post-formation, corporations have three main avenues for financing: (i) selling additional equity; (ii) borrowing money; and (iii) generating funds internally, such as through investment activity or the sale of goods and services at a profit. In this chapter, we explore these financing methods and tools.

A. INTRODUCTION

All corporations need money to establish, operate, and expand their businesses. A profitable corporation may draw upon internally generated funds (e.g., **retained earnings**, or the portion of a corporation's profits that it plows back into the business rather than distributes to investors) to support its business plans and activities. A corporation also may choose to raise money from external sources by selling **equity** (i.e., an ownership stake in the business), or by borrowing money from different types of lenders. On the **equity** side, corporations sell **equity securities** (generally, stock) to investors to raise money. The holders of equity securities have an interest, or ownership stake, in the corporation, and the capital received by a corporation in return for issuance of equity securities is called **equity capital**. Corporate stock meets the legal definition of a **security** for purposes of federal and state securities laws. We discuss the meaning of the term "security" under the federal securities laws and rules applicable to sales of corporate securities (including stock) in more detail in Chapter 13. We also discuss equity securities in Section B below.

Key Concepts

- Financing through the sale of additional equity
- Financing through debt
- Financing through internally generated funds
- Issues affecting capital structure

297

Capital Markets and Capital Structure

The term "capital markets" refers to markets where capital funds (debt and equity) are purchased and sold. The term generally is understood to include organized markets and exchanges such as the New York Stock Exchange or the NASDAQ stock market, as well as markets where private placements of debt and equity investments are traded.

Although the terms "stocks" and "bonds" are sometimes referred to in the same breath, these two types of instruments are very different from each other. A shareholder who owns equity securities is an owner of the corporation. As owners, shareholders typically have the right to vote on various corporate issues and to receive distributions of corporate profits (called dividends). Shareholders also generally have a **residual claim**, or the right to receive the net assets, if any, of the corporation upon dissolution and liquidation. Lenders and bondholders, on the other hand, are creditors of the corporation, not owners. While lenders and bondholders are entitled to be repaid the amount borrowed by the corporation at the agreed-on time and under the agreed-on terms, they generally are not entitled to vote or receive dividends, nor do they have the shareholder's residual claim on the corporation's assets upon dissolution and liquidation. Taken together, a corporation's mix of equity and debt makes up its **capital structure**.

Corporations also may borrow money to finance business activities. Corporations that access **capital markets** to borrow money issue corporate IOUs known as **bonds**. Bonds entitle the holder to repayment of the principal amount borrowed and the payment of interest. As with stock, corporate bonds usually meet the legal definition of a security; thus, bond offerings generally are subject to the federal and state securities law requirements discussed in Chapter 13. Corporations also may take on indebtedness in the form of a direct loan from a bank or other lender. Bank loans typically do not meet the legal definition of a security; thus, they usually are not subject to the securities laws discussed in Chapter 13. The capital received by a corporation in return for issuance of a debt security is known as **debt capital**. We discuss bonds (and other debt instruments) and loans in Section C below. (A brief introduction to financial statements is provided in Appendix D.)

B. EQUITY

1. Introduction

When an **investor** makes an **equity investment** in a corporation, she becomes a **shareholder** or **stockholder** — that is, an owner whose stake in the business is represented by **shares of stock**. As you will recall from Chapter 6, a corporation must identify the number and class(es) of shares that the corporation is authorized to issue in its articles of incorporation. The shares identified in the articles are referred to as **authorized shares** of the corporation. Shares that have been issued to shareholders (and not repurchased or "redeemed" by the corporation) are referred to as **outstanding shares**. Thus, shareholders of a corporation hold **authorized, issued, outstanding shares**. Large corporations can have significant numbers of outstanding shares. For example, as of 2016, General Mills, Inc. had 594 million shares of common stock issued and outstanding, and as of 2016, Chevron Corp. had approximately 2 billion common shares issued and outstanding.

The differences in the terms "authorized," "issued," and "outstanding" are important because corporations may only pay **dividends**, or distributions of earnings to shareholders, on outstanding shares, meaning the shares currently held by shareholders. Similarly, only outstanding shares are eligible to vote at shareholder meetings. Shares are issued and outstanding unless they are reacquired, redeemed, converted, or canceled by the corporation. Stock reacquired by the corporation (often because the shareholder exercised a right to compel the corporation to repurchase or redeem the stock) may be restored to the status of authorized but unissued shares, or may, in some states, be classified as **treasury stock**. Treasury stock is stock that is re-acquired by the issuing company and is thus available for retirement or resale. Treasury stock is viewed as issued, but is not considered outstanding, because it is not held by investors but rather by the corporation itself. Thus, treasury stock is not entitled to voting rights or to share in dividends, and it is not included in computing a corporation's number of outstanding shares. Treasury stock also is not entitled to receive any distribution of the corporation's net assets upon dissolution.

2. Par Value and No Par Value Stock

As noted in Chapter 6, the **par value** of stock is the nominal or face value set for each share, as set forth in the articles of incorporation. Traditionally, par value is the minimum amount for which stock can be issued. Thus, if the par value is $10, a share of stock can be issued for $10 or any amount in excess of this, but cannot be issued for an amount less than $10. Par value is not equivalent to market value. In fact, because par value is usually so low, corporations hope that market value is far in excess of par value, though this may not always turn out to be the case. For example, the par value of the common stock of General Mills, Inc. is 10 cents, while the par value of the common stock of Chevron Corp. is 75 cents. The par value of the common stock of the social gaming company Zynga is $0.00000625. As of March 8, 2016, the common stock of these corporations was trading at $59.95 (General Mills), $88.74 (Chevron), and $2.19 (Zynga). Check to see where these stocks are trading when you read this chapter to compare par value to market value.

Historically, corporations were required to set a par value for their shares. Now, however, in most states, corporations have the option of stating a par value for the stock in the articles of incorporation or stating that there will be no par value. The MBCA typifies the modern trend in not requiring any par value to be stated in the articles of incorporation. *See* MBCA § 2.02(a) and (b). Shares without a par value set forth in the articles, referred to as **no par value shares**, can be sold for whatever price the directors fix, so long as the price is reasonable. *See* MBCA § 6.21(c) (providing that before a corporation issues shares, the board must determine that the consideration is adequate). In those states that do not require that a par value be specified in the articles, statutes often provide that par value is deemed to be a certain amount—for example, $1—for certain purposes. For example, California imposes a statutory par value of $1 per share solely for the purpose of determining taxes and fees. Delaware bases its annual franchise tax on the number of authorized shares or par value of shares. For corporations having no par value stock the authorized shares method will always result in the lesser tax. As of this writing, Delaware rules provides that corporations with 5,000 or fewer authorized shares must pay an annual franchise tax of $175.00, with each additional 10,000 shares or portions thereof resulting in an additional $75.00 in franchise taxes.

For corporations using the assumed par value method to calculate franchise taxes, the corporation must provide figures for all issued shares (including treasury shares) and total gross assets in the spaces provided in the corporation's annual franchise tax report. Total gross assets means the "total assets" reported on IRS Form 1120, Schedule L relative to the company's fiscal year ending the calendar year of the report. The tax rate under this method is $350.00 per million or portion of a million. If the assumed par value capital is less than $1,000,000, the tax is calculated by dividing the assumed par value capital by $1,000,000 then multiplying that result by $350.00.

The example below is taken from the Delaware Department of State, Division of Corporations' website.[1] The example is for a corporation having 1,000,000 shares of stock with a par value of $1.00 and 250,000 shares of stock with a par value of $5.00, gross assets of $1,000,000.00 and issued shares totaling 485,000 using the assumed par value capital method.

1. Divide total gross assets by total issued shares carrying to 6 decimal places. The result is your "assumed par." Example: $1,000,000 assets divided by 485,000 issued shares = $2.061856 assumed par.
2. Multiply the assumed par by the number of authorized shares having a par value of less than the assumed par. Example: $2.061856 assumed par multiplied by 1,000,000 shares = $2,061,856.
3. Multiply the number of authorized shares with a par value greater than the assumed par by their respective par value. Example: 250,000 shares multiplied by $5.00 par value = $1,250,000.
4. Add the results of #2 and #3 above. The result is the assumed par value capital. Example: $2,061,856 plus $1,250,000 = $3,311 956 assumed par value capital.
5. Figure the annual franchise tax due by dividing the assumed par value capital, rounded up to the next million if it is over $1,000,000, by 1,000,000 and then multiply by $350.00. Example: 4 x $350.00 = $1,400.00

As of the date of writing, Delaware law provides that the minimum franchise tax for a Delaware corporation is $175.00 for corporations using the authorized shares method, and a minimum tax of $350.00 for corporations using the assumed par value capital method. All corporations using either method will have a maximum tax of $180,000.00, according to Delaware law.

Some general corporate accounting principles are affected by issuance of par value shares and no par value shares. If shares with a par value of $15 are in fact sold for $15 each, all of the amount received by the corporation is placed in an account referred to as **stated capital**. Any amount received for shares over and above the par value amount is called **capital surplus** and is placed in a capital surplus account. If the stock has no par value, the directors can sell the stock at any price they determine, so long as the corporation receives adequate consideration for the shares; the board can then allocate the proceeds to the stated capital account and to the capital surplus account. For example, if no par value stock is issued for $25 per share, the directors can allocate $5 to stated capital and $20 to capital surplus.

---

[1]This material currently is available at https://corp.delaware.gov/frtaxcalc.shtml.

The advantage of a large capital surplus account is that most state statutes permit corporations to repurchase their own shares only if there is sufficient money in the capital surplus account to make the purchase. Moreover, in many states, dividends cannot be paid from the stated capital account. Instead, dividends typically are paid from the surplus account. The existence of no par value stock thus gives the directors the flexibility to create a large capital surplus account for these purposes. Note, however, that because the MBCA has eliminated the concept of par value, the concept of stated capital is likewise eradicated, and the corporation can allocate the consideration received when the stock is issued as the directors deem appropriate.

3. Consideration for Shares

Those who wish to purchase shares must give appropriate consideration for the shares (cash, property). Upon receipt of the consideration, the corporation will issue or deliver the shares to the investor. To ensure that corporations were adequately capitalized, the older view required that the consideration given for shares generally be in cash. Promissory notes and agreements to provide services in the future generally were not acceptable. The MBCA and most modern statutes have changed this rule. According to MBCA § 6.21(b) and most modern state corporations statutes, shares may be issued for consideration consisting of any tangible or intangible property or benefit to the corporation, including cash, promissory notes, services performed, contracts for services to be performed, or other securities of the corporation. This very flexible standard allows for almost anything to be exchanged for shares, so long as there is some benefit to the corporation. Thus, a corporation can issue stock in exchange for a patent or a promise by the corporation's president to work for the corporation for two years, or even the release of a claim against the corporation. (That said, a corporation likely cannot issue all of its stock for future services or promissory notes inasmuch as the corporation requires a certain amount of cash to meet its needs.)

To ensure that an individual who pledges a note or services as consideration actually pays the note, or performs the services, the corporation may place the shares in an **escrow account**, or an account where the shares are held until the conditions of their issuance to the shareholders are satisfied, or it may otherwise restrict the transfer of shares until the investor has complied with his obligations respecting consideration. If tangible or intangible property or services are given as consideration, the board generally will appraise or determine the value of such contributions, and issue stock accordingly. A few states continue to require that the consideration be in the form of cash, property, or already performed services.

Just as stock can be **watered** by issuance for less cash than par value, it can also be watered if the corporation

Watered Stock

In general, shares issued for less than the par value are referred to as **watered stock** (or sometimes **discount** or **bonus stock**). The term "watered stock" derives from an unscrupulous practice of cattle drovers who, before the sale of their cattle stock, would feed the cattle large amounts of salt. The salt, in turn, caused the cattle to drink gallons of water, thereby increasing their weight and consequent market price. Thus, the watered cattle stock wasn't worth its purchase price. In the corporate context, watered stock also is not worth its purchase price.

does not receive adequate property or services in return for stock issued. Some jurisdictions have determined that the holder of watered stock enjoys no rights with respect to the watered stock and can be subject to liability for the difference between what was paid and par value. Most jurisdictions, however, have adopted the modern approach found in the MBCA. Under MBCA § 6.21(c), once the board determines what consideration should be paid for the stock, that determination generally is deemed conclusive as far as adequacy is concerned, subject to directors' compliance with fiduciary obligations. Once the corporation receives the consideration for which the board of directors authorized the issuance of shares, the shares are "fully paid and nonassessable." *See* MBCA § 6.21(d). Thus, under the modern view, the recipient of watered stock has simply gotten a good deal on the stock and can participate in voting and other issues just as other shareholders can without being liable to the corporation or creditors for any additional sums (assuming no fraud exists). MBCA § 6.22 provides that an individual who purchases shares from a corporation is not liable to the corporation or to its creditors except to pay the consideration required for issuance of the shares.

4. Classes of Stock

Common Stock

Although corporations law statutes generally do not use or define the term **common stock**, this term is understood to mean stock that has (i) full, unlimited voting rights; and (ii) the right to receive the net assets of the corporation upon dissolution (the so-called **residual claim**). The articles of incorporation *must* authorize one or more classes of shares that together have unlimited voting rights and one or more classes of shares that together are entitled to receive the net assets, if any, of the corporation upon dissolution. *See* MBCA § 6.01(b). This ensures that the corporation will have shareholders who can vote on corporate action and receive the net assets of the corporation in the event it dissolves. If the corporation does not specify in its articles of incorporation the type of stock to be issued and only one class of stock is authorized, it will be common stock by default. The board of directors must approve any issuance of common stock.

Holders of common stock usually enjoy the following rights:

> ### The Residual Interest
>
> Common shareholders' **residual interest** in or residual claim on the enterprise means that they have the last right to be paid in the event the corporation is liquidated. In practical terms, this means that common stockholders are entitled to the remains of the corporation after other senior groups (e.g., creditors, bondholders, and preferred shareholders) are satisfied.

Voting Rights

Each outstanding share of common stock typically is entitled to one vote on each matter subject to a shareholder vote, with fractional shares entitled to corresponding fractional votes. *See* MBCA §§ 7.21(a) and 6.04(c). It is possible for a corporation to have more than one class of common stock. In fact, many tech companies feature dual or triple class structures. For example, the certificate of incorporation of Alphabet Inc. authorizes the corporation to issue both Class A and Class B common stock, with Class A shareholders having one vote per share, and Class B shareholders having ten votes per share. This structure — called **dual capitalization** — allows Larry Page and Sergey Brin (the two founders of the company formerly known as Google, and now known as Alphabet) to maintain a majority of voting power, despite not owning a majority of the company's outstanding shares. Likewise, when Facebook, Inc. went public in May 2012, its registration statement disclosed that while each share of its Common A stock was entitled to one vote, each share of its Class B common stock was entitled to ten votes, with the Common B stockholders holding 96 percent of the voting power of the corporation. Facebook's founder, Mark Zuckerberg, was stated as holding about 57 percent of the voting power of the corporation, giving him "the ability to control the outcome of matters submitted to our stockholders for approval, including the election of our directors." Groupon and Zynga have similar capital structures. As a general rule, while different classes of common stock may have different rights from one another, every shareholder within the same class is treated the same. Note, however, that MBCA § 6.01(e) and a few states allow corporations to vary rights of shareholders *within the same class* if such variations are set forth in the articles of incorporation.

Distribution Rights

There are two main types of shareholder distributions — **dividends** and **repurchases**. A **dividend** is a transfer of cash or other property (other than the corporation's own shares) by the corporation to its shareholders on a pro rata basis. For example, if an individual owns 18 percent of the Class A common stock of the corporation, and the board lawfully declares a dividend for shareholders holding Class A common stock, the shareholder will be entitled to 18 percent of whatever distribution is declared by the board of directors for Common A shareholders. Common shareholders thus receive distributions in the same proportion that their share ownership bears to the total number of common shares issued and outstanding.

The articles of incorporation establish the relative rights of different classes of stock to receive a dividend. There is no requirement that a corporation ever declare a dividend to its common shareholders, however; instead, it is within the board's discretion to declare (or not declare) a dividend, subject to any restrictions set forth in the articles of incorporation and the state's corporations code. *See* MBCA § 6.40. For example, boards generally can declare a dividend for common stockholders only if the preferred shareholders (discussed below) have received their distributions. This is because preferred shareholders generally enjoy a dividend preference over common stockholders, as discussed below.

Moreover, a corporation may not distribute dividends to common shareholders if the distribution would cause the corporation to become **insolvent**, or if the distribution would cause the corporation's liabilities plus the liquidation preferences of any preferred stock it has outstanding to exceed the corporation's assets. *See* MBCA § 6.40(c). There are different ways of measuring insolvency. MBCA § 6.40(c)(1) speaks to the concept of **equity insolvency**, or the corporation's inability to satisfy obligations as they become due. Comment 2 to MBCA § 6.40 provides guidelines for applying the equity insolvency test. Subsection (2) of MBCA § 6.40(c) speaks to the concept of **balance sheet insolvency**, or insolvency that arises when a corporation's total liabilities exceed its total assets. Several non-MBCA states use a **legal capital test** for regulating the declaration and distribution of dividends. For example, § 170(a) of the Delaware General Corporation Law provides that "[t]he directors of every corporation, subject to any restrictions contained in its certificate of incorporation, may declare and pay dividends upon the shares of its capital stock either (1) out of its surplus . . . or (2) in case there shall be no such surplus, out of its net profits for the fiscal year in which the dividend is declared and/or the preceding fiscal year." These solvency tests protect creditors who need to be assured that the corporation will pay its obligations to them before making distributions to shareholders.

A second type of distribution — stock **repurchase** — occurs when a corporation buys back stock from its shareholders. As with dividends, stock repurchases are subject to board approval and may be made at the board's discretion, subject to the solvency and other requirements set forth for distributions in the state's corporations code. *See, e.g.*, MBCA § 6.40(c). Unlike the payment of dividends, the repurchase of stock by the corporation generally does not need to be proportional as between shareholders. That said, as we discuss in Chapter 10, there are instances when a corporation may be required to ensure that minority shareholders have equal access to a stock repurchase plan offered to majority or controlling shareholders. *Cf. Donahue v. Rodd Electrotype Co. of New England, Inc.*, 328 N.E.2d 505 (Mass. 1975).

In deciding whether to make a distribution of any kind, directors must act on an informed basis, in good faith, and in a manner that the director reasonably believes to be in the best interest of the corporation. *See, e.g.*, MBCA § 8.30. For example, under the MBCA, directors who pay dividends or repurchase shares in circumstances that violate statutory requirements may be held personally liable, unless the directors can demonstrate that they acted on an informed basis, in good faith, and in a manner that the director reasonably believed to be in the best interests of the corporation. MBCA §§ 8.30, 8.33. To reduce the risk of personal liability (and to ensure that directors are acting on an informed basis), boards often will commission a **solvency opinion** from an investment bank if there is any question as to whether a distribution is statutorily permissible. A solvency opinion is a financial opinion that addresses the solvency of an entity in preparation for a corporation financing or other transaction (here, a potential distribution). Solvency opinions typically address solvency of the entity using one or more of the tests referenced above both as of the date of contemplated transaction (i.e., immediately before the transaction occurs) and giving effect to the contemplated transaction.

Liquidation Rights

Upon **liquidation** of the corporation, the corporation must satisfy its creditors and bondholders first before distributing a proportionate share of the corporation's net assets to shareholders. Corporations thus may distribute assets to shareholders upon liquidation only if (and after) the corporation has satisfied debts and obligations owed to creditors. As noted previously, common shareholders are "junior" among shareholders with respect to the distribution of assets in that they receive net assets only after any preferred shareholders (discussed below) have been satisfied.

Other Rights

In addition to the rights of common shareholders already described, common shareholders may have preemptive rights, or a first opportunity right to purchase newly-issued shares on a pro rata basis. As discussed in Chapter 6, preemptive rights allow shareholders to maintain their ownership stake — so, for example, a shareholder with preemptive rights who owns a 20 percent stake in a corporation has the option of purchasing the number of shares in any new offering necessary to maintain that 20 percent ownership stake. Common shareholders also may have **cumulative voting rights**, or voting rights that allow shareholders to multiply the number of shares owned by the number of directors being elected and to cast these votes as they like. We discuss cumulative voting in greater detail in Chapter 8.

Preferred Stock

As with common stock, state corporations codes generally do not use or define the term **preferred stock**. The term generally is understood to refer to stock that has a preference over common stock in the payment of dividends (a **dividend preference**), or in the distribution of assets upon liquidation (a **liquidation preference**), or both. The creation and issuance of preferred stock must be authorized by the articles of incorporation. Here is a provision from the Amended and Restated Articles of Incorporation of Microsoft Corporation authorizing the issuance of preferred stock:

4.2 Issuance of Preferred Shares

The Board of Directors is hereby authorized from time to time, without shareholder action, to provide for the issuance of Preferred Shares in one or more series not exceeding in the aggregate the number of Preferred Shares authorized by these Articles of Incorporation, as amended from time to time; and to determine with respect to each such series the voting powers, if any (which voting powers, if granted, may be full or limited), designations, preferences, and relative, participating, option, or other special rights, and the qualifications, limitations, or restrictions relating thereto, including without limiting the generality of the foregoing, the voting rights relating to Preferred Shares of any series (which may be one or more votes per share or a fraction of a vote per share, which may vary over time, and which may be applicable generally or only upon the happening and continuance of stated events or conditions), the rate of dividend to which holders of Preferred Shares of any series may be entitled (which may be cumulative or noncumulative), the rights of holders of Preferred Shares of any series in the event of liquidation, dissolution, or winding up of the affairs of the Corporation, the rights, if any, of holders of Preferred Shares of any series to convert or exchange such Preferred Shares of such series for shares of any other class or series of capital stock or for any other securities, property, or assets of the Corporation or any subsidiary (including the determination of the price or prices or the rate or rates applicable to such rights to convert or exchange and the adjustment thereof, the time or times during which the right to convert or exchange shall be applicable, and the time or times during which a particular price or rate shall be applicable), whether or not the shares of that series shall be redeemable, and if so, the terms and conditions of such redemption, including the date or dates upon or after which they shall be redeemable, and the amount per share payable in case of redemption, which amount may vary under different conditions and at different redemption dates, and whether any shares of that series shall be redeemed pursuant to a retirement or sinking fund or otherwise and the terms and conditions of such obligation.

Preferred stock generally has the features discussed below.

Voting Rights

So long as there is one class of shares that has unlimited voting rights, other classes (including classes of preferred stock) may have special, limited, or no voting rights. One reason that preferred shareholders may have no voting rights (or limited or special voting rights) is that preferred stockholders generally negotiate for — and obtain, as a condition of their investment — desired rights and protections via contract in the stockholder agreement. For example, in addition to the liquidation and distribution preference, venture capitalists who receive preferred stock in exchange for their investment in a company may negotiate for (i) the right to **convert** their preferred stock to common stock; (ii) **anti-dilution protections** (protections that restrict the corporation's ability to dilute the preferred stockholders' ownership stake in the business); (iii) mandatory or optional redemption schedules; (iv) the right to elect one or more board representatives; or (v) other and special voting rights or preferences. Special voting rights could include voting rights that are contingent or conditional upon the occurrence of certain events, such as failure of the directors to declare a dividend for some period of time.

Distribution Rights

A common feature of preferred stock designed to attract investors is a **preference in distributions**. In many cases, preferred stockholders are entitled to **cumulative distributions**, meaning that if the distribution is not paid to preferred shareholders during any given year, the distribution simply adds up, so that the corporation is required to pay out the distribution to preferred stockholders in future years, before any distributions are paid to common stockholders. This cumulative dividend is generally built into the stock itself. For example, the articles of incorporation might provide that each share of preferred stock is entitled to a $5 annual cumulative dividend. Assume a preferred stockholder owns 100 shares of stock. Each year the stockholder is entitled to a distribution of $500. If the corporation does not have sufficient profits to pay this dividend for three years, the distribution continues to accumulate. In year four, the corporation must pay the preferred stockholder $2,000 ($500 for the current year's preference plus $1,500 arrearage) before any distributions can be made to common shareholders. A **noncumulative distribution** means that the dividend preference does not accumulate. If the corporation has insufficient profits to pay a distribution to our shareholder for three years, the shareholder can expect nothing for those three years. In year four, the corporation must pay the preferred stockholder $500 (the one year dividend preference amount) before distributions are made to other shareholders.

The distribution preference can be expressed in terms of dollars (e.g., "each share of preferred stock is entitled to receive $10 per share each year before any distributions can be made to any other shareholders") or in terms of ownership interest (e.g., "each share of preferred stock is entitled to receive 10 percent of the preferred stock's par value [or stated value] each year before any distributions can be made to any other shareholders"). For example, in late 2005, Blockbuster announced it planned to issue 150,000 shares of preferred stock for $1,000 a share, which would pay a dividend of 7.5 percent a year. Similarly, in late 2008, Warren Buffett's company Berkshire Hathaway, Inc. and certain of its affiliates purchased 50,000 shares of the Goldman Sachs Group, Inc's 10 percent Cumulative Perpetual Preferred Stock, Series G, having a liquidation value of $100,000 per share (and carrying an annual dividend of 10 percent), along with a warrant to purchase 43,478,260 shares of Goldman Sachs Company's voting common stock, par value $0.01 per share, for an aggregate purchase price of $5.0 billion in cash. See Exhibit 7.1 for an excerpt from an SEC filing from Goldman Sachs concerning this transaction.

EXHIBIT 7.1	**Item 3.03 from Goldman Sachs Form 8-K Dated September 23, 2008: Material Modification of the Rights of Security Holders**

The Goldman Sachs Group, Inc. (the "Company") has agreed to issue and sell, and Berkshire Hathaway Inc. and certain affiliates (the "Investor") have agreed to purchase, (1) 50,000 shares of the Company's 10% Cumulative Perpetual Preferred Stock, Series G, having a liquidation value of $100,000 per share ("Preferred Stock"), and (2) a Warrant (the "Warrant") to purchase 43,478,260 shares of the Company's voting common stock, par value $0.01 per share ("Common Stock"), for an aggregate purchase price of $5.0 billion in cash.

Dividends on the Preferred Stock will accrue on the liquidation value at a rate per annum of 10% but will be paid only when, as and if declared by the Company's Board of Directors out of legally available funds. At any time when such dividends have not been paid in full, the unpaid amounts will accrue dividends at the same 10% rate and the Company will not be permitted to pay dividends or other distributions on, or to repurchase, any of the outstanding Common Stock or any of the Company's outstanding preferred stock of any series. Subject to the approval of the Board of Governors of the Federal Reserve System, the Preferred Stock may be redeemed by the Company at any time, in whole or in part, at a redemption price of 110% of the liquidation value to be redeemed plus any accrued, unpaid dividends. The Preferred Stock has no maturity date and will rank senior to the outstanding Common Stock (and pari passu with the Company's other outstanding series of preferred stock) with respect to the payment of dividends and distributions in liquidation.

As long as at least 10,000 shares of the Preferred Stock remain outstanding, the Preferred Stock, voting as a separate class, will have the right to approve any future issuance of preferred stock ranking senior to the Preferred Stock, and any amendment of the certificate of incorporation or future merger, reclassification or similar event in which the rights and other terms of the Preferred Stock (or successor securities) are substantially modified.

Subject to certain limited exceptions, the Preferred Stock and the Warrant are not transferrable for five years, and the shares of Common Stock issuable on exercise of the Warrant may be transferred at any time but only in public offerings and other public market sales, or in private transactions, that do not involve the transfer to any single purchaser or group of more than 3.5% of the outstanding Common Stock. So long as the Investor owns at least 10,000 shares of Preferred Stock, in the event of a spin-off of a business by the Company, a portion of the Preferred Stock owned by the Investor will be exchanged for preferred stock in the spun-off business, based on the relative value of the Company and the spun-off business.

The Warrant is exercisable at the holder's option at any time and from time to time, in whole or in part, for five years at an exercise price of $115 per share of the Common Stock. The exercise price and the number of shares issuable on exercise of the Warrant are subject to antidilution adjustments for stock splits, reclassifications, noncash distributions, extraordinary cash dividends, pro rata repurchases of Common Stock, business combination transactions, and certain issuances of Common Stock (or securities convertible into or exercisable for Common Stock) at a price (or having a conversion or exercise price) that is less than 95% of the market price of the Common Stock at the pricing of the securities issuance. The Investor has agreed that it will not increase its beneficial ownership of the outstanding Common Stock above 14.9%. (At the date of issuance, the Warrant will be exercisable for approximately 9.0% of the post-exercise outstanding Common Stock.)

These securities have not been registered under the Securities Act of 1933 and are being issued and sold in a private placement pursuant to Section 4(2) thereof. The Company has agreed to enter into a registration rights agreement affording the Investor certain registration rights.

The transaction is expected to close on or about October 1, 2008.

Preferred stock can also be **participating preferred stock**, meaning that the preferred shareholder has the right to participate in other distributions, if any, declared by the board of directors, in addition to enjoying a distribution preference as described above. Participating preferred dividends thus allow preferred shareholders to share with the common shareholders when the corporation has had an exceptional year and large distributions of the corporation's profits are made. Preferred shareholders would receive their cumulative or noncumulative distribution and then would share in the other distribution made by the corporation, as well. Participating preferred dividends are somewhat rare and, if they exist, are usually paid to the preferred shareholders after the common shareholders have received their distribution of the corporation's earnings.

However they are structured, distributions, especially the cumulative distributions, can allow preferred shareholders to predict their income from their stock holdings with some degree of certainty. Preferred shareholders should remember, however, that if the corporation has a record year, and the directors declare significant distributions to the common shareholders, preferred shareholders might actually receive less than the common shareholders, since their rights are limited to the agreed-on and stated distribution fixed by the articles and the stock certificate.

Liquidation Rights

In addition to preferential distribution rights, holders of preferred stock also may be entitled to a stated distribution upon liquidation of the corporation. For example, the articles may provide that upon liquidation, the preferred stockholders are entitled to be paid $85 per share for each share of preferred stock together with interest thereon at 5 percent per year, before any other shareholders may receive assets in liquidation (but after creditors are paid). Similarly, the articles may provide that the liquidation preference is some percentage of par value, for example, "full par value plus 10 percent." After the preferred shareholders have been fully satisfied in the agreed-on amount, they might also share with the common shareholders in receiving net assets upon liquidation.

Conversion Rights

As noted above, preferred shareholders may be given the **right to convert** their preferred shares into cash, indebtedness, or shares of some other class or series, usually common shares, either at an agreed-on price or at an agreed-upon ratio. The articles of incorporation must authorize a sufficient number of shares to accommodate this right of conversion, and the corporation must have an adequate number of authorized but unissued shares to allow preferred shareholders to exercise their conversion rights. Moreover, the articles of incorporation should contain all terms and conditions relating to the conversion process, including the conversion formula and the procedures for conversion. Conversion rights may be subject to some contingency. For example, they might be exercisable only after some specified period of time or only in the event the corporation has not paid a dividend for two or more consecutive years.

Conversion rights are commonly coupled with **anti-dilution provisions**. Say a corporation with a book value of $100,000 has 4 shareholders, each of whom owns 100 of the 400 shares of stock outstanding. Each shareholder thus has 25 percent of the available voting power, and the book value of the stock is $250. If the corporation issues additional shares to a new investor — say 100 shares for $10,000 — the voting power of the existing shareholders will be diluted. Book value is diluted because the new shareholder paid less than book value for his shares, and voting power will be diluted because of the increase in the number of outstanding shares. (Whereas the existing shareholders formerly held 25 percent of voting power (100 shares owned/400 shares outstanding), they now hold only 20 percent (100 shares owned/500 shares outstanding).) An anti-dilution provision provides some protection against dilution by, for example, adjusting the conversion price via a mathematical formula. Be aware that these provisions can be complex and require both care and expertise in drafting.

Redemption Rights

Preferred stock also may be issued with **redemption rights** (sometimes referred to as a **call** or **callable shares**) by which the corporation has the power to reacquire or call back all or a portion of the shares from the shareholders. The right of redemption may be exercised by the board of directors at its option, such as when the distributions required to be given to shareholders of cumulative preferred stock become too much of a financial burden on the corporation, and the corporation desires to stem the flow of cash paid each year to the preferred stockholders. The amount to be paid when the corporation redeems the shares (typically, a percentage of the par value of the stock together with any accrued and unpaid distributions or the original purchase price of the stock plus one year's dividends) is governed by the articles of incorporation. The articles will contain all other terms relating to the redemption, such as when it may be exercised, the period of notice required to be given to the shareholder, and whether the redemption will be partial (and relate only to some of the stock owned by the preferred shareholder) or will be total, in which case all of the stock owned by the preferred shareholder can be called back by the corporation.

To ensure sufficient funds to repurchase the redeemable preferred stock, the corporation will usually establish a separate account, called the **sinking fund**, into which the corporation, over time, deposits funds for redemption purposes, for "retiring the stock." The sinking fund cannot be used for other purposes, such as the payment of expenses or distributions.

Rights of redemption may also be given to the preferred shareholder. In this case, the shareholder has the right, exercisable at her option, to compel the corporation to redeem or buy back the shares, if it has sufficient funds in the sinking fund to do so, upon the terms and conditions provided in the articles of incorporation. This particular right of redemption is referred to as a **put** and offers a preferred shareholder the advantage of having a ready buyer if the shareholder cannot sell the stock on the market.

When a corporation reacquires shares through redemption (either through the corporation's call for the stock or the shareholder's put), it will usually cancel the shares and restore them to the status of authorized but unissued shares. The effect is as if the original issuance of stock to the shareholder had never taken place. This is the MBCA approach. *See* MBCA § 6.31(a). These shares can thereafter be reissued. The transfer agent is responsible for recording the cancellation of the shares. MBCA § 6.31(b) provides that if the articles of incorporation prohibit the reissue of such reacquired shares, the number of authorized shares is reduced by the number of shares reacquired. In such a case, the directors must file a statement with the secretary of state setting forth the name of the corporation, the reduction in the number of authorized shares (itemized by class and series), and the total number of authorized shares (itemized by class and series) remaining after reduction. The statement is treated as an amendment to the articles of incorporation without the necessity of shareholder approval. See Exhibit 7.2 for a statement of cancellation of non-reissuable shares.

EXHIBIT 7.2	Illinois Statement of Cancellation of Non-Reissuable Shares

FORM **BCA 9.05** (rev. Dec. 2003)
STATEMENT OF CANCELLATION
OF NON-REISSUABLE SHARES
Business Corporation Act

Secretary of State
Department of Business Services
501S. Second St., Rm. 350
Springfield, IL 62756
217-782-6961
www.cyberdriveillinois.com

Remit payment in the form of a
check or money order payable
to Secretary of State.

_____ File #_____   Filing Fee: $5   Approved: _____

– – – – **Submit in duplicate** – – – – **Type or Print clearly in black ink** – – – – **Do not write above this line** – – – –

1. Corporate Name: _____

2. The Corporation has acquired and cancelled its own shares, and the Articles of Incorporation prohibit the re-issuance of such shares.

3. Number of shares cancelled and redemption or purchase price:

Class	Series	Par Value	Number of Shares Cancelled	Redemption or Purchase Price	Date of Cancellation
_____	_____	_____	_____	_____	_____

	BEFORE CANCELLATION				AFTER CANCELLATION		
	Class	Series	Par	Number	Class	Series	Par	Number
4. Number of authorized shares:								
5. Number of issued shares:								
6. Paid-in capital:	$_____				$_____			

7. The undersigned Corporation has caused this statement to be signed by a duly authorized officer who affirms, under penalties of perjury, that the facts stated herein are true and correct. All signatures must be in **BLACK INK**.

Dated _____ , _____   _____
                 Month Day   Year   Exact Name of Corporation

           _____
                Any Authorized Officer's Signature

           _____
                Name and Title (type or print)

NOTE: This form is applicable only where the Articles of Incorporation provide that shares redeemed or purchased shall be cancelled and shall not be re-issued. Upon such redemption and cancellation of shares, the paid-in capital of the Corporation is deemed to be reduced by that part of the paid-in capital which was represented by the shares so cancelled. The filing of this statement operates as an amendment to the Articles of Incorporation and reduces the number of shares of the class so redeemed which the Corporation is authorized to issue by the number of shares so redeemed and cancelled.

Printed by authority of the State of Illinois. January 2015 - 1 - C 150.12

In brief, the MBCA approach is that shares reacquired by a corporation automatically "bump up" the number of shares the corporation can thereafter issue unless the articles prohibit such reissue, in which case the reacquired shares are canceled by reducing the number of shares that the corporation's articles authorize it to issue.

As an alternative either to canceling the shares and reissuing them or canceling the shares and not reissuing them, in some states, the corporation can place the reacquired shares in its treasury. These treasury shares are viewed as authorized and issued but not outstanding. Thus, as noted, they do not carry any rights to voting or distributions, but they do count in determining how close the corporation is to issuing its limit of authorized shares, and they can be sold for less than par value. The MBCA has eliminated the concept of treasury shares and merely provides that a corporation can acquire its own shares, which then automatically constitute authorized but unissued shares. *See* MBCA § 6.31(a). Many states have similar provisions.

Sample Template Documents

Students who plan to work with start-up, venture capital–backed businesses may wish to take a look at the template legal documents — including the term sheet, preferred stock purchase agreement, the management rights letter, the voting agreement, the investor rights agreement, and the right of first refusal and co-sale agreement — prepared by and for the National Venture Capital Association, currently available via http://nvca.org/resources/model-legal-documents. To become familiar with common features of preferred stock, for example, review the Model Term Sheet available at the NVCA website address listed here, and compare the sample terms with the rights and preferences discussed in this section of the chapter.

Electing Directors

Preferred stock often provides holders with the right to elect a specified number of directors to the corporation's board.

Protective Provisions

Protective provisions prohibit the corporation from taking certain specified actions — say, issuing a security that is senior to existing preferred stock with respect to rights and preferences, selling all or substantially all of the corporation's assets, etc. — without the approval of the preferred stockholders. See Exhibit 7.1 for an example of a protective provision.

Other Rights

Just as common shareholders may have preemptive rights (rights of first refusal to newly issued stock) or cumulative voting rights in elections for directors, preferred shareholders may have these rights, as well. See Exhibit 7.3 for a chart comparing common and preferred stock.

Case Preview

TCV VI, L.P. v. TradingScreen Inc.

As noted above, the various rights and privileges held by preferred shareholders generally are reflected in the governing contracts (i.e., preferred stockholder agreement and related legal documents). What happens when contractually negotiated rights or privileges bump up against statutory rights or mandates? In *TCV VI, L.P. v. TradingScreen Inc.*, the Delaware Chancery Court considered whether there are any statutory or common law restrictions or limitations on the right of preferred stockholders to exit their investments under a mandatory redemption provision contained in a corporation's charter. In reading this case, think about the following questions:

1. What are redemption rights?
2. What Delaware statutory and common law restrictions on redemption are in play in this case?
3. Why was there a "tension" between the charter provision concerning redemption and statutory and common law rules respecting redemption?
4. What, if anything, could plaintiffs have done to avoid the statutory and common law restrictions at issue?

TCV VI, L.P. v. TradingScreen Inc.
C.A. No. 10164-VCN, 2015 WL 1598045 (Del. Ch. Mar. 27, 2015)*

NOBLE, Vice Chancellor.**

This case deals with the tension between a charter provision providing for the mandatory redemption of preferred stock and Delaware's statutory and common law restrictions on redemption. Plaintiffs hold preferred stock in Defendant TradingScreen, Inc. ("TradingScreen" or the "Company"). When Plaintiffs attempted to exercise their rights under TradingScreen's charter to require TradingScreen to purchase their shares, TradingScreen claimed that it could only fund a partial redemption because fully meeting Plaintiffs' demands would threaten the Company's ability to continue as a going concern. Plaintiffs have moved for judgment on the pleadings that TradingScreen has breached its charter obligations. At issue is the scope of the limitations on TradingScreen's obligation to redeem Plaintiffs' stock.

I. BACKGROUND

TradingScreen is a Delaware corporation providing electronic trading solutions. TradingScreen was founded by Defendant Philippe Buhannic ("Buhannic"), the Company's current Chief Executive Officer and Chairman of its Board of Directors (the "Board"). Defendants Piero Grandi ("Grandi") and Pierre Schroeder ("Schroeder") are TradingScreen directors.

A. The Series D Purchase Agreement

Plaintiffs TCV VI, L.P., TCV Member Fund L.P. (collectively, the "TCV Funds"), and Continental Investors Fund LLC ("Continental") have held TradingScreen

---

*After the Chancery Court denied the preferred stockholders' motion for judgment on the pleadings, the preferred stockholders sought an interlocutory appeal. The Delaware Supreme Court refused the appeal. *TCV VI, L.P. v. TradingScreen Inc.*, 115 A.3d 1216 (Del. 2015).
**Most footnotes omitted for purposes of brevity.

stock since 2007. On August 7 of that year, Plaintiffs and TradingScreen entered into the TradingScreen Inc. Series D Convertible Preferred Stock Purchase Agreement (as amended, the "Series D Purchase Agreement"). The TCV Funds purchased 4,340,398 shares of Series D Preferred Stock ("Preferred Stock") for a total purchase price of $65,931,947.74. Continental purchased 425,663 shares for a total price of $6,465,948.67.

As a result, the TCV Funds acquired 60.43%, and Continental 5.97%, of TradingScreen's Preferred Stock, which was created on September 12, 2007, when TradingScreen filed an amended and restated certificate of incorporation (the "Charter") with the Delaware Secretary of State. Section 7 of the Charter governs redemption of that stock.

Section 7.1 provides that beginning three months prior to the fifth anniversary of the issuance of the Preferred Stock, if the holders of a majority of the Preferred Stock (the "Majority Holders," *i.e.*, the TCV Funds) so request, then TradingScreen must assist the requesting Preferred Stockholders in selling their shares on satisfactory terms and conditions. If no buyer will purchase the Preferred Stock on acceptable conditions during the following nine months, then the Majority Holders may require TradingScreen to purchase all or a portion of their shares by delivering written notice identifying the number of shares they wish redeemed. All other Preferred Stockholders can participate in the redemption by delivering similar written notice.

Section 7.1.2 prescribes the process for setting the price that TradingScreen must pay for the shares. The Majority Holders and TradingScreen must first negotiate in good faith in an attempt to determine the Preferred Stock's fair market value. If no agreement is reached for twenty days following the redemption notice, then a mutually acceptable independent financial adviser determines the stock's fair market value.

Thirty days after a determination of fair market value (the "Redemption Date"), TradingScreen must redeem all shares for which it received valid redemption notices. However, any Preferred Stockholder who had submitted redemption notices may withdraw all or a portion of its request until the business day preceding the Redemption Date. The purchase of shares remaining subject to redemption must occur in three equal installments on the Redemption Date's six month, twelve month, and eighteen month anniversaries.

Further, if TradingScreen defaults on any payments due under Section 7.1.2, then interest accrues on all amounts owed at an annual percentage rate of 13%.

B. Plaintiffs Exercise Their Redemption Rights

On June 12, 2012, the TCV Funds, as Majority Holders, requested TradingScreen to assist them in selling all of their Preferred Stock. TradingScreen's Board formed a special committee (the "Special Committee") to handle this request and related matters. The TCV Funds subsequently could not find a satisfactory buyer; thus, on March 14, 2013, they delivered written notice to TradingScreen demanding that the Company purchase their stock. On March 19, 2013, Continental delivered a similar written notice.

Because the TCV Funds and TradingScreen were unable to agree on the Preferred Stock's fair market value, they engaged [redacted] to make that determination. On

February 5, 2014, [redacted] concluded that TradingScreen was worth $[redacted] million and the fair market value per share of Preferred Stock was $[redacted].

After [redacted]'s valuation, the TCV Funds decided, consistent with the Charter, to withdraw a portion of their shares from their redemption request. After these withdrawals, 4,030,398 shares remained subject to redemption. At the determined price of $[redacted], in order to redeem fully the TCV Funds's shares, TradingScreen would need to pay them $[redacted] in three equal installments of $[redacted].

On September 5, 2014, Plaintiffs delivered to TradingScreen stock certificates for the shares they wished redeemed. In response, Buhannic, TradingScreen's CEO, informed them that

> On September 4, 2014, the Special Committee of the Board of Directors of TradingScreen met in order to determine the amount of funds legally available for the redemption of shares of Series D Preferred Stock that have been the subject of redemption notices. At the meeting, the Special Committee received a presentation from AlixPartners, LLP, the Special Committee's financial advisor in connection with the redemption ("AlixPartners"), to assist it in determining the funds legally available for redemption.

The Special Committee had retained AlixPartners "to, among other things, provide analyses of TradingScreen's current and projected financial condition to assist the Special Committee in its determination of the extent to which the Company may make a payment to preferred stockholders without impairing the Company's ability to continue as a going concern." AlixPartners had presented the Special Committee with a 52-page report and (sic)

> After hearing and reviewing the presentation, asking questions and deliberating, the Special Committee determined that TradingScreen currently has $7,200,000 legally available for a partial redemption of shares of the Series D Preferred Stock, and therefore approved a resolution for the Company to redeem at this time $7,200,000 worth of shares of Series D Preferred Stock that have been noticed for redemption at the redemption price of $[redacted] per share. . . . The Special Committee also determined that it will meet on a regular basis, and no less than quarterly, to determine the amount of funds legally available for TradingScreen to make an additional payments [sic] in partial redemption of the shares of Series D Preferred Stock that have been the subject of redemption notices.

Based on its conclusion that it only had $7,200,000 legally available for redemption, TradingScreen proposed to make pro rata redemptions, and sent checks payable to the Plaintiffs in accordance with that determination.

Taking exception to the Special Committee's conclusions, the TCV Funds sent TradingScreen a letter on September 9, 2014, asserting that the Company had defaulted on its obligation under the Charter to pay the full one-third installment for the shares submitted for redemption. The TCV Funds demanded immediate payment and threatened legal action if TradingScreen did not comply within ten days. They also claimed that, pursuant to the Charter, interest would accrue at an annual rate of 13% on any unpaid amounts due. Because they viewed TradingScreen's failure to pay in full as a default under the Charter, the TCV Funds demanded that the Company make adequate assurances that it would make full redemptions on the second and third installment dates.

TradingScreen responded that it was acting in compliance with the Charter and Delaware law. According to TradingScreen, Delaware law imposes limitations "which require that any redemption of shares be made only out of legally available funds." The Special Committee had determined that $7,200,000 was the maximum amount available for redemption without jeopardizing the Company's ability to continue to operate as a going concern. TradingScreen argues that redemptions beyond this amount would violate Delaware law. Therefore, TradingScreen asserts that it has not defaulted on its obligations and that the Charter's interest provision is inapplicable. It has "assured [the TCV Funds] that TradingScreen will continue to redeem shares of its Series D Preferred Stock in accordance with the [Charter] and consistent with its obligations under applicable law."

C. Current Proceedings

Plaintiffs have moved for judgment on the pleadings on the first two of their six counts. Count I alleges that TradingScreen breached the Charter by failing to honor its redemption provision. According to Plaintiffs, the Charter is an unambiguous, binding, and enforceable contract. They followed its detailed procedure to require TradingScreen to redeem their shares. The first redemption installment of $[redacted] was due on September 7, 2014. However, TradingScreen failed to pay in full, claiming that it only had $7.2 million of "funds legally available." A provision limiting redemption to "funds legally available" is found nowhere in the Charter.

Plaintiffs contend that Section 160 of the Delaware General Corporation Law (the "DGCL"), which limits a corporation's ability to purchase shares of its own capital stock to the corporation's statutory surplus, is the only restriction on TradingScreen's obligation to comply with the Charter's explicit language. TradingScreen supposedly has more than sufficient statutory surplus and readily available cash to redeem all of Plaintiffs' tendered shares. By refusing to do so, it has allegedly breached its obligations under the Charter.

In response, Defendants argue that the common law restricts TradingScreen's ability to redeem the Preferred Stock. According to them, TradingScreen cannot redeem shares if doing so would threaten its ability to continue operating as a going concern. Because the Special Committee exercised its business judgment in determining the maximum value of shares that TradingScreen can redeem without threatening its business operations, Defendants contend that the Company has not defaulted on its payment obligations. By extension, the 13% annual interest rate has not been triggered.

However, Plaintiffs believe that TradingScreen must pay interest on all amounts overdue, regardless of whether TradingScreen's failure to pay constitutes a contractual breach. Count II requests a declaratory judgment to this effect.

II. ANALYSIS

A. *The Procedural Standard of Review*

. . .

B. *Limitations Beyond Section 160 Restrict TradingScreen's Ability to Redeem the Preferred Stock*

Plaintiffs' main argument rests on the inaccurate premise that Section 160 of the DGCL provides the only limitation on TradingScreen's obligation to redeem their shares. While Section 160 prohibits corporations that are balance-sheet insolvent from making redemptions, a corporation can satisfy Section 160's test despite being cash-flow insolvent (or at risk of becoming cash-flow insolvent), *i.e.*, unable to pay its debts as they come due. In such a case, law extraneous to Section 160 limits the scope of permissible redemptions.

1. *Section 160's Limitation on Stock Redemption*

Section 160 prohibits a corporation from "[p]urchas[ing] or redeem[ing] its own shares of capital stock for cash or other property when the capital of the corporation is impaired or when such purchase or redemption would cause any impairment of the capital of the corporation." "A repurchase impairs capital if the funds used in the repurchase exceed the amount of the corporation's 'surplus,' defined by 8 Del. C. § 154 to mean the excess of net assets over the par value of the corporation's issued stock." Net assets are calculated by subtracting total liabilities from total assets.

Section 160 thus limits a corporation's ability to purchase shares of its own capital stock to its surplus. This test prohibits certain distributions to stockholders, "but instead of using insolvency as the cut-off, the line is drawn at the amount of the corporation's capital." Section 160 protects a corporation's creditors—while preferred stock possesses characteristics of both debt and equity, the rights of all stockholders, including preferred, are subordinate to the rights of the creditors.

Plaintiffs argue that TradingScreen's net asset value is at least $[redacted] million, and after deducting for the par value of issued stock, the Company's statutory surplus is more than sufficient to redeem their shares. Having supposedly established that Section 160 is no impediment to redemption, Plaintiffs assert that they are entitled to judgment on the pleadings because the explicit language of TradingScreen's Charter sets no further limitation on their redemption rights.

2. *Common Law Limitations on Stock Redemption*

Whether Plaintiffs would be entitled to judgment on the pleadings if Section 160 were the only restriction on TradingScreen's ability to redeem their shares is irrelevant; "[o]utside the DGCL, a wide range of statutes and legal doctrines [can] restrict a corporation's ability to use funds."[20] Case law spanning the last century makes clear that "*in addition* to the strictures of Section 160, the undoubted weight of authority teaches that

---

[20]*ThoughtWorks*, 7 A.3d at 985. *See also* William W. Bratton & Michael L. Wachter, *A Theory of Preferred Stock*, 161 U. Pa. L. Rev. 1815, 1866 n.216 (2013) (observing that the view "that 'legally available' derived its exclusive meaning from reference to the legal capital rules . . . is utterly lacking in support from the cases").

a corporation cannot purchase its own shares of stock when the purchase diminishes the ability of the company to pay its debts, or lessens the security of its creditors."

ThoughtWorks dealt with a preferred stock redemption provision that explicitly provided that redemptions could only be made "out of any funds legally available therefore." This Court rejected the argument that the term "funds legally available" equates to statutory surplus.

> A corporation may be insolvent under Delaware law either when its liabilities exceed its assets, or when it is unable to pay its debts as they come due. . . . Although a corporation cannot be balance-sheet insolvent and meet the requirements of Section 160, a corporation can nominally have surplus from which redemptions theoretically could be made and yet be unable to pay its debts as they come due. The common law prohibition on redemptions when a corporation is or would be rendered insolvent restricts a corporation's ability to redeem shares under those circumstances, giving rise to yet another situation in which "funds legally available" differs from "surplus."

TradingScreen's Charter, unlike ThoughtWorks's, does not explicitly restrict redemptions to those that can be made out of "funds legally available." However, in *ThoughtWorks,* this Court noted that were such language omitted from a corporation's charter, "a comparable limitation would be implied by law." Restrictions that are comparable, though likely not identical, to the constraints identified in *ThoughtWorks* therefore limit TradingScreen's ability to make redemptions.[25]

It is true that "[t]he rules of construction which are used to interpret contracts and other written instruments are applicable when construing corporate charters." However, while Delaware stockholders "may by contract embody in the charter a provision departing from the [default] rules of the common law," they are not permitted to "transgress . . . a public policy settled by the common law or implicit in the General Corporation Law itself." Given that stockholders cannot contravene Delaware common law by explicitly including a conflicting provision in a corporate charter, they clearly cannot do so implicitly.

By urging the Court to limit its analysis to the Charter's contractual language, Plaintiffs fail to appreciate the hybrid legal status of preferred stock. Plaintiffs are holders of equity, not debt, and "[a]uthority spanning three different centuries adverts to and enforces limitations on the ability of preferred stockholders to force redemption." Partly because of the potential restrictions on mandatory redemption, investors have developed various instruments to satisfy their investment goals. However, Plaintiffs chose to invest in an equity instrument governed by certain common law and statutory rules.

Accordingly, TradingScreen may only "legally" deploy funds for stock redemptions if doing so does not "violat[e] Section 160 or other statutory or common law restrictions, including the requirement that the corporation be able to continue as a going concern and not be rendered insolvent by the distribution." To continue as a going concern, a corporation needs sufficient resources to operate for the foreseeable future without the threat of liquidation.

---

[25]For example, a corporation might lack funds yet have the legal capacity to redeem stock because it has a large surplus. Such a corporation could redeem shares in exchange for other corporate property. Alternatively, a corporation may have funds that are not "legally available." *Id.* at 984. While the omission of the phrase "funds legally available" from TradingScreen's Charter may broaden the sources of assets that TradingScreen could use to redeem stock, *i.e.,* no "funds" limitation applies, the stock cannot be redeemed if TradingScreen cannot do so "legally."

It should be noted that in affirming this Court's judgment in *ThoughtWorks,* the Supreme Court deemed it unnecessary to conclude whether this Court correctly found that "funds legally available" are distinct from statutory surplus. However, this Court's rationale for distinguishing "funds legally available" from statutory surplus remains persuasive and the Court will not now depart from the thoughtful and detailed analysis laid out in that opinion. Delaware law is clear that preferred stock "remains subject to the statutory and common law limitations that apply to equity."

C. There Are Material Factual Issues Regarding TradingScreen's Legal Ability to Make a Redemption

TradingScreen's Special Committee has concluded that the Company cannot simultaneously satisfy Plaintiffs' redemption demands in full and continue to operate as a going concern, paying its debts as they become due. TradingScreen retained AlixPartners "to assist the Special Committee in its determination of the extent to which the Company may make a payment to preferred stockholders without impairing the company's ability to continue as a going concern." Based on AlixPartners's presentation and consultation with management and legal counsel, the Special Committee determined that TradingScreen had $7.2 million of funds legally available for redemption. The Special Committee made these funds available for a pro rata partial redemption and "also determined . . . [to] meet on a regular basis, and no less than quarterly, to determine the amount of funds legally available for TradingScreen to make an additional payments [sic] in partial redemption of the shares of Series D Preferred Stock that have been the subject of redemption notices."

. . .

Whether or not the Special Committee validly concluded that a full redemption would destroy TradingScreen's ability to continue as a going concern is a factual question that cannot be decided on the pleadings. Plaintiffs' motion must be denied as to their breach of contract claim under Count I because (i) the common law restricts TradingScreen's ability to redeem its shares when doing so would damage its ability to continue as a going concern and (ii) the Special Committee undertook a facially valid process finding that a full redemption would impair TradingScreen's continuing viability.

. . .

III. CONCLUSION

Most of Plaintiffs' argument rests on their mistaken belief that Section 160 of the DGCL provides the only limitation on TradingScreen's obligation to pay for its shares of Preferred Stock. However, this Court has recognized common law restrictions on stock redemptions that are independent of, and in addition to, the DGCL's explicit provisions. TradingScreen's Special Committee purports to have exercised its business judgment in determining how much stock it can purchase while continuing forward as a going concern. While Plaintiffs may question the Special Committee's process and its conclusions, they cannot successfully do so on a motion pursuant to Court of Chancery Rule 12(c). Further, because the Court cannot conclude that TradingScreen defaulted on any payments owed to the Plaintiffs, a declaratory judgment that interest has begun to accrue is unwarranted. For these reasons, Plaintiffs' Motion for Judgment on the Pleadings is denied.

An implementing order will be entered.

Post-Case Follow-Up

The Chancery Court's holding in *TradingScreen* suggests that lawyers ought to consider whether there are limits on the right of preferred stockholders to exit their investments using contractually negotiated mandatory redemption provisions, especially in situations where the corporation is in financial distress. Preferred stockholders seeking to protect exit rights thus may wish to consider a number of strategies to protect contractually negotiated exit rights:

- *Consider using an unincorporated investment vehicle.* Unincorporated entities such as LLCs generally are not subject to all of the restrictions governing repurchase that apply in the corporations context. Preferred stockholders may wish to investigate whether their investment and related goals can be achieved using an unincorporated entity — recognizing, of course, that there are a range of benefits and costs to be considered.
- *Consider whether to purchase debt instead of preferred stock.* Debt investments can be structured to mirror the benefits of an equity investment, while providing for a right of repayment that would not be subject to the availability of surplus or other "legally available funds." While there are potential complications and technicalities to consider, along with attendant costs to private orderings, purchasing debt might be a way to accomplish financial goals while avoiding some of the pitfalls that the preferred stockholders encountered in the *TradingScreen* case.
- *Pay attention to the fiduciary duties of directors.* In other rulings, Delaware courts have noted the contractual nature of preferred stock and suggested that the fiduciary duties that directors owe to preferred stockholders may be more limited than those owed to common stockholders. (We discuss fiduciary duties owed by directors in more detail in Chapter 9.) Delaware courts also have suggested that when directors weigh the interests of preferred stockholders against those of common stockholders, they generally ought to favor the interests of common stockholders, even if at the expense of the interests of preferred stockholders. The tension between common and preferred stockholders is in play in any case where costs associated with the redemption of preferred stock could affect the viability of the common stock interests. This potential tension should be on the radar screen for preferred stockholders at the planning phase.

TCV VI, L.P. v. TradingScreen Inc.: Real Life Application

You represent a venture capital investment fund interested in investing in Acme, Inc., a start-up biotechnology company that is incorporated in Delaware. While

Acme is a "hot" start-up, the company will need to raise millions of dollars to develop and test its product — a drug used to treat obesity — before it can begin marketing the drug. Your clients want mandatory redemption rights. After reviewing the *TradingScreen* case and the practice pointers referenced above, prepare an agenda for your meeting with your clients and a memorandum outlining (i) strategies to achieve the fund's business goals; and (ii) potential risks associated with the ability to exercise redemption rights.

Series of Stock

The board of directors can classify any unissued shares into a new class or **series** of shares if the authority to do so is provided in the articles of incorporation. *See* MBCA § 6.02. This approach allows the directors to tailor stock to suit then-prevailing market conditions quickly without requiring shareholder approval. Thus, corporations might have more than one class of shares, and, in turn, each class can be further divided into one or more series. This means that corporations may have several different classes of stock — Common A, Common B, and Common C, as well as Preferred A and Preferred B — and may create series of stock within a class — Common A, Series A, and Series B — with each group having rights, limitations, and preferences that make it different from any other type. This is handy for corporations that anticipate conducting multiple rounds of preferred stock financing and that may need to tweak the rights and privileges associated with the various rounds.

Note that while the rights of the *classes* must be set forth in the articles (or the articles must be amended to set forth the specific rights and preferences of each class), stock generally can be created in a *series* within a class without the necessity of first amending the articles or obtaining shareholder approval, so long as the articles pre-authorize the creation of the series stock. For this reason, the allowance of **series stock** by the articles of incorporation is sometimes referred to as a "**blank check**" given to the directors permitting them to establish a series and to fix its rights and preferences. Although the articles need not be amended to allow the creation of a series, prior to actual issuance of the stock the directors must file a statement (or possibly an amendment of the corporation's articles) with the secretary of state containing basic information about the new series, such as its rights, limitations, and preferences. No shareholder approval is needed for the statement, which operates as an amendment to the articles of incorporation. Some states, including Pennsylvania, provide forms on their websites for notifying the secretary of state of the establishment of the new class or series. Once the directors determine the relative rights of the series stock and file the statement, they may then issue the stock.

In reality, the distinction between, for example, common and preferred stock and Series A and Series B stock is somewhat artificial. The use of various labels does not affect the fundamental principle that some types of stock might have rights and preferences that others do not, no matter what they are called. The key element to understanding series stock is that if the articles of incorporation pre-authorize such, a corporation can, without shareholder approval, create new classes of shares or divide existing classes into one or more series to respond to current market conditions by quickly raising capital.

Share Subscriptions, Stock Options, Rights, and Warrants

A **share subscription** is simply an agreement whereby a party offers to purchase stock in a corporation. These subscriptions can be entered into prior to the corporation's existence (pre-incorporation share subscriptions) or after incorporation. As this suggests, one can become a shareholder in a corporation by acquiring stock from the corporation or another shareholder, subject to any restrictions on transfer arising under state corporation law (discussed in Chapter 10) or the federal securities laws (discussed in Chapter 13).

MBCA § 6.24 provides that a corporation may issue options, rights, or warrants for the purchase of its shares (or other securities). There are many different types of options; we will focus on **stock options** here. Broadly speaking, a stock option is an agreement whereby the corporation gives a party the right to purchase a specified number of shares from the corporation at a specified price during or at a specified time period. Stock options are often granted to key employees of the corporation. If the option price is fixed at $30 per share and the corporation's stock is traded on the market for $50 per share at the time the option may be exercised, the option would allow its holder to purchase a specified number of the shares at $30 per share, thus giving the option holder a tremendous economic benefit. The option holder, of course, may allow the option to expire without exercising it.

A **right** is a short-term (often 30 or 45 days) option granted to an existing shareholder, allowing the shareholder the opportunity to purchase additional shares in the future at a price set lower than the stock's current market value.

A **warrant** is a long-term option, usually with an option period longer than one year (and often for several years). Warrants are often issued when the corporation borrows money; they may make the transaction more attractive to the lender and "sweeten" the transaction. For example, in 2008, when Berkshire Hathaway infused General Electric with billions of dollars of cash, Berkshire Hathaway not only received GE preferred stock with a 10 percent dividend, but also warrants to buy $3 billion in GE common stock at $22.50 per share at any time within the next five years. Just one year before the transaction, GE's stock was trading at more than $40 per share. Options and warrants are usually transferable, but they do not have voting rights or distribution rights. Some corporations have warrants that are publicly traded on the national exchanges.

5. Stock Certificates

Corporations can issue stock without physically delivering a certificate to the shareholder. Shares issued without the formality of stock certificates are called **uncertificated shares**. The ownership of such shares is recorded in the corporate books and is called a "book entry." Owners of uncertificated stock have the same rights as owners of stock evidenced by paper certificates. The move away from physical certificates to electronic book entry is generally called **dematerialization**. In fact, in today's volatile and modern stock market, many investors never possess actual stock certificates. For today's modern public corporations, for example, with stocks that trade rapidly day-to-day via exchanges and in various other markets, the use of actual stock certificates is uncommon. In some instances, purchasers request actual paper certificates when stock is bought as a gift, for example, for a graduation or birthday present. Some corporations charge a modest fee for issuance of a paper stock certificate or issue paper certificates only when a certain number of shares are purchased.

Neither Congress nor the securities industry favors paper certificates. To reduce public interest, many corporations no longer offer beautiful engraved certificates, but rather issue plain paper certificates. About 400 publicly traded companies, including AT&T and Visa, simply no longer print paper certificates. The SEC has asked for public comment on whether the agency should mandate destruction of old certificates. Historians and collectors have been adamantly opposed.

When actual certificates are used, their content and form is controlled by state statute. MBCA § 6.25 provides that share certificates must provide the following information:

a. The name of the issuing organization and the state law under which it is organized;
b. The name of the person to whom the share is issued; and
c. The number and class of shares (and the designation of the series, if any).

> ### Scripophily
>
> The collecting of historic stocks and bonds is known as scripophily. Certificate No. 3 of Buffalo Bill's Wild West and Pawnee Bill's Great Far East Show recently sold for $15,000, and stock certificates signed by Enron's late CEO Kenneth Lay fetch about $300 as of the time of this writing, demonstrating the high level of public interest in historical and collectible stock certificates. Although the Walt Disney Company had previously stated that it would never eliminate paper certificates, which were decorated with the company's famous cartoon characters, it ceased offering its colorful certificates in 2013 (although it does provide a "certificate of acquisition").

If uncertificated shares are issued, within a reasonable amount of time after issuance, the corporation must send the shareholder a written statement including the information required to be set forth on certificates.

Book entry (or paperless shares) may now be held through the **Direct Registration System**, which allows the shares to be registered in a stockholder's name on the corporation's books and either the corporation or its transfer agent (discussed below) holds the security in book-entry form. The purchaser receives dividends, annual reports, and account statements directly from the corporation. This system allows stockholders to electronically move the stock from the company's books for sale or to a broker for easy transfer of the stock.

Shares may also be held in **street name,** meaning they are registered and held by the buyer's brokerage firm, which is listed on the corporation's books. The brokerage company will credit the buyer's account with any dividends paid and send the buyer the corporation's annual reports, proxy forms, and so forth.

When shares certificates are issued, they must be signed (either manually or by facsimile signature or autopen) by two officers of the corporation, generally the president and the secretary. The seal may be impressed on the face of the certificate, although this is not required. Issuance of new certificates in a small corporation is typically performed by the corporate secretary or treasurer. In large corporations, however, this task would be daunting and is therefore often performed by a **transfer agent,** usually a bank, trust company, or financial institution that has a supply of blank certificates with facsimile signatures of the officers. The transfer agent also records transfer of shares and may act as the corporate **registrar,** and maintain the list of shareholders (as required by MBCA § 16.01(c)). Some transfer agents are professional companies dedicated to handling all transactions with regard to stock ownership, recordkeeping, and dividend payments. For example, American Stock Transfer & Trust Company of New York City has been serving as a transfer agent and registrar for more than 40 years and represents such companies as Revlon as of the time of this writing. The company also designs and prints proxy cards for corporate elections and maintains corporate records of shares outstanding to pay dividends and to ensure shares are not issued in excess of the number of authorized shares.

If corporations issue only one class of stock, the content of the certificate will be as already described. If more than one class of stock is authorized by the articles of incorporation, the preferences, limitations, and rights of each class must be summarized on the certificate. Alternatively, the certificate may state that the corporation will furnish this information without charge to any shareholder upon written request. If there is no certificate, the corporation will send the shareholders a written statement with the appropriate information.

Because the certificate is not what is owned but merely represents ownership of an interest in a corporation, the loss, theft, or destruction of a stock certificate is not critical. When the shareholder provides an affidavit to the corporation stating that the certificate is lost and cannot be found, or has been stolen or destroyed, the corporation or its transfer agent will cancel the original certificate and issue a duplicate. Some corporations require the shareholder to provide a bond in an amount adequate to protect the corporation if the lost certificate is later presented by an innocent purchaser.

On occasion, shareholders own fractions of shares. This generally occurs when the corporation declares a share dividend. For example, if the corporation declares a dividend of 1 share for every 100 owned, the owner of 150 shares would be entitled to receive 1.5 shares. If the state corporations code allows fractional shares, the corporation may issue a certificate for a fraction of a share. The owner of this fractional share will be entitled to fractional voting rights and dividends and to participate in the assets of the corporation upon liquidation. The MBCA authorizes the payment of cash to a shareholder for the value of fractional shares. MBCA § 6.04(a).

Alternatively, and at the discretion of the board of directors, the corporation can issue scrip rather than a stock certificate for the fractional share. **Scrip** is a document or certificate evidencing ownership of a partial share. The certificate must be conspicuously labeled "scrip." When the shareholder has accumulated sufficient scrip to total one share, the scrip may be surrendered to the corporation for a certificate evidencing one full share. Scrip is transferable but generally does not carry voting, dividend, or liquidation rights. MBCA § 6.04(c). Thus, the difference between fractional shares and scrip is that the holder of scrip is not entitled to exercise any shareholder rights. Scrip is often issued with the requirement that it be exchanged for a full share within some specified period of time or it will be void.

For quick reference, the following exhibit summarizes and compares typical features of common and preferred stock.

EXHIBIT 7.3	Comparison of Usual Features of Common and Preferred Stock	
	Common Stock	**Preferred Stock**
Voting rights	Usually one vote per share	Voting rights may or may not exist; articles will specify. Voting rights are rare, though protections generally are negotiated and set forth in a stockholders' agreement.
Distribution rights	No right to distributions; distributions declared in discretion of board and corporation must be solvent	Distributions are usually "guaranteed" via the stockholder's agreement and may be cumulative, meaning that if profits do not permit a distribution or the corporation is insolvent, the right to distribution carries over until the corporation can pay it. Shareholders may have participating preferred stock, meaning that they participate in regularly declared dividends in addition to their cumulative or noncumulative distribution.
Liquidation rights	Shareholders receive assets after distribution to creditors and then to preferred shareholders.	Shareholders receive assets after creditors and before common shareholders; distribution may be guaranteed or specified in articles.
Conversion rights	No conversion rights	Shareholders may have right to convert their preferred shares into some other type of equity (usually common stock).
Redemption rights	No redemption rights	Shareholders may be forced to sell their stock back to corporation or may have the power to compel corporation to purchase their stock at agreed-on price.

C. DEBT

In addition to issuing additional equity securities to raise capital, corporations also may borrow money to finance operations and future growth. When a corporation borrows money from a bank or other financial institutions, an investment fund, or from members of the public, it is engaging in **debt financing**. Fundamentally, debt financing refers to the process of getting a loan, which the business must pay back with interest. While debt (and debt instruments) do not create or reflect an ownership interest in the corporation, there are circumstances when being a creditor (versus an owner) may have its advantages. For example, in bankruptcy proceedings, debt has priority over equity upon liquidation, meaning that creditors of a debtor corporation will be paid back before any monies go to stockholders. If the debtor corporation's assets are insufficient to pay all debts, or if payments to creditors exhaust the debtor corporation's available resources, equity holders may receive nothing upon liquidation.

1. Promissory Notes

Although there are many different types of loans and debts securities (some of which are discussed below), all loans typically are evidenced by a **promissory note**. Promissory notes may take the form of a **demand note**, meaning that no specific time is stated for repayment and the creditor has the right to demand repayment by the corporation at any time, or they may set out a repayment schedule. Promissory notes generally contain the identity of the lender and borrower, the principal amount of the loan, the interest rate, and repayment schedule, if applicable. Promissory notes also may include other terms as well, such as provisions providing for installment payments of principal, interest, or both; or an **acceleration** clause, or provision providing that in the event the debtor misses any payment, the creditor can declare the entire balance to be immediately payable. Some notes also contain a **confession of judgment**, or a provision that allows the creditor to obtain an immediate judgment in court against the debtor in the event of a default. In this case, the corporation agrees that an immediate judgment may be taken against it in the event of its default, without the necessity of a trial. Because such a provision does not allow the debtor corporation to assert any defenses as to why it has not repaid the debt, some states prohibit confessions of judgment. Exhibit 7.4 shows a form of unsecured promissory note.

EXHIBIT 7.4   Unsecured Promissory Note

$20,000	January 1, 2015

For value received, the undersigned, Simmons Corp., a corporation organized and existing under the laws of the State of California, promises to pay to Paul J. Higgins at 2725 Delaney Circle, Los Angeles, California, the sum of Twenty Thousand Dollars ($20,000) with interest from January 1, 2015 until paid, at the rate of five percent (5%) per annum, all due and payable on December 31, 2018. Should suit be commenced or an attorney employed to enforce the terms of this note, Simmons Corp. agrees to pay such additional sum as the court might order reasonable as attorneys' fees. Principal and interest payable in lawful money of the United States. This note may be paid in full without any penalty charges. The undersigned hereby waives demand, presentment, and protest, and notices thereof and agrees to remain bound hereunder notwithstanding any extension, modification, or waiver by the holder of this note.

Simmons Corp.

By:_____

Title: _____

2. Loan Agreement

In addition to the promissory note, many loans also have a loan agreement. A loan agreement is a contract between the lender and borrower that typically includes representations and warranties (often called "reps" or "reps and warranties" for short) and covenants by the borrower. Reps and warranties are assertions of fact. In loan agreements, reps and warranties often relate to the accuracy and completeness of financial statements and financial projections that the borrower provided to the seller during the due diligence process.

Covenants are promises by the borrower to do something (affirmative covenants), or to forbear from doing something (negative covenants). In loan agreements, affirmative covenants may relate to an obligation to maintain insurance, to pay taxes, to comply with rules and regulations relating to the operation of the business, to provide certain disclosures, and the like. Negative covenants often restrict the corporation's ability to make distributions, make large capital distributions, incur additional indebtedness, and the like. Reps and warranties and covenants are heavily negotiated, particularly in larger, more complex deals. Often, the breach of a covenant constitutes an event of default, entitling the lender to accelerate the loan and declare all principal and interest immediately due and payable.

3. Types of Debt

While all debt fundamentally involves a loan that must be paid back with interest, there are many different varieties of debt instruments. Here are a few comparatively common types of debt used by corporations:

- ■ *Bonds.* Corporate bonds are a type of **debt security** issued to investors (e.g., insurance companies, mutual funds, individual investors). Bonds generally are **secured** by a business's assets (secured versus unsecured debt is discussed below), and bondholders are entitled to the repayment of their principal loan amount, plus interest paid at a specific rate, known as the **coupon**. Bonds specify the principal amount due (sometimes called the **face value**), the interest required, the date of repayment (often called the **maturity date**), and the property pledged to secure repayment of the loan. If debt is **secured**, the creditor will have rights to some

What Is Due Diligence?

Due diligence, for present purposes, refers to the practice of examining the business, business practices, financial performance, individuals, etc., involved in a potential transaction partner or potential counterparty prior to finalizing a deal.

Sandbagging

In the world of high-stakes mergers and acquisitions, a buyer "sandbags" a seller when the buyer knows the seller has materially breached a warranty, but closes the deal anyway, and then brings a breach of contract/warranty action post-closing. Traditionally, courts required the buyer to prove that it relied upon the warranty and that it did not know of the breach pre-closing to prevail. More recently, courts in some jurisdictions have permitted the buyer to sue without regard to its knowledge of pre-closing breaches in certain circumstances. Although courts appear willing to allow private ordering (i.e., contracting around default rules) respecting warranties and any alleged breach of warranty, the law respecting sandbagging varies from jurisdiction to jurisdiction and is unsettled in certain jurisdictions. To avoid unexpected or unintended results, lawyers should be sure to research the law in all relevant jurisdictions when considering whether and under what circumstances a buyer who is aware of (or concerned about) a material breach of a warranty will be able to bring a claim for breach of warranty post-closing. *See* Charles K. Whitehead, *Sandbagging: Default Rules and Acquisition Agreements,* 36 Del. J. Corp. L. 1081 (2011).

specified corporate property (e.g., trademarks, real estate, accounts receivable) in the event of a default in payment by the corporation.

- **Junk bonds.** The term "junk" bonds is a colloquialism used to refer to debt financing raised by a business through the sale of bonds with a credit rating that falls below "investment grade" because of the substantial risk of default by the borrower. There are several major rating agencies — Standard & Poors, Moody's, and FitchRatings are well-known examples — and each agency has its own rating system or "key" reflecting what constitutes investment grade. Junk bonds carry higher interest rates than investment grade products to compensate investors for taking on higher credit risk, or risk of default. Junk bonds are less colorfully known as **high-yield bonds** or **non-investment grade bonds**.

- **Debenture.** A debenture is similar to a bond, but is unsecured (i.e., not backed by **collateral,** i.e., assets pledged to the lender until the loan is repaid). If a debt is **unsecured**, the creditor has no right automatically to proceed against any specific corporate asset upon default by the corporation and thus must sue and obtain a judgment against the corporation to receive repayment of the debt. With a judgment in hand, a debenture holder may be able to proceed against corporate assets, but collection via this mechanism is fraught with risk. Debentures are typically long-term obligations, often with a term in excess of ten years.

- **Mortgage note.** In some instances, the property pledged by the corporation is real estate, for example, a parcel of land. In the event of a default, the creditor has the right to sell the property to satisfy the debt. The document evidencing the corporation's obligations and identifying the real estate as the collateral is called a **mortgage note** or **mortgage bond**. This mortgage does not differ significantly from any other type of mortgage. For example, if an individual purchases a house for $450,000 and pays $90,000 down, the remainder of the purchase price, $360,000, often must be borrowed from a bank. The bank will lend this money only on the condition that the home/real estate serve as security or collateral for repayment of the loan. That way, if the home buyer does not make the required monthly payments, the bank can take back, or foreclose on, the house, and sell it, and hopefully collect the $360,000 borrowed by the home buyer. In a corporate scenario, the corporation will usually be obligated to keep the property it has pledged in good condition, to insure it, to pay the taxes due thereon, and to keep it free and clear of other encumbrances.

- **Commercial paper.** Commercial paper is short-term, unsecured loans, the proceeds of which will be used to fund "current transactions" (e.g., operating expenses, inventory, and receivables). Maturities for commercial paper range from 2 to 270 days, with both the definition of "current transactions" and the 270-day limit derived from federal regulations.

- **Accounts receivable.** An accounts receivable loan is a loan secured by the business's accounts receivable, meaning money owed to the business from its customers.

- **Trade debt.** Trade debt is also known as accounts payable, and it refers to money owed to a **trade creditor,** or supplier or other creditor of the business for goods or services sold by the creditor and purchased by the corporation on credit.

- *Inventory loan.* An inventory loan is a loan secured by the corporation's inventory of finished goods.
- *Equipment lease.* A lease is a financing transaction in which a finance company buys a piece of equipment selected by a business, then leases the equipment to the business in exchange for lease payments. There are accounting nuances associated with these transactions, so experts should be involved when deciding whether to characterize equipment lease financing as a debt for accounting purposes.
- *Line of credit.* A line of credit is a form of pre-authorized loan, up to a certain maximum amount, which the corporation can draw from on a variable basis, as its capital needs fluctuate.
- *Redeemable debt security.* Redeemable debt security can be paid off or redeemed prior to its stated **date of maturity**.
- *Subordinated debt security.* Subordinated debt security is junior in order of payment to another debt having priority over it.

When the corporation's obligation to repay money is secured, or backed by a pledge of **collateral**, the creditor can seize the collateral if the corporation defaults. In addition to real estate, a corporation also can pledge personal property such as machinery, equipment, inventory, or accounts receivable as collateral. Trademarks, patents, and copyrights can also be pledged as security for a loan. As an example of such a pledge, in late 2006 Ford Motor Company pledged a variety of assets (including its manufacturing plants and certain trademarks and patents) as collateral when it borrowed $18 billion from banks, which was the first time the company had used its assets as collateral. Analysts noted that Ford had to seek some secured financing because deep losses had made other borrowing alternatives nearly impossible.

When personal property or fixtures constitute the security for the loan, a document called a **security agreement** is executed by the corporation and the creditor. The creditor must file a **financing statement** with the secretary of state or county recorder to provide notice of the security interest claimed in the property. See Exhibit 7.5 for a copy of the New York Commercial Code Financing Statement, Form UCC-1. The financing statement specifies and itemizes the specific personal property pledged by the corporation. A well-advised bank or other creditor usually conducts a "UCC search" before extending credit to ensure that the borrower has not already encumbered that property with debt that would take priority over the new bank or other creditor. Timely filing of financing statements is thus important both to give notice to other potential creditors and to protect the filing creditor's rights. Obtaining information about financing statements on file with the secretary of state is easily accomplished by filing a simple request for information. In most states, however, the information is available online, at no cost, at the home

> ### Practice Pointers for UCC Searches
>
> A bank or other creditor should perform a UCC search at the start of negotiations, then update that search as the deal unfolds and prior to finalizing deal terms to ensure that the new bank or other creditor obtains the priority that it expects. Also, it is important to conduct a UCC search at both the secretary of state and local levels (e.g., county, or wherever real estate records are set) to ensure that the search is comprehensive.

EXHIBIT 7.5   **UCC Financing Statement**

UCC FINANCING STATEMENT
FOLLOW INSTRUCTIONS (front and back) CAREFULLY

A. NAME & PHONE OF CONTACT AT FILER [optional]

B. SEND ACKNOWLEDGMENT TO: (Name and Address)

Print	Reset

THE ABOVE SPACE IS FOR FILING OFFICE USE ONLY

1. DEBTOR'S EXACT FULL LEGAL NAME - insert only one debtor name (1a or 1b) - do not abbreviate or combine names

1a. ORGANIZATION'S NAME			
OR 1b. INDIVIDUAL'S LAST NAME	FIRST NAME	MIDDLE NAME	SUFFIX
1c. MAILING ADDRESS	CITY	STATE / POSTAL CODE	COUNTRY

1d. **SEE INSTRUCTIONS** Not Applicable	ADD'L INFO RE ORGANIZATION DEBTOR	1e. TYPE OF ORGANIZATION	1f. JURISDICTION OF ORGANIZATION	1g. ORGANIZATIONAL ID #, if any ☐ NONE

2. ADDITIONAL DEBTOR'S EXACT FULL LEGAL NAME - insert only one debtor name (2a or 2b) - do not abbreviate or combine names

2a. ORGANIZATION'S NAME			
OR 2b. INDIVIDUAL'S LAST NAME	FIRST NAME	MIDDLE NAME	SUFFIX
2c. MAILING ADDRESS	CITY	STATE / POSTAL CODE	COUNTRY

2d. **SEE INSTRUCTIONS** Not Applicable	ADD'L INFO RE ORGANIZATION DEBTOR	2e. TYPE OF ORGANIZATION	2f. JURISDICTION OF ORGANIZATION	2g. ORGANIZATIONAL ID #, if any ☐ NONE

3. SECURED PARTY'S NAME (or NAME of TOTAL ASSIGNEE of ASSIGNOR S/P) - insert only one secured party name (3a or 3b)

3a. ORGANIZATION'S NAME			
OR 3b. INDIVIDUAL'S LAST NAME	FIRST NAME	MIDDLE NAME	SUFFIX
3c. MAILING ADDRESS	CITY	STATE / POSTAL CODE	COUNTRY

4. This FINANCING STATEMENT covers the following collateral:

5. ALTERNATIVE DESIGNATION [if applicable]: ☐ LESSEE/LESSOR   ☐ CONSIGNEE/CONSIGNOR   ☐ BAILEE/BAILOR   ☐ SELLER/BUYER   ☐ AG. LIEN   ☐ NON-UCC FILING

6. ☐ This FINANCING STATEMENT is to be filed [for record] (or recorded) in the REAL ESTATE RECORDS.   Attach Addendum   [if applicable]   7. Check to REQUEST SEARCH REPORT(S) on Debtor(s) [ADDITIONAL FEE]   [optional]   ☐ All Debtors   ☐ Debtor 1   ☐ Debtor 2

8. OPTIONAL FILER REFERENCE DATA

FILING OFFICE COPY — UCC FINANCING STATEMENT (FORM UCC1) (REV. 05/22/02) page of the state's secretary of state. Those seeking to protect a creditor must search under the debtor's proper legal name.

There are limits on a corporation's ability to pledge assets as collateral. For example, real property pledged must not be over-secured by the corporation, or repeatedly pledged as collateral for loans exceeding the value of the property. To ensure the corporation does not over-secure or over-collateralize its property, the mortgage will be recorded with the county recorder where the real estate is located. This recordation provides potential creditors notice of previous mortgages placed on the property.

4. Common Features of Debt Securities

Because investors can always place their money in banks and receive interest thereon, a corporation might introduce various features or provisions in its debt securities to induce investors to loan money to the corporation rather than simply placing it in a bank account. Higher rates of interest may be offered than those paid by banks, but other features can also be offered to make the debt security attractive to an investor.

Redemption Terms

Most creditors do not want a debtor to pay off a debt prior to the stated maturity date. The profit made by a creditor is in the interest paid rather than in the repayment of the principal amount borrowed. Therefore, the corporation might include favorable **redemption terms** in the debt security and might agree not to redeem or call the debt security before its stated maturity date, not to redeem the debt during some specified period, or to pay a penalty or premium to the creditor if the debt is redeemed prior to its date of maturity. Generally, this prepayment penalty will decline as the loan matures. Prepayment penalties assure the lender or debt security holder that it will receive the bargained-for interest. Otherwise, if the debt was negotiated at a 5 percent rate of interest, and the interest rate later fell to 3 percent, the corporation would redeem the debt and renegotiate another loan at the then-prevailing rate of 3 percent, thereby depriving the first creditor of the 5 percent interest it planned on receiving over the life of the loan. The corporation may create a sinking fund to use for purposes of redeeming or retiring debt.

Convertible Debt and Conversion Terms

Debt securities may be **convertible** into equity securities, or shares of the corporation. Such a feature would allow the creditor to trade in debt for shares evidencing ownership in the corporation. It might be that the corporation is doing extremely well and the debtor would love to buy stock but does not have sufficient liquid assets (cash) to do so. A right of conversion thus allows the creditor to purchase stock without using actual cash; the purchase price is funded by turning in the debenture (unsecured debt) or bond (secured debt). For example, in September

2014, Twitter announced that it planned to raise as much as $650 million from institutional investors by offering notes that would be convertible into shares or cash, at Twitter's option. Twitter announced that it intended to use the proceeds in connection with general corporate purposes.

On the other hand, a company may want to eliminate debt to make itself stronger. For example, in March 2009, Ford Motor Company announced that bondholders could convert their bonds for a combination of both cash and stock. In so doing, Ford sought to revamp its balance sheet and reduce the cash drain associated with repayment, and thereby weather weak auto sales. To induce bondholders to convert, Ford offered a cash premium as well as its previously agreed-upon conversion rate for common stock.

Convertible instruments also are attractive in certain deals involving start-up businesses. Because convertible notes begin their life as debt instruments, they allow the business to raise capital without having to set an equity valuation. Both the investor and the start-up may wish to defer questions of valuation to avoid impeding subsequent financings from other investors — e.g., a subsequent investor who believes that an earlier equity valuation was too high may be reluctant to invest. Using a convertible note also gives the corporation the option of potentially paying back the cash for a period of time prior to taking in permanent equity capital. Convertible debt typically is used for smaller rounds of financing at the early stages of a company's life.

If a corporation issues numerous bonds to the public at once (rather than simply executing bonds sporadically), the corporation may appoint a trustee to act on behalf of the various creditors. The trustee is usually an institutional lender or commercial bank. In the event of a default by the corporation, the trustee will represent the interests of all of the creditors in seizing the property securing the corporation's debt. The trustee's rights and responsibilities and the terms of the securities, the obligations of the corporate issuer, and the rights of creditors are set forth in an agreement called a **trust indenture** (or simply, "indenture"). The use of a disinterested trustee is an advantage to both the corporation and the creditor. In the event of a default, the corporation will have the advantage of dealing with only one party, the trustee, rather than with numerous creditors, and the creditors have the advantage of having a representative act for them, rather than having to pursue their claims individually. In many cases the trustee is the trust department of a bank or other financial institution. In 1939, Congress passed the Trust Indenture Act (15 U.S.C. §§ 77aaa et seq.) to regulate the public offering of notes, bonds, and debentures, generally those in excess of $10 million. The act requires a corporate issuer to prepare and file a registration statement with the Securities and Exchange Commission to provide information about the proposed issuance. Additionally, trustees must be qualified and file a separate statement with the SEC signifying the trustee's compliance with various eligibility and standard of conduct rules.

Priority and Subordination Rights

A corporation may borrow money over a period of time, and the debtors will know their place in the payment line in the event the corporation defaults in repaying its debts. They may receive payment before (or have priority over) some creditors, and may be paid after (or be **subordinate** to) others. A corporation can entice a creditor to loan it money by inserting a clause into the debenture or bond stating that the debt cannot be subordinated to any other debt. The debt security holder thus knows its debt must be paid first. Alternatively, the debenture or bond might state that the debt is subordinate to any future borrowing by the corporation. Typically, a creditor would agree to accept such a disadvantageous position only in return for favorable interest rates, redemption terms, or conversion terms.

In some instances, a creditor might be willing to lend money to a corporation only if its debt has priority over all others then existing. This will pose problems if various debt security holders already occupy first, second, and third places in the payment line. The corporation might need to approach these existing debt security holders and ask them to agree to occupy second, third, and fourth places (i.e., subordinate their debt) so the corporation can secure needed financing. The debt security holders might agree to do this if it appears the corporation is struggling financially and this influx of new capital is crucial for the corporation's continued existence. The existing debt security holders might also bargain for more favorable interest rates, redemption terms, or conversion terms in return for subordinating their debts to that of the new creditor.

Note that priority and subordination only become critical to lenders when the corporation defaults in paying back its loans. So long as the corporation is current in making its loan payments, lenders may not be concerned with which one of them is most senior. If the corporation defaults in making its payments, however, and lawsuits are filed or the corporation dissolves or goes bankrupt, the various priority and subordination terms in the loan agreements and bonds will determine which lenders have seniority over others.

Voting Rights

In most states, and under the MBCA, only shares are entitled to vote. MBCA § 7.21. *See also* Exhibit 7.6 for comparison of equity securities and debt securities. Some jurisdictions (including Delaware) authorize the articles of incorporation to allow debt security holders to vote on certain issues, such as election of directors, amendment of the articles of incorporation, and mergers. In Delaware, if bondholders are to vote, that must be provided for in the certificate of incorporation. Del. Code Ann. tit. 8, § 221.

Bond Trends and Curiosities

In mid-2013, Apple Inc. issued $17 billion worth of bonds (ranging from 3 to 30 years) for the first time since the 1990s to raise money to then pass along to shareholders in the form of dividends and stock buybacks. At the time, this bond offering was the largest in U.S. history, although it was surpassed in late 2013 with Verizon's sale of $49 billion worth of bonds.

Some insurance companies have begun issuing "catastrophe bonds," which are linked to specific types of disasters, such as hurricanes. If no disaster occurs during the bond period (often three years), the investor receives her money back (with a high yield). If a disaster does occur, the insurance company uses the "cat bond" money to pay victims of the disaster, and the bondholder receives nothing. Buyers of one bond that provided payouts for claims related to the 2011 earthquake in Japan lost all their money.

In mid-2014, a company in London offered a four-year bond that not only paid 8 percent but also offered weekly burritos at its fast-food outlets. Money for the "burrito bonds" was accepted through online crowdfunding sites.

EXHIBIT 7.6 Comparison of Equity and Debt Securities	
Equity Securities ("Stock")	**Debt Securities ("Bonds")**
Shareholder is an owner of the corporation and is entitled to vote and receive distributions, if earnings permit.	Bondholder is an outside creditor of the corporation and is entitled to timely repayment of the debt.
Issuance of shares produces cash for the corporation.	Issuance of bonds produces cash for the corporation.
Issuance of shares dilutes power of existing shareholders but costs the corporation nothing.	Issuance of bonds does not dilute power of existing shareholders but bonds must be repaid.
If corporation is insolvent, no distributions are paid to any shareholder.	Bondholder will be entitled to periodic payments of interest and principal, or repayment of debt.
Corporation cannot deduct distributions to shareholders (and distributions are taxed to the shareholder recipients).	Corporation can deduct interest paid to bondholders and reduce taxable income.
In event of liquidation, shareholders receive assets after debts owed to outside creditors/bondholders are satisfied.	In event of liquidation, bondholders receive assets before shareholders.

D. THE LAWYER'S ROLE: NEGOTIATING DEBT OR EQUITY FINANCING

When negotiating financing deals, lawyers often work from or toward a **term sheet** — that is, a non-binding list of deal terms — as an early step in working toward a more formal, written agreement. Term sheets are designed to facilitate negotiations and drafting of the deal documents. They allow the parties to identify and discuss key terms during the negotiation process, surface potential roadblocks, and the like. Lawyers must, however, be sensitive to the fact that clients rarely want to be bound by a term sheet. Instead, clients typically wish to be bound only when both parties agree to, and sign, mutually acceptable operative deal documents. Consequently, be sure to remember what you learned in your first-year contracts class when drafting or using a term sheet! If your client does not wish to be bound by a term sheet, note early and often that the term sheet does not constitute a binding commitment on the part of either party. In addition, make it clear that the parties will not be bound unless and until they agree to and sign operative deal documents. For reference, see the disclaimer in the sample term sheet prepared by the National Venture Capital Association (NVCA), currently available at http://nvca.org/resources/model-legal-documents:*

---

*The NVCA form contains the following important caveats, which we quote in full here:

(i) This sample document is the work product of a national coalition of attorneys who specialize in venture capital financings, working under the auspices of the NVCA. This document is intended to serve as a starting point only, and should be tailored to meet your specific requirements. This document should not be construed as legal advice for any particular facts or circumstances. Note that this sample document presents an array of (often mutually exclusive) options with respect to particular deal provisions;

This Term Sheet summarizes the principal terms of the Series A Preferred Stock Financing of [_____], Inc., a [Delaware] corporation (the "**Company**"). In consideration of the time and expense devoted and to be devoted by the Investors with respect to this investment, the No Shop/Confidentiality [and Counsel and Expenses] provisions of this Term Sheet shall be binding obligations of the Company whether or not the financing is consummated. No other legally binding obligations will be created until definitive agreements are executed and delivered by all parties. This Term Sheet is not a commitment to invest, and is conditioned on the completion of due diligence, legal review and documentation that is satisfactory to the Investors. This Term Sheet shall be governed in all respects by the laws of [_____the]. . . .

Beyond term sheets, lawyers negotiating investment deals for clients should expect vigorous negotiations over rights and obligations, and repeated rounds of drafting and editing. Take a look at the form of preferred stock purchase currently agreement prepared by and for the National Venture Capital Association, currently available at http://nvca.org/resources/model-legal-documents. The table of contents, reproduced below in Exhibit 7.7, speaks to many of the considerations and negotiation points discussed in this chapter:

EXHIBIT 7.7 **Table of Contents for National Venture Capital Association Template Series A Preferred Stock Purchase Agreement**

(ii) This term sheet maps to the NVCA Model Documents, and for convenience the provisions are grouped according to the particular Model Document in which they may be found. Although this term sheet is perhaps somewhat longer than a "typical" VC Term Sheet, the aim is to provide a level of detail that makes the term sheet useful as both a road map for the document drafters and as a reference source for the business people to quickly find deal terms without the necessity of having to consult the legal documents (assuming of course there have been no changes to the material deal terms prior to execution of the final documents).

EXHIBIT 7.7 **(continued)**

EXHIBIT 7.7   **(continued)**

E. INTERNALLY GENERATED FUNDS

Internally generated funds are funds generated by the corporation — e.g., profits generated from business activities. Instead of paying out profits to shareholders in dividends, a corporation might keep and use these so-called retained earnings to fund current or future plans. Although it might sound strange, a corporation might take on debt despite having access to internally generated funds. There are many reasons for this. In some cases, a corporation may take on debt because market demand for the corporation's debt securities allows the corporation to borrow large sums at very low cost. In February 2015, for example, Microsoft Corporation sold $10.8 billion of debt in its biggest bond sale on record, capitalizing on investor demand for Microsoft's highly rated corporate debt securities. A business also may borrow, despite having access to internally generated funds, to finance growth or expansion plans. For example, a corporation may borrow to finance the acquisition of another corporation or a particular line of business from another corporation. A business also might decide to take on debt despite having internally generated funds to address cash flow issues. For example, a business that does the bulk of its business over the holiday season may borrow during the spring and fall to pay for manufacturing costs associated with producing goods in time for the holiday season.

F. CAPITAL STRUCTURE

In thinking about how businesses use equity, debt, and internally generated funds, keep in mind the concept of **capital structure**. As noted above, a corporation's capital structure refers to the particular mix of debt and equity that the business uses to finance its operations and its plans for future growth. Capital structure is a complicated and at times controversial subject, and it often is more of a business and finance question than a legal issue. That said, a cursory introduction to capital structure is useful for lawyers:

- *Selling additional equity can dilute existing shareholders.* When a company raises money by issuing and selling equity, existing shareholders may be **diluted**. As noted above, dilution refers to a reduction in ownership percentage caused by the issuance of new stock. For example, assume that you own 100 shares of a corporation that has 5,000 shares issued and outstanding. Further assume that the corporation authorizes and issues 500 additional shares to a new investor. After this transaction, your stake in the business is diluted — instead of owning 2 percent of the business (100 divided by 5,000), you now own 1.8 percent of the business (100 divided by 5,500). Dilution may be worth it — the "new money" may be critical to the business's operations or plans for future growth, and the new investor might bring sought-after expertise, contacts, etc. That said, dilution can impact control and governance structures. A diluted shareholder may no longer own a controlling stake in the business, for example. If the business had raised money by borrowing instead of selling additional equity, existing shareholders' ownership stake in the business would be unaffected.

- *Debt and associated repayment obligations can become onerous.* Debt obligates the corporation to pay back the principal, or amount borrowed, plus interest. When a business is flush with cash, meeting repayment obligations may not be a problem. If times become tough, however, the business may find it difficult to meet repayment obligations. When repayment obligations become onerous, they can drain a business of its cash, cause the business to violate covenants to lenders, or cause the business become subject to penalty provisions in loan documents, etc. So, while debt financing does not present the dilution issues associated with equity, repayment obligations can strain financial resources during difficult times.

- *Debt, leverage, and risk.* Financial leverage is another consequence of debt financing. Financial leverage refers to the relationship of a corporation's debt to equity in its capital structure. As a general rule, the more long-term debt a corporation takes on, the greater its financial leverage. Shareholders benefit from leverage when the return on borrowed money exceeds costs associated with the borrowing and repaying of the debt. For example, assume a business buys a piece of property for $500,000, putting 20 percent down at the time of purchase ($100,000) and borrowing the remaining amount due ($400,000) at 5 percent interest. If the real estate market does well, and the company is able to sell the property six months later for $550,000, it will be able to pay back the loan, and still clear $30,000 ($550,000 — $400,000 (loan amount) — $20,000 (interest) — $100,000 (down payment)). If the real estate market crashes, however, and the corporation is forced by economic circumstances to sell the property at a price lower than the purchase price the corporation could lose money on the deal. Borrowing to purchase assets (or, borrowing against assets) thus has the potential to magnify gains and losses, and may contribute to a corporation's financial risk.

- *Priority.* As noted above, the claims of creditors have priority over equity in the liquidation or bankruptcy of the company. This priority means that in the event of a bankruptcy or liquidation, creditors (including debt holders) are entitled to be paid in full before anything is paid to the business's equity holders.
- *Tax treatment and interest.* Interest payments on debt are generally tax deductible by the borrower. This tax treatment has the effect of reducing the effective rate of interest paid by the borrower for corporations that generate taxable income. Corporations do not get to deduct cash distributions made to equity holders.

Mindful of these issues and considerations, businesses often prefer debt to equity financing — usually because of the lack of dilution, leverage possibilities, and the tax treatment of interest. That said, there is a tipping point for most businesses, or a point when a corporation's level of indebtedness gives rise to increased risk of default or financial strain as a result of repayment obligations. When such a tipping point is reached, the business may find it difficult to meet repayment obligations or to borrow more money for repayment obligations on reasonable terms. In addition, certain businesses and industries (e.g., emerging companies) tend to use equity rather than debt because they do not have the cash flow or hard assets necessary to secure debt financing on reasonable terms. To the extent lenders are willing to loan money to such businesses, they may require personal guarantees by founders or other protections as a condition to the distribution of funds. These and other considerations will impact your clients' use of debt, equity, and internally generated funds to finance operations. Your job as the lawyer often is to help your client think through the implications of debt versus equity versus internally generated funds with respect to issues such as dilution, ownership and control, governance, fiduciary obligation, and the like.

G. SECURITIES OFFERINGS

The sale of corporate securities, whether stocks or bonds, is subject to regulation by applicable state laws, as well as by the federal securities laws, including the

Small Business and Capital Formation

Rules governing the offer and sales of securities — particularly for small businesses — are both technical and ever-changing. The Securities and Exchange Commission has established an online resource center for small businesses that contains, among other things, information about fundraising. The resource center currently is available at https://www.sec.gov/info/smallbus.shtml. The SEC's summary is merely a starting point, however, and lawyers involved in securities offerings must be well versed in federal and state laws governing the offer, purchase, and sale of securities.

Securities Act of 1933 and the Securities Exchange Act of 1934. All of these laws are designed to protect the public from fraud and unfair business practices while still promoting capital formation. We provide an introduction to the federal and state securities laws governing the offer, purchase, and sale of securities in Chapter 13. Because an exhaustive survey of the rules governing the issuance and sale of securities is beyond the scope of this book, we urge you to take a course in securities regulation.

Chapter Summary

- To raise money, corporations may issue stock (equity securities which evidence an ownership interest in the corporation), borrow money, or use internally generated funds.
- Corporations may issue common and preferred stock.
- A share of common stock is the basic ownership unit in a corporation. Common stockholders have voting rights and hold a residual interest in the corporation, or the right to be paid upon liquidation after obligations to creditors and preferred stockholders have been satisfied.
- Preferred stockholders enjoy one or more preferences over common stockholders — typically, a dividend or liquidation preference, or both.
- Corporations may take on indebtedness via direct loan from a bank or other lender or through the issuance of debt securities such as corporate bonds. In either case, debt carries the obligation to repay principal and typically the obligation to pay interest.
- Debt is generally evidenced by a promissory note. Lenders and debtors also may enter into a loan agreement, which may contain representations and warranties or covenants.
- Corporations also may use internally generated funds, including retained earnings, to fund operations or plans for future growth.
- Capital structure refers to the corporation's mix of debt and equity.

Applying the Concepts

1. Access the website of the SEC and review the Form 10-K for Twitter, Inc. filed on March 6, 2014. How many shares of stock is the company authorized to issue?

2. Access the website of the SEC and review the Form 10-K for Facebook, Inc. filed on January 31, 2014.

   a. What are the rights of the holders of Class B common stock?
   b. What is the par value of Class A and Class B common stock?

    c. What are the voting rights of the Class C capital stock authorized in the corporation's amendment to its articles of incorporation?

3. Access the website of the SEC and review Form 10-K for the Walt Disney Company filed on November 20, 2013. How many shares of common stock were outstanding?

4. Access the website for Wal-Mart Stores, Inc. Select "Investors" and then "FAQs." Who is Walmart's transfer agent?

5. Access the searchable UCC database for Colorado. Conduct a UCC search on Augusta, Inc. and locate the UCC financing statement. Who is the secured party? What appliances are covered by the statement? When will the statement lapse?

6. Clark Holdings, Inc. issued callable bonds to Mason and Olivia. The bonds carry an interest rate of 5 percent.

    a. Mason's bond is unsecured, and Olivia's bond is secured by corporate equipment, including various computers. If the corporation defaults in payment of its bonds, what are Mason's and Olivia's rights?

    b. Mason and Olivia want to vote at the next shareholders' meeting and also wish to receive notices of dividends the corporation plans to issue. Are they entitled to these rights? Discuss.

    c. The current market interest rate is 3 percent. What might the corporation do to save itself money?

7. Crawford Enterprises, Inc. wishes to raise money but does not want to dilute the power of its current shareholders. What might the corporation consider?

Business Organizations in Practice

1. Evan's stock certificate states the following: "The shareholder shall have a right to receive an annual dividend of five percent of the stated value of the share represented by this certificate, cumulating." Draft a letter to Evan explaining what this provision means.

2. Nina's stock certificate for her Preferred A stock states that she has annual cumulative dividends and a liquidation preference over common stock but no voting rights.

    a. Draft a letter to Nina explaining the dividend and liquidation-related rights associated with her stock.

    b. Is the lack of voting rights a disadvantage for Nina? Why or why not? Prepare an outline so that you can discuss this issue with Nina.

3. NanoTech Corp. is a start-up company that hopes to commercialize technology developed by Sara and Jin, both of whom are professors at Nano PolyTech Institute, a university. Sara and Jin formed a corporation last year, and they currently own a majority stake in the business, represented by shares of common stock. Mountain Ventures, a leading venture capital firm, is considering making an equity investment in NanoTech.

   a. For purposes of this question only, assume that you represent Mountain Ventures. Assume that if Mountain invests, it will receive preferred stock. Review the model term sheet and Series A Preferred Stock purchase agreement prepared by and for the National Venture Capital Association referenced earlier in this chapter. Identify at least five rights and protections for Mountain that you would recommend including in the preferred stockholders' agreement.

   b. For the purposes of this question only, assume that you represent the company in its negotiations with Mountain Ventures. Assume that the company wants Mountain as an investor and has agreed to issue preferred stock to Mountain in exchange for its investment. Further assume, however, that the company is a "hot" start-up, giving it at least some leverage in its negotiations with Mountain. Review the model term sheet and Series A Preferred Stock purchase agreement prepared by and for the National Venture Capital Association referenced earlier in this chapter. Identify at least five rights and protections favorable to the company that you would recommend including in the preferred stockholders' agreement.

Introduction to Corporate Governance

In this chapter, we examine foundational corporate governance rules and structures, focusing on the "architecture" of corporate governance; the rights, roles, and obligations of key stakeholders (i.e., shareholders, directors, and officers); and the mechanics of meetings and voting. Corporate governance is shaped by a **hierarchy of control**. The corporations code of the state in which the corporation was chartered sits at the top of this hierarchy, followed by the corporation's charter, its bylaws, and the authority of the board of directors, officers, and employees. Corporate governance also is shaped by the **centralized management** system introduced in Chapter 6 that separates ownership of the corporation from control of the enterprise. Under this system, the **board of directors** has the statutory right and obligation to manage and control the business and affairs of the corporation. Although the **shareholders** are the owners of the corporation, they do not have statutory management or control rights; instead, shareholders participate in governance indirectly, through the election of directors and by voting on a limited list of items (i.e., so-called **fundamental changes** to corporate structure). Corporate **officers**, in turn, serve at the pleasure of the board. They are responsible for overseeing day-to-day affairs and implementing board decisions and policies.

There are a few caveats and reminders that we would like you to keep in mind as you work through this chapter. First, although corporations statutes draw sharp distinctions between the roles, rights, and responsibilities of stockholders, directors, and officers, lines between these groups may become blurred in closely held corporations. This

Key Concepts

- Hierarchy of corporate control
- Shareholders' role in governance and mechanics of shareholder meeting and voting
- Board of directors' role in governance and mechanics of director meetings and voting
- Role of corporate officers
- Contents of charter and bylaws and role in governance

is because in closely held corporations, the stockholders often serve as directors, officers, and employees of the corporation in addition to their ownership role. We discuss closely held corporations in more detail in Chapter 10. Second, this chapter focuses on governance structures and mechanics. Be sure to review Chapters 9, 10, and 11 for a discussion of important substantive rights and obligations associated with the director, officer, and shareholder roles, paying particular attention to fiduciary obligations that attach to the director, officer, and controlling shareholder roles. Finally, remember that federal securities laws and regulations play an important role in corporate governance. We touch upon one aspect of the federal securities law regime here — namely, the proxy system and rules and mechanics of shareholder voting. We address relevant federal and state securities law issues in more detail in Chapter 13.

A. HIERARCHY OF CORPORATE CONTROL

As noted in the introduction, corporate governance is subject to a hierarchy of control. As reflected in Exhibit 8.1, the corporations code of the state of incorporation sits atop this hierarchy, trumping individual corporate charters, bylaws, and the actions and decisions of boards, officers, and employees. This means that if a corporation enacts a charter or bylaw provision that is prohibited by the state corporations code, the provision at issue is invalid. Similarly, if a corporation enacts a bylaw provision that conflicts with a charter provision, the bylaw provision is invalid. The state corporations code, the corporation's charter, and its bylaws, in turn, trump the authority of the board of directors, the corporation's officers, and its employees.

With this hierarchy in mind, we will now examine the roles, rights, and obligations of the three main stakeholders involved in corporate governance — that is, shareholders, directors, and officers — focusing on governance rules, structures, and mechanics.

EXHIBIT 8.1   **Hierarchy of Corporate Control**

B. SHAREHOLDERS

1. Introduction

As noted in Chapter 6, state corporations codes establish a centralized management structure for corporations as a statutory matter. This structure separates ownership of the corporation from control of the enterprise. The board of directors is vested with the right (and the obligation) to manage the business. Shareholders (or stockholders, a synonymous term)[1] are the corporation's owners, but they do *not* have a statutory right to control the business and affairs of the corporation. Instead, shareholders participate indirectly in corporate governance through the exercise of shareholder voting rights. Corporate officers implement board policies and decisions and typically manage day-to-day operations.

The shareholder franchise (i.e., shareholder voting rights) has been characterized as the ideological underpinning upon which the legitimacy of director managerial power rests. *See, e.g., Blasius Indus., Inc. v. Atlas Corp.*, 564 A.2d 651, 659 (Del. Ch. 1988). Indeed, as then-Chancellor Allen famously commented in the *Blasius Industries* case:

> The shareholder franchise is the ideological underpinning upon which the legitimacy of directorial power rests. Generally, shareholders have only two protections against perceived inadequate business performance. They may sell their stock (which, if done in sufficient numbers, may so affect security prices as to create an incentive for altered managerial performance), or they may vote to replace incumbent board members.
>
> It has, for a long time, been conventional to dismiss the stockholder vote as a vestige or ritual of little practical importance. It may be that we are now witnessing the emergence of new institutional voices and arrangements that will make the stockholder vote a less predictable affair than it has been. Be that as it may, however, whether the vote is seen functionally as an unimportant formalism, or as an important tool of discipline, it is clear that it is critical to the theory that legitimates the exercise of power by some (directors and officers) over vast aggregations of property that they do not own. Thus, when viewed from a broad, institutional perspective, it can be seen that matters involving the integrity of the shareholder voting process involve consideration not present in any other context in which directors exercise delegated power.

Id. at 659 (footnote omitted).

For all its importance as an ideological matter, however, shareholder voting rights are actually quite limited. Shareholders have a statutory right to elect directors. They also have statutory voting rights with respect to certain fundamental changes to corporate structure, typically (i) amendments to the corporate charter; (ii) shareholder-initiated amendments to corporate bylaws; (iii) certain types of

---

[1] The Model Business Corporations Act, or MBCA, uses the term "shareholder," whereas the Delaware General Corporation Law, or DGCL, uses the term "stockholder." While the terms are synonymous, some attorneys use the term shareholder when forming or referring to a corporation in a jurisdiction that follows the MBCA, and the term stockholder when forming or referring to a Delaware corporation.

mergers; (iv) sales of all (or substantially all) corporate assets not in the ordinary course of business; and (v) dissolution of the corporation. Although a corporation's charter or bylaws may expand the list of items subject to a vote of shareholders, the formal expansion of shareholder voting rights is not prevalent, at least with respect to common stockholders. Additionally, although the board of directors of a corporation may choose to put an issue to a shareholder vote — for example, the approval of a conflict of interest transaction — putting non-required items to a shareholder vote is not an everyday occurrence, either. In practical terms, centralized management and the allocation of control power to the board means that there are many important decisions about the company's strategy, finances, etc., as to which shareholders have no statutory right to be heard.

What options do shareholders have if they become unhappy with the board's management of the corporation? As the *Blasius* excerpt cited above suggests, shareholders may try to vote directors associated with objectionable policies or decisions out of office. Particularly in the case of large, public companies, however, it can be difficult for individual shareholders who own only a small stake in the corporation to have an impact on director elections. Shareholders of public companies also have rights under the proxy system established by the federal securities laws to vote on certain management proposals and also to put certain shareholder-initiated proposals before shareholders, as discussed below and in Chapter 13. Once again, however, it can be difficult for shareholders owning only a small stake in the corporation to effect change through the proxy system. Shareholders also may take an activist approach to share ownership, and may use voting rights, the proxy system, and public relations strategies to press for change. Even for large or sophisticated investors, however, battles with management over the direction of the corporation may prove costly, time-consuming, and ultimately frustrating. Finally, if all else fails, shareholders may be able to "vote with their feet" — that is, sell their shares and invest in a different corporation. Oftentimes, however, there are costs and other difficulties associated with exiting a position in a particular stock. As this suggests, just as shareholders' voting rights are limited, shareholders' avenues for influencing the board and thus the direction of the corporation are limited, too.

Case Preview

Schnell v. Chris-Craft Industries, Inc.

Given shareholders' important — but limited — voting rights, maintaining a proper balance in the allocation of power between shareholders and the board is a key issue in corporate governance law. *Schnell v. Chris-Craft Industries* gives us insight into that balancing act. *Schnell* involved a dispute between dissident shareholders and management over the timing of the annual meeting. When management pushed back the date of the annual stockholders meeting, arguably to delay a shareholder vote, the dissident shareholders sued for injunctive relief. When reading *Schnell*, consider how the court balances the importance of the shareholder franchise with the board's right to manage the corporation.

1. Management argued that it strictly complied with the Delaware General Corporation Law (DGCL) in changing the annual meeting date at issue. Assuming that was true, why wasn't compliance with "the rules" enough to carry the day? Isn't compliance with the DGCL all that is required of directors to satisfy their obligation to the corporation and its stockholders? Why or why not?

2. What do you make of the court's statement that "inequitable action does not become permissible simply because it is legally possible"? What did management do that was "inequitable," in the view of the court?

Schnell v. Chris-Craft Industries, Inc.
285 A.2d 437 (Del. 1971)

HERRMANN, Justice (for the majority of the Court):*

This is an appeal from the denial by the Court of Chancery of the petition of dissident stockholders for injunctive relief to prevent management from advancing the date of the annual stockholders' meeting from January 11, 1972, as previously set by the by-laws, to December 8, 1971.

. . .

It will be seen that the Chancery Court considered all of the reasons stated by management as business reasons for changing the date of the meeting; but that those reasons were rejected by the Court below in making the following findings:

"I am satisfied, however, in a situation in which present management has disingenuously resisted the production of a list of its stockholders to plaintiffs or their confederates and has otherwise turned a deaf ear to plaintiffs' demands about a change in management designed to lift defendant from its present business doldrums, management has seized on a relatively new section of the Delaware Corporation Law for the purpose of cutting down on the amount of time which would otherwise have been available to plaintiffs and others for the waging of a proxy battle. Management thus enlarged the scope of its scheduled October 18 directors' meeting to include the by-law amendment in controversy after the stockholders' committee had filed with the S.E.C. its intention to wage a proxy fight on October 16.

Thus plaintiffs reasonably contend that because of the tactics employed by management (which involve the hiring of two established proxy solicitors as well as a refusal to produce a list of its stockholders, coupled with its use of an amendment to the Delaware Corporation Law to limit the time for contest), they are given little chance, because of the exigencies of time, including that required to clear material at the S.E.C., to wage a successful proxy fight between now and December 8. * * *."

In our view, those conclusions amount to a finding that management has attempted to utilize the corporate machinery and the Delaware Law for the purpose

---

*Footnotes have been omitted for purposes of brevity.

of perpetuating itself in office; and, to that end, for the purpose of obstructing the legitimate efforts of dissident stockholders in the exercise of their rights to undertake a proxy contest against management. These are inequitable purposes, contrary to established principles of corporate democracy. The advancement by directors of the by-law date of a stockholders' meeting, for such purposes, may not be permitted to stand. Compare *Condec Corporation v. Lunkenheimer Company*, Del. Ch., 230 A.2d 769 (1967).

When the by-laws of a corporation designate the date of the annual meeting of stockholders, it is to be expected that those who intend to contest the reelection of incumbent management will gear their campaign to the by-law date. It is not to be expected that management will attempt to advance the date in order to obtain an inequitable advantage in the contest.

Management contends that it has complied strictly with the provisions of the new Delaware Corporation Law in changing the by-law date. The answer to that contention, of course, is that inequitable action does not become permissible simply because it is legally possible.

. . . We agree with the rule of *American Hardware* that, in the absence of fraud or inequitable conduct, the date for a stockholders' meeting and notice thereof, duly established under the by-laws, will not be enlarged by judicial interference at the request of dissident stockholders solely because of the circumstance of a proxy contest. That, of course, is not the case before us.

We are unable to agree with the conclusion of the Chancery court that the stockholders' application for injunctive relief here was tardy and came too late. The stockholders learned of the action of management unofficially on Wednesday, October 27, 1971; they filed this action on Monday, November 1, 1971. Until management changed the date of the meeting, the stockholders had no need of judicial assistance in that connection. There is no indication of any prior warning of management's intent to take such action; indeed, it appears that an attempt was made by management to conceal its action as long as possible. Moreover, stockholders may not be charged with the duty of anticipating inequitable action by management, and of seeking anticipatory injunctive relief to foreclose such action, simply because the new Delaware Corporation Law makes such inequitable action legally possible.

Accordingly, the judgment below must be reversed and the cause remanded, with instruction to nullify the December 8 date as a meeting date for stockholders; to reinstate January 11, 1972 as the sole date of the next annual meeting of the stockholders of the corporation; and to take such other proceedings and action as may be consistent herewith regarding the stock record closing date and any other related matters.

Post-Case Follow-Up

Although the *Schnell* court appeared to recognize an equitable constraint on management's ability to use the "machinery" of the Delaware corporate law to interfere with shareholder voting rights, the statutory authority of the board to manage the business and affairs of the corporation makes it difficult for shareholders successfully to challenge board actions based on an alleged abridgment of shareholder voting rights. The *Blasius* decision and its progeny reflect some of these challenges. In *Blasius*, a dissident investor (Blasius Industries) sought to take control of Atlas Corp. over the objections of Atlas's incumbent board. At the time the dispute erupted, the Atlas board had 7 members, despite authorization for 15 directors in the corporation's charter. Although the board was supposed to be "staggered," Atlas's failure to authorize and seat a full complement of 15 directors meant that the staggered structure was not protected. Staggered boards are discussed below. For current purposes, it is enough to understand that with a staggered board, not all directors are up for election each year. By having only 7 directors, when the charter authorized 15, Atlas was vulnerable to a dissident shareholder (or shareholders), who could petition to amend the bylaws, increase the size of the board to 15, and elect 8 new board members to fill the newly created slots, and thereby take control of the board and the company.

One day, Blasius Industries showed up and tried to do just that. Touting what the incumbent board believed to be a speculative business plan, and seeking to take control of the company, Blasius Industries offered to pay Atlas stockholders cash up front for their shares with the promise of an additional reward later if Blasius's business strategy worked out.

As Blasius was seeking to implement its strategy, the Atlas board was in the midst of executing its own corporate restructuring strategy. The Atlas board was legitimately troubled by Blasius's bid for control, believing that Blasius's business plan would cause great injury to the corporation. Recognizing that their earlier failure to attend to the classified board structure had given Blasius an opening, Atlas filled two vacancies on the board. Although the court found that the two newly elected directors were well qualified and independent, the court also found that the effect of their election was to prevent Blasius from electing a new board majority, except by fighting through the classified board structure and winning two elections over an extended time frame.

Faced with the resistance of the Atlas board, Blasius challenged the board's actions, alleging that Atlas's board impermissibly had interfered with shareholders' statutory right to elect directors. While declining to hold that board action taken for the sole or primary purpose of thwarting a shareholder vote is *per se* invalid, Chancellor Allen held that board actions undertaken for this purpose are subject to exacting scrutiny. In particular, Chancellor Allen held that even when a board of directors is acting in subjective good faith, it must provide a "compelling justification" for its actions when it acts "for the primary purpose of interfering with the effectiveness of a stockholder vote." 564 A.2d at 659.

As this language suggests, the "trigger" for review under the *Blasius* compelling justification standard is extreme, *see Yucaipa American Alliance Fund II, L.P v. Riggio*, 1 A.3d 310, 326-36 (Del. Ch. 2010), because the standard applies only when directors "act[ ] for the primary purpose of thwarting the exercise of a shareholder vote." *Id.* at 330-31. In the years since *Blasius* was decided, litigants generally have not been able to convince courts that their boards acted for the primary purpose of interfering with the effectiveness of a shareholder vote.[1] As a result,

---

[1] In addition, the Delaware Supreme Court subsequently rejected the *Blasius* standard for those cases where a plurality plus governance policy requires directors to tender resignations. *City of Westland Police & Fire Ret. Sys. v. Axcelis Techs., Inc.*, 1 A.3d 281, 288-89 (Del. 2010).

shareholders generally have not been able to convince courts that the exacting standard of review in *Blasius* ought to be applied. So, while cases like *Schnell* and *Blasius* recognize the importance of protecting the shareholder franchise against board overreaching, it is important to remember that any challenge to board action will be filtered through the lens of the board's statutory right to manage the business and affairs of the corporation.

2. Shareholder Meetings

For a vote at a shareholder meeting to be valid, the corporation generally must provide **notice** of the meeting in accordance with the applicable corporations law statute and any charter or bylaw provisions, a **quorum** must be present (as defined by the statute and, where applicable, any charter or bylaw provisions), and shareholders must vote in accordance with rules contained in the applicable corporations code and any charter or bylaw provisions. These concepts and requirements are discussed below.

Annual Meetings

MBCA § 7.01 and most state statutes require that corporations hold **annual meetings** of shareholders. Voting for directors occurs at the annual meeting, along with voting on any matters submitted to shareholders at that time. Under the MBCA, shareholders may apply to a court to order a meeting if one has not been held within 6 months of the end of the corporation's fiscal year or 15 months after the last annual meeting. MBCA § 7.03. These rules reflect the legislative policy that because shareholders are not involved in the day-to-day operation of the corporation, they must be provided with some minimum of information about the corporation and an annual opportunity to vote on directors up for election.

The time and date of annual meetings is usually provided in the corporate bylaws. A typical bylaw provision might specify that "annual meetings of shareholders shall be held the first Monday of May of each calendar year." Most corporations hold their annual meetings in the spring (April, May, or June) because this allows sufficient time for corporate accounting and payment of taxes to be accomplished. In fact, so many meetings are held at this time of year that it is referred to as "proxy season." Exhibit 8.2 contains an excerpt from the bylaws of General Electric Company referencing an April date for the corporation's annual meeting.

EXHIBIT 8.2   **Excerpt, Article VII, Bylaws of General Electric Company**

Meeting of Shareholders

A. Meetings of shareholders may be held at such time and in such place within or without the State of New York as the Board of Directors may determine, and the annual statutory meeting required by Section 602(b) of the New York Business Corporation Law shall be held on the fourth Wednesday in April of each year, or as the Board of Directors may from time to time otherwise determine.

Application Exercise 1

You represent Javassana, Inc., a newly formed Delaware corporation that operates a combination coffee shop and yoga studio. Draft a provision for Javassana's bylaws addressing the logistics and requirements for shareholder meetings.

Special Meetings

Special meetings are shareholder meetings held between annual meetings. Shareholders must have some mechanism to call meetings between the annual meetings to investigate fraud, abuse, or mismanagement. For example, if a corporation's annual meeting is in April, and the shareholders discover embezzlement in June, they should not have to wait until the next annual meeting in April to discuss this critical matter. A special meeting allows the shareholders to meet between the annual meetings to discuss and consider matters of interest. Similarly, corporate management might need to call a special meeting to discuss and vote on unanticipated matters, such as an offer to merge with another corporation.

Most state statutes provide the terms and conditions on which special meetings may be called. Section 7.02 of the MBCA is typical of most statutes. It provides that the board of directors of a corporation may call a special meeting or that shareholders owning 10 percent or more of the outstanding stock entitled to vote at the meeting may demand in writing that the corporation call a special meeting. Additionally, any person authorized to do so in the corporation's articles of incorporation or its bylaws may call a special meeting. The demand is made upon the secretary of the corporation. In general, only such transactions or topics as are described in the notice of the special meeting may be considered. Statutory rules for special meetings normally are supplemented by corporate bylaws. Exhibit 8.3 contains an excerpt from the General Electric bylaws concerning special meetings of shareholders.

EXHIBIT 8.3   **Excerpt, Article VII, Bylaws of General Electric Company**

B. Special meetings of the shareholders may be called by the Board, or by the Secretary upon the written request therefor of shareholders holding ten percent of the then issued stock of the Company entitled to vote generally in the election of directors, filed with the Secretary. A shareholder request for a special meeting shall state the purpose(s) of the proposed meeting and shall include the information required for business to be properly brought by a shareholder before the annual meeting of shareholders as set forth in this Article VII with respect to any director nominations or other business proposed to be presented at such special meeting and as to the shareholder(s) requesting such meeting. Business transacted at a special meeting requested by shareholders shall be limited to the purpose(s) stated in the request; provided, however, that nothing in these By-Laws shall prohibit the Board of Directors from submitting matters to the shareholders at any special meeting requested by shareholders.

Place of Meetings

The bylaws may designate the location of annual or special meetings. Alternatively, and as is more common, the bylaws may provide that the directors can determine the location of meetings. If no location is specified in the bylaws, the meetings will take place at the corporation's principal office. Some larger corporations rotate their meetings to allow shareholders across the country to attend. Thus, one year's meeting may be held in Atlanta, and the next year's meeting may be held in Dallas. Older statutes required that all meetings be held in the state of incorporation. Modern statutes usually permit meetings to be held in any location, provided proper notice is given.

Notice of Meetings

All jurisdictions require that shareholders receive notice of all meetings, including both annual and special meetings. The pertinent state statutes and corporate charter and bylaws must be reviewed to ensure the notice requirements are followed. Notice requirements can be very detailed and should be scrutinized carefully to avoid having a meeting declared invalid. In general, small corporations tend to act informally and will often provide notice by telephone or e-mail, if permitted by statute and the corporate bylaws. Larger corporations act in a more form or manner and provide written notices to all shareholders entitled to receive notice. Generally, either the corporate secretary or the registrar prepares and sends notices.

Shareholders Entitled to Notice

Unless the state corporations code or the articles of incorporation require otherwise, the corporation generally is only required to give notice to shareholders entitled to vote at a meeting. Thus, if the holders of Preferred A stock have nonvoting shares, they will not be entitled to notice of a meeting to elect directors. Generally, only issued and outstanding shares vote.

To determine the particular shareholders who will receive notice, the corporate bylaws will usually establish a **record date** (some date selected in advance of a meeting) and any persons owning shares eligible to vote on the matter at issue on that record date will be entitled to notice of the meeting. Many bylaws provide that the record date will be 30 days before the meeting; any shareholders whose names are "on the books" on that date will be entitled to receive notice. These shareholders are sometimes called the **holders of record** or **record holders**. If the bylaws do not provide for fixing a record date, MBCA § 7.05 states that the record date will be the day before the first notice is delivered to shareholders.

Because the record date is set in advance of the meeting, a shareholder might be entitled to receive notice and to vote even though she no longer owns any shares in the corporation at the time of the meeting. For example, assume the bylaws of Hunter Development Corp. fix the date of the annual meeting as May 1 of each year. The bylaws also provide that any person who owns shares 30 days prior to any meeting is entitled to notice of and to vote at the meeting. If Francie Hoffman owns 100 shares on April 1, she will be entitled to receive notice and to vote. If Francie sells her shares to her sister on April 4, Francie will still receive notice of the meeting and generally will still be eligible to vote at the meeting.

This is because when a corporation determines the shareholders entitled to receive notice, it is as if the corporation takes a snapshot of its list of shareholders *on that given date.* Those individuals whose names are on the list receive notice and they may vote. Shareholders who buy stock in the corporation after the record date and before the meeting date, in this case between April 1 and May 1, may simply be out of luck. (Note, however, that it may be possible for these purchasers to negotiate a lower price for the shares or to require, as a condition of purchase, that they be empowered to vote the shares at the meeting.) This notice prerequisite is similar to that underlying voter registration. One must be "on the books" by a certain date before an election to vote. An individual who moves to a new county may simply miss the cut-off date for registration and be unable to vote in the next election. The rules relating to record dates likewise exist for the orderly administration of corporate matters.

Contents and Timing of Notice

MBCA § 7.05(a) provides that the notice to shareholders shall specify the date, time, and place of each meeting. The notice must be given no fewer than 10 nor more than 60 days before the meeting date. These time limits provide protection to shareholders by ensuring that they get adequate advance notice so they can make arrangements to attend but not so much advance notice that they forget about the meeting.

Notice of a special meeting must describe the purpose for which the meeting is called. *See* MBCA § 7.05(c). Some jurisdictions require that all notices for all meetings describe the purpose for which the meeting is called, but the MBCA rule is similar to that in most jurisdictions in providing that only notices for special meetings must specify the purpose (unless extraordinary matters, such as amendment to the articles of incorporation or dissolution will be voted on, in which case the notice of an annual meeting must describe its purposes). *See id.* Erring on the side of caution, most corporations specify the purposes of all meetings, whether annual or special.

Delivery of Notice

According to MBCA § 1.41, written notice by a corporation to its shareholders is effective when deposited in the mail (if mailed prepaid and correctly addressed) or when transmitted electronically to the shareholder in a manner authorized by the shareholder, such as by e-mail. Alternatively, notice may be delivered in person, or by telephone or voice mail, in which case it is effective when received.

Defective Notice

If the corporation fails to meet its obligations with regard to sending appropriate notice to the appropriate shareholders within the specified period, the meeting is invalid and can be attacked by any shareholder who failed to receive proper notice. Because rescheduling the meeting, preparing new notices, and transporting the directors and officers to another meeting can be expensive, there are two alternatives corporations can use to save an otherwise invalid meeting. First, a shareholder may sign a written waiver of notice, expressly waiving the right to receive notice. This waiver is effective whether signed before or after the meeting. Second, a shareholder may consent in writing to action taken at the meeting and thereby ratify the proceedings. A shareholder's attendance at a meeting is deemed a waiver of notice unless the shareholder objects to the holding of the meeting as it commences. MBCA § 7.06. See Exhibit 8.4 for a typical notice of an annual shareholders' meeting.

EXHIBIT 8.4   **Sample Notice of Annual Meeting of Shareholders**

Notice is hereby given that the Annual Meeting of Shareholders of FTB, Inc. will be held in Room Three, Fifth Floor, 5 Park Avenue East, New York, New York 10048, on May 28, 2015, at 9:00 A.M., Eastern Standard Time, for the following purposes:

1) To elect five (5) directors to serve until the next annual meeting or until their successors shall have been elected and qualified;
2) To ratify the appointment of Ernst & Young LLP as the Company's independent registered public accountants for the fiscal year ending December 31, 2015;
3) To act upon a shareholder proposal with respect to the distribution of quarterly reports; and
4) To consider such other business as may properly come before the meeting or any adjournment thereof.

Only shareholders of record at the close of business on April 1, 2015, are entitled to notice of and to vote at the meeting or any adjournments thereof.

April 14, 2015   By order of the Board of Directors
New York, New York   William V. Curtis,
                                        Secretary

As a precautionary matter, many corporations instruct the corporate secretary to prepare an affidavit or certificate of mailing to verify that all notices were properly and timely delivered. Such a certificate is similar in effect to the document signed by process servers who verify in writing that a summons and complaint were properly served upon a defendant and which protects against defendants' claims that they never received the documents. In nearly all cases, a corporation's certificate of mailing will be presumptive evidence that notices were properly prepared and delivered.

Application Exercise 2

Continuing with your representation of Javassana, and drawing upon the bylaw provision that you drafted above, draft a notice of annual meeting of shareholders.

Annual Reports

When a corporation (particularly a public corporation) sends out the notice of the annual shareholders' meeting, it usually includes a formal **annual report**, often a professional and glossy magazine-style presentation explaining the company's performance. Typical sections include a letter from the board's chair, financial reviews (summarizing sales, profit, income, cash flow, liabilities, and shareholders' equity), charts showing stock performance, brief biographies and pictures of the board members, and other information of interest to the shareholders. As part of the continuing trend of utilizing technology, many companies now post these reports as well as webcasts of previous annual meetings on their websites.

Shareholder Lists

After the record date has been determined, the corporation will prepare an alphabetical list of shareholders entitled to receive notice. The list must be arranged by voting groups and provide the address of each shareholder as well as the number of shares held by each shareholder. The list must be made available for inspection by any shareholder beginning two business days after notice of the meeting is given and must remain open for inspection during any meeting. The list will be available at the corporation's principal office or at a place identified in the meeting notice (for larger corporations, likely the office of the registrar). Shareholders (or their agents or attorneys) have the right to inspect and copy the list upon written demand. MBCA § 7.20. The rationale for making the list available to all shareholders is to encourage discussion among shareholders. Additionally, shareholders may wish to band together and agree to vote as a group to achieve certain goals.

Quorum

No action can be taken at any shareholder meeting unless a certain minimum number of shareholders, a **quorum**, is present. MBCA § 7.25 provides that unless the articles specify otherwise, a quorum is a majority of votes entitled to be cast on a given matter. Thus, if 100 shares are entitled to vote on amending the articles of incorporation, holders representing at least 51 of those shares (a majority of 100) must be present for the meeting to be held. If fewer than 51 shares are present at the meeting, the meeting cannot be held and will have to be rescheduled. This will cause great expense to the corporation because it will be required to provide new notices to all shareholders, reserve a location for another meeting, make arrangements for management to attend the new meeting, and so forth.

Many states allow corporations to modify the requirements for a quorum by providing such in the articles of incorporation, so long as the quorum is not so low as to be unfair. Most states allow such modification so long as a quorum is not less than one-third of the shares entitled to vote. In such a case, if 100 shares were outstanding and entitled to vote on an issue, at least 34 shares (one-third of 100) must be present for the meeting to go forward.

Quorum requirements prevent small factions of shareholders from controlling all shareholder action. For example, if a corporation had 100 outstanding shares entitled to vote, and the quorum was one-eighth, a shareholder owning only 13 shares could control a meeting and its outcome. The typical provision that a majority of outstanding shares constitutes a quorum ensures that action is not taken unless some reasonable and fair number of shareholders have the opportunity to consider the matter.

Once a quorum is established, it cannot be destroyed by a group of shareholders who walk out of a meeting (perhaps for the purpose of preventing action being taken on a certain matter). Once a share is represented at a meeting, it is deemed present for quorum purposes for the remainder of the meeting and any adjournment thereof. MBCA § 7.25(b).

Proxies

Most states and the MBCA allow shareholders to vote by proxy if they are unable or do not wish to attend a meeting. A **proxy** is a written authorization instructing another person (often members of the company's management) to vote one's shares on one's behalf. The word *proxy* is also used to refer to the person who will act in place of the shareholder. The closest analogy to a proxy form is an absentee ballot. Voters who are unable to be present for voting on election day may vote by absentee ballot. Similarly, shareholders who cannot attend shareholder meetings may vote by proxy. Some corporations send notices to shareholders reminding them of their ability to exercise voting rights via the proxy system. Exhibit 8.5 contains an example of such a notice.

EXHIBIT 8.5   Sample Notice Regarding Proxy Voting
No matter how many shares you own, please sign, date, and mail your proxy now, or vote by phone or the Internet, especially if you do not plan to attend the meeting. A majority is required by law. Therefore, it is important that you vote so that your corporation will not have to bear the expense of another solicitation of proxies. You may revoke your proxy at any time prior to its exercise by delivering to the secretary of the corporation a written revocation of proxy or by attending the meeting and voting in person.   FTB, Inc.

The proxy creates an agent-principal relationship between the parties. The shareholder, as the principal, authorizes another, the agent, to vote his shares. The proxy may be specific and authorize the agent (or **proxy holder**) to vote a certain way on specific issues. If such specific instructions are given, the proxy holder must so vote. This type of proxy is referred to as a **limited proxy**. Alternatively, the proxy may authorize the proxy holder to cast the shareholder's votes in the proxy holder's discretion on any issue properly arising at the meeting. This type of proxy is referred to as a **general proxy**. See Exhibit 8.6 for an example of a general proxy.

EXHIBIT 8.6 **General Proxy**

I hereby appoint Edward L. Goodman or Virginia Nelson Andrews my agent with full power to vote and act for me at their discretion upon any business, including the election of directors, at any meeting of the shareholders of FTB, Inc. or any adjournment thereof, held during the term of this proxy at which I am not present in person.

This proxy shall be valid for one year unless sooner revoked by me by delivering to the secretary of the corporation a written revocation of this proxy.

All previous proxies are hereby revoked.

_____   _____
Date   Signature

Proxies may generally be revoked by the shareholder at any time before they are voted. If the proxy does not state its duration, it will automatically expire 11 months after it is received by the corporation. *See* MBCA § 7.22(c). This provision ensures that shareholders grant new proxies for each annual shareholders' meeting. One type of proxy that is irrevocable is that granted to an individual who has purchased the shareholder's shares or has agreed to do so. Thus, in the event a shareholder sells shares after the record date and grants the new owner a proxy, this proxy cannot be revoked. Proxies are revoked by delivering a written revocation of proxy to the secretary of the corporation, delivering a subsequently dated proxy, or by attending the meeting and voting in person.

Proxies are most often used and needed for large corporations with numerous shareholders. For example, General Electric Company had nearly 460,000 shareholder accounts of record as of early 2016. There is no stadium or facility that can accommodate such a large group, and oftentimes shareholders holding only a few shares are disinclined to spend the time and money required to attend the annual meeting. Thus, most shareholders vote by proxy rather than voting in person at the meeting. The Securities Exchange Act of 1934 regulates the form and content of proxies for corporations whose stock is traded on an exchange or "over the counter" if the company has at least 500 shareholders and assets of at least $10 million. The proxy form is accompanied by a proxy statement issued by the corporation. The proxy statement includes certain required information about the matters being voted on at the meeting. We discuss the form and content of proxy materials in more detail in Chapter 13.

Proxies may be solicited by corporate management to elect management's slate of directors. In some cases, insurgent or dissident shareholders will also solicit shareholders for proxies to elect candidates favored by the insurgents or for changes in corporate policy desired by them. Each side will set forth its views in its proxy statement, which is distributed to all shareholders. A fight for control of the company reflected in competing proxy statements (or competing proposals in the company's proxy statement) is known colloquially as a **proxy fight** or **proxy contest**. Proxy contests often occur in connection with a hostile takeover when an acquiring company attempts to convince shareholders to install new managers who will be in favor of the takeover. In one 2014 proxy contest, Casablanca Capital LP, an investment advisory firm, toppled the board of directors of Cliffs Natural Resources Inc. after a six-month proxy fight. Casablanca argued to shareholders that the then-present board of Cliffs had not provided tangible growth, and ultimately Casablanca successfully placed six hand-selected directors on the Cliffs board. A newer trend is to use the Internet as part of proxy contest strategies. In the Cliffs proxy contest, Casablanca created a website entitled "FixCliffs.com" to promote its views. Some companies actively use message boards and social media to communicate with their supporters as well. We discuss proxy contests in more detail in Chapter 11, where we examine changes in corporate structure and corporate combinations.

Shareholder Action Without a Meeting

MBCA § 7.04(a) and all state statutes allow shareholders to take action without formally meeting if shareholders consent in writing. This allows business to be conducted without the expense of holding meetings. Action can be taken without a meeting if all shareholders entitled to vote on the issue consent to the proposed action in writing. The corporate secretary prepares a document called a **written consent action** or a "unanimous consent by shareholders in lieu of meeting" and distributes it to the shareholders for signature. Alternatively, rather than being required to obtain all signatures on one document, the secretary can prepare separate documents and send one to each shareholder. Once signed by the last shareholder, the measure is effective. Shareholders can also consent to action electronically by e-mail, if the state corporations code so permits and the corporation's bylaws so provide. Action by written consent is primarily designed to simplify corporate formalities for smaller corporations when it might be difficult for shareholders to get together for meetings.

Although the majority of states and the MBCA historically have required that the consent be unanimous, a growing number of states, including Delaware and Illinois, allow for written consent by the minimum number of shares that would be required to take such action at a meeting (usually a majority). In fact, a recent amendment to the MBCA allows a corporation to permit shareholder action by written consent by a majority vote (rather than unanimous vote) if the articles of incorporation so provide. MBCA § 7.04(b). Such a provision allows larger and publicly traded corporations to take actions more expeditiously and without the necessity of a meeting. When action is taken by less than unanimous written consent, the MBCA requires that notice of the action be given to nonconsenting shareholders. The rationale for the preference in most states for unanimous consent is that in the absence of a meeting, there is no opportunity for open discussion. Thus, without such discussion, most states insist that *all* shareholders be in agreement with the action proposed to be taken. See Exhibit 8.7 illustrating a form of written consent action.

EXHIBIT 8.7	**Written Consent in Lieu of Shareholders' Meeting**

The undersigned, constituting a majority of the shareholders of FTB, Inc., a Delaware corporation, and acting pursuant to Del. Code Ann. tit. 8, § 228(a) and Article VIII of the bylaws of the corporation, hereby take the following action as if present at a meeting duly called pursuant to proper notice.

RESOLVED, that Article I of the Certificate of Incorporation shall be amended to read as follows: The name of the corporation is FTB Access Link, Co.

RESOLVED, that Article III of the Certificate of Incorporation be amended to read as follows: The aggregate number of shares that the corporation shall have authority to issue is 100,000 shares of common stock.

The officers and directors of the corporation are authorized to take all appropriate action to effect these Resolutions.

Date:_____   _____
                                                                          Signature
Date: _____   _____
                                                                          Signature
Date: _____   _____
                                                                          Signature
Date: _____   _____
                                                                          Signature

3. Modern Trends

Modern technology is having a significant effect on the conduct of shareholder meetings and shareholder action. Effective January 1, 2009, under new SEC "notice and access" rules, all publicly traded companies are required to post their proxy materials (namely, the proxy statement and the annual report) on a website and then provide their shareholders with notice of the availability of these proxy materials 40 days before the meeting. Companies must also mail paper copies or send copies to shareholders by e-mail upon request. Shareholders can also now vote by telephone (by calling a toll-free number, identifying themselves by entering a control number located on a voting instruction card sent to them, and then following recorded instructions) or by accessing a website and voting. The method of voting electronically via the Internet is often called **e-proxy voting**. Broadridge Financial Solutions, Inc. has reported that by the 2013 proxy season, nearly 75 percent of the voting retail shares of publicly traded companies voted by Internet.

The statutes of some states, including California, Delaware, and New York, specifically permit shareholders of companies incorporated in those states to authorize others to act as proxies by transmission of a telegram, cablegram, or other means of electronic transmission, thus explicitly recognizing e-proxies. One site, ProxyVote, is particularly active in serving as a monitor for e-proxies cast in various shareholder matters.

These advances not only help the corporation reduce printing and postage costs (which have been estimated to total more than $1 billion each year for publicly traded corporations), but due to the ease of e-proxy voting, they greatly enhance (or have the potential to enhance) shareholder participation in corporate governance. Moreover, shareholders are increasingly using the Internet to discuss the merits of various corporate activities. For example, when USA Networks, Inc. was considering a merger with Lycos, Inc., USA executives routinely reviewed chat room conversations. When those conversations revealed a high level of shareholder concern over the proposed merger, USA killed the deal. The Internet is thus able to unite investors who once met only at annual meetings, if then. Whereas previously individual investors often threw away their notices of meetings and proxy cards, or forgot to vote, the ease of voting by telephone or through the use of e-proxies promotes shareholder involvement and activism. Companies have discovered that shareholders who receive electronic communications are more likely to vote than those who receive paper notices.

That said, although nearly one-half of the states, including Delaware, allow corporations to hold meetings solely by electronic means rather than in a physical location, corporations have been slow to use exclusively virtual meetings. The MBCA allows such virtual meetings but still requires that the meeting occur at a physical location. MBCA § 7.09. Similarly, the MBCA and these states allow shareholders to participate in meetings by remote communication, such as through telephone conference calls or the Internet. Generally, statutes provide that shareholders may vote electronically at such meetings if the corporation has implemented a process to verify that each person participating remotely is a shareholder and provides such shareholders a reasonable opportunity to participate in the meeting by voting and communicating. Although the benefits of such virtual meetings would seem to be increased shareholder participation and lower costs, many shareholder activists oppose them, believing such virtual meetings reduce dialogue among shareholders and allow management to avoid shareholder confrontation.

Although Delaware and other states have allowed remote-only meetings since 2000, in the 10 years between 2000 and 2010, only 12 corporations held remote-only meetings, according to one commentator. Lisa M. Fairfax, *Virtual Shareholder Meetings Reconsidered*, 40 Seton Hall L. Rev. 1367, 1396 (2010). Recently, however, analysts are noting an uptick in virtual meetings, with 35 purely virtual meetings in 2013 and 32 "hybrid" virtual meetings, which combine an in-person meeting with audio or video broadcasts. *See* http://proxypulse.broadridge.com.

At present, several companies, including Starbucks Coffee Company and McDonald's Corporation, broadcast their annual shareholder meetings in live webcasts. They also videotape those meetings to permit later viewing via the Internet. Some allow their shareholders to participate in the meeting by submitting questions by e-mail. Another new trend, which has been adopted by MBCA § 1.44 and SEC rule, is to allow the delivery of a single annual report and proxy statement (and other reports) to shareholders who share the same last name and address, unless contrary instructions are received from a shareholder. This practice, known as **householding**, is designed to reduce printing and postage costs.

All of these efforts, from posting reports online, to allowing voting telephonically and via the Internet, to the holding of virtual meetings, serve to promote the laudable goal of shareholder participation in matters of corporate governance and result in increased efficiency and cost savings to corporations.

Application Exercise 3

Review the most recent General Electric proxy materials, and determine what methods shareholders may use to access proxy materials and exercise voting rights.

4. Voting Rights

There are different types of shareholder voting: straight voting, cumulative voting, class voting, contingent voting, and disproportionate voting. We discuss these types of voting below.

Straight Voting

Generally, and unless the articles of incorporation provide otherwise, each share of record is entitled to one vote for each director's position to be filled or for each issue being considered. Thus, if Andrews owns 100 shares of stock and five directors are being elected, Andrews may cast 100 votes either for or against each of the nominees. He could not cast 90 votes for one candidate and 10 votes for another. This is referred to as **straight** (or *statutory*) **voting** (or sometimes as the "one share-one vote" rule) and is the most common type of voting exercised by shareholders. Some jurisdictions and MBCA § 6.04(c) allow fractional shares to exercise fractional voting rights. For example, due to a share dividend, a shareholder may have 100.5 shares of stock. Under straight voting, the shareholder would be entitled to 100.5 votes.

Cumulative Voting

Cumulative voting is a type of voting designed to make it more likely that there will be some representation of minority shareholders on the board of directors. If cumulative voting rights exist, each share is multiplied by the number of vacancies to be filled. The votes may then be cast in any manner desired by the shareholder. For example, if Andrews owns 100 shares of OmniWorld, Inc. and five directors are being elected, cumulative voting would allow Andrews 500 votes to cast however he likes, whereas straight voting would allow him only 100 votes for each director. Thus, under both straight and cumulative voting, Andrews has a total of 500 votes to cast. In cumulative voting, however, Andrews can cast all 500 votes for one candidate, or 250 votes for each of two candidates, or any other combination. In cumulative voting, all directors stand for election at the same moment, whereas in straight voting, each director is elected one at a time. The result of cumulative voting is to give minority shareholders a chance to elect at least one director who may be responsive to their needs.

To maximize the advantage of cumulative voting, minority shareholders tend to concentrate all of their votes on one candidate rather than spread the votes among the board and thereby dilute the impact of cumulative voting. For example, assume OmniWorld, Inc. has 1,000 shares outstanding. Its articles provide for cumulative voting. Further assume that the minority shareholders, Andrews and Baker, together own 400 shares, and the majority shareholders, Carter, Dowell, and Edwards together own 600 shares. Three directors are being elected. The candidates are Taylor, Tyler, and Tuttle (candidates the majority shareholders would like to see elected), and O'Brien, whom the minority shareholders would like to elect. If straight voting exists, the majority shareholders will always be able to elect the directors; they will "win" every time.

Under cumulative voting, the minority shareholders, Andrews and Baker, can elect one person to the board who they hope will represent their interests. If voting cumulatively, Andrews and Baker will have 1,200 shares to vote (400 shares multiplied by three vacancies to be filled). The majority shareholders will have 1,800 shares to vote (600 shares multiplied by three vacancies to be filled). If Andrews and Baker dump all 1,200 of their votes on their candidate, O'Brien will be elected. Although the majority shareholders have 1,800 votes, these votes must be divided somehow between their three choices for candidates. No matter which way the majority shareholders divide up their votes, they will elect two directors and the minority shareholders will be able to elect O'Brien if they cast all their votes for O'Brien (see Exhibit 8.8). Cumulative voting generally requires cohesion and agreement among minority shareholders in order to take advantage of its benefits.

Cumulative voting may be provided for in a corporation's articles of incorporation, or it may be mandated by the state's corporations statutes. Most jurisdictions allow corporations to adopt cumulative voting in director elections but use straight voting as the default rule. Cumulative voting applies *only* to the election of directors and not to any other corporate issues, such as voting for mergers, dissolutions, or amendments to the articles of incorporation. We also discuss cumulative voting as a minority shareholder protection strategy in Chapter 10.

| EXHIBIT 8.8 | Cumulative Voting |

EXHIBIT 8.8 Cumulative Voting

Ballot	Majority Shareholders			Minority Shareholders	
	Taylor	Tyler	Tuttle	O'Brien	
1	1,300	400	100	1,200	Elected: Taylor, Tyler & O'Brien
2	601	600	599	1,200	Elected: Taylor, Tyler & O'Brien
3	1,500	200	100	1,200	Elected: Taylor, Tyler & O'Brien

In a few states, such as Arizona and California, cumulative voting is mandatory (Arizona), or mandatory for non-public corporations (California). Fewer than about 10 percent of publicly traded companies provide for cumulative voting. In most states, and according to MBCA § 7.28(b), it is permissive, meaning that the articles of incorporation may provide for cumulative voting; if not provided for in the articles of incorporation, cumulative voting does not exist. In many instances, shareholders wishing to assure election of a representative to the board will examine the shareholder voting list (often kept at the office of the registrar) to identify and locate shareholders with whom they can band together to exercise their voting power.

The impact of cumulative voting can be diluted by decreasing the number of directorships (if only one director is being elected, Andrews and Baker have a total of 400 votes rather than the 1,200 votes they would have if three directors are being elected) or by **staggering** the board so that not all directors are elected at the same time. MBCA § 8.06 provides that the terms of directors may be classified or staggered by dividing the total number of directors into two or three groups, so that one-half or one-third are elected at each annual meeting. The U.S. Senate is a prototypical stagger system: All senators have a term of six years yet only one-third of the group stands for election every two years. If a nine-member board is staggered or classified into three groups of three directors (a common approach), rather than having 3,600 votes (400 × 9) to cast were all nine directors elected at one time, Andrews and Baker would have a total of 1,200 votes (400 × 3) because only three directors are elected every two years.

To ensure that majority shareholders do not defeat the effect of cumulative voting by immediately removing a director elected by minority shareholders, states and corporations mandating cumulative voting usually permit removal of a director only upon cumulative voting as well. Thus, the director cannot be removed if the number of votes sufficient to elect him under cumulative voting is voted against his removal. *See* MBCA § 8.08(c).

Class Voting

If one or more classes or series of shares exist, classes may vote as a separate unit or block, depending on the language of the relevant state corporations code and the language of the corporation's charter, bylaws, and any relevant shareholder agreement(s). For example, Common A and Common B shareholders may be one group or class for purposes of voting on amendment of the articles of incorporation and Common C and Common D shareholders are a group or class for voting on other issues, such as election of some or all of the directors.

Contingent Voting

Some shares vote only upon occurrence of a certain contingency or event. For example, the articles of incorporation might provide that Preferred A shareholders can vote for directors only in those years in which dividends are not distributed.

Disproportionate Voting

Disproportionate voting exists when one class has voting power disproportionate to that of another. For example, if Common A shareholders have two votes per share and Common B shareholders have one vote per share, disproportionate voting would exist. The voting rules of Alphabet Inc. give founders Sergey Brin and Larry Page disproportionate voting rights, as set forth in the following excerpts from Alphabet's charter. See Exhibit 8.9.

> **EXHIBIT 8.9**   **Excerpts, Article IV, Alphabet Inc. Charter**
>
> Section 2. Common Stock. A statement of the designations of each class of Common Stock and the powers, preferences and rights and qualifications, limitations or restrictions thereof is as follows:
>
> (a) Voting Rights.
> (i) Except as otherwise provided herein or by applicable law, the holders of shares of Class A Common Stock and Class B Common Stock shall at all times vote together as one class on all matters (including the election of directors) submitted to a vote or for the consent of the stockholders of the Corporation.
> (ii) Each holder of shares of Class A Common Stock shall be entitled to one (1) vote for each share of Class A Common Stock held as of the applicable date on any matter that is submitted to a vote or for the consent of the stockholders of the Corporation.
> (iii) Each holder of shares of Class B Common Stock shall be entitled to ten (10) votes for each share of Class B Common Stock held as of the applicable date on any matter that is submitted to a vote or for the consent of the stockholders of the Corporation.
>
> . . .
>
> (i) As used in this Section 2(f), the following terms shall have the following meanings:
> (1) "Founder" shall mean either Larry Page or Sergey Brin, each as a natural living person, and "Founders" shall mean both of them.
> (2) "Class B Stockholder" shall mean (a) the Founders, (b) the registered holder of a share of Class B Common Stock of Google Inc. on July 6, 2004 (the "Effective Time"), (c) each natural person who Transferred shares of Class B Common Stock of Google Inc. (or securities convertible into or exchangeable for shares of Class B Common Stock of Google Inc.) prior to the Effective Time to a Permitted Entity that, as of the Effective Time, complies with the applicable exception for such Permitted Entity specified in Section 2(f)(iii)(2), and (d) the initial registered holder of any shares of Class B Common Stock of Google Inc. that were originally issued by the Corporation after the Effective Time.

Nonvoting Stock

Nonvoting stock may be authorized and issued so long as full voting rights reside in at least one class of shares.

Conducting the Meeting

At the meeting, items on the agenda are presented in the form of resolutions, which the shareholders then vote on. Most states provide that approval by a majority vote is required to take action. (Some matters, however, such as amending the articles of incorporation or mergers, might require the affirmative vote of a super-majority, perhaps two-thirds approval, if the articles or bylaws so provide.) In many corporations, sufficient proxies are received before the actual meeting so that results are known in advance and the meeting is a formality.

Counting Votes: Majority and Plurality Voting

In general, there are two ways to count votes with respect to voting requirements: **majority voting** (in which a measure or candidate must receive a majority or at least 51 percent of the affirmative votes) and **plurality voting** (in which a measure or candidate only needs to get more votes for than against). In Delaware and most states, as well as under MBCA § 7.28, **directors** are elected by a **plurality** of votes unless the corporation's articles provide otherwise. In this context, plurality means that the candidates who receive the largest number of votes are elected, up to the maximum number of director slots up for election, even if those candidates do not receive a majority of "yes" votes. In an election in which two candidates are running for director, the candidate who receives the greatest number of votes is said to have a majority. If, however, there are more than two candidates, the person who receives the greatest number of votes has a plurality, but that person does not have a majority unless he receives more than one-half of all votes cast. For example, if Amanda and Ted are vying for a director's position (100 shares are voting) and Amanda gets 60 votes and Ted gets 40, Amanda received a majority of the votes (namely, more than one-half of the votes cast). If, however, Mike is also running, and Amanda receives 45 votes, Ted receives 30 votes, and Mike receives 25 votes, Amanda has won by a plurality. She cannot win by majority vote unless she receives at least 51 votes. Generally, "plurality voting" means that more "for" votes are cast in favor of a nominee than for other nominees, without counting the number of votes "against" or withheld. The issue of electing directors by a plurality rather than by a majority vote is a controversial matter, and a number of shareholder proposals have sought to require majority rather than plurality voting in elections for directors.

Under MBCA § 7.25(c), unless the corporation's charter or the corporations code require a greater number of affirmative votes, a measure (other than election of directors) passes when the votes for it cast within the voting group exceed the votes against it cast within the voting group regardless of abstentions. This allows a measure to pass without receiving a majority vote. For example, if 100 voting shares are outstanding, at least 51 must be present for a quorum to exist. If 51 shares are present and corporations statutes require a majority vote to take action, at least 26 of those shares must approve a certain action. Under the MBCA approach, however, the measure could pass with fewer than 26 votes if 20 shares voted in favor, 18 shares voted against the action, and 13 shares abstained (because abstentions are not counted). In an extreme case, a measure could receive only one vote "for" it with all other votes withheld or abstaining, and yet be enacted under plurality voting.

The MBCA approach, providing that a measure is approved if the votes cast in favor of it exceed the votes cast in opposition, is not followed in some states, which require that for a measure to be approved, it must receive a majority vote.

For example, under § 216 of the DGCL, unless a different requirement is set forth in another section of the DGCL or in the corporation's charter or bylaws, "the affirmative vote of the majority of shares present in person or represented by proxy at the meeting and entitled to vote on the subject matter shall be the act of the stockholders." In effect, this standard requires a majority of a quorum.

It is important to remember that certain code provisions or the corporate charter may alter voting requirements within limits set by the state corporations code. For example, it is often the case that certain mergers and sales of all (or substantially all) corporate assets must be approved by a super-majority of shareholders rather than a simple majority. For this reason, it is important that you consult both the applicable corporations statute and the corporation's organic documents to determine whether shareholders have a right to vote on a particular issue, and if so, what voting requirements apply. See Exhibit 8.10 for a sample ballot.

EXHIBIT 8.10 **Sample Ballot**

FTB, Inc.

1. Election of directors

Steven A. Butler	For ____	Against____	Abstain____
Ellen J. Jamison	For ____	Against____	Abstain____
Jacob N. Sanders	For ____	Against____	Abstain____
2. Ratification of independent auditors	For ____	Against____	Abstain____
3. Policy on board diversity	For ____	Against____	Abstain____

The Board of Directors recommends a vote AGAINST Item 4.

4. Executive compensation factors	For ____	Against____	Abstain____

Signature_____ Date_____

Shareholder Voting Agreements

In addition to advocating for cumulative voting, shareholders also may enter into voting agreements or form voting trusts to maximize or concentrate their voting power.

A *voting agreement*, sometimes called a **pooling agreement**, is an agreement among shareholders that specifies the manner in which they will vote. Shareholders may agree to cast their votes in a certain way on various matters or to pool their shares and cast them as they agree by majority agreement on a case-by-case basis. Such an agreement allows shareholders to band together to seek control. There is comparatively little regulation of vote pooling agreements, but it is important to review the applicable corporations code carefully to make sure that any requirements are satisfied. MBCA § 7.31 simply provides that two or more shareholders may agree on the manner in which they will vote their shares by signing an agreement for that purpose. The MBCA also states that the agreement is specifically enforceable, meaning that a court can order a shareholder to act as previously agreed on in the voting agreement.

A **voting trust** is a written agreement by which shareholders transfer their rights to vote to a trustee who is instructed to vote their shares on their behalf according to the terms of a written trust agreement. The shareholders surrender their shares to the trustee who then becomes the record holder of the shares for purposes of receiving notice and voting. Most states regulate the formation and operation of voting trusts. MBCA § 7.30 specifies the manner of creating a voting trust. Failure to follow the statutory requirements usually invalidates the trust. The terms of the trust may allow the trustee to exercise her independent judgment when voting, or may require the trustee to obtain a consensus of a certain percentage of the beneficial owners of the shares, or may require the trustee to vote in a certain manner.

Under MBCA § 7.30(a), a voting trust agreement must be delivered to the corporation. Thus, the corporation may know in advance how the shares subject to the trust will be voted. On the other hand, a pooling agreement is a private agreement between its parties, and the corporation will generally have no knowledge of its existence or terms. Moreover, whereas voting trusts are generally limited to some specified period of duration, often ten years, pooling agreements may last indefinitely, depending on the terms of the agreement and any applicable provision(s) of the state corporations code.

When the shareholders relinquish their stock certificates in a voting trust situation, they will receive **voting trust certificates**, which generally are freely transferable, although the new owner will be bound by the terms of the trust agreement. The shareholders retain their rights to dividends and other rights associated with share ownership, and the trustee is substituted for the shareholders only for the purposes of receiving notices of meetings and voting at those meetings. In the pooling agreement situation, new purchasers may or may not take shares subject to the terms of the agreement; the agreement itself will address this matter.

Shares that are subject to any type of voting agreement must generally be marked with a **legend** on the certificate indicating that they are subject to the terms of a restrictive agreement. Typically, the legend provides either the terms of the agreement or states that the agreement will be provided upon request. The legend usually warns that any transaction whereby shares are attempted to be transferred in violation of the agreement is not sufficient to transfer ownership, and the purported new owner will not be recognized for any purpose.

A trustee appointed under a voting trust agreement is subject to fiduciary duties and is usually compensated with a fee for services rendered. Typically, the trust agreement provides that the trustee is not liable for errors in business judgment and will be indemnified for acts of ordinary negligence but will be liable for acts of gross negligence or recklessness. There may be more than one trustee appointed. If so, a mechanism should be established to resolve disputes that could arise among trustees.

Although a voting trust agreement is more expensive and complex than a pooling agreement and will usually involve payment of a fee to the trustee, it lends more certainty in that the shareholders will not have any power to "go back on their word" and vote contrary to terms of the trust inasmuch as they no longer have any power to vote their shares. With a pooling agreement, a rogue shareholder could decide to breach the agreement and vote contrary to its terms. Although other shareholders can sue for breach of contract and apply to a court to compel the shareholder to vote according to the agreement, a voting trust eliminates the possibility of such events even occurring.

Meetings for Publicly Traded Companies

In most instances, the conduct of a shareholders' meeting for a publicly traded company is substantially similar to the conduct of any shareholders' meeting; however, a great deal more planning and paperwork is involved. For example, dissident shareholders may make proposals (within the corporation's stated deadlines and SEC rules), which must be set forth in the company's proxy statement, as discussed in Chapter 13. Similarly, a great deal of public company shareholder voting occurs via proxy rather than in person. Many publicly traded companies use the services of a professional shareholder communications company whose services include distributing shareholder materials and tallying proxy voting by conventional print form, by telephone, and by Internet proxy voting, to manage and assist with shareholder proxy voting.

Meetings of publicly traded companies are usually held in hotel meeting rooms or convention facilities, which are able to accommodate a large group of shareholders. Corporate management usually works with the legal team in preparing a "script" for the chairperson to ensure that appropriate announcements are made, resolutions are voted on, and remarks about the company's performance are included.

Minutes of Meeting

The corporation's secretary usually has the responsibility for taking **minutes** of the shareholders' meetings. There is no one statutorily required format for minutes. Some law firms provide their smaller corporate clients with "canned" or prepared minutes, allowing the secretary to merely fill in the blanks and indicate action taken at a meeting. Larger corporations tend to keep more detailed minutes. Similarly, statutes seldom address the actual manner of conducting the meeting. Many larger corporations follow *Robert's Rules of Order*, although following parliamentary procedure is not required, and many experts believe *Robert's Rules of Order* is overly complicated. Cases and statutes rarely address how meetings are to be conducted, and no uniform set of rules exists today regarding the conduct of meetings. As a result, a subcommittee of the Business Law Section of the American Bar Association has prepared a handbook of guidelines for the conduct of shareholder meetings. It can be ordered from the ABA through its website. MBCA § 7.08(c) provides merely that the rules adopted for and the conduct of the meeting must be fair to shareholders.

To provide protection against later challenges, the minutes should include a variety of recitals: that notice was properly given to all shareholders entitled to receive notice or that the shareholders properly waived notice, that a quorum was present, that a measure passed by sufficient vote, and so forth. The minutes reflect action taken at the meeting and provide an overview rather than a verbatim transcript of what was uttered at the meeting. See Exhibit 8.11 for sample minutes of an annual shareholders' meeting.

EXHIBIT 8.11 Sample Minutes of Annual Meeting of Shareholders

An annual meeting of the shareholders of Tech Management Team, Inc., a Delaware corporation, was held on May 1, 2015, at 10:00 A.M., in the Spanish Ballroom of the Fairmont Olympic Hotel, 411 University Street, Seattle, Washington, for the purpose of electing directors of the corporation, voting on the approval of Ernst & Young LLP as independent registered public accountants of the corporation, and to transact such other business properly before the meeting.

Daniel J. Sullivan, Chief Executive Officer, acted as Chair, and Diana Hendrix acted as Secretary.

At 10:00 A.M. the Chair called the meeting to order.

The Secretary announced that the meeting was called pursuant to Del. Code Ann. tit. 8, § 211 and Article VII of the bylaws of the corporation.

The Secretary announced that the meeting was held pursuant to notice properly given as required under the laws of the State of Delaware and the bylaws of the corporation, or that notice had been waived by those entitled to receive notice under the bylaws. Copies of any written waivers executed by those persons entitled to receive notice will be attached to the minutes of this meeting by the Secretary.

The Secretary read the minutes of the last annual meeting of shareholders. The minutes were approved and placed in the minute book.

The Secretary announced that an alphabetical list of the names of shareholders and the number of shares held by each was available for inspection by any person in attendance at the meeting.

The Secretary announced that a quorum was present at the meeting.

All of the directors of the corporation were present at the meeting. The following other persons were present: James K. Eckmann, Chief Financial Officer of the corporation, Susan M. Baker, representative of the corporation's registrar and transfer agent, American Stock Transfer & Trust Company, LLC, and Harry S. Hunter, election inspector appointed by the corporation's registrar and transfer agent, American Stock Transfer & Trust Company, LLC.

The reports of the President and Chief Financial Officer were presented to the shareholders and were placed in the corporate minute book.

The Chairman then called for the election of directors of the corporation.

Upon motion duly made, seconded, and carried, the following persons were elected to the board of directors of the corporation, to serve as directors until their successors are elected at the next annual meeting of shareholders of the corporation and qualify:

Lisa Black

Christopher Wagner

Kenneth Lyons

William Brady

Patricia E. Moore

EXHIBIT 8.11 **(continued)**

The Chair then called for the approval of Ernst & Young as independent registered public accountants of the corporation.

Upon motion duly made, seconded, and carried, Ernst & Young LLP was appointed as independent registered public accountants of the corporation upon the terms and conditions set forth in the Notice of this Annual Meeting of Shareholders and placed in the minute book.

There being no further business before the meeting, on motion duly made, seconded, and unanimously carried, it was adjourned.

Date: _____   _____
                                          Diana Hendrix, Secretary

C. DIRECTORS

1. Introduction

As you know, under state corporations codes, the business and affairs of a corporation are to be managed by or under the direction of the board of directors. *See, e.g.,* MBCA § 8.01(b); DGCL § 141(a). We discuss requirements for board and committee service, director duties, and the mechanics of board meetings below.

2. Number and Qualifications of Directors

Although a few states continue to require at least three directors, the more modern approach, and that of most states and the MBCA, is to require only one director. *See* MBCA § 8.03(a). Corporations having more than one director typically have an odd number (five, seven, or nine) to minimize the possibility of a deadlock. Some bylaws provide that the corporation can have a variable range board — for example, no fewer than three and no more than nine directors. While statutes generally do not set a maximum number of directors, having an unusually large board tends to makes management difficult and cumbersome. Directors usually can increase or decrease the size of the board by amending the bylaws (or the charter, if provisions establishing the size of the board are contained therein), but the corporation can never have fewer directors than required by state statute. *See* MBCA § 8.03. Directors who are also officers, employees, or significant shareholders of the corporation are sometimes called **inside directors**, and those who have no other relationship with the corporation beyond the director role are often called **outside directors.**

In terms of qualifications, whereas the older statutes required that directors be residents of the state of incorporation, the modern view is that directors need not be residents of the state of incorporation or shareholders of the corporation, unless the articles or bylaws so require. *See* MBCA § 8.02(a) and (c). The articles or bylaws can set minimum and maximum age standards and residency requirements, but the trend is to avoid such limitations. To ensure that directors have the legal capacity to enter into contracts, directors should have attained the age of majority, namely 18 years of age.

A recent trend is to require public company directors to meet additional requirements. For example, the New York Stock Exchange requires that corporations listed on the NYSE have a majority of independent directors, as set forth in the following excerpt from the NYSE Listed Company Manual. See Exhibit 8.12.

EXHIBIT 8.12	New York Stock Exchange Listed Company Manual, Sections 303A.01 and 303A.02

303A.01 Independent Directors

Listed companies must have a majority of independent directors.

Commentary: Effective boards of directors exercise independent judgment in carrying out their responsibilities. Requiring a majority of independent directors will increase the quality of board oversight and lessen the possibility of damaging conflicts of interest.

Amended: November 25, 2009 (NYSE-2009-89).

303A.02 Independence Tests

In order to tighten the definition of "independent director" for purposes of these standards:

(a)(i) No director qualifies as "independent" unless the board of directors affirmatively determines that the director has no material relationship with the listed company (either directly or as a partner, shareholder or officer of an organization that has a relationship with the company).

(ii) In addition, in affirmatively determining the independence of any director who will serve on the compensation committee of the listed company's board of directors, the board of directors must consider all factors specifically relevant to determining whether a director has a relationship to the listed company which is material to that director's ability to be independent from management in connection with the duties of a compensation committee member, including, but not limited to:

(A) the source of compensation of such director, including any consulting, advisory or other compensatory fee paid by the listed company to such director; and

(B) whether such director is affiliated with the listed company, a subsidiary of the listed company or an affiliate of a subsidiary of the listed company.

Commentary: It is not possible to anticipate, or explicitly to provide for, all circumstances that might signal potential conflicts of interest, or that might bear on the materiality of a director's relationship to a listed company (references to "listed company" would include any parent or subsidiary in a consolidated group with the listed company). Accordingly, it is best that boards making "independence" determinations broadly consider all relevant facts and circumstances. In particular, when assessing the materiality of a director's relationship with the listed company, the board should consider the issue not merely from the standpoint of the director, but also from that of persons or organizations with which the director has an affiliation. Material relationships can include commercial, industrial, banking, consulting, legal, accounting, charitable and familial relationships, among others. However, as the

EXHIBIT 8.12   **(continued)**

concern is independence from management, the Exchange does not view ownership of even a significant amount of stock, by itself, as a bar to an independence finding.

When considering the sources of a director's compensation in determining his independence for purposes of compensation committee service, the board should consider whether the director receives compensation from any person or entity that would impair his ability to make independent judgments about the listed company's executive compensation. Similarly, when considering any affiliate relationship a director has with the company, a subsidiary of the company, or an affiliate of a subsidiary of the company, in determining his independence for purposes of compensation committee service, the board should consider whether the affiliate relationship places the director under the direct or indirect control of the listed company or its senior management, or creates a direct relationship between the director and members of senior management, in each case of a nature that would impair his ability to make independent judgments about the listed company's executive compensation.

Disclosure Requirement: The listed company must comply with the disclosure requirements set forth in Item 407(a) of Regulation S-K.

Additionally, directors serving on the audit committee of a New York Stock Exchange–listed company must meet certain financial literacy requirements, as set forth in the following excerpt from the NYSE Listed Company Manual. See Exhibit 8.13.

EXHIBIT 8.13   **New York Stock Exchange Listed Company Manual, Section 303A.07 Audit Committee Additional Requirements**

(a) The audit committee must have a minimum of three members. All audit committee members must satisfy the requirements for independence set out in Section 303A.02 and, in the absence of an applicable exemption, Rule 10A-3(b)(1).

Commentary: Each member of the audit committee must be financially literate, as such qualification is interpreted by the listed company's board in its business judgment, or must become financially literate within a reasonable period of time after his or her appointment to the audit committee. In addition, at least one member of the audit committee must have accounting or related financial management expertise, as the listed company's board interprets such qualification in its business judgment. While the Exchange does not require that a listed company's audit committee include a person who satisfies the definition of audit committee financial expert set out in Item 407(d)(5)(ii) of Regulation S-K, a board may presume that such a person has accounting or related financial management expertise.

Because of the audit committee's demanding role and responsibilities, and the time commitment attendant to committee membership, each prospective audit committee member should evaluate carefully the existing demands on his or her time before accepting this important assignment.

Disclosure Requirement: If an audit committee member simultaneously serves on the audit committees of more than three public companies, the board must determine that

EXHIBIT 8.13   **(continued)**

such simultaneous service would not impair the ability of such member to effectively serve on the listed company's audit committee and must disclose such determination either on or through the listed company's website or in its annual proxy statement or, if the listed company does not file an annual proxy statement, in its annual report on Form 10-K filed with the SEC. If this disclosure is made on or through the listed company's website, the listed company must disclose that fact in its annual proxy statement or annual report, as applicable, and provide the website address.

In addition to any requirements imposed by state statute or other governmental or regulatory body or stock exchange, a corporation's organic documents may establish additional requirements for director service.

3. Director Duties

Functions Commonly Associated with Directors

Under MBCA § 8.01, directors (through the board) are voted with the authority to exercise all corporate powers. *See also* DGCL § 141. Although state statutes generally are permissive in defining board functions, there are several groups of functions commonly associated with corporate boards:

- Select, evaluate and (when appropriate) replace corporate officers (or, the management team);
- determine officer and senior management compensation;
- review and approval of financial objectives, strategies and plans, such as when to issue or reacquire stock, when to seek out loans (or issue corporate debt instruments);
- provide advice and counsel to management on important policies, strategies, business plans, etc.;
- select and recommend slate of directors for shareholder approval;
- initiate extraordinary matters such as mergers or the purchase or sale of corporate assets;
- exercise responsibility for corporate operations, including entering into contracts and buying and selling real and personal property; and
- review adequacy of internal controls.

In the case of a public corporation, MBCA § 8.01 provides that the board's oversight responsibilities include attention to the following matters:

- business performance and plans;
- major risks;
- performance and compensation of senior management;
- policies and practices that foster compliance with law;

- preparation of financial statements;
- effectiveness of internal controls;
- arrangements for providing timely and adequate information to directors; and
- composition of board and its committees, taking into account the important role of independent directors.

Committees

The board of directors has the authority to delegate some of its functions to various committees. A majority of all directors must approve the creation of a committee. Any such committee will often have at least one member of the board serving on it. As stated in Exhibit 8.13, a committee of a corporation listed on the NYSE may be required to have a specific number of directors. These committees assist the board by carrying out certain ordinary corporate activities. MBCA § 8.25 ensures that committees exercise only limited authority by prohibiting them from taking the following actions, which are non-delegable because they substantially affect shareholders: authorizing distributions, amending the bylaws, filling vacancies on the board, or approving certain matters that only shareholders may approve, such as mergers or dissolutions. The delegation of certain duties to committees does not relieve directors of their responsibilities and duties inasmuch as they are expected to select and supervise carefully those to whom duties have been delegated.

Due to the complexity of managing a large corporation in today's global economy, many corporations have established a variety of committees to deal more efficiently with specific concerns of the corporation. Some of the more common committees are as follows:

- *Executive committee*: Acts on board matters when board cannot and acts on matters specifically delegated to committee by entire board;
- *Audit committee*: Reviews financial matters, selects corporate auditors, and supervises audits of corporate accounts;
- *Nominating and governance committee*: Assists the directors in identifying and nominating candidates for elections of directors and oversees corporate governance;
- *Corporate responsibility committee*: Provides guidance on matters relating to the corporation's social responsibilities;
- *Compensation committee*: Reviews and approves compensation for senior executives (both cash and noncash, such as stock options); and
- *Special litigation committee*: Determines whether corporation should initiate or act to terminate litigation.

In the wake of the recent financial crisis and recession, an increasing number of corporations have created committees charged with identifying, monitoring, and managing risks to the corporation. For example, as set forth in Exhibit 8.14, the charter of the General Electric Risk Committee states that the committee shall have the following authority and responsibilities:

EXHIBIT 18.14   **Excerpt, General Electric Company Risk Committee Charter**

1. To review, and, as applicable, approve the Company's and GE Capital's risk governance framework, risk assessment and risk management practices, and the policies and processes for risk assessment and risk management. For GE Capital, this shall also include review and approval of significant policies and processes that management uses to manage enterprise, strategic, operational, market, credit and liquidity risks and for capital planning.

2. To review and, as applicable, approve the Company's and GE Capital's risk appetite and key policies on the establishment of risk objectives, tolerances and limits, as well as the policies and processes for monitoring and mitigating such risks.

3. To discuss with management, including GE Capital's chief risk officer and its head of credit review, the Company's and GE Capital's risk assessment and risk management policies and processes. The committee or its chairman shall also meet separately with GE Capital's chief risk officer and its head of credit review as the committee deems appropriate.

4. To receive periodic reports from management on the metrics used to measure, monitor and manage risks, including management's views on acceptable and appropriate levels of exposures.

5. To receive reports from the Company's corporate audit staff and GE Capital's internal audit and credit review functions on the results of risk management and credit reviews and assessments.

6. To review the status of financial services regulatory exams and ongoing reviews relating to GE Capital, as applicable.

7. To review periodic reports on selected risk topics as the committee deems appropriate.

8. To review the independence, authority, and effectiveness of the risk management function, including staffing level and staff qualifications.

9. To approve the appointment and, when and if appropriate, replacement of GE Capital's chief risk officer and its head of credit review, each of whom shall functionally report to the chairman of the committee.

10. To discharge any other duties or responsibilities delegated to the committee by the board.

4. Election, Term, Vacancies, and Removal of Directors

Election

The initial directors may be named in the articles of incorporation. If not, the initial board will be elected at the corporation's first organizational meeting. Those directors will serve until the corporation's first annual shareholders' meeting. The directors will then be elected at the first annual meeting and at every annual meeting thereafter, unless their terms are **staggered**. *See* MBCA § 8.06.

As noted above, directors may be elected by **majority** or **plurality** vote. Majority voting requires that a candidate receive more than 50 percent of the votes cast to be elected. Under plurality voting, candidates receiving the most number of votes win, even if that candidate does not receive a majority of votes cast.

In recent years there has been a trend in public corporations toward majority voting. In 2006, only 16 percent of the S&P 500 had majority voting; by 2013, more than 80 percent of the companies had adopted majority voting. Nevertheless, in smaller companies, directors are typically elected by a plurality of votes. In recent years, some corporations have adopted bylaw provisions that require, or otherwise provide for, the resignation of a director who receives more votes cast against him than in favor of his election in an uncontested director election. Exhibit 8.15 is a provision from the bylaws of General Electric to this effect.

EXHIBIT 8.15   **Excerpt, Article IIC General Electric Bylaws**

Election of Directors. In any non-contested election of directors, any incumbent director nominee who receives a greater number of votes cast against his or her election than in favor of his or her election shall immediately tender his or her resignation, and the Board of Directors shall decide, through a process managed by the Board committee responsible for director nominations and excluding the nominee in question, whether to accept the resignation at its next regularly scheduled Board meeting. The Board's explanation of its decision shall be promptly disclosed on Form 8-K filed with the Securities and Exchange Commission (SEC).

If the articles authorize dividing the shares into classes, the articles may also authorize the election of all or some directors by one or more classes. *See* MBCA § 8.04. Thus, if there are three classes of stock, Common A shareholders might elect three directors, Common B shareholders might elect three directors, and Common C shareholders might elect three directors. Such an arrangement may well promote minority representation on the board because Common A shareholders might own only a small percentage of the corporation's stock (the articles having specified that the corporation can issue only a certain number of shares of Common A stock) but will be guaranteed they can elect one-third of the board.

Term

Under default rules, directors typically stand for election each year, *see, e.g.*, MBCA § 8.04, unless terms are staggered. *See, e.g.*, MBCA §§ 8.04, 8.05, 8.06. Under a **staggered** or **classified system**, the directors do not all face election at the same time; instead, their terms are divided into classes or are staggered, with only one class up for election in any given year. *See* MBCA §§ 8.05, 8.06. Staggered or classified boards arguably provide some continuity of expertise for corporations inasmuch as the entire board of directors will not be replaced at one time, and the directors can focus on long-term goals rather than having to fear ouster. Additionally, a staggered board makes a hostile takeover more difficult because it will take the acquirer some amount of time to replace all directors with her own hand-picked selections. Critics argue that classified boards serve to entrench directors and deter acquisition bids that might enhance shareholder value, however, and further argue that annually elected directors are more accountable to shareholders.

Vacancies

If a vacancy occurs in the board of directors due to resignation, retirement, or death, or if a new position is created pursuant to amendment of the corporate articles or bylaws, the vacancy will be filled either by action of the shareholders or of the remaining directors, unless the articles of incorporation provide otherwise. *See, e.g.,* MBCA § 8.10(a). Most bylaws provide that the remaining directors may select a replacement to fill such a vacancy. If numerous vacancies exist, perhaps due to the simultaneous deaths of directors in an accident, if the remaining directors do not constitute a quorum, they may nevertheless fill vacancies by a majority vote of all directors remaining in office. *See, e.g.,* MBCA § 8.10(a)(3). The new director appointed to fill the vacancy usually "steps into the shoes" of his predecessor and serves for the remainder of the predecessor's term. Directors may resign at any time by providing written notice to the corporation.

Removal

At common law, directors, once elected by the shareholders, could be removed from their positions only "for cause." The "cause" was typically fraud or dishonesty. The modern approach provided by MBCA § 8.08 and by most state statutes now allows shareholders to remove directors either with or without cause (unless the articles provide otherwise). "Cause" not only includes fraud or dishonesty but also generally encompasses breach of duty and incompetence. The theory underlying the modern policy is that the shareholders own the corporation and they thus have the right at any time to determine who should manage it. This allows the shareholders greater flexibility because it is often difficult to prove fraud or dishonesty. Thus, if the shareholders elect directors in April, they can remove some or even all of those directors at any time thereafter without waiting for the next annual meeting. Vacancies created when shareholders remove directors are usually filled by shareholder vote.

Under MBCA § 8.08(d), a director may be removed by the shareholders only at a special meeting called for the purpose of removing him. The meeting notice must state that the purpose or one of the purposes of the meeting is removal of the director. *Id.* Generally, a director can be removed only by vote of the shareholders who were entitled to elect him. *See, e.g.,* MBCA § 8.08(b). Thus, if director Smith is elected by Common A shareholders, only Common A shareholders can remove Smith. When cumulative voting is authorized, a director cannot be removed if the number of votes sufficient to elect him under cumulative voting is voted against removal. MBCA § 8.08(c). Thus, if 100 shares would have been sufficient to elect a director under cumulative voting, then the director cannot be removed if 100 shares vote against removal. This ensures that the interests of minority shareholders who cumulatively vote are not circumvented by removal of a director by majority vote immediately after election.

In the event that shareholders cannot muster sufficient votes to remove a director who is also a majority shareholder (because the director has sufficient votes to block his own removal), shareholders (or the board of directors) can apply to court for removal. *See, e.g.,* MBCA § 8.09. In this case, removal by the court is dependent on proof of the director's fraudulent conduct or gross abuse of authority and a showing that removal is in the best interest of the corporation. *Id.* Generally, directors cannot remove other directors, although some states allow directors to remove directors who have been convicted of a felony or have been adjudged to be of unsound mind.

Section 141(k) of the Delaware corporations code provides as follows with respect to director removal:

> Any director or the entire board of directors may be removed, with or without cause, by the holders of a majority of the shares then entitled to vote at an election of directors, except as follows:
>
> (1) Unless the certificate of incorporation otherwise provides, in the case of a corporation whose board is classified as provided in subsection (d) of this section, stockholders may effect such removal only for cause; or
>
> (2) In the case of a corporation having cumulative voting, if less than the entire board is to be removed, no director may be removed without cause if the votes cast against such director's removal would be sufficient to elect such director if then cumulatively voted at an election of the entire board of directors, or, if there be classes of directors, at an election of the class of directors of which such director is a part.
>
> Whenever the holders of any class or series are entitled to elect 1 or more directors by the certificate of incorporation, this subsection shall apply, in respect to the removal without cause of a director or directors so elected, to the vote of the holders of the outstanding shares of that class or series and not to the vote of the outstanding shares as a whole.

In December 2015, the Delaware Court of Chancery held that a corporation without a classified board or cumulative voting may not restrict stockholders' ability to remove directors without cause. *In re Vaalco Energy S'holder Litig.,* C.A. No. 11775-VCL (Dec. 21, 2015). In 2009, Vaalco's stockholders approved an amendment to the company's certificate of incorporation to declassify the board but left in place provisions in the corporation's bylaws and charter providing that directors could be removed only for cause. When an activist investor launched a consent solicitation to remove four members of the board, Vaalco responded that any such written consent would be null and void because its directors could only be removed from office for cause. Stockholder plaintiffs sued, arguing that under § 141(k) of the DGCL, stockholders have the right to remove directors without cause unless the company has a staggered board or cumulative voting. In a transcript ruling, the Court of Chancery agreed with the plaintiffs, and invalidated those terms of Vaalco's charter and bylaws that provided that directors could be removed only for cause. Shortly thereafter, Vaalco reportedly reached a resolution with the activist investor, so the Delaware Supreme Court did not have occasion to pass upon the issue in dispute.

5. Directors' Meetings

The management of the corporation is accomplished by the directors acting as a unit — that is, the board — (rather than individually) at **meetings** (or by **unanimous written consent,** as discussed below). Few statutes give guidance regarding the notice and conduct of directors' meetings. Thus, the mechanics of most directors' meetings are governed by the charter and the bylaws of the corporation.

Regular Meetings

Most boards meet at regularly scheduled intervals, whether once a week, once a month, or once a quarter. These scheduled meetings are called regular meetings, and the board conducts its regular business and manages the corporation at these meetings. Although there is no requirement to do so, many corporations also hold annual board of directors' meetings immediately following the shareholders' annual meeting. New officers are often appointed at this annual directors' meeting. Details regarding the timing and other logistics of board meetings typically are spelled out in the bylaws. Exhibit 8.16 contains an excerpt from the bylaws of Alphabet Inc. concerning regular meetings of directors.

EXHIBIT 8.16	Excerpt, Section 3.6, Bylaws of Alphabet Inc.

3.6 REGULAR MEETINGS.

Regular meetings of the Board may be held with at least five business days prior notice at such time and at such place as shall from time to time be determined by the Board.

Special Meetings

A special meeting is any meeting held between regular meetings. Special meetings are typically called to discuss matters that cannot wait until the next regular meeting, such as time-sensitive and significant potential corporate transactions. Provisions relating to who is authorized to call a special meeting (generally, the chair of the board) will be found in the bylaws. Exhibit 8.17 contains an excerpt from the bylaws of Alphabet Inc. concerning special meetings.

EXHIBIT 8.17   **Excerpt, Section 3.7, Bylaws of Alphabet Inc.**

3.7 SPECIAL MEETINGS; NOTICE.

Special meetings of the Board for any purpose or purposes may be called at any time by the chairman of the Board, the chief executive officer, the secretary or any two directors. The person(s) authorized to call special meetings of the Board may fix the place and time of the meeting.

Notice of the time and place of special meetings shall be:

(i) delivered personally by hand, by courier or by telephone;
(ii) sent by United States first-class mail, postage prepaid;
(iii) sent by facsimile; or
(iv) sent by electronic mail,

directed to each director at that director's address, telephone number, facsimile number or electronic mail address, as the case may be, as shown on the corporation's records.

If the notice is (i) delivered personally by hand, by courier or by telephone, (ii) sent by facsimile or (iii) sent by electronic mail, it shall be delivered or sent at least twenty-four (24) hours before the time of the holding of the meeting. If the notice is sent by United States mail, it shall be deposited in the United States mail at least four days before the time of the holding of the meeting. Any oral notice may be communicated either to the director or to a person at the office of the director who the person giving notice has reason to believe will promptly communicate such notice to the director. The notice need not specify the place of the meeting if the meeting is to be held at the corporation's principal executive office nor the purpose of the meeting.

Place of Meetings

The place of the meeting, whether regular or special, may be specified in the bylaws or may be determined by the directors. Meetings need not be held in the state of incorporation and generally can be held anywhere. If no specific location is provided in the bylaws, at the end of each regular meeting, the board should specify the location of the next regular meeting.

Notice of Meetings

Generally, directors are not entitled to notice of regular meetings. *See* MBCA § 8.22. Because it is their duty to manage the corporation, they are expected to know when the board regularly meets. Thus, providing notice of a regular meeting is as unneeded as a phone call from an employer to an employee each morning reminding the employee to come to work. MBCA § 8.22(b) provides that unless the articles or bylaws provide otherwise, special meetings require two days' advance notice of the date, time, and place of the meeting. Other statutes merely require that reasonable advance notice be given of special meetings. As always, be sure to check the relevant state statute and bylaw provisions respecting meeting logistics.

Waiver of Notice

Directors can give up or waive their right to receive notice of any meeting either before or after the meeting. The waiver must be in writing, signed, and filed with the minutes or other corporate records. See Exhibit 8.18 for a sample waiver of notice by a director. A director's attendance at a meeting constitutes a waiver, unless the director attends the meeting for the purpose of objecting to the meeting. Such an objection must be made at the beginning of any meeting.

EXHIBIT 8.18   **Waiver of Notice of Meeting by Director**

The undersigned, a director of FTB, Inc., a Delaware corporation, hereby waives notice of and consents to the holding of a special meeting of the board of directors of FTB, Inc., held on May 28, 2015, at 1024 Fifteenth Street, N.W., Washington, D.C. 20005 at 10:00 A.M. for the purpose of selecting officers for FTB, Inc.

Date: _____

_____
Signature

The stringent and detailed provisions relating to notice for shareholders are somewhat relaxed with regard to notice for directors. The rationale is generally that because the directors manage the corporation, they have access to information relating to the corporation's affairs and need little protection. Shareholders, on the other hand, participate in corporate affairs only by voting, and are therefore entitled to greater protection to ensure their limited rights of participation are safeguarded.

Case Preview

Klaassen v. Allegro Development Corp.

Klaassen v. Allegro Development Corp. involves a dispute between the plaintiff director/CEO/controlling shareholder of a corporation and the corporation's other directors. After relations between the plaintiff and defendants soured over concerns about the plaintiff's management style and the corporation's performance, the defendant directors voted to oust the plaintiff as CEO at a regular board meeting. The plaintiff raised a number of objections to his ouster as CEO, including a lack of notice and defendant directors' use of allegedly deceptive tactics. In reading the case, consider the following questions:

1. Under default Delaware corporate law rules, is a director entitled to notice of a regular meeting of the board of directors?
2. Did Allegro's bylaws vary default rules regarding notice and meetings of the board of directors?
3. Was Klaassen entitled to notice of, or an agenda for, the meeting where the board voted to oust him as CEO?
4. Did Klaassen's status as a director, chief executive officer, and controlling shareholder give him an equitable right to notice of the board meeting where he was ousted as CEO?
5. Did it matter that the director defendants allegedly discussed Klaassen's potential ouster at special meetings that occurred prior to the meeting where the board voted to oust Klaasen as CEO?
6. What is acquiescence? How, if at all, did Klaassen's alleged acquiescence affect his wrongful ouster claim?
7. What is the difference between void and voidable board action?

Klaassen v. Allegro Development Corp.
106 A.3d 1035 (Del. 2014)

Jacobs, Justice:*

I. INTRODUCTION

Plaintiff-below/appellant Eldon Klaassen ("Klaassen") appeals from a Court of Chancery judgment in this proceeding brought under 8 Del. C. § 225. The judgment determined that Klaassen is not the *de jure* chief executive officer ("CEO") of Allegro Development Corporation ("Allegro"). Klaassen claimed that the remaining Allegro directors (collectively, the "Director Defendants"), in removing him as CEO, violated an equitable notice requirement and also improperly employed deceptive tactics. After a trial and without addressing its merits, the Court of Chancery held that the claim was barred under the equitable doctrines of laches and acquiescence.

We affirm the Court of Chancery judgment. We hold that, to the extent that Klaassen's claim may be cognizable, it is equitable in nature. Therefore, Klaassen's removal as CEO was, at most, voidable and subject to the equitable defenses of laches and acquiescence. We further conclude that the Court of Chancery properly found that Klaassen acquiesced in his removal as CEO, and is therefore barred from challenging that removal.

---

*Most footnotes have been omitted for purposes of brevity.

II. FACTUAL AND PROCEDURAL BACKGROUND

A. Facts

Allegro, a Delaware corporation headquartered in Dallas, Texas, is a provider of energy trading and risk management software. From the time that Klaassen founded Allegro in 1984, he has been Allegro's CEO, and until 2007, owned nearly all of Allegro's outstanding shares.

(1) The Series A Investment

In 2007, at which time Allegro was valued at approximately $130 million, Klaassen and Allegro solicited capital infusions from prospective investors. As a result, Allegro entered into transactions with North Bridge Growth Equity 1, L.P. and Tudor Ventures III, L.P. (collectively, the "Series A Investors") in late 2007 and early 2008. In those transactions those investors received Series A Preferred Stock of Allegro in exchange for an investment of $40 million. Currently, the Series A Investors own all of Allegro's Series A Preferred Stock, and Klaassen holds the majority of Allegro's Common Stock. As part of that transaction the Series A Investors, together with Klaassen and Allegro, entered into a Stockholders' Agreement (the "Stockholders' Agreement"). In addition, Allegro amended and restated both its certificate of incorporation (the "Charter") and its bylaws (the "Bylaws").

Those three documents created a framework under which Klaassen and the Series A Investors would share control of Allegro's board of directors (the "Board"). Under the Bylaws, Allegro would be governed by a seven member Board. Under the Charter, the holders of Series A Preferred Stock (voting as a separate class) became entitled to elect three directors, and the holders of Common Stock (voting as a separate class) became entitled to elect one director. The remaining three directors would be elected as provided by Section 9.2 of the Stockholders' Agreement, under which Allegro's CEO would serve as a director, and in his capacity as CEO, would designate two outside directors, subject to the approval of the Series A Investors. The two outside directors would ultimately be elected by the holders of Series A Preferred Stock and Common Stock, voting together as a group.

Although the governing documents provided for a seven member Board, in actuality Klaassen and the Series A Investors settled on a five member Board. From 2010 until November 1, 2012, that Board consisted of Michael Pehl and Robert Forlenza (the "Series A Directors"), George Patrich Simpkins, Jr. and Raymond Hood (the "Outside Directors"), and Klaassen (as the CEO director). During that period, Klaassen, as the majority common stockholder, did not elect a director, nor did the Series A Investors elect a third director.

In negotiating the terms of their investment, the Series A Investors also obtained certain guarantees regarding their eventual exit from Allegro, which was to occur in 2012. At any time after December 20, 2012, the Series A Investors could require Allegro to redeem all outstanding Series A Preferred shares. The redemption price would be the greater of: (i) the Fair Market Value (as defined in the Charter), or (ii) the original issue price, plus, in either case, any accrued or declared but unpaid dividends. If the company were sold, the Series A Investors would receive an initial liquidation preference equal to two times their original $40 million investment, plus all unpaid accrued or declared dividends. The Series A Investors could not, however, force a sale of Allegro for less than $390 million without Klaassen's consent, so long as he held at least 33% of Allegro's outstanding capital stock.

(2) Events Leading to Klaassen's Termination

Not long after the Series A Investors became shareholders, Allegro began falling short of its financial performance projections. A 2007 private placement memorandum circulated by Allegro had projected revenues of $61 million in 2008, $75 million in 2009, and $85 million in 2010. In fact, Allegro generated only $46 million in revenue in 2008, $37.5 million in 2009, and less than $35 million in 2010. Although Allegro met its targets for the first three quarters of 2011, the company's fourth quarter performance was a "disaster," and the first quarter of 2012 was similarly disappointing.

Not surprisingly, the Series A Directors, and later the Outside Directors, became discontented with Klaassen's performance as a manager. After the Series A investment transaction, Allegro hired Chris Larsen as chief operating officer to address the Series A Investors' concerns about Klaassen's management. Ten months later, Mr. Larsen resigned, citing difficulty working with Klaassen. While Allegro's financial performance continued to falter, the Series A Directors became particularly frustrated with Klaassen's inability to provide the Board with accurate information. In 2012, only four days before the end of Allegro's best sales quarter to date, Klaassen fired Allegro's senior vice president of sales — disregarding the Board's request to wait until after the quarter's end, and acting without any succession plan in place. Finally, in September 2012, Allegro's chief marketing officer resigned, citing Klaassen's leadership style as the reason.

As frustration with Klaassen mounted, in 2012 the Board began exploring ways to address the Series A Investors' redemption right.[15] At some point before the July 19, 2012 Board meeting, Klaassen proposed that Allegro buy out the Series A Investors' Preferred Stock investment for $60 million. Initially the Series A Investors had demanded $92 million — the approximate value of their initial liquidation preference — but at a July 31, 2012 Board meeting they reduced their demand to $80 million. At that same meeting, Klaassen made a presentation about Allegro's financial performance, apparently hoping to make his $60 million offer to the Series A Investors appear more attractive. Instead, all that Klaassen accomplished was to highlight Allegro's poor performance as compared to its industry peers. As a result, Mr. Forlenza (a Series A Director) concluded that the only viable path for the Series A Investors to achieve a profitable exit was to "grow" the company before exiting.

(3) Klaassen's Termination

In late summer 2012, the Board began seriously to consider replacing Klaassen as CEO. After the July 19 Board meeting, the Outside Directors discussed (with Klaassen), Klaassen's unwillingness to compromise with the Series A Investors. Mr.

---

[15]Klaassen maintained that he would not approve a third-party sale to facilitate the Series A Investors' exit unless that sale generated at least $100 million for him personally (Internal citations omitted).

Hood pointedly told Klaassen that with three director votes, the Board could remove him as CEO.[21] After Klaassen's July 31 Board meeting presentation, Messrs. Pehl and Forlenza (the Series A Directors) became more convinced that Klaassen had to be replaced. In an August 7, 2012 conference call, Messrs. Pehl, Forlenza, Hood, and Simpkins discussed the possibility of replacing Klaassen. Shortly after that call, Mr. Hood asked Baker Botts LLP (legal counsel for the Outside Directors) for advice about the ramifications of replacing Klaassen. On August 17, 2012, the Director Defendants spoke once again.

In mid-September 2012, Messrs. Simpkins and Hood met with Klaassen. Both warned Klaassen that his tenure as CEO was "in jeopardy."[26] . . . [B]y mid-October, the four Director Defendants (Pehl, Forlenza, Hood, and Simpkins) decided to replace Klaassen at the next regularly scheduled Board meeting on November 1, 2012. Those four directors held two preparatory conference calls — on October 19 and October 26 — and asked Baker Botts to prepare a draft resolution removing Klaassen as CEO. The Director Defendants decided not to forewarn Klaassen that they planned to terminate him, because they were concerned about how Klaassen would react while still having access to Allegro's intellectual property, bank accounts, and employees.[30]

On November 1, 2012, before the Board meeting, Mr. Hood emailed Klaassen, asking if Chris Ducanes, Allegro's general counsel, could attend the Board meeting to discuss the Series A redemption issue. Klaassen agreed. Mr. Hood later admitted that that email was "false" because, in fact, Mr. Ducanes' presence was needed to implement Klaassen's termination immediately after Klaassen was informed.

All five directors attended the November 1, 2012 Board meeting. Also attending were Messrs. Ducanes, and Jarett Janik, Allegro's chief financial officer. Toward the end of the meeting, the Director Defendants asked Messrs. Ducanes, Janik, and Klaassen to leave the room to allow the Director Defendants to meet in executive session. During the executive session, the Director Defendants confirmed their decision to remove and replace Klaassen. They then recalled Messrs. Ducanes and Janik, and informed them that Mr. Hood would be replacing Klaassen as CEO. Thereafter, Klaassen returned to the meeting, at which point Mr. Pehl informed Klaassen that the Board was removing him as CEO. The Board then voted on the resolution (prepared by Baker Botts) that removed Klaassen and appointed Hood as interim CEO, with the Director Defendants voting in favor and Klaassen abstaining.

(4) Post-Termination Events

After his removal as CEO, Klaassen initially offered to help Mr. Hood learn about the industry and Allegro's operations. In early to mid-November 2012, Klaassen also began negotiating the terms of a consulting agreement, under which he would serve

---

[21]Klaassen immediately confirmed with Allegro's general counsel that the Board had the power to terminate Klaassen. (Internal citations omitted).

[26]During his dinner with Klaassen, Simpkins advised Klaassen on what he needed to do to remain CEO. In September, Klaassen re-confirmed with Allegro's general counsel and outside counsel (Gibson Dunn & Crutcher LLP) that the Board had the authority to terminate Klaassen as CEO. (Internal citations omitted).

[30]Klaassen suggests that he was given no notice of the removal plans because the Director Defendants were concerned that he (Klaassen) would pre-empt those plans by changing the composition of the Board. (Internal citations omitted).

as an "Executive Consultant" to Allegro, reporting to Allegro's CEO. The draft consulting agreement expressly precluded Klaassen from holding himself out to third parties as an Allegro employee or agent.[39] . . .

. . . On December 29, 2012, all five directors executed a revised written consent removing Mr. Hood from the audit committee and appointing Klaassen to the audit and compensation committees. As a member of the compensation committee, Klaassen provided feedback on Mr. Hood's employment agreement, and also participated in vetting candidates for Hood's future management team.

In late 2012, Klaassen began expressing displeasure about his termination as CEO. In an email Hood sent in late November 2012, Hood remarked that "Eldon has not accepted his fate." On November 29, 2012, Klaassen emailed ExxonMobil (a major Allegro client), informing Exxon that Allegro was in the midst of a "bitter" shareholder dispute and that the company had become "dysfunctional." Klaassen also began hosting events for Allegro employees, at which he criticized Allegro management and spread rumors of other employee terminations.

On June 5, 2013, Klaassen sent a letter to Messrs. Ducanes, Pehl, and Forlenza, claiming that his (Klaassen's) removal as CEO was invalid. Klaassen also delivered two written consents (in his capacity as majority shareholder) that purported to: (i) remove Messrs. Simpkins and Hood as outside directors; (ii) elect John Brown as the common director; and (iii) elect Dave Stritzinger and Ram Velidi as outside directors.

B. The Court Of Chancery Decision

On June 5, 2013, Klaassen filed an action in the Court of Chancery under 8 Del. C. § 225 for a declaration that: (i) Klaassen was the lawful CEO of Allegro; (ii) Messrs. Simpkins and Hood had been effectively removed as Allegro directors; and that (iii) Messrs. Brown, Stritzinger and Velidi had been validly elected as Allegro directors. Klaassen challenged his removal as CEO on two separate grounds. First, he claimed that a majority of the Director Defendants had breached their fiduciary duty of loyalty by firing him. Second, Klaassen claimed that his November 1, 2012 termination was invalid, because the Director Defendants did not give him advance notice of (and employed deception in carrying out) their plan to terminate him before holding the November 1 Board meeting.

The Director Defendants defended, on the merits, the validity of Klaassen's removal as CEO. They also raised the equitable defenses of laches and acquiescence, claiming that under either or both doctrines Klaassen was barred from challenging his removal.

After a trial and post-trial briefing, the Court of Chancery issued a memorandum opinion on October 11, 2013, holding that because Klaassen's challenge to his removal as CEO was grounded in equity, that challenge was subject to the Director Defendants' equitable defenses. The court further found that Klaassen's challenge was barred by the equitable doctrines of laches and acquiescence. Finally, the court determined that Klaassen had validly removed Mr. Simpkins and had validly elected Mr. Brown, but that his removal of Mr. Hood and the election of Messrs. Stritzinger and Velidi were legally invalid.

---

[39]The negotiations, however, halted, and the parties never entered into the consulting agreement. (Citations omitted).

On October 23, 2013 Klaassen appealed to this Court from that judgment, and moved for expedited scheduling, which this Court granted on October 24, 2013. On November 7, 2013, the Court of Chancery issued a "Status Quo Opinion," continuing in effect part of the pre-trial status quo order in force during the pendency of the Chancery litigation.

III. THE PARTIES' CONTENTIONS AND STANDARD OF REVIEW

A. *The Contentions on Appeal*

Klaassen claims that the Court of Chancery reversibly erred in finding that he was barred by the equitable doctrines of laches and acquiescence from challenging his removal as CEO. Specifically, Klaassen argues that in effecting his removal, the Director Defendants gave him no advance notice of their plans to remove him at the November 1, 2012 Board meeting and, moreover, employed deception in calling that meeting, all in violation of "core Delaware corporate law precepts." As a consequence, (Klaassen urges), his removal as CEO was void (as distinguished from voidable), and as a result his challenge to that removal was not subject to equitable defenses. Klaassen further claims that because the Director Defendants violated the Bylaws by not giving Klaassen notice of special meetings held in advance of the November 1 Board meeting, his removal as CEO was void on that ground as well. Finally, Klaassen claims that even if his removal was only voidable, the Court of Chancery erred in finding that Klaassen's claim was barred under the doctrines of laches and acquiescence.

B. *The Issues and the Standard of Review*

Klaassen's challenge to his removal rests on two separate claims of wrongdoing by the Director Defendants: first, the lack of advance notice to Klaassen of their plan to terminate him; and second, the use of deception in carrying out that plan. The first claim requires us to decide whether Klaassen's claim — that the Director Defendants were required to give him advance notice of their plan to remove him as CEO at the November 1 Board meeting — is cognizable under Delaware law. We conclude that it is not. The remaining two issues relate solely to Klaassen's "deception" claim. They are: (1) whether Klaassen's deception-based claim is subject to equitable defenses, and (2), if so, whether that claim is barred by the doctrines of laches and/or acquiescence.

This Court reviews questions of law *de novo.* We will not overturn the Court of Chancery's factual findings unless they are clearly erroneous. A trial court's application of equitable defenses presents a mixed question of law and fact.

IV. ANALYSIS

A. *The Director Defendants Did Not Violate Any Notice Requirements*

(1) *No Notice Required for Regular Board Meeting*

Klaassen claims that the Board's action to remove him as CEO taken at the November 1 meeting was invalid, because he (Klaassen) received no advance notice that his possible termination would be considered at that meeting. This claim lacks merit. Klaassen was terminated at a regular meeting of Allegro's Board. It is settled Delaware law that corporate directors are not required to be given notice of regular board meetings. There being no such notice requirement, it follows that there is no default requirement that directors be given advance notice of the specific agenda items to be addressed at a regular board meeting.[58] Nor do any notice provisions of Allegro's Bylaws override that default rule. Therefore, the Director Defendants violated no default rule of Delaware law, or any provision of Allegro's Bylaws, by not giving Klaassen advance notice of their plan to terminate him at the November 1 regular Board meeting.

(2) Klaassen's Contrary Arguments

Klaassen contends that four Court of Chancery decisions — *Koch v. Stearn*,[59] *VGS, Inc. v. Castiel*,[60] *Adlerstein v. Wertheimer*,[61] and *Fogel v. U.S. Energy Systems, Inc.*[62] — establish the rule that a director who also is a shareholder or officer of a corporation is entitled to advance notice of any matter to be considered at a board meeting, that may affect that director's specific interests. Three of those cases (*Koch, Adlerstein,* and *Fogel*) involved corporations, and in those cases the disputed board actions all occurred at special — not regular — board meetings.[64] Those decisions, therefore, do not support Klaassen's claim. *VGS* is likewise inapplicable. *VGS* involved a limited liability company ("LLC"). Two of the LLC's three managers had

---

[58]*See* 1 R. Franklin Balotti & Jesse A. Finkelstein, The Delaware Law of Corporations & Business Organizations § 4.8[A] (3d ed. 2014). A director defendant's duty of care may limit the actions he may take at a regular meeting. *See, e.g., Smith v. Van Gorkom*, 488 A.2d 858, 872-73 (Del. 1985), *overruled on other grounds by Gantler v. Stephens*, 965 A.2d 695 (Del. 2009).

[59]1992 WL 181717 (Del. Ch. July 28, 1992), *vacated by Stearn v. Koch*, 628 A.2d 44 (Del. 1993). *Koch* involved the removal, by the corporation's board at a special meeting, of a corporation's CEO (Stearn) who also held a majority of the corporation's common stock. The Court of Chancery (in a decision vacated by this Court) held that Stearn's removal was void because the notice of the special meeting was silent as to any possible consideration of Stearn's removal as CEO, thereby depriving Stearn of the opportunity to protect himself by changing the composition of the board (as the controlling shareholder) before the special meeting.

[60]2000 WL 1277372 (Del. Ch. Aug. 31, 2000). *VGS* involved a dispute between the managers of an LLC — Sahagen, who controlled 25% of the LLC's member interests, and Castiel, who controlled the remaining 75%. By non-unanimous written consent (as permitted by the LLC's operating agreement), two of the LLC's three managers (including Sahagen) effected a merger with a new Delaware corporation that essentially reversed Sahagen's and Castiel's ownership interests — without notice to Castiel. The Court of Chancery held that by effecting the merger without giving advance notice to Castiel (who could have removed one of the managers approving the merger), the managers violated their duty of loyalty to Castiel, and the merger was therefore invalid.

[61]2002 WL 205684 (Del. Ch. Jan. 25, 2002). *Adlerstein* involved a corporate board's approval, at a special meeting, of an investment proposal that issued preferred stock to an outside investor and thereby deprived one of the corporation's directors (Adlerstein) of voting control in his capacity as a corporate shareholder. Adlerstein was given no advance notice that the investment proposal would be presented or voted on at that meeting. The Court of Chancery held that the board's approval of the investment proposal "must be undone" because the failure to give Adlerstein advance notice of the investment proposal amounted to "trickery" and precluded Adlerstein from pre-empting the board's action by removing (in his capacity as a stockholder) the other corporate directors.

[62]2007 WL 4438978 (Del. Ch. Dec. 13, 2007). *Fogel* involved the purported removal (at a special meeting of the corporation's board) of a corporation's CEO (Fogel), who was vested with the authority to call a special meeting of the corporation's shareholders. The Court of Chancery held that no board meeting had actually taken place, and therefore the removal was ineffective. Alternatively, the court held that by not giving Fogel notice of the planned termination, the remaining directors tricked Fogel into attending the special meeting. In so doing, the court explained, the directors prevented Fogel from exercising his right to call a special shareholder meeting where the shareholders could have removed those directors adverse to Fogel.

[64]Unlike with regular meetings, directors must be given notice of special meetings. *See Lippman*, 95 A. at 898 ("It is, of course, fundamental that a special meeting held without due notice to all the directors is not lawful. . . .").

acted by non-unanimous written consent with no prior notice to the third manager. The effect of the challenged action was to deprive the third manager (in his capacity as an LLC member) of his majority ownership interest in the LLC. *VGS* is distinguishable factually from the circumstances presented here, and we view its holding as limited to its facts.

Next Klaassen argues that the Director Defendants failed to give him advance notice of multiple special meetings held before the November 1 regular Board meeting. That failure (Klaassen argues) violated both Allegro's Bylaws and Delaware law requiring advance notice for special meetings. This argument is unavailing, because (as the Court of Chancery found) the complained-of action — Klaassen's termination — did not occur at any pre-November 1 "special meetings." Rather, it occurred at the November 1 regular meeting of Allegro's Board. Although the Director Defendants may have discussed and prepared to terminate Klaassen before the November 1 meeting, they took no official Board action until they voted on the termination resolution at that meeting. For these reasons, Klaassen's advance notice claim fails.

B. Klaassen's Deception Claim Is Barred by Acquiescence

We turn next to Klaassen's deception-based claim, and uphold the Vice Chancellor's determination that that claim is barred by the equitable doctrine of acquiescence. Klaassen's claim that he was deceived by the Director Defendants during the November 1 Board meeting is equitable in nature. That being the case, any Board action that violated the Board's equitable obligations would be at most voidable and, as such, subject to equitable defenses. Lastly, we conclude that the Court of Chancery correctly found that Klaassen acquiesced in his removal as Allegro's CEO. Because a finding of acquiescence is sufficient to uphold the Court of Chancery's judgment, we do not reach or address the separate issue of whether Klaassen's claim is also barred by laches.

(1) Klaassen's Deception Claim Implicates Board Action That Is Voidable, Not Void

Klaassen claims that the Board action removing him as CEO at the November 1 meeting was invalid, because the Director Defendants employed deceptive tactics — namely, offering false reasons for rescheduling that meeting, and providing a false explanation for Mr. Ducanes' presence at that meeting. Our courts do not approve the use of deception as a means by which to conduct a Delaware corporation's affairs, and nothing in this Opinion should be read to suggest otherwise.[68] Here, however, we need not address the merits of Klaassen's deception claim, because we find, as did the Court of Chancery, that Klaassen acquiesced in his removal as CEO.

---

[68]*See, e.g., Schnell v. Chris-Craft Indus., Inc.,* 285 A.2d 437, 439 (Del. 1971) ("[I]nequitable action does not become permissible simply because it is legally possible.").

Klaassen challenges his removal as a violation of "generally accepted notions of fairness." A claim of that kind is equitable in character.[70] A fundamental principle of our law is that "he who seeks equity must do equity." Consequently, a plaintiff's equitable claim against a defendant may be defeated, in a proper case, by the plaintiff's inequitable conduct towards that defendant. It follows that board action taken in violation of equitable principles is voidable, not void, because "[o]nly voidable acts are susceptible to . . . equitable defenses."

This result is congruent with the well-established distinction between void and voidable corporate actions. As this Court discussed in *Michelson v. Duncan*, "[t]he essential distinction between voidable and void acts is that the former are those which may be found to have been performed in the interest of the corporation but beyond the authority of management, as distinguished from acts which are *ultra vires*, fraudulent or gifts or waste of corporate assets."

Klaassen contends, nonetheless, that the rule in Delaware is otherwise, because *Koch, VGS, Adlerstein,* and *Fogel* dictate that a board action carried out by means of deception is *per se* void, not voidable. Klaassen's argument finds arguable support in the language of those decisions. Regrettably, in writing those opinions, the authors may have been less than precise in their use of the terms "void" and "voidable." In *Fogel* and *Koch,* for example, the court stated that where deception is employed in the course of a board meeting, any action taken thereat is "void." Yet, in both opinions, the court implicitly acknowledged that the infirm board action was curable if the aggrieved director acquiesced by participating in the board meeting. The disconnect between the use of the term "void" and the acknowledgement that the deceptive action was curable (and, thus, voidable), renders these cases infirm as precedent on this specific issue. To the extent that those decisions can fairly be read to hold that board action taken in violation of an equitable rule is void, however, we overrule them.

(2) Klaassen Acquiesced in His Removal as CEO

Finally, having determined that Klaassen's deception claim is voidable and properly subject to equitable defenses, we address whether the Court of Chancery correctly found that Klaassen's claim was barred by the doctrine of acquiescence. We conclude that the court correctly so found. A claimant is deemed to have acquiesced in a complained-of act where he:

> has full knowledge of his rights and the material facts and (1) remains inactive for a considerable time; or (2) freely does what amounts to recognition of the complained of act; or (3) acts in a manner inconsistent with the subsequent repudiation, which leads the other party to believe the act has been approved.

---

[70]*See Hollinger Int'l, Inc. v. Black,* 844 A.2d 1022, 1077-78 (Del. Ch. 2004), *aff'd sub nom., Black v. Hollinger Int'l Inc.,* 872 A.2d 559 (Del. 2005) ("[T]here are two types of corporate law claims. The first is a legal claim, grounded in the argument that corporate action is improper because it violates a statute, the certificate of incorporation, a bylaw or other governing instrument, such as a contract. The second is an equitable claim, founded on the premise that the directors or officers have breached an equitable duty that they owe to the corporation and its stockholders."); *see also Pepsi-Cola Bottling Co. v. Woodlawn Canners, Inc.,* 1983 WL 18017, at *13 (Del. Ch. Mar. 14, 1983) ("The inequitable use of an otherwise legal right can be made subject to redress."). To the extent that Klaassen's deception claim stems from alleged fiduciary duty violations, it is also equitable in nature. *See QC Commc'ns Inc. v. Quartarone,* 2013 WL 1970069, at *1 (Del. Ch. May 14, 2013) ("[The complaint] states a claim for breach of fiduciary duty, an equitable claim — perhaps *the* quintessential equitable claim.").

For the defense of acquiescence to apply, conscious intent to approve the act is not required, nor is a change of position or resulting prejudice.

Klaassen does not claim that he lacked full knowledge of either his rights or the material facts. Accordingly, the narrow question is whether Klaassen's conduct amounted, in the eyes of the law, to recognition and acceptance of his removal as Allegro's CEO. We hold that it did. Shortly after his removal, Klaassen (without protest) helped Mr. Hood transition to his new role as CEO. Klaassen also negotiated a consulting agreement (which never came into effect) providing that he would report to Allegro's CEO and that Klaassen would not hold himself out as an Allegro employee or agent. Later, Klaassen proclaimed that he would hold Mr. Hood (as CEO) responsible for Allegro's performance, commented on Hood's employment contract, executed a written consent removing Hood from the audit committee due to Hood's role as CEO, and served as a compensation committee member. Whatever may have been Klaassen's subjective intent, his conduct objectively evidenced that he recognized and accepted the fact that he was no longer Allegro's CEO.

. . .

V. CONCLUSION

For the foregoing reasons, the Court of Chancery judgment is affirmed. Jurisdiction is not retained.

Post-Case Follow-Up

On April 1, 2014, DGCL § 204 of the DGCL took effect. This section (an amendment to the DGCL) was designed to address the power of the Court of Chancery to remedy voidable corporate acts and also to provide a nonjudicial option to address certain such situations. Section 204 provides, in pertinent part, as follows:

(a) Subject to subsection (f) of this section, no defective corporate act or putative stock shall be void or voidable solely as a result of a failure of authorization if ratified as provided in this section or validated by the Court of Chancery in a proceeding brought under § 205 of this title.

(b)(1) In order to ratify 1 or more defective corporate acts pursuant to this section (other than the ratification of an election of the initial board of directors pursuant to paragraph (b)(2) of this section), the board of directors of the corporation shall adopt resolutions stating:

(A) The defective corporate act or acts to be ratified;

(B) The date of each defective corporate act or acts;

(C) If such defective corporate act or acts involved the issuance of shares of putative stock, the number and type of shares of putative stock issued, and the date or dates upon which such putative shares were purported to have been issued;

(D) The nature of the failure of authorization in respect of each defective corporate act to be ratified; and

(E) That the board of directors approves the ratification of the defective corporate act or acts.

Klaassen v. Allegro Development Corp.: Real Life Applications

You represent Acme, Inc., a Delaware corporation. Earlier today, Acme's CEO called you on the telephone and explained that she and the rest of Acme's board have profound disagreements over the strategy and the direction of the company. The CEO asks whether the rest of the board has the power to oust her as CEO. As the CEO also serves as a director, she asks whether she can be ousted from her director role, as well. Acme's board is not staggered, and the corporation's charter does not alter default rules respecting director removal or notice.

a. Does the telephone call raise any ethical issues for you as Acme's lawyer?
b. Does the board have the power to oust the CEO from her executive role?
c. Does the board have the power to remove the CEO from the board of directors? Does it matter whether the removal is for cause? Without cause?
d. Assume that the board convenes a regularly scheduled meeting where the directors vote to oust the CEO from her executive role. The CEO did not receive prior notice of this meeting. Was the vote to remove the CEO ineffective for lack of notice? What if the meeting had been a special meeting of the board?

Quorum

Directors cannot take action at any meeting unless a **quorum** is present. Generally, a quorum consists of a majority of the number of directors as fixed in the articles or bylaws. Although the articles or bylaws may provide that a greater number than a majority is needed for a quorum, they may not provide that a quorum consists of less than one-third of the prescribed number of directors. MBCA § 8.24. Assume the bylaws of a corporation prescribe that there shall be nine directors. Unless other provisions exist, a quorum will be five directors (regardless of board vacancies). Once five board members are present, action may be taken. These quorum requirements are typically relaxed with regard to filling vacancies. If the number of directors remaining in office is insufficient to constitute a quorum, the directors may fill a vacancy by the affirmative vote of those directors remaining.

Conducting the Meeting

Action is taken by directors at meetings by majority vote, unless the articles or bylaws require approval by a greater number of directors. Assuming a nine-member board, once a quorum is established, in this case five members, action may be taken by a majority of those present (in this case, three). Each director is entitled to one vote on each issue presented at the meeting. Because the number of directors is manageable, a showing of hands or a voice vote is usually acceptable. Action taken at meetings is by resolutions passed by the board of directors. According to MBCA § 8.24(d), a director who is present at a meeting when action is taken is presumed to have agreed with the action unless his dissent is entered in the minutes. Thus, if the vote is not unanimous, each director's respective vote should be reflected in the minutes of the meeting so that if liability arises with respect to action taken by the board, it can be readily determined which directors, if any, violated their duties to the corporation.

The modern statutes recognize the difficulty of gathering a quorum for a meeting, and, therefore, most states (and the MBCA) permit directors to be present at meetings through conference calls or any other means of communication by which the parties may simultaneously hear each other. These statutes would therefore likely permit directors' meetings via the Internet. *See, e.g.,* MBCA § 8.30(b). Many corporations use videoconferencing to conduct directors' meetings.

Proxies

Generally, directors cannot act or vote by proxy. As discussed in more detail in Chapter 9, directors have a fiduciary duty to the corporation and must make a fully informed decision using their personal judgment. Thus, they cannot delegate these duties to a proxy.

Minutes

Minutes of directors' meetings are usually taken and signed by the corporate secretary. There is no required format for minutes, but they should reflect the action taken on each matter or resolution presented and should recite that notice was properly given, or that directors have signed appropriate waivers of notice (which are then placed in the minute book), that a quorum was present, and that certain actions were taken. They should include details of any other pertinent matters. See Exhibit 8.19 for typical minutes of a directors' meeting.

EXHIBIT 8.19 **Sample Minutes of Regular Meeting of Board of Directors**

A regular meeting of the Board of Directors of FTB, Inc., a Delaware Corporation (the "Corporation"), was held on Tuesday, June 2, 2015, at 9:00 A.M. at the principal offices of the Corporation located at 1024 Fifteenth Street, N.W., Washington D.C. 20005.

The following persons, constituting all of the Directors of the Corporation, were present at the meeting: Lisa Black, Christopher Wagner, Kenneth Lyons, William Brady, and Patricia E. Moore.

The Chairman of the Board of the Corporation, Frederick G. Tellam, presided as Chairman of the meeting, and Diana Hendrix acted as its Secretary.

The Chairman called the meeting to order and stated that a quorum of directors was present for the meeting.

The Secretary announced that the meeting was called pursuant to Article IX of the Bylaws.

The Secretary read the minutes of the last regular meeting of the Board of Directors. The minutes were approved and placed in the corporate minute book.

EXHIBIT 8.19   **(continued)**

A discussion was had on the proposed lease for the Corporation's offices in Maryland, the Corporation's financial status, including the need for additional sums for operating expenses, and dividends to be paid on the outstanding common shares of the Corporation.

After motions duly made, seconded, and carried, the following resolutions were unanimously adopted by the Board of Directors:

RESOLVED, that the proposed lease between the Corporation and Josephine LaPointe for the premises located at 511 State Street, Baltimore, Maryland, is commercially reasonable and in the best interests of the Corporation and the lease is approved.

RESOLVED, that the Treasurer of the Corporation is authorized to borrow on behalf of the Corporation from one or more banks or other lending institutions such amount as the Treasurer determines necessary to meet the operating needs of the Corporation, and on such terms as the Treasurer may determine, but in no event may the Treasurer borrow more than the sum of $300,000 in total.

RESOLVED, the Corporation shall pay a cash dividend from its capital surplus to those persons identified as owners of its common shares on its books as of June 2, 2015, in the amount of $1.50 per share. The payment date for said dividend shall be July 10, 2015.

The officers were instructed to take appropriate action to effect the purposes of these resolutions.

There being no further business before the meeting, on motion duly made, seconded, and unanimously carried, it was adjourned.

Date: _____   _____
                                              Diana Hendrix, Secretary

6. Directors' Action Without a Meeting

Recognizing the difficulty of getting directors together for a meeting, all states (and MBCA § 8.21) permit directors to take action without a meeting if they unanimously consent in writing. Written consents are popular both for large corporations whose directors may reside in different places and for small corporations that might not take the time to have formal meetings for each action taken. This is a now a very common method of taking board action. The procedure and format of the written consent action for directors is nearly identical to that for shareholders. A document expressing the action to be taken is circulated to all directors for signature. Alternatively, the directors can sign counterparts or separate documents that are then compiled and placed in the minute book. Delaware allows its directors to act by electronic transmission, thus allowing written consents to be effected through e-mail. See Exhibit 8.20 for a sample action by written consent of directors. Written consents generally are effective as of the last-dated signature.

EXHIBIT 8.20 **Sample Action by Written Consent of Directors**

The undersigned, constituting all of the Directors of FTB, Inc. (the "Corporation"), hereby take the following actions by written consent pursuant to Del. Code Ann. tit. 8, § 141(f) and Article IV of the bylaws of the Corporation as if present at a meeting duly called pursuant to notice.

RESOLVED, the Directors approve the hiring of Celia G. Spencer as General Counsel for the Corporation, effective March 2, 2015, to perform such duties and at a salary as determined by the President of the Corporation.

RESOLVED, the Certificate of Incorporation shall be amended to change the name of the Corporation to FTB Access Link, Co. and to increase the aggregate number of common shares which may be issued by the Corporation to 100,000, said actions to be voted on by the shareholders of the Corporation pursuant to a special meeting to be called therefor by the President of the Corporation.

The officers of the Corporation are hereby authorized to take appropriate action to effect the purposes of these resolutions.

Date: _____   _____
                                                                          Lisa Black

Date: _____   _____
                                                                   Christopher Wagner

Date: _____   _____
                                                                       Kenneth Lyons

Date: _____   _____
                                                                        William Brady

Date: _____   _____
                                                                      Patricia E. Moore

7. Compensation of Directors

The older view was that directors were not required to be compensated merely for serving as directors. Directors were typically shareholders who, having a substantial financial stake in the corporation's affairs, would be amply rewarded through dividends and growth of the corporation. Most statutes now allow for compensation of directors pursuant to the articles or bylaws or pursuant to action by shareholders or even by the board itself. The MBCA and most states provide that directors may fix their own compensation unless the articles or bylaws provide otherwise. MBCA § 8.11. The safeguard against directors establishing inappropriately high compensation for themselves is provided by the fiduciary duties owed by directors, the directors' liability for self-dealing, and the shareholders' ability to remove directors. Most modern large corporations fix a substantial annual sum to be paid to directors as compensation, as well as a significant stipend, often $1,000, per meeting. Courts are reluctant to interfere with director compensation, and a complaining shareholder must generally prove that the compensation is excessive when compared to that paid to others in similar businesses. Publicly traded corporations must disclose the compensation paid to their top five executives over the past three years. Compensation might include not only salary, but also grants of stock, stock options, enhanced benefits, and bonuses.

D. OFFICERS

1. Introduction

Corporate officers are responsible for implementing board policies and decisions. The traditional **officers** of a corporation are president, vice president, secretary, and treasurer. A corporation may have more or fewer officers, if needed. The officers carry out day-to-day corporate activities and are selected, supervised, and removed by the board of directors.

2. Qualifications, Appointment, and Tenure

Some statutes require that the president or chief executive officer be a director. Most statutes, however, impose no qualifications or restrictions on those who can serve as officers. Officers are typically selected or appointed by the board of directors, although some jurisdictions allow the shareholders to elect officers. See Exhibit 8.21 for a sample resolution appointing officers.

EXHIBIT 8.21 **Resolution Appointing Officers**

RESOLVED, effective immediately, the following persons are appointed to serve in the following corporate offices, at the pleasure of the Board of Directors, at the annual salary set forth next to their names.

President: Francis Fisher	$100,000
Vice President: Timothy J. Mislock	$85,000
Secretary: Nicola Pellegrini	$75,000
Treasurer: James Crittenden	$75,000

Each officer shall have the duties specified in the bylaws and as may be designated by the Board of Directors of the Corporation.

Details regarding officers often are included in corporate bylaws. Exhibit 8.22 contains an excerpt from the General Electric bylaws concerning the appointment of officers.

EXHIBIT 8.22   **Excerpt, Article VI, General Electric Bylaws**

Article IV
Officers
A. As determined by the Board of Directors, the officers of this Company shall include:

1. A Chairman of the Board, who shall be chosen by the Directors from their own number. The Chairman of the Board shall be the Chief Executive Officer of the Company and in that capacity shall have general management, subject to the control of the Board of Directors, of the business of the Company, including the appointment of all officers and employees of the Company for whose election or appointment no other provisions is made in these By-laws; he shall also have the power, at any time, to discharge or remove any officer or employee of the Company, subject to the action thereon of the Board of Directors, and shall perform all other duties appropriate to this office. The Chairman of the Board shall preside at all meetings of Directors, and he may at any time call any meeting of the Board of Directors; he may also at his discretion call or attend any meeting of any committee of the Board, whether or not a member of such committee.

2. One or more Vice Chairmen, who shall also be chosen by the Directors. The Board may designate one or more of the Vice Chairmen to be Executive Officers of the Company accountable to the Chief Executive Officer.

3. A President of the Company, who shall be chosen by the Directors from their own number. The office of President will normally be vested in the Chairman of the Board, provided, however, that in the discretion of the Board, the position of President may be established independent of, but accountable to, the Chairman during transition periods.

4. Two or more Vice Presidents, one or more of whom may also be designated Executive Vice Presidents or Senior Vice Presidents accountable to the Chief Executive Officer.

5. A Chief Financial Officer, who shall be the principal financial officer of the Company, and who shall have such duties as the Board, by resolution, shall determine. In the absence or disability of the Chief Financial Officer, the Chairman of the Board may designate a person to exercise the powers of such office.

6. A Controller and a Treasurer who shall be officers of the Company. The Controller and Treasurer shall perform such duties as may be assigned by the Chief Financial Officer. In the absence or disability of the Controller or Treasurer, the Chairman of the Board may designate a person to execute the powers of such office.

7. A Secretary, who shall record in proper books to be kept for that purpose and have custody of the minutes of the meetings of the shareholders of the Company and of meetings of the Board of Directors and of committees of the Board (other than the compensation committee) and who shall be responsible for the custody and care of the seal of the Company. He shall attend to the giving and serving of all notices of the Company and perform such other duties as may be imposed upon him by the Board of Directors. The Secretary may appoint an Associate Secretary and Attesting Secretaries, each of whom shall have the power to affix and attest the corporate seal of the Company, and to attest the execution of documents on behalf of th (sic) Company and who shall perform such other duties as may be assigned by the Secretary; and in the absence or disability of the Secretary, the Associate Secretary may be designated by the Chairman to exercise the powers of the Secretary.

8. Such other officers as the Board may from time to time appoint.

It is often said that officers serve "at the pleasure of the board," meaning the directors have the authority to remove officers at any time, either with or without cause. *See* MBCA § 8.43(b). Some officers, however, serve pursuant to an employment contract. In such case, removal of an officer contrary to the terms of the contract subjects the corporation to damages caused by the breach. In most instances, boards who remove officers must continue to pay them their contractually stipulated salary, much the same way some coaches of athletic teams are "bought out" of their contracts. In fact, MBCA § 8.44 expressly states that an officer's removal does not affect the officer's contract with the corporation. An officer may generally resign at any time by simply delivering notice of the resignation to the board of directors. Directors select replacements to fill vacancies in offices. Some senior officers may be allowed by the board of directors to appoint other inferior officers or assistant officers.

3. Officers' Functions

The range of functions performed by the officers is extremely broad. In general, officers perform whatever functions are delegated to them by the directors. In large corporations, the board of directors may establish a policy or goal and then charge the officers with achieving the objective. For example, the board of a large corporation engaged in the manufacture of cars may determine that the corporation should introduce a new sports car into the market. The officers may be told, in effect, "Make it happen." The officers would then engage engineers, commission market studies, approve advertising, and perform all other tasks so that the board's goal is met.

MBCA § 8.41 provides that officers have the authority and shall perform the duties set forth in the bylaws or the duties prescribed by the directors. Typically, the only functions statutorily imposed on officers are that one of the officers shall have the responsibility for preparing minutes of the meetings of directors and shareholders and maintaining and authenticating records for the corporation (e.g., maintaining the articles and bylaws of the corporation).

One common duty performed by various officers, especially by corporate secretaries, is to certify that certain facts are true or documents are correct. These certificates are often provided in connection with a corporate transaction such as a sale of assets or a merger. The officer will certify that copies of articles and bylaws are true and correct, that the president's signature is valid, and that various resolutions were passed to approve the transaction. If time elapses between the date of the certificate and the date of the closing of the transaction, the officer may be asked to provide a **bringdown certificate** verifying that no changes have occurred since the date of the original certificate, so as to assure the other party or a state agency that there have been no material changes in the corporation's status or documents since the original certificate was issued.

4. Titles of Officers

The MBCA does not require any specific officers. Some states, however, do require specific officers. The corporation's bylaws may describe the officers desired, or the board of directors may appoint officers as needed. While the most common officers are president, vice president, secretary, and treasurer, a corporation is not limited by these titles and is free to create other officer positions with other titles. For example, a large corporation may have a treasurer, a chief financial officer, and a comptroller, each with specific duties relating to the financial affairs of the corporation. (The excerpt of General Electric's bylaws reproduced at Exhibit 8.22 provides for a Treasurer, CFO, and Controller.) Many corporations create officer positions by adding to the title "assistant" or "executive," such as assistant secretary, executive vice president, and so forth. Under the modern approach, and that taken by the MBCA, one person may simultaneously hold more than one corporate office. A few states, however, prohibit the same person from acting as president and secretary, generally because those are the two officers whose signatures are usually required when stock certificates are issued.

President

The president of a corporation generally presides at directors' and shareholders' meetings and performs all duties assigned by the board of directors. Often, the president acts as general manager of the corporation.

Vice President

The vice president acts in the place of the president in his absence and assists the president. Some large corporations will have numerous vice presidents, with various titles such as senior vice president, vice president of marketing, vice president of human resources, administrative vice president, and the like.

Secretary

The corporation's secretary usually has the responsibility for taking minutes of meetings of directors and shareholders and ensuring the minute book is kept in proper condition. The corporate secretary may retain custody of the corporate seal, maintain the list of shareholders, authenticate documents, and prepare and furnish other reports, correspondence, and notices, such as notices of shareholders' meetings.

Treasurer

The treasurer is the fiscal officer of the corporation and has responsibility for receiving, maintaining, and disbursing corporate funds, paying taxes, and maintaining and preparing financial records.

Other Officers

Many corporations appoint a **chief executive officer** (CEO) who will supervise all of the other officers, preside over meetings of directors and shareholders, and have primary responsibility for managing the corporation. A **chair** of the board, if appointed, is a board member who presides at directors' meetings and performs such duties as may be assigned by the board. In public companies, a recent trend is to separate the positions of chair and CEO. In fact, ProxyMonitor.org reported that in 2014, shareholders commonly proposed that their corporations separate such positions, primarily to ensure more transparency and independence. Those who advocate that the positions should be combined typically assert that corporations should have one strong executive with clear and unambiguous authority so that the corporation is managed more effectively. A **chief financial officer** (CFO) keeps all financial records and has responsibility for receiving money on behalf of the corporation, depositing money as directed by the board, disbursing money as directed, paying taxes, and preparing various reports relating to the financial affairs of the corporation. A **chief operating officer** (COO) is responsible for overseeing the company's operations.

5. Authority of Officers

Because the authority given officers comes from the board of directors, officers are agents of the corporation. Thus, the general agency principles discussed in Chapter 2 apply to them. As agents, officers may have authority to bind the corporation. This authority can be **actual authority** (meaning express authority or direction given to them by the corporation's governing documents or the board), **apparent authority** (authority that another believes the officer possesses due to the officer's conduct or position), or **inherent authority** (authority that flows naturally from an officer's position so he can carry out his duties).

E. BYLAWS

Introduction

As our discussion thus far suggests, many of the rules relating to shareholder and board action are contained within corporate bylaws. These bylaws typically address, among other topics, notice and quorum requirements for shareholder meetings, voting standards, number and qualifications of directors, etc. When drafting and reviewing bylaws, it is important to have both the relevant state corporations code and the corporation's charter handy, as both "trump" the rules set forth in the bylaws in cases of conflict.

It is fairly common for a corporation to amend its bylaws. Under the MBCA, both the board and the shareholders have the power unilaterally to amend the bylaws. *See* MBCA § 10.20. That power can be limited, or in some cases eliminated with respect to the board (but not shareholders), via the corporation's charter or certain other provisions of the corporations code. *See id.* The rule in Delaware is slightly different. The DGCL provides that shareholders have the power unilaterally to amend bylaws, but the board does not. DGCL § 109. A corporation may confer the power to amend upon the board, however, via a charter provision. *Id.* It is typical for Delaware corporations to include a provision authorizing board-initiated amendments to the bylaws in the charter.

Case Preview	*CA, Inc. v. AFSCME Employees Pension Plan*

Shareholders' statutory right to amend bylaws enjoys a unique status under the corporate law, and you might think that the right to initiate bylaw amendments would give shareholders broad authority to exert control over corporate affairs. This is not the case, however, as the scope of permissible shareholder amendments to corporate bylaws is constrained by corporations codes and the power and responsibility of the board to manage the business and affairs of the corporation. In our next case, shareholders submitted a proposed bylaw amendment that stated that the board of directors "shall cause the corporation to reimburse a stockholder or group of stockholders (together, the "Nominator") for reasonable expenses ("Expenses") incurred in connection with nominating one or more candidates in a contested election of directors to the corporation's board of directors." In reading this case, consider the following questions:

1. On what basis did the corporation seek to exclude the proposed bylaw amendment from the company's proxy materials?
2. On what basis did the shareholders argue that the proposed bylaw should be included in the company's proxy materials?
3. What does DGCL § 109 have to say about the proper scope and contents of corporate bylaws?
4. Why did the SEC certify two questions of law to the Delaware court? What were those questions?
5. Is the proposed bylaw a proper subject of shareholder action, according to the court? Why or why not?
6. Can you explain the court's distinction between (permissible) bylaws that define processes and procedures by which corporate decisions are made and (impermissible) proposed bylaws that would mandate how the board should decide specific substantive business issues?
7. Would the bylaw, as drafted, cause CA, Inc. to violate Delaware law, according to the court? Why or why not?

CA, Inc. v. AFSCME Employees Pension Plan
953 A.2d 227 (Del. 2008)

JACOBS, Justice.*

This proceeding arises from a certification by the United States Securities and Exchange Commission (the "SEC"), to this Court, of two questions of law pursuant to Article IV, Section 11(8) of the Delaware Constitution and Supreme Court Rule 41.

. . .

I. FACTS

CA is a Delaware corporation whose board of directors consists of twelve persons, all of whom sit for reelection each year. CA's annual meeting of stockholders is scheduled to be held on September 9, 2008. CA intends to file its definitive proxy materials with the SEC on or about July 24, 2008 in connection with that meeting.

AFSCME, a CA stockholder, is associated with the American Federation of State, County and Municipal Employees. On March 13, 2008, AFSCME submitted a proposed stockholder bylaw (the "Bylaw" or "proposed Bylaw") for inclusion in the Company's proxy materials for its 2008 annual meeting of stockholders. The Bylaw, if adopted by CA stockholders, would amend the Company's bylaws to provide as follows:

> RESOLVED, that pursuant to section 109 of the Delaware General Corporation Law and Article IX of the bylaws of CA, Inc., stockholders of CA hereby amend the bylaws to add the following Section 14 to Article II:
>
> The board of directors shall cause the corporation to reimburse a stockholder or group of stockholders (together, the "Nominator") for reasonable expenses ("Expenses") incurred in connection with nominating one or more candidates in a contested election of directors to the corporation's board of directors, including, without limitation, printing, mailing, legal, solicitation, travel, advertising and public relations expenses, so long as (a) the election of fewer than 50% of the directors to be elected is contested in the election, (b) one or more candidates nominated by the Nominator are elected to the corporation's board of directors, (c) stockholders are not permitted to cumulate their votes for directors, and (d) the election occurred, and the Expenses were incurred, after this bylaw's adoption. The amount paid to a Nominator under this bylaw in respect of a contested election shall not exceed the amount expended by the corporation in connection with such election.

CA's current bylaws and Certificate of Incorporation have no provision that specifically addresses the reimbursement of proxy expenses. Of more general relevance, however, is Article SEVENTH, Section (1) of CA's Certificate of Incorporation, which tracks the language of 8 Del. C. § 141(a) and provides that:

> The management of the business and the conduct of the affairs of the corporation shall be vested in [CA's] Board of Directors.

---

*Most footnotes have been omitted for purposes of brevity.

It is undisputed that the decision whether to reimburse election expenses is presently vested in the discretion of CA's board of directors, subject to their fiduciary duties and applicable Delaware law.

On April 18, 2008, CA notified the SEC's Division of Corporation Finance (the "Division") of its intention to exclude the proposed Bylaw from its 2008 proxy materials. The Company requested from the Division a "no-action letter" stating that the Division would not recommend any enforcement action to the SEC if CA excluded the AFSCME proposal.[2] CA's request for a no-action letter was accompanied by an opinion from its Delaware counsel, Richards Layton & Finger, P.A. ("RL & F"). The RL & F opinion concluded that the proposed Bylaw is not a proper subject for stockholder action, and that if implemented, the Bylaw would violate the Delaware General Corporation Law ("DGCL").

On May 21, 2008, AFSCME responded to CA's no-action request with a letter taking the opposite legal position. The AFSCME letter was accompanied by an opinion from AFSCME's Delaware counsel, Grant & Eisenhofer, P.A. ("G & E"). The G & E opinion concluded that the proposed Bylaw is a proper subject for shareholder action and that if adopted, would be permitted under Delaware law.

The Division was thus confronted with two conflicting legal opinions on Delaware law. Whether or not the Division would determine that CA may exclude the proposed Bylaw from its 2008 proxy materials would depend upon which of these conflicting views is legally correct. To obtain guidance, the SEC, at the Division's request, certified two questions of Delaware law to this Court. Given the short time-frame for the filing of CA's proxy materials, we concluded that "there are important and urgent reasons for an immediate determination of the questions certified," and accepted those questions for review on July 1, 2008.

II. THE CERTIFIED QUESTIONS

The two questions certified to us by the SEC are as follows:

1. Is the AFSCME Proposal a proper subject for action by shareholders as a matter of Delaware law?
2. Would the AFSCME Proposal, if adopted, cause CA to violate any Delaware law to which it is subject?

III. THE FIRST QUESTION

A. Preliminary Comments

The first question presented is whether the Bylaw is a proper subject for shareholder action, more precisely, whether the Bylaw may be proposed and enacted by

---

[2]Under Sections (i)(1) and (i)(2) of SEC Rule 14a-8, a company may exclude a stockholder proposal from its proxy statement if the proposal "is not a proper subject for action by the shareholders under the laws of the jurisdiction of the company's organization," or where the proposal, if implemented, "would cause the company to violate any state law to which it is subject." *See* 17 C.F.R. § 240.14a-8.

shareholders without the concurrence of the Company's board of directors. Before proceeding further, we make some preliminary comments in an effort to delineate a framework within which to begin our analysis.

First, the DGCL empowers both the board of directors and the shareholders of a Delaware corporation to adopt, amend or repeal the corporation's bylaws. 8 Del. C. § 109(a) relevantly provides that:

> After a corporation has received any payment for any of its stock, the power to adopt, amend or repeal bylaws shall be in the stockholders entitled to vote . . . ; provided, however, any corporation may, in its certificate of incorporation, confer the power to adopt, amend or repeal bylaws upon the directors. . . . The fact that such power has been so conferred upon the directors . . . shall not divest the stockholders . . . of the power, nor limit their power to adopt, amend or repeal bylaws.

Pursuant to Section 109(a), CA's Certificate of Incorporation confers the power to adopt, amend or repeal the bylaws upon the Company's board of directors. Because the statute commands that that conferral "shall not divest the stockholders . . . of . . . nor limit" their power, both the board and the shareholders of CA, independently and concurrently, possess the power to adopt, amend and repeal the bylaws.

Second, the vesting of that concurrent power in both the board and the shareholders raises the issue of whether the stockholders' power is coextensive with that of the board, and vice versa. As a purely theoretical matter that is possible, and were that the case, then the first certified question would be easily answered. That is, under such a regime any proposal to adopt, amend or repeal a bylaw would be a proper subject for either shareholder or board action, without distinction. But the DGCL has not allocated to the board and the shareholders the identical, coextensive power to adopt, amend and repeal the bylaws. Therefore, how that power is allocated between those two decision-making bodies requires an analysis that is more complex.

Moving from the theoretical to this case, by its terms Section 109(a) vests in the shareholders a power to adopt, amend or repeal bylaws that is legally sacrosanct, *i.e.,* the power cannot be non-consensually eliminated or limited by anyone other than the legislature itself. If viewed in isolation, Section 109(a) could be read to make the board's and the shareholders' power to adopt, amend or repeal bylaws identical and coextensive, but Section 109(a) does not exist in a vacuum. It must be read together with 8 Del. C. § 141(a), which pertinently provides that:

> The business and affairs of every corporation organized under this chapter shall be managed by or under the direction of a board of directors, except as may be otherwise provided in this chapter or in its certificate of incorporation.

No such broad management power is statutorily allocated to the shareholders. Indeed, it is well-established that stockholders of a corporation subject to the DGCL may not directly manage the business and affairs of the corporation, at least without specific authorization in either the statute or the certificate of incorporation. Therefore, the shareholders' statutory power to adopt, amend or repeal bylaws is not coextensive with the board's concurrent power and is limited by the board's management prerogatives under Section 141(a).[7]

Third, it follows that, to decide whether the Bylaw proposed by AFSCME is a proper subject for shareholder action under Delaware law, we must first determine: (1) the scope or reach of the shareholders' power to adopt, alter or repeal the bylaws of a Delaware corporation, and then (2) whether the Bylaw at issue here falls within that permissible scope. Where, as here, the proposed bylaw is one that limits director authority, that is an elusively difficult task. As one noted scholar has put it, "the efforts to distinguish by-laws that permissibly limit director authority from by-laws that impermissibly do so have failed to provide a coherent analytical structure, and the pertinent statutes provide no guidelines for distinction at all." The tools that are available to this Court to answer those questions are other provisions of the DGCL and Delaware judicial decisions that can be brought to bear on this question.

B. Analysis

1.

Two other provisions of the DGCL, 8 Del. C. §§ 109(b) and 102(b)(1), bear importantly on the first question and form the basis of contentions advanced by each side. Section 109(b), which deals generally with bylaws and what they must or may contain, provides that:

> The bylaws may contain any provision, not inconsistent with law or with the certificate of incorporation, relating to the business of the corporation, the conduct of its affairs, and its rights or powers or the rights or powers of its stockholders, directors, officers or employees.

And Section 102(b)(1), which is part of a broader provision that addresses what the certificate of incorporation must or may contain, relevantly states that:

> (b) In addition to the matters required to be set forth in the certificate of incorporation by subsection (a) of this section, the certificate of incorporation may also contain any or all of the following matters:
>
> (1) Any provision for the management of the business and for the conduct of the affairs of the corporation, and any provision creating, defining, limiting and regulating the powers of the corporation, the directors and the stockholders, or any class of the stockholders . . . ; if such provisions are not contrary to the laws of this State. Any provision which is required or permitted by any section of this chapter to be stated in the bylaws may instead be stated in the certificate of incorporation.

AFSCME relies heavily upon the language of Section 109(b), which permits the bylaws of a corporation to contain "any provision . . . relating to the . . . rights or powers of its stockholders [and] directors. . . ." The Bylaw, AFSCME argues, "relates

---

[7]Because the board's managerial authority under Section 141(a) is a cardinal precept of the DGCL, we do not construe Section 109 as an "except[ion] . . . otherwise specified in th[e] [DGCL]" to Section 141(a). Rather, the shareholders' statutory power to adopt, amend or repeal bylaws under Section 109 cannot be "inconsistent with law," including Section 141(a).

to" the right of the stockholders meaningfully to participate in the process of electing directors, a right that necessarily "includes the right to nominate an opposing slate."

CA argues, in response, that Section 109(b) is not dispositive, because it cannot be read in isolation from, and without regard to, Section 102(b)(1). CA's argument runs as follows: the Bylaw would limit the substantive decision-making authority of CA's board to decide whether or not to expend corporate funds for a particular purpose, here, reimbursing director election expenses. Section 102(b)(1) contemplates that any provision that limits the broad statutory power of the directors must be contained in the certificate of incorporation.[11] Therefore, the proposed Bylaw can only be in CA's Certificate of Incorporation, as distinguished from its bylaws. Accordingly, the proposed bylaw falls outside the universe of permissible bylaws authorized by Section 109(b).

Implicit in CA's argument is the premise that *any* bylaw that in *any* respect might be viewed as limiting or restricting the power of the board of directors automatically falls outside the scope of permissible bylaws. That simply cannot be. That reasoning, taken to its logical extreme, would result in eliminating altogether the shareholders' statutory right to adopt, amend or repeal bylaws. Bylaws, by their very nature, set down rules and procedures that bind a corporation's board and its shareholders. In that sense, most, if not all, bylaws could be said to limit the otherwise unlimited discretionary power of the board. Yet Section 109(a) carves out an area of shareholder power to adopt, amend or repeal bylaws that is expressly inviolate. Therefore, to argue that the Bylaw at issue here limits the board's power to manage the business and affairs of the Company only begins, but cannot end, the analysis needed to decide whether the Bylaw is a proper subject for shareholder action. The question left unanswered is what is the scope of shareholder action that Section 109(b) permits yet does not improperly intrude upon the directors' power to manage corporation's business and affairs under Section 141(a).

It is at this juncture that the statutory language becomes only marginally helpful in determining what the Delaware legislature intended to be the lawful scope of the shareholders' power to adopt, amend and repeal bylaws. To resolve that issue, the Court must resort to different tools, namely, decisions of this Court and of the Court of Chancery that bear on this question. Those tools do not enable us to articulate with doctrinal exactitude a bright line that divides those bylaws that shareholders may unilaterally adopt under Section 109(b) from those which they may not under Section 141(a). They do, however, enable us to decide the issue presented in this specific case.

2.

It is well-established Delaware law that a proper function of bylaws is not to mandate how the board should decide specific substantive business decisions, but rather, to define the process and procedures by which those decisions are made. As the Court of Chancery has noted:

---

[11]8 Del. C. § 102(b)(1) pertinently provides that the "the certificate of incorporation may also contain . . . any provision . . . limiting . . . the powers of . . . the directors."

Traditionally, the bylaws have been the corporate instrument used to set forth the rules by which the corporate board conducts its business. To this end, the DGCL is replete with specific provisions authorizing the bylaws to establish the procedures through which board and committee action is taken. . . . [T]here is a general consensus that bylaws that regulate the process by which the board acts are statutorily authorized.

* * *

. . . I reject International's argument that that provision in the Bylaw Amendments impermissibly interferes with the board's authority under § 141(a) to manage the business and affairs of the corporation. Sections 109 and 141, taken in totality, . . . make clear that bylaws may pervasively and strictly regulate the process by which boards act, subject to the constraints of equity.

Examples of the procedural, process-oriented nature of bylaws are found in both the DGCL and the case law. For example, 8 Del. C. § 141(b) authorizes bylaws that fix the number of directors on the board, the number of directors required for a quorum (with certain limitations), and the vote requirements for board action. 8 Del. C. § 141(f) authorizes bylaws that preclude board action without a meeting.[17] And, almost three decades ago this Court upheld a shareholder-enacted bylaw requiring unanimous board attendance and board approval for any board action, and unanimous ratification of any committee action. Such purely procedural bylaws do not improperly encroach upon the board's managerial authority under Section 141(a).

The process-creating function of bylaws provides a starting point to address the Bylaw at issue. It enables us to frame the issue in terms of whether the Bylaw is one that establishes or regulates a process for substantive director decision-making, or one that mandates the decision itself. Not surprisingly, the parties sharply divide on that question. We conclude that the Bylaw, even though infelicitously couched as a substantive-sounding mandate to expend corporate funds, has both the intent and the effect of regulating the process for electing directors of CA. Therefore, we determine that the Bylaw is a proper subject for shareholder action, and set forth our reasoning below.

Although CA concedes that "restrictive procedural bylaws (such as those requiring the presence of all directors and unanimous board consent to take action) are acceptable," it points out that even facially procedural bylaws can unduly intrude upon board authority. The Bylaw being proposed here is unduly intrusive, CA claims, because, by mandating reimbursement of a stockholder's proxy expenses, it limits the board's broad discretionary authority to decide whether to grant reimbursement at all. CA further claims that because (in defined circumstances) the Bylaw mandates the expenditure of corporate funds, its subject matter is necessarily

---

[17]*See also, e.g.,* 8 Del. C. § 211(a) & (b) (bylaws may establish the date and the place of the annual meeting of the stockholders); § 211(d) (bylaws may specify the conditions for the calling of special meetings of stockholders); § 216 (bylaws may establish quorum and vote requirements for meetings of stockholders and "[a] bylaw amendment adopted by stockholders which specifies the votes that shall be necessary for the election of directors shall not be further amended or repealed by the board of directors."); § 222 (bylaws may regulate certain notice requirements regarding adjourned meetings of stockholders).

substantive, not process-oriented, and, therefore falls outside the scope of what Section 109(b) permits.

Because the Bylaw is couched as a command to reimburse ("The board of directors shall cause the corporation to reimburse a stockholder"), it lends itself to CA's criticism. But the Bylaw's wording, although relevant, is not dispositive of whether or not it is process-related. The Bylaw could easily have been worded differently, to emphasize its process, as distinguished from its mandatory payment, component. By saying this we do not mean to suggest that this Bylaw's reimbursement component can be ignored. What we do suggest is that a bylaw that requires the expenditure of corporate funds does not, for that reason alone, become automatically deprived of its process-related character. A hypothetical example illustrates the point. Suppose that the directors of a corporation live in different states and at a considerable distance from the corporation's headquarters. Suppose also that the shareholders enact a bylaw that requires all meetings of directors to take place in person at the corporation's headquarters. Such a bylaw would be clearly process-related, yet it cannot be supposed that the shareholders would lack the power to adopt the bylaw because it would require the corporation to expend its funds to reimburse the directors' travel expenses. Whether or not a bylaw is process-related must necessarily be determined in light of its context and purpose.

The context of the Bylaw at issue here is the process for electing directors — a subject in which shareholders of Delaware corporations have a legitimate and protected interest.[21] The purpose of the Bylaw is to promote the integrity of that electoral process by facilitating the nomination of director candidates by stockholders or groups of stockholders. Generally, and under the current framework for electing directors in contested elections, only board-sponsored nominees for election are reimbursed for their election expenses. Dissident candidates are not, unless they succeed in replacing at least a majority of the entire board. The Bylaw would encourage the nomination of non-management board candidates by promising reimbursement of the nominating stockholders' proxy expenses if one or more of its candidates are elected. In that the shareholders also have a legitimate interest, because the Bylaw would facilitate the exercise of their right to participate in selecting the contestants. The Court of Chancery has so recognized:

> [T]he unadorned right to cast a ballot in a contest for [corporate] office . . . is meaningless without the right to participate in selecting the contestants. As the nominating process circumscribes the range of choice to be made, it is a fundamental and outcome-determinative step in the election of officeholders. To allow for voting while maintaining a closed selection process thus renders the former an empty exercise.

* * *

---

[21]*Blasius Indus., Inc. v. Atlas Corp.*, 564 A.2d 651, 660 n.2 (Del. Ch. 1988) ("Delaware courts have long exercised a most sensitive and protective regard for the free and effective exercise of voting rights."); *Id.* at 659 ("[W]hen viewed from a broad, institutional perspective, it can be seen that matters involving the integrity of the shareholder voting process involve consideration[s] not present in any other context in which directors exercise delegated power."); *See also Unitrin, Inc. v. Am. Gen. Corp.*, 651 A.2d 1361, 1378 (Del. 1995); *MM Cos., Inc. v. Liquid Audio, Inc.*, 813 A.2d 1118 (Del. 2003); and 8 Del. C. § 211 (authorizing a shareholder to petition the Court of Chancery to order a meeting of stockholders to elect directors where such a meeting has not been held for at least 13 months).

The shareholders of a Delaware corporation have the right "to participate in selecting the contestants" for election to the board. The shareholders are entitled to facilitate the exercise of that right by proposing a bylaw that would encourage candidates other than board-sponsored nominees to stand for election. The Bylaw would accomplish that by committing the corporation to reimburse the election expenses of shareholders whose candidates are successfully elected. That the implementation of that proposal would require the expenditure of corporate funds will not, in and of itself, make such a bylaw an improper subject matter for shareholder action. Accordingly, we answer the first question certified to us in the affirmative.

That, however, concludes only part of the analysis. The DGCL also requires that the Bylaw be "not inconsistent with law." Accordingly, we turn to the second certified question, which is whether the proposed Bylaw, if adopted, would cause CA to violate any Delaware law to which it is subject.

IV. THE SECOND QUESTION

In answering the first question, we have already determined that the Bylaw does not facially violate any provision of the DGCL or of CA's Certificate of Incorporation. The question thus becomes whether the Bylaw would violate any common law rule or precept. Were this issue being presented in the course of litigation involving the application of the Bylaw to a specific set of facts, we would start with the presumption that the Bylaw is valid and, if possible, construe it in a manner consistent with the law. The factual context in which the Bylaw was challenged would inform our analysis, and we would "exercise caution [before] invalidating corporate acts based upon hypothetical injuries. . . ." The certified questions, however, request a determination of the validity of the Bylaw in the abstract. Therefore, in response to the second question, we must necessarily consider any possible circumstance under which a board of directors might be required to act. Under at least one such hypothetical, the board of directors would breach their fiduciary duties if they complied with the Bylaw. Accordingly, we conclude that the Bylaw, as drafted, would violate the prohibition, which our decisions have derived from Section 141(a), against contractual arrangements that commit the board of directors to a course of action that would preclude them from fully discharging their fiduciary duties to the corporation and its shareholders.

This Court has previously invalidated contracts that would require a board to act or not act in such a fashion that would limit the exercise of their fiduciary duties. In *Paramount Communications, Inc. v. QVC Network, Inc.*, we invalidated a "no shop" provision of a merger agreement with a favored bidder (Viacom) that prevented the directors of the target company (Paramount) from communicating with a competing bidder (QVC) the terms of its competing bid in an effort to obtain the highest available value for shareholders. We held that:

> The No-Shop Provision could not validly define or limit the fiduciary duties of the Paramount directors. To the extent that a contract, or a provision thereof, purports to require a board to act or not act in such a fashion as to limit the exercise of fiduciary duties, it is invalid and unenforceable. [. . .] [T]he Paramount directors could not contract away their fiduciary obligations. Since the No-Shop Provision was invalid, Viacom never had any vested contract rights in the provision.

Similarly, in *Quickturn Design Systems, Inc. v. Shapiro,* the directors of the target company (Quickturn) adopted a "poison pill" rights plan that contained a so-called "delayed redemption provision" as a defense against a hostile takeover bid, as part of which the bidder (Mentor Graphics) intended to wage a proxy contest to replace the target company board. The delayed redemption provision was intended to deter that effort, by preventing any newly elected board from redeeming the poison pill for six months. This Court invalidated that provision, because it would "impermissibly deprive any newly elected board of both its statutory authority to manage the corporation under 8 Del. C. § 141(a) and its concomitant fiduciary duty pursuant to that statutory mandate." We held that:

> One of the most basic tenets of Delaware corporate law is that the board of directors has the ultimate responsibility for managing the business and affairs of a corporation. [. . .] The Quickturn certificate of incorporation contains no provision purporting to limit the authority of the board in any way. The Delayed Redemption Provision, however, would prevent a newly elected board of directors from *completely* discharging its fundamental management duties to the corporation and its stockholders for six months. While the Delayed Redemption Provision limits the board of directors' authority in only one respect, the suspension of the Rights Plan, it nonetheless restricts the board's power in an area of fundamental importance to the shareholders — negotiating a possible sale of the corporation. Therefore, we hold that the Delayed Redemption Provision is invalid under Section 141(a), which confers upon any newly elected board of directors *full* power to manage and direct the business and affairs of a Delaware corporation.

Both *QVC* and *Quickturn* involved binding contractual arrangements that the board of directors had voluntarily imposed upon themselves. This case involves a binding bylaw that the shareholders seek to impose involuntarily on the directors in the specific area of election expense reimbursement. Although this case is distinguishable in that respect, the distinction is one without a difference. The reason is that the internal governance contract — which here takes the form of a bylaw — is one that would also prevent the directors from exercising their full managerial power in circumstances where their fiduciary duties would otherwise require them to deny reimbursement to a dissident slate. That this limitation would be imposed by a majority vote of the shareholders rather than by the directors themselves, does not, in our view, legally matter.

AFSCME contends that it is improper to use the doctrine articulated in *QVC* and *Quickturn* as the measure of the validity of the Bylaw. Because the Bylaw would remove the subject of election expense reimbursement (in circumstances as defined by the Bylaw) entirely from the CA's board's discretion (AFSCME argues), it cannot fairly be claimed that the directors would be precluded from discharging their fiduciary duty. Stated differently, AFSCME argues that it is unfair to claim that the Bylaw prevents the CA board from discharging its fiduciary duty where the effect of the Bylaw is to relieve the board entirely of those duties in this specific area.

That response, in our view, is more semantical than substantive. No matter how artfully it may be phrased, the argument concedes the very proposition that renders the Bylaw, as written, invalid: the Bylaw mandates reimbursement of election expenses in circumstances that a proper application of fiduciary principles could preclude. That such circumstances could arise is not far fetched. Under Delaware law, a board may expend corporate funds to reimburse proxy expenses "[w]here the controversy is concerned with a question of policy as distinguished from personnel o[r] management." But in a situation where the proxy contest is motivated by personal or petty concerns, or to promote interests that do not further, or are adverse to, those of the corporation, the board's fiduciary duty could compel that reimbursement be denied altogether.

It is in this respect that the proposed Bylaw, as written, would violate Delaware law if enacted by CA's shareholders. As presently drafted, the Bylaw would afford CA's directors full discretion to determine what *amount* of reimbursement is appropriate, because the directors would be obligated to grant only the "reasonable" expenses of a successful short slate. Unfortunately, that does not go far enough, because the Bylaw contains no language or provision that would reserve to CA's directors their full power to exercise their fiduciary duty to decide whether or not it would be appropriate, in a specific case, to award reimbursement at all.

. . .

In arriving at this conclusion, we express no view on whether the Bylaw as currently drafted, would create a better governance scheme from a policy standpoint. We decide only what is, and is not, legally permitted under the DGCL. That statute, as currently drafted, is the expression of policy as decreed by the Delaware legislature. Those who believe that CA's shareholders should be permitted to make the proposed Bylaw as drafted part of CA's governance scheme, have two alternatives. They may seek to amend the Certificate of Incorporation to include the substance of the Bylaw; *or* they may seek recourse from the Delaware General Assembly.

Accordingly, we answer the second question certified to us in the affirmative.
QUESTIONS ANSWERED.

Post-Case Follow-Up

The *CA, Inc.* case is a good "bridge" to the next chapter, because it speaks to the board's authority to manage the corporation, the permissible scope and coverage of corporate bylaws, and the board's right and obligation to exercise fiduciary duties respecting corporate business. In this regard, the bylaw at issue in *CA, Inc.* was a problem in part because it did not contain a so-called "fiduciary out," or a provision that would have allowed the board to deny reimbursement if it determined, in good faith, that paying reimbursement would cause the board to violate its fiduciary duties to the corporation.

Broadly speaking, a fiduciary out gives a corporate board the ability to depart from an agreed-upon course of conduct if the board concludes that the departure is mandated by the board's fiduciary obligation to the company and its shareholders. Fiduciary outs occur most commonly in the context of merger agreements. Merger agreements often include a "no-shop" covenant, which restricts the target company's ability to negotiate with an alternative bidder. These covenants typically require the target to terminate any existing negotiations respecting acquisition proposals, and not to initiate, solicit, or otherwise facilitate any new negotiations with respect to an acquisition proposal. A fiduciary out clause allows the target's board to engage in negotiations with respect to an acquisition proposal if the target's board determines that its fiduciary duties necessitate engaging in such negotiations. As this suggests, fiduciary outs acknowledge and have the potential to mitigate the tension between a board's continuing fiduciary duties to the corporation and its shareholders on the one hand, and the binding no-shop covenants of the merger agreement, on the other.

Although *CA, Inc.* involved a proposed bylaw amendment rather than a contractual limitation on the board's ability to exercise its independent judgment, the court's concern — that is, that the proposed bylaw stripped the board of its ability to exercise its independent judgment, consistent with its fiduciary obligation, respecting reimbursement in contested director elections — at least raises the possibility that a fiduciary out might have made a difference. At least this is a question to ponder!

CA, Inc. v. AFSCME Employees Pension Plan: Real Life Applications

1. How might you revise the bylaw in *CA, Inc.* to avoid potential conflicts with Delaware law?

2. Plaintiff Sam Smith is a shareholder and board member of Acme Corp. According to Smith, Defendant Gary Jones is Acme's former chief executive officer (CEO) and a former board member. Smith says that he and other shareholders acted by stockholder written consent to amend Acme's bylaws to allow stockholders to remove and replace corporate officers (the "Amended Bylaw"). The Amended Bylaw provides as follows:

   > **Section 5.5 Term of Office.** The elected officers of the Corporation shall be elected annually by the Board at its first meeting held after each annual meeting of stockholders. All officers elected by the Board shall hold office until the next annual meeting of the Board and until their successors are duly elected and qualified or until their earlier death, resignation, retirement, disqualification or removal from office. Any officer may be removed, with or without cause, at any time by the Board *or by the stockholders acting at an annual or special meeting or acting by written consent pursuant to Section 2.8 of these Bylaws. The Board shall, if necessary, immediately implement any such removal of an officer by the stockholders.* Any officer appointed by the Chairman of the Board or President may also be removed, with or without cause, by the Chairman of the Board or President, as the case may be, unless the Board otherwise provides. Any vacancy occurring in any elected office of the Corporation may be filled by the Board *except that any such vacancy occurring as a result of the removal of an officer by the stockholders shall be filled by the stockholders.*

The bylaws were amended last week to insert the material in bold, italicized text. Jones allegedly was removed from his officer role pursuant to the amended text. Jones claims that the amendments to the bylaws are invalid. If Jones challenges the amendments, who will prevail and why?

3. Would your answer to Question 2 change if the bylaw amendment allowed for shareholders to comment on the executive in an advisory capacity only?

Spotlight: Forum Selection Bylaws

As noted in Chapter 6, in the wake of certain Delaware court decisions, some corporations passed bylaws that predetermine the forum in which litigation involving the internal affairs of the corporation can be heard. In 2015, after several high-profile cases involving the validity and enforceability of forum selection bylaws, the Delaware legislature amended the DGCL to add § 115, which pertinently provides as follows:

> The certificate of incorporation or the bylaws may require, consistent with applicable jurisdictional requirements, that any or all internal corporate claims shall be brought solely and exclusively in any or all of the courts in this State, and no provision of the certificate of incorporation or the bylaws may prohibit bringing such claims in the courts of this State. "Internal corporate claims" means claims, including claims in the right of the corporation, (i) that are based upon a violation of a duty by a current or former director or officer or stockholder in such capacity, or (ii) as to which this title confers jurisdiction upon the Court of Chancery.

According to the synopsis of the underlying bill, § 115 confirms, as was held in *Boilermakers Local 154 Retirement Fund v. Chevron Corp.*, 73 A.2d 934 (Del. Ch. 2013), that the certificate of incorporation and bylaws of the corporation may specify, consistent with applicable jurisdictional requirement, that claims arising under the DGCL shall be brought only in the courts (including the federal courts) in Delaware. The synopsis further provides that § 115 does not address the validity of charter or bylaw provisions that select a forum other than Delaware courts as an additional forum in which intra-corporate claims may be brought, but does address — and invalidate — provisions selecting the courts in a different state, or an arbitral forum, if it would preclude litigating such claims in Delaware courts.

The Delaware legislature also addressed and prohibited fee shifting (i.e., where the "winner's" legal fees are fees are shifted to, or imposed upon, the "loser") in 2015, adding the following provisions to the DGCL (primarily to ensure that stockholders are not deterred from initiating litigation against corporations to enforce their rights):

> 102(f): The certificate of incorporation may not contain any provision that would impose liability on a stockholder for the attorneys' fees or expenses of the corporation or any other party in connection with an internal corporate claim, as defined in § 115 of this title.

and

109(b): The bylaws may contain any provision, not inconsistent with law or with the certificate of incorporation, relating to the business of the corporation, the conduct of its affairs, and its rights or powers or the rights or powers of its stockholders, directors, officers or employees. The bylaws may not contain any provision that would impose liability on a stockholder for the attorneys' fees or expenses of the corporation or any other party in connection with an internal corporate claim, as defined in § 115 of this title.

The MBCA does not address fee-shifting bylaws or charter provisions.

Chapter Summary

- Corporations are subject to a hierarchy of control, with the state corporations code sitting at the top, followed by the charter, the bylaws, the board, the officers, and the employees.
- Under state corporations statutes, corporate governance involves three groups — shareholders (the owners of the corporation), directors (the managers of the corporation), and officers (appointees of the directors).
- Although shareholders own the corporation, they do not have a statutory right to manage it; instead, they participate indirectly in governance by voting to elect (or remove) directors and by voting on certain extraordinary actions involving fundamental changes to corporate structure.
- There are two types of shareholder meetings — annual meetings (at which directors are elected), and special meetings (those held between annual meetings).
- Shareholders often vote by proxy (written instruction to another).
- Shareholders may enter into agreements to pool their votes or otherwise concentrate their voting power.
- Directors manage the corporation and are elected by shareholders.
- Directors meet in regular meetings or special meetings.
- Directors and shareholders may act without a formal meeting if they unanimously consent in writing to take action.
- Officers are appointed by directors to carry out whatever functions are assigned to them by the directors.

Applying the Concepts

1. Ryan, Inc., a privately held corporation formed in an MBCA jurisdiction, has 10,000 shares outstanding and 11 directors. Its articles provide for cumulative voting.

   a. What number constitutes a quorum of shareholders?
   b. What number constitutes a quorum of directors?

    c. If seven directors are present at a meeting, how many must vote affirmatively to declare a dividend?

    d. Jordan, a shareholder, owns 500 shares. If 11 directors are being elected, how many votes will Jordan have?

    e. If the corporation has called a shareholders' meeting to vote on amending the corporation's articles, how many votes will Jordan have?

    f. May Jordan call a special meeting of shareholders to remove a director?

    g. David, a director, would like to remove another director, Neil, because he believes Neil is not devoting as much effort and time to the corporation as he should. May David call a special meeting to remove Neil?

2. The corporation's bylaws provide for a record date of 45 days before the annual meeting. The annual meeting will be held on May 20. By what date must an individual own shares in the corporation in order to receive notice of the meeting and to vote?

3. The directors of Ryan, Inc. would like to raise the quorum requirement for a shareholders' meeting. Using the authority granted to them to amend the corporation's bylaws, the board unanimously approves a bylaw amendment raising the quorum requirement. Is the amendment valid? Would your answer be different if Ryan, Inc. was a Delaware-chartered corporation?

4. Discuss the advantages and disadvantages of a classified or staggered board of directors.

5. Access the website of the SEC. Locate its Investor Glossary. What is the definition of "proxy voting"?

6. Access California's corporations statutes. What officers must a company have in California? What section governs your answer?

7. Access the website of the SEC. Review the most recently filed annual report on Form 10-K for Facebook, Inc. Who is authorized to call a special meeting of stockholders?

8. Access the website of the SEC. Review the most recent Definitive 14A proxy statement of Amazon.com Inc. filed on April 10, 2014.

    a. How many common shares were outstanding that were entitled to vote at the annual meeting?

    b. What methods of shareholder voting are authorized?

    c. Review the annual meeting proxy card. Review shareholder proposal number 4. What does this proposal relate to, and did the board of directors recommend a vote "for" or "against" it?

9. Access the website for the SEC. Locate the Definitive 14A proxy statement for Twitter, Inc., filed on April 9, 2014.

   a. How many meetings did the board of directors hold?
   b. Briefly, what is the responsibility of the company's CEO?
   c. Is the board staggered or elected annually?
   d. How many directors are "independent," within the listing standards of the New York Stock Exchange?

10. Locate the website for the Walt Disney Company. Select "Investor Relations" and then "Corporate Governance Guidelines."
   a. What is the size of the board of directors?
   b. Must directors own stock in the company?
   c. How often does the company report on its social responsibility and diversity efforts?

11. Review the New York Business Corporations Code. Identify at least three provisions that specify shareholder voting requirements (e.g., quorum or super-majority).

Business Organizations in Practice

1. 4C, Inc. is a Delaware corporation with a non-staggered board. At a meeting of the board of directors last week, 4C adopted a bylaw provision stating that shareholders may remove directors only for cause. Is this bylaw provision valid? Write a brief memo to the board explaining why or why not.

2. Acme, Inc., is a newly formed Delaware corporation involved in mining and oil and gas exploration in areas of the world prone to conflict. Acme has retained you to advise the company on what officers and board committees it ought to have, given the risks and opportunities associated with its business. Draft a memo to the board with your recommendations.

3. Acme, Inc. is a privately held company with two controlling shareholders — a father and son — and 15 minority shareholders (also family members). The father and son also serve as the company's sole officers and directors. Citing strongly held religious beliefs, the father and son have applied for an exemption from the Affordable Care Act's contraceptive mandate. Five of the company's 15 minority shareholders oppose this request. They have submitted a proposed bylaw amendment that would require the company to comply with, and not seek an exemption from, the contraceptive mandate. Is compliance with the mandate a proper subject of a corporate bylaw, and is the proposed amendment valid?

4. Javassana, a New York corporation that operates a chain of combination coffee shops and yoga studios, has a seven-member board of directors. Last week, the

chair of the board called a special meeting to discuss a potential transaction after the CEO of a competitor proposed a merger between the two companies. The meeting was scheduled for 9:00 A.M. this morning. Although all of the directors received notice of the meeting, four directors have yet to arrive due to severe winter weather and associated travel delays. You are Javassana's general counsel. The three directors who arrived on time would like to begin meeting to discuss the proposed transaction, as all are enthusiastic supporters of the potential deal. They have asked you whether they can go ahead and discuss and vote on the proposed transaction. They report to you that the remaining directors have repeatedly expressed support for the deal in private conversations. What do you tell them?

5. Assume for purposes of this question that Javassana is a newly formed, privately held California corporation. Under default rules, will shareholders use straight or cumulative voting in the election of directors? Write a memo to the board and the company's shareholders explaining default voting rules, and giving concrete examples of the mechanics and impact of straight versus cumulative voting.

Corporate Governance: The Business Judgment Rule, Fiduciary Duties, and Governance Reforms

Having examined governance structures and voting-related rules and mechanics, we now turn to two important components of corporate governance: (i) the fiduciary duties of care and loyalty applicable to corporate directors and officers; and (ii) the business judgment rule. The **duty of care** focuses on the decision-making process. It requires officers and directors to be adequately informed and to exercise diligence when making corporate decisions. The **duty of loyalty** broadly requires directors and officers to put the interests of the corporation before personal interests. It prohibits officers and directors from usurping corporate opportunities and engaging in self-dealing transactions except in compliance with statutory and common law rules. It also requires directors to discharge corporate oversight and monitoring obligations in good faith. The **business judgment rule** is a rebuttable (but strong) presumption that corporate directors comply with their duties of care and loyalty — meaning, that they act on an informed basis, in good faith, and in the honest belief that their actions are in the best interest of the company — when making business decisions. Under the business judgment rule, a director will not be held liable for breach of fiduciary duty for a business decision — even if that decision causes a corporate loss — unless the plaintiff can show that the director's decision-making process was grossly inadequate, tainted by a lack of independence or conflict of interest, or that the

Key Concepts

- The business judgment rule
- The duty of care
- The duty of loyalty
- Fiduciary duty litigation

challenged decision was irrational. We examine each of these rules and concepts in this chapter, along with rules relating to shareholder litigation.

A. INTRODUCTION: CENTRALIZED MANAGEMENT, FIDUCIARY DUTIES, AND THE BUSINESS JUDGMENT RULE

As you learned in Chapter 8, the authority to manage the business and affairs of the corporation is vested in the board of directors. *See, e.g.*, DGCL § 141(e); New York Business Corporation Law (NYBCL) § 701. Centralizing managerial control in the board makes sense. It allows for efficient decision making by a small, collaborative, and well-informed body, and it recognizes that shareholders generally are not well positioned to get into the weeds of day-to-day corporate business. Still, there are costs and risks associated with centralized management. Directors may be tempted to slack off or to use their position or influence to put personal interests before corporate best interests. And, shareholders may find it difficult to detect or police shareholder misdeeds because they are not involved in day-to-day affairs and have only limited voting rights.

Fiduciary duties — and associated conduct standards — are a response to the potential costs and risks of corporations' director-centric, centralized management structure. Under statutory rules and common law principles, directors owe fiduciary duties of care and loyalty to the corporation and its shareholders. For example, MBCA § 8.30(b) states that "[t]he members of the board of directors or a committee of the board, when becoming informed in connection with their decision-making function or devoting attention to their oversight function, shall discharge their duties with the care that a person in a like position would reasonably believe appropriate under similar circumstances." With respect to the fiduciary duty of loyalty, MBCA §§ 8.60-8.63 establishes rules relating to conflicting interest transactions, or transactions where a director (or related person) enters into a contract with the corporation or an entity controlled by the corporation. MBCA § 8.70 establishes rules relating to the corporate opportunity doctrine, or the doctrine which states that a director cannot take for herself an opportunity that belongs to the corporation. (We discuss these topics in more detail below.) More generally, MBCA § 8.30(a) states that that "[e]ach member of the board of directors, when discharging the duties of a director, shall act: (1) in good faith, and (2) in a manner the director reasonably believes to be in the best interests of the corporation." We discuss directors' fiduciary obligations and associated conduct standards in detail below.

It is important to remember, however, that fiduciary duties and associated conduct standards do not make directors guarantors of corporate success. This is where the **business judgment rule** comes into play. If corporations codes articulate conduct standards for directors' fiduciary obligations, the business judgment rule speaks to when directors will be held liable for alleged breaches of these standards. The business judgment rule operates as a rebuttable (but strong) presumption that in making a business decision, the directors of a corporation act on an informed basis, in good faith, and in the honest belief that the action taken was in the best interests of the company. If the business judgment rule presumptions apply, the directors will not be personally liable for a decision, even if it causes or contributes to a corporate loss, unless the plaintiff can show that there was no rational basis for the decision. To rebut the business judgment rule presumption, a plaintiff challenging a decision must show that the board's decision-making process was grossly inadequate, the decision was tainted by a lack of independence or conflict of interest, or that the decision was irrational. If the plaintiff succeeds in rebutting the business judgment rule presumptions, the burden shifts to the board to demonstrate that the decision was entirely fair to the corporation.

The business judgment rule thus speaks to the risk of **hindsight bias,** or the tendency of people to view events as more predictable than they really are. When directors make a decision about strategy, new products, etc., that results in a corporate loss, hindsight bias may cause some to conclude that the decision was doomed from the start, and the losses were the inevitable result of a fiduciary breach. If directors faced liability every time a shareholder challenged loss-producing decisions, few would be willing to serve as directors, and those willing to serve might not take the calculated risks that often are necessary to establish and operate a successful business. The business judgment rule protects directors from this sort of second-guessing. It recognizes directors' fundamental right and responsibility to manage the affairs of the corporation, and it encourages productive, calculated risk taking by making it clear that directors will not be held liable for business decisions absent a showing of a fiduciary breach. We discuss shareholder litigation in Section E below.

B. DIRECTORS AND THE DUTY OF CARE

The first fiduciary duty that we will study is the duty of care. The **duty of care** is process-oriented, in that it requires directors to be adequately informed and to exercise reasonable diligence in the decision-making process. The duty of care does not speak to the substance of the challenged decision, as the following excerpt from a case involving the financial institution Citigroup Inc. makes clear:

> What should be understood, but may not widely be understood by courts or commentators who are not often required to face such questions, is that compliance with a director's duty of care can never appropriately be judicially determined by reference to *the content of the board decision* that leads to a corporate loss, apart from consideration of the good faith *or* rationality of the process employed. That is, whether a judge or jury considering the matter after the fact, believes a decision substantively wrong, or degrees of wrong extending through "stupid" to "egregious" or "irrational," provides no ground for director liability, so long as the court determines that the process employed was either rational or employed in *a good faith* effort to advance corporate interests. To employ a different rule — one that permitted an "objective" evaluation of the decision — would expose directors to substantive second guessing by ill-equipped judges or juries, which would, in the long-run, be injurious to investor interests. Thus, the business judgment rule is process oriented and informed by a deep respect for all *good faith* board decisions.

In re Citigroup S'holder Derivative Litig., 964 A.2d 106, 122 (Del. Ch. 2009).

Case Preview

Smith v. Van Gorkom

Our first case is one of the most famous cases in all of Delaware law involving the duty of care. In *Smith v. Van Gorkom*, often called the *Trans Union* case, a disgruntled former shareholder of Trans Union Corporation alleged that Trans Union's directors breached their fiduciary duties when they voted in favor of a proposal calling for the cash-out merger of Trans Union into another company. In a cash-out merger, the acquiring entity cashes out the target company shareholders by paying those shareholders a specific price per share. (In *Trans Union*, shareholders received $55 per share, which represented a substantial premium over the then-current market price of Trans Union stock.) Despite the premium reflected in the $55 per share cash-out price, however, the *Trans Union* plaintiffs alleged that the $55 per share price was too low. When reading *Trans Union*, consider the following questions:

1. What did Trans Union's board do wrong, according to the Delaware Supreme Court?
2. Why wasn't the premium (i.e., the difference between the $55 per share cash-out price in the proposed merger and the then-current market price) enough to insulate the outside directors from fiduciary duty liability?
3. What legal standard (simple negligence, gross negligence) does the court use to determine whether the board's decision breached its fiduciary duty of care?
4. What might Trans Union's board have done differently when presented with the Pritzker cash-out merger proposal to avoid breaching the fiduciary duty of care?

Smith v. Van Gorkom
488 A.2d 858 (Del. 1985)

HORSEY, Justice (for the majority):*

This appeal from the Court of Chancery involves a class action brought by shareholders of the defendant Trans Union Corporation ("Trans Union" or "the Company"), originally seeking rescission of a cash-out merger of Trans Union into the defendant New T Company ("New T"), a wholly-owned subsidiary of the defendant, Marmon Group, Inc. ("Marmon"). Alternate relief in the form of damages is sought against the defendant members of the Board of Directors of Trans Union, New T, and Jay A. Pritzker and Robert A. Pritzker, owners of Marmon.

Following trial, the former Chancellor granted judgment for the defendant directors by unreported letter opinion dated July 6, 1982. Judgment was based on two findings: (1) that the Board of Directors had acted in an informed manner so as

---

*Most footnotes have been omitted for purposes of brevity.

to be entitled to protection of the business judgment rule in approving the cash-out merger; and (2) that the shareholder vote approving the merger should not be set aside because the stockholders had been "fairly informed" by the Board of Directors before voting thereon. The plaintiffs appeal.

We hold: (1) that the Board's decision, reached September 20, 1980, to approve the proposed cash-out merger was not the product of an informed business judgment; (2) that the Board's subsequent efforts to amend the Merger Agreement and take other curative action were ineffectual, both legally and factually; and (3) that the Board did not deal with complete candor with the stockholders by failing to disclose all material facts, which they knew or should have known, before securing the stockholders' approval of the merger.

I.

The nature of this case requires a detailed factual statement. The following facts are essentially uncontradicted.

A

Trans Union was a publicly-traded, diversified holding company, the principal earnings of which were generated by its railcar leasing business. During the period here involved, the Company had a cash flow of hundreds of millions of dollars annually. However, the Company had difficulty in generating sufficient taxable income to offset increasingly large investment tax credits (ITCs). Accelerated depreciation deductions had decreased available taxable income against which to offset accumulating ITCs. The Company took these deductions, despite their effect on usable ITCs, because the rental price in the railcar leasing market had already impounded the purported tax savings.

In the late 1970's, together with other capital-intensive firms, Trans Union lobbied in Congress to have ITCs refundable in cash to firms which could not fully utilize the credit. During the summer of 1980, defendant Jerome W. Van Gorkom, Trans Union's Chairman and Chief Executive Officer, testified and lobbied in Congress for refundability of ITCs and against further accelerated depreciation. By the end of August, Van Gorkom was convinced that Congress would neither accept the refundability concept nor curtail further accelerated depreciation.

Beginning in the late 1960's, and continuing through the 1970's, Trans Union pursued a program of acquiring small companies in order to increase available taxable income. In July 1980, Trans Union Management prepared the annual revision of the Company's Five Year Forecast. This report was presented to the Board of Directors at its July, 1980 meeting. The report projected an annual income growth of about 20%. The report also concluded that Trans Union would have about $195 million in spare cash between 1980 and 1985, "with the surplus growing rapidly from 1982 onward." The report referred to the ITC situation as a "nagging problem" and, given that problem, the leasing company "would still appear to be constrained to a tax breakeven." The report then listed four alternative uses of the projected 1982-1985 equity surplus: (1) stock repurchase; (2) dividend increases; (3) a major acquisition program; and (4) combinations of the above. The sale of Trans Union was not among the alternatives.

The report emphasized that, despite the overall surplus, the operation of the Company would consume all available equity for the next several years, and concluded: "As a result, we have sufficient time to fully develop our course of action."

B

On August 27, 1980, Van Gorkom met with Senior Management of Trans Union. Van Gorkom reported on his lobbying efforts in Washington and his desire to find a solution to the tax credit problem more permanent than a continued program of acquisitions. Various alternatives were suggested and discussed preliminarily, including the sale of Trans Union to a company with a large amount of taxable income.

Donald Romans, Chief Financial Officer of Trans Union, stated that his department had done a "very brief bit of work on the possibility of a leveraged buy-out." This work had been prompted by a media article which Romans had seen regarding a leveraged buy-out by management. The work consisted of a "preliminary study" of the cash which could be generated by the Company if it participated in a leveraged buy-out. As Romans stated, this analysis "was very first and rough cut at seeing whether a cash flow would support what might be considered a high price for this type of transaction."

On September 5, at another Senior Management meeting which Van Gorkom attended, Romans again brought up the idea of a leveraged buy-out as a "possible strategic alternative" to the Company's acquisition program. Romans and Bruce S. Chelberg, President and Chief Operating Officer of Trans Union, had been working on the matter in preparation for the meeting. According to Romans: They did not "come up" with a price for the Company. They merely "ran the numbers" at $50 a share and at $60 a share with the "rough form" of their cash figures at the time. Their "figures indicated that $50 would be very easy to do but $60 would be very difficult to do under those figures." This work did not purport to establish a fair price for either the Company or 100% of the stock. It was intended to determine the cash flow needed to service the debt that would "probably" be incurred in a leveraged buy-out, based on "rough calculations" without "any benefit of experts to identify what the limits were to that, and so forth." These computations were not considered extensive and no conclusion was reached.

At this meeting, Van Gorkom stated that he would be willing to take $55 per share for his own 75,000 shares. He vetoed the suggestion of a leveraged buy-out by Management, however, as involving a potential conflict of interest for Management. Van Gorkom, a certified public accountant and lawyer, had been an officer of Trans Union for 24 years, its Chief Executive Officer for more than 17 years, and Chairman of its Board for 2 years. It is noteworthy in this connection that he was then approaching 65 years of age and mandatory retirement.

For several days following the September 5 meeting, Van Gorkom pondered the idea of a sale. He had participated in many acquisitions as a manager and director of Trans Union and as a director of other companies. He was familiar with acquisition procedures, valuation methods, and negotiations; and he privately considered the pros and cons of whether Trans Union should seek a privately or publicly-held purchaser.

Van Gorkom decided to meet with Jay A. Pritzker, a well-known corporate take-over specialist and a social acquaintance. However, rather than approaching Pritzker simply to determine his interest in acquiring Trans Union, Van Gorkom assembled a proposed per share price for sale of the Company and a financing structure by which to accomplish the sale. Van Gorkom did so without consulting either his Board or any members of Senior Management except one: Carl Peterson, Trans Union's Controller. Telling Peterson that he wanted no other person on his staff to know what he was doing, but without telling him why, Van Gorkom directed Peterson to calculate the feasibility of a leveraged buy-out at an assumed price per share of $55. Apart from the Company's historic stock market price,[5] and Van Gorkom's long association with Trans Union, the record is devoid of any competent evidence that $55 represented the per share intrinsic value of the Company.

Having thus chosen the $55 figure, based solely on the availability of a leveraged buy-out, Van Gorkom multiplied the price per share by the number of shares outstanding to reach a total value of the Company of $690 million. Van Gorkom told Peterson to use this $690 million figure and to assume a $200 million equity contribution by the buyer. Based on these assumptions, Van Gorkom directed Peterson to determine whether the debt portion of the purchase price could be paid off in five years or less if financed by Trans Union's cash flow as projected in the Five Year Forecast, and by the sale of certain weaker divisions identified in a study done for Trans Union by the Boston Consulting Group ("BCG study"). Peterson reported that, of the purchase price, approximately $50-80 million would remain outstanding after five years. Van Gorkom was disappointed, but decided to meet with Pritzker nevertheless.

Van Gorkom arranged a meeting with Pritzker at the latter's home on Saturday, September 13, 1980. Van Gorkom prefaced his presentation by stating to Pritzker: "Now as far as you are concerned, I can, I think, show how you can pay a substantial premium over the present stock price and pay off most of the loan in the first five years. * * * If you could pay $55 for this Company, here is a way in which I think it can be financed."

Van Gorkom then reviewed with Pritzker his calculations based upon his proposed price of $55 per share. Although Pritzker mentioned $50 as a more attractive figure, no other price was mentioned. However, Van Gorkom stated that to be sure that $55 was the best price obtainable, Trans Union should be free to accept any better offer. Pritzker demurred, stating that his organization would serve as a "stalking horse" for an "auction contest" only if Trans Union would permit Pritzker to buy 1,750,000 shares of Trans Union stock at market price which Pritzker could then sell to any higher bidder. After further discussion on this point, Pritzker told Van Gorkom that he would give him a more definite reaction soon.

On Monday, September 15, Pritzker advised Van Gorkom that he was interested in the $55 cash-out merger proposal and requested more information on Trans

---

[5]The common stock of Trans Union was traded on the New York Stock Exchange. Over the five year period from 1975 through 1979, Trans Union's stock had traded within a range of a high of $39 ½ and a low of $24 ¼. Its high and low range for 1980 through September 19 (the last trading day before announcement of the merger) was $38 ¼–$29 ½.

Union. Van Gorkom agreed to meet privately with Pritzker, accompanied by Peterson, Chelberg, and Michael Carpenter, Trans Union's consultant from the Boston Consulting Group. The meetings took place on September 16 and 17. Van Gorkom was "astounded that events were moving with such amazing rapidity."

On Thursday, September 18, Van Gorkom met again with Pritzker. At that time, Van Gorkom knew that Pritzker intended to make a cash-out merger offer at Van Gorkom's proposed $55 per share. Pritzker instructed his attorney, a merger and acquisition specialist, to begin drafting merger documents. There was no further discussion of the $55 price. However, the number of shares of Trans Union's treasury stock to be offered to Pritzker was negotiated down to one million shares; the price was set at $38 — 75 cents above the per share price at the close of the market on September 19. At this point, Pritzker insisted that the Trans Union Board act on his merger proposal within the next three days, stating to Van Gorkom: "We have to have a decision by no later than Sunday [evening, September 21] before the opening of the English stock exchange on Monday morning." Pritzker's lawyer was then instructed to draft the merger documents, to be reviewed by Van Gorkom's lawyer, "sometimes with discussion and sometimes not, in the haste to get it finished."

On Friday, September 19, Van Gorkom, Chelberg, and Pritzker consulted with Trans Union's lead bank regarding the financing of Pritzker's purchase of Trans Union. The bank indicated that it could form a syndicate of banks that would finance the transaction. On the same day, Van Gorkom retained James Brennan, Esquire, to advise Trans Union on the legal aspects of the merger. Van Gorkom did not consult with William Browder, a Vice-President and director of Trans Union and former head of its legal department, or with William Moore, then the head of Trans Union's legal staff.

On Friday, September 19, Van Gorkom called a special meeting of the Trans Union Board for noon the following day. He also called a meeting of the Company's Senior Management to convene at 11:00 A.M., prior to the meeting of the Board. No one, except Chelberg and Peterson, was told the purpose of the meetings. Van Gorkom did not invite Trans Union's investment banker, Salomon Brothers or its Chicago-based partner, to attend.

Of those present at the Senior Management meeting on September 20, only Chelberg and Peterson had prior knowledge of Pritzker's offer. Van Gorkom disclosed the offer and described its terms, but he furnished no copies of the proposed Merger Agreement. Romans announced that his department had done a second study which showed that, for a leveraged buy-out, the price range for Trans Union stock was between $55 and $65 per share. Van Gorkom neither saw the study nor asked Romans to make it available for the Board meeting.

Senior Management's reaction to the Pritzker proposal was completely negative. No member of Management, except Chelberg and Peterson, supported the proposal. Romans objected to the price as being too low;[6] he was critical of the timing and suggested that consideration should be given to the adverse tax consequences of an

---

[6]Van Gorkom asked Romans to express his opinion as to the $55 price. Romans stated that he "thought the price was too low in relation to what he could derive for the company in a cash sale, particularly one which enabled us to realize the values of certain subsidiaries and independent entities."

all-cash deal for low-basis shareholders; and he took the position that the agreement to sell Pritzker one million newly-issued shares at market price would inhibit other offers, as would the prohibitions against soliciting bids and furnishing inside information to other bidders. Romans argued that the Pritzker proposal was a "lock up" and amounted to "an agreed merger as opposed to an offer." Nevertheless, Van Gorkom proceeded to the Board meeting as scheduled without further delay.

Ten directors served on the Trans Union Board, five inside (defendants Bonser, O'Boyle, Browder, Chelberg, and Van Gorkom) and five outside (defendants Wallis, Johnson, Lanterman, Morgan and Reneker). All directors were present at the meeting, except O'Boyle who was ill. Of the outside directors, four were corporate chief executive officers and one was the former Dean of the University of Chicago Business School. None was an investment banker or trained financial analyst. All members of the Board were well informed about the Company and its operations as a going concern. They were familiar with the current financial condition of the Company, as well as operating and earnings projections reported in the recent Five Year Forecast. The Board generally received regular and detailed reports and was kept abreast of the accumulated investment tax credit and accelerated depreciation problem.

Van Gorkom began the Special Meeting of the Board with a twenty-minute oral presentation. Copies of the proposed Merger Agreement were delivered too late for study before or during the meeting.[7] He reviewed the Company's ITC and depreciation problems and the efforts theretofore made to solve them. He discussed his initial meeting with Pritzker and his motivation in arranging that meeting. Van Gorkom did not disclose to the Board, however, the methodology by which he alone had arrived at the $55 figure, or the fact that he first proposed the $55 price in his negotiations with Pritzker.

Van Gorkom outlined the terms of the Pritzker offer as follows: Pritzker would pay $55 in cash for all outstanding shares of Trans Union stock upon completion of which Trans Union would be merged into New T Company, a subsidiary wholly-owned by Pritzker and formed to implement the merger; for a period of 90 days, Trans Union could receive, but could not actively solicit, competing offers; the offer had to be acted on by the next evening, Sunday, September 21; Trans Union could only furnish to competing bidders published information, and not proprietary information; the offer was subject to Pritzker obtaining the necessary financing by October 10, 1980; if the financing contingency were met or waived by Pritzker, Trans Union was required to sell to Pritzker one million newly-issued shares of Trans Union at $38 per share.

Van Gorkom took the position that putting Trans Union "up for auction" through a 90-day market test would validate a decision by the Board that $55 was a fair price. He told the Board that the "free market will have an opportunity to judge whether $55 is a fair price." Van Gorkom framed the decision before the Board not

---

[7] The record is not clear as to the terms of the Merger Agreement. The Agreement, as originally presented to the Board on September 20, was never produced by defendants despite demands by the plaintiffs. Nor is it clear that the directors were given an opportunity to study the Merger Agreement before voting on it. All that can be said is that Brennan had the Agreement before him during the meeting.

as whether $55 per share was the highest price that could be obtained, but as whether the $55 price was a fair price that the stockholders should be given the opportunity to accept or reject.

Attorney Brennan advised the members of the Board that they might be sued if they failed to accept the offer and that a fairness opinion was not required as a matter of law.

Romans attended the meeting as chief financial officer of the Company. He told the Board that he had not been involved in the negotiations with Pritzker and knew nothing about the merger proposal until the morning of the meeting; that his studies did not indicate either a fair price for the stock or a valuation of the Company; that he did not see his role as directly addressing the fairness issue; and that he and his people "were trying to search for ways to justify a price in connection with such a [leveraged buy-out] transaction, rather than to say what the shares are worth." Romans testified:

> I told the Board that the study ran the numbers at 50 and 60, and then the subsequent study at 55 and 65, and that was not the same thing as saying that I have a valuation of the company at X dollars. But it was a way — a first step towards reaching that conclusion.

Romans told the Board that, in his opinion, $55 was "in the range of a fair price," but "at the beginning of the range."

Chelberg, Trans Union's President, supported Van Gorkom's presentation and representations. He testified that he "participated to make sure that the Board members collectively were clear on the details of the agreement or offer from Pritzker;" that he "participated in the discussion with Mr. Brennan, inquiring of him about the necessity for valuation opinions in spite of the way in which this particular offer was couched"; and that he was otherwise actively involved in supporting the positions being taken by Van Gorkom before the Board about "the necessity to act immediately on this offer," and about "the adequacy of the $55 and the question of how that would be tested."

The Board meeting of September 20 lasted about two hours. Based solely upon Van Gorkom's oral presentation, Chelberg's supporting representations, Romans' oral statement, Brennan's legal advice, and their knowledge of the market history of the Company's stock,[9] the directors approved the proposed Merger Agreement. However, the Board later claimed to have attached two conditions to its acceptance: (1) that Trans Union reserved the right to accept any better offer that was made during the market test period; and (2) that Trans Union could share its proprietary information with any other potential bidders. While the Board now claims to have reserved the right to accept any better offer received after the announcement of the

---

[9]The Trial Court stated the premium relationship of the $55 price to the market history of the Company's stock as follows:

> . . . the merger price offered to the stockholders of Trans Union represented a premium of 62% over the average of the high and low prices at which Trans Union stock had traded in 1980, a premium of 48% over the last closing price, and a premium of 39% over the highest price at which the stock of Trans Union had traded any time during the prior six years.

Pritzker agreement (even though the minutes of the meeting do not reflect this), it is undisputed that the Board did not reserve the right to actively solicit alternate offers.

The Merger Agreement was executed by Van Gorkom during the evening of September 20 at a formal social event that he hosted for the opening of the Chicago Lyric Opera. Neither he nor any other director read the agreement prior to its signing and delivery to Pritzker. . . .

On Monday, September 22, the Company issued a press release announcing that Trans Union had entered into a "definitive" Merger Agreement with an affiliate of the Marmon Group, Inc., a Pritzker holding company. Within 10 days of the public announcement, dissent among Senior Management over the merger had become widespread. Faced with threatened resignations of key officers, Van Gorkom met with Pritzker who agreed to several modifications of the Agreement. Pritzker was willing to do so provided that Van Gorkom could persuade the dissidents to remain on the Company payroll for at least six months after consummation of the merger.

Van Gorkom reconvened the Board on October 8 and secured the directors' approval of the proposed amendments—sight unseen. The Board also authorized the employment of Salomon Brothers, its investment banker, to solicit other offers for Trans Union during the proposed "market test" period.

The next day, October 9, Trans Union issued a press release announcing: (1) that Pritzker had obtained "the financing commitments necessary to consummate" the merger with Trans Union; (2) that Pritzker had acquired one million shares of Trans Union common stock at $38 per share; (3) that Trans Union was now permitted to actively seek other offers and had retained Salomon Brothers for that purpose; and (4) that if a more favorable offer were not received before February 1, 1981, Trans Union's shareholders would thereafter meet to vote on the Pritzker proposal.

It was not until the following day, October 10, that the actual amendments to the Merger Agreement were prepared by Pritzker and delivered to Van Gorkom for execution. As will be seen, the amendments were considerably at variance with Van Gorkom's representations of the amendments to the Board on October 8; and the amendments placed serious constraints on Trans Union's ability to negotiate a better deal and withdraw from the Pritzker agreement. Nevertheless, Van Gorkom proceeded to execute what became the October 10 amendments to the Merger Agreement without conferring further with the Board members and apparently without comprehending the actual implications of the amendments. . . .

Salomon Brothers' efforts over a three-month period from October 21 to January 21 produced only one serious suitor for Trans Union—General Electric Credit Corporation ("GE Credit"), a subsidiary of the General Electric Company. However, GE Credit was unwilling to make an offer for Trans Union unless Trans Union first rescinded its Merger Agreement with Pritzker. When Pritzker refused, GE Credit terminated further discussions with Trans Union in early January.

In the meantime, in early December, the investment firm of Kohlberg, Kravis, Roberts & Co. ("KKR"), the only other concern to make a firm offer for Trans Union, withdrew its offer under circumstances hereinafter detailed.

On December 19, this litigation was commenced and, within four weeks, the plaintiffs had deposed eight of the ten directors of Trans Union, including Van Gorkom, Chelberg and Romans, its Chief Financial Officer. On January 21,

Management's Proxy Statement for the February 10 shareholder meeting was mailed to Trans Union's stockholders. On January 26, Trans Union's Board met and, after a lengthy meeting, voted to proceed with the Pritzker merger. The Board also approved for mailing, "on or about January 27," a Supplement to its Proxy Statement. The Supplement purportedly set forth all information relevant to the Pritzker Merger Agreement, which had not been divulged in the first Proxy Statement.

On February 10, the stockholders of Trans Union approved the Pritzker merger proposal. Of the outstanding shares, 69.9% were voted in favor of the merger; 7.25% were voted against the merger; and 22.85% were not voted.

II.

We turn to the issue of the application of the business judgment rule to the September 20 meeting of the Board.

The Court of Chancery concluded from the evidence that the Board of Directors' approval of the Pritzker merger proposal fell within the protection of the business judgment rule. The Court found that the Board had given sufficient time and attention to the transaction, since the directors had considered the Pritzker proposal on three different occasions, on September 20, and on October 8, 1980 and finally on January 26, 1981. On that basis, the Court reasoned that the Board had acquired, over the four-month period, sufficient information to reach an informed business judgment on the cash-out merger proposal. The Court ruled:

> . . . that given the market value of Trans Union's stock, the business acumen of the members of the board of Trans Union, the substantial premium over market offered by the Pritzkers and the ultimate effect on the merger price provided by the prospect of other bids for the stock in question, that the board of directors of Trans Union did not act recklessly or improvidently in determining on a course of action which they believed to be in the best interest of the stockholders of Trans Union.

The Court of Chancery made but one finding; i.e., that the Board's conduct over the entire period from September 20 through January 26, 1981 was not reckless or improvident, but informed. This ultimate conclusion was premised upon three subordinate findings, one explicit and two implied. The Court's explicit finding was that Trans Union's Board was "free to turn down the Pritzker proposal" not only on September 20 but also on October 8, 1980 and on January 26, 1981. The Court's implied, subordinate findings were: (1) that no legally binding agreement was reached by the parties until January 26; and (2) that if a higher offer were to be forthcoming, the market test would have produced it, and Trans Union would have been contractually free to accept such higher offer. However, the Court offered no factual basis or legal support for any of these findings; and the record compels contrary conclusions. . . .

Under Delaware law, the business judgment rule is the offspring of the fundamental principle, codified in 8 Del. C. § 141(a), that the business and affairs of a Delaware corporation are managed by or under its board of directors. *Pogostin v. Rice,* Del. Supr., 480 A.2d 619, 624 (1984); *Aronson v. Lewis,* Del. Supr., 473 A.2d 805, 811 (1984); *Zapata Corp. v. Maldonado,* Del. Supr., 430 A.2d 779, 782 (1981). In carrying out their managerial roles, directors are charged with an unyielding fiduciary duty to the corporation and its shareholders. *Loft, Inc. v. Guth,* Del. Ch., 2 A.2d

225 (1938), *aff'd*, Del. Supr., 5 A.2d 503 (1939). The business judgment rule exists to protect and promote the full and free exercise of the managerial power granted to Delaware directors. *Zapata Corp. v. Maldonado, supra* at 782. The rule itself "is a presumption that in making a business decision, the directors of a corporation acted on an informed basis, in good faith and in the honest belief that the action taken was in the best interests of the company." *Aronson, supra* at 812. Thus, the party attacking a board decision as uninformed must rebut the presumption that its business judgment was an informed one. *Id.*

The determination of whether a business judgment is an informed one turns on whether the directors have informed themselves "prior to making a business decision, of all material information reasonably available to them." *Id.*

Under the business judgment rule there is no protection for directors who have made "an unintelligent or unadvised judgment." *Mitchell v. Highland-Western Glass,* Del. Ch., 167 A. 831, 833 (1933). A director's duty to inform himself in preparation for a decision derives from the fiduciary capacity in which he serves the corporation and its stockholders. *Lutz v. Boas,* Del. Ch., 171 A.2d 381 (1961). *See Weinberger v. UOP, Inc., supra; Guth v. Loft, supra.* Since a director is vested with the responsibility for the management of the affairs of the corporation, he must execute that duty with the recognition that he acts on behalf of others. Such obligation does not tolerate faithlessness or self-dealing. But fulfillment of the fiduciary function requires more than the mere absence of bad faith or fraud. Representation of the financial interests of others imposes on a director an affirmative duty to protect those interests and to proceed with a critical eye in assessing information of the type and under the circumstances present here. *See Lutz v. Boas, supra; Guth v. Loft, supra* at 510. *Compare Donovan v. Cunningham,* 5th Cir., 716 F.2d 1455, 1467 (1983); *Doyle v. Union Insurance Company,* Neb. Supr., 277 N.W.2d 36 (1979); *Continental Securities Co. v. Belmont,* N.Y. App., 99 N.E. 138, 141 (1912).

Thus, a director's duty to exercise an informed business judgment is in the nature of a duty of care, as distinguished from a duty of loyalty. Here, there were no allegations of fraud, bad faith, or self-dealing, or proof thereof. Hence, it is presumed that the directors reached their business judgment in good faith, *Allaun v. Consolidated Oil Co.,* Del. Ch., 147 A. 257 (1929), and considerations of motive are irrelevant to the issue before us.

The standard of care applicable to a director's duty of care has also been recently restated by this Court. In *Aronson, supra,* we stated:

> While the Delaware cases use a variety of terms to describe the applicable standard of care, our analysis satisfies us that under the business judgment rule director liability is predicated upon concepts of gross negligence. (footnote omitted)

473 A.2d at 812.

We again confirm that view. We think the concept of gross negligence is also the proper standard for determining whether a business judgment reached by a board of directors was an informed one.

In the specific context of a proposed merger of domestic corporations, a director has a duty under 8 Del. C. § 251(b), along with his fellow directors, to act in an informed and deliberate manner in determining whether to approve an agreement of merger before submitting the proposal to the stockholders. Certainly in the merger context, a director may not abdicate that duty by leaving to the shareholders alone the decision to approve or disapprove the agreement. *See Beard v. Elster,* Del. Supr., 160 A.2d 731, 737 (1960). Only an agreement of merger satisfying the requirements of 8 Del. C. § 251(b) may be submitted to the shareholders under § 251(c). *See generally Aronson v. Lewis, supra* at 811-13; *see also Pogostin v. Rice, supra.*

It is against those standards that the conduct of the directors of Trans Union must be tested, as a matter of law and as a matter of fact, regarding their exercise of an informed business judgment in voting to approve the Pritzker merger proposal.

III.

The defendants argue that the determination of whether their decision to accept $55 per share for Trans Union represented an informed business judgment requires consideration, not only of that which they knew and learned on September 20, but also of that which they subsequently learned and did over the following four-month period before the shareholders met to vote on the proposal in February, 1981. The defendants thereby seek to reduce the significance of their action on September 20 and to widen the time frame for determining whether their decision to accept the Pritzker proposal was an informed one. Thus, the defendants contend that what the directors did and learned subsequent to September 20 and through January 26, 1981, was properly taken into account by the Trial Court in determining whether the Board's judgment was an informed one. We disagree with this *post hoc* approach.

The issue of whether the directors reached an informed decision to "sell" the Company on September 20, 1980 must be determined only upon the basis of the information then reasonably available to the directors and relevant to their decision to accept the Pritzker merger proposal. This is not to say that the directors were precluded from altering their original plan of action, had they done so in an informed manner. What we do say is that the question of whether the directors reached an informed business judgment in agreeing to sell the Company, pursuant to the terms of the September 20 Agreement presents, in reality, two questions: (A) whether the directors reached an informed business judgment on September 20, 1980; and (B) if they did not, whether the directors' actions taken subsequent to September 20 were adequate to cure any infirmity in their action taken on September 20. We first consider the directors' September 20 action in terms of their reaching an informed business judgment.

A

On the record before us, we must conclude that the Board of Directors did not reach an informed business judgment on September 20, 1980 in voting to "sell" the Company for $55 per share pursuant to the Pritzker cash-out merger proposal. Our reasons, in summary, are as follows:

The directors (1) did not adequately inform themselves as to Van Gorkom's role in forcing the "sale" of the Company and in establishing the per share purchase price; (2) were uninformed as to the intrinsic value of the Company; and (3) given these circumstances, at a minimum, were grossly negligent in approving the "sale" of the

Company upon two hours' consideration, without prior notice, and without the exigency of a crisis or emergency.

As has been noted, the Board based its September 20 decision to approve the cash-out merger primarily on Van Gorkom's representations. None of the directors, other than Van Gorkom and Chelberg, had any prior knowledge that the purpose of the meeting was to propose a cash-out merger of Trans Union. No members of Senior Management were present, other than Chelberg, Romans and Peterson; and the latter two had only learned of the proposed sale an hour earlier. Both general counsel Moore and former general counsel Browder attended the meeting, but were equally uninformed as to the purpose of the meeting and the documents to be acted upon.

Without any documents before them concerning the proposed transaction, the members of the Board were required to rely entirely upon Van Gorkom's 20-minute oral presentation of the proposal. No written summary of the terms of the merger was presented; the directors were given no documentation to support the adequacy of $55 price per share for sale of the Company; and the Board had before it nothing more than Van Gorkom's statement of his understanding of the substance of an agreement which he admittedly had never read, nor which any member of the Board had ever seen.

Under 8 Del. C. § 141(e), "directors are fully protected in relying in good faith on reports made by officers." *Michelson v. Duncan,* Del. Ch., 386 A.2d 1144, 1156 (1978); *aff'd in part and rev'd in part on other grounds,* Del. Supr., 407 A.2d 211 (1979). *See also Graham v. Allis-Chalmers Mfg. Co.,* Del. Supr., 188 A.2d 125, 130 (1963); *Prince v. Bensinger,* Del. Ch., 244 A.2d 89, 94 (1968). The term "report" has been liberally construed to include reports of informal personal investigations by corporate officers, *Cheff v. Mathes,* Del. Supr., 199 A.2d 548, 556 (1964). However, there is no evidence that any "report," as defined under § 141(e), concerning the Pritzker proposal, was presented to the Board on September 20.[16] Van Gorkom's oral presentation of his understanding of the terms of the proposed Merger Agreement, which he had not seen, and Romans' brief oral statement of his preliminary study regarding the feasibility of a leveraged buy-out of Trans Union do not qualify as § 141(e) "reports" for these reasons: The former lacked substance because Van Gorkom was basically uninformed as to the essential provisions of the very document about which he was talking. Romans' statement was irrelevant to the issues before the Board since it did not purport to be a valuation study. At a minimum for a report to enjoy the status conferred by § 141(e), it must be pertinent to the subject matter upon which a board is called to act, and otherwise be entitled to good faith, not blind, reliance. Considering all of the surrounding circumstances — hastily calling the meeting without prior notice of its subject matter, the proposed sale of the Company without any prior consideration of the issue or necessity therefor, the urgent time constraints imposed

---

[16]In support of the defendants' argument that their judgment as to the adequacy of $55 per share was an informed one, the directors rely on the BCG study and the Five Year Forecast. However, no one even referred to either of these studies at the September 20 meeting; and it is conceded that these materials do not represent valuation studies. Hence, these documents do not constitute evidence as to whether the directors reached an informed judgment on September 20 that $55 per share was a fair value for sale of the Company.

by Pritzker, and the total absence of any documentation whatsoever — the directors were duty bound to make reasonable inquiry of Van Gorkom and Romans, and if they had done so, the inadequacy of that upon which they now claim to have relied would have been apparent.

The defendants rely on the following factors to sustain the Trial Court's finding that the Board's decision was an informed one: (1) the magnitude of the premium or spread between the $55 Pritzker offering price and Trans Union's current market price of $38 per share; (2) the amendment of the Agreement as submitted on September 20 to permit the Board to accept any better offer during the "market test" period; (3) the collective experience and expertise of the Board's "inside" and "outside" directors; and (4) their reliance on Brennan's legal advice that the directors might be sued if they rejected the Pritzker proposal. We discuss each of these grounds *seriatim*:

(1)

A substantial premium may provide one reason to recommend a merger, but in the absence of other sound valuation information, the fact of a premium alone does not provide an adequate basis upon which to assess the fairness of an offering price. Here, the judgment reached as to the adequacy of the premium was based on a comparison between the historically depressed Trans Union market price and the amount of the Pritzker offer. Using market price as a basis for concluding that the premium adequately reflected the true value of the Company was a clearly faulty, indeed fallacious, premise, as the defendants' own evidence demonstrates.

The record is clear that before September 20, Van Gorkom and other members of Trans Union's Board knew that the market had consistently undervalued the worth of Trans Union's stock, despite steady increases in the Company's operating income in the seven years preceding the merger. The Board related this occurrence in large part to Trans Union's inability to use its ITCs as previously noted. Van Gorkom testified that he did not believe the market price accurately reflected Trans Union's true worth; and several of the directors testified that, as a general rule, most chief executives think that the market undervalues their companies' stock. Yet, on September 20, Trans Union's Board apparently believed that the market stock price accurately reflected the value of the Company for the purpose of determining the adequacy of the premium for its sale.

In the Proxy Statement, however, the directors reversed their position. There, they stated that, although the earnings prospects for Trans Union were "excellent," they found no basis for believing that this would be reflected in future stock prices. With regard to past trading, the Board stated that the prices at which the Company's common stock had traded in recent years did not reflect the "inherent" value of the Company. But having referred to the "inherent" value of Trans Union, the directors ascribed no number to it. Moreover, nowhere did they disclose that they had no basis on which to fix "inherent" worth beyond an impressionistic reaction to the premium over market and an unsubstantiated belief that the value of the assets was "significantly greater" than book value. By their own admission they could not rely on the stock price as an accurate measure of value. Yet, also by their own admission, the Board members assumed that Trans Union's market price was adequate to serve as a basis upon which to assess the adequacy of the premium for purposes of the September 20 meeting.

The parties do not dispute that a publicly-traded stock price is solely a measure of the value of a minority position and, thus, market price represents only the value of a single share. Nevertheless, on September 20, the Board assessed the adequacy of the premium over market, offered by Pritzker, solely by comparing it with Trans Union's current and historical stock price. (*See supra* note 5 at 866.)

Indeed, as of September 20, the Board had no other information on which to base a determination of the intrinsic value of Trans Union as a going concern. As of September 20, the Board had made no evaluation of the Company designed to value the entire enterprise, nor had the Board ever previously considered selling the Company or consenting to a buy-out merger. Thus, the adequacy of a premium is indeterminate unless it is assessed in terms of other competent and sound valuation information that reflects the value of the particular business.

Despite the foregoing facts and circumstances, there was no call by the Board, either on September 20 or thereafter, for any valuation study or documentation of the $55 price per share as a measure of the fair value of the Company in a cash-out context. It is undisputed that the major asset of Trans Union was its cash flow. Yet, at no time did the Board call for a valuation study taking into account that highly significant element of the Company's assets.

We do not imply that an outside valuation study is essential to support an informed business judgment; nor do we state that fairness opinions by independent investment bankers are required as a matter of law. Often insiders familiar with the business of a going concern are in a better position than are outsiders to gather relevant information; and under appropriate circumstances, such directors may be fully protected in relying in good faith upon the valuation reports of their management. *See* 8 Del. C. § 141(e). *See also Cheff v. Mathes, supra.*

Here, the record establishes that the Board did not request its Chief Financial Officer, Romans, to make any valuation study or review of the proposal to determine the adequacy of $55 per share for sale of the Company. On the record before us: The Board rested on Romans' elicited response that the $55 figure was within a "fair price range" within the context of a leveraged buy-out. No director sought any further information from Romans. No director asked him why he put $55 at the bottom of his range. No director asked Romans for any details as to his study, the reason why it had been undertaken or its depth. No director asked to see the study; and no director asked Romans whether Trans Union's finance department could do a fairness study within the remaining 36-hour period available under the Pritzker offer.

Had the Board, or any member, made an inquiry of Romans, he presumably would have responded as he testified: that his calculations were rough and preliminary; and, that the study was not designed to determine the fair value of the Company, but rather to assess the feasibility of a leveraged buy-out financed by the Company's projected cash flow, making certain assumptions as to the purchaser's borrowing needs. Romans would have presumably also informed the Board of his view, and the widespread view of Senior Management, that the timing of the offer was wrong and the offer inadequate.

The record also establishes that the Board accepted without scrutiny Van Gorkom's representation as to the fairness of the $55 price per share for sale of the Company—a subject that the Board had never previously considered. The Board thereby failed to discover that Van Gorkom had suggested the $55 price to Pritzker and, most crucially, that Van Gorkom had arrived at the $55 figure based on calculations designed solely to determine the feasibility of a leveraged buy-out.[19] No questions were raised either as to the tax implications of a cash-out merger or how the price for the one million share option granted Pritzker was calculated.

We do not say that the Board of Directors was not entitled to give some credence to Van Gorkom's representation that $55 was an adequate or fair price. Under § 141(e), the directors were entitled to rely upon their chairman's opinion of value and adequacy, provided that such opinion was reached on a sound basis. Here, the issue is whether the directors informed themselves as to all information that was reasonably available to them. Had they done so, they would have learned of the source and derivation of the $55 price and could not reasonably have relied thereupon in good faith.

None of the directors, Management or outside, were investment bankers or financial analysts. Yet the Board did not consider recessing the meeting until a later hour that day (or requesting an extension of Pritzker's Sunday evening deadline) to give it time to elicit more information as to the sufficiency of the offer, either from inside Management (in particular Romans) or from Trans Union's own investment banker, Salomon Brothers, whose Chicago specialist in merger and acquisitions was known to the Board and familiar with Trans Union's affairs.

Thus, the record compels the conclusion that on September 20 the Board lacked valuation information adequate to reach an informed business judgment as to the fairness of $55 per share for sale of the Company.

(2)

This brings us to the post-September 20 "market test" upon which the defendants ultimately rely to confirm the reasonableness of their September 20 decision to accept the Pritzker proposal. In this connection, the directors present a two-part argument: (a) that by making a "market test" of Pritzker's $55 per share offer a condition of their September 20 decision to accept his offer, they cannot be found to have acted impulsively or in an uninformed manner on September 20; and (b) that the adequacy of the $17 premium for sale of the Company was conclusively established over the following 90 to 120 days by the most reliable evidence available—the marketplace. Thus, the defendants impliedly contend that the "market test" eliminated the need for the Board to perform any other form of fairness test either on September 20, or thereafter.

---

[19]As of September 20 the directors did not know: that Van Gorkom had arrived at the $55 figure alone, and subjectively, as the figure to be used by Controller Peterson in creating a feasible structure for a leveraged buy-out by a prospective purchaser; that Van Gorkom had not sought advice, information or assistance from either inside or outside Trans Union directors as to the value of the Company as an entity or the fair price per share for 100% of its stock; that Van Gorkom had not consulted with the Company's investment bankers or other financial analysts; that Van Gorkom had not consulted with or confided in any officer or director of the Company except Chelberg; and that Van Gorkom had deliberately chosen to ignore the advice and opinion of the members of his Senior Management group regarding the adequacy of the $55 price.

Again, the facts of record do not support the defendants' argument. There is no evidence: (a) that the Merger Agreement was effectively amended to give the Board freedom to put Trans Union up for auction sale to the highest bidder; or (b) that a public auction was in fact permitted to occur. The minutes of the Board meeting make no reference to any of this. Indeed, the record compels the conclusion that the directors had no rational basis for expecting that a market test was attainable, given the terms of the Agreement as executed during the evening of September 20. We rely upon the following facts which are essentially uncontradicted:

The Merger Agreement, specifically identified as that originally presented to the Board on September 20, has never been produced by the defendants, notwithstanding the plaintiffs' several demands for production before as well as during trial. No acceptable explanation of this failure to produce documents has been given to either the Trial Court or this Court. Significantly, neither the defendants nor their counsel have made the affirmative representation that this critical document has been produced. Thus, the Court is deprived of the best evidence on which to judge the merits of the defendants' position as to the care and attention which they gave to the terms of the Agreement on September 20.

. . .

Thus, notwithstanding what several of the outside directors later claimed to have "thought" occurred at the meeting, the record compels the conclusion that Trans Union's Board had no rational basis to conclude on September 20 or in the days immediately following, that the Board's acceptance of Pritzker's offer was conditioned on (1) a "market test" of the offer; and (2) the Board's right to withdraw from the Pritzker Agreement and accept any higher offer received before the shareholder meeting.

(3)

The directors' unfounded reliance on both the premium and the market test as the basis for accepting the Pritzker proposal undermines the defendants' remaining contention that the Board's collective experience and sophistication was a sufficient basis for finding that it reached its September 20 decision with informed, reasonable deliberation.[21] . . .

. . .

We conclude that Trans Union's Board was grossly negligent in that it failed to act with informed reasonable deliberation in agreeing to the Pritzker merger proposal on September 20; and we further conclude that the Trial Court erred as a matter of

---

[21]Trans Union's five "inside" directors had backgrounds in law and accounting, 116 years of collective employment by the Company and 68 years of combined experience on its Board. Trans Union's five "outside" directors included four chief executives of major corporations and an economist who was a former dean of a major school of business and chancellor of a university. The "outside" directors had 78 years of combined experience as chief executive officers of major corporations and 50 years of cumulative experience as directors of Trans Union. Thus, defendants argue that the Board was eminently qualified to reach an informed judgment on the proposed "sale" of Trans Union notwithstanding their lack of any advance notice of the proposal, the shortness of their deliberation, and their determination not to consult with their investment banker or to obtain a fairness opinion.

law in failing to address that question before determining whether the directors' later conduct was sufficient to cure its initial error.

. . .

VI.

To summarize: we hold that the directors of Trans Union breached their fiduciary duty to their stockholders (1) by their failure to inform themselves of all information reasonably available to them and relevant to their decision to recommend the Pritzker merger; and (2) by their failure to disclose all material information such as a reasonable stockholder would consider important in deciding whether to approve the Pritzker offer.

We hold, therefore, that the Trial Court committed reversible error in applying the business judgment rule in favor of the director defendants in this case.

On remand, the Court of Chancery shall conduct an evidentiary hearing to determine the fair value of the shares represented by the plaintiffs' class, based on the intrinsic value of Trans Union on September 20, 1980. Such valuation shall be made in accordance with *Weinberger v. UOP, Inc., supra* at 712-715. Thereafter, an award of damages may be entered to the extent that the fair value of Trans Union exceeds $55 per share.

REVERSED and REMANDED for proceedings consistent herewith.

Post-Case Follow-Up

Smith v. Van Gorkom was a controversial decision because it was the first time in memory that the directors of a public company were found to have breached their fiduciary duty of care in a case involving a substantial premium for cashed-out shareholders. In the wake of *Trans Union*, it reportedly became more difficult and expensive for corporations to obtain directors and officers (D&O) liability insurance. D&O insurance provides directors and officers with insurance coverage in the event the director or officer is sued for breach of fiduciary duty. After *Trans Union*, insurance carriers apparently viewed these policies as involving more risk than had been understood to exist prior to *Trans Union*.

Changes in the D&O insurance market post-*Trans Union* led to concerns that skilled, qualified potential directors would be unwilling to serve on boards at all, or if they agreed to serve, might be less willing to make hard decisions and take the sort of calculated business risks thought to be necessary to establish and run a business. The Delaware legislature responded to these concerns by enacting DGCL § 102(b)(7). This section of the Delaware corporations code allows corporations to exculpate directors, or protect them against liability for money damages for breaches of the duty of care, via a charter provision. It provides as follows:

(b) In addition to the matters required to be set forth in the certificate of incorporation by subsection (a) of this section, the certificate of incorporation may also contain any or all of the following matters:

(7) A provision eliminating or limiting the personal liability of a director to the corporation or its stockholders for monetary damages for breach of fiduciary duty as a director, provided that such provision shall not eliminate or limit the liability of a director: (i) For any breach of the director's duty of loyalty to the corporation or its stockholders; (ii) for acts or omissions not in good faith or which involve intentional misconduct or a knowing violation of law; (iii) under § 174 of this title; or (iv) for any transaction from which the director derived an improper personal benefit. No such provision shall eliminate or limit the liability of a director for any act or omission occurring prior to the date when such provision becomes effective. All references in this paragraph to a director shall also be deemed to refer to such other person or persons, if any, who, pursuant to a provision of the certificate of incorporation in accordance with § 141(a) of this title, exercise or perform any of the powers or duties otherwise conferred or imposed upon the board of directors by this title.

Here is an example of an exculpatory provision taken from the charter of Alphabet Inc., the Delaware corporation formed as part of the reorganization of Google:

> Section 1. To the fullest extent permitted by the General Corporation Law of Delaware as the same exists or as may hereafter be amended, a director of the Corporation shall not be personally liable to the Corporation or its stockholders for monetary damages for breach of fiduciary duty as a director. If the General Corporation Law of Delaware is amended to authorize corporate action further eliminating or limiting the personal liability of directors, then the liability of a director of the Corporation shall be eliminated to the fullest extent permitted by the General Corporation Law of Delaware, as so amended.

If a corporation has a § 102(b)(7) exculpatory provision in its charter, its directors will not be subject to liability for money damages for breaches of the duty of care, even if the directors acted with gross negligence. In fact, if a plaintiff files a lawsuit against corporate directors alleging breach of the duty of care seeking money damages, and does not allege a failure to act in good faith or other breach of the duty of loyalty, and the corporation has an exculpatory provision in its charter, the court will dismiss the complaint. To avoid dismissal, a plaintiff must (i) seek equitable relief (e.g., an order enjoining a challenged merger) and not money damages; *or* (ii) allege a claim that is not subject to exculpation under § 102(b)(7) (e.g., a claim based on breach of the duty of loyalty). See Sections C, D, and E. In the wake of Delaware's adoption of § 102(b)(7), other jurisdictions followed suit. *See, e.g.,* NYBCL § 402(b).

Smith v. Van Gorkom: Real Life Applications

1. You represent Acme, Inc., a Delaware corporation. Last week, Beta Corporation reached out to Acme and expressed interest in acquiring Acme via a cash-out merger. Under applicable corporations statutes, Acme's board is required to make a recommendation to shareholders respecting the merits of the proposed transaction. Mindful of what happened to the board in *Smith v. Van Gorkom*, identify steps that Acme's board might consider taking when assessing Beta's proposed deal.

2. Acme's board decides to ask Acme's chief financial officer to assess the financial terms of the proposed deal, including the merits of the price per share that

Can Directors Rely on Experts?

As *Trans Union* suggests, boards often call upon experts — for example, lawyers, accountants, and bankers — for advice. As a general rule, directors may rely upon experts provided their reliance is reasonable under the circumstances. *See, e.g.*, DGCL § 141(e) (stating member of the board or of a board committee) "shall, in the performance of his duties, be fully protected in relying in good faith upon the records of the corporation and upon such information, opinions, reports or statements presented to the corporation by any of the corporation's officers or employees, or committees of the board of directors, or by any other person as to matters the member reasonably believes are within such other person's professional or expert competence and who has been selected with reasonable care by or on behalf of the corporation"); MCBA §§ 8.30 (d), (e), and (f); NYBCL § 717(a); ALI Principles of Corporate Governance § 4.01(b). Directors typically must establish three things to be protected in reliance: (i) good faith; (ii) reasonable belief in the professional or expert competence of the person furnishing the report; and (iii) reasonable belief that the expert upon whom the director relies has been selected with reasonable care by or on behalf of the corporation.

Beta is prepared to offer. Board members have asked you whether they may rely upon the financial analysis of Acme's CFO. Prepare a brief memo discussing this issue for Acme.

3. Assume that Acme's board recommends that shareholders approve the transaction. A shareholder is unhappy with the proposed cash-out price and sues to enjoin the merger. Acme's charter contains an exculpation provision. Is the plaintiff's lawsuit subject to dismissal under the exculpation clause? Why or why not? What if the transaction closes, and the plaintiff sues seeking money damages associated with the cash-out per share price? Is the court likely to dismiss this claim or allow it to proceed?

4. Good Dairy, Inc. is a Delaware corporation that manufactures and sells organic yogurt and other dairy products. Since its founding ten years ago, Good Dairy has touted its commitment to purchasing milk from farmers who pledge not to administer hormones to their cows. Indeed, the company has run many advertising campaigns over the years touting its "clean and pure" milk supply. Last month, however, Good Dairy's board concluded that there is no difference between milk from cows treated with hormones and milk from cows not treated with hormones. Accordingly, the board decided that the company should begin purchasing milk from farmers who administer hormones to their cows. The board made this decision after reviewing certain scientific evidence and hearing from farmers who treat cows with hormones. They did not speak with customers or with farmers who do not use hormones.

The decision to purchase milk from cows treated with hormones led to a firestorm of negative publicity for Good Dairy — other scientists challenged the evidence, longstanding customers launched a boycott, etc. The controversy led to precipitous drop in Good Dairy's profits. Sales have yet to recover.

Last week, several large shareholders filed a derivative action against Good Dairy's directors alleging that the decision to authorize milk purchases from cows treated with hormones was a breach of fiduciary duty. If the director defendants file a motion to dismiss the complaint, citing the business judgment rule, how is the court likely to rule?

C. DUTY OF LOYALTY

The **duty of loyalty** requires directors to put the interests of the corporation and its shareholders first, before personal interests. *See* MBCA § 8.30. There are two classic duty of loyalty scenarios: (i) claims arising under the **corporate opportunity doctrine,** or the doctrine that prohibits directors from taking for themselves business opportunities that properly belong to the corporation; and (ii) claims arising from **conflicting interest transactions,** or transactions between a director (or a relative of the director or an entity owned by the director) and the corporation. We discuss these claims below.

1. The Corporate Opportunity Doctrine—Usurping a Corporate Opportunity

Under the corporate opportunity doctrine, a director may not **usurp** (i.e., take for herself) a business opportunity that properly belongs to the corporation—at least not without offering the opportunity to the corporation first. Courts have developed a variety of tests to determine whether an opportunity belongs to the corporation. These tests tend to involve highly fact-specific inquiries into the relationship (if any) between the opportunity and the corporation's business. One influential test is the **line of business test** from the seminal 1939 Delaware Supreme Court decision *Guth v. Loft,* and elaborated upon more recently in *Broz v. Cellular Information Systems, Inc.,* 673 A.2d 148, 154-55 (Del. 1996). The following excerpt from *Broz* (quoting *Guth*) discusses the line of business test and details the fact-intensive nature of the inquiry:

> The doctrine of corporate opportunity represents but one species of the broad fiduciary duties assumed by a corporate director or officer. A corporate fiduciary agrees to place the interests of the corporation before his or her own in appropriate circumstances. In light of the diverse and often competing obligations faced by directors and officers, however, the corporate opportunity doctrine arose as a means of defining the parameters of fiduciary duty in instances of potential conflict.

Duty of Care Red Flags and Best Practices

To help educate and advise clients, you may want to develop a checklist of red flags and best practices regarding the duty of care. Here are some suggested topics:

■ **Undue haste in decision making?**

While there are cases where boards must act quickly—for example, when dealing with a potential hostile takeover—be wary of a "rush to judgment." Encourage client boards to take the time necessary to gather relevant information, to consult with appropriate experts, to ask questions, and to deliberate before making a decision. If haste is not mandated by the circumstances, and the board is perceived to have rushed when making a decision, a court may question why haste was necessary, and whether the board's haste hurt the corporation and its shareholders.

■ **Lack of board preparation?**

The duty of care does not require directors to set up shop at the corporation, reading every single document prepared by every single employee every single day. That said, a failure by board members to obtain and review relevant documents in preparation for board action is a red flag. Likewise, a failure to schedule or attend board meetings can create the impression that the board has been insufficiently diligent in its decision-making process.

■ **Lack of questioning or involvement by the board?**

In addition to preparation, board members should be prepared to participate actively in the decision-making process before, during, and after board meetings. Board members are well advised to review documents carefully in preparation for meetings, to ask questions during meetings, and to meet as often and for as long as needed for robust deliberation. Failing to take these steps may be a red flag respecting board diligence.

■ **Undue or unwarranted reliance on other officers or experts?**

As noted above, reasonable reliance generally is protected. Watch out for reliance upon an "expert" who lacks the necessary skills, experience, training, etc.

■ **Failing to "paper" diligence?**

Directors should be sure to attend to corporate "housekeeping." This includes ensuring that board meeting minutes reflect the board's diligence in decision making. Failing to "paper" the record with evidence of the board's diligence may make it harder to demonstrate that the board complied with its duty of care in subsequent litigation.

The classic statement of the doctrine is derived from the venerable case of *Guth v. Loft, Inc.* In *Guth*, this Court held that:

> if there is presented to a corporate officer or director a business opportunity which the corporation is financially able to undertake, is, from its nature, in the line of the corporation's business and is of practical advantage to it, is one in which the corporation has an interest or a reasonable expectancy, and, by embracing the opportunity, the self-interest of the officer or director will be brought into conflict with that of the corporation, the law will not permit him to seize the opportunity for himself.

Guth, 5 A.2d at 510-11.

The corporate opportunity doctrine, as delineated by *Guth* and its progeny, holds that a corporate officer or director may not take a business opportunity for his own if: (1) the corporation is financially able to exploit the opportunity; (2) the opportunity is within the corporation's line of business; (3) the corporation has an interest or expectancy in the opportunity; and (4) by taking the opportunity for his own, the corporate fiduciary will thereby be placed in a position inimical to his duties to the corporation. The Court in *Guth* also derived a corollary which states that a director or officer *may* take a corporate opportunity if: (1) the opportunity is presented to the director or officer in his individual and not his corporate capacity; (2) the opportunity is not essential to the corporation; (3) the corporation holds no interest or expectancy in the opportunity; and (4) the director or officer has not wrongfully employed the resources of the corporation in pursuing or exploiting the opportunity. *Guth*, 5 A.2d at 509.

Thus, the contours of this doctrine are well established. It is important to note, however, that the tests enunciated in *Guth* and subsequent cases provide guidelines to be considered by a reviewing court in balancing the equities of an individual case. No one factor is dispositive and all factors must be taken into account insofar as they are applicable. Cases involving a claim of usurpation of a corporate opportunity range over a multitude of factual settings. Hard and fast rules are not easily crafted to deal with such an array of complex situations. As this Court noted in *Johnston v. Greene*, Del. Supr., 121 A.2d 919 (1956), the determination of "[w]hether or not a director has appropriated for himself something that in fairness should belong to the corporation is 'a factual question to be decided by reasonable inference from objective facts.' " *Id.* at 923 (quoting *Guth*, 5 A.2d at 513). . . .

Broz, 673 A.2d at 154-55 (citing *Guth v. Loft, Inc.*, 5 A.2d 503, 509-10 (Del. 1939)).

Under the *Guth/Broz* test, a corporation's "line of business" includes activities as to which the corporation has "fundamental knowledge, practical experience and an ability to pursue, which, logically and naturally, is adaptable to its business having regard for its financial position, and is consonant with its reasonable needs and aspirations for expansion. . . ." *Guth*, 5 A.2d at 514 (emphasis omitted). To satisfy the "interest" or "expectancy" factor, "there must be some tie between [the opportunity at issue] and the nature of the corporate business." *Broz*, 673 A.2d at 156 (quoting *Johnston v. Greene*, 121 A.2d 919 (Del. Ch. 1956)).

As *Broz* makes clear, a director considering whether to pursue an opportunity must analyze the situation *ex ante* to determine whether the opportunity is one that rightfully belongs to the corporation. *Broz*, 673 A.2d at 157. The *Broz* court observed that presenting the opportunity to the corporation's board first creates a kind of "safe harbor" for the director, removing the "specter" of a *post hoc* judicial determination that opportunity belonged to the corporation, and that the director or officer who failed to present the opportunity to the corporation first improperly took the opportunity for herself. *Id.* While the *Broz* court was careful to note that "it is not the law of Delaware that presentation to the board is a necessary prerequisite to a finding that a corporate opportunity has not been usurped," it observed that presentation "avoids the possibility that an error in the fiduciary's assessment of the situation will create future liability for breach of fiduciary duty." *Id.*

Case Preview

Northeast Harbor Golf Club, Inc. v. Harris

While highly influential, Delaware's line of business test is not the only iteration of the corporate opportunity doctrine. In the next case, directors of a golf club challenged the club president's acquisition of, and development plans for, land adjoining the club. (We discuss officers' fiduciary duties in Section I below. For present purposes, assume that both directors and officers are subject to the corporate opportunity doctrine.) In assessing whether the president wrongfully usurped a corporate opportunity, the court examined tests used by several jurisdictions from around the country. In reading the case, consider the following:

1. Compare the line of business test to the test used by the court in this case.
2. Under the ALI approach, what role, if any, does disclosure of the alleged opportunity by the officer or director play in deciding whether a director or officer has breached her fiduciary duty of loyalty?
3. Does it matter that the board was aware of Harris's purchase of the parcels at issue for years before it decided to sue? Should it matter?
4. Do fiduciaries have disclosure obligations respecting transactions like the one at issue in this case?

Northeast Harbor Golf Club, Inc. v. Harris
661 A.2d 1146 (Me. 1995)

ROBERTS, Justice.*

Northeast Harbor Golf Club, Inc., appeals from a judgment entered in the Superior Court (Hancock County, Atwood, J.) following a nonjury trial. The Club

*Footnotes have been omitted for purposes of brevity.

maintains that the trial court erred in finding that Nancy Harris did not breach her fiduciary duty as president of the Club by purchasing and developing property abutting the golf course. Because we today adopt principles different from those applied by the trial court in determining that Harris's activities did not constitute a breach of the corporate opportunity doctrine, we vacate the judgment.

I. THE FACTS

Nancy Harris was the president of the Northeast Harbor Golf Club, a Maine corporation, from 1971 until she was asked to resign in 1990. The Club also had a board of directors that was responsible for making or approving significant policy decisions. The Club's only major asset was a golf course in Mount Desert. During Harris's tenure as president, the board occasionally discussed the possibility of developing some of the Club's real estate in order to raise money. Although Harris was generally in favor of tasteful development, the board always "shied away" from that type of activity.

In 1979, Robert Suminsby informed Harris that he was the listing broker for the Gilpin property, which comprised three noncontiguous parcels located among the fairways of the golf course. The property included an unused right-of-way on which the Club's parking lot and clubhouse were located. It was also encumbered by an easement in favor of the Club allowing foot traffic from the green of one hole to the next tee. Suminsby testified that he contacted Harris because she was the president of the Club and he believed that the Club would be interested in buying the property in order to prevent development.

Harris immediately agreed to purchase the Gilpin property in her own name for the asking price of $45,000. She did not disclose her plans to purchase the property to the Club's board prior to the purchase. She informed the board at its annual August meeting that she had purchased the property, that she intended to hold it in her own name, and that the Club would be "protected." The board took no action in response to the Harris purchase. She testified that at the time of the purchase she had no plans to develop the property and that no such plans took shape until 1988.

In 1984, while playing golf with the postmaster of Northeast Harbor, Harris learned that a parcel of land owned by the heirs of the Smallidge family might be available for purchase. The Smallidge parcel was surrounded on three sides by the golf course and on the fourth side by a house lot. It had no access to the road. With the ultimate goal of acquiring the property, Harris instructed her lawyer to locate the Smallidge heirs. Harris testified that she told a number of individual board members about her attempt to acquire the Smallidge parcel. At a board meeting in August 1985, Harris formally disclosed to the board that she had purchased the Smallidge property. The minutes of that meeting show that she told the board she had no present plans to develop the Smallidge parcel. Harris testified that at the time of the purchase of the Smallidge property she nonetheless thought it might be nice to have some houses there. Again, the board took no formal action as a result of Harris's purchase. Harris acquired the Smallidge property from ten heirs, paying a total of $60,000. In 1990, Harris paid $275,000 for the lot and building separating the Smallidge parcel from the road in order to gain access to the otherwise landlocked parcel.

The trial court expressly found that the Club would have been unable to purchase either the Gilpin or Smallidge properties for itself, relying on testimony that the Club continually experienced financial difficulties, operated annually at a deficit, and depended on contributions from the directors to pay its bills. On the other hand, there was evidence that the Club had occasionally engaged in successful fund-raising, including a two-year period shortly after the Gilpin purchase during which the Club raised $115,000. The Club had $90,000 in a capital investment fund at the time of the Smallidge purchase.

In 1987 or 1988, Harris divided the real estate into 41 small lots, 14 on the Smallidge property and 27 on the Gilpin property. Apparently as part of her estate plan, Harris conveyed noncontiguous lots among the 41 to her children and retained others for herself. In 1991, Harris and her children exchanged deeds to reassemble the small lots into larger parcels. At the time the Club filed this suit, the property was divided into 11 lots, some owned by Harris and others by her children who are also defendants in this case. Harris estimated the value of all the real estate at the time of the trial to be $1,550,000.

In 1988, Harris, who was still president of the Club, and her children began the process of obtaining approval for a five-lot subdivision known as Bushwood on the lower Gilpin property. Even when the board learned of the proposed subdivision, a majority failed to take any action. A group of directors formed a separate organization in order to oppose the subdivision on the basis that it violated the local zoning ordinance. After Harris's resignation as president, the Club also sought unsuccessfully to challenge the subdivision. *See Northeast Harbor Golf Club, Inc. v. Town of Mount Desert,* 618 A.2d 225 (Me. 1992). Plans of Harris and her family for development of the other parcels are unclear, but the local zoning ordinance would permit construction of up to 11 houses on the land as currently divided.

After Harris's plans to develop Bushwood became apparent, the board grew increasingly divided concerning the propriety of development near the golf course. At least two directors, Henri Agnese and Nick Ludington, testified that they trusted Harris to act in the best interests of the Club and that they had no problem with the development plans for Bushwood. Other directors disagreed.

In particular, John Schafer, a Washington, D.C., lawyer and long-time member of the board, took issue with Harris's conduct. He testified that he had relied on Harris's representations at the time she acquired the properties that she would not develop them. According to Schafer, matters came to a head in August 1990 when a number of directors concluded that Harris's development plans irreconcilably conflicted with the Club's interests. As a result, Schafer and two other directors asked Harris to resign as president. In April 1991, after a substantial change in the board's membership, the board authorized the instant lawsuit against Harris for the breach of her fiduciary duty to act in the best interests of the corporation. The board simultaneously resolved that the proposed housing development was contrary to the best interests of the corporation.

The Club filed a complaint against Harris, her sons John and Shepard, and her daughter-in-law Melissa Harris. As amended, the complaint alleged that during her term as president Harris breached her fiduciary duty by purchasing the lots without providing notice and an opportunity for the Club to purchase the property and by subdividing the lots for future development. The Club sought an injunction to prevent development and also sought to impose a constructive trust on the property in question for the benefit of the Club.

The trial court found that Harris had not usurped a corporate opportunity because the acquisition of real estate was not in the Club's line of business. Moreover, it found that the corporation lacked the financial ability to purchase the real estate at issue. Finally, the court placed great emphasis on Harris's good faith. It noted her long and dedicated history of service to the Club, her personal oversight of the Club's growth, and her frequent financial contributions to the Club. The court found that her development activities were "generally . . . compatible with the corporation's business." This appeal followed.

II. THE CORPORATE OPPORTUNITY DOCTRINE

Corporate officers and directors bear a duty of loyalty to the corporations they serve. As Justice Cardozo explained the fiduciary duty in *Meinhard v. Salmon,* 249 N.Y. 458, 164 N.E. 545, 546 (1928):

> A trustee is held to something stricter than the morals of the marketplace. Not honesty alone, but the punctilio of an honor the most sensitive, is then the standard of behavior. As to this there has developed a tradition that is unbending and inveterate.

Maine has embraced this "unbending and inveterate" tradition. Corporate fiduciaries in Maine must discharge their duties in good faith with a view toward furthering the interests of the corporation. They must disclose and not withhold relevant information concerning any potential conflict of interest with the corporation, and they must refrain from using their position, influence, or knowledge of the affairs of the corporation to gain personal advantage. *See Rosenthal v. Rosenthal,* 543 A.2d 348, 352 (Me. 1988); 13-A M.R.S.A. § 716 (Supp. 1994).

Despite the general acceptance of the proposition that corporate fiduciaries owe a duty of loyalty to their corporations, there has been much confusion about the specific extent of that duty when, as here, it is contended that a fiduciary takes for herself a corporate opportunity. *See, e.g.,* Victor Brudney & Robert C. Clark, *A New Look at Corporate Opportunities,* 94 Harv. L. Rev. 998, 998 (1981) ("Not only are the common formulations vague, but the courts have articulated no theory that would serve as a blueprint for constructing meaningful rules."). This case requires us for the first time to define the scope of the corporate opportunity doctrine in Maine.

Various courts have embraced different versions of the corporate opportunity doctrine. The test applied by the trial court and embraced by Harris is generally known as the "line of business" test. The seminal case applying the line of business test is *Guth v. Loft, Inc.,* 5 A.2d 503 (Del. 1939). In *Guth,* the Delaware Supreme Court adopted an intensely factual test stated in general terms as follows:

> [I]f there is presented to a corporate officer or director a business opportunity which the corporation is financially able to undertake, is, from its nature, in the line of the corporation's business and is of practical advantage to it, is one in which the corporation has an interest or a reasonable expectancy, and, by embracing the opportunity, the self-interest of the officer or director will be brought into conflict with that of his corporation, the law will not permit him to seize the opportunity for himself.

Id. at 511. The "real issue" under this test is whether the opportunity "was so closely associated with the existing business activities . . . as to bring the transaction within that class of cases where the acquisition of the property would throw the corporate officer purchasing it into competition with his company." *Id.* at 513. The Delaware court described that inquiry as "a factual question to be decided by reasonable inferences from objective facts." *Id.*

The line of business test suffers from some significant weaknesses. First, the question whether a particular activity is within a corporation's line of business is conceptually difficult to answer. The facts of the instant case demonstrate that difficulty. The Club is in the business of running a golf course. It is not in the business of developing real estate. In the traditional sense, therefore, the trial court correctly observed that the opportunity in this case was not a corporate opportunity within the meaning of the *Guth* test. Nevertheless, the record would support a finding that the Club had made the policy judgment that development of surrounding real estate was detrimental to the best interests of the Club. The acquisition of land adjacent to the golf course for the purpose of preventing future development would have enhanced the ability of the Club to implement that policy. The record also shows that the Club had occasionally considered reversing that policy and expanding its operations to include the development of surrounding real estate. Harris's activities effectively foreclosed the Club from pursuing that option with respect to prime locations adjacent to the golf course.

Second, the *Guth* test includes as an element the financial ability of the corporation to take advantage of the opportunity. The court in this case relied on the Club's supposed financial incapacity as a basis for excusing Harris's conduct. Often, the injection of financial ability into the equation will unduly favor the inside director or executive who has command of the facts relating to the finances of the corporation. Reliance on financial ability will also act as a disincentive to corporate executives to solve corporate financing and other problems. In addition, the Club could have prevented development without spending $275,000 to acquire the property Harris needed to obtain access to the road.

The Massachusetts Supreme Judicial Court adopted a different test in *Durfee v. Durfee & Canning, Inc.,* 323 Mass. 187, 80 N.E.2d 522 (1948). The *Durfee* test has since come to be known as the "fairness test." According to *Durfee,* the

> true basis of governing doctrine rests on the unfairness in the particular circumstances of a director, whose relation to the corporation is fiduciary, taking advantage of an opportunity [for her personal profit] when the interest of the corporation justly call[s] for protection. This calls for application of ethical standards of what is fair and equitable . . . in particular sets of facts.

Id. at 529 (quoting *Ballantine on Corporations* 204-05 (rev. ed. 1946)). As with the *Guth* test, the *Durfee* test calls for a broad-ranging, intensely factual inquiry. The *Durfee* test suffers even more than the *Guth* test from a lack of principled content. It provides little or no practical guidance to the corporate officer or director seeking to measure her obligations.

The Minnesota Supreme Court elected "to combine the 'line of business' test with the 'fairness' test." *Miller v. Miller,* 301 Minn. 207, 222 N.W.2d 71, 81 (1974).

It engaged in a two-step analysis, first determining whether a particular opportunity was within the corporation's line of business, then scrutinizing "the equitable considerations existing prior to, at the time of, and following the officer's acquisition." *Id.* The *Miller* court hoped by adopting this approach "to ameliorate the often-expressed criticism that the [corporate opportunity] doctrine is vague and subjects today's corporate management to the danger of unpredictable liability." *Id.* In fact, the test adopted in *Miller* merely piles the uncertainty and vagueness of the fairness test on top of the weaknesses in the line of business test.

Despite the weaknesses of each of these approaches to the corporate opportunity doctrine, they nonetheless rest on a single fundamental policy. At bottom, the corporate opportunity doctrine recognizes that a corporate fiduciary should not serve both corporate and personal interests at the same time. As we observed in *Camden Land Co. v. Lewis,* 101 Me. 78, 97, 63 A. 523, 531 (1905), corporate fiduciaries "owe their whole duty to the corporation, and they are not to be permitted to act when duty conflicts with interest. They cannot serve themselves and the corporation at the same time." The various formulations of the test are merely attempts to moderate the potentially harsh consequences of strict adherence to that policy. It is important to preserve some ability for corporate fiduciaries to pursue personal business interests that present no real threat to their duty of loyalty.

III. THE AMERICAN LAW INSTITUTE APPROACH

In an attempt to protect the duty of loyalty while at the same time providing long-needed clarity and guidance for corporate decisionmakers, the American Law Institute has offered the most recently developed version of the corporate opportunity doctrine. Principles of Corporate Governance § 5.05 (May 13, 1992), provides as follows:

§ 505 Taking of Corporate Opportunities by Directors or Senior Executives

(a) *General Rule.* A director [§ 1.13] or senior executive [§ 1.33] may not take advantage of a corporate opportunity unless:

(1) The director or senior executive first offers the corporate opportunity to the corporation and makes disclosure concerning the conflict of interest [§ 1.14(a)] and the corporate opportunity [§ 1.14(b)];

(2) The corporate opportunity is rejected by the corporation; and

(3) Either:

(A) The rejection of the opportunity is fair to the corporation;

(B) The opportunity is rejected in advance, following such disclosure, by disinterested directors [§ 1.15], or, in the case of a senior executive who is not a director, by a disinterested superior, in a manner that satisfies the standards of the business judgment rule [§ 4.01(c)]; or

(C) The rejection is authorized in advance or ratified, following such disclosure, by disinterested shareholders [§ 1.16], and the rejection is not equivalent to a waste of corporate assets [§ 1.42].

(b) *Definition of a Corporate Opportunity.* For purposes of this Section, a corporate opportunity means:

(1) Any opportunity to engage in a business activity of which a director or senior executive becomes aware, either:

(A) In connection with the performance of functions as a director or senior executive, or under circumstances that should reasonably lead the director or senior executive to believe that the person offering the opportunity expects it to be offered to the corporation; or

(B) Through the use of corporate information or property, if the resulting opportunity is one that the director or senior executive should reasonably be expected to believe would be of interest to the corporation; or

(2) Any opportunity to engage in a business activity of which a senior executive becomes aware and knows is closely related to a business in which the corporation is engaged or expects to engage.

(c) *Burden of Proof.* A party who challenges the taking of a corporate opportunity has the burden of proof, except that if such party establishes that the requirements of Subsection (a)(3)(B) or (C) are not met, the director or the senior executive has the burden of proving that the rejection and the taking of the opportunity were fair to the corporation.

(d) *Ratification of Defective Disclosure.* A good faith but defective disclosure of the facts concerning the corporate opportunity may be cured if at any time (but no later than a reasonable time after suit is filed challenging the taking of the corporate opportunity) the original rejection of the corporate opportunity is ratified, following the required disclosure, by the board, the shareholders, or the corporate decisionmaker who initially approved the rejection of the corporate opportunity, or such decisionmaker's successor.

(e) *Special Rule Concerning Delayed Offering of Corporate Opportunities.* Relief based solely on failure to first offer an opportunity to the corporation under Subsection (a)(1) is not available if: (1) such failure resulted from a good faith belief that the business activity did not constitute a corporate opportunity, and (2) not later than a reasonable time after suit is filed challenging the taking of the corporate opportunity, the corporate opportunity is to the extent possible offered to the corporation and rejected in a manner that satisfies the standards of Subsection (a).

The central feature of the ALI test is the strict requirement of full disclosure prior to taking advantage of any corporate opportunity. *Id.,* § 5.05(a)(1). "If the opportunity is not offered to the corporation, the director or senior executive will not have satisfied § 5.05(a)." *Id.,* cmt. to § 5.05(a). The corporation must then formally reject the opportunity. *Id.,* § 505(a)(2). The ALI test is discussed at length and ultimately applied by the Oregon Supreme Court in *Klinicki v. Lundgren,* 298 Or. 662, 695 P.2d 906 (1985). As *Klinicki* describes the test, "full disclosure to the appropriate corporate body is . . . an absolute condition precedent to the validity of any forthcoming rejection as well as to the availability to the director or principal senior executive of the defense of fairness." *Id.* at 920. A "good faith but defective disclosure" by the corporate officer may be ratified after the fact only by an affirmative vote of the disinterested directors or shareholders. Principles of Corporate Governance § 5.05(d).

The ALI test defines "corporate opportunity" broadly. It includes opportunities "closely related to a business in which the corporation is engaged." *Id.,* § 5.05(b). It also encompasses any opportunities that accrue to the fiduciary as a result of her position within the corporation. *Id.* This concept is most clearly illustrated by the testimony of Suminsby, the listing broker for the Gilpin property, which, if believed by the factfinder, would support a finding that the Gilpin property was offered to

Harris specifically in her capacity as president of the Club. If the factfinder reached that conclusion, then at least the opportunity to acquire the Gilpin property would be a corporate opportunity. The state of the record concerning the Smallidge purchase precludes us from intimating any opinion whether that too would be a corporate opportunity.

Under the ALI standard, once the Club shows that the opportunity is a corporate opportunity, it must show either that Harris did not offer the opportunity to the Club or that the Club did not reject it properly. If the Club shows that the board did not reject the opportunity by a vote of the disinterested directors after full disclosure, then Harris may defend her actions on the basis that the taking of the opportunity was fair to the corporation. *Id.*, § 5.05(c). If Harris failed to offer the opportunity at all, however, then she may not defend on the basis that the failure to offer the opportunity was fair. *Id.*, cmt. to § 5.05(c).

The *Klinicki* court viewed the ALI test as an opportunity to bring some clarity to a murky area of the law. *Klinicki*, 695 P.2d at 915. We agree, and today we follow the ALI test. The disclosure-oriented approach provides a clear procedure whereby a corporate officer may insulate herself through prompt and complete disclosure from the possibility of a legal challenge. The requirement of disclosure recognizes the paramount importance of the corporate fiduciary's duty of loyalty. At the same time it protects the fiduciary's ability pursuant to the proper procedure to pursue her own business ventures free from the possibility of a lawsuit.

The importance of disclosure is familiar to the law of corporations in Maine. Pursuant to 13-A M.R.S.A. § 717 (1981), a corporate officer or director may enter into a transaction with the corporation in which she has a personal or adverse interest only if she discloses her interest in the transaction and secures ratification by a majority of the disinterested directors or shareholders. Section 717 is part of the Model Business Corporations Act, adopted in Maine in 1971. P.L. 1971, ch. 439, § 1. Like the ALI rule, section 717 was designed to "eliminate the inequities and uncertainties caused by the existing rules." Model Business Corp. Act § 41, ¶2, at 844 (1971).

IV.

. . . In these circumstances, fairness requires that we remand the case for further proceedings. Those further proceedings may include, at the trial court's discretion, the taking of further evidence.

Post-Case Follow-Up

Can a corporation waive the corporate opportunity doctrine?

One question that often arises with the corporate opportunity doctrine is whether a corporation may waive the corporate opportunity doctrine, or otherwise limit director liability for usurpation claims. In Delaware, this issue was front and center in the Chancery Court's 1989 decision *Siegman v. Tri-Star Pictures, Inc.*, CIV. A. No. 9477, 1989 WL 48746 (Del. Ch. May 5, 1989). In

Siegman, the corporation amended its charter to waive the corporate opportunity doctrine and certain fiduciary duties for some of the company's large shareholders and individuals who served on the company's board of directors. The court held that the charter amendments violated DGCL § 102(b)(7), which (as you know) allows corporations to exculpate directors from liability for money damages for breaches of the duty of care but not for breaches of the duty of loyalty.

In response to *Siegman*, the Delaware legislature added subsection 17 to § 122 of the DGCL. This section permits a corporation to "[r]enounce, in its certificate of incorporation or by action of its board of directors, any interest or expectancy of the corporation in, or in being offered an opportunity to participate in, specified business opportunities or specified classes or categories of business opportunities that are presented to the corporation or 1 or more of its officers, directors or stockholders." DGCL § 122(17). The legislative history of the amendment emphasized that the Delaware legislature intended to eliminate any uncertainty regarding the power of a corporation to renounce corporate opportunities associated with the *Siegman* holding. The legislative history further emphasizes that the amendment was designed to permit corporations to determine in advance whether a specified business opportunity or class or category of business opportunity is an opportunity of the corporation.

Does it matter whether the corporation has the financial resources to take advantage of the opportunity?

A second point of follow-up relates to the corporation's financial ability to take advantage of the opportunity. As *Broz* suggests, under Delaware's line of business test, a corporation's ability (or inability) to take financial advantage of a business opportunity is relevant to determining whether a fiduciary faces liability under the corporate opportunity doctrine. Not all jurisdictions follow this rule, with some courts holding that a corporation's financial inability to take advantage of a business opportunity is not a defense to a usurpation claim. As always, be sure to research the law in relevant jurisdictions before advising clients.

Northeast Harbor Golf Club, Inc. v. Harris: Real Life Applications

Questions 1 through 3 draw upon, and in some cases change, the facts of the *Northeast Harbor Golf Club* case.

1. You represent Harris. Assume Harris comes to you before purchasing the first parcel at issue. What advice would you give her as to whether she ought to disclose her plans to purchase the parcel to the board?

2. You represent the board of Northeast Harbor Golf Club. Assume that Harris comes to the board before purchasing the first parcel and discloses her plans to acquire the land surrounding the golf club. What steps, if any, would you advise the board to take in response to Harris's disclosure?

3. After reading Section C.2 below (Conflicting Interest Transactions), assume the following: (i) Harris becomes a director of the Golf Club; (ii) she decides to sell the parcels at issue to the Golf Club; and (iii) these events take place in a jurisdiction that follows the MBCA. What provisions in the MBCA, if any, apply to the transaction between Harris and the club? What would be the result under any such provisions?

4. Plaintiff is a one-third stockholder of Realty Corp. ("Realty"), a New York corporation that owns and operates rooming and apartment buildings in Brooklyn, New York. Defendants own the remaining stock of Realty. Realty was incorporated with adequate capital, subscribed equally by the three stockholders, all of whom are directors of the company.

As set forth in Realty's charter and bylaws, the parties formed Realty for the purpose of purchasing low-rent rooming and apartment buildings in Brooklyn, where the parties all lived at that time. Defendants had previously acquired three similar buildings in Brooklyn. Based on their positive experience, which Defendants and Plaintiff discussed in detail, Defendants urged Plaintiff (then a close friend of Defendants) to "get her feet wet" in real estate. Realty was formed as a result.

For more than ten years, Defendants managed Realty's properties while Plaintiff's spouse handled accounting and tax planning. Plaintiff knew that Defendants continued to be involved in real estate activities elsewhere in Brooklyn through their previously formed corporations. Realty was successful.

Four years ago, the parties began discussing whether they ought to sell Realty's "low-rent" buildings in order to purchase higher-priced rental properties in Park Slope (a highly desirable neighborhood in Brooklyn with quality public schools, dining, nightlife, shopping, access to public transit, green space, quality housing, safety, etc.). Realty finally decided to put its low-rent Brooklyn properties on the market three years ago, selling all of them in short order. Realty has not purchased any other low-rent properties in Brooklyn (or anywhere else) for the past three years. Last year, Realty purchased one brownstone in Park Slope. At the same time, using a separate corporation owned by Defendants (but not Plaintiff), Defendants purchased nine low-rent rooming and apartment buildings in Trenton, New Jersey.

Six months ago, Plaintiff and her spouse moved to Pennsylvania. Shortly thereafter, Realty's directors began to disagree with each other as to the accounting used for Realty's rent receipts and expenditures. After mediation failed to resolve the situation, Plaintiff filed a derivative action alleging that Defendants breached their fiduciary duties to Realty when they purchased the Trenton apartment buildings without first offering them to Realty.

At trial, Plaintiff testified that she expected Defendants to offer any low-rent properties that they found to Realty once Realty was formed. Plaintiff also testified that while she was aware that Defendants owned a number of properties outside Realty, she assumed that all such properties had been purchased prior to Realty's formation. Defendants testified that they had never promised to operate solely through Realty, and that they had never misled Plaintiff respecting non-Realty activities.

Will Plaintiff prevail? Why or why not?

2. Conflicting Interest Transactions

The second classic duty of loyalty scenario involves conflicting interest transactions. In the classic conflicting interest transaction, a director (or an entity owned by the director) enters into a transaction with the corporation. For example, assume Sam is a director of a Luxury Living, Inc. (LLI), a corporation that owns apartment buildings. Further assume that Sam also is the sole owner, officer, and director of Building Security Services, Inc. (BSS), a corporation that provides security and concierge services to apartment buildings. Assume that Sam uses his influence and position with LLI to influence LLI to enter into a contract with BSS whereby LLI hires BSS to provide security and concierge services at all LLI-owned apartment buildings. As a director of LLI, Sam has a fiduciary duty to ensure that LLI obtains the best possible services at the best possible price. As the owner, officer, and director of BSS, however, Sam also has an incentive to maximize BSS's profits for personal gain. It is, of course, possible to imagine a win-win scenario whereby BSS provides excellent service to LLI at a competitive price. But, it also is possible to imagine a scenario where Sam maximizes personal profits at LLI's expense.

At common law, transactions between the corporation and its directors were seen as a form of self-dealing, and were either per se void or voidable at the option of the corporation or its shareholders, regardless of the substance or merits of the transaction. Over time, this rule was softened to provide that such transactions were not *per se* voidable, so long as the transaction at issue was (i) approved by a majority of the corporation's disinterested directors following disclosure; and (ii) fair to the corporation.

More recently, jurisdictions have enacted statutory provisions respecting conflicting interest transactions involving directors. In general, these statutes provide that a director proposing a conflicting interest transaction bears the burden of proving that a transaction was entirely fair to the corporation, unless a "cleansing" device is used — that is, the conflict is disclosed, and the transaction is approved by a fully informed majority of disinterested and independent directors or by a fully informed majority of disinterested and independent shareholders. If a cleansing device is used, the burden shifts to the plaintiff to prove that the transaction constituted a waste of corporate assets. If a cleansing device is not used, the transaction is voidable at the corporation's option unless the director involved in the transaction proves that the transaction was entirely fair to the corporation. The change from *per se* voidability to disclosure, review, and approval by disinterested directors or shareholders reflects the reality that contracts between directors (or businesses owned or controlled by directors) and the corporation may benefit all involved. At the same time, however, the existence of a structural conflict of interest associated with the conflicted director's divided loyalties means that these types of transaction merit extra scrutiny.

For example, DGCL § 144 provides as follows:

(a) No contract or transaction between a corporation and 1 or more of its directors or officers, or between a corporation and any other corporation, partnership, association, or other organization in which 1 or more of its directors or officers, are directors or officers, or have a financial interest, shall be void or voidable solely for this reason, or solely because the director or officer is present at or participates in the meeting of the board or committee which authorizes the contract or transaction, or solely because any such director's or officer's votes are counted for such purpose, if:

(1) The material facts as to the director's or officer's relationship or interest and as to the contract or transaction are disclosed or are known to the board of directors or the committee, and the board or committee in good faith authorizes the contract or transaction by the affirmative votes of a majority of the disinterested directors, even though the disinterested directors be less than a quorum; or

(2) The material facts as to the director's or officer's relationship or interest and as to the contract or transaction are disclosed or are known to the stockholders entitled to vote thereon, and the contract or transaction is specifically approved in good faith by vote of the stockholders; or

(3) The contract or transaction is fair as to the corporation as of the time it is authorized, approved or ratified, by the board of directors, a committee or the stockholders.

(b) Common or interested directors may be counted in determining the presence of a quorum at a meeting of the board of directors or of a committee which authorizes the contract or transaction.

See also NYBCL § 713; MBCA §§ 8.60, 8.61, 8.63 (defining director's conflicting interest transaction and discussing review and approval by disinterested shareholders and directors).

To determine whether statutes like § 144 apply in the first place, and whether a vote by directors or shareholders, or both, "cleansed" the transaction at issue, it is necessary to determine whether the directors and shareholders involved in the transaction (and, where applicable, the review and approval of the transaction) are interested (or disinterested), and whether they are independent (or lack independence).

When Is a Director Interested (or Disinterested)?

Generally speaking, a director is interested if he (i) has a financial interest in a transaction such that he will receive a personal benefit from a transaction that will not be shared equally by the shareholders; or (ii) will suffer a material detriment not shared by the corporation or its shareholders. *See, e.g., Rales v. Blasband*, 643 A.2d 927, 936 (Del. 1993) (holding a director is considered interested "where he or she will receive a personal financial benefit from a transaction that is not equally shared by the stockholders. Directorial interest also exists where a corporate decision will have a materially detrimental impact on a director, but not on the corporation and the stockholders.") *See also Marx v. Akers*, 666 N.E.2d 1034 (N.Y. 1996) (holding a director is interested in a challenged or questioned transaction when that director receives a direct financial benefit from the questioned transaction that is different from the benefit received generally by all shareholders); MBCA § 8.60.

When Is a Director Independent (or Lacking Independence)?

Independence speaks to whether a director (or stockholder involved in reviewing and approving a transaction) can exercise her independent judgment with respect to the transaction at issue, or whether the director (or stockholder) is under the sway of, or unduly influenced by, the director behind the conflicting interest transaction. To establish a lack of independence, a plaintiff must show that a director or shareholder is so beholden to the conflicted director that he is unable to assess the transaction at issue on the merits, and is instead subject to extraneous considerations or influences. Although the mere fact of a personal friendship or professional or colleague relationship is, by itself, usually not enough to establish a lack of independence, "financial ties, familial affinity, a particularly close or intimate personal or business affinity or . . . evidence that in the past the relationship caused the director to act non-independently vis a vis an interested director" may be enough. *See Beam ex rel. Martha Stewart Living Omnimedia, Inc. v. Stewart*, 845 A.2d 1040, 1051 (Del. 2004). Exchange listing standards also address the issue of independence, with the New York Stock Exchange Listed Company Manual recognizing that a director's independence can be compromised by the director's own relationships and actions, of course, but also by the relationships and actions of family members. *See* N.Y.S.E. Listed Company Manual § 303A.02 Independence Tests (stating, for example, that a director is not independent if director is, or has been within the last three years, an employee of the listed company, or an immediate family member is, or has been within the last three years, an executive officer of the listed company). As this suggests, although definitions vary somewhat, a director generally will be deemed independent if she has no material relationship with the company other than board membership and no business or family ties with the company apart from the director's board service. Similar rules likely apply in the shareholder context.

When Is a Conflict Disclosed or Otherwise Known?

To invoke the cleansing devices of DGCL § 144 and other like statutes (i.e., approval by disinterested directors or shareholders), the director with the conflict must disclose (or ensure that disinterested, independent board members otherwise know) all material information concerning the conflict of interest and the transaction at issue. To satisfy this burden, the director must make meaningful disclosure of the conflict. Incomplete or misleading disclosure will not satisfy these statutes.

When Is a Transaction Entirely Fair to the Corporation?

If a cleansing device is not used the conflicted shareholder generally must prove that the challenged transaction is entirely fair to the corporation. In Delaware, entire fairness has two components—fair dealing and fair price. *See Weinberger v. UOP, Inc.*, 457 A.2d 710, 710 (Del. Super. Ct. 1983). Fair dealing "embraces questions of when the transaction was timed, how it was initiated, structured, negotiated, disclosed to the directors, and how the approvals of the directors and the stockholders were obtained." *Id.* Fair price "relates to the economic and financial considerations" of the proposed transaction. *Id.* In deciding the issue of entire fairness, courts do not emphasize price over dealing, or dealing over price: Instead, courts examine all aspects of the deal (dealing and price) as a whole. *Id.*

Voidability versus Director Liability for Breach of Fiduciary Duty

It is important to remember that statutory provisions such as DGCL § 144 speak only to the issue of whether a transaction between a corporation and an interested director is voidable. These statutory provisions do not shield interested directors from breach of duty of loyalty claims. *See, e.g., CDX Liquidating Tr. v. Venrock Assocs.,* 640 F.3d 209, 218-219 (7th Cir. 2011) (holding that disclosure of conflict does not excuse or immunize director from liability for breach of fiduciary duty).

D. *CAREMARK* CLAIMS, THE DUTY OF LOYALTY, AND ACTS OR OMISSIONS NOT IN GOOD FAITH

One of the most interesting developments in Delaware director fiduciary duty law involves so-called *Caremark* claims, or claims involving directors' oversight obligations. Thus far, we have studied fiduciary duty claims arising out of challenged decisions — for example, the board's decision to approve a transaction (*Smith v. Van Gorkom*), the president's decision to purchase land alongside a golf club (*Northeast Harbor*), and so forth. With *Caremark* claims, there is no specific challenged decision or transaction. Instead, the plaintiffs claim that the directors breached their fiduciary duty as a result of unconsidered inaction — that is, by failing to act in circumstances where action and due attention would have prevented a corporate loss. We discuss *Caremark* claims in the following section.

Case Preview

In re Caremark International Inc. Derivative Litigation

In *Caremark,* corporate employees allegedly violated anti-referral payment laws applicable to health care providers, resulting in government investigations, Caremark's indictment on multiple felony counts, and its payment of approximately $250 million in civil and criminal fines and reimbursements. The plaintiffs alleged that Caremark's directors breached their fiduciary duties by failing to ensure that the company implemented a system of internal controls designed to (i) ensure compliance with the law, and (ii) detect or prevent violations of the law by employees. When reading this case, consider the following questions:

1. What is the procedural posture of the *Caremark* case?
2. Were Caremark's directors alleged to have been involved in the wrongdoing? Were they even aware of the alleged wrongdoing, according to the complaint?

3. What did Caremark's directors allegedly do wrong, according to the plaintiffs?
4. What does the court make of the *Allis-Chalmers* case with regard to directors' oversight and monitoring responsibilities?
5. What does a plaintiff need to show to establish a breach of fiduciary duty based on alleged oversight failure under *Caremark*?

In re Caremark International Inc. Derivative Litigation
698 A.2d 959 (Del. 1996)

ALLEN, Chancellor.*

Pending is a motion pursuant to Chancery Rule 23.1 to approve as fair and reasonable a proposed settlement of a consolidated derivative action on behalf of Caremark International, Inc. ("Caremark"). The suit involves claims that the members of Caremark's board of directors (the "Board") breached their fiduciary duty of care to Caremark in connection with alleged violations by Caremark employees of federal and state laws and regulations applicable to health care providers. As a result of the alleged violations, Caremark was subject to an extensive four year investigation by the United States Department of Health and Human Services and the Department of Justice. In 1994 Caremark was charged in an indictment with multiple felonies. It thereafter entered into a number of agreements with the Department of Justice and others. Those agreements included a plea agreement in which Caremark pleaded guilty to a single felony of mail fraud and agreed to pay civil and criminal fines. Subsequently, Caremark agreed to make reimbursements to various private and public parties. In all, the payments that Caremark has been required to make total approximately $250 million.

This suit was filed in 1994, purporting to seek on behalf of the company recovery of these losses from the individual defendants who constitute the board of directors of Caremark. The parties now propose that it be settled and, after notice to Caremark shareholders, a hearing on the fairness of the proposal was held on August 16, 1996.

. . .

I. BACKGROUND

For these purposes I regard the following facts, suggested by the discovery record, as material. Caremark, a Delaware corporation with its headquarters in Northbrook, Illinois, was created in November 1992 when it was spun-off from Baxter International, Inc. ("Baxter") and became a publicly held company listed on the New York Stock Exchange. The business practices that created the problem pre-dated the spin-off. During the relevant period Caremark was involved in two main health care business segments, providing patient care and managed care services. As part of its patient care business, which accounted for the majority of Caremark's revenues,

---

*Most footnotes have been omitted for purposes of brevity.

Caremark provided alternative site health care services, including infusion therapy, growth hormone therapy, HIV/AIDS-related treatments and hemophilia therapy. Caremark's managed care services included prescription drug programs and the operation of multi-specialty group practices.

A. Events Prior to the Government Investigation

A substantial part of the revenues generated by Caremark's businesses is derived from third party payments, insurers, and Medicare and Medicaid reimbursement programs. The latter source of payments are subject to the terms of the Anti-Referral Payments Law ("ARPL") which prohibits health care providers from paying any form of remuneration to induce the referral of Medicare or Medicaid patients. From its inception, Caremark entered into a variety of agreements with hospitals, physicians, and health care providers for advice and services, as well as distribution agreements with drug manufacturers, as had its predecessor prior to 1992. Specifically, Caremark did have a practice of entering into contracts for services (*e.g.,* consultation agreements and research grants) with physicians at least some of whom prescribed or recommended services or products that Caremark provided to Medicare recipients and other patients. Such contracts were not prohibited by the ARPL but they obviously raised a possibility of unlawful "kickbacks."

As early as 1989, Caremark's predecessor issued an internal "Guide to Contractual Relationships" ("Guide") to govern its employees in entering into contracts with physicians and hospitals. The Guide tended to be reviewed annually by lawyers and updated. Each version of the Guide stated as Caremark's and its predecessor's policy that no payments would be made in exchange for or to induce patient referrals. But what one might deem a prohibited *quid pro quo* was not always clear. Due to a scarcity of court decisions interpreting the ARPL, however, Caremark repeatedly publicly stated that there was uncertainty concerning Caremark's interpretation of the law.

To clarify the scope of the ARPL, the United States Department of Health and Human Services ("HHS") issued "safe harbor" regulations in July 1991 stating conditions under which financial relationships between health care service providers and patient referral sources, such as physicians, would *not* violate the ARPL. Caremark contends that the narrowly drawn regulations gave limited guidance as to the legality of many of the agreements used by Caremark that did not fall within the safe-harbor. Caremark's predecessor, however, amended many of its standard forms of agreement with health care providers and revised the Guide in an apparent attempt to comply with the new regulations.

B. Government Investigation and Related Litigation

In August 1991, the HHS Office of the Inspector General ("OIG") initiated an investigation of Caremark's predecessor. Caremark's predecessor was served with a subpoena requiring the production of documents, including contracts between Caremark's predecessor and physicians (Quality Service Agreements ("QSAs")). Under the QSAs, Caremark's predecessor appears to have paid physicians fees for monitoring patients under Caremark's predecessor's care, including Medicare and

Medicaid recipients. Sometimes apparently those monitoring patients were referring physicians, which raised ARPL concerns.

In March 1992, the Department of Justice ("DOJ") joined the OIG investigation and separate investigations were commenced by several additional federal and state agencies.

C. Caremark's Response to the Investigation

During the relevant period, Caremark had approximately 7,000 employees and ninety branch operations. It had a decentralized management structure. By May 1991, however, Caremark asserts that it had begun making attempts to centralize its management structure in order to increase supervision over its branch operations.

The first action taken by management, as a result of the initiation of the OIG investigation, was an announcement that as of October 1, 1991, Caremark's predecessor would no longer pay management fees to physicians for services to Medicare and Medicaid patients. Despite this decision, Caremark asserts that its management, pursuant to advice, did not believe that such payments were illegal under the existing laws and regulations.

During this period, Caremark's Board took several additional steps consistent with an effort to assure compliance with company policies concerning the ARPL and the contractual forms in the Guide. In April 1992, Caremark published a fourth revised version of its Guide apparently designed to assure that its agreements either complied with the ARPL and regulations or excluded Medicare and Medicaid patients altogether. In addition, in September 1992, Caremark instituted a policy requiring its regional officers, Zone Presidents, to approve each contractual relationship entered into by Caremark with a physician.

Although there is evidence that inside and outside counsel had advised Caremark's directors that their contracts were in accord with the law, Caremark recognized that some uncertainty respecting the correct interpretation of the law existed. In its 1992 annual report, Caremark disclosed the ongoing government investigations, acknowledged that if penalties were imposed on the company they could have a material adverse effect on Caremark's business, and stated that no assurance could be given that its interpretation of the ARPL would prevail if challenged.

Throughout the period of the government investigations, Caremark had an internal audit plan designed to assure compliance with business and ethics policies. In addition, Caremark employed Price Waterhouse as its outside auditor. On February 8, 1993, the Ethics Committee of Caremark's Board received and reviewed an outside auditors report by Price Waterhouse which concluded that there were no material weaknesses in Caremark's control structure. Despite the positive findings of Price Waterhouse, however, on April 20, 1993, the Audit & Ethics Committee adopted a new internal audit charter requiring a comprehensive review of compliance policies and the compilation of an employee ethics handbook concerning such policies.

The Board appears to have been informed about this project and other efforts to assure compliance with the law. For example, Caremark's management reported to the Board that Caremark's sales force was receiving an ongoing education regarding the ARPL and the proper use of Caremark's form contracts which had been approved by in-house counsel. On July 27, 1993, the new ethics manual, expressly prohibiting payments in exchange for referrals and requiring employees to report all illegal conduct to a toll free confidential ethics hotline, was approved and allegedly disseminated. The record suggests that Caremark continued these policies in subsequent years, causing employees to be given revised versions of the ethics manual and requiring them to participate in training sessions concerning compliance with the law.

During 1993, Caremark took several additional steps which appear to have been aimed at increasing management supervision. These steps included new policies requiring local branch managers to secure home office approval for all disbursements under agreements with health care providers and to certify compliance with the ethics program. In addition, the chief financial officer was appointed to serve as Caremark's compliance officer. In 1994, a fifth revised Guide was published.

D. Federal Indictments Against Caremark and Officers

On August 4, 1994, a federal grand jury in Minnesota issued a 47 page indictment charging Caremark, two of its officers (not the firm's chief officer), an individual who had been a sales employee of Genentech, Inc., and David R. Brown, a physician practicing in Minneapolis, with violating the ARPL over a lengthy period. According to the indictment, over $1.1 million had been paid to Brown to induce him to distribute Protropin, a human growth hormone drug marketed by Caremark. The substantial payments involved started, according to the allegations of the indictment, in 1986 and continued through 1993. Some payments were "in the guise of research grants," Ind. ¶ 20, and others were "consulting agreements," Ind. ¶ 19. The indictment charged, for example, that Dr. Brown performed virtually none of the consulting functions described in his 1991 agreement with Caremark, but was nevertheless neither required to return the money he had received nor precluded from receiving future funding from Caremark. In addition the indictment charged that Brown received from Caremark payments of staff and office expenses, including telephone answering services and fax rental expenses.

In reaction to the Minnesota Indictment and the subsequent filing of this and other derivative actions in 1994, the Board met and was informed by management that the investigation had resulted in an indictment; Caremark denied any wrongdoing relating to the indictment and believed that the OIG investigation would have a favorable outcome. Management reiterated the grounds for its view that the contracts were in compliance with law.

Subsequently, five stockholder derivative actions were filed in this court and consolidated into this action. The original complaint, dated August 5, 1994, alleged, in relevant part, that Caremark's directors breached their duty of care by failing adequately to supervise the conduct of Caremark employees, or institute corrective measures, thereby exposing Caremark to fines and liability.

On September 21, 1994, a federal grand jury in Columbus, Ohio issued another indictment alleging that an Ohio physician had defrauded the Medicare program by requesting and receiving $134,600 in exchange for referrals of patients whose medical costs were in part reimbursed by Medicare in violation of the ARPL. Although unidentified at that time, Caremark was the health care provider who allegedly made such payments. The indictment also charged that the physician, Elliot Neufeld, D.O., was provided with the services of a registered nurse to work in his office at the expense of the infusion company, in addition to free office equipment.

An October 28, 1994 amended complaint in this action added allegations concerning the Ohio indictment as well as new allegations of over billing and inappropriate referral payments in connection with an action brought in Atlanta, *Booth v. Rankin*. Following a newspaper article report that federal investigators were expanding their inquiry to look at Caremark's referral practices in Michigan as well as allegations of fraudulent billing of insurers, a second amended complaint was filed in this action. The third, and final, amended complaint was filed on April 11, 1995, adding allegations that the federal indictments had caused Caremark to incur significant legal fees and forced it to sell its home infusion business at a loss.

After each complaint was filed, defendants filed a motion to dismiss. According to defendants, if a settlement had not been reached in this action, the case would have been dismissed on two grounds. First, they contend that the complaints fail to allege particularized facts sufficient to excuse the demand requirement under Delaware Chancery Court Rule 23.1. Second, defendants assert that plaintiffs had failed to state a cause of action due to the fact that Caremark's charter eliminates directors' personal liability for money damages, to the extent permitted by law.

E. Settlement Negotiations

In September, following the announcement of the Ohio indictment, Caremark publicly announced that as of January 1, 1995, it would terminate all remaining financial relationships with physicians in its home infusion, hemophilia, and growth hormone lines of business. In addition, Caremark asserts that it extended its restrictive policies to all of its contractual relationships with physicians, rather than just those involving Medicare and Medicaid patients, and terminated its research grant program which had always involved some recipients who referred patients to Caremark.

Caremark began settlement negotiations with federal and state government entities in May 1995. In return for a guilty plea to a single count of mail fraud by the corporation, the payment of a criminal fine, the payment of substantial civil damages, and cooperation with further federal investigations on matters relating to the OIG investigation, the government entities agreed to negotiate a settlement that would permit Caremark to continue participating in Medicare and Medicaid programs. On June 15, 1995, the Board approved a settlement ("Government Settlement Agreement") with the DOJ, OIG, U.S. Veterans Administration, U.S. Federal Employee Health Benefits Program, federal Civilian Health and Medical Program of the Uniformed Services, and related state agencies in all fifty states and the District of Columbia.[10] No senior officers or directors were charged with wrongdoing in the

---

[10]The agreement, covering allegations since 1986, required a Caremark subsidiary to enter a guilty plea to two counts of mail fraud, and required Caremark to pay $29 million in criminal fines, $129.9 million relating to civil claims concerning payment practices, $3.5 million for alleged violations of the Controlled Substances Act, and $2 million, in the form of a donation, to a grant program set up by the Ryan White Comprehensive AIDS Resources Emergency Act. Caremark also agreed to enter into a compliance agreement with the HHS.

Government Settlement Agreement or in any of the prior indictments. In fact, as part of the sentencing in the Ohio action on June 19, 1995, the United States stipulated that *no senior executive of Caremark participated in, condoned, or was willfully ignorant of wrongdoing in connection with the home infusion business practices.*

The federal settlement included certain provisions in a "Corporate Integrity Agreement" designed to enhance future compliance with law. The parties have not discussed this agreement, except to say that the negotiated provisions of the settlement of this claim are not redundant of those in that agreement.

Settlement negotiations between the parties in this action commenced in May 1995 as well, based upon a letter proposal of the plaintiffs, dated May 16, 1995. These negotiations resulted in a memorandum of understanding ("MOU"), dated June 7, 1995, and the execution of the Stipulation and Agreement of Compromise and Settlement on June 28, 1995, which is the subject of this action. The MOU, approved by the Board on June 15, 1995, required the Board to adopt several resolutions, discussed below, and to create a new compliance committee. The Compliance and Ethics Committee has been reporting to the Board in accord with its newly specified duties.

. . .

II. LEGAL PRINCIPLES

A. *Principles Governing Settlements of Derivative Claims*

As noted at the outset of this opinion, this Court is now required to exercise an informed judgment whether the proposed settlement is fair and reasonable in the light of all relevant factors. *Polk v. Good,* Del. Supr., 507 A.2d 531 (1986). On an application of this kind, this Court attempts to protect the best interests of the corporation and its absent shareholders all of whom will be barred from future litigation on these claims if the settlement is approved. The parties proposing the settlement bear the burden of persuading the court that it is in fact fair and reasonable. *Fins v. Pearlman,* Del. Supr., 424 A.2d 305 (1980).

B. *Directors' Duties to Monitor Corporate Operations*

The complaint charges the director defendants with breach of their duty of attention or care in connection with the on-going operation of the corporation's business. The claim is that the directors allowed a situation to develop and continue which exposed the corporation to enormous legal liability and that in so doing they violated a duty to be active monitors of corporate performance. The complaint thus does not charge either director self-dealing or the more difficult loyalty-type problems arising from cases of suspect director motivation, such as entrenchment or sale of control contexts. The theory here advanced is possibly the most difficult theory in corporation law upon which a plaintiff might hope to win a judgment. The good policy reasons why it is so difficult to charge directors with responsibility for corporate losses for an alleged breach of care, where there is no conflict of interest or no facts suggesting suspect motivation involved, were recently described in *Gagliardi v. TriFoods Int'l, Inc.,* Del. Ch., 683 A.2d 1049, 1051 (1996) (1996 Del. Ch. LEXIS 87 at p. 20).

1. *Potential liability for directoral decisions:* Director liability for a breach of the duty to exercise appropriate attention may, in theory, arise in two distinct contexts. First, such liability may be said to follow *from a board decision* that results in a loss because that decision was ill advised or "negligent." Second, liability to the corporation for a loss may be said to arise from an *unconsidered failure of the board to act* in circumstances in which due attention would, arguably, have prevented the loss. *See generally* Veasey & Seitz, *The Business Judgment Rule in the Revised Model Act . . .* 63 Texas L. Rev. 1483 (1985). The first class of cases will typically be subject to review under the director-protective business judgment rule, assuming the decision made was the product of *a process* that was *either* deliberately considered in good faith or was otherwise rational. See *Aronson v. Lewis,* Del. Supr., 473 A.2d 805 (1984); *Gagliardi v. TriFoods Int'l, Inc.,* Del. Ch., 683 A.2d 1049 (1996). What should be understood, but may not widely be understood by courts or commentators who are not often required to face such questions, is that compliance with a director's duty of care can never appropriately be judicially determined by reference to *the content of the board decision* that leads to a corporate loss, apart from consideration of the good faith *or* rationality of the process employed. That is, whether a judge or jury considering the matter after the fact, believes a decision substantively wrong, or degrees of wrong extending through "stupid" to "egregious" or "irrational," provides no ground for director liability, so long as the court determines that the process employed was either rational or employed in *a good faith* effort to advance corporate interests. To employ a different rule — one that permitted an "objective" evaluation of the decision — would expose directors to substantive second guessing by ill-equipped judges or juries, which would, in the long-run, be injurious to investor interests. Thus, the business judgment rule is process oriented and informed by a deep respect for all *good faith* board decisions.

Indeed, one wonders on what moral basis might shareholders attack a *good faith* business decision of a director as "unreasonable" or "irrational." Where a director *in fact exercises a good faith effort to be informed and to exercise appropriate judgment,* he or she should be deemed to satisfy fully the duty of attention. If the shareholders thought themselves entitled to some other quality of judgment than such a director produces in the good faith exercise of the powers of office, then the shareholders should have elected other directors. Judge Learned Hand made the point rather better than can I. In speaking of the passive director defendant Mr. Andrews in *Barnes v. Andrews,* Judge Hand said:

> True, he was not very suited by experience for the job he had undertaken, but I cannot hold him on that account. After all it is the same corporation that chose him that now seeks to charge him. . . . Directors are not specialists like lawyers or doctors. . . . They are the general advisors of the business and if they faithfully give such ability as they have to their charge, it would not be lawful to hold them liable. Must a director guarantee that his judgment is good? Can a shareholder call him to account for deficiencies that their votes assured him did not disqualify him for his office? While he may not have been the Cromwell for that Civil War, Andrews did not engage to play any such role.

In this formulation Learned Hand correctly identifies, in my opinion, the core element of any corporate law duty of care inquiry: whether there was good faith effort to be informed and exercise judgment.

2. *Liability for failure to monitor:* The second class of cases in which director liability for inattention is theoretically possible entail circumstances in which a loss eventuates not from a decision but, from unconsidered inaction. Most of the decisions that a corporation, acting through its human agents, makes are, of course, not the subject of director attention. Legally, the board itself will be required only to authorize the most significant corporate acts or transactions: mergers, changes in capital structure, fundamental changes in business, appointment and compensation of the CEO, etc. As the facts of this case graphically demonstrate, ordinary business decisions that are made by officers and employees deeper in the interior of the organization can, however, vitally affect the welfare of the corporation and its ability to achieve its various strategic and financial goals. If this case did not prove the point itself, recent business history would. Recall for example the displacement of senior management and much of the board of Salomon, Inc.; the replacement of senior management of Kidder, Peabody following the discovery of large trading losses resulting from phantom trades by a highly compensated trader; or the extensive financial loss and reputational injury suffered by Prudential Insurance as a result its junior officers misrepresentations in connection with the distribution of limited partnership interests. Financial and organizational disasters such as these raise the question, what is the board's responsibility with respect to the organization and monitoring of the enterprise to assure that the corporation functions within the law to achieve its purposes?

Modernly this question has been given special importance by an increasing tendency, especially under federal law, to employ the criminal law to assure corporate compliance with external legal requirements, including environmental, financial, employee and product safety as well as assorted other health and safety regulations. In 1991, pursuant to the Sentencing Reform Act of 1984, the United States Sentencing Commission adopted Organizational Sentencing Guidelines which impact importantly on the prospective effect these criminal sanctions might have on business corporations. The Guidelines set forth a uniform sentencing structure for organizations to be sentenced for violation of federal criminal statutes and provide for penalties that equal or often massively exceed those previously imposed on corporations. The Guidelines offer powerful incentives for corporations today to have in place compliance programs to detect violations of law, promptly to report violations to appropriate public officials when discovered, and to take prompt, voluntary remedial efforts.

In 1963, the Delaware Supreme Court in *Graham v. Allis-Chalmers Mfg. Co.,* addressed the question of potential liability of board members for losses experienced by the corporation as a result of the corporation having violated the anti-trust laws of the United States. There was no claim in that case that the directors knew about the behavior of subordinate employees of the corporation that had resulted in the liability. Rather, as in this case, the claim asserted was that the directors *ought to have known* of it and if they had known they would have been under a duty to bring the corporation into compliance with the law and thus save the corporation from the loss. The Delaware Supreme Court concluded that, under the facts as they appeared, there was no basis to find that the directors had breached a duty to be informed of the ongoing operations of the firm. In notably colorful terms, the court stated that "absent cause for suspicion there is no duty upon the directors to install and operate a corporate system of espionage to ferret out wrongdoing which they have no reason to suspect exists." The Court found that there were no grounds for suspicion in that case and, thus, concluded that the directors were blamelessly unaware of the conduct leading to the corporate liability.

How does one generalize this holding today? Can it be said today that, absent some ground giving rise to suspicion of violation of law, that corporate directors have no duty to assure that a corporate information gathering and reporting systems exists which represents a good faith attempt to provide senior management and the Board with information respecting material acts, events or conditions within the corporation, including compliance with applicable statutes and regulations? I certainly do not believe so. I doubt that such a broad generalization of the *Graham* holding would have been accepted by the Supreme Court in 1963. The case can be more narrowly interpreted as standing for the proposition that, absent grounds to suspect deception, neither corporate boards nor senior officers can be charged with wrongdoing simply for assuming the integrity of employees and the honesty of their dealings on the company's behalf. *See* 188 A.2d at 130-31.

A broader interpretation of *Graham v. Allis-Chalmers* — that it means that a corporate board has no responsibility to assure that appropriate information and reporting systems are established by management — would not, in any event, be accepted by the Delaware Supreme Court in 1996, in my opinion. In stating the basis for this view, I start with the recognition that in recent years the Delaware Supreme Court has made it clear — especially in its jurisprudence concerning takeovers, from *Smith v. Van Gorkom* through *Paramount Communications v. QVC* — the seriousness with which the corporation law views the role of the corporate board. Secondly, I note the elementary fact that relevant and timely *information* is an essential predicate for satisfaction of the board's supervisory and monitoring role under Section 141 of the Delaware General Corporation Law. Thirdly, I note the potential impact of the federal organizational sentencing guidelines on any business organization. Any rational person attempting in good faith to meet an organizational governance responsibility would be bound to take into account this development and the enhanced penalties and the opportunities for reduced sanctions that it offers.

In light of these developments, it would, in my opinion, be a mistake to conclude that our Supreme Court's statement in *Graham* concerning "espionage" means that corporate boards may satisfy their obligation to be reasonably informed concerning the corporation, without assuring themselves that information and reporting systems exist in the organization that are reasonably designed to provide to senior management and to the board itself timely, accurate information sufficient to allow management and the board, each within its scope, to reach informed judgments concerning both the corporation's compliance with law and its business performance.

Obviously the level of detail that is appropriate for such an information system is a question of business judgment. And obviously too, no rationally designed information and reporting system will remove the possibility that the corporation will violate laws or regulations, or that senior officers or directors may nevertheless sometimes be misled or otherwise fail reasonably to detect acts material to the corporation's compliance with the law. But it is important that the board exercise a good faith judgment that the corporation's information and reporting system is in concept and design adequate to assure the board that appropriate information will come to its attention in a timely manner as a matter of ordinary operations, so that it may satisfy its responsibility.

Thus, I am of the view that a director's obligation includes a duty to attempt in good faith to assure that a corporate information and reporting system, which the board concludes is adequate, exists, and that failure to do so under some circumstances may, in theory at least, render a director liable for losses caused by non-compliance with applicable legal standards. I now turn to an analysis of the claims asserted with this concept of the directors duty of care, as a duty satisfied in part by assurance of adequate information flows to the board, in mind.

III. ANALYSIS OF THIRD AMENDED COMPLAINT AND SETTLEMENT

A. *The Claims*

On balance, after reviewing an extensive record in this case, including numerous documents and three depositions, I conclude that this settlement is fair and reasonable. In light of the fact that the Caremark Board already has a functioning committee charged with overseeing corporate compliance, the changes in corporate practice that are presented as consideration for the settlement do not impress one as very significant. Nonetheless, that consideration appears fully adequate to support dismissal of the derivative claims of director fault asserted, because those claims find no substantial evidentiary support in the record and quite likely were susceptible to a motion to dismiss in all events.

In order to show that the Caremark directors breached their duty of care by failing adequately to control Caremark's employees, plaintiffs would have to show either (1) that the directors knew or (2) should have known that violations of law were occurring and, in either event, (3) that the directors took no steps in a good faith effort to prevent or remedy that situation, and (4) that such failure proximately resulted in the losses complained of, although under *Cede & Co. v. Technicolor, Inc.,* Del. Supr., 636 A.2d 956 (1994) this last element may be thought to constitute an affirmative defense.

1. *Knowing violation for statute:* Concerning the possibility that the Caremark directors knew of violations of law, none of the documents submitted for review, nor any of the deposition transcripts appear to provide evidence of it. Certainly the Board understood that the company had entered into a variety of contracts with physicians, researchers, and health care providers and it was understood that some of these contracts were with persons who had prescribed treatments that Caremark participated in providing. The board was informed that the company's reimbursement for patient care was frequently from government funded sources and that such services were subject to the ARPL. But the Board appears to have been informed by experts that the company's practices while contestable, were lawful. There is no evidence that reliance on such reports was not reasonable. Thus, this case presents no occasion to apply a principle to the effect that knowingly causing the corporation to violate a criminal statute constitutes a breach of a director's fiduciary duty. *See Roth v. Robertson,* N.Y. Sup. Ct., 64 Misc. 343, 118 N.Y.S. 351 (1909); *Miller v. American*

Tel. & Tel. Co., 507 F.2d 759 (3rd Cir. 1974). It is not clear that the Board knew the detail found, for example, in the indictments arising from the Company's payments. But, of course, the duty to act in good faith to be informed cannot be thought to require directors to possess detailed information about all aspects of the operation of the enterprise. Such a requirement would simple be inconsistent with the scale and scope of efficient organization size in this technological age.

2. *Failure to monitor*: Since it does appears that the Board was to some extent unaware of the activities that led to liability, I turn to a consideration of the other potential avenue to director liability that the pleadings take: director inattention or "negligence." Generally where a claim of directorial liability for corporate loss is predicated upon ignorance of liability creating activities within the corporation, as in *Graham* or in this case, in my opinion only a sustained or systematic failure of the board to exercise oversight — such as an utter failure to attempt to assure a reasonable information and reporting system exists — will establish the lack of good faith that is a necessary condition to liability. Such a test of liability — lack of good faith as evidenced by sustained or systematic failure of a director to exercise reasonable oversight — is quite high. But, a demanding test of liability in the oversight context is probably beneficial to corporate shareholders as a class, as it is in the board decision context, since it makes board service by qualified persons more likely, while continuing to act as a stimulus to *good faith performance of duty* by such directors.

Here the record supplies essentially no evidence that the director defendants were guilty of a sustained failure to exercise their oversight function. To the contrary, insofar as I am able to tell on this record, the corporation's information systems appear to have represented a good faith attempt to be informed of relevant facts. If the directors did not know the specifics of the activities that lead to the indictments, they cannot be faulted.

The liability that eventuated in this instance was huge. But the fact that it resulted from a violation of criminal law alone does not create a breach of fiduciary duty by directors. The record at this stage does not support the conclusion that the defendants either lacked good faith in the exercise of their monitoring responsibilities or conscientiously permitted a known violation of law by the corporation to occur. The claims asserted against them must be viewed at this stage as extremely weak.

. . .

Post-Case Follow-Up

As you now know, in dicta in *Caremark*, former Delaware Chancellor Allen noted that the fiduciary duty of care of corporate directors included a "responsibility to assure that appropriate information and reporting systems are established by management" to ensure that the corporation complies with the regulatory regimes under which it operates. *Id.* at 969-70. In the wake of the *Caremark* decision, questions arose as to whether and how this dictum would make it into the law, and, whether *Caremark*-style claims involved a duty of care breach, a duty of loyalty breach, or something else entirely.

The Delaware Supreme Court addressed these questions in its 2006 decision *Stone v. Ritter*, 911 A.2d 362 (Del. 2006). In *Stone*, the plaintiffs alleged that directors of AmSouth breached their fiduciary duties in connection with employees' failure to file suspicious activities reports as required by the federal bank secrecy act and anti-money laundering ("AML") regulations. As with *Caremark*, the plaintiffs did not allege that the directors were involved in the illegal activity, or even that they were aware of the employees' violation of the law. Indeed, the plaintiffs acknowledged in their appeal that there were no red flags and that the directors neither knew nor should have known of the violations. Plaintiffs' theory was that the directors had nevertheless violated their fiduciary duties by failing adequately to oversee the company's AML compliance procedures and by failing to ensure adequate reporting to board, thereby disabling the board from being able to effectively monitor and oversee the company's compliance activities.

In affirming the Chancery Court's dismissal of the plaintiffs' claims, the *Stone* court made three important rulings:

- First, the court confirmed that the *Caremark* dicta respecting directors' oversight obligations is the law of Delaware, stating "*Caremark* articulates the necessary conditions for assessing director oversight liability." *Stone*, 911 A.2d at 365.
- Second, the court held that the *Caremark* standard for director oversight liability draws upon the duty of loyalty and directors' obligation to act in good faith (which the court conceptualized as a component of the duty of loyalty).
- Third, the court held that to establish a *Caremark*-style claim, a plaintiff must not only prove a failure of oversight, but must also prove that such a failure was the product of a failure to discharge directorial responsibilities in good faith, in the form of an intentional dereliction of duty. *Id*. The court held that gross negligence was not enough.

These holdings are reflected in the following frequently quoted excerpt from *Stone*:

> We hold that *Caremark* articulates the necessary conditions predicate for director oversight liability: (a) the directors utterly failed to implement any reporting or information system or controls; *or* (b) having implemented such a system or controls, consciously failed to monitor or oversee its operations thus disabling themselves from being informed of risks or problems requiring their attention. In either case, imposition of liability requires a showing that the directors knew that they were not discharging their fiduciary obligations. Where directors fail to act in the face of a known duty to act, thereby demonstrating a conscious disregard for their responsibilities, they breach their duty of loyalty by failing to discharge that fiduciary obligation in good faith.

Id. at 370.

With its third holding, the *Stone* court cited with approval its then-recent decision *In re Walt Disney Co. Deriv. Litig.*, 906 A.2d 27 (Del. 2006). In *Disney*, the plaintiffs alleged that Walt Disney's board members breached their fiduciary duties when they approved a compensation package that resulted in the payment of $130 million in severance to former Disney CEO Michael Eisner only 14 months after Eisner was hired by the company. Following a bench trial, the Chancery Court entered judgment for the director defendants, holding that the business judgment rule presumptions protected directors' decisions in connection with the compensation package, and further holding that the directors had not acted in bad faith. The court had reached the issue of whether the directors had acted in bad faith because Disney's charter included a § 102(b)(7) provision that exculpated the company's directors from liability for money damages for breaches of the duty of care, but did not (and could not) exculpate the directors from liability for damages resulting from loyalty breaches or acts or omissions not in good faith. The plaintiffs challenged these holdings on a number of fronts, claiming that the Chancellor had formulated and applied an incorrect definition of what constitutes an act or omission not in good faith.

The Delaware Supreme Court rejected the *Disney* plaintiffs' arguments. The court held that a failure to act in good faith requires conduct that is qualitatively different from, and more culpable than, the conduct giving rise to a violation of the fiduciary duty of care (i.e., gross negligence). The court also cited with approval the Chancellor's discussion of examples of acts and omissions that could establish a failure to discharge directorial duties in good faith:

> A failure to act in good faith may be shown, for instance, where the fiduciary intentionally acts with a purpose other than that of advancing the best interests of the corporation, where the fiduciary acts with the intent to violate applicable positive law, or where the fiduciary intentionally fails to act in the face of a known duty to act, demonstrating a conscious disregard for his duties. There may be other examples of bad faith yet to be proven or alleged, but these three are the most salient.

In re Walt Disney Co. Deriv. Litig., 906 A.2d at 67.

Citing the *Disney* court's formulation, the *Stone* court explained that an intentional failure to act in the face of a known duty to act "describes, and is fully consistent with, the lack of good faith conduct that the *Caremark* court held was a 'necessary condition' for director oversight liability, i.e., 'a sustained or systematic failure of the board to exercise oversight — such as an utter failure to attempt to assure a reasonable information and reporting system exists. . . .'" *Id.* at 369. In so holding, the *Stone* court placed directors' oversight obligations under the duty of loyalty, and also confirmed the scienter requirement (a failure to discharge the duty of loyalty in good faith, demonstrated through proof of an intentional dereliction of duty) necessary to establish a *Caremark* claim.

In re Caremark International Inc. Derivative Litigation: Real Life Applications

Wings Airlines, Inc., is a Delaware corporation. Tragically, one of Wings' pilots flew a plane into a mountainside last year, killing everyone on board. It was later determined that the pilot had been suffering from severe mental illness in the months leading up to the crash. Pat, a Wings shareholder, has filed a lawsuit against Wings' directors for breach of fiduciary duty. The complaint acknowledges that Wings' directors were unaware of the pilot's mental health issues, but alleges that Wings had inadequate procedures for monitoring the mental health of its pilots and further alleges that if adequate procedures had been in place, Wings would have grounded the pilot prior to the accident, thereby preventing the crash. The defendants have moved to dismiss the complaint.

a. You are the clerk for the judge assigned to hear the motion to dismiss. Write a bench memo outlining what the plaintiff must allege to state a *Caremark*-style claim against the defendants.

b. Assume that Wings had a policy that required the airline to monitor the mental health of its pilots, but further assume that due to cost-cutting measures, the office in charge of monitoring pilots' mental health is severely understaffed, and unable to perform adequate monitoring tasks. Are these facts, standing alone, enough to state a *Caremark* claim against Wings' directors?

c. Review the two spotlight sections immediately below these questions. Does the information in these sections change your answer to Questions a or b?

---

1. Spotlight: *Caremark* Claims, Bad Faith, and § 102(b)(7) Exculpation Provisions

One consequence of the *Stone* court's decision to place the duty of directors' oversight obligations under the duty of loyalty (rather than the duty of care) is that § 102(b)(7) exculpation provisions no longer insulate directors from the liability for money damages for breach of *Caremark* oversight duties, provided the director defendant acted with scienter, as defined by the *Disney* and *Stone* courts. A second important consequence of the *Stone* court's decision, however, is to make it clear that *Caremark* claims are enormously difficult for plaintiffs to win due to the scienter requirement. After *Stone* and *Disney*, to successfully bring a *Caremark* claim, a plaintiff must demonstrate not only a failure of oversight by a director, but also that the failure was due to an intentional dereliction of duty — that is, a failure to act in the face of a known duty to act, demonstrating a failure to discharge directorial duties in good faith. As *Disney* and *Stone* make clear, gross negligence does not satisfy this standard. It is for this reason that *Caremark* claims repeatedly have been characterized as "possibly the most difficult theory in corporation law upon which a plaintiff might hope to win a judgment." *See, e.g., In re Caremark Int'l Deriv. Litig.*, 698 A.2d at 967.

2. Spotlight: *Caremark* Claims and Illegal versus Risky Conduct

In the years immediately following *Caremark*, plaintiffs sought to use the doctrine mainly in cases involving illegal conduct by employees. *See, e.g., Stone*, 911 A.2d 362 (failure to monitor violations of the Bank Secrecy Act); *In re Am. Int'l Grp., Inc.*, 965 A.2d 763 (Del. Ch. 2009) (failure to monitor illegal and fraudulent transactions); *David B. Shaev Profit Sharing Account v. Armstrong*, No. Civ. A. 1449-N,

2006 WL 391931 (Del. Ch. Feb. 13, 2006) (failure to monitor fraudulent business practices). This is perhaps not surprising, as *Caremark* itself had involved allegedly illegal underlying conduct. *Caremark*, 698 A.2d at 959 (concerning failure to monitor violations of the Anti-Referral Payments Law).

In the wake of the financial crisis, however, plaintiffs sought to extend the doctrine to cases where it was not as clear that employees had violated substantive law. For example, in a case involving the financial institution Goldman Sachs, plaintiffs alleged that employees had engaged in unethical and highly risky (but not necessarily illegal) trading practices, leading to massive losses. In dismissing the *Caremark* claims based on these allegations, the Delaware Chancery Court distinguished cases involving illegal conduct from those involving highly risky (and even unethical) conduct:

> As described above, the Plaintiffs must plead particularized facts suggesting that the board failed to implement a monitoring and reporting system or consciously disregarded the information provided by that system. Here, the Plaintiffs assert that the Goldman employees engaged in unethical trading practices in search of short term revenues. . . .
>
> Illegal corporate conduct is not loyal corporate conduct. "[A] fiduciary of a Delaware corporation cannot be loyal to a Delaware corporation by knowingly causing it to seek profit by violating the law." The "unethical" conduct the Plaintiffs allege here, however, is not the type of wrongdoing envisioned by *Caremark*. The conduct at issue here involves, for the most part, *legal* business decisions that were firmly within management's judgment to pursue. There is nothing intrinsic in using naked credit default swaps or shorting the mortgage market that makes these actions illegal or wrongful. These are actions that Goldman managers, presumably using their informed business judgment, made to hedge the Corporation's assets against risk or to earn a higher return. Legal, if risky, actions that are within management's discretion to pursue are not "red flags" that would put a board on notice of unlawful conduct.

In re Goldman Sachs Grp., Inc. S'holder Litig., Civil Action No. 5215-VCG, 2011 WL 4826104, at *19-20 (Del. Ch. Oct. 12, 2011) (citations omitted). Reviewing the *Goldman Sachs* case along with cases involving Citigroup and the financial/insurance company AIG, it appears as though plaintiffs must allege illegal conduct by employees to state an actionable *Caremark* claim, and not (merely) highly risky or unethical conduct to survive a motion to dismiss — even in situations where the allegedly risky and/or unethical conduct led to enormous losses. *See, e.g., In re Citigroup S'holder Deriv. Litig.*, 964 A.2d 106 (Del. Ch. 2009) (holding allegation that the corporation's directors breached their fiduciary duties by failing adequately to protect the corporation from exposure to the subprime lending market not sufficient to plead a *Caremark* claim); *In re Am. Int'l Grp., Inc.*, 965 A.2d 763, 776 (Del. Ch. 2009) (denying motion to dismiss where complaint contained well-pled allegations of pervasive, diverse, and substantial fraud involving managers at the highest level of AIG).

E. SHAREHOLDER ACTIONS

Among other rights, shareholders of a corporation have the right to institute litigation against the corporation and its officers and directors, and (in limited circumstances) on behalf of the corporation, to seek redress for wrongs committed by officers or directors. There are two types of actions that shareholders may institute in these circumstances: **direct actions**, for injury caused directly to the shareholder by the corporation, and **derivative actions**, for injury sustained by the corporation for which the corporation fails to seek redress. We provide an overview of direct and derivative actions below, then drill down on substantive and procedural requirements associated with shareholder derivative actions.

1. Overview of Direct Actions

A **direct action** is a lawsuit filed against the corporation (or officers or directors, or both) by a shareholder who has been injured by some act of the corporation. Common reasons for instituting a direct action include the corporation's refusal to distribute a dividend to a shareholder when every other member of the shareholder's class received a dividend, denial of voting rights to a particular shareholder, refusal to allow inspection of the shareholder list by a shareholder, and certain alleged violations of the federal securities laws.

If numerous shareholders are similarly situated (e.g., if an entire class of shareholders, e.g., those 1,000 individuals owning Common B stock, are wrongfully denied their voting rights), one or more of the shareholders may be able to institute a **class action** on behalf of the other shareholders. Class actions, sometimes called representative actions, promote judicial economy in that similar claims are adjudicated at the same time rather than having the 1,000 shareholders institute 1,000 separate lawsuits.

Shareholder lawsuits, particularly involving claims alleging violations of the federal securities laws, showed a dramatic increase in the 1990s. In many instances, shareholders sued on the basis that their company overstated profits, with shareholders alleging that quarterly earnings statements and forecasts as to expected performance were representations upon which they could rely. When earnings did not meet such projections, shareholders sued. For example, in 1998, the day after one company announced it was restating its revenues downward from $8.3 million to $1.4 million, 23 class actions alleging securities fraud were filed.

In an effort to reduce what some considered to be abusive securities class action filings, Congress enacted the Private Securities Litigation Reform Act (15 U.S.C. §§ 78u-4 et seq.) in late 1995 to make it harder for such shareholder suits to succeed. Its advocates had convincingly argued that the law was necessary to combat the increasingly familiar practice of initiating shareholder suits (sometimes called strike suits) the moment stock losses occurred. The 1995 Reform Act requires plaintiffs to state in specific detail any allegations of misrepresentation rather than merely alleging misconduct in general terms and then using discovery to obtain specificity and perhaps uncover claims. The Act also eliminated joint and several liability for various securities violations. This rule had previously resulted in peripheral defendants with "deep pockets," often attorneys, auditors, and underwriters, being liable for an entire judgment. Under the Act, liability is apportioned such that each party is liable only for the portion of the judgment that corresponds to its actual assigned allocation of fault. Only those who knowingly commit violations remain jointly and severally liable. Finally, the Reform Act provided a "safe harbor" by allowing companies to make certain predictions about future earnings, called **forward-looking statements**, without fear of a lawsuit if actual results differed. Generally, companies must explain the reasons that actual results might differ from the projections, such as the fact that increased competition or government regulation might cause actual earnings to be less than predicted.

The Reform Act also allows control of litigation to be assumed by the largest investor, the **lead plaintiff**, who is most capable of adequately representing the interests of the class. There is a rebuttable presumption that the party with the largest financial interest in the relief sought by the class is the most adequate plaintiff. To eliminate "professional plaintiffs," who often owned only a few share of stock, a person may be a lead plaintiff in no more than five securities class actions during any three-year period. The Stanford Securities Class Action Clearinghouse has reported that institutions (such as public pensions) now serve as lead plaintiffs in more than one-half of all cases. We discuss federal and state securities laws, including the anti-fraud provisions typically at issue in shareholder class action litigation, in more detail in Chapter 13.

2. Overview of Derivative Actions

A shareholder-initiated **derivative action** is a lawsuit brought by one or more shareholders to enforce a right or cause of action owned by the corporation, but one that the corporation will not enforce. In brief, the shareholder sues the corporation to compel it to enforce corporate rights against officers, directors, or third parties. The shareholder is not suing for injury done to herself, however; the action "derives" from the shareholder's ownership interest in the corporation, which will not sue the wrongdoer. The corporation is the injured party in a derivative suit, and the alleged wrongdoers (e.g., directors, officers) are the defendants.

Most derivative actions allege mismanagement or waste of corporate assets or breach of fiduciary duty. For example, assume that FTB, Inc. has paid excessive compensation to its directors and allows its directors to borrow money from the corporation without paying interest. A shareholder could institute a derivative suit on behalf of the corporation against the directors for mismanagement and breach of fiduciary duty. If the shareholder prevails, the shareholder does not receive any recovery because that recovery is properly owed to the corporation. The shareholder will, however, be entitled to reimbursement for the costs and expenses of bringing the action. Presumably, however, the shareholder will receive at least some indirect or ultimate benefit by the corporation having additional assets.

Because derivative actions, by their very nature, impinge on the board's authority to decide whether and when to institute litigation, derivative actions are subject to a number of procedural and substantive requirements not applicable to direct actions, including (1) standing (the contemporaneous and continuous ownership rules); and (2) demand requirements. We discuss these requirements in detail in Section E.4 below. To avoid these requirements, plaintiffs have been known to style their claims as direct rather than derivative. Our first order of business, then, is to figure out how to distinguish between direct and derivative claims.

3. Distinguishing Direct from Derivative Actions

Case Preview

Tooley v. Donaldson, Lufkin & Jenrette, Inc.

In *Tooley*, the plaintiffs brought a derivative action alleging that directors breached their fiduciary duties by agreeing to delay the closing of a transaction, causing shareholders to lose the time-value of cash paid for their shares. The defendants moved to dismiss on the grounds the claims were derivative in nature, and thus subject to dismissal, because the plaintiffs had not satisfied substantive and procedural hurdles associated with bringing a derivative action. Think about the following questions when reading this case:

1. What test does the court apply to distinguish direct from derivative claims?
2. Is the claim at issue direct or derivative under the test used by the court?
3. What is Delaware Rule 23.1, and what is its significance in derivative actions?
4. Why did the court remand the case to the Chancery Court to amend its notice of dismissal to provide for dismissal without prejudice?

Tooley v. Donaldson, Lufkin & Jenrette, Inc.
845 A.2d 1031 (Del. 2004)

VEASEY, Chief Justice:*

Plaintiff-stockholders brought a purported class action in the Court of Chancery, alleging that the members of the board of directors of their corporation breached their fiduciary duties by agreeing to a 22-day delay in closing a proposed merger. Plaintiffs contend that the delay harmed them due to the lost time-value of the cash paid for their shares. The Court of Chancery granted the defendants' motion to dismiss on the sole ground that the claims were, "at most," claims of the corporation being asserted derivatively. They were, thus, held not to be direct claims of the stockholders, individually. Thereupon, the Court held that the plaintiffs lost their standing to bring this action when they tendered their shares in connection with the merger.

Although the trial court's legal analysis of whether the complaint alleges a direct or derivative claim reflects some concepts in our prior jurisprudence, we believe

---

*Footnotes have been omitted for purposes of brevity.

those concepts are not helpful and should be regarded as erroneous. We set forth in this Opinion the law to be applied henceforth in determining whether a stockholder's claim is derivative or direct. That issue must turn *solely* on the following questions: (1) who suffered the alleged harm (the corporation or the suing stockholders, individually); and (2) who would receive the benefit of any recovery or other remedy (the corporation or the stockholders, individually)?

To the extent we have concluded that the trial court's analysis of the direct vs. derivative dichotomy should be regarded as erroneous, we view the error as harmless in this case because the complaint does not set forth *any* claim upon which relief can be granted. In its opinion, the Court of Chancery properly found on the facts pleaded that the plaintiffs have no separate contractual right to the alleged lost time-value of money arising out of extensions in the closing of a tender offer. These extensions were made in connection with a merger where the plaintiffs' right to any payment of the merger consideration had not ripened at the time the extensions were granted. No other individual right of these stockholders having been asserted in the complaint, it was correctly dismissed.

In affirming the judgment of the trial court as having correctly dismissed the complaint, we reverse only its dismissal with prejudice. We remand this action to the Court of Chancery with directions to amend its order of dismissal to provide that: (a) the action is dismissed for failure to state a claim upon which relief can be granted; and (b) that the dismissal is without prejudice. Thus, plaintiffs will have an opportunity to replead, if warranted under Court of Chancery Rule 11.

FACTS

Patrick Tooley and Kevin Lewis are former minority stockholders of Donaldson, Lufkin & Jenrette, Inc. (DLJ), a Delaware corporation engaged in investment banking. DLJ was acquired by Credit Suisse Group (Credit Suisse) in the Fall of 2000. Before that acquisition, AXA Financial, Inc. (AXA), which owned 71% of DLJ stock, controlled DLJ. Pursuant to a stockholder agreement between AXA and Credit Suisse, AXA agreed to exchange with Credit Suisse its DLJ stockholdings for a mix of stock and cash. The consideration received by AXA consisted primarily of stock. Cash made up one-third of the purchase price. Credit Suisse intended to acquire the remaining minority interests of publicly-held DLJ stock through a cash tender offer, followed by a merger of DLJ into a Credit Suisse subsidiary.

The tender offer price was set at $90 per share in cash. The tender offer was to expire 20 days after its commencement. The merger agreement, however, authorized two types of extensions. First, Credit Suisse could unilaterally extend the tender offer if certain conditions were not met, such as SEC regulatory approvals or certain payment obligations. Alternatively, DLJ and Credit Suisse could agree to postpone acceptance by Credit Suisse of DLJ stock tendered by the minority stockholders.

Credit Suisse availed itself of both types of extensions to postpone the closing of the tender offer. The tender offer was initially set to expire on October 5, 2000, but Credit Suisse invoked the five-day unilateral extension provided in the agreement. Later, by agreement between DLJ and Credit Suisse, it postponed the merger a second time so that it was then set to close on November 2, 2000.

Plaintiffs challenge the second extension that resulted in a 22-day delay. They contend that this delay was not properly authorized and harmed minority stockholders while improperly benefitting AXA. They claim damages representing the time-value of money lost through the delay.

THE DECISION OF THE COURT OF CHANCERY

The order of the Court of Chancery dismissing the complaint, and the Memorandum Opinion upon which it is based, state that the dismissal is based on the plaintiffs' lack of standing to bring the claims asserted therein. Thus, when plaintiffs tendered their shares, they lost standing under Court of Chancery Rule 23.1, the contemporaneous holding rule. The ruling before us on appeal is that the plaintiffs' claim is derivative, purportedly brought on behalf of DLJ. The Court of Chancery, relying upon our confusing jurisprudence on the direct/derivative dichotomy, based its dismissal on the following ground: "Because this delay affected all DLJ shareholders equally, plaintiffs' injury was not a special injury, and this action is, thus, a derivative action, at most."

Plaintiffs argue that they have suffered a "special injury" because they had an alleged contractual right to receive the merger consideration of $90 per share without suffering the 22-day delay arising out of the extensions under the merger agreement. But the trial court's opinion convincingly demonstrates that plaintiffs had no such contractual right that had ripened at the time the extensions were entered into:

> *Here, it is clear that plaintiffs have no separate contractual right to bring a direct claim, and they do not assert contractual rights under the merger agreement.* First, the merger agreement specifically disclaims any persons as being third party beneficiaries to the contract. Second, any contractual shareholder right to payment of the merger consideration did not ripen until the conditions of the agreement were met. The agreement stated that Credit Suisse Group was not required to accept any shares for tender, or could extend the offer, under certain conditions—one condition of which included an extension or termination by agreement between Credit Suisse Group and DLJ. *Because Credit Suisse Group and DLJ did in fact agree to extend the tender offer period, any right to payment plaintiffs could have did not ripen until this newly negotiated period was over. The merger agreement only became binding and mutually enforceable at the time the tendered shares ultimately were accepted for payment by Credit Suisse Group.* It is at that moment in time, November 3, 2000, that the company became bound to purchase the tendered shares, making the contract mutually enforceable. *DLJ stockholders had no individual contractual right to payment until November 3, 2000, when their tendered shares were accepted for payment.* Thus, they have no contractual basis to challenge a delay in the closing of the tender offer up until November 3. *Because this is the date the tendered shares were accepted for payment, the contract was not breached and plaintiffs do not have a contractual basis to bring a direct suit.*

Moreover, no other individual right of these stockholder-plaintiffs was alleged to have been violated by the extensions.

That conclusion could have ended the case because it portended a definitive ruling that plaintiffs have no claim whatsoever on the facts alleged. But the defendants chose to argue, and the trial court chose to decide, the standing issue, which is predicated on an assertion that this claim is a derivative one asserted on behalf of the corporation, DLJ.

The Court of Chancery correctly noted that "[t]he Court will independently examine the nature of the wrong alleged and any potential relief to make its own determination of the suit's classification. . . . Plaintiffs' classification of the suit is not binding." The trial court's analysis was hindered, however, because it focused on the confusing concept of "special injury" as the test for determining whether a claim is derivative or direct. The trial court's premise was as follows:

> In order to bring a *direct* claim, a plaintiff must have experienced some "special injury." [citing *Lipton v. News Int'l,* 514 A.2d 1075, 1079 (Del. 1986)]. A special injury is a wrong that "is separate and distinct from that suffered by other shareholders, . . . or a wrong involving a contractual right of a shareholder, such as the right to vote, or to assert majority control, which exists independently of any right of the corporation." [citing *Moran v. Household Int'l Inc.,* 490 A.2d 1059, 1070 (Del. Ch. 1985), *aff'd* 500 A.2d 1346 (Del. 1986 [1985])].

In our view, the concept of "special injury" that appears in some Supreme Court and Court of Chancery cases is not helpful to a proper analytical distinction between direct and derivative actions. We now disapprove the use of the concept of "special injury" as a tool in that analysis.

THE PROPER ANALYSIS TO DISTINGUISH BETWEEN DIRECT AND DERIVATIVE ACTIONS

The analysis must be based solely on the following questions: Who suffered the alleged harm—the corporation or the suing stockholder individually—and who would receive the benefit of the recovery or other remedy? This simple analysis is well imbedded in our jurisprudence, but some cases have complicated it by injection of the amorphous and confusing concept of "special injury."

The Chancellor, in the very recent *Agostino* case, correctly points this out and strongly suggests that we should disavow the concept of "special injury." In a scholarly analysis of this area of the law, he also suggests that the inquiry should be whether the stockholder has demonstrated that he or she has suffered an injury that is not dependent on an injury to the corporation. In the context of a claim for breach of fiduciary duty, the Chancellor articulated the inquiry as follows: "Looking at the body of the complaint and considering the nature of the wrong alleged and the relief requested, has the plaintiff demonstrated that he or she can prevail without showing an injury to the corporation?" We believe that this approach is helpful in analyzing the first prong of the analysis: what person or entity has suffered the alleged harm? The second prong of the analysis should logically follow.

A BRIEF HISTORY OF OUR JURISPRUDENCE

The derivative suit has been generally described as "one of the most interesting and ingenious of accountability mechanisms for large formal organizations." It enables a stockholder to bring suit on behalf of the corporation for harm done to the corporation. Because a derivative suit is being brought on behalf of the corporation, the recovery, if any, must go to the corporation. A stockholder who is directly injured, however, does retain the right to bring an individual action for injuries affecting his or her legal rights as a stockholder. Such a claim is distinct from an injury caused to the corporation alone. In such individual suits, the recovery or other relief flows directly to the stockholders, not to the corporation.

Determining whether an action is derivative or direct is sometimes difficult and has many legal consequences, some of which may have an expensive impact on the parties to the action. For example, if an action is derivative, the plaintiffs are then required to comply with the requirements of Court of Chancery Rule 23.1, that the stockholder: (a) retain ownership of the shares throughout the litigation; (b) make presuit demand on the board; and (c) obtain court approval of any settlement. Further, the recovery, if any, flows only to the corporation. The decision whether a suit is direct or derivative may be outcome-determinative. Therefore, it is necessary that a standard to distinguish such actions be clear, simple and consistently articulated and applied by our courts.

. . .

. . . The proper analysis has been and should remain that stated in *Grimes*; *Kramer* and *Parnes*. That is, a court should look to the nature of the wrong and to whom the relief should go. The stockholder's claimed direct injury must be independent of any alleged injury to the corporation. The stockholder must demonstrate that the duty breached was owed to the stockholder and that he or she can prevail without showing an injury to the corporation.

STANDARD TO BE APPLIED IN THIS CASE

In this case it cannot be concluded that the complaint alleges a derivative claim. There is no derivative claim asserting injury to the corporate entity. There is no relief that would go the corporation. Accordingly, there is no basis to hold that the complaint states a derivative claim.

But, it does not necessarily follow that the complaint states a direct, individual claim. While the complaint purports to set forth a direct claim, in reality, it states no claim at all. The trial court analyzed the complaint and correctly concluded that it does not claim that the plaintiffs have any rights that have been injured. Their rights have not yet ripened. The contractual claim is nonexistent until it is ripe, and that claim will not be ripe until the terms of the merger are fulfilled, including the extensions of the closing at issue here. Therefore, there is no direct claim stated in the complaint before us.

Accordingly, the complaint was properly dismissed. But, due to the reliance on the concept of "special injury" by the Court of Chancery, the ground set forth for the dismissal is erroneous, there being no derivative claim. That error is harmless, however, because, in our view, there is no direct claim either.

CONCLUSION

For purposes of distinguishing between derivative and direct claims, we expressly disapprove both the concept of "special injury" and the concept that a claim is necessarily derivative if it affects all stockholders equally. In our view, the tests going forward should rest on those set forth in this opinion.

We affirm the judgment of the Court of Chancery dismissing the complaint, although on a different ground from that decided by the Court of Chancery. We reverse the dismissal with prejudice and remand this matter to the Court of Chancery to amend the order of dismissal: (a) to state that the complaint is dismissed on the ground that it does not state a claim upon which relief can be granted; and (b) that the dismissal is without prejudice.

Because our determination that there is no valid claim whatsoever in the complaint before us was not argued by the defendants and was not the basis of the ruling of the Court of Chancery, the interests of justice will be best served if the dismissal is without prejudice, and plaintiffs have an opportunity to replead if they have a basis for doing so under Court of Chancery Rule 11. This result — permitting plaintiffs to replead — is unusual, but not unprecedented.

Post-Case Follow-Up

Many actions involving alleged violations of the federal securities laws and alleged fiduciary duty breaches spawn both derivative and direct actions. The federal securities laws generally do not preempt claims asserted under state law (including claims for breach of fiduciary duty). Consequently, shareholders may seek to vindicate different rights and to enforce different obligations through direct and derivative claims.

Tooley v. Donaldson, Lufkin & Jenrette, Inc.: Real Life Applications

In each of the following examples, determine whether the suit would be direct or derivative and explain your reasoning:

a. Dry Cleaners, Inc., founded in 2010, operates dry cleaning businesses around the country. Last year, Dry Cleaners was fined millions of dollars by federal and state environmental protection agencies for allowing perchloroethylene (known as PERC), a solvent, to contaminate groundwater supplies near some Dry Cleaners locations. In 2009, the National Academy of Sciences classified PERC as a likely human carcinogen. Brockovich, a Dry Cleaners shareholder, sues Dry Cleaners' directors for failing to implement and oversee a system of controls designed to prevent groundwater contamination.

b. Sam is a well-known commercial real estate developer with long-time experience in the grocery industry. Sam recently joined the board of Organix, Inc., an organic grocery store and caterer. Although Organix is operating in a relatively small space today, the business is going very well, and the board (including Sam) recently voted in favor of an expansion plan that calls for the purchase of land for, and the construction of, a new warehouse and distribution center, new stores around the city, etc. Last week, one of Sam's industry contacts told Sam that a large parcel of land just off the highway was about to go on the market. The land was a perfect location for a warehouse distribution center. Sam immediately approached the seller and purchased the land for himself. Che, an Organix shareholder, learns of Sam's purchase and sues Sam for breach of fiduciary duty.

c. Sara is a shareholder of Solea, Inc., a publicly held manufacturer of solar-powered chargers for consumer electronics (e.g., phones, tablets, etc.). Solea's board recently approved a cash-out merger proposal whereby Solea shareholders received $35 dollars per share. Although $35 per share represented a substantial premium over the market price of Solea stock, Sara believes (based on analysis of financial and market data), that the cash-out price was too low. Sara sues the board for breach of fiduciary duty.

d. Amina owns Class A shares of Healthmedicus, Inc., a medical device company. Class A shares are participating preferred stock, meaning that Class A shareholders are (i) entitled to receive dividends; and (ii) also have the right to participate with common stockholders in any distributions. Last year, Healthmedicus failed to honor Class A shareholders' participation rights. Amina sues.

4. Derivative Action Requirements

Having examined how to distinguish direct from derivative actions, we now discuss the procedural and substantive requirements applicable to derivative actions.

Standing

As a general rule, a plaintiff must satisfy the contemporaneous ownership rule (which requires that a shareholder own stock at the time of the complained-of incident) and the continuous ownership rule (which requires that the plaintiff own stock all through the litigation). The following excerpt from the Delaware case *Lewis v. Anderson* speaks to this requirement:

> The short answer [to the question of standing] is that to this date § 327 in conjunction with Chancery Court Rule 23.1 and § 259 have been nearly universally construed as fully applicable to a question of post-merger standing to carry on a derivative suit. In the context of a corporate merger, the following authorities hold that a derivative shareholder must not only be a stockholder at the time of the alleged wrong and at time of commencement of suit but that he must also maintain shareholder status throughout the litigation. *Heit v. Tenneco, Inc.*, D. Del., 319 F. Supp. 884 (1970); *Schreiber v. Carney*, Del. Ch., 447 A.2d 17 (1982); *Harff v. Kerkorian*, Del. Ch., 324 A.2d 215 (1974); *Braasch v. Goldschmidt*, Del. Ch., 199 A.2d 760 (1964). The purpose of such a rule is well established: to eliminate abuses associated with a derivative suit. *Harff v. Kerkorian*, supra, at 218.

Lewis v. Anderson, 477 A.2d 1040, 1046 (Del. 1984). *See also* DGCL § 327; Del. Ch. R. 23.1.

For a helpful discussion of the difference between the contemporaneous ownership rule and the continuous ownership rule, see Malaika M. Eaton, Leonard J. Feldman & Jerry C. Chiang, *The Continuous Ownership Requirement in Shareholder Derivative Litigation: Endorsing a Common Sense Application of Standing and Choice-of-Law Principles*, 47 Willamette L. Rev. 1 (2010).

Ownership sometimes is defined statutorily. *See, e.g.*, NYBCL § 626(a) (stating that "[a]n action may be brought in the right of a domestic or foreign corporation to procure a judgment in its favor, by a holder of shares or of voting trust certificates of the corporation or of a beneficial interest in such shares or certificates.").

Where there is no statutory definition, courts generally define share ownership in an expansive manner. That said, ownership and standing can become very complicated very quickly. For example, mergers can cause a derivative plaintiff to lose standing if the plaintiff ceases to be a shareholder in the relevant corporation as a result of the transaction. As there are certain exceptions and nuances to the contemporaneous and continuous ownership rules, it is worth researching the law in the jurisdiction relevant to your matter on this point. *See, e.g., Lewis v. Anderson*, 477 A.2d at 1046, n.10 (holding there are two recognized exceptions to the requirement of contemporaneous ownership in a merger: (i) where the merger itself is the subject of a claim of fraud and (ii) where the merger is in reality a reorganization that does not affect the plaintiff's ownership).

The Demand Requirement—Rule 23.1

Along with standing, shareholders seeking to bring a derivative action on behalf of the corporation generally must comply with pre-filing **demand requirements**. In Delaware, these requirements are set forth in Chancery Court Rule 23.1. Pre-filing demand requirements are a nod to centralized management and the principle that the board's managerial authority includes the right to decide whether and when to institute litigation. The demand requirement codifies the rule that shareholders must either make a demand upon the board before filing suit, giving the board an opportunity to decide whether to institute litigation, or they must plead facts showing that demand ought to be excused because the directors are incapable of making an impartial decision about whether to pursue litigation.

In Delaware, the demand requirement is set forth in Chancery Court Rule 23.1, which states as follows:

> (a) In a derivative action brought by one or more shareholders or members to enforce a right of a corporation or of an unincorporated association, the corporation or association having failed to enforce a right which may properly be asserted by it, the complaint shall allege that the plaintiff was a shareholder or member at the time of the transaction of which the plaintiff complains or that the plaintiff's share or membership thereafter devolved on the plaintiff by operation of law. The complaint shall also *allege with particularity the efforts*, if any, made by the plaintiff to *obtain the action the plaintiff desires* from the directors or comparable authority and *the reasons for the plaintiff's failure to obtain the action or for not making the effort.*

See Del. Ch. R. 23.1 (emphasis added).

This language has been interpreted to mean that a plaintiff must make a fundamental decision prior to filing suit: *Either make a pre-suit demand* upon the board, presenting the allegations to the board and requesting that they bring suit, *or plead facts showing that demand ought to be excused as futile.* If a shareholder makes a demand, and the demand is refused, the business judgment rule presumptions apply to the board's refusal to bring a lawsuit. And, in any subsequent litigation over demand refusal, the shareholder plaintiff will be deemed to have conceded that a majority of board is disinterested and independent. Taken together, these rules mean that if a plaintiff challenges the board's refusal to bring suit following a shareholder demand, the court will examine only whether the board had a rational basis for its decision to refuse the demand.

Not surprisingly, the difficulty of establishing wrongful refusal leads most plaintiffs to sue without making a pre-suit demand, and to litigate the issue of demand excused futility. To establish that demand ought to be excused as futile under Rule 23.1, a plaintiff must plead with particularity facts meeting one of two tests discussed below, depending on the alleged misconduct at issue. Rule 23.1's particularity requirement is notably strict: Pleadings must set forth particularized factual statements that are essential to the complaint. Notice pleading is not good enough, and a wordy complaint larded with conclusory language will not satisfy Rule 23.1.

Aronson Test: Demand Futility and Board Decisions

If a plaintiff is challenging a board decision, the plaintiffs must satisfy the *Aronson* test for demand futility. *See Aronson v. Lewis*, 473 A.2d 805, 811-12 (Del. 1984). Under the *Aronson* test, a plaintiff must plead particularized factual allegations that raise a reasonable doubt that (1) the directors are disinterested and independent; *or* (2) the challenged transaction was otherwise the product of a valid exercise of business judgment. *Id.* at 814.* A plaintiff successfully pleads demand futility under the first prong of *Aronson* if she alleges particularized facts that create a reasonable doubt as to the disinterestedness and independence of a *majority* of directors. The standards for director interest are essentially the same as those discussed above in relation to director conflicting interest transactions. Notably, a plaintiff cannot make a majority of the board interested merely by naming all of the directors as defendants in the lawsuit. Only a director defendant who faces a substantial likelihood of personal liability will be deemed interested, and to meet this standard, a plaintiff must show that the conduct at issue is "so egregious on its face that . . . a substantial likelihood of director liability . . . exists." *Id.* at 815. The standards for director independence are essentially the same as those discussed above in connection with director conflicting interest transactions, as well.

To successfully plead demand futility under second prong of *Aronson*, a plaintiff must allege particularized facts creating a reasonable doubt that a majority of

---

*In *Aronson*, the court's language suggested that plaintiffs would have to satisfy both prongs of the test referenced above. In *Brehm v. Eisner*, 746 A.2d 244, 256 (Del. 2000), however, the court clarified that the two-prong test is disjunctive, meaning a plaintiff need only satisfy one of the prongs for demand to be excused.

the board (i) was adequately informed when making the challenged decision; or (ii) honestly and in good faith believed that the challenged decision was in the best interest of the corporation and its shareholders. Note that if a corporation's charter includes a § 102(b)(7) exculpatory provision, plaintiffs also must plead particularized facts that demonstrate the directors acted with scienter — that is, for example, that there was an intentional dereliction of duty or conscious disregard for responsibilities amounting to bad faith.

Focusing on independence, the Delaware Supreme Court's opinion in *Martha Stewart* offers insight into the contextual nature of the independence inquiry. *See Beam ex rel. Martha Stewart Living Omnimedia, Inc. v. Stewart*, 845 A.2d 1040 (Del. 2004). The plaintiffs alleged that Martha Stewart breached her fiduciary duties in connection with her sale of ImClone stock. The Chancery Court dismissed the complaint because it found that plaintiffs had not made a pre-suit demand under Rule 23.1 and because the court also found that the plaintiffs had failed to plead particularized facts showing that demand upon the bowel to institute litigation against Stewart ought to be excused as futile. The plaintiffs appealed. With respect to independence and demand futility, the Delaware Supreme Court observed as follows:

> The key principle upon which this area of our jurisprudence is based is that the directors are entitled to a *presumption* that they were faithful to their fiduciary duties. In the context of presuit demand, the burden is upon the plaintiff in a derivative action to overcome that presumption. The Court must determine whether a plaintiff has alleged particularized facts creating a reasonable doubt of a director's independence to rebut the presumption at the pleading stage. If the Court determines that the pleaded facts create a reasonable doubt that a majority of the board could have acted independently in responding to the demand, the presumption is rebutted for pleading purposes and demand will be excused as futile.
>
> A director will be considered unable to act objectively with respect to a presuit demand if he or she is interested in the outcome of the litigation or is otherwise not independent. A director's interest may be shown by demonstrating a potential personal benefit or detriment to the director as a result of the decision. "In such circumstances, a director cannot be expected to exercise his or her independent business judgment without being influenced by the . . . personal consequences resulting from the decision." The primary basis upon which a director's independence must be measured is whether the director's decision is based on the corporate merits of the subject before the board, rather than extraneous considerations or influences. This broad statement of the law requires an analysis of whether the director is disinterested in the underlying transaction and, even if disinterested, whether the director is otherwise independent. More precisely in the context of the present case, the independence inquiry requires us to determine whether there is a reasonable doubt that any one of these three directors is capable of objectively making a business decision to assert or not assert a corporate claim against Stewart.

Independence Is a Contextual Inquiry

Independence is a fact-specific determination made in the context of a particular case. The court must make that determination by answering the inquiries: independent from whom and independent for what purpose? To excuse presuit demand in this case, the plaintiff has the burden to plead particularized facts that create a reasonable doubt sufficient to rebut the presumption that either Moore, Seligman or Martinez was independent of defendant Stewart.

In order to show lack of independence, the complaint of a stockholder-plaintiff must create a reasonable doubt that a director is not so "beholden" to an interested director (in this case Stewart) that his or her "discretion would be sterilized." Our jurisprudence explicating the demand requirement

> is designed to create a balanced environment which will: (1) on the one hand, deter costly, baseless suits by creating a screening mechanism to eliminate claims where there is only a suspicion expressed solely in conclusory terms; and (2) on the other hand, permit suit by a stockholder who is able to articulate particularized facts showing that there is a reasonable doubt either that (a) a majority of the board is independent for purposes of responding to the demand, or (b) the underlying transaction is protected by the business judgment rule.

The "reasonable doubt" standard "is sufficiently flexible and workable to provide the stockholder with 'the keys to the courthouse' in an appropriate case where the claim is not based on mere suspicions or stated solely in conclusory terms."

Personal Friendship

A variety of motivations, including friendship, may influence the demand futility inquiry. But, to render a director unable to consider demand, a relationship must be of a bias-producing nature. Allegations of mere personal friendship or a mere outside business relationship, standing alone, are insufficient to raise a reasonable doubt about a director's independence. In this connection, we adopt as our own the Chancellor's analysis in this case:

> [S]ome professional or personal friendships, which may border on or even exceed familial loyalty and closeness, may raise a reasonable doubt whether a director can appropriately consider demand. This is particularly true when the allegations raise serious questions of either civil or criminal liability of such a close friend. Not all friendships, or even most of them, rise to this level and the Court cannot make a *reasonable* inference that a particular friendship does so without specific factual allegations to support such a conclusion.

The facts alleged by Beam regarding the relationships between Stewart and these other members of MSO's board of directors largely boil down to a "structural bias" argument, which presupposes that the professional and social relationships that naturally develop among members of a board impede independent decisionmaking. This Court addressed the structural bias argument in *Aronson v. Lewis*:

> Critics will charge that [by requiring the independence of only a majority of the board] we are ignoring the structural bias common to corporate boards throughout America, as well as the other unseen socialization processes cutting against independent discussion and decisionmaking in the boardroom. The difficulty with structural bias in a demand futile case is simply one of establishing it in the complaint for purposes of Rule 23.1. We are satisfied that discretionary review by the Court of Chancery of complaints alleging specific facts pointing to bias on a particular board will be sufficient for determining demand futility.

Id. at 1048-51 (internal citations omitted).

Rules *Test: Demand Futility and* Caremark *Claims*

If a plaintiff wishes to challenge allegedly unconsidered inaction by the board (i.e., bring a *Caremark* claim), the plaintiff must satisfy the test for demand futility set forth in *Rales v. Blasband*, 634 A.2d 927 (Del. 1993). To properly plead demand futility under *Rales*, a plaintiff must allege particularized facts that create a reasonable doubt that, at the time the complaint is filed, the board of directors could have exercised its independent and disinterested business judgment in responding to a demand. (This is, in effect, prong (1) of the *Aronson* test. Prong (2) does not apply because there is no challenged decision.) The *Rales* standard focuses on whether the board that would be addressing the demand can consider the demand on its merits impartially without being influenced by improper considerations.

Case Preview 	### *In re Citigroup Inc. Shareholder Derivative Litigation*

The next case, involving the financial institution Citigroup, offers an opportunity to examine these standards and tests in context. In *Citigroup*, plaintiffs alleged that the corporation's directors breached their fiduciary duties by failing to properly monitor and manage the risks associated with Citigroup's activities in the subprime lending market and by failing properly to disclose Citigroup's exposure to subprime assets. As is true of many derivative actions, the *Citigroup* case resulted in a long and complicated decision. For present purposes, we have excerpted sections of the opinion concerned with the motion to dismiss under Rule 23.1. When reading the case, consider the following questions:

1. What did Citigroup's directors allegedly do wrong?
2. How does the business judgment rule fit into the court's holding?
3. Are Rule 23.1 pleading requirements more or less rigorous than notice pleading requirements?
4. What impact, if any, does the presence of a § 102(b)(7) exculpation provision have on Rule 23.1 pleading requirements?
5. What is the *Aronson* test for demand futility? When does it apply?
6. What is the *Rales* test for demand futility? When does it apply?
7. What is the basis for the court's holding?

In re Citigroup Inc. Shareholder Derivative Litigation
964 A.2d 106 (Del. Ch. 2011)

CHANDLER, Chancellor.*

This is a shareholder derivative action brought on behalf of Citigroup Inc. ("Citigroup" or the "Company"), seeking to recover for the Company its losses arising

---

*Most footnotes have been omitted for purposes of brevity.

from exposure to the subprime lending market. Plaintiffs, shareholders of Citigroup, brought this action against current and former directors and officers of Citigroup, alleging, in essence, that the defendants breached their fiduciary duties by failing to properly monitor and manage the risks the Company faced from problems in the subprime lending market and for failing to properly disclose Citigroup's exposure to subprime assets. Plaintiffs allege that there were extensive "red flags" that should have given defendants notice of the problems that were brewing in the real estate and credit markets and that defendants ignored these warnings in the pursuit of short term profits and at the expense of the Company's long term viability.

Plaintiffs further allege that certain defendants are liable to the Company for corporate waste for (1) allowing the Company to purchase $2.7 billion in subprime loans from Accredited Home Lenders in March 2007 and from Ameriquest Home Mortgage in September 2007; (2) authorizing and not suspending the Company's share repurchase program in the first quarter of 2007, which allegedly resulted in the Company buying its own shares at "artificially inflated prices"; (3) approving a multi-million dollar payment and benefit package for defendant Charles Prince, whom plaintiffs describe as largely responsible for Citigroup's problems, upon his retirement as Citigroup's CEO in November 2007; and (4) allowing the Company to invest in structured investment vehicles ("SIVs") that were unable to pay off maturing debt.

Pending before the Court is defendants' motion (1) to dismiss or stay the action in favor of an action pending in the Southern District of New York (the "New York Action") or (2) to dismiss the complaint for failure to state a claim under Court of Chancery Rule 12(b)(6) and for failure to properly plead demand futility under Court of Chancery Rule 23.1. For the reasons set forth below, the motion to stay or dismiss in favor of the New York Action is denied. The motion to dismiss is denied as to the claim in Count III for waste for approval of the November 4, 2007 Prince letter agreement. All other claims are dismissed for failure to adequately plead demand futility pursuant to Rule 23.1.

. . .

C. Plaintiffs' Claims

Plaintiffs allege that defendants are liable to the Company for breach of fiduciary duty for (1) failing to adequately oversee and manage Citigroup's exposure to the problems in the subprime mortgage market, even in the face of alleged "red flags" and (2) failing to ensure that the Company's financial reporting and other disclosures were thorough and accurate. As will be more fully explained below, the "red flags" alleged in the eighty-six page Complaint are generally statements from public documents that reflect worsening conditions in the financial markets, including the subprime and credit markets, and the effects those worsening conditions had on market participants, including Citigroup's peers.

III. THE MOTION TO DISMISS UNDER RULE 23.1

A. The Legal Standard for Demand Excused

The decision whether to initiate or pursue a lawsuit on behalf of the corporation is generally within the power and responsibility of the board of directors. This follows from the "cardinal precept of the General Corporation Law of the State of Delaware . . . that directors, rather than shareholders, manage the business and affairs of the corporation." Accordingly, in order to cause the corporation to pursue litigation, a shareholder must either (1) make a pre-suit demand by presenting the allegations to the corporation's directors, requesting that they bring suit, and showing that they wrongfully refused to do so, or (2) plead facts showing that demand upon the board would have been futile. Where, as here, a plaintiff does not make a pre-suit demand on the board of directors, the complaint must plead with particularity facts showing that a demand on the board would have been futile. The purpose of the demand requirement is not to insulate defendants from liability; rather, the demand requirement and the strict requirements of factual particularity under Rule 23.1 "exist[ ] to preserve the primacy of board decisionmaking regarding legal claims belonging to the corporation."

. . .

Under the familiar *Aronson* test, to show demand futility, plaintiffs must provide particularized factual allegations that raise a reasonable doubt that "(1) the directors are disinterested and independent [or] (2) the challenged transaction was otherwise the product of a valid exercise of business judgment." Where, however, plaintiffs complain of board inaction and do not challenge a specific decision of the board, there is no "challenged transaction," and the ordinary *Aronson* analysis does not apply. Instead, to show demand futility where the subject of the derivative suit is not a business decision of the board, a plaintiff must allege particularized facts that "create a reasonable doubt that, as of the time the complaint is filed, the board of directors could have properly exercised its independent and disinterested business judgment in responding to a demand."

In evaluating whether demand is excused, the Court must accept as true the well pleaded factual allegations in the Complaint. The pleadings, however, are held to a higher standard under Rule 23.1 than under the permissive notice pleading standard under Court of Chancery Rule 8(a). To establish that demand is excused under Rule 23.1, the pleadings must comply with "stringent requirements of factual particularity" and set forth "particularized factual statements that are essential to the claim." "A prolix complaint larded with conclusory language . . . does not comply with these fundamental pleading mandates."

Plaintiffs have not alleged that a majority of the board was not independent for purposes of evaluating demand. Rather, as to the claims for waste asserted in Count III, plaintiffs allege that the approval of certain transactions did not constitute a valid exercise of business judgment under the second prong of the *Aronson* test. Plaintiffs allege that demand is futile as to Counts I, II, and IV because the director defendants are not able to exercise disinterested business judgment in responding to a demand because their failure of oversight subjects them to a substantial likelihood of personal liability. According to plaintiffs, the director defendants face a substantial threat of personal liability because their conscious disregard of their duties and lack of proper supervision and oversight caused the Company to be overexposed to risk in the subprime mortgage market.

Demand is not excused solely because the directors would be deciding to sue themselves. Rather, demand will be excused based on a possibility of personal director liability only in the rare case when a plaintiff is able to show director conduct that is "so egregious on its face that board approval cannot meet the test of business judgment, and a substantial likelihood of director liability therefore exists."

B. *Demand Futility Regarding Plaintiffs' Fiduciary Duty Claims*

Plaintiffs' argument is based on a theory of director liability famously articulated by former-Chancellor Allen in *In re Caremark*. Before *Caremark*, in *Graham v. Allis-Chalmers Manufacturing Company,* the Delaware Supreme Court, in response to a theory that the Allis-Chalmers directors were liable because they should have known about employee violations of federal anti-trust laws, held that "absent cause for suspicion there is no duty upon the directors to install and operate a corporate system of espionage to ferret out wrongdoing which they have no reason to suspect exists." Over thirty years later, in the context of approval of a settlement of a class action, former-Chancellor Allen took the opportunity to revisit the duty to monitor under Delaware law. In *Caremark,* the plaintiffs alleged that the directors were liable because they should have known that certain officers and employees were violating the federal Anti-Referral Payments Law. In analyzing these claims, the Court began, appropriately, by reviewing the duty of care and the protections of the business judgment rule.

With regard to director liability standards, the Court distinguished between (1) "*a board decision* that results in a loss because that decision was ill advised or 'negligent' " and (2) "an *unconsidered failure of the board to act* in circumstances in which due attention would, arguably, have prevented the loss." In the former class of cases, director action is analyzed under the business judgment rule, which prevents judicial second guessing of the decision if the directors employed a rational process and considered all material information reasonably available — a standard measured by concepts of gross negligence. As former-Chancellor Allen explained:

> What should be understood, but may not widely be understood by courts or commentators who are not often required to face such questions, is that compliance with a director's duty of care can never appropriately be judicially determined by reference to *the content of the board decision* that leads to a corporate loss, apart from consideration of the good faith *or* rationality of the process employed. That is, whether a judge or jury considering the matter after the fact, believes a decision substantively wrong, or degrees of wrong extending through "stupid" to "egregious" or "irrational," provides no ground for director liability, so long as the court determines that the process employed was either rational or employed in *a good faith* effort to advance corporate interests. To employ a different rule — one that permitted an "objective" evaluation of the decision — would expose directors to substantive second guessing by ill-equipped judges or juries, which would, in the long-run, be injurious to investor interests. Thus, the business judgment rule is process oriented and informed by a deep respect for all *good faith* board decisions.

In the latter class of cases, where directors are alleged to be liable for a failure to monitor liability creating activities, the *Caremark* Court, in a reassessment of the holding in *Graham,* stated that while directors could be liable for a failure to monitor, "only a sustained or systematic failure of the board to exercise oversight — such as an utter failure to attempt to assure a reasonable information and reporting system exists — will establish the lack of good faith that is a necessary condition to liability."

In *Stone v. Ritter,* the Delaware Supreme Court approved the *Caremark* standard for director oversight liability and made clear that liability was based on the concept of good faith, which the *Stone* Court held was embedded in the fiduciary duty of loyalty and did not constitute a freestanding fiduciary duty that could independently give rise to liability. As the *Stone* Court explained:

> *Caremark* articulates the necessary conditions predicate for director oversight liability: (a) the directors utterly failed to implement any reporting or information system or controls; *or* (b) having implemented such a system or controls, consciously failed to monitor or oversee its operations thus disabling themselves from being informed of risks or problems requiring their attention. In either case, imposition of liability requires a showing that the directors knew that they were not discharging their fiduciary obligations. Where directors fail to act in the face of a known duty to act, thereby demonstrating a conscious disregard for their responsibilities, they breach their duty of loyalty by failing to discharge that fiduciary obligation in good faith.

Thus, to establish oversight liability a plaintiff must show that the directors *knew* they were not discharging their fiduciary obligations or that the directors demonstrated a *conscious* disregard for their responsibilities such as by failing to act in the face of a known duty to act. The test is rooted in concepts of bad faith; indeed, a showing of bad faith is a *necessary condition* to director oversight liability.

1. *Plaintiffs' Caremark Allegations*

Plaintiffs' theory of how the director defendants will face personal liability is a bit of a twist on the traditional *Caremark* claim. In a typical *Caremark* case, plaintiffs argue that the defendants are liable for damages that arise from a failure to properly monitor or oversee employee misconduct or violations of law. For example, in *Caremark* the board allegedly failed to monitor employee actions in violation of the federal Anti-Referral Payments Law; in *Stone,* the directors were charged with a failure of oversight that resulted in liability for the company because of employee violations of the federal Bank Secrecy Act.

In contrast, plaintiffs' *Caremark* claims are based on defendants' alleged failure to properly monitor Citigroup's *business risk,* specifically its exposure to the subprime mortgage market. In their answering brief, plaintiffs allege that the director defendants are personally liable under *Caremark* for failing to "make a good faith attempt to follow the procedures put in place or fail[ing] to assure that adequate and proper corporate information and reporting systems existed that would enable them to be fully informed regarding Citigroup's risk to the subprime mortgage market." Plaintiffs point to so-called "red flags" that should have put defendants on notice of the problems in the subprime mortgage market and further allege that the board should have been especially conscious of these red flags because a majority of the directors (1) served on the Citigroup board during its previous Enron related conduct and (2) were members of the ARM Committee and considered financial experts.

Although these claims are framed by plaintiffs as *Caremark* claims, plaintiffs' theory essentially amounts to a claim that the director defendants should be personally liable to the Company because they failed to fully recognize the risk posed by subprime securities. When one looks past the lofty allegations of duties of oversight and red flags used to dress up these claims, what is left appears to be plaintiff shareholders attempting to hold the director defendants personally liable for making (or allowing to be made) business decisions that, in hindsight, turned out poorly for the Company. Delaware Courts have faced these types of claims many times and have developed doctrines to deal with them — the fiduciary duty of care and the business judgment rule. These doctrines properly focus on the decision-making process rather than on a substantive evaluation of the merits of the decision. This follows from the inadequacy of the Court, due in part to a concept known as hindsight bias,[50] to properly evaluate whether corporate decision-makers made a "right" or "wrong" decision.

The business judgment rule "is a presumption that in making a business decision the directors of a corporation acted on an informed basis, in good faith and in the honest belief that the action taken was in the best interests of the company." The burden is on plaintiffs, the party challenging the directors' decision, to rebut this presumption. Thus, absent an allegation of interestedness or disloyalty to the corporation, the business judgment rule prevents a judge or jury from second guessing director decisions if they were the product of a rational process and the directors availed themselves of all material and reasonably available information. The standard of director liability under the business judgment rule "is predicated upon concepts of gross negligence."

Additionally, Citigroup has adopted a provision in its certificate of incorporation pursuant to 8 Del. C. § 102(b)(7) that exculpates directors from personal liability for violations of fiduciary duty, except for, among other things, breaches of the duty of loyalty or actions or omissions not in good faith or that involve intentional misconduct or a knowing violation of law. Because the director defendants are "exculpated from liability for certain conduct, 'then a serious threat of liability may only be found to exist if the plaintiff pleads a *non-exculpated* claim against the directors based on particularized facts.' " Here, plaintiffs have not alleged that the directors were interested in the transaction and instead root their theory of director personal liability in bad faith.

The Delaware Supreme Court has stated that bad faith conduct may be found where a director "intentionally acts with a purpose other than that of advancing the best interests of the corporation, . . . acts with the intent to violate applicable positive law, or . . . intentionally fails to act in the face of a known duty to act, demonstrating a conscious disregard for his duties." More recently, the Delaware Supreme Court held that when a plaintiff seeks to show that demand is excused because directors face a substantial likelihood of liability where "directors are exculpated from liability

---

[50]"Hindsight bias is the tendency for people with knowledge of an outcome to exaggerate the extent to which they believe that outcome could have been predicted." Hal R. Arkes & Cindy A. Schipani, *Medical Malpractice v. The Business Judgment Rule: Differences in Hindsight Bias,* 73 Or. L. Rev. 587, 587 (1994).

except for claims based on 'fraudulent,' 'illegal' or 'bad faith' conduct, a plaintiff must also plead particularized facts that demonstrate that the directors acted with scienter, *i.e.,* that they had 'actual or constructive knowledge' that their conduct was legally improper." A plaintiff can thus plead bad faith by alleging with particularity that a director *knowingly* violated a fiduciary duty or failed to act in violation of a *known* duty to act, demonstrating a *conscious* disregard for her duties.

Turning now specifically to plaintiffs' *Caremark* claims, one can see a similarity between the standard for assessing oversight liability and the standard for assessing a disinterested director's decision under the duty of care when the company has adopted an exculpatory provision pursuant to § 102(b)(7). In either case, a plaintiff can show that the director defendants will be liable if their acts or omissions constitute bad faith. A plaintiff can show bad faith conduct by, for example, properly alleging particularized facts that show that a director *consciously* disregarded an obligation to be reasonably informed about the business and its risks or *consciously* disregarded the duty to monitor and oversee the business.

The Delaware Supreme Court made clear in *Stone* that directors of Delaware corporations have certain responsibilities to implement and monitor a system of oversight; however, this obligation does not eviscerate the core protections of the business judgment rule — protections designed to allow corporate managers and directors to pursue risky transactions without the specter of being held personally liable if those decisions turn out poorly. Accordingly, the burden required for a plaintiff to rebut the presumption of the business judgment rule by showing gross negligence is a difficult one, and the burden to show bad faith is even higher. Additionally, as former-Chancellor Allen noted in *Caremark,* director liability based on the duty of oversight "is possibly the most difficult theory in corporation law upon which a plaintiff might hope to win a judgment." The presumption of the business judgment rule, the protection of an exculpatory § 102(b)(7) provision, and the difficulty of proving a *Caremark* claim together function to place an extremely high burden on a plaintiff to state a claim for personal director liability for a failure to see the extent of a company's business risk.

To the extent the Court allows shareholder plaintiffs to succeed on a theory that a director is liable for a failure to monitor business risk, the Court risks undermining the well settled policy of Delaware law by inviting Courts to perform a hindsight evaluation of the reasonableness or prudence of directors' business decisions. Risk has been defined as the chance that a return on an investment will be different tha[n] expected. The essence of the business judgment of managers and directors is deciding how the company will evaluate the trade-off between risk and return. Businesses — and particularly financial institutions — make returns by taking on risk; a company or investor that is willing to take on more risk can earn a higher return. Thus, in almost any business transaction, the parties go into the deal with the knowledge that, even if they have evaluated the situation correctly, the return could be different than they expected.

It is almost impossible for a court, in hindsight, to determine whether the directors of a company properly evaluated risk and thus made the "right" business decision. In any investment there is a chance that returns will turn out lower than expected, and generally a smaller chance that they will be far lower than expected.

When investments turn out poorly, it is possible that the decision-maker evaluated the deal correctly but got "unlucky" in that a huge loss — the probability of which was very small — actually happened. It is also possible that the decision-maker improperly evaluated the risk posed by an investment and that the company suffered large losses as a result.

Business decision-makers must operate in the real world, with imperfect information, limited resources, and an uncertain future. To impose liability on directors for making a "wrong" business decision would cripple their ability to earn returns for investors by taking business risks. Indeed, this kind of judicial second guessing is what the business judgment rule was designed to prevent, and even if a complaint is framed under a *Caremark* theory, this Court will not abandon such bedrock principles of Delaware fiduciary duty law. With these considerations and the difficult standard required to show director oversight liability in mind, I turn to an evaluation of the allegations in the Complaint.

a. The Complaint Does Not Properly Allege Demand Futility for Plaintiffs' Fiduciary Duty Claims

In this case, plaintiffs allege that the defendants are liable for failing to properly monitor the risk that Citigroup faced from subprime securities. While it may be possible for a plaintiff to meet the burden under some set of facts, plaintiffs in this case have failed to state a *Caremark* claim sufficient to excuse demand based on a theory that the directors did not fulfill their oversight obligations by failing to monitor the business risk of the company.

The allegations in the Complaint amount essentially to a claim that Citigroup suffered large losses and that there were certain warning signs that could or should have put defendants on notice of the business risks related to Citigroup's investments in subprime assets. Plaintiffs then conclude that because defendants failed to prevent the Company's losses associated with certain business risks, they must have consciously ignored these warning signs or knowingly failed to monitor the Company's risk in accordance with their fiduciary duties. Such conclusory allegations, however, are not sufficient to state a claim for failure of oversight that would give rise to a substantial likelihood of personal liability, which would require particularized factual allegations demonstrating bad faith by the director defendants.

Plaintiffs do not contest that Citigroup had procedures and controls in place that were designed to monitor risk. Plaintiffs admit that Citigroup established the ARM Committee and in 2004 amended the ARM Committee charter to include the fact that one of the purposes of the ARM Committee was to assist the board in fulfilling its oversight responsibility relating to policy standards and guidelines for risk assessment and risk management. The ARM Committee was also charged with, among other things, (1) discussing with management and independent auditors the annual audited financial statements, (2) reviewing with management an evaluation of Citigroup's internal control structure, and (3) discussing with management Citigroup's major credit, market, liquidity, and operational risk exposures and the steps taken by management to monitor and control such exposures, including Citigroup's risk assessment and risk management policies. According to plaintiffs' own allegations, the ARM Committee met eleven times in 2006 and twelve times in 2007.

Plaintiffs nevertheless argue that the director defendants breached their duty of oversight either because the oversight mechanisms were not adequate or because the director defendants did not make a good faith effort to comply with the established oversight procedures. To support this claim, the Complaint alleges numerous facts that plaintiffs argue should have put the director defendants on notice of the impending problems in the subprime mortgage market and Citigroup's exposure thereto. Plaintiffs summarized some of these "red flags" in their answering brief as follows:

- the steady decline of the housing market and the impact the collapsing bubble would have on mortgages and subprime backed securities since as early as 2005;
- December 2005 guidance from the FASB staff — "The FASB staff is aware of loan products whose contractual features may increase the exposure of the originator, holder, investor, guarantor, or servicer to risk of nonpayment or realization.";
- the drastic rise in foreclosure rates starting in 2006;
- several large subprime lenders reporting substantial losses and filing for bankruptcy starting in 2006;
- billions of dollars in losses reported by Citigroup's peers, such as Bear Stearns and Merrill Lynch.

Plaintiffs argue that demand is excused because a majority of the director defendants face a substantial likelihood of personal liability because they were charged with management of Citigroup's risk as members of the ARM Committee and as audit committee financial experts and failed to properly oversee and monitor such risk. As explained above, however, to establish director oversight liability plaintiffs would ultimately have to prove bad faith conduct by the director defendants. Plaintiffs fail to plead any particularized factual allegations that raise a reasonable doubt that the director defendants acted in good faith.

The warning signs alleged by plaintiffs are not evidence that the directors consciously disregarded their duties or otherwise acted in bad faith; at most they evidence that the directors made bad business decisions. The "red flags" in the Complaint amount to little more than portions of public documents that reflected the worsening conditions in the subprime mortgage market and in the economy generally. Plaintiffs fail to plead "particularized facts suggesting that the Board was presented with 'red flags' alerting it to potential misconduct" at the Company. That the director defendants knew of signs of a deterioration in the subprime mortgage market, or even signs suggesting that conditions could decline further, is not sufficient to show that the directors were or should have been aware of any wrongdoing at the Company or were consciously disregarding a duty somehow to prevent Citigroup from suffering losses. Nothing about plaintiffs' "red flags" supports plaintiffs' conclusory allegation that "defendants have not made a good faith attempt to assure that adequate and proper corporate information and reporting systems existed that would enable them to be fully informed regarding Citigroup's risk to the subprime mortgage market." Indeed, plaintiffs' allegations do not even specify how the board's oversight mechanisms were inadequate or how the director defendants knew of these inadequacies and consciously ignored them. Rather, plaintiffs seem to hope the Court will accept the conclusion that since the Company suffered large losses, and since a properly functioning risk management system would have avoided such losses, the directors must have breached their fiduciary duties in allowing such losses.

Moving from such general ipse dixit syllogisms to the more specific, plaintiffs argue that the director defendants, and especially those nine directors who were on the board at the time, "should have been especially sensitive to the red flags in the marketplace in light of the Company's prior involvement in the Enron Corporation debacle and other financial scandals earlier in the decade." Plaintiffs also allege that the director defendants should have been especially alert to the dangers of transactions involving SIVs because SIVs were involved in Citigroup's transactions with Enron that resulted in liability for the Company. Plaintiffs allege that Citigroup helped finance transactions that allowed Enron to hide its true financial condition and resulted in Citigroup paying approximately $120 million in penalties and disgorgement as well as agreeing to new risk management procedures designed to prevent similar conduct.

Plaintiffs fail in their attempt to impose some sort of higher standard of liability on the director defendants that were on Citigroup's board at the time of its involvement with Enron. . . .

. . .

The Complaint and plaintiffs' answering brief repeatedly make the conclusory allegation that the defendants have breached their duty of oversight, but nowhere do plaintiffs adequately explain what the director defendants actually did or failed to do that would constitute such a violation. Even while admitting that Citigroup had a risk monitoring system in place, plaintiffs seem to conclude that, because the director defendants (and the ARM Committee members in particular) were charged with monitoring Citigroup's risk, then they must be found liable because Citigroup experienced losses as a result of exposure to the subprime mortgage market. The only factual support plaintiffs provide for this conclusion are "red flags" that actually amount to nothing more than signs of continuing deterioration in the subprime mortgage market. These types of conclusory allegations are exactly the kinds of allegations that do not state a claim for relief under *Caremark*.

To recognize such claims under a theory of director oversight liability would undermine the long established protections of the business judgment rule. It is well established that the mere fact that a company takes on business risk and suffers losses — even catastrophic losses — does not evidence misconduct, and without more, is not a basis for personal director liability. That there were signs in the market that reflected worsening conditions and suggested that conditions may deteriorate even further is not an invitation for this Court to disregard the presumptions of the business judgment rule and conclude that the directors are liable because they did not properly evaluate business risk. What plaintiffs are asking the Court to conclude from the presence of these "red flags" is that the directors failed to see the extent of Citigroup's business risk and therefore made a "wrong" business decision by allowing Citigroup to be exposed to the subprime mortgage market.

This Court's recent decision in *American International Group, Inc. Consolidated Derivative Litigation* demonstrates the stark contrast between the allegations here and allegations that are sufficient to survive a motion to dismiss. In *AIG,* the Court faced a motion to dismiss a complaint that included "well-pled allegations of pervasive, diverse, and substantial financial fraud involving managers at the highest levels of AIG." In concluding that the complaint stated a claim for relief under Rule 12(b)(6), the Court held that the factual allegations in the complaint were sufficient to support an inference that AIG executives running those divisions knew of and approved much of the wrongdoing. The Court reasoned that huge fraudulent schemes were unlikely to be perpetrated without the knowledge of the executive in charge of that division of the company. Unlike the allegations in this case, the defendants in *AIG* allegedly failed to exercise reasonable oversight over pervasive *fraudulent* and *criminal* conduct. Indeed, the Court in *AIG* even stated that the complaint there supported the assertion that top AIG officials were leading a "criminal organization" and that "[t]he diversity, pervasiveness, and materiality of the alleged financial wrongdoing at AIG is extraordinary."

Contrast the *AIG* claims with the claims in this case. Here, plaintiffs argue that the Complaint supports the reasonable conclusion that the director defendants acted in bad faith by failing to see the warning signs of a deterioration in the subprime mortgage market and failing to cause Citigroup to change its investment policy to limit its exposure to the subprime market. Director oversight duties are designed to ensure reasonable reporting and information systems exist that would allow directors to know about and prevent wrongdoing that could cause losses for the Company. There are significant differences between failing to oversee employee fraudulent or criminal conduct and failing to recognize the extent of a Company's business risk. . . .

. . .

2. *Plaintiffs' Disclosure Allegations*

Plaintiffs argue that demand is excused as futile because the director defendants face a substantial likelihood of personal liability for violating their duty of disclosure and would therefore be unable to exercise independent and disinterested business judgment in responding to a demand. Plaintiffs allege that the director defendants violated their duty of disclosure by, among other things, failing to properly disclose the value of certain financial instruments, placing underperforming assets in SIVs without fully disclosing the risk that Citigroup might have to bring the assets back onto its balance sheet, and failing to properly account for guarantees, specifically the liquidity puts that allowed buyers of CDOs to sell the products back to Citigroup at face value. Plaintiffs argue that the "red flags" alleged in the Complaint lead to a reasonable inference that the director defendants, and particularly the ARM Committee members, knew that certain disclosures regarding the Company's exposure to subprime assets were misleading.

"[E]ven in the absence of a request for shareholder action, shareholders are entitled to honest communication from directors, given with complete candor and in good faith." When there is no request for shareholder action, a shareholder plaintiff can demonstrate a breach of fiduciary duty by showing that the directors "*deliberately* misinform[ed] shareholders about the business of the corporation, either directly or by a public statement." Citigroup's certificate of incorporation exculpates the director defendants from personal liability for violations of fiduciary duty except for, among other things, breaches of the duty of loyalty and acts or omissions not in good faith or that involve intentional misconduct or knowing violation of law. Thus, to show a substantial likelihood of liability that would excuse demand, plaintiffs must plead particularized factual allegations that "support the inference that the disclosure violation was made in bad faith, knowingly or intentionally." Additionally, directors of Delaware corporations are fully protected in relying in good faith on the reports of officers and experts.

The factual allegations in the Complaint are not sufficient to allow me to reasonably conclude that the director defendants face a substantial likelihood of liability that would prevent them from impartially considering a demand. This is so for at least three reasons. First, plaintiffs fail to allege with sufficient specificity the actual misstatements or omissions that constituted a violation of the board's duty of disclosure. The Complaint merely alleges, in general and conclusory terms, that the director defendants did not adequately disclose certain risks faced by the Company — for example, the risks posed by Citigroup's SIVs and the liquidity puts that allowed purchasers of CDOs to sell the instruments back to Citigroup at face value. The Complaint does not identify any actual disclosure that was misleading or any statement that was made misleading as a result of an omission of a material fact. Instead, plaintiffs allege, for instance, that the Citigroup board "abdicated its fiduciary duties by not disclosing information on the fair value of VIEs, CDOs and SIVs" and that "the ARM Committee abdicated its fiduciary duties . . . to ensure the integrity of Citigroup's financial statements and financial reporting process, including earnings press releases and financial information provided to analysts and rating agencies."

In other words, the disclosure allegations in the complaint do not meet the stringent standard of factual particularity required under Rule 23.1. They fail to allege with particularity which disclosures were misleading, when the Company was obligated to make disclosures, what specifically the Company was obligated to disclose, and how the Company failed to do so. This information is critical because to establish a threat of director liability based on a disclosure violation, plaintiffs must plead facts that show that the violation was made knowingly or in bad faith, a showing that requires allegations regarding what the directors knew and when. Without knowing when and how the alleged disclosure violations occurred, it is impossible to determine if the directors made the misstatements or omissions knowingly or in bad faith. As a result, the disclosure allegations in the complaint do not meet the stringent requirements of factual particularity under Rule 23.1.

Second, the Complaint does not contain specific factual allegations that reasonably suggest sufficient board involvement in the preparation of the disclosures that would allow me to reasonably conclude that the director defendants face a substantial likelihood of personal liability. Plaintiffs do not allege facts suggesting that the director defendants prepared the financial statements or that they were directly responsible for the misstatements or omissions. The Complaint merely alleges that Citigroup's financial statements contained false statements and material omissions and that the director defendants reviewed the financial statements pursuant to their responsibilities under the ARM Committee charter. Thus, I am unable to reasonably conclude that the director defendants face a substantial likelihood of liability.

Third, and perhaps most importantly, the Complaint does not sufficiently allege that the director defendants had knowledge that any disclosures or omissions were false or misleading or that the director defendants acted in bad faith in not adequately informing themselves. Plaintiffs have not alleged particular facts showing that the director defendants were even aware of any misstatements or omissions. Instead, plaintiffs conclusorily assert that the members of the ARM Committee, as financial experts, knew the relevant accounting standards, knew or should have known the extent of the Company's exposure to the subprime mortgage market, and are therefore responsible for alleged false statements or omissions in Citigroup's financial statements. Instead of providing factual allegations regarding the knowledge or bad faith of the individual director defendants, the Complaint makes broad group allegations about the director defendants or the members of the ARM Committee. A determination of whether the alleged misleading statements or omissions were made with knowledge or in bad faith requires an analysis of the state of mind of the individual director defendants, and plaintiffs have not made specific factual allegations that would allow for such an inquiry. Plaintiffs' alleged "red flags," which amount to nothing more than indications of worsening economic conditions, do not support a reasonable inference that the director defendants approved or disseminated the financial disclosures knowingly or in bad faith. Merely alleging that there were signs of problems in the subprime mortgage market is not sufficient to show that the director defendants knew that Citigroup's disclosures were false or misleading. The allegations are not sufficiently specific to Citigroup or to the director defendants to meet the strict pleading requirements of Rule 23.1.

. . .

C. Demand Futility Allegations Regarding Plaintiffs' Waste Claims

Count III of the Complaint alleges that certain of the defendants are liable for waste for (1) approving the Letter Agreement dated November 4, 2007 between Citigroup and defendant Prince; (2) allowing the Company to purchase over $2.7 billion in subprime loans from Accredited Home Lenders at one of its "fire sales" in March 2007 and from Ameriquest Home Mortgage in September 2007; (3) approving the buyback of over $645 million worth of the Company's shares at artificially inflated prices pursuant to a repurchase program in early 2007; and (4) allowing the Company to invest in SIVs that were unable to pay off maturing debt.

Demand futility is analyzed under *Aronson* when plaintiffs have challenged board action or approval of a transaction. With regard to the claims based on the approval of the Letter Agreement and the repurchase of Citigroup stock, plaintiffs do not argue that a majority of the director defendants were not disinterested and independent. Rather, plaintiffs argue that demand is excused under the second prong of the *Aronson* analysis, which requires that the plaintiffs plead particularized factual allegations that raise a reasonable doubt a[s] to whether "the challenged transaction was otherwise the product of a valid exercise of business judgment."

Delaware law provides stringent requirements for a plaintiff to state a claim for corporate waste, and to excuse demand on grounds of waste the Complaint must allege particularized facts that lead to a reasonable inference that the director defendants authorized "an exchange that is so one sided that no business person of ordinary, sound judgment could conclude that the corporation has received adequate consideration." The test to show corporate waste is difficult for any plaintiff to meet; indeed, "[t]o prevail on a waste claim . . . the plaintiff must overcome the general presumption of good faith by showing that the board's decision was so egregious or irrational that it could not have been based on a valid assessment of the corporation's best interests."

1. *Approval of the Stock Repurchase Program*

Plaintiffs' claim for waste for the board's approval of the stock repurchase program falls far short of satisfying the standard for demand futility. Plaintiffs allege that "in spite of its prior buybacks below $50 per share and in spite of the Company's expanding losses and declining stock price, Citigroup repurchased 12.1 million shares during the first quarter of 2007 at an average price of $53.37." Plaintiffs then claim that at the time the buyback of Citigroup stock was halted, the stock was trading at $46 per share. Plaintiffs conclude that the director defendants "authorized and did not suspend the Company's share repurchase program, which resulted in the Company's buying back over $645 million worth of the Company's shares at artificially inflated prices."

Specifically, plaintiffs argue the following:

> As set forth in the Complaint, the Director Defendants recklessly failed to consider and account for the subprime lending crisis, the Company's exposure to falling CDO values by virtue of its liquidity puts, and the collective impact on the Company's billions in warehoused subprime loans. Consequently, the Director Defendants are not entitled to the presumption of business judgment and are liable for waste for approving the buyback of over $645 million worth of the Company's shares at artificially inflated prices pursuant to the repurchase program. Under the circumstances, the repurchase program should have been suspended, and would have saved the Company hundreds of millions of dollars. The magnitude of the Director Defendants' utter failure to properly inform themselves of the Company's dire straits has only been highlighted by the Company's recent historically low share prices.

To say the least, this argument demonstrates that the Complaint utterly fails to state a claim for waste for the board's approval of the stock repurchase. Plaintiffs seem to completely ignore the standard governing corporate waste under Delaware law — a standard that requires that plaintiffs plead facts overcoming the presumption of good faith by showing "an exchange that is so one sided that no business person of ordinary, sound judgment could conclude that the corporation has received adequate consideration." Plaintiffs attempted to meet this standard by alleging that the director defendants approved a repurchase of Citigroup stock *at the market price*. Other than a conclusory allegation, plaintiffs have alleged nothing that would explain how buying stock at the market price — the price at which presumably ordinary and rational businesspeople were trading the stock — could possibly be so one sided that no reasonable and ordinary business person would consider it adequate consideration. Again, plaintiffs merely allege "red flags" and then conclude that the board is liable for waste because Citigroup repurchased its stock before the stock dropped in price as a result of Citigroup's losses from exposure to the subprime market. In short, the Complaint states no particularized facts that would lead to any inference that the board's approval of the stock repurchase constituted corporate waste. Accordingly, plaintiffs have not adequately alleged demand futility as to this claim pursuant to Rule 23.1.

. . .

IV. CONCLUSION

Citigroup has suffered staggering losses, in part, as a result of the recent problems in the United States economy, particularly those in the subprime mortgage market. It is understandable that investors, and others, want to find someone to hold responsible for these losses, and it is often difficult to distinguish between a desire to blame *someone* and a desire to force those responsible to account for their wrongdoing. Our law, fortunately, provides guidance for precisely these situations in the form of doctrines governing the duties owed by officers and directors of Delaware corporations. This law has been refined over hundreds of years, which no doubt included many crises, and we must not let our desire to blame someone for our losses make us lose sight of the purpose of our law. Ultimately, the discretion granted directors and managers allows them to maximize shareholder value in the long term by taking risks without the debilitating fear that they will be held personally liable if the company experiences losses. This doctrine also means, however, that when the company suffers losses, shareholders may not be able to hold the directors personally liable.

For the foregoing reasons, the motion to dismiss or stay in favor of the New York Action is denied. Defendants' motion to dismiss is denied as to the claim in Count III of the Complaint for waste for approval of the November 4, 2007 Prince letter agreement. All other claims in the complaint are dismissed for failure to adequately plead demand futility pursuant to Court of Chancery Rule 23.1.

An Order has been entered consistent with this Opinion.

ORDER

For the reasons set forth in this Court's Opinion entered in this case on this date, it is

ORDERED:

1. The motion to dismiss or stay in favor of the New York Action is denied;

2. Counts I, II, and IV of the Consolidated Second Amended Derivative Complaint are hereby dismissed pursuant to Court of Chancery Rule 23.1; and

3. Defendants' motion to dismiss is denied as to the claim in Count III of the Complaint for waste for the board's approval of the November 4, 2007 letter agreement between Citigroup, Inc. and defendant Charles Prince. All other claims in Count III of the Complaint are hereby dismissed pursuant to Court of Chancery Rule 23.1.

Post-Case Follow-Up

A number of the cases that we study in this chapter arose from the recent financial crisis. As these cases continue to wend their way through the system, we are seeing new litigation trends, such as the focus on illegal (versus risky) conduct in the context of *Caremark* claims.

In a recent twist, some shareholders have brought derivative actions alleging that directors breached their fiduciary duties by failing to implement adequate information security policies, allowing data breaches and theft of customer information, and causing the corporation's stock to decrease in value. For example, in the wake of Target Corporation's data breach in late 2013, shareholder-plaintiffs filed derivative suits against the company's directors and officers, alleging breach of fiduciary duty and waste of corporate assets. The complaints in these actions generally allege that the failure to prevent the breach and (in some cases) the failure promptly to notify affected consumers damaged the company and caused it to be sued by numerous consumers and to suffer other reputational and financial losses.

In the current environment, lawyers are well advised to highlight the issue of cyber security risks for their corporate clients. Among other issues, lawyers and clients might want to consider the following issues and questions respecting cyber security risk:

- Who should examine cyber security risks? The entire board? A committee?
- Does the board need to hire experts to consult on cyber security issues?
- Does the company have a threat or disaster response plan for cyber security events?
- What cyber security training does the company give its employees?
- What "cyber due diligence" does the company perform with respect to its third-party service providers, such as independent contractors and vendors?
- Has the company performed an analysis of its systems and procedures to assess vulnerability to cyber attacks?

F. *ZAPATA* AND SPECIAL LITIGATION COMMITTEES

Rule 23.1 and demand futility litigation do not tell the whole story of derivative action practice. Even if a court finds that demand would be futile, such that it therefore is excused, the corporation and the board have one more opportunity to take control of the potential lawsuit. This last "bite at the apple" derives from the practice of appointing a special litigation committee, or SLC. An SLC is a board committee comprising directors who are independent and disinterested with respect to the subject of the derivative lawsuit. (If necessary, the company may add directors who meet the independence and disinterestedness criteria to compose the SLC.) Once the SLC is appointed, the board will then empower the SLC to investigate the plaintiff's allegations and to make a recommendation as to whether the corporation should institute litigation. If the SLC recommends that the corporation pursue the lawsuit, it generally will take control of the litigation, with the result that the stockholder-plaintiff will no longer be driving the bus. If the SLC concludes that litigation is not in the best interest of the company, it will move to dismiss the plaintiff's claim on behalf of the company, once again leaving the plaintiff-shareholder on the sidelines.

Notably, however, the decision by an SLC to seek dismissal generally is not afforded the protections of the business judgment rule. Instead, the SLC and its recommendations (including the recommendation of filing a motion to dismiss) are subject to scrutiny. In Delaware, courts apply a two-step test set forth in *Zapata Corp. v. Maldonado*, 430 A.2d 779 (Del. 1980). Under the *Zapata* test, the court first inquires into the independence and good faith of the committee, the diligence of its investigation, and the support for its conclusion respecting whether to pursue the litigation sought by the plaintiff. The court may allow limited discovery for this inquiry. Instead of applying business judgment rule presumptions to this inquiry, however, the corporation (not the challenging shareholder) bears the burden of proving the SLC's independence, good faith, and the reasonableness of its investigation. If the court is satisfied as to these issues, the court may, in its discretion, proceed to the next step. Under the second step of the *Zapata* test, the court is charged with determining whether the SLC's motion to dismiss the litigation should be granted. Once again, business judgment rule presumptions do not rule the day. Instead, in making a determination as to whether an SLC-initiated motion to dismiss should be granted, the court may apply its own independent business judgment. According to *Zapata*, the second step is intended to thwart instances where the corporation's actions meet the criteria of step one, but the result does not appear to satisfy its spirit, or is used in situations where the court concludes that granting the motion to dismiss would prematurely terminate inquiry into the stockholder's grievance.

G. MODERN PRACTICE: INSURANCE, STATUTORY LIMITATIONS, AND INDEMNIFICATION

Fearing litigation, many prospective directors and officers refuse to serve unless the corporation procures **director and officer liability insurance** (or "D&O" insurance) to insure against claims made against directors and officers. In most instances, such insurance provides for attorneys' fees and costs incurred in defending directors and officers against claims made for breaches of duty. Moreover, most policies will pay the amount of a judgment rendered against the director or officer if the director or officer acted in good faith. Willful, reckless, fraudulent, or illegal acts are rarely insured. The cost of D&O insurance is very high, and for some matters, such as patent infringement protection, it is nearly prohibitively expensive.

Due to rising insurance costs and the increased litigation against directors and officers, many states have enacted statutes allowing corporations to limit the exposure of directors. The California and Delaware statutes are typical of many. As discussed above in the context of Delaware's § 102(b)(7), these statutes state that the certificate of incorporation may include a provision eliminating or limiting the personal monetary liability of a director to the corporation or to its shareholders (but not to third parties) for certain claims. The limitation is not available for breach of the director's duty of loyalty, for unlawful distribution of dividends, for acts or omissions not in good faith or that involve intentional misconduct or a knowing violation of the law, for any transaction from which the director derived an improper benefit, or, in California, for acts or omissions that constitute an unexcused pattern of inattention that amounts to abdication of the director's duty to the corporation or its shareholders. Cal. Corp. Code § 204(10); Del. Code Ann. tit. 8, § 102(b)(7). Other states have adopted different approaches, such as imposing a ceiling for damages against directors.

In addition, corporations also may agree to **indemnify** or reimburse directors or officers from liability and expenses incurred in defending a lawsuit brought against them. Generally, corporations will indemnify corporate management only if the directors and officers acted in good faith and in a manner reasonably believed to be in the corporation's best interests. MBCA § 8.52 provides that a corporation must indemnify reasonable expenses incurred by a director who was successful in defending an action brought against her due to alleged acts or omissions as a director. On the other hand, MBCA § 8.51(d) prohibits a corporation from indemnifying a director if she is adjudged liable to the corporation in a derivative action that results in a judgment against the director or in a proceeding in which a director is adjudged liable for receiving an improper financial benefit. *See also* DGCL § 145.

H. CORPORATE SCANDALS AND GOVERNANCE REFORMS

1. Introduction

On October 16, 2001, Enron announced the disappearance of approximately $1 billion of net worth from its balance sheet. The Enron scandal was the first of many at the start of this century that staggered financial markets. Following Enron, WorldCom admitted to improper accounting procedures that caused its stock to plunge nearly 100 percent, and Tyco International also acknowledged questionable accounting methods, causing its stock to drop approximately 60 percent. Coupled with the shattering of reputations of the accounting firm Arthur Andersen, the charges against wealthy investor and media mogul Martha Stewart, the parading of corporate wrongdoers in handcuffs, and the bursting of the investment bubble in the stock market in 2001 (which triggered an economic recession), investor confidence in corporate America and the financial markets was severely shaken.

2. Some Suspected Causes of the Scandals

What caused the boom and the bust and these corporate scandals of the early 2000s? A variety of theories have been advanced, including the following:

- *Excessive compensation.* In the late 1990s, cash salaries and bonuses significantly decreased for senior executives at major companies. The total value of pay packages increased, however, with most compensation coming in the form of stock options. To ensure that the options remained valuable, companies inflated earnings so that the stock price would remain high. Because a plunge in stock price would cause the options to become worthless, companies disguised their losses and focused more on short-term growth than long-term corporate stability.

■ *Expensing of stock options.* Under generally accepted accounting principles, stock options (unlike salaries and bonuses) were not counted as corporate expenses. Thus, a company might issue as many options as it desired and would not have to deduct any money from the earnings reported to shareholders. Once again, this led to granting of mega-options to senior executives. In 2005, a new accounting rule by the Financial Accounting Standards Board took effect, requiring that stock options be counted as an expense against earnings. Some number of companies limited or stopped issuing stock options as a consequence of these reforms.

■ *Board conflicts of interest.* Members of boards of directors lacked independence due to familial and business relationships with corporate wrongdoers.

■ *Lack of accounting oversight.* Auditors such as Arthur Andersen not only provided accounting services to corporations but also provided significant consulting services. These auditing firms were thus less likely to challenge a company's financial practices for fear they would lose lucrative consulting contracts. These conflicts of interest thus caused many auditors to look the other way in the face of questionable accounting practices.

■ *Euphoria and hype.* As the obsession with the stock market grew in the 1990s, business and financial reporters and stock analysts became cheerleaders for questionable stocks. Analysts, in particular, were encouraged to "hype" a stock and rate it as a "buy" to please prospective banking clients. Individual investors then bought stock based on these hyped recommendations, which the analysts often acknowledged as phony.

■ *Greed.* In a money culture in which Jeffrey Skilling, Enron's CEO, told his employees, "All that matters is money," the stage was set for the collapse of the bubble. Kenneth Lay of Enron exercised stock options worth more than $200 million shortly before Enron's collapse. In many other companies as well, stock prices were maintained by accounting devices just long enough to allow senior managers to cash in hundreds of millions of dollars of stock options. Investors must also take some responsibility, as they were also caught up in the cycle of greed, demanding steady earnings. So long as the market kept rising, the investors were also content to look the other way. As one expert stated, a confluence of all of these factors worked together to create the "perfect storm" of fraud, corruption, boom, and bust.

3. The Fallout

The total cost to investors and the economy of the events of the early 2000s is not fully known. What is known is that thousands of employees lost their jobs, thousands of workers who owned shares in their companies in retirement plans lost their savings, numerous executives went to prison, Enron and WorldCom agreed to settlements of $7.2 and $6.2 million, respectively, and investor confidence in the economy was severely shaken. One report estimated that U.S. citizens lost more than $200 billion in savings, jobs, and retirement funds. As to the fallout to corporations and their executives:

- Arthur Andersen has collapsed.
- L. Dennis Kozlowski of Tyco was found guilty of fraud, larceny, and conspiracy and served eight years in prison.
- WorldCom founder Bernard J. Ebbers was sentenced to 25 years in prison for fraud and conspiracy.
- In May 2006, former Enron executives Kenneth Lay and Jeffrey Skilling were found guilty of multiple counts of conspiracy and fraud. Skilling is serving a 14-year sentence. Lay died shortly after his trial, and his convictions were later vacated. In all, 16 Enron executives pleaded guilty to crimes.
- In June 2003, Sam Waksal of ImClone Systems was fined more than $4 million and then served five years for insider trading.
- Martha Stewart, lifestyle maven and close friend of Sam Waksal, was found guilty of obstructing justice and lying to investigators. She served five months in prison and was released in early 2005. She rejoined the board of directors of Martha Stewart Living Omnimedia, Inc. in September 2011, after the expiration of the SEC's five-year ban on her serving as a director of a public company.
- Conseco, Inc., WorldCom, Global Crossing, Enron, Tyco, Rite Aid, and Adelphia all filed petitions under the U.S. Bankruptcy Act.

4. Reform and the Sarbanes-Oxley Act

In response to these events and developments, a number of proposals relating to corporate governance were implemented and advanced. The Sarbanes-Oxley Act of 2002 (15 U.S.C. §§ 7201 et seq.) (SOX), containing a number of important reforms, was signed into law in mid-2002. This section summarizes some of the more important SOX provisions relating to corporate governance. We discuss some of these provisions in more detail in Chapter 13.

- *Oversight board.* SOX created the Public Company Accounting Oversight Board, a nonprofit corporation rather than a government agency, to establish auditing, quality control, and ethics standards, and to conduct investigations and take disciplinary actions against accountants. The creation of PCAOB ended 100 years of self-regulation and established independent oversight of public company auditors.
- *Auditor independence.* SOX limits the scope of consulting services that accounting firms can provide to their public company audit clients. This provision prevents auditors from controlling the entire financial reporting system at a company.
- *Conflicts of interest.* SOX requires company insiders to notify the SEC of company stock transactions promptly, prohibits stock transfers by management

during certain periods, and forbids personal loans by companies to certain senior managers. SOX also deals with conflicts of interest by analysts by forbidding investment banking staff from supervising the research of analysts.

■ *Audit committees.* SOX provides for strong audit committees, all of whose members must be independent from company management.

■ *Certification and accountability.* To improve corporate accountability, CEOs and CFOs must certify that company financial statements fairly present their companies' financial condition. Issuers must also publish information in their annual reports assessing the effectiveness of their internal financial reporting control structure and procedures. Smaller public companies (those with market values of less than $75 million) and "emerging growth companies" (those whose total gross annual revenues are less than $1 billion) need not have an independent auditor attest to the effectiveness of a company's internal controls over financial reporting.

■ *Expanded SEC review.* SOX requires the SEC to review public filings of publicly traded companies at least once every three years.

■ *Broader sanctions.* SOX imposes tough jail sentences for securities fraud and extends the statute of limitations for securities fraud, allows the SEC to bar directors and officers from serving on public company boards if they are found to be "unfit" for service in a public company, and provides that debts of individuals that arise from civil and criminal penalties imposed as a result of securities fraud violations may not be discharged in bankruptcy.

In the wake of Enron and SOX, a number of companies and entities have voluntarily imposed even more far-reaching reforms, including the following:

■ Although SOX requires the SEC to review filings of publicly traded companies at least once every three years, the SEC has committed to more frequent monitoring.

■ Partly to comply with new SOX requirements, in mid-2002, the New York Stock Exchange and NASDAQ adopted stricter standards for companies listed on their exchanges, including a requirement that boards of directors consist of a majority of independent directors; that independent directors oversee director nominations, corporate governance, and compensation; an expansion of duties and responsibilities for audit committees; and a requirement that the companies adopt a code of conduct.

■ Many publicly traded companies have exceeded the NYSE and NASDAQ reforms. For example, a recent survey by the Business Roundtable (an association of CEOs of leading corporations) reported that nine out of ten companies have boards that are at least 80 percent independent, although the exchange requirements call only for a majority of independent directors.

Although there is still great public enthusiasm about the reforms engendered by SOX, criticism remains. Many companies incur extremely high audit fees and increased turnover among their financial executives. Some critics (including President Obama's Jobs Council) have argued that parts of the law require executives to spend too much time on reporting requirements rather than on leading their companies.

At the same time, some commentators believe that the SOX reforms did not go far enough. At the end of the day, commentators generally agree that SOX has enhanced transparency of the audit process and increased investor confidence, but at a cost. As corporations remain in the public eye, expect continued debate over SOX-related reforms.

5. The 2007-2008 Financial Crisis

SOX is not, of course, the end of the story. Even as SOX-driven reforms were still being implemented, public confidence in the financial markets was further shaken in 2008 with the collapse of the Bear Stearns Companies, insurance giant American International Group, Inc. (AIG), Lehman Brothers, and Washington Mutual Bank; the placing of Fannie Mae and Freddie Mac under federal conservatorship; and the government bailout plan or rescue of troubled financial institutions in the amount of $700 billion, which was approved in October 2008.

Experts have cited numerous causes for these failures, including lack of government oversight, reckless speculation, greed, and the housing and credit crises. In particular, experts have focused on the fact that during the housing boom of the early 2000s, lenders relaxed standards for homebuyers and made subprime loans to these buyers. These risky loans were then packaged into pools, purchased by Wall Street, and then securitized and sold to buyers. When the housing market slowed and their interest rates moved upward, homeowners were unable to make their mortgage payments and defaulted on their loans. Lenders and banks then became the "owners" of real estate worth less than what was owed for it. As losses mounted, loans became more difficult to obtain, causing a credit crunch. Without loans, spending slows, causing a further slowdown in the economy.

In 2011, the U.S. Senate, issuing its 635-page report on its inquiry into the financial crisis, concluded that "the crisis was not a natural disaster, but the result of high risk, complex financial products; undisclosed conflicts of interest; and the failure of regulators, the credit rating agencies, and the market itself to rein in the excesses of Wall Street." In response to the financial crisis, Congress and the executive branch took a number of actions, including the following: establishing the Troubled Asset Relief Program (TARP), which authorized the expenditure of up to $700 billion to stop financial institutions from collapsing and further damaging the U.S. economy; creating various programs by the Federal Reserve to provide assistance to U.S. and

What Is Securitization?

Securitization is the process of transforming an illiquid asset into a security. For example, assume a lender originates loans, such as loans to homeowner. The lender may then sell or assign certain assets associated with the loan, such as repayment of principal, to a special purpose vehicle or SPV. The SPV then issues debt, dividing up the benefits (and risks) among investors on a pro-rata basis. In this way, a group of consumer loans can be transformed into a publicly-issued debt security. A security is tradable, and it is therefore more liquid than the underlying loan or receivables. Securitization of assets has the potential of lower risk, added liquidity, and improved economic efficiency. That said, there are costs and risks associated with securitization as well, including risks arising from default or impairment of the underlying loan obligations.

foreign financial institutions to promote liquidity and prevent financial collapse; and passing of the Dodd-Frank Act, discussed below.

Some of the provisions in the American Recovery and Reinvestment Act of 2009 (the Obama administration's "stimulus bill") included the following measures, aimed at promoting the long-term health of American companies: pay caps on senior officers of companies that received massive government assistance; provisions allowing the government to review bonuses and compensation paid to senior executives at companies that received federal bailout money to determine whether such payments should be clawed back; and provisions allowing shareholders whose companies received federal bailout money to provide advisory votes on executive compensation, namely, "say on pay" votes.

6. The Dodd-Frank Act

The Dodd-Frank Wall Street Reform and Consumer Protection Act ("Dodd-Frank Act"), signed into law in July 2010 in the wake of the 2007-2008 crash and the resulting recession, represents the most significant overhaul of financial regulation in generations. Although its 500 sections and nearly 850 pages primarily affect the financial services industries, Dodd-Frank does affect corporate compensation and governance for large, publicly traded companies in several significant ways (although as of the writing of this text, not all of the Dodd-Frank rules have been implemented by the SEC). Some examples of governance-related reforms are listed below:

- *Independent compensation committees.* Companies that list their stock on national exchanges must require that compensation committees include only independent directors. Advisors to such committees must also be independent.
- *Say on pay and frequency votes.* Companies must provide shareholders with non-binding votes on executive compensation at least once every three years. Companies are also required to hold an advisory "frequency" vote at least once every six years in order to allow shareholders to decide how often they would like to be presented with the say on pay vote (every year, every other year, or once every three years).
- *Golden parachute disclosures.* Companies soliciting votes to approve merger or acquisition transactions must provide disclosure of certain golden parachute compensation arrangements and, in certain circumstances, conduct a separate shareholder advisory vote to approve the golden parachute compensation arrangements.
- *Disclosure format for compensation.* Larger publicly traded companies must disclose the substance of executive compensation packages and must provide charts that compare their executive compensation with the financial performance of the company and disclose the ratio of CEO pay to the median pay of the company's employees.
- *Clawbacks.* Public companies must adopt policies to recover or "claw back" executive compensation if it is based on erroneous financial information.

7. Governance Guidelines

Perhaps in response to increased shareholder activism and lawsuits, the past several years have witnessed a trend in the adoption by public companies of formal written guidelines dealing with corporate governance. General Motors Company was an early mover, adopting guidelines in 1994, and most large companies are following. In many instances, the guidelines are drafted by institutional investors who have issued statements, called **governance guidelines**, on how they want their investees to operate. Both TIAA-CREF and the California Public Employees' Retirement System have issued such statements to the corporations in which they invest heavily. Although the investors cannot force the corporations to implement the guidelines, the guidelines have spurred many companies to enact guidelines of their own.

Some guidelines suggested by institutional investors call for the following:

- clear definitions of director relationships to determine when directors are independent rather than subject to a conflict of interest involving other companies or family members;
- boards that are composed of a majority of independent directors;
- diversity in boards of directors;
- periodic reviews by corporations of their processes and structures to provide a "checkup" as to how well the corporation is operating;
- establishment of standards for director attendance at meetings so that failure to attend a certain percentage of meetings will render a director ineligible for further renomination to the board;
- performance reviews of individual board members and of the boards themselves;
- linking of executive compensation to company performance;
- mandatory retirement age for directors; and
- mandatory stock ownership by directors to ensure directors' interests are closely aligned with those of shareholders (with some guidelines setting actual targets, for example, requiring directors to own stock worth five times their annual compensation).

Microsoft Corp. has adopted a number of these guidelines in its formal Corporate Governance Guidelines, including a requirement that a substantial majority of its board be independent; that outside directors should retire at age 75; that a review of the CEO's performance be conducted annually; and that audit committees consist entirely of independent directors.

8. Spotlight: Hot Topics and Trends in Governance

With shareholders becoming increasingly activist, there are a number of additional reforms and trends in corporate governance practice, including the following:

- Shareholder proposals asking for additional disclosure on corporate political contributions and lobbying activities;

- Shareholder proposals calling for a chair who is independent and separate from the company's CEO;
- Shareholder proposals relating to climate change and other social and environmental issues;
    - For example, in 2014, nearly 60 percent of shareholder proposals related to climate change and other sustainability risks. Other proposals relate to shareholder requests that companies disclose their animal testing policies and their policies on human rights abuses in the locations where their companies operate.
- Stock ownership guidelines for top managers, often requiring the director or executive officer to hold stock valued at a certain percentage of his base salary;
- Shareholder proposals and recommendations that directors be elected by majority rather than plurality vote;
- Shareholder proposals that would make it easier for shareholders to oust directors;
    - For example, in 2006, Lockheed Martin Corp. adopted a rule allowing shareholders to remove a member of its board by majority vote; previously, the corporation had required an 80 percent vote by shareholders to remove a director.
- A move away from using a staggered or classified board of directors toward electing all directors at the same time, often called "declassification";
    - Shareholders have successfully argued that electing directors annually rather than every two or three years makes board members more responsive to them and more accountable for missteps. In 2002, more than 70 percent of public companies staggered their boards; by the end of 2013, only 11 percent had a staggered or classified board.
- New disclosure rules that require executives to explain their compensation in more detail;
    - Publicly traded companies must now provide more information in their proxy statements about the value of options and stock granted to their top five executives as well as a total compensation figure that includes all forms of cash and noncash pay (which would allow shareholders to compare pay from one company to another).
- Shareholder activism has accelerated with the use of the Internet, which allows shareholders to communicate with each other. Activists have created blogs, used Twitter, and even launched campaigns on YouTube to promote their agendas.

I. RIGHTS AND DUTIES OF OFFICERS

Finally, although we have focused principally on directors in this chapter, it is worth noting that corporate officers owe fiduciary duties to the corporation and its shareholders, as well. We have included a brief section examining the rights and responsibilities of officers here. (We address the fiduciary duties of controlling shareholders in the next chapter.)

1. Authority of Officers

Because the authority given officers comes from the board of directors, officers are agents of the corporation. Thus, the general agency principles discussed in Chapter 2 apply to them. As agents, officers may have authority to bind the corporation. This authority can be **actual authority** (meaning express or implied actual authority or direction given to the officer by the corporation's governing documents or the board), **apparent authority** (authority derived from the corporation's representations to third parties), or **inherent authority** (authority that flows naturally from an officer's position so he can carry out his duties). Review our discussion in Chapter 2 of agency law principles, as necessary, when considering whether an officer acted with authority, thereby binding the corporation.

2. Officers' Standard of Conduct, Liability, and Indemnification

Officers usually are subject to the same duties of care and loyalty imposed on directors. Like directors, they are protected by the business judgment rule and, therefore, liability is usually founded on acts (or omissions) of gross negligence or other acts and omissions not in good faith. Thus, as with directors, courts generally will not second-guess officers' decisions so long as there was some reasonable basis for the decision. Also, as with directors, officers are entitled to rely on advice and reports given by others, so long as that reliance is reasonable.

The standard of conduct required of directors and of officers under the MBCA is highly similar. Officers are required to discharge their duties in good faith, with the care that a person would exercise under similar circumstances, and in a manner reasonably believed to be in the best interest of the corporation. So long as directors and officers perform their duties in compliance with these requirements, they will not be liable for any action taken by them as a director or an officer. MBCA §§ 8.30 and 8.42. The various provisions relating to indemnification of directors for liability and litigation costs and expenses apply equally to officers. Similarly, the corporation may purchase and maintain insurance on behalf of any officer or other agent to insure against liability asserted against or incurred by the officer or other agent. Note well, however, that exculpation provisions may not apply to officers, so be sure to check relevant state law.

Chapter Summary

- Corporate governance involves three groups of people: shareholders (the owners of the corporation), directors (the managers of the corporation), and officers (appointees of the directors).
- Under centralized management, directors have the authority to manage and oversee corporate affairs.

■ Directors owe fiduciary duties of care and loyalty to the corporation and its shareholders.

■ Directors will usually be protected from liability under the business judgment rule, so long as the directors acted loyally, in good faith, and with due care.

■ Shareholders may initiate action against the corporation or its officers and directors. Direct actions allege direct harm to a shareholder, while derivative actions allege the corporation has sustained harm and has failed to enforce its own cause of action.

■ Derivative actions are subject to a number of substantive and procedural rules, including standing requirements and Rule 23.1 demand requirements.

■ Officers are subject to the same fiduciary duties as directors and may rely on the business judgment rule.

Applying the Concepts

1. Ryan Inc. ("Ryan") has been planning to buy a pharmaceutical company, Pharm Inc. ("Pharm"), which is developing a new drug to treat arthritis. Various scientists, doctors, and experts evaluated Pharm's reports, lab work, and progress on the drug during the due defence process. After Ryan purchased Pharm (for a significant amount of money), however, the FDA delayed approval of the drug, and another company has begun marketing a similar drug, making the purchase of Pharm either unnecessary or problematic. Some disgruntled shareholders would like to sue the directors for their decision in buying Pharm. Discuss whether the directors might have liability for their decision.

2. Using the facts in Question 1, would your answer be different if the directors' decision to purchase Pharm was made after merely reviewing Pharm's website?

3. Abel, Bobbi, and Carmen are the sole directors and shareholders of Feet, Inc., a Delaware corporation that owns and operates retail shoe stores across the country.

   In addition to being a director of the company, Abel also is a licensed real estate broker and sole director and shareholder of Abel's Realty Ltd. In June, the directors of Feet, Inc. (with Abel participating) voted to enter into a contract with Abel's Realty Ltd. pursuant to which Abel was to identify possible locations for a new Feet, Inc. retail store. Prior to the vote, Abel disclosed to Bobbi and Carmen that he was the sole shareholder and director of Abel's Realty. The vote was two to one, with Carmen voting against the contract. The written contract provided that if Abel's Realty Ltd. located a suitable store for Feet, Inc. to purchase, Abel's Realty Ltd. would receive a customary commission of 6 percent of the sales price when the transaction closed.

   Abel soon found a suitable store at a favorable price, and in October, Feet, Inc. contracted to purchase the store. Unfortunately, just before the deal was to close, Carmen passed away. Unhappy for a variety of reasons, Carmen's heirs challenged the Feet-Abel's Realty Ltd. contract. Carmen's heirs also sued Abel for breach of fiduciary duty.

a. Is the Feet-Abel Realty Ltd. contract void? Voidable?
b. Is Abel liable for breach of fiduciary duty?

4. Acme Corp. is a New York corporation that has adopted default rules set forth in the NYBCL with respect to issues of corporate governance. Acme's board consists of nine directors. Last month, Acme conducted its regularly scheduled quarterly board meeting, the meeting having been properly noticed pursuant to the company's bylaws. Four of Acme's board members attended the meeting; the remaining board members (all of whom live in Boston) were unable to attend or participate electronically in the meeting due to severe weather conditions. At the meeting, after extensive and well-informed deliberations, the directors voted unanimously in favor of entering into a contract with Walmart involving Walmart's business in Mexico. This was the biggest contract of this sort in Acme's history. None of Acme's directors engaged in self-dealing, or otherwise acted disloyally, in connection with the decision.

a. Sally, a director, has learned of this contract and is dismayed. She is concerned about an alleged bribery scandal involving Walmart's Mexican operations, which has been reported extensively in the papers in recent months, and she fears that Acme could become enmeshed in Walmart's legal troubles. If Sally challenges the board's unanimous decision, what is the likely outcome? If a shareholder sues the directors for going forward with the contract under the circumstances alleged, what is the likely outcome?
b. Assume for purposes of this question only that the board was unable to meet in person due to the snow storm. Further assume that seven of Acme's nine directors approved the contract via written consent after receiving a copy of the proposed contract via e-mail. If Sarah, a stockholder, sues for breach of fiduciary duty, is she likely to prevail? Why or why not?
c. Would your answer to either 4.a or 4.b be the same (or different) if Acme's charter contained an exculpation clause under DGCL § 102(b)(7)?

5. Alpha, Beta, and Chi are software developers, and officers and directors of Database Solutions, Inc. ("Database"), a New York corporation that is in the business of creating database tools. Adco, Inc. is a start-up business that is developing software that uses complex algorithms to track how users interact with websites.

Two months ago, Adco's CEO approached Database about creating a set of database tools for Adco. Adco's CEO explained that while Adco did not have the cash on hand to pay for the work, he had firm commitments from leading venture capital firms to invest millions of dollars in the business as soon as Adco's new software package was ready for commercial release. Consequently, Adco's CEO asked whether Database would do the work — which was complicated and likely to cost upwards of $100,000 — on credit, with a promise to pay in full (plus interest) once Adco's next round of funding closed. Adco's CEO represented that the closing was scheduled to take place two months later.

Knowing that Adco was a "hot" start-up that had attracted a lot of attention from the venture capital community, Alpha, Beta, and Chi unanimously agreed to take on the work provided they could get comfortable with Adco's financial position. Recognizing that it was a risk to perform such a large project entirely on credit, Alpha, Beta, and Chi decided that it was a good idea to investigate Adco's financial condition and to run a credit check before signing the development contract with Adco. When Alpha, Beta, and Chi explained this to Adco's CEO, he said no problem, but told Database's directors the sooner the background check was completed, the better, so that Adco could get its product to market (and close on new financing) as quickly as possible. He also mentioned that several other database firms in town were jockeying for Adco's business.

Because Alpha has a background in banking, accounting, and finance, Alpha, Beta, and Chi agreed that Alpha would handle the background check. (Alpha had performed similar tasks in the past for Database without incident.) Anxious to get started, Alpha falsely told Beta and Chi that he had obtained and reviewed Adco's financial statements and credit reports, and that based on his review, he believed Database should proceed with the work. In fact, Alpha had not reviewed Adco's financial information. He had spoken with a few friends in the high-tech industry, who repeated what Adco's CEO had said—that is, that Adco was a hot start-up that had attracted funding and a lot of attention from the venture capital community. Had Alpha investigated, he would have learned that Adco was running on fumes, with very little cash, and that Adco's relationship with its financial backers was strained.

Having heard from Alpha that everything checked out, Beta and Chi agreed to proceed without further inquiry. They signed a development agreement with Adco on behalf of Database, and Database spent many hours creating a database tool for Adco. Two months after beginning the project, Database's work was done. Alpha, Beta, and Chi immediately called Adco to let the CEO know the database tools were ready, and to arrange for their delivery and receipt of payment. After stalling for several days, Adco's CEO finally admitted that the company no longer had access to venture capital funding, and that Adco therefore would be unable to pay. Shocked, Alpha, Beta, and Chi learned that Adco had failed to pay a number of vendors in town recently and that the company had lost its venture capital funding and was struggling financially because the CEO had used investor funds for personal expenses.

a. A Database shareholder has sued Alpha for breach of fiduciary duty. Is Alpha likely to be held liable for breach of fiduciary duty in connection with the Adco project?

b. Which of the following answers best describes the liability risk (if any) that Beta and Chi face as a result of their role in the Adco project?
   i. Because Beta and Chi were independent and disinterested with respect to the decision to take on the Adco business, they cannot be held liable for Database's losses on the Adco contract.
   ii. Beta and Chi were independent, disinterested, and entitled to rely (and did reasonably rely) on Alpha's representations regarding his investigation

into Adco's financial condition; thus, they will not be held liable for Database's losses on the Adco contract.

iii. Beta and Chi may be held liable for breaching the duty of care because they were negligent in relying upon Alpha's representations regarding the credit check.

iv. Beta and Chi may be held liable for failing to act in good faith because they caused Database to compete with other firms for Adco's business without confirming that the work would be profitable for Database.

Business Organizations in Practice

You represent American Group, Inc. ("American") (a publicly held Delaware corporation), which owns and operates a global set of businesses involving health care, finance and information, and environmental technologies. American's capital structure is as follows: Parent Corp. ("Parent") owns 60 percent of American's issued and outstanding common stock. Parent is a privately held Delaware corporation that is wholly owned by Owen Owner ("Owner"). The remaining 40 percent of American's stock is owned by various shareholders, including Pat Plaintiff.

For the past several years, American's health care division has been expanding rapidly, due largely to sales of American's new, high-tech diagnostic imaging and scanning devices. At the last board meeting, one of American's directors suggested that the company purchase a factory from Parent for $30 million (the "Factory Transaction") to accelerate the production of scanners.

American's board consists of six directors: (i) Owen Owner, who serves as chair of the board; (ii) Paula President ("President"), who serves as American's president, for which she receives an annual salary of $500,000 plus benefits and bonuses; (iii) Anna Attorney ("Attorney"), a lawyer who regularly represents American; (iv) Priya Professor ("Professor"), a university professor who teaches at the local law and business schools; (v) Elba Economist ("Economist"), an economist with a Ph.D. in finance; and (vi) Dan Doctor ("Doctor"), a medical doctor and experienced health care industry executive. Professor, Economist, and Doctor have no obvious financial connection to Owner, Parent, or American, other than serving on American's board for nominal director fees, though they knew Owner (and each other) socially before they joined American's board through work on charitable boards and the alumni network of their undergraduate institution. American's corporate charter contains a provision stating that members of its board of directors are exculpated from liability to American and its stockholders to the maximum extent permitted by applicable corporate law.

a. American's board has asked you to prepare a memo outlining steps the company should take when considering the Factory Transaction. What points and suggestions would you make in such a memo?

b. American's board has asked you to prepare a memo outlining liability risk, if any, that board members might face in connection with the proposed

Factory Transaction. Can you advise board members on this issue under applicable ethical rules?

c. Can you advise the company as to the risk of derivative litigation should the board vote in favor of the Factory Transaction?

Assume the transaction closes, and further assume that through DCGL § 220, Pat Plaintiff obtains corporate books and records substantiating all of the facts listed above, including those regarding the capital structure of American and Owner, the composition of American's board, and facts (1)-(8) concerning the Factory Transaction:

1. The Factory Transaction was approved by American's entire board, not a special committee consisting solely of independent directors.

2. The terms of the Factory Transaction were negotiated by President on behalf of American and by Owner on behalf of Parent.

3. Prior to approval, American's board had obtained an appraisal estimating the value of the factory at $25-$30 million.

4. The appraisal was performed by Banker & Co., an investment bank that has performed work for Parent and Owner. (In fact, Banker has received over $20 million in fees from Parent and Owner in the past five years.)

5. General market conditions appear to contradict an appraised value of even $25 million for the factory, and to suggest a value of approximately $20 million.

6. American's board was aware of the relationship between Parent, Owner, and Banker when it hired Banker to conduct the appraisal, and it believed that Banker's knowledge and experience would help it perform an accurate and cost-effective appraisal;

7. Parent's initial offer to sell the factory was for $30 million, and American's board made a counteroffer of $25 million that was rejected by Parent. American's board then approved the $30 million offer.

8. The American board did not consider any alternative sites or factories to purchase.

Based on these facts, Pat Plaintiff instructs his lawyer to file a complaint for breach of fiduciary duty on behalf of American in the Delaware Court of Chancery against Owner and all of the directors of American.

a. Should Pat's lawyer make a demand on the board or should the lawyer allege facts showing that demand ought to be excused as futile? Why?

b. Assume Pat's lawyer alleges demand futility. Should the court dismiss the claim? Or, should the court allow it to proceed? Why?

Unfortunately for American, the Factory Transaction is not its only problem. Days after Pat files his complaint, the Securities and Exchange Commission, the Department of Justice and several state Attorneys General file suit against American based on American's alleged involvement in a scheme to manipulate the LIBOR. The conduct at issue occurred at American's banking division ("American Bank").

The LIBOR (a/k/a the London Interbank Offered Rate) is one of several benchmarks that banking institutions use to set the interest rates for lending between banks. Each morning a panel of large banks reports the interest rates they would pay to borrow from other banks. After removing the highest and lowest figures, the reported interest rates are averaged. The LIBOR benchmarks are used as the reference rate for a wide variety of financial instruments, including forward rate agreements, short-term interest futures contracts, interest rate swaps and inflation swaps, floating rate notes, syndicated loans, and variable rate mortgages, among many others.

Although press reports sometimes refer to the LIBOR as though it were a single figure, the LIBOR actually consists of a series of benchmarks, representing interest rates for 15 different maturities in 10 different currencies. (The currencies are the Australian dollar, the Canadian dollar, the Swiss franc, the Danish kroner, the euro, the British pound, the Japanese yen, the New Zealand dollar, the Swedish krona, and the U.S. dollar.) Different banks participate in the reporting panels for the different currencies and the lineup of panel participants has changed over time. Three U.S. banks currently participate on LIBOR panels, including American Bank (American's banking subsidiary, which is part of the company's financial division). The rates reported by LIBOR panel participants are publicly available and widely scrutinized as evidence of reporting banks' financial condition.

As early as August 2007, regulators and academics began to raise questions about the reliability of the LIBOR. The concerns surfaced in very public fashion during the spring of 2008, when the *Wall Street Journal* published two articles raising questions about the integrity of LIBOR panel members' reporting. The first article, which was published on April 16, 2008 and entitled "Bankers Cast Doubt on Key Rate Amid Crisis," reported concerns that LIBOR was "sending false signals" and potentially was "becoming unreliable" because "some banks [allegedly] don't want to report high rates they're paying for short term loans because they don't want to tip off the market that they're desperate for cash."

On May 29, 2008, the *Wall Street Journal* published a second article, entitled "Study Casts Doubt on Key Rate," which reported that "banks have been reporting significantly lower borrowing costs for the London interbank offered rate, or Libor, than what another market measure suggests they should be." The *Journal* compared the panel banks reported borrowing rates to the costs of insuring the banks against default, two measures that historically moved in synch with one another. The *Journal* determined that the two rates had diverged materially during the crisis in ways that suggested that some banks might be "low balling their borrowing rates to avoid looking desperate for cash." The participating banks were reporting similar borrowing rates even when the default insurance market was suggesting widely diverging market perceptions about the various banks' financial health.

These developments and growing concerns about the LIBOR led to regulatory investigations in a variety of different countries, including the United States. According to the lawsuits eventually filed by the Securities and Exchange Commission, the Department of Justice and various State Attorneys General against American Bank, personnel in American Bank's LIBOR department knowingly caused American Bank to report artificially low borrowing rates, thereby misrepresenting American Bank's financial condition. The lawsuits alleged that employees in American Bank's LIBOR group were encouraged to report low rates by the firm's compensation program, which rewarded employees for identifying cost savings and business generation protocols. (Reporting lower LIBOR rates allowed American to borrow money at lower rates, resulting in significant cost savings, especially during the height of the recent economic crisis. The lower rates also suggested to the market that American Bank was on sounder financial footing than it actually was, allowing American Bank to "win" certain deals.) The various lawsuits did not allege that American's board members knew of wrongdoing, or even that they had access to "red flags" regarding American Bank's involvement in the alleged LIBOR scandal.

Based on the facts set forth above, Pat's lawyer amends the complaint to allege that American's board members breached their fiduciary duties to American by failing to ensure that American had an effective system of internal controls in place to prevent manipulation of the LIBOR. Although the amended complaint took the position that the American Bank's employees engaged in illegal acts, it also argued that even if the employees' conduct was not technically illegal, American's directors breached their fiduciary duties by approving a flawed compensation plan that encouraged false reporting and by failing to identify and monitor risks associated with American's participation on the LIBOR panel.

a. Should Pat make a demand on the board respecting the LIBOR claim, or should Pat allege demand futility?

b. If Pat alleges demand futility, what standard will the court use to assess futility?

c. Does Pat have a viable *Caremark* claim against the board? Why or why not?

Shareholder Rights and Protections and Close Corporations

Having examined default corporate governance structures, rules, and procedures in Chapters 8 and 9, we now turn our attention to certain stockholder rights and protections. Some stockholder rights and protections are immutable. For example, stockholders typically have an immutable right to inspect certain corporate documents. Other rights and protections are negotiated, and depend upon shareholders' relative bargaining power. For example, most jurisdictions set default quorum and voting requirements for board or shareholder action, but allow shareholders some flexibility to alter these rules via negotiation — for example, a minority shareholder with some bargaining power might wish to negotiate for super-majority or unanimous voting for certain corporate actions to avoid being "out-voted" by majority shareholders every time. Still other rights and protections play out differently in the context of close corporations (i.e., privately held companies with a limited number of shareholders). For example, shareholders in close corporations may owe fiduciary duties to the corporation and its other shareholders, whereas non-controlling shareholders in larger, publicly traded corporations generally do not. In this chapter, we review these and other immutable and negotiated shareholder rights and protections, with a particular focus on how these rights and protections play out in the context of close corporations.

Key Concepts

- Stockholder inspection rights
- Majority or controlling versus minority stockholders
- Characteristics and governance rules for close corporations
- Heightened fiduciary obligations for stockholders in close corporations
- Negotiated stockholder rights and protections

A. IMMUTABLE RIGHTS

Shareholder Informational and Inspection Rights

We begin our study of governance-related shareholder rights, obligations, and pro ders have the right to be informed of the affairs of the corporation. At common law shareholders enjoyed a right to inspect corporate books and records, including the list of shareholders, bylaws, minutes of meetings, and so forth, qualified by the requirement that the inspection be in good faith. Examples of bad faith or improper purposes were examination of the list of shareholders for personal business reasons (such as to solicit customers for the shareholder's own business), appropriation of trade secrets to sell to competitors, or pursuing a stockholder's individual political goals.

Today, most states have enacted statutes that specifically authorize the inspection of books and records by shareholders (or their agents or attorneys). Some of these statutes provide an absolute right to inspect records such as articles, bylaws, and minutes of shareholders' meetings. Inspection of other records (such as minutes of directors' meetings) must be for a "proper purpose." *See* MBCA § 16.02. Many of these statutes also provide that a shareholder may inspect corporate books and records so long as the inspection is for a purpose "reasonably related" to one's interest as a shareholder. Most states impose a waiting period on the shareholders. Some statutes provide that inspection may not be permitted unless the shareholder owns a specified number of shares (often 5 percent) or has owned shares for a specified period of time. These limitations ensure corporations are not overburdened with demands from shareholders who may own only a few shares. Generally, a proper purpose includes a desire to determine if the corporation is being managed properly or to communicate with other shareholders; an improper purpose would be one designed to harm the corporation or intended for the shareholder's personal benefit.

Although the corporation is usually free to require that the inspection be done upon prior notice and during reasonable business hours and that the shareholder pay the reasonable costs for copies of documents, the articles of incorporation cannot contravene the state statutes. If the corporation wrongfully refuses inspection, it can be subject to monetary penalties, and a court may grant a request by a shareholder for an injunction requiring inspection.

Case Preview

Quantum Technology Partners IV, L.P. v. Ploom, Inc.

Delaware's DGCL § 220 is one of the best known—and most frequently litigated—state shareholder informational and inspection statutes. In part, this is because Delaware courts routinely remind shareholder litigants to exercise § 220 inspection rights prior to instituting litigation. *Quantum Technology Partners* does a great job walking through the requirements of a Delaware § 220 action. In 2009,

Quantum (a limited partnership that invested in early-stage information technology and life sciences companies) invested in Ploom. The investment did not go as well as the parties had hoped, so beginning at least as early as 2012, Quantum sought to divest itself of (i.e., sell) its Ploom holdings and exit the investment. To facilitate such a transaction, Quantum requested information about Ploom's financial condition. When Ploom refused to share the requested information, Quantum filed a § 220 action. In addition to keeping track of the ins and outs of § 220, consider what this case says about the difficulties that can arise when a stockholder in a privately held corporation seeks to exit its investment. When reading this case, consider the following questions:

1. Why did Quantum want access to the information at issue?
2. What are the substantive and procedural requirements associated with exercising informational and inspection rights under § 220?
3. Are there differences in the standards that apply to shareholder requests for access to a corporation's ledger, or list of stockholders on one hand, and other corporate documents on the other?
4. What is a "proper purpose" for inspection under § 220?
5. Why is information relevant to valuation particularly important for a shareholder in a privately held company?
6. What is the proper scope of inspection under § 220? Are informational and inspection rights akin to discovery rights under state or federal discovery rules?

Quantum Technology Partners IV, L.P. v. Ploom, Inc.
C.A. No. 9054-ML, 2014 WL 2156622 (Del. Ch. May 28, 2014)

LeGrow, Master*

This books and records dispute highlights the difficulties that arise when a stockholder in a privately held corporation seeks to exit that investment and demands access to books and records that the stockholder intends to use both to value his stock and to allow prospective purchasers to evaluate an offer. Overlaid on this dispute, variations of which have played out many times in this Court, are additional complications associated with the competitive nature of the company's business and a complete breakdown in trust between the parties.

Although the company professes an interest in allowing the stockholder to divest his holdings, those representations ring hollow when considered in the context of the unreasonable positions taken by the company regarding both the scope of the inspection it would permit and the terms of a confidentiality order it would accept. A more tempered approach likely would have resulted in a settlement more palatable to the company than the inspection I recommend. Instead, the antagonism between

---

*Footnotes have been omitted for purposes of brevity.

parties required trial on, and resolution of, the validity of the plaintiff's purpose, the books and records the plaintiff is entitled to inspect, and the confidentiality terms attendant to the inspection.

For the reasons that follow, I conclude that the plaintiff is entitled to inspect the bulk of the books and records requested in the demand, subject to a confidentiality agreement containing the terms described in this report, and I recommend that the Court enter inspection and confidentiality orders consistent with this report. This is my final report in this matter.

I. BACKGROUND

The plaintiff, Quantum Technology Partners IV, L.P. ("Quantum") is a Delaware limited partnership that invests in early-stage information technology and life sciences companies and is a record holder of 1,433,658 shares of stock of the defendant, Ploom, Inc. ("Ploom" or the "Company"). Quantum operates as a venture capital firm structured as a "pledge fund" wherein the firm identifies and contracts to invest in projects before soliciting and securing financing from individual partners of the fund. Quantum's general partner is Quantum Technology Management Company IV, LLC ("Quantum LLC"), which is a Delaware limited liability company whose sole managing member is Barry Dickman. Quantum LLC and two of Quantum's limited partners have interests in Quantum's Ploom shares.

Ploom is a privately held Delaware corporation incorporated in 2007, which has as its primary line of business the development, design, manufacture, sale, and distribution of "alternative" tobacco products, including handheld tobacco vaporizers or smokeless tobacco delivery systems. Ploom is part of an emerging market for such products, which includes many of the world's largest tobacco product producing companies.

A. Quantum's Initial Investment in Ploom

Following informal discussions, Quantum and Ploom executed the Series A-3 Preferred Stock Purchase Agreement (the "Purchase Agreement"), dated June 22, 2009. In the Purchase Agreement, Ploom agreed to authorize the issuance and sale of 1,674,460 shares of convertible Series A-3 Preferred Stock ("Preferred Stock"), with 1,004,675 shares earmarked for purchase by Quantum in two closings. The Purchase Agreement required Quantum to close first on 390,707 shares of Preferred Stock for an aggregate price of $350,000.41 (the "First Closing"), followed by a second closing within a specified period of time for an additional 613,968 shares of Preferred Stock for $550,000.52. In addition, the Purchase Agreement provided that Quantum could purchase, without obligation, remaining additional shares that Ploom had not yet sold to another investor.

. . .

B. The Parties Execute the Amended Purchase Agreement

Quantum completed the First Closing, but was unable to secure sufficient funds from its partners to complete the second closing. On September 30, 2009, to facilitate further investment, the parties executed the Agreement Regarding Series A-3 Preferred Stock Purchase Agreement (the "Amended Purchase Agreement"). That agreement revised the portions of the Purchase Agreement that concerned all transactions other than the First Closing and required that, on October 1, 2009, "[Quantum] shall purchase . . . an additional 156,283 shares of [Preferred Stock], for an aggregate price of $140,000.35" (the "Second Closing") and, thereafter, required Quantum to close on Preferred Stock in two further tranches: (i) 223,261 shares for $200,000.11 (the "Third Closing"); and (ii) 178,609 shares for $160,000.27 (the "Fourth Closing"). If Quantum completed all these required closings, it could purchase up to 675,366 additional shares, or a lesser amount if fewer shares were available.

Quantum completed the Second and Third Closings under the Purchase Agreement, but was unable to secure sufficient financing from its partners to make the Fourth Closing. Ploom's trust in Quantum faltered.

. . .

C. Quantum's Efforts to Divest Itself of Its Ploom Holdings

Since at least January 2012, Dickman actively has sought potential buyers of Quantum LLC's interest in Quantum's Ploom stock, and, in so doing, he has made at least one express offer. In July 2013, Dickman offered to sell to a personal creditor, Rick Lazansky, all of Quantum LLC's interests in Quantum's holdings in Ploom, in consideration for Lazansky forgiving an outstanding promissory note held by Lazansky (the "Lazansky Offer"). In addition, the Lazansky Offer gave Lazansky the right to force Quantum LLC to repurchase the shares under certain circumstances. To date, Lazansky has not agreed to the terms offered by Dickman, at least in part because Lazansky is skeptical of the price offered by Dickman. Dickman has continued exploring sell terms with Lazansky even up to November 2013. In addition to making the Lazansky Offer, Dickman solicited buy leads from his industry contacts, including those connected to the tobacco industry generally. His contacts identified several potentially interested buyers, but all the parties required additional information regarding Ploom's financials before proceeding to negotiate terms.

In March and August of 2013, Quantum requested by letter access to certain of Ploom's financial information, which Quantum claimed to need to value its interest in the Company. Ploom agreed to provide some of the requested information in response to Quantum's March 2013 request, subject to Quantum's agreement that the information it received would be subject to Section 3.4 of the IRA, which — as described below — precluded Quantum from providing any of the information to a prospective purchaser. There is no evidence in the record that, in attempting to sell Quantum LLC's interest in the Ploom shares, Dickman improperly has divulged any of Ploom's confidential or proprietary information; indeed, Dickman has informed at least one potential buy lead that he will provide confidential information only after gaining approval from this Court.

D. The Demand; Ploom's Refusal

On October 21, 2013, Quantum delivered to Ploom a demand to inspect Ploom's books and records pursuant to 8 Del. C. § 220 (the "Demand"). Citing this Court's decision in *Schoon v. Troy Corp,* Quantum also attached to the Demand a proposed confidentiality agreement.

On October 27, Ploom, through Monsees, responded to the Demand, challenging the propriety of (1) Quantum's purpose, (2) the scope of documents it demanded to inspect, and (3) the proposed confidentiality agreement. As to Quantum's purpose, Ploom noted that, in prior demands, Quantum's stated purpose was to "ascertain the value of its shares" only, yet the most recent Demand states an additional purpose, *i.e.,* to "value [Quantum's] shares *for sale.*" In addition, Ploom suggested that the Demand was part of an "ongoing effort to make itself a nuisance so that perhaps Ploom or Ploom's investors will become frustrated and want to repurchase [Quantum's] shares." On these bases, Ploom alleged that Quantum's stated purpose was improper or illusory.

Regarding the scope of Quantum's demanded inspection, Ploom refused to produce all the documents except (1) "a list of all of [Ploom's] stockholders . . . with the names and addresses of the stockholders, but . . . [no] other information"; (2) Ploom's "last unaudited annual financial statements, those for 2012"; and (3) Ploom's "latest 409A valuation," on the basis that the Demand exceeded the bounds of Delaware law. In addition, Ploom asserted that the 2012 409A Valuation that it already had produced sufficiently reflected all the demanded financial information, and that, in any event, the Demand could not be used to circumvent Quantum's loss of its contractual information rights under Section 3 of the IRA, the scope of which probably would have been wider than under Section 220.

Finally, Ploom rejected outright Quantum's proposed confidentiality agreement, stating affirmatively that "Ploom will not permit the disclosure of its confidential information to third parties" because "shar[ing such] information with third parties and even 'Highly Confidential Information' with Ploom competitors . . . is absurd for a technology company, as Quantum is aware. . . ." On this issue, Ploom also noted that Quantum already is bound by the confidentiality terms contained in Section 3.4 of the IRA. In view of this letter, Quantum commenced this suit on October 31, 2013.

· · ·

B. Inspection Standard

Stockholders of Delaware corporations enjoy a qualified statutory right to inspect the corporation's stock ledger, a list of its stockholders, and its other books and records. Inspection rights first "were recognized at common law because, '[a]s a matter of self-protection, the stockholder was entitled to know how his agents were conducting the affairs of the corporation.'" This common law right was codified in 1967 in 8 Del. C. § 220, which imposes both procedural and substantive requirements on a stockholder proceeding under that Section.

To satisfy Section 220's procedural requirements, *i.e.,* its "form and manner" requirements, demand must be made in writing, under oath, and must state the stockholder's purpose for making it. In addition, a demand must be directed to the corporation at its registered office in Delaware or at its principal place of business, and, if demand is made through an agent or attorney, it must be "accompanied by a power of attorney or such other writing which authorizes the attorney or other agent to so act on behalf of the stockholder."

Where the corporation refuses to permit the demanded inspection, or fails to reply within five business days after demand has been made, the stockholder may petition this Court in a summary proceeding to compel such inspection. In all instances, it is incumbent on the petitioner to establish its ownership of stock in the target corporation and its compliance with the statute's form and manner requirements. Where the stockholder seeks to inspect the corporation's stock ledger or list of stockholders, Section 220 imposes on the corporation opposing such inspection the burden of establishing that the stockholder's purpose is improper. On the other hand, where the stockholder seeks to inspect books and records *other* than the corporation's stock ledger or list of stockholders, it is the stockholder who must establish the propriety of the stated purpose.

C. *The Proper Purpose Requirement*

A stockholder's purpose is "proper" if it is "reasonably related to such person's interest as a stockholder." In addition, the purpose must not be adverse to the company, nor may the information be requested "out of sheer curiosity, unrelated to any legitimate interest of the stockholder, or where the sole purpose of the inspection is to harass the corporation." Stockholders may have multiple purposes for demanding inspection of a corporation's books and records, and the Court may inquire into the *bona fides* of the stockholder's primary purpose. Once the Court determines that the stockholder's primary purpose is proper, however, the existence or propriety of any secondary purposes is irrelevant, except that, as discussed herein, any such secondary purposes may be relevant in determining the scope of the inspection.

It is settled law that the valuation of one's shares is a valid purpose to inspect books and records. Because minority stockholders of privately held corporations "do not receive the mandated, periodic disclosures associated with a publicly held corporation, [those stockholders] face certain unique risks." Minority stockholders in private corporations may "have a legitimate need to inspect the corporation's books and records to value their investment, in order to decide whether to buy additional shares, sell their shares, or take some other action to protect their investment." In addition, where the alleged purpose is to explore a possible sale of stock, Section 220(c) does not require the stockholder to have taken concrete steps to sell the stockholder's shares before relying on that purpose as a basis for seeking inspection.

Even if a stockholder states a proper purpose, he is entitled to inspect only those records that are "essential and sufficient" to achieve his purpose. A document is "essential" under Section 220 if "it addresses the crux of the shareholder's purpose," and the "information the document contains is unavailable from another source." Put another way, stockholders seeking to inspect books and records must specifically and discretely identify, with "rifled precision," the documents sought. This inquiry necessarily depends on the context of each case.

In defining the scope of an inspection, the Court may consider whether the corporation previously furnished information to stockholders, and any ulterior motives of the stockholder demanding inspection. Thus, the stockholder generally cannot compel inspection to the extent the information already has been received.

D. Quantum Has Stated a Proper Purpose

Quantum has demanded to inspect certain of Ploom's books and records to: "(1) determine the value of its Ploom shares, (2) solicit buyers of its Ploom shares, and (3) evaluate offers to purchase its Ploom shares."

Quantum must be in a position to value its Ploom shares before Quantum can solicit buyers and evaluate purchase offers. Although Quantum previously sought and received limited financial information in order to value its shares, Dickman credibly testified at trial that the information is both stale and incomplete. In addition, the information Ploom previously provided Quantum is subject to strict confidentiality terms that prohibit Quantum from sharing the information with potential purchasers. For those reasons, the information Quantum previously received does not alter my analysis of either the propriety of Quantum's purpose or the scope of the inspection that should be permitted.

In addition, although he has not received any concrete offers, the record amply demonstrates that Dickman actually has pursued potential buyers of Quantum LLC's interests in Quantum's Ploom stock. One of Quantum's contacts, in fact, has indicated its intent to negotiate sale terms in the near future. Ploom asserts, however, that Quantum instituted this action to harass the Company into repurchasing Quantum's shares. I find this position unpersuasive, in part, because of the record evidence demonstrating Dickman's intent to sell Quantum LLC's interests to a third party. In addition, throughout trial, Dickman testified credibly and in detail why each of the categories of the demanded information — which Ploom has refused to produce — is essential to the valuation of Quantum's holdings in Ploom. This is in sharp contrast to the facts in *Neely v. Oklahoma Publishing Co.,* where the stockholder plaintiff sought a thorough examination of "*any and all company records and minutes*" to "ascertain that price which would be in her best interest to ask of a prospective buyer," even after she already had received considerable documentation.

E. The Scope of Quantum's Inspection

Because the Demand states a proper purpose, Quantum is entitled to inspect the books and records that are essential and sufficient to its purpose. In all, Quantum has demanded to inspect nine categories of documents. I address each of the categories *seriatim*.

As an initial matter, however, I find unpersuasive Ploom's contention that it should not be compelled to make available for inspection certain sensitive and proprietary information, ostensibly because Ploom does not trust that Quantum will protect Ploom's confidentiality, or because Ploom does not wish to concede ground in potential repurchase negotiations with Quantum. The record demonstrates, and Ploom has failed to refute, that Quantum has abided by its past agreement to maintain the confidentiality of Ploom's sensitive information. Ploom has not cited any case in support of the proposition that this Court should curtail a stockholder's statutory right to inspect books and records that, although necessary and essential to the valuation of its shares, would diminish the company's ability to preserve its higher ground in arm's length negotiations to repurchase shares from the petitioning stockholder. Without more, whether Ploom intrinsically trusts Quantum is irrelevant. Moreover, to the extent that certain information, if divulged to third parties, would be detrimental to Ploom, those concerns are addressed by entry of a proper confidentiality order.

1. The Stockholder List

The first category of Quantum's demand seeks "[a] complete record or list of the record holders of Ploom's common stock, certified by Ploom or its transfer agent, showing the name, address, and number of shares registered in the name of each such holder as of the date hereof." Ploom has agreed to provide Quantum with a complete list of Ploom's stockholders as of the date of the Demand. For the reasons explained below, the information Ploom provides in response to this category should be current as of, or close to, the date of inspection, not the date of the Demand.

2. Ploom's Annual Financial Statements

Quantum next demands to inspect "Ploom's audited annual financial statements for each of the last three fiscal years and, to the extent that audited financial statements are not available, Ploom's unaudited annual financial statements for each of the last three fiscal years." Ploom has agreed to provide Quantum with unaudited annual financial statements for 2010 and 2011 and its audited annual financial statement for 2012 when it becomes available. As explained in Section II.E.9., I find that Quantum also is entitled to inspect Ploom's audited annual financial statement for 2013, or, to the extent an audited financial statement is not available, the 2013 unaudited annual financial statement.

3. Ploom's Periodic Financial Statements

Category 3 of the Demand seeks "Ploom's periodic financial statements for all periods [following] the last financial statement produced in response to [Category] 2." Ploom has agreed to provide Quantum with the Company's quarterly financial statement for the quarter ending September 30, 2013, to be in the same form as its annual financial statements. This agreement, however, has been rendered stale by the passage of time. Because Ploom almost certainly has prepared its 2013 financial statement, which I have concluded it should produce, the only quarterly statement at issue at this point is the first quarter of 2014.

Ploom's agreement to provide quarterly financial statements post-dating its last annual statement extends, with the passage of time, to the first quarter of 2014, and even if Ploom's stipulation cannot fairly be read in that way, Quantum has established that quarterly statements for the periods after the last annual statement are essential to its stated purpose. Specifically, Dickman has explained—and Ploom has not refuted—that Ploom's finances and business fluctuate unpredictably. I disagree, however, with Dickman's assertion that Quantum requires monthly financial statements for the purpose of remaining "current" even after the latest quarterly financial statement has been made available. Although monthly financial statements may be desirable or helpful, Quantum has not demonstrated that monthly financial statements are essential to its valuation of Ploom. In addition, Quantum has not shown that Ploom formally produces such reports in the ordinary course of business.

4. Tax Returns

In category 4 of the Demand, Quantum seeks "Ploom's federal and state income tax returns for each of the last three fiscal years." Quantum contends that Ploom's tax returns are essential to valuing the Company because the returns likely will contain certain key information not available in Ploom's financial statements, such as: (1) statements of royalty income; (2) information relating to Ploom's international activities undertaken with JTI; and (3) Ploom's net operating losses. In addition, because Ploom has not yet completed an audit, Dickman explained that Ploom's tax returns are the "next best thing as far as a proxy for the signature [of an officer]," which is important to potential buyers. Although the availability of audited financial statements for 2012 (and, presumably, 2013) addresses the latter issue, Quantum has shown that the absence of certain key information from the financial statements makes the tax returns necessary to valuation and sale of the stock.

5. Valuations

Quantum next seeks to inspect "[a]ll valuations of Ploom, its stock, or its assets created, developed, or disseminated from January 1, 2011, through the date [of the Demand]." Ploom maintains that it "should not be required to incur the burden of producing [these] documents so [Quantum] can [validate] its own valuation," although Ploom has agreed to provide Quantum with the Company's next 409A valuation, when available. As noted, Quantum possesses Ploom's 2012 409A Valuation. Quantum, however, contends that, although some of the information contained in the report is useful, its overall design is governed by its purpose — to establish a strike price for Ploom's option grants — which renders the valuation within it not comparable to the value placed on the stock in an arms-length transaction. In addition, I credit Dickman's testimony that the 2012 409A Valuation that Ploom already has produced is out-of-date and that Quantum requires more current information to establish a present value for sale.

In short, I find that Quantum sufficiently has demonstrated that documents associated with this category, including, but not limited to, the next available 409A valuation, are essential to achieving its primary purpose. I also find, however, that Quantum's request for *all* valuations "created, developed, or disseminated," is too broadly framed. For example, taken literally, Quantum has demanded valuations that were created but never finalized, or that might pertain to particular assets that are not essential to Quantum's purpose of valuing its stock in Ploom. This Court may, in view of its authority to "protect the corporation's legitimate interests and to prevent possible abuse of the shareholder's right of inspection," prescribe any limitations or conditions with reference to the inspection. I therefore find that Quantum is entitled to inspect only those valuations that Ploom created or developed *and* that actually were disseminated by or to Ploom's officers or directors, even if only internally, for the purpose of assessing Ploom's value or the value of its assets.

6. Forecasts and Projections

The sixth category of the Demand seeks "All financial forecasts or projections for Ploom created, developed, or disseminated from January 1, 2011, through the date [of the Demand]." In support of its request for information in this category, Quantum contends that the management projections, *e.g.*, anticipated growth rates, sales, earnings, and margins comprising these documents are, perhaps, "the biggest indicator [of] the value of the stock for a small company." The relative value of this information is heightened in the context of early stage development companies. For its part, Ploom argues that the information sought in this request would be redundant of the information in the 2012 409A Valuation and Ploom's 2012 year-end unaudited financial statement, and in any event, Quantum can look to historical information or publicly available market analyst reports to assess Ploom's relative position in the larger e-cigarette and tobacco markets.

Quantum is entitled to the information sought in this category. The importance of forecasts and projections to valuation of a company is so basic that it does not require citation. Quantum also has shown that other forecasts or projections, apart from those in a 409A valuation, are essential to valuing and selling the stock. The purpose of a 409A valuation raises questions about its reliability as a source for valuing stock in an arms-length sale. In addition, Ploom has not demonstrated that the information contained in the 2012 409A Valuation sufficiently reflects all the types of information that are essential for Quantum to value its shares in Ploom as a going concern. Nor has Ploom demonstrated how historical information or publicly available market analyses are an analogue to actual management forecasts.

I recommend to the Court, however, that Quantum's inspection of documents in this category be limited in the same manner as recommended in category 5, particularly in view of the category 6's equally broad language. That is, Quantum should be entitled to inspect those forecasts and projections that Ploom created or developed *and* that actually were disseminated by or to Ploom's officers or directors, even if only internally, for the purpose of addressing management's outlook on Ploom's business.

7. Transactions Involving Ploom's Stock

Category 7 of the Demand seeks "[a]ll materials relating or referring to any transaction involving Ploom's stock, whether or not Ploom was a party to such transaction, from January 1, 2011, through the date [of the Demand]," while category 8 seeks "[a]ll materials relating, referring, or constituting any offer or proposal to buy or sell Ploom's stock, whether or not such proposals were directed to Ploom, from January 1, 2011, through the date [of the Demand]." Quantum seeks the information requested in categories 7 and 8 because "the price at which an asset changes hands is highly probative of its value." In support of its position, Quantum cites this Court's decision in *Gotham Partners, L.P. v. HallwoodRealty Partners, L.P.*, where the Court noted that "[i]n the real world, market prices matter and are usually considered the best evidence of value." For its part, Ploom maintains that Quantum seeks documents in these categories merely to serve as a helpful crosscheck to Quantum's internal valuations. Ploom therefore maintains this information is not *essential* to Quantum's stated purpose.

Quantum has established that the information demanded in these categories is essential to achieving its primary purpose, particularly given the rather narrow market for Ploom's stock, the Company's relatively short existence, and the fact it only recently has begun marketing products. I therefore recommend that the Court compel the inspection, but I agree with Ploom that these requests are overly broad. I recommend that, in both categories 7 and 8, the Court replace the language "relating, referring, or constituting" with "sufficient to reflect the terms of."

8. The JTI Documents

The final request in the Demand is by far the most contentious, and calls for "[a]ll materials relating, referring, or constituting contracts or agreements between Ploom and [JTI], and each of their respective subsidiaries and affiliates." Quantum contends this information is critical to valuing Quantum's shares in Ploom because the nature and terms of Ploom's contractual relationship with JTI — one of Japan's largest tobacco companies — could determine an investor's outlook on Ploom's value. For example, Dickman explained that, if JTI has a contractual right to acquire Ploom, or if JTI contractually were slated to stop paying royalties to Ploom, the terms of Ploom's agreements with JTI could affect an investor's perceived value of Ploom and its business. On the other hand, for at least three reasons, Ploom urges this Court not to compel it to make this information available for Quantum's inspection. First, Ploom contends that the nature and value of its relationship with JTI sufficiently is reflected in Ploom's historical and projected financial information. Second, Ploom reasons inspection should not be ordered in view of Ploom's contractual obligation to JTI not to divulge it. Finally, Ploom argues that disclosure of the terms of the JTI agreements, whether inadvertently or by a mischievous third party, would be disastrous for Ploom.

I find Ploom's position more persuasive. In *Neely v. Oklahoma Publishing Co.*, this Court was presented with a similarly probing stockholder request, and observed:

> If the standard is limited to that which is sufficient and essential, then obviously it stops short of including all books and records of a corporation . . . or, stated another way, it stops short of all books and records which the petitioning stockholder, in his or her personal opinion, deems to be essential. The one thing that the opposing experts [who testified in this case] agreed upon is that there is no such thing as a precise market value of stock in a company whose stock is not publicly traded. Even so, to attempt to reach the ultimate of near-precision, it can be assumed that one can never get enough information unless he is given access to everything. When this is measured against plaintiff's position that she would like to sell if the right deal comes along even though she has nothing definite in mind now, her demand becomes one to be advised of all internal affairs of the corporation and to be kept current on a monthly basis hereafter just in case. To honor the extent of her demand under these circumstances would virtually transform her into an ex officio member of the board of directors simply because she has decided to rid herself of her stock.

Here, although Quantum credibly has articulated that confirmation of certain aspects of Ploom's contractual relationship with JTI would be helpful, it has not demonstrated that such information is essential. For example, Dickman expressed a desire for information concerning whether JTI is contractually permitted to reduce its royalty payments to Ploom upon certain specified events. Information of that nature should, at least implicitly, be baked into the forecasts and projections requested in category 6. In addition, the value of the JTI relationship reasonably should be reflected in the other documents that Quantum is entitled to inspect pursuant to this action. Although this result limits Quantum's ability to collect every morsel of probative information concerning Ploom's prospects, the incremental value of this information to Quantum's purpose is outweighed both by Ploom's contractual obligation to maintain its confidentiality and by the relative harm associated with an unintended leak or a misuse of the information in issue.

I therefore recommend that the Court deny Quantum's Demand as to category 9. I also recommend, however, that the Court do so without prejudice, such that Quantum may make a new demand if it can demonstrate that potential purchasers are refusing to proceed without access to such contracts, or some other concrete need that outweighs the Company's strong interest in protecting the information from disclosure.

9. Time Periods Governing Inspection

Finally, the parties disagree about the time period that should govern the scope of Quantum's inspection. Although the Demand seeks books and records as of the date of the Demand, imposing such a time limitation would be both inequitable and self-defeating given the passage of time. Ploom's delay and its decision to force a trial in this matter have rendered that date stale. Having concluded that Quantum has stated a proper purpose in seeking to value and market its shares, the Supreme Court's decision in *Carroll* instructs that the information provided must be current to achieve that purpose.

As to documents associated with categories 2, 3, and 4, I find that Quantum has demonstrated its need for documents covering the previous three fiscal years. As to categories 2 and 4, Quantum is entitled to inspect the relevant documents from 2011, 2012, and 2013. As to the documents demanded in category 3, Quantum is entitled to inspect Ploom's quarterly financial statements, to the extent they exist, "for all periods subsequent to the last financial statement produced in response to [category 2]."

As to categories 5, 6, 7, and 8, Quantum is entitled to inspect such documents with a beginning date of January 1, 2012, rather than January 1, 2011. Dickman acknowledged that Ploom's business and finances are volatile and rapidly changing. In light of that volatility, and the fluid nature of financial information generally, Quantum has not demonstrated that the information embedded in valuations, forecasts, or stock purchase offers or transaction documents reaching back to 2011 are essential to calculating Ploom's current value.

Finally, in keeping with the Supreme Court's decision in *Carroll*, and in view of the difficulties in selling stock in an early stage, close corporation, I recommend that the Court retain jurisdiction over this action for one year to allow Quantum to present not more than two petitions to inspect and copy necessary books and records for updated information to facilitate the valuation and sale of its stock.

· · ·

6. The Production of Books and Records

It is more than disappointing that the parties could not even agree on a time-frame for production of the books and records Ploom must produce for inspection. Quantum argues that five business days are sufficient, while Ploom proposes a ten business day time frame. Reasonable minds might have, for example, suggested the parties meet in the middle. The parties instead wasted time and money briefing a difference of five business days. Paragraph 2 of the confidentiality order should state: "[w]ithin eight business days following the entry of this Order, Ploom shall produce or make available to Quantum books and records as ordered by the Court of Chancery." That paragraph also should require information that is current as of the date of the Court's order, and should, as set forth in Section II.E.9, provide Quantum with a right to make two requests for updated information within a year of entry of the confidentiality order.

. . .

CONCLUSION

For the foregoing reasons, I recommend that the Court order Ploom to produce its books and records for inspection, consistent with the parameters identified in this report and subject to Quantum executing a confidentiality agreement containing the terms outlined above. This is my final report and exceptions may be taken in accordance with Court of Chancery Rule 144.

Post-Case Follow-Up

The "Garner" exception and documents protected by the attorney-client privilege. One of the most contentious § 220 actions in recent years involves the retailing giant Wal-Mart and allegations of bribery relating to Wal-Mart's Mexican operations. *Wal-Mart Stores, Inc. v. Ind. Elec. Workers Pension Tr. Fund IBEW*, 95 A.3d 1264 (Del. 2014). One of the issues in the case was whether documents protected by the attorney-client privilege are exempt from production under § 220. In an en banc decision issued after a significant amount of litigation, the Delaware Supreme Court ordered Wal-Mart to produce certain documents about the alleged scandal. *Id.* In so holding, the court recognized an exception to the rule that documents protected by the attorney-client privilege do not need to be produced. This exception is referred to as the *Garner* exception after a case of that name from the Fifth Circuit. In *Garner v. Wolfinbarger*, 430 F.2d 1093 (5th Cir. 1970), the Fifth Circuit Court of Appeals recognized a fiduciary exception to the attorney-client privilege when it held that "[t]he attorney-client privilege still has viability for the corporate client. The corporation is not barred from asserting it merely because those demanding information enjoy the status of stockholders. But where the corporation is in suit against its stockholders on charges of acting inimically to stockholder interests, protection of those interests as well as those of the corporation and of the public require that the availability of the privilege be subject to the right of the stockholders to show cause why it should not be invoked in the particular instance." *Id.* at 1103-04. The Fifth Circuit listed several factors that should be considered when evaluating whether the plaintiff has met its "good cause" burden, including (i) the number of shareholders and the percentage of stock they represent; (ii) the bona fides of the shareholders; (iii) the nature of the shareholders' claim and whether it is obviously colorable; (iv) the apparent necessity or desirability of the shareholders having the information and the availability of it from other sources; (v) whether, if the shareholders' claim is of wrongful action by the corporation, the alleged action is criminal, illegal but not criminal, or of doubtful legality; (vi) whether the communication is of advice concerning the litigation itself; (vii) the extent to which the communication is identified versus the extent to which the shareholders are blindly fishing; and (viii) the risk of revelation of trade secrets or other information in whose confidentiality the corporation has an interest in protecting or maintaining for independent reasons. *Id.* at 1104. The *Garner* holding thus allows stockholders of a corporation to invade the corporation's attorney-client privilege in order to prove fiduciary breaches by those in control of the corporation upon showing good cause.

In *Wal-Mart*, the Delaware Supreme Court held that the *Garner* doctrine is applicable in a § 220 action, and futher held that attorney-client privilege therefore does not bar production, or is subject to an exception, if the requesting stockholder needs otherwise inaccessible information to sue a director for breach of fiduciary duty. *Wal-Mart Stores, Inc.*, 95 A.3d at 1278. The court further held, however, that in a § 220 proceeding, the necessary and essential inquiry described in *Quantum Partners* — namely, whether the need for access to records is necessary and essential to the shareholder — must precede any privilege inquiry because the necessary and essential inquiry is dispositive of the threshold question — of the scope of document production to which the plaintiff is entitled under § 220. *Id.* (holding documents are "necessary and essential" pursuant to a § 220 demand if they address the "crux of the shareholder's purpose" and if that information "is unavailable from another source"). *Id.* at 1271 & nn. 9 & 10 (citations omitted). Whether documents are necessary and essential "is fact specific and will necessarily depend on the context in which the shareholder's inspection demand arises." *Id.*

Quantum Technology Partners IV, L.P. v. Ploom, Inc.: Real Life Applications

Dean, a shareholder in Acme Corp. (a Delaware corporation), is concerned that employees of one of Acme's overseas subsidiaries sought to bribe a foreign government official in order to win a contract for Acme. Assume that such conduct, if true, would constitute a violation of the Foreign Corrupt Practices Act. Based on stories in the press, Dean believes (reasonably) that the scandal dates back four years. Dean has only been a shareholder for two years. Dean sends a § 220 demand to Acme that complies with all relevant rules seeking documents dating back four years. Acme refuses to produce records created before Dean became a shareholder.

a. Is Dean barred from requesting documents created before he became a share-holder? (You will need to research Delaware law to answer this question.)

b. What if Dean is seeking the requested documents not only because he believes the corporation has been mismanaged but also because he never liked the CEO for entirely personal reasons having nothing to do with the CEO's performance at Acme? Is Dean's dislike for the CEO grounds for refusing his § 220 demand?

c. What if Dean demands access to documents relating to alleged defects in Acme's products? If Acme refuses, is a court likely to grant Dean's request?

B. DISTINGUISHING BETWEEN CONTROLLING VERSUS MINORITY SHAREHOLDERS, AND CLOSE CORPORATIONS

In Sections C-E, we discuss shareholder rights, obligations, and protections that are not immutable and that tend to play out differently for different types of shareholders and different types of corporations. There are two main reasons for these differences. First, certain rights, obligations, and protections are negotiated, and thus depend on the balance of power between controlling shareholders on one hand and minority shareholders on the other. Second, certain rights, obligations, and protections are more common in (and, in some cases, available only to stockholders of) so-called close corporations. We define and discuss these terms in Sections B.1 and B.2, then turn to the rights, obligations, and protections at issue in Sections C-E.

1. Controlling versus Minority Shareholders

A **majority shareholder** is a stockholder who owns a majority stake (i.e., more than 50 percent) in the corporation. Majority stockholders generally are presumed to be **controlling stockholders**, because their majority ownership stake — and attendant voting control — gives them the right to control the business and affairs of the corporation under default rules. *See In re Crimson Expl. Inc. Stockholder Litig.*, C.A. No. 8541-VCP, 2014 WL 5449419, at *10 (Del. Ch. Oct. 24, 2014) ("Not surprisingly, Delaware law treats a majority stockholder as a controlling stockholder.") (citations omitted).

A non-majority stockholder may be a controlling shareholder despite owning less than a majority stake in the corporation if that stockholder has the ability to exercise actual control over the business and affairs of the corporation. *See id.* ("Exceeding the 50% mark . . . is only one method of determining whether a stockholder controls the company. A stockholder who 'exercises control over the business affairs of the corporation' also qualifies as a controller.") Such control generally is the result of relationships between the controlling shareholder and the corporation and its other directors. *See Kahn v. Lynch Commc'n Sys., Inc.*, 638 A.2d 1110, 1113-15, 1121-22 (Del. 1994) (finding that a 43 percent stockholder was a controlling stockholder where that stockholder threatened to vote down other issues if the board did not approve a merger between the corporation and the controlling shareholder). In its 2014 decision *In re Crimson Exploration Inc.*, the Delaware Chancery Court examined ten significant Delaware cases where the plaintiffs alleged control by non-majority stockholders who owned from 27.7 percent to 49+ percent of shares. *See In re Crimson Expl. Inc. Stockholder Litig.*, 2014 WL 5449419, at *10. The court concluded that "the cases do not reveal any sort of linear, sliding-scale approach whereby a larger share percentage makes it substantially more likely that the court will find the stockholder was a controlling stockholder. Instead, the scatter-plot nature of the holdings highlights the importance and fact-intensive nature of the actual control factor." *Id.* (observing that in *In re Cysive, Inc. Shareholder Litigation*, 836 A.2d 531 (Del. Ch. 2003), the court held that a 35 percent stockholder was controlling, while in *In re Western National Corp. Shareholder Litigation*, No. 15927, 2000 WL 710192 (Del. Ch. May 22, 2000), the court held that a 46 percent stockholder lacked control). The court observed that these cases "show that a large blockholder will not be considered a controlling stockholder unless they actually control the board's decisions about the challenged transaction." *Id.* at *12. With a non-majority shareholder, then, the key question is whether the shareholder has the ability to exercise actual control over the business and affairs of the corporation.

Minority stockholders are stockholders who, individually and in the aggregate, own less than 50 percent of the shares of the corporation. Particularly where there is a majority or controlling shareholder, minority shareholders suffer from certain vulnerabilities. For example, whereas a majority shareholder generally can assure election of the shareholder's preferred slate of directors (assuming straight voting, as discussed in Chapter 8), a minority shareholder may be unable to elect (or unseat) even a single director due to lack of voting power. Likewise, whereas a majority shareholder can cause the corporation to issue a dividend or to buy back shares (subject to fiduciary restraints discussed in Section E below), a minority shareholder generally cannot compel the corporation to buy back her shares or to issue a dividend due to a lack of voting power. More generally, minority shareholders may be faced with controlling shareholders who are tempted to use their influence, position, and voting power to control the corporation to drain corporate earnings by paying exorbitant salaries to favored insiders, to deprive minority shareholders of corporate offices and employment, or to engage in other oppressive conduct toward minority shareholders. Minority shareholders lack the voting power to direct corporate affairs in this fashion.

2. Closely Held Corporations

What Is a Close Corporation?

The risks and vulnerabilities associated with owning a minority stake in a corporation may be particularly acute for minority shareholders in a close corporation. A **close corporation** (or **closely held corporation** or **statutory close corporation** in jurisdictions that provide for this option) is a corporation whose stock is not publicly traded but is instead held by a small group of shareholders, often family members or friends. In most instances, these shareholders are involved in the

Close Corporations versus LLCs versus LLPs

The late Larry Ribstein, a leading scholar of unincorporated entities, said that close corporations reflect a kind of "adolescent identity crisis," sitting between partnerships (the dominant form initially) and LLCs and other unincorporated entities (dominant today). Larry Ribstein, *Close Corporation Remedies and the Evolution of the Closely Held Firm*, 33 W. New Eng. L. Rev. 531, 536 (2011). As you know from Chapter 3, partnership rules initially were designed for small enterprises where partners worked together in the business and were bound to each other by family relationships and other close social ties in addition to their business dealings. Default partnership rules (e.g., equal right to participate in management, unlimited personal liability) reflect this environment. Close corporations are like partnerships in many respects. Owners often are bound to each other by family or social ties and, as with partnerships, owners of close corporations often manage the business and affairs of the corporation. While the corporate form offers limited liability, the "mechanics" of governance (e.g., formal meetings, voting, reports, etc.) and the separation of ownership and control built into corporate governance statutes often fit uneasily with the realities of how closely held firms tend to operate. The result is a disconnect between corporate formalities and corporate governance rules on one hand and the more partnership-like day-to-day operations of close corporations on the other. Courts and legislatures eventually recognized the need for some customization of the corporate form for close corporations. In Ribstein's view, however, close corporations remain an evolutionary "dead end," especially

management of the corporation, as it is common for stockholders in a closely held corporation also to serve as officers, directors, or employees. On occasion a close corporation may be referred to as a closely held corporation, which is defined by the IRS as a corporation that is not a personal service corporation and that has 50 percent or more of its stock held by five or fewer individuals. Such a closely held corporation may or may not have elected to be treated as a statutory close corporation under its state laws, as discussed below.

As is true of corporations generally, close corporations are governed in the first instance by the corporations code of the state in which the close corporation is formed. Only a few U.S. states, including California, Delaware, and Illinois, have special statutes to address the needs of these smaller owner-managed corporations, and corporations formed pursuant to these statutes are known as **statutory close corporations**. These statutes permit, but do not require, qualifying corporations to opt into the statutory close corporation regime by electing statutory close corporation status and complying with formation and notice requirements. For example, DGCL § 342 defines a statutory close corporation as a privately held corporation organized under the Delaware close corporation statute that meets the listed criteria (e.g., no more than 30 stockholders):

(a) A close corporation is a corporation organized under this chapter whose certificate of incorporation contains the provisions required by § 102 of this title and, in addition, provides that:

(1) All of the corporation's issued stock of all classes, exclusive of treasury shares, shall be represented by certificates and shall be held of record by not more than a specified number of persons, not exceeding 30; and

(2) All of the issued stock of all classes shall be subject to 1 or more of the restrictions on transfer permitted by § 202 of this title; and

(3) The corporation shall make no offering of any of its stock of any class which would constitute a "public offering" within the meaning of the United States Securities Act of 1933 [15 U.S.C. §§ 77a et seq.] as it may be amended from time to time.

(b) The certificate of incorporation of a close corporation may set forth the qualifications of stockholders, either by specifying classes of persons who shall be entitled to be holders of record of stock of any class, or by specifying classes of persons who shall not be entitled to be holders of stock of any class or both.

(c) For purposes of determining the number of holders of record of the stock of a close corporation, stock which is held in joint or common tenancy or by the entireties shall be treated as held by 1 stockholder.

Other states do not provide for statutory close corporations in their corporatations codes. Instead, close corporations are required to follow all of the statutes relating to corporations, except where statutes or case law have liberalized requirements, carved out exceptions to rules, or allowed for greater flexibility for non-public corporations. See the discussion of management flexibility in Section D below for one such example. As a general rule, the statutory regime for statutory close corporations is substantially more liberal in a variety of ways than is mainstream corporate law. Yet, courts frequently grant comparable benefits to non-statutory close corporations. *See, e.g., Ramos v. Estrada,* 10 Cal. Rptr. 2d 833 (Ct. App. 1992). This potential for flexibility with regard to certain governance rules is a benefit of the close corporation form.

Finally, the American Bar Association approved a Model Statutory Close Corporation Supplement (MSCCS) to the MBCA designed to be adopted in states to govern the formation and operation of close corporations. A number of states followed the approach of the MSCCS, though it has since been discontinued.

in cases where the corporation's founders/owners do not fully anticipate problems that can arise upon breakup or exit. Larry Ribstein, *The Rise of the Unincorporation* 102 (2010). Perhaps it is not surprising, then, that the increasing popularity of the limited liability partnership (LLP) and limited liability company (LLC) forms, now recognized in all states, appears to have resulted in fewer close corporations being formed compared to LLPs and LLCs. This is because the LLP and LLC forms offer the benefits of the partnership form — for example, pass-through taxation, limited liability, and the flexibility to (more easily) customize management and governance rules to meet business needs and realities — along with benefits of the corporate form (e.g., limited liability). Consequently, even though MBCA § 7.32 and many state statutes allow shareholders in non-public corporations greater flexibility to tailor the operation and governance of their corporation to suit business needs, the LLC and LLP are preferred. See Exhibit 10.1 for a comparison of close corporations to LLCs, which are discussed in more detail in Chapter 12.

EXHIBIT 10.1 **Comparison of Close Corporations to LLCs**

	Close Corporation	LLC
Number of Members	Limited to 25, 35, or 50 by statute	No limit on number of members
Management	Shareholders may manage if all agree to such.	Management is always flexible.
Restrictions on Transfer	By statute, there are always restrictions on the transfer of interests.	No restrictions, per se; transferee becomes full member if operating agreement provides or all members agree.
Taxation	Double taxation (unless all shareholders agree to and the entity is eligible for S treatment)	Single, pass-through taxation

Common Characteristics of Close Corporations

Whether formed pursuant to a close corporation statute or not, close corporations tend to share a number of features in common, including the following:

- Close corporations are not publicly traded.
- There often is a limit on the number of shareholders in a statutory close corporation. Some states permit up to 50 shareholders, whereas other states restrict the number of shareholders to 25, 30, or 35.
- All or most of the shareholders participate in the management of the corporation (and the corporation typically functions informally, similar to a general partnership).
- Shareholders typically enter into agreements restricting the transfer of shares so that "outsiders" cannot easily enter the entity and upset the working relationships of the family members and friends in the close corporation. Under the MSCCS and in states following the MSCCS, restrictions on transfers of shares are automatic, and the corporation is given a right of first refusal to purchase any shares a shareholder may wish to sell. (We discuss share transfer restrictions in greater detail in Section D.2 below.)
- There is no readily available market for the shares of a close corporation.

Spotlight: Veil Piercing and Close Corporations

As you will recall from our Chapter 1 discussion of piercing the corporate veil, (traditional) veil piercing occurs when courts put aside the liability shield of the corporate form and hold the corporation's shareholders liable for debts and obligations of the enterprise. In deciding whether to pierce the corporate veil, courts consider shareholder control over the corporation and a failure to observe corporate formalities, among other factors. Since shareholder control over the enterprise and informality are hallmarks of close corporations, one might wonder whether close corporations are inherently vulnerable to veil piercing. Certainly, a review of case law suggests that veil piercing is more common with close corporations. This likely is because close corporations are more likely to have a dominant shareholder who is able to gain control of the enterprise and misuse it for fraudulent or inequitable purposes compared to non-close corporations where the presence of other shareholders may deter such conduct. Plaintiffs seeking to pierce the veil of a close corporation thus should not rely solely upon shareholder involvement in management or the corporation's failure to comply with all corporate formalities as grounds for relief. Instead, plaintiffs should plead facts showing that challenged shareholders engaged in conduct justifying veil piercing — that is, that they took control of the corporation and used it to perpetrate a fraud or to engage in inequitable conduct. *See, e.g., Agway, Inc. v. Brooks,* 790 A.2d 438, 442 (Vt. 2001) ("While it is doubtful that the court would have equitable cause to pierce the corporate veil merely because a closely held corporation did not follow corporate formalities, '[e]quity . . . will not blindly accept mere corporate form over the actual substance

EXHIBIT 10.2 **Delaware Close Corporation Certificate of Incorporation**

STATE *of* DELAWARE
CERTIFICATE *of* INCORPORATION
A CLOSE CORPORATION
Of

(name of corporation)

• **First:** The name of this Corporation is _____
_____.

• **Second:** Its Registered Office in the State of Delaware is to be located at _____
_____Street, in the City of _____
County of _____ Zip Code_____.
The Registered Agent in charge thereof is_____
_____.

Third: The nature of business and the objects and purposes proposed to be transacted, promoted and carried on, are to engage in any lawful act or activity for which corporations may be organized under the General Corporation Law of Delaware.

• **Fourth:** The amount of the total stock of this corporation is authorized to issue is
_____ shares (number of authorized shares) with a par value
of _____ per share.

• **Fifth:** The name and mailing address of the incorporator are as follows:
Name_____
Mailing Address_____
_____ Zip Code_____

• **Sixth:** All of the Corporation's issued stock of all classes, exclusive of treasury shares, shall be represented by certificates and shall be held of record by not more than a specified number of persons, not exceeding 30.

• **Seventh:** All of the issued stock of all classes shall be subject to 1 or more of the restrictions on transfer permitted by Section 202 of the General Corporation Law of State of Delaware.

• **Eighth:** The Corporation shall make no offering of any of its stock of any class which would constitute a "public offering" within the meaning of the United States Securities Act of 1933 as it may be amended from time to time.

• **I, The Undersigned,** for the purpose of forming a corporation under the laws of the State of Delaware, do make, file and record this Certificate, and do certify that the facts herein stated are true, and I have accordingly hereunto set my hand this
_____ day of _____, A.D._____.

BY: _____
(Incorporator)

NAME:_____
(type or print)

of the transactions involved.' . . . In this case there was substantial evidence of not only a lack of corporate formality, but more significantly, of the fact that Brooks Farm, Inc. was a mere corporate strawman for the Brooks Brothers Farm partnership and John and Mark Brooks's personal businesses — without assets, capital, or purpose beyond evading contract liability. We will uphold a trial court decision to pierce the corporate veil where it has done so, as in this case, to correct the use of the corporate form to evade legitimate claims of judgment creditors.").

Formation of Close Corporations

A corporation may incorporate as a close corporation in states that provide for statutory close corporation status. See Exhibit 10.2 for Delaware's form for incorporation of a close corporation. Alternatively, a corporation that has been in existence may amend its articles of incorporation to elect close corporation status in states where this designation exists. In all other respects, a close corporation is formed in the same way as any corporation — i.e., by filing of articles of incorporation. The articles of incorporation for a close corporation must generally recite that the corporation is being formed as a close corporation. Additionally, most states (and the MSCCS) require that the stock certificates for a close corporation contain a conspicuous notice or legend alerting potential purchasers that the corporation is a close corporation and that the rights of shareholders may differ materially from those of shareholders in other corporations.

When the articles of incorporation are filed with the secretary of state, they will be reviewed for compliance with the pertinent state statutes and will be approved. Any other requirement imposed for the formation of corporations, such as publication of the articles in newspapers or recording of the articles with county clerks, must generally be followed.

A close corporation may terminate its status by an amendment to its articles of incorporation, approved by a two-thirds shareholders' vote, ending its status as a close corporation. Status as a close corporation will automatically terminate if any of the conditions required of a close corporation is breached, for example, if the corporation "goes public." Alternatively, the close corporation may terminate as would any other corporation, such as by voluntary or involuntary dissolution.

C. HEIGHTENED OBLIGATIONS FOR SHAREHOLDERS IN CLOSE CORPORATIONS

As all of this suggests, shareholders in close corporations stand in a delicate balance with one another. On one hand, close corporations offer shareholders the ability to work collaboratively together to build their businesses. At the same time, however, because close corporations typically involve small groups of individuals familiar with one another, and because almost all shareholders are actively involved in managing the business, close corporations may carry a heightened risk of dissension and in-fighting. Heightened fiduciary duties are one strategy for dealing with these opportunities and tensions.

Heightened Fiduciary Duties for Controlling Shareholders

Case Preview

Donahue v. Rodd Electrotype Company of New England, Inc.

In the next case, a minority shareholder of a closely held corporation alleged that the son of the controlling shareholder caused the corporation to purchase shares from the controlling shareholder in violation of fiduciary duties owed to the plaintiff. In reading the case, be alert to the following issues and questions:

1. Is there one single legal definition of close corporations?
2. What are the defining characteristics of close corporations, according to the court?
3. In what ways are close corporations like partnerships?
4. What is a "freeze-out"?
5. Why are minority shareholders in a close corporation vulnerable to freeze-out tactics?
6. Does the heightened fiduciary duty standard announced in *Donahue* apply to majority stockholders only? Must minority stockholders comply with heightened fiduciary duties, as well?
7. What if the share purchase plan at issue had been provided for in the corporation's charter, bylaws, or shareholder agreement(s)? May a close corporation purchase stock from one stockholder without offering others an equal opportunity to participate if the other stockholders consent in advance via a charter provision, a bylaw provision, or a shareholders' agreement?

Donahue v. Rodd Electrotype Company of New England, Inc.
328 N.E.2d 505 (Mass. 1975)

Tauro, Chief Justice.*

The plaintiff, **Euphemia Donahue**, a minority stockholder in the Rodd Electrotype Company of New England, Inc. (Rodd Electrotype), a Massachusetts corporation, brings this suit against the directors of Rodd Electrotype, Charles H. Rodd,

---

*Most footnotes have been omitted for purposes of brevity.

Frederick I. Rodd and Mr. Harold E. Magnuson, against Harry C. Rodd, a former director, officer, and controlling stockholder of Rodd Electrotype and against Rodd Electrotype (hereinafter called defendants). The plaintiff seeks to rescind Rodd Electrotype's purchase of Harry Rodd's shares in Rodd Electrotype and to compel Harry Rodd "to repay to the corporation the purchase price of said shares, $36,000, together with interest from the date of purchase." The plaintiff alleges that the defendants caused the corporation to purchase the shares in violation of their fiduciary duty to her, a minority stockholder of Rodd Electrotype.

The trial judge, after hearing oral testimony, dismissed the plaintiff's bill on the merits. He found that the purchase was without prejudice to the plaintiff and implicitly found that the transaction had been carried out in good faith and with inherent fairness. The Appeals Court affirmed with costs. . . .

The case is before us on the plaintiff's application for further appellate review.

. . .

The evidence may be summarized as follows: In 1935, the defendant, Harry C. Rodd, began his employment with Rodd Electrotype, then styled the Royal Electrotype Company of New England, Inc. (Royal of New England). At that time, the company was a wholly-owned subsidiary of a Pennsylvania corporation, the Royal Electrotype Company (Royal Electrotype). Mr. Rodd's advancement within the company was rapid. The following year he was elected a director, and, in 1946, he succeeded to the position of general manager and treasurer.

In 1936, the plaintiff's husband, Joseph Donahue (now deceased), was hired by Royal of New England as a "finisher" of electrotype plates. His duties were confined to operational matters within the plant. Although he ultimately achieved the positions of plant superintendent (1946) and corporate vice president (1955), Donahue never participated in the "management" aspect of the business.

In the years preceding 1955, the parent company, Royal Electrotype, made available to Harry Rodd and Joseph Donahue shares of the common stock in its subsidiary, Royal of New England. Harry Rodd took advantage of the opportunities offered to him and acquired 200 shares for $20 a share. Joseph Donahue, at the suggestion of Harry Rodd, who hoped to interest Donahue in the business, eventually obtained fifty shares in two twenty-five share lots priced at $20 a share. The parent company at all times retained 725 of the 1,000 outstanding shares. One Lawrence W. Kelley owned the remaining twenty-five shares.

In June of 1955, Royal of New England purchased all 725 of its shares owned by its parent company. The total price amounted to $135,000. Royal of New England remitted $75,000 of this total in cash and executed five promissory notes of $12,000 each, due in each of the succeeding five years. Lawrence W. Kelley's twenty-five shares were also purchased at this time for $1,000. A substantial portion of Royal of New England's cash expenditures was loaned to the company by Harry Rodd, who mortgaged his house to obtain some of the necessary funds.

The stock purchases left Harry Rodd in control of Royal of New England. Early in 1955, before the purchases, he had assumed the presidency of the company. His 200 shares gave him a dominant eighty per cent interest. Joseph Donahue, at this time, was the only minority stockholder.

Subsequent events reflected Harry Rodd's dominant influence. In June, 1960, more than a year after the last obligation to Royal Electrotype had been discharged, the company was renamed the Rodd Electrotype Company of New England, Inc. In 1962, Charles H. Rodd, Harry Rodd's son (a defendant here), who had long been a company employee working in the plant, became corporate vice president. In 1963, he joined his father on the board of directors. In 1964, another son, Frederick I. Rodd (also a defendant), replaced Joseph Donahue as plant superintendent. By 1965, Harry Rodd had evidently decided to reduce his participation in corporate management. That year Charles Rodd succeeded him as president and general manager of Rodd Electrotype.

From 1959 to 1967, Harry Rodd pursued what may fairly be termed a gift program by which he distributed the majority of his shares equally among his two sons and his daughter, Phyllis E. Mason. Each child received thirty-nine shares. Two shares were returned to the corporate treasury in 1966.

We come now to the events of 1970 which form the grounds for the plaintiff's complaint. In May of 1970, Harry Rodd was seventy-seven years old. The record indicates that for some time he had not enjoyed the best of health and that he had undergone a number of operations. His sons wished him to retire. Mr. Rodd was not averse to this suggestion. However, he insisted that some financial arrangements be made with respect to his remaining eighty-one shares of stock. A number of conferences ensued. Harry Rodd and Charles Rodd (representing the company) negotiated terms of purchase for forty-five shares which, Charles Rodd testified, would reflect the book value and liquidating value of the shares.

A special board meeting convened on July 13, 1970. As the first order of business, Harry Rodd resigned his directorship of Rodd Electrotype. The remaining incumbent directors, Charles Rodd and Mr. Harold E. Magnuson (clerk of the company and a defendant and defense attorney in the instant suit), elected Frederick Rodd to replace his father. The three directors then authorized Rodd Electrotype's president (Charles Rodd) to execute an agreement between Harry Rodd and the company in which the company would purchase forty-five shares for $800 a share ($36,000).

The stock purchase agreement was formalized between the parties on July 13, 1970. Two days later, a sale pursuant to the July 13 agreement was consummated. At approximately the same time, Harry Rodd resigned his last corporate office, that of treasurer.

Harry Rodd completed divestiture of his Rodd Electrotype stock in the following year. As was true of his previous gifts, his later divestments gave equal representation to his children. Two shares were sold to each child on July 15, 1970, for $800 a share. Each was given ten shares in March, 1971. Thus, in March, 1971, the shareholdings in Rodd Electrotype were apportioned as follows: Charles Rodd, Frederick Rodd and Phyllis Mason each held fifty-one shares; the Donahues held fifty.

A special meeting of the stockholders of the company was held on March 30, 1971. At the meeting, Charles Rodd, company president and general manager, reported the tentative results of an audit conducted by the company auditors and reported generally on the company events of the year. For the first time, the Donahues learned that the corporation had purchased Harry Rodd's shares. According to the minutes of the meeting, following Charles Rodd's report, the Donahues raised questions about the purchase. They then voted against a resolution, ultimately adopted by the remaining stockholders, to approve Charles Rodd's report. Although the minutes of the meeting show that the stockholders unanimously voted to accept a second resolution ratifying all acts of the company president (he executed the stock purchase agreement) in the preceding year, the trial judge found, and there was evidence to support his finding, that the Donahues did not ratify the purchase of Harry Rodd's shares. . . .

A few weeks after the meeting, the Donahues, acting through their attorney, offered their shares to the corporation on the same terms given to Harry Rodd. Mr. Harold E. Magnuson replied by letter that the corporation would not purchase the shares and was not in a financial position to do so. This suit followed.

In her argument before this court, the plaintiff has characterized the corporate purchase of Harry Rodd's shares as an unlawful distribution of corporate assets to controlling stockholders. She urges that the distribution constitutes a breach of the fiduciary duty owed by the Rodds, as controlling stockholders, to her, a minority stockholder in the enterprise, because the Rodds failed to accord her an equal opportunity to sell her shares to the corporation. The defendants reply that the stock purchase was within the powers of the corporation and met the requirements of good faith and inherent fairness imposed on a fiduciary in his dealings with the corporation. They assert that there is no right to equal opportunity in corporate stock purchases for the corporate treasury. For the reasons hereinafter noted, we agree with the plaintiff and reverse the decree of the Superior Court. However, we limit the applicability of our holding to "close corporations," as hereinafter defined. Whether the holding should apply to other corporations is left for decision in another case, on a proper record.

A. Close Corporations. In previous opinions, we have alluded to the distinctive nature of the close corporation (e.g., *Brigham v. M. & J. Corp.*, 352 Mass. 674, 678, 227 N.E.2d 915 (1967); see *Samia v. Central Oil Co. of Worcester*, 339 Mass. 101, 112-113, 158 N.E.2d 469 (1959)), but have never defined precisely what is meant by a close corporation. There is no single, generally accepted definition. Some commentators emphasize an "integration of ownership and management" (Note, Statutory Assistance for Closely Held Corporations, 71 Harv. L. Rev. 1498 (1958)), in which the stockholders occupy most management positions. *Kruger v. Gerth*, 16 N.Y.2d 802, 806, 263 N.Y.S.2d 1, 210 N.E.2d 355 (1965) (Fuld, J., dissenting). Foreward, 18 Law & Contemp. Prob. 433 (1953). See *Helms v. Duckworth*, 101 U.S. App. D.C. 390, 249 F.2d 482, 486 (1957). Others focus on the number of stockholders and the nature of the market for the stock. In this view, close corporations have few stockholders; there is little market for corporate stock. The Supreme Court of Illinois adopted this latter view in *Galler v. Galler*, 32 Ill. 2d 16, 203 N.E.2d 577 (1965): "For our purposes, a close corporation is one in which the stock is held in a few hands, or in a few families, and wherein it is not at all, or only rarely, dealt in by buying or selling." Id. at 27, 203 N.E.2d at 583. Accord, *Brooks v. Willcuts*, 78 F.2d 270, 273 (8th Cir. 1935). See, generally, F. H. O'Neal, Close Corporations: Law and Practice, § 1.02 (1971). We accept aspects of both definitions. We deem a close corporation to the typified by: (1) a small number of stockholders; (2) no ready market for the corporate stock; and (3) substantial majority stockholder participation in the management, direction and operations of the corporation.

As thus defined, the close corporation bears striking resemblance to a partnership. Commentators and courts have noted that the close corporation is often little more than an "incorporated" or "chartered" partnership.[12] *Ripin v. United States Woven Label Co.*, 205 N.Y. 442, 447, 98 N.E. 855, 856 (1912) ("little more (though not quite the same as) than chartered partnerships"). *Clark v. Dodge*, 269 N.Y. 410, 416, 199 N.E. 641 (1936). Hornstein, Stockholders' Agreements in the Closely Held Corporation, 59 Yale L.J. 1040 (1950). Hornstein, Judicial Tolerance of the Incorporated Partnership, 18 Law & Contemp. Prob. 435, 436 (1953). Cf. *Barrett v. King*, 181 Mass. 476, 479, 63 N.E. 934 (1902). The stockholders "clothe" their partnership "with the benefits peculiar to a corporation, limited liability, perpetuity and the like." *In the Matter of Surchin v. Approved Bus. Mach. Co., Inc.*, 55 Misc., 2d 888, 889, 286 N.Y.S.2d 580, 581 (Sup. Ct. 1967). In essence, though, the enterprise remains one in which ownership is limited to the original parties or transferees of their stock to whom the other stockholders have agreed,[13] in which ownership and management are in the same hands, and in which the owners are quite dependent on one another for the success of the enterprise. Many close corporations are "really partnerships, between two or three people who contribute their capital, skills, experience and labor." *Kruger v. Gerth*, 16 N.Y.2d 802, 805, 263 N.Y.S.2d 1, 3, 210 N.E.2d 355, 356 (1965) (Desmond, C.J., dissenting). Just as in a partnership, the relationship among the stockholders must be one of trust, confidence and absolute loyalty if the enterprise is to succeed. Close corporations with substantial assets and with more numerous stockholders are no different from smaller close corporations in this regard. All participants rely on the fidelity and abilities of those stockholders who hold office. Disloyalty and self-seeking conduct on the part of any stockholder will engender bickering, corporate stalemates, and, perhaps, efforts to achieve dissolution. See *Lydia E. Pinkham Medicine Co. v. Gove*, 303 Mass. 1, 20 N.E.2d 482 (1939); *In the Matter of Radom & Neidorff, Inc.*, 307 N.Y. 1, 119 N.E.2d 563, rearg. den., 307 N.Y. 701, 120 N.E.2d 865 (1954); *Kruger v. Gerth*, 16 N.Y.2d 802, 263 N.Y.S.2d 1, 210 N.E.2d 355 (1965); *In the Matter of Gordon & Weiss, Inc.*, 32 A.D.2d 279, 301 N.Y.S.2d 839, app. withdrawn, 25 N.Y.2d 959 (1969).

In *Helms v. Duckworth*, 101 U.S. App. D.C. 390, 249 F.2d 482 (1957), the United States Court of Appeals for the District of Columbia Circuit had before it

---

[12]The United States Internal Revenue Code gives substantial recognition to the fact that close corporations are often merely incorporated partnerships. The so called Subchapter S, 26 U.S.C. §§ 1371-1379 (1970), enables "small business corporations," defined by the statute (26 U.S.C. § 1371(a) (1970)), to make an election which generally exempts the corporation from taxation (26 U.S.C. § 1372(b)(1) (1970)) and causes inclusion of the corporation's undistributed, as well as distributed, taxable income in the gross income of the stockholders for the year (26 U.S.C. § 1373(a) (1970)). This is essentially the manner in which partnership earnings are taxed. See 26 U.S.C. § 701 (1970).

[13]The original owners commonly impose restrictions on transfers to stock designed to prevent outsiders who are unacceptable to the other stockholders from acquiring an interest in the close corporation. These restrictions often take the form of agreements among the stockholders and the corporation or by-laws which give the corporation or the other stockholders a right of "first refusal" when any stockholder desires to sell his shares. See *Albert E. Touchet, Inc. v. Touchet*, 264 Mass. 499, 502, 163 N.E. 184 (1928); Hornstein, Stockholders' Agreements in the Closely Held Corporation, 59 Yale L.J. 1040, 1048-1049 (1950). In a partnership, of course, a partner cannot transfer his interest in the partnership so as to give his assignee a right to participate in the management or business affairs of the continuing partnership without the agreement of the other partners. G.L. c. 108A, § 27. See *Hazen v. Warwick*, 256 Mass. 302, 308, 152 N.E. 342 (1926).

a stockholders' agreement providing for the purchase of the shares of a deceased stockholder by the surviving stockholder in a small "two-man" close corporation. The court held the surviving stockholder to a duty "to deal fairly, honestly, and openly with . . . (his) fellow stockholders." Id. at 487. Judge Burger, now Chief Justice Burger, writing for the court, emphasized the resemblance of the two-man close corporation to a partnership: "In an intimate business venture such as this, stockholders of a close corporation occupy a position similar to that of joint adventurers and partners. While courts have sometimes declared stockholders 'do not bear toward each other that same relation of trust and confidence which prevails in partnerships,' this view ignores the practical realities of the organization and functioning of a small 'two-man' corporation organized to carry on a small business enterprise in which the stockholders, directors, and managers are the same persons" (footnotes omitted). Id. at 486.

Although the corporate form provides the above-mentioned advantages for the stockholders (limited liability, perpetuity, and so forth), it also supplies an opportunity for the majority stockholders to oppress or disadvantage minority stockholders. The minority is vulnerable to a variety of oppressive devices, termed "freezeouts," which the majority may employ. See, generally, Note, Freezing Out Minority Shareholders, 74 Harv. L. Rev. 1630 (1961). An authoritative study of such "freeze-outs" enumerates some of the possibilities: "The squeezers (those who employ the freeze-out techniques) may refuse to declare dividends; they may drain off the corporation's earnings in the form of exorbitant salaries and bonuses to the majority shareholder-officers and perhaps to their relatives, or in the form of high rent by the corporation for property leased from majority shareholders . . . ; they may deprive minority shareholders of corporate offices and of employment by the company; they may cause the corporation to sell its assets at an inadequate price to the majority shareholders . . . ." F. H. O'Neal and J. Derwin, Expulsion or Oppression of Business Associates, 42 (1961). In particular, the power of the board of directors, controlled by the majority, to declare or withhold dividends and to deny the minority employment is easily converted to a device to disadvantage minority stockholders. See *Hayden v. Beane*, 293 Mass. 347, 199 N.E. 755 (1936); *Lydia E. Pinkham Medicine Co. v. Gove*, 303 Mass. 1, 11-12, 20 N.E.2d 482 (1939); *Casson v. Bosman*, 137 N.J. Eq. 532, 45 A.2d 807 (Ct. E. & A. 1946); *Patton v. Nicholas*, 154 Tex. 385, 393, 279 S.W.2d 848 (1955). Cf. *Taylor v. Standard Gas & Elec. Co.*, 306 U.S. 307, 323, 59 S. Ct. 543, 83 L. Ed. 669 (1939).

The minority can, of course, initiate suit against the majority and their directors. Self-serving conduct by directors is proscribed by the director's fiduciary obligation to the corporation. *Elliott v. Baker*, 194 Mass. 518, 523, 80 N.E. 450 (1907). *Sagalyn v. Meekins, Packard & Wheat, Inc.*, 290 Mass. 434, 438, 195 N.E. 769 (1935). However, in practice, the plaintiff will find difficulty in challenging dividend or employment policies. Such policies are considered to be within the judgment of the directors. This court has said: "The courts prefer not to interfere . . . with the sound financial management of the corporation by its directors, but declare as general rule that the declaration of dividends rests within the sound discretion of the directors, refusing to interfere with their determination unless a plain abuse of discretion is made to appear." *Crocker v. Waltham Watch Co.*, 315 Mass. 397, 402, 53 N.E.2d 230, 233 (1944). Accord, *Daniels v. Briggs*, 279 Mass. 87, 95, 180 N.E. 717 (1932). See *Fernald v. Frank Ridlon*

Co., 246 Mass. 64, 71-72, 140 N.E. 421 (1923); *Perry v. Perry*, 339 Mass. 470, 479, 160 N.E.2d 97 (1959). Judicial reluctance to interfere combines with the difficulty of proof when the standard is "plain abuse of discretion" or bad faith, see *Perry v. Perry*, supra, to limit the possibilities for relief. Although contractual provisions in an "agreement of association and articles of organization" (*Crocker v. Waltham Watch Co.*, supra, 315 Mass. at 401, 53 N.E.2d at 233) or in by-laws (*Lydia E. Pinkham Medicine Co. v. Gove*, supra), have justified decrees in this jurisdiction ordering dividend declarations, generally, plaintiffs who seek judicial assistance against corporate dividend or employment policies do not prevail. See *Fernald v. Frank Ridlon Co.*, 246 Mass. 64, 140 N.E. 421 (1923); *Daniels v. Briggs*, supra; *Perry v. Perry*, supra; *Conviser v. Simpson*, 122 F. Supp. 205 (D. Md. 1954); *Berwald v. Mission Dev. Co.*, 40 Del. Ch. 509, 185 A.2d 480 (Sup. Ct. 1962); *Moskowitz v. Bantrell*, 41 Del. Ch. 177, 190 A.2d 749 (Sup. Ct. 1963); *Casson v. Bosman*, 137 N.J. Eq. 532, 45 A.2d 807 (Ct. E. & A. 1946); Note, Minority Shareholder Suits to Compel Declaration of Dividends, 64 Harv. L. Rev. 299, 300 (1950); Note, Minority Shareholders' Power to Compel Declaration of Dividends in Close Corporations — A New Approach, 10 Rutgers L. Rev. 723, 724 (1956). But see *Dodge v. Ford Motor Co.*, 204 Mich. 459, 170 N.W. 668 (1919); *Patton v. Nicholas*, 154 Tex. 385, 279 S.W.2d 848 (1955).

Thus, when these types of "freeze-outs" are attempted by the majority stockholders, the minority stockholders, cut off from all corporation-related revenues, must either suffer their losses or seek a buyer for their shares. Many minority stockholders will be unwilling or unable to wait for an alteration in majority policy. Typically, the minority stockholder in a close corporation has a substantial percentage of his personal assets invested in the corporation. *Galler v. Galler*, 32 Ill. 2d 16, 27, 203 N.E.2d 577 (1965). The stockholder may have anticipated that his salary from his position with the corporation would be his livelihood. Thus, he cannot afford to wait passively. He must liquidate his investment in the close corporation in order to reinvest the funds in income-producing enterprises.

At this point, the true plight of the minority stockholder in a close corporation becomes manifest. He cannot easily reclaim his capital. In a large public corporation, the oppressed or dissident minority stockholder could sell his stock in order to extricate some of his invested capital. By definition, this market is not available for shares in the close corporation. In a partnership, a partner who feels abused by his fellow partners may cause dissolution by his "express will . . . at any time" (G.L. c. 108A, § 31(1)(b) and (2)) and recover his share of partnership assets and accumulated profits. *Fisher v. Fisher*, 349 Mass. 675, 678, 212 N.E.2d 222 (1965). *Fisher v. Fisher*, 352 Mass. 592, 594-595, 227 N.E.2d 334 (1967). G.L. c. 108A, § 38. If dissolution results in a breach of the partnership articles, the culpable partner will be liable in damages. G.L. c. 108A, § 38(2)(a) II. By contrast, the stockholder in the close corporation or "incorporated partnership" may achieve dissolution and recovery of his share of the enterprise assets only by compliance with the rigorous terms of the applicable chapter of the General Laws. *Rizzuto v. Onset Cafe, Inc.*, 330 Mass. 595, 597-598, 116 N.E.2d 249 (1953). "The dissolution of a corporation which is a creature of the Legislature is primarily a legislative function, and the only authority courts have to deal with this subject is the power conferred upon them by the Legislature." *Leventhal v. Atlantic Fin. Corp.*, 316 Mass. 194, 205, 55 N.E.2d 20, 26 (1944). To secure dissolution of the ordinary close corporation subject to G.L. c. 156B, the stockholder, in the absence of corporate deadlock, must own at least fifty per cent of the shares (G.L. c. 156B, § 99(a)) or have the advantage of a favorable provision in the articles of organization (G.L. c. 156B, § 100(a)(2)). The minority stockholder, by definition lacking fifty per cent of the corporate shares, can never "authorize" the corporation to file a petition for dissolution under G.L. c. 156B, § 99(a), by his own vote. He will seldom have at his disposal the requisite favorable provision in the articles of organization.

Thus, in a close corporation, the minority stockholders may be trapped in a disadvantageous situation. No outsider would knowingly assume the position of the disadvantaged minority. The outsider would have the same difficulties. To cut losses, the minority stockholder may be compelled to deal with the majority. This is the capstone of the majority plan. Majority "freeze-out" schemes which withhold dividends are designed to compel the minority to relinquish stock at inadequate prices. See *Lydia E. Pinkham Medicine Co. v. Gove*, 303 Mass. 1, 12, 20 N.E.2d 482 (1939); *Mansfield Hardwood Lumber Co. v. Johnson*, 263 F.2d 748, 746 (5th Cir.), reh. den., 268 F.2d 317 (5th Cir.), cert. den., 361 U.S. 885, 80 S. Ct. 156, 4 L. Ed. 2d 120 (1959); *Cochran v. Channing Corp.*, 211 F. Supp. 239, 242-243 (S.D.N.Y. 1962); *Gottfried v. Gottfried*, 73 N.Y.S.2d 692, 695 (Sup. Ct. 1947); *Patton v. Nicholas*, 154 Tex. 385, 393, 279 S.W.2d 848 (1955). When the minority stockholder agrees to sell out at less than fair value, the majority has won.

Because of the fundamental resemblance of the close corporation to the partnership, the trust and confidence which are essential to this scale and manner of enterprise, and the inherent danger to minority interests in the close corporation, we hold that stockholders[17] in the close corporation owe one another substantially the same fiduciary duty in the operation of the enterprise[18] that partners owe to one another. In our previous decisions, we have defined the standard of duty owed by partners to one another as the "utmost good faith and loyalty." *Cardullo v. Landau*, 329 Mass. 5, 8, 105 N.E.2d 843 (1952); *DeCotis v. D'Antona*, 350 Mass. 165, 168, 214 N.E.2d 21 (1966). Stockholders in close corporations must discharge their management and stockholder responsibilities in conformity with this strict good faith standard. They may not act out of avarice, expediency or self-interest in derogation of their duty of loyalty to the other stockholders and to the corporation.

---

[17]We do not limit our holding to majority stockholders. In the close corporation, the minority may do equal damage through unscrupulous and improper "sharp dealings" with an unsuspecting majority. See *Helms v. Duckworth*, 101 U.S. App. D.C. 390, 249 F.2d 482 (1957).

[18]We stress that the strict fiduciary duty which we apply to stockholders in a close corporation in this opinion governs only their actions relative to the operations of the enterprise and the effects of that operation on the rights and investments of other stockholders. We express no opinion as to the standard of duty applicable to transactions in the shares of the close corporation when the corporation is not a party to the transaction. Cf. Andrews, The Stockholder's Right to Equal Opportunity in the Sale of Shares, 78 Harv. L. Rev. 505 (1965). Compare *Perlman v. Feldmann*, 219 F.2d 173 (2d Cir.), cert. den. 349 U.S. 952, 75 S. Ct. 880, 99 L. Ed. 1277 (1955) with *Zahn v. Transamerica Corp.*, 162 F.2d 36 (3d Cir. 1947).

We contrast[19] this strict good faith standard with the somewhat less stringent standard of fiduciary duty to which directors and stockholders[20] of all corporations must adhere in the discharge of their corporate responsibilities. Corporate directors are held to a good faith and inherent fairness standard of conduct (*Winchell v. Plywood Corp.*, 324 Mass. 171, 177, 85 N.E.2d 313 (1949)) and are not "permitted to serve two masters whose interests are antagonistic." *Spiegel v. Beacon Participations, Inc.*, 297 Mass. 398, 411, 8 N.E.2d 859, 904 (1937). "Their paramount duty is to the corporation, and their personal pecuniary interests are subordinate to that duty." *Durfee v. Durfee & Canning, Inc.*, 323 Mass. 187, 196, 80 N.E.2d 522, 527 (1948).

The more rigorous duty of partners and participants in a joint adventure,[21] here extended to stockholders in a close corporation, was described by then Chief Judge Cardozo of the New York Court of Appeals in *Meinhard v. Salmon*, 249 N.Y. 458, 164 N.E. 545 (1928): "Joint adventurers, like copartners, owe to one another, while the enterprise continues, the duty of the finest loyalty. Many forms of conduct permissible in a workaday world for those acting at arm's length, are forbidden to those bound by fiduciary ties. . . . Not honesty alone, but the punctilio of an honor the most sensitive, is then the standard of behavior." Id. at 463-464, 164 N.E. at 546.

Application of this strict standard of duty to stockholders in close corporations is a natural outgrowth of the prior case law. In a number of cases involving close corporations, we have held stockholders participating in management to a standard of fiduciary duty more exacting than the traditional good faith and inherent fairness standard because of the trust and confidence reposed in them by the other stockholders. . . .

. . .

In these and other cases (e.g., *Sher v. Sandler*, 325 Mass. 348, 353, 90 L.E.2d 536 (1950); *Mendelsohn v. Leather Mfg. Corp.*, 326 Mass. 226, 233, 93 N.E.2d 537 (1950)), we have imposed a duty of loyalty more exacting than that duty owed by a director to his corporation (*Spiegel v. Beacon Participations, Inc.*, 297 Mass. 398, 410-411, 8 N.E.2d 895 (1937)) or by a majority stockholder to the minority in a public corporation because of facts particular to the close corporation in the cases. In the instant case, we extend this strict duty of loyalty to all stockholders in close corporations. The circumstances which justified findings of relationships of trust and confidence in these particular cases exist universally in modified form in all close corporations. . . .

. . .

---

[19]Several scholarly articles have suggested that the standard of duty of stockholding officers in close corporations may be more demanding than the standard applicable to their counterparts in publicly-held corporations. See Brudney and Chirelstein, Fair Shares in Corporate Mergers and Takeovers, 88 Harv. L. Rev. 297, 325 n. 60 (1974); Note, Corporate Opportunity in the Close Corporation — A Different Result? 56 Geo. L.J. 381 (1967).

[20]The rule set out in many jurisdictions is: "The majority has the right to control; but when it does so, it occupies a fiduciary relation toward the minority, as much so as the corporation itself or its officers and directors." *Southern Pac. Co. v. Bogert*, 250 U.S. 483, 487-488, 39 S. Ct. 533, 535, 64 L. Ed. 1099 (1919). Accord, e.g., *Jones v. H. F. Ahmanson & Co.*, 1 Cal. 3d 93, 108, 81 Cal. Rptr. 592, 460 P.2d 464 (1969); *Allied Chem. & Dye Corp. v. Steel & Tube Co. of America*, 14 Del. Ch. 1, 12, 120 A. 486 (Ch. 1923); *Kavanaugh v. Kavanaugh Knitting Co.*, 226 N.Y. 185, 195, 123 N.E. 148 (1919); *Zahn v. Transamerica Corp.*, 162 F.2d 36, 42 (3d Cir. 1947). See generally Berle, "Control" in Corporate Law, 58 Col. L. Rev. 1212, 1222 (1958).

[21]We have indicated previously that the duty owed by partners inter sese and that owed by coadventurers inter sese are substantially identical. *Cardullo v. Landau*, 329 Mass. 5, 8, 105 N.E.2d 843 (1952); *DeCotis v. D'Antona*, 350 Mass. 165, 168, 214 N.E.2d 21 (1966).

B. Equal Opportunity in a Close Corporation. Under settled Massachusetts law, a domestic corporation, unless forbidden by statute, has the power to purchase its own shares. . . . An agreement to reacquire stock "(is) enforceable, subject, at least, to the limitations that the purchase must be made in good faith and without prejudice to creditors and stockholders." *Scriggins v. Thomas Dalby Co.*, supra. *Winchell v. Plywood Corp.*, supra, at 174-175, 85 N.E.2d 313, 315. When the corporation reacquiring its own stock is a close corporation, the purchase is subject to the additional requirement, in the light of our holding in this opinion, that the stockholders, who, as directors or controlling stockholders, caused the corporation to enter into the stock purchase agreement, must have acted with the utmost good faith and loyalty to the other stockholders.

To meet this test, if the stockholder whose shares were purchased was a member of the controlling group, the controlling stockholders must cause the corporation to offer each stockholder an equal opportunity to sell a ratable number of his shares to the corporation at an identical price.[24] Purchase by the corporation confers substantial benefits on the members of the controlling group whose shares were purchased. These benefits are not available to the minority stockholders if the corporation does not also offer them an opportunity to sell their shares. The controlling group may not, consistent with its strict duty to the minority, utilize its control of the corporation to obtain special advantages and disproportionate benefit from its share ownership. . . .

The benefits conferred by the purchase are twofold: (1) provision of a market for shares; (2) access to corporate assets for personal use. By definition, there is no ready market for shares of a close corporation. The purchase creates a market for shares which previously had been unmarketable. It transforms a previously illiquid investment into a liquid one. If the close corporation purchases shares only from a member of the controlling group, the controlling stockholder can convert his shares into cash at a time when none of the other stockholders can. Consistent with its strict fiduciary duty, the controlling group may not utilize its control of the corporation to establish an exclusive market in previously unmarketable shares from which the minority stockholders are excluded. . . .

The purchase also distributes corporate assets to the stockholder whose shares were purchased. Unless an equal opportunity is given to all stockholders, the purchase of shares from a member of the controlling group operates as a preferential distribution of assets. In exchange for his shares, he receives a percentage of the contributed capital and accumulated profits of the enterprise. The funds he so receives are available for his personal use. The other stockholders benefit from no such access to corporate property and cannot withdraw their shares of the corporate profits and capital in this manner unless the controlling group acquiesces. Although the purchase price for the controlling stockholder's shares may seem fair to the corporation and

---

[24]Of course, a close corporation may purchase shares from one stockholder without offering the others an equal opportunity if all other stockholders give advance consent to the stock purchase arrangements through acceptance of an appropriate provision in the articles of organization, the corporate by-laws (see *Brown v. Little Brown & Co. (Inc.)* 269 Mass. 102, 168, N.E. 521 (1929)), or a stockholder's agreement. Similarly, all other stockholders may ratify the purchase. Cf. *George H. Gilbert Mfg. Co. v. Goldfine*, 317 Mass. 681, 685, 59 N.E.2d 461 (1945); *Winchell v. Plywood Corp.*, 324 Mass. 171, 176-177, 85 N.E.2d 313 (1949).

other stockholders under the tests established in the prior case law . . . the controlling stockholder whose stock has been purchased has still received a relative advantage over his fellow stockholders, inconsistent with his strict fiduciary duty — an opportunity to turn corporate funds to personal use.

The rule of equal opportunity in stock purchases by close corporations provides equal access to these benefits for all stockholders. We hold that, in any case in which the controlling stockholders have exercised their power over the corporation to deny the minority such equal opportunity, the minority shall be entitled to appropriate relief.[25] To the extent that language in *Spiegel v. Beacon Participations, Inc.*, 297 Mass. 398, 431, 8 N.E.2d 895 (1937), and other cases suggests that there is no requirement of equal opportunity for minority stockholders when a close corporation purchases shares from a controlling stockholder, it is not to be followed.

C. Application of the Law to this Case. We turn now to the application of the learning set forth above to the facts of the instant case.

The strict standard of duty is plainly applicable to the stockholders in Rodd Electrotype. Rodd Electrotype is a close corporation. Members of the Rodd and Donahue families are the sole owners of the corporation's stock. In actual numbers, the corporation, immediately prior to the corporate purchase of Harry Rodd's shares, had six stockholders. The shares have not been traded, and no market for them seems to exist. Harry Rodd, Charles Rodd, Frederick Rodd, William G. Mason (Phyllis Mason's husband), and the plaintiff's husband all worked for the corporation. The Rodds have retained the paramount management positions.

Through their control of these management positions and of the majority of the Rodd Electrotype stock, the Rodds effectively controlled the corporation. In testing the stock purchase from Harry Rodd against the applicable strict fiduciary standard, we treat the Rodd family as a single controlling group. We reject the defendants' contention that the Rodd family cannot be treated as a unit for this purpose. From the evidence, it is clear that the Rodd family was a close-knit one with strong community of interest. . . . Harry Rodd had hired his sons to work in the family business, Rodd Electrotype. As he aged, he transferred portions of his stock holdings to his children. Charles Rodd and Frederick Rodd were given positions of responsibility in the business as he withdrew from active management. In these circumstances, it is realistic to assume that appreciation, gratitude, and filial devotion would prevent the younger Rodds from opposing a plan which would provide funds for their father's retirement.

Moreover, a strong motive of interest requires that the Rodds be considered a controlling group. When Charles Rodd and Frederick Rodd were called on to

---

[25]Under the Massachusetts law, "(n)o stockholder shall have any pre-emptive right to acquire stock of the corporation except to the extent provided in the articles of organization or in a by-law adopted by and subject to amendment only by the stockholders." G.L. c. 156B, § 20. We do not here suggest that such pre-emptive rights are required by the strict fiduciary duty applicable to the stockholders of close corporations. However, to the extent that a controlling stockholder or other stockholder, in violation of his fiduciary duty, causes the corporation to issue stock in order to expand his holdings or to dilute holdings of other stockholders, the other stockholders will have a right to relief in court. Even under the traditional standard of duty applicable to corporate directors and stockholders generally, this court has looked favorably upon stockholder challenges to stock issues which, in violation of a fiduciary duty, served personal interests of other stockholder/directors and did not serve the corporate interest. . . .

represent the corporation in its dealings with their father, they must have known that further advancement within the corporation and benefits would follow their father's retirement and the purchase of his stock. The corporate purchase would take only forty-five of Harry Rodd's eighty-one shares. The remaining thirty-six shares were to be divided among Harry Rodd's children in equal amounts by gift and sale. Receipt of their portion of the thirty-six shares and purchase by the corporation of forty-five shares would effectively transfer full control of the corporation to Frederick Rodd and Charles Rodd, if they chose to act in concert with each other or if one of them chose to ally with his sister. Moreover, Frederick Rodd was the obvious successor to his father as director and corporate treasurer when those posts became vacant after his father's retirement. Failure to complete the corporate purchase (in other words, impeding their father's retirement plan) would have delayed, and perhaps have suspended indefinitely, the transfer of these benefits to the younger Rodds. They could not be expected to oppose their father's wishes in this matter. Although the defendants are correct when they assert that no express agreement involving a quid pro quo — subsequent stock gifts for votes from the directors — was proved, no express agreement is necessary to demonstrate the identity of interest which disciplines a controlling group acting in unison. . . .

On its face, then, the purchase of Harry Rodd's shares by the corporation is a breach of the duty which the controlling stockholders, the Rodds, owed to the minority stockholders, the plaintiff and her son. The purchase distributed a portion of the corporate assets to Harry Rodd, a member of the controlling group, in exchange for his shares. The plaintiff and her son were not offered an equal opportunity to sell their shares to the corporation. In fact, their efforts to obtain an equal opportunity were rebuffed by the corporate representative. As the trial judge found, they did not, in any manner, ratify the transaction with Harry Rodd.

Because of the foregoing, we hold that the plaintiff is entitled to relief. Two forms of suitable relief are set out hereinafter. The judge below is to enter an appropriate judgment. The judgment may require Harry Rodd to remit $36,000 with interest at the legal rate from July 15, 1970, to Rodd Electrotype in exchange for forty-five shares of Rodd Electrotype treasury stock. . . . In the alternative, the judgment may require Rodd Electrotype to purchase all of the plaintiff's shares for $36,000 without interest. In the circumstances of this case, we view this as the equal opportunity which the plaintiff should have received. Harry Rodd's retention of thirty-six shares, which were to be sold and given to his children within a year of the Rodd Electrotype purchase, cannot disguise the fact that the corporation acquired one hundred per cent of that portion of his holdings (forty-five shares) which he did not intend his children to own. The plaintiff is entitled to have one hundred per cent of her forty-five shares similarly purchased.

· · ·

WILKINS, Justice (concurring).

I agree with much of what the Chief Justice says in support of granting relief to the plaintiff. However, I do not join in any implication (see, e.g., footnote 18 and the associated text) that the rule concerning a close corporation's purchase of a controlling stockholder's shares applies to all operations of the corporation as they affect minority stockholders. That broader issue, which is apt to arise in connection with salaries and dividend policy, is not involved in this case. The analogy to partnerships may not be a complete one.

Post-Case Follow-Up

In *Wilkes v. Springside Nursing Home, Inc.*, 353 N.E.2d 657 (Mass. 1976), the Massachusetts Supreme Judicial Court had occasion to consider its *Donahue* doctrine in a case involving an alleged breach of fiduciary duty arising from (i) the termination of a stockholder/employee of a close corporation; and (ii) the decision to vote that stockholder/employee out as an officer and director. Citing *Donahue*, the *Wilkes* court noted the "strict obligation on the part of majority stockholders in a close corporation to deal with the minority with the utmost good faith and loyalty." *Id.* at 663. The court also observed, however, that "untempered application of the strict good faith standard enunciated in *Donahue* to cases such as the one before us will result in the imposition of limitations on legitimate action by the controlling group in a close corporation which will unduly hamper its effectiveness in managing the corporation in the best interests of all concerned." *Id.* The court further held the "majority, concededly, have certain rights to what has been termed 'selfish ownership' in the corporation which should be balanced against the concept of their fiduciary obligation to the minority." *Id.*

To effect this balance, the court held that when a minority stockholder brings suit against the majority alleging breach of the strict good faith duty owed under *Donahue*, the court should "carefully analyze" the actions taken by controlling shareholders to determine whether the majority can demonstrate a "legitimate business purpose" for its actions. *Id.* In asking this question, the court recognized that the control group "must have some room to maneuver in establishing the business policy of the corporation. It must have a large measure of discretion, for example, in declaring or withholding dividends, deciding whether to merge or consolidate, establishing the salaries of corporate officers, dismissing directors with or without cause, and hiring and firing corporate employees." *Id.* When a business purpose is advanced by the majority, the minority must then have the opportunity to demonstrate that the same legitimate objective could have been achieved through an alternative course of action less harmful to the minority's interest. *Id.* In the event of a dispute, the court must weigh the legitimate business purpose, if any, against the practicability of a less harmful alternative. *Id.*

Delaware, fiduciary duties, and close corporations. As you likely gathered from the court's discussion in *Donahue*, the duty of utmost good faith and loyalty described in *Donahue* draws heavily upon partnership principles, and is even more exacting than the fiduciary duties owed by officers and directors to the corporation, and the duties owed by controlling shareholders in conflict of interest transactions as discussed in Chapter 11. Many U.S. jurisdictions have followed the *Donahue* approach, imposing heightened fiduciary duties on shareholders—particularly controlling shareholders—of closely held corporations. Delaware is a notable exception. In *Nixon v. Blackwell*, 626 A.2d 1366 (Del. 1993), the Delaware Supreme Court declined to create any "special, judicially-created rules to 'protect' minority stockholders of closely-held Delaware corporations." *Id.* at 1379. The court directed minority shareholders concerned about the possibility of oppression by controlling shareholders to engage in pre-investment bargaining, commenting that "[t]he tools of good corporate practice are designed to give a purchasing minority stockholder the opportunity to bargain for protection before parting with consideration." *Id.* at 1380. The court further held that "[i]t would do violence to normal corporate practice and our corporation law to fashion an ad hoc ruling which would result in a court-imposed stockholder buy-out for which the parties had not contracted." *Id.*

Donahue v. Rodd Electrotype Company of New England, Inc.: *Real Life Applications*

Zed Corp. is a privately held corporation located in Massachusetts. Four members of the Sims family own 75 percent of Zed's stock — Sylvia Sims and Sam Sims (a married couple) and their two children. Sylvia, the matriarch of the Sims family, also serves as chief executive officer and chair of the board of directors. Juanita Garcia owns the remaining 25 percent. Juanita also serves as chief financial officer of the company and is a director.

a. Sylvia is nearing retirement and would like to arrange for her children, who have been working in the business for many years, to buy out her interest in the company. As controlling shareholders, the Sims family has the voting power necessary to approve this transaction. The Sims family believes it is in the best interest of the company to buy out Sylvia for both corporate and family reasons. The Sims family does not plan on offering a buyout to any other shareholders. May the Sims family proceed with Sylvia's buyout? Are there any constraints or considerations that they ought to keep in mind?

b. Assume for purposes of this question that Sylvia's buyout must be approved by all of the company's shareholders due to a charter provision requiring unanimous director and shareholder consent to such transactions. Further assume that Juanita has refused to consent because she feels underappreciated by Sylvia and because she fears that she will be forced out of the company once the children (and not Sylvia) are in control. May Juanita refuse to consent to the buyout? Are there any constraints or considerations that Juanita ought to keep in mind when deciding whether to consent to the transaction?

D. NEGOTIATED RIGHTS, PROTECTIONS, AND OBLIGATIONS

In this section, we examine opportunities for negotiated rights, protections, and obligations for shareholders. As we have addressed a number of these issues in earlier chapters, we begin by summarizing issues, default rules, and opportunities for flexibility in chart form (Exhibit 10.3) first. We then "spotlight" several points in Sections D.2 and D.3 below.

EXHIBIT 10.3			

EXHIBIT 10.3 — Summary of Shareholder Rights, Obligations, and Protections: Default Rules and Alternatives

Issue	Default Rule	Opportunity for Negotiated Protection	Comments
Shareholder election of directors	In most states, directors are elected by straight voting. Under a **straight voting system**, a minority shareholder lacks the power to elect even one director. Because controlling shareholders tend to prefer straight voting, a corporation incorporated in one of those states normally will opt out of cumulative voting through charter provision. (Note: Cumulative voting is the default rule in some states—e.g., California.)	In jurisdictions that use straight voting as the default, corporations may opt out of straight voting, and into **cumulative voting**, via a charter provision. *See, e.g.,* DGCL § 214.	As discussed in Section 2.4 of Chapter 8, cumulative voting provides some protection for minority shareholders because it may make it possible for minority shareholders to elect at least one director.
Preemptive rights	Preemptive rights give existing shareholders the opportunity (but not the obligation) to purchase a proportionate stake in a new offering of securities. Preemptive rights thus allow a shareholder to avoid having his ownership stake diluted as a result of new issuances. Under default rules, shareholders generally do *not* have preemptive rights.	A corporation may elect to give shareholders preemptive rights via a charter provision. *See* DGCL § 102(b)(3); MBCA § 6.30(h).	Preemptive rights are disfavored by many corporations because they can operate as a constraint on new investment. Some investors may be unwilling to invest if they cannot obtain a controlling stake in the business, and preemptive rights enjoyed by existing investors can prevent a new investor from obtaining a controlling stake. Instead of giving statutory preemption rights to investors, corporations may instead give certain shareholders—particularly preferred shareholders—contractual rights of first refusal. Contractual rights of first refusal can accomplish the goal of preemptive rights (allowing the shareholder "first dibs" on new issuances) without having to deal with the formality of a charter provision.

EXHIBIT 10.3   **(continued)**

Issue	Default Rule	Opportunity for Negotiated Protection	Comments
Higher quorum and voting requirements	State corporations codes generally provide that unless the charter states otherwise, a majority of the votes entitled to be cast on the matter by shareholders (or, a group of shareholders) shall constitute a quorum. *See, e.g.,* MBCA § 7.25. If a quorum exists, action on a matter (other than the election of directors) by a voting group is approved if the votes cast within the voting group favoring the action exceed the votes cast opposing the action, unless the charter requires a greater number of affirmative votes. *See, e.g.,* MBCA § 7.25.	Corporations codes generally allow corporations to provide for a greater quorum and voting requirement than is provided for under default rules. *See, e.g.,* MBCA § 7.27.	Default quorum and voting rules generally allow majority shareholders to control corporate decision making. Increasing quorum and voting requirements can have the effect of requiring at least some minority shareholders (i) to be "present" for purposes of the vote; or (ii) to vote in favor of the action at issue. Increasing the voting requirement to two-thirds of outstanding shares is called a **super-majority** voting requirement. **Unanimous** voting requirements also may be used. Super-majority or unanimous requirements typically apply, if at all, to "big ticket" items such as dissolution, sales of substantially all assets, mergers, etc. Such requirements can have the effect of giving a minority shareholder **veto power**.
Buyout rights/ obligations	Under statutory default rules, neither the corporation nor its shareholders have the obligation to buy out a shareholder who wants to exit his investment. Particularly for minority shareholders in closely held corporations, this can mean that they are "locked into" their investment.	Shareholders may negotiate buyout, buy-sell, and other similar agreements whereby the shareholder is able (or required) to offer his shares to the corporation first, if the shareholder wishes to exit.	Lawyers drafting and negotiating these types of agreements would do well to consider how the departing shareholder's interest in the corporation will be valued. Valuation — particularly valuation of a minority stake in a privately held close corporations — is tricky business, and lawyers are well advised to consult with valuation experts (along with reviewing statutes and case law discussing valuation) at the time of drafting and when such rights are exercised.

EXHIBIT 10.3 (continued)

Issue	Default Rule	Opportunity for Negotiated Protection	Comments
Employment	Under default rules, shareholders do not have a statutory or common law right to employment with the corporation.	Shareholders can negotiate a contract of employment with the corporation.	It is common for an individual making an investment in a corporation—particularly a closely held corporation—to expect that the corporation will employ her. Indeed, for minority shareholders (who do not control the corporation and generally cannot force the corporation to issue dividends), employment may be an important part of the shareholder's economic relationship with the company. Shareholders—particularly minority shareholders—thus are well advised to enter into employment agreements that address the employee/shareholder's rights and obligations.
Dividends	Under default rules, the board is vested with the discretion to decide whether, when, and in what amount(s) to issue dividends. This means that minority shareholders generally cannot force the board to declare a dividend, even if the corporation is wildly profitable.	Minority shareholders may negotiate a dividend policy in connection with their investment. Such policies typically provide that the corporation will pay cash dividends to shareholders at regular intervals and in agreed-upon amounts (or, calculated according to an agreed-upon formula).	Be sure to review relevant statutes and case law, as there are limits on the board's discretion to authorize the payment of dividends.
Centralized management and shareholder agreements respecting management	Under default rules, control of the corporation and managerial authority are vested in the board of directors. Shareholders generally are not involved in day-to-day management.	The MBCA and many statute statutes permit stockholders of close corporations to enter into shareholder agreements to allow shareholders to play a greater role in management and operations without running afoul of rules that otherwise would vest such authority in the board of directors.	Compared to their public-company counterparts, the lines between directors and shareholders tend to be less well defined in close corporations. Often, this is because the owners of close corporations also serve as officers and directors of the entity. The statutes allowing for agreements respecting managerial authority recognize this reality.

EXHIBIT 10.3 **(continued)**

Issue	Default Rule	Opportunity for Negotiated Protection	Comments
Dissolution of the corporation, deadlock, and concerns about oppression of minority shareholders	Default rules generally provide for voluntary dissolution upon a vote of shareholders (with voting requirements set forth in the relevant corporations code) and may also provide for dissolution in cases of deadlock (again, with voting requirements set forth in corporations codes).	Some state statutes provide additional opportunities to minority shareholders of close corporations to seek judicial dissolution in cases involving fraud, illegal, or oppressive conduct by majority shareholders.	As we discuss in Section E below, minority shareholders of close corporations may be particularly vulnerable to oppression by the majority. Recognizing this, some state statutes afford minority shareholders in close corporations additional grounds for seeking judicial dissolution.

1. Documenting Shareholder Protections

Negotiated shareholder protections (including those reflected in the chart above) generally are documented in the corporation's charter, bylaws, or shareholder agreements. Sometimes the location is dictated by statute — for example, in states that use straight voting for directors as the default rule, a corporation wishing to adopt cumulative voting for directors must do so in its charter. Absent a statutory mandate, however, corporations generally like to memorialize negotiated rights and protections in a shareholder agreement. Corporations prefer to use shareholder agreements as opposed to the charter because charters are public documents and because charters can be difficult to amend. As between bylaws and shareholder agreements, bylaws generally are more "public" (or, at least subject to disclosure or requests for disclosure) compared to shareholder agreements. Shareholder agreements thus generally are a more private, and more flexible, way to document negotiated terms.

2. Spotlight: Share Transfer Restrictions

Shareholders in a closely held corporation typically will enter into an agreement among shareholders to restrict or limit their ability to transfer (or **alienate**) their ownership interests in the corporation. Because the close corporation almost always involves a group of individuals well known to each other either through family ties or friendship, the group will be reluctant to allow "outsiders" in who might change the dynamics of the organization. Therefore, shareholders in close corporations typically enter into agreements whereby they agree to certain restrictions placed on their ability to sell their shares. The restrictions also may help ensure that a corporation maintains its S status (if S status has been elected) so that it is not subject to double taxation. Because one of the fundamental rights of a property owner is to sell or dispose of that property as she wishes, restraints on alienation are carefully scrutinized by courts to ensure they are not unreasonable.

Generally speaking, restrictions on the transfer of shares may be placed in the articles of incorporation, the bylaws, or in a private agreement among the shareholders or between the shareholders and the corporation. As there are often notice requirements, be sure to consult the corporations code in the relevant jurisdiction for any requirements respecting the contents and placement of share transfer restrictions. For example, **buy-sell agreements** generally spell out contractually negotiated share transfer restrictions in that they establish terms governing a departing shareholder's sale of her stock to the corporation. The MSCCS model provided that the restriction on transfers of shares was automatic. In jurisdictions that take this approach, shareholders do not have a great deal of liquidity because there is no ready market for their shares.

The most common restriction on the transfer of shares is a **right of first refusal**. The shareholders enter into an agreement, either with each other or with the corporation, whereby they agree that before they can sell their shares to any outsider, either the corporation or the shareholders, or both, shall have the right to purchase the shares on the same terms as any third party who has made an offer for the shares. Only if the corporation and other shareholders decline to purchase the shares may they then be sold to the outsider. Any transfer of the shares in violation of such an agreement is ineffective.

There are two types of agreements for the sale of a shareholder's interest upon the death or disability of the shareholder. A **cross-purchase agreement** provides for the purchase of the shareholder's interest from her or her estate by the remaining shareholders. Under a cross-purchase agreement, each shareholder takes out a life or disability policy on the life of each of the other shareholders. Upon a shareholder's death or disability, each other shareholder then has funds from the insurance policy to purchase a portion of the deceased or disabled shareholder's shares. A cross-purchase agreement arrangement is not particularly effective if there are more than a few shareholders; in this case, there are too many insurance policies to buy and maintain.

The other type of agreement is generally referred to as an **entity purchase agreement**, or *stock redemption agreement*. In this case, the corporate entity itself is the beneficiary under the terms of an insurance policy, and in the event of the death or disability of a shareholder, the corporate entity receives the insurance proceeds and then purchases the deceased or disabled shareholder's interest. Under an entity purchase or stock redemption agreement, the corporation simply pays the premiums for and owns a single policy on the life of each shareholder.

Case Preview

F.B.I. Farms, Inc. v. Moore

While restraints on alienation are common in close corporations, there are some limits on the stockholders' ability to engage in private ordering. The next case examines some of these limits. When reading the case, consider the following questions:

1. Are restraints on alienation a function of statute? Common law? Contract? All of the above?
2. What is a consent restraint?
3. Why does the court conclude that the buyer who purchased Linda's interest at the foreclosure sale acquired the shares at issue subject to restraints on alienation?
4. Does it matter whether the buyer at the foreclosure sale had notice of the restrictions?
5. What factors do courts typically examine to decide whether a consent restraint is reasonable?

F.B.I. Farms, Inc. v. Moore
798 N.E.2d 440 (Ind. 2003)

Boehm, Justice.*

We hold that as a general proposition, restrictions on corporate share transfers may require approval of the transfer by the corporation's Board of Directors, at least in a family-owned corporation. Although generally valid against purchasers with notice of them, such restrictions may not prevent a creditor from foreclosing a lien on the shares, but a purchaser who buys at a foreclosure sale with notice of the restrictions acquires the shares subject to the restrictions. We also hold that if shares are subject to a right of first refusal, and the holder of the right has notice of the foreclosure, the holder cannot exercise the right against a purchaser at a foreclosure sale after the purchaser has taken title to the shares without objection from the holder of the rights.

FACTUAL AND PROCEDURAL BACKGROUND

F.B.I. Farms, Inc., was formed in 1976 by Ivan and Thelma Burger, their children, Linda and Freddy, and the children's spouses. Each of the three couples transferred a farm and related machinery to the corporation in exchange for common stock in the corporation. At the time, Birchell Moore was married to Linda. Linda and Moore deeded a jointly-owned 180-acre farm to F.B.I., and 2,507 shares were issued to Moore and one to Linda. These 2,508 shares represented approximately fourteen percent of the capitalization of F.B.I.

In 1977, the Board of Directors of F.B.I. consisted of Moore, Ivan, Freddy and Linda. The minutes of a 1977 meeting of the Board recite that the following restrictions on the transfer of shares were "adopted":

> 1) No stock of said corporation shall be transferred, assigned and/or exchanged or divided, unless or until approved by the Directors thereof;

---

*Most footnotes have been omitted for purposes of brevity

2) That if any stock be offered for sale, assigned and/or transferred, the corporation should have the first opportunity of purchasing the same at no more than the book value thereof;

3) Should said corporation be not interested, and could not economically offer to purchase said stock, any stockholder of record should be given the next opportunity to purchase said stock, at a price not to exceed the book value thereof;

4) That if the corporation was not interested in the stock, and any stockholders were not interested therein, then the same could be sold to any blood member of the family. Should they be desirous of purchasing the same, then at not more than the book value thereof.

Linda's marriage to Moore was dissolved in 1982. As part of the dissolution proceedings, Linda was awarded all of the F.B.I. shares and Moore was awarded a monetary judgment in the amount of $155,889.80, secured by a lien on Linda's shares.

F.B.I. filed for bankruptcy protection in 1989 and emerged from Chapter 11 Bankruptcy in 1991. Moore's judgment against Linda remained unsatisfied, and in April 1998 he sought a writ of execution of his lien. The corporation, through its counsel, responded with a letter to Moore's counsel demanding payment of the $250,700 subscription price for the 2,507 shares that were initially issued to Moore but had since been transferred to Linda. Moore obtained the writ of execution in June 1999, and in October 1999 the corporation, again through counsel, sent a letter to Moore purporting to cancel the 2,507 shares for failure to pay the subscription price. A sheriff's sale went forward and in February 2000 Moore purchased all 2,924 shares owned by Linda at the time for $290,450.67.

In December 2000 Moore instituted this suit against F.B.I., its shareholders, and Linda seeking a declaratory judgment that the attempted cancellation of the shares by the defendants was invalid, that Moore properly retained ownership of the shares, and that the shares were unencumbered by restrictions and were freely transferable. Moore also sought dissolution of the corporation, injunctive relief against alleged fraudulent practices by the defendants, and monetary damages. The trial court granted Moore's motion for partial summary judgment, finding (1) the shares were not "lawfully cancelled"; (2) Moore was the "lawful owner" of the disputed stock; (3) the restriction in paragraph one of the agreement requiring approval by F.B.I.'s directors for a share transfer was "manifestly unreasonable"; and, (4) the provision in paragraph four of the agreement giving "blood members" the option to purchase after the corporation and shareholders was "manifestly unreasonable" and unenforceable. The trial court's findings included those rendering the order appealable as a final judgment pursuant to Indiana Trial Rule 54(B).

On appeal, the Court of Appeals held that the transfer restrictions barred only voluntary transfers. *F.B.I. Farms, Inc. v. Moore,* 769 N.E.2d 688, 696 (Ind. Ct. App. 2002). Because the sheriff's sale effectuated an involuntary transfer of Linda's shares, Moore, as the purchaser of the shares, acquired the shares. *Id.* at 692. Although the court found that future transfers of stock would be subject to the restrictions in Moore's hands, it also affirmed the trial court's finding that the two disputed restrictions were manifestly unreasonable. *Id.* at 695-96. The court reasoned that the several tumultuous years of dispute between the parties rendered the restriction requiring director approval before transfer unreasonable, and the reference to "blood members" of the family was sufficiently ambiguous that that restriction was unenforceable. *Id.* at 694-96. We granted transfer.

. . .

I. TRANSFER RESTRICTIONS

A. *General Principles*

Most of the issues in this case are resolved by the Indiana statute governing share transfer restrictions. Indiana Code section 23-1-26-8 essentially mirrors Model Business Corporation Act § 6.27, which authorizes restrictions on the transfer of shares. The Indiana statute reads as follows:

(a) The articles of incorporation, bylaws, an agreement among shareholders, or an agreement between shareholders and the corporation may impose restrictions on the transfer or registration of transfer of shares of any class or series of shares of the corporation. A restriction does not affect shares issued before the restriction was adopted unless the holders of the shares are parties to the restriction agreement or voted in favor of the restriction.

(b) A restriction on the transfer or registration of transfer of shares is valid and enforceable against the holder or a transferee of the holder if the restriction is authorized by this section and its existence is noted conspicuously on the front or back of the certificate or is contained in the information statement required by section 7(b) [Ind. Code 23-1-26-7(b)] of this chapter. Unless so noted, a restriction is not enforceable against a person without knowledge of the restriction.

(c) A restriction on the transfer or registration of transfer of shares is authorized:

(1) to maintain the corporation's status when it is dependent on the number or identity of its shareholders;

(2) to preserve exemptions under federal or state securities law; or

(3) for any other reasonable purpose.

(d) A restriction on the transfer or registration of transfer of shares may, among other things:

(1) obligate the shareholder first to offer the corporation or other persons (separately, consecutively, or simultaneously) an opportunity to acquire the restricted shares;

(2) obligate the corporation or other persons (separately, consecutively, or simultaneously) to acquire the restricted shares;

(3) require the corporation, the holders of any class of its shares, or another person to approve the transfer of the restricted shares, if the requirement is not manifestly unreasonable; or

(4) prohibit the transfer of the restricted shares to designated persons or classes of persons, if the prohibition is not manifestly unreasonable. . . .

Corporate shares are personal property. At common law, any restriction on the power to alienate personal property was impermissible. *Doss v. Yingling*, 95 Ind. App. 494, 500, 172 N.E. 801, 803 (1930). Despite this doctrine, Indiana, like virtually all jurisdictions, allows corporations and their shareholders to impose restrictions on transfers of shares. The basic theory of these statutes is to permit owners of a corporation to control its ownership and management and prevent outsiders from inserting themselves into the operations of the corporation. *Id.* at 502-03, 172 N.E. 801;

12 William Meade Fletcher et al, *Fletcher Cyclopedia of the Law of Private Corporations,* § 5454 (1996). Chief Justice Holmes stated the matter succinctly a century ago: "Stock in a corporation is not merely property. It also creates a personal relation analogous otherwise than technically to a partnership. . . . [T]here seems to be no greater objection to retaining the right of choosing one's associates in a corporation than in a firm." *Barrett v. King,* 181 Mass. 476, 63 N.E. 934, 935 (1902). As applied to a family-owned corporation, this remains valid today.

Transfer restrictions are treated as contracts either between shareholders or between shareholders and the corporation.[1] *Doss,* 95 Ind. App. at 502, 172 N.E. at 803; *Butner v. United States,* 440 U.S. 48, 55, 99 S. Ct. 914, 59 L.Ed.2d 136 (1979) (the validity and enforcement of restrictions are governed by state law just like any other contract); *Boston Safe Deposit & Trust Co., et al. v. North Attleborough Chapter of the Am. Red Cross, et al.,* 330 Mass. 114, 111 N.E.2d 447, 449 (1953) (restrictions in the articles of organization are binding on a shareholder by reason of the contract made with the corporation when she accepted the certificates of stock containing the printed restrictions). Apart from any statutory requirements, restrictions on transfer are to be read, like any other contract, to further the manifest intention of the parties. Because they are restrictions on alienation and therefore disfavored, the terms in the restrictions are not to be expanded beyond their plain and ordinary meaning. 12 Fletcher § 5455 (1996).

For a party to be bound by share transfer restrictions, that party must have notice of the restrictions. I.C. § 23-1-26-8(b) (1998). Here, the restrictions on transfer of F.B.I. shares were neither "noted conspicuously" on the certificates nor contained in the information statement referred to in Indiana Code 23-1-26-8(b), but there is no doubt that Moore, the buyer at the sheriff's sale, had notice of the restrictions. He was therefore bound by them. *State ex rel. Hudelson v. Clarks Hill Tel. Co.,* 139 Ind. App. 507, 510, 218 N.E.2d 154, 156 (1966).

Finally, a closely held corporation is a "corporation in which all of the outstanding stock is held by just a few individuals, or by a small group of persons belonging to a single family." J.R. Kemper, *Validity of "Consent Restraint" on Transfer of Shares of Close Corporation,* 69 A.L.R.3d 1327, 1328 (1976). In 1977, F.B.I. plainly fell within that description; it was owned by six individuals, all members of a single family. Closely held corporations have a viable interest in remaining the organization they envision at incorporation and transfer restrictions are an appropriate means of maintaining the status quo.

---

[1]The Indiana statute provides that restrictions are valid if included in the articles, the bylaws, an agreement among shareholders or an agreement between the corporation and shareholders. I.C. § 23-1-26-8(a) (1998). None of these was done here. However, no one challenges the restrictions as defective in their initial adoption. At least as to Moore, who approved them as a director and had actual knowledge of them, under these circumstances, the restrictions constitute a contract as to all of those shareholders who approved the adoption of the restrictions. *Shortridge v. Platis,* 458 N.E.2d 301, 304 (Ind. Ct. App. 1984) (a buy-sell restriction is analyzed by the court as a contract); 18A Am. Jur. 2d *Corporations* § 687 (1985) (courts sustain a restriction whether valid as a bylaw or not, on the ground that it constitutes a valid agreement between the stockholders and the corporation, particularly as applied to stockholders who assent to, or participate in, the adoption of the bylaw).

B. Rights of First Refusal

Paragraphs (2) and (3) of the restrictions created rights of first refusal in F.B.I. and its shareholders. A transfer in violation of restrictions is voidable at the insistence of the corporation. *Groves v. Prickett,* 420 F.2d 1119, 1122 (9th Cir. 1970). F.B.I. and its shareholders argue that Moore should have been obliged to offer the shares to the corporation or a shareholder pursuant to those provisions. Moore responds, and the Court of Appeals agreed, that he was not a shareholder until he purchased the shares at the sheriff's sale. He contends he therefore had no power to offer the shares. This misses the point that before Linda could transfer her shares, she was obliged to offer them to F.B.I. and the other shareholders. Moore was on notice of that requirement. Moore, as the buyer, had the right to demand that Linda initiate the process to exercise or waive the right to first refusal.

Thus, if the corporation had insisted on its right of first refusal, Linda would have been obliged to sell to F.B.I. (or its shareholders). And Moore, as a buyer on notice of the restrictions, had the right to insist that that process go forward. But the corporation and its shareholders were aware of the sheriff's sale and did nothing to assert the right of first refusal. They cannot sit back and let the sale go forward, await future events, then claim a right to purchase on the same terms as Moore. *McCroden v. Case,* 602 N.W.2d 736, 743-44 (S.D. 1999) (transfer restriction is waived by stockholder's failure to exercise "first option" preemptive rights); *Calton v. Calton,* 118 N.C. App. 439, 456 S.E.2d 520, 523 (1995) (no justiciable controversy existed where no shareholder exercised the right to purchase stock, intended to exercise the right, or was even financially able to do so at the time the action was filed; shareholders waived any right to object to the transfers where they had knowledge of both the testators death and the restrictions contained on the stock certificates, no shareholder asked to purchase any of the stock, and shareholders waited eighteen months to file an action); *Puro v. Puro,* 40 A.D.2d 784, 337 N.Y.S.2d 586, 587 (N.Y. App. Div. 1972) (transfer restrictions are not self-executing). In sum, F.B.I. and its shareholders had rights of first refusal, but failed to exercise them. As a result, the sale to Moore proceeded as if the shares had been offered and the corporation refused the opportunity. To hold otherwise would be to give F.B.I. and its shareholders a perpetual option to purchase but no obligation to do so. Having failed to demand their right to buy at the time of the sale, the rights of first refusal gave them no ability to upset the sale conducted by the sheriff.

C. Restrictions on Transfer with Board Approval

The restrictions "adopted" in paragraphs (1) and (4) are more problematic. Indiana's statute, reflecting the common law, requires that restrictions on share transfers be reasonable. I.C. § 23-1-26-8(c)(3), (d)(3), and (d)(4). The general common law doctrine surrounding evaluation of the reasonableness of restrictions is well established. A restriction is reasonable if it is designed to serve a legitimate purpose of the party imposing the restraint and the restraint is not an absolute restriction on the recipient's right of alienability. Bernard F. Cataldo, *Stock Transfer Restrictions and the Closed Corporation,* 37 Va. L. Rev. 229, 232-33 (1951). The Indiana statute is somewhat more generous in allowing restrictions on classes of buyers unless "manifestly unreasonable." I.C. 23-1-26-8(d)(4). Several factors are relevant in determining the reasonableness of any transfer restriction, including the size of the corporation, the degree of restraint upon alienation; the time the restriction was to continue in effect, the method to be used in determining the transfer price of shares, the likelihood of the restriction's contributing to the attainment of corporate objectives, the possibility that a hostile stockholder might injure the corporation, and the probability of the restriction's promoting the best interests of the corporation. 18A Am. Jur. 2d *Corporations* § 683 (1985). At one extreme, a restriction that merely prescribes procedures that must be observed before stock may be transferred is not unreasonable. *State ex rel. Howland v. Olympia Veneer Co.,* 138 Wash. 144, 244 P. 261 (1926). At the other end of the spectrum, restrictions that are fraudulent, oppressive, unconscionable, *Tourtelott v. Chestnuts Salon,* No. 00-5496 2001 R.I. Super. LEXIS 19 at * 6 (R.I. Sup. Ct. Jan. 17, 2001), 2001 WL 91393, or the result of a breach of the fiduciary duty that shareholders in a close corporation owe to one another, will not be upheld. *Cressy v. Shannon Cont'l Corp.,* 177 Ind. App. 224, 378 N.E.2d 941, 945 (1978); 12 Fletcher § 5455 (1996). The restrictions on F.B.I.'s shares, like most, are somewhere in the middle. They impose substantive limitations on transfer, but are not alleged to be the result of fraud or breach of fiduciary duty.

The trial court, in its order granting partial summary judgment, concluded that the restriction precluding transfer without Board approval was reasonable at the time that it was adopted, but the lengthy and difficult history between the parties had rendered the restriction unreasonable. Under basic contract law principles, the reasonableness of a term of a contract is evaluated at the time of its adoption. *First Fed. Sav. Bank v. Key Mkts.,* 559 N.E.2d 600, 603 (Ind. 1990). The same is true of share transfer restrictions. As a result, evaluating the reasonableness of the restrictions in light of subsequent developments is inappropriate. For that reason, we do not agree that the restriction requiring director approval became unreasonable based upon events and disputes within the family that occurred after the restrictions had been adopted. To be sure, the parties find themselves in a difficult dispute as is sometimes the case in a family business following a dissolution. But when F.B.I. was formed and the family farms were effectively pooled, the shareholders agreed that the Board would be permitted to restrict access to the shares. To the extent that restriction devalues the shares in the hands of any individual shareholder by reason of lack of transferability, it is the result of the bargain they struck. The policy behind enforcement of these restrictions is to encourage entering into formal partnerships by permitting all parties to have confidence they will not involuntarily end up with an undesired co-venturer. Presumably for that reason, the statute permits a restriction that requires a transferee to be approved by the Board of Directors, and to that extent may severely limit transferability.

A "consent restriction" such as this has been considered unreasonable by some courts. 2 Cox, Hazen, O'Neal *Corporations* § 14.10 (2002); Harry G. Henn & John R. Alexander, *Laws of Corporations,* § 281 (1983). However, the General Assembly has allowed precisely this type of restriction in Indiana Code section 23-1-26-8(d)(3). That section provides that transfer restrictions may require the approval of "the corporation, the holders of any class of its shares, or another person" before the shares may be transferred. Board approval is one permissible way of implementing approval by "the Corporation" under this section. *See also Wright v. Iredell Telephone Co.,* 182 N.C. 308, 108 S.E. 744, 747 (1921) (upholding a restriction requiring the approval of the corporation's directors).

D. Restrictions on Transfer Except to "Blood Members of the Family"

We also find the "blood-member" restriction to be enforceable as protecting a viable interest. *Mathews v. United States,* 226 F. Supp. 1003, 1009 (E.D.N.Y. 1964) (recognized "intact family ownership" as an interest worth protecting by a restriction). These are family farmers in corporate form. It is apparent from the nature of the corporation that the Burger family had an interest in maintaining ownership and operation of F.B.I. in the hands of family members. Although one may quibble with the terminology, and there may be some individuals where status as blood members is debatable, we think it plain enough that all parties to this dispute either are or are not blood members of the Burger family. All are either direct descendants of Ivan or spouses of Ivan or of one of his children.

II. ATTEMPTED CANCELLATION OF THE SHARES

F.B.I. took the position that the subscription price for Linda's shares had not been paid and therefore the shares were cancelled. The trial court rejected the claim that the shares had been cancelled. We agree that F.B.I.'s effort in 1989 to cancel the shares in the face of the impending sheriff's sale has little merit. The shares were issued in 1977 in exchange for the 180-acre farm Linda and Moore contributed to F.B.I. That is surely sufficiently substantial consideration to eliminate any claim that there was no consideration for the shares, and its initial valuation was a matter of wide discretion for the Board. I.C. § 23-1-26-2(c).

III. RESTRICTIONS AS APPLIED TO INVOLUNTARY TRANSFERS

The Court of Appeals held that the restrictions on Linda's shares did not apply by their terms to the sheriff's sale and, as a result, did not bar the sheriff's sale to Moore. We agree that Moore acquired the shares at the sheriff's sale, but not because the restrictions were inapplicable by their terms.

The Court of Appeals relied on cases stating that involuntary transfers fall within the terms of a restriction only if the language of the restrictions specifically identifies them. *F.B.I. Farms,* 769 N.E.2d at 692. This doctrine has been developed largely in cases involving intestate transfers by a decedent, *Stern v. Stern,* 146 F.2d 870, 870 (D.C. Cir. 1945), and in marriage dissolution proceedings where a transfer is made to a spouse. *Castonguay v. Castonguay,* 306 N.W.2d 143, 146 (Minn. 1981).

The sheriff's sale where Moore purchased Linda's shares was an involuntary transfer. Transfers ordered incident to marriage dissolutions and transfers under intestate law may also be deemed involuntary. We think the governing principle is not the same for all forms of "involuntary" transfers. The language of the restrictions in this case does not specifically refer to involuntary transfers of any kind. Rather, it seems to contemplate restricting all transfers, voluntary and involuntary, by providing that no stock of the corporation should be "transferred, assigned, exchanged, divided, or sold" without complying with the restrictions. The intent of the parties is thus rather plain: to restrict ownership to the designated group, and to preclude transfer by any means. The question is whether that intent should be permitted to prevail in the face of countervailing policies.

Transfer by intestacy is in some sense involuntary, but it may also be viewed as a voluntary act of the decedent who had the option to leave a will. If a transfer could not be made by gift during lifetime, for example, to an offspring regarded by other shareholders as an undesirable partner, we see no reason to permit it at death by the decedent's choice to die intestate. There are, however, forms of involuntary transfers that a private agreement may not prevent because the agreement would unreasonably interfere with the rights of third parties. In a dissolution, the interests of the spouse require permitting transfer over the stated intent of the parties. Similarly, creditors of the shareholder cannot be stymied by a private agreement that renders foreclosure of a lien impossible. For that reason, we agree with the trial court that the sheriff's sale transferred the shares to Moore despite the restrictions. Transfer restrictions cannot preclude transfer in a foreclosure sale and thereby leave creditors without recourse. This does not turn on a doctrine of construction. Rather we hold that requiring an explicit bar specifically naming transfer by intestacy or by testamentary disposition should not be necessary. If the language purports to bar all transfers, and by its terms would apply to intestacy, devise or any other means of transfer, it should be given effect unless the restriction violates some policy.

Although we agree with Moore that he could purchase the shares at the sale, it is also the case that he purchased the shares with knowledge of the restrictions. We conclude that he could not acquire more property rights than were possessed by Linda as his seller. U.C.C. § 8-302 (1994) (the purchaser of an investment security acquires the rights in the security his transferor had or had actual authority to convey). The shares in Linda's hands were valued with restrictions in place, and therefore it is not unfair to her creditors that a purchaser at a foreclosure sale acquire the disputed shares subject to the same restrictions, and with whatever lessened value that produces. To be sure, the effect of such a restriction may be to make the shares unmarketable to any buyer. But the creditor retains the option to bid at the sale and, if successful, succeed to the shareholders' interest. The creditor then gets the assets the debtor used to secure the underlying obligation. If the creditor wants collateral free of restrictions, the creditor must negotiate for that at the outset of the arrangement.

CONCLUSION

We affirm the trial court's ruling that F.B.I. Farms did not cancel the shares prior to the sheriff's sale where Moore reacquired them. We also uphold the trial court's finding that the transfer restrictions did not prevent the sheriff's sale, and that the transfer restrictions remain applicable to the shares in Moore's hands. We reverse the trial court's ruling that the two disputed transfer restrictions are unreasonable and therefore unenforceable, and find that the director-approval and blood-member restrictions are reasonable and enforceable. The case is remanded for further proceedings consistent with this opinion.

. . .

Post-Case Follow-Up

As the *F.B.I. Farms* case notes, consent restraints are subject to conflicting authority. The following excerpt from the New York case *Rafe v. Hinden*, 288 N.Y.S.2d 662 (App. Div. 1968) (internal citations omitted) speaks to this issue:

> There is a conflict of authority in other States on the subject of the validity of a restriction on the transfer of stock in a close corporation without the consent of either all or a stated percentage of the other stockholders or the board of directors of the corporation.
>
> In *Longyear v. Hardman*, 219 Mass. 405, 106 N.E. 1012, it was held that a provision in a certificate of incorporation that none of the shares of stock shall be sold without the consent of the holders of three quarters of the stock was not palpably unreasonable or unconscionable because in a small business corporation there is a personal relation analogous to a partnership and there should be retained the right to choose one's associates; harmony of purpose and of business methods and ideals among stockholders may be a significant element in success.
>
> In *Wright v. Iredell Tel. Co.*, 182 N.C. 308, 108 S.E. 744, it was held that a provision in a certificate of incorporation that shares of stock shall not be transferred unless approved by the directors was valid, where the board of directors had acted in good faith and in the absence of allegation or proof of arbitrary, oppressive, or unreasonable conduct.
>
> In *Tracey v. Franklin*, 31 Del. Ch. 477, 67 A.2d 56, 11 A.L.R.2d 990, affg. 30 Del. Ch. 407, 61 A.2d 780, it was held that a provision whereby two stockholders in a close corporation agreed not to sell their shares, except on the consent of both, was invalid because a restraint on alienation of property is against public policy; and that the fact that two stockholders wish to solidify ownership in themselves is not a legally sufficient purpose to justify the restraint on alienation. . . .
>
> In New York certificates of stock are regarded as personal property and are subject to the rule that there be no unreasonable restraint on alienation. . . .
>
> A provision in a lease against subletting without the landlord's consent permits the lessor to refuse arbitrarily to consent, for any reason or for no reason, unless the lease provides that the lessor's consent shall not be unreasonably withheld. . . . The same rule is applicable to assignments of certificates of stock, where the consent of another stockholder to the assignment is required.
>
> The legend on the stock certificate at bar contains no provision that the individual defendant's consent may not be unreasonably withheld. Since the individual defendant is thus given the arbitrary power to forbid a transfer of the shares of stock by the plaintiff, the restriction amounts to annihilation of property. The restriction is not only not reasonable, but it is against public policy and, therefore, illegal. It is an unwarrantable and unlawful restraint on the sale of personal property, the sale and interchange of which the law favors, and in restraint of trade.

Id. at 664-65. As statutory and common law rules respecting restraints on alienation vary from jurisdiction to jurisdiction, be sure to research applicable rules when drafting or litigating any share transfer restrictions.

F.B.I. Farms, Inc. v. Moore: Real Life Application

Sarah is considering investing in Acme Corp., a New York corporation. After inspecting the relevant corporate documents, she sees the following language: "No shareholder of Acme may sell or otherwise transfer his or her shares to any third party without the consent of Acme's board of directors. Such consent may be withheld for any reason, or no reason at all." Sarah asks you whether this consent restraint is reasonable. After researching New York law, please advise Sarah. As Sarah's lawyer, are there any revisions to the consent constraint that you might suggest?

3. Spotlight: Operation of Close Corporations and Management Flexibility

As noted above, close corporations tend to operate more informally than large, publicly held corporations, and shareholders often serve as officers, directors, and employees (in addition to their role as shareholders) and are involved in day-to-day operations. The less formal, less director-centric governance of many closely held corporations in practice has the potential to run afoul of the centralized management structure embedded in state statutes. Recognizing this, many states allow shareholders of close corporations to opt into a more flexible governance structure. For example, § 623(b) and (c) of the New York Business Corporation Law allow close corporations to include provisions in their charters respecting shareholder involvement in management. Note well, however, that these provisions apply only to non-public corporations:

> (b) A provision in the certificate of incorporation otherwise prohibited by law because it improperly restricts the board in its management of the business of the corporation, or improperly transfers to one or more shareholders or to one or more persons or corporations to be selected by him or them, all or any part of such management otherwise within the authority of the board under this chapter, shall nevertheless be valid:
>> (1) If all the incorporators or holders of record of all outstanding shares, whether or not having voting power, have authorized such provision in the certificate of incorporation or an amendment thereof; and
>> (2) If subsequent to the adoption of such provision, shares are transferred or issued only to persons who had knowledge or notice thereof or consented in writing to such provision.
> (c) A provision authorized by paragraph (b) shall be valid only so long as no shares of the corporation are listed on a national securities exchange or regularly quoted in an over-the-counter market by one or more members of a national or affiliated securities association.

The MBCA likewise authorizes agreements among shareholders of non-public corporations respecting shareholder involvement in management. As with New York's statute, the MBCA thus recognizes that shareholders of close corporations may desire a more flexible governance structure, without a strict separation of management and control:

MBCA § 7.32. SHAREHOLDER AGREEMENTS

(a) An agreement among the shareholders of a corporation that complies with this section is effective among the shareholders and the corporation even though it is inconsistent with one or more other provisions of this Act in that it:

(1) eliminates the board of directors or restricts the discretion or powers of the board of directors;

(2) governs the authorization or making of distributions whether or not in proportion to ownership of shares, subject to the limitations in section 6.40;

(3) establishes who shall be directors or officers of the corporation, or their terms of office or manner of selection or removal;

(4) governs, in general or in regard to specific matters, the exercise or division of voting power by or between the shareholders and directors or by or among any of them, including use of weighted voting rights or director proxies;

(5) establishes the terms and conditions of any agreement for the transfer or use of property or the provision of services between the corporation and any shareholder, director, officer or employee of the corporation or among any of them;

(6) transfers to one or more shareholders or other persons all or part of the authority to exercise the corporate powers or to manage the business and affairs of the corporation, including the resolution of any issue about which there exists a deadlock among directors or shareholders;

(7) requires dissolution of the corporation at the request of one or more of the shareholders or upon the occurrence of a specified event or contingency; or

(8) otherwise governs the exercise of the corporate powers or the management of the business and affairs of the corporation or the relationship among the shareholders, the directors and the corporation, or among any of them, and is not contrary to public policy.

(b) An agreement authorized by this section shall be:

(1) as set forth (A) in the articles of incorporation or bylaws and approved by all persons who are shareholders at the time of the agreement or (B) in a written agreement that is signed by all persons who are shareholders at the time of the agreement and is made known to the corporation;

(2) subject to amendment only by all persons who are shareholders at the time of the amendment, unless the agreement provides otherwise; and

(3) valid for 10 years, unless the agreement provides otherwise.

(c) The existence of an agreement authorized by this section shall be noted conspicuously on the front or back of each certificate for outstanding shares or on the information statement required by section 6.26(b). If at the time of the agreement the corporation has shares outstanding represented by certificates, the corporation shall recall the outstanding certificates and issue substitute certificates that comply with this subsection. The failure to note the existence of the agreement on the certificate or information statement shall not affect the validity of the agreement or any action taken pursuant to it. Any purchaser of shares who, at the time of purchase, did not have knowledge of the existence of the agreement shall be entitled to rescission of the purchase. A purchaser shall be deemed to have knowledge of the existence of the agreement if its existence is noted on the certificate or information statement for the shares in compliance with this subsection and, if the shares are not represented by a certificate, the information statement is delivered to the purchaser at or prior to the time of purchase of the shares. An action to enforce the right of rescission authorized by this subsection must be commenced within the earlier of 90 days after discovery of the existence of the agreement or two years after the time of purchase of the shares.

(d) An agreement authorized by this section shall cease to be effective when the corporation becomes a public corporation. If the agreement ceases to be effective for any reason, the board of directors may, if the agreement is contained or referred to in the corporation's articles of incorporation or bylaws, adopt an amendment to the articles of incorporation or bylaws, without shareholder action, to delete the agreement and any references to it.

(e) An agreement authorized by this section that limits the discretion or powers of the board of directors shall relieve the directors of, and impose upon the person or persons in whom such discretion or powers are vested, liability for acts or omissions imposed by law on directors to the extent that the discretion or powers of the directors are limited by the agreement.

(f) The existence or performance of an agreement authorized by this section shall not be a ground for imposing personal liability on any shareholder for the acts or debts of the corporation even if the agreement or its performance treats the corporation as if it were a partnership or results in failure to observe the corporate formalities otherwise applicable to the matters governed by the agreement.

(g) Incorporators or subscribers for shares may act as shareholders with respect to an agreement authorized by this section if no shares have been issued when the agreement is made.

MBCA § 7.32. Note that if shareholders act like directors in managing the corporation, they generally will be subject to the liabilities and fiduciary duties of directors.

In the past, courts disfavored shareholder agreements that vested managerial authority in an individual or body other than the board of directors. *See, e.g., McQuade v. Stoneham*, 189 N.E. 234 (N.Y. 1934) (holding "stockholders may not, by agreement among themselves, control the directors in the exercise of judgment vested in them by virtue of their office to elect officers and fix salaries. . . . Directors may not by agreements entered into by stockholders abrogate their independent judgment."). More recently, however, the MBCA and state legislatures have added provisions to corporations codes like those cited above validating shareholder agreements respecting management. *See also* DGCL § 350 (providing that a "written agreement among the stockholders of a close corporation holding a majority of the outstanding stock entitled to vote, whether solely among themselves or with a party not a stockholder, is not invalid, as between the parties to the agreement, on the ground that it so relates to the conduct of the business and affairs of the corporation as to restrict or interfere with the discretion or powers of the board of directors. The effect of any such agreement shall be to relieve the directors and impose upon the stockholders who are parties to the agreement the liability for managerial acts or omissions which is imposed on directors to the extent and so long as the discretion or powers of the board in its management of corporate affairs is controlled by such agreement.").

Note that a shareholder agreement intended to fall under these kinds of statutory authorizations generally must meet certain requirements. For example, agreements intended to fall under MBCA § 7.32's safe harbor must be set forth in the corporation's charter or bylaws and approved by all persons who are shareholders at the time of the agreement or approved in a written agreement that is signed by all persons who are shareholders at the time of the agreement and is made known to the corporation. *See* MBCA § 7.32. In addition, the existence of the agreement must be noted conspicuously on the front or back of each certificate for outstanding shares or in the information statement required under § 6.26(b). *Id.* That said, § 7.32 is styled as a safe harbor provision for shareholders agreements containing provisions that otherwise might conflict with generally applicable corporate law statutes. Failure to comply with these requirements does not mean that a shareholders' agreement is automatically unenforceable under § 7.32. It just means the agreement does not fall within the § 7.32 safe harbor.

E. JUDICIAL DISSOLUTION OF CLOSE CORPORATIONS

Although we address the termination of corporate existence more generally in Chapter 11, we highlight one method of terminating corporate existence here — namely, judicial dissolution — because some jurisdictions have special rights, protections, or procedures relating to the judicial dissolution of close corporations. As we have observed throughout this chapter, special rules applicable to close corporations reflect the delicate balance that can exist between controlling shareholders of close corporations and shareholders holding a minority stake. For example, a common scenario that can threaten the continued existence of a close corporation is deadlock among directors or shareholders that results in corporate paralysis. Another common scenario that can lead to strife is oppressive conduct by controlling shareholders designed to "freeze out" minority shareholders or conduct designed to put pressure on minority shareholders to exit their investment.

Depending on the circumstances and the law of the applicable jurisdiction, dissatisfied shareholders may be able to initiate court action to seek relief. A court might appoint a custodian or provisional director until deadlocked issues are resolved and the corporation's business can again be conducted for the advantage of the shareholders. A court also might appoint a custodian to manage corporate business to protect the interests of shareholders or might order a forced buyout of shares of oppressed minority shareholders. If all else fails, the most drastic remedy is a court-ordered involuntary dissolution; it is a last resort, which is appropriate only after other approaches to resolving the dispute have failed. In this section, we examine some of the special rules and procedures applicable to the judicial dissolution of close corporations.

Judicial Dissolution and Minority Shareholders in Close Corporations

Although a corporation may be dissolved any time after it is formed, voluntary dissolutions can be tricky in the close corporation context — especially in situations where directors act fraudulently or waste corporate assets or where directors associated with a control group are opposed to dissolution. Negligent (or worse) directors are not likely to pass a resolution to dissolve a corporation they are in the process of looting, and, if the directors own stock in the corporation, the unanimous shareholder consent often needed to effect a voluntary dissolution is impossible to obtain, because acting in their capacity as shareholders, the directors will not vote for dissolution. In situations such as these, a shareholder can institute a legal action and request that a court dissolve the corporation. To prevail, the shareholder must generally establish one of the following:

1. The directors are deadlocked in managing the business affairs of the corporation and irreparable injury is being suffered or threatened to the corporation to the detriment of the shareholders;
2. Corporate management has acted in an illegal, oppressive, or fraudulent manner;
3. The shareholders are deadlocked and have failed to elect directors at two successive annual meetings; or
4. The corporate assets are being wasted or misapplied.

For example, § 14.30(a)(2) of the MBCA states that a court may dissolve a corporation whose shares are not listed on a stock exchange; quoted on a system owned by the NASD; or held by at least 300 shareholders and having shares with a market value of at least $20 million in a proceeding initiated by a shareholder in the following circumstances:

> (2) in a proceeding by a shareholder if it is established that:
> (i) the directors are deadlocked in the management of the corporate affairs, the shareholders are unable to break the deadlock, and irreparable injury to the corporation is threatened or being suffered, or the business and affairs of the corporation can no longer be conducted to the advantage of the shareholders generally, because of the deadlock;
> (ii) the directors or those in control of the corporation have acted, are acting, or will act in a manner that is illegal, oppressive, or fraudulent;
> (iii) the shareholders are deadlocked in voting power and have failed, for a period that includes at least two consecutive annual meeting dates, to elect successors to directors whose terms have expired; or
> (iv) the corporate assets are being misapplied or wasted;

As another example, in New York, shareholders representing 20 percent or more of the votes of the outstanding shares of privately held companies have the right to seek judicial dissolution in cases of fraud or illegal or oppressive conduct:

> The holders of shares representing twenty percent or more of the votes of all outstanding shares of a corporation, other than a corporation registered as an investment company under an act of congress entitled "Investment Company Act of 1940," no shares of which are listed on a national securities exchange or regularly quoted in an over-the-counter market by one or more members of a national or an affiliated securities association, entitled to vote in an election of directors may present a petition of dissolution on one or more of the following grounds:
> (1) The directors or those in control of the corporation have been guilty of illegal, fraudulent or oppressive actions toward the complaining shareholders;
> (2) The property or assets of the corporation are being looted, wasted, or diverted for non-corporate purposes by its directors, officers or those in control of the corporation.

NYBCL § 1104-a. In deciding whether to grant a petition seeking judicial dissolution under this provision, New York courts must take into account whether liquidation is the only way for the petitioners to obtain a fair return on their investment and whether liquidation is reasonably necessary for the protection of the rights and interests of a substantial number of the shareholders of the company. *See* NYBCL § 1104-a. Moreover, under § 1118 of the NYBCL, controlling shareholders may be able to avoid dissolution through a statutory buyout mechanism. *See* NYBCL § 1118.

The ability of a shareholder to bring an action for involuntary dissolution typically is available only if the corporation's stock is not publicly traded. This is because shareholders of corporations whose stock is publicly traded are protected because they can sell their shares on the open market.

Case Preview

In re Judicial Dissolution of Kemp & Beatley, Inc.

Although statutes such as the New York Business Corporation Law provision cited above reference oppressive and fraudulent conduct as grounds for judicial dissolution of qualifying close corporations, these statutes often do not define or discuss what constitutes oppressive or fraudulent conduct as a statutory matter. Instead, we must look to the common law to see what these terms mean. Reviewing the case law, minority shareholder oppression often involves (i) an owner-operated business that does not pay stock dividends; (ii) where the controlling shareholder terminates the minority shareholder's employment, thereby cutting the minority shareholder off from salary, bonus, etc.; and (iii) where the controlling shareholder also removes the minority shareholder from the board, thereby preventing the minority shareholder from having any voice in management. When reading the next case, be on the lookout for facts such as these, and consider the following questions:

1. Does the New York statute define what constitutes oppressive or fraudulent conduct?
2. How did the referee define these terms?
3. What did the defendants allegedly do wrong, according to the plaintiffs? What about the dividend policy was alleged to be oppressive or fraudulent?
4. Why did the referee conclude that dissolution was warranted?
5. According to the Court of Appeals, did the courts below abuse their discretion in finding that dissolution was the only feasible means whereby the petitioners might reasonably expect to obtain a fair return on their investment? Why or why not?
6. The court states that "[m]ajority conduct should not be deemed oppressive simply because the petitioner's subjective hopes and desires in joining the venture are not fulfilled. Disappointment alone should not necessarily be equated with oppression." What do you make of this?

7. What do you make of the court's statement that "oppression should be deemed to arise only when the majority conduct substantially defeats expectations that, objectively viewed, were both reasonable under the circumstances and were central to the petitioner's decision to join the venture"?
8. What is the reasonable expectation standard?

In re Judicial Dissolution of Kemp & Beatley, Inc.
473 N.E.2d 1173 (N.Y. 1984)

COOKE, Chief Judge.*

When the majority shareholders of a close corporation award *de facto* dividends to all shareholders except a class of minority shareholders, such a policy may constitute "oppressive actions" and serve as a basis for an order made pursuant to section 1104-a of the Business Corporation Law dissolving the corporation. In the instant matter, there is sufficient evidence to support the lower courts' conclusion that the majority shareholders had altered a long-standing policy to distribute corporate earnings on the basis of stock ownership, as against petitioners only. Moreover, the courts did not abuse their discretion by concluding that dissolution was the only means by which petitioners could gain a fair return on their investment.

I

The business concern of Kemp & Beatley, incorporated under the laws of New York, designs and manufactures table linens and sundry tabletop items. The company's stock consists of 1,500 outstanding shares held by eight shareholders. Petitioner Dissin had been employed by the company for 42 years when, in June 1979, he resigned. Prior to resignation, Dissin served as vice-president and a director of Kemp & Beatley. Over the course of his employment, Dissin had acquired stock in the company and currently owns 200 shares.

Petitioner Gardstein, like Dissin, had been a long-time employee of the company. Hired in 1944, Gardstein was for the next 35 years involved in various aspects of the business including material procurement, product design, and plant management. His employment was terminated by the company in December 1980. He currently owns 105 shares of Kemp & Beatley stock.

Apparent unhappiness surrounded petitioners' leaving the employ of the company. Of particular concern was that they no longer received any distribution of the company's earnings. Petitioners considered themselves to be "frozen out" of the company; whereas it had been their experience when with the company to receive a distribution of the company's earnings according to their stockholdings, in the form of either dividends or extra compensation, that distribution was no longer forthcoming.

---

*Footnotes have been omitted for purposes of brevity.

Gardstein and Dissin, together holding 20.33% of the company's outstanding stock, commenced the instant proceeding in June 1981, seeking dissolution of Kemp & Beatley pursuant to section 1104-a of the Business Corporation Law. Their petition alleged "fraudulent and oppressive" conduct by the company's board of directors such as to render petitioners' stock "a virtually worthless asset." Supreme Court referred the matter for a hearing, which was held in March 1982.

Upon considering the testimony of petitioners and the principals of Kemp & Beatley, the referee concluded that "the corporate management has by its policies effectively rendered petitioners' shares worthless, and * * * the only way petitioners can expect any return is by dissolution." Petitioners were found to have invested capital in the company expecting, among other things, to receive dividends or "bonuses" based upon their stock holdings. Also found was the company's "established buy-out policy" by which it would purchase the stock of employee shareholders upon their leaving its employ.

The involuntary-dissolution statute (Business Corporation Law, § 1104-a) permits dissolution when a corporation's controlling faction is found guilty of "oppressive action" toward the complaining shareholders. The referee considered oppression to arise when "those in control" of the corporation "have acted in such a manner as to defeat those expectations of the minority stockholders which formed the basis of [their] participation in the venture." The expectations of petitioners that they would not be arbitrarily excluded from gaining a return on their investment and that their stock would be purchased by the corporation upon termination of employment, were deemed defeated by prevailing corporate policies. Dissolution was recommended in the referee's report, subject to giving respondent corporation an opportunity to purchase petitioners' stock.

Supreme Court confirmed the referee's report. It, too, concluded that due to the corporation's new dividend policy petitioners had been prevented from receiving any return on their investments. Liquidation of the corporate assets was found the only means by which petitioners would receive a fair return. The court considered judicial dissolution of a corporation to be "a serious and severe remedy." Consequently, the order of dissolution was conditioned upon the corporation's being permitted to purchase petitioners' stock. The Appellate Division affirmed, without opinion. 99 A.D.2d 445, 471 N.Y.S.2d 245.

At issue in this appeal is the scope of section 1104-a of the Business Corporation Law. Specifically, this court must determine whether the provision for involuntary dissolution when the "directors or those in control of the corporation have been guilty of * * * oppressive actions toward the complaining shareholders" was properly applied in the circumstances of this case. We hold that it was, and therefore affirm.

II

Judicially ordered dissolution of a corporation at the behest of minority interests is a remedy of relatively recent vintage in New York. Historically, this State's courts were considered divested of equity jurisdiction to order dissolution, as statutory prescriptions were deemed exclusive (see *Hitch v. Hawley,* 132 N.Y. 212, 217, 30 N.E. 401). Statutes permitting judicial dissolution of corporations either limited the types of corporations under their purview (see L. 1817, ch. 146, §§ 1-4; see, also, *Matter of Niagara Ins. Co.,* 1 Paige Ch. 258) or restricted the parties who could petition for dissolution to the Attorney-General, or the directors, trustees, or majority shareholders of the corporation (see *Hitch v. Hawley,* 132 N.Y., at pp. 218-219, 30 N.E. 401, *supra;* see, generally, Business Corporation Law, §§ 1101-1104).

Minority shareholders were granted standing in the absence of statutory authority to seek dissolution of corporations when controlling shareholders engaged in certain egregious conduct. . . . Predicated on the majority shareholders' fiduciary obligation to treat all shareholders fairly and equally, to preserve corporate assets, and to fulfill their responsibilities of corporate management with "scrupulous good faith," the courts' equitable power can be invoked when "it appears that the directors and majority shareholders 'have so palpably breached the fiduciary duty they owe to the minority shareholders that they are disqualified from exercising the exclusive discretion and the dissolution power given to them by statute.' " . . . True to the ancient principle that equity jurisdiction will not lie when there exists a remedy at law . . . , the courts have not entertained a minority's petition in equity when their rights and interests could be adequately protected in a legal action, such as by a shareholder's derivative suit. . . .

Supplementing this principle of judicially ordered equitable dissolution of a corporation, the Legislature has shown a special solicitude toward the rights of minority shareholders of closely held corporations by enacting section 1104-a of the Business Corporation Law. That statute provides a mechanism for the holders of at least 20% of the outstanding shares of a corporation whose stock is not traded on a securities market to petition for its dissolution "under special circumstances" (see Business Corporation Law, § 1104-a, subd. [a]). The circumstances that give rise to dissolution fall into two general classifications: mistreatment of complaining shareholders (subd. [a], par. [1]), or misappropriation of corporate assets (subd. [a], par. [2]) by controlling shareholders, directors or officers.

Section 1104-a (subd. [a], par. [1]) describes three types of proscribed activity: "illegal," "fraudulent," and "oppressive" conduct. The first two terms are familiar words that are commonly understood at law. The last, however, does not enjoy the same certainty gained through long usage. As no definition is provided by the statute, it falls upon the courts to provide guidance. . . .

The statutory concept of "oppressive actions" can, perhaps, best be understood by examining the characteristics of close corporations and the Legislature's general purpose in creating this involuntary-dissolution statute. It is widely understood that, in addition to supplying capital to a contemplated or ongoing enterprise and expecting a fair and equal return, parties comprising the ownership of a close corporation may expect to be actively involved in its management and operation. . . . The small ownership cluster seeks to "contribute their capital, skills, experience and labor" toward the corporate enterprise. . . .

As a leading commentator in the field has observed: "Unlike the typical shareholder in a publicly held corporation, who may be simply an investor or a speculator and cares nothing for the responsibilities of management, the shareholder in a close corporation is a co-owner of the business and wants the privileges and powers that go with ownership. His participation in that particular corporation is often his principal or sole source of income. As a matter of fact, providing employment for himself may have been the principal reason why he participated in organizing the corporation. He may or may not anticipate an ultimate profit from the sale of his interest, but he normally draws very little from the corporation as dividends. In his capacity as an officer or employee of the corporation, he looks to his salary for the principal return on his capital investment, because earnings of a close corporation, as is well known, are distributed in major part in salaries, bonuses and retirement benefits." (O'Neal, Close Corporations [2d ed.], § 1.07, at pp. 21-22 [n. omitted].)

Shareholders enjoy flexibility in memorializing these expectations through agreements setting forth each party's rights and obligations in corporate governance. . . . In the absence of such an agreement, however, ultimate decision-making power respecting corporate policy will be reposed in the holders of a majority interest in the corporation (see, e.g., Business Corporation Law, §§ 614, 708). A wielding of this power by any group controlling a corporation may serve to destroy a stockholder's vital interests and expectations.

As the stock of closely held corporations generally is not readily salable, a minority shareholder at odds with management policies may be without either a voice in protecting his or her interests or any reasonable means of withdrawing his or her investment. This predicament may fairly be considered the legislative concern underlying the provision at issue in this case; inclusion of the criteria that the corporation's stock not be traded on securities markets and that the complaining shareholder be subject to oppressive actions supports this conclusion.

Defining oppressive conduct as distinct from illegality in the present context has been considered in other forums. The question has been resolved by considering oppressive actions to refer to conduct that substantially defeats the "reasonable expectations" held by minority shareholders in committing their capital to the particular enterprise. . . . This concept is consistent with the apparent purpose underlying the provision under review. A shareholder who reasonably expected that ownership in the corporation would entitle him or her to a job, a share of corporate earnings, a place in corporate management, or some other form of security, would be oppressed in a very real sense when others in the corporation seek to defeat those expectations and there exists no effective means of salvaging the investment.

Given the nature of close corporations and the remedial purpose of the statute, this court holds that utilizing a complaining shareholder's "reasonable expectations" as a means of identifying and measuring conduct alleged to be oppressive is appropriate. A court considering a petition alleging oppressive conduct must investigate what the majority shareholders knew, or should have known, to be the petitioner's expectations in entering the particular enterprise. Majority conduct should not be deemed oppressive simply because the petitioner's subjective hopes and desires in joining the venture are not fulfilled. Disappointment alone should not necessarily be equated with oppression.

Rather, oppression should be deemed to arise only when the majority conduct substantially defeats expectations that, objectively viewed, were both reasonable under the circumstances and were central to the petitioner's decision to join the venture. It would be inappropriate, however, for us in this case to delineate the contours of the courts' consideration in determining whether directors have been guilty of oppressive conduct. As in other areas of the law, much will depend on the circumstances in the individual case.

The appropriateness of an order of dissolution is in every case vested in the sound discretion of the court considering the application (see Business Corporation Law, § 1111, subd. [a]). Under the terms of this statute, courts are instructed to consider both whether "liquidation of the corporation is the only feasible means" to protect the complaining shareholder's expectation of a fair return on his or her investment and whether dissolution "is reasonably necessary" to protect "the rights or interests of any substantial number of shareholders" not limited to those complaining (Business Corporation Law, § 1104-a, subd. [b], pars. [1], [2]). Implicit in this direction is that once oppressive conduct is found, consideration must be given to the totality of circumstances surrounding the current state of corporate affairs and relations to determine whether some remedy short of or other than dissolution constitutes a feasible means of satisfying both the petitioner's expectations and the rights and interests of any other substantial group of shareholders (see, also, Business Corporation Law, § 1111, subd. [b], par. [1]).

By invoking the statute, a petitioner has manifested his or her belief that dissolution may be the only appropriate remedy. Assuming the petitioner has set forth a prima facie case of oppressive conduct, it should be incumbent upon the parties seeking to forestall dissolution to demonstrate to the court the existence of an adequate, alternative remedy (cf. *Baker v. Commercial Body Bldrs.*, 264 Or. 614, 507 P.2d 387, *supra*; *White v. Perkins*, 213 Va. 129, 189 S.E.2d 315). A court has broad latitude in fashioning alternative relief, but when fulfillment of the oppressed petitioner's expectations by these means is doubtful, such as when there has been a complete deterioration of relations between the parties, a court should not hesitate to order dissolution. Every order of dissolution, however, must be conditioned upon permitting any shareholder of the corporation to elect to purchase the complaining shareholder's stock at fair value (see Business Corporation Law, § 1118).

One further observation is in order. The purpose of this involuntary dissolution statute is to provide protection to the minority shareholder whose reasonable expectations in undertaking the venture have been frustrated and who has no adequate means of recovering his or her investment. It would be contrary to this remedial purpose to permit its use by minority shareholders as merely a coercive tool (see Davidian, *op. cit.*, 56 St. John's L. Rev. 24, 59-60, and nn. 159-160). Therefore, the minority shareholder whose own acts, made in bad faith and undertaken with a view toward forcing an involuntary dissolution, give rise to the complained-of oppression should be given no quarter in the statutory protection (cf. *Mardikos v. Arger*, 116 Misc. 2d 1028, 1032, 457 N.Y.S.2d 371, *supra*).

III

There was sufficient evidence presented at the hearing to support the conclusion that Kemp & Beatley had a long-standing policy of awarding *de facto* dividends based on stock ownership in the form of "extra compensation bonuses." Petitioners, both of whom had extensive experience in the management of the company, testified to this effect. Moreover, both related that receipt of this compensation, whether as true dividends or disguised as "extra compensation," was a known incident to ownership of the company's stock understood by all of the company's principals. Finally, there was uncontroverted proof that this policy was changed either shortly before or shortly after petitioners' employment ended. Extra compensation was still awarded by the company. The only difference was that stock ownership was no longer a basis for the payments; it was asserted that the basis became services rendered to the corporation. It was not unreasonable for the fact finder to have determined that this change in policy amounted to nothing less than an attempt to exclude petitioners from gaining any return on their investment through the mere recharacterization of distributions of corporate income. Under the circumstances of this case, there was no error in determining that this conduct constituted oppressive action within the meaning of section 1104-a of the Business Corporation Law.

Nor may it be said that Supreme Court abused its discretion in ordering Kemp & Beatley's dissolution, subject to an opportunity for a buy-out of petitioners' shares. After the referee had found that the controlling faction of the company was, in effect, attempting to "squeeze-out" petitioners by offering them no return on their investment and increasing other executive compensation, respondents, in opposing the report's confirmation, attempted only to controvert the factual basis of the report. They suggested no feasible, alternative remedy to the forced dissolution. In light of an apparent deterioration in relations between petitioners and the governing shareholders of Kemp & Beatley, it was not unreasonable for the court to have determined that a forced buy-out of petitioners' shares or liquidation of the corporation's assets was the only means by which petitioners could be guaranteed a fair return on their investments.

Accordingly, the order of the Appellate Division should be modified, with costs to petitioners-respondents, by affirming the substantive determination of that court but extending the time for exercising the option to purchase petitioners-respondents' shares to 30 days following this court's determination.

. . .

Post-Case Follow-Up

Because dissolution is such a drastic remedy, MBCA § 14.34 and many state statutes provide that if a shareholder petitions to dissolve the corporation for one of the grounds just specified, as an alternative to dissolution, the corporation or another shareholder(s) may elect to purchase all of the shares owned by the complaining shareholder at their fair market value. *See, e.g.,* NYBCL § 1118 ("In any proceeding brought pursuant to section eleven hundred four-a of this chapter, any other shareholder or shareholders or the corporation may, at any time within ninety days after the filing of such petition or at such later time as the court in its discretion may allow, elect to purchase the shares owned by the petitioners at their fair value and upon such terms and conditions as may be approved by the court, including the conditions of paragraph (c) herein. An election pursuant to this section shall be irrevocable unless the court, in its discretion, for just and equitable considerations, determines that such election be revocable.”). Although the election to purchase a complaining shareholder's shares in lieu of dissolution requires a fairly elaborate procedure, it affords a method of protecting a disputing shareholder and yet continuing the corporation for those who wish to see it continue in existence. Other non-dissolution remedies may be available as well, depending on the relevant statutory and common law.

A relatively new provision of the MBCA allows a shareholder to obtain involuntary dissolution in the event the corporation has abandoned its business, but those in control of the corporation have unreasonably delayed in liquidating it and distributing its assets (which may occur if the directors in power wish to continue receiving their salaries). MBCA § 14.30(a)(5). Shareholders may seek to dissolve the corporation on the basis of abandonment even if it is publicly traded.

In re Judicial Dissolution of Kemp & Beatley, Inc.: Real Life Applications

Salwe, Inc. is a Maryland corporation formed by respondents Clark and Jodi, a married couple. Salwe's business is acting as a corporate "head hunter" for the technology industry — meaning that Salwe recruits information technology professionals for placement as consultants at government agencies and private employers. Clark and Jodi were the only shareholders at the time of Salwe's formation, and they served as Salwe's only directors and officers during the first year of Salwe's corporate life.

One year after Salwe was formed, petitioner David joined the business in a "handshake deal." The parties agreed that David would be a 45 percent shareholder and further agreed that he would be responsible for sales and business development. David was made an officer and director of the company, but he never had a formal, written employment agreement with Salwe.

One year into his relationship with Salwe, David formally subscribed to a pre-existing stockholders' agreement. (Clark and Jodi had signed this agreement at the time of formation.) The agreement included a provision requiring any shareholder whose employment was terminated "for good cause" to sell his shares to the corporation or to the remaining shareholders.

For several years, Salwe's business grew and prospered due largely to its success in obtaining federal government contracts. Unfortunately, however, the relationship between David on one hand, and Clark and Jodi on the other, soured over money, hiring, and other issues. In 2014, Clark and Jodi reduced David's salary, citing David's allegedly poor job performance. In 2015, after the parties failed to reach terms on a negotiated buyout of David's shares, Clark and Jodi fired David, citing David's allegedly poor job performance as grounds for his termination.

David filed suit in Maryland state court shortly thereafter. David asserted a direct claim against Salwe for unpaid salary and distributions based upon his status as an employee and shareholder. David also asserted derivative claims against Clark and Jodi on behalf of Salwe alleging breach of fiduciary duty based on upon his termination (which David alleged was unjustified and harmful to the corporation) and the alleged diversion of corporate funds by Clark and Jodi for their personal use. For relief, David sought, alternatively, (i) reinstatement as an employee; or (ii) judicial dissolution of Salwe. Clark and Jodi filed a counterclaim alleging that David had been fired for good cause (poor job performance) and arguing that he was required to sell his stock to the company under the terms of the stockholders' agreement.

In support of his petition for judicial dissolution, David argued that Clark and Jodi had engaged in oppressive conduct — that is, firing David because he had refused to sell his shares of Salwe to the company or Clark and Jodi. David also argued that his job performance had been exemplary and that claims to the contrary were a pretext and retaliation for his refusal to sell his shares. The parties agree that Maryland law applies.

1. Does the Maryland corporations code address whether and under what circumstances a minority shareholder in a closely held corporation may petition for judicial dissolution?
2. Is David eligible to bring an action for judicial dissolution under Maryland Code, Corporations & Associations § 3-413?
3. What grounds will support an action for judicial dissolution under § 343?
4. Assume for purposes of this question that David is able to establish that Clark and Jodi engaged in oppressive conduct. Is the court required to grant David's petition for judicial dissolution?
5. Assume for purposes of this question that David is able to establish that Clark and Jodi engaged in oppressive conduct. Do you think the court is likely to order David's reinstatement as an employee?

Dissolution over the Objections of Minority Shareholders

In corporations in which directors hold large amounts of stock, it may be possible for the directors to force a dissolution over the wishes of minority shareholders. For example, assume a corporation has five directors, three of whom own stock in the corporation in a total amount of 52 percent. The remaining 48 percent of the stock is held by 100 individuals. The three powerful directors could compel a dissolution: Because they constitute a majority of the board, they can pass a directors' resolution recommending dissolution; because they own more than a majority of the outstanding stock, as shareholders their affirmative vote is sufficient to approve a dissolution. If the corporation's business is extremely profitable, these three director-shareholders may decide to force a voluntary dissolution, pay off the 100 individual shareholders, and re-form a corporation by themselves to do the same business and thereby keep all of the profits. Alternatively, as discussed, the director-shareholders could form a new corporation owned solely by them and merge the old corporation into the new one. Under the plan of merger, shareholders of the old corporation will receive cash only; they do not continue as shareholders in the new survivor corporation. This type of oppression is called a **freeze-out** or **squeeze-out**. As noted above, the risk of a freeze-out or squeeze-out, or other oppressive conduct, is particularly acute with close corporations, given the balance of power between controlling and minority shareholders under default rules. Because a freeze-out may be patently inequitable to the minority shareholders, some courts will prevent or enjoin dissolutions or mergers that have the effect of oppressing minority shareholders and have no legitimate business purpose.

Chapter Summary

■ Shareholders have statutory or common law rights, or both, to inspect certain corporate records.

■ Controlling shareholders are shareholders who have the power to exercise control over the corporation and its business, generally through their control of the board of directors or voting power or both. Majority shareholders are presumed to have the power to control the corporation. Shareholders owning less than 50 percent of the corporation's shares *may* be controlling shareholders if they have the ability to exercise actual control over the corporation. Minority shareholders are shareholders who own, individually and in the aggregate, less than 50 percent of the corporation's shares.

■ A close corporation is a corporation owned by a small number of shareholders who often are bound together by family and social (in addition to business) ties. Close corporation statutes generally limit the number of shareholders in a statutory close corporation to 50 or fewer. Close corporations often impose restrictions on the transfer of shares by shareholders. Close corporations also are generally allowed more flexibility in governance and operations compared to other business corporations.

■ Some state corporations codes provide for statutory close corporations. Corporations may elect statutory close corporation status in these jurisdictions via charter provisions. Other jurisdictions do not provide for statutory close corporation elections, but may include statutory provisions relating to management, judicial dissolution, etc., available only to non-public companies.

■ Shareholders in close corporations owe heightened fiduciary duties to the corporation and its other shareholders.

■ As non-controlling shareholders, minority shareholders (particularly minority shareholders in close corporations) are vulnerable to freeze-out or squeeze-out tactics and oppression by controlling shareholders. Minority shareholders may seek to address vulnerabilities associated with their minority ownership stake via negotiated rights and protections such as cumulative voting, heightened quorum or voting requirements, etc.

■ Shareholders may be able to initiate a dissolution in certain circumstances, such as director or shareholder deadlock, waste of assets, or fraud by directors. In lieu of ordering a dissolution, in some states a court can allow the complaining shareholder's shares to be purchased by the corporation or its other shareholders.

Applying the Concepts

1. Do New York, California, and Texas grant shareholders a statutory right to inspect corporate documents?

2. Elliott owns 5 percent of Beta Corp., a close corporation formed in a state that follows the MBCA. Elliot has decided to sell his shares. Where should Elliot look to find out whether there are any restrictions on his proposed share transfer?

3. Sam and Dave each own 50 percent of Zed Corp., a Delaware corporation. Sam and Dave have reached an impasse about whether to dissolve the corporation — Sam would like to dissolve the corporation, but Dave has refused to agree to this. Assume that the charter is silent as to the rights of either shareholder to seek judicial dissolution, and further assume that the parties' shareholder agreement does not address this issue, either. What, if any, options does Sam have under Delaware law?

4. Chiro, Inc. is a Delaware corporation that has elected statutory close corporation treatment via a charter provision. Does Delaware law allow shareholders in Chiro to specify when, and under what circumstances, shareholders may effect a voluntary dissolution of Chiro?

5. Does the Delaware close corporation statute allow for the appointment of a custodian for a close corporation?

6. Under Delaware law, do shareholders have preemptive rights under default rules?

7. Under Delaware law, do shareholders have cumulative voting rights in director elections under default rules?

8. What alternatives to dissolution does the Maryland Court of Appeals recognize in *Bontempo v. Lare*, 119 A.3d 791 (Md. 2015)?

9. In New Jersey, what is the fee to file a certificate of dissolution? What information is required in Paragraph 4?

10. What is the fee in Pennsylvania to file Articles of Dissolution (After Commencement of Business)? What information is required?

11. Conduct a business search in Ohio through the secretary of state's "Business Filing Portal."

   a. What is the status of Brent Johnson Supermarket, Inc.?
   b. Why does the corporation have this status?
   c. What percentage of the shareholder voting power authorized this action?

Business Organizations in Practice

1. You represent Sue, a director and shareholder owning 22 percent of the shares of Beta Corp., a privately held New York corporation. Members of the Smith family own the remaining 78 percent of the company.

   Although Sue previously worked at Beta's offices in a senior executive position, she was fired last year following a dispute with Bob Smith. Bob is the son of Dan Smith. Dan has served as CEO for the past 15 years. Since Sue was fired, Beta has hired several members of the Smith family members as consultants, paying them lucrative consulting fees. Over the same period, Beta has stopped paying dividends to shareholders. Although Sue has petitioned to be re-hired, and also petitioned for the resumption of dividends payments, Beta has refused. Sue believes that the Smith family is trying to freeze her out of the company.

   Sue has hired you to examine her options. Investigate the following issues and draft a memo to sue explaining the state of affairs:

   a. Can Sue force Beta to re-hire her? Assume Sue previously served as an at-will employee and did not have an employment contract with Beta.
   b. Can Sue force Beta to issue dividends?
   c. Is Sue entitled to petition for judicial dissolution under NYBCL § 1104?
   d. Is Sue entitled to petition for judicial dissolution under NYBCL § 1104-a?
   e. What standard/test is a New York court likely to use if Sue contends that she is entitled to judicial dissolution due to oppressive conduct by the Smith family?
   f. Assume for purposes of this question only that Beta is a Delaware corporation. Is Sue entitled to petition for judicial dissolution based on oppressive conduct?

2. Sally, an entrepreneur with chemistry and biology degrees from a leading university, has formed a Delaware corporation to commercialize technology designed to treat obesity. Evan Smith, a well-known Silicon Valley entrepreneur, would like to invest in Sally's company. Evan tells Sally that he wants preemptive rights. Sally asks for your advice.

   a. Will Evan have preemptive rights under default rules?
   b. Should Sally grant Evan preemptive rights? Why or why not?
   c. Are there alternatives that might meet Evan's needs, but still maintain a degree of flexibility in the event Sally's company wants to raise money from professional investors in the future?

3. Terry is a director and minority shareholder in Seria, Inc., a close corporation formed in Massachusetts. Before investing in Seria, Terry negotiated for certain protections, including heightened quorum and voting requirements for board action. Among other provisions, Seria's charter and bylaws state that any agreement to sell all or substantially all of the company's assets must be approved by

all directors. Last week, Seria's board met to consider whether to sell all of the company's assets to Able, Inc., a competitor. Seria's board has seven directors. All but Terry voted in favor of the transaction. Terry did not have a particularly good reason for his vote. He simply was annoyed at the other directors after years of perceived slights, and his financial condition was such that he personally did not need the money that the shareholders stood to receive for their interest in Seria if the transaction went through.

The other directors have hired you to see what, if any, options they might have to overcome Terry's opposition. In preparing to meet with your clients, investigate the following issues:

a. Are there any constraints — including fiduciary or equitable constraints — on Terry's right to exercise veto power (via the unanimous consent requirement)?

b. Would it matter if Terry honestly believed that the transaction was not in the best interest of the company?

4. John founded Forum, Inc., a New York corporation, 20 years ago. Cindy, a licensed engineer, began working at Forum 19 years ago. Cindy became a director of the company (along with John) one year after she began working there. Forum is a construction company.

Ten years ago, as part of a succession plan, John's daughter Eve and Cindy's son Joe joined the business as co-managers. Five years ago, John transferred 75 percent of Forum's stock to Eve and 25 percent of Forum's stock to Cindy (with the idea that Cindy would later transfer the shares to her son Joe). John and Cindy continued to serve as directors after the transfer of share ownership.

Unfortunately, relations between the families soured last year after the tragic death of another of John's sons — Al. Al was a brilliant engineer, and he had been pegged to join Forum as soon as he obtained his masters in civil engineering. Within a few months after Al's death, John told Cindy that he wanted to dissolve Forum. Cindy opposed dissolution. Eventually, things became so dysfunctional that Cindy asked John to buy her out. John refused.

In January 2016, John removed Cindy as director and gave Cindy notice that her employment would be terminated the next month. On February 29, 2016 — one day before her employment was formally terminated — Cindy commenced a proceeding for judicial dissolution of Forum under § 1104-a of the New York Business Corporation Law. Cindy alleged that John engaged in the following conduct, which she alleged to be oppressive: (i) removing Cindy as director; (ii) replacing Cindy as corporate secretary with a member of John's family; (iii) terminating Cindy's employment; (iv) following Cindy's termination, restricting her access to her work computer and e-mail; (v) restricting Cindy's access to customers and employees; (vi) holding secret off-site staff meetings with Forum personnel in which John accused Cindy of improprieties; (vi)firing Cindy's son and dismissing other employees perceived to be loyal to Cindy after refusing Cindy's buyout offer; and (viii) paying himself a $350,000 bonus but paying nothing to Cindy or her son.

a. Assume that Cindy had retained you to negotiate her relationship with Forum *before* she began working with the company.

    i. Would you advise Cindy to enter into an employment agreement with Forum? What, if any, provisions might you advise Cindy to include in an employment agreement?

    ii. What, if any, minority shareholder protections might you advise Cindy to seek via the articles of incorporation, the bylaws, or a shareholders' agreement?

b. Is Cindy eligible to bring an action for judicial dissolution under § 1104-a, given that she owns 25 percent of Forum's stock?

c. Is Cindy's son eligible to bring an action for judicial dissolution based upon his termination?

d. What is the standard for judicial dissolution in New York?

e. Assume you are Cindy's lawyer. What facts would you cite in support of Cindy's petition for judicial dissolution?

f. Assume you are John's lawyer. What facts would you cite in opposition to Cindy's petition?

g. Six months into the litigation, John files a motion seeking to buy out Cindy's interest in Forum. What section of the New York corporations code is John likely to proceed under with regard to this petition? Is John's petition likely to be successful?

h. Assume that Cindy believes John has caused Forum to understate its revenues in an effort to reduce the value of Cindy's stake in the company, should he be permitted to buy out Cindy's interest. Discuss whether there are any steps that Cindy can take prior to litigation to get information about Forum's financial performance.

Changes in the Corporate Structure and Corporate Combinations

Although shareholders do not "get a vote" on day-to-day corporate matters, there are some matters that involve such significant changes to the structure of the corporation that shareholder approval is required. These matters are often referred to as extraordinary matters, and the list of extraordinary matters includes (i) amending of the articles of incorporation; (ii) most mergers, consolidations, share exchanges, and sales of all or substantially all corporate assets; and (iii) dissolution of the corporation. In this chapter, we examine these extraordinary matters, paying particular attention to corporate combinations — both friendly and hostile. One note to students who wish to practice in the area of mergers and acquisitions: Our coverage in this chapter is at an overview level. As with tax, we suggest that you take a course devoted to business combinations (e.g., mergers and acquisitions, corporate transactions) for more in-depth coverage.

Key Concepts

- Amending articles of incorporation and corporate bylaws
- Corporate combinations, including mergers, consolidations, asset purchases, stock purchases, and share exchanges
- Sale of all or substantially all assets (ordinary course versus non-ordinary course transactions)
- Consensual, or friendly, deals versus hostile takeovers
- Tender offers
- Proxy battles
- Transactions involving controlling shareholders
- Domestications and conversions
- Termination of corporate existence

A. AMENDING AND RESTATING THE ARTICLES OF INCORPORATION

1. Reasons for Amending Articles of Incorporation

According to most state statutes and MBCA § 10.01, a corporation may amend its articles (or "charter" or "certificate," if so called by the state) at any time to add or change a provision that was permitted or required in the original articles or to delete any provision not required to be included in the articles of incorporation. Other states identify a list of acceptable amendments in the state's corporations code. The most common reasons for amending the articles are changing the corporation's name and increasing the number of shares the corporation is authorized to issue. The sole test for the validity of an amendment is whether the provision could lawfully have been included (or in the case of a deletion, omitted from) the charter as of the effective date of the amendment.

2. Procedure for Amending Articles

If no shares have yet been issued, the directors or incorporators can amend the articles by themselves. *See, e.g.,* MBCA § 10.02. In addition, some states and the MBCA allow the directors to make certain amendments to the articles without shareholder approval. In general, these amendments are for routine matters that do not affect the basic rights of shareholders. For example, MBCA § 10.05 provides that the board, acting alone, can adopt the following amendments: extending the duration of the corporation; deleting the names and addresses of the initial directors; deleting the name and address of the initial agent for service of process if a statement of change has been filed with the secretary of state; increasing the number of authorized shares to effect a stock split or share dividend (if the corporation has only one class of shares); or changing the corporate name by substituting the words "corporation," "incorporated," "company," or "limited" or the abbreviations "inc.," "co.," "ltd.," or "corp.," for a similar word or abbreviation or by adding, deleting, or changing a geographic attribute for the name.

The most common procedure for amending the articles, however, is discussion of the proposed amendment by the board of directors and then adoption by the board of a resolution setting forth the text of the proposed amendment and directing that it be submitted for shareholder approval. *See, e.g.,* MBCA § 10.03. The board may act at a meeting by majority vote, or may act by written consent, which most states require to be unanimous. *See, e.g.,* MBCA §§ 10.03(a); 8.21. For a sample resolution to amend articles of incorporation, see Exhibit 11.1.

EXHIBIT 11.1   **Resolution to Amend Articles**

> RESOLVED, that Article 1 of the Articles of Incorporation for the Company be amended to read as follows: The name of the corporation is Taylor Visions, Inc.
>
> RESOLVED, that Article 4 of the Articles of Incorporation be deleted in its entirety.
>
> RESOLVED, that Article 6 of the Articles of Incorporation for the Company be added as follows: The holders of shares of the Company shall have preemptive rights to purchase shares issued by the Company from time to time in the respective ratio which the number of shares held by each holder at the time of any issue bears to the total number of shares outstanding at the time of any issue.

If the amendment is required to be approved by the shareholders, the corporation must notify the shareholders of the meeting at which the amendment is to be submitted for approval. Appropriate notice of any such meeting must be given to all shareholders, even those not entitled to vote. The notice of any meeting that will consider an amendment to the articles of incorporation must state the purpose of the meeting and must set forth the text of the proposed amendment. *See, e.g.,* MBCA § 10.03(d). The amendment may be voted on by the shareholders at their annual meeting or at a special meeting. If a class of shareholders has nonvoting stock, and a proposed amendment would affect their rights (e.g., by canceling their preemptive rights), those shareholders must also be allowed to vote on the amendment.

Under the MBCA, the shareholder vote on a proposed amendment to the corporate charter is subject to those rules set forth in the charter and those determined by the board under § 10.03(c). No shareholder has a vested right in any provision of the articles (including provisions relating to management, control, capital structure, dividend entitlement, or purpose or duration of the corporation) such that his individual approval is required before an amendment can be accomplished. *See* MBCA § 10.01(b). Previous versions of the Model Act required first a two-thirds approval and then a majority approval by shareholders. MBCA §§ 7.25 and 10.03(e) now provide that the amendment will be approved if a quorum consisting of at least a majority of votes entitled to be cast on the amendment exists and more votes are cast in favor of it than against it. Most states require a simple majority vote. A few states, however, including Maryland, still require two-thirds approval by shareholders. If the original articles provided that amendments to the articles can only be accomplished by a certain percentage, for example, 75 percent, these requirements will apply unless and until the restrictions or requirements are amended in accordance with governing statutes and charter provisions. If shareholders are allowed to act by written consent, this procedure may also be used to effect an amendment to the articles of incorporation. Finally, be sure to pay attention to voting rules that apply when a corporation has more than one class of shares outstanding. *See, e.g.,* MBCA § 10.04.

3. Articles of Amendment

After the amendment has been approved by the shareholders, the corporation must prepare and file **articles of amendment** (or a **certificate of amendment**) with the secretary of state. Almost all states provide forms for articles of amendment. Most states and MBCA § 10.06(5) also require that the amendment recite that the original articles were amended pursuant to state statute and that the requisite shareholder vote was received or that shareholder approval was not needed. See Exhibit 11.2 for sample articles of amendment.

Rather than require that the entire articles be redrafted, most states allow corporations to simply set forth the text of the new amendment. The articles are then filed with the secretary of state together with the requisite filing fee. After examination of the articles of amendment, the secretary of state will issue a certificate of amendment, or return a copy of the articles of amendment stamped "approved." Any requirements relating to the original articles must also be complied with when amending articles. For example, if the original articles were required to be published or filed with a county clerk, the amended articles must be also. If the amendment changes the corporation's name or authorized number of shares, new stock certificates and a new corporate seal should be obtained.

In some circumstances, a minority of states allow shareholders who dissented from amending the articles to have their shares bought by the corporation at their fair market value. This right to dissent and have one's shares appraised and bought out is generally triggered only by an amendment that seriously impairs or adversely affects one's shares, such as an amendment abolishing some preferential right, preemptive rights, or a right to vote. The MBCA approach is to allow appraisal rights for private (not publicly traded) corporations only when an amendment reduces the number of shares of a shareholder to a fraction of a share, and the corporation will have the obligation or right to repurchase the fractional share from the shareholder, such as is the case when a reverse stock split is accomplished. *See* MBCA § 13.02(a)(4).

If the only change to the articles is a change of corporate name, consider whether the same result can be accomplished by allowing the corporation to do business under a fictitious business name. The cumbersome and somewhat expensive amendment procedure can be avoided by simply filing a fictitious business name statement with the secretary of state or local county clerk. The fictitious business name will allow the corporation to use a name different from the one it was incorporated under without necessitating a formal amendment to the articles of incorporation.

Corporate name changes should be undertaken with all of the precautions used when selecting the original corporate name: A search should be conducted to ensure the name is not confusingly similar to another, a check with the secretary of state should be conducted to ensure the name is available, and, if available, the name should be reserved during the amendment process.

An amendment to a corporation's articles does not affect the rights of any third parties. For example, the fact that a corporation changes its name does not release the corporation from a debt owed to a creditor who originally contracted with the differently named corporation. The corporate debtor remains the same — only its name has changed. Finally, if the corporation is doing business in any other jurisdictions, their state statutes should be reviewed to determine whether an amendment to the articles triggers any filing requirements in the other jurisdictions.

EXHIBIT 11.2 **Washington Articles of Amendment**

Page 1 of 1

Office of the Secretary of State
Corporations & Charities Division

Washington Profit Corporation
See attached detailed instructions

☐ **Filing Fee $30.00**

☐ **Filing Fee with Expedited Service $80.00**

This Box For Office Use Only

UBI Number:

ARTICLES OF AMENDMENT
Chapter 23B.10 RCW

SECTION 1
NAME OF CORPORATION: *(as currently recorded with the Office of the Secretary of State)*

_____

SECTION 2

AMENDMENTS were adopted on this **DATE:** _____

SECTION 3
ARTICLES OF AMENDMENT WERE ADOPTED BY: *(please check <u>one</u> of the following)*

☐   Board of Directors *(shareholder action was not required)*

☐   Duly approved by shareholders in accordance with 23B.10.030 and 23B.10.040 RCW

☐   Incorporators *(shareholder action was not required)*

SECTION 4
AMENDMENTS TO ARTICLES ON FILE: *(if necessary, attach additional information)*

_____

SECTION 5
EFFECTIVE DATE OF ARTICLES OF AMENDMENT: *(please check <u>one</u> of the following)*

☐   Upon filing by the Secretary of State

☐   Specific Date: _____ *(Specified effective date must be within 90 days AFTER the Articles of Amendment have been filed by the Office of the Secretary of State)*

SECTION 6
SIGNATURE *(see instructions page)*
This document is hereby executed under penalties of perjury, and is, to the best of my knowledge, true and correct.

X _____

| Signature | Printed Name/Title | Date | Phone Number |

Profit Corporation - Amendment   Washington Secretary of State   Revised 07/10

Application Exercise 1

You represent Acme Corp., a Delaware corporation that manufactures computer motherboards. Acme would like to amend its articles of incorporation to increase the number of shares authorized to be issued in connection with a proposed merger between Acme and Beta Corp. Acme also would like to change its name to Zeirat, Inc. for reasons having to do with sales and marketing. Prepare a checklist of steps necessary to effect these amendments and prepare all necessary documents.

4. Restating the Articles of Incorporation

Over a period of time, a corporation may amend its articles several times. If each document filed with the secretary of state contains only the amending language rather than setting forth all of the articles, the articles may become difficult to read. For example, if a corporation filed its original articles in 2000 and thereafter amended them three times, anyone attempting to review the articles would need to compare all four documents. Therefore, all states allow a corporation to restate its articles by combining the original articles with any later amendments into one clean document that supersedes all previous documents.

Because the **restated articles** of incorporation do not include any changes, but are rather a composite of previously approved amendments, shareholder approval is not necessary to restate articles of incorporation (unless a change to the articles is being made at the same time, in which case, the required procedure for amendments must be followed). The directors will approve a restatement either by majority vote at a meeting or by written consent, and then the entire text of the articles, including any changes, additions, or deletions made since filing of the original articles, will be prepared and filed with the secretary of state accompanied by a filing fee.

Mechanics of Board-Initiated Bylaw Amendments

In most states, amendment of the bylaws is performed by the directors acting at a meeting or acting by written consent. The minutes of the meeting or written consent action setting forth the change should be placed in the minute book. The section of the minute book containing the bylaws should also reflect the change. Either an entire new set of bylaws should be prepared and marked "Bylaws — Amended as of _____" or the new bylaw provision should be prepared on a separate piece of paper marked "Amendment to Bylaw No. _____, amended as of _____" and inserted at the end of the bylaws. Just as the original bylaws did not require filing with the secretary of state, the amended bylaws need not be filed with the secretary of state.

B. AMENDING THE BYLAWS OF THE CORPORATION

For the most part, changes in the corporation's bylaws are easily accomplished. Unless the state statute, the articles, or the bylaws themselves require shareholder participation, the bylaws may in many cases be amended solely by the directors. If shareholder approval is required, a simple majority vote is generally sufficient. The bylaws may be amended to change the date of the annual meeting of shareholders, to change the duties of the corporate treasurer, to add an officer, and so forth.

Note, however, that it is important to review state law, the corporation's articles, and its bylaws to see whether there are any wrinkles to the bylaw amendment process. Delaware's rules are instructive. The DGCL specifically allows for corporations to add to, and amend, their bylaws. *See* DGCL § 109. But, shareholders may be involved in this process. Specifically, under DGCL § 109(a), once a corporation receives any payment for any of its stock, stockholders entitled to vote have "the power to adopt, amend or repeal bylaws." DGCL § 109(a) also allows corporations to give the board of directors the power to add to and amend the bylaws. But, the directors' authority to adopt, amend, or repeal the company's bylaws does not restrict the stockholders' ability to change the bylaws. This is because § 109(a) specifically provides: "The fact that such power has been so conferred upon the directors or governing body [to modify the bylaws] . . . shall not divest the stockholders or members of the power, nor limit their power to adopt, amend or repeal bylaws." This means that the stockholders may repeal or amend bylaws that the directors adopted. Stockholders may also adopt bylaws of their own to aid in the governance of a corporation. Stockholders also, of course, have the right to vote or not vote for directors who adopt, amend, or repeal bylaws. *See also* New York Business Corporation Law (NYBCL) § 601.

Application Exercise 2

You represent Acme Corp., a Delaware corporation engaged in mining and energy exploration in several nations in Africa and Eastern Europe. Acme has decided to appoint a chief risk officer and to form a risk committee of the board of directors to help the company identify and mitigate risks associated with political instability in countries where Acme has mining or energy exploration operations, as well as to identify and mitigate financial risks (e.g., currency risk, interest rate risk) associated with doing business in foreign countries. This is Acme's first chief risk officer. The risk committee of the board is new as well, and the existing bylaws of the company do not provide express authorization for either the chief risk officer or any board committees. While the board believes that both actions are consistent with the board's power and obligation to oversee the affairs of the company, the board has voted in favor of amending the bylaws to reflect the new executive post and board committee. Prepare a checklist of steps necessary to effect the bylaw amendments, and prepare all necessary paperwork.

C. CORPORATE COMBINATIONS

Corporate combinations also implicate shareholder voting and approval rights. Corporations may take control of other corporations or increase or decrease their size by a variety of means. One corporation might be merged into another, with all of the merged corporation's assets and property transferred to the survivor corporation. A corporation may purchase the assets of another corporation, or sell all or substantially all of its own assets. One corporation may acquire enough stock in another corporation to assume control of that corporation. The corporations involved in these transactions are usually called **constituents**, and these transactions, or **corporate combinations**, may result in fundamental changes to the ownership, structure, and governance of the corporation. Because these changes can affect significant rights of shareholders, all are subject, to varying degrees, to the requirement of shareholder approval.

The reasons why such combinations take place are as varied as the means to accomplish the combination. A corporation may wish to acquire some special process or technology owned by another corporation; to diversify and expand its product line; or to rid itself of a competitor. A corporation also may seek to sell lines of business (or other assets) to raise cash. Oftentimes, these goals can only be accomplished by merger, consolidation, a share exchange, acquisition of assets, or acquisition of stock. Most of the time, these types of transactions are **friendly**, meaning the management of all constituent entities vote in favor of the deal. Sometimes, however, a transaction is **hostile**. A transaction is hostile if the board of directors of the **target** (i.e., the firm that has been identified as attractive for potential takeover by a potential acquirer, or **bidder**) does not want to be acquired by the bidder. We discuss the nuts and bolts of corporate combinations, focusing on friendly deals, in Section C. We discuss hostile takeovers in Section D. Finally, as a practice pointer, we note that mergers and similar transactions involving larger companies often raise antitrust issues. The Federal Trade Commission and the Department of Justice review such combinations to ensure competition is not impaired. We discuss antitrust issues in Section F.

1. Mergers and Consolidations

Mergers

A **merger** is a combination of two or more constituent corporations into a single entity. Because the merger process is controlled by statute, mergers are often referred to as **statutory mergers**. Generally speaking, merger statutes provide that the following steps must occur before the constituent corporations will be able to consummate a merger: (i) the boards of directors of the bidder and target must approve the plan of merger; (ii) the shareholders of the constituent corporations generally must approve the plan of merger; and (iii) articles of merger must be filed with the secretary of state.

In the classic merger scenario, Corporation A combines with Corporation B. At the conclusion of the combination, one of the corporations (assume Corporation A) will cease to exist. The survivor, Corporation B, will acquire everything previously owned by Corporation A: its assets, its contracts, its rights, its debts, its obligations, and usually its shareholders. In the example given, Corporation A is referred to as the **merged corporation**, the **disappearing corporation**, or the

extinguished corporation. Corporation B is called the **survivor**. Mergers can take place between two or more domestic corporations or between domestic and foreign corporations, so long as the laws of each corporation's state of incorporation are followed. A merger between different business entities (e.g., a corporation and a partnership or limited liability company) is called a **cross-species merger** (or **interspecies merger**). MBCA § 11.02 and most states recognize such cross-species mergers. There are several variations on the classic merger, including the direct merger, the forward triangular merger, and the reverse triangular merger. We discuss these structures in the following section.

Varieties of Merger

In a **direct merger**, the target merges into and with the bidder. As Exhibit 11.3 reflects, under the relevant merger statutes and as set forth in the agreement and plan of merger, the following occurs upon consummation of a direct merger: (i) the target's assets and liabilities are transferred to the bidder by operation of law;

EXHIBIT 11.3   **Direct Merger Transaction**

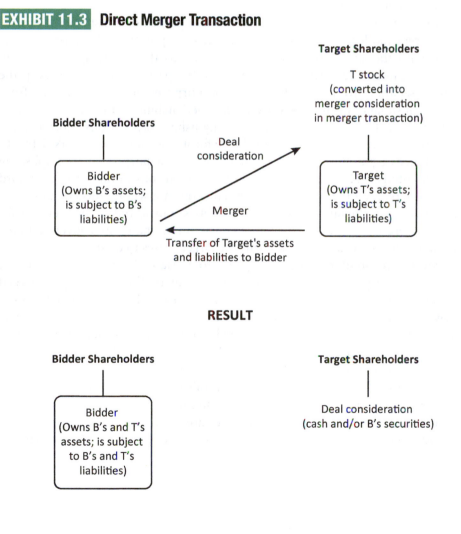

(ii) the target's outstanding shares are converted into the specified deal consideration; and (iii) the target ceases to exist.

Upstream and downstream mergers involve mergers between parent corporations and their subsidiaries. A corporation owned or formed by another corporation is called a **subsidiary**. The creator corporation is called the **parent**. On occasion, the parent may wish to merge the subsidiary back into itself, perhaps to eliminate the costs and paperwork involved in maintaining two corporations. If the parent owns at least 90 percent of the stock of the subsidiary, the MBCA and most states allow the merger to take place without approval of the shareholders of either the parent or the subsidiary. Unless the charter of the parent or subsidiary provides otherwise, approval of the subsidiary's shareholders (or its directors) is not needed because they do not have sufficient voting power to block the merger. Approval of the parent's shareholders generally is not required either because the decision is viewed as an ordinary business decision within the province of the parent's board. *See, e.g.*, MBCA § 11.05. This type of merger is called a **short-form merger**. When the subsidiary merges into the parent and the parent is the survivor, it is called an upstream merger. When the parent merges into the subsidiary and the subsidiary is the survivor, it is called a downstream merger.

A **forward triangular merger** involves three parties or constituent corporations: a parent-bidder, its subsidiary, and a target corporation. The target merges into and with the subsidiary, with the subsidiary as the surviving corporation. Rather than directly acquiring the target itself, the parent may wish to keep the subsidiary separate from it for diversification purposes or to protect itself from either the subsidiary's or the newly acquired target's liabilities. In a classic or direct merger, the parent would be liable for the extinguished corporation's debts. In a triangular merger, the subsidiary remains liable for its own and the target's debts. In many instances, a parent creates a subsidiary for the sole purpose of accomplishing a triangular merger. Thus, as Exhibit 11.4 shows, upon consummation of a forward triangular merger, (i) the target's business ends up in a wholly owned subsidiary of the bidder, with the target's assets and liabilities transferred to the merger subsidiary by operation of law; (ii) the target's outstanding shares are converted to the agreed-upon deal consideration; and (iii) the target ceases to exist.

A **reverse triangular merger** is similar to a triangular merger, except that rather than the target being merged into the subsidiary, the subsidiary is merged into and with the target and the subsidiary ceases to exist. The target then becomes the new subsidiary of the parent. This transaction may be used when the target's leases and other contracts cannot be assigned or transferred to another party; with a reverse triangular merger, the target remains a party to the leases or other contracts, yet the parent reaps their benefits. Thus, upon consummation of a reverse triangular merger, (i) the target ends up as a wholly owned subsidiary of the bidder; (ii) the target's outstanding shares are converted into the agreed-upon deal consideration; (iii) the merger subsidiary's shares are converted into target common stock; and (iv) the merger subsidiary ceases to exist. See Exhibit 11.5 for a diagram of a reverse triangular merger.

 **Forward Triangular Merger Transaction**

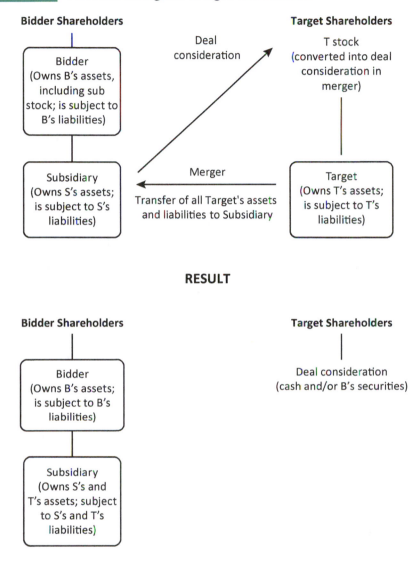

Consolidations

A **consolidation** is similar to a merger. In this type of transaction, however, two or more corporations combine and form an entirely new corporation, a different legal entity from either of the two constituent corporations. Upon consummation of a corporate combination structured as a consolidation, all of the combining constituent corporations cease to exist. The newly formed corporation acquires everything previously owned by the constituents: their assets, contracts, rights, liabilities, and shareholders. In a classic consolidation scenario, Corporation A combines with Corporation B to form Corporation X.

EXHIBIT 11.5 **Reverse Triangular Merger Transaction**

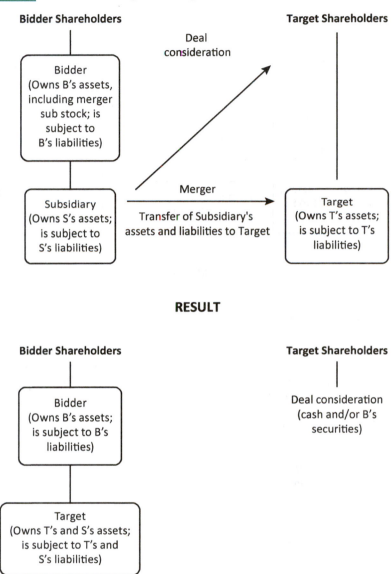

Note that the result of a consolidation can be effected by merger. For example, a parent may create a subsidiary corporation. The parent, subsidiary, and target enter into an agreement to merge whereby they agree that the parent and the target will merge into the newly formed subsidiary, which was created for the express purpose of surviving the transaction. Because it is nearly always advantageous for one of the constituent corporations in a transaction to survive and because the effect of a consolidation can be achieved through such a merger, the MBCA and some states no longer recognize consolidations. See Exhibit 11.6 for a summary chart showing varieties of mergers and a consolidation.

EXHIBIT 11.6   Summary Chart: Mergers and Consolidations

Merger

Upstream Merger

Parent + Subsidiary = Parent

Downstream Merger

Parent + Subsidiary = Subsidiary

Triangular Merger

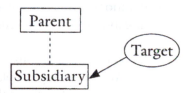

Target merges into parent's
   subsidiary and target is
   extinguished

Reverse Triangular Merger

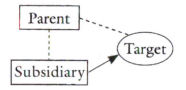

Subsidiary merges into
   target and subsidiary
   is extinguished and
   target becomes new
   subsidiary of parent

CONSOLIDATION

Procedures for Effecting Mergers and Consolidations

Mergers and consolidations may be completed in various ways, as dictated by the merger statutes in the relevant jurisdiction. The following procedures, requirements, and issues typically arise with transactions structured as mergers.

Director and Shareholder Approval

The first step in the merger or consolidation process is negotiation between or among the constituent corporations involved. These preliminary negotiations usually lead to a **letter of intent**, or a letter-form document setting forth the basic understanding and intent of the parties. The letter of intent will eventually be replaced with a formal, definitive agreement; however, the letter is sufficiently detailed to outline the key terms of the transaction. The negotiation process itself can be complex and take several months.

The constituent corporations must then prepare a **plan of merger**. The content of the plan of merger is generally regulated by statute. For example, MBCA § 11.02(c) provides that the plan of merger must set forth the following:

1. the names of the constituents and the name of the surviving corporation;
2. the terms and conditions of the merger;
3. the manner and basis of converting the shares of the disappearing corporation into shares or other securities of the survivor (or, if desired, the manner of converting the shares of the extinguished corporation into cash, thereby allowing shareholders to be cashed out); and
4. any amendments that will be required to be made to the survivor's articles of incorporation such as a name change or creation of a new class of stock.

The plan of merger will likely include other provisions as well, such as a description of authorized capital of the constituent corporations, provisions relating to assets being transferred, and a description of any litigation in which the constituents are involved.

The plan of merger is then submitted to the board of directors of each constituent corporation for its approval. *See, e.g.,* MBCA § 11.04(a). After adopting the plan of merger, the boards of the constituent corporations may be required to submit the plan for shareholder approval. *See, e.g.,* MBCA § 11.04(b). The boards of directors must recommend the plan of merger (unless, because of conflict of interest or other circumstances, the board determines it should make no recommendation), and the shareholders entitled to vote must then decide whether to approve the plan. *See, e.g.,* MBCA § 11.04(d), (e), (f), and (g). Unless this activity takes place at or near the time of the annual meeting, the corporations will likely call special meetings of shareholders for approval. *See, e.g.,* MBCA § 11.04(d). The notice of any meeting must specify that the purpose of the meeting is to consider the plan of merger. The notice must include a copy or summary of the plan of merger. *Id.*

The modern approach is to require a simple majority approval by the shareholders; a few states, however, including Maryland, require two-thirds approval. The MBCA approach is similar to its approach on amendments to the articles of incorporation: The merger will be approved if more votes are cast in favor of it than against it. *See* MBCA §§ 11.04(e), 7.25. Some states permit nonvoting shares of stock to vote on the merger. All shareholders, however, must receive notice of the meeting, whether or not they are entitled to vote. MBCA § 11.04(d). Furthermore, the notice must state whether the shareholders will have appraisal rights (discussed later). If so, shareholders must be provided copies of the statutes relating to appraisal rights. This is another situation in which it is important to review the charter of all constituent entities to make sure that there are no heightened quorum or voting requirements relating to extraordinary transactions such as mergers and consolidations.

Approval by shareholders of all constituent corporations generally is required due to the dramatic impact a merger (or consolidation) has on the shareholders. The corporation owned by the shareholders of the merging corporation will be extinguished; such an extraordinary matter should be approved by the owners of that corporation. The corporation owned by the shareholders of the survivor corporation will likely be taking on debts, liabilities, and other obligations of the extinguished corporation; such potentially significant developments should be approved by shareholders of the surviving entity. Additionally, share ownership in the survivor will be affected because the survivor must absorb shareholders of the extinguished corporation and issue them shares of the survivor. This issuance of shares to the newcomers might cause a shift in power and control among the shareholders of the survivor. Shareholder approval is important for these reasons, also. If the shareholders of the extinguished corporation receive cash rather than shares in the survivor, the survivor's shareholders will be affected by what will likely be a large outlay of cash. In either scenario, their approval is required.

Exceptions to Requirement of Shareholder Approval

There are two exceptions to the requirement that shareholders of all constituent corporations must approve a merger.

- *Short-form merger.* A merger between a parent and subsidiary (or between two of the parent's subsidiaries) need not be approved by the shareholders of *either* corporation (or by the directors of the subsidiary) if the parent owns at least 90 percent of the outstanding stock of its subsidiary. MBCA § 11.05. This is the short-form merger discussed earlier. Shareholder approval is not needed because if the parent owns 90 percent or more of the subsidiary's stock and it desires that the subsidiary be extinguished, the parent has the necessary votes to make that happen. Voting by the subsidiary's shareholders would be a superfluous exercise. Similarly, voting by the parent's shareholders is not needed because the recapture of the subsidiary by the parent does not materially affect their share ownership. The short-form merger must still be approved by the parent's directors.
- *Small-scale merger.* A merger need not be approved by the shareholders of the *survivor* corporation if very little of the survivor's stock (namely, less than 20 percent of its outstanding shares) needs to be transferred to the shareholders of the extinguished corporation. Such a **small-scale merger** simply does not have a great impact on the survivor's shareholders because their power and control will not be significantly diluted. Thus, they need not approve it. *See* MBCA §§ 621(f), 11.04(h).

These exceptions to the requirement of shareholder approval rest on the same premise: Shareholder approval of a merger is not needed when either the merger cannot be prevented or when the transaction has little impact on the survivor's shareholders.

Delaware versus the MBCA and the Voting Rights of Shareholders of the Bidder

There is an important distinction between the MBCA and the Delaware General Corporate Law respecting the voting rights of shareholders of the bidder corporation.

Under the MBCA, the right of shareholders of the bidder corporation to vote on the deal depends on how much stock, if any, the bidder corporation will be issuing in the deal. This is because MBCA § 6.21(f)(1)(ii) states that shareholders of the bidder have the right to vote on the proposed transaction if shares, other securities, or rights are issued for consideration (rather than cash or cash equivalents) and if the bidder will be issuing shares equal to more than 20 percent of its outstanding voting power pre-deal. The right of bidder shareholders to vote on a proposed merger thus depends on the type and amount of deal consideration under MBCA-style regimes.

The DGCL also uses a 20 percent rule, but this rule only applies to a deal structured as a direct merger. *See* DGCL § 251(f). The 20 percent rule does not apply to a triangular merger under Delaware law because the Delaware merger statute provides a shareholder vote, if at all, only to the shareholders of a constituent corporation or a corporation that is a party to the merger for corporate law purposes. In triangular mergers, the bidder is not a party to the merger — instead, the merger is by and between target and the merger subsidiary. This means that under Delaware law (unlike the MBCA), there are several ways to structure a transaction that do not require an affirmative vote (or, indeed any vote) by shareholders of the bidder, including an asset purchase (discussed in Section C.3 below), stock purchase (discussed in Section C.4 below), a triangular merger, or by using cash consideration in a direct merger.

Finally, whatever the voting requirements under state law and the corporation's organic documents, when a transaction involves a publicly traded company, counsel should be sure to check rules established by the exchange where the company's stock is listed to confirm whether there are any additional shareholder voting requirements.

Appraisal Rights of Dissenting Shareholders

It is possible that some shareholders may be adamantly opposed to a merger in circumstances where the requisite number of shareholders vote in favor of the proposed transaction. These shareholders might have philosophical or moral objections to one or more of the constituents involved, they might believe the deal is fundamentally ill advised, etc. To address the concerns of these shareholders, state corporations codes afford **appraisal rights** to dissenting shareholders in certain circumstances, or the right to have their shares appraised and to receive the fair value of their shares as of the date of the merger in cash. As a general rule, appraisal rights are dissenting shareholders' exclusive statutory remedy.

Dissenting shareholders must follow a fairly complex procedure to be entitled to, and exercise, appraisal rights. In the MBCA, appraisal rights are discussed in Chapter 13. MBCA § 13.02 sets forth the circumstances when a shareholder is entitled to appraisal rights — namely, (i) consummation of qualifying merger transactions; (ii) consummation of certain share exchanges; (iii) consummation of a qualifying disposition of corporate assets; (iv) certain amendments to the articles of incorporation; (v) transactions entitled to appraisal rights under the corporation's charter, bylaws, or board resolution; (vi) consummation of certain corporation domestications, (vii) consummation of a conversion of the corporation to nonprofit status; and (viii) consummation of conversion of the corporation to an unincorporated entity. *Id.*

Generally, the notice of the meeting at which the vote on the relevant transaction will occur must state whether shareholders are or are not entitled to assert appraisal rights and, if so, must include a copy of the relevant statutes. *See, e.g.*, MBCA § 13.20. If a shareholder wishes to assert appraisal rights, the shareholder must deliver a written notice of intent to demand payment for her shares. *See, e.g.*, MBCA § 13.21. This notice must be delivered to the corporation before the vote on the merger is held, and the shareholder must not vote in favor of the merger. *Id.* Within ten days after the shareholders' meeting authorizing the merger, the corporation must deliver a written appraisal notice to any shareholder who previously provided written notice of an intent to demand payment. *See, e.g.*, MBCA § 13.22. The corporation must include a form for the dissenter to use to demand payment. The shareholder must return the form by a certain date; however, the shareholder must be given not less than 40 and not more than 60 days, per MBCA § 13.22. The corporation must estimate the fair value of the shares. *See, e.g.*, MBCA § 13.24. The ultimate payment made to the shareholder must equal or exceed this estimate. Shareholders surrender their certificates upon payment to them of the fair value of their shares.

Assuming the shareholder complies with these requirements, the corporation will pay each dissenter the fair value of her shares as of the time immediately prior to the merger announcement together with accrued interest. The payment will be accompanied by financial statements of the corporation. Any appreciation or depreciation of the stock in anticipation of the transaction will be excluded. Shareholders who are dissatisfied with the corporation's payment or offer must follow procedures set forth in the relevant corporations code when asserting their objections. *See, e.g.*, MBCA § 13.26. Generally speaking, if the dissenting shareholder objects to the corporation's valuation of the shares, and the parties cannot reach agreement, the corporation will institute a judicial proceeding to determine the fair value of the shares. Unless the dissenting shareholder strictly and timely complies with the various statutory requirements, the corporation has no duty to pay the value of the shares. A shareholder may withdraw from the appraisal process and thereby decline to exercise any appraisal rights.

In a short-form merger in which a parent regains its subsidiary, although the subsidiary's shareholders are not entitled to vote on the transaction, within ten days after the transaction becomes effective, the parent must notify the subsidiary's shareholders that the merger has become effective. *See* MBCA § 11.05. Section 13.02(i) of the MBCA states that appraisal rights are not available "if the corporation [which is a party to a merger] is a subsidiary and the merger is governed by Section 11.05." MBCA § 13.02.

Some states allow partial appraisal rights so that a shareholder may dissent regarding some shares owned and be cashed out with respect to those shares, and remain a shareholder as to the remainder of the shares. Generally, however, a shareholder must demand appraisal for all of the shares of a class or series that the shareholder owns. Appraisal rights generally are not provided to the survivor's shareholders in a small-scale merger (because they do not vote on the transaction).

Most states, including Delaware, do not allow dissent and appraisal rights if the shares are listed on a national securities exchange or if there are at least 2,000 shareholders of a class of shares. The basis for this "market out" exception is that if the shares are listed on a national exchange or if there are at least 2,000 shareholders, or both, there should be ready and available buyers for the dissenter's shares. The approach of MBCA § 13.02(b) is substantially similar. The market itself will provide fair value for the shares, thus making appraisal rights unnecessary.

Articles of Merger

After the merger has been approved by the requisite shareholder vote, a certificate or articles of merger must be prepared and filed with the secretary of state. The articles may set forth or attach the plan of merger and a statement regarding the approval of the plan of merger by the shareholders. If shareholder approval was not required, the articles of merger must so state. See Exhibit 11.7 for an example of a certificate of merger. Some states require that the plan of merger be certified as approved and then filed with the secretary of state. A filing fee is required. Additionally, just as the original articles of incorporation and amended articles of incorporation might need to be published or filed with a county recorder, so may the articles of merger. New stock certificates and a new seal might need to be ordered.

The articles of incorporation of the survivor are deemed amended in accordance with the plan of merger; thus, there is often no requirement for the survivor to file a separate amendment of its articles of incorporation although most corporations do so to ensure their articles are current and can be read without reference to other documents. The secretary of state will examine the articles of merger, ensure that all taxes and fees have been paid, and then issue a certificate of merger. Many states allow a corporation to specify a later effective date for the merger so that simultaneous transactions may be completed in other states.

Upon the effective date of the merger, the merged corporation ceases to exist, and the survivor takes over all of the extinguished corporation's assets, properties, personnel, shareholders, debts, obligations, and liabilities. The shareholders of the extinguished corporation, unless they have dissented and exercised their appraisal rights, will be issued shares of the survivor in return for their shares in the extinguished corporation according to the plan of merger, or, as discussed earlier, they may be cashed out.

Modern Trends in Mergers and Consolidations

One of the more modern twists on mergers and consolidations is the **roll-up**, a combination of several companies. Roll-ups became very popular in the 1990s. In a roll-up, an entrepreneur buys various companies in an industry, combines them, takes the resulting entity public, and then goes on a buying binge of other companies. In theory, the resulting economies of scale of the combined companies would increase earnings, enhancing the roll-up's stock price, thus enabling additional acquisitions. Unfortunately, what many entrepreneurs discover is that buying companies is relatively easy but integrating them into one smooth operating unit with reliable financial controls is much harder. At present, many roll-ups have disappeared or are struggling to survive. The projected economies of scale seldom materialized, and the roll-ups were often marked by redundancies and in-fighting. Since late 1999, Wall Street has been skeptical of roll-ups, and most companies have adopted a more traditional strategy for growth: A larger public company buys a

EXHIBIT 11.7   California Certificate of Merger

OBE MERG

State of California
Secretary of State

Certificate of Merger

(California Corporations Code sections
1113(g), 3203(g), 6019.1, 8019.1, 9640, 12540.1, 15911.14, 16915(b) and 17710.14)

IMPORTANT — Read all instructions before completing this form.	This Space For Filing Use Only

1. NAME OF SURVIVING ENTITY	2. TYPE OF ENTITY	3. CA SECRETARY OF STATE FILE NUMBER	4. JURISDICTION
5. NAME OF DISAPPEARING ENTITY	6. TYPE OF ENTITY	7. CA SECRETARY OF STATE FILE NUMBER	8. JURISDICTION

9. THE PRINCIPAL TERMS OF THE AGREEMENT OF MERGER WERE APPROVED BY A VOTE OF THE NUMBER OF INTERESTS OR SHARES OF EACH CLASS THAT EQUALED OR EXCEEDED THE VOTE REQUIRED. *(IF A VOTE WAS REQUIRED, SPECIFY THE CLASS AND THE NUMBER OF OUTSTANDING INTERESTS OF EACH CLASS ENTITLED TO VOTE ON THE MERGER AND THE PERCENTAGE VOTE REQUIRED OF EACH CLASS. ATTACH ADDITIONAL PAGES, IF NEEDED.)*

SURVIVING ENTITY			DISAPPEARING ENTITY		
CLASS AND NUMBER	AND	PERCENTAGE VOTE REQUIRED	CLASS AND NUMBER	AND	PERCENTAGE VOTE REQUIRED

10. IF EQUITY SECURITIES OF A PARENT PARTY ARE TO BE ISSUED IN THE MERGER, CHECK THE APPLICABLE STATEMENT.

☐ No vote of the shareholders of the parent party was required.   ☐ The required vote of the shareholders of the parent party was obtained.

11. IF THE SURVIVING ENTITY IS A DOMESTIC LIMITED LIABLITY COMPANY, LIMITED PARTNERSHIP, OR PARTNERSHIP, PROVIDE THE REQUISITE CHANGES (IF ANY) TO THE INFORMATION SET FORTH IN THE SURVIVING ENTITY'S ARTICLES OF ORGANIZATION, CERTIFICATE OF LIMITED PARTNERSHIP OR STATEMENT OF PARTNERSHIP AUTHORITY RESULTING FROM THE MERGER. ATTACH ADDITIONAL PAGES, IF NECESSARY.

12. IF A DISAPPEARING ENTITY IS A DOMESTIC LIMITED LIABLITY COMPANY, LIMITED PARTNERSHIP, OR PARTNERSHIP, AND THE SURVIVING ENTITY IS NOT A DOMESTIC ENTITY OF THE SAME TYPE, ENTER THE PRINCIPAL ADDRESS OF THE SURVIVING ENTITY.

PRINCIPAL ADDRESS OF SURVIVING ENTITY	CITY AND STATE	ZIP CODE

13. OTHER INFORMATION REQUIRED TO BE STATED IN THE CERTIFICATE OF MERGER BY THE LAWS UNDER WHICH EACH CONSTITUENT OTHER BUSINESS ENTITY IS ORGANIZED. ATTACH ADDITIONAL PAGES, IF NECESSARY.

14. STATUTORY OR OTHER BASIS UNDER WHICH A FOREIGN OTHER BUSINESS ENTITY IS AUTHORIZED TO EFFECT THE MERGER.	15. FUTURE EFFECTIVE DATE, IF ANY
	_____ - _____ - _____
	(Month) (Day) (Year)

16. ADDITIONAL INFORMATION SET FORTH ON ATTACHED PAGES, IF ANY, IS INCORPORATED HEREIN BY THIS REFERENCE AND MADE PART OF THIS CERTIFICATE.

17. I CERTIFY UNDER PENALTY OF PERJURY UNDER THE LAWS OF THE STATE OF CALIFORNIA THAT THE FOREGOING IS TRUE AND CORRECT OF MY OWN KNOWLEDGE. I DECLARE I AM THE PERSON WHO EXECUTED THIS INSTRUMENT, WHICH EXECUTION IS MY ACT AND DEED.

SIGNATURE OF AUTHORIZED PERSON FOR THE SURVIVING ENTITY	DATE	TYPE OR PRINT NAME AND TITLE OF AUTHORIZED PERSON
SIGNATURE OF AUTHORIZED PERSON FOR THE SURVIVING ENTITY	DATE	TYPE OR PRINT NAME AND TITLE OF AUTHORIZED PERSON
SIGNATURE OF AUTHORIZED PERSON FOR THE DISAPPEARING ENTITY	DATE	TYPE OR PRINT NAME AND TITLE OF AUTHORIZED PERSON
SIGNATURE OF AUTHORIZED PERSON FOR THE DISAPPEARING ENTITY	DATE	TYPE OR PRINT NAME AND TITLE OF AUTHORIZED PERSON

For an entity that is a business trust, real estate investment trust or an unincorporated association, set forth the provision of law or other basis for the authority of the person signing: _____

OBE MERGER-1 (REV 01/2016)	APPROVED BY SECRETARY OF STATE

Clear Form   Print Form

smaller public or private company in its industry, integrates it completely, and then pursues another.

Another feature of the modern merger landscape is the fairness opinion. In almost all mergers, the boards of directors of the parties in the transaction will obtain a **fairness opinion** from investment bankers or other experts. The fairness opinion verifies that the consideration offered by the bidder is within the appropriate fair market value range for the target and that the terms of the transaction are fair to the shareholders from a financial perspective. These fairness opinions are used to demonstrate that the boards have met their fiduciary duties to act with due care. Due to a concern that sometimes the parties issuing the fairness opinions were also acting as advisors in the transaction (and thus might be tempted to determine the transaction was "fair" regardless of its merits), in late 2007, the SEC adopted new regulations requiring those issuing fairness opinions to make certain disclosures to shareholders if there are or could be conflicts of interest by those issuing the fairness opinion.

Another recent merger trend is the **reverse merger**, in which a company purchases a "shell" or defunct American company listed on one of the national exchanges, merges with it, and adopts its ticker symbol, thus allowing the acquiring company to become a publicly traded company with access to U.S. investors and the ability to raise money without the necessity of complying with rigorous laws and SEC standards and scrutiny for companies that "go public." In many instances, Chinese companies were the acquirer, thus leading to the term "Chinese reverse merger." After investors alleged accounting irregularities and numerous federal securities class-action lawsuits were filed in 2011 by investors in the China-based companies, in 2011, the SEC warned investors to be alert for potential abuses and adopted new regulations that require the post-merger company to produce financial and other information. Moreover, a company must now wait at least one year after a reverse merger before it seeks to list on an exchange. These new regulations and other crackdowns have significantly slowed the reverse merger trend.

As noted in Chapter 6, over the last several years, a number of U.S. companies have "inverted" through mergers with foreign companies, largely for tax planning reasons. Many commentators predicted that Treasury/IRS notices issued in September 2014 and November 2015 would impede inversion transactions by making it more difficult to invert and by reducing the advantages of becoming an inverted company. Some deals fell apart after the September 2014 notice, and each of the notices led to the restructuring of some deals. Inversions did not cease entirely, however, and as noted in Chapter 6, in April 2016, the Treasury Department released additional reforms designed to make inversions even more difficult. As inversions remain an area of focus, be sure to review the latest releases from the Treasury Department and the IRS before advising a client in this technical and still-changing area of the law.

The opposite of mergers are **divisions**, which involve the split of a domestic entity into two or more companies, with assets and liabilities allocated among the resulting companies. A number of corporate giants have split off business lines or created two companies, with each company having its own distinct mission. For example, in late 2014, Hewlett-Packard proposed a split that would create one company focused on personal computers and printers and a second company focused on tech services. After a year-long process, the company was split in two separate corporations. Similarly, in late 2014, at the urging of activist investor Carl Icahn, eBay agreed to split off PayPal, which it had acquired in 2002 for $1.5 billion, into a separately traded company. This transaction has since closed. Such divisions and splits often produce employee layoffs.

Another feature of the modern mergers and acquisitions landscape, at least for large companies, is shareholder challenges to mergers. The U.S. Chamber Institute for Legal Reform reported in 2013 that lawsuits were filed in more than 90 percent of all corporate mergers and acquisitions valued at $100 million or more since 2010. These lawsuits typically allege that the directors violated their fiduciary duties by failing to achieve maximum value for shareholders. Rather than delay the transaction, companies often settle these cases. Thus, companies remain interested in fee-shifting bylaw provisions (see Chapter 8), or bylaws which would shift the burden of litigation costs and attorneys' fees to an unsuccessful litigant. As noted in Chapter 8, fee-shifting bylaws are an area of legislative focus in some jurisdictions, so be sure to check state law.

In 2004 the Uniform Law Commission (ULC) together with the American Bar Association promulgated a Model Entity Transactions Act to provide a comprehensive framework for changing entity forms, from mergers to share exchanges to conversions and domestications. At the time of the writing of this text, it has only been adopted in Alaska, Arizona, Connecticut, the District of Columbia, Idaho, Kansas, and Pennsylvania. The text of the act is available on the ULC website at www.uniformlaws.org.

2. Share Exchanges

Another way in which a corporation can gain control of another corporation is through a share exchange. In a **share exchange** (sometimes called an **interest exchange**), one corporation acquires all of the shares of one or more classes of another corporation (the target). The acquiring corporation receives all of the target's shares, and the target's shareholders receive shares of the acquirer, cash, or a combination thereof. Both corporations may continue to exist; the target's shareholders exchange all of their shares for shares in the

Merger Trends

After several years of relatively flat activity, mergers surged during 2014 and 2015. Analysts point to a number of reasons for the increase in merger deals over the past couple of years, including low interest rates, which make it easy to borrow needed money for acquisitions; tax benefits that make merging into foreign companies attractive; the stockpiles of cash many corporations have on hand; and the surge in stock market prices, making it easy for an acquirer to buy another company using only stock (rather than cash); enhanced confidence in the strength of the U.S. economy and the strength of the merger market; and consolidation in certain market sectors.

Merger Trivia

- Mergers and acquisitions activity is usually seen as a sign of economic health because companies usually will not transact significant deals if they anticipate an economic slowdown.

- After a six-year slump in merger activity that began in 2007, just before the financial crisis, merger activity staged a comeback in 2014 as companies looked for ways to spend the record amounts of cash they were holding. Merger activity in the first half of 2014 amounted to $786 billion, nearly reaching 2007's record of $880.7 billion.

- The most active sectors for mergers and acquisitions are telecommunications, health care, and utilities and energy.

- The 2013 merger between American Airlines and US Airways produced the world's largest airline.

acquiring corporation (in which case the target may become the subsidiary of the acquiring corporation), for cash, or for shares in the acquiring corporation or some other corporation. Many of the procedural formalities of a merger must be complied with, namely, approval of a plan of exchange by directors of both corporations and by shareholders of the target corporation, provision of appraisal rights to dissenting shareholders, and filing of articles or a certificate of share exchange with the secretary of state. Generally, shareholders of the acquiring corporation do not vote on the transaction because it is viewed as a business decision within the decision-making authority of their board of directors. At the conclusion of a merger, the survivor owns all of the extinguished entity's assets and is liable for its obligations. In contrast, at the conclusion of a share exchange, the acquiring corporation does not necessarily become the owner of the target corporation's assets or become liable for its obligations; the terms of the plan of share exchange will control. See Exhibit 11.8 for a diagram of a share exchange.

3. Purchase of Assets

A corporation may gain control of another or combine with another by purchasing all or substantially all of its assets, both tangible and intangible. The selling corporation may be paid for its assets in cash or in stock of the acquiring corporation. At the end of the transaction, the acquiring corporation owns additional assets, and the selling corporation may be a mere shell, owning nothing other than the cash or shares it has recently received. After it has paid its liabilities and distributed the proceeds of the sale to its shareholders, it may dissolve. See Exhibit 11.9 for a diagram of an asset purchase. In an asset purchase, the acquiring corporation, in effect, "goes shopping," picking and choosing the assets it desires. It seldom, if ever, agrees to assume any liability of the target corporation, which continues its existence and retains responsibility for its obligations and liabilities. (As discussed in Section C.6, in some cases, parties are unable to avoid responsibility for liabilities associated with acquired assets.) See Exhibit 11.9 for a diagram of an asset purchase.

An **asset purchase** also affords a corporation the opportunity to buy assets of an unincorporated entity, such as a partnership or a limited liability company. Because state statutes relating to mergers, consolidations, and share exchanges often refer to constituent corporations, a corporation cannot merge with a partnership or other noncorporate entity in those states. A corporation can, however, purchase the assets of a partnership or other noncorporate entity.

Because there is no change in the status of the legal entity of the acquiring corporation and it is simply buying additional assets, it typically need not secure the approval of its shareholders. The transaction is viewed as within the purview of the directors, who have the sole authority to manage the business affairs of the corporation.

EXHIBIT 11.8 **Share Exchange Transaction**

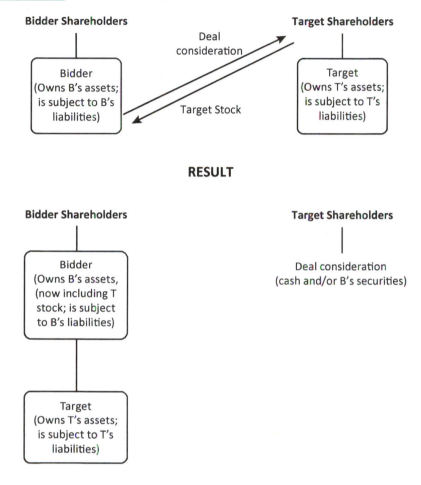

A purchase of assets may be more advantageous than a merger to an acquiring corporation; the purchase of another corporation's assets typically does not require approval by the purchaser's shareholders, and, in most cases, the seller retains its liabilities, having sold only its assets. Moreover, generally, no public filings or amendments to articles are necessitated by the asset transaction.

A mere mortgage or pledge by a corporation of its assets as security to ensure or guarantee repayment of a loan is not viewed as a sale of assets maintain. Thus, there is no need for shareholder approval. When the borrowing corporation repays the loan, the mortgage or pledge of the assets will be released and the corporation may continue its ordinary business. (A form of asset purchase agreement is provided in Appendix E.)

EXHIBIT 11.9   **Asset Purchase Transaction**

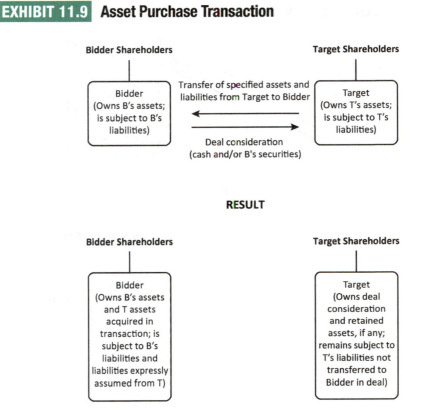

4. Purchase of Stock

A **stock purchase** is similar to an asset acquisition; however, in this transaction, the acquiring corporation (or acquiring individual) purchases all or substantially all of another corporation's stock rather than its assets. Stock purchases are memorialized in a stock purchase agreement executed by and between the bidder and the target company's shareholders. Although the target technically does not need to be a party to the agreement (because the transaction is between the bidder and the target's stockholders), the bidder typically will require the target to be party to the stock purchase agreement so that the target makes contractually enforceable representations and warranties regarding its business. The transaction documents generally will require the boards of both the target and the bidder to approve the deal, but the target company's shareholders do not get a formal vote on the transaction. This is because each shareholder makes an individual decision about whether to sell his stock to the bidder in a transaction structured as a stock purchase. The target corporation usually becomes a subsidiary of the acquiring corporation or may merge into it and the acquiring corporation will then be responsible for the debts and liabilities of the corporation whose stock is being acquired. See Exhibit 11.10 for a diagram of a stock purchase.

EXHIBIT 11.10 **Stock Purchase Transaction**

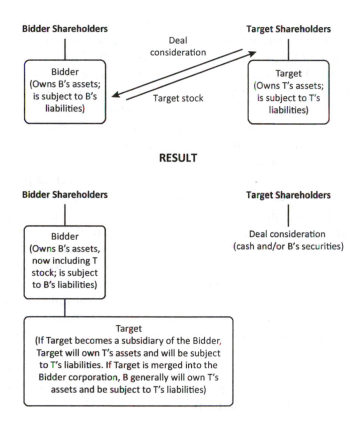

Many stock acquisition transactions involve negotiations between the management of the constituent corporations. The board of directors of the acquiring corporation seldom needs approval of its shareholders because the board is acting in the ordinary scope of business activities in determining that purchasing the stock is in the acquiring corporation's best interest. The management of the corporation whose stock is being acquired will pass a resolution recommending that the shareholders sell their stock to the acquiring corporation. Of course, the shareholders are free to decide whether or not to sell their stock. Stock acquisitions can be difficult to effect when there are numerous shareholders in the target corporation.

The procedures in a consensual stock purchase closely parallel those in mergers, consolidations, and asset purchases. Negotiations will be followed by a letter of intent, which is then followed by a definitive stock purchase agreement that each party signs. At the date of closing, stock in the seller will be transferred to the acquirer, and the acquirer will pay the appropriate purchase price to the seller. The acquirer now controls the destiny of the target and may decide to dissolve the target, allow the target to function as a subsidiary, or merge with the target.

5. Sale of All or Substantially All Assets

Most state statutes provide that a selling corporation must obtain shareholder approval if it sells, leases, or otherwise disposes of all or substantially all of its assets. Such a sale would impair its ability to carry out its business. Therefore, the selling corporation must have approval by its board of directors and its shareholders and, in most states, must offer appraisal rights to its dissenting shareholders. MBCA § 12.02 no longer uses the phrase "all or substantially all of its assets." Instead MBCA § 12.02 requires shareholder approval if a disposition or sale of assets would leave the corporation without a "significant continuing business activity." Under the MBCA, generally, a significant business activity exists if the continuing activity represents at least 25 percent of the seller's assets and either 25 percent of income before taxes or revenue from continuing operations. *See id.* If so, the selling corporation is conclusively presumed to have retained a significant continuing business activity, and it need not obtain its shareholders' approval. *Id.*

The procedure for effecting the purchase and sale of all or substantially all assets closely parallels the procedure for effecting mergers and consolidations because the result for the selling corporation is similar to that for an extinguished corporation in a merger — namely, discontinuation of its business operations. After a period of initial negotiation and a letter of intent setting forth the basic terms of the transaction, the board of directors of the selling corporation recommends the transaction and then directs that it be voted on by the shareholders, either at an annual meeting or a special meeting. All shareholders, even nonvoting shareholders, are entitled to notice of the meeting, which must state that the purpose of the meeting is to consider the sale of the corporation's assets. *See, e.g.,* MBCA § 12.02(g). The board must recommend that the shareholders approve the sale of the corporate assets. A description of the transaction must accompany the notice. The approval requirement is a simple majority in most states and a two-thirds approval in some states. The MBCA approach is similar to its approach on amendments to the articles of incorporation and mergers: The sale of assets will be approved if more votes are cast in favor of it than against it. MBCA §§ 7.25(c) and 12.02.

Most states and the MBCA require appraisal rights for dissenting shareholders of the selling corporation (unless the shareholders will be "cashed out" within one year or unless the corporation's shares are publicly traded). *See, e.g.,* MBCA § 13.02(a). An **asset purchase agreement** will be prepared and signed by both parties. This agreement will identify the parties, list the assets being sold, disclose any pending claims or litigation involving the seller, provide for the method and terms of payment, specify a date and place for closing, and include provisions in the event of either party's default. Examples of a form of asset purchase agreement are available at www.onecle.com. Unless the articles of incorporation of either corporation will be amended (perhaps to reflect a corporate name change), generally there are no state filings necessary. If either corporation is a § 12 reporting company under the federal securities laws, it must report this material event to the SEC. (Note: We define and discuss § 12 reporting companies in Chapter 13. For our purposes here, it is enough to know that large publicly traded companies generally are § 12 reporting companies.)

It is important to distinguish a sale of all or substantially all of a corporation's assets that is in the ordinary course of the corporation's business from a sale of all or substantially all of a corporation's assets that is not in the ordinary course of business. This is because a sale of all or substantially all of the assets in the ordinary course of a corporation's business generally does not require shareholder approval. *See, e.g.,* MBCA § 12.01(1) For example, a real estate company can sell all of its inventory of properties without requiring shareholder approval because this is exactly the type of business activity the corporation should be conducting. Shareholder approval is required, however, if there is a sale, lease, exchange, or disposition of all or substantially all of a corporation's assets *not* within the ordinary course of business such that the corporation is left without a significant continuing business activity.

6. Structuring Considerations

The choice of deal structure (and, thus the type of consideration) is driven by a number of factors, including the following: tax considerations; liabilities and liability risk associated with the entity, business, or assets being acquired; issues relating to the assignment of key contracts; and sometimes, licensing and regulatory issues.

Federal Income Tax Considerations

Taxable versus Non-Taxable Deals

For federal income tax purposes, with the exception of a deal structured as an asset purchase, target shareholders are treated as having sold target stock in exchange for the deal consideration. As a consequence, if a deal is taxable, a target shareholder will be required to recognize a gain in the year the deal closes if the shareholder receives consideration in excess of her **basis** in the target stock. (For present purposes, basis is generally what the shareholder paid for the stock.)

Non-Taxable Deals (Really, Tax-Deferred)

In tax terminology and in many states, mergers, consolidations, and share exchanges are all called **reorganizations**. The various types of reorganizations have different names and different tax consequences. For example, the IRS calls mergers and consolidations **Type A Reorganizations**. An exchange of shares is referred to as a **Type B Reorganization**, and an acquisition of substantially all of the assets of another corporation in exchange for shares of the acquirer is called a **Type C Reorganization**. The Internal Revenue Code provides varying tax treatment for these different types of reorganizations. As always, consider taking business taxation and corporate transactions courses and consulting with experts before practicing in this area.

A deal qualifies as a tax-free reorganization under IRC § 368 if it meets relevant IRS criteria. As a general rule, a deal will not qualify as a tax-free reorganization unless a significant portion of the deal consideration is composed of bidder stock. If a deal does qualify as a tax-free reorganization, target shareholders will not have to recognize gain with respect to the bidder stock until the shareholder sells the bidder stock. (As this suggests, tax-free really just means tax-deferred.) Tax planning and IRS rules and requirements thus may impact choice of deal structure.

Managing Liability Risk

When a corporation decides to make a bid for another corporation (however the deal is structured), it generally will perform extensive due diligence respecting the liabilities of the target. Many of these liabilities will be known and quantifiable — for example, wages owed to employees, outstanding bank loans, outstanding debts owed to trade creditors, and the like. The bidder can factor these liabilities into the purchase price the bidder is willing to pay. For example, if a bidder is considering acquiring a target that owes a substantial debt to a creditor, the bidder will generally try to negotiate to reduce its purchase price by the amount of the outstanding debt. The bidder also may factor known liabilities into structuring decisions, as liabilities flow to their acquirer by operation of law in some circumstances, as discussed above.

Contingent and unknown liabilities are another story. A **contingent liability** is a liability that might — or might not — come due, depending on what happens in the future. The classic contingent liability is a pending lawsuit against the target. If the lawsuit is decided in the target's favor, the target may not be liable for any damages. If the lawsuit is decided or resolved in a way that is unfavorable to the target, however, the target may be subject to damages or other liabilities. Even if a bidder does extensive due diligence about pending or threatened lawsuits, it can be difficult to predict the likely outcome of litigation (and the likelihood of — and likely amount of — any award of damages).

An **unknown liability** is even trickier. An unknown liability is one that is not known to exist at the time the parties are negotiating their deal. For example, a target's product or services may be subject to product liability claims in the future for defects that are not yet manifest or that have not yet caused harm. Likewise, a target's business or operations may have adverse environmental impacts that have not yet been identified. Liabilities not yet known to exist are, not surprisingly, difficult to factor in when negotiating structure and deal terms.

Because liabilities — known, contingent, and unknown — can have a dramatic impact on the economics of a corporate combination, bidders consider liability when choosing a deal structure and when pricing a deal. This is because different structures have very different implications for both bidders and targets when it comes to liabilities.

- If the deal is structured as a direct merger, the bidder succeeds to all of the liabilities of the target by operation of law.
- If the bidder purchases the target's stock (whether through a stock purchase or share exchange), the bidder does not assume the target's liabilities as a formal legal matter. Because the target keeps its liabilities, and the bidder becomes the owner of the target upon consummation of a stock purchase or share exchange, however, the bidder will want to take the target's liabilities into account when pricing the deal.

■ In a triangular merger (whether forward or reverse), the target's liabilities end up in a wholly owned subsidiary of the buyer. Thus, as with a stock purchase and share exchange, the bidder must pay attention to the target's liabilities as a practical matter, at least with respect to pricing, as the owner of the subsidiary where those liabilities reside.

■ If a bidder purchases the target's assets, the bidder will generally list the assets that it is acquiring on a schedule to the asset purchase agreement. The bidder/purchaser also will specifically list the liabilities that it is — and is not — assuming as part of the deal. Bidder/purchasers typically state in the asset purchase agreement that they are not purchasing any contingent or unknown liabilities. As discussed in the following segment below, however, this type of structuring and private ordering is not an absolute protection against liabilities associated with the acquired assets.

Asset Purchases and Successor Liability

Under most state laws and common law principles, a corporation that purchases the assets of another company is not liable for the seller's liabilities unless the purchaser expressly or impliedly assumed the seller's liability. But, there are limits to this sort of private ordering.

■ Certain federal environmental laws impose liability for environmental damage on all owners/operators of a business or property, even if the environmental damage occurred before the purchaser acquired the property or business at issue, the purchaser excluded environmental liabilities from the list of acquired liabilities in the asset purchase agreement, and the purchaser specifically disclaimed unscheduled environmental liabilities in deal documents.

■ A company that purchases another company's assets may be liable as a successor employer for purposes of federal labor and employment law if there is substantial continuity between the entities. *See, e.g., Golden State Bottling v. NLRB*, 414 U.S. 168, 182 n.5, 185 (1973) (finding successor liability theory in National Labor Relations Act (NLRA) case justified, citing need for avoidance of labor strife, prevention of deterrent effect on exercise of NLRA § 7 rights, and protection for victimized employees).

■ Courts also will not be constrained by private ordering if the transaction, though styled as an asset purchase, amounts to a consolidation or merger of the two corporations, or if the transfer of assets to the purchaser is for the fraudulent purpose of escaping liability for the seller's debts. (This is the de facto merger doctrine discussed in Section C.7 below.)

■ Courts also will look beyond private ordering if the successor is a mere continuation of the seller. *See, e.g., Ray v. Alad Corp.*, 560 P.3d 3 (Cal. 1977).

■ Relatedly, a few courts have recognized a "product line" exception to the rule that liabilities do not travel to the buyer in an asset purchase deal whereby the purchaser of a manufacturing business that continues the output of the seller's line of products may be held liable in tort for product defects in certain circumstances. *See, e.g., id.*

Teed v. Thomas & Betts Power Solutions, L.L.C.

In the following case, employees brought an action for overtime pay against their employer under the Fair Labor Standards Act (FLSA). The facts are bit complicated, so we have included a brief summary here. The district judge allowed the plaintiffs to substitute a new entity (Thomas & Betts Power Solutions, LLC) for the original defendants because the defendant's corporate parent (Thomas & Betts Corporation) had purchased the assets of Packard, the business that allegedly had engaged in the FLSA violations, and had placed Packard's assets in a wholly owned subsidiary, the substituted defendant. By virtue of the substitution, Thomas & Betts LLC was the entity against which the plaintiffs sought damages for Packard's alleged violations of their rights under the Fair Labor Standards Act. Thomas & Betts LLC objected to being substituted, and its objection, rejected by the district court, is the sole basis of the appeal excerpted below. In a nutshell, the question on appeal is whether Thomas & Betts LLC is, as the district court held, liable by virtue of the doctrine of successor liability for whatever damages might be owed the plaintiffs as a result of Packard's alleged violations. When reading the case, consider the following questions:

1. In the first paragraph, Judge Posner questions why the parent company at issue was made a defendant in the case in the first place, noting that "a parent corporation is not liable for violations of the Fair Labor Standards Act by its subsidiary unless it exercises significant authority over the subsidiary's employment practices." Why do you think Judge Posner says this? Think back to your reading on piercing the corporate veil in Chapter 1.
2. What type of transaction is at issue? Merger? Consolidation? Stock purchase? Share exchange?
3. What is successor liability?
4. What is the default rule regarding successor liability for transactions structured as asset purchases, according to the court?
5. Is there a difference between state law regarding successor liability generally, and liability that is based on a violation of a federal statute relating to labor relations or employment? What is the successor liability rule for claims arising under federal labor and employment statutes, according to the court?
6. What does the court say about the potential interplay between the successor liability rule for alleged violations of the federal labor and employment statute and in bankruptcy cases?

Teed v. Thomas & Betts Power Solutions, L.L.C.
711 F.3d 763 (7th Cir. 2013)

POSNER, Circuit Judge.

Before us are appeals in two closely related collective actions for overtime pay under the Fair Labor Standards Act; for simplicity we'll pretend that they are just one suit and that there is just one appeal. The original named defendants were JT Packard & Associates, the plaintiff's employer, and Packard's parent, S.R. Bray Corp. We don't know why the parent was made a defendant. It was not the plaintiffs' employer, and a parent corporation is not liable for violations of the Fair Labor Standards Act by its subsidiary unless it exercises significant authority over the subsidiary's employment practices. *In re Enterprise Rent-A-Car Wage & Hour Employment Practices Litigation,* 683 F.3d 462, 469 (3d Cir. 2012); cf. *Antenor v. D & S Farms,* 88 F.3d 925, 935-36 (11th Cir. 1996). The record doesn't indicate that Bray exercised such authority over Packard's employment practices.

But this is an aside. What is important is that the district judge allowed the plaintiffs to substitute Thomas & Betts Power Solutions, LLC, for the original defendants, the reason being that its parent, Thomas & Betts Corporation, had bought Packard's assets and placed them in a wholly owned subsidiary, the substituted defendant. Essentially that company is Packard renamed, and we'll continue to refer to it under that name when we are talking about the company as a company; when we are talking about it as the substituted defendant we'll call it Thomas & Betts.

By virtue of the substitution, Thomas & Betts is the entity against which the plaintiffs seek damages for Packard's alleged violations of their rights under the Fair Labor Standards Act when Packard was owned by Bray. Thomas & Betts objected to being substituted, and its objection, rejected by the district court, is the sole basis of the appeal, which is from a final judgment for some $500,000 in damages, attorneys' fees, and costs, pursuant to a settlement agreement that is conditional however on the outcome of this appeal. We must decide whether Thomas & Betts is, as the district court held, liable by virtue of the doctrine of successor liability for whatever damages may be owed the plaintiffs as a result of Packard's alleged violations.

When a company is sold in an asset sale as opposed to a stock sale, the buyer acquires the company's assets but not necessarily its liabilities; whether or not it acquires them is the issue of successor liability. Most states limit such liability, with exceptions irrelevant to this case, to sales in which a buyer (the successor) expressly or implicitly assumes the seller's liabilities. Wisconsin, the state whose law would apply if the underlying claim were based on state law, is such a state. *Columbia Propane, L.P. v. Wisconsin Gas Co.,* 261 Wis. 2d 70, 661 N.W.2d 776, 784 (2003). But when liability is based on a violation of a federal statute relating to labor relations or employment, a federal common law standard of successor liability is applied that is more favorable to plaintiffs than most state-law standards to which the court might otherwise look. See, e.g., *John Wiley & Sons, Inc. v. Livingston,* 376 U.S. 543, 548-49, 84 S. Ct. 909, 11 L. Ed. 2d 898 (1964) (Labor Management Relations Act); *Golden State Bottling Co. v. NLRB,* 414 U.S. 168, 184-85, 94 S. Ct. 414, 38 L. Ed. 2d

388 (1973) (National Labor Relations Act); *Wheeler v. Snyder Buick, Inc.,* 794 F.2d 1228, 1236 (7th Cir. 1986) (Title VII); *Upholsterers' Int'l Union Pension Fund v. Artistic Furniture,* 920 F.2d 1323, 1327 (7th Cir. 1990) (ERISA); *EEOC v. G-K-G, Inc.,* 39 F.3d 740, 747-48 (7th Cir. 1994) (Age Discrimination in Employment Act); *Sullivan v. Dollar Tree Stores, Inc.,* 623 F.3d 770, 781 (9th Cir. 2010) (Family and Medical Leave Act); cf. *Musikiwamba v. ESSI, Inc.,* 760 F.2d 740, 746 (7th Cir. 1985) (42 U.S.C. § 1981 — racial discrimination in contracting). In particular, a disclaimer of successor liability is not a defense.

We must consider whether the federal standard applies when liability is based on the Fair Labor Standards Act, and if so whether, properly applied, the standard authorized the imposition of successor liability in this case.

Packard provided, and continues under its new ownership by Thomas & Betts to provide, maintenance and emergency technical services for equipment designed to protect computers and other electrical devices from being damaged by power outages. All of Packard's stock was acquired in 2006 by Bray, though Packard retained its name and corporate identity and continued operating as a stand-alone entity. The workers' FLSA suit was filed two years later.

Several months after it was filed, Bray defaulted on a $60 million secured loan that it had obtained from the Canadian Imperial Bank of Commerce and that Packard, Bray's subsidiary, had guaranteed. To pay as much of the debt to the bank as it could, Bray assigned its assets — including its stock in Packard, which was its principal asset — to an affiliate of the bank. The assets were placed in a receivership under Wisconsin law and auctioned off, with the proceeds going to the bank. Thomas & Betts was the high bidder at the auction, paying approximately $22 million for Packard's assets. One condition specified in the transfer of the assets to Thomas & Betts pursuant to the auction was that the transfer be "free and clear of all Liabilities" that the buyer had not assumed, and a related but more specific condition was that Thomas & Betts would not assume any of the liabilities that Packard might incur in the FLSA litigation. After the transfer, Thomas & Betts continued to operate Packard much as Bray had done (and under the same name, as we noted), and indeed offered employment to most of Packard's employees.

If Wisconsin state law governed the issue of successor liability, Thomas & Betts would be off the hook because of the conditions. But as we said, they do not control, or even figure, when the federal standard applies. As usually articulated, that standard requires consideration of the following factors instead (see *Wheeler v. Snyder Buick, Inc., supra,* 794 F.2d at 1236; *Musikiwamba v. ESSI, Inc., supra,* 760 F.2d at 750-51):

(1) Whether the successor had notice of the pending lawsuit, which Thomas & Betts unquestionably had when it bought Packard at the receiver's auction; this is a factor favoring successor liability.

(2) Whether the predecessor (Packard or Bray — remember that both were defendants originally) would have been able to provide the relief sought in the lawsuit before the sale. The answer is no, because of Packard's and Bray's insolvency caused by Bray's defaulting on the bank loan. The answer counts against successor liability by making such liability seem a windfall to plaintiffs. But this depends on how long before the sale one looks.

(3) Whether the predecessor could have provided relief after the sale (again no — Packard had been sold, with the proceeds of the sale going to the bank, along with Bray's remaining assets). The predecessor's inability to provide relief favors successor liability, as without it the plaintiffs' claim is worthless.

(4) Whether the successor can provide the relief sought in the suit — Thomas & Betts can — without which successor liability is a phantom (this is a "goes without saying" condition, not usually mentioned).

(5) Whether there is continuity between the operations and work force of the predecessor and the successor, as there is in this case, which favors successor liability on the theory that nothing really has changed.

Judges tend to be partial to multifactor tests, which they believe discipline judicial decisionmaking, providing objectivity and predictability. But this depends on whether the factors making up the test are clear, whether they are valid, whether each is weighted so that the test can be applied objectively even if the factors don't all line up on one side of the issue in every case (they don't in this case, for example), and whether the factors are exhaustive or illustrative — if the latter, the test is open-ended, hence indefinite. The federal standard does not satisfy all these criteria. But applying a slight variant of the standard, the district judge concluded that there was successor liability in this case, and her analysis is thoughtful and persuasive.

We reach the same conclusion that she did, though by a slightly different route. We suggest that successor liability is appropriate in suits to enforce federal labor or employment laws — even when the successor disclaimed liability when it acquired the assets in question — unless there are good reasons to withhold such liability. Lack of notice of potential liability — the first criterion in the federal standard as usually articulated — is an example of such a reason. We'll examine other possible reasons applicable to this case shortly; but first we need to decide whether a federal standard should ever apply when the source of liability is the Fair Labor Standards Act.

The idea behind having a distinct federal standard applicable to federal labor and employment statutes is that these statutes are intended either to foster labor peace, as in the National Labor Relations Act, or to protect workers' rights, as in Title VII, and that in either type of case the imposition of successor liability will often be necessary to achieve the statutory goals because the workers will often be unable to head off a corporate sale by their employer aimed at extinguishing the employer's liability to them. This logic extends to suits to enforce the Fair Labor Standards Act. "The FLSA was passed to protect workers' standards of living through the regulation of working conditions. 29 U.S.C. § 202. That fundamental purpose is as fully deserving of protection as the labor peace, anti-discrimination, and worker security policies underlying the NLRA, Title VII, 42 U.S.C. § 1981, ERISA, and MPPAA." *Steinbach v. Hubbard,* 51 F.3d 843, 845 (9th Cir. 1995). In the absence of successor liability, a violator of the Act could escape liability, or at least make relief much more difficult to obtain, by selling its assets without an assumption of liabilities by the buyer (for such an assumption would reduce the purchase price by imposing a cost on the buyer) and then dissolving. And although it can be argued that imposing successor liability in such a case impedes the operation of the market in companies by increasing the cost to the buyer of a company that may have violated the FLSA, it's not a strong argument. The successor will have been compensated for bearing the liabilities by paying less for the assets it's buying; it will have paid less because the net value of the assets will have been diminished by the associated liabilities.

There are better arguments against having a federal standard for labor and employment cases, besides the general objections to multifactor tests that we noted earlier: applying a judge-made standard amounts to judicial amendment of the statutes to which it's applied by adding a remedy that Congress has not authorized; implied remedies (that is, remedies added by judges to the remedies specified in statutes) have become disfavored; and borrowing state common law, especially a common law principle uniform across the states, to fill gaps in federal statutes is an attractive alternative to creating federal common law, an alternative the Supreme Court adopted for example in *United States v. Bestfoods,* 524 U.S. 51, 62-64, 118 S. Ct. 1876, 141 L. Ed. 2d 43 (1998), in regard to the liability of a corporation under the Superfund law for a subsidiary's violations. But Thomas & Betts does not ask us to jettison the federal standard; it just asks us not to "extend" it to the Fair Labor Standards Act. Yet none of the concerns that we've just listed regarding the filling of holes in a federal statute with federal rather than state common law looms larger with respect to the Fair Labor Standards Act than with respect to any other federal labor or employment statute. The issue is not extension but exclusion.

Thomas & Betts argues that the Act imposes liability only on "employers," 29 U.S.C. §§ 203(d), 216(b), and Thomas & Betts was not the employer of the suing workers when the Act was violated. But that is equally true when successor liability is imposed in a Title VII case, as the case law requires. It argues that Wisconsin has an interest in this case because it too has minimum wage and overtime laws. But states also have their own laws, paralleling Title VII, forbidding employment discrimination. It points out that most FLSA suits are brought by individuals for the recovery of individual damages rather than by the government (though in fact the Department of Labor brings many), but likewise most Title VII suits are private rather than public. It argues that violations of the FLSA are "victimless," because no one is compelled to work for a company that violates that Act. Neither is anyone forced to work for a company that discriminates on grounds forbidden by Title VII, such as race and sex. Yet there are victims of the violations in both FLSA and Title VII cases — workers who would be paid higher wages if their employer complied with the FLSA and workers who would have better jobs and working conditions if their employer complied with Title VII. Moreover, there is an interest in legal predictability that is served by applying the same standard of successor liability either to all federal statutes that protect employees or to none — and "none" is not an attractive option at our level of the judiciary, given all the cases we cited earlier.

And so the federal standard applies to this case. But was it properly applied? The argument that it was not focuses on Packard's financial situation before it was sold to Thomas & Betts. Remember that Bray owed the bank $60 million and couldn't pay; that its only valuable asset was Packard; and that Packard was worth little more than a third of what Bray owed the bank. So only the happenstance of Packard's acquisition by Thomas & Betts could enable the plaintiffs to obtain relief.

But it might seem that to allow that relief would enable the plaintiffs, whose wage claims are unsecured, to obtain a preference over a senior creditor, namely the bank, which had a secured claim. Thomas & Betts would have bid less at the auction had it known it would have to pay the workers' FLSA claims, and so the bank would have obtained less money from the sale. It is true that as soon as Bray defaulted, the bank could have foreclosed on Packard's assets because they were the security for the bank's loan; the workers' claim to those assets was unsecured and therefore subordinate to the banks' claim. But the bank would no more want to own Packard, a nonfinancial company, than to own the houses of defaulting mortgagors whose mortgages it forecloses. It would want to sell Packard; and if it sold it as a going concern, a buyer subject to successor liability would not pay as much as it would if it didn't bear that liability. As a result the bank's secured claim would in effect become junior to the workers' unsecured claim by the amount by which that claim depressed the price that the successor would pay for Packard.

That is a good reason not to apply successor liability after an insolvent debtor's default, whether its assets were sold in bankruptcy or outside (by a receiver, for example, as in this case): to apply the doctrine in such a case might upend the priorities of competing creditors. See *In re Trans World Airlines*, 322 F.3d 283, 290, 292-93 (3d Cir. 2003); Douglas G. Baird, *The Elements of Bankruptcy* 227-28 (5th ed. 2010). It's an example of a good reason not mentioned in conventional formulations of the federal standard for not imposing successor liability. But it doesn't figure in this appeal. Thomas & Betts has not urged it. It says that it didn't discount its bid for Packard because of the workers' claims; this both suggests that it didn't anticipate successor liability and may explain why the bank has not complained about the imposition of that liability.

Thomas & Betts argues that to allow the plaintiffs to obtain relief gives them a "windfall." They had no right to expect that Packard would be sold, at least as a going concern; and had it not been sold, but instead continued under Bray's ownership, or broken up and its assets sold piecemeal, the bank loan would have precluded their obtaining any relief. Had Packard remained an operating subsidiary of Bray, its net income (about $5 million a year) would have belonged to the bank, while if its assets had been sold piecemeal there is no successor liability, because of the lack of continuity between predecessor and successor; for when a company is broken up and its assets sold piecemeal, there is no successor to transfer the company's liability to. But to allow Thomas & Betts to acquire assets without their associated liabilities, thus stiffing workers who have valid claims under the Fair Labor Standards Act, is equally a "windfall."

Thomas & Betts argues finally, with support in *Musikiwamba v. ESSI, Inc., supra*, 760 F.2d at 751, that allowing the workers to enforce their FLSA claims against the successor, in a case such as this in which the predecessor cannot pay them, complicates the reorganization of a bankrupt. Seeing the handwriting on the wall and wanting to minimize the impact of the reorganization on them (in loss of employment or benefits), the workers might decide to file a flurry of lawsuits, whether or not well grounded, hoping to substitute a solvent acquirer for their employer as a defendant in the suits. The prospect thus created of increased liability might scare off prospective buyers of the assets. But there is no suggestion of such a tactic by workers in this case; if there were, it would be another good reason for denying successor liability.

Still another concern is that an insolvent company, seeking to maximize its value, might decide not to sell itself as a going concern but instead to sell off its assets piecemeal, even if the company would be worth more as a going concern than as a pile of dismembered assets. In the latter case there would be as we said no successor liability, and successor liability depresses the going-concern value of the predecessor, so the insolvent company might be better off even though it was destroying value by not selling itself as a going concern. Once a firm is in Chapter 7 bankruptcy (or in a Chapter 11 bankruptcy in which a trustee is appointed), or receivership, it is "owned" by the trustee (or receiver), whose sole concern is with maximizing the net value of the debtor's estate to creditors (and maybe to other claimants — including shareholders, if the estate is flush enough to enable all the creditors' claims to be satisfied in full). *In re Taxman Clothing Co.,* 49 F.3d 310, 315 (7th Cir. 1995); *In re Central Ice Cream Co.,* 836 F.2d 1068, 1072 (7th Cir. 1987). With immaterial exceptions, the trustee in a Chapter 7 bankruptcy (or, we assume, a receiver) must sell the debtor's assets for the highest price he can get. 11 U.S.C. § 704(a)(1); *In re Moore,* 608 F.3d 253, 263 (5th Cir. 2010); *In re Atlanta Packaging Products, Inc.,* 99 B.R. 124 (Bankr. N.D. Ga. 1988). He may not cut the price so that some junior creditor can enforce a claim not against the debtor's assets but against a third party, the successor, in this case Thomas & Betts. The trustee would be required to sell the assets piecemeal if that would yield more money for the creditors as a whole (to be allocated among them according to their priorities) than sale as a going concern would, even if some creditors would be harmed because successor liability would have been extinguished, and even if economic value would have been destroyed.

But this is a theoretical rather than a practical objection. Since most firms' assets are worth much more as a going concern than dispersed, successor liability will affect the choice between the two forms of sale in only a small fraction of cases. Lynn M. LoPucki & Joseph W. Doherty, "Bankruptcy Fire Sales," 106 Mich. L. Rev. 1, 5 (2007).

With these chimeras set to one side, there is no good reason to reject successor liability in this case — the default rule in suits to enforce federal labor or employment laws. (For remember that the successor's disclaimer of liability is not a good reason in such a case.) Packard was a profitable company. It went on the auction block not because it was insolvent but because it was the guarantor of its parent's bank loan and the parent defaulted. Had Packard been sold before Bray got into trouble, imposition of successor liability would have been unexceptionable; Bray could have found a buyer for Packard willing to pay a good price even if the buyer had to assume the company's FLSA liabilities. Those liabilities were modest, after all. Remember that the parties have agreed to settle the workers' suit (should we affirm the district court) for only about $500,000, though doubtless there was initial uncertainty as to what the amount of a judgment or settlement would be; in addition, Thomas & Betts incurred attorneys' fees to defend against the suit. Nevertheless had Packard been sold before Bray got into trouble, imposition of successor liability would have been unexceptionable, and we have not been given an adequate reason why its having been sold afterward should change the result.

AFFIRMED.

Post-Case Follow-Up

Courts often apply the **substantial continuity** test to determine whether a successor entity ought to be held responsible for a predecessor's liabilities arising under federal labor and employment law. Courts applying this test typically look to factors set forth in the seminal Sixth Circuit case *EEOC v. McMillan*, 503 F.2d 1086, 1094 (6th Cir. 1974). In that case, the court cited the following factors as relevant to determining whether (or not) to impose successor liability on an entity purchasing the assets of another business: (1) whether the successor company had prior notice of the charge or pending lawsuit; (2) the ability of the predecessor to provide relief; (3) whether there has been substantial continuity of business operations; (4) whether the new employer uses the same facilities; (5) whether the new employer uses the same or substantially the same work force; (6) whether the new employer uses the same or substantially the same supervisory personnel; (7) whether the same jobs exist under substantially the same working conditions; (8) whether the new employer uses the same machinery, equipment, and methods of production; and (9) whether the new employer produces the same product.

Teed v. Thomas & Betts Power Solutions, L.L.C.: Real Life Applications

You represent Acme, Inc. in its negotiations with Zed, Inc. Zed manufactures respirators (masks) used by workers to prevent lung damage that might otherwise result from the use of paints and pesticides. Acme explains that it wants to structure a transaction with Zed as an asset purchase agreement, because it is concerned about the potential for product defect tort claims. While Zed has not been sued to date, Acme is concerned that Zed's products are relatively new and that workers may yet claim that Zed's respirators did not adequately protect them against lung damage.

a. Prepare a schedule for the asset purchase addressing the disposition of liability for tort claims arising out of the use or operation of Zed's respirators. Your schedule should make it clear that Acme has not agreed to assume these liabilities.

b. Prepare a letter for the client explaining whether, and under what circumstances, a court might hold Acme responsible for damages caused by product defects notwithstanding the schedule that you prepared in response to Question 1.a.

c. What, if anything, might you advise Acme to do to address and mitigate risks associated with unknown product defect claims?

Shareholder Voting Issues

Shareholder voting rights also may impact deal structuring. As noted above, except for deals structured as stock purchases and short-form mergers, shareholders of the target corporation get to vote on the corporate combinations discussed in this chapter. The voting rights of the shareholders of the bidder generally turn on how the deal is structured. For example, under Delaware's 20 percent rule, codified at DGCL § 251(f) and discussed above, there are several ways to structure a deal that do not require a bidder vote, including an asset purchase agreement, stock purchase, triangular merger, or by using cash consideration in a direct merger. Under the MBCA, bidder shareholders get to vote on a proposed acquisition if the bidder issues shares that are equal to more than 20 percent of the bidder's outstanding pre-deal voting power. *See* MBCA § 6.21(f)(1)(ii) (providing that an issuance of shares or other securities convertible into or rights exercisable for shares, in a transaction or a series of integrated transactions, requires approval of the shareholders, at a meeting at which a quorum consisting of at least a majority of the votes entitled to be cast on the matter exists, if "the voting power of shares that are issued and issuable as a result of the transaction or series of integrated transactions will comprise more than 20% of the voting power of the shares of the corporation that were outstanding immediately before the transaction").

At a minimum, target shareholder voting rights mean that the boards of the bidder and target generally cannot force a transaction over the objections of target company shareholders. Nothing requires shareholders to go along with a corporate combination, after all, even if it is recommended by management. Since bidder shareholder rights vary depending on state law and the transaction at issue, lawyers need to identify relevant rules, assess risks associated with having to deal with both buyer and seller shareholder voting rights, if applicable, and then execute any required shareholder vote.

Appraisal Rights

As noted above, appraisal rights provide qualifying dissenting shareholders the option of having the corporation buy back their shares for cash at fair value as determined by the court. Under the MBCA, appraisal rights are available to dissenting shareholders in transactions structured as a share exchange, sale of all or substantially all assets, and merger. *See* MBCA § 13.02(a). Only certain mergers trigger appraisal rights under the DGCL. Appraisal rights can cause issues for deals intended to be structured as tax-free reorganizations. This is because the cash paid to shareholders may count as "boot"—that is, cash that can be paid out in a tax-free reorganization under IRS rules—and having too much "boot" may make the transaction ineligible for tax-free treatment under IRS rules. Furthermore, the target and bidder must consider the amount of the cash payments that will need to be made to dissenting shareholders. A deal with significant shareholder opposition—and thus large numbers of potentially dissenting shareholders—may prove to be too expensive (or, alternatively, not economically advantageous enough) to justify going forward.

Contract Assignment

Another issue that can impact structuring relates to assignment and delegation rules arising under contract law. As is true for many businesses, a target corporation may be a party to large numbers of contracts. The general rule under contracts law is that many types of contracts and contract rights are freely assignable. Thus, if a contract is silent on the issue of assignment, default contract rules will apply, and those rules generally (but not always) permit assignment.

There are exceptions to the rule that contracts and contract rights are freely assignable, however, and these exceptions have implications for certain corporate combinations. First, contracts often contain clauses limiting or prohibiting assignment or delegation. If a contract contains an anti-assignment clause, a bidder/potential acquirer will not be able to step into the shoes of the target if the deal is structured as an asset purchase. This is because an asset purchase, by definition, constitutes an assignment. While assignment *may* be possible if the deal is structured as something other than an asset purchase — for example, a forward or reverse triangular merger — the right to assign will depend on the precise language of any anti-assignment or anti-delegation clause, and there is a risk that the seller/potential target acquirer may not be able to assign rights or delegate duties under a contract impacted by a proposed corporate combinaton. Second, certain types of contracts and contract rights are not freely assignable as a matter of substantive law. For example, certain types of patent, copyright, and trademark licenses are not freely assignable (or, if they are assignable, the assignment documents must include specified statutory language). Likewise, personal services contracts generally are not freely assignable, either. It is possible to include language in contracts that makes it easier to assign contractual rights (assuming assignment is legally permissible) in connection with a transaction. The bidder/potential acquirer should be careful to review key contracts during the due diligence process, however, as risks associated with contract assignment or delegation may impact both structuring and pricing.

Governmental Approvals and Licensing Requirements

A final issue related to assignment that may influence structuring relates to licensing requirements or governmental approvals. In some cases, assignment is not possible because the buyer lacks a license or governmental approval necessary to be a party to a contract. In addition to reviewing key contracts for anti-assignment clauses or change of control provisions, lawyers also should identify regulatory requirements associated with assignment or performance under key contracts.

Anti-Assignment Provisions, Change of Control Provisions

Here is an example of an anti-assignment provision:

Licensee shall not assign any of its rights under this Agreement, except with the prior written consent of the Licensor. Any and all assignments of rights are prohibited under this section, whether voluntary or involuntary, by merger, consolidation, dissolution, operation of law, or by any other manner. For purposes of this provision, (i) any "change of control" is deemed an assignment of right; and (ii) "merger" refers to any merger in which the Licensee participates, whether it is the surviving or disappearing corporation.

Here is an example of a change of control provision:

A change of control for purposes of this Agreement shall mean any (a) merger, reorganization, share exchange, consolidation, business combination, private purchase, recapitalization, or other transaction involving the Licensee as a result of which (i) the stockholders or owners of the Licensee immediately preceding the transaction would hold less than 50% of the outstanding shares of, or less than 50% of the outstanding voting power of the ultimate company resulting from such transaction immediately after consummation thereof; or (ii) any person or group would hold 50% or more of the outstanding shares or voting power of the ultimate company resulting from such transaction immediately after the consummation thereof; (b) the direct or indirect acquisition by any Person or group of beneficial ownership, or the right to acquire beneficial ownership, or formation of any group which beneficially owns or has the right to acquire beneficial ownership, of more than 50% of either the outstanding voting power of the outstanding shares of Licensee, in each case on a fully diluted basis; (c) the purchase or license by the Licensee of any part, division, or asset of a company that is directly competitive with any licensed product; or (d) the adoption of a plan relating to the liquidation or dissolution of the Licensee.

7. De Facto Merger Doctrine and Freeze-Outs

As noted above, the **de facto merger doctrine** is an exception to the general rule that a corporation that purchases the assets of another company is not liable for the seller's liabilities unless the purchaser expressly or impliedly assumed the predecessor's liability. Broadly speaking, the de facto merger doctrine allows courts to treat an acquisition as a merger if it is a merger "in fact," although it might not be a merger in name. Under the doctrine, a corporation must comply with all of the formalities of a merger — board approval, shareholder approval, and appraisal rights for dissenters — if a transaction has the effect of a merger, no matter what the parties involved choose to call it.

A merger undertaken for the purpose of "**freezing out**" minority shareholders may be enjoined or set aside by a court if there is no legitimate business purpose for the transaction other than to oppress minority shareholders. Such a freeze-out (or "squeeze-out") often occurs when a corporation is profitable and directors who are also holders of a majority of the corporation's stock wish to eliminate other shareholders. They thus form a new corporation owned solely by them and merge the old corporation into the new one. Under the plan of merger, shareholders of the old corporation will receive cash but will not continue as shareholders in the new corporation, thus being frozen out of their corporation.

8. Limitation of Shareholder Remedies, Creditor Rights

Shareholders have very limited remedies to oppose a merger, share exchange, or purchase of assets once it has been approved. For example, under newly adopted MBCA § 13.40, shareholders cannot attempt to enjoin or set aside one of these transactions once it has been approved unless there was some fundamental flaw in the process by which the transaction was approved, it was procured by fraud, or involved a conflict of interest. Absent such evidence, a dissenting shareholder may be limited to appraisal rights (where available).

As for creditors of a corporation involved in a corporate combination, the sale of all or substantially all of a corporation's assets may trigger certain requirements of Article 6 of the Uniform Commercial Code or state law provisions relating to **bulk sales**, i.e. the sale or transfer of more than one-half of a company's inventory and equipment outside the scope of its ordinary course of business. To protect creditors of the selling corporation, the bulk sales provisions require that creditors of the selling corporation be given notice of the intended transfer. Noncompliance with the bulk sales requirements may entitle a creditor to damages. The pertinent state statutes should be consulted to determine if the selling corporation must comply with its state's bulk sales requirements, especially because many states have repealed or revised Article 6 (primarily because with today's technology and credit reporting advances, creditors are better able to evaluate risk and protect themselves).

D. HOSTILE TAKEOVERS

1. Introduction

Most proposed combinations go forward — or not — on a consensual basis: After a period of negotiation, the management of the constituent firms either comes to terms, or disagrees on the transaction, in which case the transaction usually dies. Sometimes, though, combinations occur without the consent of the management of the target corporation. Combinations that are not consented to by the target's management usually are referred to as **hostile takeovers**. In a hostile takeover, the aggressor or bidder goes over the head of the target's management and courts the shareholders directly, promising management changes and often offering attractive consideration for the shareholders' stock as inducements. There are two primary methods of conducting a hostile takeover: a **tender offer** or a **proxy fight**. We discuss both of these methods below, along with common defensive measures put in place by incumbent boards in response to a contest for corporate control.

2. Preparing for the Takeover

Assume that both the aggressor and the target are publicly traded corporations. The aggressor's first step might be to build up a war chest of cash to finance the acquisition. It may borrow money or even sell some of its assets to acquire cash. The aggressor may collect information about the target, its management, and its operations to confirm that a takeover of the target is a sound decision. The aggressor must then evaluate whether it wishes to attempt a consensual acquisition and deal with the target's management or whether it should appeal directly to the target's shareholders. Each technique has advantages and disadvantages. An approach to the target's management could yield significant accurate information about the target so that the aggressor does not pay too much for acquiring the target. On the other hand, if the target's management believes it is threatened, it might take immediate steps to thwart the transaction. An approach directly to the shareholders could result in overpaying for their stock, yet it has the distinct advantage of surprise, which may make it difficult for the target's management to take action to defend itself.

Assume the aggressor decides to proceed by surprise. It may begin purchasing the target's stock on the open market. Because a purchase of more than 5 percent of a class of stock of a publicly traded company generally requires disclosure and filings with the SEC, the aggressor often purchases up to 4.9 percent of the target's outstanding shares. This is called the **foothold**, **toehold**, or **creeping tender offer**. An acute target will notice that its stock is being actively traded and that the increased trading is causing its stock to rise in value. The target might thus suspect an aggressor is planning a takeover, but it might not know the identity of the aggressor at this time. The target could begin adopting defensive strategies to ward off the anticipated aggressor.

3. The Tender Offer

Rather than continuing to purchase shares anonymously on the open market, after it obtains its toehold, the aggressor may publicly announce a cash offer for as much of the target's stock as it needs to acquire all or majority control, in this case, 45.2 percent of the target's stock (45.2 percent + 4.9 percent = 50.1 percent). This is the formal tender offer. In SEC parlance, "a tender offer is a broad solicitation by a company or a third party to purchase a substantial percentage of a company's . . . shares or units for a limited period of time. The offer is at a fixed price, usually at a premium over the current market price, and is customarily contingent on shareholders tendering a fixed number of their shares or units." *See* Securities and Exchange Commission, Fast Answers, Tender Offer, https://www.sec.gov/answers/tender.htm. In less technical terms, a tender offer is a public announcement made directly to the target's shareholders, specifying the identity of the bidder, the price at which the aggressor will purchase the stock, the amount of stock it wishes to purchase, the date by which the shares must be tendered by the target's shareholders, and the identification of the place where the shares are to be tendered.

For example, the aggressor may offer to buy 45.2 percent of the target's stock, at $50 per share, the offer to expire in 45 business days. If the aggressor acquires 45.2 percent of the stock, it will have sufficient power to replace the majority of the target's board of directors and thereby effectively control the target corporation. If insufficient shares are tendered to give the aggressor 45.2 percent of the target's stock, the aggressor will return all the tendered shares and might decide not to proceed. At this point, the aggressor has invested only the amount of its toehold and some costs in attempting the takeover. During the tender offer period, another aggressor corporation might enter the fray and offer to buy the toehold from the first aggressor. The first aggressor may sell this to the second at a substantial profit. The second aggressor will then proceed with the takeover.

Setting the price for the tender offer is highly complex. The aggressor needs to make the offer high

Characteristics of Tender Offers

Tender offers typically are structured as stock purchases, and they usually include some or all of the following characteristics and techniques: (i) public announcement of tender offer purchasing program coupled with active solicitation of target shareholders; (ii) significant and rapid accumulation of target company stock by bidder/acquirer prior to and/or accompanying announcement of tender offer; (iii) offer to purchase target company stock from stockholders at a price higher than the then-prevailing market price; (iv) offer that is contingent upon shareholders' tender of a specific number of shares (with both a minimum and a maximum number of shares specified); (v) offer open for a limited period of time; and (vi) offerees thus encouraged or pressured to tender shares.

enough to induce shareholders to tender their shares yet not so high as to be excessive and wasteful. Many tender offers range from 30 percent to 50 percent above the market price of the stock. Tender offers can be partial in nature, in which case the bidder attempts to acquire only a majority interest in the corporation, or they can be full, in which case the bidder offers to buy all of the outstanding shares of the corporation. The bidder may offer cash only or a combination of cash and its own shares.

Regulation of hostile takeovers, including tender offers, is accomplished through § 13(d) of the Securities Exchange Act of 1934 regulating the reporting of acquisitions of stock that result in ownership of more than 5 percent of a class of stock, § 14(d) of the 1934 Act regulating the making of tender offers, and the **Williams Act**, passed in 1968, which is basically a series of refinements to § 13 and § 14 of the 1934 Act that apply to § 12 reporting companies. The intent of the Williams Act is to impose some structure and rules for tender offers and eliminate fraud by requiring certain disclosures by both aggressors and targets. It protects shareholders from their own management as well as from the individuals and entities seeking to effect a hostile takeover. Additionally, many states have enacted legislation regulating takeovers of their domestic corporations, often to discourage takeovers of locally based corporations that contribute significantly to the state's economy.

Some of these federal and state rules focus on reporting and disclosure obligations. For example, because consummation of a tender offer would result in the aggressor owning more than 5 percent of a class of stock, the aggressor must comply with reporting and disclosure requirements of § 14(d) of the 1934 Act. The aggressor must file the appropriate statement with the SEC, identifying itself, the source of the money being used to purchase the target's stock, how much of the target's stock it owns, and any plans it has for the target (such as liquidating it, selling its assets, merging it with another corporation, and so forth) in the event the tender offer is successful. The statement is filed with the SEC on the date of the commencement of the tender offer. A copy must be delivered to the target and to any exchange (such as NYSE) on which the target's stock is traded. Tender offer materials must also be delivered to the target's stockholders at the time the bidder provides them with detailed instructions on how to tender their shares. The company that is the subject of the takeover must file its response to the tender offer with the SEC and provide a copy of the response to its shareholders within ten business days. The response indicates if the target company recommends acceptance or rejection of the tender offer. The aggressor may continue to purchase stock during the tender offer period. Announcement of the tender offer is often done by advertisement or press release and is said to put the target "into play."

The tender offer rules also contain substantive and procedural protections for target company shareholders. For example, the Williams Act requires that the tender offer remain open for at least 20 business days. Shareholders must be given a right to withdraw their tenders, and all shareholders must be treated equally. If the shares tendered exceed the amount specified in the tender offer, the offer is **oversubscribed**. To avoid a stampede by shareholders to sell their stock without adequate time for reflection, the Williams Act requires that an oversubscribed tender offer must be effected on a pro rata basis rather than a "first come, first

Rules Governing Tender Offers

Regulations promulgated under the Securities Exchange Act of 1934 contain certain structural and procedural rules designed to protect target company shareholders in a tender offer situation. For example, Exchange Act rules impose a 20-day minimum offering period; allow shareholders to revoke their tenders during the offering period; provide for pro rata purchases from shareholders in the event a tender offer is oversubscribed; state that all shareholders must be able to participate in the tender offer; and further state that all shareholders must get the best price offered by the bidder (which matters in situations where the bidder later sweetens the offer to get more shareholders to tender). The SEC's tender offer rules generally do not apply to tender offers that, if consummated, will result in ownership of 5 percent or less of the target's outstanding shares, which are called "mini-tender offers."

served" basis. Thus, the aggressor cannot simply elect to purchase the first shares tendered to it. For example, if the aggressor needs to purchase 10 million shares, and 12 million shares are actually tendered, it cannot buy the first 10 million tendered; it must purchase 10,000,000/12,000,000 (or 5/6) of each tender. Alternatively, the aggressor can elect to purchase all 12 million shares tendered. During the period the tender offer is open, the aggressor cannot negotiate with individual shareholders or make purchases other than according to the tender offer. Once the tender offer period expires, however, it can negotiate privately with shareholders in attempts to acquire more shares.

When a tender offer is made and the target is put into play, other investors may begin trading in the target's shares. For example, as soon as the tender offer is announced, speculators might begin buying the target's stock so that they can then tender the stock to the aggressor and make an immediate profit. This behavior is called **risk arbitrage**, and although it is hugely speculative, it can also be hugely lucrative. The danger to the risk arbitrageurs (the arbs), of course, is that insufficient shares will be tendered or some other force might make the aggressor's bid unsuccessful, leaving the risk arbitrageur holding stock that it paid dearly for in a target that is still weak and poorly managed.

4. Post-Tender Offer Transactions

If the aggressor abandons its takeover bid, much of the stock of the target might be in the hands of the risk arbitrageurs or other speculators who recently bought stock in the target only to make a profit and not for any desire to control the target, improve its management, or make it more profitable. Thus, if the tender offer is unsuccessful, either the aggressor or some other third party may deal directly with the risk arbitrageurs and other speculators to purchase the target's stock from them. This practice is called a **street sweep**, the reference being to Wall Street.

If the tender offer is successful and the aggressor acquires a controlling interest in the target, the aggressor usually thereafter attempts to gain even more stock, with the ideal being ownership of 100 percent of the target's outstanding stock. No matter how attractive the offer is, however, some individual shareholders will refuse to sell their shares. To obtain 100 percent ownership, the aggressor will proceed with a **mop up** or **back end transaction**, essentially a short-form merger, to obtain total ownership of the target's stock. Because there are so few shareholders left, they are powerless to stop a merger initiated by the target with its controlling shares of stock. Although these holdouts might have appraisal rights as dissenters (assuming the stock is not publicly traded), often the appraisal right is not as attractive as the tender offer, thus encouraging shareholders to accept promptly the terms of the tender offer rather than being forced to sell their shares at a less attractive price later.

Ideally, bidders would like to obtain at least 90 percent of the target's shares in the tender offer so that they can quickly gain the remaining 10 percent through a short-form merger. In many instances, achieving this 90 percent threshold is a merger condition, such that if the acquiring company does not acquire sufficient shares to reach this level, it need not complete the transaction. SEC rules allow bidders to give a "subsequent offering period" (after expiration of the initial 20-day tender offer period) to the target's shareholders to give them a second opportunity to tender their shares now that they understand that the takeover is inevitable. So long as appropriate notice is given of the subsequent offering period, bidders can then use the procedure to gain additional shares and perhaps effect a short-form merger.

In fact, the two-step approach (tender offer followed by a back-end short-form merger when the acquirer owns at least 90 percent of the target's outstanding stock) is a common one. In another scenario, called the "top up option," if an acquiring company does not obtain the requisite number of shares to reach the 90 percent threshold needed to effect a short-form merger, it is then permitted to acquire newly issued shares of the target in order to reach this threshold number and then effect a short-form merger.

5. Proxy Fights

As an alternative to a hostile takeover by tender offer, an aggressor corporation might solicit the target's shareholders with a proposal that they vote for the aggressor's slate of directors and managers. This is the so-called **proxy battle** or **proxy fight**. In a proxy fight, the bidder/acquirer tries to take over the target's board of directors by getting people friendly to the bidder (and the bidder's plans for the corporation) elected to fill a majority of board seats. This method is called a proxy fight, or proxy battle, because shareholder voting in public companies generally occurs by proxy; both management and the aggressor will be attempting to obtain proxies from shareholders for election of their own directors. If the aggressor is successful, it effectively obtains control of the target through controlling the majority of the board. Once it has control of the board, it may dismantle defensive measures (discussed below) and negotiate a consensual merger. In general, it is more difficult to obtain control of a corporation through a proxy fight than through a tender offer, primarily because it is difficult to induce shareholders to vote out management. Shareholders would much rather be induced with the profit they can make by tendering their shares at above-market prices to the aggressor. As with tender offers, proxy fights are regulated by the federal securities laws.

6. Defensive Strategies

Corporations have developed a number of strategies to avoid being taken over. These **takeover defenses** may be developed even before a tender offer is made or a proxy battle is initiated to discourage a takeover bid in the first place, or they may be adopted after a tender offer has been made, in an attempt by the target to defeat the aggressor. As discussed below, defensive measures undertaken in response to a contest for corporate control are the subject of frequent litigation. We describe some common defensive measures first, then discuss the heightened standard of review applied to such defensive measures under Delaware fiduciary duty law.

Pre-Tender Offer Defenses

Provisions instituted before a takeover bid are generally designed to make the target less attractive to would-be aggressors. These provisions are usually called **shark repellents** or **porcupine provisions** and are included in a corporation's articles or bylaws:

- A **staggered** or **classified board** of directors might be introduced together with a provision that directors can only be removed "for cause." This approach means that it could take the aggressor several years to acquire control of the target's board. Of course, if the bidder acquires all or nearly all of the outstanding shares, it might be able to amend the articles to "unstagger" the board, assuming shareholder approval can be obtained.
- Bylaw provisions calling for a **super-majority vote** (perhaps two-thirds or more) by shareholders to approve a merger, unseat directors, or amend bylaws tend to discourage hostile takeover attempts.
- The corporation may grant directors, officers, and key employees **golden parachutes** requiring that these individuals, if ousted, must be compensated in some extraordinary amount. The golden parachutes might make the takeover too expensive for the aggressor, as these contractual requirements must be satisfied by the aggressor before installing its own key people. Severance contracts for lower level employees are sometimes called **tin parachutes** (or even *lead parachutes*). Note that under the Dodd-Frank Act, companies soliciting votes to approve merger or acquisition transactions must provide disclosure of certain golden parachute compensation arrangements and, in certain circumstances, conduct a separate shareholder advisory vote to approve the golden parachute compensation arrangements.
- The target can make itself unattractive by selling off certain assets or divisions, acquiring debt, or distributing a huge cash dividend to its shareholders. Thus, the aggressor will be forced to acquire a cash-poor target with few desirable assets.
- The target might adopt a **poison pill** defense, also known as a **shareholder rights plan.** This defense is extremely popular and has been widely adopted. The poison pill defense is implemented by directors as part of an anti-takeover program and is triggered by a tender offer made by a bidder. Once the tender offer

is announced or an acquisition reaches certain limits (often 15 percent), the target's shareholders are automatically given additional rights, including increased voting rights, the right to acquire additional shares or bonds of the target at bargain prices (often 50 percent below market value), or the right to turn in shares for cash if the takeover is successful. These rights granted to the shareholders make acquisition of control by a bidder far more difficult and nearly prohibitively expensive. Once shareholders exercise their rights to purchase more stock at the bargain prices and acquire massive amounts of stock, shares owned by the incoming bidder become more diluted. As poison pills can be complicated, we offer a few summary points here. We recommend that you take a course in mergers and acquisitions if you intend to practice in this area.

- Poison pills are a consequence of the different treatment of mergers and tender offers under Delaware corporate law. Both tender offers and mergers are extraordinary transactions that, if consummated, threaten equivalent impacts on the corporation and its shareholders — namely, a change in control. But, mergers and tender offers are treated differently when it comes to board involvement. Under DGCL § 251, board approval and recommendation are required before shareholders have the opportunity to vote on or even consider a merger proposal. In contrast, the board has no statutory role in responding to tender offers. Poison pills are an attempt to address the board's lack of involvement in tender offers, in that they make it more difficult for an aggressor to force a change of control over the objections of the incumbent board.

- Historically, poison pills have been adopted by boards of directors without shareholder approval. They usually include both "**flip-in**" and "**flip-over**" components. A flip-in clause allows shareholders to purchase stock in their own company (at a discount) once the bidder acquires a certain percentage of the company's shares; a flip-over clause (also called a **flip-out** clause) allows shareholders to purchase stock (at a discount) in the bidder after a takeover occurs.

- Because aggressors might seize control of a board of directors and then deactivate the poison pill to avoid the shareholders' rights, would-be targets have adopted the variations or refinements to poison pill defenses. For these and other reasons, there are now many different kinds of poison pills, and there is a robust body of case law discussing the propriety of various poison pill terms and devices.

  - A **dead-hand poison pill** is one that can only be deactivated by the directors who established it (or their designated successors). The dead-hand pill is also called a **continuing director plan**. In many instances, directors eliminate the dead-hand by redeeming the purchase rights from shareholders by paying them a small fee. The dead-hand pill protects the target's current board because it can only be deactivated by those who continue after a takeover. Some states, notably Delaware, have held that dead-hand pills are invalid because they result in two different classes of directors: those who can deactivate the dead-hand and those who cannot. Moreover, dead-hand pills wrest too much control from shareholders.

  - A **slow-hand poison pill** is one that bars newly elected directors from deactivating or redeeming the pill for some limited period of time, often six months.

- A **no-hand poison pill** provides that no director can remove the pill if control of the board changes hands. Some states, including Delaware, have held slow-hand and no-hand pills invalid on the basis that they impermissibly interfere with directors' abilities to manage the corporation.
- A **chewable poison pill** is one that is more palatable to shareholders and is one of short duration (often three or five years rather than the often ten-year term of a standard poison pill), is triggered only when a significant number of shares are purchased by a bidder (often 20 percent rather than the trigger threshold of 10 percent or 15 percent for most poison pills), and allows a takeover to proceed if it is fully financed and all cash, even if the incumbent board opposes it. Chewable poison pills are a recent innovation that appeals to shareholders.

Shareholders sometimes dislike poison pills because they have the potential to thwart a takeover that the shareholders desire. In recent years, activist shareholders have been successful in getting corporate management to give them a voice in decisions relating to poison pills. For example, any poison pill adopted by General Electric Co. must be ratified by its shareholders within 12 months. In other modern trends, companies adopt poison pill plans of shorter duration (often five years rather than ten) or wait to adopt the pill until one is needed in response to a particular hostile bid (sometimes called the "morning after pill"). Many companies now obtain shareholder approval before adopting a poison pill plan or provide that the pill will automatically terminate if not approved by shareholders at their next annual meeting.

Post-Tender Offer Defenses

Once a tender offer has been made, the target can implement a variety of defenses in an attempt to thwart the aggressor. Some of these defenses are as follows:

- The target might attempt to find another more compatible corporation with which to merge. The third party is called the **white knight** because its function is to save the target from the enemy aggressor, often called the **black knight**.
- The target might turn the tables and make a tender offer to acquire the aggressor. This is the **Pac-Man** defense, because its effect is to eat up the opposition.
- The target could begin selling off some of its most valuable assets to make itself less attractive to the aggressor. This is the **crown jewel** defense.
- The target could engage in a **scorched earth** battle by selling off its crown jewels, loading itself up with debt, or having an immediate and sudden departure of all of the target's management, in an effort to avoid capture.
- The target might use the **Jonestown** defense and effectively commit suicide by going into bankruptcy or destroying itself to avoid a takeover.
- The target could quickly purchase another corporation engaged in a business competitive to the aggressor's business, thereby creating antitrust problems for the aggressor.
- The management of the target might enter into a so-called **suicide pact** or **people pill**, whereby managers agree that if any one of them is fired or demoted after

a takeover, they will all resign. Such an en masse walkout leaves the aggressor without any stability or continuity in management.

■ Management of the target might routinely recommend against the takeover and refuse to deactivate its poison pill, using the **just say no** defense. If this approach is consistent with the board's fiduciary duties, it is valid.

■ The target could attempt a **self-tender**, a purchase of its own shares on the open market or from its own shareholders, to prevent the aggressor from acquiring control. Such a self-tender is subject to various SEC rules imposing disclosure requirements on the target much the same way that disclosure is required of an aggressor.

As with poison pills, these strategies and techniques have been the subject of frequent and intense litigation.

7. *Unocal* and Enhanced Scrutiny of Defensive Measures

Ordinarily, a board's decision to enter into (or, not enter into) a transaction is subject to the business judgment rule. This is because it ordinarily is up to the board to decide whether (or not) to enter into a transaction, and whether (or not) to implement measures such as a staggered board. When a board implements a defensive measure in response to a contest for corporate control, however, there is a concern that the board is acting out of a desire to entrench existing management, and to preserve its own power, rather than acting in the best interests of the shareholders and the corporation. To address this (at a minimum) structural conflict of interest, the Delaware courts have developed an enhanced scrutiny standard of review for defensive measures implemented in response to a contest for corporate control.

Case Preview

Unocal Corp. v. Mesa Petroleum Co.

The goal of the enhanced scrutiny standard, first announced in the next case — *Unocal Corp. v. Mesa Petroleum Co.* — is to ensure that directors are acting in the corporation's best interest and not failing to comply with fiduciary duties. When reading *Unocal*, consider the following questions:

1. Who is Mesa? What is a greenmailer?
2. What did Mesa offer Unocal's shareholders?
3. What did Unocal's board do in response to Mesa's tender offer?
4. Why did Unocal's board decide to oppose a deal with Mesa?
5. What test or standard does the court apply to determine whether a board's decision to implement defensive measures in response to a contest for corporate control complies with the board's fiduciary obligations to the corporation and its shareholders?
6. Why doesn't the business judgment rule apply?
7. Did Unocal's board breach its fiduciary duties? Why or why not?

Unocal Corp. v. Mesa Petroleum Co.
493 A.2d 946 (Del. 1985)

MOORE, Justice.*

We confront an issue of first impression in Delaware — the validity of a corporation's self-tender for its own shares which excludes from participation a stockholder making a hostile tender offer for the company's stock.

The Court of Chancery granted a preliminary injunction to the plaintiffs, Mesa Petroleum Co., Mesa Asset Co., Mesa Partners II, and Mesa Eastern, Inc. (collectively "Mesa"), enjoining an exchange offer of the defendant, Unocal Corporation (Unocal) for its own stock. The trial court concluded that a selective exchange offer, excluding Mesa, was legally impermissible. We cannot agree with such a blanket rule. The factual findings of the Vice Chancellor, fully supported by the record, establish that Unocal's board, consisting of a majority of independent directors, acted in good faith, and after reasonable investigation found that Mesa's tender offer was both inadequate and coercive. Under the circumstances the board had both the power and duty to oppose a bid it perceived to be harmful to the corporate enterprise. On this record we are satisfied that the device Unocal adopted is reasonable in relation to the threat posed, and that the board acted in the proper exercise of sound business judgment. We will not substitute our views for those of the board if the latter's decision can be "attributed to any rational business purpose." *Sinclair Oil Corp. v. Levien*, Del. Supr., 280 A.2d 717, 720 (1971). Accordingly, we reverse the decision of the Court of Chancery and order the preliminary injunction vacated.

I.

The factual background of this matter bears a significant relationship to its ultimate outcome.

On April 8, 1985, Mesa, the owner of approximately 13% of Unocal's stock, commenced a two-tier "front loaded" cash tender offer for 64 million shares, or approximately 37%, of Unocal's outstanding stock at a price of $54 per share. The "back-end" was designed to eliminate the remaining publicly held shares by an exchange of securities purportedly worth $54 per share. However, pursuant to an order entered by the United States District Court for the Central District of California on April 26, 1985, Mesa issued a supplemental proxy statement to Unocal's stockholders disclosing that the securities offered in the second-step merger would be highly subordinated, and that Unocal's capitalization would differ significantly from its present structure. Unocal has rather aptly termed such securities "junk bonds."[3]

---

*Most footnotes have been omitted for purposes of brevity.

[3] Mesa's May 3, 1985 supplement to its proxy statement states:

(i) following the Offer, the Purchasers would seek to effect a merger of Unocal and Mesa Eastern or an affiliate of Mesa Eastern (the "Merger") in which the remaining Shares would be acquired for a combination of subordinated debt securities and preferred stock; (ii) the securities to be received by Unocal shareholders in the Merger would be subordinated to $2,400 million of debt securities of Mesa Eastern, indebtedness incurred to refinance up to $1,000 million of bank debt which was incurred by affiliates of Mesa Partners II to purchase Shares and to pay related interest and expenses and all then-existing debt of Unocal; (iii) the

Unocal's board consists of eight independent outside directors and six insiders. It met on April 13, 1985, to consider the Mesa tender offer. Thirteen directors were present, and the meeting lasted nine and one-half hours. The directors were given no agenda or written materials prior to the session. However, detailed presentations were made by legal counsel regarding the board's obligations under both Delaware corporate law and the federal securities laws. The board then received a presentation from Peter Sachs on behalf of Goldman Sachs & Co. (Goldman Sachs) and Dillon, Read & Co. (Dillon Read) discussing the bases for their opinions that the Mesa proposal was wholly inadequate. Mr. Sachs opined that the minimum cash value that could be expected from a sale or orderly liquidation for 100% of Unocal's stock was in excess of $60 per share. In making his presentation, Mr. Sachs showed slides outlining the valuation techniques used by the financial advisors, and others, depicting recent business combinations in the oil and gas industry. The Court of Chancery found that the Sachs presentation was designed to apprise the directors of the scope of the analyses performed rather than the facts and numbers used in reaching the conclusion that Mesa's tender offer price was inadequate.

Mr. Sachs also presented various defensive strategies available to the board if it concluded that Mesa's two-step tender offer was inadequate and should be opposed. One of the devices outlined was a self-tender by Unocal for its own stock with a reasonable price range of $70 to $75 per share. The cost of such a proposal would cause the company to incur $6.1-6.5 billion of additional debt, and a presentation was made informing the board of Unocal's ability to handle it. The directors were told that the primary effect of this obligation would be to reduce exploratory drilling, but that the company would nonetheless remain a viable entity.

The eight outside directors, comprising a clear majority of the thirteen members present, then met separately with Unocal's financial advisors and attorneys. Thereafter, they unanimously agreed to advise the board that it should reject Mesa's tender offer as inadequate, and that Unocal should pursue a self-tender to provide the stockholders with a fairly priced alternative to the Mesa proposal. The board then reconvened and unanimously adopted a resolution rejecting as grossly inadequate Mesa's tender offer. Despite the nine and one-half hour length of the meeting, no formal decision was made on the proposed defensive self-tender.

On April 15, the board met again with four of the directors present by telephone and one member still absent. This session lasted two hours. Unocal's Vice President of Finance and its Assistant General Counsel made a detailed presentation of the proposed terms of the exchange offer. A price range between $70 and $80 per share was considered, and ultimately the directors agreed upon $72. The board was also

---

corporation surviving the Merger would be responsible for the payment of all securities of Mesa Eastern (including any such securities issued pursuant to the Merger) and the indebtedness referred to in item (ii) above, and such securities and indebtedness would be repaid out of funds generated by the operations of Unocal; (iv) the indebtedness incurred in the Offer and the Merger would result in Unocal being much more highly leveraged, and the capitalization of the corporation surviving the Merger would differ significantly from that of Unocal at present; and (v) in their analyses of cash flows provided by operations of Unocal which would be available to service and repay securities and other obligations of the corporation surviving the Merger, the Purchasers assumed that the capital expenditures and expenditures for exploration of such corporation would be significantly reduced.

advised about the debt securities that would be issued, and the necessity of placing restrictive covenants upon certain corporate activities until the obligations were paid. The board's decisions were made in reliance on the advice of its investment bankers, including the terms and conditions upon which the securities were to be issued. Based upon this advice, and the board's own deliberations, the directors unanimously approved the exchange offer. Their resolution provided that if Mesa acquired 64 million shares of Unocal stock through its own offer (the Mesa Purchase Condition), Unocal would buy the remaining 49% outstanding for an exchange of debt securities having an aggregate par value of $72 per share. The board resolution also stated that the offer would be subject to other conditions that had been described to the board at the meeting, or which were deemed necessary by Unocal's officers, including the exclusion of Mesa from the proposal (the Mesa exclusion). Any such conditions were required to be in accordance with the "purport and intent" of the offer.

Unocal's exchange offer was commenced on April 17, 1985, and Mesa promptly challenged it by filing this suit in the Court of Chancery. On April 22, the Unocal board met again and was advised by Goldman Sachs and Dillon Read to waive the Mesa Purchase Condition as to 50 million shares. This recommendation was in response to a perceived concern of the shareholders that, if shares were tendered to Unocal, no shares would be purchased by either offeror. The directors were also advised that they should tender their own Unocal stock into the exchange offer as a mark of their confidence in it.

Another focus of the board was the Mesa exclusion. Legal counsel advised that under Delaware law Mesa could only be excluded for what the directors reasonably believed to be a valid corporate purpose. The directors' discussion centered on the objective of adequately compensating shareholders at the "back-end" of Mesa's proposal, which the latter would finance with "junk bonds." To include Mesa would defeat that goal, because under the proration aspect of the exchange offer (49%) every Mesa share accepted by Unocal would displace one held by another stockholder. Further, if Mesa were permitted to tender to Unocal, the latter would in effect be financing Mesa's own inadequate proposal.

On April 24, 1985 Unocal issued a supplement to the exchange offer describing the partial waiver of the Mesa Purchase Condition. On May 1, 1985, in another supplement, Unocal extended the withdrawal, proration and expiration dates of its exchange offer to May 17, 1985.

Meanwhile, on April 22, 1985, Mesa amended its complaint in this action to challenge the Mesa exclusion. A preliminary injunction hearing was scheduled for May 8, 1985. However, on April 23, 1985, Mesa moved for a temporary restraining order in response to Unocal's announcement that it was partially waiving the Mesa Purchase Condition. After expedited briefing, the Court of Chancery heard Mesa's motion on April 26.

On April 29, 1985, the Vice Chancellor temporarily restrained Unocal from proceeding with the exchange offer unless it included Mesa. The trial court recognized that directors could oppose, and attempt to defeat, a hostile takeover which they considered adverse to the best interests of the corporation. However, the Vice Chancellor decided that in a selective purchase of the company's stock, the corporation bears the burden of showing: (1) a valid corporate purpose, and (2) that the transaction was fair to all of the stockholders, including those excluded.

Unocal immediately sought certification of an interlocutory appeal to this Court pursuant to Supreme Court Rule 42(b). On May 1, 1985, the Vice Chancellor declined to certify the appeal on the grounds that the decision granting a temporary restraining order did not decide a legal issue of first impression, and was not a matter to which the decisions of the Court of Chancery were in conflict.

However, in an Order dated May 2, 1985, this Court ruled that the Chancery decision was clearly determinative of substantive rights of the parties, and in fact decided the main question of law before the Vice Chancellor, which was indeed a question of first impression. We therefore concluded that the temporary restraining order was an appealable decision. However, because the Court of Chancery was scheduled to hold a preliminary injunction hearing on May 8 at which there would be an enlarged record on the various issues, action on the interlocutory appeal was deferred pending an outcome of those proceedings.

In deferring action on the interlocutory appeal, we noted that on the record before us we could not determine whether the parties had articulated certain issues which the Vice Chancellor should have an opportunity to consider in the first instance. These included the following:

a) Does the directors' duty of care to the corporation extend to protecting the corporate enterprise in good faith from perceived depredations of others, including persons who may own stock in the company?
b) Have one or more of the plaintiffs, their affiliates, or persons acting in concert with them, either in dealing with Unocal or others, demonstrated a pattern of conduct sufficient to justify a reasonable inference by defendants that a principle objective of the plaintiffs is to achieve selective treatment for themselves by the repurchase of their Unocal shares at a substantial premium?
c) If so, may the directors of Unocal in the proper exercise of business judgment employ the exchange offer to protect the corporation and its shareholders from such tactics? *See Pogostin v. Rice,* Del. Supr., 480 A.2d 619 (1984).
d) If it is determined that the purpose of the exchange offer was not illegal as a matter of law, have the directors of Unocal carried their burden of showing that they acted in good faith? *See Martin v. American Potash & Chemical Corp.,* 33 Del. Ch. 234, 92 A.2d 295 at 302.

After the May 8 hearing the Vice Chancellor issued an unreported opinion on May 13, 1985 granting Mesa a preliminary injunction. . . .

. . .

On May 13, 1985 the Court of Chancery certified this interlocutory appeal to us as a question of first impression, and we accepted it on May 14. The entire matter was scheduled on an expedited basis.

II.

The issues we address involve these fundamental questions: Did the Unocal board have the power and duty to oppose a takeover threat it reasonably perceived to be harmful to the corporate enterprise, and if so, is its action here entitled to the protection of the business judgment rule?

Mesa contends that the discriminatory exchange offer violates the fiduciary duties Unocal owes it. Mesa argues that because of the Mesa exclusion the business judgment rule is inapplicable, because the directors by tendering their own shares will derive a financial benefit that is not available to *all* Unocal stockholders. Thus, it is Mesa's ultimate contention that Unocal cannot establish that the exchange offer is fair to *all* shareholders, and argues that the Court of Chancery was correct in concluding that Unocal was unable to meet this burden.

Unocal answers that it does not owe a duty of "fairness" to Mesa, given the facts here. Specifically, Unocal contends that its board of directors reasonably and in good faith concluded that Mesa's $54 two-tier tender offer was coercive and inadequate, and that Mesa sought selective treatment for itself. Furthermore, Unocal argues that the board's approval of the exchange offer was made in good faith, on an informed basis, and in the exercise of due care. Under these circumstances, Unocal contends that its directors properly employed this device to protect the company and its stockholders from Mesa's harmful tactics.

III.

We begin with the basic issue of the power of a board of directors of a Delaware corporation to adopt a defensive measure of this type. Absent such authority, all other questions are moot. Neither issues of fairness nor business judgment are pertinent without the basic underpinning of a board's legal power to act.

The board has a large reservoir of authority upon which to draw. Its duties and responsibilities proceed from the inherent powers conferred by 8 Del. C. § 141(a), respecting management of the corporation's "business and affairs." Additionally, the powers here being exercised derive from 8 Del. C. § 160(a), conferring broad authority upon a corporation to deal in its own stock. From this it is now well established that in the acquisition of its shares a Delaware corporation may deal selectively with its stockholders, provided the directors have not acted out of a sole or primary purpose to entrench themselves in office. *Cheff v. Mathes,* Del. Supr., 199 A.2d 548, 554 (1964); *Bennett v. Propp,* Del. Supr., 187 A.2d 405, 408 (1962); *Martin v. American Potash & Chemical Corporation,* Del. Supr., 92 A.2d 295, 302 (1952); *Kaplan v. Goldsamt,* Del. Ch., 380 A.2d 556, 568-569 (1977); *Kors v. Carey,* Del. Ch., 158 A.2d 136, 140-141 (1960).

Finally, the board's power to act derives from its fundamental duty and obligation to protect the corporate enterprise, which includes stockholders, from harm reasonably perceived, irrespective of its source. *See e.g. Panter v. Marshall Field & Co.,* 646 F.2d 271, 297 (7th Cir. 1981); *Crouse-Hinds Co. v. Internorth, Inc.,* 634 F.2d 690, 704 (2d Cir. 1980); *Heit v. Baird,* 567 F.2d 1157, 1161 (1st Cir. 1977); *Cheff v. Mathes,* 199 A.2d at 556; *Martin v. American Potash & Chemical Corp.,* 92 A.2d at 302; *Kaplan v. Goldsamt,* 380 A.2d at 568-69; *Kors v. Carey,* 158 A.2d at 141; *Northwest Industries, Inc. v. B.F. Goodrich Co.,* 301 F. Supp. 706, 712 (M.D. Ill. 1969). Thus, we are satisfied that in the broad context of corporate governance, including issues of fundamental corporate change, a board of directors is not a passive instrumentality.

Given the foregoing principles, we turn to the standards by which director action is to be measured. In *Pogostin v. Rice,* Del. Supr., 480 A.2d 619 (1984), we held that the business judgment rule, including the standards by which director conduct is judged, is applicable in the context of a takeover. *Id.* at 627. The business judgment rule is a "presumption that in making a business decision the directors of a corporation acted on an informed basis, in good faith and in the honest belief that the action taken was in the best interests of the company." *Aronson v. Lewis,* Del. Supr., 473 A.2d 805, 812 (1984) (citations omitted). A hallmark of the business judgment rule is that a court will not substitute its judgment for that of the board if the latter's decision can be "attributed to any rational business purpose." *Sinclair Oil Corp. v. Levien,* Del. Supr., 280 A.2d 717, 720 (1971).

When a board addresses a pending takeover bid it has an obligation to determine whether the offer is in the best interests of the corporation and its shareholders. In that respect a board's duty is no different from any other responsibility it shoulders, and its decisions should be no less entitled to the respect they otherwise would be accorded in the realm of business judgment. *See also Johnson v. Trueblood,* 629 F.2d 287, 292-293 (3d Cir. 1980). There are, however, certain caveats to a proper exercise of this function. Because of the omnipresent specter that a board may be acting primarily in its own interests, rather than those of the corporation and its shareholders, there is an enhanced duty which calls for judicial examination at the threshold before the protections of the business judgment rule may be conferred.

This Court has long recognized that:

> We must bear in mind the inherent danger in the purchase of shares with corporate funds to remove a threat to corporate policy when a threat to control is involved. The directors are of necessity confronted with a conflict of interest, and an objective decision is difficult.

Bennett v. Propp, Del. Supr., 187 A.2d 405, 409 (1962). In the face of this inherent conflict directors must show that they had reasonable grounds for believing that a danger to corporate policy and effectiveness existed because of another person's stock ownership. *Cheff v. Mathes,* 199 A.2d at 554-55. However, they satisfy that burden "by showing good faith and reasonable investigation. . . ." *Id.* at 555. Furthermore, such proof is materially enhanced, as here, by the approval of a board comprised of a majority of outside independent directors who have acted in accordance with the foregoing standards. *See Aronson v. Lewis,* 473 A.2d at 812, 815; *Puma v. Marriott,* Del. Ch., 283 A.2d 693, 695 (1971); *Panter v. Marshall Field & Co.,* 646 F.2d 271, 295 (7th Cir. 1981).

IV.

A.

In the board's exercise of corporate power to forestall a takeover bid our analysis begins with the basic principle that corporate directors have a fiduciary duty to act in the best interests of the corporation's stockholders. *Guth v. Loft, Inc.,* Del. Supr., 5 A.2d 503, 510 (1939). As we have noted, their duty of care extends to protecting the corporation and its owners from perceived harm whether a threat originates from third parties or other shareholders. But such powers are not absolute. A corporation does not have unbridled discretion to defeat any perceived threat by any Draconian means available.

The restriction placed upon a selective stock repurchase is that the directors may not have acted solely or primarily out of a desire to perpetuate themselves in office. *See Cheff v. Mathes,* 199 A.2d at 556; *Kors v. Carey,* 158 A.2d at 140. Of course, to this is added the further caveat that inequitable action may not be taken under the guise of law. *Schnell v. Chris-Craft Industries, Inc.,* Del. Supr., 285 A.2d 437, 439 (1971). The standard of proof established in *Cheff v. Mathes* and discussed *supra* at page 16, is designed to ensure that a defensive measure to thwart or impede a takeover is indeed motivated by a good faith concern for the welfare of the corporation and its stockholders, which in all circumstances must be free of any fraud or other misconduct. *Cheff v. Mathes,* 199 A.2d at 554-55. However, this does not end the inquiry.

B.

A further aspect is the element of balance. If a defensive measure is to come within the ambit of the business judgment rule, it must be reasonable in relation to the threat posed. This entails an analysis by the directors of the nature of the takeover bid and its effect on the corporate enterprise. Examples of such concerns may include: inadequacy of the price offered, nature and timing of the offer, questions of illegality, the impact on "constituencies" other than shareholders (i.e., creditors, customers, employees, and perhaps even the community generally), the risk of nonconsummation, and the quality of securities being offered in the exchange. *See* Lipton and Brownstein, *Takeover Responses and Directors' Responsibilities: An Update,* p. 7, ABA National Institute on the Dynamics of Corporate Control (December 8, 1983). While not a controlling factor, it also seems to us that a board may reasonably consider the basic stockholder interests at stake, including those of short term speculators, whose actions may have fueled the coercive aspect of the offer at the expense of the long term investor. Here, the threat posed was viewed by the Unocal board as a grossly inadequate two-tier coercive tender offer coupled with the threat of greenmail.

Specifically, the Unocal directors had concluded that the value of Unocal was substantially above the $54 per share offered in cash at the front end. Furthermore, they determined that the subordinated securities to be exchanged in Mesa's announced squeeze out of the remaining shareholders in the "back-end" merger were "junk bonds" worth far less than $54. It is now well recognized that such offers are a classic coercive measure designed to stampede shareholders into tendering at the first tier, even if the price is inadequate, out of fear of what they will receive at the back end of the transaction. Wholly beyond the coercive aspect of an inadequate two-tier tender offer, the threat was posed by a corporate raider with a national reputation as a "greenmailer."[13]

---

[13]The term "greenmail" refers to the practice of buying out a takeover bidder's stock at a premium that is not available to other shareholders in order to prevent the takeover. The Chancery Court noted that "Mesa has made tremendous profits from its takeover activities although in the past few years it has not been successful in acquiring any of the target companies on an unfriendly basis." Moreover, the trial court specifically found that the actions of the Unocal board were taken in good faith to eliminate both the inadequacies of the tender offer and to forestall the payment of "greenmail."

In adopting the selective exchange offer, the board stated that its objective was either to defeat the inadequate Mesa offer or, should the offer still succeed, provide the 49% of its stockholders, who would otherwise be forced to accept "junk bonds," with $72 worth of senior debt. We find that both purposes are valid.

However, such efforts would have been thwarted by Mesa's participation in the exchange offer. First, if Mesa could tender its shares, Unocal would effectively be subsidizing the former's continuing effort to buy Unocal stock at $54 per share. Second, Mesa could not, by definition, fit within the class of shareholders being protected from its own coercive and inadequate tender offer.

Thus, we are satisfied that the selective exchange offer is reasonably related to the threats posed. It is consistent with the principle that "the minority stockholder shall receive the substantial equivalent in value of what he had before." *Sterling v. Mayflower Hotel Corp.,* Del. Supr., 93 A.2d 107, 114 (1952). *See also Rosenblatt v. Getty Oil Co.,* Del. Supr., 493 A.2d 929, 940 (1985). This concept of fairness, while stated in the merger context, is also relevant in the area of tender offer law. Thus, the board's decision to offer what it determined to be the fair value of the corporation to the 49% of its shareholders, who would otherwise be forced to accept highly subordinated "junk bonds," is reasonable and consistent with the directors' duty to ensure that the minority stockholders receive equal value for their shares.

V.

Mesa contends that it is unlawful, and the trial court agreed, for a corporation to discriminate in this fashion against one shareholder. It argues correctly that no case has ever sanctioned a device that precludes a raider from sharing in a benefit available to all other stockholders. However, as we have noted earlier, the principle of selective stock repurchases by a Delaware corporation is neither unknown nor unauthorized. *Cheff v. Mathes,* 199 A.2d at 554; *Bennett v. Propp,* 187 A.2d at 408; *Martin v. American Potash & Chemical Corporation,* 92 A.2d at 302; *Kaplan v. Goldsamt,* 380 A.2d at 568-569; *Kors v. Carey,* 158 A.2d at 140-141; 8 Del. C. § 160. The only difference is that heretofore the approved transaction was the payment of "greenmail" to a raider or dissident posing a threat to the corporate enterprise. All other stockholders were denied such favored treatment, and given Mesa's past history of greenmail, its claims here are rather ironic.

However, our corporate law is not static. It must grow and develop in response to, indeed in anticipation of, evolving concepts and needs. Merely because the General Corporation Law is silent as to a specific matter does not mean that it is prohibited. *See Providence and Worcester Co. v. Baker,* Del. Supr., 378 A.2d 121, 123-124 (1977). In the days when *Cheff, Bennett, Martin* and *Kors* were decided, the tender offer, while not an unknown device, was virtually unused, and little was known of such methods as two-tier "front-end" loaded offers with their coercive effects. Then, the favored attack of a raider was stock acquisition followed by a proxy contest. Various defensive tactics, which provided no benefit whatever to the raider, evolved. Thus, the use of corporate funds by management to counter a proxy battle was approved. *Hall v. Trans-Lux Daylight Picture Screen Corp.,* Del. Ch., 171 A. 226 (1934); *Hibbert v. Hollywood Park, Inc.,* Del. Supr., 457 A.2d 339 (1983). Litigation, supported by corporate funds, aimed at the raider has long been a popular device.

More recently, as the sophistication of both raiders and targets has developed, a host of other defensive measures to counter such ever mounting threats has evolved and received judicial sanction. These include defensive charter amendments and other devices bearing some rather exotic, but apt, names: Crown Jewel, White Knight, Pac Man, and Golden Parachute. Each has highly selective features, the object of which is to deter or defeat the raider.

Thus, while the exchange offer is a form of selective treatment, given the nature of the threat posed here the response is neither unlawful nor unreasonable. If the board of directors is disinterested, has acted in good faith and with due care, its decision in the absence of an abuse of discretion will be upheld as a proper exercise of business judgment.

To this Mesa responds that the board is not disinterested, because the directors are receiving a benefit from the tender of their own shares, which because of the Mesa exclusion, does not devolve upon *all* stockholders equally. *See Aronson v. Lewis,* Del. Supr., 473 A.2d 805, 812 (1984). However, Mesa concedes that if the exclusion is valid, then the directors and all other stockholders share the same benefit. The answer of course is that the exclusion is valid, and the directors' participation in the exchange offer does not rise to the level of a disqualifying interest. The excellent discussion in *Johnson v. Trueblood,* 629 F.2d at 292-293, of the use of the business judgment rule in takeover contests also seems pertinent here.

Nor does this become an "interested" director transaction merely because certain board members are large stockholders. As this Court has previously noted, that fact alone does not create a disqualifying "personal pecuniary interest" to defeat the operation of the business judgment rule. *Cheff v. Mathes,* 199 A.2d at 554.

Mesa also argues that the exclusion permits the directors to abdicate the fiduciary duties they owe it. However, that is not so. The board continues to owe Mesa the duties of due care and loyalty. But in the face of the destructive threat Mesa's tender offer was perceived to pose, the board had a supervening duty to protect the corporate enterprise, which includes the other shareholders, from threatened harm.

Mesa contends that the basis of this action is punitive, and solely in response to the exercise of its rights of corporate democracy. Nothing precludes Mesa, as a stockholder, from acting in its own self-interest. *See e.g., DuPont v. DuPont,* 251 Fed. 937 (D. Del. 1918), *aff'd* 256 Fed. 129 (3d Cir. 1918); *Ringling Bros.-Barnum & Bailey Combined Shows, Inc. v. Ringling,* Del. Supr., 53 A.2d 441, 447 (1947); *Heil v. Standard Gas & Electric Co.,* Del. Ch., 151 A. 303, 304 (1930). *But see, Allied Chemical & Dye Corp. v. Steel & Tube Co. of America,* Del. Ch., 120 A. 486, 491 (1923) (majority shareholder owes a fiduciary duty to the minority shareholders). However, Mesa, while pursuing its own interests, has acted in a manner which a board consisting of a majority of independent directors has reasonably determined to be contrary to the best interests of Unocal and its other shareholders. In this situation, there is no support in Delaware law for the proposition that, when responding to a perceived harm, a corporation must guarantee a benefit to a stockholder who is deliberately provoking the danger being addressed. There is no obligation of self-sacrifice by a corporation and its shareholders in the face of such a challenge.

Here, the Court of Chancery specifically found that the "directors' decision [to oppose the Mesa tender offer] was made in the good faith belief that the Mesa tender offer is inadequate." Given our standard of review under *Levitt v. Bouvier*, Del. Supr., 287 A.2d 671, 673 (1972), and *Application of Delaware Racing Association*, Del. Supr., 213 A.2d 203, 207 (1965), we are satisfied that Unocal's board has met its burden of proof. *Cheff v. Mathes*, 199 A.2d at 555.

VI.

In conclusion, there was directorial power to oppose the Mesa tender offer, and to undertake a selective stock exchange made in good faith and upon a reasonable investigation pursuant to a clear duty to protect the corporate enterprise. Further, the selective stock repurchase plan chosen by Unocal is reasonable in relation to the threat that the board rationally and reasonably believed was posed by Mesa's inadequate and coercive two-tier tender offer. Under those circumstances the board's action is entitled to be measured by the standards of the business judgment rule. Thus, unless it is shown by a preponderance of the evidence that the directors' decisions were primarily based on perpetuating themselves in office, or some other breach of fiduciary duty such as fraud, overreaching, lack of good faith, or being uninformed, a Court will not substitute its judgment for that of the board.

In this case that protection is not lost merely because Unocal's directors have tendered their shares in the exchange offer. Given the validity of the Mesa exclusion, they are receiving a benefit shared generally by all other stockholders except Mesa. In this circumstance the test of *Aronson v. Lewis*, 473 A.2d at 812, is satisfied. *See also Cheff v. Mathes*, 199 A.2d at 554. If the stockholders are displeased with the action of their elected representatives, the powers of corporate democracy are at their disposal to turn the board out. *Aronson v. Lewis*, Del. Supr., 473 A.2d 805, 811 (1984). *See also* 8 Del. C. §§ 141(k) and 211(b).

With the Court of Chancery's findings that the exchange offer was based on the board's good faith belief that the Mesa offer was inadequate, that the board's action was informed and taken with due care, that Mesa's prior activities justify a reasonable inference that its principle objective was greenmail, and implicitly, that the substance of the offer itself was reasonable and fair to the corporation and its stockholders if Mesa were included, we cannot say that the Unocal directors have acted in such a manner as to have passed an "unintelligent and unadvised judgment." *Mitchell v. Highland-Western Glass Co.*, Del. Ch., 167 A. 831, 833 (1933). The decision of the Court of Chancery is therefore REVERSED, and the preliminary injunction is VACATED.

Post-Case Follow-Up

The all holders rule. In 1986, the SEC amended Exchange Act Rule 13e-4(f)(8)(i) to include the so-called all holders rule, or the rule providing that an issuer tender offer must be open to all security holders. This rule, had it been in effect at the time of *Unocal*, would have prevented Unocal from excluding Mesa from its self-tender offer. The SEC also adopted Exchange Act Rule 14d-10 at that time to include an all holders rule applicable to non-issuer tender offers.

The Unocal *test.* If a board wants to implement defensive measures in response to a hostile takeover attempt, it must satisfy the enhanced scrutiny standard described in *Unocal* and its progeny. Under the first prong of the *Unocal* test, a board must have reasonable grounds for believing that a tender offer presents a danger to corporate policy and effectiveness. The board's belief is more likely to be found reasonable if it is based upon a good faith, reasonable investigation into the tender offer (and the goals and plans of the persons or entities behind the tender offer). The reasonableness of the board's belief is materially enhanced when the investigation involves independent directors and consultation with legal and financial advisers.

Under the second prong of *Unocal,* the court will examine whether the board's response to the takeover attempt is reasonable in light of the threat posed. Defensive measures are disproportionate, and thus unreasonable, if they are coercive or preclusive. A measure is coercive if it is aimed at forcing down upon stockholders a management-sponsored alternative to a hostile tender offer. A measure is preclusive if deprives stockholders of the right to receive all tender offers or precludes a bidder from seeking control by fundamentally restricting proxy contests or otherwise.

Poison pills implemented in response to a hostile takeover attempt are judged under the *Unocal* test. The target's board must identify a threat to company policy and effectiveness that supports adoption of a poison pill. And, the pill's operation must be proportional in relation to threat. The pill (in combination with other defensive structures) cannot be preclusive of shareholders' exercise of voting rights, and thus must not have the effect of preventing (ever, and under any circumstances) a successful proxy contest. The pill, in concert with other defensive measures, also cannot be coercive, and thus cannot have the effect of cramming down management's preferred alternative.

Unocal Corp. v. Mesa Petroleum Co.: Real Life Applications

Acme Corp. is a Delaware corporation that operates an online classified ad service that allows users to post items and services for sale. Although Acme is a publicly traded for-profit company, Acme's chief executive officer (who is also the company's founder and controlling shareholder) has always been public interest-minded. On several occasions over the past few years, Acme's CEO has caused Acme to make decisions that some believe put public interest concerns above shareholder wealth maximization.

Last week, the CEO of Raptor Inc. called Acme's CEO to discuss the possibility of a merger. Acme's CEO dislikes Raptor's CEO for personal reasons having to do with differences of political opinion.

After rejecting the possibility of a merger outright, Acme's CEO called the company's lawyers and instructed them to prepare an aggressive shareholder rights plan, or poison pill, designed to make it difficult (if not impossible) for Raptor to acquire control of Acme. Acme's CEO then asked board members to approve the implementation of the poison pill via unanimous written consent. The board members complied and immediately returned signed consents without convening a board meeting.

a. If a plaintiff challenges the decision of Acme's board to adopt and implement a poison pill as a breach of fiduciary duty, what standard of review will apply?
b. Is the plaintiff likely to prevail? Why or why not?

8. *Revlon* Duties

Prior to the time a sale of the corporation (and thus a change in control) becomes inevitable, the board's duty focuses on protecting shareholders from an inadequate bid. This is why, for example, a corporation is not required to do a consensual deal and may resist a hostile takeover attempt (subject to *Unocal* enhanced scrutiny) if the board in good faith believes that a transaction is not in the best interest of shareholders.

At some point, however, a change in control may become inevitable. The incumbent board may decide that a corporate combination is in the shareholders' best interest on its own initiative or in response to an unsolicited offer. At the point when the firm's sale becomes inevitable, the incumbent board's duty switches from protecting shareholders from inadequate bids to maximizing the sale price. This is because when a sale becomes inevitable, the board's duty is to get the best possible deal for shareholders in the transaction.

Case Preview

Revlon, Inc. v. MacAndrews & Forbes Holdings, Inc.

In *Revlon*, the Delaware Supreme Court examined directors' obligations when a change of control becomes inevitable. When reading the case, consider the following questions:

1. What are *Revlon* duties?
2. When do they attach?
3. If a board's reaction to a hostile takeover attempt is found to constitute only a defensive measure, and not an abandonment of the corporation's continued existence, do *Revlon* duties apply? Or, does *Unocal* apply?
4. What defensive measures did Revlon implement to ward off Pantry Pride?
5. What test or level of scrutiny did the court apply to determine whether Revlon's board had breached its fiduciary duties in responding to the Pantry Pride takeover attempt? May a corporation consider the impact of a takeover threat on constituencies other than (or, in addition to) shareholders, according to the court?
6. What, if anything, did the Revlon board do wrong?

Revlon, Inc. v. MacAndrews & Forbes Holdings, Inc.
506 A.2d 173 (Del. 1986)

MOORE, Justice:*

In this battle for corporate control of Revlon, Inc. (Revlon), the Court of Chancery enjoined certain transactions designed to thwart the efforts of Pantry Pride, Inc. (Pantry Pride) to acquire Revlon. The defendants are Revlon, its board of directors, and Forstmann Little & Co. and the latter's affiliated limited partnership (collectively, Forstmann). The injunction barred consummation of an option granted Forstmann to purchase certain Revlon assets (the lock-up option), a promise by Revlon to deal exclusively with Forstmann in the face of a takeover (the no-shop provision), and the payment of a $25 million cancellation fee to Forstmann if the transaction was aborted. The Court of Chancery found that the Revlon directors had breached their duty of care by entering into the foregoing transactions and effectively ending an active auction for the company. The trial court ruled that such arrangements are not illegal *per se* under Delaware law, but that their use under the circumstances here was impermissible. We agree. *See MacAndrews & Forbes Holdings, Inc. v. Revlon, Inc.,* Del. Ch., 501 A.2d 1239 (1985). Thus, we granted this expedited interlocutory appeal to consider for the first time the validity of such defensive measures in the face of an active bidding contest for corporate control. Additionally, we address for the first time the extent to which a corporation may consider the impact of a takeover threat on constituencies other than shareholders. *See Unocal Corp. v. Mesa Petroleum Co.,* Del. Supr., 493 A.2d 946, 955 (1985).

In our view, lock-ups and related agreements are permitted under Delaware law where their adoption is untainted by director interest or other breaches of fiduciary duty. The actions taken by the Revlon directors, however, did not meet this standard. Moreover, while concern for various corporate constituencies is proper when addressing a takeover threat, that principle is limited by the requirement that there be some rationally related benefit accruing to the stockholders. We find no such benefit here.

Thus, under all the circumstances we must agree with the Court of Chancery that the enjoined Revlon defensive measures were inconsistent with the directors' duties to the stockholders. Accordingly, we affirm.

I.

The somewhat complex maneuvers of the parties necessitate a rather detailed examination of the facts. The prelude to this controversy began in June 1985, when Ronald O. Perelman, chairman of the board and chief executive officer of Pantry Pride, met with his counterpart at Revlon, Michel C. Bergerac, to discuss a friendly acquisition of Revlon by Pantry Pride. Perelman suggested a price in the range of $40-50 per share, but the meeting ended with Bergerac dismissing those figures as considerably below Revlon's intrinsic value. All subsequent Pantry Pride overtures

*Most footnotes have been omitted for purposes of brevity.

were rebuffed, perhaps in part based on Mr. Bergerac's strong personal antipathy to Mr. Perelman.

Thus, on August 14, Pantry Pride's board authorized Perelman to acquire Revlon, either through negotiation in the $42-$43 per share range, or by making a hostile tender offer at $45. Perelman then met with Bergerac and outlined Pantry Pride's alternate approaches. Bergerac remained adamantly opposed to such schemes and conditioned any further discussions of the matter on Pantry Pride executing a standstill agreement prohibiting it from acquiring Revlon without the latter's prior approval.

On August 19, the Revlon board met specially to consider the impending threat of a hostile bid by Pantry Pride.[3] At the meeting, Lazard Freres, Revlon's investment banker, advised the directors that $45 per share was a grossly inadequate price for the company. Felix Rohatyn and William Loomis of Lazard Freres explained to the board that Pantry Pride's financial strategy for acquiring Revlon would be through "junk bond" financing followed by a break-up of Revlon and the disposition of its assets. With proper timing, according to the experts, such transactions could produce a return to Pantry Pride of $60 to $70 per share, while a sale of the company as a whole would be in the "mid 50" dollar range. Martin Lipton, special counsel for Revlon, recommended two defensive measures: first, that the company repurchase up to 5 million of its nearly 30 million outstanding shares; and second, that it adopt a Note Purchase Rights Plan. Under this plan, each Revlon shareholder would receive as a dividend one Note Purchase Right (the Rights) for each share of common stock, with the Rights entitling the holder to exchange one common share for a $65 principal Revlon note at 12% interest with a one-year maturity. The Rights would become effective whenever anyone acquired beneficial ownership of 20% or more of Revlon's shares, unless the purchaser acquired all the company's stock for cash at $65 or more per share. In addition, the Rights would not be available to the acquiror, and prior to the 20% triggering event the Revlon board could redeem the rights for 10 cents each. Both proposals were unanimously adopted.

Pantry Pride made its first hostile move on August 23 with a cash tender offer for any and all shares of Revlon at $47.50 per common share and $26.67 per preferred share, subject to (1) Pantry Pride's obtaining financing for the purchase, and (2) the Rights being redeemed, rescinded or voided.

The Revlon board met again on August 26. The directors advised the stockholders to reject the offer. Further defensive measures also were planned. On August 29, Revlon commenced its own offer for up to 10 million shares, exchanging for each share of common stock tendered one Senior Subordinated Note (the Notes) of $47.50 principal at 11.75% interest, due 1995, and one-tenth of a share of $9.00 Cumulative

---

[3]There were 14 directors on the Revlon board. Six of them held senior management positions with the company, and two others held significant blocks of its stock. Four of the remaining six directors were associated at some point with entities that had various business relationships with Revlon. On the basis of this limited record, however, we cannot conclude that this board is entitled to certain presumptions that generally attach to the decisions of a board whose majority consists of truly outside independent directors. *See Polk v. Good & Texaco,* Del. Supr., ___ A.2d ___, ___ (1986); *Moran v. Household International, Inc.,* Del. Supr., 500 A.2d 1346, 1356 (1985); *Unocal Corp. v. Mesa Petroleum Co.,* Del. Supr., 493 A.2d 946, 955 (1985); *Aronson v. Lewis,* Del. Supr., 473 A.2d 805, 812, 815 (1984); *Puma v. Marriott,* Del. Ch., 283 A.2d 693, 695 (1971).

Convertible Exchangeable Preferred Stock valued at $100 per share. Lazard Freres opined that the notes would trade at their face value on a fully distributed basis. Revlon stockholders tendered 87 percent of the outstanding shares (approximately 33 million), and the company accepted the full 10 million shares on a pro rata basis. The new Notes contained covenants which limited Revlon's ability to incur additional debt, sell assets, or pay dividends unless otherwise approved by the "independent" (non-management) members of the board.

At this point, both the Rights and the Note covenants stymied Pantry Pride's attempted takeover. The next move came on September 16, when Pantry Pride announced a new tender offer at $42 per share, conditioned upon receiving at least 90% of the outstanding stock. Pantry Pride also indicated that it would consider buying less than 90%, and at an increased price, if Revlon removed the impeding Rights. While this offer was lower on its face than the earlier $47.50 proposal, Revlon's investment banker, Lazard Freres, described the two bids as essentially equal in view of the completed exchange offer.

The Revlon board held a regularly scheduled meeting on September 24. The directors rejected the latest Pantry Pride offer and authorized management to negotiate with other parties interested in acquiring Revlon. Pantry Pride remained determined in its efforts and continued to make cash bids for the company, offering $50 per share on September 27, and raising its bid to $53 on October 1, and then to $56.25 on October 7.

In the meantime, Revlon's negotiations with Forstmann and the investment group Adler & Shaykin had produced results. The Revlon directors met on October 3 to consider Pantry Pride's $53 bid and to examine possible alternatives to the offer. Both Forstmann and Adler & Shaykin made certain proposals to the board. As a result, the directors unanimously agreed to a leveraged buyout by Forstmann. The terms of this accord were as follows: each stockholder would get $56 cash per share; management would purchase stock in the new company by the exercise of their Revlon "golden parachutes"; Forstmann would assume Revlon's $475 million debt incurred by the issuance of the Notes; and Revlon would redeem the Rights and waive the Notes covenants for Forstmann or in connection with any other offer superior to Forstmann's. The board did not actually remove the covenants at the October 3 meeting, because Forstmann then lacked a firm commitment on its financing, but accepted the Forstmann capital structure, and indicated that the outside directors would waive the covenants in due course. Part of Forstmann's plan was to sell Revlon's Norcliff Thayer and Reheis divisions to American Home Products for $335 million. Before the merger, Revlon was to sell its cosmetics and fragrance division to Adler & Shaykin for $905 million. These transactions would facilitate the purchase by Forstmann or any other acquiror of Revlon.

When the merger, and thus the waiver of the Notes covenants, was announced, the market value of these securities began to fall. The Notes, which originally traded near par, around 100, dropped to 87.50 by October 8. One director later reported (at the October 12 meeting) a "deluge" of telephone calls from irate noteholders, and on October 10 the Wall Street Journal reported threats of litigation by these creditors.

Pantry Pride countered with a new proposal on October 7, raising its $53 offer to $56.25, subject to nullification of the Rights, a waiver of the Notes covenants, and the election of three Pantry Pride directors to the Revlon board. On October 9, representatives of Pantry Pride, Forstmann and Revlon conferred in an attempt to negotiate the fate of Revlon, but could not reach agreement. At this meeting Pantry Pride announced that it would engage in fractional bidding and top any Forstmann offer by a slightly higher one. It is also significant that Forstmann, to Pantry Pride's exclusion, had been made privy to certain Revlon financial data. Thus, the parties were not negotiating on equal terms.

Again privately armed with Revlon data, Forstmann met on October 11 with Revlon's special counsel and investment banker. On October 12, Forstmann made a new $57.25 per share offer, based on several conditions.[6] The principal demand was a lock-up option to purchase Revlon's Vision Care and National Health Laboratories divisions for $525 million, some $100-$175 million below the value ascribed to them by Lazard Freres, if another acquiror got 40% of Revlon's shares. Revlon also was required to accept a no-shop provision. The Rights and Notes covenants had to be removed as in the October 3 agreement. There would be a $25 million cancellation fee to be placed in escrow, and released to Forstmann if the new agreement terminated or if another acquiror got more than 19.9% of Revlon's stock. Finally, there would be no participation by Revlon management in the merger. In return, Forstmann agreed to support the par value of the Notes, which had faltered in the market, by an exchange of new notes. Forstmann also demanded immediate acceptance of its offer, or it would be withdrawn. The board unanimously approved Forstmann's proposal because: (1) it was for a higher price than the Pantry Pride bid, (2) it protected the noteholders, and (3) Forstmann's financing was firmly in place. The board further agreed to redeem the rights and waive the covenants on the preferred stock in response to any offer above $57 cash per share. The covenants were waived, contingent upon receipt of an investment banking opinion that the Notes would trade near par value once the offer was consummated.

Pantry Pride, which had initially sought injunctive relief from the Rights plan on August 22, filed an amended complaint on October 14 challenging the lock-up, the cancellation fee, and the exercise of the Rights and the Notes covenants. Pantry Pride also sought a temporary restraining order to prevent Revlon from placing any assets in escrow or transferring them to Forstmann. Moreover, on October 22, Pantry Pride again raised its bid, with a cash offer of $58 per share conditioned upon nullification of the Rights, waiver of the covenants, and an injunction of the Forstmann lock-up.

On October 15, the Court of Chancery prohibited the further transfer of assets, and eight days later enjoined the lock-up, no-shop, and cancellation fee provisions of the agreement. The trial court concluded that the Revlon directors had breached their duty of loyalty by making concessions to Forstmann, out of concern for their liability to the noteholders, rather than maximizing the sale price of the company for the stockholders' benefit. *MacAndrews & Forbes Holdings, Inc. v. Revlon, Inc.,* 501 A.2d at 1249-50.

---

[6]Forstmann's $57.25 offer ostensibly is worth $1 more than Pantry Pride's $56.25 bid. However, the Pantry Pride offer was immediate, while the Forstmann proposal must be discounted for the time value of money because of the delay in approving the merger and consummating the transaction. The exact difference between the two bids was an unsettled point of contention even at oral argument.

II.

To obtain a preliminary injunction, a plaintiff must demonstrate both a reasonable probability of success on the merits and some irreparable harm which will occur absent the injunction. *Gimbel v. Signal Companies,* Del. Ch., 316 A.2d 599, 602 (1974), *aff'd,* Del. Supr., 316 A.2d 619 (1974). Additionally, the Court shall balance the conveniences of and possible injuries to the parties. *Id.*

A.

We turn first to Pantry Pride's probability of success on the merits. The ultimate responsibility for managing the business and affairs of a corporation falls on its board of directors. 8 Del. C. § 141(a). In discharging this function the directors owe fiduciary duties of care and loyalty to the corporation and its shareholders. *Guth v. Loft, Inc.,* 23 Del. Supr. 255, 5 A.2d 503, 510 (1939); *Aronson v. Lewis,* Del. Supr., 473 A.2d 805, 811 (1984). These principles apply with equal force when a board approves a corporate merger pursuant to 8 Del. C. § 251(b); *Smith v. Van Gorkom,* Del. Supr., 488 A.2d 858, 873 (1985); and of course they are the bedrock of our law regarding corporate takeover issues. *Pogostin v. Rice,* Del. Supr., 480 A.2d 619, 624 (1984); *Unocal Corp. v. Mesa Petroleum Co.,* Del. Supr., 493 A.2d 946, 953, 955 (1985); *Moran v. Household International, Inc.,* Del. Supr., 500 A.2d 1346, 1350 (1985). While the business judgment rule may be applicable to the actions of corporate directors responding to takeover threats, the principles upon which it is founded — care, loyalty and independence — must first be satisfied. *Aronson v. Lewis,* 473 A.2d at 812.

If the business judgment rule applies, there is a "presumption that in making a business decision the directors of a corporation acted on an informed basis, in good faith and in the honest belief that the action taken was in the best interests of the company." *Aronson v. Lewis,* 473 A.2d at 812. However, when a board implements anti-takeover measures there arises "the omnipresent specter that a board may be acting primarily in its own interests, rather than those of the corporation and its shareholders . . ." *Unocal Corp. v. Mesa Petroleum Co.,* 493 A.2d at 954. This potential for conflict places upon the directors the burden of proving that they had reasonable grounds for believing there was a danger to corporate policy and effectiveness, a burden satisfied by a showing of good faith and reasonable investigation. *Id.* at 955. In addition, the directors must analyze the nature of the takeover and its effect on the corporation in order to ensure balance — that the responsive action taken is reasonable in relation to the threat posed. *Id.*

B.

The first relevant defensive measure adopted by the Revlon board was the Rights Plan, which would be considered a "poison pill" in the current language of corporate takeovers — a plan by which shareholders receive the right to be bought out by the corporation at a substantial premium on the occurrence of a stated triggering event. *See generally Moran v. Household International, Inc.,* Del. Supr., 500 A.2d 1346 (1985). By 8 Del. C. §§ 141 and 122(13), the board clearly had the power to adopt the measure. *See Moran v. Household International, Inc.,* 500 A.2d at 1351. Thus, the focus becomes one of reasonableness and purpose.

The Revlon board approved the Rights Plan in the face of an impending hostile takeover bid by Pantry Pride at $45 per share, a price which Revlon reasonably concluded was grossly inadequate. Lazard Freres had so advised the directors, and had also informed them that Pantry Pride was a small, highly leveraged company bent on a "bust-up" takeover by using "junk bond" financing to buy Revlon cheaply, sell the acquired assets to pay the debts incurred, and retain the profit for itself. In adopting the Plan, the board protected the shareholders from a hostile takeover at a price below the company's intrinsic value, while retaining sufficient flexibility to address any proposal deemed to be in the stockholders' best interests.

To that extent the board acted in good faith and upon reasonable investigation. Under the circumstances it cannot be said that the Rights Plan as employed was unreasonable, considering the threat posed. Indeed, the Plan was a factor in causing Pantry Pride to raise its bids from a low of $42 to an eventual high of $58. At the time of its adoption the Rights Plan afforded a measure of protection consistent with the directors' fiduciary duty in facing a takeover threat perceived as detrimental to corporate interests. *Unocal,* 493 A.2d at 954-55. Far from being a "show-stopper," as the plaintiffs had contended in *Moran,* the measure spurred the bidding to new heights, a proper result of its implementation. *See Moran,* 500 A.2d at 1354, 1356-67.

Although we consider adoption of the Plan to have been valid under the circumstances, its continued usefulness was rendered moot by the directors' actions on October 3 and October 12. At the October 3 meeting the board redeemed the Rights conditioned upon consummation of a merger with Forstmann, but further acknowledged that they would also be redeemed to facilitate any more favorable offer. On October 12, the board unanimously passed a resolution redeeming the Rights in connection with any cash proposal of $57.25 or more per share. Because all the pertinent offers eventually equalled [sic] or surpassed that amount, the Rights clearly were no longer any impediment in the contest for Revlon. This mooted any question of their propriety under *Moran* or *Unocal.*

C.

The second defensive measure adopted by Revlon to thwart a Pantry Pride takeover was the company's own exchange offer for 10 million of its shares. The directors' general broad powers to manage the business and affairs of the corporation are augmented by the specific authority conferred under 8 Del. C. § 160(a), permitting the company to deal in its own stock. *Unocal,* 493 A.2d at 953-54; *Cheff v. Mathes,* 41 Del. Supr. 494, 199 A.2d 548, 554 (1964); *Kors v. Carey,* 39 Del. Ch. 47, 158 A.2d 136, 140 (1960). However, when exercising that power in an effort to forestall a hostile takeover, the board's actions are strictly held to the fiduciary standards outlined in *Unocal.* These standards require the directors to determine the best interests of the corporation and its stockholders, and impose an enhanced duty to abjure any action that is motivated by considerations other than a good faith concern for such interests. *Unocal,* 493 A.2d at 954-55; *see Bennett v. Propp,* 41 Del. Supr. 14, 187 A.2d 405, 409 (1962).

The Revlon directors concluded that Pantry Pride's $47.50 offer was grossly inadequate. In that regard the board acted in good faith, and on an informed basis, with reasonable grounds to believe that there existed a harmful threat to the corporate enterprise. The adoption of a defensive measure, reasonable in relation to the threat posed, was proper and fully accorded with the powers, duties, and responsibilities conferred upon directors under our law. *Unocal,* 493 A.2d at 954; *Pogostin v. Rice,* 480 A.2d at 627.

D.

However, when Pantry Pride increased its offer to $50 per share, and then to $53, it became apparent to all that the break-up of the company was inevitable. The Revlon board's authorization permitting management to negotiate a merger or buy-out with a third party was a recognition that the company was for sale. The duty of the board had thus changed from the preservation of Revlon as a corporate entity to the maximization of the company's value at a sale for the stockholders' benefit. This significantly altered the board's responsibilities under the *Unocal* standards. It no longer faced threats to corporate policy and effectiveness, or to the stockholders' interests, from a grossly inadequate bid. The whole question of defensive measures became moot. The directors' role changed from defenders of the corporate bastion to auctioneers charged with getting the best price for the stockholders at a sale of the company.

III.

This brings us to the lock-up with Forstmann and its emphasis on shoring up the sagging market value of the Notes in the face of threatened litigation by their holders. Such a focus was inconsistent with the changed concept of the directors' responsibilities at this stage of the developments. The impending waiver of the Notes covenants had caused the value of the Notes to fall, and the board was aware of the noteholders' ire as well as their subsequent threats of suit. The directors thus made support of the Notes an integral part of the company's dealings with Forstmann, even though their primary responsibility at this stage was to the equity owners.

The original threat posed by Pantry Pride — the break-up of the company — had become a reality which even the directors embraced. Selective dealing to fend off a hostile but determined bidder was no longer a proper objective. Instead, obtaining the highest price for the benefit of the stockholders should have been the central theme guiding director action. Thus, the Revlon board could not make the requisite showing of good faith by preferring the noteholders and ignoring its duty of loyalty to the shareholders. The rights of the former already were fixed by contract. *Wolfensohn v. Madison Fund, Inc.,* Del. Supr., 253 A.2d 72, 75 (1969); *Harff v. Kerkorian,* Del. Ch., 324 A.2d 215 (1974). The noteholders required no further protection, and when the Revlon board entered into an auction-ending lock-up agreement with Forstmann on the basis of impermissible considerations at the expense of the shareholders, the directors breached their primary duty of loyalty.

The Revlon board argued that it acted in good faith in protecting the noteholders because *Unocal* permits consideration of other corporate constituencies. Although such considerations may be permissible, there are fundamental limitations upon that prerogative. A board may have regard for various constituencies in discharging its responsibilities, provided there are rationally related benefits accruing to the stockholders. *Unocal*, 493 A.2d at 955. However, such concern for non-stockholder interests is inappropriate when an auction among active bidders is in progress, and the object no longer is to protect or maintain the corporate enterprise but to sell it to the highest bidder.

Revlon also contended that by *Gilbert v. El Paso Co.*, Del. Ch., 490 A.2d 1050, 1054-55 (1984), it had contractual and good faith obligations to consider the noteholders. However, any such duties are limited to the principle that one may not interfere with contractual relationships by improper actions. Here, the rights of the noteholders were fixed by agreement, and there is nothing of substance to suggest that any of those terms were violated. The Notes covenants specifically contemplated a waiver to permit sale of the company at a fair price. The Notes were accepted by the holders on that basis, including the risk of an adverse market effect stemming from a waiver. Thus, nothing remained for Revlon to legitimately protect, and no rationally related benefit thereby accrued to the stockholders. Under such circumstances we must conclude that the merger agreement with Forstmann was unreasonable in relation to the threat posed.

A lock-up is not *per se* illegal under Delaware law. Its use has been approved in an earlier case. *Thompson v. Enstar Corp.*, Del. Ch., ___ A.2d ___ (1984). Such options can entice other bidders to enter a contest for control of the corporation, creating an auction for the company and maximizing shareholder profit. Current economic conditions in the takeover market are such that a "white knight" like Forstmann might only enter the bidding for the target company if it receives some form of compensation to cover the risks and costs involved. Note, *Corporations-Mergers — "Lock-up" Enjoined Under Section 14(e) of Securities Exchange Act — Mobil Corp. v. Marathon Oil Co.*, 669 F.2d 366 (6th Cir. 1981), 12 Seton Hall L. Rev. 881, 892 (1982). However, while those lock-ups which draw bidders into the battle benefit shareholders, similar measures which end an active auction and foreclose further bidding operate to the shareholders' detriment. Note, *Lock-up Options: Toward a State Law Standard*, 96 Harv. L. Rev. 1068, 1081 (1983).

Recently, the United States Court of Appeals for the Second Circuit invalidated a lock-up on fiduciary duty grounds similar to those here. *Hanson Trust PLC, et al. v. ML SCM Acquisition Inc., et al.*, 781 F.2d 264 (2nd Cir. 1986). Citing *Thompson v. Enstar Corp., supra*, with approval, the court stated:

> In this regard, we are especially mindful that some lock-up options may be beneficial to the shareholders, such as those that induce a bidder to compete for control of a corporation, while others may be harmful, such as those that effectively preclude bidders from competing with the optionee bidder. 781 F.2d at 274.

In *Hanson Trust*, the bidder, Hanson, sought control of SCM by a hostile cash tender offer. SCM management joined with Merrill Lynch to propose a leveraged buy-out of the company at a higher price, and Hanson in turn increased its offer. Then, despite very little improvement in its subsequent bid, the management group sought a lock-up option to purchase SCM's two main assets at a substantial discount.

The SCM directors granted the lock-up without adequate information as to the size of the discount or the effect the transaction would have on the company. Their action effectively ended a competitive bidding situation. The Hanson Court invalidated the lock-up because the directors failed to fully inform themselves about the value of a transaction in which management had a strong self-interest. "In short, the Board appears to have failed to ensure that negotiations for alternative bids were conducted by those whose only loyalty was to the shareholders." *Id.* at 277.

The Forstmann option had a similar destructive effect on the auction process. Forstmann had already been drawn into the contest on a preferred basis, so the result of the lock-up was not to foster bidding, but to destroy it. The board's stated reasons for approving the transactions were: (1) better financing, (2) noteholder protection, and (3) higher price. As the Court of Chancery found, and we agree, any distinctions between the rival bidders' methods of financing the proposal were nominal at best, and such a consideration has little or no significance in a cash offer for any and all shares. The principal object, contrary to the board's duty of care, appears to have been protection of the noteholders over the shareholders' interests.

While Forstmann's $57.25 offer was objectively higher than Pantry Pride's $56.25 bid, the margin of superiority is less when the Forstmann price is adjusted for the time value of money. In reality, the Revlon board ended the auction in return for very little actual improvement in the final bid. The principal benefit went to the directors, who avoided personal liability to a class of creditors to whom the board owed no further duty under the circumstances. Thus, when a board ends an intense bidding contest on an insubstantial basis, and where a significant by-product of that action is to protect the directors against a perceived threat of personal liability for consequences stemming from the adoption of previous defensive measures, the action cannot withstand the enhanced scrutiny which *Unocal* requires of director conduct. *See Unocal,* 493 A.2d at 954-55.

In addition to the lock-up option, the Court of Chancery enjoined the no-shop provision as part of the attempt to foreclose further bidding by Pantry Pride. *MacAndrews & Forbes Holdings, Inc. v. Revlon, Inc.,* 501 A.2d at 1251. The no-shop provision, like the lock-up option, while not *per se* illegal, is impermissible under the *Unocal* standards when a board's primary duty becomes that of an auctioneer responsible for selling the company to the highest bidder. The agreement to negotiate only with Forstmann ended rather than intensified the board's involvement in the bidding contest.

It is ironic that the parties even considered a no-shop agreement when Revlon had dealt preferentially, and almost exclusively, with Forstmann throughout the contest. After the directors authorized management to negotiate with other parties, Forstmann was given every negotiating advantage that Pantry Pride had been denied: cooperation from management, access to financial data, and the exclusive opportunity to present merger proposals directly to the board of directors. Favoritism for a white knight to the total exclusion of a hostile bidder might be justifiable when the latter's offer adversely affects shareholder interests, but when bidders make relatively similar offers, or dissolution of the company becomes inevitable, the directors cannot fulfill their enhanced *Unocal* duties by playing favorites with the contending factions. Market forces must be allowed to operate freely to bring the target's shareholders the best price available for their equity.[16] Thus, as the trial court ruled, the shareholders' interests necessitated that the board remain free to negotiate in the fulfillment of that duty.

The court below similarly enjoined the payment of the cancellation fee, pending a resolution of the merits, because the fee was part of the overall plan to thwart Pantry Pride's efforts. We find no abuse of discretion in that ruling.

IV.

Having concluded that Pantry Pride has shown a reasonable probability of success on the merits, we address the issue of irreparable harm. . . . We are satisfied that the plaintiff has shown the need for an injunction to protect it from irreparable harm, which need outweighs any harm to the defendants.

V.

In conclusion, the Revlon board was confronted with a situation not uncommon in the current wave of corporate takeovers. A hostile and determined bidder sought the company at a price the board was convinced was inadequate. The initial defensive tactics worked to the benefit of the shareholders, and thus the board was able to sustain its *Unocal* burdens in justifying those measures. However, in granting an asset option lock-up to Forstmann, we must conclude that under all the circumstances the directors allowed considerations other than the maximization of shareholder profit to affect their judgment, and followed a course that ended the auction for Revlon, absent court intervention, to the ultimate detriment of its shareholders. No such defensive measure can be sustained when it represents a breach of the directors' fundamental duty of care. *See Smith v. Van Gorkom,* Del. Supr., 488 A.2d 858, 874 (1985). In that context the board's action is not entitled to the deference accorded it by the business judgment rule. The measures were properly enjoined. The decision of the Court of Chancery, therefore, is

AFFIRMED.

Post-Case Follow-Up

Like *Unocal, Revlon* is an enhanced scrutiny standard, meaning that the reasonableness required of directors under *Revlon* is more stringent than the rational basis standard applied under the business judgment rule. Under *Revlon,* enhanced scrutiny requires (i) a judicial determination regarding the adequacy of the decision-making process employed by the directors, including the information on which the directors based their decision; and (ii) judicial examination of the reasonableness of the directors' actions in light of the circumstances then existing. Ultimately, under

---

[16]By this we do not embrace the "passivity" thesis rejected in *Unocal. See* 493 A.2d at 954-55, nn. 8-10. The directors' role remains an active one, changed only in the respect that they are charged with the duty of selling the company at the highest price attainable for the stockholders' benefit.

Revlon, the board has the burden of proving that it was adequately informed and acted reasonably.

In subsequent decisions, the Delaware courts have made it clear there is no single path or set of required steps that a board must take to comply with *Revlon* duties. Instead, directors must follow a path of reasonableness in their effort to maximize shareholder returns in a change of control transaction.

Also, in subsequent opinions, the Delaware courts have made it clear that *Revlon* duties do not attach simply because a corporation is "in play" — i.e., when market participants believe the corporation is (or is likely to be) a target for solicited or unsolicited offers, or both. Instead, the duty to seek the best available value for shareholders applies only when a company embarks upon a transaction — on its own initiative or in response to an unsolicited offer — that will result in a change in control. Among other scenarios, this can occur when a corporation initiates an active bidding process whereby the corporation puts itself up for sale, or when a corporation, in response to a hostile bid, abandons long-term strategy and looks for a friendly bidder that will break up the company. The focus of *Revlon* is on change of control transactions — whether through a sale of control or breakup of the corporate entity.

A related point is that one corporation's desire to take over another corporation — whether through a consensual or hostile transaction — is not enough to trigger *Revlon* duties. Indeed, a corporation can "just say no" in response to friendly or hostile overtures if it believes that saying no is in the best interest of the corporation. The decision to negotiate with (or, not negotiate with) a third party respecting a consensual transaction likely will be judged according to the business judgment rule. Any defensive measures implemented to ward off a hostile takeover will be judged under *Unocal. See Airgas v. Air Prods. & Chems., Inc.*, 16 A.3d 48 (Del. Ch. 2011).

State Anti-Takeover Statutes

In *CTS Corp. v. Dynamics Corporation of America*, 481 U.S. 69 (1987), the Supreme Court held that the Williams Act did not preempt Indiana's Control Share Acquisition Act, an anti-takeover statute that conditioned acquisition of control of a corporation on approval of a majority of the preexisting disinterested shareholders. In the wake of *CTS Corp.*, a number of states adopted various forms of anti-takeover legislation. For example, NYBCL § 912 requires a five-year waiting period for any person acquiring a 20 percent or more interest in a New York corporation before that person can engage in a "business combination" with that corporation, unless that person obtains approval from the board of directors prior to obtaining the 20 percent interest. DGCL § 203 requires a three-year waiting period before any person acquiring 15 percent of a Delaware corporation may engage in a business combination as defined by the statute, unless that person acquires 85 percent of the corporation in a single transaction or obtains the approval of two-thirds of the disinterested shareholders and approval of the board of directors.

Revlon, Inc. v. MacAndrews & Forbes Holdings, Inc.: Real-Life Applications

Acme Corp. and Beta Corp. are Delaware corporations. Both are involved in the computer component manufacturing business. Two months ago, Beta's CEO called Acme's CEO to explore the possibility of a merger of the two companies. Acme's CEO agreed to take the proposal under advisement. For the next two months, Acme's board and executive team evaluated the possibility of merger. They retained lawyers to evaluate potential deal structures, consulted with investment bankers to examine valuation and pricing issues, and also consulted extensively with internal and external industry experts regarding both companies' businesses and potential market opportunities. At the conclusion of this process, Acme's board voted not to pursue a merger with Beta.

a. If Acme's board is sued for breach of fiduciary duty for its decision not to pursue a transaction with Beta, what standard of review will govern?

b. Is the plaintiff likely to prevail? Why or why not?

9. Takeover Terminology

You might already have noticed that much of the terminology used in describing hostile takeovers and the defenses thereto has war-like connotations. First, the aggressor builds up a war chest to acquire the target. The target institutes a number of defensive strategies to avoid being captured, including adopting poison pill defenses, suicide pacts, and scorched earth tactics. A number of other colorful terms are also used in the jargon of hostile takeovers. Among them are the following:

Bear hug: An approach by the aggressor to the target after the aggressor has acquired its toehold. The aggressor meets with the target's management and makes clear that if the target does not cooperate in the transaction, the aggressor will pursue a hostile takeover. The target is often offered a generous price per share to induce it to cooperate.

Blitz: A "lightning," no-notice strike against a target sufficiently forceful that the target is so overwhelmed it cannot adopt any defenses. Blitzes, midnight raids, and Saturday night specials (discussed later) are less common due to Williams Act requirements that a tender offer be open for at least 20 days.

Greenmail: A kind of legal corporate blackmail in which an aggressor threatens to take over a target, and then sells the toehold back to the target at an inflated price. The target thus "buys" peace from the aggressor who has made money at *not*

Constituency Statutes

In the 1980s, a wave of hostile takeover attempts caused some to lobby state legislatures for statutory authority to consider interests other than corporate profitability and shareholder wealth maximization when making decisions about potential mergers or acquisitions. As part of these efforts, there was discussion of whether corporate directors could or should consider potential impacts of merger and acquisition activity — for example, job loss, plant closures — on constituencies such as employees and the surrounding community. Since that time, about 40 states have adopted so-called other constituency or non-shareholder constituency statutes. These statutes typically state that directors may, in certain circumstances, in considering the best interests of the corporation, consider impacts on constituencies such as shareholders, employees, suppliers, customers, and creditors of the corporation.

Most non-shareholder constituency statutes are permissive, meaning directors may, but are not required to, take non-shareholder interests into account in evaluating any action that has the potential to result in a change of control of the corporation. For example, § 717(b) of the NYBCL provides as follows:

(b) In taking action, including, without limitation, action which may involve or relate to a change or potential change in the control of the corporation, a director shall be entitled to consider, without limitation, (1) both the long-term and the short-term interests of the corporation and its shareholders and (2) the effects that the corporation's actions may have in the short-term or in the long-term upon any of the following:

(i) the prospects for potential growth, development, productivity and profitability of the corporation;

(ii) the corporation's current employees;

(iii) the corporation's retired employees and other beneficiaries receiving or entitled to receive retirement, welfare or similar benefits from or pursuant to any plan sponsored, or agreement entered into, by the corporation;

(iv) the corporation's customers and creditors; and

(v) the ability of the corporation to provide, as a going concern, goods, services, employment opportunities and employment benefits and otherwise to contribute to the communities in which it does business.

The New York statute makes it clear, however, that this statute does not create any duties owed by directors to any person or entity

being successful at its takeover attempt. To discourage greenmail, high taxes are imposed on greenmail money. Moreover, overpaying a troublesome investor for his shares might raise questions about the corporation's use of its financial resources. Under some state laws, greenmail is illegal.

Killer bees: Attorneys, advisors, and public relations teams retained by the target to fight off the takeover.

Midnight raid: A raid by an aggressor after the afternoon closing of the New York Stock Exchange and concluded before the resumption of trading in the morning by securing firm commitments from large institutional shareholders of the target to sell sufficient stock so that the aggressor can obtain control of the target before the target is even aware a raid has begun.

Nuclear war: A hostile takeover involving numerous large publicly traded companies.

Preemptive strike: An extremely attractive offer made by an aggressor with the intent of obtaining immediate control of a target and blocking any other bidders.

Saturday night special: A raid by an aggressor made over a weekend so that the target has difficulty marshaling its management forces. Some experts recommend that companies identify and establish a permanent takeover team, even before a tender offer is made, specifically to ward off and respond to a Saturday night special.

Standstill agreement: An agreement by an aggressor not to purchase any more shares of the target for some specified period of time, perhaps several years. The standstill agreement is usually part of the peace pact entered into between an aggressor and the target when the aggressor accepts greenmail to stay away from the target.

Stock watch: An early warning system employed by corporations to detect fluctuations in the market that might warn them of action by aggressors.

Strike team: The aggressor's legal counsel, investment advisors, public relations teams, and so forth.

E. LEVERAGED BUYOUTS AND SHARE REPURCHASES

A corporation may decide to "go private" through a transaction called the **leveraged buyout** (LBO). To avoid a takeover by an aggressor, management of a target might offer to purchase all of its publicly held shares from its own shareholders. Because of the enormous amount of cash required to buy out all of the existing shareholders, the money used is borrowed or leveraged against the target's own assets, which are used to finance the purchase, with management pledging various corporate assets as security or collateral for repayment of the debts. In some instances, a new entity may be created by management and investors. This new entity borrows the money needed for the buyout and uses the funds to purchase all of the outstanding shares.

In some transactions, after the buyout is complete and management (and perhaps other investors) owns all of the stock of the corporation, unneeded assets are sold to reduce the corporation's debt. Then the corporation will "go public" by offering shares at a price higher than management paid for the shares when it went private. If successful, this technique results in great profits for management as well as reduction of the corporation's debt. In other instances, the debt taken on by the corporation to finance the buyout of all shareholders is so crippling that the corporation does not survive.

Some companies buy back their own stock on the open market (or from their shareholders), primarily to increase demand for the shares to push the stock price up. A stock buyback strategy increases earnings per share because it reduces the number of shares outstanding in the marketplace. These buybacks are usually referred to as **share repurchases**. Additionally, if a company purchases a great number of its own shares, it can be more difficult and expensive for an aggressor to take it over. Note that share repurchases may implicate both state corporate law and federal securities law issues, including requirements associated with Rule 10(b)-18 promulgated under the '34 Act.

to consider or afford any particular weight to impact upon any of the listed constituencies nor does it abrogate duties owed to the corporation and its shareholders. *See* NYBCL § 717(b) ("Nothing in this paragraph shall create any duties owed by any director to any person or entity to consider or afford any particular weight to any of the foregoing or abrogate any duty of the directors, either statutory or recognized by common law or court decisions."). Notably, Delaware has not adopted a non-shareholder constituency statute.

Trends in Hostile Takeovers

According to lawyers from Wachtell, Lipton, Rosen & Katz, a New York law firm with one of the nation's leading mergers and acquisitions practices, hostile and unsolicited M&A have increased in recent years, from $145 billion of bids, representing 5 percent of total M&A volume, in 2013 to $563 billion of bids, representing 11 percent of total volume, in 2015. *See* Andrew R. Brownstein, Mergers and Acquisitions — 2016, https://corpgov.law.harvard.edu/2016/02/10/mergers-and-acquisitions-2016/#more-72455. Notable recent bids identified by the Wachtell lawyers include 21st Century Fox's $80 billion offer for Time Warner; Cigna's bid for Anthem (resulting in an agreed $54 billion merger); Mylan's $35 billion bid for Perrigo (which was defeated), and Teva's $40 billion bid for Mylan (ultimately withdrawn); DISH Network's $26 billion bid for Sprint Nextel (ultimately withdrawn); and Energy Transfer Equity's bid for Williams Companies (resulting in an agreed $38 billion combination). *Id.*

F. GOVERNMENTAL REGULATION

In addition to rules set forth in state corporations statutes and the federal securities laws and associated regulations, other substantive bodies of law may come into play with corporate combinations. For example, the federal government has the authority to review mergers and acquisitions under the Clayton Act (15 U.S.C. §§ 12 et seq.) to ensure that such transactions do not impair competition and result in monopolies. The **Hart-Scott-Rodino Antitrust Improvements Act** of 1976 (HSR) (15 U.S.C. § 18a) requires that parties to certain merger transactions file premerger notification with the government and wait for a certain period before closing a transaction. The waiting period, generally 30 days, allows the government to review the transaction and take action, if needed, to protect competition. The waiting period can be shortened on request.

Generally, although there are several exceptions, as of 2016, if the acquiring party will hold more than $78.2 million of the acquired party's stock or assets (or the transaction is larger than $312.6 million, regardless of the size of either party), each party must complete a premerger notification form providing certain information about the parties and the transaction and file it with the Federal Trade Commission (FTC) and the Department of Justice. The FTC typically reviews mergers in energy, health care, chemicals, computer hardware, biotech, and other industries. The Department of Justice reviews mergers in media and entertainment, financial services and insurance, telecommunications, and travel. Small acquisitions, acquisitions involving small parties, and other types of acquisitions that are less likely to affect competition are excluded from the coverage of HSR and need not be reported. The filing fee for the premerger notification form ranges from $45,000 for transactions between $78.2 and $156.3 million to $280,000 for transactions of $781.5 million or more. If the government does not object to the transaction or does not request additional information, the parties may proceed once the waiting period expires.

In its Annual Report to Congress for 2013, the FTC reported 1,326 transactions. Despite the number of mergers, government challenges remain few. For example, in 2013, the FTC and the Department of Justice together challenged only 38 transactions. When a transaction is challenged, the parties often enter into consent agreements, agreeing to divest certain assets, or they may restructure the transaction or even abandon it. For example, the Department of Justice challenged the $1 billion acquisition of US Airways by American Airlines in 2013 because the proposed transaction would have reduced competition and raised prices for consumers. To settle these concerns, the parties agreed to divest several slots and gates at airports around the country. The FTC may also challenge a consummated merger; in 2003, it ordered a party to unwind a completed acquisition. Fines for HSR violations can run up to $16,000 per day.

G. CONTROLLING SHAREHOLDER TRANSACTIONS

Another important topic that we cover in this chapter is the level of judicial scrutiny that applies when a minority shareholder challenges a controlling shareholder conflicted transaction. Controllers engage in a conflicted transaction when the controller stands on both sides of the deal or when the controller competes with the common stockholders for consideration. One controller conflict of interest transaction scenario that has received attention in the courts lately is when a controlling shareholder of a public company seeks to buy out minority shareholders and take the company private. A key question in these cases is whether the court will apply the business judgment rule or the so-called entire fairness standard (a standard that may sound familiar from our discussion of director conflicting interest transactions in Chapter 9), when assessing whether the controller breached fiduciary obligations owed to the corporation and its minority shareholders.

Case Preview

Kahn v. M & F Worldwide Corp.

In the next case, MacAndrews & Forbes Holdings, Inc. — a 43 percent stockholder in M & F Worldwide Corp. — sought to acquire the 17 percent of M & F common stock that it did not already own in order to buy out the minority shareholders and then take M & F private. From the outset, MacAndrews & Forbes made its proposal contingent upon two conditions. First, it required the merger to be negotiated and approved by a special committee of independent M & F directors. Second, it required that the deal be approved by a majority of stockholders not affiliated with MacAndrews & Forbes. In an earlier case, the Delaware Supreme Court had held that when a transaction involving self-dealing by a controlling stockholder is challenged, the applicable standard of review is entire fairness. The question for the *Kahn* court was whether entire fairness — or some other standard (specifically, the business judgment rule) — ought to apply to the controller buyout at issue, given the shareholder protective conditions referenced above. When reading the case, consider the following:

1. How was the deal at issue structured?
2. Why do you think MacAndrews & Forbes conditioned the deal on the procedural protections referenced above?
3. What is the entire fairness standard?
4. How does the entire fairness standard compare to the enhanced scrutiny standards applied in *Revlon* and *Unocal*?
5. How does the entire fairness standard compare to the business judgment rule?
6. What standard or test does the court apply to the transaction at issue? Why?
7. How is this case distinguishable from *Kahn v. Lynch Communication Systems, Inc.*?
8. When does the standard for the type of transaction at issue switch from entire fairness to the business judgment rule?

Kahn v. M & F Worldwide Corp.
88 A.3d 635 (Del. 2014)

HOLLAND, Justice:*

This is an appeal from a final judgment entered by the Court of Chancery in a proceeding that arises from a 2011 acquisition by MacAndrews & Forbes Holdings, Inc. ("M & F" or "MacAndrews & Forbes") — a 43% stockholder in M & F Worldwide Corp. ("MFW") — of the remaining common stock of MFW (the "Merger"). From the outset, M & F's proposal to take MFW private was made contingent upon two stockholder-protective procedural conditions. First, M & F required the Merger to be negotiated and approved by a special committee of independent MFW directors (the "Special Committee"). Second, M & F required that the Merger be approved by a majority of stockholders unaffiliated with M & F. The Merger closed in December 2011, after it was approved by a vote of 65.4% of MFW's minority stockholders.

The Appellants initially sought to enjoin the transaction. They withdrew their request for injunctive relief after taking expedited discovery, including several depositions. The Appellants then sought post-closing relief against M & F, Ronald O. Perelman, and MFW's directors (including the members of the Special Committee) for breach of fiduciary duty. Again, the Appellants were provided with extensive discovery. The Defendants then moved for summary judgment, which the Court of Chancery granted.

Court of Chancery Decision

The Court of Chancery found that the case presented a "novel question of law," specifically, "what standard of review should apply to a going private merger conditioned upfront by the controlling stockholder on approval by both a properly empowered, independent committee and an informed, uncoerced majority-of-the-minority vote." The Court of Chancery held that business judgment review, rather than entire fairness, should be applied to a very limited category of controller mergers. That category consisted of mergers where the controller voluntarily relinquishes its control — such that the negotiation and approval process replicate those that characterize a third-party merger.

The Court of Chancery held that, rather than entire fairness, the business judgment standard of review should apply "if, *but only if:* (i) the controller conditions the transaction on the approval of both a Special Committee and a majority of the minority stockholders; (ii) the Special Committee is independent; (iii) the Special Committee is empowered to freely select its own advisors and to say no definitively; (iv) the Special Committee acts with care; (v) the minority vote is informed; and (vi) there is no coercion of the minority."

The Court of Chancery found that those prerequisites were satisfied and that the Appellants had failed to raise any genuine issue of material fact indicating the

---

*Most footnotes have been omitted for purposes of brevity.

contrary. The court then reviewed the Merger under the business judgment standard and granted summary judgment for the Defendants.

Appellants' Arguments

The Appellants raise two main arguments on this appeal. First, they contend that the Court of Chancery erred in concluding that no material disputed facts existed regarding the conditions precedent to business judgment review. The Appellants submit that the record contains evidence showing that the Special Committee was not disinterested and independent, was not fully empowered, and was not effective. The Appellants also contend, as a legal matter, that the majority-of-the-minority provision did not afford MFW stockholders protection sufficient to displace entire fairness review.

Second, the Appellants submit that the Court of Chancery erred, as a matter of law, in holding that the business judgment standard applies to controller freeze-out mergers where the controller's proposal is conditioned on both Special Committee approval and a favorable majority-of-the-minority vote. Even if both procedural protections are adopted, the Appellants argue, entire fairness should be retained as the applicable standard of review.

Defendants' Arguments

The Defendants argue that the judicial standard of review should be the business judgment rule, because the Merger was conditioned *ab initio* on two procedural protections that together operated to replicate an arm's-length merger: the employment of an active, unconflicted negotiating agent free to turn down the transaction; and a requirement that any transaction negotiated by that agent be approved by a majority of the disinterested stockholders. The Defendants argue that using and *establishing* pretrial that both protective conditions were extant renders a going private transaction analogous to that of a third-party arm's-length merger under Section 251 of the Delaware General Corporation Law. That is, the Defendants submit that a Special Committee approval in a going private transaction is a proxy for board approval in a third-party transaction, and that the approval of the unaffiliated, noncontrolling stockholders replicates the approval of all the (potentially) adversely affected stockholders.

FACTS

MFW and M & F

MFW is a holding company incorporated in Delaware. Before the Merger that is the subject of this dispute, MFW was 43.4% owned by MacAndrews & Forbes, which in turn is entirely owned by Ronald O. Perelman. MFW had four business segments. Three were owned through a holding company, Harland Clarke Holding Corporation ("HCHC"). They were the Harland Clarke Corporation ("Harland"), which printed bank checks; Harland Clarke Financial Solutions, which provided technology products and services to financial services companies; and Scantron Corporation, which manufactured scanning equipment used for educational and other purposes. The fourth segment, which was not part of HCHC, was Mafco Worldwide Corporation, a manufacturer of licorice flavorings.

The MFW board had thirteen members. They were: Ronald Perelman, Barry Schwartz, William Bevins, Bruce Slovin, Charles Dawson, Stephen Taub, John Keane, Theo Folz, Philip Beekman, Martha Byorum, Viet Dinh, Paul Meister, and Carl Webb. Perelman, Schwartz, and Bevins were officers of both MFW and MacAndrews & Forbes. Perelman was the Chairman of MFW and the Chairman and CEO of MacAndrews & Forbes; Schwartz was the President and CEO of MFW and the Vice Chairman and Chief Administrative Officer of MacAndrews & Forbes; and Bevins was a Vice President at MacAndrews & Forbes.

The Taking MFW Private Proposal

In May 2011, Perelman began to explore the possibility of taking MFW private. At that time, MFW's stock price traded in the $20 to $24 per share range. MacAndrews & Forbes engaged a bank, Moelis & Company, to advise it. After preparing valuations based on projections that had been supplied to lenders by MFW in April and May 2011, Moelis valued MFW at between $10 and $32 a share.

On June 10, 2011, MFW's shares closed on the New York Stock Exchange at $16.96. The next business day, June 13, 2011, Schwartz sent a letter proposal ("Proposal") to the MFW board to buy the remaining MFW shares for $24 in cash. The Proposal stated, in relevant part:

> The proposed transaction would be subject to the approval of the Board of Directors of the Company [*i.e.*, MFW] and the negotiation and execution of mutually acceptable definitive transaction documents. It is our expectation that the Board of Directors will appoint a special committee of independent directors to consider our proposal and make a recommendation to the Board of Directors. *We will not move forward with the transaction unless it is approved by such a special committee. In addition, the transaction will be subject to a non-waivable condition requiring the approval of a majority of the shares of the Company not owned by M & F or its affiliates.* . . .

> . . . In considering this proposal, you should know that in our capacity as a stockholder of the Company we are interested only in acquiring the shares of the Company not already owned by us and that in such capacity we have no interest in selling any of the shares owned by us in the Company nor would we expect, in our capacity as a stockholder, to vote in favor of any alternative sale, merger or similar transaction involving the Company. If the special committee does not recommend or the public stockholders of the Company do not approve the proposed transaction, such determination would not adversely affect our future relationship with the Company and we would intend to remain as a long-term stockholder.

> . . .

> In connection with this proposal, we have engaged Moelis & Company as our financial advisor and Skadden, Arps, Slate, Meagher & Flom LLP as our legal advisor, and we encourage the special committee to retain its own legal and financial advisors to assist it in its review.

MacAndrews & Forbes filed this letter with the U.S. Securities and Exchange Commission ("SEC") and issued a press release disclosing substantially the same information.

The Special Committee Is Formed

The MFW board met the following day to consider the Proposal. At the meeting, Schwartz presented the offer on behalf of MacAndrews & Forbes. Subsequently, Schwartz and Bevins, as the two directors present who were also directors of MacAndrews & Forbes, recused themselves from the meeting, as did Dawson, the CEO of HCHC, who had previously expressed support for the proposed offer.

The independent directors then invited counsel from Willkie Farr & Gallagher — a law firm that had recently represented a Special Committee of MFW's independent directors in a potential acquisition of a subsidiary of MacAndrews & Forbes — to join the meeting. The independent directors decided to form the Special Committee, and resolved further that:

> [T]he Special Committee is empowered to: (i) make such investigation of the Proposal as the Special Committee deems appropriate; (ii) evaluate the terms of the Proposal; (iii) negotiate with Holdings [*i.e.*, MacAndrews & Forbes] and its representatives any element of the Proposal; (iv) negotiate the terms of any definitive agreement with respect to the Proposal (it being understood that the execution thereof shall be subject to the approval of the Board); (v) report to the Board its recommendations and conclusions with respect to the Proposal, including a determination and *recommendation as to whether the Proposal is fair and in the best interests of the stockholders of the Company other than Holdings* and its affiliates and should be approved by the Board; and (vi) determine to elect not to pursue the Proposal....
>
> . . .
>
> ... [T]he Board shall not approve the Proposal without a prior favorable recommendation of the Special Committee....
>
> ... [T]he Special Committee [is] empowered to retain and employ legal counsel, a financial advisor, and such other agents as the Special Committee shall deem necessary or desirable in connection with these matters....

The Special Committee consisted of Byorum, Dinh, Meister (the chair), Slovin, and Webb. The following day, Slovin recused himself because, although the MFW board had determined that he qualified as an independent director under the rules of the New York Stock Exchange, he had "some current relationships that could raise questions about his independence for purposes of serving on the Special Committee."

ANALYSIS

What Should Be the Review Standard?

Where a transaction involving self-dealing by a controlling stockholder is challenged, the applicable standard of judicial review is "entire fairness," with the defendants having the burden of persuasion. In other words, the defendants bear the ultimate burden of proving that the transaction with the controlling stockholder was entirely fair to the minority stockholders. In *Kahn v. Lynch Communication Systems, Inc.*, however, this Court held that in "entire fairness" cases, the defendants may shift the burden of persuasion to the plaintiff if either (1) they show that the transaction was approved by a well-functioning committee of independent directors; or (2) they show that the transaction was approved by an informed vote of a majority of the minority stockholders.

This appeal presents a question of first impression: what should be the standard of review for a merger between a controlling stockholder and its subsidiary, where the merger is conditioned *ab initio* upon the approval of both an independent, adequately-empowered Special Committee that fulfills its duty of care, and the uncoerced, informed vote of a majority of the minority stockholders. The question has never been put directly to this Court.

Almost two decades ago, in *Kahn v. Lynch,* we held that the approval by *either* a Special Committee *or* the majority of the noncontrolling stockholders of a merger with a buying controlling stockholder would shift the burden of proof under the entire fairness standard from the defendant to the plaintiff. *Lynch* did not involve a merger conditioned by the controlling stockholder on both procedural protections. The Appellants submit, nonetheless, that statements in *Lynch* and its progeny could be (and were) read to suggest that even if both procedural protections were used, the standard of review would remain entire fairness. However, in *Lynch* and the other cases that Appellants cited, *Southern Peru* and *Kahn v. Tremont,* the controller did not give up its voting power by agreeing to a non-waivable majority-of-the-minority condition. That is the vital distinction between those cases and this one. The question is what the legal consequence of that distinction should be in these circumstances.

The Court of Chancery held that the consequence should be that the business judgment standard of review will govern going private mergers with a controlling stockholder that are conditioned *ab initio* upon (1) the approval of an independent and fully-empowered Special Committee that fulfills its duty of care and (2) the uncoerced, informed vote of the majority of the minority stockholders.

The Court of Chancery rested its holding upon the premise that the common law equitable rule that best protects minority investors is one that encourages controlling stockholders to accord the minority both procedural protections. A transactional structure subject to both conditions differs fundamentally from a merger having only one of those protections, in that:

> By giving controlling stockholders the opportunity to have a going private transaction reviewed under the business judgment rule, a strong incentive is created to give minority stockholders much broader access to the transactional structure that is most likely to effectively protect their interests. . . . That structure, it is important to note, is critically different than a structure that uses only *one* of the procedural protections. The "or" structure does not replicate the protections of a third-party merger under the DGCL approval process, because it only requires that one, and not both, of the statutory requirements of director and stockholder approval be accomplished by impartial decisionmakers. The "both" structure, by contrast, replicates the arm's-length merger steps of the DGCL by "requir[ing] two independent approvals, which it is fair to say serve independent integrity-enforcing functions."

Before the Court of Chancery, the Appellants acknowledged that "this transactional structure is the optimal one for minority shareholders." Before us, however, they argue that neither procedural protection is adequate to protect minority stockholders, because "possible ineptitude and timidity of directors" may undermine the special committee protection, and because majority-of-the-minority votes may be unduly influenced by arbitrageurs that have an institutional bias to approve virtually any transaction that offers a market premium, however insubstantial it may be. Therefore, the Appellants claim, these protections, even when combined, are not sufficient to justify "abandon[ing]" the entire fairness standard of review.

With regard to the Special Committee procedural protection, the Appellants' assertions regarding the MFW directors' inability to discharge their duties are not supported either by the record or by well-established principles of Delaware law. As the Court of Chancery correctly observed:

> Although it is possible that there are independent directors who have little regard for their duties or for being perceived by their company's stockholders (and the larger network of institutional investors) as being effective at protecting public stockholders, the court thinks they are likely to be exceptional, and certainly our Supreme Court's jurisprudence does not embrace such a skeptical view.

Regarding the majority-of-the-minority vote procedural protection, as the Court of Chancery noted, "plaintiffs themselves do not argue that minority stockholders will vote against a going private transaction because of fear of retribution." Instead, as the Court of Chancery summarized, the Appellants' argued as follows:

> [Plaintiffs] just believe that most investors like a premium and will tend to vote for a deal that delivers one and that many long-term investors will sell out when they can obtain most of the premium without waiting for the ultimate vote. But that argument is not one that suggests that the voting decision is not voluntary, it is simply an editorial about the motives of investors and does not contradict the premise that a majority-of-the-minority condition gives minority investors a free and voluntary opportunity to decide what is fair for themselves.

Business Judgment Review Standard Adopted

We hold that business judgment is the standard of review that should govern mergers between a controlling stockholder and its corporate subsidiary, where the merger is conditioned *ab initio* upon both the approval of an independent, adequately-empowered Special Committee that fulfills its duty of care; and the uncoerced, informed vote of a majority of the minority stockholders. We so conclude for several reasons.

First, entire fairness is the highest standard of review in corporate law. It is applied in the controller merger context as a substitute for the dual statutory protections of disinterested board and stockholder approval, because both protections are potentially undermined by the influence of the controller. However, as this case establishes, that undermining influence does not exist in every controlled merger setting, regardless of the circumstances. The simultaneous deployment of the procedural protections employed here create a countervailing, offsetting influence of equal — if not greater — force. That is, where the controller irrevocably and publicly disables itself from using its control to dictate the outcome of the negotiations and the shareholder vote, the controlled merger then acquires the shareholder-protective characteristics of third-party, arm's-length mergers, which are reviewed under the business judgment standard.

Second, the dual procedural protection merger structure optimally protects the minority stockholders in controller buyouts. As the Court of Chancery explained:

> [W]hen these two protections are established up-front, a potent tool to extract good value for the minority is established. From inception, the controlling stockholder knows that it cannot bypass the special committee's ability to say no. And, the controlling stockholder knows it cannot dangle a majority-of-the-minority vote before the special committee late in the process as a deal-closer rather than having to make a price move.

Third, and as the Court of Chancery reasoned, applying the business judgment standard to the dual protection merger structure:

> . . . is consistent with the central tradition of Delaware law, which defers to the informed decisions of impartial directors, especially when those decisions have been approved by the disinterested stockholders on full information and without coercion. Not only that, the adoption of this rule will be of benefit to minority stockholders because it will provide a strong incentive for controlling stockholders to accord minority investors the transactional structure that respected scholars believe will provide them the best protection, a structure where stockholders get the benefits of independent, empowered negotiating agents to bargain for the best price and say no if the agents believe the deal is not advisable for any proper reason, plus the critical ability to determine for themselves whether to accept any deal that their negotiating agents recommend to them. A transactional structure with both these protections is fundamentally different from one with only one protection.

Fourth, the underlying purposes of the dual protection merger structure utilized here and the entire fairness standard of review both converge and are fulfilled at the same critical point: price. Following *Weinberger v. UOP, Inc.,* this Court has consistently held that, although entire fairness review comprises the dual components of fair dealing and fair price, in a non-fraudulent transaction "price may be the preponderant consideration outweighing other features of the merger." The dual protection merger structure requires two price-related pretrial determinations: first, that a fair price was achieved by an empowered, independent committee that acted with care; and, second, that a fully-informed, uncoerced majority of the minority stockholders voted in favor of the price that was recommended by the independent committee.

The New Standard Summarized

To summarize our holding, in controller buyouts, the business judgment standard of review will be applied *if and only if:* (i) the controller conditions the procession of the transaction on the approval of both a Special Committee and a majority of the minority stockholders; (ii) the Special Committee is independent; (iii) the Special Committee is empowered to freely select its own advisors and to say no definitively; (iv) the Special Committee meets its duty of care in negotiating a fair price; (v) the vote of the minority is informed; and (vi) there is no coercion of the minority.

. . .

This approach is consistent with *Weinberger, Lynch* and their progeny. A controller that employs and/or establishes only one of these dual procedural protections would continue to receive burden-shifting within the entire fairness standard of review framework. Stated differently, unless *both* procedural protections for the minority stockholders are established *prior to trial*, the ultimate judicial scrutiny of controller buyouts will continue to be the entire fairness standard of review.

Having articulated the circumstances that will enable a controlled merger to be reviewed under the business judgment standard, we next address whether those circumstances have been established as a matter of undisputed fact and law in this case.

Dual Protection Inquiry

To reiterate, in this case, the controlling stockholder conditioned its offer upon the MFW Board agreeing, *ab initio*, to both procedural protections, *i.e.,* approval by a Special Committee and by a majority of the minority stockholders. For the combination of an effective committee process and majority-of-the-minority vote to qualify (jointly) for business judgment review, each of these protections must be effective singly to warrant a burden shift.

We begin by reviewing the record relating to the independence, mandate, and process of the Special Committee. In *Kahn v. Tremont Corp.,* this Court held that "[t]o obtain the benefit of burden shifting, the controlling stockholder must do more than establish a perfunctory special committee of outside directors."

Rather, the special committee must "function in a manner which indicates that the controlling stockholder did not dictate the terms of the transaction and that the committee exercised real bargaining power 'at an arms-length.' " As we have previously noted, deciding whether an independent committee was effective in negotiating a price is a process so fact-intensive and inextricably intertwined with the merits of an entire fairness review (fair dealing and fair price) that a pretrial determination of burden shifting is often impossible. Here, however, the Defendants have successfully established a record of independent committee effectiveness and process that warranted a grant of summary judgment entitling them to a burden shift prior to trial.

We next analyze the efficacy of the majority-of-the-minority vote, and we conclude that it was fully informed and not coerced. That is, the Defendants also established a pretrial majority-of-the-minority vote record that constitutes an independent and alternative basis for shifting the burden of persuasion to the Plaintiffs.

. . .

To evaluate the parties' competing positions on the issue of director independence, the Court of Chancery applied well-established Delaware legal principles. To show that a director is not independent, a plaintiff must demonstrate that the director is "beholden" to the controlling party "or so under [the controller's] influence that [the director's] discretion would be sterilized." Bare allegations that directors are friendly with, travel in the same social circles as, or have past business relationships with the proponent of a transaction or the person they are investigating are not enough to rebut the presumption of independence.

A plaintiff seeking to show that a director was not independent must satisfy a materiality standard. The court must conclude that the director in question had ties to the person whose proposal or actions he or she is evaluating that are sufficiently substantial that he or she could not objectively discharge his or her fiduciary duties. Consistent with that predicate materiality requirement, the existence of some financial ties between the interested party and the director, without more, is not disqualifying. The inquiry must be whether, applying a subjective standard, those ties were *material,* in the sense that the alleged ties could have affected the impartiality of the individual director.

. . .

The record supports the Court of Chancery's holding that none of the Appellants' claims relating to Webb, Dinh or Byorum raised a triable issue of material fact concerning their individual independence or the Special Committee's collective independence.

The Special Committee Was Empowered

It is undisputed that the Special Committee was empowered to hire its own legal and financial advisors, and it retained Willkie Farr & Gallagher LLP as its legal advisor. After interviewing four potential financial advisors, the Special Committee engaged Evercore Partners ("Evercore"). The qualifications and independence of Evercore and Willkie Farr & Gallagher LLP are not contested.

Among the powers given the Special Committee in the board resolution was the authority to "report to the Board its recommendations and conclusions with respect to the [Merger], including a determination and recommendation as to whether the Proposal is fair and in the best interests of the stockholders. . . ." The Court of Chancery also found that it was "undisputed that the [S]pecial [C]ommittee was empowered not simply to 'evaluate' the offer, like some special committees with weak mandates, but to negotiate with [M & F] over the terms of its offer to buy out the noncontrolling stockholders. This negotiating power was accompanied by the clear authority to say no definitively to [M & F]" and to "make that decision stick." MacAndrews & Forbes promised that it would not proceed with any going private proposal that did not have the support of the Special Committee. Therefore, the Court of Chancery concluded, "the MFW committee did not have to fear that if it bargained too hard, MacAndrews & Forbes could bypass the committee and make a tender offer directly to the minority stockholders."

The Court of Chancery acknowledged that even though the Special Committee had the authority to negotiate and "say no," it did not have the authority, as a practical matter, to sell MFW to other buyers. MacAndrews & Forbes stated in its announcement that it was not interested in selling its 43% stake. Moreover, under Delaware law, MacAndrews & Forbes had no duty to sell its block, which was large enough, again as a practical matter, to preclude any other buyer from succeeding unless MacAndrews & Forbes decided to become a seller. Absent such a decision, it was unlikely that any potentially interested party would incur the costs and risks of exploring a purchase of MFW.

Nevertheless, the Court of Chancery found, "this did not mean that the MFW Special Committee did not have the leeway to get advice from its financial advisor about the strategic options available to MFW, including the potential interest that other buyers might have *if MacAndrews & Forbes was willing to sell.*" The undisputed record shows that the Special Committee, with the help of its financial advisor, did consider whether there were other buyers who might be interested in purchasing MFW, and whether there were other strategic options, such as asset divestitures, that might generate more value for minority stockholders than a sale of their stock to MacAndrews & Forbes.

The Special Committee Exercised Due Care

The Special Committee insisted from the outset that MacAndrews (including any "dual" employees who worked for both MFW and MacAndrews) be screened off from the Special Committee's process, to ensure that the process replicated arm's-length negotiations with a third party. In order to carefully evaluate M & F's offer, the Special Committee held a total of eight meetings during the summer of 2011.

From the outset of their work, the Special Committee and Evercore had projections that had been prepared by MFW's business segments in April and May 2011. Early in the process, Evercore and the Special Committee asked MFW management to produce new projections that reflected management's most up-to-date, and presumably most accurate, thinking. Consistent with the Special Committee's determination to conduct its analysis free of any MacAndrews influence, MacAndrews — including "dual" MFW/MacAndrews executives who normally vetted MFW projections — were excluded from the process of preparing the updated financial projections. Mafco, the licorice business, advised Evercore that all of its projections would remain the same. Harland Clarke updated its projections. On July 22, 2011, Evercore received new projections from HCHC, which incorporated the updated projections from Harland Clarke. Evercore then constructed a valuation model based upon all of these updated projections.

The updated projections, which formed the basis for Evercore's valuation analyses, reflected MFW's deteriorating results, especially in Harland's check-printing business. Those projections forecast EBITDA for MFW of $491 million in 2015, as opposed to $535 million under the original projections.

On August 10, Evercore produced a range of valuations for MFW, based on the updated projections, of $15 to $45 per share. Evercore valued MFW using a variety of accepted methods, including a discounted cash flow ("DCF") model. Those valuations generated a range of fair value of $22 to $38 per share, and a premiums paid analysis resulted in a value range of $22 to $45. MacAndrews & Forbes's $24 offer fell within the range of values produced by each of Evercore's valuation techniques.

Although the $24 Proposal fell within the range of Evercore's fair values, the Special Committee directed Evercore to conduct additional analyses and explore strategic alternatives that might generate more value for MFW's stockholders than might a sale to MacAndrews. The Special Committee also investigated the possibility of other buyers, *e.g.,* private equity buyers, that might be interested in purchasing MFW. In addition, the Special Committee considered whether other strategic options, such as asset divestitures, could achieve superior value for MFW's stockholders. Mr. Meister testified, "The Committee made it very clear to Evercore that we were interested in any and all possible avenues of increasing value to the stockholders, including meaningful expressions of interest for meaningful pieces of the business."

The Appellants insist that the Special Committee had "no right to solicit alternative bids, conduct any sort of market check, or even consider alternative transactions." But the Special Committee did just that, even though MacAndrews' stated unwillingness to sell its MFW stake meant that the Special Committee did not have the practical ability to market MFW to other buyers. The Court of Chancery properly concluded that despite the Special Committee's inability to solicit alternative bids, it *could* seek Evercore's advice about strategic alternatives, including *values that might be available if MacAndrews was willing to sell.*

Although the MFW Special Committee considered options besides the M & F Proposal, the Committee's analysis of those alternatives proved they were unlikely to achieve added value for MFW's stockholders. The Court of Chancery summarized the performance of the Special Committee as follows:

> [t]he special committee did consider, with the help of its financial advisor, whether there were other buyers who might be interested in purchasing MFW, and whether there were other strategic options, such as asset divestitures, that might generate more value for minority stockholders than a sale of their stock to MacAndrews & Forbes.

On August 18, 2011, the Special Committee rejected the $24 a share Proposal, and countered at $30 per share. The Special Committee characterized the $30 counteroffer as a negotiating position. The Special Committee recognized that $30 per share was a very aggressive counteroffer and, not surprisingly, was prepared to accept less.

On September 9, 2011, MacAndrews & Forbes rejected the $30 per share counteroffer. Its representative, Barry Schwartz, told the Special Committee Chair, Paul Meister, that the $24 per share Proposal was now far less favorable to MacAndrews & Forbes — but more attractive to the minority — than when it was first made, because of continued declines in MFW's businesses. Nonetheless, MacAndrews & Forbes would stand behind its $24 offer. Meister responded that he would not recommend the $24 per share Proposal to the Special Committee. Later, after having discussions with Perelman, Schwartz conveyed MacAndrews's "best and final" offer of $25 a share.

At a Special Committee meeting the next day, Evercore opined that the $25 per share *price was fair* based on generally accepted valuation methodologies, including DCF and comparable companies analyses. At its eighth and final meeting on September 10, 2011, the Special Committee, although empowered to say "no," instead unanimously approved and agreed to recommend the Merger at a price of $25 per share.

Influencing the Special Committee's assessment and acceptance of M & F's $25 a share price were developments in both MFW's business and the broader United States economy during the summer of 2011. For example, during the negotiation process, the Special Committee learned of the underperformance of MFW's Global Scholar business unit. The Committee also considered macroeconomic events, including the downgrade of the United States' bond credit rating, and the ongoing turmoil in the financial markets, all of which created financing uncertainties.

In scrutinizing the Special Committee's execution of its broad mandate, the Court of Chancery determined there was no "evidence indicating that the independent members of the special committee did not meet their duty of care. . . ." To the contrary, the Court of Chancery found, the Special Committee "met frequently and was presented with a rich body of financial information relevant to whether and at what *price* a going private transaction was advisable." The Court of Chancery ruled that "the plaintiffs d[id] not make any attempt to show that the MFW Special Committee failed to meet its duty of care. . . ." Based on the undisputed record, the Court of Chancery held that, "there is no triable issue of fact regarding whether the [S]pecial [C]ommittee fulfilled its duty of care." In the context of a controlling stockholder merger, a pretrial determination that the *price* was negotiated by an empowered independent committee that acted with care would shift the burden of persuasion to the plaintiffs under the entire fairness standard of review.

Majority of Minority Stockholder Vote

We now consider the second procedural protection invoked by M & F — the majority-of-the-minority stockholder vote. Consistent with the second condition imposed by M & F at the outset, the Merger was then put before MFW's stockholders for a vote. On November 18, 2011, the stockholders were provided with a proxy statement, which contained the history of the Special Committee's work and recommended that they vote in favor of the transaction at a price of $25 per share.

The proxy statement disclosed, among other things, that the Special Committee had countered M & F's initial $24 per share offer at $30 per share, but only was able to achieve a final offer of $25 per share. The proxy statement disclosed that the MFW business divisions had discussed with Evercore whether the initial projections Evercore received reflected management's latest thinking. It also disclosed that the updated projections were lower. The proxy statement also included the five separate price ranges for the value of MFW's stock that Evercore had generated with its different valuation analyses.

Knowing the proxy statement's disclosures of the background of the Special Committee's work, of Evercore's valuation ranges, and of the analyses supporting Evercore's *fairness opinion,* MFW's stockholders — representing more than 65% of the minority shares — approved the Merger. In the controlling stockholder merger context, it is settled Delaware law that an uncoerced, informed majority-of-the-minority vote, without any other procedural protection, is itself sufficient to shift the burden of persuasion to the plaintiff under the entire fairness standard of review. The Court of Chancery found that "the plaintiffs themselves do not dispute that the majority-of-the-minority vote was fully informed and uncoerced, because they fail to allege any failure of disclosure or any act of coercion."

Both Procedural Protections Established

Based on a highly extensive record, the Court of Chancery concluded that the procedural protections upon which the Merger was conditioned — approval by an independent and empowered Special Committee and by a uncoerced informed majority of MFW's minority stockholders — had *both* been undisputedly established *prior to trial.* We agree and conclude the Defendants' motion for summary judgment was properly granted on all of those issues.

Business Judgment Review Properly Applied

We have determined that the business judgment rule standard of review applies to this controlling stockholder buyout. Under that standard, the claims against the Defendants must be dismissed unless no rational person could have believed that the merger was favorable to MFW's minority stockholders. In this case, it cannot be credibly argued (let alone concluded) that no rational person would find the Merger favorable to MFW's minority stockholders.

Conclusion

For the above-stated reasons, the judgment of the Court of Chancery is affirmed.

Post-Case Follow-Up

Delaware is not the only jurisdiction to consider what standard of review ought to apply to "going private" transactions involving controlling shareholders. On November 20, 2014, the New York Appellate Division, First Department, in a case of first impression under New York law, ruled in favor of Kenneth Cole in a case involving a challenge to a going private transaction involving Kenneth Cole Productions, Inc. (KCP). *In re Kenneth Cole Prods. S'holder Deriv. Litig.*, 998 N.Y.S.2d 1 (App. Div. 2014). Cole controlled approximately 89 percent of KCP's voting power and owned a 46 percent economic interest in KCP. The Appellate Division found that the business judgment standard of review — and not the entire fairness standard — applied to judicial review of breach of fiduciary claims because the transaction had been structured at the outset with dual protections of an independent special committee review and the vote of a "majority of the minority" shareholders. On May 5, 2016, the New York Court of Appeals affirmed the Appellate Division order, expressly adopting the standard of review announced in *Kahn v. M&F Worldwide Corp.*, 88 A.3d 635, 648-49 (Del. 2014). *In re Kenneth Cole Prods. S'holder Deriv. Litig.*, 2016 WL 2350133 (N.Y. May 5, 2016).

Kahn v. M & F Worldwide Corp.: Real Life Applications

You represent Sarah Smith. Smith owns 52 percent of Smithworld, Inc., a publicly traded Delaware corporation. Smith is by far the largest individual shareholder of Smithworld, and she exercises actual control over the management and day-to-day affairs of the corporation. In recent years, Smith has come to the conclusion that having minority shareholders is more trouble than it is worth. She also believes — correctly — that taking Smithworld private would dramatically reduce legal and accounting expenses, as Smithworld would no longer incur the registration, disclosure, and reporting obligations applicable to a public company. Smith has hired you to advise her on executing a controller buyout — that is, a transaction whereby Smith would buy out Smithworld's minority shareholders and then take the company private.

a. If you are counsel to Smithworld, can you advise Smith with respect to the proposed transaction?

b. Smithworld's board currently consists exclusively of directors with deep personal and professional ties to Smith. Will Smith be able to take advantage of the business judgment standard announced in *Kahn*?

c. What would Smith need to do to ensure that the transaction is subject to review under the business judgment rule?

d. Assume for purpose of this question only that Smithworld is able to increase the size of the board and create a committee consisting solely of independent directors. What steps should the committee take when assessing Smith's proposal and negotiating with Smith?

H. DOMESTICATION AND ENTITY CONVERSION

Chapter 9 of the MBCA provides a series of procedures allowing corporations to change their state of incorporation (domestication) and also allowing corporations to become different business structures (entity conversion). For example, a corporation may change its structure and become a limited liability company, as AOL did in 2006, changing from America Online Inc. to AOL LLC (although AOL has since become a Delaware corporation). Both domestication and entity conversion may be accomplished by merger with a wholly owned subsidiary. For example, an Ohio corporation could create and then merge into a Texas corporation, with the Texas corporation surviving. This requires, however, that the Ohio corporation be wound up and dissolved. Domestications and entity conversions allow this same result to be accomplished directly, without the need for one entity to dissolve, thereby saving time and money. Not all states recognize domestications or conversions.

1. Domestication

Domestication allows a corporation to change its state of incorporation and be governed by the laws of another state. For example, a corporation formed in Pennsylvania may decide to "go public" and prefer to be a Delaware corporation because of the state's flexible and permissive statutes. Similarly, tax savings might justify a change in the state of incorporation.

As with the other changes in corporate structure discussed in this chapter, the process begins with the board of directors, which adopts a **plan of domestication** that contains the terms and conditions of the transaction, indicates whether any amendments to the articles are necessitated, and specifies the manner and basis of reclassifying shares based on the laws of the new state of domestication. The plan of domestication is then submitted to the shareholders for their approval (with the directors' recommendation that the shareholders approve the plan). The corporation must notify all shareholders (whether or not they are entitled to vote) of the meeting at which the plan will be submitted for approval, and the notice of the meeting must state its purpose and must include a copy or summary of the plan. Under the MBCA, if a quorum is present, the plan will be approved if more votes are cast in favor of it than against it. Many states, however, require majority approval.

The corporation will then prepare **articles of domestication** (sometimes called a certificate of domestication) and file them with the secretary of state in the new jurisdiction in which the corporation is to be domesticated and surrender its original charter or articles of incorporation to the former state of incorporation.

Domestication has no effect on the corporation's debts, assets, or liabilities, and after the domestication, the corporation remains the same, except that its state of incorporation has changed.

2. Entity Conversion

MBCA § 9.50 permits corporations to change their structures to unincorporated associations. For example, an Arizona corporation could become a limited liability partnership (LLP) or limited liability company (LLC). Similarly, the reverse could occur: An LLP or LLC may become a corporation. A business corporation may convert to a nonprofit corporation. Such changes are called **entity conversions**.

The process of effecting an entity conversion is nearly identical to that for effecting a domestication. The converting entity must adopt a **plan of entity conversion**, which sets forth the terms and conditions of the conversion, identifies the type of entity the new business will be, and sets forth the manner and basis of converting shares into other interests. For the purposes of this discussion, we will assume that a California corporation is converting to a California LLC. After adoption by the board, the board must submit the plan to the shareholders for their approval (together with the board's recommendation that the shareholders approve the plan). All shareholders must be notified of the meeting at which the plan is to be submitted for approval. The notice must state that the purpose is to consider the plan of entity conversion and must include a copy or summary of the plan. Although most states require approval by a majority of shareholders entitled to vote, the MBCA provides that the plan is approved if more shareholders vote for it than against it. Because some former shareholders might now face personal liability (e.g., if a corporation converts to a general partnership), each person who would become subject to such personal liability must sign a separate written consent. Shareholders of a business corporation that is converting to a noncorporate or nonprofit form have appraisal rights. After the conversion has been adopted and approved, **articles of entity conversion** will be prepared and filed with the state. The articles must provide that the plan was duly approved by the shareholders. A corporation that converts to a foreign unincorporated form must then surrender its articles or charter. As is the case with domestication, entity conversion does not affect the company's contracts, liabilities, and so forth.

I. TERMINATION OF CORPORATE EXISTENCE

1. Overview: Termination of Corporate Existence

Absent a specified period of duration, a corporation will continue in existence until it is expressly dissolved. Just as a corporation can only be created by strict compliance with state statutes, it can only be terminated or dissolved in accordance with state statutes, as well. Merely ceasing to conduct business will not terminate a corporation's status as a legal entity. Termination of the corporation's existence as a legal entity is referred to as **dissolution**. There are three types of dissolution: **voluntary dissolution**, initiated by the directors, or occasionally, the shareholders; **administrative dissolution**, initiated by the secretary of state for technical defaults (such as failure to pay taxes); and **involuntary** or **judicial dissolution**, initiated by the state, shareholders, or creditors. Cal. Corp. § 1900.

2. Voluntary Dissolution

A corporation may be dissolved even before shares have been issued to any shareholders or before it has commenced business. *See, e.g.*, MBCA § 14.01. In this case, if no directors have been named, the incorporators who formed the corporation will dissolve it. *Id.* Otherwise, the initial directors will dissolve the corporation. *Id.*

In most cases, however, a corporation dissolves after it has named directors, appointed officers, issued shares, and conducted business. Once shares have been issued, shareholders must approve the decision to dissolve because shareholders are the owners of the corporation, and a dissolution is a fundamental change to their corporation. *See, e.g.*, MBCA § 14.02. A voluntary decision to dissolve the corporation may originate with the directors (or, in some states, with the shareholders). Typically, though, the decision to dissolve voluntarily is initiated by the directors. As the managers of the corporation, they are in the best position to know whether dissolution is called for or whether the corporation should continue its operations. The directors will propose dissolution, and this will be approved at a directors' meeting, by majority vote, or by written consent, which usually must be unanimous. The directors will usually prepare a plan of dissolution. The directors will recommend dissolution to the shareholders and must call a special meeting of shareholders to vote on the proposed dissolution (unless the matter can be considered at an annual meeting). Notice of the special meeting must generally be given to all shareholders, whether or not they ordinarily have voting rights. The notice must state that the purpose of the meeting is to consider dissolution.

The modern approach, followed in Delaware, is to require a simple majority vote of shareholders to approve dissolution (unless the corporation's articles require a greater vote). *See* DGCL § 275. The MBCA provides that a proposal to dissolve requires the approval of the shareholders at a meeting at which quorum consisting of at least a majority of the votes entitled to be cast exists. *See* MBCA § 14.02(e).

Some states, however, including Maryland, require two-thirds approval by shareholders. Some states allow all shareholders to vote; others allow only shareholders holding voting stock to vote on the dissolution. Shareholders are seldom given any right to dissent and have their shares appraised; they will share in any assets remaining after creditors have been satisfied.

In some states, the next step in the dissolution process is for the corporation to file a notice with the secretary of state indicating its intent to dissolve. The MBCA does not require this public notice but simply provides that after dissolution is authorized, the corporation may dissolve by filing articles of dissolution with the secretary of state. Some states require that all creditors of the corporation also receive a notice stating the corporation's intent to dissolve. Alternatively, many jurisdictions allow the **notice of intent to dissolve** to be published in a legal newspaper in the county in which the corporation's principal office is located. The purpose of these notices is to inform the public and the corporation's creditors that the corporation is dissolving; this allows corporate creditors and other claimants to submit claims for debts owed to them.

Some states, such as Delaware, allow shareholders to initiate a voluntary dissolution. *See* DGCL § 275(c). In most instances, when a voluntary dissolution originates with the shareholders, unanimous approval is required. The shareholders can act by unanimous written consent. The requirement for unanimous consent is based on the fact that because shareholders do not manage the corporation, they are not likely to be in the best position to evaluate whether dissolution is wise. On the other hand, if *all* of the owners of the corporation agree that it should be dissolved, there is no logical reason it should not be. In California, however, shareholders may voluntarily elect to dissolve their corporation upon a simple majority vote.

Articles of Dissolution

After dissolution has been approved by both the directors and the shareholders, articles of dissolution (or a certificate of dissolution) are prepared and filed with the secretary of state in the state of incorporation. Most states provide forms for the articles of dissolution. See Exhibit 11.11 for a sample certificate of dissolution. The articles must generally set forth the following items:

- the name of the corporation;
- the date dissolution was authorized; and
- that the dissolution was approved by the requisite shareholder vote (or that the corporation has not issued shares and therefore it is being dissolved by the incorporators).

In some states, such as California, the corporation must also state that all of its known debts and liabilities have been paid or provided for and that its known assets have been distributed to the persons entitled thereto.

The articles of dissolution are filed in the office of the secretary of state with the appropriate filing fee. The secretary of state will usually require that the corporation submit appropriate documentation showing it does not owe any outstanding taxes to the state. Most states supply forms for such tax clearance. Failure to provide the

EXHIBIT 11.11   **Sample Certificate of Dissolution**

DISS STK

State of California
Secretary of State

Domestic Stock Corporation
Certificate of Dissolution

There is no fee for filing a Certificate of Dissolution.

IMPORTANT – Read instructions before completing this form.

This Space For Filing Use Only

Corporate Name   (Enter the name of the domestic stock corporation exactly as it is of record with the California Secretary of State.)

1. Name of corporation

Required Statements   (The following statements are required by statute and should not be altered.)

2. A final franchise tax return, as described by California Revenue and Taxation Code section 23332, has been or will be filed with the California Franchise Tax Board, as required under the California Revenue and Taxation Code, Division 2, Part 10.2 (commencing with Section 18401). The corporation has been completely wound up and is dissolved.

Debts & Liabilities   (Check the applicable statement. Note: Only one box may be checked.)

3. ☐ The corporation's known debts and liabilities have been actually paid.

☐ The corporation's known debts and liabilities have been paid as far as its assets permitted.

☐ The corporation's known debts and liabilities have been adequately provided for by their assumption and the name and address of the assumer is _____ .

☐ The corporation's known debts and liabilities have been adequately provided for as far as its assets permitted.

(Specify in an attachment to this certificate (incorporated herein by this reference) the provision made and the address of the corporation, person or governmental agency that has assumed or guaranteed the payment, or the name and address of the depositary with which deposit has been made or other information necessary to enable creditors or others to whom payment is to be made to appear and claim payment.)

☐ The corporation never incurred any known debts or liabilities.

Assets   (Check the applicable statement. Note: Only one box may be checked.)

4. ☐ The known assets have been distributed to the persons entitled thereto.

☐ The corporation never acquired any known assets.

Election   (Check the "YES" or "NO" box, as applicable. Note: If the "NO" box is checked, a Certificate of Election to Wind Up and Dissolve pursuant to Corporations Code section 1901 must be filed prior to or together with this Certificate of Dissolution.)

5. The election to dissolve was made by the vote of all the outstanding shares.   ☐ YES   ☐ NO

Verification & Execution   (If additional signature space is necessary, the dated signature(s) with verification(s) may be made on an attachment to this certificate. Any attachments to this certificate are incorporated herein by this reference.)

6. The undersigned constitute(s) the sole director or a majority of the directors now in office. I declare under penalty of perjury under the laws of the State of California that the matters set forth in this certificate are true and correct of my own knowledge.

_____
Date

_____   _____
Signature of Director   Type or Print Name of Director

_____   _____
Signature of Director   Type or Print Name of Director

_____   _____
Signature of Director   Type or Print Name of Director

DISS STK (REV 01/2013)   APPROVED BY SECRETARY OF STATE tax clearance form will result in rejection of the articles of dissolution. Additionally, the corporation must notify the Internal Revenue Service (using Form 966) within 30 days after a resolution to dissolve that it is dissolving and make arrangements to pay federal taxes. Once the secretary of state reviews and approves the articles, the corporation ceases to exist for the purpose of doing any business other than winding up. If the corporation has been authorized to transact business in other states, it should withdraw its certificate of authority in those states.

Revocation of Dissolution

Almost all states allow corporations to revoke the decision to dissolve by filing articles of revocation of dissolution. Revocation must be approved by the board and then the requisite vote of shareholders. MBCA § 14.04 allows a corporation to revoke its decision to dissolve within 120 days of the effective date of the dissolution, in which case it is as if dissolution never occurred.

MBCA Approach

The MBCA and many states require only one publicly filed document to effect dissolution, the articles of dissolution, and the corporation is dissolved on the effective date of the articles of dissolution. *See* MBCA § 14.03(b). After the articles of dissolution are filed, the corporation is referred to as a "dissolved corporation," but it continues its existence only for the purpose of winding up and liquidating its business and affairs. The corporation then proceeds to liquidate by disposing of its known claims and unknown claims and distributing the balance of its assets to its shareholders. Thus, in this approach, dissolution precedes liquidation. There is no statutorily required period within which liquidation must be completed, although it is obviously in the corporation's interest to proceed with liquidation in an expeditious manner.

In other states, such as California, voluntary dissolution is initiated by a publicly filed notice of the corporation's intent or election to dissolve, and then to complete the dissolution process, articles or a certificate of dissolution must be filed, which must recite that all known debts and liabilities have been paid and that assets have been distributed to shareholders. In states following this approach, liquidation precedes formal dissolution. This approach would seem to provide more comfort to both creditors and shareholders because the corporation is not allowed to dissolve unless its directors state under penalty of perjury that debts and liabilities have been taken care of and assets have been distributed to those entitled to them. See Sections 3 and 4 of Exhibit 11.11.

3. Administrative Dissolution

Grounds and Procedure for Administrative Dissolution

Nearly all states and the MBCA recognize a type of dissolution that is less serious than involuntary dissolution. In these states, the secretary of state will dissolve a corporation for one of the following reasons: its failure to pay taxes or file annual reports; failure to have a registered agent for some period of time (often 60 days) or to notify the secretary of state that its registered agent or office have changed; or for continuing to operate after the corporation's period of duration expires. *See, e.g.*, MBCA § 14.20. Grounds of this nature are often called technical — or administrative — defaults. Many states provide written notice to the corporation of technical defaults and give the corporation an opportunity to cure the defaults. If it does not do so, it will be administratively dissolved, and it cannot carry on any routine business except that necessary to wind up and liquidate its affairs.

Reinstatement After Administrative Dissolution

Most states and MBCA § 14.22 allow a corporation to apply for **reinstatement** or revival within a certain period of time (two years under the MBCA) after it has been dissolved on technical grounds. The corporation must cure the default. Reinstatement is retroactive so that after reinstatement, the corporation may continue doing business as if the administrative dissolution had never occurred. Not all states allow reinstatement. If the prior name of the corporation is no longer available, it must select a new name and file an amendment to its original articles of incorporation. See Exhibit 11.12 for an application for reinstatement. A decision by the secretary of state to deny an application for reinstatement may be appealed to the courts. Generally, only corporations dissolved for technical grounds may be reinstated.

4. Involuntary or Judicial Dissolution

State statutes also allow for the dissolution of corporations even when dissolution is not desired by the board of directors. This is referred to as an **involuntary dissolution** or, because the dissolution proceeding is brought before a court, an involuntary dissolution is also called a **judicial dissolution**. A corporation can be forced to dissolve against its will by the state, unsatisfied creditors, or by its shareholders. If a court determines that there are grounds for dissolution shown by the state, creditors, or shareholders, it will enter a decree of dissolution specifying the effective date of the dissolution. The decree will be provided to the secretary of state by the clerk of the court, and the secretary of state will then file the decree in its records. The court will then order winding up and liquidation of the corporation's business and affairs and notification of its creditors and claimants.

Practice Pointer: Keep a Docket Calendar for Corporate Clients

Because a corporation can be dissolved by the state for failure to file annual reports and pay taxes, you should be sure to maintain an accurate docket or calendar for all corporate clients. Although many states provide reminder notices to corporations that annual reports are due, clients are often so busy they neglect to file the report on time. Use your docket to remind clients of the critical deadline for filing the annual report.

EXHIBIT 11.12   **Illinois Application for Reinstatement**

FORM **BCA 12.45/13.6** (rev. Dec. 2003)
APPLICATION FOR REINSTATEMENT
DOMESTIC/FOREIGN CORPORATIONS
Business Corporation Act

Secretary of State
Department of Business Services
501 S. Second St., Rm. 350
Springfield, IL 62756
217-782-1837 (foreign)
217-785-5782 or 217-782-5797 (domestic)
www.cyberdriveillinois.com

Remit payment in the form of a cashier's
check, certified check, money order,
Illinois attorney's check payable to
Secretary of State.

See notes on back.

_____ File #_____   **Filing Fee: $200**   Approved: _____

— — — — **Submit in duplicate** — — — — **Type or Print clearly in black ink** — — — — **Do not write above this line** — — — —

1. a. Corporate Name as of date of issuance of Certificate of Dissolution or Revocation:

    _____

    b. Corporate Name if changed: (See Note 2.)

    _____

    c. If a foreign corporation having authority under an assumed corporate name restriction, the Assumed Corporate Name:
        (See Note 3.) _____

    _____

2. State of Incorporation: _____

3. Date Certificate of Dissolution or Revocation issued: _____

4. Name and Address of Illinois Registered Agent and the Illinois Registered Office upon reinstatement:
    NOTICE: Completion of Item 4 does not constitute a registered agent or office change. (See Note 4.)

    Registered Agent _____
                                First Name   Middle Name   Last Name

    Registered Office _____
                Number   Street   Suite # (P.O. Box alone is unacceptable)
                                      IL
                City   ZIP Code   County

5. This application is accompanied by all delinquent report forms together with the filing fees, franchise taxes, license fee and penalties required. (See Note 1.)

6. The undersigned corporation has caused this application to be signed by a duly authorized officer who affirms, under penalties of perjury, that the facts stated herein are true and correct. (All signatures must be in **BLACK INK.**)

    Dated _____ , _____   _____
              Month   Day   Year   Exact Name of Corporation

    _____
    Any Authorized Officer's Signature

    _____
    Name and Title (type or print)

Printed by authority of the State of Illinois. April 2015 — 2.5M — C 89.25

Action by the State

Corporations exist only by virtue of the authority of the state of incorporation. Because a state always has the power and authority to ensure compliance with its laws, a corporation can be dissolved by its creator, the state of incorporation. An action for involuntary dissolution is usually brought in the name of the state attorney general, the individual in each state charged with enforcing the laws of the state. Generally, the grounds for dissolution by the state include the following:

1. procuring the articles of incorporation through fraud; or
2. exceeding or abusing the authority given to the corporation by the state.

See, e.g., MBCA § 14.30. Generally, reinstatement is not available after a judicial dissolution.

Action by a Creditor

A creditor of the corporation may institute a proceeding for judicial dissolution of a corporation. Typically, the creditor must establish that the corporation is insolvent and that the creditor has either received a judgment against the corporation for the claim or the corporation has acknowledged in writing that the claim is owed. Once the creditor has established either or both of these facts, the court may order a winding up and dissolution of the corporation so that the creditor may be paid the money owed to it. During liquidation, the expenses of liquidation will be paid first, then creditors will be paid, and then the corporation's remaining assets (if any) will be distributed to shareholders on a pro rata basis in accordance with their ownership interest and in accordance with any preferences. Because creditors' claims must be paid before assets are distributed to shareholders upon dissolution, the creditor may believe it is in his best interest to force a dissolution and thereby collect some amount of the claim rather than no amount at all if the corporation is refusing to satisfy the debt. In many cases, a creditor might simply initiate a bankruptcy petition against the corporation rather than petitioning to dissolve the corporation.

Action by Shareholder(s)

We discussed special judicial dissolution rules applicable to close corporations in some states in Chapter 10. We also referenced MBCA rules regarding voluntary dissolution by shareholders above. Here, we wish to note only that some state statutes include authorization for judicial dissolution upon a by petition some — but not all — shareholders in cases other than oppression or fraudulent or illegal conduct by the majority shareholders of a close corporation — for example, where the board or shareholders are deadlocked. Here is an example from New York:

§ 1104. Petition in case of deadlock among directors or shareholders.
(a) Except as otherwise provided in the certificate of incorporation under section

613 (Limitations on right to vote), the holders of shares representing one-half of the votes of all outstanding shares of a corporation entitled to vote in an election of directors may present a petition for dissolution on one or more of the following grounds:

(1) That the directors are so divided respecting the management of the corporation's affairs that the votes required for action by the board cannot be obtained.

(2) That the shareholders are so divided that the votes required for the election of directors cannot be obtained.

(3) That there is internal dissension and two or more factions of shareholders are so divided that dissolution would be beneficial to the shareholders.

(b) If the certificate of incorporation provides that the proportion of votes required for action by the board, or the proportion of votes of shareholders required for election of directors, shall be greater than that otherwise required by this chapter, such a petition may be presented by the holders of shares representing more than one-third of the votes of all outstanding shares entitled to vote on non-judicial dissolution under section 1001 (Authorization of dissolution).

(c) Notwithstanding any provision in the certificate of incorporation, any holder of shares entitled to vote at an election of directors of a corporation, may present a petition for its dissolution on the ground that the shareholders are so divided that they have failed, for a period which includes at least two consecutive annual meeting dates, to elect successors to directors whose terms have expired or would have expired upon the election and qualification of their successors.

NYBCL § 1104. Remember that in some states (and, sometimes in the context of closely held corporations only), a court can allow or require the complaining shareholder's shares to be purchased in lieu of ordering judicial dissolution. *See, e.g.,* NYBCL § 1118 (applicable to close corporations). Be sure to research the corporations code of the relevant jurisdiction to determine whether a buy-out in lieu of dissolution is an option.

J. LIQUIDATION

1. Introduction

Closely associated with dissolution is completing the corporation's business, paying creditors, and distributing remaining assets to shareholders. This process of wrapping up the business affairs of the corporation is called **liquidation**. Liquidation generally involves the following activities:

a. collecting assets;
b. disposing of properties that will not be distributed to shareholders;
c. discharging liabilities or making provisions for discharging liabilities; and
d. distributing the remaining property to the shareholders according to their respective interests.

See MBCA § 14.05.

Once a corporation has filed its notice of intent to dissolve (or, in many states, its articles of dissolution), it continues business only for the purpose of liquidating and cannot conduct ordinary or additional business. As discussed above, some states, such as California, will not allow a corporation to end its legal existence unless liquidation has been accomplished. Thus, in those states, the corporation must wind up its business affairs before a certificate of dissolution will be issued. Under MBCA § 14.09, directors have a duty to discharge any claims against the corporation and may only distribute assets to shareholders after payment of creditors' claims. A breach of this duty may lead to personal liability.

2. Nonjudicial Liquidation

When dissolution is voluntary (initiated by the directors with shareholder approval or unanimously agreed to by the shareholders) or administrative, corporate officers and directors will liquidate the corporation. Contracts will be completed, creditors will be notified to submit their claims, and assets will be collected. State statutes do not generally impose any specific time limit within which the liquidation must be completed. Even in a voluntary dissolution, the corporation may request judicial supervision of liquidation if it believes such is appropriate.

3. Judicial Liquidation

A judicial dissolution initiated by the state, shareholders, or creditors is often caused by the directors' failure to manage the corporation properly, by fraud, or by waste of the corporate assets. Because a court therefore cannot place confidence in corporate management to conduct liquidation properly, the court generally appoints a receiver whose function is to receive the assets of the corporation and distribute them to the creditors and shareholders. Some jurisdictions refer to the individual or company appointed to oversee the winding up process as the court-appointed liquidator. The receiver will be compensated for services rendered in effecting an orderly liquidation. The court may also appoint a separate custodian to manage the business and affairs of the corporation during this time.

4. Claims Against the Corporation

There are two types of claims that must be discharged or resolved by a dissolving corporation: **known claims** (those claims, debts, and obligations the corporation knows about) and **unknown claims** (claims that have not yet matured or been made against the corporation, for example, claims for injuries that may be sustained in the future due to a defective product the corporation has made). Corporations cannot use dissolutions to avoid contractual obligations. For example, if the corporation is a party to a long-term employment contract, it must satisfy the obligations thereunder, at least as to money to be paid to the employee, unless the terms of the contract contemplate dissolution and excuse performance by the corporation in the event of a dissolution.

Known Claims

The MBCA provides an orderly process for disposing of claims against the corporation. As to known claims, the corporation may notify the claimants in writing of the dissolution, inform the creditor or claimant where to submit the claim, provide at least 120 days for the creditor to make the claim, and inform the creditor the claim will be barred if not timely submitted to the corporation. If the creditor does not submit the claim in a timely fashion, the claim will be barred. If a claim is submitted and the corporation rejects it, the claimant must institute legal action within 90 days of rejection of the claim to enforce the claim or it will be barred. MBCA § 14.06.

Unknown Claims

To ensure that unknown claims are also discharged, MBCA § 14.07 provides that the corporation may place in a newspaper of general circulation a notice of dissolution stating that the claim will be barred unless an action to enforce the claim is brought within three years of publication of the notice. In some states, the notice must be posted on the corporation's website. If the corporation's assets have been distributed before the claim is made, shareholders may be liable, but only to the extent of assets distributed to them. If the corporation was dissolved because of a merger or consolidation, a creditor is usually able to enforce a claim against the surviving corporation. In many states, the articles of dissolution must recite that no debt remains unpaid or that the corporation's debts and liabilities have been adequately provided for by their assumption by certain individuals or companies whose addresses are provided. Corporations may provide for such unknown claims by purchasing insurance or setting aside a portion of assets. Alternatively, under MBCA § 14.08, a corporation may initiate a court proceeding to establish an amount that should be set aside for unknown claims. Once this is done, neither the corporation nor any shareholders have any liability for any unknown claims.

K. DISTRIBUTIONS TO SHAREHOLDERS

After all debts have been discharged and any expenses of liquidation have been paid, and assuming any assets remain, the shareholders are entitled to receive a distribution, generally called a **liquidation distribution**. This is the shareholder's residual interest in the enterprise. Corporate assets are typically converted to "liquid" form, namely cash, and the shareholders will receive cash payments. Alternatively, they may receive assets. If there are preferred shareholders whose shares have a liquidation preference (i.e., they are first in line with respect to liquidating distributions), those preferences must be honored. Shareholders participate in the distribution in accordance with their ownership interests; if a shareholder owns 23 percent of the common stock of a corporation, the shareholder will be entitled to receive 23 percent of any liquidation distribution made to common shareholders. Shareholders must report these distributions to the Internal Revenue Service.

Note that a shareholder receiving a liquidation distribution is treated as though the shareholder sold his shares for an amount equal to the liquidating distribution. Thus, they will get "share or exchange" treatment (and thus capital gains treatment) as opposed to (dividend) distribution (and thus ordinary income) treatment.

Shareholders are not entitled to appraisal rights arising out of a dissolution inasmuch as all shareholders are equally affected by a dissolution. Their sole right is to receive a distribution, if sufficient assets remain after payment of liquidation costs and creditors' claims.

Chapter Summary

- Significant changes to a corporation typically require shareholder approval.
- A corporation generally can amend its articles at any time by resolution of the directors followed by shareholder approval. A corporation may restate its articles to create one composite document superseding prior amendments; shareholder approval is unnecessary because nothing new is being added to the articles.
- Amending corporate bylaws is typically handled by directors, but it is important to review state law to determine if, when, and how shareholders are involved in the bylaw amendment process.
- A merger is the combination of two or more corporations into one corporate entity. The survivor succeeds to all of the business, debts, liabilities, and assets of the extinguished corporation. Generally, shareholders of all constituent corporations must approve the transaction, though there are exceptions to this rule.
- A consolidation is the combination of two or more corporations and the formation of an entirely new entity that succeeds to all of the business, debts, liabilities, and assets of the consolidating corporations. Shareholders of both corporations generally must approve the transaction.
- Shareholders of privately held corporations who dissent from a merger or consolidation generally have the right to have their shares appraised and purchased from them at fair value, though there are some exceptions to this rule.
- In a share exchange, the target's shareholders exchange their shares for cash or shares in the acquiring corporation.
- As an alternative to a merger, one corporation can purchase all or substantially all of another's assets. Liabilities are generally not purchased, though there are circumstances when substantive law overrides structuring and private ordering decisions.
- Corporate combinations can be consensual or hostile. The two principal methods of effecting a hostile takeover are tender offers and proxy fights.
- Corporations may enact a variety of defenses to ward off a takeover. One of the most popular defenses is a poison pill or shareholder rights plan, by which shareholders are given extra voting rights or rights to purchase more shares at fire sale prices once a tender offer is announced.
- The *Unocal* and *Revlon* cases speak to directors' obligations in connection with hostile takeover attempts and transactions that will result in a sale of the corporation or change in corporate control. *Unocal* calls for enhanced judicial scrutiny

of takeover defenses, and *Revlon* requires directors to maximize shareholder returns when sale of the corporation becomes inevitable. Both the *Unocal* and *Revlon* standards of review are more searching than review under the business judgement rule.

■ Controller buyouts of Delaware corporations are subject to review under the entire fairness standard, except in cases where the transaction is conditioned upon certain shareholder protective devices.

■ Corporations may change their state of incorporation (domestication) and may convert to another business structure, such as converting to an LLC (entity conversion).

■ Dissolution refers to termination of the corporate entity's existence, whereas liquidation refers to termination of the corporation's business and affairs.

■ Corporations can dissolve voluntarily (usually by action of the directors, which is then approved by shareholders), administratively (for technical defaults such as failure to pay taxes), or involuntarily or judicially (by action by the state, shareholders, or creditors). If dissolution is voluntary, articles of dissolution will be filed with the state. If dissolution is involuntary, a court will enter a decree of dissolution.

■ If dissolution is voluntary, corporate management will oversee liquidation; if dissolution is involuntary or judicial, a court will supervise liquidation.

■ An administrative dissolution may be initiated by the state for technical reasons (such as a corporation's failure to file annual reports or pay taxes). A corporation that is dissolved for such reasons can generally apply to be reinstated.

■ Creditors can initiate a dissolution if the corporation is insolvent and their claim is undisputed. The court will order winding up and liquidation so the creditor may be paid the money owed to it.

■ Shareholders may be able to initiate a dissolution in certain circumstances, such as director or shareholder deadlock, waste of assets, or fraud by directors. In lieu of ordering a dissolution, in some states a court can allow the complaining shareholder's shares to be purchased.

■ During liquidation, the expenses of liquidation will be paid, creditors will be paid, and then remaining assets will be distributed to shareholders on a pro rata basis in accordance with any preferences.

Applying the Concepts

1. TechCom Inc., a Delaware corporation, has decided to combine with Geo Industries, Inc. Use the MBCA to answer the following questions:

   a. Assume Geo will be extinguished at the end of the transaction. Which corporation's shareholders, if any, must vote on the transaction? Why?

   b. Assume that in the above transaction, TechCom had 100,000 outstanding shares, and at the conclusion of the transaction, it would need to issue 15,000 shares to the shareholders of Geo. Would your answer to Question 1.a change? Discuss.

    c. Assume that the transaction is approved by both constituents. Alex, a shareholder of TechCom, is opposed to the transaction. Does Alex have any remedies? Discuss.

    d. Would your answer to Question 1.c change if TechCom's stock were traded on NASDAQ?

    e. Discuss how having a staggered board, golden parachutes for its ten most senior executives, and a poison pill might discourage the acquisition of Geo by TechCom.

    f. Three months after the transaction is concluded, TechCom decided to change its name to TechTransfer Corp., to increase its authorized number of shares so that it may declare a stock split, and to change the date of its annual shareholders' meeting. Discuss the procedure by which TechCom will accomplish these changes and shareholder approval issues, if any.

2. TechCom has decided to acquire certain manufacturing plants owned by Smart Vision, Inc. These manufacturing plants constitute about 40 percent of Smart Vision's assets and produce about 70 percent of Smart Vision's revenue. Identify the type of transaction involved, discuss shareholder approval issues (if any), and discuss which entity will repay Smart Vision's current loan from Wells Fargo Bank.

3. What is the fee in New York for a for-profit corporation to file a certificate of amendment?

4. What is the fee in Pennsylvania for filing a certificate of merger relating to three parties or constituents? Review the form of certificate. What information is required in Section Five?

5. Access the website of the SEC and locate the "Tender Offer Statement by Third Party" filed on September 10, 2014 by Dollar General Corporation.

    a. What filing fee was paid?

    b. Briefly describe the terms of the offer.

6. Does Pennsylvania have a nonshareholder constituency statute?

7. Are there any limitations on the board's ability to amend a corporation's bylaws under California law?

8. What is the best deal structure if a buyer is worried that purchasers of the target's products may suffer injuries as result of product defects?

Business Organizations in Practice

1. Acme Corp., a corporation formed in a jurisdiction that follows the MBCA, has agreed to acquire Zed Corp. in a reverse triangular merger. The deal consideration consists of Acme common stock and debt securities. Acme's common stock trades on the NASDAQ stock market. Acme plans to issue $35 million shares of common stock in the deal. Zed also was formed in a jurisdiction that follows the MBCA, and its shares are also traded on the NASDAQ stock market.

   a. You represent Zenia, an Acme shareholder who is unhappy with the proposed transaction. Write a brief memo to Zenia discussing whether she has appraisal rights.
   b. A colleague represents Tim, a Zed stockholder, who is unhappy with the proposed deal, as well. Does Tim have appraisal rights?
   c. You represent Acme. Advise Acme's board as to whether Acme's shareholders get to vote on the deal.
   d. Do Zed's shareholders get to vote on the deal?

2. Sandy is a shareholder in Salwe, Inc., a privately held corporation formed in a jurisdiction that follows the MBCA. Last month, Salwe's board voted in favor of a merger with Aurelius Corp. That transaction subsequently was approved by two-thirds of Salwe's shareholders. Under the MBCA and according to Salwe's charter, this satisfied necessary voting requirements. Sandy is adamantly opposed to the transaction and would like to be bought out. Assume for purposes of this question that Sandy has appraisal rights under the MBCA.

   a. Prepare a checklist outlining Salwe's statutory obligations respecting appraisal rights. Prepare all necessary documents.
   b. Prepare a checklist laying out the steps that Sandy must take to exercise appraisal rights.

3. MA, Inc. is a small, privately held New York corporation with directors — Shanna, Sue, Juanita, Sanjay, and Zane. MA's bylaws provide that any amendments to the bylaws must be approved by all five of the corporation's directors. This provision was voted into the corporation's bylaws by the company's shareholders.

   Sue recently had a falling out with the other directors. She has dissented from a number of proposed bylaw amendments, much to the frustration of the other directors, and she has refused to resign from the board.

   Last week, at a board meeting, MA's board members voted four to one to delete the unanimous voting requirement from the bylaws. Write a letter to Sue explaining whether or not the board has the power to amend the bylaws over Sue's objections.

4. 4C, Inc., a privately held corporation formed in a jurisdiction that follows the MBCA, would like to amend its charter to increase the number of authorized shares and permit the issuance of preferred stock, in anticipation of receiving

a round of venture capital financing. You are 4C's outside counsel. Consult the MBCA and draft a checklist of steps that the company will need to take to amend the charter.

5. Assume that all of 4C's directors support amending the charter. The next regularly scheduled board meeting is not for several months, and the directors live all over the country. Can 4C obtain the directors' consent to the charter amendment via written consent (rather than through in-person voting at a board meeting)? If so, draft a unanimous written consent for the board members.

6. Assume that 4C just held its annual meeting last month. Further assume that at the meeting, several shareholders expressed reservations about management and the direction of the company.

   a. Does 4C need shareholder approval to amend the charter?
   b. Is it likely that 4C will be able to obtain shareholder approval via written consent?
   c. If 4C is not able to obtain shareholder approval via written consent, how can or should the company put the amendment to a shareholder vote?
   d. Draft a notice for a special meeting of shareholders to consider and vote on the proposed charter amendment.
   e. What voting rules and requirements are likely to apply to the shareholder vote?
   f. 4C anticipates that many of its shareholders will not attend the shareholder meeting in person. Draft a proxy form for those shareholders.
   g. Assume shareholders vote in favor of the amendments. Will you need to file the amendments with the secretary of state? When will the amendments become effective?

Limited Liability Companies

Like registered limited liability partnerships and registered limited liability limited partnerships, the limited liability company (LLC) is a fairly new form of business organization. LLCs are a hybrid: They combine attractive features of corporations (e.g., limited liability for owners) with attractive features of partnerships (e.g., pass-through taxation and the opportunity to customize management and governance rules). In this chapter, we discuss the characteristics of this increasingly popular form of business association, focusing on the formation requirements, management and governance rules, the contents and role of the LLC operating agreement, and the LLC liability shield.

A. WHAT IS A LIMITED LIABILITY COMPANY?

A **limited liability company** (LLC) is an unincorporated entity formed pursuant to a state LLC statute that provides (i) limited liability for owners (called members), while still allowing members to participate fully in the management of the business; (ii) pass-through taxation; and (iii) the opportunity to customize most internal management and governance and rules via the LLC operating agreement. On occasion, the LLC form has been referred to as a statutory partnership association, partnership association, or limited partnership association. Limited liability company, however, is the most frequently used name for this type of entity.

Key Concepts

- Definition and characteristics of the limited liability company form
- The LLC operating agreement
- The LLC liability shield
- Rights and responsibilities of LLC members with respect to the LLC, other members, and third parties

The LLC Revolution

The explosion in growth in the number of LLCs is staggering. Wyoming adopted the first LLC statute in the nation in 1975. After the Internal Revenue Service issued a ruling in 1998 allowing LLCs to be classified as partnerships or disregarded entities for tax purposes, states began adopting LLC statutes in earnest. By 1996, all 50 states and the District of Columbia had enacted legislation recognizing LLCs, and by 2007, more LLCs were formed than corporations in 46 states. As a measure of the popularity of LLCs, the number of new LLCs formed in the United States now outpaces the number of new corporations created by nearly two to one. LLC formations now outpace the number of new limited partnerships formed by more than 34 to 1, as well. *See, e.g.,* Rodney D. Chrisman, *LLCs Are the New King of the Hill: An Empirical Study of the Number of New LLCs, Corporations, and LPs Formed in the United States Between 2004-2007 and How LLCs Were Taxed for Tax Years 2002-2006*, 15 Fordham J. Corp. & Fin. L. 459, 460, 462 (2010). For a discussion of the history and the origins of the LLC form, *see* William J. Carney, *Limited Liability Companies: Origins and Antecedents*, 66 U. Colo. L. Rev. 855, 857 (1995).

LLCs versus LLPs

Both the LLC and LLP forms provide owners with a liability shield and the opportunity to participate in management. How do lawyers and business people decide which of these two forms to use, then? The traditional professions (e.g., law, accounting, and medicine) make up the majority of LLPs (with some PLLCs thrown in), whereas businesses in "emerging" professions (e.g., computer consulting, marketing, and management services) tend to adopt the LLC form, according to some commentators. *See* Conrad S. Ciccotello & Terry Grant, *Professionals as Commercial Institutions: An Analysis of Evolving Organizational Forms*, 7 J. Legal Stud. Bus. 1, 2, 8 (2000). The rationale for this breakdown may be that professional services firms historically have used the partnership form, so the LLP form may feel familiar and comfortable to individuals from these fields. Emerging professions do not have historical associations with the partnership form, and may prefer the default rules and the liability shield of the LLC. *Id.* at 25.

Economic considerations also may help to explain entity choice. For example, although Texas was the first state to recognize LLPs, the state requires an application and imposes an annual fee of $200 for each LLP partner. Thus, a law firm with 200 partners would pay $40,000 annually to be recognized as an LLP in Texas, whereas a firm organized as a professional limited liability corporation, or PLLC, would not have such a requirement. *See* Robert W. Hamilton, *Professional Partnerships in the United States*, 26 J. Corp. L. 1045, 1053-1054 (2001). A more recent study affirmed that the cost of forming the entity is an important feature in explaining entity choice. *See* Daniel M. Hausermann, *For a Few Dollars Less: Explaining State to State Variation in Limited Liability Company Popularity*, 20 U. Miami Bus. L. Rev. 1, 3 (2011). The same article also noted that LLC formations first surpassed incorporations in 2004, and since that time have remained the most popular business entity in the United States. *See id.* at 4.

Other distinctions between the LLP and LLC forms may be important to particular clients:

■ LLCs can be managed by appointed managers (who need not be members of the LLC), whereas LLPs are generally co-managed by all of their partners.

■ In the case of an LLP, if the parties' agreement fails to address the sharing of profits and losses, profits and losses will be shared equally regardless of contributions (i.e., the partnership model). In the case of an LLC, profits and losses are allocated in the same ratio as the members' unreturned contributions (i.e., the corporate model) under some state LLC statutes, although the Uniform Limited Liability Company Act and many states provide for equal distributions in the absence of an agreement to the contrary.

■ All states allow a one-person LLC, making it attractive for sole proprietors to convert to LLCs and thereby achieve protection from personal liability. Because LLPs are a form of partnership, they must always have at least two partners.

■ Under the Uniform Limited Liability Company Act and many state statutes, not-for-profit businesses may operate as LLCs, whereas the LLP, as a form of partnership, must be operated with the expectation of making a profit.

■ The LLC form is similar to investment vehicles recognized in other countries — primarily Germany, France, Portugal, Saudi Arabia, Switzerland, Japan, and several South American and Central American nations. Due to our increasingly global economy, the "familiarity" of the LLC form to overseas counterparts may make the LLC an attractive form of business organization for certain foreign investors. For example, the LLC form may be familiar to investors from certain Latin American countries, which recognize a business similar to an LLC that is referred to as a *limitada*. Similarly, the *GmbH* business entity recognized in Germany, Austria, and other Central European countries is analogous to American LLCs.

Ultimately, the selection of one entity over another ought to be based upon consideration of a number of issues, including liability, taxation, organizational custom, entity-level fees and taxes, and (of course) client-specific needs and goals.

B. WHAT LAW GOVERNS LIMITED LIABILITY COMPANIES?

1. The Uniform Limited Liability Company Act

As a general rule, the formation and internal affairs of a limited liability company are governed by the limited liability company statute of the state in which the LLC files its **certificate of organization (a/k/a articles of organization)** — a document that is analogous to the articles or certificate of incorporation in the corporate context. *See* Uniform Limited Liability Company Act (ULLCA) § 104 (providing, in pertinent part, that the law of the state of organization governs) (1) the internal affairs of a limited liability company; and (2) the liability of a member as member and a manager as manager for a debt, obligation, or other liability of a limited liability company. To illustrate rules and concepts relating to LLCs, we reference the current version of the ULLCA in this chapter — that is, the ULLCA-2006 (as modified in 2011 and 2013).[1] It is important to note, however, that while the Uniform Law Commission (ULC) has adopted and periodically has amended the uniform

---

[1] As with the uniform acts referenced in Chapters 3, 4, and 5. We cite to the latest version of the ULLCA currently available on the Uniform Law Commission website.

Uniform Limited Liability Company Act

The 2011 and 2013 amendments to the ULLCA were enacted as part of the Harmonization of Business Entity Acts (HBEA) project. These amendments updated and harmonized the language in the ULLCA with similar provisions in other uniform and model unincorporated entity acts. The latest version of the ULLCA that we cite here is available on the Uniform Law Commission website.

LLC Act, fewer than half of the states (Alabama, California, Florida, Idaho, Iowa, Minnesota, Nebraska, New Jersey, North Dakota, South Dakota, Utah, Vermont, Washington, and Wyoming) and the District of Columbia follow the current version of the ULLCA. The remaining jurisdictions are mixed, with some state statutes drawing upon older versions of the uniform act, and others drawing upon a mix of uniform act language and non-standard statutory provisions. As this suggests, there is considerable variability in state LLC statutes. As always, we urge you to become familiar with the LLC statute in your home jurisdiction and jurisdictions in which you practice.

When selecting a state of organization, the Delaware LLC regime tends to be attractive to business owners who wish to engage in sophisticated planning. This is because the Delaware LLC statute (as interpreted and described by the Delaware courts) is contract-centric, giving business owners significant flexibility to customize management, governance, and financial rules to meet business needs. Smaller LLCs with operations concentrated in a single state — especially those that do not need all of the "bells and whistles" of the Delaware statute — are more likely to be formed in the state in which the LLC has its headquarters or does most of its business.

2. Series LLCs

Though we do not catalog all of the differences between the ULLCA and state LLC statutes, we do want to note one point of distinction. The revised ULLCA does not provide for **series LLCs**, as do some state statutes. Under a series LLC, a "master" LLC can create within itself one or more series of members, managers, interests, or assets. Although contained within the master LLC, each series can have its own separate assets, have its own separate group of members, and be responsible for its own obligations. Each series provides limited liability to its series members, and each series is an entity separate from other series and also separate from the LLC itself (thus affording limited liability protection for each series in the event another series incurs debts or obligations, just as subsidiaries of a corporation are each liable for their own debts but not the debts of each other). The series concept is recognized in a few states (including Delaware, Iowa, Texas, and Utah), but after much debate and discussion, the Uniform Law Commission decided not to allow for the creation of the series LLC in the revised 2006 Act.

3. The Operating Agreement

As with partnerships, the LLC operating agreement is a key source for LLC management and governance rules. This is because LLC statutes (like partnership statutes) not only contain default rules, but also give members the flexibility to customize default rules via the operating agreement. Consequently, as with partnerships, the default rules in state LLC statutes typically apply only when (i) the operating agreement is silent on a matter covered by a default rule; (ii) the parties fail to agree on a modification of a default rule; or (iii) the matter involves a limited list of non-waivable or non-modifiable matters. Otherwise, as between the operating agreement and statutory default rules, the operating agreement governs. Section 105(a) of the ULLCA reflects this approach, and establishes the primacy of the operating agreement, stating as follows:

> (a) Except as otherwise provided in subsections (c) and (d), the operating agreement governs:
>> (1) relations among the members as members and between the members and the limited liability company;
>> (2) the rights and duties under this [act] of a person in the capacity of manager;
>> (3) the activities and affairs of the company and the conduct of those activities and affairs; and
>> (4) the means and conditions for amending the operating agreement.
> (b) To the extent the operating agreement does not provide for a matter described in subsection (a), this [act] governs the matter.

As with the RUPA discussed in Chapter 3, § 105(c) of the ULLCA also identifies a list of non-waivable and non-modifiable matters:

> (c) An operating agreement may not:
>> (1) vary the law applicable under Section 104;
>> (2) vary a limited liability company's capacity under Section 109 to sue and be sued in its own name;
>> (3) vary any requirement, procedure, or other provision of this [act] pertaining to:
>>> (A) registered agents; or
>>> (B) the [secretary of state], including provisions pertaining to records authorized or required to be delivered to the [secretary of state] for filing under this [act];
>> (4) vary the provisions of Section 204;
>> (5) alter or eliminate the duty of loyalty or the duty of care, except as otherwise provided in subsection (d);
>> (6) eliminate the contractual obligation of good faith and fair dealing under Section 409(d), but the operating agreement may prescribe the standards, if not manifestly unreasonable, by which the performance of the obligation is to be measured;
>> (7) relieve or exonerate a person from liability for conduct involving bad faith, willful or intentional misconduct, or knowing violation of law;
>> (8) unreasonably restrict the duties and rights under Section 410, but the operating agreement may impose reasonable restrictions on the availability and use of information obtained under that section and may define appropriate remedies, including liquidated damages, for a breach of any reasonable restriction on use;

(9) vary the causes of dissolution specified in Section 701(a)(4);

(10) vary the requirement to wind up the company's activities and affairs as specified in Section 702(a), (b)(1), and (e);

(11) unreasonably restrict the right of a member to maintain an action under [Article] 8;

(12) vary the provisions of Section 805, but the operating agreement may provide that the company may not have a special litigation committee;

(13) vary the right of a member to approve a merger, interest exchange, conversion, or domestication under Section 1023(a)(2), 1033(a)(2), 1043(a)(2), or 1053(a)(2);

(14) vary the required contents of a plan of merger under Section 1022(a), plan of interest exchange under Section 1032(a), plan of conversion under Section 1042(a), or plan of domestication under Section 1052(a); or

(15) except as otherwise provided in Sections 106 and 107(b), restrict the rights under this [act] of a person other than a member or manager.

C. TAXATION

Under default rules, single-owner LLCs are **disregarded as a separate entity** for federal income tax purposes, meaning that they are treated as an entity not separate from its single owner for income tax purposes. LLCs with at least two members are classified as partnerships for tax purposes under default rules, resulting in **pass-through** tax treatment as the default rule. Under both disregarded entity and partnership taxation regimes, members declare their share of the LLC income on their individual federal tax returns and pay tax at whatever rate is appropriate. Losses sustained by members of LLCs generally may be used to offset other income and thereby decrease members' tax liability. As is the case with general partnerships, limited partnerships, and limited liability partnerships, the LLC (whether a single-member or multiple-member LLC) may elect to be classified as an association taxable as a corporation by "checking the box" on its tax form (see Exhibit 3.5). If an LLC does not formally declare its election, by default, it will have the tax status of a disregarded entity or partnership, depending on the number of member-owners.

D. HOW ARE LLCS CREATED?

The Certificate or Articles of Organization

An LLC is created when a document called the **articles of organization** (or the **certificate of organization**, per the ULLCA) is filed with the appropriate state agency, usually the secretary of state, and when at least one person becomes a member of the LLC. *See* ULLCA § 201. The ULLCA requires only a "bare bones" certificate of organization. *See* ULLCA § 201(b) (stating a certificate of organization must state (1) the name of the limited liability company, which must comply with certain naming requirements; (2) the street and mailing addresses of the company's principal office; and (3) the name and street and mailing addresses in the state of the company's registered agent). Many state statutes require a bit more, including the following information:

1. the name of the company (including any required abbreviations or signals);
2. the address of the initial designated office;
3. the name and street address of the initial agent who will receive service of process (which cannot be a post office box);
4. the name and address of each organizer; and
5. a statement regarding how the entity is to be managed (e.g., whether it will be managed by one or more persons or all members).

By way of example, Exhibit 12.1 contains the form of Articles of Organization for California LLCs.

In many states, after review of the articles of organization and acceptance of the required fee, the secretary of state will issue a certificate of organization for the LLC recognizing the existence of the business. Some states have additional requirements at the formation stage — for example, New York has a publication requirement. *See, e.g.,* N.Y. Ltd. Liab. Co. § 206.

E. VOTING AND GOVERNANCE RULES

1. The Operating Agreement

The LLC operating agreement serves as a foundational contract among the entity's owners, and it is the first place that you should look to determine the management, governance, and financial rules and structures of an existing LLC. If you are creating an LLC, the operating agreement is the place where you should specify those rules.

In a few states (including New York), the operating agreement must be a written agreement; most states and the ULLCA allow an oral agreement. *See* ULLCA § 102(13). Even if an oral agreement is permitted, however, you should prepare a written operating agreement for your clients. Putting the operating agreement in writing is important because unwritten, vague, or ambiguous terms can lead to discord and litigation. Careful drafting also can help avoid the need for amendments to the operating agreement. Amending the operating agreement often requires approval of

---

The De Facto Corporation Doctrine and LLCs

Under the *de facto corporation doctrine,* a court may (but is not required to) treat a business as a corporation for liability purposes, despite technical non-compliance with formation requirements, if the owners/founders make a colorable attempt to comply with formation requirements. Some courts have held that this de facto corporation doctrine applies to LLCs. *See, e.g., In re Estate of Hausman,* 921 N.E.2d 191, 193 (N.Y. 2009) ("The parties do not dispute, and both courts below concluded, that the *de facto corporation* doctrine is applicable to limited liability companies. We agree. The statutory schemes of the Business Corporation Law and the Limited Liability Company Law are very similar, and we see no principled reason why the de facto corporation doctrine should not apply to both corporations and limited liability companies.") (emphasis added). In jurisdictions that apply the de facto corporation doctrine to LLCs, a court may recognize a business entity as an LLC despite technical non-compliance with statutory formation requirements, provided the owners of the business make a colorable attempt to comply with those formation requirements. As lawyers, however, it is better not to rely upon the "relief valve" of substantial compliance. *See id.* Instead, strive for strict compliance with statutory formation rules.

EXHIBIT 12.1   **California LLC Articles of Organization**

LLC-1	**Articles of Organization of a Limited Liability Company (LLC)**

To form a limited liability company in California, you can fill out this form, and submit for filing along with:

- A **$70** filing fee.
- A separate, non-refundable **$15** service fee also must be included, if you **drop off** the completed form.

Important! LLCs in California may have to pay a minimum $800 yearly tax to the California Franchise Tax Board. For more information, go to https://www.ftb.ca.gov.

LLCs may not provide "professional services," as defined by California Corporations Code sections 13401(a) and 13401.3.

Note: *Before submitting the completed form,* you should consult with a private attorney for advice about your specific business needs.

This Space For Office Use Only

For questions about this form, go to *www.sos.ca.gov/business/be/filing-tips.htm.*

LLC Name (List the proposed LLC name exactly as it is to appear on the records of the California Secretary of State.)

① _____

Proposed LLC Name

The name **must** include: LLC, L.L.C., Limited Liability Company, Limited Liability Co., Ltd. Liability Co. or Ltd. Liability Company; and **may not** include: bank, trust, trustee, incorporated, inc., corporation, or corp., insurer, or insurance company. For general entity name requirements and restrictions, go to www.sos.ca.gov/business/be/name-availability.htm.

Purpose

② The purpose of the limited liability company is to engage in any lawful act or activity for which a limited liability company may be organized under the California Revised Uniform Limited Liability Company Act.

LLC Addresses

③ a. _____ **CA** ____

Initial Street Address of Designated Office in CA - Do not list a P.O. Box   City (no abbreviations)   State   Zip

b. _____

Initial Mailing Address of LLC, if different from 3a   City (no abbreviations)   State   Zip

Service of Process (List a California resident or a California registered corporate agent that agrees to be your initial agent to accept service of process in case your LLC is sued. You may list any adult who lives in California. You may **not** list an LLC as the agent. **Do not** list an address if the agent is a California registered corporate agent as the address for service of process is already on file.)

④ a. _____

Agent's Name

b. _____ **CA** ____

*Agent's Street Address (if agent is **not** a corporation) - Do not list a P.O. Box*   City (no abbreviations)   State   Zip

Management (Check only one.)

⑤ The LLC will be managed by:

☐ One Manager   ☐ More Than One Manager   ☐ All Limited Liability Company Member(s)

This form must be signed by each organizer. If you need more space, attach extra pages that are 1-sided and on standard letter-sized paper (8 1/2" x 11"). All attachments are made part of these articles of organization.

▶ _____   _____

Organizer - Sign here   *Print your name here*

Make check/money order payable to: **Secretary of State**	*By Mail*	*Drop-Off*
Upon filing, we will return one (1) uncertified copy of your filed document for free, and will certify the copy upon request and payment of a $5 certification fee.	Secretary of State Business Entities, P.O. Box 944228 Sacramento, CA 94244-2280	Secretary of State 1500 11th Street., 3rd Floor Sacramento, CA 95814

Corporations Code §§ 17701.04, 17701.08, 17701.13, 17702.01, Revenue and Taxation Code § 17941
LLC-1 (REV 01/2014)

2014 California Secretary of State
www.sos.ca.gov/business/be

[Clear Form] [Print Form]

all LLC members (unless the operating agreement provides otherwise), and such approval can be difficult to obtain, so it is better to avoid having to rewrite terms post-formation due to drafting errors or omissions. Unlike the certificate of organization, the operating agreement is a private document and is not filed with any state agency.

2. Member-Managed versus Manager-Managed

Among other provisions, the operating agreement should address how the LLC will be managed. Under the ULLCA and state LLC statutes, LLCs may be **member-managed** or **manager-managed**, at the members' election. In a **member-managed** LLC, each member, by default, has equal rights respecting the management and conduct of LLC business. *See* ULLCA § 407. Member-managed LLCs are thus similar to partnerships from a management perspective. (As discussed below, a key difference between the LLC and the limited partnership form in certain jurisdictions is that the members of a member-managed LLC are able to participate fully in the management of the LLC while still enjoying the protections of the liability shield.) Under the ULLCA, there is a presumption that LLCs are member-managed, unless the organizing documents provide otherwise. *See* ULLCA § 407.

For an LLC with numerous members, being member-managed may prove cumbersome. Therefore, some LLCs may elect a management committee, board of managers, or other similar structure, in much the same way that a corporation is managed by its board of directors. This type of LLC is referred to as a **manager-managed LLC**. Since manager-managed is not the default rule under all state LLC statutes, members who prefer this governance structure generally must specify it as such in their operating agreement. Note that managers do not have to be members of the LLC. This feature may prove helpful in family businesses where the combination of business and family relationships can lead to discord. Family members who wish to avoid intra-family conflict may prefer to delegate management duties to a professional manager. If managers are to be elected, the operating agreement must indicate how often elections will be held and how notice of these election meetings will be given to the members. The members also need to decide the term for each manager, whether it be yearly or some longer term, such as three years.

Case Preview

Goldstein v. Pikus

As is true of general partnerships, it is usually a good idea to avoid an equal division (e.g., 50/50) of authority when it comes to LLC management. This is because an equal allocation of authority can lead to disputes — and litigation — if relations between members with equal control rights sour. In addition, it is also a good idea to review LLC operating agreements for consistency, since conflicting or confusing provisions also can lead to discord and litigation. Finally, it is important to remember that modifications to LLC operating agreements should be made in writing, in a manner that is consistent with the operating agreement.

Goldstein v. Pikus involves a series of disputes between LLC managers with equal voting rights. When reading this case, consider the following questions:

1. What role, if any, did the allocation of voting power play in the dispute between the parties?
2. What could Pikus have done if, as he argued, the parties orally modified the operating agreement?
3. What impact, if any, do the quoted provisions of the operating agreement have on the resolution of the parties' dispute?

Goldstein v. Pikus

2015 N.Y. Slip Op. 31455(U) (Sup. Ct. N.Y Cnty. July 20, 2015)

Hon. CHARLES E. RAMOS, J.S.C.*

. . .

These actions arise out of the ongoing disputes between Stuart D. Goldstein (Goldstein) and Jeffrey S. Pikus (Pikus), the two Managers of Ten Sheridan Associates, LLC (the Company), a New York limited liability company, with respect to the management, operation, and control of the Company and its sole asset, a mixed-use apartment building located at 10 Sheridan Square in Manhattan (the Property).

. . .

On December 10, 1996, Pikus formed the Company to serve as a vehicle for the purchase of the Property. On December 11, 1996, the Company entered into an agreement to purchase the Property, a transaction opportunity that was obtained by Pikus. The Property, which was constructed sometime during the 1920's, is a landmarked, 14-story mixed-use building containing approximately 73 residential apartments, a large number of which are studios, and all of which currently are rent regulated.

In order to complete the purchase of the Property, the Company needed to obtain additional funds and/or investors. To this end, Pikus and Goldstein were introduced, and Goldstein agreed to try to procure investors and/or to provide such additional funds as necessary to complete the purchase of the Property. Pikus and Goldstein thereafter executed a written agreement, dated January 9, 1997, memorializing the terms of their agreements and understandings with regard to the purchase and management of the Property and the operation of the Company.

Under the terms of the Syndication Agreement, the parties agreed that they would attempt to syndicate up to 50% of the Company. Pikus and Goldstein also agreed that they would both be the managers of the Company with equal voting

---

*For purposes of brevity, footnotes and citations to the record have been omitted.

rights, and that as soon as practicable after executing the Syndication Agreement, the parties would execute an operating agreement for the operation and management of the Company.

The parties further agreed that Goldstein, or any management company controlled by him, would be retained as the managing agent to manage the Property for an annual management fee, and that "of that fee [Pikus] shall be paid by [Goldstein] an annual supervisor fee equal to 37.5% of the management fee." In addition, the parties agreed that any additional fees earned by the managing agent, other than the management fee, would be divided equally between Pikus and Goldstein.

. . .

Under section 5.1 (a) of the Operating Agreement, the "right to manage, control and conduct the business of the Company" is vested exclusively in the Managers, who must be Class A Members. The Operating Agreement designates Pikus and Goldstein to serve as the Company's Managers. This section further provides that

> "[a]ll decisions affecting the Company, its policy and management shall be made by the Managers including but not limited to, the purchase, sale, finance, mortgage, lease of any real estate or personal property of the Company, and the Members agree to abide by any such decision[.]"

However, section 5.2 of the Operating Agreement provides that

> "In carrying out Section 5.1. the Managers shall have the power to delegate their authority to qualified Persons. Any such delegation of authority may be rescinded at any time by the Managers. The Managers hereby designate SDG Management Corp., or a successor entity directly or indirectly controlled by Goldstein, ('Goldstein') as Managing Agent for the Premises. The Managing Agent, on consent of the Managers, shall receive remuneration customarily paid for the services rendered, including, but not limited to, disposition, refinancing fees, construction management fees and leasing commissions. The Managing Agent shall have the authority as is generally given to a Managing Agent including, without limitation, the right to enter into, make and perform any and all contracts, leases and other agreements related to the management of the Premises, whether or not such agreements are with persons or entities affiliated with any Member. The Managing Agent shall take all necessary action to maintain the Premises in first class condition and to maximize the value of the Premises. The Managing Agent shall maintain the books and records of the Premises in good and accurate order and shall make all required filings with the necessary agencies and parties. The Managing Agent shall make all reasonable and usual repair to the Premises. Upon the death, incompetency, resignation, or bankruptcy of either Manager, the remaining Manager shall have the right to designate the Managing Agent for the Premises[.]"

Section 5.1(c) provides that, "[e]xcept as is otherwise specifically provided [in the Operating Agreement], all determinations or consents to be made or actions to be taken by the Managers shall require the action of all the Managers." Additionally, section 5.6 (b) of the Operating Agreement provides that, notwithstanding anything to the contrary in the agreement or the LLCL, the Managers shall not "liquidate or dissolve the Company, in whole or in part" without the unanimous consent of the Class A Members.

. . .

The record reflects that beginning no later than late 2012 and/or early 2013, various disputes arose between Goldstein and Pikus over the management and control of the Property, with each accusing the other of various wrongdoing with respect to the management of the Property. The disputes have since expanded to include the issues of who is authorized to manage the Property under the Company's governing documents, and which agreements constitute the Company's governing documents.

Essentially, Pikus alleges that although the Company's Operating Agreement, as written, designates SDG as the sole Managing Agent of the Property, during the first 17 years of the Company's existence, it was Pikus who actually managed the Property and oversaw virtually all facets of the Property's operation.

Pikus alleges that, pursuant to the provisions agreed to in the 1997 Syndication Agreement, the Company was to retain Goldstein and/or his management company to manage the Property "under Pikus's supervision," for which Pikus was to be paid 37.5% of the management fee and 50% of any additional fees.

Pikus alleges that sometime after the Company acquired the Property in March 1997, the "parties" orally modified the Operating Agreement "so that it was consistent with the [Syndication] Agreement's provisions pertaining to the management of the Property—i.e., that Pikus would actively supervise the management of the Property and would be paid 37.5% of the management fee and 50% of any additional fees." Defendants allege that in reliance on this Oral Modification, Pikus managed the Property for 17 years, for which Goldstein caused Pikus to be paid the aforementioned fees until April 18, 2014.

Defendants allege that, as a result of the disagreements and disputes that have since arisen between the two Managers, on April 18, 2014, Goldstein took actions that effectively froze Pikus out of the management of the Property and of the Company, and ceased paying Pikus his share of the management fee.

Defendants allege that these Manager disputes arose only after Pikus began objecting to an alleged scheme by Goldstein to use the Company's assets for his family's benefit. Defendants allege that, as part of this scheme, Goldstein caused the Company to rent apartments at the Property to two of his children, Darin and Danielle Goldstein, each a Class B Member of the Company, through below market rate "sweetheart leases."

In addition to the low rent, defendants allege that these "sweetheart leases" were intended to afford Goldstein's children the exclusive right to purchase their apartments, at insider prices, if and/or when the Property is converted into condominiums.

. . .

The Goldstein plaintiffs dispute defendants' claim that the Company's Operating Agreement had been orally modified, and thus that Pikus, rather than SDG, had been the manager of the Property.

Plaintiffs allege that, with the exception of certain major decisions, such as whether to sell or refinance the property, the Operating Agreement expressly delegates all of the Managers' responsibility for the day-to-day management of the Property to SDG, not Pikus. Plaintiffs allege that SDG has performed as the Managing Agent of the Property since the acquisition of the Property, and that between then and April 18, 2014, SDG had paid a monthly consulting fee to Pikus for assisting, as needed, in the management of the Property.

Plaintiffs allege that on April 18, 2014, SDG was forced to terminate Pikus's consultancy after Pikus allegedly embarked on a clandestine campaign to artificially inflate the Company's rent roll and stockpile vacant units, in order to increase the value of his interest in the Company, in the event that the Property were sold or refinanced.

Plaintiffs allege that as part of this scheme, Pikus began intentionally delaying the renovation of vacant apartments, and then demanding that unnecessary, expensive, and duplicative apartment renovations be performed to enable the Company to set higher, but ultimately unachievable, apartment rents. Plaintiffs allege that Pikus's actions caused a depletion in the Company's operating account, and were taken solely as part of Pikus's undisguised desire and effort to cash in on his minority membership interest in the Company, by forcing a premature sale or refinancing of the Property.

Plaintiffs allege that Pikus also has attempted to usurp SDG's authority as Managing Agent of the Property, and has engaged in conduct that has interfered with SDG's ability to manage the Property.

Plaintiffs contend that Pikus's misconduct and misbehavior escalated after Goldstein twice rebuffed Pikus's demands/suggestions that the Company sell and/or refinance the Property. Plaintiffs allege that it was only after Pikus, through his newly retained counsel, began accusing Goldstein and SDG of breaching their fiduciary duties to the Company and threatening them with litigation, that Goldstein and SDG terminated Pikus's consultancy and commenced the Goldstein Action.

In the Goldstein Action complaint, plaintiffs seek, inter alia, (1) a declaration with respect to the status of the Company's Operating Agreement and the rights of the various parties to manage the Property and Company under the terms of that agreement (First Cause of Action); (2) a permanent injunction enjoining Pikus from interfering or participating in SDG's management of the Property (Second Cause of Action); and, damages arising out of Pikus's alleged breach of his fiduciary duty (Third Cause of Action).

Defendants since have asserted thirteen counterclaims/cross claims (hereinafter, counterclaims) against the plaintiffs and Danielle Goldstein (added as an additional defendant), seeking (1) indemnification from the Company for the losses and expenses that Pikus has and will incur as a result of plaintiff's lawsuit (First Counterclaim); (2) a declaration that Pikus is entitled to manage the Property based on the Oral Modification of the Operating Agreement (Second, Third, and Fourth Counterclaims); (3) damages against Stuart, Darin and Danielle Goldstein for breach of their fiduciary duty with respect to the "sweetheart leases" (Fifth Counterclaim); (4) a declaration that the "sweetheart leases" are null and void as ultra vires (Sixth Counterclaim); (5) damages against Goldstein for breach of his fiduciary duty with respect to allegedly excessive construction fees paid to a Goldstein-controlled construction company (Seventh Counterclaim); (6) damages against Goldstein for breach of section 5.3 of the Operating Agreement, by failing to comply with the various laws and regulations of certain state entities (Eighth Counterclaim); (7) damages against all of the individual plaintiffs for breach of their fiduciary duty in commencing this action, the alleged sole purpose of which was to pressure Pikus to sell his membership interest for a depressed price (Ninth Counterclaim); (8) damages against Goldstein for breach of section 7.3 of the Operating Agreement, by refusing to make the Company's complete books and records available to Pikus for inspection (Tenth Counterclaim); (9) an accounting from Goldstein and SDG (Eleventh Counterclaim); (10) damages against Goldstein for breach of the Syndication Agreement and the Oral Modification of the Operating Agreement, by failing to pay Pikus his percentage of SDG's management fee since April 2014 (Twelfth Counterclaim); and, (11) a declaratory judgment removing Goldstein as a Manager of the Company, and declaring that Pikus is the sole Manager (Thirteenth Counterclaim).

. . .

DISCUSSION

. . .

As the parties have produced no other evidence to demonstrate that any other agreement might exist relating to the operations of the Company and its members, or to raise an issue of fact in this regard, plaintiffs' motion for summary judgment on their first cause of action is granted to the extent of declaring that the Company's Operating Agreement is the primary and controlling document with respect to the Company's operations.

In this regard, LLCL § 417 (a) provides that the members of an LLC "shall adopt a written operating agreement relating to the business of the company, the conduct of its affairs and the rights and powers of its members." "The operating agreement is, therefore, the primary document defining the rights of members, the duties of managers and the financial arrangements of the limited liability company" (*Willoughby Rehabilitation and Health Care Ctr., LLC v. Webster*, 13 Misc 3d 1230(A) *4, 2006 NY Slip Op 52067[U] [Sup Ct, Nassau County 2006], *affd* 46 AD3d 801 [2d Dept 2007], citing Rich, Practice Commentaries, 32A Limited Liability Company Law Section 1.A, p. 4, [McKinney's, 2006]).

Additionally, as under the terms of the Operating Agreement, the Managers expressly delegated their authority to manage the Property to SDG alone (Operating Agreement § 5.2), plaintiffs also are entitled to a declaration that SDG, and not Pikus, has the authority to manage the Property under the Operating Agreement.

. . .

Unless the wrongful acts of a managing member, although sufficient to give rise to a derivative claim, are contrary to the contemplated functioning and purpose of the limited liability company, they do not provide a basis for judicial dissolution (*Matter of 1545 Ocean Ave., LLC*, 72 AD3d at 132).

Thus, without more, the allegations of overreaching and breach of fiduciary duty by Goldstein do not provide the requisite grounds for dissolution of this limited liability company. . . .

Post-Case Follow-Up

As *Goldstein* suggests, lawyers representing LLCs or their owner-members should discuss voting power and the allocation of managerial control early and often. Failing to articulate clear, consistent voting and control rules in the operating agreement can lead to expensive, time-consuming, and contentious litigation. Failing to ensure that parties are "behaving" in ways that are consistent with the operating agreement also can lead to disputes.

Goldstein v. Pikus: Real Life Applications

You represent a business person seeking to form an LLC with a colleague who is also a long-time friend. Your client informs you that she and her colleague get along famously, and have never had a dispute that they failed to resolve. Accordingly, the client asks you to prepare an operating agreement that divides voting power and managerial control on a 50/50 basis.

a. Would you advise your client to allocate voting power and managerial control in this fashion?

b. After reviewing subsection 3 (Meetings and Voting) below, what, if any, alternatives might you propose?

3. Meetings and Voting

In addition to the management structure, the operating agreement also should address requirements and procedures relating to meetings and voting. Most state statutes and the ULLCA do not impose requirements for meetings of an LLC. Thus, the operating agreement should specify how often regular meetings will be held, where they will be held, and the procedure for providing notice of the meetings to the members. The operating agreement also should specify how special meetings can be called to discuss urgent issues, such as an offer by a third party to buy the LLC business.

With respect to voting and decision making, most ordinary-course business decisions are made by majority vote of the members (if the LLC is member-managed) or by majority vote of the managers (if the LLC is managed by a board of managers LLCs) under default rules. *See* ULLCA § 407(b) (rules for member-managed LLCs); § 407(c) (rules for manager-managed LLCs). Extraordinary matters, such as amending the operating agreement, consenting to dissolve the LLC, or agreeing to sell all of the LLC's assets, often require unanimous approval of all members. Under ULLCA § 407(b), voting and management is on an equal basis, meaning one member one vote (unless the operating agreement provides otherwise), but many states, such as California, follow the "corporate model" — if meaning the operating agreement is silent, voting is in proportion to ownership interests in the LLC.

4. Agency and Authority

As you will recall from Chapter 3, in a general partnership, all partners are agents of the partnership for the purpose of partnership business. LLCs take a different approach. Under § 301 of the ULLCA, "[a] member [of an LLC] is not an agent of a limited liability company solely by reason of being a member." The LLC operating agreement thus should specify who is authorized to act on behalf of the LLC in a manner consistent with the LLC's management structure (member-managed or manager-managed), and also should specify the nature and extent of authority and any limitations on that authority. For example, members of an LLC may decide to restrict managers from borrowing money in excess of a certain amount, selling certain assets, or making certain purchases unless a majority of the members approve or unless the managers unanimously agree. If the operating agreement is silent as to member or manager authority, under the ULLCA, the following activities require consent of all members: amendment of the operating agreement or undertaking an act that is not in the ordinary course of the company's business (e.g., a merger). *See* ULLCA § 407. Borrowing from general partnership law, the ULLCA also provides that an LLC may file a statement of authority to indicate which members have authority to perform certain acts, such as purchasing real property. *See* ULLCA § 302. LLC members also can file statements of denial concerning member authority.

5. Fiduciary Duties and Fiduciary Waivers

Members are well advised to consider fiduciary matters when drafting or entering into an LLC operating agreement. As you will recall from Chapter 3, in a general partnership, all partners owe fiduciary duties to the partnership and fellow partners. In LLCs, managing members typically owe duties of care and loyalty to the LLC and to the manager's fellow members. For example, § 409 of the ULLCA provides as follows:

> (c) The fiduciary duty of loyalty of a member in a member-managed limited liability company includes the duties:
>> (1) to account to the company and hold as trustee for it any property, profit, or benefit derived by the member:
>>> (A) in the conduct or winding up of the company's activities and affairs;
>>> (B) from a use by the member of the company's property; or
>>> (C) from the appropriation of a company opportunity;
>> (2) to refrain from dealing with the company in the conduct or winding up of the company's activities and affairs as or on behalf of a person having an interest adverse to the company; and
>> (3) to refrain from competing with the company in the conduct of the company's activities and affairs before the dissolution of the company.

See also Salm v. Feldstein, 799 N.Y.S.2d 104 (App. Div. 2005) ("As the managing member of the company and as a co-member with the plaintiff, the defendant owed the plaintiff a fiduciary duty to make full disclosure of all material facts."). Non-managing members generally do not owe fiduciary duties, but they may owe contractual duties of good faith and fair dealing. *See* ULLCA § 409(d).

The question of whether LLC members can expand, limit, or even eliminate fiduciary obligations of fellow members is complicated and has been the subject of both statutory and judicial attention. Under § 105(d) of the ULLCA, members may agree via the operating agreement to alter a member's duty of care and loyalty, provided that such private ordering is not manifestly unreasonable:

> (d) Subject to subsection (c)(7), without limiting other terms that may be included in an operating agreement, the following rules apply:
> (1) The operating agreement may:
> (A) specify the method by which a specific act or transaction that would otherwise violate the duty of loyalty may be authorized or ratified by one or more disinterested and independent persons after full disclosure of all material facts; and
> (B) alter the prohibition in Section 405(a)(2) so that the prohibition requires only that the company's total assets not be less than the sum of its total liabilities.
> (2) To the extent the operating agreement of a member-managed limited liability company expressly relieves a member of a responsibility that the member otherwise would have under this [act] and imposes the responsibility on one or more other members, the agreement also may eliminate or limit any fiduciary duty of the member relieved of the responsibility which would have pertained to the responsibility.
> (3) If not manifestly unreasonable, the operating agreement may:
> (A) alter or eliminate the aspects of the duty of loyalty stated in Section 409(b) and (i);
> (B) identify specific types or categories of activities that do not violate the duty of loyalty;
> (C) alter the duty of care, but may not authorize conduct involving bad faith, willful or intentional misconduct, or knowing violation of law; and
> (D) alter or eliminate any other fiduciary duty.

Section 105(e) speaks to the court's ability to decide when a term in an operating agreement is manifestly unreasonable and thus subject to invalidation:

> (e) The court shall decide as a matter of law whether a term of an operating agreement is manifestly unreasonable under subsection (c)(6) or (d)(3). The court:
> (1) shall make its determination as of the time the challenged term became part of the operating agreement and by considering only circumstances existing at that time; and
> (2) may invalidate the term only if, in light of the purposes, activities, and affairs of the limited liability company, it is readily apparent that:
> (A) the objective of the term is unreasonable; or
> (B) the term is an unreasonable means to achieve the term's objective.

See also ULLCA § 409. Under these rules, if desired, an LLC operating agreement could (for example) allow members to compete with the business of the LLC by altering or eliminating aspects of the duty of loyalty, as set forth in § 105(a) and (d). Intentional misconduct or knowing violations of law cannot be permitted by the operating agreement, however, and members may include provisions in the operating agreement to remove or expel members or managers for certain acts of misconduct.

Apart from the uniform act, leading business law jurisdictions also have wrestled with fiduciary duties and fiduciary waivers in the LLC context. The *Auriga* case from Delaware is instructive. We will start with the Chancery Court opinion. In *Auriga Capital Corp. v. Gatz Props, LLC*, 40 A.3d 839 (Del. Ch. 2012), the Delaware Chancery Court examined a self-dealing transaction by the manager and controlling member of an LLC. The LLC at issue was majority-controlled by William Gatz and his family, and it was formed as an investment vehicle to develop and lease a property (also controlled by Gatz) to be used as a public golf course. A Gatz-controlled entity was manager of the LLC. The LLC subleased the property to an operator that was unable to generate a profit. Knowing that the operator was close to terminating the sublease, Gatz commissioned an appraisal that showed the land was worth more if developed for real estate purposes than if used as a golf course. In an effort to reacquire the property for development, Gatz rejected a third party's offers to take over the LLC's long-term lease and structured what the court found to be a "sham" auction of the LLC. The winner of the auction was Gatz, who purchased the LLC for significantly less than the amount offered by the third party. Minority members sued, claiming that Gatz had breached both statutory and contractual fiduciary obligations.

The Chancery Court held that the Delaware LLC statute imposed default equitable fiduciary duties on the managers and controlling members of an LLC. The court reasoned that (i) fiduciary duties are owed in the corporate context; (ii) § 18-1104 of the Delaware LLC Act, which stated, "[i]n any case not provided for in this chapter, the rules of law and equity, including the law merchant, shall govern," provided an equitable fiduciary backstop and governed situations not specifically addressed by the LLC Act; (iii) under traditional equitable principles, the manager of an LLC fits comfortably within traditional definitions of a fiduciary; and (iv) the legislative history, in the court's view, supported its interpretation. The court acknowledged that the Delaware LLC Act permits parties to an LLC agreement to modify or disclaim default principles, but suggested that eliminating default fiduciary duties entirely would upset the expectations of those currently party to LLC agreements, and would make Delaware a less attractive place for LLC investors.

The Delaware Supreme Court took a decidedly different approach. While the supreme court agreed that the Gatz-controlled manager of the LLC had breached its fiduciary duties, the supreme court held that the breach arose from terms in the operating agreement and not as a result of statutory default obligations. The supreme court found that the members of the LLC had contracted for an entire fairness obligation via the operating agreement and held that neither party had asked the Chancery Court to decide the issue of whether default fiduciary duties existed in the LLC context or whether such duties applied to the case. The supreme court thus held that the Chancery Court could have — and should have — decided the case without recourse to a discussion of default fiduciary duties and further held that the Chancery Court's statements regarding default statutory fiduciary duties should be regarded as dictum and without any precedential value.

In the wake of the Delaware Supreme Court's opinion in *Auriga*, the Delaware legislature modified DLLCA § 18-1104 as follows (the new language is underscored):

> In any case not provided for in the chapter, the rules of law and equity, including the rules of law and equity relating to fiduciary duties and the law merchant, shall govern.

The Synopsis to the proposed bill elaborated on the amendment:

> Section 8. The amendment to Section 18-1104 confirms that in some circumstances fiduciary duties not explicitly provided for in the limited liability company agreement apply. For example, a manager of a manager-managed limited liability company would ordinarily have fiduciary duties even in the absence of a provision in the limited liability company agreement establishing such duties. Section 18-1101(c) continues to provide that such duties may be expanded, restricted or eliminated by the limited liability company agreement.

In light of this amendment, it now appears that a manager of a manager-managed LLC ordinarily owes fiduciary duties (even in the absence of an express provision in the LLC operating agreement providing for such duties), but those duties are subject to private ordering, and may be expanded, contracted, or even eliminated via the operating agreement, under the Delaware LLC Act. The Delaware Chancery Court's holding in the post-*Auriga* case *Feeley v. NHAOGC, LLC*, 62 A.3d 649 (Del. Ch. 2012), suggests as much. In that case, the Chancery Court held that if the LLC operating agreement does not expressly disclaim fiduciary duties, then managing members will owe such duties.

Pappas v. Tzolis, 982 N.E.2d 576 (N.Y. 2012), from the New York Court of Appeals (New York's highest court) also is instructive. In *Pappas*, the New York Court of Appeals considered whether to enforce a contractual waiver of fiduciary duties among LLC members entered into post-formation, in connection with a buyout transaction. The dispute in *Pappas* related to an LLC formed to acquire and manage a long-term lease for a building in downtown Manhattan. Shortly after forming the LLC, significant business disputes arose among the three members, and one member (Tzolis) offered to buy out the other two for $1.5 million, or 20 times what they had contributed to the LLC only a year earlier. The other members accepted the offer. Seven months later, Tzolis assigned the LLC's long-term lease to a developer for $17.5 million — or more than 200 times the departing members' initial investment. Not surprisingly, the former LLC members sued. The members alleged that even before the buyout, Tzolis had been negotiating with the developer and had failed to disclose these negotiations to the other members of the LLC in violation of fiduciary duties allegedly owed to them. Tzolis moved to dismiss.

The Court of Appeals affirmed dismissal of complaint, noting that in the buyout documents, the departing members certified that they (i) had performed their own due diligence; (ii) had engaged legal counsel to advise them; (iii) were not relying on any representation other than those set forth in the documents; and (iv) certified that Tzolis had no fiduciary duty to them in connection with the buyout. Based on these facts, the court of appeals held Tzolis owed no duty to the departing members to disclose his alleged negotiations with the developer. In reaching this conclusion, the Court of Appeals noted that the complaint's allegations revealed an "antagonistic" relationship between the members in the year leading up to the buyout:

> [P]laintiff's own allegations make it clear that at the time of the buyout, the relationship between the parties was not one of trust, and reliance on Tzolis' representations as a fiduciary would not have been reasonable. . . . Therefore, crediting plaintiffs' allegations, the release [fiduciary waiver] contained in the Certificate is valid, and plaintiffs cannot prevail on their cause of action alleging breach of fiduciary duty.

The court also noted that the plaintiffs were "sophisticated businessmen represented by counsel," and found that Tzolis's offer to buy plaintiffs' membership interests for 20 times what they had paid a year earlier, in the context of the antagonism between the parties, made it "obvious" that plaintiffs "needed to use care to reach an independent assessment of the value of the lease."

Pappas suggests that fiduciary duties may be waived by post-formation contract in New York, at least in circumstances where the relationship between members has become antagonistic, and the parties are sophisticated, represented by counsel, and demonstrate an understanding of the relinquished rights. The *Pappas* case is fact-intensive, however, and it is not clear whether the court's holding reflects a broad authorization for private ordering or whether the holding will be applied in a more limited fashion. Moreover, the *Pappas* court did not have occasion to address the interplay (if any) between the waivers in the buyout agreement and § 417 of New York's LLC statute, which provides that an LLC operating agreement

> may set forth a provision eliminating or limiting the personal liability of managers to the limited liability company or its members for damages for any breach of duty in such capacity, provided that no such provision shall eliminate or limit: (1) the liability of any manager if a judgment or other final adjudication adverse to him or her establishes that his or her acts or omissions were in bad faith or involved intentional misconduct or a knowing violation of law or that he or she personally gained in fact a financial profit or other advantage to which he or she was not legally entitled or that with respect to a distribution the subject of subdivision (a) of section five hundred eight of this chapter his or her acts were not performed in accordance with section four hundred nine of this article; or (2) the liability of any manager for any act or omission prior to the adoption of a provision authorized by this subdivision.

Given the varied approaches reflected in the ULLCA, state statutes, and in cases like *Auriga* and *Pappas*, you should be sure to (i) investigate the law in your home jurisdiction to determine default rules and opportunities for private ordering as to fiduciary obligations and the contractual covenant of good faith and fair dealing;

(ii) consult with your clients respecting their hopes and expectations as to fiduciary matters; and (iii) exercise care when drafting operating agreements, buyout agreements, and any (other) post-formation contracts between or among members.

6. Additional Governance Issues

In addition to provisions respecting management, voting, and fiduciary matters, LLC operating agreements often contain a number of other provisions that may have an impact on governance and relations between members. For example, the operating agreement may provide that members cannot transfer their interest in the LLC without offering it first to existing members of the LLC. (As with partnership agreements, we strongly recommend that LLC agreements explicitly address member exit.) LLC agreements also may provide for the purchase of life insurance for each member so that if a member dies, insurance proceeds are available to pay the decedent's estate for purchase of the interest of the decedent. The operating agreement also may provide for a dispute resolution mechanism, the application of specific accounting rules, reimbursement for expenses, expulsion of managers, amendments to the operating agreement, meetings of the members, whether written ballots are required or voice votes are sufficient, whether members must be present in person or may vote by proxy, and any other matters pertinent to the operation and governance of the LLC. Finally, the operating agreement may incorporate state statutory or ULLCA provisions allowing LLC members access to the LLC's records and books. Although the ULLCA does not require the LLC to maintain any specific records (unlike a limited partnership, which is required to maintain specified documents for review), the LLC is required to furnish records and information concerning its business and affairs that would be reasonably needed by a member to exercise rights and perform duties. The member's right to these LLC records and information may not be unreasonably restricted by the operating agreement. *See* ULLCA § 105. (The specific contents of the operating agreement are discussed below in Section O of this chapter.)

F. LLC LIABILITY RULES

Limited Liability and Management Rights

Under default rules, the members of an LLC cannot be held personally liable for the debts or obligations of the business based solely on their status as members. *See* ULLCA § 304 (stating a "debt, obligation, or other liability of a limited liability company is solely the debt, obligation, or other liability of the company. A member or manager is not personally liable, directly or indirectly, by way of contribution or otherwise, for a debt, obligation, or other liability of the company solely by reason of being or acting as a member or manager. This subsection applies regardless of the dissolution of the company."). This rule applies even as to members who participate in

Veil Piercing and the LLC

While LLCs offer a robust liability shield, recall from Chapter 1 that some courts have applied veil piercing (and reverse veil piercing) in the LLC context. Be sure to research the law in your home jurisdiction on this issue before advising clients.

management. Members may, however, be held liable for their own misconduct, *see* ULLCA § 301(b), and judgment creditors can obtain a charging order from a court requiring the LLC to pay over distributions to a tort or contract creditor of a member.

The LLC liability shield has several important advantages over the liability shield for LLPs and LPs discussed in Chapters 4 and 5. For example, although limited partners in a limited partnership enjoy limited liability, their protection hinges on their passivity with regard to management in certain jurisdictions. With an LLC, members can be active in management *and* retain their limited liability. In addition, although LLP statutes in full shield jurisdictions protect partners from personal liability for LLP obligations not flowing from their own misconduct, in two states (Louisiana and South Carolina), the protection from liability is partial, and thus only relates to claims for a co-partner's wrongful acts, leaving LLP partners with personal liability for other LLP obligations, such as those arising under contract. By contrast, the LLC form affords full protection for its members from all personal liability for LLC obligations, whether arising in tort or contract.

G. MEMBERS' INTERESTS IN THE LLC

Transferability of LLC Interests; Potential for Practical Constraints on the Admission of New Members

Like partnership statutes, most state LLC statutes and the ULLCA provide that a member's right to LLC distributions is a type of personal property. *See, e.g.,* ULLCA § 501. Therefore, assuming the operating agreement does not provide otherwise, a member may transfer or assign her right to distributions. As with partnerships, however, the assignment of distribution rights typically carries with it only the assignor's right to allocated profits. Such an assignment does not entitle the transferee/assignee to become a member of the LLC, or to participate in LLC management as a member, unless the operating agreement so provides, or other members consent. *See* ULLCA § 502(a)(3).

H. ALLOCATION OF DISTRIBUTIONS

The uniform act provides for equal allocation of distributions to members, *see* ULLCA § 404(a), but many state LLC statutes provide for pro rata distributions: To confirm allocations for an existing LLC, first check the operating agreement. If the operating agreement is silent, then consult the governing state LLC statute.

I. DISSOCIATION AND DISSOLUTION OF LLCS

LLC dissolution rules draw upon both partnership and corporation law principles. Recall that under the RUPA, not every partner dissociation from a general partnership causes a dissolution, winding up, and termination of the partnership. Instead, in many instances, a departing or dissociating partner's interest will be purchased by the partnership, and the partnership business will continue as a going concern. The ULLCA takes a similar approach. Under the ULLCA, although many events (such as an individual LLC member's death or bankruptcy) will cause a dissociation of that member, far fewer events require dissolution and winding up of the LLC. In brief, ULLCA §§ 601, 602, 603, and 701 contain default rules respecting dissociation, dissolution, and winding up.

1. Events Causing Dissociation

A member may withdraw or dissociate according to terms specified in the operating agreement or the articles of organization. *See* ULLCA § 602. If no specific provisions are set forth, a member may generally withdraw from the LLC upon giving notice to the LLC. *See* ULLCA § 601 ("A person has the power to dissociate as a member at any time, rightfully or wrongfully, by withdrawing as a member by express will under Section 602(1)."). Even if a dissociation is wrongful (because it is in breach of a term of the operating agreement), the member will be able to dissociate nonetheless. A wrongfully dissociating member may, however, face liability for damages caused by a wrongful dissociation. There are a few other circumstances that will result in dissociation:

- An event occurs that has been agreed to in the operating agreement;
- A member is expelled;
- A member files for bankruptcy (in a member-managed LLC); or
- A member dies.

See ULLCA § 602. The usual effect of a dissociation is that the member no longer has the right to participate in the management of the LLC. Notably, the LLC generally will be unaffected by the dissociation and will continue in business despite the dissociation of a member.

2. Events Causing Dissolution

As is true under the RUPA, the dissociation of a member does not automatically result in the dissolution of an LLC and the requirement of winding up. Rather, under the ULLCA, an LLC will dissolve only if any of the following events occur:

- An event occurs that has been specified in the operating agreement;
- All members consent to dissolve (note that some states, including California and New York, provide for dissolution on majority vote and do not require unanimity);
- Ninety days pass with no LLC members; or

■ A judicial decree is entered that it is not reasonably practicable to carry on the LLC business or that the managers are acting fraudulently, illegally, or in a manner that is oppressive and harmful to the applicant.

See ULLCA § 701. Generally, upon the dissolution of an LLC, the LLC must file articles of termination or dissolution with the state in which it was formed (and in any other states in which it is conducting business).

3. Winding Up

In winding up, assets must first be applied to discharge any obligations to creditors, including members of the LLC who are creditors. *See* ULLCA § 702. Any surplus will then be paid to the LLC members in accordance with their rights to distributions. After distributing its assets, the LLC then terminates its existence by filing articles of termination or dissolution with the secretary of state. The articles of termination or dissolution must contain the name of the LLC, the date of the dissolution, and a statement that the company's business has been wound up, its obligations satisfied or otherwise provided for, and its legal existence has been terminated. See Exhibit 12.2 for a sample form of the articles of dissolution required in Illinois.

Under the ULLCA and most state statutes, failure to file an annual report or pay any fees or taxes when due will result in an **administrative dissolution** of the LLC. An LLC may be reinstated by the secretary of state (usually within two years) upon compliance with the annual report requirements or payment of appropriate fees or taxes. Reinstatement may be retroactive to the date of the dissolution, and if so, the LLC may resume its activities as if no dissolution had occurred.

Case Preview

In re 1545 Ocean Avenue, LLC

As with partnerships and corporations, there are two main types of LLC dissolution — judicial dissolution and nonjudicial dissolution. In the following case, an LLC member petitioned the court for entry of an order of judicial dissolution. Consider the following questions when reading this case:

1. What does the New York LLC statute say about judicial dissolution of an LLC? Is the availability of judicial dissolution principally a question of contract, or statute, or both?
2. How does the New York standard for judicial dissolution of an LLC compare with the New York standard for judicial dissolution of a corporation? Is deadlock grounds for the judicial dissolution of an LLC under the New York statute?
3. How does the New York standard for judicial dissolution compare with the ULLCA standard?
4. What does "not reasonably practicable" mean, according to the court?

EXHIBIT 12.2 Illinois LLC Articles of Dissolution Form

Form **LLC-35.15** May 2012 **Secretary of State** Department of Business Services Limited Liability Division 501 S. Second St., Rm. 351 Springfield, IL 62756 217-524-8008 www.cyberdriveillinois.com **Payment may be made by check payable to Secretary of State. If check is returned for any reason this filing will be void.**	Illinois **Limited Liability Company Act** **Articles of Dissolution** **SUBMIT IN DUPLICATE** Type or Print Clearly This space for use by Secretary of State. **Filing Fee:** $100 **Approved:**	FILE # This space for use by Secretary of State.

1. Limited Liability Company Name:_____

2. Address to which a copy of any process against the Limited Liability Company that may be served on the Secretary of State may be mailed:

   _____

   _____

   _____

3. All debts, obligations and liabilities of the Limited Liability Company have been paid and discharged or adequate provision has been made therefor.

4. All remaining property and assets of the Limited Liability Company have been distributed among the members in accordance with their respective rights and interest.

5. There are no suits pending against the company in any court or that adequate provision has been made for the satisfaction of any judgment, order or decree that may be entered against it in any pending suit.

6. The undersigned affirms, under penalties of perjury, having authority to sign hereto, that these Articles of Dissolution are to the best of my knowledge and belief, true, correct and complete.

Dated _____, _____
                                    Month & Day   Year

_____
Signature

_____
Name and Title (type or print)

RETURN TO: (Please type or print clearly.)

_____
Name if a Company or other Entity
and whether a member or manager of the LLC.

_____
Name

_____
Street

_____
City, State, ZIP Code

Printed by authority of the State of Illinois. May 2012 — 1 — LLC 9.6

In re 1545 Ocean Avenue, LLC

893 N.Y.S.2d 590 (App. Div. 2010)

Austin, J.

On this appeal, we are asked to determine whether the Supreme Court properly granted the petition of Crown Royal Ventures, LLC (hereinafter Crown Royal), to dissolve 1545 Ocean Avenue, LLC (hereinafter 1545 LLC). For the following reasons, we answer in the negative and reverse the order of the Supreme Court.

I

1545 LLC was formed in November 2006 when its Articles of Organization were filed with the Department of State. On November 15, 2006, two membership certificates for 50 units each were issued respectively to Crown Royal and the appellant, Ocean Suffolk Properties, LLC (hereinafter Ocean Suffolk).

On the same date that the membership certificates were issued, an operating agreement was executed by Ocean Suffolk and Crown Royal. The operating agreement provided for two managers; Walter T. Van Houten (hereinafter Van Houten), who was a member of Ocean Suffolk, and John J. King, who was a member of Crown Royal. Each member of 1545 LLC contributed 50% of the capital which was used to purchase premises known as 1545 Ocean Avenue in Bohemia (hereinafter the property) on January 5, 2007. 1545 LLC was formed to purchase the property, rehabilitate an existing building, and build a second building for commercial rental (hereinafter Building A and B, respectively).

It was agreed by Van Houten and King that they would solicit bids from third parties to perform the necessary demolition and construction work to complete the project. Van Houten, who owns his own construction company, Van Houten Construction (hereinafter VHC), was permitted to submit bids for the project, subject to the approval of the managers.

Ocean Suffolk alleges that when there were no bona fide bidders, the managers agreed to allow VHC to perform the work, while Crown Royal maintains that VHC began demolition and reconstruction on Building A without King's consent. In rehabilitating the existing building, Van Houten claims that he discovered and remediated various structural flaws with the claimed knowledge and approval of King or another member of Crown Royal.

King wanted architect Gary Bruno to review the blueprints upon which VHC began demolition since it had been started without the necessary building permits. In addition, King claimed that VHC did not have the proper equipment to efficiently do the excavation and demolition work, causing the billing to be greater than necessary. VHC billed 1545 LLC the sum of $97,322.27 for this work. King claims that he agreed 1545 LLC would pay VHC's invoice on the condition that it would no longer unilaterally do work on the site. Notwithstanding King's demand, VHC continued working on the site. Despite his earlier protests, King did nothing to stop it.

Thereafter, Bruno applied to the Town of Islip for the necessary building permits. The Suffolk County Department of Health required an environmental review whereby a so-called "hot spot" was detected by an environmental engineering firm which proposed to remediate it for $6,500. F & E, the company recommended by

Crown Royal to do the remediation work, estimated that the cost for the environmental remediation work would be about $6,675. King claims that Van Houten objected to F & E and had another firm do a separate evaluation without King's approval, while Van Houten asserts that although F & E eventually charged $8,229.63 for its work, payment to F & E by 1545 LLC was made with his approval. Moreover, Van Houten claimed that the separate evaluation was paid for by Ocean Suffolk out of its own account.

Following this incident, King contended that tensions between King and Van Houten escalated. King asserted that things could not continue as they were or else the project would not be finished in an economical or timely manner. King claimed that Van Houten refused to meet on a regular basis; that he proclaimed himself to be a "cowboy"; and that Van Houten stated he would "just get it done." Nevertheless, King acknowledged that the construction work undertaken by VHC was "awesome."

By April 2007, King announced that he wanted to withdraw his investment from 1545 LLC. He proposed to have all vendors so notified telling them that Van Houten was taking over the management of 1545 LLC. As a result, Van Houten viewed King as having resigned as a manager of 1545 LLC.

Ultimately, King sought to have Ocean Suffolk buy out Crown Royal's membership in 1545 LLC or, alternatively, to have Crown Royal buy out Ocean Suffolk. In the interim, King had his attorney send a "stop work" request to Van Houten.

There ensued discussions regarding competing proposals for the buy-out of the interest of each member by the other. No satisfactory resolution was realized. Nevertheless, despite disagreement among the members during this difficult period, VHC continued to work unilaterally on the site so that the project was within weeks of completion when this proceeding was commenced whereby further work by Van Houten was enjoined.

II

Article 4.1 of the operating agreement provides that "[a]t any time when there is more than one Manager, any one Manager may take any action permitted under the Agreement, unless the approval of more than one of the Managers is expressly required pursuant to the [operating agreement] or the [Limited Liability Company Law, hereinafter LLCL]."

Article 4.12 of the operating agreement entitled, "Regular Meetings," does not require meetings of the Managers with any particular regularity. Meetings may be called without notice as the Managers may "from time to time determine."

Article 7.4 of the operating agreement provides, "any matter not specifically covered by a provision of the [operating agreement], including without limitation, dissolution of the Company, shall be governed by the applicable provisions of the [LLCL]." Accordingly, dissolution of 1545 LLC is governed by LLCL article VII.

III

This proceeding was commenced by order to show cause and verified petition seeking the dissolution of 1545 LLC and related relief. The sole ground for dissolution cited by Crown Royal is deadlock between the managing members arising from

Van Houten's alleged violations of various provisions of article 4 of the operating agreement. There was no allegation of fraud or frustration of the purpose of 1545 LLC on the part of Ocean Suffolk, Van Houten, and VHC.

Answering the petition, Van Houten, on behalf of his company and Ocean Suffolk, denied the allegations in the petition and set forth their claim that they did business in accordance with the operating agreement. Van Houten alleged that the only significant dissension among the members arose from the inability of the parties to agree on a buy-out of each other's interest in 1545 LLC. Significantly, Van Houten alleged, without dispute, that the renovation of Building A was within three to four weeks of completion when this proceeding was commenced.

Van Houten also contended that, as a result of King's resignation as a managing member, Crown Royal could not reasonably claim that a deadlock existed. Moreover, there is no evidence that King complied with article 4.8 of the operating agreement by submitting a written resignation. Nevertheless, by May 10, 2007, in anticipation of a buy-out of the Crown Royal interest in the venture, the parties were operating as if Van Houten was the sole managing member of 1545 LLC. Indeed, throughout the negotiations for the buy-out, the renovation work on Building A continued.

IV

LLCL 702 provides for judicial dissolution as follows:

"On application by or for a member, the Supreme Court in the judicial district in which the office of the limited liability company is located may decree dissolution of a limited liability company *whenever it is not reasonably practicable to carry on the business* in conformity with the articles of organization or operating agreement" (emphasis added).

The LLCL came into being in 1994. Many of its provisions were amended in 1999 (L. 1999, ch. 420) to track changes in federal tax code treatment of such entities (*see Mahler, When Limited Liability Companies Seek Judicial Dissolution, Will the Statute Be Up to the Task?*, 74 N.Y. St. BJ 5 [June 2002]). Such amendments included changes in how the withdrawal of a member was to be treated (LLCL 606) and events of dissolution which relate back to the operating agreement (LLCL 701).

Although various provisions of the LLCL were amended, LLCL 702 was neither modified nor amended in 1999. In declining to amend LLCL 702, the Legislature can only have intended the dissolution standard therein provided to remain the sole basis for judicial dissolution of a limited liability company (*see* McKinney's Statutes §§ 74, 153, 191). Phrased differently, since the Legislature, in determining the criteria for dissolution of various business entities in New York, did not cross-reference such grounds from one type of entity to another, it would be inappropriate for this Court to import dissolution grounds from the Business Corporation Law or Partnership Law to the LLCL.

Despite the standard for dissolution enunciated in LLCL 702, there is no definition of "not reasonably practicable" in the context of the dissolution of a limited liability company. Most New York decisions involving limited liability company dissolution issues have avoided discussion of this standard altogether (*see e.g. Matter of*

Extreme Wireless, 299 A.D.2d 549, 550, 750 N.Y.S.2d 520; *Matter of Horning v. Horning Constr., LLC,* 12 Misc. 3d 402, 816 N.Y.S.2d 877; *Matter of Spires v. Lighthouse Solutions, LLC,* 4 Misc. 3d 428, 778 N.Y.S.2d 259).

Such standard, however, is not to be confused with the standard for the judicial dissolution of corporations (*see* Business Corporation Law §§ 1104, 1104-a) or partnerships (*see* Partnership Law § 62) (*see Widewaters Herkimer Co., LLC v. Aiello,* 28 A.D.3d 1107, 1108, 817 N.Y.S.2d 790 [Appellate Division, Fourth Department, held that the defendants did not plead the requisite grounds for dissolution of a limited liability company in pleading the corporate dissolution standard of "oppressive conduct"]; *see also Matter of Horning v. Horning Constr., LLC,* 12 Misc.3d at 413, 816 N.Y.S.2d 877 [holding that LLCL 702 was "more stringent" than corporate or partnership dissolution standards]).

The Business Corporation Law applies to "every domestic corporation and to every foreign corporation which is authorized to do business in this state" and also to "a corporation of any type or kind, formed for profit under any other chapter of the laws of this state *except a chapter of the consolidated laws* " (Business Corporation Law § 103[a]; emphasis added). The grounds for judicial dissolution of a corporation are set forth in article 11 of the Business Corporation Law.

Partnership Law § 10(2) states that "any association formed under any other statute of this state . . . is not a partnership under this chapter." The bases for dissolution of a partnership are clearly enumerated in Partnership Law §§ 62, 63.

Limited liability companies thus fall within the ambit of neither the Business Corporation Law nor the Partnership Law.

The language of LLCL 702 appears to be borrowed from Revised Partnership Law § 121-802 (dissolution is authorized when it is "not reasonably practicable to carry on the business in conformity with the partnership agreement") and Partnership Law § 63(1)(d), in which dissolution is permitted, inter alia, where a partner's conduct of the partnership business makes it "not reasonably practicable to carry on the business in partnership with him." While there are no New York cases which interpret and apply this standard in the context of limited partnerships, it has been held to mean that, without more, disagreements between the partners with regard to the accounting of the entity are insufficient to warrant dissolution (*see Red Sail Easter Ltd. Partners, L.P. v. Radio City Music Hall Productions, Inc.,* 1992 WL 251380, *5-6 [Del. Ch. 1992]).

The LLCL also clarifies its scope by defining "limited liability company" as "an unincorporated organization of one or more persons having limited liability . . . other than a partnership or trust" (LLCL 102[m]). Thus, the existence and character of these various entities are statutorily dissimilar as are the laws relating to their dissolution (*compare* Business Corporation Law art. 11; Partnership Law §§ 62, 63; LLCL 702). Indeed, it was found to be improper to apply partnership dissolution standards to a cause for dissolution of a limited liability company (*see Matter of Spires v. Lighthouse Solutions,* 4 Misc. 3d at 431, 778 N.Y.S.2d 259).

In the absence of applying Business Corporation Law or Partnership Law dissolution factors to the analysis of what is "not reasonably practicable," the standard for dissolution under LLCL 702 remains unresolved in New York. However, LLCL 702 is clear that unlike the judicial dissolution standards in the Business Corporation Law and the Partnership Law, the court must first examine the limited liability company's operating agreement (*see Matter of Spires v. Lighthouse Solutions, LLC,* 4 Misc. 3d at 432, 778 N.Y.S.2d 259) to determine, in light of the circumstances presented, whether it is or is not "reasonably practicable" for the limited liability company to continue to carry on its business in conformity with the operating agreement (*id.* at 433, 778 N.Y.S.2d 259). Thus, the dissolution of a limited liability company under LLCL 702 is initially a contract-based analysis.

Section 102(u) of the LLCL defines "operating agreement" as "any written agreement of the members concerning the business of a limited liability company and the conduct of its affairs." LLCL 417(a) mandates that the operating agreement contain "provisions not inconsistent with law . . . relating to (i) the business of the limited liability company, (ii) the conduct of its affairs and (iii) the rights, powers, preferences, limitations or responsibilities of its members [and] managers." Where an operating agreement, such as that of 1545 LLC, does not address certain topics, a limited liability company is bound by the default requirements set forth in the LLCL (*see Matter of Spires v. Lighthouse Solutions, LLC,* 4 Misc. 3d at 436-437, 778 N.Y.S.2d 259; 1545 LLC operating agreement art. 7.4).

The operating agreement of 1545 LLC does not contain any specific provisions relating to dissolution. It provides only in article 1.5 that "(t)he Company's term is perpetual from the date of filing of the Articles of Organization . . . unless the Company is dissolved."

Crown Royal argues for dissolution based on the parties' failure to hold regular meetings, failure to achieve quorums, and deadlock. The operating agreement, however, does not require regular meetings or quorums (*see* 1545 LLC operating agreement arts. 4.2, 4.13). It only provides, in article IV, § 4.12, for meetings to be held at such times as the managers may "from time to time determine." The record demonstrates that the managers, King and Van Houten, communicated with each other on a regular basis without the formality of a noticed meeting which appears to conform with the spirit and letter of the operating agreement and the continued ability of 1545 LLC to function in that context.

King and Van Houten did not always agree as to the construction work to be performed on the 1545 LLC property. King claims that this forced the parties into a "deadlock." "Deadlock" is a basis, in and of itself, for judicial dissolution under Business Corporation Law § 1104. However, no such independent ground for dissolution is available under LLCL 702. Instead, the court must consider the managers' disagreement in light of the operating agreement and the continued ability of 1545 LLC to function in that context.

It has been suggested that judicial dissolution is only available when the petitioning member can show that the limited liability company is unable to function as intended or that it is failing financially (*see Schindler v. Niche Media Holdings,* 1 Misc. 3d 713, 716, 772 N.Y.S.2d 781). Neither circumstance is demonstrated by the petitioner here. On the contrary, the purpose of 1545 LLC was feasibly and reasonably being met.

The "not reasonably practicable" standard for dissolution of limited liability companies and partnerships has been examined in other jurisdictions. In Delaware, the Chancery Court has observed, "Given its extreme nature, judicial dissolution is a limited remedy that this court grants sparingly" (*Matter of Arrow Inv. Advisors, LLC,* 2009 WL 1101682, *2 [Del. Ch. 2009]). In Virginia, dissolution is only available when the business cannot continue "in accord with its . . . operating agreement" (*Dunbar Group, LLC v. Tignor,* 267 Va. 361, 367, 593 S.E.2d 216, 218 [2004] [serious differences of opinion among the members and the managers and the commingling of funds was insufficient to warrant a finding that it was not reasonably practicable for the company to continue]). However, where the economic purpose of the limited liability company is not met, dissolution is appropriate (*see Kirksey v. Grohmann,* 754 N.W.2d 825 [S.D. 2008]). Several courts take the view that the "not reasonably practicable" standard should be read as "capable of being done logically and in a reasonable, feasible manner" (*Taki v. Hami,* 2001 WL 672399, *6 [Mich. App. 2001] [dissolution granted where the two partners had not spoken in years and there were allegations of violence and expulsion]), or as "one of reasonable practicability, not impossibility" (*PC Tower Ctr., Inc. v. Tower Ctr. Dev. Assoc. L.P.,* 1989 WL 63901, *6 [Del. Ch. 1989]).

Here, a single manager's unilateral action in furtherance of the business of 1545 LLC is specifically contemplated and permitted. Article 4.1 of the 1545 LLC Operating Agreement states:

> "At any time when there is more than one Manager, *any one manager may take any action permitted under the Agreement,* unless the approval of more than one of the Managers is expressly required pursuant to the Agreement or the Act" (emphasis added).

This provision does not require that the managers conduct the business of 1545 LLC by majority vote. It empowers each manager to act autonomously and to unilaterally bind the entity in furtherance of the business of the entity. The 1545 LLC operating agreement, however, is silent as to the issue of manager conflicts. Thus, the only basis for dissolution can be if 1545 LLC cannot effectively operate under the operating agreement to meet and achieve the purpose for which it was created. In this case, that is the development of the property which purpose, despite the disagreements between the managing members, was being met. As the Delaware Chancery Court noted in *Matter of Arrow Inv. Advisors, LLC,* "The court will not dissolve an LLC merely because the LLC has not experienced a smooth glide to profitability or because events have not turned out exactly as the LLC's owners originally envisioned; such events are, of course, common in the risk-laden process of birthing new entities in the hope that they will become mature, profitable ventures. In part because a hair-trigger dissolution standard would ignore this market reality and thwart the expectations of reasonable investors that entities will not be judicially terminated simply because of some market turbulence, dissolution is reserved for situations in which the LLC's management has become so dysfunctional or its business purpose so thwarted that it is no longer practicable to operate the business, such as in the case of a voting deadlock or where the defined purpose of the entity has become impossible to fulfill."

. . .

"Dissolution of an entity chartered for a broad business purpose remains possible upon a strong showing that a confluence of situationally specific adverse financial, market, product, managerial, or corporate governance circumstances make it nihilistic for the entity to continue" (2009 WL 1101682, *2-3 [Del. Ch. 2009]).

Here, the operating agreement avoids the possibility of "deadlock" by permitting each managing member to operate unilaterally in furtherance of 1545 LLC's purpose.

V

After careful examination of the various factors considered in applying the "not reasonably practicable" standard, we hold that for dissolution of a limited liability company pursuant to LLCL 702, the petitioning member must establish, in the context of the terms of the operating agreement or articles of incorporation, that (1) the management of the entity is unable or unwilling to reasonably permit or promote the stated purpose of the entity to be realized or achieved, or (2) continuing the entity is financially unfeasible.

VI

Dissolution is a drastic remedy (*see Matter of Arrow Inv. Advisors, LLC*, 2009 WL 1101682, *2 [Del. Ch. 2009]). Although the petitioner has failed to meet the standard for dissolution enunciated here, there are numerous other factors which support the conclusion that dissolution of 1545 LLC is inappropriate under the circumstances of this case.

First, the dispute between King and Van Houten was not shown to be inimicable to achieving the purpose of 1545 LLC (*see e.g. Haley v. Talcott*, 864 A.2d 86, 94 [Del. Ch. 2004] [Delaware's "not reasonably practicable" standard "has the obvious purpose of providing an avenue of relief when an LLC cannot continue to function in accordance with its chartering agreement"]). Indeed, the test is "whether it is 'reasonably practicable' to carry on the business of the [LLC], and not whether it is 'impossible' " (*Fisk Ventures, LLC v. Segal*, 2009 WL 73957, *3 [Del. Ch. 2009], *affd.* 984 A.2d 124 [Del. Supr. 2009]).

King never objected to the quality of Van Houten's construction work, but only to its expense. The work on Building A was all but complete when this proceeding was commenced. King approved and praised it. Further, the parties were operating in conformity with the operating agreement.

Second, there is a remedy available in the LLCL to regulate Van Houten's conduct. LLCL 411 permits a limited liability company to avoid contracts entered into between it and an interested manager, or another limited liability company in which a manager has a substantial financial interest, unless the manager can prove the contract was fair and reasonable. Crown Royal took no action under LLCL 411 here. Beyond complaining about the cost of VHC's work and seeking to withdraw from 1545 LLC, the record is clear that Crown Royal ratified, albeit grudgingly at times, Van Houten's unilateral efforts.

The notion that 1545 LLC could void the contract with VHC in its entirety may serve as a check on Van Houten's unilaterally hiring his own company for future construction work on the property, and may result in Van Houten being made to disgorge excess moneys paid in derogation of 1545 LLC's best interest at the time of the accounting of the members. In any event, a fair reading of LLCL 702 demonstrates that an application to dissolve 1545 LLC does not flow from a claim under LLCL 411.

Finally, if Crown Royal is truly aggrieved by Van Houten's actions as manager, the Court of Appeals has found that a derivative claim is available (*see Tzolis v. Wolff,* 10 N.Y.3d 100, 855 N.Y.S.2d 6, 884 N.E.2d 1005). Nevertheless, such remedy cannot serve as the basis for dissolution unless the wrongful acts of a managing member which give rise to the derivative claim are contrary to the contemplated functioning and purpose of the limited liability company.

VII

"The appropriateness of an order for dissolution of the limited liability company is vested in the sound discretion of the court hearing the petition" (*Matter of Extreme Wireless,* 299 A.D.2d 549, 550, 750 N.Y.S.2d 520, citing LLCL 702). However, in applying the standard for dissolution of a limited liability company, upon a review of the evidence submitted, we conclude that the Supreme Court did not providently exercise its discretion in granting the petition for dissolution. Thus, the order of the Supreme Court should be reversed, the petition denied, and the proceeding dismissed.

DILLON and MILLER, JJ., concur.

Post-Case Follow-Up

The remedy of judicial dissolution continues to be important in the LLC context for several reasons — controlling owners may feud with minority owners, buyout rights may not be present, and dissociated LLC members may be left with non-managing equity interests, etc. Without a cash-out right, LLC members may need a default judicial exit route. Most LLC statutes, including Delaware and New York, authorize judicial dissolution only when it is not reasonably practicable to carry on the business in conformity with the parties' agreement. The ULLCA and a minority of states also provide for judicial dissolution when a majority or controlling member engages in oppressive conduct toward minority members.

Courts in both Delaware and New York have construed their LLC statutes as authorizing judicial dissolution only when the purpose of the entity, as defined in the operating agreement, can no longer be achieved. *See, e.g., In re Seneca Invs., LLC,* 970 A.2d 259 (Del. Ch. 2008). Does this mean courts will never look outside the four corners of an LLC operating agreement when deciding whether its purpose is no longer achievable, then? What if the LLC has no written agreement? In the June 2014 opinion, *Meyer Natural Foods LLC v. Duff,* C.A. No. 9703-VCN (Del. Ch. June 4, 2015), Vice Chancellor Noble dissolved a Delaware LLC at the request of its 51 percent managing member, notwithstanding the absence of operational deadlock or any genuine dispute that the LLC's business could be carried on profitably in conformity with the LLC agreement's broadly defined purpose, which was to engage in the business of marketing, distributing, and selling natural beef products. Why dissolution? The court found that the minority owner had terminated a supply agreement between the LLC and a beef products supplier owned by the minority member and obtained a court order stating that the supplier could compete with the LLC following the termination of the supply agreement. Although the LLC agreement made no mention of the supply agreement and contained an integration clause, the supply agreement stated that it was a "condition to" the LLC agreement, and the LLC agreement referenced non-compete covenants. Under these circumstances, Vice Chancellor Noble held that "[l]imiting the analysis to the purpose clause of the LLC Agreement would resolve the dispute on a technicality. . . . Fundamentally, the Court looks to the match between the company's purpose and its reasonable current and future activities. . . . Given that the purpose of [the LLC] was to market and sell natural beef supplied by [the Respondents] according to [petitioner's] specifications, the Court concludes that it is no longer reasonably practicable to operate [the LLC] in line with this vision. . . . [The LLC] cannot achieve its purpose when Respondents do not believe restrictive covenants apply to them and the Output and Supply Agreement has been terminated. The Court has determined that the purpose of [the LLC] was to operate a 'joint venture business' based on a supply and distribution arrangement, but Respondents' entities no longer provide [the LLC] with cattle." *Id.* at 15-17. *See also Natanel v. Cohen*, 988 N.Y.S.2d 524 (Sup. Ct. 2014).

In re 1545 Ocean Avenue, LLC: Real Life Applications

1. Review the LLC judicial dissolution statute in (i) the ULLCA; (ii) the New York LLC Act; and (iii) the Delaware LLC Act.
   a. How are they alike?
   b. How are they different?
   c. What role, if any, does oppression by a majority or controlling member play in the statutory standard for judicial dissolution under these statutes?

2. Assume you represent a minority member in a New York LLC. Your client believes that the majority member(s) have engaged in oppressive conduct designed to freeze out minority members. The LLC is profitable. Is your client likely to be successful if he files a petition for judicial dissolution of the LLC?

3. You represent a business person seeking to form an LLC with a colleague. The initial focus of the business will be real estate development, as your client and her colleague intend to redevelop properties.. The LLC is to be formed in a jurisdiction that follows the ULLCA.
   a. Consider how you might define the purpose of the LLC in the operating agreement.
   b. Consider what type of governance and voting rights your client might want to include in the operating agreement to reduce the risk of deadlock.
   c. Prepare a memo and talking points for your client concerning potential cash-out/buy-sell provisions for the operating agreement.

d. Prepare a memo and talking points for your client respecting the rules concerning judicial dissolution. Will your client be able to petition for judicial dissolution if relations with the co-member deteriorate?

J. ACTIONS BY LLC MEMBERS

Just as partners in a limited partnership and corporate shareholders may initiate direct action for injury sustained by them, a member of an LLC also may maintain a direct action if personally injured by the LLC or co-members. The question of whether the derivative action remedy (to enforce an obligation due to the LLC) is or ought to be available in the LLC context is controversial, and state legislatures and courts have taken different approaches to this issue. Some state legislatures have provided for derivative actions via statute. In other jurisdictions, courts have allowed derivative actions despite the absence of express statutory authorization. To the extent LLC members are permitted to proceed via derivative action, they must comply with procedural and substantive requirements relating to derivative actions set forth in state statutory and common law.

Case Preview

Tzolis v. Wolff

In this case, New York's highest court wrestled with whether to allow an LLC member to bring a derivative action. When reading *Tzolis*, consider the following questions:

1. Does the New York LLC statute speak to whether members can bring a derivative action?
2. What is the court's holding, and what is its rationale for its holding?
3. Consider reading the full dissent in this case. What do you make of the dissent's review of the legislative history underlying the New York LLC statute?

Tzolis v. Wolff
884 N.E.2d 1005 (N.Y. 2008)

SMITH, J.*

We hold that members of a limited liability company (LLC) may bring derivative suits on the LLC's behalf, even though there are no provisions governing such suits in the Limited Liability Company Law.

---
* Footnotes omitted for purpose of brevity.

FACTS AND PROCEDURAL HISTORY

Pennington Property Co. LLC was the owner of a Manhattan apartment building. Plaintiffs, who own 25% of the membership interests in the LLC, bring this action "individually and in the right and on behalf of" the company. Plaintiffs claim that those in control of the LLC, and others acting in concert with them, arranged first to lease and then to sell the LLC's principal asset for sums below market value; that the lease was unlawfully assigned; and that company fiduciaries benefitted personally from the sale. Plaintiffs assert several causes of action, of which only the first two are in issue here: The first cause of action seeks to declare the sale void, and the second seeks termination of the lease.

Supreme Court dismissed these causes of action. It held that they could not be brought by plaintiffs individually, because they were "to redress wrongs suffered by the corporation" (12 Misc. 3d 1151[A], 2006 N.Y. Slip Op 50851[U], *4, 2006 WL 1310621). It also held, following *Hoffman v. Unterberg*, 9 A.D.3d 386, 780 N.Y.S.2d 617 (2d Dept. 2004), that "New York law does not permit members to bring derivative actions on behalf of a limited liability company" (*id.* at *5). The Appellate Division, concluding that derivative suits on behalf of LLCs are permitted, reversed (39 A.D.3d 138, 829 N.Y.S.2d 488 [1st Dept. 2007]), and granted two defendants permission to appeal on a certified question. We now affirm the Appellate Division's order.

DISCUSSION

The issue is whether derivative suits on behalf of LLCs are allowed. The basis for appellants' argument that they are not is the Legislature's decision, when the Limited Liability Company Law was enacted in 1994, to omit all reference to such suits. We hold that this omission does not imply such suits are prohibited. We base our holding on the long-recognized importance of the derivative suit in corporate law, and on the absence of evidence that the Legislature decided to abolish this remedy when it passed the Limited Liability Company Law in 1994.

I

The derivative suit has been part of the general corporate law of this state at least since 1832. It was not created by statute, but by case law. Chancellor Walworth recognized the remedy in *Robinson v. Smith*, 3 Paige Ch. 222 (1832), because he thought it essential for shareholders to have recourse when those in control of a corporation betrayed their duty. Chancellor Walworth applied to a joint stock corporation — then a fairly new kind of entity — a familiar principle of the law of trusts: that a beneficiary (or "cestui que trust") could bring suit on behalf of a trust when a faithless trustee refused to do so. Ruling that shareholders could sue on behalf of a corporation under similar circumstances, the Chancellor explained:

> "The directors are the trustees or managing partners, and the stockholders are the cestui que trusts, and have a joint interest in all the property and effects of the corporation. . . . And no injury the stockholders may sustain by a fraudulent breach of trust, can, upon the general principles of equity, be suffered to pass without a remedy. In the language of Lord Hardwicke, in a similar case [*Charitable Corp. v. Sutton*,

2 Atk. 400, 406 (Ch. 1742)], 'I will never determine that a court of equity cannot lay hold of every such breach of trust. I will never determine that frauds of this kind are out of the reach of courts of law or equity; for an intolerable grievance would follow from such a determination.' " (3 Paige Ch. at 232.)

Eventually, the rule that derivative suits could be brought on behalf of ordinary business corporations was codified by statute (*see* Business Corporation Law § 626[a]). But until relatively recently, no similar statutory provision was made for another kind of entity, the limited partnership; again, the absence of a statute did not prevent courts from recognizing the remedy. In *Klebanow v. New York Produce Exch.,* 344 F.2d 294 (2d Cir. 1965, Friendly, J.), the Second Circuit Court of Appeals held that limited partners could sue on a partnership's behalf. For the Second Circuit, the absence of a statutory provision was not decisive because the court found no "clear mandate *against* limited partners' capacity to bring an action like this" (*id.* at 298 [emphasis added]). We agreed with the holding of *Klebanow* in *Riviera Congress Assoc. v. Yassky,* 18 N.Y.2d 540, 547, 277 N.Y.S.2d 386, 223 N.E.2d 876 (1966, Fuld, J.), relying, as had Chancellor Walworth long before, on an analogy with the law of trusts:

> "There can be no question that a managing or general partner of a limited partnership is bound in a fiduciary relationship with the limited partners . . . and the latter are, therefore, *cestuis que trustent.* . . . It is fundamental to the law of trusts that *cestuis* have the right, 'upon the general principles of equity' (*Robinson v. Smith,* 3 Paige Ch. 222, 232) and 'independently of [statutory] provisions' (*Brinckerhoff v. Bostwick,* 88 N.Y. 52, 59), to sue for the benefit of the trust on a cause of action which belongs to the trust if 'the trustees refuse to perform their duty in that respect.' (*Western R.R. Co. v. Nolan,* 48 N.Y. 513, 518. . . .)"

After *Klebanow* and *Riviera* were decided, the Partnership Law was amended to provide for derivative actions by limited partners (*see* Partnership Law § 115-a [1]).

We now consider whether to recognize derivative actions on behalf of a third kind of entity, the LLC, as to which no statutory provision for such an action exists. In addressing the question, we continue to heed the realization that influenced Chancellor Walworth in 1832, and Lord Hardwicke 90 years earlier: When fiduciaries are faithless to their trust, the victims must not be left wholly without a remedy. As Lord Hardwicke put it, to "determine that frauds of this kind are out of the reach of courts of law or equity" would lead to "an intolerable grievance" (*Charitable Corp. v. Sutton,* 2 Atk. at 406).

To hold that there is no remedy when corporate fiduciaries use corporate assets to enrich themselves was unacceptable in 1742 and in 1832, and it is still unacceptable today. Derivative suits are not the only possible remedy, but they are the one that has been recognized for most of two centuries, and to abolish them in the LLC context would be a radical step.

Some of the problems such an abolition would create may be seen in the development of New York law since the Limited Liability Company Law, omitting all reference to derivative suits, was passed in 1994. Several courts have held that there is no derivative remedy for LLC members (*see Hoffman v. Unterberg,* 9 A.D.3d 386, 780 N.Y.S.2d 617 [2d Dept. 2004]; *Lio v. Mingyi Zhong,* 10 Misc. 3d 1068[A], 2006 N.Y.

Slip Op. 50016[U], 2006 WL 37044 [Sup. Ct., N.Y. County 2006]; *Schindler v. Niche Media Holdings,* 1 Misc. 3d 713, 716, 772 N.Y.S.2d 781 [Sup. Ct., N.Y. County 2003]). But since the Legislature obviously did not intend to give corporate fiduciaries a license to steal, a substitute remedy must be devised. Perhaps responding to this need, some courts have held that members of an LLC have their own, direct claims against fiduciaries for conduct that injured the LLC—blurring, if not erasing, the traditional line between direct and derivative claims (*see Matter of Marciano [Champion Motor Group, Inc.],* 2007 N.Y. Slip Op. 34071[U], *4, 2007 WL 4473342 [Sup. Ct., Nassau County 2007]; *Out of the Box Promotions LLC v. Koschitzki,* 15 Misc. 3d 1134[A], 2007 N.Y. Slip Op 50973[U], *7, 2007 WL 1374501 [Sup. Ct., Kings County 2007]; *Lio,* 2006 N.Y. Slip Op 50016[U], at *4). Similarly, Supreme Court's decision in this case upheld several of plaintiffs' claims that are not in issue here, characterizing the claims as direct, though they might well be derivative under traditional analysis (*see generally,* Kleinberger, *Direct Versus Derivative and The Law of Limited Liability Companies,* 58 Baylor L. Rev. 63 [2006]).

Substituting direct remedies of LLC members for the old-fashioned derivative suit—a substitution not suggested by anything in the language of the Limited Liability Company Law—raises unanswered questions. Suppose, for example, a corporate fiduciary steals a hundred dollars from the treasury of an LLC. Unquestionably he or she is liable to the LLC for a hundred dollars, a liability which could be enforced in a suit by the LLC itself. Is the same fiduciary also liable to each injured LLC member in a direct suit for the member's share of the same money? What, if anything, is to be done to prevent double liability? No doubt, if the Legislature had indeed abolished the derivative suit as far as LLCs are concerned, we could and would answer these questions and others like them. But we will not readily conclude that the Legislature intended to set us on this uncharted path.

II

As shown above, courts have repeatedly recognized derivative suits in the absence of express statutory authorization (*Robinson v. Smith,* 3 Paige Ch. 222 [1832]; *Klebanow v. New York Produce Exch.,* 344 F.2d 294 [2d Cir. 1965]; *Riviera Congress Assoc. v. Yassky,* 18 N.Y.2d 540, 277 N.Y.S.2d 386, 223 N.E.2d 876 [1966]). In light of this, it could hardly be argued that the mere absence of authorizing language in the Limited Liability Company Law bars the courts from entertaining derivative suits by LLC members. It is argued, however, by appellants and by our dissenting colleagues, that here we face not just legislative silence, but a considered legislative decision not to permit the remedy. The dissent finds, in the legislative history of the Limited Liability Company Law, a "legislative bargain" to the effect that derivative suits on behalf of LLCs should not exist (dissenting op. at 113, 855 N.Y.S.2d at 14, 884 N.E.2d at 1013). We find no such thing. For us, the most salient feature of the legislative history is that no one, in or out of the Legislature, ever expressed a wish to *eliminate,* rather than limit or reform, derivative suits.

The Legislature clearly did decide not to enact a statute governing derivative suits on behalf of LLCs. An Assembly-passed version of the bill that became the Limited Liability Company Law included an article IX, entitled "Derivative Actions." In the Senate-passed version, and the version finally adopted, the article was deleted, leaving a conspicuous gap; in the law as enacted, the article following article VIII is article X. Nothing in the legislative history discusses the omission. Our only source of information on the reason for it is a sentence written by the author of the Practice Commentaries on the Limited Liability Company Law: "Because some legislators had raised questions about the derivative rights provisions, to avoid jeopardizing passage of the balance of the entire law, Article IX was dropped" (Rich, Practice Commentaries, McKinney's Cons. Laws of N.Y., Book 32/32A, Limited Liability Company Law, at 181 [2007]). Nothing tells us what the "questions" were, or why they would have jeopardized the bill's passage.

The dissent attempts to fill this gap by reviewing some other events preceding the passage of the legislation. The dissent points out that New York politicians in 1993 and 1994 wanted to improve "New York's overall business climate" (dissenting op. at 110, 855 N.Y.S.2d at 12, 884 N.E.2d at 1011), and that among the proposed means of doing so were "bills . . . to *modify the treatment of* derivative lawsuits and authorize limited liability companies" (*id.,* quoting Blackman, Corporate Update, *Move Over Delaware! Making New York Incorporation-Friendly,* NYLJ, Dec. 16, 1993, at 5, col. 2 [emphasis added]). But the dissent cites no evidence, and we know of none, that anyone ever suggested doing away with derivative suits entirely — a radical step, as we have already pointed out, and one that might be expected to harm the "business climate" more than help it.

In fact, the reforms of derivative suits that were under discussion in 1993-1994 came nowhere near to abolition. They were, in substance, proposals to codify and expand on our decision in *Auerbach v. Bennett,* 47 N.Y.2d 619, 419 N.Y.S.2d 920, 393 N.E.2d 994 (1979), holding that a decision by disinterested directors to terminate a derivative suit would be honored by the courts (*see* Blackman, NYU, Dec. 16, 1993, at 5, col. 2). All three of the bills introduced to reform derivative suits began with an endorsement of such suits in principle:

> "The legislature finds and declares it to be the public policy of the state of New York to maintain the shareholder derivative suit proceeding as a remedy for shareholders on behalf of New York corporations because such suits, when meritorious, serve as an important deterrent against breaches of fiduciary duties by directors of such corporations." (*See* NY Senate Bill S6222 [introduced Dec. 15, 1993]; NY Senate Bill S6222-A [amended Dec. 17, 1993]; NY Assembly Bill A8938 [Dec. 17, 1993]).

The connection, if any, between the proposed reforms of derivative suits and the fate of proposed article IX of the Limited Liability Company Law is obscure. It seems to be true that the Senate favored a bill from which article IX was absent, and that the Assembly acquiesced in the Senate's preference. But this does not prove that any legislator, much less the Legislature as a whole, thought that the absence of article IX would render derivative suits nonexistent — an extreme result that no legislator is known to have favored. We simply do not know what consequences the legislators expected to follow from the omission. It is possible that some legislators did expect — though no one expressed the expectation — that there would be no derivative suits. It is possible that some legislators expected the courts to follow the established case law, and to recognize derivative suits in the absence of a "clear mandate against" doing so (*Klebanow,* 344 F.2d at 298); one witness at a legislative public hearing did express that expectation (statement of Howard N. Lefkowitz, chair of Committee on Corporation Law, Association of Bar of City of NY, Transcript of Assembly Public Hearing on Limited Liability Company Legislation, June 11, 1992, at 133). It is possible that the Senate expected one thing, and the Assembly the other. It is even possible that neither expected anything, except that the problem would cease to be the Legislature's and become the courts'. The legislative history is, in short, far too ambiguous to permit us to infer that the Legislature intended wholly to eliminate, in the LLC context, a basic, centuries-old protection for shareholders, leaving the courts to devise some new substitute remedy.

The dissent says that, in upholding the right of LLC members to sue derivatively, we leave that right "unfettered by the prudential safeguards against abuse that the Legislature has adopted . . . in other contexts" (dissenting op. at 121, 855 N.Y.S.2d at 20, 884 N.E.2d at 1019). But the right to sue derivatively has never been "unfettered," and the limitations on it are not all of legislative origin. The case in which derivative suits originated, *Robinson v. Smith,* held that such a suit could be brought only on "a sufficient excuse" — i.e., a showing that those in control of the corporation "refused to prosecute" because they were themselves the wrongdoers, or were in "collusion with" them (3 Paige Ch. at 232, 233). Later cases reaffirmed the rule that a derivative action could not be brought "unless it is necessary because of the neglect and refusal of the corporate body to act" (*see e.g. Continental Sec. Co. v. Belmont,* 206 N.Y. 7, 15, 99 N.E. 138 [1912]). The statutes governing ordinary business corporations and limited partnerships now reflect the existence of that rule, requiring the complaint in a derivative suit to allege "the efforts of the plaintiff to secure the initiation of such action . . . or the reasons for not making such effort" (Business Corporation Law § 626[c]; Partnership Law § 115-a[3]). Other statutory provisions impose other limitations (*see* Business Corporation Law § 626[b]; Partnership Law § 115-a [2] [contemporaneous ownership of plaintiff's interest]; Business Corporation Law § 627; Partnership Law § 115-b [posting security for expenses]). What limitations on the right of LLC members to sue derivatively may exist is a question not before us today. We do not, however, hold or suggest that there are none.

Finding no clear legislative mandate to the contrary, we follow *Robinson, Klebanow* and *Riviera* in concluding that derivative suits should be recognized even though no statute provides for them. We therefore hold that members of LLCs may sue derivatively (*accord Bischoff v. Boar's Head Provisions Co. Inc.,* 436 F. Supp. 2d 626 [S.D.N.Y. 2006]; *Weber v. King,* 110 F. Supp. 2d 124 [E.D.N.Y. 2000]; *contra Pennacchio ex rel. Old World Brewing Co., Inc. v. Powers,* 2007 WL 446355, 2007 U.S. Dist LEXIS 8051 [E.D.N.Y. 2007]).

Accordingly, the order of the Appellate Division, insofar as appealed from, should be affirmed with costs and the certified question answered in the affirmative.

READ, J. (dissenting).

The result in this case is unique in the annals of the Court of Appeals. Never before has a majority of the Court read into a statute provisions or policy choices that the enacting Legislature unquestionably considered and rejected. I respectfully dissent.

· · ·

CONCLUSION

The enacting (not a subsequent) Legislature considered and explicitly rejected language authorizing the very result that plaintiffs have successfully sought from the judiciary in this case. Fourteen years after the fact the majority has unwound the legislative bargain. The proponents of derivative rights for LLC members — who were unable to muster a majority in the Senate — have now obtained from the courts what they were unable to achieve democratically. Thanks to judicial fiat, LLC members now enjoy the right to bring a derivative suit. And because created by the courts, this right is unfettered by the prudential safeguards against abuse that the Legislature has adopted when opting to authorize this remedy in other contexts (*see* Business Corporation Law §§ 626, 627; Partnership Law §§ 115-a, 115-b).

Presumably, those businesses electing to organize as LLCs relied on what the Limited Liability Company Law says, and counted on the New York judiciary to interpret the statute as written. Instead, the majority has effectively rewritten the law to add a right that the Legislature deliberately chose to omit. For a Court that prides itself on resisting any temptation to usurp legislative prerogative, the outcome of this appeal is curious. I respectfully dissent.

Chief Judge KAYE and Judges CIPARICK and PIGOTT concur with Judge SMITH; Judge READ dissents in a separate opinion in which Judges GRAFFEO and JONES concur.

Order, insofar as appealed from, affirmed, with costs, and certified question answered in the affirmative.

Post-Case Follow-Up

The derivative remedy came to the LLC world via limited partnerships. Although the derivative action remedy was not specifically authorized in the original version of Uniform Limited Partnership Act (and was not recognized in some early cases), courts from 1960s onward began to allow derivative actions in the limited partnership context. The first statutory provisions addressing the availability of derivative actions in the limited partnership context appeared in New York and Delaware, and the derivative remedy entered the uniform limited partnership law in 1976. When LLC statutes began to appear, drafters used the emerging limited partnership approach as a model when thinking about derivative actions in the LLC context. Today, the derivative remedy is present in approximately 75 percent of LLC statutes and is included in the ULLCA. *See* ULLCA § 802.

K. CONVERSIONS, MERGERS, AND DOMESTICATIONS

Under Article 10 of the ULLCA, a general partnership or limited partnership or other entity (such as a corporation) may convert to an LLC (or vice versa) either by unanimous vote or by the appropriate vote required by their respective agreements. After the **conversion** is approved by the entity, it will file its articles of conversion with the secretary of state. The articles must state that the entity was converted from a different type of organization, its former name, and a statement that it was approved by the appropriate vote.

Additionally, an LLC may merge with or into nearly any other business entity, including another LLC, a corporation, a general or limited partnership, or other domestic or foreign entity. A plan of merger must address various issues relating to the merger, and the plan must be approved by the membership of all merging entities. After approval of all parties, articles of merger must be filed with the secretary of state. Conversions, mergers, and domestications do not affect property owned by the converting, merging, or domesticating entity or any of its debts and obligations, and the new or surviving entity will retain liability for any obligations that existed prior to the transaction. Thus, conversions, mergers, and domestications cannot be used to evade liability. Finally, a foreign LLC may become a domestic LLC (or vice versa) by adopting a plan of **domestication** and filing articles of domestication, similar to the articles of merger and conversion described earlier.

Note that an LLC may transact business in a state other than the one in which it was formed. Generally, the LLC must file an application to transact business in the new state and must submit a certificate of its good standing from the state of formation. See Exhibit 12.3 for a sample application to transact business in another state. Before filing the application for authority to do business in the foreign state, carefully review that state's statutes to ensure that the LLC is in fact required to qualify in the foreign state. Review the state statutes as to what constitutes "transacting business," as well. For example, under ULLCA § 905, the following activities, among others, do not constitute transacting business: maintaining or defending a lawsuit, having LLC meetings, maintaining bank accounts, or conducting an isolated transaction. Thus, engaging in such activities would not require an LLC to file an application in the foreign state.

Failure to obtain the certificate to transact business in another state will preclude the LLC from maintaining a lawsuit in the state, might subject it to monetary penalties, and may provide a basis upon which the state's attorney general could bring an action against the LLC to prevent it from doing business in the state. In many states, the LLC may reserve its name even before doing business by filing certain forms with the secretary of state. The name reservation holds the proposed name of the LLC in the foreign state for some stated period of time, often several months.

L. PROFESSIONAL LIMITED LIABILITY COMPANIES

Although the ULLCA and most states allow LLCs to be formed for any lawful purpose (although many states do not allow an LLC to offer insurance or banking services), some states (including New York) have added separate statutes specifically permitting professional firms (such as those offering legal, medical, and accounting

EXHIBIT 12.3 Montana Foreign LLC Application for Registration

STATE OF MONTANA

Prepare, sign, submit with an original signature and filing fee.
This is the minimum information required.

CERTIFICATE of AUTHORITY
of FOREIGN LIMITED LIABILITY COMPANY
APPLICATION
(35-8-1003, MCA)

(This space for use by the Secretary of State only)

MAIL: **LINDA McCULLOCH**
               Secretary of State
               P.O. Box 202801
               Helena, MT 59620-2801
PHONE: (406) 444-3665
FAX: (406) 444-3976
WEB SITE: sos.mt.gov

Required Filing Fee: $70.00
☐ 24 Hour Priority Handling check box and Add $20.00
☐ 1 Hour Expedite Handling check box and **Add $100.00**

Please Check One Box: ☐Foreign Limited Liability Company ☐Foreign Professional Limited Liability Company

1. The name of the limited liability company is:

_____

   Please Note: Must contain the words "limited liability company", "limited co." "or an abbreviation. If professional, must contain the words "professional limited liability company", or an abbreviation.

2. State of organization: _____

3. The date of its organization is (Month/Day/Year) _____ and the period of duration is: _____

4. The name and address of the registered office/agent **in Montana**:
   Appointment of the Registered Agent is confirmation of the agent's consent.

   Name: _____

   Street Address (required): _____

   Mailing Address: _____

   City: _____ State: **MT** Zip Code: _____

5. The business mailing address of the principal office is: _____

   City: _____ State: _____ Zip Code: _____

6. The LLC is managed by (check one) a ☐**Manager or** by its ☐**Members**.

7. Name and business address of current **managing** Managers or **managing** Members are (attach a list if necessary):

   _____

   _____

8. If a Professional Limited Liability Company, the services to be rendered: _____

9. **I, HEREBY SWEAR AND AFFIRM,** under penalty of law, that the facts contained in this document are true and that this entity has complied with the organizational laws in the jurisdiction in which it is organized and that it exists in that jurisdiction.

   Applicant Signature: _____ DATE: _____

   Daytime Contact Phone: _____ Email: _____

services) to organize as **professional limited liability companies** (PLLCs). Typically, the statutes provide that the professionals retain liability for their own negligence and that of others under their supervision. Nevertheless, the PLLC protects the members' personal assets from obligations of the PLLC itself. Membership in the PLLC is usually restricted to licensed professionals, and the name of the business must indicate by some signal (usually "PLLC") that the entity is a professional limited liability company. In some states, the PLLC is created by a mere statement in the standard form for LLC articles of organization that the entity will operate as a PLLC. Other states provide separate documents for formation of PLLCs. California does not allow professionals to be organized as LLCs.

M. FAMILY LIMITED LIABILTY COMPANIES

A newer trend is the rise of a family LLC (similar to a family limited partnership, discussed in Chapter 5). Like FLiPs, family LLCs are designed to achieve certain tax and estate planning objectives. One famous example of a family LLC is Bill Gates's Cascade Investment LLC, which manages a portion of the Gates family money.

N. LOW-PROFIT LIMITED LIABILITY COMPANY (L3C)

A new form of hybrid entity was created in Vermont in 2008, the **low-profit limited liability company** (usually called an "L3C"). The entity is a for-profit entity with explicit social purposes, such as promoting affordable public housing, alternative energy sources, or some other charitable or social purpose goal. These businesses engage in profit-making activities to achieve their social goals; profit making is secondary to their stated social mission. Unlike a traditional charity, however, the L3C may distribute its profits, after taxes, to its owners. These for-profit businesses use business practices to achieve their social goals.

These new entities are able to attract capital and investment money from foundations and other socially conscious investors. In general, foundations have two alternatives for spending their money: They can give grants (in which case they do not earn any return on the money) or they can make program-related investments, called PRIs, in which case they invest in low-profit ventures and potentially earn a return. Because of burdensome IRS regulations relating to PRIs, most foundations have avoided investing in for-profit ventures due to the uncertainty of whether they would qualify as PRIs. If a venture does not qualify as a PRI, the foundation could be subject to fines.

Enter the L3C, which is expressly formed to further a social goal and whose operating agreement specifically delineates its PRI-qualified purpose, making it easier for foundations to invest in such entities. The states that have recognized L3Cs have typically amended their limited liability company statutes to allow for L3Cs. The L3C's articles of organization must indicate that it intends to qualify as a low-profit limited liability company and that no significant purpose of the company is the production of income or the appreciation of property. It must use an appropriate signal as part of its name (such as "L3C"). The L3C form is not widely used, however, and the American Bar Association Limited Liability Company Committee has recommended that that states *not* enact L3C legislation, primarily because certain tax issues still remain unresolved and because other business structures may accomplish the same goals as L3Cs.

O. CONTENTS OF THE OPERATING AGREEMENT

In addition to addressing the management and governance rules discussed above, LLC operating agreements also should contain (at least) the basic information described in the following subsections. Standard contractual provisions (such as indemnification provisions, choice of law provisions, choice of venue, amendement provisions, etc.) should also be included. In this regard, the Joint Venture Agreement shown in Appendix D may be a useful starting point when thinking about such provisions.

1. Name of the LLC

The operating agreement must specify a name. As with any business name, the LLC's name cannot be deceptively similar to that of another business such that there would be a likelihood of confusion in the marketplace. A search should be conducted to ensure the name is available and a check made of the state statutes to determine what signal, such as "L.L.C." or "L.C.," must be used in the business name. The ULLCA provides that the name include "limited liability company," or "limited company," or the abbreviation "L.L.C.," "LLC," "L.C.," or "LC." Most states and the ULLCA allow a new LLC to reserve a name during the formation period by filing an application (with a fee) to reserve the name. The reservation is valid for some period of time, often 90 days, during which another LLC may not file articles of organization using that name. See Exhibit 12.4 for a sample form of the application to reserve a name used in New York. The LLC can also operate under an assumed name, just as a sole proprietor, partnership, or corporation can. The state simply needs to be informed of the assumed name the LLC has elected. The full name of the LLC, with its signal indicating adoption of the LLC form, should appear on all signage, correspondence, stationery, websites, business cards, and other documents of the LLC to provide notice to the public that the entity is operating as an LLC.

2. Names and Addresses of Members

The names and addresses of all members should be provided so that notices and information can be communicated to the members. Corporations and other business entities may be members of LLCs, and they are deemed notified at the addresses provided.

3. Purpose

The purpose of the LLC should be stated. The purpose clause should be broad enough so that the LLC can expand and grow without requiring amendment of

EXHIBIT 12.4 New York LLC Application for Name Reservation

Application for Reservation of Name
Under §205 of the Limited Liability Company Law

NYS Department of State
Division of Corporations, State Records and
Uniform Commercial Code
One Commerce Plaza, 99 Washington Avenue
Albany, NY 12231-0001
www.dos.ny.gov

PLEASE TYPE OR PRINT

APPLICANT'S NAME AND STREET ADDRESS

NAME TO BE RESERVED

RESERVATION IS INTENDED FOR (CHECK ONE)

☐ New domestic limited liability company
(The Limited Liability Company Law requires that the name end with "Limited Liability Company," "LLC" or "L.L.C.")

☐ New domestic professional service limited liability company
(The name must end with "Professional Limited Liability Company" or "Limited Liability Company" or an abbreviation in §1212(b) of the Limited Liability Company Law.)

☐ Existing foreign limited liability company intending to apply for authority to do business in New York State

☐ Existing foreign professional service limited liability company intending to apply for authority to do business in New York State

☐ Change of name of an existing domestic or an authorized foreign limited liability company

☐ A person intending to form a foreign limited liability company which will apply for authority to do business in this state

☐ Existing foreign limited liability company intending to apply for authority to do business in New York State whose name is not available for use in New York State and must use a fictitious name

☐ Authorized foreign limited liability company intending to change its fictitious name under which it does business in this state

☐ Authorized foreign limited liability company which has changed its name in its jurisdiction, such new name not being available for use in New York State

---

X _____

Signature of applicant, applicant's attorney or agent
(If attorney or agent, so specify)

Typed/printed name of signer

INSTRUCTIONS:

1. Upon filing this application, the name will be reserved for 60 days and a certificate of reservation will be issued.
2. The certificate of reservation, which will be in the form of a receipt, must be returned with and attached to the articles of organization, application for authority, certificate of amendment or with a cancellation of the reservation.
3. The name used must be the same as appears in the reservation.
4. A $20 fee payable to the Department of State must accompany this application.

NOTE: In all applications for existing domestic and foreign limited liability companies, the applicant must be the limited liability company.

DOS-1233 (Rev. 10/12)

Page 1 of 1

the operating agreement. In most states, a general clause stating that the purpose of the LLC is to engage in any business lawful in the state is acceptable. Generally, an LLC may be formed for any lawful purpose (including operating as a nonprofit entity), although most states prohibit insurance and banking companies, with their significant potential liability to consumers, from operating as LLCs. As previously discussed, California prohibits professionals from operating as LLCs. We discussed the purpose requirement, and its relation to LLC dissolution, above.

4. Address

The principal place of business of the LLC should be provided so that members and others can provide communications to the LLC.

5. Term

Most states and the ULLCA provide that if no specific term is set forth in the operating agreement, the LLC will have perpetual existence.

6. LLC Powers

The operating agreement should indicate the powers of the LLC and the activities in which it may engage. Some state LLC statutes provide a model list of powers of LLCs, including the power to sue and be sued in the LLC name; to purchase, own, use, lease, or sell real or personal property; to make contracts; to lend money; to elect managers and appoint officers; and to establish compensation plans for members and managers. This listing of LLC powers is similar to that provided by statutes applying to corporations and is an example of borrowing of corporate concepts by LLC statutes. The ULLCA eliminates this list of powers and provides simply that LLCs have the power to do all things necessary or convenient to carry out their activities. *See* ULLCA §§ 108, 109.

7. Financial Provisions

The initial contributions to the LLC should be identified. As with a partnership, these contributions may be present or future cash, services, or property. *See* ULLCA § 402. A separate contribution agreement is advisable to help the contributing member and the LLC avoid misunderstandings or disputes regarding the valuation of contributed property, the status of contributed property should the LLC dissolve, and the like. Circumstances that will require additional contributions of capital should be set forth. The general rule is that additional contributions must be made in proportion to the initial capital contributions. This section of the operating agreement also should discuss the distribution of assets, namely, the percentage to be allocated to each member and when distributions will be made. Generally, distributions to members cannot be made if such would preclude the LLC from paying its obligations as they come due.

EXHIBIT 12.5 Quick Reference: Unincorporated Business Structures

	Sole Proprietorship	General Partnership	Limited Partnership	Limited Liability Partnership	Limited Liability Company
Types of Members	Individuals only	No restrictions	No restrictions	No restrictions	No restrictions
Number of Members Required	One only	At least two	At least two, one general partner and one limited partner	At least two	One or more members
Administrative Formalities of Organization	None	None	Filing of certificate of limited partnership required	Filing of application of LLP required	Filing of articles of organization required
Management	Managed solely by sole proprietor	Managed jointly by all general partners	Managed solely by general partners	Generally managed jointly by all LLP partners	Can be member-managed or managed by appointed managers
Liability	Unlimited personal liability	Unlimited personal liability	General partners have unlimited personal liability; limited partners personally liable only to extent of investment	LLP partners are always protected from personal liability for their co-partners' torts; in 49 jurisdictions, no personal liability for co-partners' acts whether arising in tort or contract	Members personally liable only to extent of investment (but professionals retain liability for their own negligence)
Transferability of All Ownership Rights	None; new sole proprietorship created upon transfer	Only partner's economic interest is transferable; assignee becomes partner only if agreement so provides or all other partners consent	Economic interest is assignable; assignee becomes partner only if agreement provided or all partners consent	Economic interest is assignable; assignee becomes partner only if agreement so provides or all other partners consent	Economic interest is transferable; transferee becomes member only if agreement so provides or all LLC members consent
Ability to Do Business in Other States	Yes	Yes	Yes, if authorized by foreign state	Yes, if authorized by foreign state	Yes, if authorized by foreign state

EXHIBIT 12.5	Quick Reference: Unincorporated Business Structures				
	Sole Proprietorship	**General Partnership**	**Limited Partnership**	**Limited Liability Partnership**	**Limited Liability Company**
Continuity of Life	No; terminates upon death of sole proprietor	Under RUPA, only certain dissociations cause dissolution and winding up	LP can survive withdrawal of limited partner (and general partner if all consent), so long as there is always at least one limited partner and at least one general partner	Only certain dissociations cause a dissolution and winding up	Dissolution occurs only if operating agreement requires such, all members consent, 90 days pass with no members, or after judicial order
Taxation	Income taxed directly to sole proprietor*	Income taxed directly to all partners*	Income taxed directly to all partners*	Income taxed directly to all partners*	Income taxed directly to all members*
Right to Bring Derivative Action	No	No	Yes	No	Yes

*Under IRS "check-the-box" regulations, the entity may elect to be taxed as a corporation at corporate tax levels.

Chapter Summary

- LLCs are hybrids, drawing upon attractive features of corporations (e.g., limited liability) and those of partnerships (e.g., flexible, customizable management, and pass-through taxation).
- LLCs offer their members full protection from personal liability whether arising in tort or contract. Only the LLC itself is liable for debts and obligations (although members retain liability for their own wrongful conduct).
- LLCs can be managed by their members ("member-managed") or by appointed managers ("manager-managed").
- Voting and management and control rules should be spelled out in the operating agreement.
- LLCs can be formed only by compliance with state statutes, which mandate the filing of articles of organization with the state agency.
- LLCs are governed in the first instance by their operating agreements, which usually are (and should be) in writing. If the operating agreement is silent on various matters, the pertinent state LLC statute will control.
- While there is a uniform LLC act, state LLC statutes are highly variable, and case law tends to be less robust for LLCs compared to partnerships and corporations, so it is important that you research the law in your home jurisdiction when forming LLCs and advising clients.

Applying the Concepts

1. What is the default rule regarding LLC voting (e.g., per capita, pro rata) in Texas? California? North Carolina?

2. Is oppression by a majority or controlling member a basis for judicial dissolution under the LLC statute in Texas? California? North Carolina?

3. Modern Furniture LLC, a member-managed LLC with four members, owes $40,000 to one of its furniture suppliers. Having fallen on hard times, the LLC does not have enough money to pay this debt. The supplier has sued the LLC and all of its members, arguing that the members took delivery of the furniture, and incurred the debt, knowing the LLC would be unable to pay. Who is liable for payment of the money owed to the supplier? Are there any circumstances under which members could be held personally liable for the debt to the supplier?

4. Leslie is a member (along with Fran) in SolPanels, LLC, an LLC formed in a jurisdiction that follows the ULLCA that is engaged in the solar power business. Leslie needs a break from the business and would like to transfer her interest in the LLC to her sibling, Morgan.

   a. May Leslie transfer her interest?
   b. If Leslie transfers her interest, will the LLC dissolve?
   c. What rights, if any, will Morgan have respecting profits generated by SolPanels?
   d. What rights, if any, will Morgan have respecting LLC management and governance?

5. Sugo is a New York limited liability company (LLC) formed by Smith and Jones, each of whom owns a 50 percent interest. Sugo was formed to market goods and services to mobile telephone users via their cellular phones. Despite equal ownership interests, Jones assumed the titles and responsibilities of chief executive officer and president of Sugo.

   Shortly after forming Sugo, and at the solicitation of Jones, Dan provided $100,000 in "seed money" to Sugo. Upon receipt of the seed money, Sugo entered into a number of contracts, including a joint venture agreement with Latin World Entertainment (LWE) to develop and distribute mobile media content for the Latino/Latina market.

   Smith alleges that shortly after Sugo and LWE entered into their joint venture, Jones embarked upon a plan to dilute Smith's interest in Sugo. Initially, Jones asked Smith reduce her ownership stake in Sugo in order give Dan a significant equity stake in the business. Smith alleges that when she refused to dilute her interest unless Jones diluted his interest by an equal amount, Jones began plotting with Dan to misappropriate the business opportunities afforded by the LWE joint venture. Smith also alleges that after she refused to dilute her interest, Jones sought to dissolve Sugo over Smith's objections. Two weeks ago, Jones abandoned his role and functions at Sugo and froze the cash assets of Sugo without the consent of Smith.

Shortly before Jones abandoned his role at Sugo, Jones and Dan formed Rip Road, LLC, and Rip Road, Inc. (collectively "Rip Road"). Jones is the chief executive officer and president of Rip Road and Dan is the vice president of finance and strategy. Immediately after its formation, Rip Road entered into agreements to develop and distribute mobile media content for the Latino/Latina market, including a deal with LWE. Neither Jones nor Dan advised Smith or Sugo of the creation of Rip Road, or of Rip Road's efforts respecting the Latino/Latina market. Following Rip Road's formation, LWE and other businesses elected to work with Rip Road (and not Sugo) on projects relating to the Latino/Latina market. This caused Sugo to fall on hard times, since the Sugo-LWE joint venture was Sugo's main asset.

a. Assume Smith has sued Jones for misappropriation and seeks the imposition of a constructive trust on any profits made by Rip Road relating to the Latino/Latina market. (Note: a constructive trust arises when one party obtains property by wrongful conduct and is said to hold it for the benefit of its rightful owner.) Will Smith win? Does the answer to this question depend on the language of Sugo's operating agreement? Why or why not?

b. Assume that Jones came to you before forming Sugo. Further assume that Jones explained that while he was very enthusiastic about Sugo's prospects, he wanted to retain the flexibility to work with others on business opportunities involving the Latino/Latina market. What advice, if any, might you give to Jones regarding Sugo's structure, the operating agreement, and Sugo's business?

6. Plaintiffs Whitewater LLC ("Whitewater") and High Peaks Ventures, LLC ("High Peaks") filed suit against Defendants, two minority members of Whitewater. Plaintiffs allege that Defendants breached Whitewater's LLC operating agreement when they failed to make required contributions in response to capital calls. (Note: A capital call refers to the legal right of an investment firm to demand a portion of the total amount promised to the firm by an investor over time, as specific investment opportunities become available.)

Under the LLC operating agreement, Whitewater and High Peaks had broad authority to issue capital calls in amounts and upon dates of their choosing, and it is undisputed that Defendants failed to contribute capital in response to several such calls. Citing the operating agreement (which states that members who fail to contribute capital in response to capital calls shall be required to sell their membership interests to the majority member at an agreed-upon price), Plaintiffs seek a declaration that Whitewater and High Peaks have the right to acquire Defendants' membership interests in Whitewater at the price specified in the LLC agreement.

Defendants filed an answer denying liability and a counterclaim seeking judicial dissolution of Whitewater based on High Peaks's allegedly oppressive conduct. Defendants allege that Plaintiffs issued capital calls at times and in amounts without considering Defendants' financial condition, causing Defendants to experience financial difficulties. The operating agreement recites (and does not modify) the New York LLC statute with respect to judicial dissolution.

a. Plaintiffs have moved to dismiss the dissolution counterclaim. Will Plaintiffs prevail?

b. What if this case were decided under the ULLCA dissolution statute?

Business Organizations in Practice

1. You are an associate at a law firm. Anna, Ben, and Carly retain you to draft a certificate of organization and a written operating agreement for their web design and database development business, which they would like to form and operate as an LLC. Anna plans to contribute $30,000 to the business, Ben plans to contribute $100,000, and Carly plans to contribute $20,000. Carly also plans to contribute several servers (a type of computer that the business will use to store and manage data and provide web services) to the venture. Assume that the LLC is being formed in a jurisdiction that follows the ULLCA.

   a. May Carly contribute servers to the business? If so, what (if any) issues should you consider when memorializing Carly's contribution?

   b. Anna, Ben, and Carly ask you to allocate voting power based on each member's initial contributions to the business. Draft a provision for the operating agreement that accomplishes this goal. How does this compare with the default rule regarding voting power under the ULLCA?

2. After you finish meeting with Anna, Ben, and Carly, Anna pulls you aside to explain that she wants to manage the business day to day because she thinks that Ben and Carly are wonderful designers but terrible business people. She is worried that Ben and Carly will spend profits unwisely and demand excessive distributions, so she asks you to make sure that she has managerial control over all matters, whether ordinary course or not.

   a. What ethical issues, if any, does this conversation raise under your state's ethical rules?

   b. If you allocate voting according to ownership interest, and say nothing about ordinary course versus non-ordinary course activities, will Anna have control over all matters?

   c. Assume for purposes of this question that Ben and Carly agree with Anna's assessment of their business skills, and further agree (upon advice of personal counsel) that Anna should have managerial control over all matters, whether ordinary course or not. Draft provision(s) for the operating agreement that will accomplish this goal.

   d. Assume that Ben and Carly are generally on board with allowing Anna to manage the LLC day to day (upon advice of personal counsel), but would like to limit Anna's authority to engage in certain transactions, including the purchase or rental of any real estate. Assume that Anna agrees with these limitations (upon advice of personal counsel). What might the LLC consider doing to address these limits on Anna's authority to act on behalf of the LLC?

3. Anna, Ben, and Carly call you up two weeks after the initial meeting to explain that they want to bring Isaac into the LLC. Isaac is a brilliant designer and is beloved by clients but has no capital to contribute to the LLC. What rules govern the admission of new members under the ULLCA?

4. Assume that the LLC has been successful, and would like to make a distribution of $500,000 in profits. How will these profits be allocated and (if the partners so desire) distributed under the ULLCA? What about the default rules of your home jurisdiction as assigned by your professor?

5. You are an associate at a law firm. Sue Stein, a successful business person, has asked about forming a family limited partnership or a family LLC for estate and tax planning purposes. You are meeting with her next week. Research the differences between these two forms of organizations, and prepare an outline and memo for your conversation with Sue.

i3

Securities Regulation in Business Organizations: Securities Offerings, Anti-Fraud Rules, Corporate Governance Reforms, and the Proxy System

Investors in corporations are protected not only by state statutes relating to the formation, operation, and management of corporations, but also by various federal and state laws that govern the offer, purchase, and sale of securities and shareholder voting procedures. For example, the Securities Act of 1933 and regulations promulgated thereunder contain registration and disclosure requirements for securities offerings and anti-fraud rules relating to the offer and sale of securities. The Securities Exchange Act of 1934 and regulations promulgated thereunder regulate the buying and selling of securities subsequent to their original issuance

Key Concepts

- Registration, disclosure, and anti-fraud rules associated with the Securities Act of 1933
- Registration, disclosure, and anti-fraud rules associated with the Securities Exchange Act of 1934
- The proxy system
- The Sarbanes-Oxley Act of 2000 and the Dodd-Frank Wall Street Reform and Consumer Protection Act and their impact on registration, reporting, and corporate governance rules
- Exchange listing requirements
- State blue sky laws

Ferdinand Pecora, the Pecora Hearings, and the Origins of the Federal Securities Laws

In 1932, after learning that a so-called bear raid — a move to drive stock prices down for profit — was in the offing, Herbert Hoover launched an investigation into the stock market. For its first witness, the Senate Banking and Currency Committee called the president of the New York Stock Exchange, Richard Whitney. Whitney was a bond dealer with close ties to the nation's elite, including J.P. Morgan and Company (the storied Wall Street firm). Whitney believed no reform was necessary. "You gentlemen are making a great mistake," he reportedly informed the senators. "The Exchange is a perfect institution." Edward J. Perkins, *Wall Street to Main Street: Charles Merrill and Middle Class Investors* 136 (Cambridge University Press 1999).

After the Democrats took over the committee, Whitney and the Wall Street elites met their match in the committee's newly appointed chief counsel Ferdinand Pecora. If Whitney represented the "white shoe" banking and finance establishment, Pecora was his polar opposite. A Sicilian-born New Yorker, Pecora reportedly was forced to drop out of school in his teens after his father was injured in a work-related accident. Pecora eventually got a job as a law clerk and later obtained his law degree and passed the bar, becoming one of just a few first-generation Italian lawyers in New York City. After landing a job as an assistant district attorney, Pecora established a reputation as a smart, honest, and tenacious prosecutor.

Pecora made the hearings about more than an investigation

and shareholder voting procedures. The '34 Act also established conduct standards for certain securities industry professionals and called for the creation of the Securities and Exchange Commission, the federal agency charged with protecting investors, maintaining fair, orderly, and efficient markets, and facilitating capital formation. The '34 Act also contains antifraud rules. Two other federal statutes codified in the federal securities laws (among other places) — the Sarbanes-Oxley Act of 2002 and the Dodd-Frank Wall Street Reform and Consumer Protection Act — also contain rules relating to securities offerings, financial reporting obligations, and corporation governance. In this chapter, we examine rules, rights, and obligations arising under federal and state securities statutes and regulations, paying particular attention to those arising under the federal securities laws and the associated regulatory regime.

A. INTRODUCTION TO SECURITIES OFFERINGS

Prior to the stock market crash of October 29, 1929, and the subsequent Great Depression, corporations desiring to sell stock to the public simply distributed securities by having agents sell stock on commission. There was no federal regulation of securities offerings — the Securities and Exchange Commission did not exist yet, and the federal securities laws had not yet been enacted. Regulation at the state level was either limited or non-existent, as well.

The 1929 crash and subsequent Great Depression provided the impetus for a public examination of the nation's securities markets and industry practices surrounding securities offerings. After reports of speculative and unscrupulous trading practices came to light, and in the wake of Congressional hearings that exposed corruption on Wall Street, the public clamored for action. Congress responded by passing the **Securities Act of 1933** ("the Securities Act," "the 1933 Act," or "the '33 Act"), also referred to as the "truth in securities" law. The following year, Congress enacted the **Securities Exchange Act of 1934** ("the Exchange Act," "the 1934 Act," or "the '34 Act"), which created the **Securities and Exchange Commission (SEC)**, an independent federal agency charged with investor protection and the promotion of fair and efficient capital markets, and given responsibility for rulemaking and other tasks related to the administration of the '33 and '34 Acts.

B. SECURITIES OFFERINGS AND THE SECURITIES ACT OF 1933

1. Definition of a Security

Registration of securities offerings is a fundamental tenet of the modern system of securities regulation. Under the Securities Act of 1933, all **securities** offered for sale in the United States must be **registered** with the SEC or must qualify for an **exemption** from registration. 15 U.S.C. §§ 77a et seq. Section 2(a)(1) of the Securities Act defines security as follows:

> (1) The term "security" means any note, stock, treasury stock, security future, security-based swap, bond, debenture, evidence of indebtedness, certificate of interest or participation in any profit-sharing agreement, collateral-trust certificate, preorganization certificate or subscription, transferable share, investment contract, voting-trust certificate, certificate of deposit for a security, fractional undivided interest in oil, gas, or other mineral rights, any put, call, straddle, option, or privilege on any security, certificate of deposit, or group or index of securities (including any interest therein or based on the value thereof), or any put, call, straddle, option, or privilege entered into on a national securities exchange relating to foreign currency, or, in general, any interest or instrument commonly known as a "security," or any certificate of interest or participation in, temporary or interim certificate for, receipt for, guarantee of, or warrant or right to subscribe to or purchase, any of the foregoing.

of the causes of the crash or the rumors of a bear run. He used the hearings as an opportunity to expose greed, corruption, and self-dealing on Wall Street. The high point of the hearings came when Pecora looked at the House of Morgan. Pecora's investigators turned up a "preferred list" of highly placed Americans allowed by J.P. Morgan and Company to buy low and sell high on insider information. The testimony of the powerful banker J.P. Morgan, Jr. also caused a public outcry after Morgan admitted that he and many of his partners had not paid any income taxes in 1931 and 1932. With the Pecora hearings fanning public outrage, it became possible for FDR to achieve his promise of financial reform: Congress enacted the Securities Act of 1933 and the Securities Exchange Act of 1934. We discuss the '33 and '34 Acts below.

Ferdinand Pecora, © Bettmann/CORBIS

Section 3(a)(10) of the Securities Exchange Act of 1934 includes a similar definition.

As this definition suggests, certain instruments automatically (or, almost automatically) qualify as a security under § 2(1) — e.g., stock, bonds, debentures, options, etc. Section 2(1) does not, however, limit the reach of the securities laws only to these familiar products. Instead, the definition contains several "catch-all" references designed to catch transactions and products that the issuer/seller might not denominate as a security, but which ought to be treated as such under applicable rules.

For example, both the Exchange Act and the Advisers Act define "security" to include an "investment contract." 15 U.S.C. §§ 78c(a)(10), 80b-2(a)(18). The Supreme Court has defined an investment contract broadly to include (1) an investment of money; (2) in a common enterprise; (3) with an expectation of profits to be derived solely from the efforts of others. *SEC v. W.J. Howey Co.*, 328 U.S. 293, 298-99 (1946). In deciding whether a product or transaction constitutes an investment contract under the *Howey* test, courts disregard form in favor of substance and focus on economic realities rather than the parties' usage. *See United Hous. Found., Inc. v. Forman*, 421 U.S. 837, 848 (1975). If an instrument, transaction, or scheme qualifies as a security under the *Howey* test, the issuer must comply with the federal securities laws (including any applicable registration requirements), whether or not the issuer calls the transaction, instrument, or scheme a security, and even if the issuer affirmatively represents that the offering does not constitute a security for purposes of the federal securities laws. Thus, while the typical securities offering scenario involves a corporation issuing **equity securities** (e.g., stock) or **debt securities** (e.g., bonds), *Howey* and its progeny make it clear that entities other than corporations can offer securities, and that instruments, transactions, and investment schemes other than stocks or bonds can qualify as securities under the federal securities laws.

Case Preview

Securities and Exchange Commission v. Mutual Benefits Corp.

Oftentimes, when the Securities and Exchange Commission brings an enforcement action alleging fraud in connection with the offer, purchase, or sale of an instrument, transaction, or investment scheme, the first line of defense for the defendant/respondent is that the SEC does not have jurisdiction because the product or investment scheme at issue is not a security. The following case examines whether a product known as a viatical life settlement is a security under the *Howey* test. A viatical life settlement refers to the sale of a policy owner's existing life insurance policy to a third party for more than its cash surrender value, but less than its net death benefit. The point of a viatical life settlement generally is to provide a chronically ill individual with needed cash to pay for medical expenses. The third party purchaser of the policy pays the premiums and receives the benefit when the original insured dies. When reading the case, consider the following questions:

1. What are the elements of the *Howey* test, according to the court?
2. Must a plaintiff prove that profits were derived "solely" from the efforts of others under the court's interpretation of the *Howey* test?
3. What is horizontal privity? What is vertical privity?
4. Does this court follow the holding of the D.C. Circuit in *SEC v. Life Partners*, 87 F.3d 536 (D.C. Cir. 1996), with respect to whether a viatical settlement is a security? Why or why not?

Securities and Exchange Commission v. Mutual Benefits Corp.
323 F. Supp. 2d 1337 (S.D. Fla. 2004)

MORENO, District Judge.*

Before the Court is an action commenced by the Securities and Exchange Commission for the violation of various federal securities regulations in the trade of life insurance policies of terminally ill people. Presently, the Court is called upon to decide whether the sale of these "viatical settlements" is beyond the scope of the federal securities laws. Specifically, Defendants contend that investments in viatical settlements are not investment contracts and as a result, the Securities and Exchange Commission has no jurisdiction to assert its claims. The Court here finds that, in light of the underlying principles of the federal securities laws, investments in viatical settlements are covered by the federal securities laws.

I. BACKGROUND

Defendant Mutual Benefit Corporation ("MBC") is a Florida corporation, formed in 1994 and located in Fort Lauderdale, Florida. Defendants Joel and Leslie Steinger are alleged principals of MBC. Defendant Peter Lombardi is president and sole shareholder of MBC.

. . .

A. Viatical Settlement Industry

A viatical settlement is a transaction in which a terminally or chronically ill insured ("viator") sells the benefits of his life insurance policy to a third party in return for a lump-sum cash payment equal to a percentage of the policy's face value. Viatical settlement providers purchase the policies from individual viators. Once purchased, these viatical settlement providers typically sell fractionalized interests in these policies to investors.

B. MBC's Activities

MBC is a viatical settlement provider.[2] MBC engages in both the procurement of viatical settlements and the sale of fractional interests in them to investors. Beginning in 1994 and extending to May, 2004, over 29,000 investors nationwide have invested over $1 billion in interests of viatical settlements offered by MBC. From the procurement of the settlements to the sale to investors, MBC undertook a number of activities.

With respect to the procurement of the viatical settlements, MBC located the policies, negotiated purchase prices, bid on policies, and obtained life expectancy evaluations of individual viators. In addition, it appears that MBC created the legal documents needed to conclude the transactions.

---

*Most footnotes have been omitted for purposes of brevity.

[2]MBC is also a life settlement provider. The only distinction between life settlements and viatical settlements is that in life settlements, the insured is not terminally or chronically ill. For purposes of this order, the Court does not distinguish between viatical and life settlements.

In order to sell the viatical settlements to investors, MBC solicited funds from investors directly and through agents. Investors were asked to identify a desired maturity date and submit a purchase agreement. MBC promised rates of return ranging from 12% to 72%. The rate of return was dependent upon the term of the investment, which was determined by the life expectancy evaluation. If the viator lives beyond his life expectancy, the term of the investment is extended and the premiums must either be paid from new investor funds assigned to other policies or by additional funds from the original investors.

Finally, following the placement of investor funds, MBC, through VSI, would pay the premiums, monitor the health of viators, collect the benefits upon death, and distribute the proceeds to investors.

C. SEC Enforcement

Plaintiff SEC filed its Complaint for Injunctive and Other Relief on May 3, 2004, alleging violations of various federal securities laws. . . .

II. LEGAL ANALYSIS

The narrow issue before the Court is whether investments in viatical settlements constitute securities. Defendants petition the Court to dismiss the present action because they argue such investments are not covered by the federal securities laws, and as a result, this Court lacks subject matter jurisdiction. After carefully reviewing the numerous pleadings from the parties and surveying the relevant statutory and jurisprudential sources on the topic of the definition of a security, the Court has come to the conclusion that investments in viatical settlements constitute investment contracts, and as such, fall under the coverage of the federal securities laws.

. . .

B. Historical Background of the Federal Securities Laws

From September 1, 1929 through the end of October of the same year, the aggregate value of stocks listed on the NYSE fell from $89 billion to $18 billion. Enacted in the early 1930's, the federal securities laws came in direct response to the stock market crash of late 1929 and the resulting depression that forged a political consensus in Congress to regulate securities. As noted by the Supreme Court, " '[i]t requires but little appreciation . . . of what happened in this country during the 1920's and 1930's to realize how essential it is that the highest ethical standards prevail' in every facet of the securities industry." *SEC v. Capital Gains Research Bureau*, 375 U.S. 180, 186, 84 S. Ct. 275, 11 L. Ed. 2d 237 (1963) (*quoting Silver v. New York Stock Exchange*, 373 U.S. 341, 366, 83 S. Ct. 1246, 10 L. Ed. 2d 389 (1963)). Underpinning the complicated statutory framework of the federal securities laws are two unifying principles, repeated time and again in numerous Supreme Court opinions, that serve to guide courts in interpreting the law's application. After a survey of the relevant case law, the Court has identified the principle of flexibility in the law's application and the principle of full disclosure in the law's remedial thrust.

First and foremost, the federal securities laws were drafted and have consistently been interpreted from the perspective that flexibility in the law's applicability is paramount. In its seminal case on the interpretation of the term "investment contract," the Supreme Court declared that Congress purposefully gave a broad definition to what constitutes a security. *SEC v. W.J. Howey Company*, 328 U.S. 293, 299, 66 S. Ct. 1100, 90 L. Ed. 1244 (1946) (warning that the "statutory policy of affording broad protection to investors is not to be thwarted by unrealistic and irrelevant formulae"); *see also Tcherepnin v. Knight*, 389 U.S. 332, 336, 88 S. Ct. 548, 19 L. Ed. 2d 564 (1967) (noting that "remedial legislation should be construed broadly to effectuate its purposes"), *Pinter v. Dahl*, 486 U.S. 622, 652, 108 S. Ct. 2063, 100 L. Ed. 2d 658 (1988). Moreover in *Reves v. Ernst & Young*, the Court explained that the securities laws should be interpreted "against the backdrop of what Congress was attempting to accomplish in enacting the Securities Acts." 494 U.S. 56, 63, 110 S. Ct. 945, 108 L. Ed. 2d 47 (1990). Through *Howey* and its progeny, the Supreme Court has consistently repeated the interpretive principle that courts should determine the contours of the term "security" from the posture that substance should be elevated over form, with a special sensitivity to the economic reality of the transaction, not its formal characteristics. *See Tcherepnin*, 389 U.S. at 336, 88 S. Ct. 548.

In addition to the principle of flexibility, the second unifying principle of the federal securities laws for courts to consider is the strong preference for full disclosure. Indeed, the remedial thrust of the federal securities laws is to establish full disclosure, not risk-free investment. *See SEC v. Capital Gains Research Bureau*, 375 U.S. 180, 186, 84 S. Ct. 275, 11 L. Ed. 2d 237 (1963) (holding that the primary purpose of the federal securities laws is to "substitute a philosophy of full disclosure for the philosophy of *caveat emptor*"); *see also Tcherepnin*, 389 U.S. at 336, 88 S. Ct. 548.

Prior to the adoption of the federal securities laws, there existed a divergence of opinion on the remedial goal of any securities regulation. The split of opinion was divided between those who sought to impose a merit standard on securities and those who preferred a disclosure requirement. Eventually, the disclosure philosophy gained political momentum and became the principle remedial thrust of the federal securities laws. An important advocate of the philosophy of full disclosure was Louis D. Brandeis, who wrote, in his seminal piece, *Other People's Money*, that "[s]unlight is said to be the best of disinfectants; electric light the most efficient policeman." Tempering the policies of flexibility and full disclosure, the Court recognizes that Congress did not aim to create a broad federal remedy for fraud. *Marine Bank v. Weaver*, 455 U.S. 551, 556, 102 S. Ct. 1220, 71 L. Ed. 2d 409 (1982).

C. *Defining the Scope of the Federal Securities Laws*

Under the Securities Act of 1933, Congress defined a "security" as including investment contracts. 15 U.S.C. § 77b(a)(1). The term "investment contract" was derived from various state legislation that predated the federal securities laws in what were called "blue sky laws." 1 L. Loss & J. Seligman, *Securities Regulation* 31-43 (3d ed. 1998). Indeed the first securities regulation in the nation began at the turn of the twentieth century with the enactment of the "blue sky laws."[6] Under these early state regulations, an investment contract was defined as a transaction that placed capital "in a way intended to secure income or profit from its employment." *State v. Gopher Tire & Rubber Co.,* 146 Minn. 52, 177 N.W. 937, 938 (1920).

Like the state legislatures that first attempted to regulate investment contracts under the "blue sky laws," Congress also refused to narrowly define the term "investment contract" in favor of offering great latitude to courts to "meet the countless and variable schemes devised by those who seek the use of money of others on the promise of profits." *Howey,* 328 U.S. at 299, 66 S. Ct. 1100. The Supreme Court in *Howey* set out the classic test for determining when a transaction is properly characterized as an investment contract that falls within the ambit of the federal securities laws. *See SEC v. Edwards,* 540 U.S. 389, 124 S. Ct. 892, 896, 157 L. Ed. 2d 813 (2004); *see also* Cristina Moreno, Comment, *Discretionary Accounts,* 32 Miami L. Rev. 401, 405 (1977). Moreover, the Eleventh Circuit has interpreted the *Howey* test to comprise the following three elements: (1) an investment of money; (2) a common enterprise; and (3) the expectation of profits derived solely from the efforts of others. *Unique Financial Concepts, Inc.,* 196 F.3d at 1199 (*citing Villeneuve v. Advanced Business Concepts Corp.,* 698 F.2d 1121, 1124 (11th Cir. 1983), *aff'd en banc,* 730 F.2d 1403 (11th Cir. 1984)).

Specifically, Defendants move the Court to dismiss the present action for lack of subject matter jurisdiction because investments in viatical settlements fail to meet the second and third elements of the test set forth in *Howey.*

1. Commonality

Defendants contend that investments in viatical settlements do not satisfy the second prong of *Howey,* requiring that the investment be in a common enterprise. Specifically, Defendants argue that "horizontal commonality" is not present in investments in viatical settlements because the necessary interdependency among investors is lacking.

The Court notes however that there exists a split among the circuits on the appropriate test for commonality. The Defendants cite the precedent from the Seventh Circuit in support of the more stringent requirement of "horizontal commonality." Defendants' Motion to Dismiss at 13 (*citing Wals v. Fox Hills Dev. Corp.,* 24 F.3d 1016 (7th Cir. 1994)). However, the Eleventh Circuit has adopted the test of "vertical commonality," which does not require the pooling of investor funds or the *pro rata* distribution of profits. *See Unique Financial Concepts,* 196 F.3d 1195, 1199 n.4 (11th Cir. 1999).

Under the vertical commonality standard, all that is required is for the success of the investors to be dependent on the success of the investment promoters' efforts to secure a return. *Id.* at 1200. Here, investors' return is highly dependent on MBC's efforts because the investors rely on MBC's skill in locating, negotiating, bidding, and evaluating policies. As a result, the Court finds that investments in viatical

---

[6]The term appears to have originated from the speculative schemes that these early laws intended to prevent that "had no more basis than so many feet of blue sky." *State v. Gopher Tire & Rubber Co.,* 146 Minn. 52, 177 N.W. 937, 938 (1920) (*citing Hall v. Geiger-Jones Co.* 242 U.S. 539, 550, 37 S. Ct. 217, 61 L. Ed. 480 (1917)).

settlements satisfy the commonality requirement of *Howey*, as interpreted by the Eleventh Circuit.

2. Expectation of Profits Derived Solely from the Efforts of Others

Defendants second and more substantial contention is that investments in viatical settlements do no[t] satisfy *Howey*'s third prong. On this issue, the Court holds that investments in viatical settlements satisfy the third prong of *Howey* that there be an expectation of profits derived solely from the efforts of others. In light of the principles informing the federal securities laws, repeated time and again by the Supreme Court, coupled with the nature of the relationship between the promoters and the investors in viatical settlements, the Court is convinced that the nature of the transaction is an investment contract.

(a) Promoters' efforts versus external market forces

In order to satisfy the third prong of *Howey*, investments must be substantively passive and depend on the "entrepreneurial or managerial efforts of others." *United Housing Foundation, Inc. v. Forman*, 421 U.S. 837, 852, 95 S. Ct. 2051, 44 L. Ed. 2d 621 (1975). The key determination is whether it is the promoters' efforts, not that of the investors, that form the "essential managerial efforts which affect the failure or success of the enterprise." *Unique Financial Concepts*, 196 F.3d at 1201 (*citing SEC v. Glenn W. Turner Enterprises, Inc.*, 474 F.2d 476, 482 (9th Cir. 1973)).

It is important to note that the original requirement that profits be derived "solely" from the efforts of others has been modified by later opinions to include only that the efforts of others be merely predominant. The Eleventh Circuit has adopted the view that the inquiry is "whether the efforts made by those other than the investor are the undeniably significant ones, those essential managerial efforts which affect the failure or success of the enterprise." *Unique Financial Concepts*, 196 F.3d at 1201 (adopting the reasoning of *SEC v. Koscot Interplanetary, Inc.*, 497 F.2d 473, 483 (5th Cir. 1974)).

Taken together, the case law seems to indicate that the key question for a court in assessing whether a transaction satisfies the third prong of *Howey* is to determine whether profits are derived from the activities of the promoter or rather, the operation of external market forces beyond the control of the promoter. The obvious reason for making such a distinction is because the securities laws disclosure requirements will only protect investments that depend on the efforts of promoters, not those that depend on the operation of external market forces. *See SEC v. G. Weeks Securities, Inc.*, 678 F.2d 649, 652 (6th Cir. 1982). Defendants here contend that with respect to investments in viatical settlements, profits are determined by the purely external force of the time of the viator's death.

Without question, the timing of the viator's death is of great consequence in the realization of the investors' profits. However, investors' profits are not determined by the timing of the viator's death. Rather, profits from investments in viatical settlements are determined by whether MBC's life expectancy evaluation is correct. Here, MBC located policies, evaluated viators' life expectancies, bid on policies, and negotiated the purchase price of policies. The profitability of investments in these viatical settlements is wholly determined by the efforts of the promoters in evaluating life expectancies. In investments in viatical settlements, the investor only chooses the desired term of investment. MBC matches the investors' funds with viators' policy whose life expectancies match the investors' desired term of investment. The longer a viator lives beyond his life expectancy, as evaluated by MBC, the lower the investors' profits. The investors plainly rely on MBC's life expectancy evaluations.

(b) *Life Partners'* bright-line rule

Defendants urge the Court to follow the D.C. Circuit opinion of *SEC v. Life Partners, Inc.,* 87 F.3d 536 (D.C. Cir. 1996), which created a bright-line rule that promoters' entrepreneurial and managerial efforts must occur post-purchase in order to satisfy the third prong of *Howey.* Of special import is the fact that *Life Partners* is the only federal appellate court to decide the issue of whether an investment in a viatical settlement is a security.

Nevertheless, the Court is uncomfortable with the bright-line rule enunciated by the D.C. Circuit and must decline Defendants' invitation to adopt a rule that is inconsistent with the policies underlying the federal securities laws and misconceives the nature of investments in viatical settlements.[9] Bright-line rules are discouraged in the context of federal securities laws for the reason that they tend to create loopholes that can be used by the clever and dishonest. Indeed, the bright-line rule enunciated in *Life Partners* created a loophole, which became the Defendants' corporate structure model. Anthony Livoti, trustee for MBC, testified in his deposition that the "attorneys of Mutual Benefits were cognizant of the SEC vs. Life Partners case." Livoti depo. at 12. Indeed counsel for MBC, Michael McNerney, testified at the evidentiary hearing that MBC attempted to restructure certain portions of their operations to conform to the D.C. Circuit's ruling in *Life Partners.* See also Livoti depo. at 12-13.

The Supreme Court gave the following rationale for the statutory and jurisprudential policy of flexibility in the context of determining the coverage of the federal securities laws:

> Such an approach has the corresponding advantage, though, of permitting the SEC and the courts sufficient flexibility to ensure that those who market investments are not able to escape the coverage of the Securities Acts by creating new instruments that would not be covered by a more determinate definition. *Reves,* 494 U.S. at 63 n.2, 110 S. Ct. 945.

Further, in arriving at its bright-line rule distinguishing between pre and post purchase activities, the D.C. Circuit relied heavily on the Ninth Circuit case of *Noa v. Key Futures, Inc.,* 638 F.2d 77 (1980). However, the investments in *Noa* appear factually dissimilar from investments in viatical settlements. *Noa* involved investments

---

[9]Although *Life Partners* is the only federal appellate decision on the issue, the Court notes that other courts have refused to follow *Life Partners*[.] *See, e.g., Wuliger v. Christie,* 310 F. Supp. 2d 897 (N.D. Ohio 2004) (rejecting the D.C. Circuit's analysis as unpersuasive).

in silver bars which the promoter had located, promised to store, and promised to repurchase at the published spot price. *Life Partners,* 87 F.3d at 546 (describing facts of *Noa v. Key Futures, Inc.,* 638 F.2d 77 (1980)). The Ninth Circuit found that the investments' profitability depended on the external market forces affecting the silver market. *Noa,* 638 F.2d at 79-80. Remarkably, the D.C. Circuit read into the holding of *Noa* implicit support for the irrelevance of pre-purchase efforts. *Life Partners,* 87 F.3d at 546. Indeed, a fair reading of *Noa* reveals no such distinction between pre and post-purchase activities.

Finally, at closing argument, Defendants advanced the position that rejecting the *Life Partners* approach and adopting a flexible interpretation of the definition of an investment contract would be the equivalent of this Court's substitution of its own will for that of Congress. The Court disagrees with Defendants' well-argued position. The Court rejects *Life Partners'* bright-line rule not out of a wish to substitute its will over that of Congress, but rather, in fidelity to the statutory and jurisprudential principles that underpin the federal securities laws. Informing the Court's decision is the Supreme Court's declaration that: "[o]ne could question whether, at the expense of the goal of clarity, Congress overvalued the goal of avoiding manipulation by the clever and dishonest. If Congress erred, however, it is for that body, and not this Court, to correct its mistake." *Reves,* 494 U.S. at 63 n.2, 110 S. Ct. 945. In light of the language of *Reves,* the Court must reject the bright-line rule laid down by judges in *Life Partners* in order to effectuate the mandate of Congress.

III. CONCLUSION

In holding that investments in viatical settlements constitute securities for purposes of the federal securities laws, the Court has endeavored to rule in accordance with the underpinning principles of the federal securities laws laid out by Congress and interpreted time and again by the highest court in the land, the Supreme Court. Essentially the inquiry turns on whether the profits from the investment are derived predominantly from the efforts of others. In light of the significant entrepreneurial and managerial efforts involved in locating, negotiating, and performing life expectancy evaluations, the Court is convinced that investments in viatical settlements constitute investment contracts under the classic standard set out in *Howey* and as a result, fall under the coverage of the federal securities laws. Accordingly, it is

ADJUDGED that Defendants' Motion to Dismiss for Lack of Subject Matter Jurisdiction (D.E. No. 100), filed on *June 3, 2004* is DENIED. Further, it is

ADJUDGED that pursuant to 28 U.S.C. § 1292(b), the Court hereby certifies that this order involves a controlling question of law as to which there is substantial ground for difference of opinion and that an immediate appeal from this order may materially advance the ultimate termination of the action.

Post-Case Follow-Up

On appeal, the Eleventh Circuit affirmed the district court's ruling, stating, in pertinent part, as follows:

> We decline to adopt the test established by the *Life Partners* court. We are not convinced that either *Howey* or *Edwards* require such a clean distinction between a promoter's activities prior to his having use of an investor's money and his activities thereafter. The rule set forth in *Howey* and reiterated in *Edwards* directs us to broadly apply the Security Acts of 1993 and 1994 to all "schemes devised by those who seek the use of the money of others on the promise of profits." *Howey*, 328 U.S. at 299, 66 S. Ct. at 1103; *see also Tcherepnin v. Knight*, 389 U.S. 332, 336, 88 S. Ct. 548, 553, 19 L. Ed. 2d 564 (1967) ("[I]n searching for the meaning and scope of the word 'security' in the Act[s], form should be disregarded for substance and the emphasis should be on economic reality.").
>
> While it may be true that the "solely on the efforts of the promoter or a third party" prong of the *Howey* test is more easily satisfied by post-purchase activities, there is no basis for excluding pre-purchase managerial activities from the analysis. *See Life Partners*, 87 F.3d at 551 (Wald, J., dissenting). Significant pre-purchase managerial activities undertaken to insure the success of the investment may also satisfy *Howey*. *See id.* Indeed, investment schemes may often involve a combination of both pre- and post-purchase managerial activities, both of which should be taken into consideration in determining whether *Howey*'s test is satisfied. Courts have found investment contracts where significant efforts included the pre-purchase exercise of expertise by promoters in selecting or negotiating the price of an asset in which investors would acquire an interest. *See Sec. & Exch. Comm'n v. Eurobond Exch., Ltd.,* 13 F.3d 1334 (9th Cir. 1994) (involving interests in foreign treasury bonds); *Gary Plastic Packaging Corp. v. Merrill Lynch, Inc.,* 756 F.2d 230 (2d Cir. 1985) (involving interests in certificate of deposit program); *Glen-Arden Commodities, Inc. v. Costantino,* 493 F.2d 1027 (2d Cir. 1974) (involving investments in warehouse receipts for whiskey).
>
> . . .
>
> MBC thus offered what amounts to a classic investment contract. Investors were offered and sold an investment in a common enterprise in which they were promised profits that were dependent on the efforts of the promoters. This is true regardless of which specific MBC purchase agreement form is at issue. Whether the investors were offered a longer or shorter window in which to withdraw funds from escrow, whether the life-expectancy evaluation was actually performed before or after closing, and despite certain differences in how premiums were paid, all investors here relied on the pre- and post-purchase managerial efforts of MBC to make a profit on the investment in viatical settlement contracts. The investors here relied on MBC to identify terminally ill insureds, negotiate purchase prices, pay premiums, and perform life expectancy evaluations critical to the success of the venture. The flexible test we are instructed to apply by *Howey* and *Edwards* covers these activities, qualifying MBC's viatical settlement contracts as "investment contracts" under the Securities Acts of 1933 and 1934.

SEC v. Mutual Benefits Corp., 408 F.3d 737, 743-46 (11th Cir. 2005).

In *Reves v. Ernst & Young*, 494 U.S. 56 (1990), the Supreme Court considered whether demand notes issued by a farmer's cooperative were securities within the meaning of § 3(a)(10) of the '34 Act. In concluding that the notes were securities, the Court adopted the so-called family resemblance approach used by the Second Circuit. The family resemblance approach begins with a presumption that any note with a term of more than nine months is a security within the meaning of the federal securities laws. The Second Circuit then developed a list of notes that it decided were not obviously securities. Under the Second Circuit's family resemblance test, an issuer could rebut the presumption that a note is a security if it can show that the note in question "bear[s] a strong family resemblance" to an item on the judicially crafted list of exceptions. *See, e.g., Chem. Bank v. Arthur Andersen & Co.,* 726 F.2d 930, 939 (2d Cir. 1984). *Reves* concluded that to determine whether an instrument denominated as a note is a security, courts are to apply the family resemblance test as refined by the Supreme Court. Under this test, an instrument denominated as a note is presumed to be a security, and that presumption may be rebutted only by a showing that the note bears a strong resemblance (in terms of four factors identified by the court) to one of the enumerated categories of instruments deemed not to constitute securities. The four factors call for a court to do the following: (i) examine the transaction to assess the motivations that would prompt a reasonable seller and buyer to enter into it (e.g., profit motive? intended use of proceeds?); (ii) examine the plan of distribution of the instrument (e.g., is there common trading for speculation?); (iii) examine the reasonable expectations of the investing public; and (iv) examine whether some factor such as the existence of another regulatory scheme significantly reduces the risk of the instrument, thereby rendering application of securities acts unnecessary.

Securities and Exchange Commission v. Mutual Benefits Corp.: Real Life Applications

1. You represent Zed Corp., a newly formed entity that seeks to develop a documentary film about immigration reform. Zed's founders are recent college graduates who currently work for advocacy organizations involved in immigration reform; while they have deep experience dealing with immigration reform efforts, they do not have the money to develop the film by themselves. Zed's founders would like to post a project to Kickstarter seeking potential funders. Kickstarter, a benefit corporation, states that its mission is to help artists, musicians, and creators find the resources they need to make their projects a reality. In exchange for pledges of money, Zed's creators offer to send funders a DVD of the documentary once it is complete. Is Zed offering to sell securities to potential investors in the project? (Hint: Take a look at the discussion of crowdfunding in Section B.4 below.)

2. Junior owns and operates a hardware store in upstate New York. At the beginning of the winter season, Junior purchased a large number of snow blowers on credit. Unfortunately for Junior, this winter has been very mild, with little if any snowfall. When the snow blowers did not sell, Junior fell behind on his bills. The business now owes the snow blower manufacturer $5,000. On January 1, 2016, Ray (the owner of the snow blower manufacturer) makes Junior sign a document styled as a "promissory note" with the following terms:

Principal amount due: $5,000
Maturity: Payment of principal and interest due on October 1, 2016
Interest rate: 15% per annum

Is the note a security? Why or why not?

2. Registration Requirements for Securities Offerings

For securities offerings required to be registered, an issuer must complete and file the form of **registration statement** provided by the SEC, namely Form S-1. See Exhibit 13.1 for an excerpt from Form S-1. Since 1993, registration forms must be filed electronically with the SEC through its **EDGAR** (Electronic Data Gathering, Analysis, and Retrieval) database. The main part (or Part I) of the registration statement is called the **prospectus**. It is this document that must be provided to any investors. The prospectus describes the securities being sold, provides background information about the issuing corporation and its directors and officers, and describes the investment so that all investors can fully evaluate the potential risks involved in purchasing the security.

The registration statement provides essential facts, including the following:

a. a description of the security offered for sale;
b. a description of the issuer's business and properties, as well as risk factors that might affect the offering;
c. a description of the management of the issuer;
d. intended use of the proceeds; and
e. financial statements audited by certified independent accountants.

Part II of the registration statement includes "additional information" about the company and the offering and remains on file with the SEC for public inspection.

Once the registration statement is filed electronically with the SEC (with the appropriate fee), it becomes a matter of public record. The SEC will respond to the registration statement in a "comment letter" within 30 days, and the company may be required to file clarifying amendments to its registration statement. The SEC does not evaluate the merits of offerings, or opine on whether purchasing the security being offered is a good idea (or not) for any individual investor; instead, the SEC merely declares registration statements "effective" when they are deemed to satisfy SEC disclosure rules.

The time between the filing of a registration statement until it is declared effective is called the "**quiet period**" or "**waiting period**." During this period, the federal securities laws limit what information a company and related parties can release to the public. For example, oral offers between interested investors and the issuer corporation may take place, although actual sales cannot occur. Limited advertising can also take place in the form of **tombstone ads**, called such because of the black border surrounding the advertisement. Tombstone ads (now often published electronically) merely announce that securities are being issued by a corporation;

| EXHIBIT 13.1 | **Excerpt, Form S-1** |

UNITED STATES
SECURITIES AND EXCHANGE COMMISSION
Washington, D.C. 20549

OMB APPROVAL	
OMB Number:	3235-0065
Expires:	March 31, 2018
Estimated average burden hours per response	.........972.32

FORM S-1
REGISTRATION STATEMENT UNDER THE SECURITIES ACT OF 1933

_____

(Exact name of registrant as specified in its charter)

_____

(State or other jurisdiction of incorporation or organization)

_____

(Primary Standard Industrial Classification Code Number)

_____

(I.R.S. Employer Identification Number)

_____

(Address, including zip code, and telephone number,
including area code, of registrant's principal executive offices)

_____

(Name, address, including zip code, and telephone number,
including area code, of agent for service)

_____

(Approximate date of commencement of proposed sale to the public)

If any of the securities being registered on this Form are to be offered on a delayed or continuous basis pursuant to Rule 415 under the Securities Act of 1933 check the following box: ☐

If this Form is filed to register additional securities for an offering pursuant to Rule 462(b) under the Securities Act, please check the following box and list the Securities Act registration statement number of the earlier effective registration statement for the same offering. ☐

If this Form is a post-effective amendment filed pursuant to Rule 462(c) under the Securities Act, check the following box and list the Securities Act registration statement number of the earlier effective registration statement for the same offering. ☐

If this Form is a post-effective amendment filed pursuant to Rule 462(d) under the Securities Act, check the following box and list the Securities Act registration statement number of the earlier effective registration statement for the same offering. ☐

Indicate by check mark whether the registrant is a large accelerated filer, an accelerated filer, a non-accelerated filer, or a smaller reporting company. See the definitions of "large accelerated filer," "accelerated filer" and "smaller reporting company" in Rule 12b-2 of the Exchange Act.

Large accelerated filer ☐   Accelerated filer ☐

Non-accelerated filer ☐ (Do not check if a smaller reporting company)   Smaller reporting company ☐

SEC 870 (01-16   Persons who are to respond to the collection of information contained in this form are not required to respond unless the form displays a currently valid OMB control number.

they are not considered prospectuses and thus need not comply with the '33 Act's registration requirements.

Exceeding the SEC's permissible forms of communications, called "**gun jumping**," is prohibited. Concerns about gun jumping can impact securities offerings. For example, in April 2004, approximately one week before Google Inc. filed its IPO registration statement with the SEC, the company's co-founders gave an interview to *Playboy* magazine. Four months later, the interview appeared in the magazine with the cover title *The Google Guys: America's Newest Billionaires*. While the SEC did not delay the much-anticipated IPO, Google included the text of the article as an appendix to the prospectus and, as a consequence, assumed prospectus liability for the article's contents under § 12 of the '33 Act. Perhaps mindful of the specter of prospectus liability, Google (and its lawyers) proceeded with care. After careful review of the article's text, Google appended an addendum correcting what it believed were factual inaccuracies. The company also included a risk factor in the prospectus, which disclosed that, while Google "would contest vigorously any claim that a violation of the Securities Act occurred," the company could be subject to rescission claims if its involvement in the *Playboy* article were held by a court to violate the Securities Act. After the effective date of the registration statement, a corporation can commence full-scale sales and promotional efforts.

3. Sales of Unregistered Securities

If a securities offering is required to be registered, but the issuer fails to do so, those who offer the securities for sale face the possibility of liability under the '33 Act. The SEC can prosecute issuers and sellers who sell unregistered, non-exempt securities under § 5 of the '33 Act. To prove a violation of § 5, the plaintiff must prove three elements: (1) an offer or sale of a security; (2) that was not registered pursuant to § 5 of the Securities Act (but was required to be registered); and (3) use by the sellers of the mail or other facilities of interstate commerce. Section 5 is a strict liability statute: It does not require proof of scienter (i.e., intent to deceive or defraud) but instead looks to whether without the defendant's participation, the transaction still would have taken place. Under § 20(b) of the '33 Act, the SEC can seek injunctions if the '33 Act has been violated or if a violation is imminent. As for private litigants, § 5 and § 12(a)(1) allow certain purchasers of unregistered non-exempt offerings to sue sellers. As long as the purchaser can prove a direct link between the purchaser and the seller, and the suit is within the statute of limitations, the purchaser may obtain rescission with interest, or damages if the investor sold his securities for less than he purchased them.

4. Exemptions from Registration for Securities Offerings

The exhaustive coverage of the '33 Act's requirements is moderated by a number of exemptions from registration. Generally speaking, these exemptions are intended to make it easier and less expensive for small businesses to raise capital while still ensuring some level of investor protection. To understand how the exemptions work, it is helpful to first distinguish between **public offerings** and **non-public** or **private offerings**, also known as **private placements**. This is because most public offerings do not qualify for the exemptions from registration discussed below.

Public Offerings

Although the term "public offering" is not defined in the securities laws, a corporation generally will be deemed to conduct a public offering if it sells its shares to members of the public at large. The first offering of the corporation's stock to the public is referred to as the **initial public offering** (IPO). There are many benefits to "going public" — issuers can raise capital, diversify their shareholder base, and generate publicity for their businesses. But, there are downsides (or, at least, responsibilities and consequences) associated with being a public company, too. The influx of new shareholders may result in a loss of control and power by existing shareholders. The costs of going public and complying with the various regulations imposed on public corporations are significant. Additionally, public corporations tend to be subject to more scrutiny compared to their privately held counterparts. For example, after a corporation goes public, the corporation's financial history and past and future financial performance will be open for inspection and discussion by the public due to SEC disclosure and reporting requirements. For all of these reasons, although many companies choose to "go public," some large, well-known corporations choose to remain privately held — for example, Mars, Inc., the candy maker, which has annual revenues of more than $75 billion and 75,000 employees, is a private company.

Non-public or Private Offerings

Traditionally, a non-public offering is an offering that is not made to the public at large. In the seminal 1953 case *SEC v. Ralston Purina Co.*, 346 U.S. 119 (1953) the Supreme Court examined what it means to conduct a private versus a public offering, citing the language and legislative intent behind the private offering exemption set forth in § 4(a)(2) of the '33 Act. The SEC later adopted and refined rules relating to offerings to help clarify when an offering is eligible for the § 4(a)(2) private offering exemption, shedding further light on the differences between public and private offerings. The SEC's rulemaking efforts culminated in the adoption of Rule 506 of Regulation D in 1982. Rule 506 (which is discussed below) serves as a safe harbor for § 4(a)(2), meaning that if an offering complies with the conditions set forth in Rule 506, the offering will be deemed a private offering that is eligible for the § 4(a)(2) exemption from registration.

With this background in mind, we will now examine exemptions from registration established by the '33 Act.

Exemptions for Certain Securities

The Securities Act provides that certain classes of securities are exempt from the registration requirements of the Act. Among them are securities issued by the

United States or state governments and banks, securities of nonprofit organizations, securities issued by savings and loan associations, and securities issued only to persons residing within a single state by a company organized in that state.

Exemptions for Limited Offerings Under Regulation D

The '33 Act also contains exemptions for limited offerings, or offerings involving smaller amounts of money or those made in a limited manner. In particular, under the SEC's Regulation D and Rules 504, 505, and 506 promulgated thereunder, there are three types of offerings that are exempt from the SEC registration requirements. The Regulation D exemptions are often referred to as "**private placement**" exemptions, with securities offered pursuant to these exemptions through so-called **private placement offerings** (PPO) or **private placement memorandum** (PPM), because these types of offerings do not involve offering securities to the public at large. In contrast to the filing and disclosure requirements applicable to public offerings, the only filing requirement under each of these exemptions is the requirement to file a notice on Form D (see Exhibit 13.2) with the SEC. The notice on Form D must be filed within 15 days after the first sale of securities in the offering. Many states also require the filing of a Form D notice in a Regulation D offering. The main purpose of the Form D filing is to notify federal (and state) authorities of the amount and nature of the offering being undertaken in reliance upon Regulation D.

The Regulation D exemptions generally distinguish between so-called accredited and non-accredited investors. An **accredited investor** is an individual with a net worth in excess of $1 million (excluding the value of the person's home) or yearly income in excess of $200,000 ($300,000 jointly with a spouse), banks, principals of the issuers, and other similarly sophisticated investors. A **non-accredited investor** is an investor who does not meet these net worth requirements. Accredited investors are presumed to be sufficiently knowledgeable (or, at least better able to withstand a financial loss), and thus better positioned to take on risks associated with offerings of this sort, which can be very risky.

Rule 504, sometimes referred to as the "seed capital exemption," permits an eligible issuer to sell securities in any 12-month period for a total price up to $1 million without registration. Under Rule 504, a corporation may offer and sell securities to an unlimited number of persons. There are no specific limits on the number of so-called non-accredited investors who may participate. The securities sold pursuant to Rule 504 are **restricted securities,** or securities issued in private offerings that must be held by purchasers for a certain period of time before they may be resold.

Traditionally, issuers were not permitted to use general solicitation or advertising (such as television, radio, or newspaper ads) to market securities offered under the Rule 504 exemption. And, purchasers of restricted securities were not permitted to sell them without SEC registration or using another exemption. A corporation may, however, use the Rule 504 exemption for a public offering of its securities with general solicitation and advertising, and investors will receive non-restricted securities, under one of the following circumstances:

EXHIBIT 13.2 **Excerpt, Form D**

FORM D	**U.S. Securities and Exchange Commission**	OMB APPROVAL
Notice of Exempt Offering of Securities	Washington, DC 20549	OMB Number: 3235-0076
	(See instructions beginning on page 5)	Expires: September 30, 2016

Intentional misstatements or omissions of fact constitute federal criminal violations. See 18 U.S.C. 1001.

Estimated average burden hours per response: 4.00

Item 1. Issuer's Identity

Name of Issuer

Jurisdiction of Incorporation/Organization

Previous Name(s) ☐ None

Entity Type (Select one)
- ☐ Corporation
- ☐ Limited Partnership
- ☐ Limited Liability Company
- ☐ General Partnership
- ☐ Business Trust
- ☐ Other (Specify)

Year of Incorporation/Organization (Select one)
- ○ Over Five Years Ago
- ○ Within Last Five Years (specify year)
- ○ Yet to Be Formed

(If more than one issuer is filing this notice, check this box ☐ and identify additional issuer(s) by attaching Items 1 and 2 Continuation Page(s).)

Item 2. Principal Place of Business and Contact Information

Street Address 1

Street Address 2

City

State/Province/Country

ZIP/Postal Code

Phone No.

Item 3. Related Persons

Last Name

First Name

Middle Name

Street Address 1

Street Address 2

City

State/Province/Country

ZIP/Postal Code

Relationship(s): ☐ Executive Officer ☐ Director ☐ Promoter

Clarification of Response (if necessary)

(Identify additional related persons by checking this box ☐ and attaching Item 3 Continuation Page(s).)

Item 4. Industry Group   (Select one)

- ○ **Agriculture**
- **Banking and Financial Services**
  - ○ Commercial Banking
  - ○ Insurance
  - ○ Investing
  - ○ Investment Banking
  - ○ Pooled Investment Fund

    If selecting this industry group, also select one fund type below and answer the question below:
  - ○ Hedge Fund
  - ○ Private Equity Fund
  - ○ Venture Capital Fund
  - ○ Other Investment Fund

    Is the issuer registered as an investment company under the Investment Company Act of 1940? ○ Yes ○ No
  - ○ Other Banking & Financial Services

- ○ **Business Services**
- **Energy**
  - ○ Electric Utilities
  - ○ Energy Conservation
  - ○ Coal Mining
  - ○ Environmental Services
  - ○ Oil & Gas
  - ○ Other Energy
- **Health Care**
  - ○ Biotechnology
  - ○ Health Insurance
  - ○ Hospitals & Physicians
  - ○ Pharmaceuticals
  - ○ Other Health Care
- ○ **Manufacturing**
- **Real Estate**
  - ○ Commercial

- ○ Construction
- ○ REITS & Finance
- ○ Residential
- ○ Other Real Estate
- ○ **Retailing**
- ○ **Restaurants**
- **Technology**
  - ○ Computers
  - ○ Telecommunications
  - ○ Other Technology
- **Travel**
  - ○ Airlines & Airports
  - ○ Lodging & Conventions
  - ○ Tourism & Travel Services
  - ○ Other Travel
- ○ **Other**

- It sells in accordance with a state law that requires the public filing and delivery to investors of a substantive disclosure document; or

- it sells in accordance with a state law that requires registration and disclosure document delivery and also sells in a state without those requirements, so long as the company delivers to all purchasers the disclosure documents mandated by a state in which it is registered; or

- it sells exclusively according to state law exemptions that permit general solicitation and advertising, so long as sales are made only to accredited investors.

Rule 505 exempts from registration offerings of less than $5 million in any 12-month period. Under this exemption, a corporation may sell to an unlimited number of accredited investors and up to 35 other persons who do not need to satisfy the sophistication or wealth standards associated with accredited investors. General advertising may not be used to sell the securities, and purchasers may not resell the securities for one year. Thus, these purchasers are buying for investment purposes and not for resale.

Under Rule 505, if the offering involves any purchasers who are not accredited investors, the issuer must give those purchasers disclosure documents that generally contain the same information as that which is included in a registration statement for a registered offering. There are also financial statement requirements that apply to Rule 505 offerings involving purchasers who are not accredited investors. For instance, if financial statements are required, they must be audited by a certified public accountant. The issuer may decide what information to give to accredited investors, so long as it does not violate the anti-fraud prohibitions of the federal securities laws. If the company provides information to accredited investors, it must make this information available to the non-accredited investors as well.

Rule 506 provides two different ways of conducting a securities offering that is exempt from registration: Rule 506(b) and Rule 506(c). Rule 506(b) is a longstanding rule. Rule 506(c) was added in 2013 to implement a statutory mandate under the Jumpstart Our Business Startups (JOBS) Act of 2012, passed to increase access by emerging growth companies to public capital markets.

Rule 506(b) is a "safe harbor" for the non-public offering exemption in § 4(a)(2) of the Securities Act, which means it provides specific requirements that, if followed, establish that the transaction falls within the § 4(a)(2) exemption. Rule 506 does not limit the amount of money a company can raise or the number of accredited investors it can sell securities to, but to qualify for the safe harbor, the issuing corporation must (i) not use general solicitation or advertising to market the securities; (ii) not sell securities to more than 35 non-accredited investors (unlike Rule 505, all non-accredited investors, either alone or with a purchaser representative, must meet the legal standard of having sufficient knowledge and experience in financial and business matters to be capable of evaluating the merits and risks of the prospective investment); (iii) give non-accredited investors specified disclosure documents that generally contain the same information as provided in registered offerings (the company is not required to provide specified disclosure documents to accredited investors, but, if it does provide information to accredited investors, it must also make this information available to the non-accredited investors); (iv) be available to answer questions from prospective purchasers who are non-accredited investors; and (v) provide the same financial statement information as required under Rule 505.

Rule 506(c) was implemented pursuant to § 201(a) of the JOBS Act to eliminate the prohibition on using general solicitation under Rule 506 for offerings meeting certain criteria. Specifically, under Rule 506(c), issuers may offer securities through means of general solicitation if (i) all purchasers in the offering are accredited investors; (ii) the issuer takes reasonable steps to verify their accredited investor status; and (iii) certain other conditions in Regulation D are satisfied.

Exemption for Small Entity Issuers Under Regulation A

Regulation A is a limited exemption from registration for certain public offerings, generally used by smaller companies or issuers in earlier stages of development. Securities in a Regulation A offering can be offered publicly, using general solicitation and advertising, and sold to purchasers irrespective of their status as accredited investors. Securities sold in a Regulation A offering are not considered "restricted securities" for purposes of aftermarket resales.

In March 2015, in order to implement § 401 of the JOBS Act (and to help newly developing companies raise funds more efficiently), the SEC amended Regulation A by creating two offering tiers: Tier 1, for offerings of up to $20 million in a 12-month period; and Tier 2, for offerings of up to $50 million in a 12-month period. For offerings of up to $20 million, companies can elect to proceed under the requirements for either Tier 1 or Tier 2. The amendments became effective on June 19, 2015. There are certain basic requirements applicable to both Tier 1 and Tier 2 offerings, including company eligibility requirements, bad actor disqualification provisions, disclosure, and other matters. Additional requirements apply to Tier 2 offerings, including limitations on the amount of money a non-accredited investor may invest in a Tier 2 offering, requirements for audited financial statements, and the filing of ongoing reports. As the Regulation A requirements associated with the JOBS Act are relatively new as of this writing, lawyers are well advised (as always) to work through them carefully before recommending or conducting a securities offering pursuant to this exemption.

Exemption for Intrastate Offerings

To facilitate the financing of local business operations, **intrastate offerings** (offerings only within one state) are also exempt from the registration and disclosure requirements of the '33 Act. This exemption applies only if the following conditions are met: (i) the issuer must be organized in and doing business in the state in which the offers and sales are made; and (ii) the offering may only be made to residents of that state. There is no limit on the size of the offering or the number of purchasers. Note, however, that although an intrastate offering is exempt from the registration requirements of the 1933 Act, it is likely to be subject to state securities laws and any registration and disclosure requirements arising under those laws.

Shelf Registrations

A **shelf registration** permits an issuer to file a registration statement for a new issue, which is prepared up to three years in advance of any sale of the securities. The securities may be offered on an immediate, continuous, or delayed basis. A shelf registration complies with SEC requirements beforehand and can then be "taken off the shelf" when the company needs funds or when market conditions are more favorable. Under SEC rules adopted in late 2005, the shelf registration process has been significantly streamlined. Companies that are defined as "well-known seasoned issuers" (which typically means a company that routinely files timely reports with the SEC and has at least $700 million in market value or has issued at least $1 billion in securities in the last three years) may use new "automatic" registration and have their registration statement become effective without SEC review, using their "core" or "base" prospectus (supplemented by more specific information following once details of the offering are known), thus permitting numerous offerings based on the same registration. About one-third of companies that offer their stock publicly fall into the category of "well-known seasoned issuers." Thus, issuers with proven track records may offer securities immediately after filing the shelf registration statement without waiting for SEC review. New shelf registrations must be filed every three years.

Crowdfunding

The JOBS Act required the SEC to develop new rules permitting capital raising by "**crowdfunding**." Crowdfunding is a means of raising money by attracting relatively small individual contributions from a large number of people. In recent years, crowdfunding websites have proliferated to raise funds for charities, artistic endeavors, and businesses. These sites did not, however, offer securities, such as an ownership interest or share of profits in a business (recall our real life application question in Section B.1); instead, money was contributed in the form of donations or in return for the product being made. The JOBS Act created an exemption from the registration requirements of the Securities Act that provides for a form of securities crowdfunding. In October 2015, the SEC — finally, some might say — adopted crowdfunding rules. We have summarized certain of these rules below, but once again urge students to take a course in securities regulation for a more detailed examination of these issues:

- *Limitation on capital raised.* An issuer is able to raise a maximum aggregate amount of $1 million through crowdfunding offerings over the course of a rolling 12-month period. Any amounts raised pursuant to other Securities Act exemptions during that period would not count toward this $1 million limit.
- *Limits on investment.* The aggregate amount of securities sold to any one investor during the 12-month period preceding the date of a transaction is capped at a specified level based on the annual income or net worth of the investor.
  - Investors with annual income or net worth of less than $100,000 are permitted to invest up to the greater of (i) $2,000 or (ii) 5 percent of the lesser of their annual income or net worth.

- Investors with both annual income and net worth equal to or more than $100,000 are permitted to invest up to 10 percent of the lesser of their annual income or net worth.
- During the 12-month period, the aggregate amount of securities sold to an investor through all crowdfunding offerings cannot exceed $100,000.

- *Issuer eligibility.* The crowdfunding exemption is not available to certain issuers, including foreign companies, companies that are subject to reporting requirements under the Exchange Act, certain investment companies, companies that are disqualified under the disqualification rules (modeled on the "bad actor" rules under Rule 506 of Regulation D), companies that have failed to comply with the annual reporting requirements during the two years immediately preceding the filing of the offering statement, and companies that have no specific business plan or have indicated their business plan is to engage in a merger or acquisition with an unidentified company or companies. So-called SPACs (special purpose acquisition companies) and other blind pool arrangements are excluded, as well.

- *Issuer disclosure requirements.* Issuers are required to provide disclosure, including financial information, to the SEC, investors, and the relevant brokers or funding portals. These disclosures are required to be filed with the SEC via EDGAR on new Form C.

- *Restrictions on resales.* The crowdfunding rules impose a one-year lock-up on the securities sold, subject to certain limited exceptions, including resales to the issuer, to an accredited investor, to a member of the family of the purchaser, or as part of a registered offering.

- *Crowdfunding platforms.* An offering of securities under Regulation Crowdfunding is required to be conducted through an intermediary — either a broker or a "**funding portal**." A "funding portal" is a new type of intermediary that performs limited functions in connection with the offer and sale of securities under the crowdfunding exemption.

- *Additional requirements for funding portals.* Funding portals are required to register with the SEC by filing a form ("Form Funding Portal") with information consistent with, but less extensive than, the information required for broker-dealers on Form BD. They are also required to be a member of FINRA (the Financial Industry Regulatory Authority) or any other national securities association registered under § 15A of the Exchange Act. They are, however, exempt from the requirement to register as a broker-dealer under the Exchange Act.

- *Limitation on advertising terms of offering.* Under the final rule, an issuer can publish a notice advertising the terms of an offering pursuant to the crowdfunding exemption and certain factual information about the issuer (similar to the "tombstone ads" permitted under Rule 134 of the Securities Act), provided that the notice includes the address of the intermediary's platform on which additional information about the issuer and the offering may be found. Other advertising is not permitted.

- *Liability.* Securities Act § 4A(c) provides that an issuer will be liable to a purchaser of its securities in a transaction exempted by § 4(a)(6) if the issuer, in the offer or sale of the securities, makes an untrue statement of a material fact or omits to state a material fact required to be stated or necessary in order to make the statements, in light of the circumstances under which they were made, not misleading, provided that the purchaser did not know of the untruth or omission, and the issuer does not sustain the burden of proof that such issuer did not know, and in the exercise of reasonable care could not have known, of the untruth or omission. In the adopting release, the SEC specifically declined to exempt funding portals (or any intermediaries) from the statutory liability provision of § 4A(c), or to interpret these rules as categorically excluding such intermediaries, and instead noted that the determination of "issuer" liability for an intermediary will turn on applicable facts and circumstances.

■ *Exemption from § 12(g).* Holders of securities offered pursuant to the crowd-funding exemption do not count toward the threshold number of holders that would require a company to register with the SEC under § 12(g) of the Exchange Act (discussed below) if the issuer is current in its annual reporting obligations, retains the services of a registered transfer agent, and has less than $25 million in total assets at the end of its most recently completed fiscal year. The crowdfunding rules are meant to provide smaller companies with innovative ways to raise capital and yet still give investors the protections they need. Some experts have expressed concerns, however, that the requirements imposed on these issuers under crowdfunding rules may make it difficult for newer or smaller entities to take advantage of this fundraising vehicle.

Direct Public Offerings

Some company offerings that are exempt from registration requirements are called "**direct public offerings**" (in contrast to "initial public offerings") because shares are offered directly to prospective investors, bypassing the traditional underwriting process used in an IPO. Because there is no underwriting investment bank to serve as a "gatekeeper" that conducts due diligence and provides research, the issuer itself retains sole liability for misrepresentations. In many cases, money is raised from a company's employees, suppliers, and its principals' friends, similar to crowdfunding.

Exemption for Non-Issuers

As noted above, the registration requirements of the '33 Act apply to every sale of securities unless there is an exemption from registration. What about small investors who ask their brokers to sell their shares of stock in a company such as Ford Motor Company? The '33 Act provides an exemption for transactions by any person who is not an issuer, underwriter, or dealer. Because individual investors are not issuers (such as Ford), underwriters (those who assist Ford in selling its shares to the public), or **dealers** (those engaged in the business of selling securities), they may freely resell their shares without any registration.

Going Private

On occasion, a company might "**go private**," or move from public ownership to private ownership. Dell Inc. went private in late 2013 after all of its outstanding shares were purchased by its founder Michael Dell and another investor. Michael Dell has stated that going private has allowed the company to focus first on long-term corporate strategy and innovation rather than satisfying short-term shareholder demands for quarterly profit increases, which was the case when Dell was a public company. Similarly, H.J. Heinz Co. went private in 2013, with its shares purchased by Warren Buffet's Berkshire Hathaway and another investment company for $27.5 billion.

5. Anti-Fraud Provisions of the 1933 Act

Section 17(a) of the '33 Act is a broad anti-fraud provision, and it is designed to protect investors from fraud, deceit, material misrepresentations and omissions, half-truths, and so forth in the offer and sale of securities. Section 17(a) states, in pertinent part, as follows:

> (a) It shall be unlawful for any person in the offer or sale of any securities (including security-based swaps) or any security-based swap agreement (as defined in section 3(a)(78) of the Securities Exchange Act) by the use of any means or instruments of transportation or communication in interstate commerce or by use of the mails, directly or indirectly —
>> (1) to employ any device, scheme, or artifice to defraud, or
>> (2) to obtain money or property by means of any untrue statement of a material fact or any omission to state a material fact necessary in order to make the statements made, in light of the circumstances under which they were made, not misleading; or
>> (3) to engage in any transaction, practice, or course of business which operates or would operate as a fraud or deceit upon the purchaser.

Unlike § 5, which imposes liability on issuers and other sellers for sales of unregistered non-exempt securities, § 17(a) applies to *any* offer or sale of securities — whether public or private, exempt or non-exempt, and regardless of the size of the offering. The only jurisdictional hook is the requirement that the violators must have used the mails or interstate commerce instrumentalities. The SEC has the power to investigate and bring actions against violators of the '33 Act and may also impose fines. Criminal violations (which might trigger fines or imprisonment) are referred to the Department of Justice for prosecution. Aggrieved investors or shareholders may also bring actions under certain of the anti-fraud provisions of the '33 Act. Note that § 17(a)(1) requires proof of scienter, or intent to deceive or defraud, whereas § 17(a)(2) and (a)(3) do not. *See Aaron v. SEC*, 446 U.S. 680 (1980) (scienter not required for subsections (a)(2) and (a)(3) of § 17); *accord Design Time, Inc. v. Synthetic Diamond Tech., Inc.*, 674 F. Supp. 1564 (N.D. Ind. 1987). (Note: We discuss scienter in the context of § 10(b) of the '34 Act and Rule 10b-5 promulgated thereunder below. As a general rule, the same principles of law apply to scienter in the context of § 17(a)(1) of the '33 Act.)

In addition to § 17(a), Section 11 of the '33 Act gives purchasers a right of action against the issuer and designated individuals (directors, partners, underwriters, and so forth) for material misstatements or omissions in registration statements. 15 U.S.C. § 77k(a). This section provides, in pertinent part, as follows:

> In case any part of the registration statement, when such part became effective, contained an untrue statement of a material fact or omitted to state a material fact required to be stated therein or necessary to make the statements therein not misleading, any person acquiring such security . . . [may] sue.

Unlike § 17(a)(1), the buyer need not prove that the defendant acted with scienter, or an intent to deceive or defraud, to sustain a claim under § 11. *Herman & MacLean v. Huddleston*, 459 U.S. 375, 381-82 (1983).

Section 12(a)(2) of the '33 Act creates liability for any person who offers or sells a security by means of a prospectus or oral communication that includes a material misstatement or omission. 15 U.S.C § 77l(a)(2). The Supreme Court has interpreted § 12(a)(2) to contemplate a "buyer-seller relationship not unlike traditional contractual privity." *Pinter v. Dahl*, 486 U.S. 622, 642 (1988). Liability extends only to the "immediate sellers" of securities and "those who solicit purchasers to serve their own financial interests or those of the securities owner." *Me. State Ret. Sys. v. Countrywide Fin. Corp.*, No. 2:10-CV-0302 MRP, 2011 WL 4389689, at *9 (C.D. Cal. May 5, 2011) (citations omitted). Section 12(a)(2) "imposes liability without requiring proof of either fraud or reliance." *In re WorldCom, Inc. Sec. Litig.*, 346 F. Supp. 2d 628, 659 (S.D.N.Y. 2004).

Section 15 of the '33 Act creates liability for control persons for violations of the securities law by the controlled entity. To make out a claim for control-person liability under § 15 of the Securities Act, plaintiffs must allege "(a) a primary violation by a controlled person, and (b) control by the defendant of the primary violator." *In re Global Crossing, Ltd. Secs. Litig.*, No. 02 Civ. 910, 2005 WL 2990646, at *7 (S.D.N.Y. Nov. 7, 2005). Control entails "'the power to direct or cause the direction of the management and policies of a person, whether through the ownership of voting securities, by contract, or otherwise.'" *SEC v. First Jersey Sec., Inc.*, 101 F.3d 1450, 1472-73 (2d Cir. 1996) (quoting 17 C.F.R. § 240.12b-2). To prevail on a § 15 claim, "[a] plaintiff is required to prove actual control, not merely control person status." *In re IPO Sec. Litig.*, 241 F. Supp. 2d 281, 352 (S.D.N.Y. 2003) (emphasis omitted).

Historically, many of the SEC's high-profile enforcement actions under the anti-fraud provisions of the '33 and '34 Acts (discussed below) have involved publicly traded companies. Recently, however, SEC Chair Mary Jo White reminded market participants that the SEC is concerned about the private markets as well, especially with regard to "**unicorns**," private start-up firms with valuations that exceed $1 billion. In a March 2016 speech, SEC Chair Mary Jo White cited a study that estimated that there were more than 50 unicorn financings in the last three quarters of 2015. White emphasized that the SEC's challenge is to ensure, as it does with all transactions, that the information supplied to investors (including employees of the unicorns, who are often paid in stock and options) is accurate and complete. The SEC has wide-ranging authority under anti-fraud rules, including Section 17(a) of the '33 Act and Section 10(b) and Rule 10b-5 of the '34 Act (discussed below), to combat fraud in public and private securities transactions. Thus, with unicorns, the concern is to determine whether the prestige associated with reaching sky-high valuations drives unicorns to try to appear more valuable than they actually are. This pressure is similar to that encountered by public companies to meet projections they make to the market, with the attendant risk of financial reporting irregularities and problems. Because the risk of distortion and inaccuracy is amplified with start-up companies, which typically have limited operating histories and far less robust internal controls and governance procedures than most public companies, White signaled that the SEC intends to exercise oversight to ensure that the unicorns do not manipulate their accounting and financial reporting practices to meet investors' expectations and projections.

At the time of writing, Theranos, Inc., a well-known Silicon Valley unicorn, has been in the news due to questions surrounding the company's technology, lab practices, and disclosures to investors. Theranos purports to have developed a new type of blood testing technology that allows users to perform a range of medical tests using only a few drops drawn from the patient's finger, at a fraction of the cost of conventional blood tests. Press reports have raised questions about Theranos's claims, and various federal and state agencies reportedly have launched probes into Theranos's technology and its disclosures to investors and government officials. Theranos has denied wrongdoing, and has said that it will cooperate fully with these investigations. Nevertheless, Theranos's recent troubles serve as a sobering reminder of the importance of ensuring that information supplied to investors and potential investors is accurate and complete, whether the company in question is publicly traded or privately held but funded by investors eager to find the next unicorn.

The '33 Act does, of course, contain defenses to liability. For example, because a host of individuals will be involved in the preparation of the registration statement, and not all of them will have access to all pertinent information, persons (other than the issuer) are not liable for certain misstatements or omissions if they can prove they conducted **due diligence** in preparing the statement; that is, they conducted a reasonable investigation and had reasonable grounds to believe the statement at issue was true and accurate and did not know (or have reason to know) of the alleged misstatement or omission. *See, e.g., In re WorldCom, Inc. Sec. Litig.*, 346 F. Supp. 2d at 660 (quoting *Royal Am. Managers, Inc. v. IRC Holding Corp.*, 885 F.2d 1011, 1019 (2d Cir. 1989)) ("No liability lies under section 12(2) where the defendant did not know, and in the exercise of reasonable care could not have known, of [the alleged] untruth or omission.") (citation and internal quotation marks omitted).

C. SECONDARY TRADING AND THE REGULATION OF MARKETS AND SECURITIES INDUSTRY PROFESSIONALS UNDER THE SECURITIES EXCHANGE ACT OF 1934

1. Introduction

Whereas the '33 Act is concerned with the initial offering of securities, the **Securities Exchange Act of 1934** (15 U.S.C. §§ 78a et seq.) ("the Exchange Act" or "the '34 Act") focuses on the distribution of securities after their initial issuance and the reporting of information by publicly held companies. The '34 Act also provides for the regulation and registration of those involved in the sale and trading of securities such as brokers, dealers, and exchanges. Additionally, the '34 Act created the SEC and authorizes it to investigate fraud, manipulation, and other undesirable trading practices in the market.

2. Registration and Exemptions Under the '34 Act

Unless an exemption exists, a company is required to register securities under § 12 of the Exchange Act if (i) the securities are listed on a national exchange, such as the New York Stock Exchange; (ii) the company has total assets of $10 million or more and a class of equity securities held of record by (a) 2,000 or more persons or (b) 500 or more persons who are not accredited investors (increased from a previous strict limit of 500 shareholders pursuant to the JOBS Act); or (iii) the company has filed a registration statement under the Securities Act that became effective. *See* Exchange Act § 12(b). For purposes of determining numbers of shareholders, employees who receive their shares pursuant to an employee compensation plan or those who receive their shares through crowdfunding are not "counted" against the threshold limit. Companies that are required to register securities under these provisions are often called **Section 12 companies**, **registered companies**, or **reporting companies**. For example, well-known companies such as McDonald's, Coca-Cola Company, General Electric, and FedEx are § 12 companies subject to compliance with the registration and disclosure requirements of the '34 Act. The JOBS Act's increase of the 500 shareholder limit (to 2,000 shareholders) was intended to allow smaller companies to raise capital without facing the burdens and costs of going public.

The registration statement required of § 12 companies under the 1934 Act is similar to that required under the 1933 Act. The statement (Form 10) is filed with the appropriate exchange and with the SEC. See Exhibit 13.3 below. It includes information about the corporation, the securities offered, the financial structure and finances of the business, management of the issuer, executive compensation, and so forth. Registration is generally effective 60 days after filing the application. The registration under the 1933 Act is done prior to offering securities for sale. The registration under the 1934 Act is primarily for reporting purposes.

 **Excerpt, Form 10**

OMB APPROVAL	
OMB Number:	3235-0064
Expires:	May 31, 2017
Estimated average burden hours per response. 215	

UNITED STATES
SECURITIES AND EXCHANGE COMMISSION
Washington, D.C. 20549

FORM 10

GENERAL FORM FOR REGISTRATION OF SECURITIES
Pursuant to Section 12(b) or (g) of The Securities Exchange Act of 1934

_____

(Exact name of registrant as specified in its charter)

_____

(State or other jurisdiction of incorporation or organization)   (I.R.S. Employer Identification No.)

_____

(Address of principal executive offices)   (Zip Code)

Registrant's telephone number, including area code _____

Securities to be registered pursuant to Section 12(b) of the Act:

Title of each class   Name of each exchange on which
to be so registered   each class is to be registered

_____   _____

_____   _____

Securities to be registered pursuant to Section 12(g) of the Act:

_____

(Title of class)

_____

(Title of class)

Indicate by check mark whether the registrant is a large accelerated filer, an accelerated filer, a non-accelerated filer, or a smaller reporting company. See the definitions of "large accelerated filer," "accelerated filer" and "smaller reporting company" in Rule 12b-2 of the Exchange Act.

Large accelerated filer ☐   Accelerated filer ☐
Non-accelerated filer ☐ (Do not check if a smaller reporting company)   Smaller reporting company ☐

 SEC 1396 (02-08)

EDGAR and Access to Corporate Filings

Registration statements, periodic reports and event-driven reports including those on Forms 8-K, 10-Q, and 10-K, and other forms are all available on EDGAR for public review for both domestic and foreign companies. The EDGAR system collects, indexes, and accepts submissions by companies that are required by law to file various materials with the SEC. Companies that must submit documents to the SEC must submit them electronically to the EDGAR system in a specialized format. The process is generally called "Edgarizing" a document. Generally, documents are available for public review within minutes after they are filed on ED-GAR. To access a company's filings, one may use the company's name, **ticker symbol**, or a unique identifier assigned to companies by the SEC, called a Central Index Key Number or CIK. A ticker symbol is the letters that identify a security for trading purposes — for example, the ticker symbol of Facebook, Inc. is FB. It is possible to limit search results by date to request documents filed after a certain date or to limit results by types of filings, so as to access only a Form 10-K, for example. In addition to EDGAR, public companies also have a section of their website devoted to investor relations. Oftentimes, corporations post SEC filings, press releases, earnings information, and other documents relevant to investors and potential investors there, as well.

3. Periodic and Event-Driven Reporting Requirements

Section 12 reporting companies must file a variety of reports with the SEC. These include periodic reports, annual reports, quarterly reports, and certain event-driven reports. Falsification of reports can result in the imposition of criminal penalties. The SEC typically allows smaller reporting companies to use simplified reports and to have additional time to file various reports. Larger companies are subject to stricter reporting requirements.

Form 8-K, often called a **current report**, is used to report the occurrence of any material events or corporate changes that are of importance to investors or security holders and that have previously not been reported by the registrant. Thus, a merger, bankruptcy, or resignation of a director would be reported on Form 8-K. Reforms have increased the number and type of events required to be reported and also shortened the time period for reporting.

Form 10-Q is a quarterly report. It includes unaudited financial statements and provides a continuing view of the company's financial position, quarter by quarter, over the course of the year. The report must be filed for each of the three fiscal quarters of the company's fiscal year and is due within 40 days of the close of the quarter for large accelerated filers (companies with a worldwide market value or "public float" of $700 million or more) and accelerated filers (companies that have at least $75 million but less than $700 million in public float) or 45 days of the close of the quarter for all other filers. The fourth quarterly report is subsumed into the annual report on Form 10-K. "Smaller reporting companies" (those with less than $75 million in public float or annual revenues of less than $50 million) use a more simplified disclosure. More than 45 percent of reporting companies are eligible for these simplified disclosure reports.

Form 10-K is the annual report filed with the SEC. It must include audited financial statements and comprehensive information about the company, its management, and its securities, as well as disclosure of the identity and compensation for directors and highly compensated executives, and a complete management discussion and analysis of the company's financial condition. This annual report must be filed within 60 days after the end of the company's fiscal year for large accelerated filers, 75 days for accelerated filers, and 90 days for all other filers. Smaller reporting companies use a simplified disclosure. Form 10-K is different from the annual report to shareholders that a company sends to its shareholders when it holds its annual shareholders' meeting.

4. Event-Driven Reporting, Internal Controls, and Certification Requirements Under Sarbanes-Oxley

The **Sarbanes-Oxley Act of 2002** (SOX) was enacted in the wake of accounting frauds uncovered at several well-known (and formerly high-flying companies), including the energy company Enron and the telecommunications company World-Com. Among other provisions, SOX reformed requirements respecting the content, timing, and accuracy and reliability of reports filed on Forms 10-K, 10-Q, and 8-K.

Internal Controls Reporting

Section 404 (and rules promulgated thereunder) is one of SOX's most well-known reforms. It requires covered firms to include an internal controls report in their annual reports on Form 10-K that "state[s] the responsibility of management for establishing and maintaining an adequate internal control structure and procedures for financial reporting" and that contains "an assessment . . . of the effectiveness of the internal control structure and procedures of the issuer for financial reporting." In addition, SOX § 404(b) requires auditors to "attest to, and report on, the assessment made by management of the issuer." See Exhibit 13.4 for an example of such a report by Apple Inc.

EXHIBIT 13.4	**Excerpt from Annual Report on Form 10-K for Apple Inc. for Fiscal Year Ended September 26, 2015**

Evaluation of Disclosure Controls and Procedures

Based on an evaluation under the supervision and with the participation of the Company's management, the Company's principal executive officer and principal financial officer have concluded that the Company's disclosure controls and procedures as defined in Rules 13a-15(e) and 15d-15(e) under the Securities Exchange Act of 1934, as amended (the "Exchange Act") were effective as of September 26, 2015 to provide reasonable assurance that information required to be disclosed by the Company in reports that it files or submits under the Exchange Act is (i) recorded, processed, summarized and reported within the time periods specified in the Securities and Exchange Commission rules and forms and (ii) accumulated and communicated to the Company's management, including its principal executive officer and principal financial officer, as appropriate to allow timely decisions regarding required disclosure.

Inherent Limitations over Internal Controls

The Company's internal control over financial reporting is designed to provide reasonable assurance regarding the reliability of financial reporting and the preparation of financial statements for external purposes in accordance with U.S. generally accepted accounting principles ("GAAP"). The Company's internal control over financial reporting includes those policies and procedures that:

(i)   pertain to the maintenance of records that, in reasonable detail, accurately and fairly reflect the transactions and dispositions of the Company's assets;

(ii)   provide reasonable assurance that transactions are recorded as necessary to permit preparation of financial statements in accordance with GAAP, and that the Company's receipts and expenditures are being made only in accordance with authorizations of the Company's management and directors; and

(iii) provide reasonable assurance regarding prevention or timely detection of unauthorized acquisition, use, or disposition of the Company's assets that could have a material effect on the financial statements.

Management, including the Company's Chief Executive Officer and Chief Financial Officer, does not expect that the Company's internal controls will prevent or detect all errors and all fraud. A control system, no matter how well designed and operated, can provide only reasonable, not absolute, assurance that the objectives of the control system are met. Further, the design of a control system must reflect the fact that there are resource constraints, and the benefits of controls must be considered relative to their costs. Because of the inherent limitations in all control systems, no evaluation of internal controls can provide absolute assurance that all control issues and instances of fraud, if any, have been detected. Also, any evaluation of the effectiveness of controls in future periods are subject to the risk that those internal controls may become inadequate because of changes in business conditions, or that the degree of compliance with the policies or procedures may deteriorate.

Management's Annual Report on Internal Control over Financial Reporting

The Company's management is responsible for establishing and maintaining adequate internal control over financial reporting (as defined in Rule 13a-15(f) under the Exchange Act). Management conducted an assessment of the effectiveness of the Company's internal control over financial reporting based on the criteria set forth in Internal Control—Integrated Framework issued by the Committee of Sponsoring Organizations of the Treadway Commission (2013 framework). Based on the Company's assessment, management has concluded that its internal control over financial reporting was effective as of September 26, 2015 to provide reasonable assurance regarding the reliability of financial reporting and the preparation of financial statements in accordance with GAAP. The Company's independent registered public accounting firm, Ernst & Young LLP, has issued an audit report on the Company's internal control over financial reporting, which appears in Part II, Item 8 of this Form 10-K.

Changes in Internal Control over Financial Reporting

There were no changes in the Company's internal control over financial reporting during the fourth quarter of 2015, which were identified in connection with management's evaluation required by paragraph (d) of rules 13a-15 and 15d-15 under the Exchange Act, that have materially affected, or are reasonably likely to materially affect, the Company's internal control over financial reporting.

The biggest criticism of § 404 relates to cost — businesses (especially smaller businesses) have argued that complying with § 404 is enormously expensive. Responding to these criticisms, the Dodd-Frank Wall Street Reform and Consumer Protection Act permanently exempted certain entities (namely, smaller reporting companies) from compliance with § 404(b).

Enhanced, and More Timely, Disclosure on Form 8-K

SOX also enhanced reporting requirements associated with reports on Form 8-K. In particular, SOX § 409 requires public companies to "disclose to the public on a rapid and current basis such additional information concerning material changes in the financial condition or operations of the issuer . . . as the [SEC] determines, by rule, is necessary or useful for the protection of investors and in the public interest." Through SOX-related rulemaking, the SEC added to the list of events that trigger an obligation to file a report on Form 8-K and decreased the deadline for filing an 8-K. For example, one such amendment requires covered companies to disclose their entry into or material amendment of a material definitive agreement not made in the ordinary course of business.

Certifications: Reliability and Accuracy of Corporate Disclosures

SOX also contains a number of provisions that speak to the reliability and accuracy of corporate disclosures. In particular, § 302 requires senior officers to certify in each report submitted on Forms 10-K and 10-Q that (i) the report is free of material misstatements of fact or materially misleading omissions; and (ii) the report fairly presents the financial condition and results of operations of the company. Covered officers also must certify that they are responsible for establishing and maintaining the company's internal controls, have evaluated these controls, and have reported to the company's auditor and audit committee all significant deficiencies in the design or operation of these controls. This provision carries with it the possibility of personal liability for certifiers, including fines and jail time. See Exhibits 13.5 and 13.6 for examples of such certifications by Apple Inc.

Other SOX Reforms

As noted in Chapter 9, SOX also included a number of other important reforms relating to corporate governance, including (i) the creation of the Public Company Accounting Oversight Board; (ii) reforms relating to auditor independence; (iii) rules relating to stock transactions by company insiders; (iv) rules prohibiting investment staff from supervising the work of research analysts; (v) rules relating to the independence of audit committee members; (vi) rules requiring enhanced SEC review of certain corporate filings; and (vii) additional or enhanced sanctions for certain violations of the federal securities laws. Section 10(b) of the '34 Act and Rule 10b-5.

EXHIBIT 13.5 | # Section 302 Certification, Excerpt from Annual Report on Form 10-K of Apple Inc. for Fiscal Year Ended September 26, 2015

Exhibit 31.1

CERTIFICATION

I, Timothy D. Cook, certify that:

1. I have reviewed this annual report on Form 10-K of Apple Inc.;

2. Based on my knowledge, this report does not contain any untrue statement of a material fact or omit to state a material fact necessary to make the statements made, in light of the circumstances under which such statements were made, not misleading with respect to the period covered by this report;

3. Based on my knowledge, the financial statements, and other financial information included in this report, fairly present in all material respects the financial condition, results of operations and cash flows of the Registrant as of, and for, the periods presented in this report;

4. The Registrant's other certifying officer(s) and I are responsible for establishing and maintaining disclosure controls and procedures (as defined in Exchange Act Rules 13a-15(e) and 15d-15(e)) and internal control over financial reporting (as defined in Exchange Act Rules 13a-15(f) and 15d-15(f)) for the Registrant and have:

    (a) Designed such disclosure controls and procedures, or caused such disclosure controls and procedures to be designed under our supervision, to ensure that material information relating to the Registrant, including its consolidated subsidiaries, is made known to us by others within those entities, particularly during the period in which this report is being prepared;

    (b) Designed such internal control over financial reporting, or caused such internal control over financial reporting to be designed under our supervision, to provide reasonable assurance regarding the reliability of financial reporting and the preparation of financial statements for external purposes in accordance with generally accepted accounting principles;

    (c) Evaluated the effectiveness of the Registrant's disclosure controls and procedures and presented in this report our conclusions about the effectiveness of the disclosure controls and procedures, as of the end of the period covered by this report based on such evaluation; and

    (d) Disclosed in this report any change in the Registrant's internal control over financial reporting that occurred during the Registrant's most recent fiscal quarter (the Registrant's fourth fiscal quarter in the case of an annual report) that has materially affected, or is reasonably likely to materially affect, the Registrant's internal control over financial reporting; and

5. The Registrant's other certifying officer(s) and I have disclosed, based on our most recent evaluation of internal control over financial reporting, to the Registrant's auditors and the audit committee of the Registrant's board of directors (or persons performing the equivalent functions):

    (a) All significant deficiencies and material weaknesses in the design or operation of internal control over financial reporting which are reasonably likely to adversely affect the Registrant's ability to record, process, summarize, and report financial information; and

    (b) Any fraud, whether or not material, that involves management or other employees who have a significant role in the Registrant's internal control over financial reporting.

Date: October 28, 2015

By: /s/ Timothy D. Cook
_____
Timothy D. Cook
Chief Executive Officer

EXHIBIT 13.6 | # Section 906 Certification, Excerpt from Annual Report on Form 10-K of Apple Inc. for Fiscal Year Ended September 26, 2015

Exhibit 32.1

CERTIFICATIONS OF CHIEF EXECUTIVE OFFICER AND CHIEF FINANCIAL OFFICER
PURSUANT TO
18 U.S.C. SECTION 1350,
AS ADOPTED PURSUANT TO
SECTION 906 OF THE SARBANES-OXLEY ACT OF 2002

I, Timothy D. Cook, certify, as of the date hereof, pursuant to 18 U.S.C. Section 1350, as adopted pursuant to Section 906 of the Sarbanes-Oxley Act of 2002, that the Annual Report of Apple Inc. on Form 10-K for the fiscal year ended September 26, 2015 fully complies with the requirements of Section 13(a) or 15(d) of the Securities Exchange Act of 1934 and that information contained in such Form 10-K fairly presents in all material respects the financial condition and results of operations of Apple Inc. at the dates and for the periods indicated.

Date: October 28, 2015

By: /s/ Timothy D. Cook
_____
Timothy D. Cook
Chief Executive Officer

I, Luca Maestri, certify, as of the date hereof, pursuant to 18 U.S.C. Section 1350, as adopted pursuant to Section 906 of the Sarbanes-Oxley Act of 2002, that the Annual Report of Apple Inc. on Form 10-K for the fiscal year ended September 26, 2015 fully complies with the requirements of Section 13(a) or 15(d) of the Securities Exchange Act of 1934 and that information contained in such Form 10-K fairly presents in all material respects the financial condition and results of operations of Apple Inc. at the dates and for the periods indicated.

Date: October 28, 2015

By: /s/ Luca Maestri
_____
Luca Maestri
Senior Vice President,
Chief Financial Officer

A signed original of this written statement required by Section 906 has been provided to Apple Inc. and will be retained by Apple Inc. and furnished to the Securities and Exchange Commission or its staff upon request.

5. Anti-Fraud Provisions of the 1934 Act

Like the '33 Act, the '34 Act also contains anti-fraud provisions. The most important and broadly drafted of these provisions is § 10(b). This section makes it unlawful to "use or employ, in connection with the purchase or sale of any security . . . any manipulative or deceptive device or contrivance in contravention of [the] rules and regulations" that the SEC prescribes. 15 U.S.C. § 78j. Rule 10b-5, which implements § 10(b), provides as follows:

> It shall be unlawful for any person, directly or indirectly . . . :
>   (a) To employ any device, scheme, or artifice to defraud,
>   (b) To make any untrue statement of a material fact or to omit to state a material fact necessary in order to make the statements made, in the light of the circumstances under which they were made, not misleading, or
>   (c) To engage in any act, practice, or course of business which operates or would operate as a fraud or deceit upon any person, in connection with the purchase or sale of any security.

17 C.F.R. § 240.10b-5.

It is important to remember that § 10(b) and Rule 10b-5 apply to the purchase and sale of *any* security, not just the securities of large, publicly traded companies. To state a claim for securities fraud under § 10(b) and Rule 10b-5, a plaintiff must allege that each defendant (1) made misstatements or omissions of material fact, (2) with scienter, (3) in connection with the purchase or sale of securities, (4) upon which the plaintiff relied, and (5) that the plaintiff's reliance was the proximate cause of its injury. *See, e.g., ATSI Comm'ns, Inc. v. Shaar Fund, Ltd.*, 493 F.3d 87, 105 (2d Cir. 2007). Like § 17(a) of the '33 Act, § 10(b) has an interstate commerce jurisdictional requirement.

There is a robust body of case law surrounding § 10(b) and Rule 10b-5, in part because § 10(b) can be enforced by the SEC, the Department of Justice, and by private plaintiffs through an implied private right of action. *See, e.g., Blue Chip Stamps v. Manor Drug Stores*, 421 U.S. 723, 730 (1975) (reading § 10(b) and Rule 10b-5 as providing injured persons with a private right of action to sue for damages suffered through those provisions' violation). We offer a brief overview of the elements of a claim under § 10(b) and Rule 10b-5 here, but urge you to take a course in securities regulation for a deeper dive into these materials.

Misstatements or Omissions

The first element of a claim under § 10(b) and Rule 10b-5 is a misstatement or omission of material fact. A misstatement is a statement not in accord with the facts. As for omissions, the Supreme Court has held that "[s]ilence, absent a duty to disclose, is not misleading under Rule 10b-5." *Basic Inc. v. Levinson*, 485 U.S. 225, 239 n.17 (1988); *see also Chiarella v. United States*, 445 U.S. 222, 230 (1980). Rather, "an omission is actionable under the securities laws only when the corporation is subject to a duty to disclose the omitted facts." *In re Time Warner Inc. Sec. Litig.*, 9 F.3d 259, 267 (2d Cir. 1993); *see Glazer v. Formica Corp.*, 964 F.2d 149, 157 (2d Cir. 1992). Such a duty may arise when there is "a corporate insider trad[ing] on confidential information," a "statute or regulation requiring disclosure," or a corporate statement that would otherwise be "inaccurate, incomplete, or misleading." *Glazer*, 964 F.2d at 157 (quoting *Backman v. Polaroid Corp.*, 910 F.2d 10, 12 (1st Cir. 1990) (en banc)); *accord Oran v. Stafford*, 226 F.3d 275, 285-86 (3d Cir. 2000).

Materiality

A misstatement or omission is not actionable under § 10(b) or Rule 10b-5 unless it is **material**. A fact is material if there is a substantial likelihood that a reasonable shareholder would consider it important in making an investment decision. *See TSC Indus., Inc. v. Northway, Inc.*, 426 U.S. 438, 449 (1976) (defining material omission for purposes of § 14 of the '34 Act); *see also Basic Inc. v. Levinson*, 485 U.S. at 224, 232 (adopting *TSC Industries'* materiality standard for actions under § 10(b) and Rule 10b-5). An omitted fact is material if there is "a substantial likelihood that the disclosure of the omitted fact would have been viewed by the reasonable investor as having significantly altered the total mix of information made available." *TSC Indus., Inc.*, 426 U.S. at 449 (internal quotations omitted).

Scienter

To state a claim under § 10(b) and Rule 10b-5, a plaintiff must establish that the defendant made the challenged misstatement or omission with scienter. *See Ernst & Ernst v. Hochfelder*, 425 U.S. 185 (1976). The scienter requirement derives from the language of § 10(b), which references manipulative or deceptive devices and contrivances. *See, e.g., Santa Fe Indus., Inc. v. Green*, 430 U.S. 462, 473 (1977) ("The language of § 10(b) gives no indication that Congress meant to prohibit any conduct not involving manipulation or deception.). To satisfy the scienter requirement, the plaintiff must plead and prove that the defendant made the challenged misstatement or omission with a mental state embracing an intent to deceive or defraud. *Ernst & Ernst*, 425 U.S. at 193, n.12.

In its 2007 opinion *Tellabs, Inc. v. Makor Issues & Rights, Ltd.*, 551 U.S. 308, 313-14 (2007), the Supreme Court observed that "[e]very Court of Appeals that has considered the issue has held that a plaintiff may meet the scienter requirement by showing that the defendant acted intentionally or recklessly, though the Circuits differ on the degree of recklessness required." While the *Tellabs* Court did not reach the question whether recklessness satisfies the scienter requirement, it did not disturb the case law from the courts of appeals holding that proof of recklessness is sufficient to satisfy the scienter requirement. Generally speaking, recklessness has been defined for purposes of § 10(b) and Rule 10b-5 as conduct constituting such an extreme departure from ordinary care that, under the circumstances, it presented a danger of misleading the plaintiff that was either known to the defendant or was so obvious that the defendant must have been aware of it. *See, e.g., Ottman v. Hanger Orthopedic Grp., Inc.*, 353 F.3d 338, 343-45 (4th Cir. 2003); *Sundstrand Corp. v. Sun Chem. Corp.*, 553 F.2d 1033, 1044-45 (7th Cir. 1977).

In 1995, Congress passed the Private Securities Litigation Reform Act (PSLRA) in order to curb § 10(b) litigation that was described by critics as abusive and lawyer-driven. The PSLRA amended the Exchange Act to require a plaintiff proceeding under § 10(b) and Rule 10b-5 to plead "with particularity facts giving rise to a strong inference that the defendant acted with the required state of mind" — that is, scienter. The PSLRA did not define or specify what would qualify as a strong inference. In the *Tellabs, Inc.* case, the Supreme Court held that to qualify as strong, an inference of scienter must be more than merely plausible or reasonable — it must be cogent and at least as compelling as any opposing inference of nonfraudulent intent. *Tellabs, Inc.*, 551 U.S. at 313-14. Under this standard, a complaint can survive a motion to dismiss "only if a reasonable person would deem the inference of scienter cogent and at least as compelling as any opposing inference one could draw from the facts alleged." *Id.* The Court further held that a court must assess a plaintiff's scienter allegations holistically in determining whether the plaintiff has met the requisite strong inference pleading standard.

In Connection with the Purchase or Sale of Securities

Courts traditionally have interpreted the "in connection with" requirement broadly to include any false or misleading statements that were made "in a manner reasonably calculated to influence the investing public." *SEC v. Texas Gulf Sulphur Co.*, 401 F.2d 833, 862 (2d Cir. 1968). Misstatements or omissions do not need to be specifically directed to investors to be actionable; instead, they need only be disseminated in a medium upon which a reasonable investor would rely. Consequently, material misstatements and omissions in communications ranging from SEC filings to press releases, blog posts, and even tweets may be actionable under § 10(b) and Rule 10b-5.

As for the purchase or sale requirement, the Supreme Court has held that § 10(b) and Rule 10b-5 apply only to actual purchases or sales of securities. Nonpurchasers and nonsellers do not have standing to bring an action under Rule 10b-5. *See Blue Chip Stamps*, 421 U.S. at 723. Thus, an action cannot be brought by one who alleges, "I would have sold my stock if I had known the facts the corporation did not disclose." Generally, courts have been concerned that allowing such claims would open the floodgates to litigation.[1]

Reliance

To state a claim under § 10(b) and Rule 10b-5, a private plaintiff must plead and prove reliance — meaning, the plaintiff must show that the material misrepresentation or omission was a substantial factor in causing the plaintiff to enter into the securities transaction(s) at issue. In its 1988 decision in *Basic Inc. v. Levinson*, 485 U.S. 244 (1988), the Supreme Court held that investors could satisfy the reliance requirement through the so-called **fraud on the market** presumption, or a presumption that the price of stock traded in an efficient market reflects all public material information. The fraud on the market presumption maintains that the market price of shares reflects all publicly available information, including material misrepresentations. This presumption is particularly important in securities fraud class actions where, as the *Basic* Court recognized, requiring proof of direct reliance by every securities fraud plaintiff would eliminate the possibility of class relief because individual

---

[1] Some (but not all) states recognize so-called holder claims — i.e., claims brought by investors who allege that they were wrongfully induced to hold stock — as a matter of state law. *See, e.g., Grant Thornton LLP v. Prospect High Income Fund*, 314 S.W.3d 913, 926 (Tex. 2010) ("In a 'holder' claim, the plaintiff alleges not that the defendant wrongfully induced the plaintiff to purchase or sell stock, but that the defendant wrongfully induced the plaintiff

issues would necessarily overwhelm the common issues required for maintaining a class. *Basic* created a rebuttable presumption of reliance premised upon the fraud on the market theory, holding that when an investor buys or sells stock at the market price, his reliance may be presumed, if he is able to plead that (1) the alleged misrepresentations were publicly known; (2) they were material; (3) the stock was traded in an efficient market; and (4) the plaintiff traded in the stock in the relevant period. If the link between the misrepresentation and the price the plaintiff paid is severed, the presumption will not apply.

In the 2014 Supreme Court case *Halliburton Co. v. Erica P. John Fund, Inc.*, 134 S. Ct. 2391 (2014), Haliburton challenged the presumption of class-wide reliance, arguing that *Basic* should be overruled. In the alternative, Haliburton argued that a plaintiff should be required to prove that a defendant's misrepresentation affected the stock price in order to obtain the presumption of reliance. Halliburton also argued that a defendant should be permitted to rebut the presumption of reliance with evidence of a lack of price impact prior to the class certification or merits stage of a class action.

The Supreme Court rejected Halliburton's argument for the elimination of *Basic*'s presumption of reliance. The Court noted that the standard for overruling Supreme Court precedent is high — a "special justification" is required, not just an argument that the decision is wrong. Haliburton's arguments did not, in the Court's view, meet this standard. Second, the Court rejected arguments that the economic underpinnings of the *Basic* decision were wrong or outmoded, pointing out that the *Basic* Court had understood and considered disagreements over the economic theory. Finally, the Court cited the rebuttable nature of the presumption, holding that the *Basic* standard protects alleged securities law violators by acknowledging the possibility that a misrepresentation may not impact a stock price by permitting defendants to rebut the presumption.

Economic Loss

To satisfy this element, a plaintiff must plead and prove actual economic loss as a result of the alleged fraud.

Loss Causation

In addition to proving economic loss, a private plaintiff also must plead and prove loss causation to state a claim under § 10(b) and Rule 10b-5. This element requires a plaintiff to prove that the economic harm that it allegedly suffered occurred as a result of the alleged misrepresentations or omissions, and that the resulting damages were a foreseeable consequence of the challenged misstatements or omissions. *See Dura Pharm., Inc. v. Broudo*, 544 U.S. 336 (2005). In *Dura*, the Supreme Court reversed a Ninth Circuit ruling that had held that a plaintiff in a securities fraud class action under § 10(b) of the '34 Act could satisfy the loss causation requirement merely by pleading that the price of the security on the date

to continue holding his stock. As a result, the plaintiff seeks damages for the diminished value of the stock, or the value of a forfeited opportunity, allegedly caused by the defendant's misrepresentations."). The Delaware Supreme Court recently held that holder claims are direct rather than derivative in nature because they are personal to the stockholder and thus do not belong to the corporation. *Citigroup Inc. v. AHW Investment Partnership*, No. 641, 2015, 2016 WL 2994902, *9-10 (Del. May 24, 2016).

of purchase was inflated because of the alleged misrepresentations — without any showing that subsequent price declines or trading losses were actually caused by the allegedly false statements. In reversing the Ninth Circuit, the Supreme Court held that in fraud on the market cases, "an inflated purchase price will not itself constitute or proximately cause the relevant economic loss." *Id.* at 341. Thus, while an inflated stock price at the time of purchase may turn out to be "necessary condition" of any economic loss, it is not, standing alone, sufficient to prove that the defendant's fraud or misleading statement proximately caused the plaintiff's economic loss for purposes of the loss causation requirement of § 10(b). *Id.* at 343. Although the Court did not specifically identify precisely how loss causation must be pleaded, it cited with approval various authorities requiring pleading and proof of a loss resulting from a stock price decline upon disclosure of the fraud.

6. Spotlight: Insider Trading

Plaintiffs (including the SEC) have used § 10(b) of the '34 Act and Rule 10b-5 to target a wide variety of unscrupulous practices, including **insider trading**. Insider trading occurs when a person buys or sells a security based on material non-public information. There are two different theories, or types, of insider trading cases — **traditional**, or **classical theory** cases and **misappropriation theory** cases. Under the "traditional" or "classical theory," a corporate insider violates § 10(b) when he trades in the securities of his corporation on the basis of material, non-public information. Trading on such information is a "deceptive device" for purposes of § 10(b) because it breaches the "relationship of trust and confidence between the shareholders of a corporation and those insiders who have obtained confidential information by reason of their position within that corporation." *Chiarella v. United States*, 445 U.S. 222, 228 (1980).

The idea behind the classical theory is that corporate insiders are in a position to know critical matters affecting the corporation and the value of its stock, such as plans to merge, technological advances and discoveries, as well as events likely to have an adverse impact upon the corporation. If these insiders purchase stock, knowing the stock is about to soar in value due to a recent discovery, they receive a benefit from their position not available to other investors. Similarly, if the insiders sell their stock, knowing that a future public announcement will cause the stock to fall, they abuse their position to the detriment of others. When an insider receives a personal benefit, in the form of gains realized or losses avoided, not available to uninformed purchasers or sellers of the company's stock, she breaches a duty owed to shareholders. Consequently, under the classical theory of insider trading, an insider has an obligation to disclose or abstain — that is, to disclose the material non-public information the insider has gained by virtue of her position to the public or refrain from trading.

Under the **misappropriation theory**, § 10(b) is violated when a corporate outsider "misappropriates confidential information for securities trading purposes in breach of a duty owed to the source of the information." *United States v. O'Hagan*, 521 U.S. 642, 652 (1997). This qualifies as a "deceptive device" under § 10(b) because the outsider trades on confidential information entrusted to him for non-trading purposes, and thereby "defrauds the principal of the exclusive use of that information." *Id.* Consequently, under the misappropriation theory, an outsider entrusted with confidential information must either refrain from trading or must disclose to the principal that he plans to trade on the information. *Id.* at 665 n.6. The misappropriation theory thus is "designed to protect the integrity of the security markets against abuses by 'outsiders' to a corporation who have access to confidential information that will affect the corporation's security price when revealed, but who owe no fiduciary or other duty to the corporation's shareholders." *Id.* at 653.

As with any action under § 10(b), a plaintiff alleging unlawful insider trading must show the defendant acted intentionally to deceive, manipulate, or defraud; mere negligence on the part of a defendant is not sufficient. In addition, a plaintiff alleging insider trading must establish that the fact at issue was material. Some examples of facts held to be material are a significant drop in corporate profits, management's decision to pay a dividend, an agreement for the sale of corporate assets, and critical discoveries. In one well-known case, *SEC v. Texas Gulf Sulphur Co.*, 401 F.2d 833 (8th Cir. 1968), for example, a company discovered significant mineral deposits. The news was leaked to the media and the company then downplayed the discovery with a misleading press release. During this period, various officers, directors, and employees of the company purchased stock. When the announcement of the mineral deposit was eventually made public, the value of the stock increased, and the insiders who had previously purchased stock received a windfall in the increased value of their stock. The company was sued by the SEC as well as by individuals who sold their stock after reading the press release, believing the corporation had not made a significant discovery. The court held that all of the transactions by the corporate insiders were in violation of Rule 10b-5.

Insider trading allegations are common in shareholder lawsuits. Because insider trading undermines investor confidence in the fairness and integrity of the securities markets, the SEC has treated the detection and prosecution of insider trading violations as one of its enforcement priorities. The SEC regularly brings cases against (i) corporate officers, directors, and employees who traded the corporation's securities after learning of significant, confidential corporate developments; (ii) friends, business associates, family members, and other so-called **tippees** of such officers, directors, and employees, who traded the securities after receiving such information; (iii) employees of law, banking, brokerage, and printing firms who were given such information to provide services to the corporation whose securities they traded; (iv) government employees who learned of such information because of their employment by the government; and (v) other persons who misappropriated, and took advantage of, confidential information from their employers. As this list suggests, the list of insiders, tippees, and misappropriators includes not only directors and officers but anyone entrusted with corporate information for the corporation's purposes, such as attorneys, accountants, and bankers. Liability may result from affirmative misrepresentations of a material fact, nondisclosure of a material fact, or misappropriation of such information.

Case Preview

United States v. O'Hagan

In the next case — *O'Hagan* — the Supreme Court recognized the misappropriation theory as a basis for insider trading liability. In reading the case, consider the following questions:

1. What are the differences between the classical and misappropriation theories of insider trading liability?
2. Does the Court apply the misappropriation theory? Why or why not? Could O'Hagan have been held liable under the classical theory?
3. To state a claim under the misappropriation theory against O'Hagan, does the government have to prove that O'Hagan breached a duty owed to the corporation that issued the securities involved in the case?
4. Would the government have used the misappropriation theory if O'Hagan had been assigned to work on the corporate transaction at issue?
5. If you were on the management committee of a law firm, what (if any) internal controls or compliance procedures might you adopt in response to a case like *O'Hagan*?

United States v. O'Hagan
521 U.S. 642 (1997)

Justice GINSBURG delivered the opinion of the Court.*

This case concerns the interpretation and enforcement of § 10(b) and § 14(e) of the Securities Exchange Act of 1934, and rules made by the Securities and Exchange Commission pursuant to these provisions, Rule 10b-5 and Rule 14e-3(a). Two prime questions are presented. The first relates to the misappropriation of material, nonpublic information for securities trading; the second concerns fraudulent practices in the tender offer setting. In particular, we address and resolve these issues: (1) Is a person who trades in securities for personal profit, using confidential information misappropriated in breach of a fiduciary duty to the source of the information, guilty of violating § 10(b) and Rule 10b-5? (2) Did the Commission exceed its rulemaking authority by adopting Rule 14e-3(a), which proscribes trading on undisclosed information in the tender offer setting, even in the absence of a duty to disclose? Our answer to the first question is yes, and to the second question, viewed in the context of this case, no.

I

Respondent James Herman O'Hagan was a partner in the law firm of Dorsey & Whitney in Minneapolis, Minnesota. In July 1988, Grand Metropolitan PLC (Grand

---

*Most footnotes have been omitted for purposes of brevity.

Met), a company based in London, England, retained Dorsey & Whitney as local counsel to represent Grand Met regarding a potential tender offer for the common stock of the Pillsbury Company, headquartered in Minneapolis. Both Grand Met and Dorsey & Whitney took precautions to protect the confidentiality of Grand Met's tender offer plans. O'Hagan did no work on the Grand Met representation. Dorsey & Whitney withdrew from representing Grand Met on September 9, 1988. Less than a month later, on October 4, 1988, Grand Met publicly announced its tender offer for Pillsbury stock.

On August 18, 1988, while Dorsey & Whitney was still representing Grand Met, O'Hagan began purchasing call options for Pillsbury stock. Each option gave him the right to purchase 100 shares of Pillsbury stock by a specified date in September 1988. Later in August and in September, O'Hagan made additional purchases of Pillsbury call options. By the end of September, he owned 2,500 unexpired Pillsbury options, apparently more than any other individual investor. See App. 85, 148. O'Hagan also purchased, in September 1988, some 5,000 shares of Pillsbury common stock, at a price just under $39 per share. When Grand Met announced its tender offer in October, the price of Pillsbury stock rose to nearly $60 per share. O'Hagan then sold his Pillsbury call options and common stock, making a profit of more than $4.3 million.

The Securities and Exchange Commission (SEC or Commission) initiated an investigation into O'Hagan's transactions, culminating in a 57-count indictment. The indictment alleged that O'Hagan defrauded his law firm and its client, Grand Met, by using for his own trading purposes material, nonpublic information regarding Grand Met's planned tender offer. *Id.*, at 8. According to the indictment, O'Hagan used the profits he gained through this trading to conceal his previous embezzlement and conversion of unrelated client trust funds. *Id.*, at 10. O'Hagan was charged with 20 counts of mail fraud, in violation of 18 U.S.C. § 1341; 17 counts of securities fraud, in violation of § 10(b) of the Securities Exchange Act of 1934 (Exchange Act), 48 Stat. 891, 15 U.S.C. § 78j(b), and SEC Rule 10b-5, 17 CFR § 240.10b-5 1996); 17 counts of fraudulent trading in connection with a tender offer, in violation of § 14(e) of the Exchange Act, 15 U.S.C. § 78n(e), and SEC Rule 14e-3(a), 17 CFR § 240.14e-3(a) (1996); and 3 counts of violating federal money laundering statutes, 18 U.S.C. §§ 1956(a)(1)(B)(i), 1957. See App. 13-24. A jury convicted O'Hagan on all 57 counts, and he was sentenced to a 41-month term of imprisonment.

A divided panel of the Court of Appeals for the Eighth Circuit reversed all of O'Hagan's convictions. 92 F.3d 612 (1996). Liability under § 10(b) and Rule 10b-5, the Eighth Circuit held, may not be grounded on the "misappropriation theory" of securities fraud on which the prosecution relied. *Id.*, at 622. The Court of Appeals also held that Rule 14e-3(a) — which prohibits trading while in possession of material, nonpublic information relating to a tender offer — exceeds the SEC's § 14(e) rulemaking authority because the Rule contains no breach of fiduciary duty requirement. *Id.*, at 627. The Eighth Circuit further concluded that O'Hagan's mail fraud and money laundering convictions rested on violations of the securities laws, and therefore could not stand once the securities fraud convictions were reversed. *Id.*, at 627-628. Judge Fagg, dissenting, stated that he would recognize and enforce the misappropriation theory, and would hold that the SEC did not exceed its rulemaking authority when it adopted Rule 14e-3(a) without requiring proof of a breach of fiduciary duty. *Id.*, at 628.

Decisions of the Courts of Appeals are in conflict on the propriety of the misappropriation theory under § 10(b) and Rule 10b-5, see *infra* this page and n.3, and on the legitimacy of Rule 14e-3(a) under § 14(e), see *infra,* at 25. We granted certiorari, 519 U.S. 1087, 117 S. Ct. 759, 136 L. Ed. 2d 695 (1997), and now reverse the Eighth Circuit's judgment.

II

We address first the Court of Appeals' reversal of O'Hagan's convictions under § 10(b) and Rule 10b-5. Following the Fourth Circuit's lead, see *United States v. Bryan,* 58 F.3d 933, 943-959 (1995), the Eighth Circuit rejected the misappropriation theory as a basis for § 10(b) liability. We hold, in accord with several other Courts of Appeals, that criminal liability under § 10(b) may be predicated on the misappropriation theory.

A

In pertinent part, § 10(b) of the Exchange Act provides:

"It shall be unlawful for any person, directly or indirectly, by the use of any means or instrumentality of interstate commerce or of the mails, or of any facility of any national securities exchange —

. . .

"(b) To use or employ, in connection with the purchase or sale of any security registered on a national securities exchange or any security not so registered, any manipulative or deceptive device or contrivance in contravention of such rules and regulations as the [Securities and Exchange] Commission may prescribe as necessary or appropriate in the public interest or for the protection of investors." 15 U.S.C. § 78j(b).

The statute thus proscribes (1) using any deceptive device (2) in connection with the purchase or sale of securities, in contravention of rules prescribed by the Commission. The provision, as written, does not confine its coverage to deception of a purchaser or seller of securities, see *United States v. Newman,* 664 F.2d 12, 17 (C.A.2 1981); rather, the statute reaches any deceptive device used "in connection with the purchase or sale of any security."

Pursuant to its § 10(b) rulemaking authority, the Commission has adopted Rule 10b-5, which, as relevant here, provides:

"It shall be unlawful for any person, directly or indirectly, by the use of any means or instrumentality of interstate commerce, or of the mails or of any facility of any national securities exchange,

"(a) To employ any device, scheme, or artifice to defraud, [or]

. . .

"(c) To engage in any act, practice, or course of business which operates or would operate as a fraud or deceit upon any person,

"in connection with the purchase or sale of any security." 17 CFR § 240.10b-5 (1996).

Liability under Rule 10b-5, our precedent indicates, does not extend beyond conduct encompassed by § 10(b)'s prohibition. See *Ernst & Ernst v. Hochfelder*, 425 U.S. 185, 214, 96 S. Ct. 1375, 1391, 47 L. Ed. 2d 668 (1976) (scope of Rule 10b-5 cannot exceed power Congress granted Commission under § 10(b)); see also *Central Bank of Denver, N.A. v. First Interstate Bank of Denver, N. A.*, 511 U.S. 164, 173, 114 S. Ct. 1439, 1446, 128 L. Ed. 2d 119 (1994) ("We have refused to allow [private] 10b-5 challenges to conduct not prohibited by the text of the statute.").

Under the "traditional" or "classical theory" of insider trading liability, § 10(b) and Rule 10b-5 are violated when a corporate insider trades in the securities of his corporation on the basis of material, nonpublic information. Trading on such information qualifies as a "deceptive device" under § 10(b), we have affirmed, because "a relationship of trust and confidence [exists] between the shareholders of a corporation and those insiders who have obtained confidential information by reason of their position with that corporation." *Chiarella v. United States*, 445 U.S. 222, 228, 100 S. Ct. 1108, 1114, 63 L. Ed. 2d 348 (1980). That relationship, we recognized, "gives rise to a duty to disclose [or to abstain from trading] because of the 'necessity of preventing a corporate insider from . . . tak[ing] unfair advantage of . . . uninformed . . . stockholders.'" *Id.*, at 228-229, 100 S. Ct., at 1115 (citation omitted). The classical theory applies not only to officers, directors, and other permanent insiders of a corporation, but also to attorneys, accountants, consultants, and others who temporarily become fiduciaries of a corporation. See *Dirks v. SEC*, 463 U.S. 646, 655, n. 14, 103 S. Ct. 3255, 3262, 77 L. Ed. 2d 911 (1983).

The "misappropriation theory" holds that a person commits fraud "in connection with" a securities transaction, and thereby violates § 10(b) and Rule 10b-5, when he misappropriates confidential information for securities trading purposes, in breach of a duty owed to the source of the information. . . . Under this theory, a fiduciary's undisclosed, self-serving use of a principal's information to purchase or sell securities, in breach of a duty of loyalty and confidentiality, defrauds the principal of the exclusive use of that information. In lieu of premising liability on a fiduciary relationship between company insider and purchaser or seller of the company's stock, the misappropriation theory premises liability on a fiduciary-turned-trader's deception of those who entrusted him with access to confidential information.

The two theories are complementary, each addressing efforts to capitalize on nonpublic information through the purchase or sale of securities. The classical theory targets a corporate insider's breach of duty to shareholders with whom the insider transacts; the misappropriation theory outlaws trading on the basis of nonpublic information by a corporate "outsider" in breach of a duty owed not to a trading party, but to the source of the information. The misappropriation theory is thus designed to "protec[t] the integrity of the securities markets against abuses by 'outsiders' to a corporation who have access to confidential information that will affect th[e] corporation's security price when revealed, but who owe no fiduciary or other duty to that corporation's shareholders." *Ibid.*

In this case, the indictment alleged that O'Hagan, in breach of a duty of trust and confidence he owed to his law firm, Dorsey & Whitney, and to its client, Grand Met, traded on the basis of nonpublic information regarding Grand Met's planned tender offer for Pillsbury common stock. App. 16. This conduct, the Government charged, constituted a fraudulent device in connection with the purchase and sale of securities.[5]

B

We agree with the Government that misappropriation, as just defined, satisfies § 10(b)'s requirement that chargeable conduct involve a "deceptive device or contrivance" used "in connection with" the purchase or sale of securities. We observe, first, that misappropriators, as the Government describes them, deal in deception. A fiduciary who "[pretends] loyalty to the principal while secretly converting the principal's information for personal gain," . . . "dupes" or defrauds the principal. See Aldave, Misappropriation: A General Theory of Liability for Trading on Nonpublic Information, 13 Hofstra L. Rev. 101, 119 (1984).

. . .

Deception through nondisclosure is central to the theory of liability for which the Government seeks recognition. As counsel for the Government stated in explanation of the theory at oral argument: "To satisfy the common law rule that a trustee may not use the property that [has] been entrusted [to] him, there would have to be consent. To satisfy the requirement of the Securities Act that there be no deception, there would only have to be disclosure." Tr. of Oral Arg. 12; see generally Restatement (Second) of Agency §§ 390, 395 1958) (agent's disclosure obligation regarding use of confidential information).[6]

The misappropriation theory advanced by the Government is consistent with *Santa Fe Industries, Inc. v. Green,* 430 U.S. 462, 97 S. Ct. 1292, 51 L. Ed. 2d 480 (1977), a decision underscoring that § 10(b) is not an all-purpose breach of fiduciary duty ban; rather, it trains on conduct involving manipulation or deception. See *id.,* at 473-476, 97 S. Ct., at 1300-1302. In contrast to the Government's allegations in this case, in *Santa Fe Industries,* all pertinent facts were disclosed by the persons charged with violating § 10(b) and Rule 10b-5, see *id.,* at 474, 97 S. Ct., at 1301; therefore, there was no deception through nondisclosure to which liability under those provisions could attach, see *id.,* at 476, 97 S. Ct., at 1302. Similarly, full disclosure forecloses liability under the misappropriation theory: Because the deception essential to the misappropriation theory involves feigning fidelity to the source of information, if the fiduciary discloses to the source that he plans to trade on the nonpublic information,

---

[5]The Government could not have prosecuted O'Hagan under the classical theory, for O'Hagan was not an "insider" of Pillsbury, the corporation in whose stock he traded. Although an "outsider" with respect to Pillsbury, O'Hagan had an intimate association with, and was found to have traded on confidential information from, Dorsey & Whitney, counsel to tender offeror Grand Met. Under the misappropriation theory, O'Hagan's securities trading does not escape Exchange Act sanction, as it would under Justice Thomas' dissenting view, simply because he was associated with, and gained nonpublic information from, the bidder, rather than the target.

[6]Under the misappropriation theory urged in this case, the disclosure obligation runs to the source of the information, here, Dorsey & Whitney and Grand Met. Chief Justice Burger, dissenting in *Chiarella,* advanced a broader reading of § 10(b) and Rule 10b-5; the disclosure obligation, as he envisioned it, ran to those with whom the misappropriator trades. 445 U.S., at 240, 100 S. Ct., at 1120-1121 ("a person who has misappropriated nonpublic information has an absolute duty to disclose that information or to refrain from trading"); see also *id.,* at 243, n.4, 100 S. Ct., at 1122 n.4. The Government does not propose that we adopt a misappropriation theory of that breadth.

there is no "deceptive device" and thus no § 10(b) violation — although the fiduciary-turned-trader may remain liable under state law for breach of a duty of loyalty.[7]

We turn next to the § 10(b) requirement that the misappropriator's deceptive use of information be "in connection with the purchase or sale of [a] security." This element is satisfied because the fiduciary's fraud is consummated, not when the fiduciary gains the confidential information, but when, without disclosure to his principal, he uses the information to purchase or sell securities. The securities transaction and the breach of duty thus coincide. This is so even though the person or entity defrauded is not the other party to the trade, but is, instead, the source of the nonpublic information. See Aldave, 13 Hofstra L. Rev., at 120 ("a fraud or deceit can be practiced on one person, with resultant harm to another person or group of persons"). A misappropriator who trades on the basis of material, nonpublic information, in short, gains his advantageous market position through deception; he deceives the source of the information and simultaneously harms members of the investing public. See *id.,* at 120-121, and n.107.

The misappropriation theory targets information of a sort that misappropriators ordinarily capitalize upon to gain no-risk profits through the purchase or sale of securities. Should a misappropriator put such information to other use, the statute's prohibition would not be implicated. The theory does not catch all conceivable forms of fraud involving confidential information; rather, it catches fraudulent means of capitalizing on such information through securities transactions.

The Government notes another limitation on the forms of fraud § 10(b) reaches: "The misappropriation theory would not . . . apply to a case in which a person defrauded a bank into giving him a loan or embezzled cash from another, and then used the proceeds of the misdeed to purchase securities." Brief for United States 24, n.13. In such a case, the Government states, "the proceeds would have value to the malefactor apart from their use in a securities transaction, and the fraud would be complete as soon as the money was obtained." *Ibid.* In other words, money can buy, if not anything, then at least many things; its misappropriation may thus be viewed as sufficiently detached from a subsequent securities transaction that § 10(b)'s "in connection with" requirement would not be met. *Ibid.*

. . .

The misappropriation theory comports with § 10(b)'s language, which requires deception "in connection with the purchase or sale of any security," not deception of an identifiable purchaser or seller. The theory is also well tuned to an animating purpose of the Exchange Act: to insure honest securities markets and thereby promote investor confidence. See 45 Fed. Reg. 60412 (1980) (trading on misappropriated information "undermines the integrity of, and investor confidence in, the securities markets"). Although informational disparity is inevitable in the securities markets, investors likely would hesitate to venture their capital in a market where trading based on misappropriated nonpublic information is unchecked by law. An investor's informational disadvantage vis-à-vis a misappropriator with material,

---

[7]Where, however, a person trading on the basis of material, nonpublic information owes a duty of loyalty and confidentiality to two entities or persons — for example, a law firm and its client — but makes disclosure to only one, the trader may still be liable under the misappropriation theory.

nonpublic information stems from contrivance, not luck; it is a disadvantage that cannot be overcome with research or skill. . . .

In sum, considering the inhibiting impact on market participation of trading on misappropriated information, and the congressional purposes underlying § 10(b), it makes scant sense to hold a lawyer like O'Hagan a § 10(b) violator if he works for a law firm representing the target of a tender offer, but not if he works for a law firm representing the bidder. The text of the statute requires no such result. The misappropriation at issue here was properly made the subject of a § 10(b) charge because it meets the statutory requirement that there be "deceptive" conduct "in connection with" securities transactions.

. . .

Chiarella involved securities trades by a printer employed at a shop that printed documents announcing corporate takeover bids. See 445 U.S., at 224, 100 S. Ct., at 1112. Deducing the names of target companies from documents he handled, the printer bought shares of the targets before takeover bids were announced, expecting (correctly) that the share prices would rise upon announcement. In these transactions, the printer did not disclose to the sellers of the securities (the target companies' shareholders) the nonpublic information on which he traded. See *ibid.* For that trading, the printer was convicted of violating § 10(b) and Rule 10b-5. We reversed the Court of Appeals judgment that had affirmed the conviction. See *id.,* at 225, 100 S. Ct., at 1113.

. . .

Chiarella thus expressly left open the misappropriation theory before us today. Certain statements in *Chiarella,* however, led the Eighth Circuit in the instant case to conclude that § 10(b) liability hinges exclusively on a breach of duty owed to a purchaser or seller of securities. See 92 F.3d, at 618. The Court said in *Chiarella* that § 10(b) liability "is premised upon a duty to disclose arising from a relationship of trust and confidence *between parties to a transaction,*" 445 U.S., at 230, 100 S. Ct., at 1115 (emphasis added), and observed that the printshop employee defendant in that case "was not a person in whom the sellers had placed their trust and confidence," see *id.,* at 232, 100 S. Ct., at 1117. These statements rejected the notion that § 10(b) stretches so far as to impose "a general duty between all participants in market transactions to forgo actions based on material, nonpublic information," *id.,* at 233, 100 S. Ct., at 1117, and we confine them to that context. The statements highlighted by the Eighth Circuit, in short, appear in an opinion carefully leaving for future resolution the validity of the misappropriation theory, and therefore cannot be read to foreclose that theory.

Dirks, too, left room for application of the misappropriation theory in cases like the one we confront. *Dirks* involved an investment analyst who had received information from a former insider of a corporation with which the analyst had no connection. See 463 U.S., at 648-649, 103 S. Ct., at 3258-3259. The information indicated that the corporation had engaged in a massive fraud. The analyst investigated the fraud, obtaining corroborating information from employees of the corporation. During his investigation, the analyst discussed his findings with clients and investors, some of whom sold their holdings in the company the analyst suspected of gross wrongdoing. See *id.,* at 649, 103 S. Ct., at 3258-3259.

The SEC censured the analyst for, *inter alia,* aiding and abetting § 10(b) and Rule 10b-5 violations by clients and investors who sold their holdings based on the nonpublic information the analyst passed on. See *id.,* at 650-652, 103 S. Ct., at 3259-3260. In the SEC's view, the analyst, as a "tippee" of corporation insiders, had a duty under § 10(b) and Rule 10b-5 to refrain from communicating the nonpublic information to persons likely to trade on the basis of it. See *id.,* at 651, 655-656, 103 S. Ct., at 3261-3262. This Court found no such obligation, see *id.,* at 665-667, 103 S. Ct., at 3266-3268, and repeated the key point made in *Chiarella:* There is no " 'general duty between all participants in market transactions to forgo actions based on material, nonpublic information.' " 463 U.S., at 655, 103 S. Ct., at 3261 (quoting *Chiarella,* 445 U.S., at 233, 100 S. Ct., at 1117); see Aldave, 13 Hofstra L. Rev., at 122 (misappropriation theory bars only "trading on the basis of information that the wrongdoer converted to his own use in violation of some fiduciary, contractual, or similar obligation to the owner or rightful possessor of the information").

No showing had been made in *Dirks* that the "tippers" had violated any duty by disclosing to the analyst nonpublic information about their former employer. The insiders had acted not for personal profit, but to expose a massive fraud within the corporation. See 463 U.S., at 666-667, 103 S. Ct., at 3267-3268. Absent any violation by the tippers, there could be no derivative liability for the tippee. See *id.,* at 667, 103 S. Ct., at 3267-3268. Most important for purposes of the instant case, the Court observed in *Dirks:* "There was no expectation by [the analyst's] sources that he would keep their information in confidence. Nor did [the analyst] misappropriate or illegally obtain the information. . . ." *Id.,* at 665, 103 S. Ct., at 3267. *Dirks* thus presents no suggestion that a person who gains nonpublic information through misappropriation in breach of a fiduciary duty escapes § 10(b) liability when, without alerting the source, he trades on the information.

Last of the three cases the Eighth Circuit regarded as warranting disapproval of the misappropriation theory, *Central Bank* held that "a private plaintiff may not maintain an aiding and abetting suit under § 10(b)." 511 U.S., at 191, 114 S. Ct., at 1455. We immediately cautioned in *Central Bank* that secondary actors in the securities markets may sometimes be chargeable under the securities Acts: "Any person or entity, including a lawyer, accountant, or bank, who employs a manipulative device or makes a material misstatement (or omission) *on which a purchaser or seller of securities relies* may be liable as a primary violator under 10b-5, assuming . . . the requirements for primary liability under Rule 10b-5 are met." *Ibid.* (emphasis added). The Eighth Circuit isolated the statement just quoted and drew from it the conclusion that § 10(b) covers only deceptive statements or omissions on which purchasers and sellers, and perhaps other market participants, rely. See 92 F.3d, at 619. It is evident from the question presented in *Central Bank,* however, that this Court, in the quoted passage, sought only to clarify that secondary actors, although not subject to aiding and abetting liability, remain subject to primary liability under § 10(b) and Rule 10b-5 for certain conduct.

Furthermore, *Central Bank*'s discussion concerned only private civil litigation under § 10(b) and Rule 10b-5, not criminal liability. *Central Bank*'s reference to purchasers or sellers of securities must be read in light of a longstanding limitation on private § 10(b) suits. In *Blue Chip Stamps v. Manor Drug Stores*, 421 U.S. 723, 95 S. Ct. 1917, 44 L. Ed. 2d 539 (1975), we held that only actual purchasers or sellers of securities may maintain a private civil action under § 10(b) and Rule 10b-5. We so confined the § 10(b) private right of action because of "policy considerations." *Id.*, at 737, 95 S. Ct., at 1926. In particular, *Blue Chip Stamps* recognized the abuse potential and proof problems inherent in suits by investors who neither bought nor sold, but asserted they would have traded absent fraudulent conduct by others. See *id.*, at 739-747, 95 S. Ct., at 1927-1931; see also *Holmes v. Securities Investor Protection Corporation*, 503 U.S. 258, 285, 112 S. Ct. 1311, 1326-1327, 117 L. Ed. 2d 532 1992) (O'Connor, J., concurring in part and concurring in judgment); *id.*, at 289-290, 112 S. Ct., at 1328-1329 (Scalia, J., concurring in judgment). Criminal prosecutions do not present the dangers the Court addressed in *Blue Chip Stamps*, so that decision is "inapplicable" to indictments for violations of § 10(b) and Rule 10b-5. *United States v. Naftalin*, 441 U.S. 768, 774, n. 6, 99 S. Ct. 2077, 99 S. Ct., at 2082, 60 L. Ed. 2d 624 (1979); see also *Holmes*, 503 U.S., at 281, 112 S. Ct., at 1324-1325 (O'Connor, J., concurring in part and concurring in judgment) ("[T]he purchaser/seller standing requirement for private civil actions under § 10(b) and Rule 10b-5 is of no import in criminal prosecutions for willful violations of those provisions.").

In sum, the misappropriation theory, as we have examined and explained it in this opinion, is both consistent with the statute and with our precedent. Vital to our decision that criminal liability may be sustained under the misappropriation theory, we emphasize, are two sturdy safeguards Congress has provided regarding scienter. To establish a criminal violation of Rule 10b-5, the Government must prove that a person "willfully" violated the provision. See 15 U.S.C. § 78ff(a). Furthermore, a defendant may not be imprisoned for violating Rule 10b-5 if he proves that he had no knowledge of the Rule. See *ibid.* O'Hagan's charge that the misappropriation theory is too indefinite to permit the imposition of criminal liability, see Brief for Respondent 30-33, thus fails not only because the theory is limited to those who breach a recognized duty. In addition, the statute's "requirement of the presence of culpable intent as a necessary element of the offense does much to destroy any force in the argument that application of the [statute]" in circumstances such as O'Hagan's is unjust. *Boyce Motor Lines, Inc. v. United States*, 342 U.S. 337, 342, 72 S. Ct. 329, 331-332, 96 L. Ed. 367 (1952).

The Eighth Circuit erred in holding that the misappropriation theory is inconsistent with § 10(b). The Court of Appeals may address on remand O'Hagan's other challenges to his convictions under § 10(b) and Rule 10b-5.

III

We consider next the ground on which the Court of Appeals reversed O'Hagan's convictions for fraudulent trading in connection with a tender offer, in violation of § 14(e) of the Exchange Act and SEC Rule 14e-3(a). A sole question is before us as to these convictions: Did the Commission, as the Court of Appeals held, exceed its rulemaking authority under § 14(e) when it adopted Rule 14e-3(a) without requiring a showing that the trading at issue entailed a breach of fiduciary duty? We hold that the Commission, in this regard and to the extent relevant to this case, did not exceed its authority.

The governing statutory provision, § 14(e) of the Exchange Act, reads in relevant part:

> "It shall be unlawful for any person . . . to engage in any fraudulent, deceptive, or manipulative acts or practices, in connection with any tender offer. . . . The [SEC] shall, for the purposes of this subsection, by rules and regulations define, and prescribe means reasonably designed to prevent, such acts and practices as are fraudulent, deceptive, or manipulative." 15 U.S.C. § 78n(e).

Section 14(e)'s first sentence prohibits fraudulent acts in connection with a tender offer. This self-operating proscription was one of several provisions added to the Exchange Act in 1968 by the Williams Act, 82 Stat. 454. The section's second sentence delegates definitional and prophylactic rulemaking authority to the Commission. Congress added this rulemaking delegation to § 14(e) in 1970 amendments to the Williams Act. See § 5, 84 Stat. 1497.

Through § 14(e) and other provisions on disclosure in the Williams Act, Congress sought to ensure that shareholders "confronted by a cash tender offer for their stock [would] not be required to respond without adequate information." *Rondeau v. Mosinee Paper Corp.*, 422 U.S. 49, 58, 95 S. Ct. 2069, 2076, 45 L. Ed. 2d 12 (1975); see *Lewis v. McGraw,* 619 F.2d 192, 195 (C.A.2 1980) (*per curiam*) "very purpose" of Williams Act was "informed decisionmaking by shareholders"). As we recognized in *Schreiber v. Burlington Northern, Inc.,* 472 U.S. 1, 105 S. Ct. 2458, 86 L. Ed. 2d 1 (1985), Congress designed the Williams Act to make "disclosure, rather than court imposed principles of 'fairness' or 'artificiality,' . . . the preferred method of market regulation." *Id.,* at 9, n.8, 105 S. Ct., at 2463 n.8. Section 14(e), we explained, "supplements the more precise disclosure provisions found elsewhere in the Williams Act, while requiring disclosure more explicitly addressed to the tender offer context than that required by § 10(b)." *Id.,* at 10-11, 105 S. Ct., at 2464.

Relying on § 14(e)'s rulemaking authorization, the Commission, in 1980, promulgated Rule 14e-3(a). That measure provides:

> "(a) If any person has taken a substantial step or steps to commence, or has commenced, a tender offer (the 'offering person'), it shall constitute a fraudulent, deceptive or manipulative act or practice within the meaning of section 14(e) of the [Exchange] Act for any other person who is in possession of material information relating to such tender offer which information he knows or has reason to know is nonpublic and which he knows or has reason to know has been acquired directly or indirectly from:
> "(1) The offering person,
> "(2) The issuer of the securities sought or to be sought by such tender offer, or
> "(3) Any officer, director, partner or employee or any other person acting on behalf of the offering person or such issuer, to purchase or sell or cause to be purchased or sold any of such securities or any securities convertible into or exchangeable for any such securities or any option or right to obtain or to dispose of any of the foregoing securities, unless within a reasonable time prior to any purchase or sale such information and its source are publicly disclosed by press release or otherwise." 17 CFR § 240.14e-3(a) (1996).

As characterized by the Commission, Rule 14e-3(a) is a "disclose or abstain from trading" requirement. 45 Fed. Reg. 60410 (1980). The Second Circuit concisely described the Rule's thrust:

> "One violates Rule 14e-3(a) if he trades on the basis of material nonpublic information concerning a pending tender offer that he knows or has reason to know has been acquired 'directly or indirectly' from an insider of the offeror or issuer, or someone working on their behalf. Rule 14e-3(a) is a disclosure provision. It creates a duty in those traders who fall within its ambit to abstain or disclose, *without regard to whether the trader owes a pre-existing fiduciary duty* to respect the confidentiality of the information." *United States v. Chestman,* 947 F.2d 551, 557 (1991) (en banc) (emphasis added), cert. denied, 503 U.S. 1004, 112 S. Ct. 1759, 118 L. Ed. 2d 422 (1992)....

. . .

In sum, it is a fair assumption that trading on the basis of material, nonpublic information will often involve a breach of a duty of confidentiality to the bidder or target company or their representatives. The SEC, cognizant of the proof problem that could enable sophisticated traders to escape responsibility, placed in Rule 14e-3(a) a "disclose or abstain from trading" command that does not require specific proof of a breach of fiduciary duty. That prescription, we are satisfied, applied to this case, is a "means reasonably designed to prevent" fraudulent trading on material, nonpublic information in the tender offer context. See *Chestman,* 947 F.2d, at 560 ("While dispensing with the subtle problems of proof associated with demonstrating fiduciary breach in the problematic area of tender offer insider trading, [Rule 14e-3(a)] retains a close nexus between the prohibited conduct and the statutory aims."); accord, *Maio,* 51 F.3d, at 635, and n.14; *Peters,* 978 F.2d, at 1167. Therefore, insofar as it serves to prevent the type of misappropriation charged against O'Hagan, Rule 14e-3(a) is a proper exercise of the Commission's prophylactic power under § 14(e).

Post-Case Follow-Up

Under the misappropriation theory, the plaintiff must plead and prove that the violator obtained the material non-public information at issue in breach of a duty owed to the source of the information. This duty may arise out of a traditional fiduciary duty or a duty of trust and confidence similar to those characterized by traditional fiduciary duties. One question that has arisen over the years is whether family relations constitute — or, can give rise to — relationships of trust and confidence. In *United States v. Chestman,* 947 F.2d 551 (2d Cir. 1991) — decided six years before *O'Hagan* — the president of the Waldbaum supermarket chain told his sister Shirley about the pending acquisition of the company. Shirley told her daughter Susan, Susan told her husband Keith, and Keith shared the information with his stock broker, Chestman. Chestman traded on the information. The SEC sued Chestman, arguing that a duty of trust and confidence existed between Susan and Keith as husband and wife. Chestman was convicted, but the Second Circuit reversed the conviction, finding that no fiduciary relationship existed between a husband and wife absent some additional element. The court held that "a fiduciary duty cannot be imposed unilaterally by entrusting a person with confidential information," even if that person is a family member. *Id.* at 567.

Following *O'Hagan*, the SEC promulgated and adopted Exchange Act Rule 10b5-2. This rule includes a non-exhaustive list of examples of relationship of trust and confidence for the purposes of the misappropriation theory:

> (b) *Enumerated "duties of trust or confidence."* For purposes of this section, a "duty of trust or confidence" exists in the following circumstances, among others:
>
> (1) Whenever a person agrees to maintain information in confidence;
>
> (2) Whenever the person communicating the material nonpublic information and the person to whom it is communicated have a history, pattern, or practice of sharing confidences, such that the recipient of the information knows or reasonably should know that the person communicating the material nonpublic information expects that the recipient will maintain its confidentiality; or
>
> (3) Whenever a person receives or obtains material nonpublic information from his or her spouse, parent, child, or sibling; provided, however, that the person receiving or obtaining the information may demonstrate that no duty of trust or confidence existed with respect to the information, by establishing that he or she neither knew nor reasonably should have known that the person who was the source of the information expected that the person would keep the information confidential, because of the parties' history, pattern, or practice of sharing and maintaining confidences, and because there was no agreement or understanding to maintain the confidentiality of the information.

Tipper/Tippee Liability

In addition to the insider who trades, so-called **tippees** (those who receive tips from insiders in violation of a breach of duty, knowing the information is nonpublic) can be subject to insider trading liability. **Tippers** (those insiders giving tips) can be held liable, as well. Even subtippees of tippees have been held liable. Depending on the facts, tippers and tippees may be held liable for insider trading under the classical or misappropriation theories or under the Williams Act's prohibition on insider trading contained in Rule 14e-3, discussed below.

Case Preview

United States v. Newman

In the next case, two remote tippees appealed from judgments of conviction entered against them on insider trading charges. The government alleged that the defendants had participated in an unlawful insider trading scheme by trading in securities based on inside information obtained from analysts at various hedge funds and investment firms. The government alleged that the analysts had illicitly obtained the inside information from employees of publicly traded companies. As the basis for their appeal, the defendants argued that the district court erred in failing to instruct the jury that it must find that the tippee knew that the insider disclosed confidential information in exchange for a personal benefit. In reading the case, consider the following questions:

1. What did the defendants do wrong, according to the government?
2. What is a remote tippee?
3. Under what (if any) circumstances will a remote tippee be held liable for or found guilty of insider trading?
4. What constitutes a personal benefit, according to the court?

United States v. Newman
773 F.3d 438 (2d Cir. 2014)

BARRINGTON D. PARKER, Circuit Judge*:

Defendants-appellants Todd Newman and Anthony Chiasson appeal from judgments of conviction entered on May 9, 2013, and May 14, 2013, respectively in the United States District Court for the Southern District of New York (Richard J. Sullivan, J.) following a six-week jury trial on charges of securities fraud in violation of sections 10(b) and 32 of the Securities Exchange Act of 1934 (the "1934 Act"), 48 Stat. 891, 904 (codified as amended at 15 U.S.C. §§ 78j(b), 78ff), Securities and Exchange Commission (SEC) Rules 10b-5 and 10b5-2 (codified at 17 C.F.R. §§ 240.10b-5, 240.10b5-2), and 18 U.S.C. § 2, and conspiracy to commit securities fraud in violation of 18 U.S.C. § 371.

The Government alleged that a cohort of analysts at various hedge funds and investment firms obtained material, nonpublic information from employees of publicly traded technology companies, shared it amongst each other, and subsequently passed this information to the portfolio managers at their respective companies. The Government charged Newman, a portfolio manager at Diamondback Capital Management, LLC ("Diamondback"), and Chiasson, a portfolio manager at Level Global Investors, L.P. ("Level Global"), with willfully participating in this insider trading scheme by trading in securities based on the inside information illicitly obtained by this group of analysts. On appeal, Newman and Chiasson challenge the sufficiency of the evidence as to several elements of the offense, and further argue that the district court erred in failing to instruct the jury that it must find that a tippee knew that the insider disclosed confidential information in exchange for a personal benefit.

We agree that the jury instruction was erroneous because we conclude that, in order to sustain a conviction for insider trading, the Government must prove beyond a reasonable doubt that the tippee knew that an insider disclosed confidential information *and* that he did so in exchange for a personal benefit. Moreover, we hold that the evidence was insufficient to sustain a guilty verdict against Newman and

---

*Footnotes have been omitted for purposes of brevity.

Chiasson for two reasons. *First,* the Government's evidence of any personal benefit received by the alleged insiders was insufficient to establish the tipper liability from which defendants' purported tippee liability would derive. *Second,* even assuming that the scant evidence offered on the issue of personal benefit was sufficient, which we conclude it was not, the Government presented no evidence that Newman and Chiasson knew that they were trading on information obtained from insiders in violation of those insiders' fiduciary duties.

Accordingly, we reverse the convictions of Newman and Chiasson on all counts and remand with instructions to dismiss the indictment as it pertains to them with prejudice.

BACKGROUND

This case arises from the Government's ongoing investigation into suspected insider trading activity at hedge funds. . . .

At trial, the Government presented evidence that a group of financial analysts exchanged information they obtained from company insiders, both directly and more often indirectly. Specifically, the Government alleged that these analysts received information from insiders at Dell and NVIDIA disclosing those companies' earnings numbers before they were publicly released in Dell's May 2008 and August 2008 earnings announcements and NVIDIA's May 2008 earnings announcement. These analysts then passed the inside information to their portfolio managers, including Newman and Chiasson, who, in turn, executed trades in Dell and NVIDIA stock, earning approximately $4 million and $68 million, respectively, in profits for their respective funds.

Newman and Chiasson were several steps removed from the corporate insiders and there was no evidence that either was aware of the source of the inside information. With respect to the Dell tipping chain, the evidence established that Rob Ray of Dell's investor relations department tipped information regarding Dell's consolidated earnings numbers to Sandy Goyal, an analyst at Neuberger Berman. Goyal in turn gave the information to Diamondback analyst Jesse Tortora. Tortora in turn relayed the information to his manager Newman as well as to other analysts including Level Global analyst Spyridon "Sam" Adondakis. Adondakis then passed along the Dell information to Chiasson, making Newman and Chiasson three and four levels removed from the inside tipper, respectively.

With respect to the NVIDIA tipping chain, the evidence established that Chris Choi of NVIDIA's finance unit tipped inside information to Hyung Lim, a former executive at technology companies Broadcom Corp. and Altera Corp., whom Choi knew from church. Lim passed the information to co-defendant Danny Kuo, an analyst at Whittier Trust. Kuo circulated the information to the group of analyst friends, including Tortora and Adondakis, who in turn gave the information to Newman and Chiasson, making Newman and Chiasson four levels removed from the inside tippers.

Although Ray has yet to be charged administratively, civilly, or criminally, and Choi has yet to be charged criminally, for insider trading or any other wrongdoing, the Government charged that Newman and Chiasson were criminally liable for insider trading because, as sophisticated traders, they must have known that information was disclosed by insiders in breach of a fiduciary duty, and not for any legitimate corporate purpose.

At the close of evidence, Newman and Chiasson moved for a judgment of acquittal pursuant to Federal Rule of Criminal Procedure 29. They argued that there was no evidence that the corporate insiders provided inside information in exchange for a personal benefit which is required to establish tipper liability under *Dirks v. S.E.C.,* 463 U.S. 646, 103 S. Ct. 3255, 77 L. Ed. 2d 911 (1983). Because a tippee's liability derives from the liability of the tipper, Newman and Chiasson argued that they could not be found guilty of insider trading. Newman and Chiasson also argued that, even if the corporate insiders had received a personal benefit in exchange for the inside information, there was no evidence that they knew about any such benefit. Absent such knowledge, appellants argued, they were not aware of, or participants in, the tippers' fraudulent breaches of fiduciary duties to Dell or NVIDIA, and could not be convicted of insider trading under *Dirks*. In the alternative, appellants requested that the court instruct the jury that it must find that Newman and Chiasson knew that the corporate insiders had disclosed confidential information for personal benefit in order to find them guilty.

The district court reserved decision on the Rule 29 motions. With respect to the appellants' requested jury charge, while the district court acknowledged that their position was "supportable certainly by the language of *Dirks*," . . . it ultimately found that it was constrained by this Court's decision in *S.E.C. v. Obus*, 693 F.3d 276 (2d Cir. 2012), which listed the elements of tippee liability without enumerating knowledge of a personal benefit received by the insider as a separate element. . . . Accordingly, the district court did not give Newman and Chiasson's proposed jury instruction. Instead, the district court gave the following instructions on the tippers' intent and the personal benefit requirement:

> Now, if you find that Mr. Ray and/or Mr. Choi had a fiduciary or other relationship of trust and confidence with their employers, then you must next consider whether the [G]overnment has proven beyond a reasonable doubt that they intentionally breached that duty of trust and confidence by disclosing material[,] nonpublic information for their own benefit.

Tr. 4030.

On the issue of the appellants' knowledge, the district court instructed the jury:

> To meet its burden, the [G]overnment must also prove beyond a reasonable doubt that the defendant you are considering knew that the material, nonpublic information had been disclosed by the insider in breach of a duty of trust and confidence. The mere receipt of material, nonpublic information by a defendant, and even trading on that information, is not sufficient; he must have known that it was originally disclosed by the insider in violation of a duty of confidentiality.

Tr. 4033:14-22.

On December 17, 2012, the jury returned a verdict of guilty on all counts. The district court subsequently denied the appellants' Rule 29 motions.

On May 2, 2013, the district court sentenced Newman to an aggregate term of 54 months' imprisonment, to be followed by one year of supervised release, imposed a

$500 mandatory special assessment, and ordered Newman to pay a $1 million fine and to forfeit $737,724. On May 13, 2013, the district court sentenced Chiasson to an aggregate term of 78 months' imprisonment, to be followed by one year of supervised release, imposed a $600 mandatory special assessment, and ordered him to pay a $5 million fine and forfeiture in an amount not to exceed $2 million. This appeal followed.

DISCUSSION

Newman and Chiasson raise a number of arguments on appeal. Because we conclude that the jury instructions were erroneous and that there was insufficient evidence to support the convictions, we address only the arguments relevant to these issues. We review jury instructions *de novo* with regard to whether the jury was misled or inadequately informed about the applicable law. *See United States v. Moran-Toala,* 726 F.3d 334, 344 (2d Cir. 2013).

I. The Law of Insider Trading

Section 10(b) of the 1934 Act, 15 U.S.C. § 78j(b), prohibits the use "in connection with the purchase or sale of any security . . . [of] any manipulative or deceptive device or contrivance in contravention of such rules and regulations as the Commission may prescribe. . . ." Although Section 10(b) was designed as a catch-all clause to prevent fraudulent practices, *Ernst & Ernst v. Hochfelder,* 425 U.S. 185, 202-06, 96 S. Ct. 1375, 47 L. Ed. 2d 668 (1976), neither the statute nor the regulations issued pursuant to it, including Rule 10b-5, expressly prohibit insider trading. Rather, the unlawfulness of insider trading is predicated on the notion that insider trading is a type of securities fraud proscribed by Section 10(b) and Rule 10b-5. *See Chiarella v. United States,* 445 U.S. 222, 226-30, 100 S. Ct. 1108, 63 L. Ed. 2d 348 (1980).

A. The "Classical" and "Misappropriation" Theories of Insider Trading

The classical theory holds that a corporate insider (such as an officer or director) violates Section 10(b) and Rule 10b-5 by trading in the corporation's securities on the basis of material, nonpublic information about the corporation. *Id.* at 230, 100 S. Ct. 1108. Under this theory, there is a special "relationship of trust and confidence between the shareholders of a corporation and those insiders who have obtained confidential information by reason of their position within that corporation." *Id.* at 228, 100 S. Ct. 1108. As a result of this relationship, corporate insiders that possess material, nonpublic information have "a duty to disclose [or to abstain from trading] because of the 'necessity of preventing a corporate insider from . . . tak[ing] unfair advantage of . . . uninformed . . . stockholders.'" *Id.* at 228-29, 100 S. Ct. 1108 (citation omitted).

In accepting this theory of insider trading, the Supreme Court explicitly rejected the notion of "a general duty between all participants in market transactions to forgo actions based on material, nonpublic information." *Id.* at 233, 100 S. Ct. 1108. Instead, the Court limited the scope of insider trading liability to situations where the insider had "a duty to disclose arising from a relationship of trust and confidence between parties to a transaction," such as that between corporate officers and share-holders. *Id.* at 230, 100 S. Ct. 1108.

An alternative, but overlapping, theory of insider trading liability, commonly called the "misappropriation" theory, expands the scope of insider trading liability to certain other "outsiders," who do not have any fiduciary or other relationship to a corporation or its shareholders. Liability may attach where an "outsider" possesses material non-public information about a corporation and another person uses that information to trade in breach of a duty owed to the owner. *United States v. O'Hagan,* 521 U.S. 642, 652-53, 117 S. Ct. 2199, 138 L. Ed. 2d 724 (1997); *United States v. Libera,* 989 F.2d 596, 599-600 (2d Cir. 1993). In other words, such conduct violates Section 10(b) because the misappropriator engages in deception by pretending "loyalty to the principal while secretly converting the principal's information for personal gain." *Obus,* 693 F.3d at 285 (citations omitted).

B. Tipping Liability

The insider trading case law, however, is not confined to insiders or misappro-priators who trade for their own accounts. *Id.* at 285. Courts have expanded insider trading liability to reach situations where the insider or misappropriator in posses-sion of material nonpublic information (the "tipper") does not himself trade but discloses the information to an outsider (a "tippee") who then trades on the basis of the information before it is publicly disclosed. *See Dirks,* 463 U.S. at 659, 103 S. Ct. 3255. The elements of tipping liability are the same, regardless of whether the tipper's duty arises under the "classical" or the "misappropriation" theory. *Obus,* 693 F.3d at 285-86.

In *Dirks,* the Supreme Court addressed the liability of a tippee analyst who received material, nonpublic information about possible fraud at an insurance com-pany from one of the insurance company's former officers. *Dirks,* 463 U.S. at 648-49, 103 S. Ct. 3255. The analyst relayed the information to some of his clients who were investors in the insurance company, and some of them, in turn, sold their shares based on the analyst's tip. *Id.* The SEC charged the analyst Dirks with aiding and abetting securities fraud by relaying confidential and material inside information to people who traded the stock.

In reviewing the appeal, the Court articulated the general principle of tipping liability: "Not only are insiders forbidden by their fiduciary relationship from per-sonally using undisclosed corporate information to their advantage, but they may not give such information to an outsider for the same improper purpose of exploiting the information for their personal gain." *Id.* at 659, 103 S. Ct. 3255 (citation omitted). The test for determining whether the corporate insider has breached his fiduciary duty "is whether the insider personally will benefit, directly or indirectly, from his disclosure. Absent some personal gain, *there has been no breach of duty. . . ." Id.* at 662, 103 S. Ct. 3255 (emphasis added).

The Supreme Court rejected the SEC's theory that a recipient of confidential information (i.e. the "tippee") must refrain from trading "whenever he receives inside information from an insider." *Id.* at 655, 103 S. Ct. 3255. Instead, the Court held that "[t]he tippee's duty to disclose or abstain is derivative from that of the insider's duty."

Id. at 659, 103 S. Ct. 3255. Because the *tipper's* breach of fiduciary duty requires that he "personally will benefit, directly or indirectly, from his disclosure," *id.* at 662, 103 S. Ct. 3255, a tippee may not be held liable in the absence of such benefit. Moreover, the Supreme Court held that a tippee may be found liable "only when the insider has breached his fiduciary duty . . . *and* the tippee knows or should know that there has been a breach." *Id.* at 660, 103 S. Ct. 3255 (emphasis added). In *Dirks,* the corporate insider provided the confidential information in order to expose a fraud in the company and not for any personal benefit, and thus, the Court found that the insider had not breached his duty to the company's shareholders and that Dirks could not be held liable as tippee.

E. *Mens Rea*

Liability for securities fraud also requires proof that the defendant acted with scienter, which is defined as "a mental state embracing intent to deceive, manipulate or defraud." *Hochfelder,* 425 U.S. at 193 n.12, 96 S. Ct. 1375. In order to establish a criminal violation of the securities laws, the Government must show that the defendant acted "willfully." 15 U.S.C. § 78ff(a). We have defined willfulness in this context "as a realization on the defendant's part that he was doing a wrongful act under the securities laws." *United States v. Cassese,* 428 F.3d 92, 98 (2d Cir. 2005) (internal quotation marks and citations omitted); *see also United States v. Dixon,* 536 F.2d 1388, 1395 (2d Cir. 1976) (holding that to establish willfulness, the Government must "establish a realization on the defendant's part that he was doing a wrongful act . . . under the securities laws" and that such an act "involve[d] a significant risk of effecting the violation that occurred.") (quotation omitted).

II. *The Requirements of Tippee Liability*

The Government concedes that tippee liability requires proof of a personal benefit to the insider. Gov't Br. 56. However, the Government argues that it was not required to prove that Newman and Chiasson knew that the insiders at Dell and NVIDIA received a personal benefit in order to be found guilty of insider trading. Instead, the Government contends, consistent with the district court's instruction, that it merely needed to prove that the "defendants traded on material, nonpublic information they knew insiders had disclosed in breach of a duty of confidentiality. . . ." Gov't Br. 58.

In support of this position, the Government cites *Dirks* for the proposition that the Supreme Court only required that the "tippee know that the tipper disclosed information in *breach of a duty.*" *Id.* at 40 (citing *Dirks,* 463 U.S. at 660, 103 S. Ct. 3255) (emphasis added). In addition, the Government relies on dicta in a number of our decisions post-*Dirks,* in which we have described the elements of tippee liability without specifically stating that the Government must prove that the tippee knew that the corporate insider who disclosed confidential information did so for his own personal benefit. *Id.* at 41-44 (citing, *inter alia, United States v. Jiau,* 734 F.3d 147, 152-53 (2d Cir. 2013); *Obus,* 693 F.3d at 289; *S.E.C. v. Warde,* 151 F.3d 42, 48-49 (2d Cir. 1998)). By selectively parsing this dictum, the Government seeks to revive the absolute bar on tippee trading that the Supreme Court explicitly rejected in *Dirks.*

Although this Court has been accused of being "somewhat Delphic" in our discussion of what is required to demonstrate tippee liability, *United States v. Whitman,* 904 F. Supp. 2d 363, 371 n.6 (S.D.N.Y. 2012), the Supreme Court was quite clear in *Dirks. First,* the tippee's liability derives *only* from the tipper's breach of a fiduciary duty, *not* from trading on material, non-public information. *See Chiarella,* 445 U.S. at 233, 100 S. Ct. 1108 (noting that there is no "general duty between all participants in market transactions to forgo actions based on material, nonpublic information"). *Second,* the corporate insider has committed no breach of fiduciary duty unless he receives a personal benefit in exchange for the disclosure. *Third,* even in the presence of a tipper's breach, a tippee is liable only if he knows or should have known of the breach.

While we have not yet been presented with the question of whether the tippee's knowledge of a tipper's breach requires knowledge of the tipper's personal benefit, the answer follows naturally from *Dirks. Dirks* counsels us that the exchange of confidential information for personal benefit is not separate from an insider's fiduciary breach; it *is* the fiduciary breach that triggers liability for securities fraud under Rule 10b-5. For purposes of insider trading liability, the insider's disclosure of confidential information, standing alone, is not a breach. Thus, without establishing that the tippee knows of the personal benefit received by the insider in exchange for the disclosure, the Government cannot meet its burden of showing that the tippee knew of a breach.

The Government's overreliance on our prior dicta merely highlights the doctrinal novelty of its recent insider trading prosecutions, which are increasingly targeted at remote tippees many levels removed from corporate insiders. By contrast, our prior cases generally involved tippees who directly participated in the tipper's breach (and therefore had knowledge of the tipper's disclosure for personal benefit) or tippees who were explicitly apprised of the tipper's gain by an intermediary tippee. *See, e.g., Jiau,* 734 F.3d at 150 ("To provide an incentive, Jiau promised the tippers insider information for their own private trading."); *United States v. Falcone,* 257 F.3d 226, 235 (2d Cir. 2001) (affirming conviction of remote tipper where intermediary tippee paid the inside tipper and had told remote tippee "the details of the scheme"); *Warde,* 151 F.3d at 49 (tipper and tippee engaged in parallel trading of the inside information and "discussed not only the inside information, but also the best way to profit from it"); *United States v. Mylett,* 97 F.3d 663 (2d Cir. 1996) (tippee acquired inside information directly from his insider friend). We note that the Government has not cited, nor have we found, a single case in which tippees as remote as Newman and Chiasson have been held criminally liable for insider trading.

Jiau illustrates the importance of this distinction quite clearly. In *Jiau,* the panel was presented with the question of whether the evidence at trial was sufficient to prove that the tippers personally benefitted from their disclosure of insider information. In that context, we summarized the elements of criminal liability as follows:

> (1) the insider-tippers . . . were entrusted the duty to protect confidential information, which (2) they breached by disclosing [the information] to their tippee . . . , who (3) knew of [the tippers'] duty and (4) still used the information to trade a security or further tip the information for [the tippee's] benefit, and finally (5) the insider-tippers benefited in some way from their disclosure.

Jiau, 734 F.3d at 152-53 (citing *Dirks,* 463 U.S. at 659-64, 103 S. Ct. 3255; *Obus,* 693 F.3d at 289). The Government relies on this language to argue that Jiau is merely the most recent in a string of cases in which this Court has found that a tippee, in order to be criminally liable for insider trading, need know only that an insider-tipper disclosed information in breach of a duty of confidentiality. Gov't Br. 43. However, we reject the Government's position that our cursory recitation of the elements in *Jiau* suggests that criminal liability may be imposed on a defendant based only on knowledge of a breach of a duty of confidentiality. In *Jiau,* the defendant knew about the benefit because she provided it. For that reason, we had no need to reach the question of whether knowledge of a breach requires that a tippee know that a personal benefit was provided to the tipper.

In light of *Dirks,* we find no support for the Government's contention that knowledge of a breach of the duty of confidentiality without knowledge of the personal benefit is sufficient to impose criminal liability. Although the Government might like the law to be different, nothing in the law requires a symmetry of information in the nation's securities markets. The Supreme Court explicitly repudiated this premise not only in *Dirks,* but in a predecessor case, *Chiarella v. United States.* In *Chiarella,* the Supreme Court rejected this Circuit's conclusion that "the federal securities laws have created a system providing equal access to information necessary for reasoned and intelligent investment decisions . . . because [material non-public] information gives certain buyers or sellers an unfair advantage over less informed buyers and sellers." 445 U.S. at 232, 100 S. Ct. 1108. The Supreme Court emphasized that "[t]his reasoning suffers from [a] defect . . . [because] not every instance of financial unfairness constitutes fraudulent activity under § 10(b)." *Id. See also United States v. Chestman,* 947 F.2d 551, 578 (2d Cir. 1991) (Winter, J., concurring) ("[The policy rationale [for prohibiting insider trading] stops well short of prohibiting all trading on material nonpublic information. Efficient capital markets depend on the protection of property rights in information. However, they also require that persons who acquire and act on information about companies be able to profit from the information they generate. . . .")]. Thus, in both *Chiarella* and *Dirks,* the Supreme Court affirmatively established that insider trading liability is based on breaches of fiduciary duty, not on informational asymmetries. This is a critical limitation on insider trading liability that protects a corporation's interests in confidentiality while promoting efficiency in the nation's securities markets.

As noted above, *Dirks* clearly defines a breach of fiduciary duty as a breach of the duty of confidentiality in exchange for a personal benefit. *See Dirks,* 463 U.S. at 662, 103 S. Ct. 3255. Accordingly, we conclude that a tippee's knowledge of the insider's breach necessarily requires knowledge that the insider disclosed confidential information in exchange for personal benefit. In reaching this conclusion, we join every other district court to our knowledge — apart from Judge Sullivan — that has confronted this question. *Compare United States v. Rengan Rajaratnam,* No. 13-211 (S.D.N.Y. July 1, 2014) (Buchwald, J.); *United States v. Martoma,* No. 12-973 (S.D.N.Y. Feb. 4, 2014) (Gardephe, J.); *United States v. Whitman,* 904 F. Supp. 2d 363, 371 (S.D.N.Y. 2012) (Rakoff, J.); *United States v. Raj Rajaratnam,* 802 F. Supp. 2d 491, 499 (S.D.N.Y. 2011) (Holwell, J.); *State Teachers Retirement Bd. v. Fluor Corp.,* 592 F. Supp. 592, 594 (S.D.N.Y. 1984) (Sweet, J.), *with United States v. Steinberg,* No. 12-121,

21 F. Supp. 3d 309, 316, 2014 WL 2011685 at *5 (S.D.N.Y. May 15, 2014) (Sullivan, J.), and *United States v. Newman*, No. 12-121 (S.D.N.Y. Dec. 6, 2012) (Sullivan, J.).

Our conclusion also comports with well-settled principles of substantive criminal law. As the Supreme Court explained in *Staples v. United States*, 511 U.S. 600, 605, 114 S. Ct. 1793, 128 L. Ed. 2d 608 (1994), under the common law, *mens rea*, which requires that the defendant know the facts that make his conduct illegal, is a necessary element in every crime. Such a requirement is particularly appropriate in insider trading cases where we have acknowledged "it is easy to imagine a . . . trader who receives a tip and is unaware that his conduct was illegal and therefore wrongful." *United States v. Kaiser*, 609 F.3d 556, 569 (2d Cir. 2010). This is also a statutory requirement, because only "willful" violations are subject to criminal provision. *See United States v. Temple*, 447 F.3d 130, 137 (2d Cir. 2006) (" 'Willful' repeatedly has been defined in the criminal context as intentional, purposeful, and voluntary, as distinguished from accidental or negligent").

In sum, we hold that to sustain an insider trading conviction against a tippee, the Government must prove each of the following elements beyond a reasonable doubt: that (1) the corporate insider was entrusted with a fiduciary duty; (2) the corporate insider breached his fiduciary duty by (a) disclosing confidential information to a tippee (b) in exchange for a personal benefit; (3) the tippee knew of the tipper's breach, that is, he knew the information was confidential and divulged for personal benefit; and (4) the tippee still used that information to trade in a security or tip another individual for personal benefit. *See Jiau*, 734 F.3d at 152-53; *Dirks*, 463 U.S. at 659-64, 103 S. Ct. 3255.

In view of this conclusion, we find, reviewing the charge as a whole, *United States v. Mitchell*, 328 F.3d 77, 82 (2d Cir. 2003), that the district court's instruction failed to accurately advise the jury of the law. The district court charged the jury that the Government had to prove: (1) that the insiders had a "fiduciary or other relationship of trust and confidence" with their corporations; (2) that they "breached that duty of trust and confidence by disclosing material, nonpublic information"; (3) that they "personally benefited in some way" from the disclosure; (4) "that the defendant . . . knew the information he obtained had been disclosed in breach of a duty"; and (5) that the defendant used the information to purchase a security. Under these instructions, a reasonable juror might have concluded that a defendant could be criminally liable for insider trading merely if such defendant knew that an insider had divulged information that was required to be kept confidential. But a breach of the duty of confidentiality is not fraudulent unless the tipper acts for personal benefit, that is to say, there is no breach unless the tipper "is in effect selling the information to its recipient for cash, reciprocal information, or other things of value for himself. . . ." *Dirks*, 463 U.S. at 664, 103 S. Ct. 3255 (quotation omitted). Thus, the district court was required to instruct the jury that the Government had to prove beyond a reasonable doubt that Newman and Chiasson knew that the tippers received a personal benefit for their disclosure.

The Government argues that any possible instructional error was harmless because the jury could have found that Newman and Chiasson inferred from the circumstances that some benefit was provided to (or anticipated by) the insiders. Gov't Br. 60. We disagree.

An instructional error is harmless only if the Government demonstrates that it is "clear beyond a reasonable doubt that a rational jury would have found the defendant guilty absent the error[.]" *Neder v. United States*, 527 U.S. 1, 17-18, 119 S. Ct. 1827, 144 L. Ed. 2d 35 (1999); *accord Moran-Toala*, 726 F.3d at 345; *United States v. Quattrone*, 441 F.3d 153, 180 (2d Cir. 2006). The harmless error inquiry requires us to view whether the evidence introduced was "uncontested and supported by overwhelming evidence" such that it is "clear beyond a reasonable doubt that a rational jury would have found the defendant guilty absent the error." *Neder*, 527 U.S. at 18, 119 S. Ct. 1827. Here both Chiasson and Newman contested their knowledge of any benefit received by the tippers and, in fact, elicited evidence sufficient to support a contrary finding. Moreover, we conclude that the Government's evidence of any personal benefit received by the insiders was insufficient to establish tipper liability from which Chiasson and Newman's purported tippee liability would derive.

III. *Insufficiency of the Evidence*

As a general matter, a defendant challenging the sufficiency of the evidence bears a heavy burden, as the standard of review is exceedingly deferential. *United States v. Coplan*, 703 F.3d 46, 62 (2d Cir. 2012). Specifically, we "must view the evidence in the light most favorable to the Government, crediting every inference that could have been drawn in the Government's favor, and deferring to the jury's assessment of witness credibility and its assessment of the weight of the evidence." *Id.* (citing *United States v. Chavez*, 549 F.3d 119, 124 (2d Cir. 2008)). Although sufficiency review is *de novo*, we will uphold the judgments of conviction if "any rational trier of fact could have found the essential elements of the crime beyond a reasonable doubt." *Id.* (citing *United States v. Yannotti*, 541 F.3d 112, 120 (2d Cir. 2008) (emphasis omitted); *Jackson v. Virginia*, 443 U.S. 307, 319, 99 S. Ct. 2781, 61 L. Ed. 2d 560 (1979)). This standard of review draws no distinction between direct and circumstantial evidence. The Government is entitled to prove its case solely through circumstantial evidence, provided, of course, that the Government still demonstrates each element of the charged offense beyond a reasonable doubt. *United States v. Lorenzo*, 534 F.3d 153, 159 (2d Cir. 2008).

However, if the evidence "is nonexistent or so meager," *United States v. Guadagna*, 183 F.3d 122, 130 (2d Cir. 1999), such that it "gives equal or nearly equal circumstantial support to a theory of guilt and a theory of innocence, then a reasonable jury must necessarily entertain a reasonable doubt," *Cassese*, 428 F.3d at 99. Because few events in the life of an individual are more important than a criminal conviction, we continue to consider the "beyond a reasonable doubt" requirement with utmost seriousness. *Cassese*, 428 F.3d at 102. Here, we find that the Government's evidence failed to reach that threshold, even when viewed in the light most favorable to it.

The circumstantial evidence in this case was simply too thin to warrant the inference that the corporate insiders received any personal benefit in exchange for their tips. As to the Dell tips, the Government established that Goyal and Ray were not "close" friends, but had known each other for years, having both attended business school and worked at Dell together. Further, Ray, who wanted to become a Wall Street analyst like Goyal, sought career advice and assistance from Goyal. The evidence further showed that Goyal advised Ray on a range of topics, from discussing the qualifying examination in order to become a financial analyst to editing Ray's résumé and sending it to a Wall Street recruiter, and that some of this assistance began before Ray began to provide tips about Dell's earnings. The evidence also established that Lim and Choi were "family friends" that had met through church and occasionally socialized together. The Government argues that these facts were sufficient to prove that the tippers derived some benefit from the tip. We disagree. If this was a "benefit," practically anything would qualify.

We have observed that "[p]ersonal benefit is broadly defined to include not only pecuniary gain, but also, *inter alia,* any reputational benefit that will translate into future earnings and the benefit one would obtain from simply making a gift of confidential information to a trading relative or friend." *Jiau,* 734 F.3d at 153 (internal citations, alterations, and quotation marks deleted). This standard, although permissive, does not suggest that the Government may prove the receipt of a personal benefit by the mere fact of a friendship, particularly of a casual or social nature. If that were true, and the Government was allowed to meet its burden by proving that two individuals were alumni of the same school or attended the same church, the personal benefit requirement would be a nullity. To the extent *Dirks* suggests that a personal benefit may be inferred from a personal relationship between the tipper and tippee, where the tippee's trades "resemble trading by the insider himself followed by a gift of the profits to the recipient," *see* 463 U.S. at 664, 103 S. Ct. 3255, we hold that such an inference is impermissible in the absence of proof of a meaningfully close personal relationship that generates an exchange that is objective, consequential, and represents at least a potential gain of a pecuniary or similarly valuable nature. In other words, as Judge Walker noted in *Jiau,* this requires evidence of "a relationship between the insider and the recipient that suggests a *quid pro quo* from the latter, or an intention to benefit the [latter]." *Jiau,* 734 F.3d at 153.

While our case law at times emphasizes language from *Dirks* indicating that the tipper's gain need not be *immediately* pecuniary, it does not erode the fundamental insight that, in order to form the basis for a fraudulent breach, the personal benefit received in exchange for confidential information must be of some consequence. For example, in *Jiau,* we noted that at least one of the corporate insiders received something more than the ephemeral benefit of the "value[ ] [of] [Jiau's] friendship" because he also obtained access to an investment club where stock tips and insight were routinely discussed. *Id.* Thus, by joining the investment club, the tipper entered into a relationship of *quid quo pro* with Jiau, and therefore had the opportunity to access information that could yield future pecuniary gain. *Id.; see also SEC v. Yun,* 327 F.3d 1263, 1280 (11th Cir. 2003) (finding evidence of personal benefit where tipper and tippee worked closely together in real estate deals and commonly split commissions on various real estate transactions); *SEC v. Sargent,* 229 F.3d 68, 77 (1st Cir. 2000) (finding evidence of personal benefit when the tipper passed information to a friend who referred others to the tipper for dental work).

Here the "career advice" that Goyal gave Ray, the Dell tipper, was little more than the encouragement one would generally expect of a fellow alumnus or casual acquaintance. *See, e.g.,* J.A.2080 (offering "minor suggestions" on a resume), J.A.2082 (offering advice prior to an informational interview). Crucially, Goyal testified that he would have given Ray advice without receiving information because he routinely did so for industry colleagues. Although the Government argues that the jury could have reasonably inferred from the evidence that Ray and Goyal swapped career advice for inside information, Ray himself disavowed that any such *quid pro quo* existed. Further, the evidence showed Goyal began giving Ray "career advice" over a year before Ray began providing any insider information. Tr. 1514. Thus, it would not be possible under the circumstances for a jury in a criminal trial to find beyond a reasonable doubt that Ray received a personal benefit in exchange for the disclosure of confidential information. *See, e.g., United States v. D'Amato*, 39 F.3d 1249, 1256 (2d Cir. 1994) (evidence must be sufficient to "reasonably infer" guilt).

The evidence of personal benefit was even more scant in the NVIDIA chain. Choi and Lim were merely casual acquaintances. The evidence did not establish a history of loans or personal favors between the two. During cross examination, Lim testified that he did not provide anything of value to Choi in exchange for the information. Tr. 3067-68. Lim further testified that Choi did not know that Lim was trading NVIDIA stock (and in fact for the relevant period Lim did not trade stock), thus undermining any inference that Choi intended to make a "gift" of the profits earned on any transaction based on confidential information.

Even assuming that the scant evidence described above was sufficient to permit the inference of a personal benefit, which we conclude it was not, the Government presented absolutely no testimony or any other evidence that Newman and Chiasson knew that they were trading on information obtained from insiders, or that those insiders received any benefit in exchange for such disclosures, or even that Newman and Chiasson consciously avoided learning of these facts. As discussed above, the Government is required to prove beyond a reasonable doubt that Newman and Chiasson knew that the insiders received a personal benefit in exchange for disclosing confidential information.

It is largely uncontroverted that Chiasson and Newman, and even their analysts, who testified as cooperating witnesses for the Government, knew next to nothing about the insiders and nothing about what, if any, personal benefit had been provided to them. Adondakis said that he did not know what the relationship between the insider and the first-level tippee was, nor was he aware of any personal benefits exchanged for the information, nor did he communicate any such information to Chiasson. Adondakis testified that he merely told Chiasson that Goyal "was talking to someone within Dell," and that a friend of a friend of Tortora's would be getting NVIDIA information. Tr. 1708, 1878. Adondakis further testified that he did not specifically tell Chiasson that the source of the NVIDIA information worked at NVIDIA. Similarly, Tortora testified that, while he was aware Goyal received information from someone at Dell who had access to "overall" financial numbers, he was not aware of the insider's name, or position, or the circumstances of how Goyal obtained the information. Tortora further testified that he did not know whether Choi received a personal benefit for disclosing inside information regarding NVIDIA.

The Government now invites us to conclude that the jury could have found that the appellants knew the insiders disclosed the information "for some personal reason rather than for no reason at all." Gov't Br. 65. But the Supreme Court affirmatively rejected the premise that a tipper who discloses confidential information necessarily does so to receive a personal benefit. *See Dirks,* 463 U.S. at 661-62, 103 S. Ct. 3255 ("All disclosures of confidential corporate information are not inconsistent with the duty insiders owe to shareholders"). Moreover, it is inconceivable that a jury could conclude, beyond a reasonable doubt, that Newman and Chiasson were aware of a personal benefit, when Adondakis and Tortora, who were more intimately involved in the insider trading scheme as part of the "corrupt" analyst group, disavowed any such knowledge.

Alternatively, the Government contends that the specificity, timing, and frequency of the updates provided to Newman and Chiasson about Dell and NVIDIA were so "overwhelmingly suspicious" that they warranted various material inferences that could support a guilty verdict. Gov't Br. 65. Newman and Chiasson received four updates on Dell's earnings numbers in the weeks leading up to its August 2008 earnings announcement. Similarly, Newman and Chiasson received multiple updates on NVIDIA's earnings numbers between the close of the quarter and the company's earnings announcement. The Government argues that given the detailed nature and accuracy of these updates, Newman and Chiasson must have known, or deliberately avoided knowing, that the information originated with corporate insiders, *and* that those insiders disclosed the information in exchange for a personal benefit. We disagree.

Even viewed in the light most favorable to the Government, the evidence presented at trial undermined the inference of knowledge in several ways. The evidence established that analysts at hedge funds routinely estimate metrics such as revenue, gross margin, operating margin, and earnings per share through legitimate financial modeling using publicly available information and educated assumptions about industry and company trends. For example, on cross-examination, cooperating witness Goyal testified that under his financial model on Dell, when he ran the model in January 2008 without any inside information, he calculated May 2008 quarter results of $16.071 billion revenue, 18.5% gross margin, and $0.38 earnings per share. Tr. 1566. These estimates came very close to Dell's reported earnings of $16.077 billion revenue; 18.4% gross margin, and $0.38 earnings per share. Appellants also elicited testimony from the cooperating witnesses and investor relations associates that analysts routinely solicited information from companies in order to check assumptions in their models in advance of earnings announcements. Goyal testified that he frequently spoke to internal relations departments to run his model by them and ask whether his assumptions were "too high or too low" or in the "ball park," which suggests analysts routinely updated numbers in advance of the earnings announcements. Tr. 1511. Ray's supervisor confirmed that investor relations departments routinely assisted analysts with developing their models.

Moreover, the evidence established that NVIDIA and Dell's investor relations personnel routinely "leaked" earnings data in advance of quarterly earnings. Appellants introduced examples in which Dell insiders, including the head of Investor Relations, Lynn Tyson, selectively disclosed confidential quarterly financial information arguably similar to the inside information disclosed by Ray and Choi to establish relationships with financial firms who might be in a position to buy Dell's stock. For example, appellants introduced an email Tortora sent Newman summarizing a conversation he had with Tyson in which she suggested "low 12% opex [was] reasonable" for Dell's upcoming quarter and that she was "fairly confident on [operating margin] and [gross margin]." Tr. 568:18-581:23.

No reasonable jury could have found beyond a reasonable doubt that Newman and Chiasson knew, or deliberately avoided knowing, that the information originated with corporate insiders. In general, information about a firm's finances could certainly be sufficiently detailed and proprietary to permit the inference that the tippee knew that the information came from an inside source. But in this case, where the financial information is of a nature regularly and accurately predicted by analyst modeling, and the tippees are several levels removed from the source, the inference that defendants knew, or should have known, that the information originated with a corporate insider is unwarranted.

Moreover, even if detail and specificity could support an inference as to the *nature* of the source, it cannot, without more, permit an inference as to that source's improper *motive* for disclosure. That is especially true here, where the evidence showed that corporate insiders at Dell and NVIDIA regularly engaged with analysts and routinely selectively disclosed the same type of information. Thus, in light of the testimony (much of which was adduced from the Government's own witnesses) about the accuracy of the analysts' estimates and the selective disclosures by the companies themselves, no rational jury would find that the tips were so overwhelmingly suspicious that Newman and Chiasson either knew or consciously avoided knowing that the information came from corporate insiders or that those insiders received any personal benefit in exchange for the disclosure.

In short, the bare facts in support of the Government's theory of the case are as consistent with an inference of innocence as one of guilt. Where the evidence viewed in the light most favorable to the prosecution gives equal or nearly equal circumstantial support to a theory of innocence as a theory of guilt, that evidence necessarily fails to establish guilt beyond a reasonable doubt. *See United States v. Glenn,* 312 F.3d 58, 70 (2d Cir. 2002). Because the Government failed to demonstrate that Newman and Chiasson had the intent to commit insider trading, it cannot sustain the convictions on either the substantive insider trading counts or the conspiracy count. *United States v. Gaviria,* 740 F.2d 174, 183 (2d Cir. 1984) ("[W]here the crime charged is conspiracy, a conviction cannot be sustained unless the Government establishes beyond a reasonable doubt that the defendant had the specific intent to violate the substantive statute.") (internal quotation marks omitted). Consequently, we reverse Newman and Chiasson's convictions and remand with instructions to dismiss the indictment as it pertains to them.

CONCLUSION

For the foregoing reasons, we vacate the convictions and remand for the district court to dismiss the indictment with prejudice as it pertains to Newman and Chiasson.

Post-Case Follow-Up

On October 13, 2015, the Supreme Court denied cert in *United States v. Newman*, 773 F.3d 438 (2d Cir. 2014), *cert. denied*, 136 S. Ct. 242 (2015). Without further commentary, the Justices declined to consider the government's challenge to the Second Circuit's decision overturning the insider trading convictions of two hedge fund portfolio managers. The Supreme Court's denial means that the Second Circuit's decision — characterized by the government as a "roadmap for unscrupulous traders" — stands.

United States v. Newman: Real Life Applications

Sam Smith is married to Terry Jones. Jones is the president of School Software, Inc., a publisher and distributor of educational software whose stock is quoted on the NASDAQ National Market System and whose option contracts are traded on the Chicago Board Options Exchange (CBOE). Smith is a real estate agent.

On January 27, 2016, Jones attended a corporate retreat at which Software's chief financial officer revealed that the company would post a loss for the current quarter. The CFO also revealed that the company was preparing a public announcement revising its earnings forecast downward. The CFO and the CEO cautioned employees not to sell any of the Software securities holdings until after the announcement, which the CFO believed (correctly) was likely to result in a decline in Software's stock price. The executive team also cautioned the retreat attendees to keep the matter confidential and informed the attendees that the negative earnings announcement would be released a few days later on February 3, 2016.

Over the weekend, Smith and Jones discussed an asset statement that Jones had prepared as part of the couple's negotiation of a division of assets. (Smith and Jones were in the process of finalizing a divorce.) Jones explained that he had assigned a value of $30 to his Software options, even though Software stock was trading at $40 at that time, because he believed that the price would drop on February 3rd following the company's release of the negative earnings announcement. Jones told Smith not to disclose the information. Smith agreed to keep it confidential.

On Monday, February 1, 2016, Smith went to work. Smith worked out of a cubicle in a space shared with several other real estate agents. Around 10:00 A.M., Smith called the attorney who was helping Smith negotiate the division of assets to discuss Jones's statement of assets. Smith told the attorney what Jones had said about the impending earnings announcement and the likely decline in Software's stock price. Another real estate agent with the firm — Shannon — overheard the conversation after she entered the brokers' shared workspace to pick up a file.

Two hours after overhearing Smith's conversation with the lawyer, Shannon called her stockbroker and placed an order to purchase put options. Put options are a contract that grants the holder the right to sell at a specified price a specific number of shares by a set date. For example, the purchaser of a Software February $40 put 100 has the right to sell 100 shares of Software at $40 to the put seller at any time until the contract expires in February. Put options are most commonly used when a purchaser of the put believes the price of the underlying stock is likely to decline. When Shannon's broker told Shannon that he knew of no reason why Software's stock price would decline, Shannon explained that based on rumors being exchanged in real estate broker circles, she wanted to buy the puts. Shannon then purchased $20,000 worth of Software put options in an amount equal to nearly half the value of Shannon's entire investment portfolio.

After the stock market closed on February 3, 2016, Software issued its negative earnings release. As expected, the price of Software's stock declined. Shannon then sold the puts, realizing a profit of $269,000, or almost a 1,300 percent return on investment.

The SEC has sued Smith and Shannon for allegedly violating § 10(b) of the Exchange Act and Rule 10b-5.

1. Smith has moved to dismiss the SEC's complaint, arguing that an individual who does not purchase or sell the stock at issue cannot be held liable under insider trading laws. Is this position correct?

2. Smith also has moved to dismiss on the grounds that individuals who are not employed by the company whose securities are at issue, and who does not otherwise qualify as a corporate insider, does not owe any duties to the issuer and thus cannot be held liable under insider trading laws. Is this position correct?

3. Shannon has moved to dismiss the SEC's complaint on the grounds that she is not a corporate insider of Software and thus did not have a duty to disclose or abstain from trading. Is Shannon's position correct?

4. Assume that the personal benefit requirement as articulated in *Newman* applies to Smith. What will the SEC have to establish respecting the intent to benefit requirement? Do you think the SEC can establish an intent to benefit in this case?

Rule 14e-3

Rule 14e-3 promulgated under the '34 Act prohibits a person from trading while in possession of material non-public information relating to a tender offer. In contrast to both the classical and misappropriation theories, Rule 14e-3 applies even if the trader did not breach a fiduciary duty or other relationship of trust and confidence in connection with the trade.

Compliance and Internal Controls

Because insider trading is so serious and causes lack of public confidence in the stock market, most large companies now appoint their own compliance officers to clear or approve trades by inside company executives who might have access to non-public information. Insider trading cases brought by the SEC historically have remained steady at about 7 percent of all of its enforcement cases. Criminal prosecutions by the Justice Department, however, have increased in the past decade.

7. Remedies and Penalties for Violation of 1934 Act

Purchasers or sellers of stock traded in violation of Rule 10b-5 have a wide array of remedies available to them. The most common remedy is to allow the defrauded party to recover "out-of-pocket" damages, namely, the difference between what the victim purchased or sold the stock for and its actual worth at the time of the deception. In certain cases, treble damages (damages up to three times any profit gained or loss avoided) can also be imposed. Criminal penalties for violations have also been enacted. Jail terms have been increased to up to 20 years, and fines have increased to up to $5 million for individuals and $25 million for firms. 15 U.S.C. § 78ff. These penalties do not affect any other actions that can be taken by the SEC or by private investors.

In 2011, the SEC broadened its then-existing bounty program and implemented new rules adopted under the Dodd-Frank Act to require the payment of significant award payments to certain whistleblowers whose information leads to a successful SEC enforcement action for *any* securities violation (if the SEC obtains sanctions of more than $1 million). The SEC then established its Office of the Whistleblower, which paid more than $28 million to whistleblowers in 2015. In September 2014, the SEC announced it was paying a single foreign tipster more than $30 million, its largest whistleblowing award on record.

In 2007, NASD (formerly the National Association of Securities Dealers) merged with the regulatory operations of the NYSE to form the **Financial Industry Regulatory Authority** (FINRA), which is responsible for the oversight of all public securities firms doing business in the United States. FINRA also regulates the securities industry, enacts and enforces its own rules as well as federal securities laws, educates investors, and provides dispute resolution services. FINRA not only can impose monetary fines, it can also expel firms and individuals from the securities industry. It also engages in continuous electronic surveillance of trading to detect abuses such as insider trading. FINRA oversees nearly every aspect of the securities industry.

8. Short-Swing Profits: § 16(b)

Section 16(b) of the 1934 Act requires all officers, all directors, and persons who are beneficial owners of more than 10 percent of any class of stock of a § 12 company to report their ownership and trading in their corporation's stock to the SEC. These individuals must report their ownership interest to the SEC and file additional reports within two business days after a change in their stock ownership. Thus, the SEC is provided with detailed records regarding purchases and sales of stock and grants of stock options to corporate insiders. This information must also be posted on the company's website, thus allowing shareholders to determine when those "in the know" have bought or sold company stock.

To ensure that insiders do not obtain any benefit from their intimate knowledge of corporate affairs, § 16 provides that any profits realized from the purchase or sale of any stock in a company by these officers, directors, or 10-percent shareholders in any six-month period shall be recaptured by the corporation. It is irrelevant whether the insider has actually used insider information; any such profits made in such a short time frame (the **"short-swing" profit**) must be disgorged to the corporation. Thus, § 16(b) imposes liability without regard to fraud or intent. The profits obtained through this short-swing trading must be disgorged to the corporation even if innocently obtained.

The SEC's 2015 annual report disclosed that it obtained $4.2 billion in disgorgement and penalties.

D. PROXY REGULATION

1. Overview

Most states and the MBCA allow shareholders to vote by proxy if they are unable or do not wish to attend a meeting. As discussed in Chapter 8, a **proxy** is a written authorization instructing another person (often members of the company's management) to vote one's shares on one's behalf. The word *proxy* is also used to refer to the person who will act in place of the shareholder. As discussed, the closest analogy to a proxy form is an absentee ballot: Voters who are unable to be present for voting on election day may vote by absentee ballot. Similarly, shareholders who cannot attend shareholder meetings may vote by proxy. Proxies are most often used and needed for large corporations with numerous shareholders where most shareholders vote by proxy rather than voting in person at the meeting.

Section 14 of the Securities Exchange Act of 1934 regulates the solicitation of proxies from shareholders of § 12 companies. The intent of § 14 is to protect shareholders from abuse by corporate management, which might mislead shareholders. The 1934 Act thus requires that any materials used to solicit shareholder votes in annual or special meetings held for the election of directors and approval of other corporate action must be filed with the SEC in advance of any such solicitation. Among other requirements, SEC regulations state that the solicitation of proxies relating to meetings at which directors will be elected must be accompanied by a written proxy statement containing specified information such as information about the management of the corporation, compensation of managers, the background of nominees, stock option grants, and any other matters being voted on. Typically, corporations provide a package of materials to shareholders in connection with management's solicitation of proxies consisting of the proxy statement, a proxy card, and the company's annual report. In this way, shareholders are given information from which to make an informed decision about matters subject to a shareholder vote. The proxy form or card is generally distributed with the notice of the meeting. See Exhibit 13.8 for an excerpt from General Electric's 2015 proxy materials summarizing the matters up for a vote, the details of the annual meeting, the various channels for obtaining information, and the mechanics of exercising voting rights. Exhibit 13.9 is the 2016 Proxy Card for Apple Inc.

EXHIBIT 13.8 **Excerpt, 2015 General Electric Proxy Statement**

Notice of 2015 Annual Meeting of Shareowners

Meeting Information

Date: April 22, 2015

Time: 10:00 a.m. Central Time

Location: Cox Convention Center,
1 Myriad Gardens,
Oklahoma City, OK 73102

March 10, 2015

Dear Shareowners:

You are invited to attend General Electric Company's 2015 Annual Meeting of Shareowners. Following a report on GE's business operations, shareowners will vote:

- to **elect** the **16 directors** named in the proxy statement for the coming year;
- to **approve** our **named executives' compensation** in an advisory vote;
- to **ratify** the selection of our **independent auditor** for 2015; and
- on the **shareowner proposals** set forth in the proxy statement, if properly presented at the meeting.

Shareowners also will transact any other business that may properly come before the meeting.

If you plan to attend the meeting, please follow the advance registration instructions under "Attending the Meeting" on page 53 to obtain an admission card. To enter the meeting, you must present this card along with photo identification.

If you are unable to attend the meeting, you may view the live webcast on our Investor Relations website at www.ge.com/investor-relations.

Cordially,

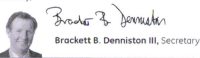

Brackett B. Denniston III, Secretary

How You Can Vote

Your vote is important. You are eligible to vote if you were a shareowner of record at the close of business on February 23, 2015. To make sure that your shares are represented at the meeting, please cast your vote as soon as possible by one of the following methods:

FOR REGISTERED HOLDERS & RSP PARTICIPANTS: *(hold shares directly with GE or through GE Retirement Savings Plan)*	FOR BENEFICIAL OWNERS: *(hold shares through broker, bank or nominee)*
Using the Internet at www.investorvote.com/GE	Using the Internet at www.proxyvote.com

Scanning this QR code to vote with your mobile device

Scanning this QR code to vote with your mobile device

Calling toll-free from the U.S., U.S. territories and Canada to 1-800-652-VOTE (8683)

Calling toll-free from the U.S., U.S. territories and Canada to 1-800-454-VOTE (8683)

Mailing your signed proxy form

Mailing your signed voting instruction form

How You Can Access the Proxy Materials Online

Important notice regarding the availability of GE's proxy materials for the 2015 annual meeting:

Please visit the websites or scan the QR codes above with your mobile device to view our interactive proxy and annual report websites and download these materials. If you received a Notice of Internet Availability of Proxy Materials, please see "How We Use the E-Proxy Process (Notice & Access)" on page 50 for more information.

The proxy statement is available at www.ge.com/proxy

The annual report is available at www.ge.com/annualreport

GE 2015 Proxy Statement

EXHIBIT 13.9 2016 Proxy Card, Apple Inc.

Apple Inc.

IMPORTANT ANNUAL MEETING INFORMATION 000004

ENDORSEMENT LINE _____ SACKPACK

MR A SAMPLE
DESIGNATION (IF ANY)
ADD 1
ADD 2
ADD 3
ADD 4
ADD 5
ADD 6

C123456789

000000000.000000 ext   000000000.000000 ext
000000000.000000 ext   000000000.000000 ext
000000000.000000 ext   000000000.000000 ext

Electronic Voting Instructions

You can vote by Internet or telephone!
Available 24 hours a day, 7 days a week!

Instead of mailing your proxy, you may choose one of the voting methods outlined below to vote your proxy.

VALIDATION DETAILS ARE LOCATED BELOW IN THE TITLE BAR.

Proxies submitted by the Internet or telephone must be received by 1:00 a.m., Eastern Time, on February 26, 2016.

Vote by Internet
• Log on to the Internet and go to
  www.investorvote.com/AAPL
• Follow the steps outlined on the secured website.

Vote by telephone
• Call toll free 1-800-652-VOTE (8663) within the USA, US territories & Canada any time on a touch tone telephone. There is NO CHARGE to you for the call.
• Follow the instructions provided by the recorded message.

Using a **black ink** pen, mark your votes with an **X** as shown in this example. Please do not write outside the designated areas.   [X]

Apple Inc. Annual Shareholder Meeting Proxy Card   1234 5678 9012 345

▼ IF YOU HAVE NOT VOTED VIA THE INTERNET OR TELEPHONE, FOLD ALONG THE PERFORATION, DETACH AND RETURN THE BOTTOM PORTION IN THE ENCLOSED ENVELOPE. ▼

A Proposals — The Board of Directors recommends a vote FOR all the listed nominees and FOR Proposals 2, 3 and 4.

1. Election of Directors:

	For	Against	Abstain		For	Against	Abstain		For	Against	Abstain
01 - JAMES BELL	☐	☐	☐	02 - TIM COOK	☐	☐	☐	03 - AL GORE	☐	☐	☐
04 - BOB IGER	☐	☐	☐	05 - ANDREA JUNG	☐	☐	☐	06 - ART LEVINSON	☐	☐	☐
07 - RON SUGAR	☐	☐	☐	08 - SUE WAGNER	☐	☐	☐				

	For	Against	Abstain		For	Against	Abstain
2. Ratification of the appointment of Ernst & Young LLP as Apple's independent registered public accounting firm for 2016	☐	☐	☐	3. An advisory resolution to approve executive compensation	☐	☐	☐
4. Approval of the amended and restated Apple Inc. 2014 Employee Stock Plan	☐	☐	☐				

B Shareholder Proposals — The Board of Directors recommends a vote AGAINST Proposals 5, 6, 7 and 8.

	For	Against	Abstain		For	Against	Abstain
5. A shareholder proposal entitled "Net-Zero Greenhouse Gas Emissions by 2030"	☐	☐	☐	6. A shareholder proposal regarding diversity among our senior management and board of directors	☐	☐	☐
7. A shareholder proposal entitled "Human Rights Review – High Risk Regions"	☐	☐	☐	8. A shareholder proposal entitled "Shareholder Proxy Access"	☐	☐	☐

IF VOTING BY MAIL, YOU MUST COMPLETE SECTIONS A - D ON BOTH SIDES OF THIS CARD.

C 1234567890   JNT   MR A SAMPLE (THIS AREA IS SET UP TO ACCOMMODATE
                          140 CHARACTERS) MR A SAMPLE AND MR A SAMPLE AND
1UPX   2575841   MR A SAMPLE AND MR A SAMPLE AND MR A SAMPLE AND
                          MR A SAMPLE AND MR A SAMPLE AND MS A SAMPLE AND

In general, anyone who solicits a proxy (whether management or shareholder groups) must fully and truthfully disclose any matters pertinent to the proxy or to the matters to be voted on. Remedies for violation include injunctions preventing solicitation or voting of the proxies as well as an award of monetary damages. Effective January 1, 2009, all publicly traded companies are required to post their proxy materials (namely, the proxy statement and the annual report) on an Internet website and then provide their shareholders with notice of the availability of these proxy materials 40 days before any meeting. Companies may also mail their proxy materials, and if shareholders request materials by mail, they must be provided at no charge.

2. Shareholder Proposals: Rules and Mechanics

Certain questions and proposals set for a shareholder vote must be included in proxy materials. There are two types of proposals that are made at shareholders' meetings for publicly traded companies: management proposals (those proposed by the company's management) and shareholder proposals (those proposed by the company's shareholders). Shareholders may circulate their own proxy materials to shareholders containing shareholder proposals (which is expensive and time consuming), or they may seek to have their proposals included in the company's proxy statements. The requirements (both procedural and substantive) for including shareholder proposals in the company's proxy materials are set forth in Rule 14a-8 promulgated under the Exchange Act. Procedural requirements include the following:

■ To be eligible to submit a proposal, the shareholder must have at least $2,000 in market value or 1 percent of the company's shares, and the shareholder must have held the stock continuously for the 12 months preceding the proposal.
■ A shareholder may not submit more than one proposal for each shareholder's meeting.
■ A proposal may not exceed 500 words.
■ Most proposals submitted for consideration at the annual meeting must be submitted at least four months prior to anniversary of the mailing date of the previous year's proxy materials.
■ Either the shareholder or the shareholder's "qualified representative" must attend the meeting at which the proposal is to be considered.

Rule 14a-8's substantive requirements for shareholder proposals include the following:

■ The proposal may not, if implemented, cause the company to violate substantive law;
■ The proposal may not address a special interest or personal grievance not applicable to other shareholders;
■ The topic of the proposal must be a proper subject for actions by shareholders under the law of the state of incorporation;
■ If the proposal relates to the company's operations, those operations must involve at least 5 percent of the company's assets, net earnings, or gross sales, *or* the operations must be "significantly related to the company's business";
■ The proposal must not violate the proxy rules;
■ The proposal may not address management functions, such as the company's ordinary business operations;
■ The proposal must not be beyond the company's power to implement;
■ The proposal may not relate to specific amounts of cash or stock dividends;
■ The proposal may not directly conflict with one of the company's own proposals that is being submitted at the same meeting; and
■ If the proposal was previously submitted within the last five years and did not receive the required percentage of votes, it may be excluded by the company.

See Exchange Act Rule 14a-8.

If a corporation wishes to exclude a proposal from its proxy materials, it typically will file a **no action letter request** with the SEC explaining why the corporation believes the proposal is excludable under Rule 14a-8. A no action letter asks the SEC's Division of Corporation Finance to confirm that it will not recommend that an enforcement action be filed against the corporation if the corporation excludes the proposal at issue. If the SEC provides no action relief, the corporation generally will exclude the proposal from its proxy materials. If the SEC declines to provide no action relief, the corporation typically will include the proposal in its proxy materials. The board of directors will then indicate in the proxy materials whether it supports or opposes the various management and shareholder proposals. The SEC maintains a searchable database of no action letter requests. As an alternative to requesting no action relief, a corporation also may seek a declaratory judgment that a shareholder proposal is excludable.

3. Shareholder Proposals: Topics and Trends

Spotlight: Shareholder Proposals Relating to Political Activity

In the wake of the Supreme Court's decision in *Citizens United v. Federal Election Commission*, 558 U.S. 310 (2010), that the government may not, consistent with First Amendment principles, suppress political speech on the basis of the speaker's corporate identity, there have been a number of shareholder proposals seeking additional disclosure respecting corporate political activities. Exhibit 13.10 contains an example of a shareholder proposal relating to political expenditures submitted by the New York City Comptroller to Cabot Oil & Gas Corp.

EXHIBIT 13.10 | **Shareholder Proposal of Comptroller of the City of New York to Cabot Oil & Gas Corporation.**

PROPOSAL 4 REPORT ON POLITICAL CONTRIBUTIONS

The Comptroller of the City of New York, Scott M. Stringer, as custodian and a trustee of the New York City Employees' Retirement System, the New York City Fire Department Pension Fund and the New York City Teachers' Retirement System, has notified us that it intends to present the following proposal at the Annual Meeting. The proponent has furnished evidence of ownership of at least $2,000 in market value of the Company's common stock for at least one year prior to the date the proposal was submitted. **The Company is not responsible for the contents of this proposal or the supporting statement and recommends that you vote AGAINST the following shareholder proposal for the reasons set forth in the Company's opposition statement following the proposal.**

RESOLVED: that the shareholders of Cabot Oil & Gas ("Cabot" or the "Company") hereby request that the Company provide a report, updated semiannually, disclosing the Company's:

1. Policies and procedures for making, with corporate funds or assets, contributions and expenditures (direct or indirect) to (a) participate or intervene in any political campaign

on behalf of (or in opposition to) any candidate for public office, or (b) influence the general public, or any segment thereof, with respect to an election or referendum.

2. Monetary and non-monetary contributions and expenditures (direct and indirect) used in the manner described in section 1 above, including:
   a. The identity of the recipient as well as the amount paid to each; and
   b. The title(s) of the person(s) in the Company responsible for decision-making.

The report shall be presented to the board of directors or relevant board committee and posted on the Company's website within 12 months from the date of the annual meeting.

STOCKHOLDER SUPPORTING STATEMENT

Almost half of Cabot's voting shareholders supported this resolution last year.

As long-term shareholders of Cabot, we support transparency and accountability in corporate spending on political activities. These include any activities considered intervention in any political campaign under the Internal Revenue Code, such as direct and indirect contributions to political candidates, parties, or organizations; independent expenditures; or electioneering communications on behalf of federal, state or local candidates.

We acknowledge that Cabot now discloses some information on its political spending on its website, including the annual aggregate amount spent on political engagement and the names of trade associations to which it belongs. We believe this is deficient since it does not disclose how much and to whom the Company gave. For example, we do not know to which candidates, parties, and committees the Company gave and how much, or if it gave to any of the "social welfare" organizations that engage in political activities.

Publicly available records show that Cabot spent at least $327,850 to intervene in elections since the 2004 election cycle. (CQ: http://moneyline.cq.com and National Institute on Money in State Politics: http://followthemoney.org)

Gaps in transparency and accountability may expose the company to reputational and business risks that could threaten long-term shareholder value. This may be especially true for Cabot, which the Political Economy Research Institute included in its Toxic 100 Water Polluters list of 2013.

Relying on publicly available data does not provide a complete picture of the Company's political spending. The proposal asks Cabot to disclose all of its political spending, including payments to trade associations and other tax exempt organizations used for political purposes. This would bring our Company in line with a growing number of its peers, including Noble Energy, Exelon Corp., and ConocoPhillips that support political disclosure and accountability and present this information on their websites.

The Company's Board and its shareholders need comprehensive disclosure to be able to fully evaluate the political use of corporate assets. We urge your support for this critical governance reform.

CABOT'S STATEMENT IN OPPOSITION TO PROPOSAL 4

Our Board of Directors has carefully considered this proposal and believes that approval of the proposed resolution is not in the best interest of Cabot or our shareholders. This is the second consecutive year we have received this proposal from the Comptroller of the City of New York. At our 2014 annual meeting, the proposal received the support of only 31% of the shares represented in person or by proxy at the meeting. Our Board believes that this vote result indicates that our shareholders support the Company's current policies and practices with respect to political contributions.

We publicly disclose our political spending on our website.

As disclosed on our website in accordance with our Policy on Political Contributions and Activities, our total corporate political contributions for 2014 were $50,000 and the total amount of our dues paid to business and trade associations to which we belong that were used for non-deductible lobbying expenses in 2014, as reported to us by the associations, were less than $250,000. Based on the 2014 shareholder vote, Cabot's existing transparency with respect to its political activities and the de minimis nature of our political contributions, the Board believes that the requested report is both unnecessary and not a productive use of Cabot's and the shareholders' resources.

We follow our Board-approved policy on political contributions.

We operate in an industry that is heavily regulated and as such, deeply affected by the political and legislative process. We strongly believe that Cabot's long-term value to our shareholders is enhanced by a business environment that protects and supports free enterprise economic policies and, in particular, the oil and gas industry. To address this business need and to provide oversight for the participation in the political process, the Board has approved a Policy on Political Contributions and Activities, which is contained in our Code of Business Conduct found on our website at www.cabotog.com/about-cabot/governance. We strictly adhere to this Policy and to all U.S. and state laws and regulations that govern political engagement for U.S. public companies.

Cabot is prohibited by its policy and by law from directly participating in federal elections or campaigns. Cabot has also never engaged in "independent expenditures," which are aimed at the general public and advocate the election or defeat of a specific candidate and were allowed by the decision of the U.S. Supreme Court in the *Citizens United* case in 2010. We participate in the political process primarily indirectly, through sponsorship of the non-partisan Cabot Oil & Gas Political Action Committee ("COGPAC"), which is financed completely through voluntary employee contributions.

From time to time, however, where allowed by state law, Cabot supports organizations that are active in the political process on a state level, state candidates or ballot initiatives, and these contributions are reported by the recipients to the appropriate state agencies and publicly available. We also disclose the total amount of these corporate political contributions on an annual basis on our website. For 2014, the total amount was $50,000. The Board believes this disclosure provides the transparency that shareholders need to make informed investment decisions in Cabot and that naming individual recipients is unnecessary and not in the best interest of Cabot or its shareholders as a whole.

We disclose all trade association memberships and lobbying expenses on our website and such expenditures are de minimis.

Consistent with our policy, we are members of business and industry trade groups that engage in collaborative activities and information sharing regarding issues that affect our industry. Some of these associations also engage in lobbying activities that seek to promote legislative solutions that are, in our judgment, sound and responsible and that advance Cabot's and our industry's business goals and interests. A list of our business and trade association memberships can be found on our website at www.cabotog.com/social-responsibility/environment-safety. The primary reason for Cabot's membership in trade associations is to further business goals and initiatives and not to fund political activities. Some of the trade associations in which we participate, however, have notified us that a small portion (generally 5% or less) of our dues paid in 2014 may have been used for non-deductible lobbying expenses. The total non-deductible portion of our dues paid to all business and trade associations in which we participate, as reported to us by those associations, is disclosed on our website each year. In 2014, such amount was less than $250,000. These expenditures are ancillary to the primary business purpose of our membership in those associations, and we believe that reasonable investors could only consider such amounts immaterial. Accordingly, our Board believes it is not necessary to report the amount of our dues, or the non-deductible portions, paid to such associations by name, as requested by the proponent.

Our Board of Directors oversees all political spending.

Finally, we believe that the proponents' stated concern regarding Cabot's exposure to reputational and business risks from participation in the political process is unfounded. Our Board receives a report at least annually, detailing all political contributions by the COGPAC, as well as all direct political contributions by Cabot, and listing recipients by name and amount. Additionally, the Chairman of the Board and CEO approves the Company's participation in, and levels of contributions to, all business and trade associations. In this way, our Board oversees our political contributions process and compliance with our policies and seeks to ensure that our participation in the political process is consistent with the best interests of the Company and our shareholders.

For the reasons stated above, the Board believes that the shareholders as a whole would not benefit from the additional report outlined in the proposal and urges that you vote against it.

THE BOARD OF DIRECTORS UNANIMOUSLY RECOMMENDS THAT YOU VOTE AGAINST APPROVAL OF THE SHAREHOLDER PROPOSAL.

Spotlight: Shareholder Proposals Relating to Proxy Access for Shareholder Nominees

Shareholders historically have desired to place their own nominees for directors on the ballot for shareholder meetings. In 2010, the SEC adopted Rule 14a-11. This rule required public companies to include in their proxy materials candidates for the board of directors nominated by eligible shareholders unless the law of the state of incorporation or the company's governing documents prohibited shareholders from nominating directors. The Business Roundtable and U.S. Chamber of Commerce challenged the rule, however, and in July 2011, the U.S. Court of Appeals for the District of Columbia vacated the rule, holding that the SEC had adopted it in violation of the Administrative Procedures Act. The SEC did not appeal the ruling. Instead, the Commission amended Rule 14a-8 to allow shareholder proposals that seek to establish a procedure for the inclusion of shareholder nominees in the company's proxy materials. In addition, both the DGCL and the MBCA were amended to specifically authorize proxy access bylaw provisions. Exhibit 13.11 contains an example of a shareholder proposal for a proxy access bylaw submitted by the Comptroller of the City of New York and included in the proxy materials of Cabot Oil & Gas Corp., followed by the statement of the board of the company recommending that shareholders vote against the proposal.

EXHIBIT 13.11 **Shareholder Proposal/Proxy Access Bylaw, Cabot Oil & Gas Corporation, 2015 Proxy Materials**

PROPOSAL 5 PROXY ACCESS

The Comptroller of the City of New York, Scott M. Stringer, as custodian and trustee of the New York City Employees' Retirement System, the New York City Police Pension Fund and custodian of the New York City Board of Education Retirement System, has notified us that it intends to present the following proposal at the Annual Meeting. The proponent has furnished evidence of ownership of at least $2,000 in market value of the Company's common stock for at least one year prior to the date the proposal was submitted. **The Company is not responsible for the contents of this proposal or the supporting statement and recommends that you vote AGAINST the following shareholder proposal for the reasons set forth in the Company's opposition statement following the proposal.**

RESOLVED: Shareholders of Cabot Oil & Gas Corporation (the "Company") ask the board of directors (the "Board") to adopt, and present for shareholder approval, a "proxy access" bylaw. Such a bylaw shall require the Company to include in proxy materials prepared for a shareholder meeting at which directors are to be elected the name, Disclosure and Statement (as defined herein) of any person nominated for election to the board by a shareholder or group (the "Nominator") that meets the criteria established below. The Company shall allow shareholders to vote on such nominee on the Company's proxy card.

The number of shareholder-nominated candidates appearing in proxy materials shall not exceed one quarter of the directors then serving. This bylaw, which shall supplement existing rights under Company bylaws, should provide that a Nominator must:

a) have beneficially owned 3% or more of the Company's outstanding common stock continuously for at least three years before submitting the nomination:

b) give the Company, within the time period identified in its bylaws, written notice of the information required by the bylaws and any Securities and Exchange Commission rules about (i) the nominee, including consent of being named in the proxy materials and to serving as director if elected; and (ii) the Nominator, including proof it owns the required shares (the "Disclosure"); and

c) certify that (i) it will assume liability stemming from any legal or regulatory violation arising out of the Nominator's communications with the Company shareholders, including the Disclosure and Statement; (ii) it will comply with all applicable laws and regulations if it uses soliciting material other than the Company's proxy materials; and (iii) to the best of its knowledge, the required shares were acquired in the ordinary course of business and not to change or influence control at the Company.

The Nominator may submit with the Disclosure a statement not exceeding 500 words in support of the nominee (the "Statement"). The Board shall adopt procedures for promptly resolving disputes over whether notice of a nomination was timely, whether the Disclosure and Statement satisfy the bylaw and applicable federal regulations, and the priority to be given to multiple nominations exceeding the one-quarter limit.

STOCKHOLDER SUPPORTING STATEMENT

We believe proxy access is a fundamental shareholder right that will make directors more accountable and contribute to increased shareholder value. The CFA Institute's 2014 assessment of pertinent academic studies and the use of proxy access in other markets similarly concluded that proxy access:

■ Would "benefit both the markets and corporate boardrooms, with little cost or disruption."

■ Has the potential to raise overall US market capitalization by up to $140.3 billion of adopted market-wide. (http://www.cfapubs.org/doi/ pdf/10.2469/ccb.v2014.n9.1)

The proposed bylaw terms enjoy strong investor support—votes for similar shareholder proposals averaged 55% from 2012 through September 2014—and similar bylaws have been adopted by companies of various sizes across industries, including Chesapeake Energy, Hewlett-Packard, Western Union and Verizon.

We urge shareholders to vote FOR this proposal.

CABOT'S STATEMENT IN OPPOSITION TO PROPOSAL 5

The Board of Directors has carefully considered this proposal and recommends a vote AGAINST this proposal. As discussed below, Cabot has already implemented proxy access for its stockholders; accordingly, the Board believes that no further action is needed, and that the form of proxy access sought by the proponent is not in the best interest of Cabot or its stockholders.

We have an established record of best governance practices, exceptional performance and strong support from our stockholders.

Our commitment to corporate governance best practices is well established and discussed throughout this proxy statement. See, for example, "Proxy Summary—Governance Highlights" above on page 9. Our stockholders have expressed continued confidence in our Board through support for each of our current director nominees in excess of 95% at each annual meeting in the last five years at which they were also nominated. This support for our Board is also expressed through the advisory vote in favor of our executive compensation programs in excess of 95% since 2011, the first year such vote was taken. Our exceptional financial and operational performance, as discussed above under "Compensation Discussion and Analysis—2014 Financial and Operational Highlights," puts us at the top of our peer group over those periods. Additionally, our total shareholder returns (TSR) for the last three and five year periods have been at the top of our current peer group, outperforming all but one of our peers in each of those periods. We believe that the strength of our Board and our corporate governance practices have contributed to the strong returns Cabot's stockholders have enjoyed over the last three and five year periods.

Our Board of Directors is responsive to stockholders.

We routinely engage with many of our stockholders to discuss their views on corporate governance, executive compensation and other matters of interest to our stockholders, and have demonstrated our willingness to respond to these concerns. As a result of this ongoing engagement, in recent years we have implemented majority voting in uncontested director elections and declassified the structure of our Board. In accordance with this practice, we sought input about proxy access from many of our significant stockholders. Based on these discussions, we found that our stockholders generally support proxy access rights for long-term stockholders as a means to increase director accountability and give stockholders a more meaningful voice in director elections. Our stockholders do not, however, have uniform views on the ownership levels and holding periods that should be required for a stockholder or group of stockholders to be eligible to include their nominees in our proxy materials, or the number of such nominees that may be included. For example, many of our stockholders expressed a willingness to support higher ownership thresholds where a company had already implemented many key corporate governance best practices and financial performance was strong.

Our Board of Directors has adopted proxy access for the benefit of all stockholders.

Due to the interest of our stockholders in proxy access, our Board considered various potential formulations of proxy access, including the provisions advocated by the proponent, taking into account feedback from many of our stockholders, the level of ownership and nature of our larger holders and the size, tenure and structure of our Board. Based upon the Board's assessment of the relative advantages and disadvantages to the stockholders and the Company of the various proxy access formulations, in March 2015, the Board of Directors amended the bylaws of the Company to implement proxy access in the form it believes is most appropriate for Cabot and its stockholders. Under the amended bylaws adopted by the Board, any stockholder or group of up to 10 stockholders that beneficially owns at least 5% of our outstanding Common Stock continuously for three years is permitted to nominate candidates for election to the Board and to require the Company to list such nominees along with the Board's nominees in the Company's proxy statement. The qualifying stockholder or group of stockholders may nominate up to 20% of the Board, rounding down to the nearest whole number of Board seats, under the proxy access provisions of the bylaws.

The proponent's version of proxy access is unnecessary and could be detrimental to stockholders as a whole.

In selecting the appropriate proxy access formulation, our Board sought to balance the desire to provide meaningful rights to stockholders who we believe are generally representative of our other long-term stockholders against the potential harm to Board effectiveness that may be caused by the nomination of directors who may pursue narrow special interests, including interests unrelated to long-term stockholder value. We believe that a 5% ownership level, as opposed to the 3% ownership level urged by the proponent, is more effective at balancing these competing goals, particularly when up to 10 stockholders may aggregate their stockholdings to reach the 5% ownership threshold. Allowing a lower ownership threshold or an unlimited number of holders to act as a group undermines the principle that we believe is shared by most of our stockholders: that the right to nominate a director using the Company's proxy statement should be available only for those who have a sufficient financial stake in the Company to cause their interests to be aligned with the interests of the stockholders as a whole. For these reasons, our Board believes that the Company's current proxy access right is in the best interests of the stockholders and that the proponent's approach is not appropriate for Cabot.

THE BOARD OF DIRECTORS UNANIMOUSLY RECOMMENDS THAT YOU VOTE AGAINST APPROVAL OF THE STOCKHOLDER PROPOSAL.

Responding to investor pressure or perhaps to thwart competing shareholder proposals, a number of companies have voluntarily adopted some form of proxy access, typically allowing investors who own at least 3 percent of a company's shares for at least three years to nominate candidates for up to 20 percent of the board's open spots. For example, on December 21, 2015, Apple Inc. amended and restated its bylaws to allow for greater proxy access for certain shareholders. The relevant excerpt from Apple's amended bylaws is contained in Exhibit 13.12.

EXHIBIT 13.12 **Section 5.15, Apple Inc. Amended and Restated Bylaws**

5.15 Proxy Access for Director Nominations

(a) Subject to the terms and conditions of these Bylaws, the Corporation shall include in its proxy materials for an annual meeting of shareholders the name and other Required Information of any Shareholder Nominee nominated for election or reelection to the Board of Directors at such annual meeting of shareholders in accordance with this Section 5.15. Capitalized terms used in this Section 5.15 shall have the meanings indicated in this Section 5.15. This Section 5.15 shall be the exclusive method for shareholders to require that the Corporation include nominees for election as a director in the Corporation's proxy materials.

(b) Definitions.

(i) "Shareholder Nominee" means any nominee for election or reelection to the Board of Directors who satisfies the eligibility requirements in this Section 5.15, and who is identified in a timely and proper Shareholder Notice.

(ii) "Shareholder Notice" means a notice that (1) complies with the requirements of this Section 5.15 and (2) is given by or on behalf of an Eligible Shareholder.

(iii) "Eligible Shareholder" means one or more shareholders or beneficial owners of shares of the Corporation that (1) expressly elect at the time of the delivery of the Shareholder Notice pursuant to this Section 5.15 to have one or more Shareholder Nominees included in the Corporation's proxy materials, (2) Own and have Owned (as defined in Section 5.15(c) below) continuously for at least three (3) years, as of the date of the Shareholder Notice, a number of shares of the Corporation that represents at least three percent (3%) of the outstanding shares entitled to vote as of the date of the Shareholder Notice (the "Required Shares"), and (3) satisfy such additional requirements as are set forth in these Bylaws, including Section 5.15(d) below. No shares may be attributed to more than one (1) group constituting an Eligible Shareholder (and no shareholder or beneficial owner, alone or together with any of its affiliates, may be a member of more than one (1) group constituting an Eligible Shareholder) under this Section 5.15.

(iv) "Required Information" means (1) the information set forth in the Schedule 14N provided with the Shareholder Notice concerning each Shareholder Nominee and the Eligible Shareholder that the Corporation determines is required to be disclosed in the Corporation's proxy materials by the applicable requirements of the Exchange Act and the rules and regulations thereunder, and (2) if the Eligible Shareholder so elects, a written statement (the "Statement") of the Eligible Shareholder, not to exceed 500 words, in support of each Shareholder Nominee, which must be provided at the same time as the Shareholder Notice for inclusion in the Corporation's proxy materials for the annual meeting of shareholders.

E. SPOTLIGHT: THE JUMPSTART OUR BUSINESS STARTUPS ACT

As discussed earlier in this chapter, the JOBS Act was enacted to make it easier for smaller companies to raise capital without being required to "go public" and thus become subject to SEC registration and reporting requirements. Among its provisions, some of which have been noted earlier in this chapter, are the following:

- Creation of a new category of issuer, called an **emerging growth company** (namely, one with total annual gross revenues of less than $1 billion), which is subject to relaxed SEC requirements in connection with initial public offerings (allowing these companies to submit draft registration statements to the SEC for confidential review) and subject to relief from various reporting and disclosure requirements, including some Sarbanes-Oxley and Dodd-Frank requirements, for up to five years after their IPOs. The phasing in of these compliance requirements is meant to encourage companies to go public and is often referred to as the "IPO on-ramp."
- Exemption from registration requirements under Regulation A for certain offerings, as discussed.
- Allowance of general advertising and solicitation in "private" offerings under Rule 506 so long as all purchasers are accredited.
- Raising of the threshold for the number of shareholders that triggers § 12 registration and reporting from 500 to 2,000 (or 500 shareholders who are not accredited). The $10 million asset threshold is maintained. This exemption allows companies to stay private for a longer period of time while they raise revenue.
- Creating an exemption from registration requirements for certain types of equity crowdfunding.

Although the JOBS Act is meant to streamline the process of going public for certain companies, such as the emerging growth companies, and reduce burdensome disclosure requirements for other companies, many critics have expressed concern that without rigorous reporting and disclosure requirements, investors will be subject to increased risk of fraud. For example, crowdfunding will allow entrepreneurs to solicit funds over the Internet from smaller investors (and allows these investors to participate in start-ups), but the anonymity of the Internet might facilitate the conning of unsophisticated investors out of their money by scam artists posing as small business owners. Many experts believe that concern about such potential fraud is the primary reason the SEC did not adopt final rules related to equity crowdfunding until October 2015.

F. SPOTLIGHT: THE DODD-FRANK ACT AND EXECUTIVE COMPENSATION

As noted in Chapter 9, the Dodd-Frank Wall Street Reform and Consumer Protection Act ("Dodd-Frank Act") represents the most significant overhaul of financial regulation in generations. Reforms relating to corporate governance include requirements a requirement of independent directors on compensation committees, "say on pay" votes on executive compensation, and additional disclosures relating to executive compensation generally and so-called "golden parachutes" required to be paid upon a corporation combination or change in corporate control.

Say on Pay

Say on pay proposals have been sought by shareholders who have wanted to rein in excessive executive compensation for years. According to the AFL-CIO, in 1980 the average CEO of a large U.S. company earned 42 times what his average employee did; by 2013, the average CEO made 331 times workers' median pay. Although the say on pay provisions of Dodd-Frank are not binding, they provide significant help to shareholders who now have a chance to voice disapproval of misguided executive compensation schemes. In fact, in April 2012, shareholders rejected Citigroup's executive compensation plan, marking the first time investors rejected a compensation plan at a major U.S. bank. Nevertheless, say on pay proposals generally receive majority approval of shareholders, indicating that companies have been effectively addressing shareholder concerns about executive pay.

In the wake of Dodd-Frank, the role of proxy advisory firms (companies that provide opinions on directors being elected, director tenure, executive pay, and other items voted on at annual meetings) has come under scrutiny. Because large institutional investors such as pension plans or mutual funds cannot possibly research every vote facing every corporation in which the funds own stock, the institutional investors began relying heavily on the recommendations of the proxy advisory firms, causing many corporations to argue that the proxy advisors wielded too much power. For example, if a proxy advisory firm determined that directors should attend 75 percent of all meetings, and a director failed to do so, the proxy advisory firm would recommend that investors vote against that director in the next election. In fact, the two largest proxy advisors issue formal annual guidelines, recommending how shareholders should vote on specific issues at their next meeting. To rein in the proxy advisors, the SEC issued new guidance in mid-2014, requiring investment funds to adopt and implement policies to ensure that proxies are voted in the best interests of their clients and strengthening the proxy advisory firms' obligations to disclose conflicts of interest. Some experts, however, remain concerned as to the influence of proxy advisors.

Recall that under the JOBS Act, a new category of business, an emerging growth company (an issuer that has total annual gross revenues of less than $1 billion) is exempt from various requirements, including the Dodd-Frank say on pay, frequency, and golden parachute votes, and is subject to scaled-back executive compensation disclosures for five years after becoming a public company.

G. STATE SECURITIES REGULATION

A company selling securities must comply with federal and state securities laws. Each state has its own statutes regulating the issuance of securities within its jurisdictional borders. Many of these state statutes predate the federal securities laws. According to *Hall v. Geiger-Jones Co.*, 242 U.S. 539, 550 (1917), these regulations were intended to prevent "speculative schemes which have no more basis than so many feet of 'blue sky.'" As a result, state laws regulating the issuance of securities are referred to as **blue sky laws**. The best known loose-leaf service containing each state's laws, recent topics, and digests of cases relating thereto is the *Blue Sky Law Reporter*, published by CCH, Incorporated. The state blue sky laws exist concurrently with the federal statutes relating to issuance and sale of securities. Therefore, a corporation wishing to go public must comply not only with the federal securities laws but also with a variety of state laws. Under the intrastate offering exemption discussed earlier, securities that are offered and sold only to persons residing in one state are exempt from federal registration, 15 U.S.C. § 77c(a)(11), and need only comply with the pertinent state's regulations.

Provisions of state blue sky laws differ widely among states. Generally, however, there are three common elements:

- *Prohibition of fraud.* Most state blue sky laws contain anti-fraud provisions highly similar to or patterned after the anti-fraud provisions of Rule 10b-5. These provisions prohibit fraud in the sale of securities.
- *Broker and dealer registration.* Most states regulate securities by regulating and licensing the persons involved in the offer and sale of securities, namely, brokers, dealers, salespersons, and so forth.
- *Registration requirements.* Most states combine securities registration requirements with other provisions to require disclosure of pertinent information by registration. Unless a valid exemption applies, the issuer must register or qualify the securities with the state corporations commissioner before sales to investors. Some states require that certain information be provided in an application to register the securities before the securities may be sold in the state. Some states evaluate the merits of the transaction and refuse to register the securities if refusal is in the public interest.

The actual process of registering securities in the states varies greatly, but most states provide three alternative approaches. In a registration by coordination scheme, if the securities have been registered under federal law, they can be issued in the state without further requirements. A copy of the prospectus filed with the SEC and other documents are provided to the state. The objective of registration by coordination is simultaneous registration of the offering with the SEC and in the states where the offering will be made. In a registration by notice filing, if a registration statement has been filed under the 1933 Act and the issuer has been engaged in business in the United States for some period of time and has a certain net worth, the issuer provides a simple notification to the state that it will be offering securities in the state. Attached to this is a copy of the latest prospectus filed with the SEC. In a registration by qualification scheme, the issuer must provide comprehensive information to the state, similar to the registration statement required under the 1933 Act. The state corporations commissioner will carefully review the statement and securities being offered, generally because there has been no federal registration of the securities. Registration by qualification is used when no other procedure or exemption is available. Generally, if an issuer has filed a registration statement with the SEC, the process of state registration is simpler than if the issuer is selling securities in the state for the first time without having filed a federal registration statement.

The Uniform Law Commission has approved a Uniform Securities Act (2002 and amended in 2005), which replaces earlier versions of the Uniform Securities Act and has been adopted in 17 states. The text of the Uniform Securities Act is available at the ULC's website. As is true of federal registration requirements, there are numerous exemptions from state blue sky laws. Some of the exemptions relate to the type of security being offered (such as securities offered by governmental institutions) and others relate to smaller issues, exempting them from the state registration requirements.

I. LISTING STANDARDS

Both the New York Stock Exchange (NYSE) and the NASDAQ stock market have listing standards that corporations must meet for their securities to be listed. Some of these standards relate to share price and other quantitative measures. As discussed in Chapter 8, other requirements relate to corporate governance issues. Examples of governance-related NYSE listing standards (including standards relating to independence as discussed in Chapter 8) are as follows:

- A listed company's board must hold regular executive sessions of non-management directors without management present.
- A majority of directors on a listed company's board must be independent, as that term is defined by exchange rules.
- A listed company must have a nominating and governance committee composed solely of independent directors.
- The compensation committee of a listed company's board must be composed of independent directors.
- The audit committee of a listed company must be composed of independent directors, and must also have at least three directors who are financially literate.

Chapter Summary

- The federal securities laws define "security" broadly to include a wide range of instruments, transactions, and investment schemes, including transactions that constitute an "investment contract."
- Under the federal securities laws, securities offerings are required to be registered with the Securities and Exchange Commission or to qualify for an exemption from registration. With limited exceptions, public offerings of securities are not eligible for an exemption from registration.
- In addition to the federal securities law regime, state "blue sky" laws also contain registration and disclosure requirements relating to securities offerings.
- The Securities Act of 1933 governs securities offerings, and it contains registration, disclosure, and anti-fraud rules.

- The Securities and Exchange Act of 1934 governs the purchase and sale of securities after their initial offering, and it contains registration, disclosure, and anti-fraud rules. These rules include period and event-driven reporting requirements for public companies.
- The JOBS Act relaxed certain restrictions on securities offerings with an eye toward making it easier for smaller companies to raise money without having to go public.
- There are two types or theories of insider trading — the classical theory and the misappropriation theory.
- The Securities and Exchange Act of 1934 regulates the proxy system of shareholder voting.
- The NYSE and the NASDAQ have listing rules relating to corporate governance, including rules relating to director independence and service on nominating and governance committees and requirements relating to service on a listed corporation's audit committee.

Applying the Concepts

1. Access corporate filings via the SEC's website (www.sec.gov). Locate and review the Current Report on Form 8-K filed by Twitter, Inc. on July 1, 2014. Briefly, why did Twitter file this current report?

2. Locate the 2015 Notice of Annual Meeting and Proxy Statement filed by General Electric. (You can locate filings via the SEC's website or via the Investor Relations Section of General Electric's website. Look for the Definitive Proxy Statement filed on Form 14A dated March 10, 2015.)

   a. What was the date, time, and location of General Electric's annual meeting of shareholders?
   b. What items were up for a shareholder vote at the annual meeting?
   c. What were the different ways shareholders can get copies of the annual meeting materials, including the proxy materials?
   d. What were the different ways that shareholders could vote?
   e. Did General Electric implement a form of proxy access for shareholders prior to the 2015 annual meeting? If so, describe GE's reforms in this area.
   f. What governance changes did General Electric make between the 2014 and 2015 annual meetings?
   g. How many directors were up for election?
   h. Did any of the director nominees qualify as independent?
   i. Locate the shareowner proposals that appear in the proxy statement. Review each proposal and the board of directors' recommendation to shareholders for each proposal.
      i. The first shareowner proposal concerns cumulative voting. Does GE's board recommend voting FOR or AGAINST this proposal? Why do you think the board made the recommendation that it did? Did shareowners

vote on a proposal relating to cumulative voting in 2014? What was the result of that vote?

 ii. Why couldn't the shareholder proposals in the proxy materials be excluded from GE's proxy materials?

 j. If a shareholder wished to submit a proposal for inclusion in the 2016 GE proxy statement, to whom should the shareholder send the proposal? By what date must the shareholder submit the proposal?

3. A corporation incorporated in California (and which conducts 90 percent of its business in California) intends to sell stock only to California residents. Must it comply with the registration requirements of the 1933 Securities Act? Discuss.

4. In June 2011, Groupon Inc. filed a registration statement with the SEC for its proposed initial public offering, or IPO. The financial media raised questions about Groupon's use of a non-GAAP accounting metric in reporting profits. Commentators also raised questions about Groupon's business model, citing low barriers to entry and the potential of deep-pocketed competitors. In August 2011, Groupon's CEO and co-founder sent an e-mail to employees that contained impassioned defenses of Groupon's business. The e-mail leaked and quickly went viral.

 a. The SEC required Groupon to include the e-mail as an amendment to the company's prospectus. Why?

 b. By including the e-mail in the prospectus, did Groupon assume liability for the e-mail's contents under any provisions of the securities laws?

5. Jacob, an officer of ABC Inc., recently learned at a company meeting that the company intends to buy a patent that is critical to its business. Jacob purchased 20,000 shares of ABC stock at $40 each. When the announcement of the patent purchase was made, the company's stock increased to $60 per share. Discuss whether Jacob has committed any violations of securities laws. Would your answer be different if Jacob had instructed his father to purchase the shares? Discuss.

6. Olivia, the treasurer of Hartridge Group, Inc., purchased 40,000 shares of stock of the company in December. In May, Olivia sold 20,000 of these shares so that she would have enough money to pay her son's college tuition. Olivia made $18,000 on the sale of the stock. Has Olivia violated any securities laws? Discuss.

7. Jenny and Taro would like to raise $500,000 from friends and family to help take their New York City–based app development business to the next level. Family members from across the country have expressed interest in backing Taro and Jenny.

 a. Does the offering have to be registered?

 b. Are any exemptions from registration potentially available?

 c. Can Jenny and Taro promote the offering via the Internet?

  d. Assume that family members in California, Texas, North Carolina, and Florida would like to invest. Do Jenny and Taro need to comply with blue sky laws in each of these states?

  e. Assume Jenny and Taro ask you about crowdfunding. What, if any, rules exist regarding the mechanics of equity crowdfunding — e.g., are there any restrictions on the size of the offering or investments, or both, by individual investors?

8. Mark, a well-known entrepreneur and TV personality, recently retained you for representation on all securities law matters. During your first meeting with Mark, you learn the following facts:

   In January of last year, Mark acquired 100,000 shares, or an 8 percent stake, of Zed.com, Inc., a publicly held company that develops human resources software that is used primarily in overseas markets. Mark's only relationship with Zed is that of shareholder; Mark is not an officer or director of the company, nor is Mark a controlling shareholder.

   In March, Zed's CEO called Mark and told him that Zed had decided to raise additional capital through a PIPE offering. PIPE stands for private investment in public equity. In a PIPE offering, investors purchase restricted shares from a company at a specified price. The company, in turn, agrees to file a resale registration statement to so that investors can resell the shares to the public. Because PIPE offerings have the potential to increase the supply of the company's stock, PIPE offerings can dilute the value of existing shares.

   During their conversation, Mark told Zed's CEO that he did not like PIPE deals because they tend to dilute existing shareholders. After a heated exchange, Mark told the CEO, "Well, now I am stuck. I can't sell, even though I am opposed to your plan."

   Shortly after this conversation, Zed's CEO told the chair of Zed's board about the conversation with Mark. The chair sent an e-mail to the entire Zed board updating them on the PIPE deal. The e-mail included the following statements:

   > Earlier today, I told Mark about the PIPE deal, asking whether or not Mark might want to participate. As expected, Mark flew off the handle and said that he planned to sell his shares — which, of course, he cannot do until we announce the PIPE deal. I arranged to send him details of the offering in case he changes his mind.

   Mark did not receive this e-mail or otherwise learn of its contents.

   The next day, Mark called the CEO requesting additional information about the planned PIPE deal. The CEO supplied Mark with the requested information. The conversation was brief, and there was no discussion of confidentiality. One minute after hanging up the phone, Mark called his broker and instructed the broker to sell his entire stake in Zed. The broker quickly liquidated Mark's position.

   One day after the broker sold Mark's position in Zed, the CEO announced the PIPE deal. Zed's stock price immediately declined by 10 percent. By selling his shares when he did, Mark avoided $500,000 in losses. Mark proactively notified the SEC that he had sold his stake in the company because Zed had decided to conduct a PIPE offering, due to the dilutive effect of the offering. The SEC responded by sending Mark a request for documents and subpoena seeking investigative testimony.

Mark tells you that he believes he was free to sell his Zed stock when he did. Research the following questions in preparation for your next meeting with Mark:

a. Is Mark at risk of being held liable for insider trading under the classical theory?

b. Is Mark at risk of being held liable for insider trading under the misappropriation theory?

c. Mark tells you that he never promised to keep the information confidential. Does that matter?

d. What if Mark had not said "I'm stuck"? Would that change your insider trading analysis?

Business Organizations in Practice

1. You represent a hot new technology company preparing for its initial public offering. The founders, recent graduates of Stanford and MIT, have used social media — for example, Twitter, YouTube, Facebook, etc. — with great skill over the years to help build the company's business. None of the founders has worked for a public company before.

Last week, the company achieved an exciting milestone — it filed a prospectus with the Securities and Exchange Commission for an initial public offering of its stock. You are concerned that the founders might inadvertently engage in gun jumping. Prepare a memo for your clients addressing the following questions:

a. Do gun jumping restrictions apply to social/new media — for example, Facebook posts, Twitter tweets, YouTube videos, etc.?

b. Depending on your answer to Question 1.a, what (if any) internal review procedures might you recommend to your clients respecting their social media activities?

c. What are the potential consequences of gun jumping respecting the timing of the company's planned IPO?

2. You work for a law firm, and you recently were appointed to your firm's risk and compliance committee. Your firm regularly does corporate transactions involving public companies. As a result, the firm's attorneys and staff often have advance notice of mergers, acquisitions, and other deals of this sort. Having read the *O'Hagan* case, you are concerned about potential insider trading liability. Draft rules and procedures to minimize the risk of unlawful insider trading by the firm's attorneys and employees.

3. You are counsel to Zed, Inc., a technology company preparing to conduct an initial public offering. Zed's securities will be listed on NASDAQ. You have been asked to help Zed make sure Zed's board members satisfy listing rules relating to qualifications and independence. Review NASDAQ's listing rules and write a memo identifying any such requirements for your client.

4. You represent The Green Fund, an investment fund that invests in energy companies with an eye toward mitigating environmental impacts associated with energy production. Two years ago, The Green Fund invested in Limestone Energy, Inc., a public company that has announced it intends to engage in hydraulic fracturing, or hydrofracking, a technique in which large amounts of water, combined with smaller amounts of chemicals and sand, are pumped under high pressure into a drilled gas well. The Green Fund is opposed to hydrofracking generally, in part because companies engaged in hydrofracking have refused to divulge the contents of the fracking solutions pumped into the wells.

   The Green Fund has asked you to draft a shareholder proposal seeking information about Limestone's hydrofracking business and operations. The Green Fund plans to submit the proposal to Limestone for inclusion in Limestone's proxy materials next year. Assume that any proposal by The Green Fund would be timely submitted. Examine SEC Rule 14a-8 and advise The Green Fund as to what, if any, proposals it might be able to make.

JOINT VENTURE AGREEMENT

This Joint Venture Agreement ("Agreement") is entered into on
_____, _____, by and among _____,
an individual residing at _____, an individual residing at
_____, and _____,
an individual residing at _____ (collectively referred
to as the "Joint Venturers").

WHEREAS, the Joint Venturers desire to form a joint venture (the "Venture")
pursuant to the laws of the State of _____ and the terms and conditions of
this Agreement;

NOW, THEREFORE, for good and valuable consideration, the receipt and sufficiency of which are hereby acknowledged, the Joint Venturers agree as follows.

1. <u>Formation and Business Purpose</u>. The parties do hereby form the Venture for
   the purpose of _____ and any purpose rea-
   sonably related thereto.

2. <u>Principal Place of Business</u>. The principal place of business of the Venture shall
   be located at _____.

3. <u>Contributions</u>. Each Joint Venturer has made the contribution set forth after
   his respective name:

<u>Name</u>	<u>Contribution</u>
_____	$_____
_____	$_____
_____	$_____

In the event additional contributions are necessary or reasonable for the operation of the Venture, the Joint Venturers shall make such additional contributions in the same proportion as their original contributions bear to the total contributions originally made to the Venture as provided herein.

4. <u>Term</u>. The Venture shall commence on the date provided hereinabove and shall continue until terminated as provided in Section 11 hereof.

5. <u>Profits and Losses</u>. The Joint Venturers agree that their interest in any gross profits and interest in any losses or liabilities that may result from the operation of the Venture shall be borne in the same proportion as their original individual contributions (together with any later contributions) bear to the total contributions made to the Venture (the "percentage of participation"). Profits made during the term of the Venture shall be distributed to each Joint Venturer in accordance with his respective percentage of participation in the Venture within ninety (90) days after the Venture's receipt of such profits, except that the Joint Venturers may decide to retain reasonable sums in bank accounts established for the Venture for operation of the business of the Venture.

6. <u>Management</u>. The Venturers shall jointly manage, control, and operate the business and affairs of the Venture and shall each have as many votes on each issue to be decided by the Venture as is equal to his percentage of participation. All issues relating to the management and operation of the Venture shall be decided by majority vote. No Joint Venturer shall have the authority to incur any debt, obligation, expense, or liability on behalf of the Venture in excess of the amount of $5000 without the prior written consent of all other Venturers. If a Venturer breaches the foregoing provision, that Venturer shall bear full responsibility and any liability arising therefrom and the remaining Joint Venturers shall have no responsibility or obligation to indemnify or reimburse the breaching Venturer for such breach.

7. <u>Admission of New Joint Venturers</u>. No new joint venturer may be admitted to the Venture without prior written approval of all Joint Venturers.

8. <u>Expenses</u>. Joint Venturers shall be entitled to be reimbursed for expenses reasonably incurred in connection with the business of the Venture.

9. <u>Return of Contributions</u>. No Joint Venturer shall have the right to withdraw his contribution or demand a return of such contribution except as provided herein.

10. <u>Liability</u>. The Joint Venturers shall have no liability to each other for any loss or damage suffered that arises out of a Joint Venturer's act or omission so long as such act or omission was in the best interests of the Venture and did not constitute gross negligence, misconduct, or a breach of this Agreement.

11. <u>Termination</u>. This Venture shall terminate and be dissolved upon the occurrence of the first of the following to occur:

a. The withdrawal, removal, or death of any Joint Venturer or the filing of a petition under the U.S. Bankruptcy Act by or for a Joint Venturer, except that in the event of any of such occurrences, the remaining Joint Venturers may agree to continue the business of the Venture.

b. The sale of all or substantially all of the assets of the Venture;

c. Completion of the purpose of the Venture; or

d. Mutual written agreement of the Joint Venturers.

12. <u>Liquidation and Distributions</u>. Upon dissolution of the Venture, the Joint Venturers shall liquidate the assets and liabilities of the Venture and shall distribute any assets as follows: after payment of all expenses, obligations, and liabilities, of whatever nature and kind of the Venture, each Joint Venturer shall receive his percentage of participation of any assets remaining.

13. <u>General Provisions</u>.

a. The books and records of the Venture shall be located at its principal place of business and shall be available for inspection by any Joint Venturer upon reasonable advance notice.

b. The bank accounts of the Venture shall be maintained at _____.

c. In the event that any provision of this Agreement is held to be invalid, such invalidity shall not affect the remainder of this Agreement.

d. In the event of a dispute between or among the Joint Venturers that cannot be amicably resolved, the Joint Venturers shall submit the dispute for binding arbitration by the American Arbitration Association.

e. This Agreement constitutes the entire agreement of the Joint Venturers with respect to the Venture and supersedes any prior oral or written agreement and can be modified only by a written agreement signed by all parties hereto.

f. No Joint Venturer may assign any interest in the Venture to any other party without the prior written consent of all other parties except that a Venturer may assign his right to receive profits or distribution to another upon written notice to the Venture.

g. Notices required or permitted to be given hereunder shall be addressed to the Venture and to each Joint Venturer at the addresses provided hereinabove. Notice shall be deemed received three (3) days after notice is deposited in the U.S. Mail, postage prepaid.

h. This Agreement shall be governed by the laws of the State of _____.

IN WITNESS WHEREOF, this Agreement is executed as of the date provided herein.

_____

_____

_____

Corporate Bylaws

◆ ◆ ◆

BYLAWS OF _____

ARTICLE I—OFFICES

Section 1.　*Registered Office:* The registered office of ____ ("the Corporation") in the State of ____ shall be ____ , County of ____ , ____ . The registered agent of the Corporation at such address shall be ____ .

Section 2.　*Other Offices:* The Corporation may also have offices at such other places, both within and without the State of ____ , as the Board of Directors may from time to time determine or the business of the Corporation may require.

ARTICLE II—MEETINGS OF SHAREHOLDERS

Section 1.　*Place of Meetings:* Meetings of shareholders shall be held at the principal office of the Corporation or at such place as may be determined from time to time by the Board of Directors.

Section 2.　*Annual Meetings:* The Corporation shall hold annual meetings of shareholders commencing with the year ____ , on such date and at such time as shall be determined from time to time by the Board of Directors, at which meeting shareholders shall elect a Board of Directors and transact such other business as may properly be brought before the meeting.

Section 3.　*Special Meetings:* Special meetings of the shareholders, for any purpose or purposes, may be called at any time by the President of the Corporation, or the Board of Directors, or shareholders holding at least ____ percent (____ %) of the issued and outstanding voting stock of the Corporation.

Business transacted at any special meeting shall be confined to the purpose or purposes set forth in the notice of the special meeting.

Section 4.　*Notice of Meetings:* Whenever shareholders are required or permitted to take any action at a meeting, a written notice of the meeting shall be provided to each shareholder of record entitled to vote at or entitled to notice of the meeting, which shall state the place, date, and hour of the meeting, and, in the case of a special meeting, the purpose or purposes for which the meeting is called.

Unless otherwise provided by law, written notice of any meeting shall be given not less than ten nor more than sixty days before the date of the meeting to each shareholder entitled to vote at such meeting.

Section 5. *Quorum at Meetings:* Shareholders may take action on a matter at a meeting only if a quorum exists with respect to that matter. Except as otherwise provided by law, a majority of the outstanding shares of the Corporation entitled to vote, represented in person or by proxy, shall constitute a quorum at a meeting of shareholders. Once a share is represented for any purpose at a meeting (other than solely to object to the holding of the meeting), it is deemed present for quorum purposes for the remainder of the meeting and the shareholders present at a duly organized meeting may continue to transact business until adjournment, notwithstanding the withdrawal of sufficient shareholders to leave less than a quorum.

The holders of a majority of the outstanding shares represented at a meeting, whether or not a quorum is present, may adjourn the meeting from time to time.

Section 6. *Proxies:* Each shareholder entitled to vote at a meeting of shareholders or to express consent or dissent to corporate action in writing without a meeting may authorize in writing another person or persons to vote for him or her by proxy, but no such proxy shall be voted or acted upon after one year from its date, unless the proxy provides for a longer period.

A duly executed proxy shall be irrevocable if it states that it is irrevocable and if, and only so long as, it is coupled with an interest sufficient in law to support an irrevocable power.

Except as otherwise provided herein or by law, every proxy is revocable at the pleasure of the shareholder executing it by communicating such revocation, in writing, to the Secretary of the Corporation.

Section 7. *Voting at Meetings:* If a quorum exists, action on a matter (other than the election of directors) is approved if the votes cast favoring the action exceed the votes cast opposing the action. Directors shall be elected by a majority of the votes cast by the shares entitled to vote in the election (provided a quorum exists).

Unless otherwise provided by law or in the Corporation's Articles of Incorporation, and subject to the other provisions of these Bylaws, each shareholder shall be entitled to one vote on each matter, in person or by proxy, for each share of the Corporation's capital stock that has voting power and that is held by such shareholder. Voting need not be by written ballot.

Section 8. *List of Shareholders:* The officer of the Corporation who has charge of the stock ledger of the Corporation shall prepare and make, at least ten days before any meeting of shareholders, a complete list of the shareholders entitled to vote at the meeting, arranged alphabetically, and showing the address of each shareholder and the number and class of shares held by each shareholder. The list shall be open to the examination of any shareholder for any purpose related to the meeting, during ordinary business hours, for a period of at least ten days before the meeting, either at a place in the city where the meeting is to be held, which place must be specified in the notice of the meeting, or at the place where the meeting is to be held. The list shall also be produced and kept available at the time and place of the meeting, for the entire duration of the meeting, and may be inspected by any shareholder present at the meeting.

Section 9.   *Consent in Lieu of Meetings:* Any action required to be taken or which may be taken at any meeting of shareholders, whether annual or special, may be taken without a meeting, without prior notice, and without a vote, if a consent in writing, setting forth the action so taken, shall be signed by the holders of all outstanding shares.

The action must be evidenced by one or more written consents, describing the action taken, signed and dated by the shareholders entitled to take action without a meeting, and delivered to the Corporation at its registered office or to the officer having charge of the Corporation's minute book.

No consent shall be effective to take the corporate action referred to in the consent unless the number of consents required to take action are delivered to the Corporation or to the officer having charge of its minute book within sixty days of the delivery of the earliest-dated consent.

Section 10.   *Conference Call:* One or more shareholders may participate in a meeting of shareholders by means of conference telephone, videoconferencing, or similar communications equipment by means of which all persons participating in the meeting can simultaneously hear each other. Participation in this manner shall constitute presence in person at such meeting.

Section 11.   *Annual Statement:* The President and the Board of Directors shall present at each annual meeting a full and complete statement of the business and affairs of the Corporation for the preceding year.

ARTICLE III—DIRECTORS

Section 1.   *Powers of Directors:* The business and affairs of the Corporation shall be managed by or under the direction of the Board of Directors, which may exercise all such powers of the Corporation and do all lawful acts and things, subject to any limitations set forth in these Bylaws or the Corporation's Articles of Incorporation.

Section 2.   *Number, Qualification, and Election:* The number of directors which shall constitute the whole board shall be not fewer than _____ nor more than _____ . Each director shall be at least 18 years of age. The directors need not be residents of the state of incorporation. Directors need not be shareholders in the Corporation. The directors shall be elected by the shareholders at the annual meeting of shareholders by the vote of shareholders holding of record in the aggregate at least a majority of the shares of stock of the Corporation present in person or by proxy and entitled to vote at the annual meeting of shareholders. Each director shall be elected for a term of _____ year[s], and until his or her successor shall be elected and shall qualify or until his or her earlier resignation or removal.

Section 3.   *Nomination of Directors:* The Board of Directors shall nominate candidates to stand for election as directors; and other candidates may also be nominated by any shareholder of the Corporation, provided such nomination[s] is submitted in writing to the Corporation's Secretary no later than _____ days prior to the meeting of shareholders at which such directors are to be elected, together with the identity of the nominator and the number of shares of the stock of the Corporation owned by the nominator.

Section 4.   *Vacancies:* Except as otherwise provided by law, any vacancy in the Board of Directors occurring by reason of an increase in the authorized number of directors or by reason of the death, withdrawal, removal, disqualification, inability to act, or resignation of a director shall be filled by the majority of directors then in office. The successor shall serve the unexpired portion of the term of his or her predecessor. Any director may resign at any time by giving written notice to the Board or the Secretary.

Section 5.   *Meetings:*

a.   Regular Meetings: Regular meetings of the Board of Directors shall be held without notice and at such time and at such place as determined by the Board.

b.   Special Meetings: Special meetings of the Board may be called by the Chairperson or the President on _____ days' notice to each director, either personally or by telephone, express delivery service, or facsimile or electronic transmission, and on _____ days' notice by mail (effective upon deposit of such notice in the mail). The notice need not specify the purpose of a special meeting.

Section 6.   *Quorum and Voting at Meetings:* A majority of the total number of authorized directors shall constitute a quorum for transaction of business. The act of a majority of directors present at any meeting at which a quorum is present shall be the act of the Board of Directors, except as provided by law, the Articles of Incorporation, or these Bylaws. Each director present shall have one vote, irrespective of the number of shares of stock, if any, he or she may hold.

Section 7.   *Committees of Directors:* The Board of Directors, by resolution, may create one or more committees, each consisting of one or more Directors. Each such committee shall serve at the pleasure of the Board. All provisions of the law of the State of _____ and these Bylaws relating to meetings, action without meetings, notice, and waiver of notice, quorum, and voting requirements of the Board of Directors shall apply to such committees and their members.

Section 8.   *Consent in Lieu of Meetings:* Any action required or permitted to be taken at any meeting of the Board of Directors or of any committee thereof, may be taken without a meeting if all members of the Board or committee, as the case may be, consent thereto in writing, such writing or writings to be filed with the minutes of proceedings of the Board or committee.

Section 9.   *Conference Call:* One or more directors may participate in meetings of the Board or a committee of the Board by any communication, including videoconference, by means of which all participating directors can simultaneously hear each other during the meeting. Participation in this manner shall constitute presence in person at such meeting.

Section 10.   *Compensation:* The Board of Directors shall have the authority to fix the compensation of directors. A fixed sum and expenses of attendance may be allowed for attendance at each regular or special meeting of the Board. No such payment shall preclude any director from serving the Corporation in any other capacity and receiving compensation therefor.

Section 11.   *Removal of Directors:* Any director or the entire Board of Directors may be removed, with or without cause, by the holders of a majority of the shares then entitled to vote at an election of directors.

ARTICLE IV—OFFICERS

Section 1.   *Positions:* The officers of the Corporation shall be a Chairperson, a President, a Secretary, and a Treasurer, and such other officers as the Board may from time to time appoint, including one or more Vice Presidents and such other officers as it deems advisable. Any number of offices may be held by the same person, except that the President and the Secretary may not be the same person. Each such officer shall exercise such powers and perform such duties as shall be set forth herein and such other powers and duties as may be specified from time to time by the Board of Directors. The officers of the Corporation shall be elected by the Board of Directors. Each of the Chairperson, President, and/or any Vice Presidents may execute bonds, mortgages, and any other documents under the seal of the Corporation, except where required or permitted by law to be otherwise executed and except where execution thereof shall be expressly delegated by the Board to some other officer or agent of the Corporation.

Section 2.   *Chairperson:* The Chairperson shall have overall responsibility and authority for management and operations of the Corporation, shall preside at all meetings of the Board of Directors and shareholders, and shall ensure that all orders and resolutions of the Board of Directors and shareholders are effected.

Section 3.   *President:* The President shall be the chief operating officer of the Corporation and shall have full responsibility and authority for management of the day-to-day operations of the Corporation. The President shall be an ex-officio member of all committees and shall have the general powers and duties of management and supervision usually vested in the office of president of a corporation.

Section 4.   *Secretary:* The Secretary shall attend all meetings of the Board and all meetings of the shareholders and shall act as clerk thereof, and record all the votes of the Corporation and prepare and keep the minutes of all its transactions in a book to be kept for that purpose, and shall perform like duties for all committees of the Board of Directors when required. The Secretary shall give, or cause to be given, notice of all meetings of the shareholders and special meetings of the Board of Directors, and shall perform such other duties as may be prescribed by the Board of Directors or President, and under whose supervision the Secretary shall be. The Secretary shall maintain the records, minutes, and seal of the Corporation and may attest any instruments signed by any other officer of the Corporation.

Section 5.   *Treasurer:* The Treasurer shall be the chief financial officer of the Corporation, shall have responsibility for the custody of the corporate funds and securities, shall keep full and accurate records and accounts of receipts and disbursements in books belonging to the Corporation, and shall keep the monies of the Corporation in a separate account in the name of the Corporation. The Treasurer shall provide to the President and directors, at the regular meetings of the Board, or whenever requested by the Board, an account of all financial transactions and of the financial condition of the Corporation.

Section 6.   *Term of Office:* The officers of the Corporation shall hold office until their successors are chosen and have qualified or until their earlier resignation or removal. Unless an officer or agent serves subject to a valid written agreement, any officer or agent elected or appointed by the Board may be removed at any time, with or without cause, by the affirmative vote of a majority of the Board of Directors. Any vacancy occurring in any office as a result of death, resignation, removal, or otherwise, shall be filled for the unexpired portion of the term, if any, by a majority vote of the Board of Directors.

Section 7.   *Compensation:* The compensation of officers of the Corporation shall be fixed by the Board of Directors.

ARTICLE V—CAPITAL STOCK

Section 1.   *Stock Certificates:* The shares of the Corporation shall be represented by certificates, provided that the Board of Directors may provide by resolution that some or all of any or all classes or series of the stock of the Corporation shall be uncertificated shares. Notwithstanding the adoption of such a resolution by the Board of Directors, every holder of stock represented by certificates and, upon request, every holder of uncertificated shares, shall be entitled to have a certificate signed in the name of the Corporation, by the Chairperson, President or any Vice President, and by the Treasurer or Secretary. Any or all of the signatures on the certificate may be by facsimile. The stock certificates of the Corporation shall be numbered and registered in the share ledger and transfer books of the Corporation as they are issued and may bear the corporate seal.

Section 2.   *Lost Certificates:* The Corporation may issue a new certificate of stock in place of any certificate previously issued and alleged to have been lost, stolen, or destroyed, and the Corporation may require the owner of the lost, stolen, or destroyed certificate, or his or her legal representative, to make an affidavit of that fact, and the Corporation may require indemnity against any claim that may be made against the Corporation on account of the alleged loss, theft, or destruction of any such certificate or the issuance of such new certificate.

Section 3.   *Transfers:* Transfers of shares shall be made on the books of the Corporation upon surrender and cancellation of the certificates therefor, endorsed by the person named in the certificate or by his or her legal representative. No transfer shall be made which is inconsistent with any provision of law, the Articles of Incorporation, or these Bylaws.

Section 4.   *Record Date:* In order that the Corporation may determine the shareholders entitled to notice of or to vote at any meeting of shareholders, or any adjournment thereof, or to take action without a meeting, or to receive payment of any dividend or other distribution, or to exercise any rights in respect of any change, conversion, or exchange of stock, or for the purpose of any other lawful action, the Board of Directors may fix a record date, which record date shall not precede the date upon which the resolution fixing the record date is adopted by the Board of Directors and shall not be less than ten nor more than fifty days before the meeting or action requiring a determination of shareholders.

If no record date is fixed by the Board of Directors:

a.   for determining shareholders entitled to notice of or to vote at a meeting, the record date shall be at the close of business on the day preceding the day on which notice is given, or, if notice is waived, at the close of business on the day preceding the day on which the meeting is held or other action taken;

b.   for determining shareholders entitled to consent to corporate action without a meeting, the record date shall be the day on which the first written consent is delivered to the Corporation in accordance with these Bylaws; and

c.   for determining shareholders for any other purpose, the record date shall be at the close of business on the day on which the Board of Directors adopts the resolution relating thereto.

ARTICLE VI—DIVIDENDS

Section 1.   *Dividends:* The Board of Directors may declare and pay dividends upon the outstanding shares of the Corporation, from time to time and to such extent as the Board deems advisable, in the manner and upon the terms and conditions provided by law and the Corporation's Articles of Incorporation.

Section 2.   *Reserves:* The Board of Directors may set apart, out of the funds of the Corporation available for dividends, said sum as the directors, from time to time, in their absolute discretion, think proper as a reserve fund for any proper purpose. The Board of Directors may abolish any such reserve in the manner it was created.

ARTICLE VII—GENERAL PROVISIONS

Section 1.   *Insurance and Indemnity:* The Corporation shall purchase and maintain insurance in a reasonable amount on behalf of any person who is or was a director, officer, agent, or employee of the Corporation against liability asserted against or incurred by such person in such capacity or arising from such person's status as such.

Subject to applicable statute, any person made or threatened to be made a party to any action, suit, or proceeding, by reason of the fact that he or she, his or her testator or intestate representative, is or was a director, officer, agent, or employee of the Corporation, shall be indemnified by the Corporation against the reasonable expenses, including attorneys' fees, actually and necessarily incurred by him or her in connection with such an action, suit, or proceeding.

Notwithstanding the foregoing, no indemnification shall be made by the Corporation if judgment or other final determination establishes that the potential indemnitee's acts were committed in bad faith or were the result of active or deliberate fraud or dishonesty or clear and gross negligence.

Section 2.   *Inspection of Corporate Records:* Any shareholder of record, in person or by attorney or other agent, shall, upon written demand under oath stating the purpose thereof, have the right during the usual hours for business to inspect for any proper purpose the Corporation's stock ledger, a list of its shareholders, and its other books and records, and to make copies or extracts therefrom. A proper purpose shall mean a purpose reasonably related to such person's interest as a shareholder. In every instance in which an attorney or other agent shall be the person seeking the right to inspection, the demand under oath shall be accompanied by a power of attorney or such other writing authorizing the attorney or other agent to so act on behalf of the shareholder. The demand under oath shall be directed to the Corporation at its registered office or its principal place of business.

Section 3.   *Fiscal Year:* The fiscal year of the Corporation shall be the calendar year.

Section 4.   *Seal:* The corporate seal shall be in such form as the Board of Directors shall approve. The seal may be used by causing it or a facsimile thereof to be impressed, affixed, or otherwise reproduced.

Section 5.   *Execution of Instruments:* All contracts, checks, drafts, or demands for money and notes and other instruments or rights of any nature of the Corporation shall be signed by such officer or officers as the Board of Directors may from time to time designate.

Section 6.   *Notice:* Whenever written notice is required to be given to any person, it may be given to such person, either personally or by sending a copy thereof through the United States mail, or by facsimile or by electronic transmission (if the person to whom notice is to be given has consented in writing to such electronic transmission), charges prepaid, to his or her address appearing on the books of the Corporation, or supplied by him or her to the Corporation for the purpose of notice. If the notice is sent by mail, it shall be deemed to have been given to the person entitled thereto when deposited in the United States mail. If the notice is sent by facsimile, it shall be deemed to have been given at the date and time shown on a written confirmation of the transmission of such facsimile communication. If the notice is sent by electronic transmission, it shall be deemed to have been given at the close of business on the day transmitted. Such notice shall specify the place, day, and hour of the meeting, and, in the case of a special meeting of shareholders, the purpose of and general nature of the business to be transacted at such special meeting.

Section 7.   *Waiver of Notice:* Whenever any written notice is required by law, or by the Articles of Incorporation or by these Bylaws, a waiver thereof in writing, signed by the person or persons entitled to such notice, whether before or after the time stated therein, shall be deemed equivalent to the giving of such notice. Except in the case of a special meeting of shareholders, neither the business to be conducted at nor the purpose of the meeting need be specified in the waiver of notice of the meeting. Attendance of a person either in person or by proxy, at any meeting, shall constitute a waiver of notice of such meeting, except where a person attends a meeting for the express purpose of objecting to the transaction of any business because the meeting was not lawfully convened or called.

Section 8.   *Amendments:* The Board of Directors shall have the power to make, adopt, alter, amend, and repeal from time to time the Bylaws of the Corporation except that the adoption, amendment, or repeal of any Bylaw regulating the election of directors shall be subject to the vote of shareholders entitled to cast at least a majority of the votes which all shareholders are entitled to cast at any regular or special meeting of the shareholders, duly convened after notice to the shareholders of that purpose.

The foregoing Bylaws were adopted by the Board of Directors on _____ .

_____

Secretary

**Written Consent in Lieu
of the Organizational Meeting**

WRITTEN CONSENT IN LIEU OF THE ORGANIZATIONAL MEETING OF THE BOARD OF DIRECTORS OF _____
(A Delaware Corporation)

Pursuant to Section 108 of Title 8 of the Delaware General Corporation Law, the undersigned, constituting all _____ (_____) of the initial director(s) of _____, a corporation organized and existing under the laws of the State of Delaware (the "Corporation"), do/does hereby consent in writing to the adoption of the following resolutions, such resolutions to have effect as if adopted at a duly held meeting of the directors of the Corporation:

RESOLVED, that the Charter issued to the Corporation by the Division of Corporation of the Delaware Department of State be filed in the minute book of the Corporation.

RESOLVED, that the Bylaws attached to this Consent are hereby adopted as the Bylaws of the Corporation.

RESOLVED, that the corporate seal, an impression of which is affixed in the margin hereof, is adopted as the corporate seal of the Corporation.

RESOLVED, that the form of stock certificate, a copy of which is attached to this Consent, is hereby adopted as the certificate for the common stock of the Corporation.

RESOLVED, that the following persons are hereby elected to the offices set forth after their respective names, to assume the duties and responsibilities fixed by the

Bylaws, each such officer to hold office until a successor is chosen and qualifies in that officer's stead, or until that officer's earlier resignation or removal:

Name	*Office*
_____	President
_____	Vice-President
_____	Treasurer
_____	Secretary

RESOLVED, that any officer of the Corporation is hereby authorized to open such bank accounts as may be necessary or appropriate to conduct the business of the Corporation with such banks or financial institutions as that officer deems necessary; and

FURTHER RESOLVED, that the corporate banking resolutions of any such bank or financial institution are hereby incorporated by reference and are adopted as if fully set forth herein.

RESOLVED, that the Corporation elects to be treated as an S corporation for income tax purposes, subject to the receipt of written consent to such election by each shareholder; and

FURTHER RESOLVED, that upon receipt of written consent of said election by each shareholder, the President is hereby authorized and directed to take any and all action necessary or desirable to comply with all of the requirements of the Internal Revenue Service for making said election.

RESOLVED, that the Corporation hereby confirms that all shares of the common stock of the Corporation issued upon acceptance of the following subscription offers shall be treated as Section 1244 stock under I.R.C. § 1244; and

RESOLVED, that the officers of the Corporation are authorized and directed to perform such actions and execute such documents as they shall deem necessary or appropriate to enable the Corporation to carry out its business in such jurisdictions as its activities make such qualification necessary or appropriate.

WHEREAS, the following person(s) has/have offered the amounts set forth next to his/her/their name(s) below in consideration of the issuance of the number of shares of the common stock, one cent ($0.01) par value per share, of the Corporation set forth below;

RESOLVED, that in consideration of the amounts indicated below, an aggregate of _____ (_____) shares of the common stock of the Corporation be and hereby are issued to the person(s) listed below, and that upon receipt from such person of the amount set forth opposite the person's name, the President and Secretary are hereby authorized and directed to issue to such person a certificate representing the number of shares set forth opposite that person's name, as follows:

Name	Shares	Consideration
_____	_____	$ _____
_____	_____	$ _____
_____	_____	$ _____

RESOLVED, that the [accrual/cash] method of accounting shall be the basis on which the Corporation computes its income and keeps its books; and

FURTHER RESOLVED, that the fiscal year of the Corporation shall be the twelve-month period ending _____.

RESOLVED, that any agreements, contracts, or obligations incurred by or on behalf of the Corporation prior to its formation are hereby ratified, effective as of the date such agreements or contracts were entered into or such obligation was incurred, and any person who acted on behalf of the Corporation in entering into any agreements or contracts or incurring any obligations is hereby expressly relieved of any liability created while so acting.

RESOLVED, that any officer of the Corporation be and hereby is authorized to pay all expenses incurred in connection with the organization of the Corporation and to reimburse the incorporators or directors for any amounts expended by them on behalf of the Corporation prior to the date hereof; and

FURTHER RESOLVED, that the Secretary of the Corporation be and hereby is authorized and directed to procure all corporate books, including books of account and stock books, required by the statutes of the State of Delaware or necessary or appropriate in connection with the business of the Corporation, and to apply in the name and on behalf of the Corporation on Form SS-4 for a Federal Employer Identification Number.

RESOLVED, that any officer of the Corporation be and hereby is authorized to take such actions and execute such documents as may be necessary, appropriate, or convenient to carry out the foregoing resolutions.

Dated as of _____ , 20 _____

_____
Name

_____
Name

_____
Name

CONSENT

I, _____ , hereby consent to my election as Director of ____, by ____, the Sole Incorporator of the Corporation.

_____   _____

Date of Execution   Name

WAIVER OF SOLE INCORPORATOR OF ____

I, ____, being the Sole Incorporator named in the Certificate of Incorporation of _____ (the "Corporation"), which Certificate of Incorporation was received and filed with the Delaware Secretary of State on ____, 20 ____, hereby waive all right, title, and interest in and to any stock or property of the Corporation and any right in the management thereof.

____   ____

Financial Statement Basics

When we discuss business, finance, and accounting concepts in our business organizations classes, students sometimes wonder why we are "taking time away from the law" to examine these topics. Some students think business, finance, and accounting topics are not relevant to their intended practice areas. Other students believe that these areas of study are relevant, but are the domain of bankers and accountants, not lawyers. (After all, as these students correctly point out, lawyers typically are not responsible for keeping their clients' books and records, preparing financial statements, executing securities trades, or building financial models to examine the financial effects of corporate combinations.) Still other students may shy away from accounting, business, and finance concepts because they are unfamiliar with — and perhaps a bit intimidated by — these areas of study.

We appreciate these concerns, and we recognize that business, finance, and accounting terminology can be unfamiliar or off-putting for law students. The reality is, however, that today's law students and lawyers need to understand core business, finance, and accounting concepts and terminology. Business, finance, and accounting issues arise in almost every practice area. A corporate lawyer representing an investor in a start-up business needs to be able to understand the economics of the proposed investment, the business's capital structure, and the business risks and opportunities in play so that she can negotiate desired investment terms and draft or comment on deal documents. A lawyer handling tax and estate planning issues for a client involved in a family business needs to be able to understand how to value the business when negotiating a buy-sell agreement. A solo practitioner needs to know enough about accounting to determine whether his law practice is operating at a profit or a loss. The list goes on and on.

With this in mind, this Appendix contains a brief introduction to financial statements. We urge you not to stop here. Students interested in developing a degree of fluency in business, finance, and accounting topics should consider taking a course (e.g., accounting for lawyers, business and finance basics for lawyers, or other similar class) in this area. Students also may want to consider reading high-quality publications that focus on business, finance, and accounting topics. And, when advising a client, there is no substitute for reading the client's financial statements, annual reports, and other similar documents for insight into the client's financial condition, business challenges, and opportunities.

A. ACCOUNTING AND GAAP

Fundamentally, accounting is a set of rules, principles, and tools used to record, measure, and track the activities of a business — e.g., the business's revenues, expenses, cash flow, assets, and liabilities. Businesses use the conventions of accounting to summarize and present this information through financial statements — specifically, the income statement, the balance sheet, and the cash flow statement. (We discuss the income statement, balance sheet, and cash flow statement below.)

Most businesses prepare their financial statements in accordance with generally accepted accounting principles, or GAAP. Public companies are required to do so. GAAP has been codified, and the Financial Accounting Standards Board (the FASB) is the organization principally responsible for articulating GAAP standards. The FASB is a nonprofit entity that has been designated by the American Institute of Certified Public Accountants (AICPA) and the Securities and Exchange Commission (SEC) as the principal arbiter of GAAP, though other entities such as the SEC and the Public Company Accounting Oversight Board (PCAOB), created by the Sarbanes-Oxley Act, also play an important role in the development and articulation of accounting standards.

B. FINANCIAL STATEMENTS

As noted above, businesses produce financial statements — (i) the income statement; (ii) the balance sheet; and (iii) the cash flow statement — to measure, track, and report on the company's economic activity and (in the case of public companies) to comply with disclosure and reporting requirements. We discuss these below.

1. The Income Statement

The income statement shows the company's financial performance over a specific period of time, thus providing important information about the company's profits and losses. The basic equation used to prepare the income statement is as follows:

$$\boxed{\text{Revenue} - \text{Expenses} = \text{Net income (or loss)}}$$

In this equation, revenue refers to the money generated by the business from the sale of products or services. Expenses are costs incurred by the business in order to generate the revenue. Net income (or loss) reflects the income or losses incurred by the business during the relevant period. Here is an example of a consolidated statement of income from the 2015 Annual Report of Exxon Mobil Corporation:

CONSOLIDATED STATEMENT OF INCOME

	Note Reference Number	2015	2014	2013
		(millions of dollars)		
Revenues and other income				
Sales and other operating revenue *(1)*		259,488	394,105	420,836
Income from equity affiliates	7	7,644	13,323	13,927
Other income		1,750	4,511	3,492
Total revenues and other income		268,882	411,939	438,255
Costs and other deductions				
Crude oil and product purchases		130,003	225,972	244,156
Production and manufacturing expenses		35,587	40,859	40,525
Selling, general and administrative expenses		11,501	12,598	12,877
Depreciation and depletion		18,048	17,297	17,182
Exploration expenses, including dry holes		1,523	1,669	1,976
Interest expense		311	286	9
Sales-based taxes *(1)*	19	22,678	29,342	30,589
Other taxes and duties	19	27,265	32,286	33,230
Total costs and other deductions		246,916	360,309	380,544
Income before income taxes		21,966	51,630	57,711
Income taxes	19	5,415	18,015	24,263
Net income including noncontrolling interests		16,551	33,615	33,448
Net income attributable to noncontrolling interests		401	1,095	868
Net income attributable to ExxonMobil		16,150	32,520	32,580
Earnings per common share *(dollars)*	12	3.85	7.60	7.37
Earnings per common share - assuming dilution *(dollars)*	12	3.85	7.60	7.37

(1) Sales and other operating revenue includes sales-based taxes of $22,678 million for 2015, $29,342 million for 2014 and $30,589 million for 2013.

The information in the Notes to Consolidated Financial Statements is an integral part of these statements.

As you can see, the consolidated income statement references notes. These notes are (as the income statement reflects) an integral part of the income statement, and the income statement should always be read in conjunction with the Notes, which explain and disclose information such as accounting methods and other matters that materially affect the financial statements.

2. The Balance Sheet

The balance sheet reports the assets, liabilities, and owners' equity of a business as of a particular day. This "snapshot" typically is taken at the end of the corporation's fiscal year. As the name suggests, the balance sheet must balance as an accounting matter. This means that assets must always equal liabilities plus equity.

$$\boxed{\text{Assets} = \text{Liabilities} + \text{Equity}}$$

Here is an example of a balance sheet from the 2015 Annual Report of Exxon Mobil Corporation. Once again, observe that the Notes are an integral part of the balance sheet.

CONSOLIDATED BALANCE SHEET

	Note Reference Number	Dec. 31 2015	Dec. 31 2014
		(millions of dollars)	
Assets			
Current assets			
Cash and cash equivalents		3,705	4,616
Cash and cash equivalents - restricted		-	42
Notes and accounts receivable, less estimated doubtful amounts	6	19,875	28,009
Inventories			
Crude oil, products and merchandise	3	12,037	12,384
Materials and supplies		4,208	4,294
Other current assets		2,798	3,565
Total current assets		42,623	52,910
Investments, advances and long-term receivables	8	34,245	35,239
Property, plant and equipment, at cost, less accumulated depreciation and depletion	9	251,605	252,668
Other assets, including intangibles, net		8,285	8,676
Total assets		336,758	349,493
Liabilities			
Current liabilities			
Notes and loans payable	6	18,762	17,468
Accounts payable and accrued liabilities	6	32,412	42,227
Income taxes payable		2,802	4,938
Total current liabilities		53,976	64,633
Long-term debt	14	19,925	11,653
Postretirement benefits reserves	17	22,647	25,802
Deferred income tax liabilities	19	36,818	39,230
Long-term obligations to equity companies		5,417	5,325
Other long-term obligations		21,165	21,786
Total liabilities		159,948	168,429
Commitments and contingencies	16		
Equity			
Common stock without par value			
(9,000 million shares authorized, 8,019 million shares issued)		11,612	10,792
Earnings reinvested		412,444	408,384
Accumulated other comprehensive income		(23,511)	(18,957)
Common stock held in treasury			
(3,863 million shares in 2015 and 3,818 million shares in 2014)		(229,734)	(225,820)
ExxonMobil share of equity		170,811	174,399
Noncontrolling interests		5,999	6,665
Total equity		176,810	181,064
Total liabilities and equity		336,758	349,493

The information in the Notes to Consolidated Financial Statements is an integral part of these statements.

3. Statement of Cash Flows

The cash flow statement shows the business's cash inflows and outflows during a specific period in time. Cash flows fall into one of three buckets: (i) cash flows from operations; (ii) cash flows from investing; and (iii) cash flows from financing activities. Here is an example of a statement of cash flows, again taken from the 2015 Annual Report of Exxon Mobil Corporation. The statement of cash flows also should be read in conjunction with the relevant Notes.

CONSOLIDATED STATEMENT OF CASH FLOWS

	Note Reference Number	2015	2014	2013
			(millions of dollars)	
Cash flows from operating activities				
Net income including noncontrolling interests		16,551	33,615	33,448
Adjustments for noncash transactions				
Depreciation and depletion		18,048	17,297	17,182
Deferred income tax charges/(credits)		(1,832)	1,540	754
Postretirement benefits expense				
in excess of/(less than) net payments		2,153	524	2,291
Other long-term obligation provisions				
in excess of/(less than) payments		(380)	1,404	(2,566)
Dividends received greater than/(less than) equity in current				
earnings of equity companies		(691)	(358)	3
Changes in operational working capital, excluding cash and debt				
Reduction/(increase) - Notes and accounts receivable		4,692	3,118	(305)
- Inventories		(379)	(1,343)	(1,812)
- Other current assets		45	(68)	(105)
Increase/(reduction) - Accounts and other payables		(7,471)	(6,639)	(2,498)
Net (gain) on asset sales	5	(226)	(3,151)	(1,828)
All other items - net	5	(166)	(823)	350
Net cash provided by operating activities		30,344	45,116	44,914
Cash flows from investing activities				
Additions to property, plant and equipment	5	(26,490)	(32,952)	(33,669)
Proceeds associated with sales of subsidiaries, property, plant				
and equipment, and sales and returns of investments	5	2,389	4,035	2,707
Decrease/(increase) in restricted cash and cash equivalents		42	227	72
Additional investments and advances		(607)	(1,631)	(4,435)
Collection of advances		842	3,346	1,124
Net cash used in investing activities		(23,824)	(26,975)	(34,201)
Cash flows from financing activities				
Additions to long-term debt	5	8,028	5,731	345
Reductions in long-term debt		(26)	(69)	(13)
Additions to short-term debt		-	-	16
Reductions in short-term debt		(506)	(745)	(756)
Additions/(reductions) in commercial paper, and debt with				
three months or less maturity	5	1,759	2,049	12,012
Cash dividends to ExxonMobil shareholders		(12,090)	(11,568)	(10,875)
Cash dividends to noncontrolling interests		(170)	(248)	(304)
Changes in noncontrolling interests		-	-	(1)
Tax benefits related to stock-based awards		2	115	48
Common stock acquired		(4,039)	(13,183)	(15,998)
Common stock sold		5	30	50
Net cash used in financing activities		(7,037)	(17,888)	(15,476)
Effects of exchange rate changes on cash		(394)	(281)	(175)
Increase/(decrease) in cash and cash equivalents		(911)	(28)	(4,938)
Cash and cash equivalents at beginning of year		4,616	4,644	9,582
Cash and cash equivalents at end of year		3,705	4,616	4,644

The information in the Notes to Consolidated Financial Statements is an integral part of these statements.

4. Additional Information

In addition to the income statement, balance sheet, and cash flow statement, public companies also include expanded financial statements containing a wealth of additional information about the company as part of their required SEC filings. These expanded financial statements generally include the following sections: (i) management discussion and analysis (MD&A), which contains a summary of the firm's operations and other important financial information; (ii) the notes to financial statements referenced above, which contain detailed information about the accounting policies used to prepare the statements; and (iii) the auditor's report, which contains the auditor's opinion respecting the fairness of the presentation of the company's financial position.

C. FINANCIAL STATEMENT ANALYSIS

Financial statements are powerful tools: Business people use them to perform various types of analyses into a business's financial condition and business prospects. For example, an investor or potential investor may use financial statements to conduct a profitability analysis to assess the past performance of a business and to make predictions about future performance. Investors and creditors (current and potential) also may use financial statements to evaluate the liquidity and solvency of a business. As you will recall from the main text, liquidity speaks to the business's ability to convert assets into cash, whereas solvency speaks to the ability of the business to meet its commitments as a going concern. Measures of liquidity and solvency thus speak to the ability of the business to meet its obligations as they come due. Financial statements also are useful for evaluating a business's leverage, or the extent to which the firm is debt financed versus equity financed.

Taken together, analysis of the income statement, balance sheet, and statement of cash flows may help a business's managers, investors, potential investors, creditors, potential creditors, business partners, and potential business partners make informed judgments about the business and its future prospects. These judgments will, in turn, inform business decisions and business activities (e.g., transactions) requiring legal work. So, while lawyers may not need to prepare financial statements or perform financial statement analyses, they do need to be able to understand and interpret these materials to represent clients involved in identifying, managing, and capitalizing upon business opportunities and risks.

APPENDIX

ASSET PURCHASE AGREEMENT

This ASSET PURCHASE AGREEMENT is dated and entered into this ___ day of_____, ____, by and between QUALITY SYSTEMS, INC., a Massachusetts corporation with its principal address at 340-A Fairfax Road, Boston, Massachusetts 01887 ("Seller") and MANAGEMENT TECHNOLOGY CONSULTANTS, INC., a Virginia corporation with its principal address at 2805 S. Lee, Suite 1200, Richmond, Virginia 22106 ("Buyer").

WITNESSETH:

WHEREAS, Seller desires to sell the Assets (as hereinafter defined) and Buyer desires to purchase the Assets from Seller, all upon the terms and subject to the conditions set forth herein.

NOW, THEREFORE, in consideration of the mutual covenants, conditions, and agreements set forth herein and for other good and valuable consideration, the receipt and sufficiency of which are hereby acknowledged, the parties hereto agree as follows:

1. DEFINITIONS

When used in this Agreement, the following terms shall have the meanings specified below:

1.1 <u>Agreement</u>. "Agreement" shall mean this Asset Purchase Agreement, together with the Schedules attached hereto and the agreements and documents specifically incorporated by reference herein, as the same may be amended from time to time in accordance with the terms hereof.

1.2 <u>Assets</u>. "Assets" shall mean all properties, assets, and rights (of every kind, nature, and description whatsoever) owned, leased, licensed, or used, or held for use by Seller, including without limitation, the Books and Records, the Contracts,

865

and those assets identified herein and specifically listed on <u>SCHEDULE A</u> hereto; provided however, the Assets shall not include accounts receivable owned by Seller as of the Closing Date.

1.3   <u>Books and Records</u>. "Books and Records" shall mean original or true and complete copies of all of the books, records, data, and information relating to the Assets, including, without limitation, all client lists, financial and accounting records, correspondence, and miscellaneous records with respect to clients and all other general correspondence, records, books, and files owned by Seller with respect to the Assets.

1.4   <u>Buyer</u>. "Buyer" shall mean Management Technology Consultants, Inc., a Virginia corporation.

1.5   <u>Closing</u>. "Closing" shall mean the closing of the sale and purchase of the Assets and the consummation of the transactions contemplated hereby.

1.6   <u>Closing Date</u>. "Closing Date" shall mean _____.

1.7   <u>Contracts</u>. "Contracts" shall mean only those contracts, agreements, leases, licenses, relationships, and commitments that are specifically listed on <u>SCHEDULE B</u> attached hereto.

1.8   <u>Purchase Price</u>. "Purchase Price" shall mean the consideration paid by Buyer pursuant to this Agreement, namely the sum of _____.

1.9   <u>Seller</u>. "Seller" shall mean Quality Systems, Inc., a Massachusetts corporation.

2. PURCHASE AND SALE

2.1   <u>Purchase and Sale of the Assets</u>

(a)   At the Closing, Seller will execute and deliver to Buyer a Bill of Sale in the form attached hereto as <u>SCHEDULE C</u> (the "Bill of Sale").

(b)   At the Closing, Buyer and Seller will execute and Seller will deliver to Buyer an Assignment and Assumption Agreement in the form attached hereto as <u>SCHEDULE D</u> (the "Assignment and Assumption Agreement").

2.2.   <u>Payment of the Purchase Price</u>. In consideration of Seller's sale, transfer, assignment, conveyance, and delivery of the Assets, Buyer hereby pays the Purchase Price to Seller and Seller hereby acknowledges receipt of the Purchase Price.

2.3   <u>Assumption of Liabilities</u>. Except as specifically set forth in the Assignment and Assumption Agreement with respect to the performance by Buyer of obligations arising under the Contracts from and after the Closing Date, Buyer does not and will not assume (i) any liability of obligation of any kind of Seller; (ii) any liability or obligation relating to the Assets; or (iii) any liability or obligation relating to performance by Seller under the Contracts prior to the Closing Date, in each case, whether absolute or contingent, accrued or unaccrued, asserted or unasserted, known or unknown, or otherwise.

2.4 <u>Allocation of Purchase Price</u>. The Purchase Price shall be allocated as is indicated on <u>SCHEDULE E</u> attached hereto and made a part hereof. The parties hereto agree that the allocation of the Purchase Price for purposes of Section 1060 of the Internal Revenue Code of 1986, as amended, shall be as set forth on <u>SCHEDULE E</u>. Seller and Buyer shall use such final allocation in all tax returns, filings, and other reports and in their respective financial statements. The parties hereto further agree that such allocation is based upon the respective fair market value of the Assets. Within thirty (30) days following the Closing Date, the parties shall sign Internal Revenue Service Form 8594 which shall reflect such allocation and each shall timely file such Form 8594 with the Internal Revenue Service.

3. CLOSING AND TERMINATION

3.1 <u>Closing</u>. The Closing shall take place on _____ , at twelve o'clock noon at the offices of Buyer given above or at such other place or by such other means as Seller and Buyer may mutually agree.

3.2 <u>Deliveries at Closing</u>.

(a) <u>By Buyer to Seller</u>. At the Closing, Buyer will deliver to Seller (i) the stock certificate(s) evidencing the Shares, endorsed in blank or with an executed blank stock transfer power attached, suitable to vest good title in Buyer to the Shares; (ii) evidence that Buyer has assumed the obligations of Seller described in Section 1.8 hereinabove; and (iii) evidence satisfactory to Seller that the Buyer has performed all obligations and complied with all covenants and agreements necessary to be performed or complied with by Buyer on or before the Closing.

(b) <u>By Seller to Buyer</u>. At the Closing, Seller will deliver to Buyer (i) good and marketable title to the Asserts; (ii) evidence satisfactory to Buyer that the representations and warranties of Seller made pursuant to this Agreement are true and correct in all material respects at and as of the Closing with the same force and effect as if such representations and warranties had been made at and as of such time and that Seller has performed all obligations and complied with all covenants and agreements necessary to be performed or complied with by Seller on or before the Closing; (iii) the fully executed Bill of Sale and Assignment and Assumption Agreement attached hereto as <u>SCHEDULES C and D</u>, respectively; and (iv) such other instruments and documents relating to the transactions contemplated by this Agreement as Buyer may reasonably request.

3.3 <u>Termination</u>. Notwithstanding anything in this Agreement to the contrary, this Agreement may be terminated in writing at any time prior to the Closing Date:

(a) without liability on the part of either party hereto (unless occasioned by reason of a material breach by a party hereto of any of its representations, warranties, or obligations hereunder) by mutual consent of the parties;

(b)   without liability on the part of either party hereto (unless occasioned by reason of a material breach by any party hereto of any of its representations, warranties, or obligations hereunder) by any of the parties if the Closing shall not have occurred on or before _____ (or such later date as may be agreed upon in writing by the parties hereto);

(c)   by Buyer if Seller shall breach any of its representations, warranties, or obligations hereunder and such breach shall not have been cured or waived and Seller shall not have provided reasonable assurance that such breach will be cured on or before the Closing Date;

(d)   by Seller if Buyer shall breach any of its representations, warranties, or obligations hereunder and such breach shall not have been cured or waived and Buyer shall not have provided reasonable assurance that such breach will be cured on or before the Closing Date; or

(e)   by Buyer if Buyer is unable to obtain the approval of or obtain financing or borrow the necessary funds from its lender, Bank of America, so it may pay the Purchase Price to Seller at the Closing as provided herein or if Bank of America refuses to approve or consent to this Agreement and the transactions contemplated hereby, Seller expressly acknowledging that such approval and consent and funding of Buyer's financing by Bank of America is an express condition precedent to Buyer's obligations hereunder and the consummation of the transactions contemplated hereby.

4.   REPRESENTATIONS AND WARRANTIES OF SELLER

Seller represents and warrants to Buyer as of the date hereof and as of the Closing Date as follows:

4.1   <u>Organization, Standing, and Qualification</u>. Seller is a corporation duly organized, validly existing, and in good standing under the laws of the Commonwealth of Massachusetts and is qualified to do business as a foreign corporation in each jurisdiction where the failure to be so qualified would have a material adverse effect on Seller.

4.2.   <u>Due Authorization</u>. Seller has full corporate power and authority to carry on its business as now being conducted and to own its Assets and Seller has full power and authority to execute and deliver this Agreement and the other agreements and instruments to be executed and delivered by it pursuant hereto. All corporate acts and other proceedings required to be taken by or on the part of Seller to authorize Seller to execute, deliver, and carry out the terms of this Agreement and the transactions contemplated hereby have been duly and properly taken, including, without limitation, effective authorization by Seller's Board of Directors and shareholders' approval, if required. This Agreement has been and each of the other agreements when executed and delivered will be as of the Closing Date, duly executed and delivered by Seller and will constitute a legal, valid, and binding obligation of Seller, enforceable in accordance with its terms.

4.3   Absence of Changes. Since the date of the signed letter of intent between the parties, there has not been and will not be:

(a)   any change in the Assets of Seller except changes that are not materially adverse to Seller;

(b)   any changes except in the ordinary course of business in the obligations of Seller;

(c)   any damage, destruction, or loss materially and adversely affecting the Assets of Seller;

(d)   any waiver or compromise by Seller of a valuable right or of a material debt owed to it;

(e)   any loans made by Seller to its employees, officers, or directors other than reasonable travel or other like advances made in the ordinary course of business;

(f)   any material increases in the compensation of Seller's employees, officers, or directors;

(g)   any borrowing by Seller; or

(h)   any distribution of the Assets of Seller.

4.4   No Conflict. The execution and delivery by Seller of this Agreement and the consummation of the transactions contemplated hereby will not violate any law, or conflict with, or result in any material breach of, or constitute a material default (or an event which with notice or lapse of time or both would become a material default) under its Articles of Incorporation or Bylaws or under any Contract or agreement to which Seller is a party or by which Seller or its Assets may be bound or affected.

4.5   Consents. No approval, authorization, consent, or other order or action of or filing with any court, administrative agency, or other governmental authority is required for the execution and delivery by Seller of this Agreement or the consummation of the transactions contemplated hereby.

4.6   Title to Properties. Seller has good, valid, and marketable title to the Assets free and clear of all security interests, liens, charges, or other encumbrances of any kind or nature ("Encumbrances"). Except as disclosed in writing to Buyer, all of the Assets, buildings, fixtures, structures, and properties owned, used, licensed, or leased by Seller are in a good state of repair, maintenance, and operating condition, and except as so disclosed, and except for normal wear and tear, there are no defects with respect thereto which would impair the day-to-day use of any such Assets, buildings, fixtures, structures, or properties.

4.7   Contracts. SCHEDULE B hereto contains an accurate and complete list of all Contracts, and accurate copies of the Contracts have been delivered to Buyer. Seller has performed each material term, covenant, and condition of each of the Contracts that is to be performed by it at or before the Closing Date. No event has occurred that would, with the passage of time or compliance with any applicable notice requirements, constitute a default by Seller, or, to the knowledge of Seller, any other party under any of the Contracts, and, to the knowledge of Seller, no party to any of the Contracts intends to cancel, terminate, or exercise any option under any of the Contracts. The Contracts were entered into in the ordinary course of business and are in full force and effect. Seller has made no prior assignment of the Contracts or any of its rights or obligations thereunder and has not bound the Buyer to any obligations or taken any other action which has not been reflected on the Books and Records of Seller and disclosed to Buyer in writing.

4.8   Subsidiaries and other Equity Interests. Except as disclosed in writing to Buyer, Seller does not presently own or control, directly or indirectly, any other corporation, association, or business entity.

4.9   No Undisclosed Liabilities. Except as have been fully and accurately disclosed in writing to Buyer, Seller has no liabilities or obligations which, individually or in the aggregate, may reasonably be expected to have an adverse effect on the value of the Assets on or after the Closing Date.

4.10   Compliance with Laws. Seller has complied with any and all federal, state, or local laws, rules, regulations, order, or decrees applicable to Seller and the Assets. Seller has not received notice of any violation of any federal, state, local, or foreign law, rule, regulation, order, or decree relating to Seller or the Assets.

4.11   Litigation and Claims. There are no claims, actions, suits, proceedings, arbitrations, or investigations pending or threatened against Seller, or any director, officer, or shareholder of Seller or the Assets and, to the best of Seller's knowledge, there is no basis for any claim, action, suit, proceeding, arbitration, or investigation, the loss of which by Seller would have a material adverse effect on Seller or the Assets.

4.12   Intellectual Property. Seller has taken all reasonable and appropriate steps required in accordance with sound business practice to establish and preserve its rights in and to all material copyright, trade secret, trademark, service mark, and other proprietary rights associated with its business, products, and technology. Seller has required all professional and technical employees and independent contractors having access to valuable non-public information of the Seller to execute agreements under which such employees and independent contractors are required to maintain the confidentiality of such information and appropriately restricting the use thereof. Seller has no knowledge of any infringement by others of any intellectual property rights of Seller. To the knowledge of Seller, the present business, activities, products, and services of the Seller or its employees or individual contractors do not infringe any intellectual property or right of any other person or entity.

4.13   Customers and Suppliers. Except as disclosed in writing to Buyer, no customer, client, or supplier of Seller has canceled or otherwise terminated, or made any threat or claim to Seller to cancel or otherwise terminate, for any reason, its relationship with Seller or has at any time after _____ materially decreased its usage of the products or services of Seller and to the best of Seller's knowledge, no such customer, client, or supplier intends to so cancel or otherwise terminate its relationship with Seller or to materially decrease its usage of Seller's products or services.

4.14   Fees and Expenses of Brokers. Seller is not committed to any liability for any brokers' or finders' fees or any similar fees in connection with this Agreement and the transactions contemplated hereby and has not retained any broker or other intermediary to act on its behalf in connection with the transactions contemplated hereby.

4.15   Insurance. Seller has insurance policies in effect sufficient for compliance with all requirements of law and all agreements to which Seller is a party.

4.16   Accuracy of Information. Neither this Agreement nor any written statement or certificate furnished or to be furnished to Buyer pursuant to this Agreement or in connection with the transactions contemplated hereby contains any untrue statement of a material fact or omits a material fact necessary to make the statements contained herein and therein not misleading and Seller has disclosed to Buyer all material facts regarding the Assets or the transactions contemplated hereby.

5.   REPRESENTATIONS AND WARRANTIES OF BUYER

Buyer represents and warrants as of the date hereof and as of the Closing Date to Seller as follows:

5.1   Organization, Standing, and Power. Buyer is a corporation duly organized, validly existing, and in good standing under the laws of the Commonwealth of Virginia.

5.2   Due Authorization. Buyer has full corporate power and authority to execute and deliver this Agreement and to consummate the transactions contemplated hereby. All corporate acts required to be taken by or on the part of Buyer to execute, deliver, and carry out this Agreement and the transactions contemplated hereby have been duly and properly taken, including, without limitation, effective authorization by Buyer's Board of Directors. This Agreement, when executed, will constitute a legal, valid, and binding obligation of Buyer, enforceable in accordance with its terms.

5.3   No Conflict. The execution and delivery by Buyer of this Agreement and the consummation of the transactions contemplated hereby will not violate any law or conflict with or result in any breach of or constitute a default (or any event which with notice or lapse of time or both would become a default) under its Articles of Incorporation or Bylaws or under any contract or agreement to which Buyer is a party.

5.4   Ownership of Shares. Buyer is the lawful record and beneficial owner of the Shares that comprise a portion of the Purchase Price, as described in Section 1.8 hereof. Buyer owns the Shares free and clear of all Encumbrances. Upon the delivery of the Shares in the manner contemplated herein, Seller will acquire the beneficial and legal, valid, and indefensible title to such Shares, free and clear of all Encumbrances.

6. ADDITIONAL COVENANTS AND AGREEMENTS

6.1 <u>Financing for Transaction</u>. In order to consummate the transactions contemplated hereby, and as an express condition precedent to Buyer's obligations hereunder, Buyer must obtain the consent of and obtain financing and borrow funds from its lender, Bank of America. Buyer will use its best efforts to secure promptly said consent, financing, and funds and will at all times keep Seller apprised of the process of obtaining such consent, financing, and funds and will provide to Seller a copy of any commitment letter for the financing of the transactions contemplated hereby.

6.2 <u>Consents Related to Contracts</u>. Seller agrees to will use its reasonable best efforts after Closing to obtain any necessary third party consents to assignment of the Contracts to Buyer.

6.3 <u>Employee Matters</u>. Buyer shall have the right, but not the obligation, to transfer employment to any employees of Seller or consultants to Seller on whatever terms Buyer may determine to propose, such employment to commence at any time on or after the Closing Date. Notwithstanding the foregoing, if Buyer offers employment to any such employees or consultants, such employees or consultants who accept employment shall each be granted options to purchase shares of stock in Buyer pursuant to the Buyer Stock Option Plan, exercisable in accordance with the normal vesting schedule applicable to Buyer's employees. Seller shall not, directly or indirectly, do any of the following:

(a) recruit or solicit, or induce or influence any other prospective employer to recruit or solicit any such employee or consultant;

(b) induce or influence any employee or consultant to pursue or consider employment or consultancy opportunities with anyone other than Buyer or to negotiate for or request terms other than those extended by Buyer; or

(c) otherwise discourage, inhibit, or interfere with any relationship or prospective relationship between Buyer and any such employee or consultant.

6.4 <u>Financial Statements</u>. From and after the Closing Date, Seller agrees to cooperate fully with Buyer and its representatives in connection with Buyer's preparation of financial statements relating to Seller, the Assets, and the transactions contemplated hereby. Such cooperation shall include, without limitation, furnishing Buyer and its representatives with access to Seller's financial and accounting records and such other information with respect to Seller, the Assets, and the transactions contemplated hereby as Buyer may reasonably request. Seller shall also instruct its accountants and representatives to cooperate fully with Buyer and its representatives and to permit Buyer and its representatives to review all materials relating to Seller, the Assets, and the transactions contemplated hereby.

6.5   <u>Maintenance of Records</u>. For a period of five (5) years following the Closing Date, Seller agrees to preserve and maintain any business, financial, accounting, and corporate records of Seller not included in the Books and Records in existence on the Closing Date.

6.6   <u>Confidentiality</u>. Seller and Buyer agree that they will keep confidential and will not disclose or divulge any confidential, proprietary, or secret information which either of them may obtain from the other unless the party providing the information gives its written consent to the release of such information, except that no such written consent shall be required (and the recipient shall be free to release such information) if such information is to be provided to the recipient's lawyer or accountant, or to an officer or director of the recipient.

6.7   <u>Conduct of Seller's Business</u>. Seller agrees that between the date hereof and the Closing Date, except as contemplated by this Agreement or by written consent of Buyer, Seller shall do the following:

(a)   operate its business only in the ordinary course consistent with prior practice;

(b)   preserve the Assets intact and use its best efforts to keep available to Buyer the services of the present employees and consultants to Seller and to preserve for Buyer the good will of Seller's suppliers, customers, clients, and any others having business relations with Seller; and

(c)   maintain in force any insurance policies applicable to the Assets.

6.8   <u>Access to Information and Confidentiality</u>. From the date of execution of this Agreement to the Closing Date, Seller will permit Buyer and its representatives the opportunity to conduct such reasonable investigation with respect to the Contracts, Assets, Books and Records, employees and consultants, business operations, and financial condition of Seller as will permit Buyer to evaluate its interest in the transactions contemplated by this Agreement. Seller will hold and will cause its representatives to hold in strict confidence (unless compelled to disclose by judicial or administrative process), all documents and information concerning Seller furnished to Buyer and all documents and information concerning Buyer furnished to Seller in connection with the transactions contemplated by this Agreement.

6.9   <u>Announcements Regarding Transaction</u>. Any announcements regarding the transactions contemplated hereby shall be made only with the prior written consent of Buyer and Seller.

6.10   <u>Transitional Assistance</u>. From the date of this Agreement to the Closing Date, Seller shall cooperate with Buyer in the orderly transfer to Buyer of Seller's Assets. Such cooperation and assistance shall include but not be limited to:

(a)   the physical transfer of any Assets;

(b)   reasonable access to and assistance from any employees of or consultants to Seller; and

(c) reasonable access to and use of the facilities and equipment of Seller during such transitional period.

6.11 <u>Non-Competition Agreements</u>. Buyer need not consummate the transactions contemplated hereby unless Seller's shareholders shall have executed and delivered on the Closing Date the Non-Competition Agreements attached hereto as <u>SCHEDULE F</u>, collectively, and the offers of employment made to them by Buyer attached hereto as <u>SCHEDULE G</u>, collectively, and which Schedules are incorporated herein by this reference.

6.12 <u>Further Assurances</u>. At any time, and from time to time after the date hereof and after the Closing Date, at Buyer's request, and without further consideration, Seller shall execute and deliver such other instruments of sale, transfer, conveyance, assignment, and confirmation and take such action as the Buyer may reasonably deem necessary or desirable in order to more effectively sell, transfer, convey, and assign to Buyer and to confirm Buyer's title to the Assets.

6.13 <u>Post-Closing Adjustment</u>. The parties hereto understand and acknowledge that in the course of consummating the transactions contemplated hereby, Seller may make certain advance payments for Assets, services, and goods that may benefit Buyer, and, similarly, the Buyer may make certain payments for services and goods that may benefit Seller. As soon as practicable after the Closing, and upon a mutual and good faith determination of any such payment which inures to the benefit of a party, said payment shall result in an immediate adjustment of the Purchase Price in such amount, which amount shall be payable by the party benefited to the other party in immediately available funds.

7. INDEMNIFICATION

7.1 <u>Buyer's Indemnification</u>. Buyer agrees to indemnify, defend, and hold harmless Seller at all times after the Closing from and against any and all claims, damages, losses, liabilities, costs, and expenses (including, without limitation, all reasonable legal fees) (collectively "Damages") to the extent such Damages arise out of, result from, or relate to:

(a) Buyer's failure to perform obligations arising under the Contracts from and after the Closing Date;

(b) a material breach of any representation or warranty of Buyer contained in this Agreement; or

(c) a material breach of any covenant or agreement made by Buyer in this Agreement.

7.2 <u>Seller's Indemnification</u>. Seller agrees to indemnify, defend, and hold harmless Buyer at all times after the Closing from and against any and all Damages to the extent such Damages arise out of, result from, or relate to:

(a) Seller's failure to perform obligations or any liabilities arising under the Contracts or relating in any way to the Assets prior to the Closing Date;

(b) a material breach of any representation or warranty of Seller contained in this Agreement; or

(c) a material breach of any covenant or agreement made by Seller in this Agreement.

7.3 Survival Period. The representations, warranties, covenants, and agreements contained in this Agreement shall survive the Closing regardless of any investigation made by or on behalf of any party hereto.

7.4 Claim for Indemnification. Any claim for indemnification must be made by written notice to the party against whom indemnification is sought. Such notice shall specify in reasonable detail the particulars of the claim for indemnity and the basis upon which indemnity is claimed.

8. ARBITRATION

The parties shall attempt to resolve any disputes arising hereunder or in connection herewith through negotiations. In the event that the parties are unable to resolve any such dispute within thirty (30) days after commencement of such negotiations, the dispute shall be resolved exclusively by binding arbitration administered by an arbitration panel in accordance with the rules and procedures of the American Arbitration Association. Any arbitration shall be conducted in Arlington, Virginia and shall be governed by the Federal Rules of Civil Procedure. The parties hereto agree to abide by all awards and decisions rendered in an arbitration proceeding in accordance with this Section 8. All such awards and decisions may be enforced in any court having jurisdiction over the person or property of the party against whom the award or decision is being enforced. The parties hereby accept and irrevocably consent, generally and unconditionally, to the jurisdiction of the state courts of Virginia or of the United States District Court for the Eastern District of Virginia for the enforcement of all awards pursuant to such arbitration.

9. GENERAL PROVISIONS

9.1 Expenses. Each party hereto shall pay its own expenses incident to this Agreement and the transactions contemplated hereby, including, without limitation, all legal and accounting fees and disbursements.

9.2 Notices. All notices required or permitted by this Agreement shall be in writing and shall be deemed to have been given when delivered personally or by messenger or by overnight delivery service, or when mailed by registered or certified United States mail, postage prepaid, return receipt requested, or when received via facsimile, in all cases addressed to the person for whom it is intended at the address set forth on the first page hereof or to such other address as a party shall have designated by notice in writing to the other party in the manner provided by this Section.

9.3   Entire Agreement; Amendment. This Agreement (including the Schedules hereto and the other agreements and documents incorporated herein by this reference) contains the entire understanding and agreement of the parties relating to the subject matter hereof and supersedes all prior oral or written agreements between the parties with respect to such matters. This Agreement may be amended only by a writing signed by each of the parties hereto.

9.4   Parties in Interest. Nothing expressed or implied in this Agreement is intended to or shall confer upon any person, firm, or entity other than the parties hereto and their permitted assignees, any rights, remedies, obligations, or liabilities under or by reason of this Agreement.

9.5   Assignment; Binding Effect. This Agreement may not be assigned by any party without the prior written consent of the other party hereto which shall not be unreasonably withheld or delayed. When assignment is so consented to, this Agreement shall be binding upon and inure to the benefit of the parties hereto and their respective successors and permitted assigns.

9.6   Governing Law. This Agreement shall be governed by and construed in accordance with the laws of the Commonwealth of Virginia regardless of the laws that might otherwise govern under applicable principles of conflicts of laws.

9.7   Severability. In the event that any provision of this Agreement shall be held invalid or unenforceable in any arbitration proceeding or by any court of competent jurisdiction, such holding shall not invalidate or render unenforceable any other provision hereof.

9.8   Counterparts. This Agreement may be executed in one or more counterparts, each of which shall be deemed to be an original and all of which together shall constitute one and the same instrument.

9.9   Waiver. A waiver by Buyer of a breach of any provision hereof or delay in enforcing any provision hereof shall not be deemed to be a waiver of any other provision or any subsequent breach. No waiver shall be valid against any party hereto unless made in writing and signed by the party against whom enforcement of such waiver is sought.

9.10   Bulk Sales Compliance. Buyer hereby waives compliance by Seller with the provisions of the bulk sales law of any jurisdiction, and Seller covenants and agrees to pay and discharge when due all claims of any governmental entities and creditors of Seller that could be asserted against Buyer by reason of such non-compliance. Seller agrees to indemnify and hold Buyer harmless from and against and shall on demand reimburse Buyer for any and all Damages suffered by Buyer by reason of Seller's failure to pay and discharge any such claims.

9.11   Voluntary Agreement. Each of the parties hereby represents that this Agreement has been fully read and understood, that each of the parties has had an opportunity to consult with its legal or financial advisors, and that this Agreement is entered into voluntarily.

9.12   <u>Subordination of Agreement</u>. THIS AGREEMENT IS SUBJECT TO THE TERMS OF THAT CERTAIN SUBORDINATION AGREEMENT ENTERED INTO BY AND AMONG SELLER, BUYER, AND BANK OF AMERICA, A COPY OF WHICH SUBORDINATION AGREEMENT IS ATTACHED HERETO AND INCORPORATED HEREIN BY THIS REFERENCE.

IN WITNESS WHEREOF, each of the parties has caused this Agreement to be duly executed on its behalf by its officers thereunto duly authorized, all as of the date first above written.

QUALITY SYSTEMS, INC.

By: _____
Name and Title: Francis P. Taylor, President

MANAGEMENT TECHNOLOGY CONSULTANTS, INC.

By: _____
Name and Title: Timothy Lyden, President

SCHEDULE A
ASSETS

SCHEDULE B
CONTRACTS

SCHEDULE C
BILL OF SALE

KNOW ALL MEN BY THESE PRESENT that, pursuant to a certain Asset Purchase Agreement, dated this _____ day of ____, 20__ (the "Purchase Agreement"), QUALITY SYSTEMS, INC., a Massachusetts corporation ("Seller") and MANAGEMENTTECHNOLOGY CONSULTANTS, INC., a Virginia corporation ("Buyer"), in consideration of the payment of the Purchase Price specified in the Purchase Agreement and for other good and valuable consideration, the receipt and sufficiency of which are hereby acknowledged, Seller does hereby sell, assign, transfer, convey, and deliver to Buyer, and to its successors and assigns, all right, title, and interest (including, without limitation, all rights of copyright and any other intellectual property rights) in and to the Assets (as defined in the Purchase Agreement), including, without limitation those assets identified in Schedule A attached hereto and made a part hereof.

TO HAVE AND TO HOLD the said described property to Buyer, and to its successors and assigns, for their exclusive use and benefit forever.

IN WITNESS WHEREOF, Seller has executed this Bill of Sale by its duly authorized officer effective as of the ____ day of _____, 20__.

QUALITY SYSTEMS, INC.

By: _____
Francis P. Taylor, President

SCHEDULE D
ASSIGNMENT AND ASSUMPTION AGREEMENT

KNOW ALL MEN BY THESE PRESENTS, that pursuant to the Asset Purchase Agreement, dated as of _____, 20__, (the "Purchase Agreement"), by and between QUALITY SYSTEMS, INC. ("Seller") and MANAGEMENT TECHNOL-OGY CONSULTANTS, INC. ("Buyer"), in consideration of the payment of the Purchase Price specified in the Purchase Agreement and for other good and valuable consideration, the receipt and sufficiency of which are hereby acknowledged, the Seller does hereby transfer, convey, and assign to Buyer all rights of the Seller under the Contracts arising from and after the Closing (as such terms are defined in the Purchase Agreement) and the Buyer does hereby assume all of the liabilities and obligations of the Seller under the Contracts arising from and after the Closing.

IN WITNESS WHEREOF, the parties have executed this Assignment and Assumption Agreement as of the _____ day of _____, 20__.

QUALITY SYSTEMS, INC.
By: _____
        Francis P. Taylor, President

MANAGEMENT TECHNOLGY
CONSULTANTS, INC.

By: _____
        Timothy Lyden, President

SCHEDULE E
ALLOCATION OF PURCHASE PRICE

SCHEDULE F
NON-COMPETITION AGREEMENTS

SCHEDULE G
OFFERS OF EMPLOYMENT

Glossary

Acceleration clause: Provision in loan agreement providing that unpaid balance will become immediately due and payable if specified events (e.g., debtor missing a single payment) occur.

Accredited investor: Rule 501 of Regulation D defines accredited investors to include the following qualifying institutions and individuals: (i) banks; (ii) savings and loan associations; (iii) broker-dealers; (iii) insurance companies; (iv) registered investment companies; (v) natural persons whose individual net worth, or joint net worth with that person's spouse, exceeds $1,000,000 (not including the person's primary residence).

Accrual method of accounting: Accounting method of listing expenses and income in business records when they are incurred or billed rather than when they are actually paid or received.

Actual authority: The grant of authority, either express or implied, by a principal to an agent.

Administrative dissolution: Dissolution of a business entity, often for technical reasons such as failing to pay taxes or file annual reports; most states allow reinstatement of the entity upon cure of defaults.

Affiliates: Subsidiaries formed by a common parent corporation.

Agency: Legal relationship formed when one party (the **agent**) agrees to act on behalf of, and subject to the control of another party (the **principal**), and the principal agrees that the agent may act on the principal's behalf, subject to the principal's control.

Agent: One who acts for or represents another, called a **principal**.

Agent for service: *See* Registered agent.

Aggressor: Corporation (or individual) attacking or wishing to acquire control over another corporation, typically called the **target**.

Alienation: The transfer of some property.

Alter ego: When corporate shareholders or other entity owners fail to respect the separate legal status of the entity, they are said to view the entity as their "alter ego," namely, a mere extension of themselves. Shareholders or owners who treat an entity as their alter ego may have personal liability imposed on them for the entity's debts under the equitable doctrine of **piercing the veil**.

Angel investors: Individuals who provide advice and seed capital to entrepreneurs seeking to launch a new business. Angel investors typically invest at an early stage of the lifecycle of a start-up enterprise.

Annual meeting: Yearly meeting of shareholders of a corporation to elect directors and conduct other business.

Annual report: Yearly form required to be filed by business entities in most states providing information about the entity.

Anti-dilution protections: Protections that restrict a corporation's ability to dilute preferred stockholders' ownership stake in the business via the issuance of new shares of stock.

Apparent authority: Authority created when the conduct of a principal causes a third party to believe an agent had authority to act for the principal.

Appraisal rights: Right of dissenting shareholders to have their shares or interests appraised, or valued, and bought out.

Arbitrageurs: Includes individuals or companies trading in a target's stock after announcement of a tender offer or trading in different stocks and bonds in different markets at the same time. Sometimes called risk arbitrageurs or simply "arbs."

Articles of amendment: Document filed with secretary of state to effect an amendment to a requiremed document — e.g., articles of amendment filed to amend a corporation's charter. Also known as a certificate of amendment in some jurisdictions.

Articles of dissolution: Document filed with the secretary of state to effect a dissolution or termination of a corporation as a legal entity. Sometimes called a certificate of dissolution.

Articles of domestication: The document filed with the state to effect a change of a corporation's or other entity's state of incorporation or formation.

Articles of entity conversion: The document filed with the state to effect a change in a business's structure.

Articles of incorporation: Document that creates a corporation. Sometimes called a **certificate of incorporation** or **charter**.

Articles of merger: Document filed with the secretary of state to effect a merger or other combination of two or more corporations.

Articles of organization: Document filed with the appropriate state official creating a limited liability company.

Asset purchase: Acquisition by one corporation of another's assets.

Assignment: Transfer of one's interest in certain rights or property.

Assumed name: *See* Fictitious business name.

At-risk limitation: Limitation of the deduction that a partner can take for losses allocated to her to the amount the partner has at risk.

Authorized shares: Shares identified in the articles of incorporation as being capable of and subject to issuance by a corporation.

Back-end transaction: *See* **Mop up**.

Bankruptcy: The condition of a person or entity being declared bankrupt under federal law.

Basis: Generally speaking, the original cost (plus out of pocket expenses) that must be reported to the IRS when an investment is sold and that must be used when calculating gains or losses on the investment.

Basis limitation: The basis limitation limits the deduction that a partner can take for partnership losses allocated to her in any particular year to the partner's adjusted basis in her partnership interest, before taking into account the partner's share of the loss.

Bear hug: Approach by an aggressor to a target after the aggressor has acquired a **toehold** in the target.

Benefit corporation: A corporation that combines profit-making with consideration of the impact of decisions on society and often the environment.

Bidder: Entity that seeks to take over, or otherwise effect a corporate combination with, another entity (known as the **target**).

Black knight: Aggressor attempting to acquire a target.

Blank check stock: Provision in articles of incorporation authorizing directors to create a new class or series of stock.

Blank stock: *See* **Series stock.**

Blitz: Lightning and no-notice strike against a target's stock so forceful that the target is sufficiently overwhelmed and cannot adopt any defenses to prevent a takeover.

Blue sky laws: State laws regulating the issuance, purchase, and sale of securities.

Board of directors: *See* **Director**.

Bond: Debt security secured by some corporate asset that can be seized by a creditor upon default by the corporation.

Bringdown certificate: Certificate of corporate officer verifying continuing accuracy of facts or documents.

Broker: Securities firm that acts on behalf of a customer, rather than trading on its own account, as does a dealer.

Bulk sale: Sale or transfer of the major portion of a company's business outside the scope of its ordinary course of business, usually triggering notices to creditors.

Business judgment rule: Court-made rule immunizing directors and officers from liability for their decisions so long as the decision had a rational basis and was made in good faith and with due care.

Buy-sell agreement: Agreement entered into by shareholders restricting the transfer or sale of their stock, which typically provides for the purchase and sale of ownership interests in the business at a price determined in accordance with the agreement upon the occurrence of certain events – e.g., the death, disability, bankruptcy or an owner or the owner's attempted transfer of her ownership interest to a third party.

Bylaws: Rules governing the management and operation of a corporation.

C-corporation: For profit corporation that is subject to double taxation under Subchapter C of the IRC. Default tax classification for for-profit corporations.

Call: Right of an entity or individual to reacquire stock issued or sold to another. For example, call rights include the right of a corporation to reacquire stock it previously issued to a shareholder (generally, a preferred shareholder).

Cancellation: Elimination of shares reacquired by a corporation.

Capital: Generally, money or property contributed to a business to fund its establishment, operations, plans for future growth, etc.

Capital surplus: Amount of consideration in excess of par value of shares that a corporation receives for its shares.

Cash dividend: Distribution of cash by a corporation to its shareholders.

Cash method of accounting: Accounting method of listing expenses and income in business records only when they are paid or received.

Centralized management: Principle of corporate governance whereby authority to manage the corporation is vested in the board of directors.

Certificate of good standing: Document issued by a secretary of state showing that a corporation is in compliance with that state's laws (also called certificate of existence).

Charging order: Order from a court requiring partnership or other entity (e.g., LLC) to pay distributions an owner would have received to the partner's or owner's creditor until a judgment is fully satisfied.

Chair: Member of board of directors who presides over board meetings.

Charter: Name used by some states to refer to a corporation's articles of incorporation.

Chewable poison pill: An anti-takeover defense; a type of poison pill that is of short duration and is triggered only when a bidder buys significant numbers of shares.

Chinese reverse merger: *See* **Reverse merger**.

Class action: Action brought by one or a few shareholders on behalf of numerous other shareholders who are similarly situated.

Class voting: Voting rights given to a class of stock.

Close corporation: Corporation whose shares are held by a few people, usually friends or relatives active in managing the business. Some flexibility typically is permitted with regard to observing corporate formalities and with respect to certain governance rules and structures. Also known as closely held corporation.

Collateral: Assets pledged to a lender until a loan is repaid.

Commingling: Combining shareholders' or owners' personal funds improperly with those of the corporation or other business entity. Liability can be imposed on shareholders or other business owners who fail to respect the corporate or business entity by commingling funds under the equitable doctrine of piercing the veil.

Common stock: Stock in a corporation that has no special features (e.g., right, privilege, or preference), as does preferred stock; usually has the right to vote and to share in liquidation dividends.

Confession of judgment: Provision contained in a promissory note entitling a creditor to obtain an immediate judgment against a debtor in default; not valid in all states.

Conflicting interest transaction: Transaction between a director (or relative of a director or entity owned by a director) and a corporation.

Consolidation: Combination of two or more corporations into a new corporate entity (example: A + B = C).

Constituency statute: Statute allowing directors to consider nonshareholder constituencies when considering takeover offers and other corporate matters.

Constituent corporations: Corporations that are parties to a merger, consolidation, or other combination.

Contingent voting: Voting that is dependent on the occurrence of some event such as default by a corporation in the payment of dividends.

Contingent liability: A liability that might – or might not – come due, depending on future developments.

Continuation agreement: An agreement between partners providing that non-withdrawing partners may continue the partnership business even after a partner withdraws from the enterprise.

Control rule: Rule applicable to limited partnerships in certain jurisdictions stating that limited partners may lose the protections of limited liability if they participate in control of the limited partnership business.

Controlling shareholder: A shareholder who owns a majority stake in a corporation or one who has the ability to control the business and affairs of a corporation.

Conversion right: (1) Right of preferred shareholders to convert preferred stock into some other security of the corporation, usually common stock; (2) right of creditors to convert debt security (bond) into equity security (shares).

Corporate opportunity doctrine: A doctrine that prohibits directors (and officers) from wrongfully usurping, or taking for themselves, business opportunities that properly belong to the corporation.

Corporation: Legal entity existing by authority of state law, owned by its shareholders, and managed by its elected directors and appointed officers.

Corporation by estoppel: Defectively formed corporation that cannot be attacked by a third party due to that party's dealing with the corporation as if it were a valid corporation; third party is estopped, or precluded, from treating the entity as anything other than a corporation.

Coupon: The interest rate on a bond that the issuer promises to pay until maturity.

Covenant: Promises by the borrower to do something (affirmative covenant) or to forbear from doing something (negative covenant) in a loan agreement.

Cross-purchase agreement: Agreement for (i) the sale of a shareholder's interest upon the death or disability of the shareholder, and (ii) the purchase of that shareholder's interest by the remaining shareholders.

Cross-purchase insurance: Insurance policies taken out by each shareholder on the life of each other shareholder to provide funds to purchase shares from a deceased shareholder's estate under a cross-purchase agreement.

Cross-species merger: Merger between corporation and some other business entity (also called an **interspecies merger**)

Crowdfunding: Generally refers to a financing method in which money is raised through soliciting relatively small individual investments or contributions from a large number of people, often via the Internet.

Crown jewel defense: Sale by a target of its valuable assets, usually to make itself unattractive to an aggressor.

Cumulative dividend: Distribution that "adds up" over time and must be paid to a preferred shareholder, when the corporation has funds to do so, before any distribution can be made to other shareholders.

Cumulative voting: In an election of directors, a type of voting whereby each share carries as many votes as there are directors' vacancies to be filled; assists minority shareholders in electing representatives to the board of directors.

Dead-hand poison pill: An anti-takeover defense; a type of poison pill that can only be deactivated by the directors who established it (also called a continuing *director plan*).

DBA: "Doing business as" statement filed with local or state authority to inform the public that business intends to "do business as" or "trade as" a fictitious business name. Also referred to as **fictitious business name statement**.

D&O Insurance (Directors and Officers Liability Insurance):   Insurance obtained for the benefit of a corporation's directors and officers to insure against claims made against them arising from the performance corporate duties.

Dealer: Securities firm that buys securities for resale to its customers; the firm trades "on its own account."

Debenture: Debt security that is unsecured, such as a simple promissory note.

Debt financing: Borrowing money to raise capital.

Debt security: Instrument meeting the definition of a security that evidences a corporation's debt to another.

De facto corporation: A corporation with a defect in its incorporation process such that it cannot have **de jure status**. So long as founders substantially complied with formation rules, however, corporate status cannot be attacked by a third party in jurisdictions that recognize the **de facto corporation doctrine**. De facto corporations are, however, subject to invalidation by the state.

De facto merger: Transaction that has the effect of a merger, even if not characterized as a merger in opesative documents, must comply with all statutory formalities pertaining to mergers.

De jure corporation: A corporation formed in substantial compliance with the laws of the state of incorporation, the validity of which cannot be attacked by any party or the state.

Demand note: Note containing no specific stated time for payment, but as to which lender can demand repayment at any time.

Dematerialization: Issuance of stock by electronic book entry rather than paper certificate.

Derivative action: Action brought by a limited partner or shareholder or other business owner (e.g., a member of an LLC) not to enforce his or her own cause of action but rather to enforce an obligation due to the business entity; the action "derives" from the claimant's ownership interest in the business entity.

Direct action: Action brought by a limited partner, LLC member, shareholder of a corporation or other entity or individual for a direct injury sustained by the claimant; for example, being refused the right to examine corporate books and records.

Direct registration: Registration of ownership of stock in the buyer's name on the issuer's books.

Director: One who directs or manages a corporation via participation on the board of directors.

Disclosed principal: Principal whose existence and identity are known to others.

Disproportionate voting: Voting rights that differ in one class from those granted to another class.

Disregarded entity: Tax treatment whereby an entity such as a sole proprietorship or single member LLC is disregarded as an entity separate from its owner for federal income tax purposes.

Dissenter's rights: *See* Appraisal rights.

Dissenting shareholder: Shareholder opposing some corporation action, such as an amendment to the articles of incorporation, merger, or consolidation.

Dissociation: The withdrawal or departure of a partner under certain partnership statutes.

Dissolution: Termination of a business organization as a legal entity, such as a partnership or corporation; may be voluntary or involuntary for a corporation.

Distribution: Direct or indirect transfer by a corporation of money or other property (other than its own shares) to or for the benefit of its shareholders, whether a distribution of corporate profits or a distribution at the time of liquidation. The older view used this term to refer to distributions to shareholders *other than* distributions of a corporation's own profits.

Dividend: Corporation's distribution of its profits to its shareholders by way of cash, property, or shares. The modern approach is to refer to any distribution as a dividend, whether a distribution of corporate profits or a distribution at the time of liquidation.

Division: The split of a domestic company into two or more companies; the opposite of a merger; also called a *split.*

Domestication: The changing of a corporation's or other entity's state of incorporation or formation.

Domestic corporation: A corporation created or incorporated in the state in which it is conducting business.

Double taxation: Taxation of corporate income at two levels: once when the corporation earns money and then again when shareholders receive distributions from the corporation. *See* **Subchapter C.**

Downstream merger: Merger of a parent and a subsidiary in which the subsidiary survives (example: P + S = S).

Due diligence: Careful review of corporate records, other documents, and transactions to ensure they are appropriate for a party and in compliance with all pertinent laws; comprehensive appraisal of a business undertaken by a prospective buyer, especially to establish its assets and liabilities and evaluate its financial condition and commercial potential.

Dummy directors: Nominal directors in the articles of incorporation, often an attorney and staff members named for the convenience of signing documents; dummies will resign at the organizational meeting and be replaced with the corporation's true directors.

Election judge: Neutral party who oversees corporate elections to determine whether a quorum is present, that proxies have been counted, and that a measure has received sufficient votes for approval.

Emerging growth company: A company with annual revenue of less than $1 billion, and which is relieved from various SEC reporting and disclosure requirements per the Jumpstart Our Business Startups Act of 2012.

Entity conversion: A business's change of its structure—for example, a conversion from a corporation to an LLC.

Entity purchase agreement: Agreement(s) providing that (i) corporation is the beneficiary of an insurance policy, (i) in the event of the death or disability of a shareholder, the corporation will receive proceeds under the policy; and (iii) corporation will then use the proceeds to purchase the shareholder's interest. Also known as a stock redemption agreement.

E-proxy voting: Method of voting electronically.

Equity financing: Issuance of shares to raise capital.

Equity insolvency test: Test to determine if dividends can be paid in which corporation must be able to pay debts as they become due.

Equity security: Security demonstrating a person's ownership interest in a corporation.

Escrow account: An account where shares are held until the conditions of their issuances to the shareholders are satisfied.

Estoppel: Prohibition imposed on a party to preclude a challenge to some fact or event because such a challenge would be inequitable based on the party's conduct.

Exempt security: Security that is exempt from compliance with registration requirements of the Securities Act of 1933.

Exempt transaction: Transaction exempt from compliance with the registration requirements of the federal securities laws.

Express authority: Authority expressly granted to agent by principal.

Exhaustion doctrine: Principle that creditors of partnership must exhaust partnership resources first, before seeking redress from individual partners. Also known as the **marshaling of assets** doctrine.

Extinguished corporation: Corporation that does not survive a merger or other combination. Sometimes called a **merged corporation** or **disappearing corporation**.

Face value: Principal amount owed by a debtor to a creditor as shown on debt instrument.

Fairness opinion: Expert opinion on valuation — i.e., the valuation of a target requested by the target's directors — to demonstrate that directors or others charged with responsibility for a potential transaction have met their fiduciary duties when pricing the deal.

Family limited partnership: A type of partnership composed of family members and designed to achieve estate and tax planning benefits (also called a **family limited liability company** if organized as such).

Fictitious business name: Name adopted for use by a person, partnership, corporation, or other business that is other than its true or legal name. Sometimes called an assumed name.

Fiduciary duties: Obligations owed by officers, directors, and others with the power to control an enterprise to act loyally, in good faith, and with due care when carrying out business duties.

Fiduciary relationship: Relationship in which a party owes duties of care and loyalty to another or to others.

Financial Industry Regulatory Authority (FINRA): The membership organization and self-regulatory organization for the broker-dealer industry in the United States.

Financing statement: Document recorded with the secretary of state or county recorder to provide notice of a security interest claimed in personal property; also called a UCC-1 form.

Fiscal year: Twelve-month reporting period adopted by a business for accounting purposes; it need not be the calendar year.

Foothold: *See* **Toehold**.

Foreign corporation: Corporation conducting business in a state other than the one in which it is incorporated. Occasionally, corporations formed outside the United States are called foreign corporations, although they are more properly termed alien corporations.

Foreign partnership: Partnership conducting business in a state other than the one in which it is organized.

Forward-looking statement: Predictions made by corporations about future earnings.

Forward Triangular merger: Merger among a parent, its subsidiary, and a target corporation whereby the subsidiary merges with the target, leaving the subsidiary as the survivor.

Flip-in clause: A clause in some **poison pills** whereby shareholders may purchase stock in their own company, at a discount, once the bidder acquires a certain percentage of the company's shares.

Flip-over clause: Also known as a flip-out clause. A clause in some **poison pills** whereby shareholders can purchase stock in the bidder at a discount after a takeover occurs.

Fractional share: A portion of a share; typically entitled to proportionate voting and distribution rights.

Franchise tax: Fee or tax imposed by a state on a business for the privilege of conducting business in the state.

Fraud on the market: Presumption available in certain securities class action lawsuits that the price of stock traded in an efficient market reflects all public material information.

Freeze-out: Impermissible tactic by directors to compel a corporate dissolution or merger to dispose of minority shareholders; sometimes called a **squeeze-out**.

Full shield state: State offering full protection from personal liability for partners in a limited liability partnership, whether arising from tort or contract.

Fundamental changes: Changes to corporate structure involving so-called extraordinary matters as to which shareholders generally have voting rights. List of extraordinary matters includes (i) amendments to articles of incorporation; (ii) most mergers, consolidations, share exchanges, sales of all or substantially all assets; and (iii) dissolution of the corporation.

Funding portal: New type of intermediary that performs limited functions in connection with the offer and sale of securities under the crowdfunding rules of the Jumpstart Our Business Startups Act of 2012.

GAAP: Generally accepted accounting principles.

General agency: Act of a partner in carrying out the usual business of the firm that will bind the partnership unless the person with whom the partner is dealing knows the partner has no authority to perform that act.

General partner: Individuals or entities managing or controlling a (general) partnership or a limited partnership.

General proxy: A proxy authorizing the proxy holder to vote a shareholder's shares in the proxy holder's discretion.

Going private: *See* **Leveraged buy-out**.

Going public: Offering securities to members of the public at large. *See* Initial public offering.

Golden parachute: Lucrative compensation package given to key corporate managers who leave or are let go by a corporation.

Governance guidelines: Formal written policies relating to management of corporations and often sought by shareholders.

Greenmail: Form of legal corporate blackmail in which an aggressor threatens to take over a target and then sells the toehold back to the target at an inflated price in return for an agreement not to take over the target.

Gun-jumping: Impermissibly exceeding SEC's permissible forms of communication during the so-called **quiet period**, or the period between the filing of a registration statement and the date upon which the registration statement is declared effective.

Harmonization of Business Entity Acts: The Harmonization of Business Entity Acts (HBEA), also referred to as the "hub," harmonizes the common or shared language and provisions of all of the uniform unincorporated entity acts — i.e., the Uniform Partnership Act, Uniform Limited Partnership Act, Uniform Limited Liability Company Act, Model Entity Transactions Act, Model Registered Agents Act, Uniform Limited Cooperative Association Act, Uniform Unincorporated Nonprofit Association Act, and Uniform Statutory Trust Entity Act. The HBEA also permits their integration into a single code of entity laws.

Hart-Scott-Rodino Antitrust Improvements Act: A federal statute requiring premerger notification to the government so it can determine if the proposed transaction would have an anticompetitive effect.

High-yield bonds: Also known as non-investment grade bonds or junk bonds, these bonds offer a higher rate of interest than investment grade products to compensate investors for taking on higher credit risk, or risk of default.

Hindsight bias: The tendency of people to view events as more predictable than they really are after the fact.

Holder of record: Owner of stock as of a particular date. *See* **Record date**.

Hostile takeover: Acquisition of a corporation against the will of its directors and shareholders.

Householding: Practice of sending only one report and proxy statement to shareholders with same surname at same address.

Illegal dividend: Dividend paid out of an unauthorized account or made while a corporation is insolvent; also called unlawful dividend.

Implied authority: Authority to perform acts customarily performed by agents, even if not expressly so directed by a principal.

Inadvertent partnership: A partnership formed through conduct — i.e., through the act of associating as the co-owners of a for-profit business — rather than through an express oral or written partnership agreement.

Incorporate: Process of forming a corporation.

Incorporator: Person who prepares and signs the articles of incorporation to form a corporation.

Indemnify: Compensating or reimbursing one who has incurred a debt or obligation on another's behalf.

Independent contractor: One who is not subject to the control and direction of another but exercises independent judgment and discretion while performing duties and activities for that party.

Independent director: Director with no family or business ties to a corporation other than service as a director.

Information returns: Documents filed with the Internal Revenue Service reporting income earned by or distributed to partners, shareholders, or other business owners.

Initial public offering: Also known as IPO, the first offering of securities to the public; usually, the offering by a corporation of its securities to the public as a means of raising capital; often referred to as going public.

Inside director: A director who is also a significant shareholder or officer of the corporation.

Insider trading: Generally refers to buying or selling a security, in breach of a fiduciary duty or other relationship of trust and confidence, while in possession of material, nonpublic information about the security. Traditional or classical theory involves trading by corporate insiders. Misappropriation theory involves trading based upon information obtained in breach of a duty of trust and confidence owed to the source of the information.

Insolvency: Inability to pay one's debts as they become due in the usual course of business or excess of liabilities over assets.

Internal affairs doctrine: Rule that state of organization governs an entity's internal affairs.

Intrastate offering: Securities offering conducted only within one state.

Inversion: Reincorporating a U.S. company in a country with a lower tax rate to reduce U.S. income taxes.

Investor: One who puts money at risk.

Involuntary dissolution: Dissolution forced on an entity, such as a partnership or corporation, through a judicial proceeding initiated by either the state or owners of the entity, or perhaps by creditors. Sometimes called judicial dissolution.

Issuance: Process of selling corporate securities.

Joint and several liability: When each member of an association is liable to pay all of a debt or obligation; when a creditor may sue all individuals in an association or pick among them to satisfy a debt or obligation.

Joint venture: Type of partnership formed to carry out a particular enterprise rather than an ongoing business.

Jonestown defense: A target that effectively commits "suicide" by destroying itself rather than be taken over by an aggressor.

Judicial dissolution: *See* **Involuntary dissolution**.

Judicial liquidation: Liquidation of a corporation that has been involuntarily dissolved by a court; often performed by a court-appointed receiver or trustee.

Jumpstart Our Business Startups (JOBS) Act: Legislation passed in 2012 to make it easier for smaller companies to raise capital.

Junk bond: Bond below investment grade. Also known as **high-yield** bond.

"Just say no" defense: Defense to corporate takeover in which target's management recommends against the takeover.

Key person policy: Insurance policy taken out on the life of a senior manager. In the event of the manager's death, the policy proceeds go to the business entity to provide sufficient funds to purchase the decedent's ownership interest in the entity.

Killer bees: Attorneys, advisors, and others retained by a target to fight off a takeover.

L3C: *See* **Low-profit limited liability company**.

Legal personality: An attribute of certain forms of organization (e.g., the corporate form) whereby the entity has a legal identity or personality that is separate from the legal identity or personality of the owners of the enterprise.

Legend: Generally, a notation on a stock certificate stating that it is subject to some restriction, typically as to transfer of stock represented by the certificate; a notation on a corporate document such as a prospectus.

Leveraged buyout: Offer by a target's management to purchase all of the publicly held shares of a target corporation that typically involves the usage of leverage. Sometimes called going private.

Liability shield: Refers to limited liability for owners. Attribute of form of organization (other than sole proprietorships and general partnerships) whereby owners are not liable for debts and obligations of enterprise based solely on status as owner.

Limited liability: Liability that is confined to that amount contributed by an investor to an enterprise; when personal assets of an investor cannot be used to satisfy business debts or obligations.

Limited liability company: New form of business enterprise, recognized in all states, offering the pass-through tax status of a partnership and the limited liability of a corporation.

Limited liability limited partnership: A limited partnership that files paperwork electing limited liability limited partnership status with the secretary of state so its general partner has no personal liability for partnership obligations. Recognized fully only in some states.

Limited liability partnership: *See* **Registered limited liability partnership**.

Limited partner: Individual or entity with an ownership interest in a limited partnership, but who does not manage or control the enterprise, and whose liability is limited to the amount contributed to the limited partnership.

Limited partnership: Partnership formed under statutory requirements that has as members one or more general partners and one or more limited partners.

Limited partnership agreement: Agreement among partners in a limited partnership, usually written, regarding the affairs of the limited partnership, the duties of the general partner, rights of limited partners, and the conduct of the business.

Limited partnership certificate: Document filed with a state agency to create a limited partnership.

Limited proxy: A proxy directing a proxy holder to vote as specified by the shareholder giving the proxy.

Line of credit: A type of preauthorized loan that the borrower draws against as needed.

Liquidation: Process of completing the affairs of a business; for corporations, the process of collecting corporate assets, discharging debts, and distributing any remains to the shareholders; may be judicial or nonjudicial. Sometimes called winding up.

Liquidation distribution: Distribution made to business owners after creditors have been paid upon dissolution of a business entity.

Liquidator: *See* **Receiver**.

Low-profit limited liability company: A new type of LLC organized for a social purpose; profit-making is secondary.

Manager-managed: Governance structure for limited liability company whereby individual manager (or board of managers) has the right to manage and control the enterprise.

Marshaling of assets: Requirement that partnership creditors must first exhaust partnership assets before attacking a partner's personal assets to satisfy a debt or obligation.

Master limited partnership: A type of limited partnership (or perhaps limited liability company) that is traded on a national securities exchange.

Maturity: The date at which a debt instrument is due and payable.

Member: Owner or investor in a limited liability company

Member-managed: Governance structure for limited liability company whereby members (i.e., owners) have equal rights to manage and control the enterprise.

Merger: Combinations of two or more corporations into one corporate entity (example: A + B = A).

Merger clause: A contractual provision that provides that the signed writing constitutes the full and final statement of the agreement between the parties; sometimes called integration clause.

Midnight raid: Raid by aggressor after the afternoon closing of a stock exchange and concluded before resumption of trading in the morning.

Mini-tender offer: A tender offer to purchase less than 5 percent of a target's outstanding shares; not subject to SEC rules relating to tender offers.

Minority discount: A discount applied when valuing a minority or non-controlling interest in a closely held enterprise.

Minority stockholders: Stockholders who, individually and in the aggregate, own less than 50 percent of the shares of a corporation. In the LLC context, the equivalent reference is minority members. In the partnership context, the equivalent reference is minority partner.

Minutes: Written summary of the proceedings at directors' or shareholders' meetings.

Model Business Corporations Act (MBCA):   Model corporations code drafted by the American Bar Association on which many individual state statutes governing corporations are based.

Mop up: Attempt by a successful aggressor to acquire 100 percent ownership of a target's stock.

Mortgage bond or note: Debt security in which a corporations pledges real estate as security for its promise to repay money borrowed from a creditor.

Name registration: Reservation and registration of a corporate name in foreign states in which the corporation intends to do business in the future.

Name reservation: Reservation of a proposed corporate or other entity name prior to filing of articles of incorporation or formation documents; generally effective for some specified period.

Name saver: Subsidiary incorporated in a state expressly to ensure a name is available for corporate parent or other entity in that state.

NASDAQ Stock Market: Computerized trading system for trading of securities

No-hand poison pill: An anti-takeover device; a poison pill that cannot be removed by any director if control of the board changes hands.

Nonaccredited investor: Investor who is not sophisticated or "accredited"; *see* **Accredited investor**.

Nonjudicial liquidation: Liquidation of an entity that has been voluntarily dissolved; in a corporation, such liquidation is performed by corporate directors and officers.

Nonprofit corporation: Corporation formed for some charitable, religious, educational, or scientific purpose or for the mutual benefit of its members, rather than for the purpose of making a profit.

No action letter: Letter requested from the SEC in which the Commission states, in response to a request, that it will not take action (civil or criminal) if the requestor engages in the activity or takes the position referenced in requestor's letter.

No par value stock: Stock having no stated minimum value; the price can be determined by a corporation's board of directors.

Novation: Legal device whereby one party is substituted for another on a contract. For pre-incorporation contracts, novation refers to the substitution of the corporation for a promoter as the responsible party.

Nuclear war: Hostile takeover involving numerous large publicly traded companies.

NYSE Euronext: Large secondary market for trading of securities; usually referred to as NYSE or New York Stock Exchange.

Officer: One appointed by a corporation's board of directors to carry out management functions as delegated by the board.

Operating agreement: Agreement governing the operation of a limited liability company. Also known as limited liability company agreement.

Opt-in provisions: State laws providing that unless preemptive rights are provided for in the articles of incorporation, they do not exist.

Option: Right to purchase securities or commodities at a specified price during a specified time period.

Opt-out provisions: State laws providing that preemptive rights exist unless specifically denied by the articles of incorporation.

Organizational meeting: First meeting of a corporation held after incorporation to finalize the incorporation process by electing directors, appointing officers, adopting bylaws, and so forth.

Outside director: Director who is not an employee or officer of the corporation.

Outstanding shares: Shares issued by a corporation and held by a shareholder.

Oversubscription: Shares tendered to an aggressor in excess of the amount requested in the aggressor's tender offer.

Over-the-counter market: Computerized securities trading network with no physical trading location for securities.

Pac-Man defense: Tender offer by a target to acquire an aggressor's stock.

Parent corporation: Corporation that creates or acquires another corporation (called a subsidiary) and holds all or a majority of its shares.

Partial shield state: A state offering limited protection from liability to partners in a limited liability partnership for acts arising out of wrongful conduct of co-partners (but not offering such protection for acts arising out of contractual obligations).

Partially disclosed principal: Principal whose existence but not specific identity is known to others.

Participating preferred stock: Stock that enjoys the right to participate in corporate distributions in addition to those "built into" the preferred stock.

Partnership: An association of two or more persons to carry on as co-owners a business for profit; often called a general partnership to distinguish it from a limited partnership.

Partnership at will: Partnership with no specific term of duration.

Partnership for a term: Partnership with a definite term of duration.

Passive activity loss limitation: Tax regulation allowing taxpayers to deduct losses from passive activities but only to the extent of the taxpayer's income from other passive activities for the year.

Par value: Minimum consideration for which a share of stock can be issued; set forth in a corporation's articles of incorporation.

Pass-through taxation: A tax treatment whereby the profits and losses of the business are allocated and passed through to the owners of the business.

Per capita: A Latin phrase literally meaning "by heads," and commonly translated as "for each person." In the context of voting in business entities, for example, per capita refers to one person/one vote.

Person: According to most statutes, a "person" is a natural individual or a business organization, such as a partnership or corporation.

Personal liability: Liability for debts and obligations in excess of that originally invested, namely, liability extending to one's personal assets.

Pick your partner principle: Principle that provides that partners may choose with whom they associate, and that the admission of new partners therefore requires the unanimous consent of all partners.

Piercing the veil: Equitable doctrine whereby the liability shield of an entity such as a corporation or (in some jurisdictions) a limited liability company is set aside, usually when it would be unjust or unfair not to do so. With traditional veil piercing, a creditor seeks to collect from the entity's owners in addition to collecting from the entity itself. With reverse veil piercing, the creditor seeks to hold the entity liability for the debt of that owner. The related doctrine of enterprise liability applies in situations where a creditor seeks to disregard the separate legal existence of multiple entities under common control to satisfy a liability owned by one entity.

Plan of domestication: The plan that provides the terms and conditions of an entity's or corporation's change of its state of incorporation.

Plan of entity conversion: The plan that provides the terms and conditions of a business's change in its structure.

Plan of merger: Blueprint for a merger containing all of the terms and conditions of a merger.

Plurality: The number of votes received by a successful candidate who does not receive a majority of votes cast in an election but who receives more than an opponent; counting only votes "for" a nominee and not counting votes "against" or withheld.

Poison pill: Defensive measures designed to thwart a hostile takeover; also called shareholder rights plan.

Pooling agreement: Agreement between or among shareholders specifying the manner in which they will vote.

Porcupine provision: *See* **Shark repellent**.

Preemptive right: The right of a shareholder to purchase newly issued stock in an amount proportionate to his or her current share ownership. Generally not available unless provided for in the corporate charter under modern corporation codes.

Preemptive strike: Highly attractive offer made by an aggressor with the intent of obtaining immediate control of a target.

Preferred stock: Corporate stock that has some right, privilege, or preference over another type of stock.

Preincorporation agreement or contract: Agreement entered into between promoters of a corporation and some third party prior to creation of the corporation; promoter is bound by the agreement.

Preincorporation share subscription: Offer by a party to purchase stock in a corporation made before the corporation is formed.

Principal: One who appoints another, called an agent, to act for or represent him or her.

Priority: Process of making one debt senior, or prior, to another (which is referred to as subordinate).

Privately held corporation: Corporation whose shares are not sold to the public but are held by a small group of investors, often family and friends.

Private placement offering: Nonpublic offering of a corporation's stock, generally exempt from the registration requirements of the Securities Act of 1933.

Private Securities Litigation Reform Act: Federal law intended to reduce frivolous shareholder securities class action lawsuits.

Process: Complaint filed in court by a plaintiff and the summons issued thereafter by the court to the party named as defendant requiring an appearance or response.

Professional corporation: Corporation formed by a person or persons practicing a certain profession, such as law, medicine, or accounting, who retain liability for their own misconduct and the misconduct of those acting under their control.

Professional limited liability company: A type of limited liability company organized by professionals who retain liability for their own negligence.

Promissory note: Document evidencing one's debt to another.

Promoter: One who plans and organizes a corporation.

Property dividend: Distribution that is not cash or shares in the issuing corporation but is generally some physical or tangible item.

Prospectus: Document that must be provided to any purchaser of securities registered under the Securities Act of 1933; it includes information relating to the corporation, its management, and the securities being issued.

Protective provision: Provision in preferred stockholders' agreement that prohibits the corporation from taking specified actions, such as issuing a security that is senior to existing preferred stock with respect to rights and preferences.

Proxy: Written authorization by a shareholder directing another to vote his or her shares.

Proxy access: The ability of a shareholder or shareholders to include desired nominees for director positions in the company's proxy materials

Proxy fight: Solicitation of a target's shareholders by management of the aggressor and management of the target to vote for each party's management slate; also called a proxy contest.

Public corporation: Corporation whose shares can be purchased and sold by members of the general public.

Public offering: Issuance of securities to the general public that generally must first be registered according to the Securities Act of 1933 (or exempt from registration).

Put: Right of a shareholder (usually, a preferred shareholder) to compel a corporation to reacquire stock issued to the shareholder.

Qualification: Process by which a corporation or entity formed in one state is authorized to transact business in another.

Qualified small business stock: Stock in certain small businesses that qualifies for tax advantages by excluding from taxable income one-half of any gain on the sale of the stock.

Quiet period: Time between filing of a registration statement and date registration statement is declared effective by the SEC.

Quorum: Minimum number of shareholders or directors required to be present at a meeting to conduct business; usually a majority.

Ratification: Acceptance or approval of a certain act; may be express or implied from conduct.

Receiver: Individual or firm appointed by a court to oversee a judicial or involuntary dissolution. Sometimes called a liquidator.

Record date: Date selected in advance of a meeting used to determine who will be entitled to notice of a meeting and who will be entitled to vote at a meeting.

Redemption right: (1) Right given to a corporation to repurchase the stock of preferred shareholders (call) or the right given to a preferred shareholder to compel the corporation to repurchase preferred stock (put); (2) Right of a corporation to pay off, or redeem, debt owed to a creditor before the stated maturity date.

Registered agent: Individual or company designated by a business to receive service of process (and perhaps other documents) on the business's behalf.

Registered limited liability partnership: Newly recognized form of partnership in which a partner has no personal liability for the misconduct of another partner (and, in 49 jurisdictions no personal liability for contractual obligations of the partnership); formed by filing an application with the appropriate state official; also called limited liability partnership.

Registered office: Principal location of a business organization identified in various state forms or filings so that third parties may contact the business.

Registrar: Bank or other institution that maintains a corporation's list of shareholders.

Registration: (1) Process of protecting a corporate or entity name in another state; (2) Process of complying with the Securities Act of 1933 for issuance of securities to the public.

Registration statement: Form or document filed with the Securities and Exchange Commission, pursuant to the federal securities laws, when securities are first offered to the public.

Regular meeting: Routinely scheduled meeting of corporate directors.

Regulations A and D: *See* **Small issues.**

Reinstatement: Process of reviving a corporation or other entity after it has been dissolved, often for a technical violation of state law, such as failure to file an annual report.

Reorganization: Tax term for mergers, consolidations, and share exchanges. There are different types of reorganization under tax rules – i.e., Type A reorganizations (mergers and consolidations), Type B reorganizations (exchange of shares), and Type C reorganizations (acquisition of all or substantially all of the assets of another corporation in exchange for shares of the acquirer.)

Representations and warranties: Assertions of fact. In the context of loan agreements, representations and warranties often relate to the accuracy and completeness of financial statements and financial projections that the borrower provided to the seller during the **due diligence** process.

Representative action: Action brought by numerous shareholders or business owners against a corporation, directors, or other entity; a class action by shareholders or business owners.

Reservation: *See* **Name reservation.**

Residual claim: The right of common stockholders to receive the net assets of the corporation upon dissolution.

Respondeat superior: Latin phrase meaning "let the master answer"; legal theory by which liability is imposed on an employer-principal for an employee-agent's acts committed in the course and scope of the employment or agency.

Restated articles of incorporation: Document filed with the secretary of state to combine previously amended articles into a more comprehensible document.

Restricted stock: Stock that must be held for a fixed period of time.

Retained earnings: Net profits accumulated and retained by a corporation rather than being distributed to owner-investors.

Reverse merger: Often, the purchase of a defunct American listed company and merging with it to avoid regulatory oversight; sometimes called a Chinese reverse merger.

Reverse triangular merger: Merger among a parent, its subsidiary, and a target corporation in which the subsidiary merges into the surviving target.

Right: A short-term option, as distinguished from a warrant, a long-term option.

Roll-up: Combination of several companies in the same industry.

Rules 504, 505 and 506: SEC rules that contain exemptions from requirement that securities must be registered prior to their offer and sale.

Safe harbor: Activities that a person or entity may engage in that do not violate a statute.

Sarbanes-Oxley Act of 2002: Federal statute enacted in the wake of accounting scandals containing rules relating to financial reporting and internal controls.

Saturday night special: Raid by an aggressor made over a weekend so the target cannot marshal its management team.

Scorched earth: Extreme and dramatic efforts by a target to ward off a hostile takeover.

S corporation: Tax classification for eligible corporations in which all income is passed through to shareholders who pay taxes at appropriate individual rates. Certain eligibility requirements must be met and maintained to qualify for S status.

Scrip: Certificate evidencing a fractional share; scrip does not typically possess voting, dividend, or liquidation rights.

Secondary trading: Traditionally, a stock exchange where established corporations trade their securities, such as the NYSE.

Secretary of State: The arm of state government charged with (among other things) processing, filing, and maintaining documents relating to businesses formed or operating in the state. Also known as department of state in some jurisdictions.

Section 12 company: Company required to register its securities pursuant to Section 12 of the Securities Exchange Act of 1934 and required to file various reports with the SEC; also called Section 12 reporting company.

Section 1224 stock: Stock that, when sold at a loss, provides certain tax advantages; the loss is treated as an ordinary rather than a capital loss. Certain requirements must be met to issue Section 1244 stock.

Secured debt or transaction: Debt secured by some corporate asset that can be seized upon the corporation's default in repayment of its loan obligation.

Securities Act of 1933:   Federal law imposing requirements on a company's original issuance of securities to the public.

Securities and Exchange Commission (SEC):   Independent federal agency charged with the regulation of securities.

Securities Exchange Act of 1934:   Federal law imposing requirements on the trading of stock, primarily the purchase and sale of securities after their original issuance; also imposes reporting requirements on corporations that trade their stock publicly. Also includes conduct rules and reporting requirement for certain financial institutions and financial services industry professionals

Security: Share or ownership interest in a corporation (equity security) or obligation of the corporation to an investor (debt security) as well as a wide range of instruments, transactions, and investment schemes.

Security agreement: Agreement between a debtor and a lender in which the debtor pledges personal property (rather than real estate) as collateral to secure repayment of the debtor's loan to the creditor.

Self-tender: Target's purchase of its own shares to prevent a hostile takeover.

Series LLC: A separate and distinct group within an LLC, which has its own members and assets; not recognized by revised Uniform Limited Liability Company Act of 2006.

Series stock: Stock issued within a class including rights and preferences different from those of other series or classes and issued without the necessity of shareholder approval; sometimes referred to as *blank stock*.

Service of process: Delivery of a summons and complaint (i.e., process) on a defendant or its agent.

Share: Units in which the proprietary interests of a corporation are divided.

Share dividend: Distribution to shareholders of the corporation's own shares.

Share exchange: Process by which the shareholders of a target exchange their shares for cash or shares of another corporation; sometimes called an interest exchange.

Shareholder: One who owns an interest in a corporation; synonymous with stockholder.

Share repurchase: The buying of its own shares from its shareholders or on the open market by a corporation; such buybacks often elevate the market value of the remaining shares.

Share subscription: Agreement whereby a party offers to purchase stock in a corporation.

Shark repellent: Attempts by a target to ward off an aggressor even before a tender offer is made. Sometimes called a porcupine provision.

Shelf registration: A registration of new stock prepared up to three years in advance of sales; registration is automatically effective for well-known seasoned issuers.

Short-form merger: Merger between a parent and its subsidiary in which the parent owns at least 90 percent of the subsidiary's stock.

Short-swing profits: Profits made by a Section 12 company's officers, directors, or principal shareholders within a six-month period, which must be disgorged to the corporation, even without a showing of insider trading or bad faith.

Sinking fund: Fund of money set aside by a corporation to enable it to redeem or reacquire shares from preferred shareholders or to pay off money borrowed by the corporation from a creditor.

Slow-hand poison pill: An anti-takeover device; a poison pill that bars newly elected directors from deactivating it for some period of time.

Small business corporation: Domestic corporation, with no more than 100 shareholders, all of whom are individuals and that meet other requirements, which may elect to be treated as an S corporation and thereby avoid double taxation.

Small issue: Offering of stock that does not exceed statutory limits and is exempt from the registration requirements of the Securities Act of 1933.

Small-scale merger: Merger not dramatically affecting the survivor corporation's shareholders that is therefore not subject to approval by the survivor's shareholders.

Sole proprietorship: Business managed and owned by one person who has sole authority for all decision-making and faces unlimited personal liability for business debts and obligations.

Solvency: Ability to pay debts as they come due.

Special allocations: Allocations of profits and losses made on a basis other than ownership interest.

Special litigation committee: Committee established by a board of directors to determine if derivative litigation is appropriate.

Seal: Device used to impress the corporation's name on certain documents.

Special meeting: Any meeting held between the annual meetings of shareholders or regular meetings of directors.

Squeeze-out: *See* **Freeze-out**.

Stagger system: Process of varying election dates for board members so that they are not all elected at same time; a stagger system reduces the effect of cumulative voting; also called classified system.

Standstill agreement: Agreement by an aggressor not to purchase more shares of the target for some specified period of time; the target may pay greenmail to the aggressor for this agreement.

Stated capital: Amount equivalent to the par value of issued stock or consideration received for stock issued without par value.

Statement of authority: An optional filing available under certain business entity statutes that provides public notice of the nature and scope of the authority of agents of the business (e.g., a partner of a partnership).

Statement of denial: An optional filing available under certain business entity statutes through which a business entity can deny the authority of an individual or entity to act on behalf of the filer. Often filed by or in connection with a withdrawing partner to indicate that the partner's authority to act on behalf of the partnership is terminated.

Statutory close corporation: A corporation that has elected to be formed pursuant to and governed by a state's close corporation statute.

Stock: *See* **Share**.

Stock certificate: Document evidencing an ownership interest in a corporation.

Stock exchange: Marketplace where securities are traded.

Stockholder: *See* **Shareholder**.

Stock option: Plan used by a corporation or agreement to compensate employees who have the right to buy the corporation's stock at certain times at fixed prices.

Stock purchase: Acquisition of stock in a corporation.

Stock watch: Early warning system used by a corporation to detect fluctuations in the market price of its shares that might warn of action by aggressors.

Straight voting: The right carried by each outstanding share of record to one vote.

Street name: The registration of stock in the name of a brokerage firm.

Street sweep: Process by which an aggressor or third party attempts to purchase stock from a risk arbitrageur or speculator in the event an aggressor's takeover bid is unsuccessful.

Strike suit: Lawsuit filed by disgruntled shareholders after a stock drop.

Strike team: Aggressor's legal counsel, advisors, public relations team, and so forth.

Subagent: An agent appointed by another agent.

Subchapter C: Default tax treatment for corporations pursuant to which corporate profits are taxed twice – once at the entity level and once at the shareholder level when profits are distributed. Commonly referred to as double taxation.

Subchapter K: Default tax treatment for partnerships whereby profits and losses of enterprise are passed through to owners.

Subchapter S: A tax treatment available to qualifying corporations whereby profits and losses of business are passed through to owners and taxed at the owner level rather than at both the entity and owner level. Contrasts with Subchapter C tax treatment.

Subordination: Process of making one debt junior, or subordinate, to another (which is said to have priority over it).

Subsidiary: Corporation formed or acquired by another corporation, called the parent. The term wholly owned subsidiary refers to a subsidiary corporation whose stock is owned entirely by its parent.

Suicide pact: Agreement by a target's management team to resign en masse in the event any one of them is fired or demoted after a hostile takeover (also called people pill).

Super-majority vote: Voting standard requiring more than a bare majority — e.g., two-thirds or more.

Surplus account: Value of corporation's net assets that is greater than its stated capital.

Survivor: Corporation that continues in existence after a merger.

Takeover: *See* **Hostile takeover**.

Target: Corporation being attacked, acquired, or subject to takeover by another corporation or some third party.

Tender offer: Public offer by an aggressor to shareholders of a target corporation seeking to acquire their shares.

The street: Nickname for Wall Street in New York City.

Tippee: One who receives a tip or information from a corporate insider about the corporation.

Tipper: Corporate insider who gives tips or information to others about the corporation's finances or operations.

Toehold: Stock of a target purchased by an aggressor wishing to take over the target, usually less than 5 percent. Sometimes called a foothold or creeping tender offer.

Tombstone ad: Limited advertising offering securities during the 20-day period between filing of a registration statement with the SEC and its effective date.

Trademark: A word, symbol, or device used to identify and distinguish one's goods or services.

Transacting business: Activities engaged in by a corporation or other entity doing business in a state other than its state of incorporation or formation that will require it to formally qualify with that host state to conduct business.

Transfer agent: Bank or other institution that physically issues or cancels stock certificates for large corporations.

Treasury stock: Stock reacquired by a corporation; it is considered issued but not outstanding.

Trust indenture: Agreement specifying a trustee's rights and responsibilities when a corporation issues numerous bonds at one time.

Ultra vires act: Act beyond the purposes and powers of a corporation. The doctrine of ultra vires is limited by modern statutes that allow a corporation to perform any lawful act and that generally prohibit the corporation or a third party from disaffirming a contract as ultra vires and void or thus voidable.

Uncertificated share: Share issued without a formal share certificate.

Undisclosed principal: Principal whose existence and identity are unknown to others.

Uniform Business Organizations Code: Comprehensive uniform code for all business entities prepared by Uniform Law Commission (ULC).

Uniform Partnership Act (2001) (Last Amended 2013): The Uniform Partnership Act (UPA) proposed by the ULC. Intended to modernize the Uniform Partnership Act of 1914, the current version of the UPA establishes a partnership as a separate legal entity. The 2011 and 2013 amendments, enacted as part of the **Harmonization of Business Entity Acts** project, harmonize the language in UPA with the language of similar provisions in the other uniform unincorporated entity acts.

Uniform Limited Liability Company Act (2006) (Last Amended 2013): The Uniform Limited Liability Company Act (ULLCA) proposed by the ULC. The ULLCA permits the formation of limited liability companies (LLCs) which provide the owners with the advantages of both corporate-type limited liability and partnership tax treatment. The 2011 and 2013 amendments, enacted as part of the **Harmonization of Business Entity Acts** project, updated and harmonize the language in this act with similar provisions in other uniform model unincorporated entity acts.

Uniform Limited Partnership Act (1997) (Last Amended 2013): The Uniform Limited Partnership Act (ULPA) proposed by the ULC. The 2011 and 2013 amendments to ULPA, enacted as part of the **Harmonization of Business Entity Acts** project, updated and harmonize the language in this act with similar provisions in the other uniform unincorporated entity acts.

Uniform Law Commission: Also known as the National Conference of Commissioners on Uniform State Laws (NCCUSL), the Uniform Law Commission is a non-partisan organization composed of lawyers (including practicing lawyers, judges, legislators and legislative staff, and law professors) that researches, drafts, and promotes the enactment of uniform state laws in areas of state law where uniformity is desirable and practical.

Unknown liability: A liability that is not known to exist.

Unlimited liability: Liability not limited to a party's investment in an enterprise but which rather may be satisfied from the investor's other assets, savings, and property.

Unsecured debt: Debt for which no property is pledged as collateral to secure repayment of the loan; in the event of default, a creditor must sue the debtor to recover money loaned to the debtor.

Upstream merger: Merger of a parent and its subsidiary in which the parent survives (example: P + S = P).

Venture capital investor: Firms that provide capital to emerging growth companies. Venture capital firms typically invest at a later stage in the lifecycle of a business compared to angel investors.

Vicarious liability: Liability imposed on another for an act that is not his or her fault; typically, it is liability imposed on an employer for an employee's torts.

Voluntary dissolution: Dissolution of an entity initiated by the entity itself; with regard to a corporation, a dissolution initiated by corporate directors or shareholders.

Voting agreement: Agreement among shareholders specifying the manner in which they will vote. Sometimes called a pooling agreement.

Voting trust: Agreement among shareholders by which they transfer their voting rights to a trustee to vote on their behalf.

Waiver of notice: Giving up the right to receive notice of some action or event, usually a meeting of directors or shareholders.

War chest: Funds collected or borrowed by an aggressor to acquire a target.

Warrant: Long-term option enabling its holder to purchase shares at a specified price during a specified time period.

Watered stock: Stock issued for less than its par value or for property or services worth less than its par value. Sometimes called discount stock or bonus stock.

White knight: Corporation that saves a target from a hostile takeover.

Williams Act: Federal statute relating to tender offers.

Winding up: *See* **Liquidation.**

Withdrawal: Request by an entity wishing to cease being qualified in a state in which it has transacted business.

Written consent: Action taken by a board of directors or shareholders without the necessity of meeting in person; most states require written consent to be unanimous.

Table of Cases

Principal cases are italicized.

Index